essentials of
SOCIOLOGY

essentials of
SOCIOLOGY

essentials of
SOCIOLOGY

GEORGE RITZER
University of Maryland

Los Angeles | London | New Delhi
Singapore | Washington DC

Los Angeles | London | New Delhi
Singapore | Washington DC

FOR INFORMATION:

SAGE Publications, Inc.
2455 Teller Road
Thousand Oaks, California 91320
E-mail: order@sagepub.com

SAGE Publications Ltd.
1 Oliver's Yard
55 City Road
London EC1Y 1SP
United Kingdom

SAGE Publications India Pvt. Ltd.
B 1/I 1 Mohan Cooperative Industrial Area
Mathura Road, New Delhi 110 044
India

SAGE Publications Asia-Pacific Pte. Ltd.
3 Church Street
#10-04 Samsung Hub
Singapore 049483

Printed in Canada

Cataloging-in-Publication Data is available from the Library of Congress.

ISBN 978-1-4833-4017-3

Acquisitions Editor: Jeff Lasser
Associate Editor: Nathan Davidson
Editorial Assistant: Lauren Johnson
Production Editor: Olivia Weber-Stenis
Copy Editor: Melinda Masson
Typesetter: C&M Digitals (P) Ltd.
Proofreader: Theresa Kay
Indexer: Sheila Bodell
Cover Designer: Gail Buschman
Marketing Manager: Erica DeLuca

This book is printed on acid-free paper.

15 16 17 18 19 10 9 8 7 6 5 4 3 2 1

*To Sue: With much love for enduring, mostly with her usual good humor intact,
all the years I was often unavailable while writing this book*

ABOUT THE AUTHOR

George Ritzer is Distinguished University Professor at the University of Maryland. Among his awards are Honorary Doctorate from La Trobe University, Melbourne, Australia; Honorary Patron, University Philosophical Society, Trinity College, Dublin; American Sociological Association's Distinguished Contribution to Teaching Award; and 2013 Eastern Sociological Society's Robin Williams Lecturer. He has chaired four sections of the American Sociological Association: Theoretical Sociology, Organizations and Occupations, Global and Transnational Sociology, and the History of Sociology. In the application of social theory to the social world, his books include *The McDonaldization of Society* (7th ed., 2013; 8th ed. forthcoming), *Enchanting a Disenchanted World* (3rd ed., 2010), and *The Globalization of Nothing* (2nd ed., 2007). He is the author of *Globalization: A Basic Text* (Blackwell, 2010; 2nd ed. forthcoming). He edited the *Wiley-Blackwell Companion to Sociology* (2012), *The Blackwell Companion to Globalization* (2008) and co-edited (with Jeff Stepnisky) the *Wiley-Blackwell Companions to Classical and Contemporary Major Social Theorists* (2012) and the *Handbook of Social Theory* (2001). He was founding editor of the *Journal of Consumer Culture*. He also edited the eleven-volume *Encyclopedia of Sociology* (2007; 2nd ed. forthcoming), the two-volume *Encyclopedia of Social Theory* (2005), and the five-volume *Encyclopedia of Globalization* (2012). He co-edited a special double issue (2012) of the *American Behavioral Scientist* on prosumption. His books have been translated into over twenty languages, with more than a dozen translations of *The McDonaldization of Society* alone.

BRIEF CONTENTS

DETAILED CONTENTS

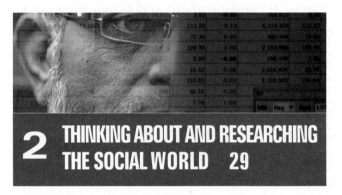

3 CULTURE 68

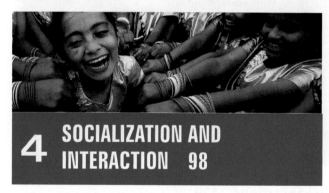

4 SOCIALIZATION AND INTERACTION 98

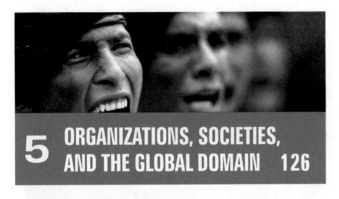

7 SOCIAL STRATIFICATION 188

8 RACE AND ETHNICITY 220

9 GENDER AND SEXUALITY 250

10 THE FAMILY 278

11 RELIGION AND EDUCATION   306

12 POLITICS AND THE ECONOMY   344

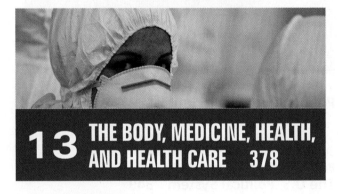

13 THE BODY, MEDICINE, HEALTH, AND HEALTH CARE   378

14 POPULATION, URBANIZATION, AND THE ENVIRONMENT   404

15 SOCIAL CHANGE, SOCIAL MOVEMENTS, AND COLLECTIVE ACTION   436

LETTER FROM THE AUTHOR

To me, the social world, as well as the discipline of sociology that studies that world, is always interesting, exciting, and ever-changing. The goal in this new, "essentials" version of my introduction to sociology is not only to introduce YOU, the student, to the field, but also to discuss what has made sociology my life-long passion. My hope is that readers of this text learn a good deal about the social world from the perspective of sociology, as well as get at least a sense of why I am so passionate about it. Please let me explain how this book is, in many ways, an expression of that passion as well as of my personal sociological journey. . . .

My initial interests in the field were the sociology of work and of organizations, but I was quickly drawn to sociological theory and how even the most classical theories were relevant to, and at play in, my everyday life . . . and yours. This interest came to fruition in the publication of *The McDonaldization of Society* in 1993 (the 7th edition of that book was published in 2013 and an 8th edition is planned). In this book I apply and expand upon the famous classic theoretical ideas of Max Weber on rationality. I saw those ideas at work in my local fast food restaurant, as well as in many other settings. The major themes addressed in *The McDonaldization of Society* are prominent in various places in this textbook.

Journalists often interview me on the ideas behind "McDonaldization" and these experiences allowed me to better appreciate "public sociology," the impact of sociologists' work on the larger public. Public sociology is of increasing importance and in this text I have highlighted the writings of not only sociologists whose work has had a significant public impact, but also the work of journalists that is implicitly, and sometimes explicitly, sociological in nature.

After the publication of *The McDonaldization of Society*, my thinking and research moved in many related and interesting directions, and these interests are manifest throughout this text. I became very interested in consumption and, more specifically, was drawn to the study of credit cards which inspired *Expressing America: A Critique of the Global Credit Card Society*. I was surprised by the number of my undergraduate students who maintained one or more credit card accounts. I was also distressed by their fears of growing indebtedness (in hindsight perhaps a harbinger of The Great Recession). Also in the area of consumption, I authored *Enchanting a Disenchanted World: Continuity and Change in the Cathedrals of Consumption*. Shopping malls, theme parks such as Disney World, Las Vegas–style casinos, and cruise ships are "cathedrals of consumption" which lure consumers and lead them to overspend and to go deeply into debt.

Later, as I reflected on my research on fast food restaurants, credit cards, and cathedrals of consumption, I was drawn to a fascinating, newly emerging area of sociology-globalization—in *The Globalization of Nothing* and *Globalization: A Basic Text*. I realized that all of the phenomena of interest to me had been invented in the United States but had rapidly spread throughout much of the world. Accordingly, this book includes a strong emphasis on globalization with the hope that students will better understand that process and better appreciate their roles within our globalized world.

Most recently, my sociological journey has led me to the Internet, especially social networking sites such as Facebook, Twitter, and Pinterest. These sites are highly rationalized (or McDonaldized), are often sites of consumption (e.g., eBay), and are all globalized (Facebook alone has over one billion users throughout the world). Throughout this book—in boxes (entitled "Digital Living") and in the narrative—the sociological implications of the Internet are discussed and explained; there is much in this topic for students to contemplate.

The above describes much of my personal sociological journey. I hope that this book will provide YOU with a starting point to begin your own personal sociological journey, to examine your social world critically, and to develop your own sociological ideas and opinions. It is my hope that this book better equips you to see the social world in a different way and more importantly to use the ideas discussed here to help to create a better world.

George Ritzer
University of Maryland

essentials of
SOCIOLOGY
x GEORGE RITZER

Join the conversation with one of sociology's best-known thinkers.

Welcome to George Ritzer's *Essentials of Sociology*. While providing a brief, but rock-solid foundation of the critical topics and concepts in sociology, Ritzer continues his exploration of today's most compelling sociological phenomena: globalization, the Internet, consumption, and his signature theme— the McDonaldization of society.

THEMES

GLOBALIZATION

Globalization continues to attract increasing attention in the field of sociology, indicated by the dramatic growth of the American Sociological Association's section on Global and Transnational Sociology. As denizens of the global age, students, like sociologists, are deeply immersed in and transformed by the innumerable effects of globalization.

THE INTERNET

The Internet's sociological significance grows by the day, even as the electronic landscape continues to change. Facebook has reached over a billion members worldwide, Twitter brings breaking news to our smartphones, and YouTube videos make and destroy careers. The impact of the Internet on the lives of students is increasing as is their ability to influence others throughout the world via the Internet.

CONSUMPTION

Consumption, which we take for granted, drives the economies and the cultures of developed and even developing countries. Consumption is a topic that has been studied extensively by sociologists in the United States and Europe. More recently it has also become a compelling sociological and public issue in modernizing countries such as China where, until now, production has been the prevailing socioeconomic concern.

MCDONALDIZATION

With restaurants in 120 countries on 6 continents, McDonald's is an indelible global business enterprise. Ritzer, recognized for his striking theory of *McDonaldization*, introduces students to the worldwide impact of a business and cultural model based on efficiency, calculability, predictability, and control.

GEORGE RITZER'S PRESENTATION OF THEORY

The text presents theory through a three-pronged approach, similar to that in most introductory sociology texts but here encompassing the most contemporary perspectives. Each theoretical category—structural/functional, conflict/critical, and inter/actionist—encompasses two or more theories, including some of the most important theories developed in the late 20th and early 21st centuries:

- *Structural/functional* theory includes structural functionalism and structuralism.

- *Conflict/critical* theory includes conflict theory, critical theory, feminist theory, queer theory, critical theories of race and racism, and postmodern theory.

- *Inter/actionist* theory includes symbolic interactionism, ethnomethodology, exchange theory, and rational choice theory.

In this *Essentials* version, some coverage of theory has been streamlined to make the text more accessible.

FEATURES

The essential content of each chapter is supported by attractive and proven features that compel reading, reinforce comprehension, and encourage critical thought. Many are completely new to this edition; all the others have been thoroughly revised and updated.

▶ **NEW** *Learning Objectives* at the beginning of each chapter preview the key topics and help students read with a purpose. The *Learning Objectives* can also help instructors plan assessment activities.

In June 2013, 30-year-old U.S. Central Intelligence Agency contractor Edward Snowden told the world that the U.S. government had been spying on its own citizens to an unsuspected degree. The National Security Agency, Snowden informed a British newspaper, had for years been accumulating data on routine phone calls made by ordinary citizens who were not suspected of any wrongdoing. Public reaction was swift and loud, with some arguing the government had gone to unwarranted lengths, breaching its citizens' privacy, while others claimed any and all steps necessary to uncover terrorist plots were defensible. Snowden, who made his revelations from Hong Kong, then fled to Russia seeking asylum.

Our lives are framed by our relationships with many different organizations and institutions.

Each aspect of this event reveals the relationship between us as individuals and the different organizations and institutions that frame our lives, such as our local and national governments. These organizations can exist only with willing members. When groups of individuals begin to question the authority and rationality of the bureaucracies that govern them, they may voice concern about, seek to change, or even rebel against them. Social order cannot be maintained if citizens refuse to adhere to society's shared laws and norms. How do governments, as institutions, react?

We've seen how technology and globalization facilitate the global flow of information, for instance, fundamentally altering the way we communicate. But this nearly instantaneous dissemination of ideas has become a bonanza for everyone, including revolutionaries, rioters, potential terrorists, and even elected governments. For instance, revelations that swiftly followed Snowden's initial leak suggested the United States had also been secretly conducting extensive monitoring of the communications of its European Union allies. Some governments, such as the United Kingdom's after a 2011 series of violent riots in London, have considered shutting down digital communication during public disturbances. Other countries, such as China, Syria, and Iran, routinely exert censorship power over their citizens' use of the Internet. Such barriers to the flow of information, as well as efforts such as Snowden's to overcome them, are of profound interest to sociologists, public figures, and social activists alike.

At the time of this writing, Snowden was marooned at the Moscow airport while he negotiated with several Latin American countries for asylum. Meanwhile the United States pressured its allies to deny him entry so he could be arrested and tried under espionage laws for revealing classified information. •

GL🌐BALIZATION

Violence against Women in India

India and much of the world were galvanized by the horrific gang rape and death of a 23-year-old Indian female medical student in New Delhi in December 2012.

The woman and a male friend had been to the movies and were seeking a ride when a bus pulled over and they were waved on board. The couple had been tricked into believing that it was a public bus. Six men, including the driver and another posing as a conductor, were out for a joy ride. The woman was harassed and her companion was beaten with a metal rod. The woman was then repeatedly raped, and she was penetrated by the metal rod as the bus circled the city. Eventually, the naked couple was dumped by the side of a highway on the outskirts of the city (Mandhana and Trivedi 2012). The woman survived for almost two weeks but then died as a result of internal injuries.

The case brought attention to a broader pattern of murder and other forms of violence against women in India, including killings over dowry disputes, sexual violence, family conflicts, and discriminatory treatment of both infant girls and elderly women (Harris 2013). Sexual harassment is common and rape is a daily occurrence in New Delhi and elsewhere in India.

This rape of the medical student was followed a month later by what was apparently a well-planned attack in the north Indian state of Punjab. A woman was assaulted after accepting a motorcycle ride from the driver of a bus on which she had been riding. He took her to a nearby village, where she

The death of a rape victim in India drew the world's attention to a widespread pattern of sexual harassment and violence against women there. Is this an Indian problem?

himself, the conductor, and four other men (Timmons and Kumar 2013).

One woman who had lived in New Delhi for 24 years described her experiences: "I wore clothes that were two sizes too large. . . . The steady thrum of whistles, catcalls, hisses, sexual innuendos and open threats continued. Packs of men . . . would thrust their pelvises at female passersby . . . In my office . . . at the doctor's office, even at a house party—I couldn't escape the intimidation (Faleiro 2013).

While violence against women has a long history in India, as well as in many other places in the world, it has been fueled

who blame their failures on the success of women (Harris 2013).

Recent rapes have attracted global attention and spurred protests and demonstrations in India (Timmons and Gottipati 2012). It remains to be seen whether anything changes, and whether Indian women will become less subject to rape and other forms of sexual violence and harassment.

Think About It

What cultural forces contribute to an atmosphere in which rape is so commonplace? What economic forces might also be contributing to this social problem in India? What needs to happen for rape and other

DIGITAL LIVING

Gender and the Internet

Sociologists interested in the early, male-dominated Internet wondered whether it allowed people to be free of ascribed statuses and identities such as gender and race (Hornsby 2013: 61–64). For example, users of MUDs ("multiuser dungeons") freely selected their name, their gender, and even their species. In *Life on the Screen*, Sherry Turkle (1995: 10) argued that identity in cyberspace may be "decentered, multiple and fragmented" and that cyberspace plays a prominent role in "eroding boundaries." Many theorists thought "gender" would be a category that would erode in cyberspace (Stone 1991).

In time, the Internet started to include equal numbers of women, and users not necessarily interested in technology but who simply wanted to use technology to socialize, to shop, and to interact. As a result, our understanding of how gender online interacts with gender offline changed. The rise of sites such as Facebook, which require people to use their real names and make it easy to post many pictures of themselves, has made gender even more prominent.

Most current research finds that women and men tend to replicate certain offline gender patterns online. Women who tend to do most of the work of kinship and socializing tend to do so online as well, and women are prominent users of social networking sites. Women interacted more

Why doesn't gender disappear in the online environment?

with their close friends and family whereas men were more likely to be searching for other people. This reflects gender patterns we see in the offline world.

Women and men portray themselves differently online, and women are rewarded for posting sexualized photographs of themselves. Female students are more likely than males to have private profiles (Lewis et al. 2011). It looks like cyberspace does not completely free us from gender, after all, and that life on the screen looks somewhat like life off the screen.

SOURCE: Printed with the permission of Zeynep Tufekci.

Think About It

Are you surprised that early predictions about the likely users of the Internet were proven wrong? What social factors drew women online in such unexpected numbers? Why do you think men's and women's different patterns of communication and social interaction in the real world have simply migrated to the Internet essentially unchanged? Could things have been different?

PUBLIC SOCIOLOGY

Andrew Cherlin on Public Sociology, in His Own Words

I have written for, and spoken to, the print and electronic media about family and demographic issues since I took a job as an assistant professor of sociology at Johns Hopkins University in the late 1970s. . . .

To write for newspapers . . . I had to learn how to (1) engage the reader's interest, (2) make a single point, and (3) present my interpretation, all in about 700 words. I also had to be willing to accept failure. During my career, I have submitted more than 20 op-ed pieces to the *New York Times*, and the editors have accepted nine of them. That's actually a good batting average . . .

My early newspaper and magazine pieces led to telephone calls from reporters who wanted a quote from an academic expert for a story they were writing. Here I had to develop another skill: how to say

something that helps the reader understand the topic in 25 words or less. It's harder than you might think to get to the heart of an issue in a sentence or two.

I have found that print (and now online) reporters can usually be trusted to put my remarks in the proper context. Many reporters cover family and demographic issues day after day, and they become quite knowledgeable. . . . Television, however, is another story. Typically, a harried producer who rarely covers the family will be given an assignment at 10:00 a.m., call me at 10:30, send a crew to film me by 2:00, and then splice five or ten seconds of my remarks into a piece that will run on the evening news at 6:30. Sometimes the producer will include nothing if the piece has to be shortened at the last minute. I often feel used and discarded by television,

in contrast to my generally positive experiences with print, online, and radio media.

Overall, though, my work with the media has served me well. It has allowed me to place my ideas before a broad audience. It has also expanded the reach of my academic work.

SOURCE: Printed with the permission of Andrew Cherlin.

Think About It

Is there a need for sociologists who study the family, as Andrew Cherlin does, to share their ideas and findings directly with the public as well as with their peers? What do family members gain from such exposure to public sociology? What about legislators and policy makers on issues affecting the family?

◀ ***Public Sociology*** boxes convincingly demonstrate that sociology is more than an academic discipline—it has tangible, real-world effects on our lives. Several are contributed by notable sociologists, who provide first-hand accounts of their commitment to public sociology.

▶ ***Active Sociology*** exercises focus on Ritzer's definition of a *prosumer* as someone who combines the acts of consumption and production. *Prosumption* happens most often online, so each chapter's exercise asks the student to investigate a particular aspect of a popular interactive website, such as Facebook, Twitter, Trip Advisor, Ancestry.com, Etsy, WebMD, YouTube, or Change.org, and respond to a specific set of thought-provoking questions about the process of participating there. These innovative exercises can serve as chapter assignments or class discussion starters.

ACTIVE SOCIOLOGY

How Good Are Your Impression Management Skills?

How do you use your own social media pages (Facebook, Twitter, Pinterest) to manage impressions in the minds of others? How do you present yourself? Do an analysis of the content of the photographs, status updates, links, and comments on one of your social media pages. What do these items say about you?

Posted content	What I think it says about me
Photographs	
Status updates	
Links	
Comments	

Identify two or three general themes, based on your analysis of your content. Then consider the following:

1. What status do you possess on the site, and what corresponding roles do you perform?

2. Where/how did you learn these things (that is, who or what were important *agents of socialization*)?

3. How does this page represent your *front stage*? How is your *back stage* different from the way you've presented yourself on the website?

▶ **Marginal glossary** definitions allow students to easily reference and master key terms.

globalization "A transplanetary *process* or set of *processes* involving increasing *liquidity* and the growing multidirectional *flows* of people, objects, places and information as well as the *structures* they encounter and create that are *barriers* to, or *expedite*, those flows" (Ritzer 2010c).

consumption The process by which people obtain goods and services.

consumer culture A culture in which the core ideas and material objects relate to consumption and in which consumption is a primary source of meaning in life.

RESISTANCE WORLDWIDE

Protests have grown in number, significance, and impact around the globe. Europeans rallied against government austerity, women in India marched against widespread sexual aggression toward women and girls, and citizens challenged corruption in China and Russia. In Brazil, even soccer fans protested the government's lavish spending on the World Cup as schools and hospitals fell into neglect. Time will tell of the impact of these demonstrations.

▲ Chilean riot police arrest a student protestor in Santiago. Students say the government is using the state education system for profiteering.

▲ Riot police in Athens (left) clash with antigovernment protestors opposed to the government's austerity plans. Police restrain Indian student protestors (right) angered by the recent rape and murder of a young college student.

▲ Amsterdam's gay community depicts Russian president Vladimir Putin in makeup in a protest against Russia's stringently enforced laws against homosexuality.

◀ In the heart of Brazil's Amazon region, some 200 peasants, including this woman carrying her child, used bows and arrows against police with tear gas and dogs in a vain protest against eviction from a privately owned tract of land.

THINKING ABOUT SOCIOLOGY

1. Are social movements and mass protests inextricably linked? Or can one occur without the other?

2. Have you ever participated, or would you participate, in a public protest? Do you feel it is an effective way of stating opposition or accomplishing change? Why or why not?

3. Essay question: The world faces a number of global threats, including overpopulation, climate change, and food and water shortages, whose impact will be serious but difficult to forecast with precision. Are mass protests an effective way to bring about global government action to reduce the impact of these events? If so, explain why and what they would accomplish, and if not, propose and defend the course of action you recommend.

▲ Evocative and visually stimulating **photo essays** at several places in the text use contemporary scenes to present sociological meditations on the social transformations wrought by the fast-food industry (pages 96–97), work in a global world (pages 218–219), "cathedrals of consumption" (pages 376–377), and protests and revolutions worldwide (pages 436–437). Each is accompanied by a new set of thoughtful discussion questions for use in class or as assignments.

ASK YOURSELF

What would your life be like in a postconsumption age? In what ways might it be better? Worse? Why?

◀ New *Ask Yourself* questions, distributed throughout the chapters, invite students to pause and reflect critically on their reading and its application to their own experience. These questions can also serve as discussion starters or in-class assignments.

▶ New *Checkpoint* summary tables conclude each major topic in the chapter. These offer students a well-organized recap of the major points for a quick interim review and comprehension check.

CHECKPOINT 1.1		MAJOR SOCIAL CHANGES SOCIOLOGISTS HAVE STUDIED
Time period	**Major social changes**	**Related issues of interest to sociologists**
Eighteenth and nineteenth centuries	Industrial Revolution	Rise of factories and blue-collar work; relationships between industry, the state, and the family.
Mid-twentieth century	Postindustrial age	White-collar work, bureaucracies, growth of the service sector.
Twenty-first century	Information age	Participation of women in the workforce, growth of unpaid labor, effects of computer technology on society and individuals.

▶ **Maps** provide geographical context and data on the global issue at hand.

▼ Dozens of appealing and thoughtfully captioned **photos** throughout the chapters support and demonstrate sociological ideas. These colorful images are drawn from a wide range of subjects to which today's students can easily relate. Many photos are new to this edition; all the captions are new and most now include a critical thinking question.

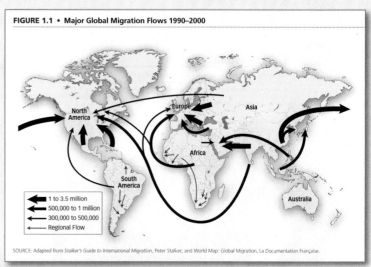

FIGURE 1.1 • Major Global Migration Flows 1990–2000

1 to 3.5 million
500,000 to 1 million
300,000 to 500,000
Regional Flow

SOURCE: Adapted from *Stalker's Guide to International Migration*, Peter Stalker; and World Map: Global Migration, La Documentation Française.

Jeri (left) and Amy Andrews holding their marriage license in Seattle after Washington state legalized same-sex matrimony in December 2012. Do you think the ability to marry is, on balance, a benefit to gays and lesbians, or a surrender to conformity?

The Hindu Holi festival, or the festival of colors, occurs in the spring and celebrates the love of Krishna and Radha.

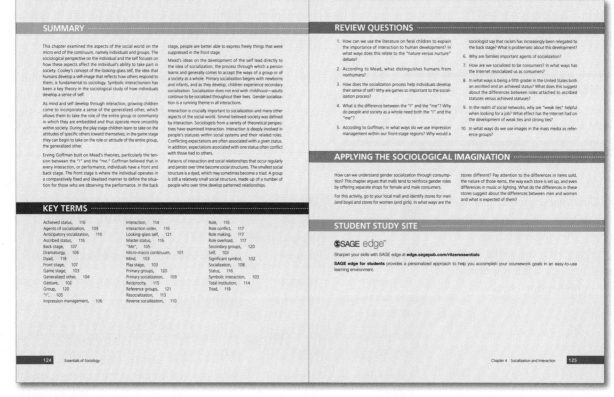

SUMMARY

This chapter examined the aspects of the social world on the micro end of the continuum, namely individuals and groups. The sociological perspective on the individual and the self focuses on how these aspects affect the individual's ability to take part in society. Cooley's concept of the looking-glass self, the idea that humans develop a self-image that reflects how others respond to them, is fundamental to sociology. Symbolic interactionism has been a key theory in the sociological study of how individuals develop a sense of self.

As mind and self develop through interaction, growing children come to incorporate a sense of the generalized other, which allows them to take the role of the entire group or community in which they are embedded and thus operate more smoothly within society. During the play stage children learn to take on the attitudes of specific others toward themselves; in the game stage they can begin to take on the role or attitude of the entire group, the generalized other.

Erving Goffman built on Mead's theories, particularly the tension between the "I" and the "me." Goffman believed that in every interaction, or performance, individuals have a front and back stage. The front stage is where the individual operates in a comparatively fixed and idealized manner to define the situation for those who are observing the performance. In the back

stage, people are better able to express freely things that were suppressed in the front stage.

Mead's ideas on the development of the self lead directly to the idea of socialization, the process through which a person learns and generally comes to accept the ways of a group or of a society as a whole. Primary socialization begins with newborns and infants, and as they develop, children experience secondary socialization. Socialization does not end with childhood—adults continue to be socialized throughout their lives. Gender socialization is a running theme in all interactions.

Interaction is crucially important to socialization and many other aspects of the social world. Simmel believed society was defined by interaction. Sociologists from a variety of theoretical perspectives have examined interaction. Interaction is deeply involved in people's statuses within social systems and their related roles. Conflicting expectations are often associated with a given status. In addition, expectations associated with one status often conflict with those tied to others.

Patterns of interaction and social relationships that occur regularly and persist over time become social structures. The smallest social structure is a dyad, which may sometimes become a triad. A group is still a relatively small social structure, made up of a number of people who over time develop patterned relationships.

REVIEW QUESTIONS

1. How can we use the literature on feral children to explain the importance of interaction to human development? In what ways does this relate to the "nature versus nurture" debate?

2. According to Mead, what distinguishes humans from nonhumans?

3. How does the socialization process help individuals develop their sense of self? Why are games so important to the socialization process?

4. What is the difference between the "I" and the "me"? Why do people and society as a whole need both the "I" and the "me"?

5. According to Goffman, in what ways do we use impression management within our front-stage regions? Why would a

sociologist say that racism has increasingly been relegated to the back stage? What is problematic about this development?

6. Why are families important agents of socialization?

7. How are we socialized to be consumers? In what ways has the Internet resocialized us as consumers?

8. In what ways is being a fifth grader in the United States both an ascribed and an achieved status? What does this suggest about the differences between roles attached to ascribed statuses versus achieved statuses?

9. In the realm of social networks, why are "weak ties" helpful when looking for a job? What effect has the Internet had on the development of weak ties and strong ties?

10. In what ways do we use images in the mass media as reference groups?

APPLYING THE SOCIOLOGICAL IMAGINATION

How can we understand gender socialization through consumption? This chapter argues that malls tend to reinforce gender roles by offering separate shops for female and male consumers.

For this activity, go to your local mall and identify stores for men (and boys) and stores for women (and girls). In what ways are the

stores different? Pay attention to the differences in items sold, the nature of those items, the way each store is set up, and even differences in music or lighting. What do the differences in these stores suggest about the differences between men and women and what is expected of them?

KEY TERMS

Achieved status, 116
Agents of socialization, 109
Anticipatory socialization, 110
Ascribed status, 116
Back stage, 107
Dramaturgy, 106
Dyad, 118
Front stage, 107
Game stage, 103
Generalized other, 104
Gesture, 102
Group, 120
"I", 105
Impression management, 106

Interaction, 114
Interaction order, 116
Looking-glass self, 121
Master status, 116
"Me", 105
Micro-macro continuum, 101
Mind, 103
Play stage, 103
Primary groups, 120
Primary socialization, 109
Reciprocity, 115
Reference groups, 121
Resocialization, 113
Reverse socialization, 110

Role, 116
Role conflict, 117
Role making, 117
Role overload, 117
Secondary groups, 120
Self, 103
Significant symbol, 102
Socialization, 108
Status, 116
Symbolic interaction, 103
Total institution, 114
Triad, 118

STUDENT STUDY SITE

$SAGE edge™

Sharpen your skills with SAGE edge at **edge.sagepub.com/ritzeressentials**

SAGE edge for students provides a personalized approach to help you accomplish your coursework goals in an easy-to-use learning environment.

▲ End-of-chapter features—**chapter summaries**, **key terms**, *Review Questions*, and *Applying the Sociological Imagination* exercises—allow readers the opportunity to think critically about the concepts they've learned in the chapter and take their learning beyond the classroom and the book.

INTERACTIVE EBOOK

An **Interactive eBook** version of *Essentials of Sociology* integrates chapter content with rich multimedia. In addition to a full electronic textbook, students can click on multimedia icons to watch video, listen to audio, read interesting articles, and much more, which creates an exciting interactive learning experience for sociologists in training.

ONLINE RESOURCES

$SAGE edge™

SAGE edge offers a robust online environment featuring an impressive array of tools and resources for review, study, and further exploration, keeping both instructors and students on the cutting edge of teaching and learning. **SAGE edge** content is open access and available on demand. Learning and teaching have never been easier!

SAGE EDGE FOR STUDENTS

www.edge.sagepub.com/ritzeressentials

SAGE edge for Students provides a personalized approach to help students accomplish their coursework goals in an easy-to-use online learning environment.

- Mobile-friendly **eFlashcards** strengthen understanding of key terms and concepts.

- Mobile-friendly practice **quizzes** allow for independent assessment by students of their mastery of course material.

- A customized online **action plan** allows students to individualize their learning experience and take advantage of the resources available to them.

- **Chapter summaries** with **learning objectives** reinforce the most important material.

- **Interactive exercises** and meaningful web links facilitate student use of internet resources, further exploration of topics, and responses to critical thinking questions.

- **EXCLUSIVE!** Access to full-text **SAGE journal articles** have been carefully selected to support and expand on the concepts presented in each chapter.

- **Reference links** pulled directly from SAGE Handbooks and Encyclopedias allow for even more in-depth research and reading.

- **Research | Social Impact links** direct students to contemporary and research-based magazine articles from the award-winning *Pacific Standard* magazine.

- Well-known **CQ Researcher Articles** are also available for even more researched resources.

- Multimedia content such as **video** and **audio** links help engage students' senses.

Journal article links

Reference links

Research | Social Impact links

CQ Researcher articles

Video links

Audio links

SAGE EDGE FOR INSTRUCTORS

Found at **www.edge.sagepub.com/ritzeressentials**

SAGE edge for Instructors supports teaching by making it easy to integrate quality content and create a rich learning environment for students.

- **Test banks**, available in both **Microsoft® Word®** and **Respondus**, provide a diverse range of pre-written options as well as the opportunity to edit any question and/or insert personalized questions to effectively assess students' progress and understanding.

- **Sample course syllabi** for semester and quarter courses provide suggested models for structuring one's course.

- Editable, chapter-specific **PowerPoint® slides** offer complete flexibility for creating a multimedia presentation.

- **EXCLUSIVE!** Access to full-text **SAGE journal articles** have been carefully selected to support and expand on the concepts presented in each chapter to encourage students to think critically.

- **Lecture notes** and **chapter summaries** highlight key concepts chapter-by-chapter to ease preparation for lectures and class discussions.

- **Discussion questions** help launch classroom conversation by prompting students to engage with the material and reinforcing important content.

- **Chapter exercises** invite lively and stimulating activities to be used in and outside of the classroom for groups or individuals.

- **In-text visuals** such as tables and figures are provided online to use in teaching aids such as PowerPoint® slides, handouts, and lecture notes.

- **Reference links** pulled directly from SAGE Handbooks and Encyclopedias allow for even more in-depth research and reading.

- **Research | Social Impact links** direct students to contemporary and research-based magazine articles from the award-winning *Pacific Standard* magazine.

- Well-known **CQ Researcher Articles** are also available for even more researched resources.

- Web resources from interesting **videos** to attention-getting **audio links** engage students' senses.

ACKNOWLEDGMENTS

I need to begin with my friends for decades, and co-authors of a previous introductory textbook, Kenneth C. W. Kammeyer and Norman R. Yetman. That book went through seven editions, the last of which was published in 1997. It was most useful to me in this text in helping to define various sociological concepts that have changed little over the years. I have also been able to build on discussions of many issues covered in that text. However, because of the passage of a decade and a half in sociology and in the social world (an eternity in both), as well as the innumerable changes in them, this text has comparatively little in common with the earlier one. Nonetheless, my perspective on sociology was strongly shaped by that book and the many insights and ideas provided by my friends and co-authors both before, during, and in the many years after writing that book.

I had worked with Becky Smith as a developmental editor on previous projects. She had done a great job with those books and she continued her good work on the first ten chapters of this book. As time grew short, the work of developmental editor was picked up by Colin Grover who finished the job in a timely and excellent fashion.

Many thanks to Olivia Weber-Stenis who amiably and capably managed the production of this book, as well as to Melinda Masson who handled the copyediting

Several undergraduate and graduate students at the University of Maryland made important contributions to this project. I would especially like to thank Chih-Chin Chen who worked long, hard and good-naturedly on various aspects of the book, especially the numerous figures to be found throughout the text. Another undergraduate, Michelle McDonough, also made important contributions to the book. Paul Dean, at the time a graduate student, but now Assistant Professor at Ohio Wesleyan, made innumerable contributions to the text, especially those aspects of it dealing with globalization. Nathan Jurgenson contributed his great expertise and experience to the parts of the text dealing with the Internet.

I would like to thank Professors Jack Levin, Andrew Cherlin, and Robert J. Brulle for writing boxes dealing with their own experiences in doing public sociology. Thanks also to contributions from P. J. Rey, William Yagatich, Jillet Sam, Zeynep Tufekci, and Margaret Austin Smith. Also to be thanked for writing first drafts of parts of chapters are Professors William Carbonaro (Education), Deric Shannon (Politics), and Lester Kurtz (Religion). A special thanks to Professor Peter Kivisto who made especially important and numerous contributions to the Essentials edition of this book. I'm especially thankful for his work on the Religion and Education chapter.

At SAGE Publications, I am especially grateful for Vice President and Editorial Director Michele Sordi's confidence in, and support for, the project. She agreed from the beginning to spend and do whatever was necessary to make this a first-class introductory sociology text. As you can see from the finished project, she was true to her word. Michele also worked closely with me in an editorial capacity to help get the project through some of its most difficult periods. Michele was a positive force and upbeat presence throughout the writing of this book and I am deeply grateful for who she is and what she has done. Brenda Carter, Executive Editorial Director at SAGE, took over Michele's role in this Essentials edition, and performed it with same level of expertise, good humor and good sense (plus she got me prime seats to a game in New York involving my beloved Yankees). New to SAGE, as well as the Essentials edition, is Jeff Lasser, Sociology Publisher, and he proved to be not only easy to work with, but a sage (pun intended) advisor on many on many of its key dimensions.

I also need to thank Nathan Davidson at SAGE. The production of the first edition of this book really took off when he took over its day-to-day management. We worked together closely for about a year on virtually every aspect of the final project. Before Nathan came on board I was in danger of being overwhelmed by the demands of finishing this book, but he provided the hard work, great organizational abilities and good sense that helped me complete it and finish it on time. Nathan continued to manage the Essentials edition of this book and, if possible, he did an even better job. While his imprint is found throughout this book, it is especially notable in the selection of an excellent set of photographs, especially the faces from across the globe that serve as openers for each chapter.

Also to be thanked in the Essentials edition is Elisa Adams who as a consultant was instrumental in creating various features of the book including Checkpoints, Ask Yourself questions, Think About It questions, photo captions, text for the photo essays, revised/expanded Active Sociology features (originally written for the first edition by Lisa Munoz), and tightening opening vignettes and chapter summaries. Sheri Gilbert is to be thanked for her work on the many permissions needed for material included in this edition. Gail Buschman did great work on the interior design and the cover for the Essentials edition of this book. Thanks to Lauren Habib and Rachael Leblond, Digital Content Editors, for their work on the ancillary materials and ebook resources.

I am particularly grateful to the following reviewers who provided enormously helpful feedback for this edition: Augustine Aryee, Fitchburg State College; William Danaher, College of Charleston; Colleen Eren, Hunter College; Tammie Foltz, Des Moines Area Community College; Laura Gibson, Brescia University; Edward Glick, Des Moines Area Community College; Colin Goff, University of Winnipeg; Kristi Hagen, Coconino Community College; Marta Henrikson, Central New Mexico Community College; Hanna Jokinen-Gordon, Florida State University; Alan Kemp, Pierce College; Lloyd Klein, CUNY York College; Ke Liang, Baruch College; Wade Luquet, Gwynedd-Mercy College; Kim MacInnis, Bridgewater State College; Mahgoub Mahmoud, Tennessee State University – Nashville; Setsuko Matsuzawa, College of Wooster; Christine McClure, Cape Cod Community College; Hosik Min, Norwich University; Gail Mosby, West Virginia State University; Megan Nielsen, Midland Lutheran College; Nirmal Niroula, Franklin University; David O'Donnell, Vermilion Community College; Godpower Okereke, Texas A & M University-Texarkana; Dan Poole, Salt Lake Community College; Teresa Roach, Florida State University; Desiree' Robertson, Mid South Community College; Amy Ruedisueli, Tidewater Community College; Luceal Simon, Wayne State University; Nicolas Simon, Eastern Connecticut State University; Rhianan Smith, Carroll College; Jennifer Solomon, Winthrop University; Paul Sturgis, Truman State University; Daniel Suh, Orange Coast College; Mary Texeira, California State University-San Bernardino; Miriam Thompson, Northwest Vista College; Okori Uneke, Winston-Salem State University; Paul Van Auken, University of Wisconsin-Oshkosh; Jonathan Van Wieren, Grand Valley State University; John Vlot, Lehigh Carbon Community College; Russell Ward, Maysville Community Tech College; Matthew Vox, Covenant College; Bernadette White, Ohlone College; Matthew Wilkinson, Coastal Carolina University; George Wilson, University of Miami ; Melisa Wingfield, Wichita Area Tech College; Elizabeth Wissinger, Borough Manhattan Community College; Robert Wonser, College of the Canyons; Susan Wortmann, Nebraska Wesleyan University.

I'm also grateful to the following reviewers, advisory board members, and class testers who provided feedback for the first edition: Sophia Krzys Acord, University of Florida; Kristian Alexander, University of Utah; Lori J. Anderson, Tarleton State University; Lester Andrist, University of Maryland; Meg Austin Smith, University of Maryland; Denise Bielby, University of California, Santa Barbara; Donna Bird, University of Southern Maine; David Daniel Bogumil, California State University, Northridge; Craig Boylstein, Coastal Carolina University; Yvonne Braun, University of Oregon; Robert Brenneman, Saint Michael's College; Rebecca Brooks, Ohio Northern University; Bradley Campbell, California State University, Los Angeles; Brenda Chaney, Ohio State University, Marion; Langdon Clough, Community College of Rhode Island, Flan; Jessica Collett, University of Notre Dame; Keri Diggins, Scottsdale Community College; Scott Dolan, University at Albany, State University of New York; Brenda Donelan, Northern State University; Gili Drori, Stanford University; Kathy Edwards, Ashland Community and Technical College; Pam Folk, North Hennepin Community College; Tammie Foltz, Des Moines Area Community College; Douglas Forbes, U.W., Stevens Point; Sarah Michele Ford, Buffalo State College; S. Michael Gaddis, University of North Carolina, Chapel Hill; Deborah Gambs, Borough Manhattan, Community College-CUNY; Gilbert Geis, University of California, Irvine; Bethany Gizzi, Monroe Community College; Barry Goetz, Western Michigan University; Roberta Goldberg, Trinity Washington University; Elizabeth Grant, Chabot College; Kristi Hagen, Chippewa Valley Technical College; James Harris, Mountain View College; Cedric Herring, University of Illinois, Chicago; Joy Honea, Montana State University Billings; John C. Horgan, Concordia University-Wisconsin; Gabe Ignatow, University of North Texas; Mike

Itashiki, Collin County Community College & University of North Texas; Wesley Jennings, University of South Florida; James R. Johnson, Southwest Indian Polytechnic Institute; Faye Jones, Mississippi Community College; Carolyn Kapinus, Ball State University; Mary Karpos, Vanderbilt University; Zeynep Kilic, University of Alaska, Anchorage; Jeanne Kimpel, Fordham University; Chuck Kusselow, River Valley Community College; Richard Lachmann, University at Albany—SUNY; Barbara LaPilusa, Montgomery College; Erin Leahey, University of Arizona; Maria Licuanan, Kent State University; John Lie, University of California, Berkeley; Cameron D. Lippard, Appalachian State University; David Lopez, California State University, Northridge; Jeanne M. Lorentzen, Northern Michigan University; Garvey Lundy, Montgomery County Community College; Aaron Major, University at Albany—SUNY; Vanessa Martinez, Holyoke Community College; Suzanne L. Maughan, University of Nebraska at Kearney; Patrick McGrady, Florida State University; Paul McLean, Rutgers University; Jeff Mullis, Emory University; Megan Nielsen, Midland University; Charles Norman, Indiana State University; Donna Philips, Bluegrass Community and Technical College; Alex Piquero, University of Texas, Dallas; Dwaine Plaza, Oregon State University; Winnie Poster, Washington University, Saint Louis; Malcolm Potter, Los Angeles Pierce College; Ekaterin Ralston, Concordia University, St. Paul; Rashawn Ray, University of California, Berkeley; P. J. Rey, University of Maryland; Adrienne Riegle, Iowa State University; David N. Sanders, Angelo State University; Mary Satian, Northern Virginia Community College; Dave Schall, Milwaukee Area Technical College; Elizabeth D. Scheel, Saint Cloud State University; Jerald Schrimsher, Southern Illinois University, Carbondale; Sandra Schroer, Muskingum University; Howard Schuman, University of Michigan; Frank Scruggs, National-Louis University; Megan Seely, Sierra College; Vincent Serravallo, Rochester Institute of Technology; Mark Sherry, The University of Toledo; Amber Shimel, Liberty University; Kristen Shorette, University of California, Irvine; Julia Spence, Johnson County Community College; Steven Stack, Wayne State University; Richard Sweeney, Modesto Junior College; Joyce Tang, CUNY Queens College; Rae Taylor, Loyola University New Orleans; Ha Thao, MiraCosta College; Santos Torres, CSU, Sacramento; Richard Tweksbury, University of Louisville; Mark Vermillion, Wichita State University; Russell Ward, Maysville Community and Technical College; Jeff Wilhelms, Rutgers University; Elizabeth Wissinger, Borough of Manhattan Community College; Rowan Wolf, Portland Community College; Susan Wortmann, Nebraska Wesleyan University; Kassia Wosick, New Mexico State University; Yuping Zhang, Lehigh University; Grace Auyang, University of Cincinnati, Raymond Walters College; Libby Barland, Lynn University; John Batsie, Parkland College; Cari Beecham, Columbia College, Chicago; Berch Berberoglu, University of Nevada, Reno; Miriam Boeri, Kennesaw State University; Ann Bullis, College of Southern Nevada; Josh Carreiro, University of Massachusetts; Susan Claxton, Georgia Highlands College; Evan Cooper, Farmingdale State College; Julie Cowgill, Oklahoma City University; David Embrick, Loyola University, Chicago; Heather Feldhaus, Bloomsburg University; Rosalind Fisher, University of West Florida; Karie Francis, University of Las Vegas, Nevada ; Joshua Gamson, University of San Francisco; Robert Garot, John Jay College of Criminal Justice; Matthew Green, College of Dupage; Gary Heidinger, Roane State Community College; Marta Henriksen, Central New Mexico Community College; Anthony Hickey, Western Carolina University; Jeanne Humble, Bluegrass Community Technical College; Dai Ito, Georgia State University ; Mike F. Jessup, Taylor University; Ellis Jones, Holy Cross University; Lloyd Klein, York College; Steve Lang, Laguardia Community College; Dongxiao Liu, Texas A&M University; Tara McKay, University of California, Los Angeles; Rohald Meneses, University of California, Pembroke; Eric Mielants, Fairfield University; Ami Moore, University of Northern Texas; Amanda Moras, Sacred Heart University ; Brigitte Neary, University of South Carolina, Spartanburg; Michael O'Connor, Hawkeye Community College; Aurea Osgood, Winona State; Johanna Pabst, Boston College; Frank Roberts, Mount San Antonio College; Lauren Ross, Temple University; Janet Ruane, Montclair State University; Matthew Sargent, Madison Area Technical College; Lynn Schlesinger, SUNY College, Plattsburgh; Sarah Scruggs, Oklahoma City University; Meena Sharma, Henry Ford Community College; Nicole Shortt, Florida Atlantic University, Boca; Chris Solario, Chemeketa Community College; William Staudenmeier, Eureka College; Kevin Sullivan, Bergen Community College; Donna Sullivan, Marshall University; Jaita Talukdar, Loyola University, New Orleans; Linda Treiber, Kennesaw State University; PJ Verrecchia, York College; Debra Welkley, California State University, Sacramento; Beau Weston, Centre College; George Wilson, University of Miami; Julie Withers, Butte College; Kassia Wosick-Correa, New Mexico State University; James Wright, Chattanooga Technical Community College; Paul Calarco, Hudson Valley Community College; Joyce Clapp, University of North Carolina, Greensboro; Tina Granger, Nicholls State University; Dan Gurash, Fairmont State University; Lee Hamilton, New Mexico State University; AJ Jacobs, East Carolina University; Barry Kass, Orange

County Community College; Stacy Keogh, University of Montana; Crystal Lupo, Auburn University; Tiffany Parsons, University of West Georgia; Lindsey Prowell Myers, Ohio State University; Michael Steinhour, Purdue University; Sheryl Switaj, Schoolcraft College; Ruth Thompson-Miller, University of Dayton; Deanna Trella, Northern Michigan University; Kristie Vise, Northern Kentucky University; Wendy Wiedenhoft Murphy, John Carroll University; Jane Young, Luzerne County Community College.

Chief Raoni before a protest at the Brazilian Congress seeking land, mining, and water rights for native Indians. A well-known defender of the rainforest, Raoni wears a traditional wooden plate stretching his lower lip. Sociologists ask how individuals like Raoni, groups like Brazil's Indians, and institutions like the government affect one another.

AN INTRODUCTION TO SOCIOLOGY IN THE GLOBAL AGE

1

LEARNING OBJECTIVES

1 Identify major social changes since the 1880s studied by sociologists.

2 Explain why sociologists today focus on trends in globalization and consumption.

3 Describe what we mean by the McDonaldization of society.

4 Explain sociology's approach to studying social life, including using the sociological imagination and examining the relationship between private troubles and public issues.

5 Differentiate between sociology's two possible purposes, science and social reform.

6 Evaluate the ways in which sociological knowledge differs from common sense.

In December 2010, street demonstrations, labor strikes, and other acts of civil resistance swept through the small North African nation of Tunisia. The demonstrators met strong resistance from the Tunisian government. Nevertheless, their protests continued into 2011, eventually resulting in the overthrow of President Ben Ali after 23 years in power.

The immediate trigger for the Tunisian protests was the self-immolation of Mohamed Bouazizi, a 26-year-old street vendor who claimed he had long been harassed and humiliated by authorities. Bouazizi set himself on fire before the rural governor's office and died in a burn and trauma center 18 days later without regaining consciousness.

However powerful the public reaction to Bouazizi's death proved to be, the sources underlying both the Tunisian revolution and the Arab Spring—the wave of social unrest and social revolution it inspired throughout the region—sprang

> ## Sociology tries to understand the individual's place in society, and society's effect on the individual.

from far more than a single act of protest. Without considering the social, political, and economic conditions of prerevolution Tunisia, it would be impossible for us to understand why Bouazizi set himself alight, and why thousands of Tunisians and others throughout the Arab world saw his act as an appropriate—and necessary—call for change. The promise of the Arab Spring has yet to be fulfilled—and the mid-2013 overthrow of Egypt's elected Islamist president Mohamed Morsi undid it, at least in part. However, the events that precipitated the unrest remain important to the Middle East, to the world as a whole, to sociology, and to you. One of the goals of this chapter, and this book, is to show you why.

By drawing on modern sociology's 200-year history while looking to the future, sociologists today can find the tools and resources to better understand where we have been, where we are, and, perhaps most importantly, where we are going. Some believe that helping people enact meaningful social change is the true end of sociology. The Tunisian protesters would certainly agree with them.

As an academic discipline, sociology has traditionally tried to understand the place of the individual—even a Tunisian street vendor—within society, and society's effect on the individual. In today's global age, however, social structures like online networks that transcend national boundaries and rapidly changing communication technologies that spread information far and wide have forever altered the ways in which we interact with each other, as well as the societies that shape us. As the world has become increasingly globalized, sociology has developed an increasingly global perspective. ●

One of the most important lessons that you will learn in your study of sociology is that what you think and do as an individual is affected by what is happening around you in groups, organizations, cultures, societies, and the world. This is especially true of social changes, even those that are global in scope and seem at first glance to be remote from you. Take, for example, the trigger of the revolution known as the Arab Spring. In 2010, as described in the introduction to this chapter, Mohamed Bouazizi, a Tunisian street vendor, burned himself to death in full public view. That set in motion a revolution in Tunisia and throughout much of the Middle East. The roots of that dramatic act of protest lay in poverty, high unemployment, an authoritarian government, and political corruption that affected Bouazizi personally. Before his actions, most Tunisians would never have risked their lives to protest against their country's repressive regime. Yet he and tens of thousands of others in other countries in the region did just that. It's likely that your impression of the Arab countries and the majority Muslim population was much different before the Arab Spring than after. You may find yourself feeling a surge of appreciation for democracy or feeling more open than before to learning about Islam or studying the Arabic language. You may even be inspired to take actions yourself in support of the kinds of changes that took place in Tunisia and in other places in the Arab world. In those senses, you and many others have felt the impact of Bouazizi's actions.

A second important sociological lesson is not only that you are affected by events but also that you are capable to some degree of having an impact on large-scale structures and processes. This can be seen as an example of the *butterfly effect* (Lorenz 1995). While generally applied to physical phenomena, the **butterfly effect** is also applicable to social phenomena (Daipha 2012). The idea is that a relatively small change in a specific location can have far-ranging, even global, effects, over both time and distance. For example, the actions of Bouazizi helped lead to the Tunisian revolution, which, in turn, led to street demonstrations and civil war elsewhere in the Arab world including Yemen, Egypt, Libya, and Syria (Kienle 2012;

Noueihed and Warren 2012). The consequences of this series of events were felt at the time and are still unfolding. However, they certainly include the major changes that took place in those societies as well as the possibility of major international political realignments. They could also make for greater or diminished opportunities for personal, social, and business relationships between people in the Arab world and in the West. Perhaps the arc of your life and career will be affected by the upheavals of the Arab Spring. More importantly, it is very possible that actions you take in your lifetime will have wide-ranging, perhaps global, effects.

This example of the relationship between people and larger social realities and changes sets the stage for the definition of the discipline to be introduced in this book: **Sociology** is the systematic study of the ways in which people are affected by, and affect, the social structures and social processes that are associated with the groups, organizations, cultures, societies, and world in which they exist.

THE CHANGING NATURE OF THE SOCIAL WORLD— AND SOCIOLOGY

Sociology deals with very contemporary phenomena, as you have seen, but it also has many longer-term interests because of its deep historical roots. In the fourteenth century, for instance, the Muslim scholar Abdel Rahman Ibn-Khaldun studied various social relationships, including those between politics and economics. Of special importance to the founding of sociology was the eighteenth- and nineteenth-century Industrial Revolution. During this "industrial age," many early sociologists concentrated on factories, the production that took place in those settings, and those who worked there, especially blue-collar, manual workers. Sociologists also came to focus on the relationship between industry and the rest of society including, for example, the state and the family.

By the middle of the twentieth century, manufacturing in the United States was in the early stages of a long decline that continues to this day. (However, manufacturing in other parts of the world, most notably China, is booming.) The United States had moved from the industrial age to the "postindustrial age" (Bell 1973; Leicht and Fitzgerald 2006). In the United States, as

butterfly effect The far-ranging or even global impact of a small change in a specific location, over both time and distance.

sociology The systematic study of the ways in which people are affected by, and affect, the social structures and social processes that are associated with the groups, organizations, cultures, societies, and world in which they exist.

Protests

Manufacturing jobs in the United States have declined in the postindustrial age. Why is industry's place in society a topic of interest to sociologists?

So, too, are the technologies—computers, smartphones—that have greatly increased the productivity of individual workers and altered the nature of their work. Just one of many examples is the current use of computer-assisted technologies to create designs for everything from electric power grids to patterned fabrics rather than drawing them by hand. In fact, it is not just work that has been affected by these new technologies; virtually everyone and everything has been affected by them. One aspect of this new technological world, Google, is so powerful that a media culture scholar has written a book titled *The Googlization of Everything* (Vaidhyanathan 2011). Thus much sociological attention has shifted to the computer and the Internet and to those who work with them (Baym 2010; DiMaggio et al. 2001; Scholz 2013).

The transition from the industrial to the postindustrial and now to the information age has important personal implications. Had you been a man who lived in the industrial age, you would have worked for money (pay), and you would have done so in order to be able to buy what you needed and wanted. Women working in the private sphere were largely uncompensated or compensated at a lower rate, as is often still the case. In the postindustrial age, it is increasingly likely that men and women are willing, or forced, to work for free (Anderson 2009; Ritzer and Jurgenson 2010; Terranova 2013), as in the case of an intern, a blogger, or a contributor to YouTube or Wikipedia. They may hope that such work will eventually have an economic payoff and perhaps even lead to a full-time job. In fact, there are many examples of individuals succeeding after starting out by "giving away" their labor. For example, members of the Los Angeles band OK Go found an audience based on free YouTube videos and then built thriving, well-paying careers.

well as the western world more generally, the center of the economy, and the attention of many sociologists, shifted from the factory to the office. That is, the focus moved from blue-collar manual work to white-collar office work (Mills 1951), as well as to the bureaucracies in which many people worked (Clegg and Lounsbury 2009; Weber [1921] 1968). Also involved was the growth of the service sector of the economy. This sector ranges all the way from high-status service providers such as physicians and lawyers to lower-status house cleaners and those who work behind the counters of fast-food restaurants.

The more recent rise of the "information age" (Castells 2010; David and Millwood 2012) can be seen as a part, or an extension, of the postindustrial age. Knowledge and information are critical in this contemporary epoch.

You may also be willing to perform this free labor because you enjoy it and because much of what is important in your life is, in any case, available free on the Internet. There is no need for you to buy newspapers when blogs are free or to buy CDs or DVDs when music and movies can be streamed or downloaded at no cost or inexpensively from the Internet. A whole range of software is also downloadable

CHECKPOINT 1.1 — MAJOR SOCIAL CHANGES SOCIOLOGISTS HAVE STUDIED

Time period	Major social changes	Related issues of interest to sociologists
Eighteenth and nineteenth centuries	Industrial Revolution	Rise of factories and blue-collar work; relationships between industry, the state, and the family.
Mid-twentieth century	Postindustrial age	White-collar work, bureaucracies, growth of the service sector.
Twenty-first century	Information age	Participation of women in the workforce, growth of unpaid labor, effects of computer technology on society and individuals.

at no cost. While all of this, and much else, is available free of charge, the problem is that the essentials of life—food, shelter, clothing—still cost money, lots of money.

CENTRAL CONCERNS FOR A TWENTY-FIRST-CENTURY SOCIOLOGY

While the social world has been changing dramatically over the last two centuries or so, and sociology has adapted to those changes, sociology has continued to focus on many of its traditional concerns. We have already mentioned industry, production, and work as long-term sociological interests; others include deviance and crime (see Chapter 7), the family (see Chapter 11), and the city (see Chapter 14). Of particular concern to many sociologists has been, and is, the issue of inequality as it affects the poor, racial and ethnic groups, women, and gays and lesbians (see Chapter 8). The bulk of this book will be devoted to these basic sociological topics and concerns. But there will also be a focus on the nontraditional and very contemporary issues of consumption, the digital world, and especially globalization.

GLOBALIZATION

No social change is as important today as globalization since it is affecting all aspects of the social world everywhere on the globe. A date marking the beginning of globalization cannot be given with any precision, and in fact is in great dispute (Ritzer 2010c, 2012). However, the concept of globalization first began to appear in the popular and academic literature around 1990. Today, globalization is a central issue in the social world as a whole as well as in sociology; globalization and talk about it are all around us. In fact, we can be said to be living in the "global age" (Albrow 1996).

A major component of any past or present definition of sociology is "society." There are about 200 societies in the world, including the United States, China, and South Africa. **Society** is a complex pattern of social relationships that is bounded in space and persists over time. It has traditionally been the largest unit of analysis in sociology. However, in the global age, societies are seen as of declining importance (Holton 2011; Meyer, Boli, and Ramirez 1997). This is the case, in part, because there are

The United States heavily patrols its border with Mexico. What influence does this policy have on the ease and volume of flows across that border?

larger transnational and global social structures that are growing in importance. These include the United Nations (UN), the European Union (EU), the Organization of the Petroleum Exporting Countries (OPEC), multinational corporations (MNCs) such as Google and ExxonMobil, and multinational nongovernmental organizations (NGOs) such as Amnesty International. In at least some cases, these transnational structures are becoming more important than individual societies. OPEC, for example, is more important to the rest of the world's well-being than are key member societies such as Abu Dhabi or even Saudi Arabia.

Social processes, like social structures, exist not only at the societal level but also at the global level, and these global processes are increasing in importance. Consider migration (see Chapter 14). People move about, or migrate, within and between societies. For example, many people have moved from the northeastern United States to the west and south, although those historically large migrations slowed dramatically with the Great Recession that began in 2007. However, in the global age, people are increasingly moving between societies (see Figure 1.1), some halfway around the world. Major examples involve people migrating from and through Mexico to the United States (Massey 2003; Ortmeyer and Quinn 2012) and from a number of Islamic societies to the West (Caldwell 2009; Voas and Fleischman 2012).

There have always been such population movements. However, in the global age people generally move around

> **society** A complex pattern of social relationships that is bounded in space and persists over time.

Border Enforcement

FIGURE 1.1 • Major Global Migration Flows 1990–2000

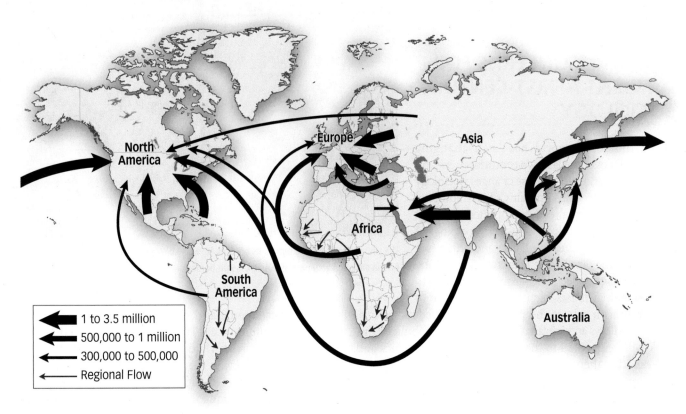

1 to 3.5 million
500,000 to 1 million
300,000 to 500,000
Regional Flow

SOURCE: Adapted from *Stalker's Guide to International Migration*, Peter Stalker; and World Map: Global Migration, La Documentation Française.

the world far more freely and travel much greater distances than ever before. Another way of saying this is that people—and much else—are more "fluid." That is, they move farther, more easily, and more quickly than ever before. The movement of products of all types is also more fluid as a result of the existence of massive container ships, jet cargo planes, and package delivery services such as FedEx and UPS. Even more fluid is the digital "stuff" you buy on the Internet when you download music, movies, and so on. And in the realm of the family, tasks once confined to the home, such as caregiving and housework, have become increasingly fluid as those who can afford to do so often outsource domestic labor (van der Lippe, Frey, and Tsvetkova 2012; Yeates 2009). More generally, that greater fluidity is manifested in the information that flows throughout the world in the blink of an eye as a result of the Internet, e-mail, and social networking sites such as Facebook and Twitter.

These flows can be expedited by structures of various types. For example, the European Union, founded in 1993, is an example of a social structure that serves to ease the flow of citizens between member nations (but not of people living outside the EU). Border restrictions among the 27 EU member nations have been reduced or eliminated completely. Similarly, the creation in 1975 of the euro has

greatly simplified economic transactions among the 17 EU countries that accept it as their currency. Another example is the fact that the continuing free flow of information on the Internet is made possible by an organization called ICANN (Internet Corporation for Assigned Names and Numbers). It handles the Net's underlying infrastructure.

There are also structures that impede various kinds of global flows. National borders, passports and passport controls (Robertson 2010; Torpey 2000, 2012), security checks, and customs controls limit the movement of people throughout the world. Such restrictions were greatly increased in many parts of the world after the terrorist attacks on September 11, 2001. This made global travel and border crossing more difficult and time-consuming. Then there are the even more obvious structures designed to limit the movement of people across borders. Examples include the fences between the United States and Mexico and between Israel and the West Bank, as well as the most recent one between Israel and Egypt, which was completed in 2013. The fences across the Mexican border, and increased border police and patrols, have led unauthorized migrants to take longer and more risky routes into the United States. One result is that more dead bodies are being discovered in the desert that spans the U.S.–Mexico border. The American Civil Liberties Union reports that border deterrence strategies have resulted in the deaths of more than 5,000 Mexican migrants since 1994 (Androff and Tavassoli 2012; Jimenez 2009). There are, of course, many other structural barriers, most notably trade barriers and tariffs, that limit the free movement of goods and services of many kinds.

In sum, **globalization** is defined by increasingly fluid global flows and the structures that expedite and impede those flows. Globalization is certainly increasing, and it brings with it a variety of both positive and negative developments (Ritzer 2010c). On one side, most people throughout the world now have far greater access to goods, services, and information from around the globe than people did during the industrial age. On the other side, a variety of highly undesirable things also flow more easily around the world such as diseases like HIV/AIDS and the adverse effects of climate change (including global warming). Also on the negative side are the flows of such forms of "deviant globalization" as terrorism, sex trafficking, and the black markets for human organs and drugs (Gilman, Goldhammer, and Weber 2011).

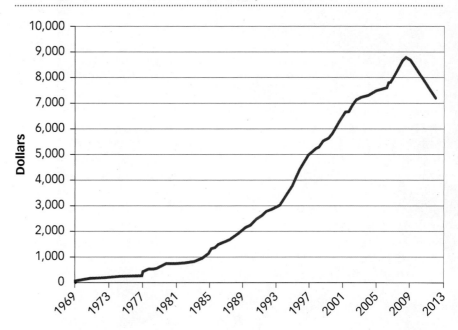

FIGURE 1.2 • U.S. Credit Card Debt, 1969–2012

SOURCE: U.S. Federal Reserve and U.S. Census Bureau.

ASK YOURSELF

Have you ever thought of your Facebook page as part of a global flow of information? In what ways does it actually fit this description? What kind of information does it reveal about you?

CONSUMPTION

Beginning in the 1950s, another major social change took place in the United States and other developed countries. The central feature of many capitalist economies began to shift from production and work to **consumption**, or the process by which people obtain and utilize goods and services. During that period, the center of the American economy shifted from the factory and the office to the shopping mall (Baudrillard [1970] 1998; Lipovetsky 2005). For many people, work and production became less important than consumption.

The dramatic increase in consumption was made possible by, among other things, increasingly available credit cards. They have now become widespread at shopping malls, on the Internet, and in many other settings. One indicator of the increase in consumption in the United States is the increase in credit card debt. As you can see in Figure 1.2, credit card debt per household grew astronomically in the early years of credit card use (the figure begins with $37 in 1969) and reached its highest point, $8,729, in 2008. It has declined somewhat since the onset of the Great Recession and was down to a still high level of $7,194 in 2012.

ASK YOURSELF

Have your consumption habits or credit card use changed over the last six months? The last three years? Do you anticipate that they will change in the next three years, and if so, how and why?

> **globalization** "A transplanetary *process* or set of *processes* involving increasing *liquidity* and the growing multidirectional *flows* of people, objects, places and information as well as the *structures* they encounter and create that are *barriers* to, or *expedite*, those flows" (Ritzer 2010c).
>
> **consumption** The process by which people obtain goods and services.

Consumption is certainly significant economically, but it is significant in other ways as well. For example, culture

Sex Trafficking

Slave Trade

Credit Card Debt

The principles that account for the success of fast-food chains like McDonald's appear to be spreading to other social institutions. Which of these principles have you observed in action?

goods from China in 1985 (U.S. Census Bureau 2013). Furthermore, the speed and convenience of Internet commerce tends to make global realities and distances irrelevant to consumers. Finally, travel to other parts of the world—a form of consumption itself—is increasingly affordable and common. A major objective of tourists is often the sampling of the food of, and the purchase of souvenirs from, foreign lands (Chambers 2010; Gmelch 2010; Mak, Lumbers, and Eves 2012).

Contemporary sociologists are devoting increasing attention to consumption in general (Sassatelli 2007) and more specifically to such phenomena as online shopping (Horrigan 2008), the behavior of shoppers in more material locales such as department stores (Miller 1998; Zukin 2004), and the development of more recent consumption sites, such as fast-food restaurants (Ritzer 2013a) and shopping malls (Ritzer 2010b).

My study of fast-food restaurants led to the development of the concept of **McDonaldization,** or the process by which the rational principles of the fast-food restaurant are coming to dominate more and more sectors of society and more societies throughout the world (see Ritzer 2010d: 275–357 for a number of critical essays on this perspective). This process leads to the creation of rational systems—like fast-food restaurants—that are characterized by the most direct and efficient means to their ends. McDonaldized systems have four defining characteristics:

• *Efficiency*. The emphasis is on the use of the quickest and least costly means to whatever end is desired. It is clear that employees of fast-food restaurants work efficiently: Burgers are cooked and assembled as if on an assembly line, with no wasted movements or ingredients. Similarly, customers are expected to spend as little time as possible in the fast-food restaurant. Perhaps the best example of efficiency is the drive-through window, a

is very much shaped by consumption, and various aspects of consumption become cultural phenomena. A good example is the iPhone, which has revolutionized culture in innumerable ways. Millions of people have bought iPhones and similar smartphones as well as the ever-increasing number of "apps" associated with them. These phones have altered how and where people meet to socialize and the ways in which they socialize. In addition, so much time is spent by the media and by people in general in discussing the implications of the iPhone and similar products (Samsung's Galaxy) that they have become central to the larger culture in which we live. Rumors about the

CHECKPOINT 1.2	CHARACTERISTICS OF GLOBALIZATION AND CONSUMPTION
Globalization is characterized by . . .	**Consumption is characterized by . . .**
Increasingly fluid flows of people, goods, and information and ideas across national boundaries.	Increasingly available credit cards (and debt), an increased focus on shopping for goods and services, and ease of online purchasing.

characteristics and release date of the next version of the iPhone continually add to its excitement.

Consumption and globalization are also deeply intertwined. Much of what we consume in the developed world comes from other countries. In 2012 alone, the United States imported $426 billion worth of goods from China; the United States imported only $4 million in

> **McDonaldization** The process by which the rational principles of the fast-food restaurant are coming to dominate more and more sectors of society and more societies throughout the world.

highly organized means for employees to dole out meals in a matter of seconds (Horovitz 2002).

- *Calculability*. You hear a lot at McDonald's about quantities: how large the food portions are—the Big Mac—and how low the prices are—the dollar breakfast. You don't hear as much, however, about the quality of the restaurant's ingredients or its products. Similarly, you may hear about how many burgers are served per hour or how quickly they are served, but you don't hear much about the skill of employees. A focus on quantity also means that tasks are often done under great pressure. This means that they are often done in a slipshod manner.

- *Predictability*. McDonaldization ensures that the entire experience of patronizing a fast-food chain is nearly identical from one geographic setting to another—even globally—and from one time to another. For example, when customers enter a McDonald's restaurant, employees ask what they wish to order, following scripts created by the corporation. For their part, customers can expect to find most of the usual menu items. Employees, following another script, can be counted on to thank customers for their order. Thus, a highly predictable ritual is played out in the fast-food restaurant.

- *Control*. In McDonaldized systems, a good deal of control is maintained through technology. French fry machines buzz when the fries are done and even automatically lift them out of the hot oil. The automatic fry machine may save time and prevent accidents, but it makes it impossible to meet a special customer request for brown, crispy fries. Similarly, the drive-through window can be seen as a technology that ensures that customers dispose of their own garbage, if only by dumping it in the backseats of their cars or on the roadside.

Paradoxically, rationality often seems to lead to its exact opposite—irrationality. Just consider the problem of roadside litter due to drive-through services at fast-food restaurants. Or the societal irrationalities in dealing with childhood obesity that has been blamed, in part, on the ubiquity of fast food. Another of the irrationalities of rationality is dehumanization. Fast-food employees are forced to work in dehumanizing jobs, which can lead to job dissatisfaction, alienation, and high turnover rates. Fast-food customers are forced to eat in dehumanizing settings, such as in the cold and impersonal atmosphere of the fast-food restaurant, in their cars, or on the move as they walk down the street. As more of the world succumbs to McDonaldization, dehumanization becomes increasingly likely.

> **technology** The interplay of machines, tools, skills, and procedures for the accomplishment of tasks.

Social change continues. The Great Recession and its continuing aftermath have altered many things, including the degree to which society is dominated by consumption. Consumption sites have experienced great difficulties. Many outdoor strip malls have emptied, and indoor malls have numerous vacant stores, including large department stores. Las Vegas, which has become a capital for the consumption of entertainment and high-end goods and services, is hurting (Nagourney 2013). Dubai, aspiring to be the consumption capital of the East, hit a financial rough spot in 2009 and has yet to recover from it. It seems possible, although highly unlikely, that even though we entered the consumption age only about half a century ago, we now may be on the verge of what could be called the "postconsumption age." While excessive consumption and the related high level of debt were key factors in causing the Great Recession, a postconsumption age would bring with it problems of its own, such as fewer jobs and a declining standard of living for many.

ASK YOURSELF

What would your life be like in a postconsumption age? In what ways might it be better? Worse? Why?

THE DIGITAL WORLD

Sociology has always concerned itself with the social aspects and implications of **technology**, or the interplay of machines, tools, skills, and procedures for the accomplishment of tasks. One example is the assembly line, a defining feature of early twentieth-century factories. Later, sociologists became interested in the automated technologies that came to define factories. However, technologies have continued to evolve considerably since then. Sociologists are now devoting an increasing amount of attention to the digital world that has emerged as a result of new technologies already mentioned in this chapter, such as computers, smartphones, the Internet, and social networking sites (Clough 2013).

It is important to note that while we discuss the digital world throughout this book, living digitally is not separate from life in the social world. In fact, the two forms of living are increasingly intersecting and in the process creating an augmented world for all involved (Jurgenson 2012). For example, the wide-scale use of smartphones allows people to text many others to let them know they are going to be at a local club. This can lead to a spontaneous social

Americans and Debt

The Internet and Thinking

The Shopping Malls of Dubai

Although we are all quite familiar with today's indoor shopping malls, there were predecessors such as the early eighteenth-century Parisian arcades (Benjamin 1999). However, the first modern, fully enclosed mall opened in Minnesota in 1956 (Ritzer 2010b). Today, shopping malls are common throughout the United States. Although the modern shopping mall was an American invention, the mall concept has been globalized, and now malls are common in other parts of the world as well. Many international malls now outshine those located in the United States. For example, at 9.6 million square feet and accommodating 1,500 retail outlets, the South China Mall, located in Dongguan, is by a wide margin the largest mall in the world (Pocock 2011). None of the world's 10 largest malls are in the United States. The United States is also no longer the leader in the most innovative, glitziest, and fanciest malls.

One locale notable for its malls is Dubai in the United Arab Emirates (UAE). Located on the coast of the Persian Gulf, Dubai covers more than 1,600 square miles, mostly desert. Among other things, the emirate has become a regional, if not global, center of consumption and has developed a thriving tourist industry (Arnold 2011). Visitors are drawn by the tallest building in the world—the Burj Khalifa—three artificial islands, and Dubai's over-the-top shopping malls.

At 3.7 million square feet in area and accommodating more than 1,200 retail outlets, the newest, largest, and most elegant of Dubai's malls is the Dubai Mall.

Yes, you can ski in Dubai. Does a society give something up when it makes such an expensive luxury possible?

Among its most notable elements is the largest gold souk, or ancient Arab bazaar, in the world. It also has a 10 million–liter aquarium behind the world's largest acrylic viewing panels (Bianchi 2010). Perhaps the most striking feature of the Dubai Mall is that, in the middle of one of the world's hottest and most arid deserts, it has an indoor ice rink, which can accommodate up to 2,000 skaters.

The Mall of the Emirates is much smaller than the Dubai Mall with only 520 shops, although it has a five-star Kempinski hotel and a 14-screen cinema complex. The Mall of the Emirates has gone further than even the Dubai Mall in thumbing its nose at the heat of the desert—the mall houses Ski Dubai, a 400-meter indoor ski slope.

The malls of Dubai are obviously involved in consumption, but they are also involved in the process of globalization in numerous ways. Copying, and being copied by, American malls, attracting visitors from many parts of the world, and being affected by global economic processes such as the Great Recession are all indicators of globalization.

Think About It

Which characteristics of McDonaldization are found in malls? Do you think malls contribute to the increased prominence of consumption in contemporary life? Why or why not? Why do you think they have become so popular abroad?

gathering at the club that would not have occurred were it not for this new technology.

The networking sites on the Internet that involve social interaction are the most obviously sociological in character (Aleman and Wartman 2008; Patchin and Hinduja 2010). These sites are important especially in the West where the percentage of Internet users based on population is highest (see Figure 1.3). However, their importance is increasing in the Middle East and North Africa as reflected in the role they played in recent social revolutions. Protesters used cell phones and the Internet to inform each other, and the world, about the evolving scene. To take another example, Facebook.com/yalaYL has become a key site where Israelis, Palestinians, and other Arabs communicate with each other about both everyday concerns and big issues such as the prospect for peace in the Middle East. This social networking takes place online while physical interaction between such people, and between their leaders, is difficult or nonexistent (Bronner 2011b).

One sociological issue related to the Internet is the impact on our lives of spending so much time interacting on social networking sites. For example, are you more likely to write term papers for your college classes using shorter sentences and more abbreviations because of your experience with texting? Consider also the impact of the 7.5 hours per day—up by a full hour in only five years—that young people between the ages of 8 and 18 spend on electronic devices of all types (Lewin 2010). In some cases, little time remains for other activities (schoolwork, face-to-face interaction).

We may also multitask among several online and off-line interactions simultaneously, such as in class or while doing homework. You may think you do a great job of multitasking, but it can actually reduce your ability to comprehend and remember and thus lower your performance on tests and other assignments (PBS 2010).

Internet technology also affects the nature of consumption. More of it is taking place on such sites as eBay and Amazon.com, and that trend is expected to continue to grow. In 2010, a Pew study found that, during an average day, 21 percent of Internet users in the United States look for information about a service or product they are thinking about buying (Jansen 2010). It is also easier for people to spend money on consumption on Internet sites than it is in the material world. It is

Technologies we take for granted today would have been unimaginable a century ago. How do they affect our lives, both positively and negatively?

FIGURE 1.3 • Internet Access by Geographic Region, 2012

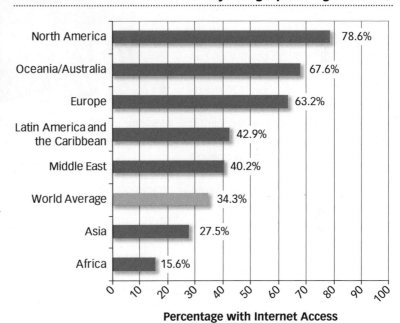

Percentage with Internet Access

Region	Percentage
North America	78.6%
Oceania/Australia	67.6%
Europe	63.2%
Latin America and the Caribbean	42.9%
Middle East	40.2%
World Average	34.3%
Asia	27.5%
Africa	15.6%

SOURCE: Bar chart showing World Internet Penetration Rates by Geographic Regions, 2012 Q2. From Internet World Stats. Copyright © 2012 Miniwatts Marketing Group. www .internetworldststs.com/stats.htm.

worth noting that these sites, as well as the Internet in general, are global in their scope. The ease with which global interactions and transactions occur on the Internet is a powerful spur to the process of globalization.

Internet Use

Online Networks

The Internet in China

In the last three decades, no country has played a larger role in changing the global economic and political landscape than China (Jacques 2009). Its economy has achieved unprecedented growth, and it became the second largest economy in the world in 2010; it is estimated it will surpass the United States as the world's largest economy as early as 2030 (Barboza 2010). However, the rising economic tide in China has not benefited everyone. Income inequality is extremely high. There are a number of recently minted billionaires and a rapidly growing middle class, but much of China's rural population and its factory workers remain very poor.

This divide extends to Internet use. Only about a third of China's population currently uses the Internet. But that's still a lot of people. In 2010, about 420 million people in China used the Internet (China Internet Network Information Center 2010). There are already more Internet "citizens" in China than there are people in the United States, and China's lead in Internet use will only increase in the future. Furthermore, Chinese Internet users are young: 70 percent are under 30 (Ye 2008). This augurs well for future Chinese involvement in the Internet.

The types of content that are available on the Internet in China are not much different from those elsewhere in the world. However, the Chinese government has made an active effort to erect a barrier— a "Great Firewall"—to stop these flows (Segan 2011). This is part of a larger effort by the Chinese government to block all flows of information in a variety of ways,

Internet use is highly unevenly distributed among the Chinese population and heavily regulated by the government. How is this different from your Internet experience?

including censorship of news, control over television, and limits on bookshops and movie theaters (Bennett 2011). Barriers on the Internet include restricted access to a large number of foreign websites such as Wikipedia, Flickr, YouTube, and sometimes Myspace ("Timeline" 2010). These restrictions illustrate the relationship between global flows and structural barriers to those flows. China's efforts to censor the Internet have resulted in a unique Internet world in China. For example, many popular online communities consist entirely of Chinese citizens. In an increasingly global world, however, how long can China maintain barriers that few, if any, other countries in the world erect (Lacharite 2002)? Although the majority of Chinese Internet users are completely oblivious to the existence of the Great Firewall (French 2008), there are many signs now of rebellion against it.

Think About It

Do you think the Chinese government will be able to keep its Internet controls in place for the long term? Why or why not? How does your understanding of globalization affect your answer?

GLOBALIZATION, CONSUMPTION, THE DIGITAL WORLD, AND YOU

The three main issues discussed above, taken singly and collectively, are of great concern not only to society in general and to sociologists but also to you as a college student. You live a good part of your life in these three interrelated domains.

As a college student, you live a truly global existence in a college or university. A significant number of your classmates come from elsewhere in the world. Your classes are increasingly being taught by teaching assistants and professors from other parts of the globe. The ideas you are learning are the most global of all, flowing freely from virtually everywhere in the world to become part of lectures and textbooks.

As consumers, you and your classmates are likely well acquainted with the college bookstore and the nearby shopping mall. In addition, on the Internet you are apt to find a nearly infinite variety of goods and services, the majority of which are likely to come from the far reaches of the world.

Finally, an increasing portion of your education is obtained the inherently global Internet through, for example, e-learning on web-based courses and online degree programs. In 2009, more than 4.6 million students were taking at least one online course (Allen and Seaman 2010). This constituted a growth rate in enrollment of 17 percent compared to a 1.2 percent growth rate for traditional courses. With the emergence of massive online open courses (MOOCs) you, and perhaps hundreds of thousands of students from around the globe, are increasingly more likely to participate in global classes and programs available on the Internet (see Chapter 17 for more on MOOCs) (Heller 2013; Lewin 2012).

Globalization, consumption, and the Internet are of great importance on their own. However, perhaps more important are the ways in which they interact with one another and interpenetrate with your life as a college student, as well as the lives of virtually everyone else.

SOCIOLOGY: CONTINUITY AND CHANGE

This chapter has emphasized recent social changes and their impact on society and on sociology, but there is

The U.S. sociologist C. Wright Mills achieved success early in life and died when he was only 46.

CHECKPOINT 1.3	THE FOUR CHARACTERISTICS OF MCDONALDIZATION
Efficiency	Emphasizes the quickest and least costly means to whatever end is desired.
Calculability	Focuses on quantity over quality and often means doing tasks under great time pressure.
Predictability	Transforms experiences into highly predictable routines that are nearly identical each time.
Control	Emphasizes automation and standardization, most often maintained through technology.

also much continuity in society, as well as in the field of sociology. This section deals with a number of traditional approaches and concerns in sociology that are of continuing relevance to even the most recent sociological issues.

THE SOCIOLOGICAL IMAGINATION

The systematic study of the social world has always required imagination on the part of sociologists. The phenomenon

ACTIVE SOCIOLOGY

Where Was It Made?

Globalization is visible everywhere, from the clothes we wear to the electronic devices that shape our everyday existence. To recognize the power of globalization, use the table below to make a list of the countries represented by the clothes you are wearing now and other personal belongings you have with you. For example, you may find that your footwear was made in Cambodia, your coat in Honduras, your T-shirt in Vietnam, and your cell phone batteries in South Korea. You may even find an item made in the United States. Most people can readily find at least 10 products made in different countries.

Many companies produce products while respecting human rights and ethical labor practices, but others impose a high human cost. Clothing, for example, is often made using child or forced labor. Select one item from your list below and research who produced it. Find out whether this manufacturer has used forced/child labor, unethical labor practices, and hazardous working conditions; share your results with the class.

Item	Where was it made?	Who made it?
Purse/backpack/tote		
Pants/jeans		
Top/T-shirt/hoodie		
Coat/jacket		
Shoes		
Hat		
Watch/jewelry		
Eyeglasses/shades		
Contents of your pockets		
Cell phone		
Cell phone batteries		
Laptop/tablet		
Other		

There are numerous tools to help you be a just consumer.

- Free2Work (http://free2work.org) has a cell phone application that helps consumers grade companies on their labor practices, reduce their "slavery footprint," and access information about how to resist all forms of human trafficking as they shop. Swipe a bar code, reduce human trafficking!

- If you discover a "slavery footprint," go to Change.org (www.change .org), which is dedicated to helping people develop and circulate online petitions on a variety of social issues.

of being able to look at the social world from different, imaginative perspectives caught the attention of the famous sociologist C. Wright Mills (1959). He argued that sociologists had a unique perspective—the **sociological imagination**—that gave them a distinctive way of looking at data or reflecting on the world around them.

In his 1956 book *The Power Elite*, Mills demonstrated the application of the sociological imagination to the political world of his day. It was dominated by the Cold War—the nonshooting "war" that existed between the United States and the Soviet Union between the end of World War II in 1945 and the fall of the Soviet Union in 1991—and by the likelihood of nuclear war between

> **sociological imagination** A unique perspective that gives sociologists a distinctive way of looking at data and reflecting on the world around them.

the United States and the Soviet Union. Mills argued that a "military-industrial complex" consisting of the military and many defense industries had come into existence in the United States. They both favored war, or at least preparedness for war, and therefore the expenditure of huge sums of taxpayer money on armaments of all types. In 1960, a few years after *The Power Elite* was published, president and former five-star general Dwight D. Eisenhower warned the nation, in his farewell presidential address, of the threats to liberty and democracy posed by the military-industrial complex, to say nothing of its role in elevating the risk of war.

Sociology requires at least as much imagination today as it did in Mills's day, and probably more, to deal with new and emerging realities. For example, the risk of global warfare, especially nuclear war, has declined with the end of the Cold War and the demise of the Soviet Union. But a military-industrial complex not only remains in place in the United States but may be more powerful than ever. Consider the simultaneous wars in Iraq and Afghanistan, to say nothing of the seemingly open-ended and perhaps never-ending "War on Terror." Some sociologists would point out that the military and defense industries want, indeed need, hundreds of billions of dollars to be spent each year on armaments of all types. The new threats that arise regularly, real or imagined, lead to ever-greater expenditures and further expansion of the military-industrial complex. In Figure 1.4, for example, you can see that U.S. military expenditures spiked dramatically

Bystanders and police race toward the site of a fatal explosion at the close of the 2013 Boston Marathon, the suspected work of two Chechen brothers inspired by overseas terrorist groups. How does the sociological imagination help us interpret the war on terror?

FIGURE 1.4 • U.S. Defense Budget, 1940–2015

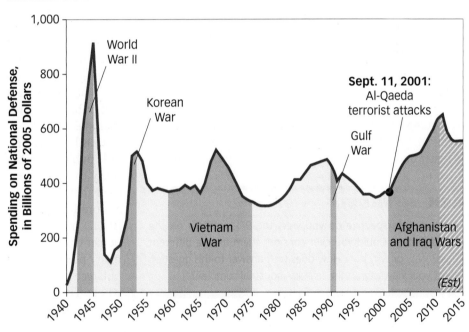

SOURCE: A Topline View of U.S. Defense Budget History from "U.S. Defense Spending: The Mismatch Between Plans and Resources," by Mackenzie Eaglen. The Heritage Foundation.

after the terrorist attacks of September 11, 2001—reflecting overlapping wars with Iraq and Afghanistan. Given the economic problems facing the United States, there is now some movement toward cutting the defense budget in future years. Whatever happens, we can be sure that a military-industrial complex will survive and fight hard against any reductions.

A very different example of the utility of a sociological imagination begins with the ideas of one of the classic thinkers in the history of sociology, Georg Simmel. Among many other things, Simmel ([1907] 1978) argued that money is crucial to a modern economy. For example, cash money allows people to be paid easily for their work and just as easily to buy goods and services. However, money

Military-Industrial Complex

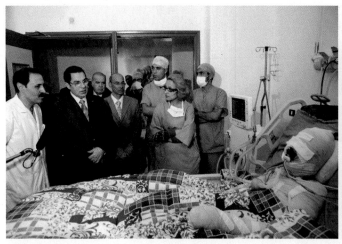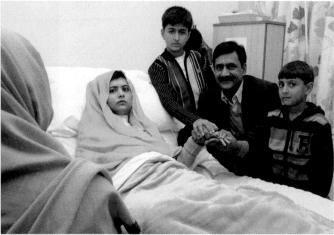

The recent private troubles of two young people became global public issues. The self-immolation and death of Tunisian vegetable seller Mohamed Al Bouazzizi (left) ignited a revolution in his country, while Malala Yousufzai (right) became an international spokesperson for the education of Pakistani girls after the Taliban shot her in the head for her beliefs.

not only speeds up consumption but also allows people to consume more than they otherwise would. While a money economy creates its own problems, it is the credit economy that nearly wrecked the American, and much of the global, economy during the Great Recession. The availability of "money" had dramatically increased with the expansion of credit for individuals, in the form of mortgage loans, auto loans, and credit cards. People not only tended to spend all of the cash (including savings) they had on hand, but they were going into more and more debt because loans were easy to obtain. Simmel's imaginative thinking on money allows us to better understand the problems created by easy credit.

ASK YOURSELF

From what perspective do you view the 9/11 attacks on the United States? Could you ever consider them from a different angle? Why or why not? How does your answer to this question reflect your views about the military-industrial complex?

Private Troubles and Public Issues

The sociological imagination may be most useful in helping sociologists see the linkage between private troubles and public issues. For example, prior to the onset of the Great Recession, the sociological imagination would have been useful in alerting society to the fact that the increasing levels of individual consumption and debt, seen at the time as private issues, would soon morph into a public issue—the near-collapse of the global economy. Credit cards can create both private troubles and public issues. A person going so deeply into debt that there is no way out other than declaring bankruptcy is experiencing a private trouble. However, private troubles become public issues

when high levels of personal debt and bankruptcy lead to such things as bank failures and even default on debts by various nations. Today, the sociological imagination could also be used to reflect on, for example, the fleeting nature of private social relationships on Facebook and Twitter and whether in the future they will lead all types of social relationships in the same direction.

Many other examples of the link between private troubles and public issues relate to young people and students. For example, ADHD—attention deficit/hyperactivity disorder—can easily be seen as a private trouble. For years, there was little public awareness of ADHD, and those who had it were likely to suffer alone. But since the 1980s, it has become clear that ADHD is also a public issue, and it is becoming a more important public issue. Children diagnosed with ADHD increased from 5.7 percent in 1997–1999 to 7.6 percent in 2006–2008 (Goodwin 2011). It is clear that many people suffer from ADHD, which creates a number of larger problems for schools, employers, and society as a whole. The fact that it has become a public issue may make ADHD less of a private trouble for some, as there is now greater public understanding of the problem and many more support groups are available.

In another example, a 2011 White House report details the fact that women are more likely to be concentrated in lower-paying jobs (U.S. Department of Commerce, Executive Office of the President, and White House Council on Women and Girls 2011). For example, in medicine, women are more likely to be general practitioners or practical nurses than they are to be highly paid surgeons. Being limited occupationally creates personal troubles for many women, such as inadequate income and job dissatisfaction. This is also a public issue, not only because the discrepancy between the sexes is unfair to women as a whole but also because society is not the beneficiary of the many contributions of which women are capable.

ASK YOURSELF

Do you agree that private choices sometimes lead to, or are part of, public issues? Can you think of an example from your own life, or the life of a family member?

The Micro–Macro Relationship

The interest in personal troubles and public issues is a specific example of a larger and more basic sociological concern with the relationship between microscopic (**micro**, or small-scale) social phenomena, such as individuals and their thoughts and actions, and macroscopic (**macro**, or large-scale) social phenomena such as groups, organizations, cultures, society, and the world, as well as the relationship between them (J. Turner 2005). For example, Karl Marx, often considered one of the earliest and most important sociologists, was interested in the relationship between what workers did and thought (micro issues) and the capitalist economic system (a macro issue) in which the workers existed.

In fact, there is a continuum that runs from the most microscopic to the most macroscopic of social realities. The definition of sociology presented at the beginning of this chapter fits this continuum quite well. Individual actions and thoughts lie on the micro end of the continuum; groups, organizations, cultures, and societies fall more toward the macro end; and worldwide structures and processes are at the most macro end of the continuum. Although in their own work, the vast majority of individual sociologists focus on only very limited segments of this continuum, the field as a whole is concerned with the continuum in its entirety as well as the interrelationships among its various components.

> **micro** Microscopic; used to describe small-scale social phenomena such as individuals and their thoughts and actions.
>
> **macro** Macroscopic; used to describe large-scale social phenomena, such as groups, organizations, cultures, society, and the globe.
>
> **dangerous giants** An entity that has agency.
>
> **agency** Individual social power and capacity for creativity; the potential to disrupt or destroy the structures in which one finds oneself.

The Agency–Structure Relationship

American sociologists tend to think in terms of the micro–macro relationship. In other parts of the world, especially in Europe, sociologists are more oriented to the agency–structure relationship. The agency–structure continuum is complex, but for our purposes we can think of agency as resembling the micro level and structure resembling the macro level.

The utility of the agency–structure terminology is that it highlights several important social realities and aspects of the field of sociology. Of greatest significance is the fact that the term *agency* gives great importance to the individual—the "agent"—as having power and a capacity for creativity (Giddens 1984). In sociological work on agency, great emphasis is placed on the individual's mental abilities and the ways in which these abilities are used to create important, if not decisive, actions.

However, these agents are seen as enmeshed in macro-level social and cultural structures that they create and by which they are constrained (King 2004). For example, as a student you help create the universities you attend, and you are constrained by them and the power they have over you. Your university can require you to do certain things (such as take specific courses in order to earn your degree) and prevent you from doing other things (such as taking courses that might be of greater interest, or even taking no courses at all). On the other hand, you as a student can act to change or overthrow those structures. You might organize student-run groups on topics of interest, such as religious rights or manga cartoons; attract many participants to the groups; and eventually prompt the university to add courses on those topics. Or perhaps you might organize students to stop enrolling in an elective course that seems irrelevant to their lives, causing that elective to be dropped from the course catalog.

Agents (you as a student, in this case) have great power. In the words of another important sociologist, Erving Goffman (1961: 81), individuals are **dangerous giants**. That is, they have **agency**, or the potential to disrupt and destroy the structures in which they find themselves. Yet often, agents do not realize the power they possess. As a result, social structures such as the university and the class you are currently taking function over long periods of time with little or no disruption by individual agents.

However, there are times, such as during the anti–Vietnam War protests of the late 1960s and early 1970s, when students have come to realize that they are dangerous giants and act to change not only the university but also the larger society (Gitlin 1993). There are far more minor, everyday actions that reflect the fact that people can be dangerous giants. Examples might include questioning a professor's argument or going to the dean to protest the excessive

Private troubles—individual issues like credit-card debt and bankruptcy.	Public issues—widespread issues like bank failures and governments defaulting on their debt.
Macro social phenomena—large-scale phenomena such as groups, organizations, cultures, society, and the world.	Micro social phenomena—small-scale social phenomena such as individuals and their thoughts and actions.
Agency—the individual's power and capacity for creativity.	Structure—macro-level social and cultural institutions that constrain agents' actions.

absences of an instructor. However, most people most of the time do not realize that they are dangerous giants—that they have the capacity to greatly alter the social structures that surround them and in which they are enmeshed.

One more distinctive thing about the agency–structure perspective is the idea that social structures are both constraining and enabling. As we will see in Chapter 2, there is a long tradition in sociology of seeing structures like the university as mainly controlling people, if not being totally oppressive. While the agency–structure perspective acknowledges and deals with these constraints, it also makes the very important point that structures enable agents (you would be one) to do things they otherwise would not be able to do. For example, it is the global structure of the Internet that allows you to communicate easily and quickly with people throughout the world. It also permits you to consume many goods and services from the comfort of your home or dorm room rather than traveling, perhaps great distances, to obtain them. Similarly, while the university constrains you in many ways, it does offer you the knowledge and skills you need to succeed, or perhaps simply to survive, in the modern world. In thinking about and critiquing the constraining power of structures, it is important to remember that those structures also enable you in many different ways.

THE SOCIAL CONSTRUCTION OF REALITY

The discussion of agency and structure leads to another basic concept in sociology: the **social construction of reality** (Berger and Luckmann 1967). People at the agency end of the continuum are seen as creating social reality, basically macro-level phenomena, through their thoughts and actions. That reality then comes to have a life of its own. That is, it becomes a structure that is partly or wholly separate from the people who created it and exist in it. Once macro phenomena have lives of their own, they constrain and even control what people do. Of course, people can refuse to accept these constraints and controls and create

new social realities. This process of individual creation of structural realities, constraint, and coercion then begins anew, in a continuing loop. It is this continuous loop that is the heart of the agency–structure and micro–macro relationships, the social world, and the field of sociology.

For example, in the realm of consumption, it is people—as designers, manufacturers, and consumers—who create the world of fashion (Entwhistle 2009). However, once the fashion world comes into existence, that world comes to have a great deal of influence over individuals who are part of that world. Famous fashion houses such as Dior and Givenchy come to dominate the industry and perpetuate their existence by continual fashion changes. These companies control people's tastes in fashion and thereby the nature of the clothing people wear. Changing fashions are highly profitable for the fashion houses. Consumers seem eager to buy the designs created by the leading fashion houses, although most often in the form of the relatively inexpensive knockoffs derived from them. The power of the fashion industry, and the nature of its products, has been analyzed by a number of sociologists (Lipovetsky [1987] 2002; Simmel [1904] 1971), most notably another of the early giants in the field, Thorstein Veblen. In *The Theory of the Leisure Class*, Veblen ([1899] 1994) criticized the high heel, and especially the skirt. He argued that women persist in wearing a skirt even though "it is expensive and hampers the wearer at every turn and incapacitates her for all useful exertion" (p. 171). Feminist theorists have extended this critique, arguing that beauty devices such as high heels help to maintain gender inequality by serving to limit women physically (Dworkin 1974; Jeffreys 2005). More subtly, these devices encourage women to engage in a never-ending project of bodily discipline aimed at attaining what in fact is an unreachable beauty ideal created by society (Bartky 1990; Wolf 2002). Were it not for the fashion industry, would as many women wear tight skirts and spike heels?

Of course, many people do not go along with the constraints of the fashion industry. They do not wear what the industry wants them to wear, and they do not change their dress because of changes in fashion induced

> **social construction of reality** The continuous process of individual creation of structural realities and the constraint and coercion exercised by those structures.

by the fashion industry. Many people have their own sense of fashion and create their own way of dressing. Others ignore fashion altogether. Of greatest importance from this perspective is the fact that the source of what is in fashion often comes not from the fashion industry but rather from the ways of dressing put together by people themselves. The latter have, in a real sense, constructed their own social reality. In fact, there is a process known as "cool hunting" (Gloor and Cooper 2007) in which scouts for the fashion industry seek out new and interesting ways of dressing, often focusing on what young people in the suburbs and in the inner city are wearing. They bring those innovative ideas back to the fashion industry, and some of them are turned into next year's fashions.

Once this happens, however, we are back to a situation where the fashion industry is controlling, or is at least attempting to control, what people wear. Many will accept the new fashion, but others, especially the "cool" kids who are sought out by the cool hunters, will not. They may well have moved on to some entirely new sense of what they want to wear. They will again attract the attention of cool hunters, and the process will begin anew.

SOCIAL STRUCTURES AND PROCESSES

Social structures are enduring and regular social arrangements, such as the family and the state. While social structures do change, they are generally not very dynamic; they change very slowly. Social processes are the dynamic and ever-changing aspects of the social world.

The elements of globalization can be divided between structures (such as the United Nations) and a variety of more specific social processes (such as the migration of people across national borders). In terms of consumption, we can think of the shopping mall (or an online mall like Amazon .com) as a structure and the shopping (or consumption) that takes place in it as a process. Finally, the Internet as a whole and social networking sites in particular are structures, while the communication and the social interaction that take place in them can be viewed as processes.

> **social structures** Enduring and regular social arrangements, such as the family and the state, based on persistent patterns of interaction and social relationships.
>
> **social processes** Dynamic and changing aspects of the social world.

Among those who create our social reality by influencing our tastes are members of the fashion industry. Are your choices as a consumer ever influenced by what is considered in or out of style?

SOCIOLOGY'S PURPOSE: SCIENCE OR SOCIAL REFORM?

Many of today's sociologists study social problems of all sorts such as poverty and crime. They also seek to use what they know in order to deal with these problems by suggesting ways of reforming society. They believe that these two activities are not necessarily distinct; they can and should be mutually enriching. While many contemporary sociologists accept this position, a division has developed over time with some sociologists focusing more on scientific research and others more engaged in activities designed to reform society and address social problems.

Sociologists who engage in "pure science" operate with the conviction that we need to better understand how the social world operates before we can change it, if that's what we want to do. That knowledge may ultimately be used by those who want to change society, or to keep it as it is, but that is not the immediate concern of the social researcher. For example, sociologists known as "ethnomethodologists" (see Chapter 2) argue that the task of the sociologist is to better understand common forms of social behavior (Rawls 2011). They research the details of everyday life such as how we know when a laugh is expected in a conversation, or when to applaud or boo during a speech. For them, the goal is purely knowledge and understanding. Other sociologists take the opposite position. C. Wright Mills, for example, was little interested in doing scientific research. He was mostly interested in such social reforms as limiting or eliminating the unwholesome and worrisome ties between

Sociology as Pure Science	Sociology as a Means of Social Reform
• The goal of study is simply knowledge and understanding of the way the social world operates.	• Public sociology should address itself to and work on behalf of many diverse publics, especially society's underdogs.
• Change is not the social researcher's immediate concern.	• Gathering knowledge to reform society enriches both activities.
• Using knowledge to effect social change might distort social behaviors.	• Some "scientific" work has been distorted by social biases.

the military and industry in the United States. He was also critical of many of the most prominent sociologists of his day for their orientation toward being pure scientists, their lack of concern for the pressing problems of the day, and their unwillingness to do anything about them. Feminist sociologists have extended the argument, pointing out that the topics and methods of objective, scientific sociology themselves sometimes reflect, and ultimately reinforce, social inequality along the lines of race, gender, and class because they are based on the assumptions of society's elite (Epstein 1988).

Until recently, scientific researchers have almost always been men. The questions about what problems were worthy of study reflected male, rather than female, interests. For example, issues more relevant to women such as rape and housework were deemed trivial and overshadowed by other issues such as achievement and power (Riger 1992). As a result, these seemingly "scientific" views of women reinforced false assumptions about male-female differences, held both men and women to supposedly universal male norms, and reproduced gender inequality (Rutherford, Vaughn-Blount, and Ball 2010).

The view that sociology has a social purpose has created renewed interest in what is now called public sociology. In contrast to professional sociology in which work is done for other sociologists, **public sociology** addresses a wide range of audiences, most of which are outside the academy. These publics include a variety of local, national, and global groups. Public sociologists write for these groups, and they can become involved in collaborative projects with them (Burawoy 2005; Clawson et al., 2007; Nyden, Hossfeld, and Nyden 2011). There have been public sociologists from the beginning of the discipline, and they have existed throughout the field's history. However, in recent decades the field has been dominated by technically oriented sociologists working out of universities and think tanks. They have done highly sophisticated work aimed, primarily, at other sociologists and sociology students with a similar orientation. This has been important work, and it has

benefited the larger public by enhancing our understanding of society. Still, many American sociologists are searching for better ways of reaching a larger public beyond the university. Interestingly, this is less of an issue in Europe where many of the leading sociologists have always been public sociologists.

In addressing the larger public, sociologists are urged to be driven more by their personal values as well as by the values (for example, democracy) of the larger society rather than by technical considerations. However, there is not just one public to be addressed, but rather a number of diverse publics. For example, young people, parents, and the aged have different issues and need to be addressed in different ways. Public sociology should not consist of sociologists' pronouncements on important issues but rather encourage a dialogue with these diverse publics. Nonetheless, most public sociologists believe that their work should be addressed to, and done on behalf of, the underdogs in society. It is often aimed at stimulating activism, solving various social problems, and helping to create a better society. A good example of the latter is the work of Eric Olin Wright (2010) on "real utopias." Wright was elected president of the American Sociological Association, and he made such utopian ideas the theme of its 2012 meetings (Wright 2013).

ASK YOURSELF

What do you believe is the best purpose of sociology: pure science or social reform? Why? Make a note to ask yourself this question again at the end of your course. Did you answer it differently?

Public sociologists engage with the public in a variety of ways, such as by writing blogs, books, and articles for a popular audience, and op-ed pieces in newspapers; by teaching as well as presenting public lectures and making TV appearances; and by working directly with groups to help them achieve their goals. In addition, sociology sometimes becomes public through the work

> **public sociology** Sociological work addressing a wide range of audiences, most of which are outside the academy, including a variety of local, national, and global groups.

George Ritzer and the McDonaldization of Society

To some I am a public sociologist (Ritzer 2006) or, as Rojek (2007) labels me, a "public intellectual." On most occasions my public sociology has involved interviews with newspaper, radio, and TV reporters. While some of them occurred in the United States, a disproportionate number of such interviews have occurred in other parts of the world, especially Great Britain. There is far greater interest in Great Britain (and in many other places) in the work of academics than there is in the United States. However, even elsewhere in the world there seems to be a decline in public interest in scholarly work by sociologists (and others).

It is not easy for scholars to do public sociology. Interestingly, it is far easier for journalists to do it, to do "pop sociology." Thus, the journalist Eric Schlosser (2001), who wrote the best-selling *Fast Food Nation*, in part influenced by my earlier book, *The McDonaldization of Society* ([1993] 2013a), has done much more public sociology, including a 2006 movie based (loosely) on his book, than I have.

Beyond the challenge of getting the attention of the popular media, it is difficult for scholars to do interviews that are reported accurately by the media. Reporters are often ill prepared having, at best, Googled a few of a scholar's writings prior to an interview. As a result, they often ask the "wrong" questions or fail to fully understand the answers. In any case, they are usually facing an imminent deadline and are forced to write up the interviews very quickly. I have often been disappointed in the way my thoughts have been translated by the media.

A bigger problem, one that is directly relevant to my work, is the tendency for reporters to "McDonaldize" their stories. Basically, this means that they seek to simplify what has been said in an interview and to avoid anything that they consider to be too complex for their readership. They want to produce what are, in effect, "News McNuggets" that in their simplicity resemble "Chicken McNuggets." Neither is fully satisfying.

Reporters are often drawn to write about the McDonaldization of society because it appears to be an idea that can be communicated simply. While I have tried to do that in my work, reporters usually go way too far in their efforts to McDonaldize the idea. As a result, much of the depth of the concept gets lost in translation.

This was particularly clear in an aborted interview with NBC TV a few years ago. The first part of the interview on McDonaldization went well, but then the reporter asked me about another of my books, *The Globalization of Nothing* (Ritzer 2007). This involves a far more difficult thesis to McDonaldize, but I plunged ahead. As I did, I could sense the reporter losing interest. At the end, she said, in effect, "Don't call us, we'll call you." I responded by saying, "Well, I guess my ideas on the globalization of nothing are not McDonaldized enough." She laughed, and said, "That's right."

The challenge for me, and all public sociologists, is to have their ideas reach the larger public without McDonaldizing them or having them be McDonaldized. That is never easy!

of nonsociologists whose thinking is shaped explicitly or implicitly by sociological knowledge and a sociological perspective. Such work is often produced by journalists in the form of newspaper articles, books released by popular presses, or website postings and blogs capable of reaching a huge public audience. The type of work discussed throughout this section will be dealt with in a series of boxes headed "Public Sociology" to be found throughout this book.

SOCIOLOGY, THE OTHER SOCIAL SCIENCES, AND COMMON SENSE

Sociology is one of the social sciences that studies various aspects of the social world. Among the others are anthropology, communication, economics, geography, political science, and psychology. Generally speaking, sociology is the broadest of these fields. Other social scientists are more likely to delve into specific aspects of the social world in much greater depth. Sociological study touches on the culture of concern to anthropologists, the nation-state of interest to political scientists, and the mental processes that are the focus of psychologists. However, that does not mean that sociology is in any sense "better" than, or conversely not as good as, the other social sciences.

Rather than compare and contrast these fields in general terms, the focus in this concluding section will be

Fast Food Nation

Public Sociology: Eric Schlosser

on the different ways in which these fields approach one of this book's signature concerns—globalization:

- Anthropology: cultural aspects of societies around the world, such as the food people eat and how they eat it, as well as the differences among cultures around the globe (Inda and Rosaldo 2008).

- Communication studies: communication across the globe, with the Internet obviously of focal concern in the contemporary world.

- Economics: production, distribution, and consumption of resources through markets and other structures that span much of the globe, especially those based on and involving money.

- Geography: spatial relationships on a global scale and mapping of those spaces (Herod 2009).

- Political science: nation-states, especially the ways in which they relate to one another around the world, as well as the way they have grown increasingly unable to control global flows of migrants, viruses, recreational drugs, Internet scams, and the like.

- Psychology: ways in which individual identities are shaped by increased awareness of the rest of the world and tensions associated with globalization (such as job loss), which may lead to individual psychological problems such as depression (Lemert and Elliott 2006).

Sociology encompasses all of these concerns, and many others, in its approach to globalization: globe-straddling cultures (such as consumer, or fast-food, culture), relationships between political systems (the European Union and its member nations, for example), communication networks (such as CNN and Al Jazeera, Twitter and Facebook), markets (for labor or stocks and bonds, for example) that cover vast expanses of the globe, the mapping of all of these, and even their impact, both good and bad, on individuals. You might want to study the other fields to get a sense of the depth of what they have to offer on specific aspects of globalization. However, if you are looking for the field that gives you the broadest possible view of all of these things, as well as the ways in which they interrelate, that field is sociology.

While sociology and the other social sciences have important differences, they are all quite different from commonsense understandings of the social world. Everyone participates in globalization in one way or another. However, few, if any, people research these phenomena in the way and to the degree that they are studied by social scientists. That research leads, among other things, to a greater understanding of the nature of globalization. For example, you probably have a sense that globalization has changed society—perhaps even an impression that it is changing your life. What you aren't likely to know are globalization's causes, linkages to other social phenomena, and largely invisible effects on society and the world. Research on the topic is also likely to yield much more insight into the pros and cons of globalization on a personal, societal, and global level. That more detailed knowledge and insight will help you, and others, more successfully navigate the accompanying changes in social processes and structures.

SUMMARY

Social changes in the last few centuries, including the Industrial Revolution, the growth of white-collar work, the increased participation of women in the labor force, and the arrival of the information age, have set the stage for sociology to come into its own. Sociology is the systematic examination of the ways in which people are affected by, and affect, the social structures and social processes associated with the groups, organizations, cultures, societies, and the world in which they exist. This book focuses especially on three powerful structural forces in the social world that have drawn the attention of contemporary sociologists—globalization, consumption, and digital technology.

As the world has become more globalized, individual societies have lost some of their significance, and larger, transnational organizations have become more prominent. Global society has also become

more fluid. People move more quickly and easily across borders, as do goods, messages, and music, to name a few.

Consumption is the process by which people obtain and utilize various goods and services. While it might seem like a positive force, sociologists have also identified some of its negative aspects. Among these are overconsumption and excessive and rising debt.

Life in the digital world and its links to life in the real world have become major topics of study for sociologists. Technology also plays an important role in consumption, particularly with the shift from a highly social shopping experience, such as in a mall with other people, to the more isolated experience of shopping online.

The McDonaldization of society brings the rational principles of the fast-food restaurant into prominence in additional sectors of society and the world. These principles are efficiency, calculability, predictability, and control.

All these changes are easier to understand using C. Wright Mills's "sociological imagination," which calls on us to look at phenomena not just from a personal perspective but also from a distinctively sociological one, a view from the outside. It is also helpful to see the relationship between private troubles and larger public issues, and to acknowledge that much of our reality is socially constructed.

Sociologists study many topics, sometimes to understand them through scientific research and sometimes to create change and reform. Many of the topics we discuss in this book are familiar to you from your daily life. Take a systematic sociological approach to understanding them. Keep in mind that sociological phenomena are all around you, and keep your own sociological imagination honed and ready as you explore the social world.

KEY TERMS

Agency, 19
Butterfly effect, 5
Consumption, 9
Dangerous giant, 19
Globalization, 7
Macro, 19

McDonaldization, 10
Micro, 19
Public sociology, 22
Social construction of reality, 20
Social processes, 21
Social structure, 21

Society, 7
Sociological imagination, 16
Sociology, 5
Technology, 11

REVIEW QUESTIONS

1. How does the aftermath of Mohamed Bouazizi burning himself to death in full public view in Tunisia in 2010 illustrate the butterfly effect? Use your sociological imagination to think of ways that your individual choices and actions have been influenced by this event.

2. Your social world is continually changing. What are some examples of new technologies that have been developed during your lifetime? How have they changed the way you interact with and relate to others?

3. How do Dubai's shopping malls reflect increasing globalization? Do you think such shopping malls lead to a sameness of culture around the world, or do they allow local areas to retain their differences?

4. What items are you most likely to buy using the Internet? How do social networking sites (Facebook, Twitter, Pinterest) influence what you consume?

5. According to C. Wright Mills, how are private troubles different from public issues? How can we use the micro–macro distinction to show how private troubles are related to public issues?

6. What is the difference between structure and agency? Within your classroom, could you be a "dangerous giant"? In what ways does your classroom enable you to do things you would not be able to do otherwise?

7. What do sociologists mean by the social construction of reality? How can you apply this perspective to better understand trends in the music industry?

8. How is George Ritzer's *McDonaldization of Society* an example of public sociology?

9. Can you think of ways in which we can use "pure science" to better understand the fast-food industry? In your opinion, what should be the goal of research?

10. How does sociology approach globalization differently than other social sciences? In your opinion, what are the advantages of using a sociological approach to understand globalization?

APPLYING THE SOCIOLOGICAL IMAGINATION ....

Twitter has emerged as a way to instantaneously share information and keep up-to-date with what is currently happening. But how can we use Twitter to make sense of the interrelated processes of globalization and consumption?

For this activity, go to Twitter.com and find the day's top trending topics worldwide. Explore these top trends by clicking on them and looking at the specific tweets. Do research on the Internet for topics mentioned in the tweets that are unfamiliar to you.

In what ways are these topics and tweets reflective of a globalized world? How are these topics and tweets related to goods and services that you consume? In what ways does Twitter facilitate the flow of information and goods globally? How does this influence the decisions and choices that individuals make at the micro level? How do these trends affect your own choices?

STUDENT STUDY SITE ....

Sharpen your skills with SAGE edge at **edge.sagepub.com/ritzeressentials**

SAGE edge for students provides a personalized approach to help you accomplish your coursework goals in an easy-to-use learning environment.

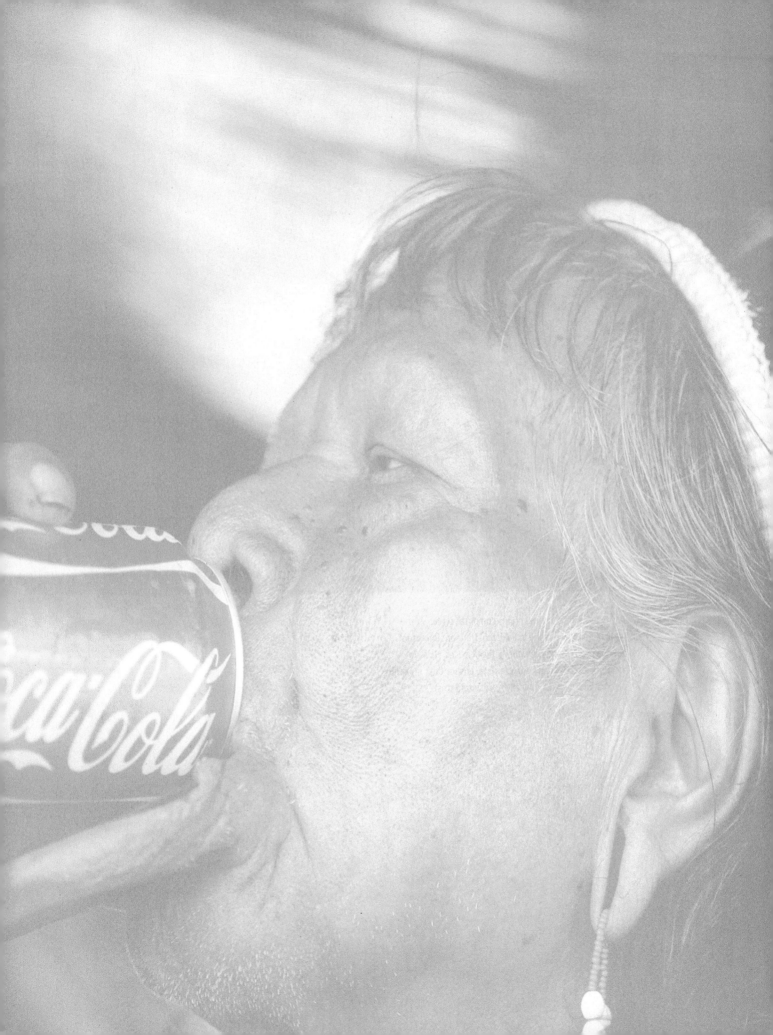

A broker monitors prices on his computer screen at the
Karachi Stock Exchange in Pakistan. Data are important
in many professions, particularly the sciences. How do
sociologists collect and analyze data, ensure their reliability
and validity, and act ethically to maintain trust?

THINKING ABOUT AND RESEARCHING THE SOCIAL WORLD

LEARNING OBJECTIVES

1 Describe the work of the classical era's social theorists, including Marx, Weber, Durkheim, and others.

2 Outline the tenets of structural/functional, conflict/critical, and inter/actionist theories.

3 Describe the scientific method.

4 Describe the various methods of sociological research and the types of questions each one can help us answer.

5 Describe how sociologists engage in secondary data analysis.

6 Identify the key issues in social research, including reliability, validity, trust, legality, and objectivity.

Humankind has made amazing advances during its short existence on Earth. From the development of agriculture to the Industrial Revolution to the advent of globalization, each generation has pushed us further into an unknown future. Many of us now enjoy longer life expectancies, improved standards of living, cheap manufactured goods, readily available food, quick and effortless communication, and the ability to travel around the world. But our advancement as a species has come at a significant ecological price.

Climate change, marked by long-term fluctuations in Earth's intricate and interwoven weather patterns, has occurred since the formation of the planet. Some fluctuations affect only specific regions, while others affect the entire world. Some span decades; others occur over millions of years. Though gradual climate change is a natural process, a growing body of careful research suggests that significant recent changes are directly attributable to human activities including fossil fuel combustion and deforestation.

> ### Sociology is a science, like—and also unlike—any other.

Despite this scientific consensus, our impact on climate change remains a hotly debated issue. If the available geological, atmospheric, and oceanographic evidence is solid enough to convince the scientific community, why do so many people remain fiercely unconvinced? Who is opposed to the notion that human actions are a major cause of climate change, and how have institutional forces influenced their personal beliefs over time?

Physical science can help us understand and explain climate change, but to understand the motivations, beliefs, and actions that affect our response to it, we need sociologists and their research methods. There are many types of social research; each can uncover unknown or even unsuspected truths about the relationship between people and climate change, as well as many other social issues. Thus, sociology is a science, like—and also unlike—any other.

Like all scientists, passionate sociologists may unintentionally let their personal feelings or their drive to succeed interfere with their research. Though we all make occasional mistakes, research methods must be ethical, reliable, and valid for their results to be widely accepted. This is especially important since contemporary sociological research often deals with heated issues like the role of people and society in climate change.

As you learn about the major types and purposes of sociological research, consider the issues and phenomena that you yourself might like to research. You might someday have an opportunity to do so. •

THEORIZING THE SOCIAL WORLD

While they are not, and should not be, clearly separated, in the two parts of this chapter we will deal with thinking about social issues (theorizing) and researching them (using sociological methods).

Theories are sets of interrelated ideas that have a wide range of application, deal with centrally important issues, and have stood the test of time (Ritzer and Stepnisky 2014). Theories have stood the test of time when they continue to be applicable to the changing social world and have withstood challenges from those who accept other theories. Sociological theories are necessary to make sense of both the innumerable social phenomena and the many highly detailed findings of sociological research. Without such theories we would have little more than knowledge of isolated bits of the social world. However, once those theories have been created, they can be applied broadly to such areas as the economy, organizations, and religion, as well as society as a whole and even the globe. The theories to be discussed in this chapter deal with very important social issues that have affected the social world for centuries, and will likely continue to affect them.

CLASSICAL SOCIOLOGICAL THEORY

These are among the most important early sociological theorists:

- *Auguste Comte* is noted for invention of the term *sociology*, development of a general theory of the social world, and interest in developing a science of sociology (Pickering 2011).

- *Harriet Martineau*, like Comte, developed a general scientific theory, although she is best known today for

Auguste Comte hoped his ideas would form the basis of a new religion of humanity with himself as high priest. Could he have expressed this ambition differently?

her feminist, women-centered sociology (Hoecker-Drysdale 2011).

- *Herbert Spencer* also developed a general, scientific theory of society, but his overriding theoretical interest was in social change, specifically evolution in not only the physical domain but also the intellectual and social domains (Francis 2011).

THE GIANTS OF CLASSICAL SOCIOLOGICAL THEORY

The theorists to be discussed in this section are the most significant of the classical era's social theorists and of the greatest continuing contemporary relevance to sociology (and other fields).

Karl Marx

Marx focused most of his attention on the structure of capitalist society. Marx defined **capitalism** as an economic system based on the fact that one group of people—the **capitalists**—owns what is needed for production,

> **theories** A set of interrelated ideas that have a wide range of application, deal with centrally important issues, and have stood the test of time.
>
> **capitalism** In Marx's view, an economic system based on one group of people (the capitalists or owners) owning what is needed for production and a second group (the proletariat or workers) owning little but their capacity for work.
>
> **capitalists** Those who own what is needed for production—factories, machines, tools—in a capitalist system.

Sociological Theorists

Herbert Spencer

Auguste Comte

Harriet Martineau was an unusual woman for her time, both in being well educated and in supporting her family with her published writing. What career might she pursue today?

FIGURE 2.1 • U.S. Income Gap, 1969–2011

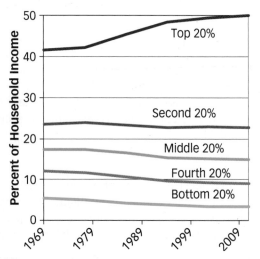

SOURCE: Data From Carmen Denavas-Walt, Bernadette D. Proctor, and Jessica C. Smith. Income, Poverty, and Health Insurance Coverage in the United States: 2012. Table A-3. Current Population Reports: Current Income. U.S. Census Bureau, U.S. Department of Commerce, September 2012.

including factories, machines, and tools. A second group—the **proletariat**, or workers—owns little or nothing, except for their capacity for work and labor. In order to work and survive, the workers must sell their labor time, primarily their working hours, to the capitalists in exchange for wages.

The capitalist system is marked by **exploitation**. The proletariat produces virtually everything but gets only a small portion of the income derived from the sale of the products. The capitalists, who do little productive work, reap the vast majority of the rewards. In other words, the capitalists exploit the workers. Furthermore, driven by the need to compete in the marketplace, the capitalists are forced to keep costs, including wages, as low as possible. As competition with other capitalists intensifies, there is pressure to reduce wages further. As a result, the proletariat barely subsists, living a miserable, animal-like existence.

In addition, the workers experience **alienation** on the job and in the workplace (Meszaros 2006). They are alienated because

- the work that they do—for example, repetitively and mechanically inserting wicks into candles or hubcaps on cars—is not a natural expression of human skills, abilities, and creativity;

- they have little or no connection to the finished product; and

- instead of working harmoniously with their fellow workers, they may be in competition, or have little or no contact, with them.

Thus, what defines people as human beings—their ability to think, to act on the basis of that thought, to be creative, to interact with other human beings—is denied to the workers in capitalism.

Over time, Marx believed, the workers' situation would grow much worse as the capitalists increased the level of exploitation and restructured the work so that the

> **proletariat** Workers as a group, or those in the capitalist system who own little or nothing except for their capacity for work (labor), which they must sell to the capitalists to survive.
>
> **exploitation** A feature of capitalism in which the workers (proletariat) produce virtually everything but get few rewards, while the capitalists, who do little, reap the vast majority of the rewards.
>
> **alienation** In a capitalist system, being unconnected to one's work, products, fellow workers, and human nature.

proletariat was even more alienated. Once the workers understood how capitalism "really" worked, especially the ways in which it worked to their detriment, they would rise up and overthrow that system. The outcome of the proletarian revolution would be the creation of a communist society.

Marx's theories about capitalism are relevant to contemporary society. For example, in the United States, a capitalist country, the gap he predicted between those at the top of the economic system and the rest of the population is huge and growing. In 2009, the top 20 percent of the population in terms of income had almost as much income as the rest of the population combined. Furthermore, as you can see in Figure 2.1, since 1969 those at the top have secured more of the income for themselves (DeNavas-Walt, Proctor, and Smith 2010). As Marx predicted, corporations today search the globe for workers willing to work for lower wages, driving down pay everywhere and reaping as much profit as possible from lower labor costs.

However, history has failed to bear out much of Marx's thinking about the demise of capitalism. Nevertheless, capitalism continues to exist, and Marx's ways of thinking about it continue to be useful.

Max Weber

Weber's best known work is *The Protestant Ethic and the Spirit of Capitalism* ([1904–1905] 1958). It is a part of his historical-comparative study of religion in various societies throughout the world (see "Historical-Comparative Method" later in this chapter). One of the main objectives in this work is to analyze the relationship between the economy and religion. Like Marx, Weber accepted the central importance of the economy in general, and of capitalism in particular, but he wanted to demonstrate the importance of other sociological variables. Marx had argued that religion is a relatively minor force that serves to distract the masses from the problems caused by capitalism. In Marx's ([1843] 1970) famous words, religion "is the opium of the people." In contrast, Weber focused on the central role played by religion in the western world's economic development.

Unlike Marx, Weber was not interested in capitalism per se. He was more interested in the broader phenomenon of **rationalization**, or the process by which social structures are increasingly characterized by the most direct and efficient means to their ends. To Weber, this process was becoming more and more common in

> **rationalization** The process by which social structures are increasingly characterized by the most direct and efficient means to their ends.

Karl Marx's work is often misunderstood, but his criticisms of capitalism, based on his humanism and idealism, are still influential today. What is your understanding of his theories?

many sectors of society. This included the economy, especially in bureaucracies and in the most rational economic system—capitalism. Capitalism is rational because, for example, of its continuous efforts to find ways to produce efficiently more profitable products with fewer inputs and simpler processes. A specific and early example of rationalization in capitalism is the assembly line in which raw materials entered the line and emerged as finished products.

Weber saw rationalization leading an "iron cage," making it increasingly difficult to escape the process. This concept gives a clear sense of his negative opinion of rationalization.

> Capitalism is today an immense cosmos into which the individual is born . . . It forces the individual . . . to conform to capitalist rules of action. (Weber [1904–1905] 1958: 54)

Harriet Martineau

Marx's Life

Marxist Theory

Max Weber, who initially studied law, suffered a nervous breakdown triggered by a fight with his father shortly before his father's death and did not work for several years. Over the course of his lifetime, however, he was extremely productive.

While Marx was optimistic and had great hope for socialism and communism, Weber was a pessimist about most things. Socialism and communism, he felt, would not eliminate or prevent the iron cage from enveloping us (Gerth and Mills 1958: 128).

Émile Durkheim

To Durkheim, the major concern of the science of sociology was **social facts.** These are macro-level phenomena, such as social structures and cultural norms and values, that stand apart from people and, more importantly, impose themselves on people. Examples include the structure and norms of your university and the U.S. government. Durkheim felt that such structures and their constraints were not only necessary but highly desirable.

Both Marx and Weber had a generally positive sense of people as thoughtful, creative, and naturally social. They criticized social structures for stifling and distorting people's innate characteristics. In contrast,

Durkheim had a largely negative view of people as being slaves to their passions. Left to their own devices, he believed, people would seek to satisfy those passions. However, the satisfaction of one passion would simply lead to the need to satisfy other passions. This endless succession of passions could never be satisfied. In Durkheim's view, passions should be limited, but people are unable to exercise this control themselves. They need social facts that are capable of limiting and controlling their passions.

The most important of these social facts is the **collective conscience**, or the set of beliefs shared by people throughout society. In Durkheim's view, the collective conscience is highly desirable not only for society but also for individuals. For example, it is good for both society and individuals that we share the belief that we are not supposed to kill one another. Without a collective conscience, murderous passions would be left to run wild. Individuals would be destroyed, of course, and so would society.

This leads us to *Suicide* (Durkheim [1897] 1951), one of the most famous research studies in the history of sociology. Because he was a sociologist, Durkheim did not focus on why any given individual committed suicide. Rather he dealt with the more collective issues of suicide rates and why one group of people had a higher rate of suicide than another. It was in many ways an ideal example of the power of sociological research. Using publicly available data, Durkheim found, for example, that suicide rates were not related to psychological and biological factors such as alcoholism or race and heredity. Rather, suicide rates were related to social factors that exert negative pressure on the individual. These include collective feelings of rootlessness and normlessness. Suicide also constitutes a threat to society, since those who commit suicide are rejecting a key aspect of the collective conscience—that one should not kill oneself.

Suicide demonstrates the power of sociology to explain one of the most private and personal of acts. Durkheim believed that if sociology could be shown to apply to suicide, it could deal with any and all social phenomena.

Durkheim differentiated among four different types of suicide. The most important one for our purposes is *anomic*

social facts Macro-level phenomena—social structures and cultural norms and values—that stand apart from and impose themselves on people.

collective conscience The set of beliefs shared by people throughout society.

anomie The feeling of not knowing what is expected of one in society or of being adrift in society without any clear, secure moorings.

suicide. **Anomie** is defined as people's feeling that they do not know what is expected of them in society, the feeling of being adrift in society without any clear or secure moorings. The risk of anomic suicide increases when people do not know what is expected of them, when society's regulation over them is low, and when their passions are allowed to run wild.

More generally, Durkheim believed that anomie was the defining problem of the modern world. This broad view appeared in another famous work by Durkheim, *The Division of Labor in Society* ([1893] 1964). Durkheim depicted a change over time in the direction of an increasing division of labor. Since people did different things, they didn't believe strongly in the same set of ideas. A weak collective conscience was a problem, Durkheim argued, because it progressively lost the power to control people's passions. Further, because of the weakened collective conscience, people were more likely to feel anomic and, among other things, were more likely to commit anomic suicide.

OTHER IMPORTANT EARLY THEORISTS

Georg Simmel, W. E. B. Du Bois, and Thorstein Veblen all had grand theories of society, and you will see references to their ideas throughout the book.

Georg Simmel

Simmel's major importance lies in his contributions to micro theory, especially the way conscious individuals interact with one another (Scaff 2011).

Simmel was interested in the *forms* taken by social interaction. One such form involves the interaction between superiors and subordinates. Simmel was also interested in the *types* of people who engage in interaction. For example, one type is the poor person, and another is the rich person. To Simmel, it is the nature of the interaction between these two types of people and not the nature of each that is of greatest importance. Therefore, poverty is not about the nature of the poor person but about the kind of interaction that takes place between poor and rich. A poor person is defined, then, not as someone who lacks money but rather as someone who receives aid from a rich person.

W. E. B. Du Bois

Du Bois is best known in sociology for his theoretical ideas (Taylor 2011). He saw a "color line" existing between whites and blacks in the United States. This barrier was physical, but it was also political in that much of the white population did not see African Americans as "true" Americans. As a result, they denied African Americans

Émile Durkheim, from a family of rabbis, spent much of his life studying religion through a sociological lens, though not as a practicing Jew. Does the study of sociology or any other science preclude holding deep religious beliefs?

many political rights, such as the right to vote. And the barrier was psychological because, among other things, African Americans found it difficult to see themselves in ways other than the ways in which white society saw them.

One of Du Bois's goals, especially in *The Souls of Black Folk* (1903), was to lift the veil of race and give whites a glimpse of "Negroes" in America. He also wanted to show blacks that they could see themselves in a different way, especially outside the view that white society had prescribed for them. Politically, he hoped for the day when the veil would be lifted forever, thereby freeing

Max Weber

Weberian Theorizing

Émile Durkheim

Do you agree with W. E. B. Du Bois's assertion that Black Americans have a "double-consciousness," a sense of being American and of being African American, and that this produces great tension for them?

do what most people consider to be work. However, the problem with conspicuous leisure is that it is often difficult for many others to witness these displays.

Over time the focus shifts for the wealthy from publicly demonstrating a waste of time to publicly demonstrating a waste of money. The waste of money is central to Veblen's most famous idea, **conspicuous consumption**. It is much easier for others to see conspicuous consumption than to see conspicuous leisure. Examples include driving around one's neighborhood in a Porsche and wearing expensive Dolce and Gabbana clothing with the D&G logo visible to all.

Veblen is important for focusing on consumption at a time when it was largely ignored by other social theorists.

CONTEMPORARY SOCIOLOGICAL THEORY

As sociology has grown as a discipline, the theories of earlier sociologists have evolved and branched out into at least a dozen newer theories. As Table 2.1 shows, these contemporary theories and the others reviewed in the rest of this chapter can be categorized under three broad headings: structural/functional, conflict/critical, and inter/actionist theories.

STRUCTURAL/FUNCTIONAL THEORIES

Structural/functional theories have evolved out of the observation and analysis of large-scale social phenomena. These phenomena include, for example, the state and the culture, the latter encompassing the ideas and objects that allow people to carry out their collective lives (see Chapter 3 for more on culture). The two major theories under the broad heading of structural/functional theories are *structural-functionalism*, which looks at both social structures and their functions, and *structuralism*, which concerns itself solely with social structures, without concern for their functions. Note that while they sound the same, structural-functionalism is one theory under the broader heading of structural/functional theories.

blacks. Another of Du Bois's important ideas is **double-consciousness**. That is, black Americans have a sense of "two-ness," of being American and being African American. Double-consciousness results in a sense among black Americans that they are characterized by "two souls, two thoughts, two unreconciled strivings; two warring ideals" (Du Bois [1903] 1966: 5). Double-consciousness obviously produces great tension for black Americans, much greater than the racial tensions felt by white Americans.

Thorstein Veblen

In his most famous book, *The Theory of the Leisure Class* (Veblen [1899] 1994), one of Veblen's main concerns was the ways in which the upper classes demonstrate their wealth.

One way is through *conspicuous leisure*, or doing things that demonstrate quite publicly that one does not need to

> **double-consciousness** Among black Americans, the sense of "two-ness," of being both black and American.
>
> **conspicuous consumption** The public demonstration of wealth, through consumption, that one is able to waste money—for example, by flaunting the use of expensive, high-status goods and services (mansions, yachts, personal assistants, etc.).

Structural-Functionalism

Structural-functionalism focuses on social structures as well as the functions that such structures perform. Structural-functionalists were influenced by, among others, the work of Émile Durkheim. Structural-functional theorists start out with a positive view of social structures (e.g., the military and the police). They also assert that those structures are desirable, necessary, and even impossible to do without. However, as you will see later, not all sociologists view social structures as completely positive.

Structural-functionalism tends to be a "conservative" theory. The dominant view is that if certain structures exist and are functional—and it is often assumed that if they exist, they are functional—they ought to be retained and conserved.

A series of well-known and useful concepts was developed by structural-functionalists, especially Robert Merton ([1949] 1968; Crothers 2011). These concepts are easily explained in the context of globalization. Specifically they can be applied to issues such as border controls and the passports needed to pass through them (Torpey 2012) as well as the physical barriers at borders, such as the wall between the United States and Mexico.

One central concept in Merton's version of structural-functionalism is **functions**. These are the observable, positive consequences of a structure that help it survive, adapt, and adjust. National borders are functional in various ways. For example, the passport controls at borders allow a country to monitor who is entering the country and to refuse entry to those it considers undesirable or dangerous.

CHECKPOINT 2.1 — LEADING EARLY THEORISTS IN SOCIOLOGY

Theorist	Major Contribution to Sociology
Karl Marx	Examined the structure of capitalist society and its exploitation of the proletariat class.
Max Weber	Focused on the central role of religion in the economic development of the West, as well as the more general issue of the rationalization of society.
Émile Durkheim	Studied social structures and cultural norms and values, including the collective conscience, that impose themselves on people and whose weakness creates anomie.
Georg Simmel	Developed micro-level theory of social interaction.
W. E. B. Du Bois	Developed a sociology of race and the idea of double-consciousness.
Thorstein Veblen	Studied consumption, and in particular conspicuous consumption, by the wealthy.

Structural-functionalism is greatly enriched when we add the concept of **dysfunctions**, which are observable consequences that negatively affect the ability of a given system to survive, adapt, or adjust. While border and

TABLE 2.1 • Major Sociological Theories

Structural/ Functional Theories	Conflict/ Critical Theories	Inter/Actionist Theories
Structural-functionalism	Conflict theory	Symbolic interactionism
Structuralism	Critical theory	Ethnomethodology
	Feminist theory	Exchange theory
	Queer theory	Rational choice theory
	Critical theories of race and racism	
	Postmodern theory	

Georg Simmel

W. E. B. Du Bois

Other Theorists

TABLE 2.2 • Foreign College Students in the U.S.: Top 10 Countries of Origin, 2011

Country of Origin	Percent
China	21.8
India	14.4
South Korea	10.1
Canada	3.8
Taiwan	3.4
Saudi Arabia	3.1
Japan	2.9
Vietnam	2.1
Mexico	1.9
Turkey	1.7

SOURCE: Adapted from Project Atlas, Atlas of Student Mobility. Institute of International Education, Inc.

passport controls clearly have functions, they also have dysfunctions. For example, after 9/11, Congress passed many immigration-related acts. As a result, it has become much more difficult for everyone to enter the United States (Kurzban 2006). This is true not only for potential terrorists but also for legitimate workers, businesspeople, and students (Kasarda and Lindsay 2011; Lowell, Bump, and Martin 2007). Table 2.2 lists the top 10 countries of origin of international students attending school in the United States.

Merton differentiated between two types of functions. The first is **manifest functions**, or positive consequences that are brought about consciously and purposely. For example, the manifest function of tariffs imposed on goods imported into the United States from elsewhere in the world is to make their prices higher compared with American-made goods and to protect U.S.-based producers. Such actions often have **latent functions**, or unintended positive consequences. For example, when foreign products become more expensive and therefore less desirable, U.S. manufacturers may produce more and perhaps better goods in the United States. In addition, more jobs for Americans would be created.

One more concept of note is the idea of **unanticipated consequences**, or consequences that are unexpected and can be either positive or, more importantly, negative. A negative unanticipated consequence of tariffs is the possibility of a trade war. China, for example, might respond to an increase in U.S. tariffs by raising its own tariffs on U.S. imports. If the United States retaliates with new and still higher tariffs, we could quickly be in the midst of an unanticipated, and probably undesirable, trade war involving the United States, China, and perhaps other nations.

Structuralism

A second structural/functional theory, **structuralism**, focuses on structures but is *not* concerned with their functions. In addition, while structural-functionalism focuses on quite visible structures such as border fences, structuralism is more interested in the social impact of hidden or underlying structures, such as the global economic order or gender relations. It adopts the view that these hidden structures determine what transpires on the surface of the social world. Thus, for example, behind-the-scenes actions of capitalists determine what positions are taken by political leaders. This perspective comes from the field of linguistics, which has largely adopted the view that the surface, the way we speak and express ourselves, is determined by an underlying grammatical system (Saussure [1916] 1966).

Marx can be seen as a structuralist because he was interested in the hidden structures that determine how capitalism works. So, for example, on the surface capitalism seems to operate to the benefit of all. However, hidden below the surface is a structure that operates mostly for the benefit of the capitalists, who exploit the workers and pay them subsistence wages. Similarly, capitalists argue that the value of products is determined by supply and demand in the market. In contrast, Marx argued that hidden beneath the surface is the fact that value comes from the labor that goes into the products and this labor comes entirely from the workers.

Similarly, Marx's frequent collaborator, Friedrich Engels ([1884] 1970), looked at relationships between women and men and theorized that the structures of capitalism and patriarchy keep women subordinated to men. Engels assumed that family structure followed an evolutionary path from primitive to modern. In the early communistic society, members had multiple sexual pairings, and the uncertainty about who had fathered a child gave women power in the family and in society. Property passed from mother to child, and women were held in high esteem.

manifest functions Positive consequences that are brought about consciously and purposely.

latent functions Unintended positive consequences.

unanticipated consequences Unexpected social effects, especially negative effects.

structuralism Social theory interested in the social impact of hidden or underlying structures.

However, as wealth began to accumulate and men gained control of agricultural production, men claimed more status. In order to guarantee the fidelity of the wife and therefore the paternity of the children, the social system evolved so that the wife was subjugated to male power and men sought to claim women as their own property. Monogamy eventually led to the even more restrictive marriage bond. Engels believed that with the advent of "marriage begins the abduction and purchase of women" (Engels [1884] 1970: 735).

Engels believed that female oppression is rooted in the hidden and underlying structure of private property rights in capitalism. As a result, he thought that the key to ending that oppression is to abolish private property. The connections he drew between gender inequality and the underlying structure of society have proved to be enduring, and many contemporary feminist theorists (see below) have built more sophisticated analyses upon them.

A structuralist approach leads sociologists to look beyond the surface for underlying structures and realities, which determine what transpires on the surface. Thus, for example, military threats made by North Korea, and its test firing of missiles, may not really be about military matters at all but instead be about its failing economic system. North Korea may hope that the symbolic expression of military power will distract its citizens, strengthen its global prestige, frighten others, and perhaps coerce other countries, especially the United States, into providing economic aid.

A very useful sociological idea in this context is **debunking**, or looking beneath and beyond surface realities (Berger 1963). For example, while the United States seems to emphasize peace, sociologists (as we have seen) have pointed out that it has a hidden and powerful military-industrial complex with a vested interest in war, or at least in preparations for war (Ledbetter, 2011; Mills 1956). Many sociologists see debunking as going to the very heart of the field (Baehr and Gordon 2012).

CONFLICT/CRITICAL THEORIES

Several different theories are discussed under this heading: conflict theory, critical theory, feminist theory, queer theory, critical theories of race and racism, and postmodern theory. They all tend to emphasize stresses, strains, and conflicts in

> **debunking** Looking beneath and beyond the surface of social structures, which are seen as facades that conceal what is truly important.
>
> **conflict theory** A set of ideas focusing on the sources of conflict within society; this theory sees society as held together by coercion and focuses on its negative aspects.

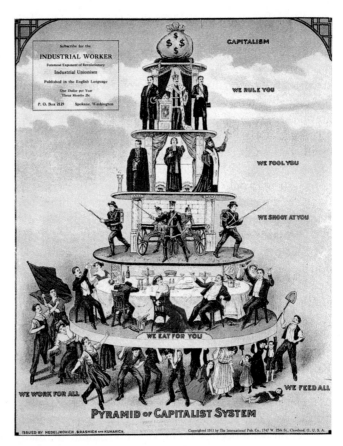

Though capitalism appears to benefit all participants, structuralists see a structure beneath its surface that benefits capitalists at workers' expense. How do you view capitalism?

society. They are critical of society in a variety of different ways, especially of the power that is exercised over less powerful members of society.

Conflict Theory

The best known of these theories is conflict theory (R. Collins 2012). It has roots in Marx's theory. Much of it can be seen as an inversion of structural-functionalism, which **conflict theory** was designed to compete with and to counteract. While structural-functionalism emphasizes what is positive about society, conflict theory focuses on its negative aspects. To the structural-functionalist, society is held together by consensus; virtually everyone accepts the social structure, its legitimacy, and its benefits. But, to the conflict theorist, society is held together by coercion. Those who are adversely affected by society, especially economically, would rebel were it not for coercive forces like the police, the courts, and the military.

Public Sociology: Karl Marx

False Consciousness

A good example of conflict theory is to be found in the work of Ralf Dahrendorf (1959). Although he was strongly influenced by Marx, he was more strongly motivated by a desire to develop a viable alternative to structural-functionalism. For example, while structural-functionalists tend to see society as static, conflict theorists emphasize the ever-present possibility of change. Where structural-functionalists see the orderliness of society, conflict theorists see dissension and conflict everywhere. Finally, structural-functionalists focus on the sources of cohesion internal to society, but conflict theorists see the coercion and power that holds together an otherwise fractious society.

Overall, conflict theorists like Dahrendorf see two basic sides to society—consensus and conflict—and believe that both are needed. Sociology therefore needs, at least in this view, two different theories: conflict theory and "consensus" (or structural-functional) theory.

Dahrendorf offers a very sociological view of authority, arguing that it resides not in individuals—Barack Obama, for example—but in positions (e.g., the presidency of the United States) and in various associations of people. In his view, those associations are controlled by a hierarchy of authority positions and the people who occupy them. However, there are many such associations in any society. Thus a person may be in authority in one type of association but be subordinate in many others.

What most interests Dahrendorf is the potential for conflict between those in positions of authority and those who are subordinate. They usually have very different interests. Like authority, those interests are not characteristics of individuals but rather are linked to the positions they hold. Thus, the top management of a corporation such as Wal-Mart is interested in making the corporation more profitable by cutting wages. In contrast, those who hold such low-level jobs as cashier or stock clerk are interested in increasing their wages to meet basic needs. Because of this inherent tension and conflict, authority within associations is always tenuous.

In general, the interests of those involved in associations are unconscious, but at times they become conscious and therefore more likely to lead to overt conflict. *Conflict groups* may form, as when a group of cashiers goes out on strike against Wal-Mart. The coalitions formed out of resistance efforts often increase cohesion among group members, further uniting them and bolstering the strength of the movement (Coser 1956). The actions of conflict groups very often change society, as well as elements of society like the Wal-Mart corporation, sometimes quite radically.

Critical Theory

While Marx's work was critical of the capitalist economy, **critical theory** shifts the focus to culture (e.g., movies, the Internet). Marx believed that culture is shaped by the economic system. In contrast, the critical school has argued that by the early twentieth century and at an ever-accelerating rate to this day, culture has succeeded in becoming important in its own right. Furthermore, in many ways it has come to be more important than the economic system. Instead of being controlled by the capitalist economy, more of us are controlled, and controlled more often, by culture, specifically by the culture industry.

The **culture industry** is the rationalized and bureaucratized structures that control modern culture. In the 1920s and 1930s, the critical theorists focused on radio, magazines, and movies. Today, movies remain important, but the focus has shifted to television and various aspects of the Internet. These are critiqued for producing, or serving as an outlet for, **mass culture**, or cultural elements that are administered by organizations, lack spontaneity, and are phony. Two features of mass culture and its dissemination by the culture industry are of great concern to critical theorists:

- *Falseness.* True culture should emanate from the people and reflect their reality, but mass culture involves prepackaged sets of ideas that falsify reality. The reality shows that dominate television today are a contemporary example of mass culture. They are presented as if they are authentic, but in fact they are scripted, highly controlled, and selectively edited.

- *Repressiveness.* The effect of mass culture is to pacify, stupefy, and repress the masses so that they are far less likely to demand social change. Those who rush home nightly to catch up on their favorite reality TV shows are unlikely to have much interest in, or time for, revolutionary activities, or even civic activities and reforms. Additionally, according to some theorists, the "culture industry" has succeeded in creating corporate brands that are globally recognized and sought after as cultural symbols (Arvidsson 2012; Lash and Lury 2007). Instead of engaging in revolutionary activities, many people are striving to keep up with, and acquire, the latest and hottest brands.

---

critical theory A set of critical ideas derived from Marxian theory but focusing on culture rather than the economy.

culture industry The rationalized and bureaucratized structures that control modern culture.

mass culture Cultural elements that are administered by large organizations, lack spontaneity, and are phony.

Do you see evidence of critical theory's ideas of falseness and repressiveness in the elements of mass culture to which you are exposed? If so, what form do they take?

Critical theory can be applied to some of the newest media forms, such as YouTube, Facebook, Twitter, and eBay (Denegri-Knott and Zwick 2012). Despite plenty of false and stupefying content on these sites, and much educational material as well, they are not controlled by large rationalized bureaucracies—at least not yet. Almost all of the content that appears on such sites is provided by those who also consume material on the sites. The sites exercise little control over content; they are arguably spontaneous and authentic. It's tempting to conclude that these new aspects of the culture industry are not assailable from a traditional critical theory perspective.

The Bollywood-style film *The Big-Hearted Will Take the Bride* had been playing at a Mumbai theater for 900 weeks by the beginning of 2013, with no end in sight. Some fans have seen the movie dozens of times. What would a critical theorist say about the respective roles of the culture industry and the public in making this the longest-running film in India's history?

Yet it could be argued that while the content is not produced by the culture industry, the content is disseminated by it. So although many websites have yet to become profitable, they have come to be worth many billions of dollars each because of investors' belief in their future profitability. More importantly, the masses are pacified, repressed, and stupefied by spending endless hours buying and selling on eBay, uploading images on Pinterest, and updating their Facebook pages and following day-to-day, even minute-by-minute, developments in the lives of others. The same could be said of Twitter's tweets, which inform us instantaneously that, for example, one of our friends has gotten a haircut or a manicure. While people do find friends, learn useful things, and may even foment revolutions on Twitter (as in the case of the "Arab Spring" uprisings in 2011), they also may spend, and likely waste, endless amounts of time on it.

Feminist Theory

Historically, male social theorists have received the most attention (one exception, mentioned above, is Harriet Martineau), and to a large extent that is still the case today. Not surprisingly, then, social theories in the main have ignored women and the distinctive problems they face (one exception is the work of Engels discussed above). A central aspect of **feminist theory** in general is the critique of patriarchy (male dominance) and the problems it poses not only for women but also for men. Feminist theory also offers ideas on how women's (and men's) situation can be bettered, if not revolutionized.

Feminist theory embraces a variety of theoretical positions (Lengermann and Niebrugge 2014; Tong 2009). One fundamental debate within feminist theory is whether or not gender inequality causes, or results from, gender differences. A few feminist theorists (Rossi 1983) believe that there are *essential* (or biologically determined) differences between men's and women's behavior, and that gender inequality is a result of the social devaluing of female characteristics (such as nurturing). But the majority of feminist scholars argue that gender differences are *socially constructed*. In other words, the differences we see between men's and women's behavior are not biologically determined but rather are created socially.

Feminist theorists who agree that gender differences are socially constructed disagree on the underlying causes. One view is that men, as the dominant group in society, have defined gender in such a way as to purposely restrain and subordinate women. Another view holds that social

> **feminist theory** A set of ideas critical of the social situation confronting women and offering solutions for improving, if not revolutionizing, their situation.

Conflict Theory

Gay Rights

Queer Theory

structures such as capitalist organizations and patriarchal families have evolved to favor men and traditionally male roles. Both structures benefit from the uncompensated labor of women, and so there is little incentive for men as a dominant group to change the status quo. Clearly these perspectives all involve a critical orientation.

There is also a broad consensus among feminist theorists that women face extraordinary problems related directly to gender inequality. As a result, equally extraordinary solutions are needed. However, feminist theorists vary in the degree to which they are willing to support dramatic, even revolutionary, changes in women's situation. Some feminist theorists suggest that the solution to gender inequality is to change social structures and institutions so they are more inclusive of women. Others argue that because those very structures and institutions create gender difference and inequality, we must first destroy them and then rebuild them in a wholly different way.

Women of color have sometimes been dissatisfied with feminist theory for not representing their interests very well. Several scholars argue that feminist theory generally reflects the perspective of white women while ignoring the unique experiences and viewpoints of women of color (Collins 2000; hooks 2000; Zinn 2012). Similarly, studies related to race tend to focus largely on the position of men. Thus many contemporary feminists have advocated scholarship that takes into account not just gender but also how it intersects with race and ethnicity, social class, and sexuality. The discussion of critical theories of race and racism provides more detail on this view.

Queer Theory

The word *queer* has conventionally been used as an umbrella term for gays, lesbians, bisexuals, and transgendered, transsexual, and intersexed persons. However, queer theory is not a theory of queers. In fact, it stands in contrast to the field of gay and lesbian studies, which focuses on homosexuality. Rather, **queer theory** is based on the idea that there are no fixed and stable identities that determine who we are (Plummer 2012). The theory also unsettles ("queers") identities that have been thought to be fixed, stable, or natural (Butler 1990). It is impossible to talk about any group of people, including those who are either gay or straight, on the basis of a single shared characteristic. Being homosexual does not mean that you have sexual relations only with those of the same sex, just as being heterosexual does not preclude other kinds of sexual relationships. Advocates of queer theory point out that modern western culture cannot be understood without critiquing modern definitions of homosexuality and heterosexuality (Sedgwick 1991).

Queer theory studies the dynamics of the relationship between heterosexuals and homosexuals, especially the exercise of power by heterosexuals over homosexuals. In this respect, queer theory is clearly a form of conflict/critical theory. In recent decades, however, homosexuals have consistently and successfully contested the blatant power of heterosexuals to control gay men's and lesbians' lives. Although some of the most serious abuses of heterosexuals' social power have waned, power continues to be exercised over homosexuals in subtler ways. For example, homosexuals often govern their own behavior (as when they avoid even mild displays of affection in public) so that heterosexuals feel comfortable.

Critical Theories of Race and Racism

Critical theories of race and racism argue that racism continues to adversely affect people of color (Outlaw 2012; Slatton and Feagin 2012). Given its history of slavery and racism, the United States has often been singled out for analysis using this theory.

Some commentators have argued that racism today is of little more than historical interest because white Americans have become "color-blind." They argue that we have come to ignore skin color when discussing social groups and that skin color is no longer used in hiring or admissions policies. However, critical theorists of race and racism disagree. They argue that while skin color has nothing to do with a person's physical or intellectual abilities, color-blindness ignores the past and present realities facing racial minorities, including the social consequences of years of racial discrimination. As a result, critics of color blindness argue that it is little more than a "new racism," a smoke screen that allows whites to practice and perpetuate racial discrimination (Bonilla-Silva 2009).

Of particular importance to work in this area is the idea of **intersectionality**. This points to the fact that people are affected, often adversely, not only by their race but also by their gender, sexual orientation, class, age, and global location. The confluence, or intersection, of these various statuses and the inequality and oppression associated with combinations of them are what matter most. Not only can't we deal with race, gender, class, and so on separately, but we also can't gain an understanding

---

queer theory A theory based on the idea that there are no fixed and stable identities (such as "heterosexual" or "homosexual") that determine who we are.

critical theories of race and racism A set of ideas arguing that race continues to matter and that racism continues to exist and adversely affect blacks and others.

intersectionality The confluence, or intersection, of various social statuses and the inequality and oppression associated with each in combination with others.

The Hijras of India

The hijras are one of India's smaller religious communities (Kalra 2012). There are about 50,000 hijras in India, mostly in the cities in the northern part of the country. Hijras tend to work and live together in communal households of five to fifteen people, operating like one large family. They share their incomes and chores. Since they are supposed to embody the power of a mother goddess, Bahuchara Mata, the main role of hijras in Indian society is a religious one. They engage in religious rituals and perform at various rites of passage (a source of their income) such as the birth of a child, weddings, and festivals in the temple. Other income is derived from begging or prostitution.

What makes hijras relevant in a discussion of queer theory is that hijras are considered neither men nor women. They represent a third gender, "one of the very few alternative gender roles currently functioning in any society" (Nanda 1999: xi). Their existence underscores gender possibilities beyond the male and female in the real world. Similar gender categories include berdaches, xaniths, and "manly hearted women" in African and American Indian societies (Lorber 1994). The hijras call into question our belief that there are only two natural, biologically based, genders.

Most hijras have neither male nor female sex organs. A few are born that way, or with both male and female sex organs (they are intersexed), but most are born males. In order to become a hijra, a person who is born with male sex organs

These hijra dancers performed at a recent conference in New Delhi intended to open a public discussion about achieving equality for members of their community. What challenges do they face?

has traditionally undergone surgery to remove both penis and testicles. That tradition is slowly changing, however, and some hijras do not undergo the surgery. In contrast to a sex change operation, no vagina is created to replace the male sex organs.

Hijras normally adopt the mannerisms of, and dress like, women. They insist that outsiders refer to them as women. Hijras who become prostitutes service a male clientele. Others become mistresses to men or marry men and refer to these men as their husbands. Marriage may occur in conjunction with, or perhaps after, a life as a prostitute.

Although they are stigmatized and often abused by the larger society, hijras have nevertheless been able to create a viable subculture, one that is able to give their lives considerable meaning.

Think About It

Does the existence and apparent viability of hijras support queer theory's assertions that there are no fixed or stable sexual identities? Why or why not? Do you believe hijras have a long-term future in India's increasingly modern, Westernized society?

of oppression by simply adding them together. For example, a poor black female lesbian faces a complex of problems different from the problems faced by a poor person or a black person or a woman or a lesbian.

ASK YOURSELF

Is your life affected by intersectionality? How many different statuses do you hold, and to which social and cultural groups do you belong?

Phenomena that were once associated almost exclusively with majority-minority relations in the United States are increasingly found elsewhere in the world. Europe, for example, has a long history of racism that includes centuries of colonialism, the African slave trade, anti-Semitism, and the Holocaust. Racial turmoil abated after World War II, but it is again on the rise—at least in part because of the large influx of immigrants in the early twenty-first century. Racist propaganda, hate speech, and incitement to violence have become much more common in recent years, notably in France, Austria, Germany, Sweden, and the United Kingdom. The main victims have been Muslims, Jews, people of North African/Arab origin, and Roma people from Central and Eastern Europe. They are largely powerless because Europe has not experienced anything like the U.S. civil rights movement, which served to mobilize and organize black Americans.

Postmodern Theory

Postmodern theory has many elements that fit well under the heading of critical theory, although it is more than critique (Lipovetsky 2005).

Postmodern theory is a theoretical orientation that is a reaction against modern theory. For example, postmodernists are opposed to the broad depictions of history and society offered by modern theorists. An example of such a narrative is Weber's theory of the increasing rationalization of the world. Instead, postmodernists tend to offer more limited, often unrelated, snapshots of the social world. In fact, postmodernists frequently deconstruct, or take apart, modern grand narratives. Postmodernists are also opposed to the scientific pretensions of much modern social theory. They adopt, instead, a nonscientific or even antiscientific approach to the social world. Postmodern theory offers a new and important way of theorizing. Postmodern social theorists look at familiar social phenomena in different ways or adopt a very different focus for their work. For example, in his study of the history of prisons, Michel Foucault ([1975] 1979) was critical of the modernist view that criminal justice had grown progressively liberal. He contended that prisons had, in fact, grown increasingly oppressive through the use of techniques such as constant, enhanced surveillance of prisoners. Similarly, in opposition to the traditional view that in the Victorian era people were sexually repressed, Foucault (1978) found instead an explosion of sexuality in the Victorian era.

Jean Baudrillard argued that we are now living in a consumer society where much of our lives is defined not by our productive work but by what we consume and how we consume it. The postmodern world is in fact characterized by **hyperconsumption**, which involves consuming more than we need, more than we really want, and more than we can afford.

ASK YOURSELF

Is there a relationship between Baudrillard's idea of hyperconsumption and critical theorists' characterization of the culture industry?

Another of Baudrillard's critical ideas that demonstrates the nature of postmodern social theory is simulation. A **simulation** is an inauthentic or fake version of something. Baudrillard saw the world as increasingly dominated by simulations. For example, when we eat at McDonald's, we consume Chicken McNuggets, or simulated chicken. It is fake in the sense that it is often not meat from one chicken, but bits of meat that come from many different chickens. When we go to Disney World, we enter via Main Street, a simulation of early America that is really a shopping mall. When we go to Las Vegas, we stay in casino hotels that are simulations of New York of the early to mid twentieth century (New York, New York) and ancient Egypt (Luxor). The idea that we increasingly consume simulations, and live a simulated life, is a powerful critique not only of consumer society but more generally of the contemporary world. That is, we are not only consuming more, but much of what we consume is fake.

INTER/ACTIONIST THEORIES

The slash between *inter* and *action(ist)* is meant to communicate the fact that we will deal with two closely related sets of theories. The first is theories that deal mainly with the interaction of two or more people (symbolic

postmodern theory A set of ideas oriented in opposition to modern theory by, for example, rejecting or deconstructing the grand narratives of modern social theory.

hyperconsumption Consumption of more than one needs, really wants, and can afford.

simulation An inauthentic or fake version of something.

interactionism, ethnomethodology, and exchange theory). The second is those that focus more on the actions of individuals (rational choice theory). A common factor among them is that they focus on the micro level of individuals and groups. This is in contrast to the theories above that focus on the macro structures of society.

Symbolic Interactionism

Symbolic interactionism is concerned with the interaction of two or more people through the use of symbols (Kotarba, Salvini, and Merryl 2010). We all engage in mutual action with many others on a daily basis, whether face-to-face or more indirectly via cell phone, e-mail, or social media. But interaction could not take place without symbols: words, gestures, and even objects that stand in for things. Symbols allow the communication of meaning among a group of people.

Although we can interact with one another without words, such as through physical gestures like the shrug of a shoulder, in the vast majority of cases we need and use words to interact. And words make many other symbols possible. For example, the Harley-Davidson brand has meaning because it symbolizes a particular type of motorcycle (Holt 2004).

Symbolic interactionism has several basic principles:

- Humans have a great capacity for thought that differentiates them from lower animals. That innate capacity is greatly shaped by social interaction. It is during social interaction that people acquire the symbolic meanings that allow them to exercise their distinctive ability to think. Those symbolic meanings in turn allow people to act and interact in ways that lower animals cannot.

- Symbolic meanings are not set in stone. People are able to modify them based on a given situation and their

For symbolic interactionists, symbols allow us to communicate meaning, but meaning is a matter of interpretation. In Hindu mythology, *svastika* is the Sanskrit name for the symbol of prosperity, which is shown here emblazoned with candles to celebrate Diwali, a festival of lights. Can you think of other symbols that have more than one meaning?

interpretation of it. The Christian cross, for example, is a symbol whose meaning can vary. Christians throughout the world define it in positive religious ways, but many in the Islamic world view it as a negative symbol. Muslims recall the twelfth- and thirteenth-century Crusades waged against their world by the Christian West.

- People are able to modify symbolic meanings because of their unique ability to think. Symbolic interactionists frame thinking as people's ability to interact with themselves. In that interaction with themselves, people are able to alter symbolic meanings. They are also able to examine various courses of action open to them in a given situation, to assess the relative advantages and disadvantages of each, and then to choose one of them.

- It is the pattern of those choices, of individual action and interaction, that is the basis of groups, larger structures such as bureaucracies, and society as a whole. Most generally, symbolic interaction is the basis of everything else in the social world.

Ethnomethodology

While symbolic interactionism deals primarily with people's interactions, it is also concerned with the mental

> **symbolic interactionism** A sociological perspective focusing on the role of symbols and how their meanings are shared and understood by those involved in human interaction.
>
> **ethnomethodology** A theory focusing on what people do rather than on what they think.

Europe's Immigration Turmoil

Youth Volunteerism

processes, such as mind and self, deeply implicated in these interactions. **Ethnomethodology** is another inter/actionist theory, but it focuses on what people *do* rather than what they think (Liu 2012). Ethnomethodologists study the way people organize everyday life.

Ethnomethodologists regard people's lives and social worlds as extraordinary practical accomplishments. For example, one ethnomethodological study of coffee drinkers attempts to understand their participation in a subculture of coffee connoisseurship (Manzo 2010). Ethnomethodologists take a different view of large-scale social structures than do structural-functionalists, who tend to see people and their actions as being highly constrained by those structures. Ethnomethodologists argue that this view tells us very little about what really goes on within structures such as courtrooms and hospitals. Rather than being constrained, people act within these structures and go about much of their business using common sense rather than official procedures. They may even adapt those structures and rules to accomplish their goals. For example, police departments have rules about categorizing deaths as homicides. However, police officers often apply their own commonsense rules rather than organizational rules in order to interpret the evidence.

The best known example of an ethnomethodological approach relates to gender (Stokoe 2006). Ethnomethodologists point out that people often erroneously think of gender as being biologically based. It is generally assumed that one does not have to do or say anything in order to be considered masculine or feminine. But, there are things we all do (for example, the way we walk) and say (for example, the tone of our voice) that allow us to accomplish being masculine or feminine. That is, being masculine and feminine is based on what people *do* on a regular basis. This is clearest in the case of those who are defined as being male or female at birth (based on biological characteristics) but then later do and say things that lead others to see them as belonging to the other gender (based on social characteristics). If this is the case for gender, a great many other facts of our everyday lives can be analyzed as accomplishments.

Exchange Theory

Like ethnomethodology, **exchange theory** is not concerned with what goes on in people's minds and how that affects behavior. Instead, exchange theorists are interested in the behavior itself and the rewards and costs associated with it (Molm, Whithama, and Melameda 2012). George Homans (1961: 13) argued that instead of studying large-scale structures, sociologists should study the "elementary forms of social life."

Exchange theorists are particularly interested in social behavior that involves two or more people engaged in a variety of tangible and intangible exchanges. For example, you can reward someone who does you a favor with a tangible gift or with more intangible words of praise. Those exchanges are not always rewarding; they also can be punitive. You could, for example, punish someone who wrongs you by slapping him.

In their actions and interactions, people are seen as rational profit seekers. Basically, people will continue on courses of action, or in interactions, in which the rewards are greater than the costs. Conversely, they will discontinue those in which the costs exceed the rewards.

While exchange theory retains an interest in the elementary forms of social behavior, over the years it has grown more concerned with how those forms lead to more complex social situations. That is, individual exchanges can become stable over time and develop into persistent **exchange relationships**. For example, because you and another person find your initial interactions rewarding, you may develop a friendship, which is one particular type of exchange relationship.

Exchange relationships rarely develop in isolation from other exchange relationships. For example, your new friend probably has other friends who are engaged in exchange relationships with one another. You may well become involved in some of those relationships. All of these exchange relationships may become so highly interconnected that they become a single network structure (Cook et al. 1983).

Rational Choice Theory

As in exchange theory, in rational choice theory people are regarded as rational, but the focus is not exchange, rewards, and costs. Rather, the basic principle in **rational choice theory** is that people act intentionally in order to achieve goals. People are seen as having purposes, as intending to do certain things. In order to achieve their goals, people have a variety of means available to them and choose among the available means on a rational basis. They choose the means that are likely to best satisfy their needs and wants (Kroneberg and Kalter 2012).

There are two important constraints on the ability to act rationally (Friedman and Hechter 1988):

- *Access to scarce resources.* It is relatively easy for those with access to lots of resources to act rationally and

> **exchange theory** A set of ideas related to the rewards and costs associated with human behavior.
>
> **exchange relationships** Stable and persistent bonds between individuals who interact, generally formed because their interactions are rewarding.
>
> **rational choice theory** A set of ideas that sees people as rational and as acting purposively to achieve their goals.

ACTIVE SOCIOLOGY

What's Trending?

How do people use and discuss sociological concepts and theories in everyday life? Go to Twitter and search for sociologists or sociological concepts mentioned in this chapter.

How do the tweets you found on Twitter add to your understanding of these topics? Choose a concept or sociologist from this chapter that interests you. Create a tweet, using the concept or person in a hashtag. Then answer the questions below and share your results with the class.

1. How many people liked or responded to your tweet?

2. Did anyone retweet it?

3. Was anyone tagged in any responses? Who, and why?

4. Describe the sociological content of any exchanges your tweet inspired.

5. Does your tweet add to the discussion about the topic? How?

---

reach their goals. Those who lack access to such resources are less likely to be able to act rationally in order to achieve their goals. For example, if you have access to money, you can rationally pursue the goal of purchasing food for dinner. However, without access to money, you will have a much harder time taking rational actions that will lead to the acquisition of food needed for dinner.

- *Requirements of social structures.* The structures in which people find themselves—businesses, schools—often have rules that restrict the actions available to those within the structures. For example, being a full-time student may limit one's ability to earn enough money to always be able to obtain the kind of food one prefers to eat.

Rational choice theorists understand that people do not always act rationally. They argue, however, that their predictions will generally hold despite these occasional deviations (Coleman 1990; Zafirovski 2013).

> **empiricism** The gathering of information and evidence using one's senses, especially one's eyes and ears, to experience the social world.

CHECKPOINT 2.2 — MAJOR TYPES OF THEORIES IN CONTEMPORARY SOCIOLOGY

Theory	Major Points
Structural/functional theories (macro level)	These theories examine social structures like the military and the police, in some cases focusing on the functions they perform.
Conflict/critical theories (macro level)	Rooted in Marx's theory, these theories analyze and criticize the role of social structures in a society held together by power and coercion.
Inter/actionist theories (micro level)	These theories focus on the interactions between two or more people, and their meaning and purpose.

RESEARCHING THE SOCIAL WORLD

Sociology is a science of the social world. Research is absolutely central to such a science. All sociologists study the research of others, and most do research of their own. Sociologists may theorize, speculate, and even rely totally on their imaginations for answers to questions about society. However, they almost always do so on the basis of data or information derived from research. Put another way, sociologists practice **empiricism**, which means that they gather information and evidence using their senses,

Sociology Majors

Life Without Laws

TABLE 2.3 • The Scientific Method

	Steps in the Research Process
1	Uncover a question in need of an answer.
2	Review the relevant literature.
3	Develop hypotheses about how phenomena relate to one another.
4	Identify a method for answering the research question.
5	Collect data.
6	Analyze the data.

especially their eyes and ears. In addition to using their senses, sociologists adopt the scientific method, or a similarly systematic approach, in search of a thorough understanding of topics of interest to sociology. They have a variety of methods at their disposal in researching and analyzing society.

THE SCIENTIFIC METHOD

The **scientific method** is a structured way of finding answers to questions about the world (Carey 2011). The scientific method employed by sociologists is much the same as in other sciences. Table 2.3 outlines the following list of steps (although in practice creative sociological research often does not rigidly adhere to them):

1. Sociologists uncover *questions in need of answers*. These questions can come from issues in the larger society, personal experiences, or topics of concern within the field of sociology. The best and most durable research often stems from issues that are important to the sociologist doing the research. Karl Marx, for example, detested the exploitation of workers that characterized capitalism. Max Weber feared the impact of bureaucracies. These powerful arguments spurred their important research on, and key insights into, these monumentally important social realities.

2. Sociologists review the *relevant literature* on the question of interest to them. For example, my work on McDonaldization (Ritzer 2013a) is based on a review of work on rationalization by Max Weber ([1921] 1968), his successors (such as Kalberg 1980), and contemporary researchers (Ram 2007). Similarly, others have reviewed

> **scientific method** A structured way to find answers to questions about the world.

my work and that of other scholars on McDonaldization (for a collection of this work, see Ritzer 2010d). They have amplified on the concept, and they have applied it to, among many other domains, religion (Drane 2001, 2008), higher education (Hayes and Wynyard 2002), social work (Dustin 2007), and Disney World (Bryman 2004).

3. Researchers often develop *hypotheses,* or educated guesses about how social phenomena can be expected to relate to one another. For example, Uri Ram (2007) hypothesized that Israeli society would grow increasingly McDonaldized, and he found evidence to support that idea. As another example, Marx hypothesized that the conflict between capitalists and workers would ultimately lead to the collapse of capitalism. However, capitalism has not collapsed. This makes it clear that hypotheses are, simply, hypotheses. They may not be confirmed by research or borne out by social developments.

4. Researchers must choose a *research method* to help them answer the research question. Sociology offers diverse methodological tools, and some are better than others for answering certain kinds of questions. For example, some sociologists are interested in how a person's social class shapes his or her opinions about social issues. They may use surveys and quantitative methods to evaluate the relationship between class position and attitudes. Other sociologists are interested in how people interpret social phenomena, and how this meaning making shapes social action. They may use qualitative methodologies such as observation to study these issues. Specifically, they might observe how two individuals interact in a romantic context, and how they interpret certain gestures, attire, and other nonverbal cues to assess the interest of the other person.

5. Researchers use their chosen method to *collect data* that can confirm, or fail to confirm, their hypotheses. Many contemporary sociologists venture out into the field to collect data through observations, interviews, questionnaires, and other means.

6. Researchers conduct an *analysis of the data* collected and their meaning in light of the hypothesis that guided the research. For example, as you learned earlier in this chapter, Émile Durkheim hypothesized that those who were involved with other people would be less likely to commit suicide than those who lived more isolated existences and were experiencing what he called anomie. That is, being integrated with other people would, in a way, "protect" an individual from suicide. Analyzing data from several nineteenth-century European countries, Durkheim

([1897] 1951) found that the suicide rates were, in fact, higher for widowed or divorced people. Those who are married are presumably more socially integrated than people in these other categories.

ASK YOURSELF

What are the advantages to sociologists of using the scientific method for research? Are there any disadvantages?

SOCIOLOGICAL RESEARCH

Sociological knowledge is derived from research using a number of different methods. In most cases, the method chosen is driven by the nature of the research question. Imagine that you are a sociologist and want to study the beliefs and behaviors of gamblers in Las Vegas. You might start by using the research method of observation. Observation can range from participating at the roulette table to watching and listening from a distance.

A more direct and focused approach would be to interview those who have come to Las Vegas to gamble. You might ask them questions about their expectations before they arrived, how those expectations related to their own previous experiences, as well as what they heard from others about their gambling experiences in Las Vegas. This would be a more efficient use of your time because it would not entail waiting around for gamblers to do or say something relevant to your research question. However, in interviews people might not be willing to talk to you about their gambling experiences, especially if they have been losing money. Furthermore, even if they are willing to talk to you, they might not give you totally honest answers.

Another technique would be to survey a group of gamblers by administering a questionnaire. However, questions for a survey are not easy to formulate. You would also need to find a good way of distributing the questionnaires to your respondents. You could hand them out to people leaving the casino. However, many may not be willing to take them especially if, as is likely, they have lost money. Even if they did take a questionnaire, they might not answer the questions or mail the questionnaire back to you. Instead of handing out the questionnaires randomly to people leaving the casino, you could be more systematic and scientific by obtaining a list of guests at a given casino hotel. However, it is highly unlikely that you would be given such private information. You could just get

a sample of people from the phone book in your hometown and mail them questionnaires, but it is unlikely that many of them would have visited Las Vegas recently. Among the relatively few who would have, only a very small number are likely to return the completed questionnaires.

You could also create an experiment. In a social science laboratory at your university, you could set up a Las Vegas–style poker table and recruit students as participants in the experiment. You could tell them that previous research has shown that most players lose most of the time. You could then ask them whether, in spite of that information, they still want to gamble at your poker table. Of greatest interest would be those who say yes. You would want to interview them before they start "gambling" at your table, observe them as they gamble, and interview them again after they have finished. Did they start out believing, despite all the evidence to the contrary, that they would win? How could they have retained such a belief in spite of all the counter-evidence? What are their feelings after gambling at your table? Did those feelings relate to whether they won or lost? How likely are they to gamble again?

Observation, interviews, surveys, and experiments, and other research methods, are all useful and important to sociologists. All have strengths but also limitations. Before examining those methods and their strengths and limitations in more detail, there is one important distinction among research methods that should be discussed.

QUALITATIVE AND QUANTITATIVE RESEARCH

One common way in which sociologists think about different research methods is by classifying them according to the kinds of data they seek to collect and analyze. Is the method essentially qualitative or quantitative?

Qualitative research involves studies done in natural settings that produce in-depth descriptive information (e.g., in respondents' own words) about the social world (Denzin and Lincoln 2011). Such research does not necessarily require statistical methods for reporting data (Marshall and Rossman 2010). Observation and open-ended interviews are two of the qualitative methods used by sociologists. These methods are used to capture descriptive information about an incredibly wide range of social phenomena. These range from people's lived experiences and feelings to the way in which organizations function in interactions between nations. By gathering information from a small number of groups and individuals, such methods often produce rich data about the social world and in-depth

> **qualitative research** Any research method that does not require statistical methods for collecting and reporting data.

Films with Research

Research Methods

Observation remains a primary investigative tool in sociology. Do you think people behave differently when they know they are being observed?

résumés applied for the same job, those with white-sounding names (such as Emily and Greg) were 50 percent more likely to get a callback than applicants with black-sounding names (such as Lakisha and Jamal) (Bertrand and Mullainathan 2004). The researchers sent out 5,000 résumés to 1,300 employers and used the responses to draw broader inferences about the population of job applicants.

Sociologists generally recognize that both methods have value. Each method has its own set of strengths and limitations in terms of what it can do to help a researcher to answer a specific question. Furthermore, there is a broad consensus that quantitative and qualitative research methods can complement one another (Ragin 1987; Riis 2012; Rueschemeyer, Stephens, and Stephens 1992). Sociologists may combine both quantitative and qualitative research methods in a single study.

OBSERVATIONAL RESEARCH

A major qualitative method is **observation**. It involves systematic watching, listening to, and recording what takes place in a natural social setting over some period of time (Hammersley 2007).

understanding of particular social processes. Sometimes they help to provide insights about new areas where little research has been done. However, because qualitative methods usually rely on small sample sizes, the findings cannot be generalized to the broader population; for this, we use quantitative methods.

Quantitative research involves the analysis of numerical data derived usually from surveys and experiments (Creswell 2008). The analysis of quantitative data on groups of people can help us to describe and to better understand important observable social realities.

Statistics is the mathematical method used to analyze numerical data. Statistics can aid researchers in two ways:

- When researchers want to see trends over time or compare differences between groups, they use **descriptive statistics**. The purpose of such statistics is to describe some particular body of data that is based on a phenomenon in the real world (Salkind 2004). For example, researchers have used survey data to track trends in educational attainment over time and then used statistical analysis to describe how educational attainment varies by race, gender, and age (Crissey 2009).

- To test hypotheses, researchers use **inferential statistics**, which allow researchers to use data from a relatively small group to speculate with some level of certainty about a larger group. Take, for example, a field experiment on labor market discrimination. It was found that when people with comparable

quantitative research Any research method that involves the analysis of numerical data derived usually from surveys and experiments.

statistics The mathematical method used to analyze numerical data.

descriptive statistics Numerical data that allow researchers to see trends over time or compare differences between groups, to describe some particular collection of data that is based on a phenomenon in the real world.

inferential statistics Numerical data that allow researchers to use data from a small group to speculate with some level of certainty about a larger group.

observation A research method that involves systematically watching, listening to, and recording what takes place in a natural social setting over some period of time.

PUBLIC SOCIOLOGY

Robert Park and "Scientific Reporting"

Robert Park (1864–1944) felt a strong need to work outside the academic world and thus started his career as a journalist. "I made up my mind to go in for experience for its own sake, to gather . . . all the joys and sorrows of the world" (Park [1927] 1973: 253). He liked to wander around and explore the social world by, for example, "'hunting down gambling houses and opium dens'" (Park [1927] 1973: 254).

Park returned to school and eventually completed his doctoral dissertation in 1904. He joined the Department of Sociology at the University of Chicago in 1914. His use of the city as a laboratory for his observational studies helped the Chicago department assume a leadership position in urban sociology.

Park demonstrates the close association between journalism and at least some forms of sociology. Throughout his life Park retained an interest in, and a passion for, the accurate description of social life. However, he grew dissatisfied with journalism because it did not fulfill his intellectual needs. In contrast to journalism, sociology draws upon theory and uses more systematic methods of data collection and analysis to understand the social world. Park's ability to use sociological methods to pursue his deep interest in reforming society and overcoming its ills, especially with regard to race relations, is an important reason to consider him a public sociologist.

Think About It

How might journalism contribute to public sociology? What are journalism's limitations as input to sociology? Do you think blogs and social networks can make the same potential contributions as traditional journalism? Why or why not?

There are several key dimensions to any type of observation in sociology:

- *Degree to which those being observed are aware that they are being observed.* This can vary from everyone involved being fully informed about the research to being observed from afar or through hidden cameras, one-way mirrors, and the like. The reality TV series *Undercover Boss* involves a kind of covert observational research.

- *Degree to which the presence of the observer affects what those being observed do.* Especially when they are aware that they are being observed, people often present themselves in the way they think the observer expects or will accept. An example would be gang members who do not engage in illegal activities in the presence of a researcher.

- *Degree to which the process is structured.* Highly structured observational research might use preset categories or a checklist to guide observations. At the other end of the spectrum, some observations seek the widest possible range of data and are totally open and unstructured.

Some of the most famous research in the history of sociology has been done using the observational method. Examples include the *Philadelphia Negro* (Du Bois [1899] 1996), *Street Corner Society* (Whyte 1943), and the *Code of the Street* as it relates to crime (E. Anderson 1999).

Participant and Nonparticipant Observation

There are two major types of observational methods. One is **participant observation** in which the researcher actually plays a role, usually a minor one, in the group or setting being observed. A participant observer might play poker in Las Vegas with the people being studied, sell books on the sidewalk in order to watch what happens on a busy city street (Duneier 1999), or become a (quasi) member of a gang (Venkatesh 2008). Kanter (1993) researched gender segregation in the corporate world of the 1970s by, among other things, participating in group discussions and meetings at a major U.S. company. Ehrenreich (2008) worked in low-wage jobs (for example, waitress) to study the experience of such low-wage work. She found that many of the women she studied were unable to meet basic living expenses including housing, transportation, and food. (See the "Public Sociology" box in Chapter 12.)

The Discovery Channel's *Dirty Jobs* is essentially an informal exercise in participant observation. The show's star,

> **participant observation** A research method in which the researcher actually plays a role, usually a minor one, in the group or setting being observed.

Participant Observation

Mike Rowe, is *not* a trained sociologist, and he is *not* trying to uncover the sociological aspects of the jobs he is studying, but he *is* a participant observer. In each episode, he actually does the job that is being examined—he is a participant—and he observes the workers as well as their dirty jobs. Among the jobs Rowe has performed and observed are "turd burner," owl vomit collector, baby chicken sexer, sheep castrator, rat exterminator, maggot farmer, and diaper cleaner.

The second observational method is **nonparticipant observation** where the sociologist plays little or no role in what is being observed. For example, Gary Fine (1987) observed Little League baseball without becoming a team member or participating in the baseball games. He was interested in learning about the organized and informal activities of young boys that helped them to become men. Fine's research included observation not just of actual games but also of the players in dugouts, at practice fields, and before and after games. While Fine did not play baseball with his research subjects, he did get to know the boys outside the baseball setting "when they were 'doing nothing'" (Fine 1987: 1). The *Real World* reality show, which began on MTV in 1992, can be seen as another example of nonparticipant observation. Of course, sociologists are not involved in this show, and the observation is not as systematic as it would be if it were a sociological study. The show is based on selecting a group of young people who have never met to live together in a house. Although a camera operator is there to record at least some of the group's activities, no outsider is present in the house to participate in those activities. The "observers" are the viewing audience. They can be seen as amateur nonparticipant observers in the sense that they "study" sociological aspects of what goes on among the residents.

There are no firm dividing lines between participant and nonparticipant observation; at times they blend imperceptibly into one another. The participant often becomes simply an observer. An example is the sociologist who begins with participant observation of a gang, hanging out with members in casual settings, but becomes a nonparticipant when illegal activities such as drug deals take place. And the nonparticipant observer sometimes becomes a participant. An example is the sociologist who is unable to avoid being asked to take sides in squabbles among members of a Little League team.

ASK YOURSELF

Do you think a participant observer risks becoming too close to the subjects under study? Why or why not? What about a nonparticipant observer? How can sociologists conducting observational research avoid possible risks?

Ethnography

Ethnography is the creation of an account of observations of what a group of people does and the way they live (Adler and Adler 2012; Hammersley 2007). It usually entails much more intensive and lengthy periods of observation than traditional sociological observation. Researchers may live for years with the groups, tribes, or subcultures (such as gamblers) being studied.

Those interested in the sociology of gender (see Chapter 9) often advocate the use of ethnographic methods because they can reveal much about the experiences of traditionally understudied and marginalized groups of women (e.g., immigrant factory workers [M. Chin 2005]; lap dancers [Colosi 2010]; and ex-convicts [Opsal 2011]). Some suggest that the personal relationships that develop between researchers and subjects in ethnographic studies makes it less likely that the results will be distorted by the power researchers exert over subjects (Bourdieu 1992). Feminist researchers are especially concerned that study participants not be coerced and exploited in the research process.

Normally ethnographies are small in scale, microscopic, and local. Researchers observe people, talk to them, and conduct interviews with them over an extended period of time. Nevertheless, the ethnographic method has now been extended to the global level. For instance, Michael Burawoy (2000) argues that a **global ethnography** is the best way to understand globalization. This is a type of ethnography that is grounded in various parts of the world and that seeks to understand globalization as it exists in people's social lives. Burawoy and his colleagues "set out from real experiences . . . of welfare clients, migrant nurses, and breast cancer activists in order to explore *their* global contexts" (Burawoy 2000: 341).

One example of a global ethnography is a study of homeless people who are able to survive by recycling some of the things they find on the street (Gowan 2000). Many of the homeless are out of work, often because of the global economic changes that have led many jobs to be outsourced to other countries. In addition, at least some of the objects the homeless recycle may have been produced outside the

nonparticipant observation A research method in which the sociologist plays little or no role in what is being observed.

ethnography Observational research, often intensive and over lengthy periods, that leads to an account of what people do and how they live.

global ethnography A type of ethnography that is "grounded" in various parts of the world and that seeks to understand globalization as it exists in people's social lives.

DIGITAL LIVING

Netnography

The basic concerns of sociology—communications, relationships, and groups—are key elements of the Internet. Not surprisingly, **netnography**, or an account of what transpires online, has become a highly relevant method for sociological research (Kozinets 2009; Turkle 1997, 2011).

For example, a netnographer might join the online fan club of a world-famous rock star in order to learn something about the relationship between a star and her fans. The researcher might be able to interact directly with the fans and the star through a Twitter feed. Netnographers can also study the use of Facebook by activists such as took place in Egypt while they were engaged in the overthrow of longtime dictator Hosni Mubarak in 2011 (Wolfsfeld, Segev, and Sheafer 2013). Membership in this emerging online community gave researchers real-time access to ongoing global communication. When the success in Egypt spawned popular social uprisings in other countries, researchers had the opportunity to study how newly emerging popular movements in one country can shape others.

Globalization, introduced in Chapter 1, is far easier to study on the Internet than it is anywhere else (Kozinets 2002). Instead of needing to be in several places around the world, netnographers who study globalization can do most, if not all, of the research from their computers. Many online communities are global in their scope, engaged in global communications, and generating global actions of various kinds (for example, efforts to deal with the causes of climate change). A great attraction of these communities to the researcher is that they can be tapped into instantly, with relatively little effort, and at no cost. However, language barriers can be a problem. It is also important to remember that people in some parts of the world are unable to access the Internet very often, very well, or even at all. Their interests are not going to be well represented online.

Think About It

What kinds of sociological research questions do you think are best answered by netnography? Do you think people will change their online behavior if they know they are being observed? Why or why not?

United States. Once they are recycled, those objects may once again find their way into new commodities that come to be distributed globally.

INTERVIEWS

While observers often interview those they are studying, they usually do so very informally. Other sociologists rely mainly, or exclusively, on **interviews** in which information is sought from participants by asking a series of questions that have been spelled out before the research is conducted (Gubrium et al. 2012). Interviews are usually conducted face-to-face, although they can be done by phone and are increasingly done via the Internet (Farrell and Peterson 2010; Fontana 2007). In addition, large-scale national surveys increasingly include interviews (Sirkin et al. 2011).

The use of interviews has a long history in sociology. One very early example is W. E. B. Du Bois's ([1899] 1996) study of the *Philadelphia Negro*. A watershed in the history of interviewing in sociology was reached during World War II when large-scale interview studies of members of the American military were conducted. Some of the data from those studies were reported in a landmark study, *The American Soldier* (Stouffer et al. 1949). More recently, Allison Pugh (2009) did intensive interviewing (and observation) of children and their families. She found that parents tend to buy things for their children in order to help them to be better integrated into groups at school and in their neighborhood. Parents continue to do so even when it is difficult for them to afford such purchases. Through these purchases, parents contribute directly to consumer culture. They also help ensure that their children will become involved in that culture.

Types of Interviews

The questions asked in an interview may be preselected and prestructured so that respondents must choose from a set of answers such as *agree* and *disagree*. Or the interview can be more spontaneous, unstructured, and completely open-ended. The latter is the case with the questions asked by those who do observational research. An unstructured interview offers no preset answers; respondents are free to say anything they want to say.

> **interviews** A research method in which information is sought from participants (respondents) who are asked a series of questions that have been spelled out, at least to some degree, before the research is conducted.
>
> **netnography** An ethnographic method in which the Internet becomes the research site and what transpires there is the sociologist's research interest.

 Feminist Ethnography   Public Sociology: Robert Part

Prestructured interviews are attractive when the researcher wants to avoid any unanticipated responses from those being studied. The interviewer attempts to

- behave in the same way in each interview;
- ask the same questions using the same words and in the same sequence;
- ask closed-ended questions where the participant must choose from a set of preselected responses;
- offer the same explanations when requested by respondents; and
- not react to the answers no matter what they might be.

Interviews conducted in this way often yield information that can be coded numerically and then analyzed statistically, as is the case with data obtained from questionnaires.

There are problems associated with prestructured interviews. First, interviewers often find it difficult to live up to the guidelines for such interviews:

- They are frequently unable to avoid reacting to answers (especially outrageous ones).

- They may use a different intonation from one interview to another.

- They may change the wording, and even the order, of the questions asked.

Second, respondents may not respond accurately or truthfully. For example, they may give answers they believe the interviewer wants to hear. Third, closed-ended questions limit the responses, possibly cutting off important, unanticipated information.

The latter problem is solved by the use of open-ended or *unstructured interviews*. The interviewer begins with only a general idea of the topics to be covered and the direction to be taken in the interview. The answers in unstructured interviews offer a good understanding of the respondents and what the issues under study mean to them. Such understandings and meanings are generally not obtained from structured interviews. However, unstructured interviews create problems of their own. For example, they may yield so much diverse information that it is hard to offer a coherent summary and interpretation of the results.

The Interview Process
Conducting interviews, especially those that are prestructured, usually involves several steps.

1. The interviewer must *gain access* to the setting being studied. This is relatively easy in some cases, such as interviewing one's friends in a local bar. However, access would likely be much more difficult if one wanted to interview one's friends on the job. They might be less eager to talk to a researcher in such settings. Some groups, such as the extremely wealthy, have the resources to insulate, even isolate, themselves. They can be quite difficult for researchers to gain access to and thus may be underrepresented in sociological research.

2. The interviewer must often seek to *locate a key informant*—a person who has intimate knowledge of the group being studied and who is willing to talk openly to the researcher about the group (Brown, Bankston, and Forsyth 2013; Rieger 2007). Key informants can help the researcher gain access to the larger group of respondents and verify information being provided by them. The latter is useful because interviewees may well provide erroneous information. In Sudhir Venkatesh's (2008) study of a Chicago housing project and its gangs, his key informant was the gang leader "J.T." Of this relationship, Venkatesh (1994: 322) says, "In the course of my fieldwork I became dependent on the continual support of J.T."

3. The interviewer must seek to *understand the language and culture* of the people being interviewed. In some cases this is very easy. For example, it is not a great problem for an academic interviewer to understand the language and culture of college students. However, it is more difficult if the academician interviews those with their own and very different language and culture. Examples might include interviews with members of motorcycle gangs or prostitutes in a brothel. In such cases, it is all too easy for the researcher to misunderstand or to impose incorrect meanings on the words of respondents.

4. The researcher must *gain the trust of the respondents and develop a rapport* with them. Establishing trust and rapport can be easy or difficult, depending on the characteristics of the researcher. Feminist scholars would point out that well-educated and relatively powerful male researchers may intimidate less privileged female respondents. Older researchers may have trouble interviewing students. In a few cases, trust need only be earned once, but in many cases, it needs to be earned over and over. And trust can easily be lost. Venkatesh had to work constantly on his rapport with J.T. and other gang members. In fact, J.T. at first thought Venkatesh might be a cop. J.T. later confessed that he was never 100 percent sure that Venkatesh was not a policeman.

ASK YOURSELF

Have you ever conducted or participated in an interview, perhaps for a job or an internship? How closely did it adhere to the guidelines mentioned here?

SURVEY RESEARCH

Survey research involves the collection of information from a population, or more usually a representative portion of a population, through the use of interviews and, most importantly, questionnaires. While some sociologists do their own surveys, most rely on data derived from surveys done by others such as the U.S. government (the U.S. Census, for example) and the National Opinion Research Center, which conducts various opinion polls.

Interviews involve questions being asked by the researcher in person or on the telephone. Every two years the General Social Survey conducts face-to-face interviews with a large sample of Americans. In contrast, **questionnaires** are self-administered, written sets of questions. While the questions can be presented to respondents on a face-to-face basis, they are more often delivered to them by mail, asked over the telephone, or presented in web-based formats. Questionnaires are now increasingly filled out on one's personal computer and over the phone (Snyder 2007).

Types of Survey

There are two broad types of survey. The first is the **descriptive survey** designed to gather accurate information about, for example, those in a group or an organization. A descriptive survey might gather data on the level of sexual activity of college students or the employment status of Americans. The best known descriptive surveys are those conducted by organizations such as Gallup, which describe preferences, beliefs, and attitudes of a given group of people.

In one example of descriptive survey research using the Internet, a survey was placed on a website designed to allow married people to find extramarital sexual partners.

> **survey research** A research methodology that involves the collection of information from a population, or more usually a representative portion of a population, through the use of interviews and, more importantly, questionnaires.
>
> **questionnaires** Self-administered, written sets of questions.
>
> **descriptive survey** A questionnaire or interview used to gather accurate information about those in a group, people in a given geographic area, or members of organizations.

This 1930 census taker uses a questionnaire to gather information. Have you ever filled out a questionnaire?

Based on a sample of more than 5,000 respondents, the data showed that females were more likely than males to engage in "sexting" (see Chapter 9) (Wysocki and Childers 2011).

For many years, the Institute for Social Research at the University of Michigan has conducted a descriptive survey of high school seniors in the United States. One of the topics has been marijuana use. As you can see in Figure 2.2, the prevalence of marijuana use among high school seniors has risen and fallen as if in waves. Marijuana use in this group peaked in 1979 (at over half of students admitting use of the drug), reached a low of 21.9 percent in 1992, and has generally been rising since then, although never approaching the 1979 level. In 2011, slightly less than 40 percent of 12th graders reported using marijuana in the previous 12 months.

The data in Figure 2.2 are derived from descriptive surveys, but what if we wanted to explain, and not just statistically describe, changes in marijuana use among high school seniors? To get at this, we would need to do

Interviews

FIGURE 2.2 • **Marijuana Use among High School Seniors in the United States, 1975–2011**

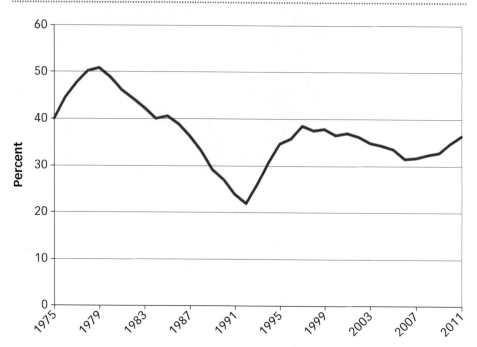

SOURCE: Adapted from Table 16: Long-term trends in Annual Prevalence of Use of Various Drugs in Grade 12 in "Monitoring the Future: A Continuing Study of American Youth," Ann Arbor, MI: The Regents of the University of Michigan, 2011.

an **explanatory survey**, which seeks to uncover potential causes of, in this case, changes in marijuana use. For example, having discovered variations in marijuana use by high school students over the years, we might hypothesize that the variation is linked to students' changing perceptions about the riskiness of marijuana use. Specifically, we might hypothesize that as students increasingly come to see marijuana as less risky, its use will go up. In this case, we would use the survey to learn more about respondents' attitudes toward and beliefs about the riskiness of marijuana use and not simply measure student use of marijuana.

Sampling

It is almost never possible to survey an entire population, such as all Americans, or all students at your college. Thus survey researchers usually need to construct a **sample**, or a representative portion of the overall population. The more careful the researcher is in avoiding biases in selecting the sample, the more the findings are likely to be representative of the whole group.

The most common way to avoid bias is to create a **random sample** in which every member of the group has an equal chance of being included. Random samples can be obtained by using a list of, for example, names of all the professors at your university. A coin is tossed for each name on the list. Those professors for whom the toss results in heads are included in the sample. More typical and efficient is the

use of random number tables, found in most statistics textbooks, to select those in the sample (Kirk 2007). In our example, each professor is assigned a number, and those whose number comes up in the random number table are included in the sample. More recently, use is being made of computer-generated random numbers. Other sampling techniques are used in survey research as well. For example, the researcher might create a **stratified sample** in which a larger group is divided into a series of subgroups and then random samples are taken within each of these groups. This ensures representation from each group in the final sample, something that might not occur if one simply did a random sample of the larger group. Thus random and stratified sampling are the safest ways of drawing accurate conclusions about a population as a whole. However, there is an element of chance in all sampling, especially random sampling, with the result that findings can vary from one sample to another. Even though sampling is the safest way of reaching conclusions about a population, errors are possible. Random and stratified sampling are depicted in Figure 2.3.

Sometimes researchers use **convenience samples**, which simply include those who are available to participate in a research project. An example would involve researchers passing out surveys to the students in their classes (Lunneborg 2007). These nonrandom samples are rarely

explanatory survey A questionnaire or interview used to uncover potential causes for some observation.

sample A representative portion of the overall population.

random sample A subset of a population in which every member of the group has an equal chance of being included.

stratified sample A sample created when a larger group is divided into a series of subgroups and then random samples are taken within each of these groups.

convenience samples Readily available groups of people who fit the criteria for participating in a research project.

FIGURE 2.3 • Random Samples and Stratified Samples

Random Sample: Survey respondents are selected randomly.

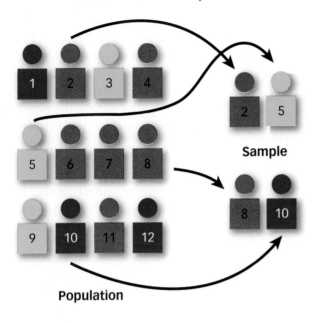

Population

Stratified Sample: The population is subdivided on the basis of some characteristic relevant to the study, and then survey respondents are randomly selected from each group.

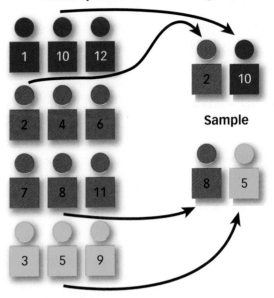

SOURCE: Reprinted with permission of Dan Kernler, Assoicate Professor of Mathematics, Elgin Community College, Elgin, IL.

ever representative of the larger population whose opinions the researcher is interested in knowing. Nonrandom samples therefore may create a substantial amount of bias in the researchers' results (Popham and Sirotnik 1973: 44). Many surveys that pop up on the Internet are suspect because the respondents are the people who happened to be at a certain website (which is likely to reflect their interests) and who felt strongly enough about the topic of the survey to answer the questions.

Research based on convenience samples is usually only exploratory. It is almost impossible to draw any definitive conclusions from such research.

EXPERIMENTS

Some sociologists perform experiments (Schaefer 2012). An **experiment** involves the manipulation of one or

> **experiment** The manipulation of a characteristic under study (an independent variable) to examine its effect on another characteristic (the dependent variable).
>
> **independent variable** In an experiment, a condition that can be independently manipulated by the researcher with the goal of producing a change in some other variable.

more characteristics in order to examine the effect of that manipulation (Kirk 2007).

Devah Pager (2009) was interested in how the background of a job applicant affects the likelihood of being called back for an interview. Pager randomly assigned fake criminal records to pairs of similar young men, one in each pair black and one white. So in each pair, one person had a criminal record and one did not, and one was white and one was not. These young men then sent résumés to companies, seeking entry-level jobs. One major finding of this experiment was that the young men believed to have a criminal record received a callback less than half as often as those of the same race believed not to have a criminal record. A second finding was that black men without criminal records received callbacks at about the same rate as white men with criminal records.

In this experiment, we can clearly see the relationship between two important elements of an experiment: independent and dependent variables. In Pager's experiment, the **independent variable**, the condition that was manipulated by the researcher, was the job applicant's combination of race and criminal background. The

Sampling

Survey on Use of Domestic Drones

Survey Flaws

RESEARCH METHODS IN SOCIOLOGY

Observation	Systematic watching, listening to, and recording of what takes place in a natural setting over time; can be participant or nonparticipant research.
Ethnography	Creation of an account of what a group of people does and how they live.
Interview	Collection of data via a series of questions, often face-to-face but also by phone or online.
Survey	Collection of information from a representative sample of the population through interviews and questionnaires.
Experiment	Manipulation of one or more characteristics to examine the effect; can be laboratory, natural, or field experiment.

dependent variable, the characteristic or measurement that resulted from the manipulation, was whether or not the applicant was called in for an interview.

There are several different types of experiments:

- *Laboratory experiments.* **Laboratory experiments** take place in controlled settings. The "laboratory" may be a classroom or a simulated environment. The setting offers the researcher great control over the selection of the participants as well as of the independent variables—the conditions to which the participants are exposed (Lucas, Graif, and Lovaglia 2008). The famous experiments by Solomon Asch on conformity (see Chapter 4) were laboratory experiments. This type of experiment can be difficult to organize and sometimes yields artificial results. However, it allows for more accurate tests of research hypotheses.

- *Natural experiments.* In **natural experiments** researchers take advantage of a naturally occurring event to study its effect on one or more dependent variables. Such experiments offer the experimenter little or no control over independent variables (De Silva et al. 2010). For example, during the Vietnam War the U.S. Army instituted a lottery to select the young men to be drafted. The men with low numbers in the lottery were drafted first; the men with high numbers had a good chance of not being drafted. The researchers had no control over the lottery or the young men's draft numbers (Walker and Willer 2007). Studying the effects of the lottery, they found that male students who had low draft numbers had more positive attitudes toward the Vietnam War than those with high numbers. The researchers also found that those with low draft numbers had higher long-term mortality rates outside the military than those who had higher numbers. The researchers hypothesized that the young men with low numbers

were more likely to suffer stress associated with knowing they were going to be drafted, and had a greater likelihood of fighting and perhaps dying in the war.

- *Field experiments.* In some natural situations, researchers are able to exert at least some control over who participates and what happens during the experiment (Bertrand and Mullainathan 2004; Pager and Western 2012). These are called **field experiments**. One of the most famous studies in the history of sociology is the "Robbers Cave" field experiment (Sherif et al. [1954] 1961). It was called that because it took place in Robbers Cave State Park in Oklahoma. The researchers controlled important aspects of what took place at the site. For example, they were able to assign the 22 boys in the study into two groups, called the Rattlers and the Eagles. The researchers were also able to create various situations that led to rivalry, bickering, and hostility between the groups. At the end of the experiment, they had each group rate the other: 53 percent of ratings of the Eagles were unfavorable, while nearly 77 percent of ratings of the Rattlers were unfavorable. Later, the researchers introduced conditions that they hoped would reduce bad feelings and friction between the groups. In fact, greater harmony between the groups was created by having them work together on tasks like securing needed water. By the end of the experiment, just 5 percent of the ratings of the Eagles were unfavorable,

dependent variable A characteristic or measurement that is the result of manipulating an independent variable.

laboratory experiments Research that occurs in a laboratory, giving the researcher great control over both the selection of the participants to be studied and the conditions to which they are exposed.

natural experiments Experiments that occur when researchers take advantage of a naturally occurring event to study its effect on one or more dependent variables.

field experiments Research that occurs in natural situations but that allows researchers to exert at least some control over who participates and what happens during the experiment.

while unfavorable ratings of the Rattlers had dropped to 23 percent.

Some observers see a bright future for experimentation in sociology, in part because of the potential to use the Internet as a site for sociological experiments (Hanson and Hawley 2011). In one Internet-based experiment, male respondents were asked to evaluate the attractiveness of digitally altered pictures of females on the basis of their perception of how overweight the women appeared to be. One finding was that respondents who were overweight were less likely to report differences in the attractiveness of the women on the basis of the women's weight (Conley and McCabe 2011).

SECONDARY DATA ANALYSIS

All of the methods discussed thus far involve the collection of new and original data, but many sociologists engage in **secondary data analysis** in which they reanalyze data collected by others. Secondary analysis can involve a wide variety of different types of data, from censuses and surveys to historical records and old transcripts of interviews and focus groups. Until recently, obtaining and using some of these secondary data sets was laborious and time-consuming. Today, however, thousands of data sets are available on the web, and they can be accessed with a few keystrokes. A number of websites provide both the data sets and statistical software to look at them in different ways (Schutt 2007).

Secondary analysis very often involves statistical analysis of government surveys and census data. The U.S. census data that are collected every 10 years—they were last collected for 2010—are a gold mine for sociologists both here and abroad. For example, a team of sociologists drew on 2000 census data to examine how the gender of managers in the workplace affects wage inequality and found that the presence of female managers did tend to reduce inequality (Cohen and Huffman 2007).

> **secondary data analysis** Reanalysis of data, often survey data, collected by others, including other sociologists.
>
> **historical-comparative research** A research methodology that contrasts how different historical events and conditions in various societies (or components of societies) lead to different societal outcomes.
>
> **ideal type** An exaggeratedly rational model that is used to study real-world phenomena.

HISTORICAL-COMPARATIVE METHOD

The goal of **historical-comparative research** is to contrast how different historical events and conditions in various societies led to different societal outcomes. The historical component involves the study of the history of societies, as well as of the major components of society such as the state, religious system, and economy. The addition of the comparative element, comparing the histories of two or more societies, or of components of societies, makes it more distinctively sociological.

One of the things that differentiates history and historical-comparative sociology is the level of historical detail. Historians go into much more detail, and collect much more original historical data, than do sociologists. In contrast, sociologists are much more interested in generalizing about society than are historians. Perhaps the best way to exemplify the difference between a historical-comparative sociologist and a historian is in the concept of the ideal type (Clegg 2007; Weber [1921] 1968). An **ideal type**, to Max Weber ([1903–1917] 1949: 90), is a "one-sided *accentuation*" of social reality. Unlike the goal of the historian, an ideal type is not meant to accurately depict reality. Rather, it is designed to help us better understand social reality. It is a sort of measuring rod. Thus, for example, Weber developed an ideal type of bureaucracy, which accentuated its rational elements. He then used that ideal type to compare organizations in different societies and time periods in terms of their degree of rationality. Not surprisingly, he concluded that organizations of the modern West are the most rational and thus best approximate the ideal type of bureaucracy.

Weber is the preeminent historical-comparative sociologist (Mahoney and Rueschmeyer 2003; Tyrell 2010; Varcoe 2007). Consider his comparison of the world's major religions and their impact on the economy. Weber did comparative analyses of the histories of Protestantism in the West, Confucianism in China, and Hinduism in India. He sought to determine which religions fostered the development of capitalism and which served to impede its development. Of course, Weber knew that capitalism had developed in the West and not in China and India. The issue, then, was what about these religions (and many other social factors) did or did not foster the emergence of capitalism. A key factor was the fact that in contrast to Protestantism, Confucianism and Hinduism did not foster rationality and efficiency and a striving for material success. Sometimes, they even served to inhibit rationality and efficiency, thus preventing the development of capitalism.

Experiments

World Values Survey

Financial Misconduct

More recent instances of historical-comparative research have covered a wide range of issues. One researcher used a historical-comparative approach to elucidate critical differences in the timing and character of modern pension systems that developed in Britain, Canada, and the United States (Orloff 1993). This analysis highlights the role played by states and political institutions.

ISSUES IN SOCIAL RESEARCH

Research conducted by sociologists raises a number of issues of great importance.

RELIABILITY AND VALIDITY

A key issue with sociological data relates to the ability to trust that findings represent the social world as accurately as possible.

Reliability involves the degree to which a given question, or another kind of measure, produces the same results time after time. In other words, would the same question asked one day get the same response from the participants or the same measurement on the scale on the following day, or week, or month? For instance, do those involved in your hypothetical study of Las Vegas gamblers give the same answers at various points in time to questions about whether or not they routinely lose money when gambling?

The other dimension of trustworthiness is **validity**, or the degree to which a question, or another kind of measure, gets an accurate response. In other words, does the question measure what it is supposed to measure? For example, suppose you asked gamblers, "When you leave Las Vegas, do you consider yourself a 'winner'?" You may be asking this question to find out whether they left Las Vegas with more money than the amount they had when they arrived. However, they may interpret the question more broadly as asking about the total experience of being in Las Vegas. Thus, even though they have lost money, they might answer yes to the question because they had a great time and consider their losses as part of the price for having such an experience. A more valid question might be: "On balance, do you win more money than you lose while gambling in Las Vegas?"

RESEARCH ETHICS

Ethics is concerned with issues of right and wrong, the choices that people make, and how they justify them (Zeni

2007). World War II and the behavior of the Nazis helped make ethics a central issue in research. The Nazis engaged in horrendous medical experiments on inmates in concentration camps (Korda 2006; Spitz 2005). This is the most outrageous example of a violation of the ethical code in the conduct of research. Another well-known example is the research conducted between 1932 and 1972 at Tuskegee Institute in Alabama on 399 poor black American men suffering from syphilis. The researchers were interested in studying the natural progression of the disease over time, but they never told the participants that they were suffering from syphilis. Despite regular visits to collect data from and about the participants, the researchers did not treat them for the disease and allowed them to suffer over long periods of time before they died painfully (Reverby 2009).

A more recent issue of research ethics is the case of Henrietta Lacks (Skloot 2011), a poor black woman who died of cervical cancer in 1951. Without her knowledge or consent, some of her tumor was removed. Cancer cells from that tumor live on today and have spawned much research and even highly successful industries. While those cells have led to a variety of medical advances, a number of ethical issues are raised by what happened to Lacks and subsequently to her family. For example, should the tumor have been removed and cancer cells reproduced without Lacks and her family knowing about, and approving of, what was intended? Would the procedures have been the same if Lacks was a well-to-do white woman? Finally, should Lacks's descendants get a portion of the earnings of the industries that have developed on the basis of her cancer cells?

No research undertaken by sociologists has caused the kind of suffering and death experienced by the people being studied in Nazi Germany or at Tuskegee Institute, or even the ethical firestorm raging around the Lacks case. Nonetheless, this is the context and background for ethical concerns about the harmful or negative effects of research on the participants in sociological research (the code of ethics of the American Sociological

> **reliability** The degree to which a given question (or another kind of measure) produces the same results time after time.
>
> **validity** The degree to which a question (or another kind of measure) gets an accurate response, or measures what it is supposed to measure.
>
> **ethics** A set of beliefs concerning right and wrong in the choices that people make and the ways those choices are justified.

Association can be found at www .asanet.org/about/ethics.cfm). There are three main areas of concern: physical and psychological harm to participants, illegal acts by researchers, and violation of participants' trust.

Physical and Psychological Harm

The first issue is concern over whether the research can actually cause participants physical harm. Most sociological research is not likely to cause such harm. However, physical harm may be an unintended consequence. In the Robbers Cave research, discussed earlier as an example of a natural experiment, competition and conflict were engendered between two groups of 12-year-old boys. The hostility reached such a peak that the boys engaged in apple-throwing fights and in raids on each other's compounds.

A much greater issue in sociological research is the possibility of psychological harm to those being studied. Even questionnaire or interview studies can cause psychological harm merely by asking people about sensitive issues such as sexual orientation, drug use, and experience with abortion. This risk is greatly increased when, unbeknownst to the researcher, a participant is hypersensitive to these issues because of a difficult or traumatic personal experience.

Some of the more extreme risks of psychological harm have occurred in experiments. The most famous example is Stanley Milgram's (1974) laboratory study of how far people will go when they are given orders by those in authority. This study was inspired by the discovery after World War II that Nazi subordinates went so far as to torture and kill innocent citizens if ordered to do so by their superiors. In the Milgram experiment, the members of one group, the "learners," were secretly paid to pretend that painful shocks were being applied to them by the other group of participants, the "teachers," who were led to believe that the shocks they thought they were applying were very real. The researcher, dressed officially in a white coat and projecting an aura of scientific respectability, would order the "teachers" to apply shocks that appeared to be potentially lethal. The "teachers" did so even though the "learners," who were in another room and not visible, were screaming with increasing intensity. The research clearly showed that if they were ordered to do so by authority figures, people would violate the social norms against inflicting pain on, and even possibly endangering the lives of, others.

By letting his subjects believe they were harming other subjects with electric shocks, Stanley Milgram attempted to learn how the Nazis were able to carry out torture and killings. Do you think most people would comply with an authority figure's orders?

Compliance is a 2012 movie based on Milgram's work. It deals with a real-life case in which a caller identified himself as a police officer investigating a theft at a McDonald's restaurant. He was able to convince the store manager to, among other things, allow a young girl working there to be strip-searched and sexually violated.

The results of the Milgram experiment (as well as events depicted in the movie) are important in many senses. We are concerned here with what the study did to the psyches of the people involved in the study. For one thing, the "teachers" came to know that they were very responsive to the dictates of authority figures, even if they were ordered to commit immoral acts. Some of them certainly realized that their behavior indicated that they were perfectly capable in such circumstances of harming, if not killing, other human beings. Such realizations had the possibility of adversely affecting the way participants viewed, and felt about, themselves. But the research has had several benefits as well, for both participants and others who have read about the Milgram studies. For example, those in powerful positions could better understand, and therefore limit, the potential impact of orders to subordinates and how far they might be willing to go in carrying them out.

Another famous study that raises similar ethical issues was conducted by Philip Zimbardo (1973). (The 2010

Social Sciences in War

Research Ethics

Philip Zimbardo's experimental recreation of prison conditions was so realistic, and the participants were so severely affected by their assigned roles, that the experiment was cut short by several weeks. Should this early cutoff have invalidated the research?

movie *The Experiment* is a fictionalized depiction of this experiment.) Zimbardo set up a prison-like structure called "Stanford County Prison" as a setting in which to conduct his experiment. Participants were recruited to serve as either prisoners or guards. The conditions in the "prison" were very realistic with windowless cells, minimal toilet facilities, and strict regulations imposed on the inmates. The guards had uniforms, badges, keys, and clubs. They were also trained in the methods of managing prisoners.

The experiment was supposed to have lasted six weeks, but it was ended after only six days. The researchers feared for the health and the sanity of those acting as prisoners. Some of the guards insulted, degraded, and dehumanized the prisoners. Only a few guards were helpful and supportive. However, even the helpful guards refused to intervene when prisoners were being abused. The prisoners could have left. However, they tended to go along with this situation, accepting both the authority of the guards and their own lowly and abused position. The ethical issues are similar to those raised by the Milgram research. Some of the guards experienced psychological distress, but it was worse for the prisoners when they realized how much they had contributed to their own difficulties. Social researchers learned that a real or perceived imbalance of power between researcher and participant may lead the participant to comply with a researcher's demands even though they cause distress. However, as in the case of Milgram's research, the Zimbardo

research yielded positive by-products, such as a greater understanding of how those put in guard positions may lose their humanity and how submissive prisoners can become.

Illegal Acts

In the course of ethnographic fieldwork, a researcher might witness or even become entangled in illegal acts. This problem often confronted Venkatesh (2008) in his research on gangs in and around a Chicago housing project. He frequently witnessed illegal acts such as drug use, drug sales, and prostitution. As we saw above, from the beginning he was suspected of being a police informant. Had he informed the police about the illegal acts he witnessed, he would have been likely to compromise his ability to continue his research. In not informing the police, he was forced to live with the fact that his silence was, at the minimum, not serving to reduce such illegal behavior.

In other cases, the researcher must weigh the sticky legal and ethical ramifications for participants. In one study of children in a nursery, the researchers witnessed an illegal act (Anspach and Mizrachi 2006). They had to decide whether or not to report it. The researchers had to juggle concerns about the criminality of the act with a desire to protect their research participants and the trust they had extended. Other concerns lingered in the background. Publishing an account of such a dramatic act might help the researchers' careers, but might also send the perpetrator of the illegal act to jail. It is possible that not informing the police, or refusing to turn over field notes, could lead to imprisonment for the researchers (Emerson 2001; Van Maanen 1983).

Violation of Trust

There are several ways that researchers can betray participants' trust in the research enterprise. For instance, the researcher might inadvertently divulge the identity of respondents even though they were promised anonymity. There is also the possibility of exploitative relationships, especially with key informants. Exploitation is of special concern in cases where there is a real or perceived imbalance of power—often related to race, class, or gender—between researcher and participant. In the Tuskegee case, for example, African American men suffered the adverse effects of the research even though syphilis is distributed throughout the larger population. Although this research should not have occurred under any circumstances, a more equitable research design would have meant that most of the participants would have been white males.

It is also a betrayal of trust for the researcher to develop inappropriate relationships with participants. One noteworthy example of this latter point is a study conducted by Erich Goode (2002) in order to better understand the stigma of obesity. He has publicly acknowledged that he had sexual relations with some of his female informants. Goode argues that because of this he was able to obtain information that may not have been obtainable by any other means. However, one must ask about the cost to his participants of obtaining knowledge in this way. One can only imagine how his participants felt when some of them discovered that Goode had an ulterior motive in having intimate relationships with them. Many of his participants were already very sensitive about their body image and their relationships with men. Because Goode's participants did not have full knowledge of his motives, they were unable to make informed choices about engaging in sexual relations with him. In this case, the power imbalance between researcher and participant led to exploitation.

The best known example of sociological research involving deception and intrusion into people's lives is Laud Humphreys's (1970) study of the homosexual activities of men in public restrooms (*tearooms*). Humphreys acted as a lookout outside tearooms and signaled men involved in anonymous acts of fellatio when members of the public or the police were approaching. He openly interviewed some of the men involved with full disclosure. However, he also noted the license numbers of some of those he observed and tracked down their addresses. Humphreys appeared at their homes a year or so later, in disguise, to interview them under false pretenses. There he uncovered one of the most important findings of his study: Over half of the men were married, with wives and families. They were involved in the tearoom trade not because they were homosexual but because sexual relations in their marriage were problematic.

Humphreys deceived these men by not telling them from the outset that he was doing research on them or, with those he interviewed under false pretenses, the true nature of the research. His research had at least the potential of revealing something that most of the participants wanted to conceal. He later admitted that if he had the chance to do the research over again, he would tell the participants about his true role and goal. But the research itself is not without merit. It helped to distinguish between homosexual acts and homosexual identity. Also, homosexuals had very difficult lives in the early 1970s. Nearly half of his participants were covertly bisexual or homosexual and faced numerous difficulties, if not danger, if they "came out." Thus, there were very strong reasons for them to keep their homosexual activity hidden. Many of these men also experienced considerable stress trying to live as married men while simultaneously engaging in impersonal homosexual activity with strangers. Humphreys's research provided some much needed insight into their lives.

OBJECTIVITY, OR "VALUE-FREE" SOCIOLOGY

Another issue relating to sociological research is whether or not researchers have been, or can be, objective. That is, do they allow personal preferences and judgments to bias their research? Many argue that value-laden research jeopardizes the entire field of sociology. The publication of such research, and public revelations about those biases, erode and could destroy the credibility of the field as a whole. In the history of sociology, this discussion is traceable, once again, to the work of Max Weber. Taken to its extreme, *value-free sociology* means preventing all personal values from affecting any phase of the research process. However, this is not what Weber intended in his work on values, and it is instructive to take a brief look at what he actually meant.

Weber was most concerned with the need for teachers, especially professors, to be value free in their lectures. This issue arose in Weber's day in Germany, at least in part because of the growing number of Marxist-oriented teachers. Many of them wished to use the classroom to express Marxist ideology and to raise the consciousness of students about the evils of capitalism. They may even have wanted to foment revolution against the capitalist system. Weber was opposed to Marxism, but he was also more generally opposed to using the classroom to express any values. He took this position

CHECKPOINT 2.5	**ISSUES IN SOCIAL RESEARCH**
Reliability	The degree to which a given question or measure produces the same results each time.
Validity	The degree to which a question or measure draws an accurate response.
Ethics	Standard by which we judge right and wrong, the choices that people make, and how they justify them.
Objectivity	Absence of personal preferences and judgments that bias research.

Methodology and Ethics

Laud Humphreys

because he felt that young students were neither mature nor sophisticated enough to see through such arguments. He believed they were also likely to be too intimidated by the position of their professors, especially in the authoritarian Germany of his day, to be able to evaluate their ideas critically. The idea of, and the need for, value freedom in the classroom seems clear and uncontestable. However, we must realize that all professors, like all other human beings, have values. Therefore, the best we can hope for is for them to strive to be as objective as possible in the classroom.

Weber did *not* take the same position with reference to research. In fact, he saw at least two roles for values in social research. The first is in the selection of a question to be researched. In that case, it is perfectly appropriate for researchers to be guided by their personal values, or the values that predominate in the society of the day.

The second is in the analysis of the results of a research study. In that analysis, sociologists can, and should, use personal and social values to help them make sense of, or to interpret, their findings. These values are an aid in interpretation and understanding. However, they are not to be used to distort purposely the findings or mislead the reader of a report on the study.

In Weber's opinion, the only place in research to be value free is in the collection of the research data. This is a rather unexceptional argument meaning that researchers should do everything they can to prevent bias in the data-collection process. Few, if any, observers would accept the opposing position that it is perfectly acceptable to engage in such distortions. Such a position would undermine all research and the scientific status and aspirations of sociology.

SUMMARY

Sociologists use theories to make sense of social phenomena. These theories help sociologists to interpret, explain, categorize, and predict social phenomena—sometimes even using theory to change the world.

Karl Marx focused the majority of his attention on macro issues, particularly the structure of capitalist society. Unlike Marx, Max Weber did not focus exclusively on the economy but considered the importance of other sociological variables, particularly religion. Émile Durkheim believed the control that social structures and cultural norms and values have over individuals is not only necessary but also desirable.

Georg Simmel focused on the micro-level issues, or interactions among individuals. W. E. B. Du Bois was a pioneering researcher of race in the United States at the turn of the twentieth century. Thorstein Veblen focused on consumption and the ways the rich show off their wealth, including through conspicuous consumption.

In contemporary sociological theory, structural/functional theories focus on large-scale social phenomena. Structural-functionalists like Robert Merton are concerned with both social structures and the functions—and dysfunctions—that such structures perform. In contrast, structuralism focuses on the social impact of hidden or underlying structures.

Conflict/critical theories tend to emphasize societal stresses, strains, and conflicts in a society held together by power and coercion. Conflict theory focuses on conflict and the ways in which it is prevented through coercion. Critical theory focuses on culture and offers a critical analysis of it. Feminist theory critiques the social situation confronting women and offers ideas on how their situation can be bettered, if not revolutionized. Queer theory addresses the relationship between heterosexuals and homosexuals but stresses the broader idea that there are no fixed and stable identities that determine who we are. Critical theories of race and racism argue that race continues to matter. They also raise the issue of oppression at the intersection of gender, race, sexual orientation, and other social statuses. Postmodern theory is similarly critical of society.

Inter/actionist theories deal with micro-level interactions among people and, to a degree, with individual action. Symbolic interactionism, for instance, is concerned with the effect of symbols, including words, on the interaction of two or more people. Ethnomethodology focuses on what people do rather than what they think and often analyzes conversations. Exchange theory, similar to ethnomethodology, studies not what people think but rather their behavior. Rational choice theory sees behavior as based on rational evaluations of goals and the means to achieve them.

Sociologists apply the scientific method. First, a sociologist finds a question that needs to be answered, then reviews the literature to see what has already been found. Next the sociologist develops a hypothesis, chooses a research method, and collects data that can confirm, or fail to confirm, the hypothesis. Finally, the researcher analyzes the data in relationship to the initial hypothesis.

Quantitative methods yield data in the form of numbers, and qualitative methods yield verbal descriptions. Observation consists of systematic watching, listening to, and recording what takes place in a natural social setting over some period of time. In interviews, respondents are asked a series of questions, usually on a face-to-face basis. Survey research collects data through interviews and questionnaires. Experimentation, less common, manipulates one or more independent variables to examine the effect on dependent variable(s).

Sociologists often also engage in secondary data analysis, in which they reanalyze data collected by others. Secondary data may consist of statistical information and historical documents and analyses.

Reliability is the degree to which a given measure produces the same results time after time, and validity is the degree to which a measure gets an accurate response. It is difficult to avoid bias altogether. However, clear and objective descriptions of research procedures will enable other researchers to evaluate and perhaps replicate them.

KEY TERMS

Alienation, 32
Anomie, 34
Capitalism, 31
Capitalists, 31
Collective conscience, 34
Conflict theory, 39
Conspicuous consumption, 36
Convenience sample, 56
Critical theories of race and racism, 42
Critical theory, 40
Culture industry, 40
Debunking, 39
Dependent variable, 58
Descriptive statistics, 50
Descriptive survey, 55
Double-consciousness, 36
Dysfunction, 37
Empiricism, 47
Ethics, 60
Ethnography, 52
Ethnomethodology, 45
Exchange relationship, 46
Exchange theory, 46
Experiment, 57

Explanatory survey, 56
Exploitation, 32
Feminist theory, 41
Field experiment, 58
Function, 37
Global ethnography, 52
Historical-comparative research, 59
Hyperconsumption, 44
Ideal type, 59
Independent variable, 57
Inferential statistics, 50
Intersectionality, 42
Interview, 53
Laboratory experiment, 58
Latent functions, 38
Manifest functions, 38
Mass culture, 40
Natural experiment, 58
Netnography, 53
Nonparticipant observation, 52
Observation, 50
Participant observation, 51
Postmodern theory, 44
Proletariat, 32

Qualitative research, 49
Quantitative research, 50
Queer theory, 42
Questionnaire, 55
Random sample, 56
Rational choice theory, 46
Rationalization, 33
Reliability, 60
Sample, 56
Scientific method, 48
Secondary data analysis, 59
Simulation, 44
Social facts, 34
Statistics, 50
Stratified sample, 56
Structural-functionalism, 37
Structuralism, 38
Survey research, 55
Symbolic interactionism, 45
Theories, 31
Unanticipated consequence, 38
Validity, 60

REVIEW QUESTIONS

1. What are theories, and how do sociologists use theories to make sense of the social world?

2. Max Weber said the world is becoming increasingly rationalized. What are the benefits and disadvantages of rationality? In what ways is McDonaldization the same as, or different from, rationalization?

3. You live in a world that is increasingly dominated by consumption. How are the items that you consume reflective of Thorstein Veblen's concept of "conspicuous consumption"?

4. What are the functions and dysfunctions of using the Internet to consume goods and services? On balance, do you think that consumption through the Internet is positive or negative?

5. What is mass culture, and why are critical theorists concerned about the dissemination of mass culture? Do you think the Internet and social networking sites are elements of mass culture and part of the traditional "culture industry"?

6. According to symbolic interactionist theory, why are symbols so important to our interactions? In what ways has language changed because of the development of the Internet?

7. What are the differences between participant and nonparticipant observational methods? How do sociologists ensure that their observations are systematic using both approaches?

8. What is the key value of conducting ethnographic research? How would a global ethnography help you to make sense of your own place in the world?

9. Some experiments allow researchers to take advantage of a naturally occurring event to study its effect on one or more dependent variables. Can you think of any recent events that might have been conducive to natural experiments?

What would be the dependent variable or variables in your example?

10. What are some ethical concerns raised by sociological research? Use specific examples from research discussed in the chapter to describe these ethical concerns.

11. What role do values play in the research process? According to Weber, when is objectivity most important?

APPLYING THE SOCIOLOGICAL IMAGINATION

How can we use surveys to describe the attitudes of all college students at your school toward globalization? Construct a survey consisting of 10 questions to determine how much students know about globalization and the extent to which they think that globalization is positive or negative. Check the Internet for surveys conducted by other researchers and organizations to see what types of questions are commonly asked to get at these sorts of questions. For your own survey, be sure to consider whether it will be structured or unstructured and whether it will be administered face-to-face, by mail, or over the web. How would you go about sampling students at your school? Why?

Once you have considered all of the above, take a convenience sample of five of your friends and administer the survey to them. What are your findings?

STUDENT STUDY SITE

ⓢSAGE edge™

Sharpen your skills with SAGE edge at **edge.sagepub.com/ritzeressentials**

SAGE edge for students provides a personalized approach to help you accomplish your coursework goals in an easy-to-use learning environment.

A Hindu holy man in Kathmandu, Nepal, applies paint to his face in preparation for the annual Shivaratri festival honoring Lord Shiva. The festival is marked by prayer and the smoking of marijuana. How much of our public behavior is governed by our culture and its values and norms?

CULTURE

3

LEARNING OBJECTIVES

1 Define culture.

2 Identify the basic elements of culture, including values and norms.

3 Discuss diversity within cultures, including the concepts of ideal and real culture, subcultures and countercultures, culture wars, and assimilation.

4 Describe emerging issues in culture such as global and consumer culture.

The term *cool* originated in fifteenth-century Africa, where the Yoruba (a Nigerian tribe) word *Itutu*, literally "cool," denoted a person who was calm and steady as cool water. Centuries later, Miles Davis's landmark 1957 jazz album *Birth of the Cool* gave new life to the term, which came to describe beat poetry, film noir, abstract expressionist art, and of course jazz.

Our ideas and attitudes that define coolness have remained constant ever since. Acting with self-assurance and awareness, even in the face of adversity, is cool. Using expressions, postures, and vocal patterns that express nonchalance and composure is cool. Dressing fashionably and using contemporary slang is cool. Mastering cutting-edge technology is cool. Being young and hip is cool. However, these specific characteristics of coolness depend entirely on our culture, and on the cultural regulations that allow us to live in harmony with others.

> **Different cultures have different norms, values, and symbols which change over time.**

Different cultures thus have different norms, values, and symbols and consider different traits and mannerisms to be cool (or uncool). These markers also change over time. The people and things we consider cool today differ remarkably from the cool icons of the mid twentieth century. Lady Gaga, Panda Bear, Keith Urban, and Nicki Minaj could be considered cool, at least for the moment. A person might work for years to be cool in the eyes of her peers, but if thrust into a new subculture such as college, she may have to start from scratch. Her iPhone 3GS might have been cool a few years ago, but it isn't anymore.

Different cultures have different norms, values, and symbols which change over time.

Because U.S. culture is generally similar across the country, coolness is not difficult to spot within our borders. Around the world, however, it takes on many forms. A mustachioed middle-aged man might be considered uncool in the United States but be an ultracool Bollywood heartthrob in parts of India. A cool attitude in China might be considered conservative and materialistic in Italy. But though coolness is culturally relative, globalization and Americanization have altered some countries' values and norms. As U.S. culture spreads around the world, U.S. coolness and cool icons are not far behind.

Coolness is, of course, just a small aspect of culture. Still, it speaks to many larger cultural issues. Who and what do you and your peers consider cool? What does that say about you and your culture? ●

As you read this chapter on culture, keep in mind that you are actually immersed in many different cultures. For example, you are likely to be involved to some degree or another in global, American, consumer, and digital culture, as well as the culture of university life. You are continually learning the rules of these and other cultures. Much of that learning happens almost effortlessly, as you live your daily life. But cultures that are new to you, such as university culture, or that are evolving rapidly, such as digital culture, are likely to require much, and continuing, effort, alertness, and flexibility on your part in order to learn how to behave in them.

Gang members make use of symbols, colors, clothing, and language to distinguish themselves. Does your school or university use visible signs of its own culture?

A DEFINITION OF CULTURE

Culture encompasses the ideas, values, practices, and material objects that allow a group of people, even an entire society, to carry out their collective lives in relative order and harmony. There are innumerable ideas, values, practices, and material objects associated with most cultures. As a result, no one individual can possibly know them all or what they all mean. But people must know at least the most basic and important elements of their culture. Knowledge of a shared culture leads people to behave in similar ways and to adopt a similar way of looking at the world.

Consider the cultures of the Bloods and the Crips, two street gangs with origins in Los Angeles in the early 1970s but now existing nationwide (Patton 1998; C. Simpson 2006). Members of the two gangs distinguish themselves from each other in a variety of ways but most notably by their defining colors—red for Bloods and blue for Crips. These colors and other symbols are very meaningful to gang members, helping them to mark territories, easily identify friends and foes, and signify their values. The meaning of these symbols was created by the group itself, and the symbols have been passed down from one gang member to another. Symbols like these may also be passed along from a gang in one locale to those situated elsewhere. Some Mexican American

> **culture** A collection of ideas, values, practices, and material objects that mean a great deal to a group of people, even an entire society, and that allow them to carry out their collective lives in relative order and harmony.

gangs—for example, La Gran Raza and La Gran Familia—have adopted ideas and objects, as well as names, such as La Eme and Nuestra Familia, from predecessors in Mexico or gangs formed in U.S. prisons.

In contrast, for those who are not members of the group, an idea, a value, a practice, or an object may have little meaning, may mean something completely different, or may even have no meaning at all. For example, to members of the general public, a spray-painted gang tag may just be a scribble defacing neighborhood property. A person wearing a red shirt is simply wearing a red shirt.

The existence of a culture and common knowledge of it are so important that newcomers to the group, especially children, are taught its basic elements early. They then expand on that knowledge as they mature and become more integral members of the group.

At the same time, culture is constantly being affected by changes both internal and external to the group. Among the *internal changes* are the average age of the population within that group, with the result that the culture increasingly reflects the needs and interests of younger or older people. For example, in the United States and other aging societies, television programs and the advertisements associated with them are more oriented to older people than is the case in societies with a large proportion of younger people (Carter and Vega 2011). A good example of this is the great popularity, especially among older viewers, of PBS's *Downton Abbey*. On the other hand,

Gangs

FIGURE 3.1 • Cellphone Use and Texting-While-Driving Laws, 2013

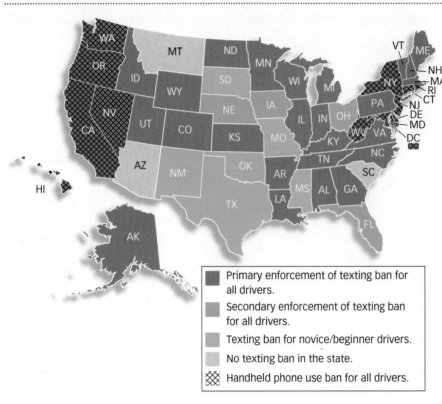

Legend:
- Primary enforcement of texting ban for all drivers.
- Secondary enforcement of texting ban for all drivers.
- Texting ban for novice/beginner drivers.
- No texting ban in the state.
- Handheld phone use ban for all drivers.

NOTE: Under secondary laws, an officer must have some other reason to stop a vehicle before citing a driver for using a cellphone. Laws without this restriction are called primary.

SOURCE: Map showing Cellphone Use and Texting While Driving Laws in "Distracted Drivers." Copyright © National Conference of State Legislatures. Reprinted with permission.

television certainly cannot and does not ignore its younger audience. The great popularity and cultural influence of HBO's *Girls* is indicative of that.

Technological innovations, among other things, are *external changes* that are likely to alter a group's culture significantly. For example, with the growth in use of smartphones, text messages have become increasingly popular, especially among young people, as a communication method, and phone conversations have become proportionally less common. Thus not only newcomers to the group, but also those who have participated for years, must constantly learn new aspects of culture and perhaps unlearn others that are no longer relevant.

The rise of the smartphone has created a whole new set of realities for which clear and firm cultural rules are not yet in place. One such rule involves what should and should not be discussed on a smartphone when others, especially strangers, are close enough that they can overhear what is being said. For example, not long ago I took an Amtrak train from Washington, DC, to New York City. Sitting behind me was a woman talking on the phone with her mother about her difficulties in getting pregnant. In another conversation with a nurse, she discussed the status of her eggs. I'm not sure

the woman would have wanted to share these experiences with a stranger like me if we were talking face-to-face. And I'm not at all sure I wanted or needed to know about this part of her life. The personal nature of smartphones, and of many of the conversations that take place on them, is often in conflict with the public setting in which the phones are used and in which the conversations occur (Humphreys 2005).

Then there is the issue of smartphone use intruding on others' consciousness. Long, loud, and frequent smartphone conversations are not a problem in the privacy of one's home, but they are a problem in public areas where there is an expectation of quietude, as at a nice restaurant. I found out for myself how rude a smartphone conversation may be perceived, and the consequences, on my return trip from New York. Amtrak now has "quiet cars" for those who do not want to be plagued by the cell phone conversations of strangers. I found myself in one, but I didn't know what it meant to be in such a car. Soon after the trip began, my wife called, and we began a conversation. Almost immediately, a man sitting a few rows in front of me jumped up and glared at me angrily, while another passenger gently tugged on my sleeve and pointed to the "quiet car" sign. I now understood its meaning and said good-bye to my wife. This illustrates the power of culture and also how we learn about new cultural elements and developments, sometimes the hard way. I no longer need to be reminded of what is expected of me in a "quiet car."

A more formal set of rules regarding talking and texting on cell phones is being developed to control their use by drivers. It has become apparent—both from insurance company statistics and from experimental research—that using a handheld cell phone while driving increases the risk of accidents (Horrey and Wickens 2006). A very active media campaign was developed—promoted by Oprah Winfrey, among others—to discourage people from using handheld cell phones while driving. As shown in Figure 3.1, several states have enacted laws against the practice, and some safety advocates are pressing for a similar federal law. If both campaigns succeed, using a handheld cell phone while driving will no longer be culturally acceptable and will in fact become illegal across the nation.

Although we generally accept and learn the various components of culture, sometimes we refuse to comply with, or even accept, them. For example, many continue to talk and text on cell phones in their automobiles even though they know that the larger culture is increasingly characterized by a negative view of such behaviors. To take a different example, premarital and extramarital sexual relationships continue to be disapproved of by traditional American culture, but many people have come to reject these ideas. Indeed, it could be argued that these forms of sexual behavior have come to be widely accepted and have, in fact, become accepted parts of the culture.

THE BASIC ELEMENTS OF CULTURE

All groups have a culture. Furthermore, culture relates to such diverse social phenomena as athletics, cooking, funeral ceremonies, courtship, medicine, marriage, sexual restrictions, bodily adornment, calendars, dancing, games, greetings, sexual taboos, hairstyles, personal names, religion, and myths. However, the specific content of each of these domains, and many more, varies from culture to culture. Cultures differ from one another mainly because each involves a unique mix of values, norms, objects, and language inherited from the past, derived from other groups, and created anew by each group.

VALUES

The broadest elements of culture are **values**, the general and abstract standards defining what a group or society as a whole considers good, desirable, right, or important. Values express the ideals of everything from a group to an entire society.

In his classic work *Democracy in America* ([1835–1840] 1969), the French writer Alexis de Tocqueville detailed what he perceived to be America's values. Among the things that Americans valued in the early nineteenth century were democracy, equality, individualism, "taste for physical comfort," spirituality, and economic prosperity. Although Tocqueville wrote about his impressions of the United States almost 200 years ago, the vast majority of Americans today would accept most, if not all, of the values he described (Crothers 2010).

> **values** General and abstract standards defining what a group or society as a whole considers good, desirable, right, or important—in short, its ideals.

French aristocrat Alexis de Tocqueville traveled the United States and studied its political systems and cultural norms. What conclusions about U.S. culture might he draw today?

CHECKPOINT 3.1	TYPES OF CHANGES THAT AFFECT CULTURAL GROUPS	
Internal		**External**
Demographics of group members, such as age.		Technology, such as smartphones.

Indeed, Americans find these values so natural and incontrovertible that they expect them to be accepted in other cultures around the world. However, such a belief has had some disappointing, even disastrous, consequences for the United States. For example, when the United States undertook invasions of Iraq and Afghanistan, one of the objectives was the creation of democratic regimes in those societies. The assumption was that Iraqis and Afghanis wanted the same kind of democracy as the one that exists in the United States.

Alexis de Tocqueville

Have you ever deliberately broken a social norm? Some of the passengers on this New York City subway are participating in an annual "No-Pants Subway Ride" event.

written down and formally enforced through institutions such as the state. Rules regarding speaking and texting on handheld smartphones while driving are examples of how informal norms may be codified into laws.

You are expected to follow the norms and obey the laws, but the consequences for failing to do so are usually very different in the two cases. If you violate the law against homicide, then you can expect to be arrested, incarcerated, and perhaps even executed. But if you fail to follow the norm of using utensils to eat your dinner and you eat instead with your fingers, all that might be expected are a few raised eyebrows and a "tsk tsk" or two from your dinner companions. However, such relatively mild reactions are not always the case. For example, violations by a gang member of a norm against fleeing a fight with another gang may lead to physical violence, death, and other not-so-subtle outcomes.

However, creating democracies in those countries has proven to be extremely difficult for a variety of reasons, including the fact that they lack a tradition of democratic government. It is extremely difficult, if not impossible, to impose a value, such as the value of democracy, on a society where it does not already exist, or where it exists in a very different form.

Researchers using data collected through the World Values Survey have found that to be the case (Welzel and Inglehart 2009). The World Values Survey has gathered data from a variety of countries around the world on individual views on gender equality; tolerance for abortion, homosexuality, and divorce; desire for autonomy over authority (for example, obedience and faith); and democratic participation over security. Respondents in countries where personal freedom is not valued highly—such as Pakistan, Jordan, and Nigeria—tend to think of antidemocratic authoritarian regimes as being democratic. The surveys also showed that citizens within these countries have little knowledge of the meaning of liberal democracy. There is little chance that American-style democracy will succeed in these countries.

Norms are reinforced through **sanctions,** which can take the form of punishments (negative sanctions) or rewards (positive sanctions). When norms are violated, punishments are used, whereas rewards are employed when norms are followed. For example, dinner companions might frown when you eat with your hands and approve when you use the right utensil. Gang members would be likely to disapprove of those who flee and praise those who stay and fight. Children who bring home report cards with lots of As and Bs may be applauded, while those whose report cards show lower grades may get a stern lecture from a parent. In other words, sanctions may be applied when norms are observed as well as when they are violated. Sometimes either positive or negative sanctions are enough to enforce norms. However, in general enforcement is more effective when positive and negative sanctions are used in tandem—when *both* the "carrot" (reward) and the "stick" (punishment) are applied. Most people follow norms primarily because sanctions are associated with them.

NORMS

Based on values, **norms** are the informal rules that guide what people do and how they live. Norms tell us what we should and should not do in a given situation (Dandaneau 2007). Many norms are informal. That is, they are not formally codified or written down in any one place. **Laws** are norms that have been codified. They are

> **norms** Informal rules that guide what a member of a culture does in a given situation and how that person lives.
>
> **laws** Norms that have been codified, or written down, and are formally enforced through institutions such as the state.
>
> **sanctions** The application of rewards (positive sanctions) or punishments (negative sanctions) when norms are accepted or violated.

ACTIVE SOCIOLOGY

What's Happening to U.S. Culture?

The McDonaldization of society reflects the U.S. values of efficiency, predictability, calculability, and control through nonhuman rather than human technology. To better understand the process of McDonaldization, describe what each of these values means to you, and give an example of the way we might see each one operating in the McDonaldization of U.S. culture.

Value	Meaning	Example of McDonaldization of U.S. culture
Efficiency		
Predictability		
Calculability		
Control through nonhuman technology		

ASK YOURSELF

What norms are operating in your classroom or your dorm or apartment? What negative sanctions have you observed when these norms are violated?

Not all norms are the same, are equally important, or carry with them the same penalties if they are violated. A distinction made over a century ago by William Graham Sumner ([1906] 1940) remains useful today. On the one hand, there are **folkways**, or norms that are relatively unimportant. Whether they are observed or violated, they carry with them few if any sanctions. For example, many college classes have norms against texting during a lecture, but the norm is frequently violated. When violations are detected by alert instructors, the negative sanctions, such as asking the student to stop or to leave the room for the rest of class, are generally mild. In contrast, **mores** (pronounced MOR-ays) are more important norms whose violation is likely to be met with severe negative sanctions. Students who use their smartphones to cheat on college exams are violating mores (as well as campus rules). If their actions are witnessed or discovered, they may be subjected to severe negative sanctions, such as failing a class and even being expelled from school. While Sumner makes a clear distinction between folkways and mores, in fact they exist

> **folkways** Norms that are relatively unimportant and, if violated, carry few if any sanctions.
>
> **mores** Important norms whose violation is likely to be met with severe sanctions.
>
> **material culture** All of the material objects that are reflections or manifestations of a culture.

along a continuum so that it is often hard to distinguish with certainty where a folkway ends and a more begins.

MATERIAL CULTURE

Values and norms exist within the realm of ideas. However, culture also takes material—that is, tangible—forms. **Material culture** encompasses all of the artifacts, the "stuff" (Molotch 2003; Steketee and Frost 2011), that are reflections or manifestations of culture (Dant 2007). A wide range of things can be included under the heading of material culture, including the clothes we wear, the homes we live in, our computers and smartphones, the toys our children play with, and even the weapons used by our military.

Culture shapes these objects. For instance, the value Americans place on economic prosperity is reflected in such material objects as games like Monopoly. This game was first patented in the mid-1930s, and its icon is a well-dressed, economically successful tycoon with a monocle, named Rich Uncle Pennybags. The winner of the game is the player who ends up with the most money and the most highly valued properties. Similarly, one of the objectives in the online virtual world Second Life is the accumulation of as many Linden Dollars—ultimately convertible to real dollars—as possible. However, unlike Monopoly, the real objective in Second Life is not to "win" by having the most money, but to "hang out" and socialize.

Material culture also shapes the larger culture in various ways. For example, in playing Monopoly, children are learning about, helping to support, and furthering a culture that values wealth and material success. To take

Folkways

Social Experiment

This Russian family is posing with all their material possessions displayed outside their home. How do your home's contents compare?

One important aspect of symbolic culture is **language**, a set of meaningful symbols that enable communication. Language, especially in its written form, allows for the storage and development of culture. Cultures with largely oral traditions do manage to accumulate culture and transmit it from one generation or group to another. However, written language is a far more effective way of retaining and expanding upon a culture.

Perhaps more importantly, language facilitates communication within a culture. Words reflect how we think and see the world. They also shape and influence culture. Suppose a time traveler from the 1950s arrived at a modern-day supermarket to buy something to eat for breakfast. Kellogg's Frosted Flakes, with a sprinkling of sugar, was a noteworthy innovation in the 1950s. However, our time traveler would be bewildered by the wide array of new brand-name breakfast cereals like Bear Naked, Count Chocula, Cap'n Crunch's Crunch Berries, Double Chocolate Cookie Crisp, Pebbles Boulders, and so on. The exotic and varied flavors we have now would be considered a marvel by someone from the 1950s. The point, however, is that having names for a large number of cereal brands allows the consumer to make much finer distinctions and judgments about breakfast and much else.

The contemporary world has given us a wealth of new words. For example, in the digital era, e-mail and advertisers gave us the word *spam* for the avalanche of unwanted messages. In the world of social networking, Twitter has given us the word *tweet* to describe the brief

a different example, the centuries-old American value of individual freedom and individualism has been greatly enhanced by the widespread adoption of such material objects as the automobile, the single-family home, and the smartphone. The latter, for example, gives us highly individualized and mobile access to the vast world available on the phone and the Internet.

SYMBOLIC CULTURE AND LANGUAGE

Symbolic culture includes the nonmaterial aspects of culture. In fact, we have already discussed two key forms of symbolic culture—values and norms. Symbolic culture is in many ways more important than material culture. However, there is no clear line between material and nonmaterial culture. Most, if not all, material phenomena have symbolic aspects, and various aspects of symbolic culture are manifest in material objects. Examples include buying American rather than Japanese or Korean automobiles as a symbol of one's patriotism; purchasing an iPad as an example of one's technological sophistication; and using cloth diapers versus disposables as a symbol of one's commitment to "green" parenting.

---

symbolic culture Aspects of culture that exist in nonmaterial forms.

language A set of meaningful symbols that makes possible the communication of culture as well as communication more generally within a given culture, and that calls out the same meaning in the person to whom an utterance is aimed as it does to the person making the utterance.

messages on that system and *hashtag* for a label to help us in searching tweets. The consumption-oriented nature of our society has also led to the creation of many new words, a large number of them brand names. For example, the *iPod* is the leading portable music device; it led to the development of the sales of *iTunes*. The *iPhone* is the leading *smartphone* (another new word), and it has led to a booming industry in *apps* (applications) of all sorts. Similarly, globalization has led to new words, including *globalization* itself, which was virtually unused prior to 1990. The boom in sending work to be performed in another country or countries has given us the term *outsourcing* (Ritzer and Lair 2007).

Words like these are shared by people all over the world and allow them to communicate with one another. Communication among people of different cultures is also easier if they share a mother tongue. African cultures use a variety of official and national languages. People in countries where French is the official language, such as Burkina Faso and Niger, can transact their business more easily with one another (assuming relations are tranquil) than when they are dealing with the African nations where Arabic or Portuguese is the primary language, such as Mauritania and Cape Verde.

Communication between cultures is never as easy or as clear as communication within a given culture. For example, the 2003 movie *Lost in Translation* deals with communication difficulties experienced by Americans in Japan. The lead, played by Bill Murray, is a famous American actor visiting Japan to do commercials. Among other things, he is unable to understand how a large number of words spoken in Japanese become, when translated for him, a very small number of English words. He seems to suspect that the translator is purposely not telling him things. He also finds himself unable to understand what the director of the commercial he is filming wants him to do, even when the directions are translated into English.

In a world dominated by consumption, communication between cultures also takes place through the viewing of common brands. However, brand names well known in some cultures may not translate well in other cultures. As a result, brands are often renamed to better reflect other cultures. Take the following list of well-known brands in the United States and elsewhere and the way they are translated into Chinese:

The world's languages display an infinite variety. This young teacher is a member of the tiny religious community called the Kalash, who live in Pakistan near the Afghanistan border. Notice the letters of the Kalasha alphabet she is writing on the blackboard.

Brand	Chinese Translation
Nike	Enduring and Persevering
BMW	Precious Horse
Heineken	Happiness Power
Coca-Cola	Tasty Fun
Marriott	10,000 Wealthy Elites

While such name changes are common, some Chinese brands are simply phonetic translations of global brands. For example, Cadillac is translated as "Ka di la ke." Although this means nothing to the Chinese, the fact that it is foreign gives it an aura of status and respectability. However, if Microsoft had used a phonetic translation of its search engine Bing, it would have been in big trouble. In Chinese, Bing translates into "disease" or "virus." Rather than be seen as disease-ridden or a carrier of a virus, Microsoft changed its Chinese name to Bi ying. This has the far more appealing meaning of "responding without fail." Peugeot did go ahead with the name Biao zhi, although it turned out that that sounds much like the Chinese slang word for prostitute. As a result, Peugeot has become the butt of a number of dirty jokes in China (Wines 2011).

Even when people share a language, communication may be difficult if their backgrounds and values are too

Buying Green

THE BASIC ELEMENTS OF CULTURE

Values	General and abstract standards defining what the group considers good, right, or important.
Norms	Informal rules that guide what people do and how they live; reinforced through positive and negative sanctions.
Material culture	Artifacts that serve as reflections or manifestations of culture, including clothing, technology, and weapons.
Symbolic culture	Nonmaterial aspects of culture, including values and norms but also language.

different. In the popular and influential HBO (2002–2008) series *The Wire,* a police major takes some inner-city youths from Baltimore (the site of the series) to a fancy restaurant. Given their lack of experience in such a restaurant, they don't understand the menu, what they are ordering, how to order it, or how to eat it. The symbolic culture that is familiar to them is far different from the symbolic culture of the restaurant.

ASK YOURSELF

Have you ever been in a situation, such as a trip abroad, in which understanding and communicating were difficult for you because you were unfamiliar with the language and symbols around you? How did you cope? Have you ever helped someone else who was in a similar situation? What did you do?

CULTURAL DIFFERENCES

As you have seen so far, we can think in terms of the culture of society as a whole (for example, American culture), and later in this chapter we will even conceive of the possibility of a global culture. But you have also seen that there is great diversity within cultures, from gang culture to Internet culture and too many other variants of culture for us to enumerate. Studying and understanding culture becomes easier, however, with the aid of a few key ideas: ideal and real culture, ideology, subculture and counterculture, culture wars, and multiculturalism.

IDEAL AND REAL CULTURE

There is often a large gap, if not a chasm, between **ideal culture,** or what the norms and values of society lead us to think people *should believe and do,* and **real culture,** or what people *actually think and do* in their everyday lives. For example, as we have seen, a major American value is

democracy. However, barely a majority of Americans bother to vote in presidential elections (58.2 percent of eligible voters voted in the 2012 election, the same figure recorded four years earlier [McDonald 2013]). (See Chapter 12.) A far smaller percentage of those who are eligible vote in state and local elections. In the 2012 presidential election, just under 60 percent of the eligible voters voted (McDonald 2013); see Figure 3.2 for the statistics for your state. Worse, very few Americans are active in politics in other ways, such as canvassing on behalf of a political party or working to get people out to vote.

In another example, the cultural ideal that mothers should be completely devoted to their children (Blair-Loy 2003; Hays 1998) often comes into conflict with the lived reality of the many women who work outside of the home and must balance their time between work and family. One area where this contradiction becomes apparent is with breast-feeding, which at least for some women is becoming a norm, once again, of motherhood (Avishai 2007; Stearns 2009, 2011). But breast-feeding is difficult or impossible for many women because it is labor- and time-intensive and because most women have jobs or other constraints in their lives. One recent study showed that women who breast-fed for more than six months suffered greater economic losses than those who did so for less time or not all (Rippeyoug and Noonan 2012). The result for an individual mother can be great ambivalence toward breast-feeding and, at times, the feeling that she has failed to live up to the standards of being a "good mom" (Blum 2000; P. Taylor, Funk, and Clark 2007).

IDEOLOGY

An *ideology* is a set of shared beliefs that explains the social world and guides people's actions. There are many ideologies in any society, and some of them become dominant. For example, in the United States, *meritocracy* is a dominant ideology involving the widely shared belief that all people have an equal chance of succeeding economically based on their hard work and skills. Many people act on the basis

> **ideal culture** Norms and values indicating what members of a society should believe in and do.
>
> **real culture** What people actually think and do in their everyday lives.

of that belief and, among other things, seek the education and training that seem to be needed to succeed.

However, even with dedication and adequate education and training, not everyone succeeds. This reflects the key fact that not all ideologies are true. For one thing, they may come from, and be true for, some groups of people (such as those in the upper classes) and not for others (those in the lower classes) (Mannheim [1931] 1936). For another, they may be outright distortions used by one group to hide reality from another group (Marx [1857–1858] 1964). In this sense, it could be argued that meritocracy is an ideology created by the upper classes to hide the fact that those in the lower classes have little or no chance of succeeding. This fact is hidden from them in order to prevent them from becoming dissatisfied and rebellious. If the lower classes accept the ideology of meritocracy, they may be more likely to blame themselves for failing rather than the upper classes or the American economic system as a whole.

SUBCULTURES

Within any culture there are **subcultures** that involve groups of people who accept much of the dominant culture but are set apart from it by one or more culturally significant characteristics. In the United States, major subcultures include the LGBT community (lesbians, gays, bisexuals, and transgendered persons), Hispanics, the Tea Party, Hasidic Jews, hip-hop fans, and youth subcultures. Muslims are becoming an increasingly important subculture in the United States (especially in cities like Detroit). They already constitute a major subculture in many European countries, most notably Great Britain.

There are subcultures in the realm of consumption as well. For example, "brand communities" develop around a particular brand-name product (Meister 2012; Muniz and O'Guinn 2001). Harley-Davidson motorcycle riders are one such subculture, with distinctive clothing, events, and norms. Brand communities have formed around a number of Apple products, such as the Macintosh computer (the "Mac") and the iPad. The members of these communities share a number of cultural elements, including norms. In the case of the Mac, for example, some community members positively sanction *jailbreaking,* a method for hacking into Apple's software in order to get around its restrictions and limitations.

Any society includes many subcultures, such as golfers or those devoted to fishing, which develop around particular styles of entertainment and fashion and share a special vocabulary. A great deal of attention has been devoted to "deviant" subcultures, such as those that involve punks, goths, and the like (Berard 2007). In Great Britain, "football hooligans," those who often engage in violence at, or surrounding, soccer matches, constitute a deviant subculture largely specific to that society (Ayres and Treadwell 2012; Dunning, Murphy, and Williams 1986). However, there are also many "straight" youth subcultures such as "straight edge" music fans who eschew alcohol and drugs (www.straightedge.com; Wood 2006).

FIGURE 3.2 • Voter Turnout for the 2012 Presidential Election

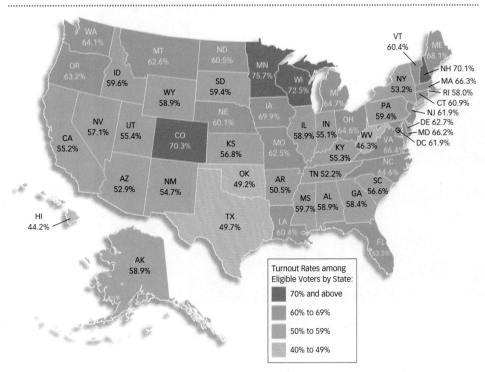

SOURCE: From Michael McDonald, "2012 General Election Turnout Rates," last updated 7/22/2013, United States Elections Project, George Mason University. Reprinted by permission of the author.

> **subcultures** A group of people who accept much of the dominant culture but are set apart from it by one or more culturally significant characteristics.

The Wire

So-called soccer hooligans are a kind of subculture often known for violent partisanship. These Turkish fans are clashing with police following an important match.

Another example of a subculture can be found in the world of skateboarders. The majority of skateboarders accept most of society's culture, norms, values, and language. But they also differ in some ways. For instance, many of them are more willing to take risks than others are. Many are involved in a new sport known as parkour where participants take risks by seeking to overcome urban obstacles such as walls and ledges (Kidder 2012). Skateboarders often use those obstacles to enhance the thrill of their activity. They also have their own vocabulary.

COUNTERCULTURES

Countercultures are groups that not only differ from the dominant culture, but whose norms and values may be incompatible with those of the dominant culture (Binkley 2007; Zellner 1995). They may, in fact, consciously and overtly act in opposition to the dominant culture. The term *counterculture* was introduced by Theodore Roszak ([1968] 1995, 1969) in the late 1960s, in reference to hippies, antiwar activists, and radical students. An even earlier example of a counterculture was the Ku Klux Klan. Klan members rejected the American value of equal treatment for all by mistreating members of various minority groups, especially black Americans. They also conducted lynchings and committed murders by other means, and in so doing they rejected the value placed on life, to say nothing of the law against murder.

Computer hackers are a contemporary example of a counterculture (Levy 2010). Many hackers simply seek to show their technical mastery of computers through relatively benign actions such as writing free computer software. However, a minority of hackers are devoted to subverting authority and negatively affecting the Internet. They write malicious code in order to disrupt or even shut down the normal operations of computers. There are many cases of break-ins to government and corporate computer systems in order to steal secret information.

In the realm of consumption, an important contemporary counterculture is formed by those who are associated with, or sympathetic to, the "voluntary simplicity movement" (Elgin 2010; Grigsby 2004). Juliet Schor (1993, 1998) has critiqued the dominant American culture's emphasis on what she calls "work and spend." That is, we are willing to work long hours in order to be able to spend a great deal on consumption. In addition, she points out the ways in which our consumer culture has led to the commercialization of childhood (see below), with advertising pervading all aspects of children's lives (Schor 2005). As a countercultural alternative, she suggests that we both work less and spend less and instead devote ourselves to more meaningful activities. Living a simpler life means avoiding overconsumption, minimizing the work needed to pay for consumption, and doing less harm to the environment.

Globalization, especially economic globalization, has also spawned a number of very active countercultural groups. They are not necessarily antiglobalization, but they favor alternative forms of globalization (R. Kahn and Kellner 2007; Pleyers 2010). In fact, many of them are part of the process of globalization. The World Social Forum (WSF) was created in 2001 after a series of antiglobalization protests, especially in Seattle in 1999. Its members come from all over the world. The WSF's slogan is "Another world is possible." That other world would be less capitalistic. It also would allow for more democratic decision making on matters that affect large portions of the world's population. Those who accept this kind of perspective are clearly part of a counterculture. They oppose the global spread of the dominant capitalist culture that prioritizes maximizing profits over democratic decision making.

> **countercultures** Groups whose cultures not only differ in certain ways from the dominant culture, but whose norms and values may be incompatible with those of the dominant culture.

PUBLIC SOCIOLOGY

Todd Gitlin and the Culture Wars

Born in 1943, Todd Gitlin is an American sociologist, journalist, novelist, and poet. He has been actively involved in the "culture wars" (see below) since his early days as a college student. In 1963–1964, he was president of Students for a Democratic Society (SDS), one of the most famous radical student movement organizations of the day. He helped organize both the first national protest against the Vietnam War and the first American demonstrations against corporate involvement in apartheid South Africa. Gitlin's view of his activist role is reflected in his quote: "I am a realist as well as an idealist, and I think that it is incumbent upon those of us in opposition to try to work within what are always arduous circumstances to stretch the limits of the possible" (Monbiot and Gitlin 2011).

Gitlin has written extensively on media and communications. His work has had an impact both on sociology and on the larger public. One of his most famous books is *The Whole World Is Watching* (1980), an analysis of major news coverage of the early days of the anti–Vietnam War movement. In this book, Gitlin draws on interviews with movement activists, news coverage, and his own experiences to analyze how the media reported on the antiwar movement and other movements. He shows that the media tend first to ignore movements, and when they finally do cover them, they selectively focus on only certain parts of the story. Despite their claims of neutrality and objectivity, they thereby distort the reality and treat these movements as abnormal social phenomena. The media help to destabilize social movements by overemphasizing their revolutionary rhetoric and distorting what they do. In supporting "moderate" societal reforms, the media further undermine more radical social movements.

Gitlin currently serves as professor of journalism and sociology at Columbia University. His social commentary has appeared in a variety of newspapers (*The New York Times, Los Angeles Times, The Washington Post, San Francisco Chronicle*), magazines (*The Nation, Mother Jones*, poetry in *The New York Review of Books*), and other outlets (National Public Radio). He also served as a member of the board of directors of Greenpeace USA from 2003 to 2006. Gitlin has sought to engage a variety of publics (including students, everyday citizens, and bystanders) by using sociological ideas to help them make better sense of the world and to imagine the range of human and social possibilities.

SOURCE: Printed with the permission of Paul Dean.

Think About It

What does Todd Gitlin mean by "stretching the limits of the possible"? Do you agree with his assessment of the media's coverage of movements? Why or why not? Can you think of other events the media first ignore and then distort?

CULTURE WARS

In the 1960s, the hippies, student radicals, and anti–Vietnam War activists vocally, visibly, and sometimes violently rejected traditional American norms and values. Among other things, they rejected unthinking patriotism and taboos against recreational drugs and sexual freedom. The term *culture wars* was used to describe the social upheavals that ensued. More generally, **culture wars** are conflicts pitting a subculture or counterculture against the dominant culture, or conflicts between dominant groups within a society. Culture wars sometimes lead to the disruption of the social, economic, and political status quo (Hunter 1992; Luker 1984).

In the United States today, the major culture war involves a series of battles between those who see themselves as on the conservative end of the sociopolitical spectrum and those who view themselves as on the liberal end. This war is largely viewed as a political battle over such things as government spending, taxes, social services, national defense, environmental measures, and so on. Conservatives generally favor less government spending, lower taxes for the wealthy, fewer entitlements for the poor, an aggressive national defense, and minimal environmental regulations. Liberals usually support higher government spending on education, health care, and services for the poor; less spending on national defense; and stricter environmental regulations.

> **culture wars** A conflict that pits subcultures and countercultures against the dominant culture or that pits dominant groups within society against each other.

 Misconceptions of Counterculture

 Debating Hip-Hop

The counterculture of the 1960s was distinguished by staunch opposition to the war in Vietnam, as expressed by these protestors. What countercultures exist in the United States today?

ASK YOURSELF

Do you think the culture war between U.S. conservatives and liberals is really a political conflict about taxes and spending, or are there underlying social norms and values at play? Give examples to explain your answer.

There are also important differences in fundamental values between these groups. Consider, for example, the long-running battle over abortion. The political battle is over legal limits to abortion and contraception. However, the underlying values have to do with one's definition of life and attitude toward women's role in society. Similarly, much heat is generated over "family values," with conservatives worrying about the decline in the traditional nuclear family, the increasing prevalence of cohabitation and single parenthood, and homosexual marriages and child adoptions. They place more emphasis on strict moral codes and self-discipline. In contrast, liberals place more

significance on empathy, openness, and fairness (McAdams et al. 2008). They tend to see these developments in the family as signs of greater acceptance of people's differences and circumstances. Within the field of sociology, in fact, there is intense debate among family scholars who argue that the family is in decline (Popenoe 1993, 2009) and those who feel the concept of the family needs to be broadened to embrace the many ways in which people experience kin connections (Biblarz and Stacey 2010; Stacey 1998) (see Chapter 11).

The conservative-liberal culture war is debated endlessly in the popular media. The media themselves tend to be increasingly divided along conservative-liberal lines. The leading media pundits are often at war with one another. In 2010, the battle spilled over into the streets of Washington, DC. Glenn Beck, at the time with Fox News, organized a conservative "Rally to Restore Honor," and a short time later Jon Stewart, liberal host of the satirical *Daily Show* on Comedy Central, reacted by organizing a "Rally to Restore Sanity." Beck's rally sought a return to America's traditional values, while the Stewart rally was aimed at moving away from extremist views.

MULTICULTURALISM AND ASSIMILATION

A great deal of attention has been paid in recent years to another aspect of cultural diversity—**multiculturalism**, or an environment in which cultural differences are accepted and appreciated both by the state and by the majority group (Kivisto 2012c; Modood 2007). These cultural groups can be based on race, ethnicity, nationality, or language. They can also be based on age and other dimensions of difference. People in the United States, for example, generally accept that young and old have their own cultural preferences. Americans generally tolerate—sometimes even celebrate—their coexistence within the larger culture.

When it comes to ethnicity or national origin, however, multiculturalism has not always been celebrated in this country. The dominant culture has been primarily interested in **assimilation**, or integrating the minority group into the mainstream. As a so-called nation of immigrants, the population of the United States has always had to resolve issues of cultural diversity. Until late in the

multiculturalism The encouragement of cultural differences within a given environment, both by the state and by the majority group.

assimilation The integration of minorities into the dominant culture.

FIGURE 3.3 • Legal Migration to the United States by Region of Origin, 1820–2009

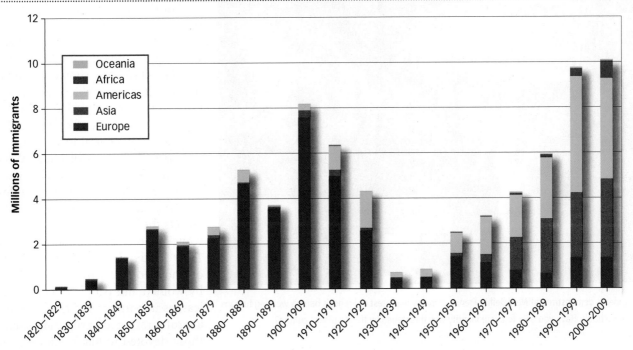

SOURCE: Data from Table 2, Persons Obtaining Legal Permanent Resident Status by Region and Selected Country of Last Residence: Fiscal Years 1820 to 2012. *Yearbook of Immigration Statistics: 2012 Legal Permanent Residents.* U.S. Department of Homeland Security.

twentieth century, most immigrants to the United States were from Europe, especially Eastern and Southern Europe (see Figure 3.3). Many of these groups did assimilate to a large degree, even if their assimilation occurred over a couple of generations. Today we do not think twice about whether or not Polish Americans or Italian Americans, for instance, are "regular" Americans.

But immigrants from the next large wave, in the 1990s and 2000s, have not assimilated so well. If you refer again to Figure 3.3, you can see that the flow of immigrants is now mostly from the Americas, with another large group from Asia. These immigrants, especially those from Mexico and China, often live in largely separate enclaves, speak their native languages, and retain their basic cultures, such as their tastes in food. It remains to be seen whether, and to what degree, they will be assimilated into mainstream culture or their culture will be accepted as a valued element of American culture.

ASK YOURSELF

If you were born in the United States, imagine yourself as an immigrant to another country, one to which you have no cultural or genealogical ties and where you know no one. What would you do on your arrival in order to survive? Would you seek out other Americans? Why or why not? Would you try to assimilate? How?

The question of multiculturalism is relatively recent for many European societies, particularly the Scandinavian countries and the Netherlands. They have traditionally been almost monocultures and even now, during a period of widespread global migration, have a smaller proportion of foreign-born residents than the United States. However, beginning in the 1950s, many European countries began to experience a labor shortage (Fassman and Munz 1992; Fielding 1989). Large numbers of people from poorer Southern European countries such as Spain and Italy migrated to Northern European countries. Later, migration flowed from less developed countries outside of Europe, such as Turkestan, other largely Islamic countries, and many African countries. The fall of the Soviet Union in 1991 brought additional Eastern Europeans from places like Albania. Many northern European governments had intended for these immigrant workers to stay only a short time. However, many of the immigrants built lives for themselves, brought their families, and chose to remain. The result is that European countries today are far more multicultural than they were several decades ago.

More recent immigrants to Europe bring with them very different cultures and a very different religion (Islam, for example) than that of the largely Christian Europe. They have also been comparatively poor. A relatively small, monocultural country like the Netherlands has had

Sikh students demonstrate at New Delhi's French embassy in protest of France's ban on wearing turbans in French schools. Have you ever felt your identity was threatened by the dominant culture?

Identity politics has played itself out not only on streets in public protests and demonstrations, but also in schools and especially in universities. In the latter, the central issue has been whether all students should be required to learn the "canon"—a common set of texts, sometimes referred to as the "great books"—and a body of knowledge long regarded as of central importance. For example, the works of Marx, Weber, and Durkheim are often thought to be the canonical texts in sociology. Minority cultures claim that the canon reflects the interests and experiences of white middle- and upper-class males. They argue that alternative bodies of knowledge, such as those created by women and people of color, are at least as important. The result has been a proliferation of programs such as those devoted to black, Chicano, and feminist studies, where the focus is on those alternative texts and bodies of knowledge. However, such programs have been the subject of much controversy and political scrutiny. For example, the Arizona secretary of education targeted racial and ethnic studies programs in a bill passed in 2010, contending that they encourage students to think of themselves as oppressed, a ruling that has been upheld by a lower court (Lacey 2011). The legal challenges to the ruling by supporters of such programs have not yet been exhausted.

trouble digesting its roughly 1 million Muslim immigrants. France has experienced riots in the suburbs of Paris that are heavily populated by poor immigrants from North Africa. In 2009, the Swiss voted to ban the building of new minarets associated with Islamic mosques. In a 2011 protest against Muslim immigration to his country, a Norwegian right-wing extremist bombed government buildings in Oslo, killing eight people. He later killed another 69 people during a shooting spree at a summer camp related to the country's ruling party. In short, European countries today have more cultural diversity than ever. However, the situation is fraught with tension, conflict, and danger as people from very different cultures, religions, and languages struggle to find a way to live side by side (J. Alexander 2013; Caldwell 2009).

Identity Politics

The goal of multiculturalism and coexistence among people of different cultures still exists. However, in recent years some minority groups have become impatient with the dominant culture's unwillingness to accept them. Instead, they have asserted their right to retain their distinctive culture and their right not to assimilate, at least totally. These groups have engaged in **identity politics** in using their power to strengthen the position of the cultural group with which they identify (Nicholson 2008; Wasson 2007). Identity politics has a long history, more recently including the black power, feminist, and gay pride movements in many parts of the world. The goal of such movements has been the creation of a true multicultural society, one that accepts minorities for who they are.

Cultural Relativism and Ethnocentrism

Multiculturalism and identity politics are closely related to **cultural relativism**. The idea is that aspects of culture such as norms and values need to be understood within the context of a person's own culture and that there are no cultural universals, or universally accepted norms and values. In this view, different cultures simply have different norms and values. There is no way to say that one set of norms and values is better than another (Weiler 2007). Thus, for example, those in western countries should not

> **identity politics** The use of a minority group's power to strengthen the position of the cultural group with which it identifies.
>
> **cultural relativism** The idea that aspects of culture such as norms and values need to be understood within the context of a person's own culture and that there are no universally accepted norms and values.

judge Islamic women's use of head scarves. Conversely, those in the Islamic world should not judge western women's baring of their midriffs.

Cultural relativism runs counter to the tendency in many cultures toward **ethnocentrism**, or the belief that the norms, values, traditions, and material and symbolic aspects of one's own culture are better than those of other cultures (S. Brown 2007b; Machida 2012). The tendency toward ethnocentrism both among subcultures within the United States and in cultures throughout the world represents a huge barrier to greater cultural understanding. However, to be fair, a belief in one's own culture can be of great value to a culture. It gives the people of that culture a sense of pride and identity. Problems arise when ethnocentrism serves as a barrier to understanding other cultures, a source of conflict among cultures, or an excuse for one culture to deny rights or privileges to another.

EMERGING ISSUES IN CULTURE

Culture is continually in the process of change, just as it is continually being transmitted from one generation to the next. Some of the ways in which today's culture is changing are worthy of further exploration in this book. In this section, we will focus on global culture, consumer culture, and cyberculture.

GLOBAL CULTURE

There are certainly major differences within American culture such as those that exist among subcultures. Yet, few would dispute the idea that it is possible to talk about American culture in general. However, discussing anything like a global culture, a culture common to the world as a whole, is not as easy. Some elements of material culture,

> **ethnocentrism** The belief that one's own group or culture—including its norms, values, customs, and so on—is superior to, or better than, others.
>
> **cultural imperialism** The imposition of one culture, more or less consciously, on other cultures.

CHECKPOINT 3.3	SOME COMPARISONS THAT DEFINE CULTURAL DIFFERENCES
Ideal culture—what our norms and values lead us to think we should believe and do.	**Real culture**—what we actually think and do.
Subculture—groups that accept much of the dominant culture but are set apart by one or more significant characteristics.	**Counterculture**—groups that not only differ from the dominant culture but hold norms and values that may be incompatible with it.
Multiculturalism—an environment in which cultural differences are accepted and appreciated by the majority group.	**Assimilation**—the integration of a cultural minority group into the mainstream.
Cultural relativism—the belief that different cultures have different norms and values, and that none are universally accepted or better than any others.	**Ethnocentrism**—the belief that the norms, values, traditions, and symbols of our own culture are better than those of others.

including hamburgers, sushi, cars, and communication technology, have spread widely around the world. However, the globalization of values, norms, and symbolic culture is not always appreciated and often cannot be easily pinpointed.

Cultural Imperialism

Many have the strong view that what affects global culture most of all is **cultural imperialism**, or the imposition of one dominant culture on other cultures (Tomlinson 1999, 2012). Cultural imperialism tends to destroy local cultures. Let us look briefly at two examples of cultural imperialism in contemporary India:

- Saris are a key element of Indian material culture. Indian saris have traditionally been made of silk and woven by hand in a process that can take as much as two months for each sari. Elaborate designs are interspersed with strands of gold thread and green silk. However, India's roughly 1 million sari makers are now threatened by machine-made saris, especially from China (Wax 2007). A culture that emphasizes inexpensive, machine-made products is imposing itself on a realm in another culture that has emphasized local products, practices, and indigenous skilled workers. In the process, the local sari-making culture is being

Consumer Culture

Cultural Imperialism

Children's Consumption of Fashion

Globalization is a profound threat to the professional letter-writer of India, as well as to many other cultural traditions.

slowly consumed cups of coffee. In contrast, in France and Italy and other countries, the historic preference has been for quickly consumed tiny cups of espresso. Starbucks stores are now located in more than 50 countries (see Figure 3.4).

Cultural imperialism certainly exists, but it would be wrong to overestimate its power. Local cultures can be quite resilient. Not all cultures suffer the fate of French movie producers and Indian sari makers and letter writers. For example:

- The powerful process of Americanization is often countered by **anti-Americanism**, which is an aversion to America in general, as well as to the influence of its culture abroad (Huntington 1996; O'Connor and Griffiths 2005).

destroyed, and the sari itself, a distinctive Indian product, is losing its unique character.

- There is also a long tradition in India of professional letter writers, or men who place themselves in prominent locations (for example, near train stations) and write letters for poor, illiterate migrants. Many of these letter writers are able to survive on the pittance they are paid for each letter. However, the spread from the West of the cell phone, and of text messaging, is rendering the professional letter writers, and the cultural traditions associated with them, obsolete.

There is certainly a great deal of cultural imperialism in the world today, with much of it associated with the United States (L. Crothers 2010; Kuisel 1993). The process of **Americanization** involves the importation by other countries of a variety of cultural elements—products, images, technologies, practices, norms, values, and behaviors—that are closely associated with the United States. One example is the American movie industry. Its popularity around the world has decimated the movie industries of many countries, including Great Britain and France. (India is one exception with its thriving Bollywood productions such as the 2009 Academy Award winner for best picture, *Slumdog Millionaire*; Rizvi 2012). Another successful American cultural export is its taste for food, especially fast food and the way in which it is eaten (quickly, with one's hands, standing up or in the car). McDonald's is a prime example, but another of note is Starbucks (B. Simon 2009), which has been surprisingly successful in exporting its model of large,

- Many cultures—Chinese and Islamic cultures, for example—have long, even ancient, histories. Those cultures have resisted at least some impositions from other cultures for centuries. They are likely to continue to resist changes that threaten their basic values and beliefs.

- Local cultures modify inputs and impositions from other cultures by integrating them with local realities and in the process pr oduce **cultural hybrids** that combine elements of both (Nederveen Pieterse 2009). Examples of hybridization include the British watching Asian rap performed by a South American in a London club owned by a Saudi Arabian; another example is the Dutch watching Moroccan women engage in Thai boxing. In the fast-food realm, McDonald's sells such hybrid foods as McChicken Korma Naan, which caters to those in Great Britain who have developed a taste

Americanization The importation by other countries of products, images, technologies, practices, norms, values, and behaviors that are closely associated with the United States.

anti-Americanism An aversion to America in general, as well as to the influence of its culture abroad.

cultural hybrids Cultural phenomena combining inputs and impositions from other cultures with local realities.

for Indian food (including the many Indians who live there); McLaks, a grilled salmon sandwich in Norway; and McHuevos, hamburgers with poached egg in Uruguay.

Thus cultural imperialism needs to be examined in the context of the counterreactions to it, the counterflows from elsewhere in the world, and the combination of the global and local to produce unique cultural elements.

CONSUMER CULTURE

American culture is a **consumer culture**, one in which the core ideas and material objects relate to consumption and in which consumption is a primary source of meaning in life (Belk 2007; Sassatelli 2007; Slater 1997). Meaning may be found in the goods and services that you buy, in the process of buying them (in shopping malls, cybermalls, etc.), in the social aspects of consumption (shopping with your friends or family), and even in the settings in which consumption takes place (the Venetian or some other Las Vegas casino hotel, eBay, etc.) (Ritzer, Goodman, and Wiedenhoft 2001). There are norms about the consumption process as well. For example, customers should wait patiently in the queue at the cashier, gamblers at a Las Vegas casino should not flaunt their winnings in front of other gamblers and should tip dealers, and so on.

Consumer culture is rather unique in the history of the world. In the past, culture has generally focused on some other aspect of social life such as religion, warfare, citizenship, or work. In fact, in the not-too-distant past in the United States and other developed countries, the core ideas and material objects of culture related to work and production. People were thought to derive their greatest meaning from their work. This was true from the Industrial Revolution until approximately 1970, when observers began to realize that developed societies, especially the United States, were beginning to derive more meaning from consumption (Baudrillard [1970] 1998). Of course, work continues to be important, as do religion, warfare, and

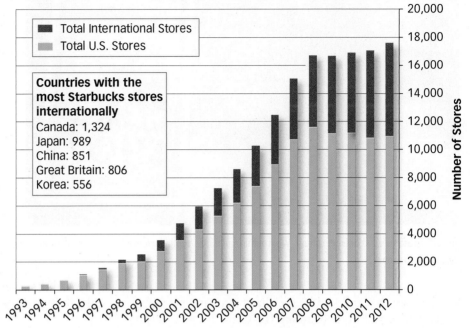

FIGURE 3.4 • Starbucks' Global Expansion: 1993–2012

Total International Stores
Total U.S. Stores

Countries with the most Starbucks stores internationally
Canada: 1,324
Japan: 989
China: 851
Great Britain: 806
Korea: 556

SOURCE: Starbucks' Global Reach, 2013. Data from "Starbucks Company Statistics: Statistic Brain." 2012 Statistic Brain Research Institute, publishing as Statistic Brain.

citizenship, but many people, especially in the developed world, now live in a culture dominated by consumption.

The roots of today's consumer culture can be traced further back in history, to when popular settings of consumption, such as large expositions, world's fairs, and department stores, began to arise (R. Williams [1982] 1991). France in the mid nineteenth century was particularly important to this development. It was the home of the trend-setting Le Bon Marché department store and several world's fairs, including the first truly international exposition. In these settings, consumption became democratized. It was no longer restricted to the aristocracy and to men. It became popular with the middle class and, as their ability to afford consumption improved, with the working class as well.

It could be said that the rise of consumer culture was linked to the rise of the modern world in the West (Campbell 1987). Today, of course, consumer culture has arguably become *the* culture of the modern West and indeed of modernity in general. But consumer culture has also globalized to a great degree. It has become firmly entrenched in such nonwestern locales as Singapore, Hong Kong, and Dubai. Japan has been called the premier consumer culture. Even in today's China, known for its production-oriented culture, hundreds of millions of its citizens are becoming more and more consumption oriented.

Children in a Consumer Culture

The most controversial aspect of consumer culture may be the involvement of children. In a consumer culture, it

> **consumer culture** A culture in which the core ideas and material objects relate to consumption and in which consumption is a primary source of meaning in life.

The United States is a consumer culture. What subtle and not-so-subtle factors influence our cultural inclination to shop?

researchers observe the way children use and respond to products and advertising messages not just in focus groups and in the lab, but also in natural settings such as school and the home. Additionally, marketers have discovered the importance of the "pester power" of children. This is the ability of children to nag their parents into buying something. It is effective not only for selling children's products but also for getting children to influence their parents' purchases. Overall, children are much more immersed in consumer culture today than ever before. They learn at an early age to value it as well as the norms involved in participating in it. As adults, then, they are very likely to fit well into a culture with consumption at its core.

is important that children be socialized into, and become actively involved in, consuming (D. Cook 2004, 2007). Consumption by children has not always been valued, however. In fact, there were once strong norms against it. Children were not considered able to make informed choices about consumption and were therefore seen as even more susceptible than adults to exploitation by advertisers and marketers.

An important change began to take place in the mid nineteenth century with the advent of department stores. Some stores offered supervised play areas so that parents could shop more easily. A key development by the mid twentieth century was children's sections in department stores; they were eventually subdivided into shops for babies, children, and teens. Also during this period, radio programs, movies, and TV shows were increasingly directed at children. Disney was a leader in this trend. TV shows of the 1950s like the Davy Crockett series (*King of the Wild Frontier*) prompted the sales of hundreds of millions of dollars' worth of simulated coonskin caps and other merchandise for children. More recently, children have come to be targeted directly by advertisers on Saturday morning TV shows and cable channels such as Nickelodeon that specialize in children's programming.

In fact, marketing aimed at children is now pervasive. For example, the Disney Company has begun directly marketing baby products, and thus the Disney brand, to new mothers in maternity wards. In schools, branded products are sold at book fairs, and corporate sponsorships adorn everything from sports stadiums to classroom supplies. Brands and logos are woven into textbook problems and examples. Market

Nontraditional Settings for Consumption

An interesting aspect of consumer culture is the way in which it has spread beyond the economy to other aspects of society. Higher education is increasingly characterized by consumer culture. Students and their parents shop around for the best colleges and the most conspicuous degrees or for the best values in a college education. College rankings, such as those published by *Kiplinger* and *U.S. News & World Report,* are big business. For-profit colleges have become a booming industry, with enterprises like the University of Phoenix and Kaplan University enrolling hundreds of thousands of students in the market for a degree on a more flexible schedule. Once enrolled in college, students shop for the best classes, or at least the best class times. Not long ago students were largely passive recipients of their education, but now they are more active consumers of it. For example, they regularly rate their professors and choose classes on the basis of the professors with the best ratings. They are also much more likely to make similar demands for up-to-date "products" and attentive service from their professors and colleges as they do on salespeople and shopping malls.

A key site of consumption is now the Internet (Miller and Slater 2000). A good portion of the time that people spend on the Internet is related to consumption, either directly (purchasing items on eBay.com, Amazon.com, or Zappos.com; Groupon's ads, its "deal of the day," and the purchase of its discount coupons; etc.) or more indirectly (buying things on Second Life with Linden Dollars or on FarmVille with real dollars). In 2000, only 22 percent

Japanese Consumer Culture

The Japanese have become avid, highly sophisticated, and well-informed mass consumers (Clammer 1997). Japanese consumers are defined by a high degree of rationality. Indeed, they may be more focused on convenience and efficiency than American consumers. Consider the central role of vending machines in Japan. Japan has the highest number of vending machines per capita in the world. They provide everything from snacks and beverages to eggs, ice, beer, umbrellas, flowers, neckties, sneakers, fresh vegetables, batteries, hot French fries, board games, pornographic magazines, and even smart cars (or, to be more precise, smart car brochures and stickers) ("14 Cool Vending Machines From Japan" 2009).

Another example of this rationality is the eagerness with which the Japanese have embraced American fast-food chains. Japan also has many fast-food chains of its own. The preference for a rationalized way of eating is clear in the popularity of the "beef bowl," Japan's contribution to fast food. A beef bowl is an all-in-one meal including beef, rice, noodles, and various other ingredients. There are three big chains of beef bowl restaurants in Japan—Sukiya, Yoshinoya, and Matsuya (Tabuchi 2010: B6).

Kura is a Japanese chain of 262 sushi restaurants. Most of the waiters in a Kura restaurant have been replaced by conveyor belts that carry sushi in its various forms to the diner (Tabuchi 2010). Similarly, sushi chefs have been largely replaced

While Japan may rival the United States in its enthusiasm for consumption, it probably surpasses it in the sophisticated variety of purchases consumers can make from vending machines.

by sushi-making robots. This is particularly striking because the traditional sushi chef was, and is, highly skilled and greatly valued.

Diners at a Kura restaurant order their own food using touch screens. They are also required to put their finished plates into a tableside bay so that the bill can be calculated automatically. Not only do the consumers at Kura "work" to produce their own meals, but unlike many of those employed in fast-food restaurants throughout the world, they seem to like the work.

Think About It

What aspect of consumer culture accounts for Japan's apparent acceptance of sushi-making robots to replace chefs whose skills are highly valued? Can you think of any similar changes taking place in U.S. consumer culture, whether in the restaurant business or elsewhere? What about income tax software, for example, or virtual dressing rooms on clothing websites?

of Americans had used the Internet to buy a product online, including books, music, toys, and clothing. By 2010, that number had increased to 52 percent (Jansen 2010). The growing importance of consumption on the Internet is reflected in the increasing amount spent on such consumption on "Cyber Monday" (the Monday after Thanksgiving). In addition, advertisements are often woven seamlessly into the content of Internet sites—even into games designed for children. Beyond that, many websites carry pop-up ads for goods or services targeted to the interests of the individuals who are viewing the site. For example, free porn sites are rife with ads for fee-based porn or other sexual services.

ASK YOURSELF

How much of the time you spend online is devoted to shopping or purchasing? Try keeping a log of your Internet use for a few days. Note how many times you went online and on how many of those occasions you bought something. Are you a typical Internet consumer? Why or why not?

It could be argued that people, especially children and teens, are becoming more immersed in consumer culture as they become more deeply enmeshed with the Internet. As a result, consumer culture is becoming an even more inescapable part of their daily lives. Furthermore, consumption on the Internet is increasingly wedded to the material world. For example, goods ordered on Amazon .com are delivered to our doors by FedEx. That level of integration is being ratcheted up even further. You can now pay for parking and rental cars using apps on smartphones. There is even an iPhone app that allows a renter to open the doors of her Zipcar, which can be rented by the hour or the day, and honk its horn.

Culture Jamming and Burning Man

Consumer culture has been threatened by organized groups actively seeking to subvert aspects of both consumer culture and the larger culture. For example, **culture jamming** involves radically transforming mass media messages, if not turning them on their heads completely (Lasn 2000). It is a form of social protest aimed at revealing underlying realities of which consumers may be unaware. The hope is that once people are made aware of these realities by culture jamming, they will change their behaviors or perhaps even band together to change those underlying realities.

The best examples of culture jamming are to be found in the magazine *Adbusters* and in media campaigns it sponsors. *Adbusters'* main targets are in the realm of consumption, especially web and magazine advertisements and billboards. The idea is to transform a corporation's ads into anticorporate, anticonsumption advertisements (Handelman and Kozinets 2007).

The following are some examples of the ways in which culture jamming turns commercial messages inside out:

- "Joe Chemo"—rather than Joe Camel—shows an emaciated version of the Camel character (who, of course, smokes Camel cigarettes) in a hospital bed undergoing chemotherapy, presumably for lung cancer caused by smoking.

- "Tommy Sheep" is a spoof of a Tommy Hilfiger ad, with sheep (presumably representing the conformists who buy such clothing) pictured in front of a huge American flag.

- "Absolute on Ice," spoofing an Absolut vodka ad, depicts the foot of a corpse (presumably killed by excessive alcohol consumption) with a toe tag.

- "True Colors of Benetton" depicts a man wearing a Benetton shirt but with wads of money stuffed in his mouth. The ad is designed to underscore the true objective of Benetton—and of all corporations in capitalist society: money and profits.

All of the above show the hidden realities (sickness, death, and other miseries) and goals (conformist consumers, obscene profits) of corporations. A broader objective is to show viewers the folly of consumer culture, which encourages the consumption of numerous harmful (cigarettes, alcohol) and wasteful (expensive clothing) goods and services.

Another effort to subvert culture is to be found in the annual weeklong event known as Burning Man held in Nevada's Black Rock Desert. Begun in 1986, it now attracts about 50,000 participants a year. It is devoted to free self-expression, community building, and the de-commodification of human relationships. As a result, cash transactions among participants are banned. More generally, it is opposed to market-based transactions (Kozinets 2002a). As opposed to the order associated with the market, Burning Man is characterized by "creative chaos" (Chen 2009). This is reflected, among other places, in the activity that gives the festival its name— the burning of an enormous effigy at the festival's close.

> **culture jamming** The radical transformation of an intended message in popular culture, especially one associated with the mass media, to protest underlying realities of which consumers may be unaware.

Steven Jones (2011) sees Burning Man as so important that it is shaping a new American counterculture.

CYBERCULTURE

The Internet is, as mentioned before, one site for the proliferation of consumer culture. It is also the site of an entirely new culture—**cyberculture** (F. Turner 2008). That is, the Internet as a whole (as well as the individual websites that it comprises) has the characteristics of all culture, including distinctive values and norms.

Some of the distinctive values within cyberculture are openness, knowledge sharing, and access. These values have their roots in the open-source software that emerged before computing became an attractive commercial opportunity. They are also rooted in the knowledge sharing and continuous improvement that were the practice when early computer professionals survived through reciprocity (Bergquist 2003). These roots have been maintained through the open-source movement, through actions against censorship, and through organizations such as the Free Software Foundation and the "copyleft" movement. These "cyber-libertarians" favor user control of information and applications and free products (Dahlberg 2010; Himanen 2001). They are in conflict with the more dominant values of profit maximization and control of the Internet by large corporations. This conflict of values, a culture war by the definition offered earlier in this chapter, goes a long way toward defining the Internet today.

Various norms have also come to be a part of cyberculture. Internet users are not supposed to hack into websites, create and disseminate spam, unleash destructive worms and viruses, maliciously and erroneously edit user-generated sites such as Wikipedia, and so on. Many norms relate to desirable behavior on the Internet. For example, creating and editing entries on Wikipedia is supposed to be taken seriously and done to the best of one's ability. Once an entry exists,

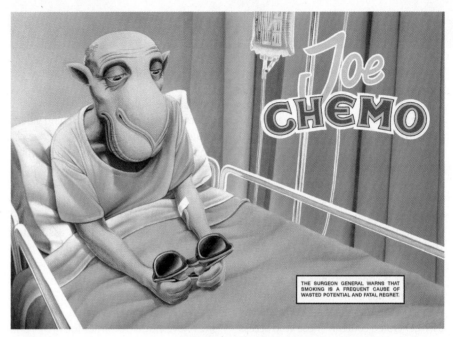

"Joe Chemo" is an example of culture jamming intended to overturn the tobacco industry's glamorous portrayal of cigarette smoking. Is this an effective way to change a cultural norm?

the many people who offer additions and deletions are expected to do so in a similar spirit. Those who purposely add erroneous information on Wikipedia will suffer the stern disapproval of other contributors to, and users of, the site. They may even be banned from Wikipedia by those who are involved in its management.

There is, of course, much more to the culture of the Internet. But the point is that cyberculture, like all cultures, is emerging and evolving as other changes take place within and around it. The biggest difference from other cultures is that, because the Internet is so new and the changes in it are so rapid, cyberculture is far more fluid than culture in general.

---

cyberculture An emerging online culture that has the characteristics of all culture, including distinctive values and norms.

prosumers A consumer who produces value in the process of consumption; one who combines the acts of consumption and production.

CHECKPOINT 3.4   **EMERGING ISSUES IN CULTURE**

Global culture	Globalization of values, cultural imperialism, Americanization, anti-Americanism.
Consumer culture	Social aspects of consumption, marketing to children, online shopping, culture jamming.

Hyper-McDonaldized Sushi

Culture Jamming

Citizen's Support for Global Capitalism

DIGITAL LIVING

Commercialization and Web 2.0

In its early years, the Internet was dominated by what has been called Web 1.0 (Ritzer and Jurgenson 2010). The early Yahoo! and AOL sites were, and still to a large extent are, two examples of Web 1.0. Basically, those who owned and controlled these sites decided on what was to be provided to those who accessed their sites. There was little or no choice. Few, if any, options were available to the user.

Web 1.0 sites continue to exist, but the Internet has come to be dominated by Web 2.0 sites. These sites are dominated by user-generated content. Those who access Web 2.0 sites are not simply consumers (as they were of Web 1.0 sites), but they are **prosumers** (Ritzer, Dean, and Jurgenson 2012) of those sites, both producing and consuming the content. While the concept of the prosumer is relatively new, it is an old idea that overlaps to a large extent with the more familiar idea of the "do-it-yourselfer" (Watson and Shove 2008). The prosumer is prominent on all of the major sites (Facebook, Myspace, Wikipedia, Second Life, Flickr, eBay, Amazon), as well as blogs and many other aspects of the Internet. Instead of simply and passively reading news stories written by others on Yahoo! or the *New York Times* website, more of us will be both creating blogs and reading, as well as commenting on, blogs written by others. Instead of merely watching videos created for the major TV networks, we will produce *and* watch the videos on YouTube. Rather than gazing at pictures produced by professional photographers, we will download our own photos on Flickr while examining those downloaded by others.

While some corporations associated with Web 2.0 (eBay, Amazon) have been hugely profitable, largely because the products they offer are not free, others have yet to generate a profit. However, many investors believe that many free sites have huge potential for profit and will be the new media giants in the coming years.

Take Facebook, for example. At the time of this writing, over 1.1 billion people in the world are on Facebook, a number that continues to grow (Cosenza 2011). It clearly costs a great deal of money to provide all of those users with the computer capacity needed to meet all of their needs (for example, to write on people's walls, to play Scrabble online), and the users pay nothing for those services. However, Facebook is already making a lot of money, and it will earn much, much more in the future.

One way in which Facebook earns money was introduced in late 2012. It is called "Gifts," where those on the network can buy presents such as babyGap pajamas and iTunes gift cards for their friends. A gift-box icon pops up when, for example, a friend's birthday or wedding anniversary is approaching. A menu of numerous gifts is then made available. Facebook receives an unknown percentage of every sale. While its cut is not public knowledge, Amazon.com gets about 15 percent for similar transactions. In addition to money earned through sales, Facebook stands to gain personal information that it uses to create still more targeted and paid advertisements (Sengupta 2012).

Think About It

While users do not pay directly for accessing Facebook, their presence allows the website to sell on-site advertising directed at them, much as U.S. television networks do. So the "price" of using this website, and many others, is the intrusion of advertising. How would the cultural experience of using the Internet be different if users paid for it directly, as we do for parking at the airport, for instance? What if the Internet were paid for by voluntary contributions, as public television and radio stations are? What if the government maintained the Internet, as it does the roads and highways?

SUMMARY

Culture encompasses the ideas, values, norms, practices, and objects that allow a group of people, or even an entire society, to carry out their collective lives with a minimum of friction. Values are the general, abstract standards defining what a group or society as a whole considers good, desirable, right, or important. Norms are the rules that guide what people do and how they live. Culture also has material and symbolic elements. Material culture encompasses all the objects and technologies that are reflections or manifestations of a culture. Symbolic culture, the nonmaterial side of culture, is best represented by language.

We are immersed in a diversity of cultures. Subcultures include people who may accept much of the dominant culture but are set apart from it by one or more culturally significant characteristics.

Countercultures are groups of people who differ in certain ways from the dominant culture and whose norms and values may be incompatible with it. Culture wars pit one subculture or counterculture against another or against the dominant culture.

Many cultures tend to be ethnocentric, in that they believe that their own norms, values, traditions, and the like are better than those of other cultures. Many times newcomers are expected to assimilate, or to replace elements of their own culture with elements of the dominant culture. A society that values multiculturalism accepts, and even embraces, the cultures of many different groups and encourages the retention of cultural differences.

Some scholars argue that globalization has increasingly led to a global culture; others attribute the growing cultural similarity around the world to cultural imperialism. In consumer culture, the core ideas and material objects relate to consumption. An increasingly important cyberculture thrives on the Internet.

KEY TERMS

Americanization,   86
Anti-Americanism,   86
Assimilation,   82
Consumer culture,   87
Counterculture,   80
Cultural hybrid,   86
Cultural imperialism,   85
Cultural relativism,   84
Culture,   71
Culture jamming,   90

Culture war,   81
Cyberculture,   91
Ethnocentrism,   85
Folkway,   75
Ideal culture,   78
Identity politics,   84
Language,   76
Law,   74
Material culture,   75
Mores,   75

Multiculturalism,   82
Norm,   74
Prosumer,   91
Real culture,   78
Sanction,   74
Subculture,   79
Symbolic culture,   75
Values   73

REVIEW QUESTIONS

1. How and why might the American value of democracy have created tensions in Iraq and Afghanistan?

2. As part of our material culture, what values do smartphones reflect? In what ways have "brand communities" or other subcultures formed around smartphones and the use of smartphones?

3. Consider the new terminology that has developed around the Internet. How does this language reflect changes in the world around us? In what ways does this new language shape the world around us?

4. Skateboarders compose a subculture because they have certain cultural differences (for example, language, dress, values) that set them apart from other groups in society. What is another example of a subculture in the United States, and what elements of this culture (both material and symbolic) make it unique?

5. How does a counterculture differ from a subculture? Is it reasonable to say that computer hackers are part of a counterculture? Can you think of other examples of countercultures?

6. What is the difference between assimilation and multiculturalism? Would you say that the United States is an assimilationist or a multiculturalist society? Would you say that multiculturalism is more a part of the ideal culture or the real culture of the United States? Why?

7. What do we mean by a global culture? Do you think the evolution of popular social networking sites such as Facebook and Twitter is related more to the evolution of a global culture or more to Americanization? In what ways are these sites reflective of cultural hybridization?

8. To what extent are you and your friends embedded in a consumer culture? How has the development of technology (the Internet, smartphones, etc.) helped create this consumer culture?

9. Do you think that culture jamming and Burning Man are significant threats to consumer culture?

10. Do you see yourself as a cyber-libertarian as far as the Internet is concerned?

APPLYING THE SOCIOLOGICAL IMAGINATION ....

Multinational chains (like McDonald's and Starbucks) are important cultural actors in an increasingly globalized world. These multinational corporations have made great efforts to promote an image and a culture around their brands. For this exercise, spend some time outside of class at an outlet of one of your favorite global chains. Pay close attention to the ways in which informal and formal norms are created in the space through decor, language, layout, and so on.

How does the physical space govern behavior within the location? How does the physical space relate to the kind of image the company is trying to create for its brand? In what ways are the norms that operate within the store reflective of the larger norms of society? Do any of the norms conflict with larger societal norms?

Do some research on the Internet to see the ways in which these stores operate differently in other countries. How do they compare and contrast? Given the similarities or differences across countries, would you say such global chains are signs of cultural imperialism or hybridization?

STUDENT STUDY SITE ....

Sharpen your skills with SAGE edge at **edge.sagepub.com/ritzeressentials**

SAGE edge for students provides a personalized approach to help you accomplish your coursework goals in an easy-to-use learning environment.

Fast Food International

Perhaps it is not surprising that the Western fast-food industry, which perfected the principles of efficiency, calculability, predictability, and control via McDonaldization, has been among the most successful global industries. Western-style fast food is now available literally anywhere in the world, despite the health dangers of many of its typical offerings.

▲ At the Robot Restaurant in Harbin, China, twenty robots cook and deliver customers' meals, displaying any of ten facial expressions and vocalizing simple welcoming statements. Though they need a two-hour charge for every five hours of work, the robots are probably more predictable than human employees and easier to control.

▲ Fast-food outlets are springing up around the world, often blending local and Western culture. This KFC store outside the Grand Mosque in Mecca, Saudi Arabia (left), serves men and women separately. An Andean woman (right) carries her child in traditional fashion for a fast-food meal at a new shopping mall in one of Peru's farming provinces.

▲ Chickens are roasted and served the traditional way, by hand, in a roadside eatery in Baghdad, Iraq, even during a sandstorm. Are any principles of McDonaldization apparent here?

"TASTE WORTH DYING FOR!"®

◄ Giant grease- and fat-laden burgers loaded with thousands of calories unapologetically dominate the menu at the controversial hospital-themed Heart Attack Grill, which opened in Chandler, Arizona (shown here), but now operates in Las Vegas.

THINKING ABOUT SOCIOLOGY

1. Would you be a regular customer at any of the food outlets shown here? Which one(s) and why?

2. Entrepreneurial food trucks now serve a variety of hot meals, often including ethnic specialties, to U.S. urban workers on their lunch breaks. What accounts for the success of these alternative forms of fast food?

3. **Essay question:** Describe some of the advantages and disadvantages of cooking simple, nutritious meals at home. Do the same for consuming fast food. Consider the economic, health, cultural, and social factors involved in both choices, and compare.

Indian schoolchildren celebrate Independence Day in the northern city of Chandigarh. Much of our personal development occurs during childhood, by means of interactions with parents, teachers, and peers in the process of socialization. What group activities characterized your childhood? What did they teach you about your society?

SOCIALIZATION AND INTERACTION

4

LEARNING OBJECTIVES

1 Describe the development of the self in the context of symbolic interaction.

2 Discuss the concept of the individual as performer, including the ideas of impression management and the front and back stages.

3 Explain the significance of socialization in childhood and adulthood.

4 Describe the key aspects of interaction with others as they relate to the socialization process.

5 Identify micro-level social structures including social networks and groups.

On February 11, 2013, during a daylong battle against 300 insurgents in the war in Afghanistan, U.S. Army Staff Sergeant Clinton Romesha "took out an enemy machine gun team . . . undeterred by his injuries." Romesha also recovered the bodies of the fallen and helped the wounded reach safety. He was awarded the Medal of Honor, the country's highest military decoration, for "extraordinary heroism above and beyond the call of duty."

Why would someone risk his or her life to save the lives of others? It is tempting to label Romesha a born hero—an individual destined for greatness. A sociologist, however, would focus instead on the way Romesha was socialized to behave as he did— by family, teachers, friends, and later the Army.

Socialization and social interaction help to shape who we are and how we act.

Although you may never face enemy gunfire, you too are who you are because of the people, institutions, and social structures that have surrounded you since birth (and even before). From the color of the blanket you were first swaddled in to the outfit you picked out today, you have been socialized to look, think, act, and interact in ways that allow you to live harmoniously with those around you. Perhaps that means playing intramural sports without embarrassing yourself . . . or perhaps it means becoming a hero.

Discovering how socialization and social interaction shape who we are and how we act, as we will do in this chapter, is the most basic level of sociological analysis. But, in fact, sociologists are concerned with everything along the micro-macro continuum, which was introduced in Chapter 1. That includes the individual's mind and self, interactions among individuals, interactions within and between groups, formally structured organizations, entire societies, and the world as a whole, as well as all the new global relationships of the "global age."

Sociology's micro-macro continuum means that rather than being clearly distinct, social phenomena tend to blend into one another, often without our noticing. For example, the interaction that takes place in a group is difficult to distinguish from the group itself. The relationships between countries are difficult to distinguish from their regional and even global connections. Everything in the social world, and on the micro-macro continuum, interpenetrates. ●

In this chapter, you'll learn how socialization and social interaction shape who we are, and, in turn, the ways in which who we are shapes how and with whom we interact. This is the most basic level of sociological analysis. But, in fact, sociologists are concerned with everything from the smallest social realities to the largest trends and developments in the social world, what is, as we saw in Chapter 1, the **micro-macro continuum** (Ritzer 1981; Ritzer and Stepinsky 2014; J. Turner 2010). This chapter and the next will introduce you, at least briefly, to the full range of sociological concerns along the micro-macro continuum. We will start with the smallest-scale social phenomena and work our way to ever-larger ones as these two chapters progress.

THE INDIVIDUAL AND THE SELF

A prime issue in sociology is what, if anything, distinguishes humans as individuals from other animals. Some would argue that it is characteristics such as a larger brain or an opposable thumb. However, most sociologists believe that the essential difference between humans and other animals is the distinctive interaction that humans are capable of having with other humans.

An important source of this view is data about individuals who grow up in social isolation and who do not experience normal human interaction during their development. For instance, we have information on cases in which children have been locked in a closet or in a single room for much, or all, of their childhood (Curtiss 1977; Davis 1940, 1947).

Of related interest is the existence of *feral,* or wild, *children*—that is, children who have been raised in the wilderness by animals (Newton 2002). A relatively recent example of a feral child is Oxana Malaya from a small village in the Ukraine (Grice, 2006; videos on her can be found on YouTube). In 1986, at age three, she crawled into a hovel housing dogs. The "Dog Girl" lived there for five years before a neighbor reported her existence. When she emerged, she could hardly speak. Like the dogs she lived with, she barked and ran about on all fours. Years later living in a home for the mentally disabled, Oxana was found to have the mental capacity of a six-year-old. Among other things, she could not spell her name or read. She was only able to communicate like other humans and talk because she had acquired some speech before she began living with dogs. She has learned to eat with her hands and to walk upright (Grice 2006; Lane 1975; Shattuck 1980).

Oxana has done better than other feral children (Lane 1975; Shattuck 1980). Feral children are generally unable to talk and to show much in the way of human emotion. Oxana, in contrast, has had boyfriends, although it is doubtful that she has the emotional ability to develop long-term relationships. The overall conclusion from the literature of feral children and those raised in isolation is that people do not become human, or at least fully human, unless they are able to interact with other people, especially at an early age.

The concept of "feral" children relates to the fundamental question of the relationship between "nature" and "nurture." The nature argument is that we are born to be the kinds of human beings that we ultimately become; it is built into our "human nature" (Settle et al. 2010). The nurture argument is that we are human beings because of the way we are raised by other human beings who teach us what it is to be human. Of course, *both* nature and nurture are important. However, the cases of feral children indicate that nurture is in many ways more important than nature in determining the human beings we become.

SYMBOLIC INTERACTION AND DEVELOPMENT OF THE SELF

As the example of feral and isolated children suggests, human development presupposes the existence of other humans and interaction with and among them. This brings us into the domain of symbolic interactionism (see Chapter 2), which developed many ideas of great relevance to this view of humans. In general, the interaction that takes place between parents and children is loaded with symbols and symbolic meaning.

One early symbolic interactionist, Charles Horton Cooley (1864–1929), explained how parents help children develop the ability to interact with others in his famous concept of the **looking-glass self**. This is the idea that as humans we develop a self-image that reflects how others respond to us. Since children's earliest interactions are typically with their parents, it is that interaction which is most important in the formation of a self-image. This helps explain why feral children and others who spent their formative years in prolonged social isolation are unlikely to form a fully developed self-image: There are no others to

> **micro-macro continuum** The range of social entities from the individual, even the mind and self, to the interaction among individuals, the groups often formed by that interaction, formally structured organizations, societies, and increasingly the global domain.
>
> **looking-glass self** The self-image that reflects how others respond to a person, particularly as a child.

Feral Children

The interactions we have with others when we are young are especially influential in our development of a sense of self, but the development process is never really over. Which group is benefiting more from their interactions at this Japanese daycare center, the children or the elderly?

respond to them. It is as we interact with others, especially when we are young, that we develop a sense of our selves.

The major thinker associated with symbolic interactionism is George Herbert Mead. We need to look into his thinking in order to deal with the issue of human development. While Mead ([1934] 1962: 7) was very concerned with the micro level (the individual, mind, self), he prioritized the social (including interaction). In fact, it is this prioritization of the social that distinguishes sociologists from psychologists in their studies of individuals and interaction. We will examine some of Mead's more general ideas before turning to his thinking on development, especially of the self.

Humans and Nonhumans

Mead distinguished between humans and nonhumans. However, both are capable of making gestures (such as by raising a limb). By **gestures**, Mead means the movements of one individual that elicit an automatic and appropriate response from another individual.

Both animals and humans are capable of not only gestures but also *conversations of gestures* whereby they use a series of gestures to relate to one another. Thus, the snarl of one dog may lead a second dog to snarl in return. That second snarl might lead the first dog to become physically ready to attack or be attacked. In terms of humans, Mead gives the example of a boxing match where the cocking of one boxer's arm might cause the other boxer to raise an arm to block the anticipated blow. That raised arm might cause the first boxer to throw a different punch or even to hold back on the punch. All of this occurs, as in the case of animals, instantaneously and with few, if any, conscious thought processes.

In addition to physical gestures, animals and humans are both capable of vocal gestures. The bark of a dog and the grunt of a human (boxer) are both vocal gestures. In both cases, a conversation of vocal gestures is possible as the bark of one dog (or the grunt of a boxer) elicits the bark (or grunt) of another. However, when humans (and animals) make a facial gesture, they cannot *see* that gesture (unless they happen to be looking in a mirror). In contrast, both animals and humans can *hear* their own vocal gestures.

It is the vocal gesture that truly begins to separate humans from animals. In humans, but not lower animals, the vocal gesture can affect the speaker as much and in the same way as the hearer. Thus, humans react to and interpret their own vocal gestures and, more importantly, their words. Furthermore, humans have a far greater ability to control their vocal gestures. We can stop ourselves from uttering sounds or saying various things, and we can alter what we say as we are saying it. Animals do not possess this capacity. In short, only humans are able to develop a language out of vocal gestures; animals remain restricted to isolated vocal gestures.

Symbolic Interaction

Of greatest importance in distinguishing humans from animals is a kind of gesture that can *only* be made by humans. Mead calls such a gesture a **significant symbol**, a gesture that arouses in the individual the same kind of response as it is supposed to elicit from those to whom the gesture is addressed. It is only with significant symbols, especially those that are vocal, that we can have communication in the full sense of the term. In Mead's view, although more and more research on animals tends to contradict it (Gerhardt and Huber 2002; Ristau 1983;

> **gesture** A movement of one animal or human that elicits a mindless, automatic, and appropriate response from another animal or human.
>
> **significant symbol** A gesture that arouses in the individual the same kind of response, although it need not be identical, as it is supposed to elicit from those to whom the gesture is addressed.

Schmitt and Fischer 2009), ants, bees, and dogs are unable to communicate by means of such symbols.

Over time, humans develop a set of vocal significant symbols, or language. *Language* involves significant symbols that call out the same meaning in the person to whom an utterance is aimed as in the person making the utterance. The utterances have meaning to all parties involved. In a conversation of gestures, only the gestures are communicated. With language, both the (vocal) gestures and the meanings are communicated. One of the key functions of language is that it makes the mind and mental processes possible. To Mead, thinking (and the mind; see below) is nothing more than internalized conversations individual humans have with themselves. Thinking involves talking to oneself. It is little different from talking to other people.

ASK YOURSELF

What did George Herbert Mead mean by saying thinking is so much like talking to yourself that it is little different from talking to other people? Do you agree with him? Why or why not? Think of some examples and counterexamples.

Symbols also make possible **symbolic interaction**. This is interaction on the basis of significant symbols. It also allows for much more complex interaction patterns than would occur where interaction is based only on gestures. Because people can think about and interpret significant symbols, they can interact with large numbers of people and make complex plans for some future undertaking. They can interpret the symbolic meaning of what others say and do and understand, for example, that some of them are acting in accord with their own plans. Animals lack the ability to make and understand complex plans.

> **symbolic interaction** Interaction on the basis of not only gestures but also significant symbols.
>
> **mind** An internal conversation that arises in relation to, and is continuous with, interactions, especially conversations that one has with others in the social world.
>
> **self** The sense of oneself as an object.
>
> **play stage** Mead's first stage in the socialization process where children learn to take on the attitudes of specific others toward themselves.
>
> **game stage** Mead's second stage in the socialization process in which a child develops a self in the full sense of the term, because it is then that the child begins to take on the role of a group of people simultaneously rather than the roles of discrete individuals.

Mind and Self

Central to Mead's ideas about the development of human beings, and the differences between humans and nonhumans, are the concepts of mind and self. As pointed out above, the **mind** is an internal conversation that arises, is related to, and is continuous with interactions, especially conversations that one has with others in the social world. Thus, the social world and its relationships and interactions precede the mind and not vice versa. This perspective stands in contrast to the conventional view that prioritizes the brain and argues that we think first and then engage in social relationships. It also differs from the view that the mind and the brain are one and the same thing. The brain is a physiological organ that exists within us, but the mind is a social phenomenon. It is part of, and would not exist without, the social world. While the brain is an intracranial phenomenon, the mind is not.

The **self** is the ability to take oneself as an object. The self develops over time. Key to the development of self is the ability to imagine being in the place of others and looking at oneself as they do. In other words, people need to take the role of others in order to get a sense of their own selves. There are two key stages in Mead's theory of how the self develops over time:

1. **Play stage.** Babies are not born with the ability to think of themselves as having a self. But as they develop, children learn to take on the attitudes of specific others toward themselves. Thus, young children play at being Mommy and Daddy, adopt Mommy's and Daddy's attitudes toward the child, and evaluate themselves as do Mommy and Daddy. However, the result is a very fragmented sense of the self. It varies depending on the specific other (for example, Mommy *or* Daddy) being taken into consideration. Young children lack a more general and organized sense of themselves.

2. **Game stage.** Children begin to develop a full sense of self when they take on the roles of a group of people simultaneously rather than the roles of discrete individuals. Each of those different roles comes to be seen as having a definite relationship to all of the others. Children develop organized personalities because of their ability to take on multiple roles, indeed the entirety of roles in a given group. The developed personality does not vary with the individual role (Mommy, Daddy) that children happen to be taking. This development allows children to function in organized groups. Most importantly, it greatly affects what they will do within a specific group.

George Herbert Mead

In the game stage of the development of the self, Mead theorized that we learn how to work with others by understanding their roles as well as our own. Do you think we ever complete this learning process?

children learn in the game stage, and they continue to implement and practice this ability throughout their lives.

The Generalized Other

Mead also developed the concept of the **generalized other**, or the attitude of the entire group or community. Individuals take the role of the generalized other. That is, they look at themselves and what they do from the perspective of the group or community. The generalized other becomes central to the development of self during the game stage. In the baseball example, the generalized other is the attitude of all teammates on a baseball field. It also likely involves the attitude of the team manager and coaches. In the classroom example, it is the attitude of the group working on the collaborative project. In the family, to take still another example, it is the attitude of all family members.

Mead offers the example of a baseball game (or what he calls "ball nine") to illustrate his point about the game stage of development. It is not enough in a baseball game for you to know what you are supposed to do in your position on the field. In order to play your position, you must know what those who play all other eight positions on the team are going to do. In other words, a player, every player, must take on the roles of all of the other players. For example, a shortstop must know that the center fielder is going to catch a particular fly ball; that he is going to be backed up by the left fielder; that because the runner on second is going to "tag up," the center fielder is going to throw the ball to third base; and that it is his job as shortstop to back up the third baseman. This ability to take on multiple roles obviously applies in a baseball game, but it applies as well in a playgroup, a work setting, and every other social setting.

To take a more contemporary example from the college classroom, students are often asked to work together on group class presentations. Each student will not only have to prepare her part of the project and presentation, but will also need to know, and coordinate with, what each of the other presenters, as well as the group as a whole, will do. One might have to know the content of each presentation and the sequence of presentations, along with the time allotted to each of them. Such group work resembles that of Mead's baseball team, where all members have to be familiar with and know the roles of all of the others involved in order to be successful as a group. This is, in essence, what

In taking on the perspectives of the generalized other, children begin developing more fully rounded and complete selves. They can view and evaluate themselves from the perspective of a group or community and not merely from the viewpoint of discrete others. To have a coherent self in the full sense of the term, as an adult one must become a member of a group or community. An adult must also be sensitive to the attitudes common to the community.

Having members who can take the role of the generalized other is also essential to the development of the group, especially in its organized activities. The group can function more effectively and efficiently because it is highly likely that individual members will understand and do what is expected of them. In turn, individuals can operate more efficiently within the group because they can better anticipate what others will do.

This discussion might lead you to think that the demands of the generalized other produce conformists. However, Mead argues that, while selves within a group share some commonalities, each self is different because each has a unique biographical history and experience. Furthermore, there are many groups and communities in society and therefore many generalized

generalized other The attitude of the entire group or community adopted by individuals.

others. Your generalized other in a baseball game is different from your generalized other in a classroom or in the family.

The "I" and the "Me"

Critical to understanding the difference between conformity and creative thinking and acting is Mead's distinction between two aspects, or phases, of the self—the "I" and the "me." Bear in mind that the "I" and the "me" are not things; they do not exist in a physical sense. We would not find the "I" or the "me" if we dissected the brain. Rather, the "I" and the "me" are subprocesses that are involved in the larger thinking process. An individual sometimes displays more of the "I" aspect of the self and sometimes more of the "me."

The **"I"** is the immediate response of an individual to others. It is that part of the self that is unconscious, incalculable, unpredictable, and creative. Neither the person nor the members of the group know in advance what that response of the "I" is going to be. The shortstop on a baseball team does not know in advance—nor do his teammates—whether he will react brilliantly to a batted ball or make an error. Similarly, a daughter at a holiday dinner does not always know in advance what she is going to say or do, and the same is true of the other family members at the dinner table. That is what makes for frequent squabbles, if not outright battles, on such family occasions. As a result of the "I," people often surprise themselves, and certainly others, because of the unexpected things they say and do.

Mead greatly values the "I" for various reasons, including the fact that it is the source of new and original responses. In addition, the "I" allows a person to realize the self fully and to develop a definite, unique personality. The "I" also gives us the capacity to have an impact on the groups and communities in which we live. Moreover, in Mead's view, some individuals, including the great figures in history, have a larger and more powerful "I." They are therefore able to have a greater impact on these entities, as well as on society and even on the globe.

The **"me"** is the organized set of others' attitudes assumed by the individual. In other words, the "me" involves the adoption by the individual of the generalized other. For example, your "I" might dispose you to introduce yourself to an attractive student in this class. However, your "me" might counter that impulse by suggesting that such a self-introduction is not considered appropriate behavior

> **"I"** The immediate response of an individual to others; the part of the self that is incalculable, unpredictable, and creative.
>
> **"me"** The organized set of others' attitudes assumed by the individual; it involves the adoption by the individual of the generalized other.

in your social group (the generalized other in this case). To Mead, the "me" involves a conscious understanding of what a person's responsibilities are to the larger group. The behaviors associated with the "me" also tend to be habitual and conventional. We all have a "me," but conformists have an overly powerful "me."

It is through the "me" that society is able to dominate the individual. In fact, Mead defines "social control" as the dominance of the "I" by the "me." Through the "me," individuals control themselves with little or no need for control by outside influences. In the "me" phase, however, individuals analyze and critique their own thoughts and actions from the point of view of the social group and what its criticisms are likely to be. Thus, in most cases, the group need not criticize individuals; they do it themselves. In other words, self-criticism is often, in reality, criticism by the larger society.

Nevertheless, people and society as a whole need both "I" and "me." For the individual, the "me" allows for a comfortable existence within various social groupings. The "I" lends some spice to what might otherwise be a boring existence. For society, the "me" provides the conformity needed for stable and orderly interaction. The "I" is the source of changes in society as it develops and adapts to the shifting environment.

It has been demonstrated that members of a given culture internalize the social sentiments considered the norm in their culture, such as attitudes toward different types of cheating; refer to those sentiments during social interaction; and maintain those sentiments within the culture over time (Heise 1979, 2007; MacKinnon and Heise 2010).

"I" and "Me" in Consumer Society. While the "me" generally provides the individual with some comfort and security, that is less the case in consumer society. The reason is that consumer society is all about change, and as a result the "me" is constantly changing. For example, one might be expected to adopt a given fashion at one time, but soon after an entirely different fashion comes to be expected. Instead of stability, "consumers must never be allowed to rest" (Bauman 1999:38). Of course, the "I" always impels the individual in unpredictable directions such as making unusual fashion decisions. However, in consumer society *both* the "I" and the "me" are at least somewhat unpredictable. This serves to make many people uneasy because they lack the comfort of a strong and stable "me."

While it is generally the case that consumer society is not conducive to a stable "me," the level of unpredictability is very much related to one's position in the stratification system. It is those in the middle class who are likely to

Language and Socialization

CHECKPOINT 4.1   CONCEPTS OF THE INDIVIDUAL AND THE SELF

The looking-glass self	Cooley's idea that we develop a self-image reflecting the way others respond to us.
The mind	An internal conversation that arises and is related to and continuous with interactions, especially with others in the social world.
The self	The ability to take our self as an object and develop a sense of who we are.
The generalized other	The attitude of the entire group or community adopted by individuals.
The "I"	The individual's immediate response to others.
The "me"	The organized set of others' attitudes that the individual assumes.

experience the most instability. As rapidly as they change, they are led to desire many more fashion changes than they can afford to make. The upper class is also confronted with a rapidly changing world of consumption. However, those in it can afford to change whenever it seems necessary. The lower class can afford little with the result that those in it are unable to change what they consume to any great degree. However, the lower class experiences the uneasiness associated with not being able to keep up with changing demands of the "me."

THE INDIVIDUAL AS PERFORMER

Erving Goffman is another important contributor to the symbolic interactionists' understanding of the self and how it develops. Goffman's work on the self is deeply influenced by Mead's thinking, especially the tension between the "I" and the "me." In Goffman's work this distinction takes the form of the tension between what we want to do spontaneously and what people expect us to do (Goffman 1959).

Goffman developed a notion of **dramaturgy**, which views an individual's social life as a series of dramatic performances akin to those that take place on a theatrical stage. To Goffman, the self is not a thing possessed by the individual but the dramatic product of the interaction between people and their audiences (Manning 2007). While many performances of the self are successful, there is always the possibility of disruption. Goffman focuses on this possibility and what people can do to prevent disruptions or to deal with them once they occur.

IMPRESSION MANAGEMENT

When people interact with others, they use a variety of techniques to control the image of themselves that they want to project during their social performances. They seek to maintain these impressions even when they encounter problems in their performances (Manning 2005). Goffman (1959) called these efforts to maintain a certain image **impression management**.

For example, in your sociology class you might typically project an image of a serious, well-prepared student. Then one night you stay up late partying and do not get the required reading done before class. When the instructor asks you a question in class, you try to maintain your image by pretending to be writing busily in your notebook rather than raising your hand. Called on nonetheless, you struggle, in vain, to give a well-thought-out, serious answer to the question. The smiles and snickers of fellow students who know that you were out partying late the night before might well disrupt the performance you are endeavoring to put on. To deflect attention from you to them, you might suggest that they try to answer the question.

ASK YOURSELF

What impression management activities do you undertake? Have they generally been successful? Do you see yourself performing more of these activities as time goes on, or fewer? Why?

While the idea of impression management is generally applied to face-to-face social interaction, it also applies to interaction on social networking sites. For example, many people constantly change the pictures on their Facebook page in order to alter the image of themselves that is conveyed to others (Cunningham, Brody, and Davis 2012).

> **dramaturgy** The view that social life is a series of dramatic performances akin to those that take place in a theater and on a stage.
>
> **impression management** People's use of a variety of techniques to control the image of themselves that they want to project during their social performances.

These photos show the actor Sacha Baron Cohen "back stage" with his family (left), and on his "front stage" (right) in costume for his role in the film *The Dictator*. Who else, besides actors, is likely to live on such wildly different front and back stages?

FRONT AND BACK STAGE

Continuing the theatrical analogy, Goffman (1959) argues that in every performance there is a **front stage**, where the social performance tends to be idealized and designed to define the situation for those who are observing it. In the example above, in class you are typically performing in your front stage. Your audience is the teacher and perhaps other students. As a rule, people feel they must present an idealized sense of themselves when they are front stage (presenting that seemingly well-thought-out answer). Because it is idealized, things that do not fit the image must be hidden. For example, you might hide the fact that you were partying the night before and are now unprepared to answer questions intelligently.

Also of concern to Goffman is the back stage. In the **back stage** people feel free to express themselves in ways that are suppressed in the front (Cahill et al. 1985). Thus, after class you might well confess to your friends in the cafeteria to partying and to faking answers to questions in class. If somehow your front-stage audience—the instructor in this case—sees your back-stage performance, your ability to maintain the impression you are trying to project in the classroom, in the front stage, is likely to become difficult or impossible in the future.

> **front stage** The part of the social world where the social performance is idealized and designed to define the situation for those who observe it.
>
> **back stage** The part of the social world where people feel free to express themselves in ways that are suppressed in the front stage.

The back stage plays a prominent role in our lives. For every one of our front-stage performances, there are one or more back stages where all sorts of things happen that we do not want to be seen in the front stage. For example, when summer camp is over, counselors are often "friended" by campers on Facebook. In order to allow the campers to stay in contact with them through Facebook, counselors might post limited, carefully edited profiles to special Facebook pages. This is, in effect, the counselors' front stage for former campers. However, the counselors might retain a back-stage version of Facebook, with profiles that the ex-campers are unable to see.

The existence of two stages, front and back, causes us all sorts of tensions and problems. We are always afraid that those in the front stage will find out about our back stage, or that elements of the back stage will intrude in the front stage.

These ideas are central to Leslie Picca and Joe Feagin's *Two-Faced Racism: Whites in the Frontstage and Backstage* (2007). White college students say and do different things depending on whether they are in their front or back stage. When they are in their back stage with friends and family, as well as with other whites, they often feel free to talk and act in a blatantly racist manner. Examples include telling racist jokes and mocking minority group members. However, when they are in their front stage in a public setting, especially with African Americans present, they may act as if they are blind to a person's color or even be gratuitously polite to African Americans. Thus,

Consumerism

Erving Goffman

Socialization

Sometimes it is difficult to distinguish between the front and back stages of a dramaturgical performance.

process that children develop a self as they learn the need, for example, to take on the role of the generalized other. Socialization almost always involves a process of interaction as those with knowledge and experience teach those with a need to acquire that knowledge or to learn from others' experiences.

While socialization occurs throughout one's lifetime, it can generally be divided into two parts. Socialization during childhood sets the course for a lifetime and has been a central focus for researchers. However, researchers have increasingly pointed up a variety of ways in which adults continue to learn how to function within their society. Erik Erikson (1994) is the scholar most responsible for promoting the idea of socialization across the life course. He proposed eight stages of socialization beginning at birth and ending at death, each based on what he described as a fundamental "existential question." For example, the final stage involves addressing the growing awareness of one's mortality and answering the question about whether or not one's life has been meaningful and major goals have been achieved.

while overt racism may have declined in the front stage of public settings, it persists in the back stage (Sallaz 2010).

While the distinction between front and back stage is important, bear in mind that these are not "real" places, nor are they rigidly separated from one another. That is, what is the front stage at one time can become the back stage at another time. Nevertheless, in general, people are most likely to perform in an idealized manner on their front stage when they are most concerned about making positive impressions. They are likely to perform more freely back stage, among those who are more accepting of less-than-ideal behavior and attitudes.

CHILDHOOD SOCIALIZATION

A central concern in the study of socialization is those who do the socializing, or the **agents of socialization** (Wunder 2007). The first and often most effective agents of socialization are the child's parents as well as other family members and friends. These are defined as primary agents of socialization. In addition, broader, less personal influences, such as the educational system, the media, and consumer culture, are important in socialization. These are defined as secondary agents of socialization. All play a part in creating an individual who

CHECKPOINT 4.2	CONCEPTS OF THE INDIVIDUAL AS PERFORMER
Dramaturgy	Goffman's idea that an individual's social life is a series of dramatic performances.
Impression management	Techniques individuals use to control the image of themselves they want to project during their social performances.
Front stage	Arena where our behavior is idealized in order to define the situation for observers.
Back stage	Arena where we feel free to express ourselves in ways suppressed on the front stage.

SOCIALIZATION

Socialization is the process by which an individual learns and generally comes to accept the ways of a group or a society of which he or she is a part. It is during the socialization

socialization The process through which a person learns and generally comes to accept the ways of a group or of society as a whole.

agents of socialization Those who do the socializing.

The Self in the Global Age

There are many things we can say about the self in an increasingly globalized world, but the focus here is on the impact on the self of the increasing mobility associated with globalization. People can now move physically with great ease throughout the world, and, perhaps more importantly, they can move even more easily digitally via e-mail, Twitter, Facebook, Skype, and the like. This mobility is of great importance in itself (Urry 2007), as well as because of its impact on the self: "The globalization of mobility extends into the core of the self" (Elliott and Urry 2010: 3).

Globalization has a variety of positive and negative effects on the self. On the positive side, the self can become more open and flexible as a result of all of the new and different experiences associated with the global age. The large number of brief interactions in the global age through, for example, meetings at airports or on planes as well as digitally can lead to a different kind of self. Such a self might be more oriented to the short-term and the episodic than to that which is long-term or even lifelong.

Of greatest concern are the negative effects of globalization, especially the great mobility associated with it, on the self. At the extreme, Lemert and Elliott (2006) see globalization as "toxic" for the individual, including the self. For

Our selves are not fixed in nature but continue to change over time. Do you think the increased mobility of modern life is a positive or a negative influence on the development of self?

example, because people are increasingly so globally mobile, they are likely to feel as if their selves are either dispersed and adrift in various places in the world or existing even more loosely in global cyberspace. Furthermore, while in the past the self was increasingly likely to be shaped by close personal relationships, it is now more likely to reflect the absence of such relationships and a sense of distance, even disconnection, from others. At the minimum, this can lead to a different kind of self than that which existed before the global age.

At the maximum, it can lead to one that is weak because it is untethered to anything that is strong and long lasting.

Think About It

Do you agree that the self today is formed more by the absence of close personal friendships and a sense of distance from others than by close personal relationships? What might be some of the negative effects of this change, if it is real? How could society counteract them?

---

can effectively operate within and shape culture. Except for education, which will be discussed in Chapter 11, we will examine each of these various agents of socialization below.

> **primary socialization** The acquisition of language, identities, gender roles, cultural routines, norms, and values from parents and other family members at the earliest stages of an individual's life.

Primary Socialization and the Family

In a process known as **primary socialization**, newborns, infants, and young children acquire language, identities, cultural routines, norms, and values as they interact with parents and other family members (Lubbers, Jaspers, and Ultee 2009). This socialization lays the foundation for later personality development (Rohlinger 2007). Early socialization performs various functions for society as well. They include equipping the young to fit better into society and the perpetuation of culture from one generation to the next.

Parents also do **anticipatory socialization**, or teaching children what will be expected of them in the future. Anticipatory socialization is how parents prepare children for the very important developmental changes (puberty, for example) that they will experience. Among the many other things that must be anticipated in family socialization is entrance into school, the work world, and life as an independent adult. Anticipatory socialization is especially important in societies and in time periods undergoing a great deal of change.

Many assumptions about primary and anticipatory socialization are changing dramatically as the nature of the family undergoes major transformations. The socialization process was thought to be rather straightforward when the ideal of the nuclear family, composed of a mother, a father, and two or more children all living in the same home, predominated throughout much of the twentieth century. Children were required to learn, at least as far as the family was concerned, that when they became adults they would go on to create the same kind of nuclear family as the one in which they grew up. However, assumptions about the goodness and inevitability of the nuclear family and the ease of the socialization process now seem impossible to accept (McLanahan 1999). This is the case because of increasing public awareness of the many problems that are associated with the nuclear family such as divorce, abuse, and unhappiness (see Chapter 11).

Then there is the expansion of many alternative family forms (e.g., single-parent households, grandparents as primary caregivers) and the increasing centrality of day care centers and their workers to the socialization process. The agencies doing the socializing today are much more complex and varied than in the era of the predominance of the nuclear family. As a result, socialization is not as straightforward as it once was thought to be. In addition, it is no longer possible to think of a seamless relationship between the agencies of socialization and the socialization process. For example, the family may be socializing its children in one way, but the day care center may be doing it very differently.

In addition, at one time socialization was seen as one-directional, for example, from parent to child. However, current thinking sees such socialization as two-directional with, for example, parents socializing children and children socializing adults, parents, and families (Gentina and Muratore 2012). For example, children tend to be far more familiar with the latest advances in digital technology, and they teach their parents much about both the technology itself and the digital culture. Another example is found in the large number of immigrant families in the United States and elsewhere. Children are more likely to learn the language and culture of their new country (often in school). As a result, they are frequently the ones to teach, or at least to try to teach, those things to parents (Mather 2009). This is **reverse socialization** where those who are normally being socialized are instead doing the socializing.

ASK YOURSELF

Have you experienced any instances of reverse socialization? For instance, have you taught your parents how to use their smartphones or set up a Facebook page, or has a younger relative or friend introduced you to the latest app like Fruit Ninja? What was this experience like?

Peers

A good deal of socialization within the schools (see Chapter 11 for a discussion of the role of schools and teachers in the process of socialization) takes place informally through interaction with fellow students. This is a situation where primary agents of socialization (peers) compete with secondary agents of socialization (teachers and other employees of the school system). Such informal socialization grows increasingly important as students progress through the school years, especially the high school years (Steinberg and Monahan 2007). Peers are also important sources of socialization outside of school, such as in scouting groups and athletic teams (Bennett and Fraser 2000; Fine 1987).

As the child matures and spends an increasing amount of time in the company of friends, peer socialization is increasingly likely to conflict with what is being taught at home and in the schools. Peer involvement in risky and delinquent behavior exerts an influence that is often at odds with the goals set forth by parents and educators (Gardner and Steinberg 2005; Haynie 2001).

Although peer socialization is especially important in, and associated with, childhood, it continues to be important throughout the life course. For example, peers help us learn what we are expected to do at college (Brimeyer, Miller, and Perucci 2006), at work (Montoya 2005), in social settings (Friedkin 2001), and in civic arenas (Dey 1997), as well as how to be sports fans (Melnick and Wann 2010).

anticipatory socialization The teaching (and learning) of what will be expected of one in the future.

reverse socialization The socialization of those who normally do the socializing—for example, children socializing their parents.

Gender

Sociologists devote a great deal of attention to gender socialization (McHale, Crouter, and Whiteman 2003; Rohlinger 2007), or the transmission of norms and values about what boys and girls can and should do. Even before babies are born, their parents start to "gender" them. In America they do so by, for example, painting rooms blue for boys and pink for girls. Parents often dress baby girls in frilly dresses and affix bows to their bald heads to signal to others that their child is a girl. These gender differences are reinforced by the toys children are likely to be given by parents—trucks and soldiers for boys, dolls and dollhouses for girls. As children grow up, they learn from their parents what behaviors are considered appropriate and inappropriate for their gender. For example, parents give girls a great deal of sympathy for crying, while boys are told to "be a man" and not cry after an injury. Boys also are expected to have an interest in sports, to play rough with each other, and to be unable to sit still. Girls, in contrast, are expected to express more "ladylike" behaviors, such as sitting quietly and sharing. Many children come to see these traditional gender expectations as natural expressions of being male or female.

The feminist movement challenged the idea that girls could not be active or that boys could not be nurturing (Lorber 2000). Today, girls are more likely to aspire to high-level careers, such as law and medicine. Some parents pride themselves on raising girls who engage in stereotypically male activities, such as team sports. Yet, many parents continue to strongly discourage boys from expressing an interest in activities that are stereotypically "for girls" (Kane 2006). Historically, traditional socialization for gender roles has been reinforced in schools, sports, and the mass media. In school, teachers and curricula tended to support traditional gender norms, and peer groups were likely to be segregated by gender (Thorne 1993). In sports, girls were channeled into different sports than boys; for example, girls tended to play softball while boys played baseball (Coakley 2007). When girls did play "male" sports, their efforts were often labeled differently, such as calling girls' football teams "powderpuff" football. The passage in 1972 of Title IX in the United States, which barred discrimination on the basis of gender in educationally based sporting activities receiving federal funding, has changed these views dramatically. Women's athletic activities in college and even in high school have become increasingly visible and, in some cases, more highly regarded as "real" sports. One of the best examples is women's basketball at the collegiate level. More generally, both men and women are now more likely to seek to build muscular and athletic bodies.

ASK YOURSELF

Why do you think traditional ideas about gender-role socialization in childhood remain strong in U.S. culture today? Do you foresee that they will ever give way to more egalitarian norms? Why or why not?

The media, especially movies, TV, and video games, have also tended to reinforce children's traditional gender role socialization. However, that, too, is changing. More television programs feature strong female characters (*Powerpuff Girls, The Good Wife, Grey's Anatomy, NCIS*), especially numerous shows featuring female cops and police chiefs (*Dexter, Dark Blue*). Female action stars (Sigourney Weaver in the *Alien* movies, Halle Berry in *X-Men*) are increasingly likely to play strong and aggressive characters. Young adult novels may also have strong female leading characters, such as Katniss Everdeen in the *Hunger Games* series.

Change is less obvious in other settings. Malls tend to reinforce traditional gender roles by offering separate shops for boys and girls, men and women. The Disney amusement parks offer highly differentiated attractions for boys ("Pirates of the Caribbean") and girls ("It's a Small World"). Most video games are aimed at boys, while girls are offered computer games focused on facial makeovers and shopping. This media emphasis on girls' and women's appearance is not new. Movies, television programming, and advertisements have been widely critiqued for decades for their unrealistic portrayal of women's bodies (Bordo 1993; Cole and Daniel 2005; Milkie 1999; Neuendorf et al. 2009). Magazines such as *Rolling Stone* are using more sexualized images of men on their covers, but there are still more such images of women. More striking is the fact that the images of women have become increasingly sexualized over time (Hatton and Trautner 2011). Many of the action heroines (for example, those in James Bond movies) continue to embody traditional male preferences for female bodies: young, attractive, and slender. Young women comparing themselves to these versions of adult Barbie dolls become anxious about their own bodies. Media images of women may also reaffirm racial stereotypes, with young women of color often sexualized or portrayed as poor and irresponsible (P. Collins 2004).

Mass Media and New Media

Until recently, much of the emphasis on the role of the mass media in socialization has been on the role played

Pressure and Creativity

Youth Political Socialization

Women and Sports

Katniss Everdeen, the bold central character of the *Hunger Games* book series (and portrayed by Jennifer Lawrence in the films), is a potential role model who defies traditional female norms. Can you think of any fictional male characters who successfully challenge traditional norms for men?

and other new digital media, the child can play video games such as *Grand Theft Auto IV*. These games engage children in simulations of antisocial activities like stealing cars and evading police chases. Clearly, the nature of the socialization implicit in such games is at odds with the lessons that parents and teachers wish to impart.

Smartphones and social networking sites play a role in socialization as well, mostly through the influence of peers. A great deal of peer socialization also takes place via sites such as Facebook and Twitter (Buckingham 2008; Watkins 2009). All of this is so new, and new forms of media are emerging so rapidly, that it is hard to know exactly what role the new media will play in socialization in the future, but their role is likely to be increasingly powerful and pervasive.

by television and the enormous number of hours per week children spend in front of their TVs (Comstock and Scharrer 2007). TV remains an important agent of socialization, especially for young children. However, it is clear that as children mature, especially in the middle and upper classes, more of their socialization is taking place via the computer, smartphones, video games, and other new and emerging technologies (Rideout, Foehr, and Roberts 2010). As Figure 4.1 shows, children and young people between the ages of 8 and 18 now spend almost 11 hours a day exposed to media of various sorts. That's an increase of more than 3 hours in the past 10 years. The percentage of young people who own their own media devices is high and, for the most part, increasing (see Figure 4.2).

Of course, a world of wonderful information is available to children on the computer via the new media. However, there are also lots of worrying things online, which children can easily find or stumble upon. In addition, access to the computer has changed the viewing experience considerably. Watching TV programs or movies is a passive activity. Even when "adult themes" are presented, the child is an observer, not a participant. However, on computers

Consumer Culture

Children need to be socialized to consume, especially to devote a significant portion of their lives to consumption. Like many other types of socialization, much of this socialization takes place early on in the family, in schools, and in peer groups. Of course, one must not ignore the role of marketing, especially to children, in learning to consume (Schor 2005).

However, much socialization now takes place in consumption sites themselves rather than in the family,

FIGURE 4.1 • Daily Exposure to Media Among 8- to 18-Year-Olds

	Time spent (hrs:min)		
	2009	2004	1999
TV content	4:29	3:51	3:47
Music/audio	2:31	1:44	1:48
Computer	1:29	1:02	:27
Video games	1:13	:49	:26
Print	:38	:43	:43
Movies	:25	:25	:18
Total media exposure	**10:45**	**8:33**	**7:29**

SOURCE: Data from Kaiser Family Foundation, 2010, "Generation M2: Media in the Lives of 8–18 Year-Olds: A Kaiser Family Foundation Study." January 2010.

schools, or advertisements. For example, preteens and teens spend a large amount of time at the shopping mall either with their families or, as they mature, more on their own and in the company of peers. Although young people may be going to a movie in the mall's multiplex or just "hanging out" there, rather than shopping, the fact remains that those activities take place in a setting devoted to shopping and consumption (Cook 2004; Rose 2010). Children readily learn the nuts and bolts of how to consume. They also learn various norms and values of consumption, especially to value consumption and shopping, as well as the goods and services acquired through those processes. There is even a game, *Mall Madness,* which socializes children into the realities of shopping at a mall. The object of the game is to be the first player to buy all six items on one's shopping list and return to the game's starting point. In other words, the winner in the game, and in much of consumer culture, is the best consumer.

Online consumption and shopping sites (such as Amazon.com and eBay.com) are also socializing agents. Navigation and buying strategies are learned at the digital retailers, and those have an effect on consumption in the brick-and-mortar world. For instance, many younger people who have grown up with online shopping are adept comparison shoppers. They are likely to compare products online and to search out the best possible deal before making a purchase. Socialization into being a consumer also reinforces lessons about race, class, and gender (Otnes and Zayre 2012). In *Inside Toyland,* Christine Williams (2006) shows that consumer choices—where to shop, what brands to buy, what products are appropriate for whom—contribute to the maintenance of social inequalities. Girls face pressures to consume beauty products that encourage them to live up to an idealized and usually unattainable level of female beauty (Wiklund et al. 2010). For example, Barbie dolls are often presented as an ideal form of the female body that is physically impossible to attain in real life. Such toys socialize children not only into a consumer culture, but into one that reproduces and reinforces harmful gender expectations.

ADULT SOCIALIZATION

While adult socialization takes place in many settings, the focus in this section is on the workplace and total institutions such as prisons.

Workplaces

A great deal of adult socialization takes place as people enter the work world and become independent of their

> **resocialization** The unlearning of old behaviors, norms, and values and the learning of new ones.

FIGURE 4.2 • Ownership of Media Devices among 12- to 17-Year-Olds

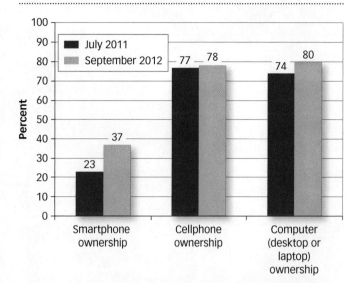

SOURCE: From Amanda Lenhart, Rich Ling, Scott Campbell, and Kristen Purcell. "Teens and Mobile Phones." Pew Internet, April 20, 2010. Pew Internet and American Life Project, Washington D.C. Reprinted with permission of Pew Internet & American Life Project.

families. At one time socialization into a workplace was a fairly simple and straightforward process. Many workers were hired for jobs in large corporations (General Motors, U.S. Steel) and remained there until they reached retirement age. Especially for those who held jobs in the lower reaches of the corporate hierarchy, socialization occurred for the most part in the early stages of a career. Today, however, relatively few workers can look forward to careers in a single position within a single company. Increasing numbers of workers change employers, jobs, and even careers with some frequency (Bernhardt et al. 2001; Legerski 2012). Each time workers change jobs, they need **resocialization** to unlearn old behaviors, norms, and values and learn new ones. One can no longer rely, assuming it was ever possible, on what one learned as a child, in school, or in early years on the job.

ASK YOURSELF

Have you ever experienced an orientation or training period in a job you have held? What occurred during this time that you could now classify as part of a workplace socialization process? How successful was it, and, thinking back, are there ways you believe it could have been done better?

Toys and Socialization

Branches of the military are total institutions. Why?

Furthermore, the Great Recession caused a record number of workers to lose their jobs (Farber 2011). Those who have been able to find new ones needed to be resocialized into them.

Total Institutions

Many adults find themselves at some point in their lives in some type of total institution (Gambino 2013; Goffman

formal resocialization in the form of being told the rules and procedures they must follow. But of far greater importance is the informal socialization that occurs over time through their interactions with guards and especially with other inmates (Walters 2003). In fact, other inmates often socialize relatively inexperienced criminals into becoming more expert criminals; prisons are often "schools for crime" (Sykes [1958] 2007; Walters 2003).

INTERACTION

Socialization generally involves **interaction**, or social engagement involving two or more individuals who perceive, and orient their actions to, one another (vom Lehn 2007). Interaction generally involves face-to-face relationships among people, but in the twenty-first century interaction is increasingly mediated by smartphones and social media.

The following sections deal with several important issues in the sociology of interaction.

SUPERORDINATE–SUBORDINATE INTERACTIONS

Georg Simmel ([1908] 1971a) saw society as being defined by interaction. Moreover, he differentiated between the forms that interaction takes and the types of people who engage in interaction. For example, one "form" of interaction is the relationship between *superordinate* and *subordinate*. This type of relationship is found in many settings and includes teacher and student in the

CHECKPOINT 4.3	SOCIALIZATION CONCEPTS
Agents of socialization	Those who socialize us.
Primary socialization	Process by which newborns, infants, and young children acquire language, identities, cultural routines, norms, and values by interacting with parents and family members.
Anticipatory socialization	Process by which parents teach children what will be expected of them in the future.
Resocialization	Process of unlearning old behaviors, norms, and values and learning new ones.

1961a). A **total institution** is a closed, all-encompassing place of residence and work set off from the rest of society that meets all of the needs of those enclosed in it.

A major example of a total institution is the prison. According to the U.S. Department of Justice (Glaze 2011), 2.27 million Americans are housed in federal and state prisons and county jails. On initial entry into prison, inmates undergo

total institution A closed, all-encompassing place of residence and work set off from the rest of society that meets all of the needs of those enclosed within it.

interaction A social engagement that involves two or more individuals who perceive, and orient their actions to, one another.

classroom; judge and defendant in the courtroom; and guard and prisoner in the jail. We tend to think of this relationship as eliminating the subordinate's independence. However, a relationship cannot exist unless subordinates have at least some freedom to be active parties to the interaction. For example, if the employee cannot react to the supervisor's direction, there is no interaction. There is only one-way communication from the supervisor to the employee. Furthermore, experimental research has demonstrated that the greater the equality in an employee-manager relationship, the greater the amount of two-way communication (Johnson, Ford, and Kaufman 2000).

Another type of superordinate–subordinate relationship analyzed by Simmel is the one between a benefactor and a "poor" person (Simmel [1908] 1971b). Simmel uniquely defined the *poor* in terms of relationships and interactions. The conventional view is that a poor person is someone who lacks resources. For Simmel, in contrast, a poor person is one who is aided by others (that is, receives charity), or at least has the right to that aid. In receiving aid, the poor person and the benefactor are involved in a specific kind of interaction in which one party gives and the other receives. That is, they are involved in an exchange relationship, although it is a highly unequal relationship.

In the movie comedy *Horrible Bosses*, three hapless friends, including Nick (Jason Bateman, right), plot to kill their abusive bosses, including the manipulative and deceitful Dave (Kevin Spacey). Fortunately most superordinate-subordinate relationships are more balanced than those portrayed in the film.

RECIPROCITY AND EXCHANGE

To those sociologists who theorize about exchange, interaction is a rational process in which those involved seek to maximize rewards and to minimize costs. Interaction is likely to persist as long as those involved find it rewarding, but it is likely to wind down or end when one or both no longer find it rewarding. An important idea in this context is the social norm of **reciprocity**, which means that those engaged in interaction expect to give and receive rewards of roughly equal value (Gouldner 1960; Molm 2010). When one party feels that the other is no longer adhering to this norm, not giving about as much as she is receiving, the relationship is likely to end.

---

reciprocity The expectation that those involved in an interaction will give and receive rewards of roughly equal value.

Studies of exchange relationships are now being challenged to find ways of dealing with virtual interaction: e-mail, social networking sites, and Skype. One researcher who has explored the effects of virtual reality on interaction in the "real" world, and vice versa, concludes that "the constantly evolving avatar [or digital representation of oneself] influences the 'real' self, who now also orients toward virtual, yet all-too-real others" (Gottschalk 2010). In other words, interactions in the digital realm and the physical realm both influence the self. Additional research questions come to mind quite readily. For example, are people compelled to cooperate to the same extent in the digital realm (such as when using e-mail communication) as they are in the material world (such as during in-person communication) (Naquin, Kurtzberg, and Belkin 2008)? However, it is important to remember that the digital and material worlds are not separate from one another, but rather interpenetrate. An important issue, then, is the connection between, for example, collaborative relationships on- and off-line (Ritzer 2013b).

"DOING" INTERACTION

Another interactionist theory of great relevance here is ethnomethodology, which focuses on people's everyday practices, especially those that involve interaction. The

Socialization in Prison

basic idea is that interaction is something that people actively "do," something that they accomplish on a day-to-day basis. For example, the simple act of walking together can be considered a form of interaction. Engaging in certain practices makes it clear that you are walking with a particular someone and not with someone else (Pantzar and Shove 2010; Ryave and Schenkein 1974). You are likely to walk close to, or perhaps lean toward, a close friend. When you find yourself walking in step with a total stranger, you behave differently. You might lean away in order to make it clear that you are not walking, in interaction, with that stranger. More complex forms of interaction require much more sophisticated practices. In the process of interaction, people create durable forms of interaction such as those that relate to gender (West and Zimmerman 1987) and the family.

INTERACTION ORDER

While every instance of interaction may seem isolated and independent of others, they are all part of what Erving Goffman (1983) called the **interaction order**. This is a social domain that is organized and orderly. The order is created informally and governed by those involved in the interaction rather than by some formal structure such as a bureaucracy and its constraints (Fine 2012; Jacobs 2007). One example of an interaction order is a group of students who form a clique and develop their own norms governing their interaction. In this thinking, Goffman is following Simmel's view that society is based, in a real sense, on interaction. In many ways, society *is* interaction.

ASK YOURSELF

What does it mean to say that society *is* interaction? Give some examples that illustrate your answer.

The interaction order can be seen in many settings and contexts. One particularly good one is the way people spontaneously form queues and wait for the doors to open at, for example, a rock concert. Some sociologists have suggested that human interaction with animals is another place to observe the interaction order (Jerolmack 2009b). In fact, there is a relatively new sociological theory—actor-network theory—that seeks to include not only animals but inanimate objects in the interaction order (Law and Hassard 1999).

STATUS AND ROLE

Status and role are key elements in the interaction order, as well as the larger structures in which such interactions often exist. A **status** is a position within a social system occupied by people. Within the university, for example, key statuses are professor and student. A **role** is what is generally expected of a person who occupies a given status (Hindin 2007). Thus, a professor is expected to show up for class, to be well prepared, to teach in an engaging manner, and so on. For their part, students are also expected to attend class, to listen and sometimes to participate, to avoid texting during class, to complete the required assignments, and to take, and pass, examinations.

The concept of status can be broken down further. One form of status is an **ascribed status**, or a position in which individuals are placed, or to which they move, but where such placement or movement has nothing to do with what people do or the nature of their capacities or accomplishments. This can be seen clearly in the realm of gender, where in all but a few cases we are categorized as a male or a female irrespective of our actions or abilities. The same point applies to age and racial status. In contrast, an **achieved status** is a position acquired by people on the basis of what they accomplish or the nature of their capacities. For example, becoming a graduate of a college or university, a spouse, a parent, and a successful entrepreneur are all achieved statuses.

Whether it is ascribed or achieved, a status can become a **master status**, or a position that is more important than any others both for the person in the position and for all others involved. Major examples of a master status are one's race or being disabled.

---

interaction order An area of interaction that is organized and orderly, but in which the order is created informally by those involved in the interaction rather than by some formal structure.

status A dimension of the social stratification system that relates to the prestige attached to people's positions within society.

role What is generally expected of a person who occupies a given status.

ascribed status A position in which individuals are placed, or to which they move, that has nothing to do with what they have done or their capacities or accomplishments.

achieved status A position acquired by people on the basis of what they accomplish or the nature of their capacities.

master status A position that is more important than any others both for the person in the position and for all others involved.

West Point graduates enjoy achieved status upon their graduation. What achieved statuses do you have or hope to have in the near future?

Roles can be congruent; that is, the expectations attached to a given status can be consistent (for example, going to class and doing your homework). But they can also come into conflict (for example, going to class and keeping up with your social life). **Role conflict** can be defined as conflicting expectations associated with a given position or multiple positions (Merton 1957). A professor who is expected to excel at both teaching and research can be seen as having role conflict. Devoting a lot of time to research can mean that a professor is ill prepared to teach her classes. A student may need to deal with the role conflict between being a student and studying and being a friend and going with buddies to see a crucial football game.

Much research has been done on the role conflicts experienced by workers with domestic obligations. Each role interferes with the ability to satisfactorily meet the expectations associated with the other role (Moore 1995). For example, working women, who still tend to be responsible for the care of children and the home, experience higher levels of stress and poorer physical health than working men (Gove and Hughes 1979; Pearlin 1989; Roehling, Hernandez Jarvis, and Swope 2005). The heavy burden of the female caretaking role inhibits women's ability to fulfill their role as caretakers of themselves.

Another role-related problem is **role overload**, in which people are confronted with more expectations than they can possibly handle. Students during final exam week are often confronted with role overload in trying to satisfy the expectations of several professors and courses. One study of the American "time crunch" and mental health suggests that feeling under time pressure is likely the active ingredient in role overload, which in turn affects people's psychological well-being (Roxburgh 2004).

There is a tendency to see roles as fixed and unchanging and as constraining on people. However, people do have the ability to engage in **role making.** That is, they have the ability to modify their roles, at least to some degree (Turner 1978). Thus, the professor in the above example might take her child to the office so that she can perform parent and teacher roles simultaneously. Researchers have noted that parents adopt a variety of work-family strategies to reduce work-family conflict (P. Becker and Moen 1999; Bianchi and Milkie 2010). Examples of such strategies include reducing work hours, turning down promotions, or negotiating trade-offs with one's partner.

MICRO-LEVEL SOCIAL STRUCTURES

Through an accumulation of persistent patterns of interaction and social relationships, individuals contribute to the creation of social structures, which are enduring and regular social arrangements (Hunt 2007). Social structures include everything from the face-to-face interaction that is characteristic of the interaction order, to networks, groups, organizations, societies, and the globe. This chapter focuses on the micro-level social structures—interpersonal relationships, social networks, and groups. Chapter 5 covers larger-scale social structures.

INTERPERSONAL RELATIONSHIPS

A good place to start a discussion of social structure is with another famous set of concepts created by Georg Simmel

> **role conflict** Conflicting expectations associated with a given position or multiple positions.
>
> **role overload** Confrontation with more expectations than a person can possibly handle.
>
> **role making** The ability of people to modify their roles, at least to some degree.

Animal Communication

Conversation Analysis

Interaction	Social engagement between two or more individuals who perceive, orient their actions to, one another.
Reciprocity	Social norm that those engaged in interaction expect to give and receive rewards of roughly equal value.
Interaction order	A social domain whose order is created informally and governed by those engaged in the interaction.

(1950) to describe the structures common to interpersonal relationships. **Dyads** are two-person groups, and **triads** are three-person groups.

Dyads are the most basic of interpersonal relationships, but they often evolve into triads—as when a couple welcomes a new child. The addition of one person to a dyad, creating a triad, would appear to be of minimal importance sociologically. After all, how important can the addition of one person be? Simmel demonstrates that no further addition of members to a group, no matter how many that might be, is as important as the addition of a single person to a dyad. A good example is the dramatic change in the husband-wife relationship caused by the arrival of a first child. Another is the powerful impact of a new lover on an intimate dyadic relationship. In cases like these, social possibilities exist in the triad that do not exist in a dyad. For example, in a triad two of the parties can form a coalition against the third. A wife and child can form a coalition against the husband. Or one member of the triad, say, the child, can take on the role of mediator or arbitrator in disputes involving the other members.

The most important point to be made about Simmel's ideas on the triad is that it is the group structure that matters, *not* the people involved in the triad or the nature of their personalities. Different people with different personalities will make one triad different from another, but it is not the nature of the people or their personalities that make the triad itself possible (Webster and Sell 2012).

SOCIAL NETWORKS

Simmel's work, especially on social forms, also informs the study of social networks (Chriss 2007; Kadushin 2012). The most basic social networks involve two or more individuals, but social networks also include groups, organizations, societies, and even global networks.

Network analysts are interested in how networks are organized and the implications of that organization for social life. They look at the nodes, or positions, occupied by individuals (and other entities) in a network, the linkages among nodes, and the importance of central nodes to other nodes in the network. Figure 4.3 demonstrates a network with low centrality and one with high centrality. In the low-centrality network, one node appears in the center, but it is actually linked to only two other nodes. The central node in the high-centrality example is far more influential. Every other node is connected to it, and there is only one link that is independent of the central node. Those who occupy positions that are central in any network have access to a great many resources and therefore have a considerable ability to gain and to exercise power in a network.

A key idea in network theory is the "strength of weak ties." We are all aware of the power of strong ties between, for example, family members or among those who belong to close-knit social groups such as gangs. However, Mark Granovetter (1973) demonstrated that those who have only weak ties with others (that is, they are just acquaintances) can have great power. While those with strong ties tend to remain within given groups, those with weak ties can more easily move between groups and thus provide important linkages among and between them (see Figure 4.4). Those with weak ties are the ones who hold together disparate groups that are themselves linked internally by strong ties.

Researchers generally find that at least half of all workers in the United States have obtained their jobs through informal means, meaning referrals, rather than formal job postings (Marsden and Gorman 2001; Pfeffer and Parra 2009). If you are looking for a job, you may want to seek out the help of friends and acquaintances who have weak ties to many groups. They are likely to have many diverse and potentially useful contacts with people you *and* your strong ties do not know at a number of different employers.

Those who are responsible for hiring need to keep in mind that access to network resources is largely dependent on one's own social position. Social network research has shown that those who are socioeconomically disadvantaged suffer deficits in both strong and weak network ties (Bian 1997; Granovetter 1973, 1974; Lin

---

dyad A two-person group.

triad A three-person group.

Facebook Relationships

You're seeing someone. It's great! It's wonderful! But is it a "real" relationship? Is it "Facebook official"? Once both partners confirm the relationship publicly via Facebook, the status change appears on your friends' (and friends of friends') Facebook home pages, and they can publish comments on the relationship if they so choose. The status remains on your profile until you change it, at which point your friends will be alerted once again that your relationship status has changed.

Had he dealt with it, French sociologist Pierre Bourdieu might have described a Facebook relationship status as a kind of "symbolic capital"—that is, a socially recognized symbol that offers status to individuals who hold it. In the case of the Facebook relationship status, it is symbolic because the status alone does not fully describe the complexity of your relationship. It merely represents—symbolizes—that you and your significant other are involved in a mutually and publicly recognized relationship. As a symbol of that relationship, it is a simplification that makes that relationship easily and widely recognizable to others. Thus, knowledge of your relationship can "travel" easily—almost like cash, or capital. You can "exchange" that symbol for resources like attention such as appearing on your friends' home pages. It can

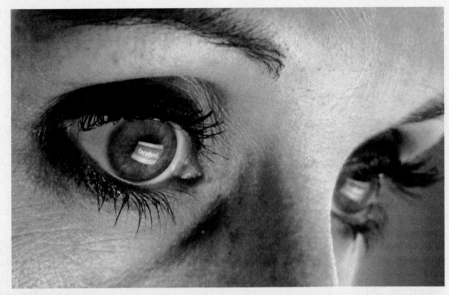

Is a relationship more real because it's been posted on Facebook? How did people let others know their personal news before Facebook?

be exchanged for claims to legitimacy or exclusivity such as marking that you and your significant other are "taken." Or, that symbol can be exchanged for claims about wrongs or grievances. For example, it becomes readily apparent to all those who see that your significant other is leaving messages for someone else that you are entitled to some comfort, encouragement, advice, or even retribution. In short, your Facebook relationship status is itself a kind of "capital" that can quickly and easily be converted into meanings that may further advantage you and shape a number of your social relationships.

Think About It

Do you have any other symbolic capital online besides your Facebook status? Do your various online presences project a consistent image? In other words, how well are you managing your front stage online?

SOURCE: Printed with the permission of Margaret Austin Smith.

1999; Lin and Bian 1991; Lin, Ensel, and Vaughn 1981; Wegener 1991). To overcome this barrier to finding talented disadvantaged workers, an employer may want to seek ties to networks that include the socioeconomically disadvantaged.

One point worth underscoring in any discussion of social networks is the importance of Internet networks, including Facebook, Skype, and Twitter. This is another domain where weak ties can be of great importance. On Facebook, for instance, you may have hundreds, even thousands, of "friends." However, it is clear that these "friendships" involve weak ties, in fact far weaker ties than analysts such as Granovetter had in mind. It is also important to note that they leave objective traces such as e-mail messages and writings on a Facebook wall. As a result, such networks are much easier to study than, for example, those that exist in face-to-face interaction, which

Social Networks

Migrant Networks

FIGURE 4.3 • Social Network Centrality

Opposite Degrees of Network Centrality

Low Network Centrality

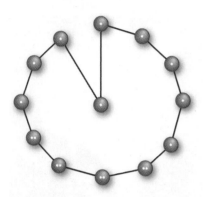

High Network Centrality

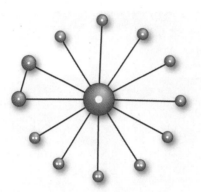

SOURCE: Reprinted by permission of S. Joshua Mendelsohn.

usually leave few material traces. This is the reason behind Snapchat, an app which allows you to arrange for traces—such as photos—to disappear after a given period of time (Wortham 2013).

FIGURE 4.4 • The Strength of Weak Ties

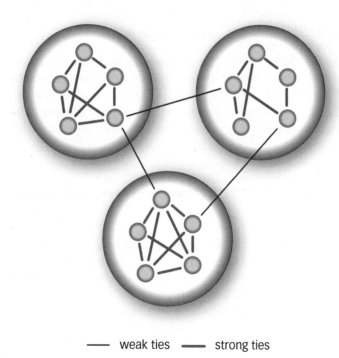

—— weak ties —— strong ties

SOURCE: Adapted from *Weak Ties in Social Networks*, Bokardo, a blog about interface and product design, Joshua Porter.

GROUPS

We have already encountered the key sociological concept of groups at several points in this chapter, especially in Simmel's ideas on the dyad and beyond. A **group** is a relatively small number of people who over time develop a patterned relationship based on interaction with one another. However, just because we see a small number of people—say, on a queue waiting to board a plane—that does not mean that they necessarily constitute a group. Most people on a queue are not likely to interact with one another, to have the time or inclination to develop patterned relationships with one another, and, if they interact, to do so beyond the time it takes to board the plane and find their seats.

Types of Groups

Several key concepts in sociology relate to groups. Consider the traditional distinction between the primary group and the secondary group (Cooley 1909). **Primary groups** are those that are small, are close-knit, and have intimate face-to-face interaction. Relationships in primary groups are personal, and people identify strongly with the groups. The family is the model of a primary group, although as we will see in Chapter 10, the family is often riddled with many conflicts, and at least some members leave the family or are driven from it. Primary groups can also take unlikely forms. A 2009 study of people in New York City who tend pigeons and fly them from the rooftop documents the formation of primary group ties among the members involved in this rare animal practice activity (Jerolmack 2009b). Such group ties can be stronger for these individuals than class and ethnic ties.

In contrast, **secondary groups** are generally large and impersonal, ties are relatively weak, members do not know one another very well, and their impact on

> **group** A relatively small number of people who over time develop a patterned relationship based on interaction with one another.
>
> **primary groups** Groups that are small, are close-knit, and have intimate face-to-face interaction.
>
> **secondary groups** Generally large, impersonal groups in which ties are relatively weak and members do not know one another very well, and whose impact on members is typically not very powerful.

PUBLIC SOCIOLOGY

Malcolm Gladwell's *Tipping Point*

Malcolm Gladwell (1963–) is a journalist who draws on many different fields, including sociology. In his best-known book, *The Tipping Point* (2000), he deals with diverse topics such as the beginning of the American Revolution, teenage suicide in Micronesia, and the dramatic drop in the crime rate in New York City in the mid-1990s. He is able to deal with so many different topics because, unlike an empirical sociologist, he does not collect any data of his own. He bases his generalizations on conversations and newspaper accounts. Indeed, he offers generalizations that few sociologists would feel comfortable making, but they are nevertheless intriguing and often quite insightful.

In *The Tipping Point* Gladwell deals with the kinds of phenomena mentioned above, and many others. He argues that they all operate like infectious diseases. They can start very small, simmer for a while, explode, and then die away. Of greatest interest to him is that "tipping point" when things suddenly, rather than gradually, either explode or die off. For example, he is interested in why an "epidemic" of teenage suicide suddenly arises, or in why a long-running crime wave seemingly peters out overnight. Much of his explanation relates to the power of word-of-mouth communication (or verbal interaction), especially in the beginning, but also at the end, of these social epidemics.

One type of person critical to the needed verbal interaction is *connectors*, or those who talk to a lot of people and are critically important in bringing them together on a specific matter. Paul Revere was successful in mobilizing people to resist the British army because as a connector he was already known to them before he took his fateful ride, and through that ride he was able to bring them together.

Gladwell's work is useful and intriguing, but like all "pop sociology," it has its scholarly limitations (Pinker 2009:12).

Think About It

Have you ever been involved in, or observed, a tipping point of the kind described by Gladwell? Have you ever served as a connector? Give personal examples of both a tipping point and acting as a connector.

---

members is typically not very powerful. Members of a local parent-teacher association would be a good example of a secondary group.

Primary and secondary group ties can occur in the same social context. For example, the primary group for servicemen and -women is usually the squad or platoon. The secondary group is typically the company, battalion, brigade, or regiment (in descending order of closeness) (Siebold 2007).

Also worth mentioning are **reference groups**, or those groups that you take into consideration in evaluating yourself. Your reference group can be one to which you belong, or it can be another group to which you do not belong but to which you nevertheless often relate (Ajrouch 2007; Merton and Kitt 1950). People often have many reference groups, and those groups can and do change over time. Knowing people's reference groups, and how they change, tells us a great deal about their behavior, attitudes, and values. We often think of reference groups in positive terms. An example would be a group of people whose success you would like to emulate. They also can be negative if they represent values or ways of life that you reject (say, neo-Nazis). The group to which one belongs is not necessarily the most powerful group in one's life.

Reference groups can be illustrated by the case of immigrants. Newly arrived immigrants are more likely to take those belonging to the immigrant culture, or even those in the country from which they came, as their reference group. In contrast, their children, second-generation immigrants, are much more likely to take as their reference group those associated with the new culture in the country to which they have immigrated (Kosic et al. 2004).

Conformity to the Group

We have seen that group members generally conform to certain aspects of the group with which they prefer to

> **reference groups** Groups that people take into consideration in evaluating themselves.

Malcom Gladwell's Tipping Point

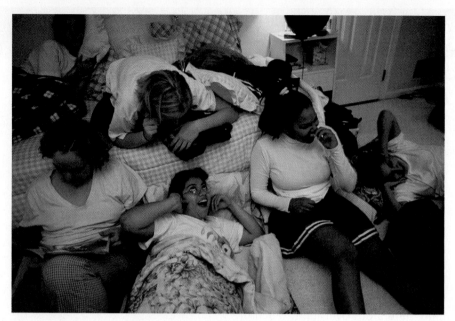

The friends with whom we are close are often members of our reference groups. Have your reference groups changed since your high school years?

identify. Some conformity is clearly necessary for a group to survive. If everyone "did his or her own thing," or went his or her own way, there would be no group. But too much conformity can have disastrous consequences. A central issue in the sociological study of groups has been the degree to which members conform to the

expectations and demands of the group despite their own misgivings. The experiments by Stanley Milgram (1974), discussed in Chapter 2, generally demonstrated that people tended to conform to authority figures who were demanding the administration of painful shocks. Groups often develop informal authority structures that can induce the kind of conformity uncovered by Milgram. Also discussed in Chapter 2 is research by Zimbardo (1973), which showed similarly troubling tendencies toward conformity.

Another series of experiments conducted by Solomon Asch (1952) showed that groups with no clear authority figure also promote conformity. He demonstrated that the power of the group is so great that it may override an individual's own judgments and perceptions (Asch 1952; Kinney 2007). In one of the experiments, groups of seven to nine students were assembled. All but one (the subject) were confederates of the researcher. All but the subject knew the details of the experiment. Only the subject believed that the experiment was investigating vision. Each group was shown two cards, one with one vertical line on it and a second with three such lines (see Figure 4.5). One of the lines on the second card was the same length as the line on the first card. The other two lines were clearly different. All the students were asked to choose the line on the comparison card that matched the single line on the reference card. As they had been instructed, the confederates chose, out loud, one of the wrong lines. The subjects were always positioned last in the group. When their turn came, about a third of them tended to conform to the group's erroneous choice and chose a wrong line. They made the wrong choice even though they apparently knew it was the wrong choice.

There is no question that some people conform to group demands, at least some of the time. Conformity is especially likely when the demands come from someone in authority in the group. However, it is important to remember that about two-thirds of the choices in the Asch conformity experiments indicated independence from the group. It is also important to note that these experiments are decades old, and many of them occurred in a period of American history more defined by conformity than is the case today.

FIGURE 4.5 • Solomon Asch's Conformity Experiment Cards

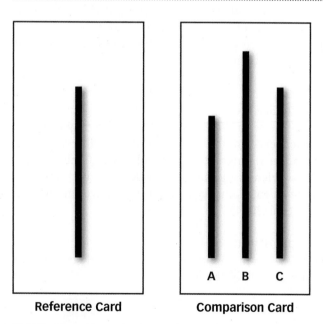

Reference Card   Comparison Card

SOURCE: Adapted from Solomon E. Asch, Opinions and Social Pressure, *Scientific American, 193* (1955), pp. 31–35.

ACTIVE SOCIOLOGY

How Good Are Your Impression Management Skills?

How do you use your own social media pages (Facebook, Twitter, Pinterest) to manage impressions in the minds of others? How do you present yourself? Do an analysis of the content of the photographs, status updates, links, and comments on one of your social media pages. What do these items say about you?

Posted content	What I think it says about me
Photographs	
Status updates	
Links	
Comments	

Identify two or three general themes, based on your analysis of your content. Then consider the following:

1. What status do you possess on the site, and what corresponding roles do you perform?

2. Where/how did you learn these things (that is, who or what were important *agents of socialization*)?

3. How does this page represent your *front stage*? How is your *back stage* different from the way you've presented yourself on the website?

Yet, obedience to authority has not disappeared. In the mid-2000s, a prank phone caller targeting fast-food restaurants across the country demonstrated the relevance of work on obedience to authority outside of the laboratory (Wolfson 2005). Posing as a police officer on the phone, the caller informed managers that one of their female employees was suspected of stealing. While some managers became suspicious of the caller's real identity, others followed his directions—even when they were asked to have the employee strip-searched. In at least one case, the employee was sexually assaulted. As mentioned in Chapter 2, these events are all dramatized in the 2012 movie *Compliance*. Incidents such as this one suggest that many people are still willing to obey authorities such as the police, even when they are asked to engage in actions at odds with their own values.

CHECKPOINT 4.5 — TYPES OF GROUPS (SMALL NUMBERS OF PEOPLE WHO DEVELOP A PATTERNED RELATIONSHIP BASED ON INTERACTIONS OVER TIME)

Dyad	Two-person group.
Triad	Three-person group.
Primary group	Small, close-knit groups with intimate face-to-face interaction.
Secondary group	Large and impersonal groups with relatively weak ties among members who do know each other very well.
Reference group	Group you take into consideration in evaluating yourself, whether you belong to it or not.

Upward Mobility

SUMMARY

This chapter examined the aspects of the social world on the micro end of the continuum, namely individuals and groups. The sociological perspective on the individual and the self focuses on how these aspects affect the individual's ability to take part in society. Cooley's concept of the looking-glass self, the idea that humans develop a self-image that reflects how others respond to them, is fundamental to sociology. Symbolic interactionism has been a key theory in the sociological study of how individuals develop a sense of self.

As mind and self develop through interaction, growing children come to incorporate a sense of the generalized other, which allows them to take the role of the entire group or community in which they are embedded and thus operate more smoothly within society. During the play stage children learn to take on the attitudes of specific others toward themselves; in the game stage they can begin to take on the role or attitude of the entire group, the generalized other.

Erving Goffman built on Mead's theories, particularly the tension between the "I" and the "me." Goffman believed that in every interaction, or performance, individuals have a front and back stage. The front stage is where the individual operates in a comparatively fixed and idealized manner to define the situation for those who are observing the performance. In the back stage, people are better able to express freely things that were suppressed in the front stage.

Mead's ideas on the development of the self lead directly to the idea of socialization, the process through which a person learns and generally comes to accept the ways of a group or of a society as a whole. Primary socialization begins with newborns and infants, and as they develop, children experience secondary socialization. Socialization does not end with childhood—adults continue to be socialized throughout their lives. Gender socialization is a running theme in all interactions.

Interaction is crucially important to socialization and many other aspects of the social world. Simmel believed society was defined by interaction. Sociologists from a variety of theoretical perspectives have examined interaction. Interaction is deeply involved in people's statuses within social systems and their related roles. Conflicting expectations are often associated with a given status. In addition, expectations associated with one status often conflict with those tied to others.

Patterns of interaction and social relationships that occur regularly and persist over time become social structures. The smallest social structure is a dyad, which may sometimes become a triad. A group is still a relatively small social structure, made up of a number of people who over time develop patterned relationships.

KEY TERMS

Achieved status, 116
Agents of socialization, 109
Anticipatory socialization, 110
Ascribed status, 116
Back stage, 107
Dramaturgy, 106
Dyad, 118
Front stage, 107
Game stage, 103
Generalized other, 104
Gesture, 102
Group, 120
"I", 105
Impression management, 106

Interaction, 114
Interaction order, 116
Looking-glass self, 121
Master status, 116
"Me", 105
Micro-macro continuum, 101
Mind, 103
Play stage, 103
Primary groups, 120
Primary socialization, 109
Reciprocity, 115
Reference groups, 121
Resocialization, 113
Reverse socialization, 110

Role, 116
Role conflict, 117
Role making, 117
Role overload, 117
Secondary groups, 120
Self, 103
Significant symbol, 102
Socialization, 108
Status, 116
Symbolic interaction, 103
Total institution, 114
Triad, 118

REVIEW QUESTIONS

1. How can we use the literature on feral children to explain the importance of interaction to human development? In what ways does this relate to the "nature versus nurture" debate?

2. According to Mead, what distinguishes humans from nonhumans?

3. How does the socialization process help individuals develop their sense of self? Why are games so important to the socialization process?

4. What is the difference between the "I" and the "me"? Why do people and society as a whole need both the "I" and the "me"?

5. According to Goffman, in what ways do we use impression management within our front-stage regions? Why would a

sociologist say that racism has increasingly been relegated to the back stage? What is problematic about this development?

6. Why are families important agents of socialization?

7. How are we socialized to be consumers? In what ways has the Internet resocialized us as consumers?

8. In what ways is being a fifth grader in the United States both an ascribed and an achieved status? What does this suggest about the differences between roles attached to ascribed statuses versus achieved statuses?

9. In the realm of social networks, why are "weak ties" helpful when looking for a job? What effect has the Internet had on the development of weak ties and strong ties?

10. In what ways do we use images in the mass media as reference groups?

APPLYING THE SOCIOLOGICAL IMAGINATION

How can we understand gender socialization through consumption? This chapter argues that malls tend to reinforce gender roles by offering separate shops for female and male consumers.

For this activity, go to your local mall and identify stores for men (and boys) and stores for women (and girls). In what ways are the

stores different? Pay attention to the differences in items sold, the nature of those items, the way each store is set up, and even differences in music or lighting. What do the differences in these stores suggest about the differences between men and women and what is expected of them?

STUDENT STUDY SITE

⑤SAGE edge™

Sharpen your skills with SAGE edge at **edge.sagepub.com/ritzeressentials**

SAGE edge for students provides a personalized approach to help you accomplish your coursework goals in an easy-to-use learning environment.

A military parade to celebrate the 200th anniversary of Venezuela's independence included these soldiers wearing face paint. The military is a prime example of the type of social organization called a bureaucracy. To how many organizations do you belong? Are any of them bureaucracies?

ORGANIZATIONS, SOCIETIES, AND THE GLOBAL DOMAIN

5

LEARNING OBJECTIVES

1 Describe the features of organizations and bureaucracies—formal, informal, gendered, and network.

2 Contrast *gemeinschaft* and *gesellschaft* societies.

3 Describe global societies in terms of nations, states, and nation-states.

In June 2013, 30-year-old U.S. Central Intelligence Agency contractor Edward Snowden told the world that the U.S. government had been spying on its own citizens to an unsuspected degree. The National Security Agency, Snowden informed a British newspaper, had for years been accumulating data on routine phone calls made by ordinary citizens who were not suspected of any wrongdoing. Public reaction was swift and loud, with some arguing the government had gone to unwarranted lengths, breaching its citizens' privacy, while others claimed any and all steps necessary to uncover terrorist plots were defensible. Snowden, who made his revelations from Hong Kong, then fled to Russia.

Our lives are framed by our relationships with many different organizations and institutions.

Each aspect of this event reveals the relationship between us as individuals and the different organizations and institutions that frame our lives, such as our local and national governments. These organizations can exist only with willing members. When groups of individuals begin to question the authority and rationality of the bureaucracies that govern them, they may voice concern about, seek to change, or even rebel against them. Social order cannot be maintained if citizens refuse to adhere to society's shared laws and norms. How do governments, as institutions, react?

We've seen how technology and globalization facilitate the global flow of information, for instance, fundamentally altering the way we communicate. But this nearly instantaneous dissemination of ideas has become a bonanza for everyone, including revolutionaries, rioters, potential terrorists, and even elected governments. For instance, revelations that swiftly followed Snowden's initial leak suggested the United States had also been secretly conducting extensive monitoring of the communications of its European Union allies (including the Prime Minister of Germany). Some governments, such as the United Kingdom's after a 2011 series of violent riots in London, have considered shutting down digital communication during public disturbances. Other countries, such as China, Syria, and Iran, routinely exert censorship power over their citizens' use of the Internet. Such barriers to the flow of information, as well as efforts such as Snowden's to overcome them, are of profound interest to sociologists, public figures, and social activists alike. ●

ORGANIZATIONS

The social world is awash with **organizations**, which are collectives purposely constructed to achieve particular ends. Examples include your college or university, which has the objective of educating you as well as your fellow students; corporations, such as Apple, Google, and Wal-Mart, whose objective is to earn profits; the International Monetary Fund (IMF), which seeks to stabilize currency exchanges throughout the world; and Greenpeace, which works to protect and conserve the global environment.

There is a particularly long and deep body of work in sociology that deals with organizations (Godwyn and Gittell 2011), much of it traceable to the thinking of Max Weber on a particular kind of organization, the bureaucracy. As you may recall, a **bureaucracy** is a highly rational organization, especially one that is very efficient. The bureaucracy is a key element of Weber's theory of the rationalization of the western world. In fact, along with capitalism, the bureaucracy best exemplifies what Weber meant by rationalization. For decades the concept of bureaucracy dominated sociological thinking about organizations, and it led to many important insights about the social world. However, as the social world has changed, so too has sociological thinking about organizations. New concepts are supplementing the concept of bureaucracy to enrich our understanding of these new realities.

BUREAUCRACIES

Throughout his work Weber created and used many "ideal types" as methodological tools to study the real world and with which to do historical-comparative analysis (see Chapter 2). One of Weber's most famous ideal types was the bureaucracy. While the ideal type of bureaucracy is primarily a methodological tool, it also gives us a good sense of the advantages of bureaucracies over other types of organizations.

The ideal-typical bureaucracy is a model of what most large-scale organizations throughout much of the twentieth century looked like, or at least tried to resemble. Figure 5.1 is an organization chart for a typical bureaucracy. A bureaucracy has the following characteristics:

> **organizations** A collective purposely constructed to achieve particular ends.
>
> **bureaucracy** A highly rational organization characterized by efficiency.

- There is a continuous series of offices, or positions, within the organization. Each office has official functions and is bound by a set of rules.

- Each office has a specified sphere of competence. Those who occupy the position are responsible for specific tasks and have the authority to handle them. Those in other relevant offices are obligated to help with those tasks.

- The offices exist in a vertical hierarchy.

- The positions have technical requirements, and those who hold those offices must undergo the needed training.

- Those who occupy the positions do not own the things needed to do the job (computers, desks, etc.). The organization provides officeholders with what they need to get the job done.

- Those who occupy a particular office—chief executive officers, for example—cannot take the office as their own; it remains part of the organization.

- Everything of formal importance—administrative acts, decisions, rules—is in writing.

The development of the bureaucracy is one of the defining characteristics of western society. In Weber's view, it was a key source of the superiority of the West over other civilizations in the operation of society as a whole as well as of its major components such as the military. Weber felt that in meeting the needs of large societies for mass administration, there is no better organizational form than, and no alternative to, the bureaucracy.

ASK YOURSELF

Have you ever been a member of a bureaucracy? How many of Weber's characteristics did it have? How well or poorly did it meet the needs of the society it was designed to serve? Why?

Authority Structures and Bureaucracy

Weber's work on bureaucracy is related to his thinking on three types of authority structures. Before getting to those

Bureaucracy

Female militia members executing a precisely choreographed march during a training session outside Beijing, China. Do the characteristics of their highly efficient and uniform organization appeal to you?

types, we need two preliminary definitions. **Domination** is the probability or likelihood that commands will be obeyed by subordinates (Weber [1921] 1968). There are degrees of domination. Strong domination involves a high probability that commands will be obeyed; domination is weak when those probabilities are low. **Authority** is a particular type of domination; it is legitimate domination. The key question, then, is what makes authority legitimate as far as subordinates are concerned.

Weber differentiates among three types of authority:

- **Rational-legal authority.** Domination is legitimated on the basis of legally enacted rules and the right of those with authority under those rules to issue commands. For example, the president of the United States has rational-legal authority because he is duly elected in accord with the country's election laws. It is also legitimate for the president in his role as commander-in-chief to issue various commands. Similarly, your professors have rational-legal authority because of the nature of their positions in, and the rules of, the university. They can, for example, demand that you read this chapter, take an exam on it, and complete other course requirements.

- **Traditional authority.** Authority based on the belief in long-running traditions is traditional authority. For example, although the pope is elected by the College of Cardinals, his authority within Catholicism is based

primarily on the long traditions associated with his position. At the university, it is traditional for senior professors with many years of service, especially those who are well known on the campus or internationally, to acquire authority in their departments as well as in the university as a whole.

- **Charismatic authority.** The third type of authority is based on the devotion of followers to what they define as the exceptional characteristics of a leader. Large numbers of people believed that Martin Luther

---

domination The probability or likelihood that commands will be obeyed by subordinates.

authority A particular type of domination: legitimate domination.

rational-legal authority Authority that is legitimated on the basis of legally enacted rules and the right of those with authority under those rules to issue commands.

traditional authority Authority based on a belief in long-running traditions.

charismatic authority Authority based on the devotion of the followers to what they define as the exceptional characteristics, such as heroism, of the leaders.

FIGURE 5.1 • Organization Chart for a Typical Bureaucracy

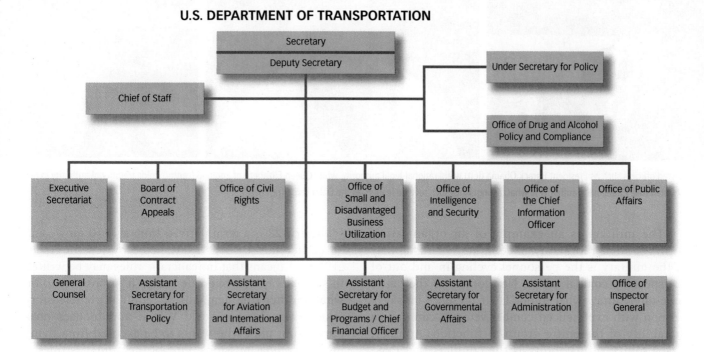

King Jr. and Mahatma Gandhi had such exceptional characteristics and, as a result, became their devoted followers. A professor who is considered to be a charismatic teacher by her students is likely to attract a large number of adoring students. Such a professor is also likely to have authority over them as well as other professors interested in learning how to improve their teaching techniques.

Each type of authority can spawn its own organizational form. However, it is rational-legal authority that is most associated with bureaucracy. In comparison to the bureaucracy, the organizations based on traditional and charismatic authority are less rational. They are, for example, less efficient than the highly efficient bureaucracy.

Rationality and Irrationality

Much sociological research on organizations in the twentieth century took Weber's highly rational model of a bureaucracy as a starting point for the study of the ways in which bureaucracies actually worked. However, much of that research found Weber's model to be unrealistic. For one

> **bounded rationality** Rationality limited by, among other things, instabilities and conflicts within most, if not all, organizations, as well as by the limited human capacity to think and act in a rational manner.

thing, there is no single organizational model. The nature of the organization and its degree of rationality are contingent on such factors as its size and the technologies that it employs (Orlikowski 2010; Pugh et al. 1968). For another, researchers found Weber's ideal-typical bureaucracy to be overly rational. This is not surprising since for Weber ([1904] 1949: 47) it was "not a *description* of reality." Weber purposely exaggerated its degree of rationality. The ideal-typical bureaucracy is a fiction designed to serve as a reference point to study real-world bureaucracies. However, researchers often overlooked the fact that this ideal type is a methodological tool and mistook it for an attempt to accurately describe bureaucracies. They concluded that, at best, real-world organizations exhibit a limited form of rationality, or what is called **bounded rationality** (Collet 2009; Simon [1945] 1976; Williamson 1975, 1985). That is, rationality is limited by the instabilities and conflicts that exist in most, if not all, organizations and the domains in which they operate (Scott 2008). It is also limited by inherent limitations on humans' capacities to think and act in a rational manner. Some members of the organization are capable of acting more rationally than others. However, none are able to operate in anything approaching the fully rational manner associated with Weber's ideal-typical organization (Cyert and March 1963).

Charismatic Authority

Elected officials such as President Barack Obama (left) wield rational-legal authority, while Queen Elizabeth of England (center) holds traditional authority in her inherited role. Charismatic authority is what distinguishes such revered leaders as the Dalai Lama (right).

The military is an example of an organization with bounded rationality. One source of instability in the military is the personnel cycling in and out of it, especially combat zones. Newcomers to the battle zone rarely know what to do. Their presence in, say, a platoon with experienced combat veterans can reduce the ability of the entire group to function. Another, larger source of instability is the conflicts that exist between branches of the armed forces, as well as between central command and those in the field. In addition, military actions are often so complex and far-reaching that military personnel cannot fully understand them or decide rationally what actions to take. This is sometimes referred to as the "fog of war" (Blight and Lang 2005).

A good deal of sociological research on bureaucracies has dealt with how the rational (that is, what is efficient) often becomes irrational (or inefficient). This is often referred to as the "irrationality of rationality," the irrationality that often accompanies the seemingly rational actions associated with the bureaucracy (Ritzer 2013a). For example, Robert Merton ([1949] 1968) and other observers found that instead of operating efficiently, bureaucracies introduce great inefficiency due to, among other things, "red tape." *Red tape* is a colloquial term for rules that a bureaucracy's employees are needlessly required to follow. It also includes unnecessary online and off-line questions to be answered and forms to be filled out by the clients of a bureaucracy. Bureaucracies generally demand far more information than they need, often to protect themselves from complaints, bad publicity, and lawsuits. Red tape also includes the telephone time wasted by keeping clients on hold and forcing them to make their way through a maze of prerecorded "customer service" options. In the end, clients often discover that they have been holding for the wrong office or, as is increasingly the case today, that they can only resolve their problem by visiting the company's website.

Catch-22 is a term derived from a 1970 movie and an earlier novel of the same name by Joseph Heller (1955). It means that bureaucratic rules may be written in such a way that one rule makes it impossible to do what another rule demands or requires. Heller's story takes place during World War II and focuses on a burned-out pilot who wants to be excused from flying further combat missions. One of the military's rules is that he can be excused from such missions if he has a doctor declare him crazy. However, there is another, contrary rule—Rule 22. It states that anyone rational enough to want to get out of combat cannot possibly be crazy. In other words, it is the ultimate in sanity to want to avoid life-threatening activities. If the pilot follows the first rule and does what is required to avoid flying combat missions, catch-22 will make it impossible for him to get out of those missions.

Lawrence J. Peter and Raymond Hull (1969) intended what they called the Peter Principle to be a humorous characterization of a tendency in bureaucratic organizations to award promotions presumably on the basis of merit. The principle can be succinctly summarized in one sentence: "Employees tend to rise to their level of incompetence." The idea behind the principle is that if an employee does well in her position, she is rewarded by being promoted to a higher level in the organization. If she does well in that new position, she once again is offered a promotion. Promotions continue in this way until the person ends up in a position of authority and responsibility for which she does not possess the required skill set. To the extent that this possibility occurs, the result is an organization in which people in key leadership positions are not up to the task, thereby hampering an organization's ability to fulfill its mission.

Parkinson's Law was similarly conceived as a humorous attempt to point to another source of irrationality in bureaucratic organizations. It was formulated by Cyril Northcote Parkinson (1955), who worked in the British civil service and thus was intimately familiar with the ways that large bureaucratic organizations functioned. Parkinson summarized the law when he wrote that "work expands so as to fill the time available for its completion." Thus, if a bureaucrat is assigned three reports to complete in a month, it will require a month's work to complete all three. If that same employee is assigned two reports during that time, it will take a month to complete two. And the task will still take a month even if the assignment calls for completing only one report.

Another source of irrationality is Robert Merton's ([1949] 1968) **bureaucratic personality**, or someone who follows the rules of the organization to such a great extent that the ability to achieve organizational goals is subverted. For example, an admissions clerk in a hospital emergency department might require incoming patients to fill out so many forms that they do not get needed medical care promptly. Similarly, a teacher might devote so much time and attention to discussing and enforcing classroom rules that little real learning takes place. A government bureaucrat might refuse welfare aid to a deserving person simply because a form was late or filled out incorrectly.

In these and in many other ways, the actual functioning of bureaucracies is at variance with Weber's ideal-typical characterization. However, it is important to remember that Weber was well aware of at least some of these possibilities. His ideal type was created as a methodological tool, *not* as an accurate description of reality.

The Informal Organization

A great deal of research in the twentieth century focused on the **informal organization**—that is, an organization as it actually functions as opposed to the way it is intended to function as depicted, for example, in Weber's ideal-typical formal bureaucracy (Blau 1963). For example, those who occupy offices lower in the bureaucratic hierarchy often have greater knowledge of and competence in specific issues than those who rank above them. Thus, fellow employees may seek the advice of the lower-level bureaucrat rather than the one who ranks higher in the authority structure. Similarly, a recent study found that

> **bureaucratic personality** A type of bureaucrat who slavishly follows the rules of the organization to such an extent that the ability to achieve organizational goals is subverted.
>
> **informal organization** An organization as it really functions as opposed to the way it is intended to function.

those interested in land conservation are more likely to be influenced by informal contacts outside a conservationist organization than by those in the organization (Prell et al. 2010). More generally, the informal organization can help to make up for inadequacies in the formal organization (Gulati and Puranam 2009). It might lead employees to take very useful actions that are ignored by the formal organization. For example, students constitute an informal network that offers advice to fellow students about which faculty members to seek out if looking for an undemanding course or a guaranteed high grade. In addition, "Greek groups" on campus often maintain exam and term paper files for use by their members.

ASK YOURSELF

What specific bureaucracy came to mind when you read about Weber's definition of this type of organization? Is there an informal organization at work there? How is it different from the formal organization? In what ways is it more effective, or less effective, than the formal one?

Employees sometimes do things that exceed what is expected of them by the organization. However, they more often do less, perhaps far less, than they are expected to do. For example, contrary to the dictates of the formal organization, the most important things that take place in an organization may never be put in writing. Employees may find it simply too time-consuming to fill out every form or document everything in writing. Instead, and contrary to the organization's rules, they may handle many tasks orally. In addition, tasks are handled orally so that if anything goes wrong, there is no damning evidence that could jeopardize careers and even the organization as a whole.

The danger of putting things in writing in organizations has only become worse in the age of digitalization. Posts to the Internet, in particular, can exist forever and be circulated widely and endlessly. This danger was pointed up in 2010 and 2011 when a global organization, WikiLeaks, released many previously unpublished official government documents, including some relating to the Afghanistan war. These documents revealed, among other things, secret ties between the Pakistan security forces and the Taliban. The public release of this information jeopardized the lives of people in Afghanistan working undercover for the United States and disrupted the already

Red Tape

Robert K. Merton

troubled Pakistan–U.S. relations. However, there are those, including those involved with WikiLeaks, who feel that secrets and secret agreements pose the greatest dangers to the lives of people. For example, it is widely believed that Pakistan's security forces are secretly helping the Taliban kill American soldiers.

An interesting app, Snapchat, attempts to deal with the problem of information remaining on the Internet forever by automatically deleting posts and photos after a few seconds. While this seems comforting, those who receive the information and photos can save them by taking screenshots. More importantly, the fact is that no such information ever really disappears. As one of the founders of Snapchat said: "'Nothing ever goes away on the Internet'" (Wortham 2013: A3).

While power is supposed to be dispersed throughout the offices in some bureaucracies, it often turns out that the organization becomes an **oligarchy**. That is, a small group of people at the top illegitimately acquire and exercise far more power than they are entitled to have. This can occur in any organization with notable examples being the leaders of the Communist Party in Soviet Russia and to this day in China. Interestingly, this undemocratic process was first described by Robert Michels ([1915] 1962) in the most unlikely of organizations—labor unions and socialist parties that supposedly prized democracy. Michels called this "the iron law of oligarchy" (Guillen 2010). Those in power manipulate the organization (by, for example, structuring elections to work to their advantage) so that they and their supporters can stay in power indefinitely. At the same time, they make it difficult for others to get or to keep power. While oligarchy certainly develops in such organizations, its occurrence is, in reality, neither iron nor a law. That is, most such organizations do not become oligarchical. Nevertheless, the tendency toward oligarchy is another important organizational process not anticipated by Weber's ideal-typical bureaucracy.

Weber's model also makes no provision for infighting within organizations. However, internal squabbles, and outright battles, are everyday phenomena within organizations. This is particularly evident in the government and other very large organizations, where one branch or office often engages in pitched turf battles with others. For example, in his book *Obama's Wars,* investigative journalist Bob Woodward (2010) revealed numerous conflicts within the Obama administration over the direction of the war in Afghanistan. Obama's own advisors clashed. For example, Vice President Joe Biden called the now-deceased Richard Holbrooke, then special representative to Afghanistan, "the most egotistical bastard I ever met" (Baker 2010: A12). There were also conflicts between Obama's advisors and others. For example,

Afghanistan commander General David Petraeus disliked Obama advisor David Axelrod because he was "a complete spin doctor" (Baker 2010: A12). In 2013, Supreme Court Justice Antonin Scalia, before the Court took up a case challenging provisions of the Voting Rights Act of 1965, declared that one of the act's provisions "is not the kind of question you can leave to Congress." He said this knowing that the act had been reauthorized by Congress four times, most recently in 2006 by a 98–0 vote in the Senate and a 390–33 vote in the House. Not surprisingly, his comments were challenged by members of Congress who accused him of judicial activism and failing to understand the proper balance of power between the three branches of government (Cummings 2013). This kind of conflict is also apparent in universities. For example, those in charge of closely related academic departments such as psychology, anthropology, and sociology often battle over increasingly scarce resources. They may even conflict over the direction of the university as a whole and what it should emphasize.

Gendered Organizations

Weber's model also does not account for discrimination within organizations. In the ideal bureaucracy, any worker with the necessary training can fill any job. However, as "gendered organization" theorists, such as Joan Acker (1990, 2009), have shown, bureaucracies do not treat all workers the same (Pager, Western, and Bonikowski 2009). Jobs often are designed for an idealized worker—one who has no other obligations except to the organization. Women, and sometimes men, who carry a larger responsibility for child rearing can have difficulty fitting this model (Williams 2001). Women may face the "competing devotions" of motherhood and work (Blair-Loy 2003; Wharton and Blair-Loy 2006). Organizations may also discriminate (consciously or unconsciously) in hiring and promotions, with white men (who tend to populate the higher levels of bureaucracies) being promoted over women and minorities (Alvesson and Billing 2009; Ortiz and Roscigno 2009). Some women in male-dominated organizations find they hit a "glass ceiling." That is, they reach a certain level of authority in a company after which there is a decline in their chances of additional promotions (Acker 2009; Appelbaum, Asham, and Argheyd 2011a, 2011b; Gorman and Kmec 2009). They can see the top—hence the "glass"—but find it difficult, if not impossible, to reach it. Within other organizations, particularly female-dominated ones, men

oligarchy An organization led by a small group of people who illegitimately acquire and exercise far more power than they are entitled to have.

can find themselves riding the "glass escalator" (Williams 1995). This is an invisible force that propels them past equally competent, or even more competent, women to positions of leadership and authority (Williams, Muller, and Kilanski 2012).

In a global context American female executives face a "double-paned" glass ceiling. There is the pane associated with the glass ceiling that exists in the employing company in the United States, and there is a second pane that is encountered when women executives seek work experience in a foreign locale of the corporation. This is a growing problem since experience overseas is an increasing requirement for top-level management positions in multinational corporations. However, corporations have typically "masculinized" these expatriate positions and thereby disadvantaged females. Among the problems experienced by women who succeed in getting these positions are sexual harassment, a lack of availability of programs (e.g., career counseling) routinely available to men, a lack of adequate mentoring, and male managers who are more likely to promote male rather than female expatriates. Much of the blame for this problem lies in the structure of the multinational corporations, and with the men who occupy high-level management positions within them. However, research has shown that female managers' greater passivity and lesser willingness to promote themselves for such expatriate management positions contributes to their difficulties (Insch, McIntyre, and Napier 2008).

While most of these ideas have been developed on the basis of studies of American organizations, they likely apply as well, or better, globally. For example, a recent study in Durban, South Africa, found that the glass ceiling exists there, as well (Kiaye and Singh 2013).

The idea of a glass ceiling relates to vertical mobility—and its absence—for women in organizations. A related concept is the "glass cage," which deals with the horizontal segregation of women (and other minorities) (Kalev 2009). The idea here is that men and women doing the same or similar jobs operate in separate and segregated parts of the organization. As in the case of the glass ceiling, women can see what is going on in other cages. However, compared to men, it is more difficult for them to move between the cages. Although the cage is made of glass, the skills and abilities of women tend to be less visible, and, as a result, stereotypes about them abound. In addition, women

What accounts for the fact that the so-called glass escalator often elevates men to positions of power in organizations, but particularly in female-dominated ones? Is this the result you would expect in such organizations?

have less communication with those outside the cage, are less likely to learn about jobs available there, are not as likely to get high-profile assignments, and are less likely to get needed training. The situation confronting women would improve if there were more collaboration across the boundaries of the glass cage. Of course, the ultimate solution involves the elimination of both the glass cage and the glass ceiling.

A third interesting idea here is that of the "glass cliff" (Ryan and Haslam 2005). The glass ceiling and the glass cage deal with barriers to the mobility of women within organizations. The glass cliff describes what can happen to women who experience upward mobility when the organization is going through hard times. The implication is that women who rise to high levels at such times end up in highly precarious positions. Of course, the same would be true of men, but Ryan and Haslam (2005) find that women are more likely than men to move into positions on boards of directors when the organization has been performing badly. This means they are more likely than males to find themselves at the edge of that organizational cliff. A disproportionate number of those women are likely to be demoted or fall off that cliff and lose their jobs.

Gendering Globalization

The International Monetary Fund (IMF) is a global organization meant to promote economic growth and reduce poverty around the world, but when its methods prove unpopular—as in Greece, where violent protests against austerity measures erupted—its entire purpose can come into question.

Problems in Organizations

The ideal-typical bureaucracy also makes no provision for an array of problems in the organization or for problematic organizations (Friedrichs 2007). However, in the real world there is no shortage of either. The most heinous example of a problematic (to put it mildly) organization is the Nazi bureaucracy responsible for the murder of 6 million Jews, and others, during the Holocaust (Bauman 1989). Al-Qaeda, the Mafia, and Mexican drug cartels, among many others, would also be considered by most people to be problematic organizations. In addition, many less developed countries in the world regard global organizations like the International Monetary Fund and the World Bank as problematic organizations because of the damaging austerity programs and other forms of "structural adjustment" they impose on recipient countries in exchange for monetary assistance and other help (Babb 2005).

Sexual harassment is one of many organizational problems (Lopez, Hodson, and Roscigno 2009) that are less spectacular than those discussed above, but are much more common. **Sexual harassment** involves unwanted sexual attention, such as sexually oriented remarks and jokes, advances, and requests that take place in the workplace or in other settings (Zippel 2007; see Chapter 9). Sexual harassment is widely practiced, and a great many women are harmed by it. Usually it takes the form of high-ranking men demanding sexual favors from those, usually women, in positions lower than them in the hierarchy. For example, there have been many allegations of sexual

harassment or abuse of female service members in the armed services. There have been mounting criticisms of the armed services for failing to react adequately to these forms of deviant behavior (Schemo 2003; Shear 2013; Verkaik 2006). More serious are cases of sexual assault. As is the case with harassment, there has been mounting evidence, as well as criticisms, of sexual assault in the military. Another example is assaults on young boys by priests and other church officials. They have caused great problems for the boys and officials who have been caught, as well as for one of the largest organizations in the world, the Catholic Church. This has been a huge problem not only because of the behavior of the priests, but also because Church officials have not done nearly enough to dismiss those responsible and make it more difficult for such assaults to occur in the future (Doyle 2003). This was a factor in the abdication of Pope Benedict XVI in early 2013.

Disasters (and other unplanned outcomes) are deeply problematic for organizations. They often occur as the result of rational organizational processes (Vaughan 1996). For example, in the 1980s the National Aeronautics and Space Administration (NASA) operated on the basis of what it considered a highly reliable and rational plan. As a result, it focused, among many other things, on a variety of quantifiable factors in order to keep the space shuttle *Challenger* on schedule for its launch. In doing so, it cut a number of corners and engaged in various economies. These actions made sense from the perspective of NASA as a rationalized organization. However, they contributed to the disaster on January 28, 1986, in which *Challenger*'s fuel tank broke apart causing the in-flight destruction of the shuttle and the death of seven crew members.

Contemporary Changes in Bureaucracy

In the last several decades bureaucratic organizations have undergone a number of important changes that do not fit well with Weber's view of organizations. For one thing, contrary to Weber's thinking on the likelihood of their growth

> **sexual harassment** Unwanted sexual attention that takes place in the workplace or other settings.

and spread, many of the largest organizations, especially industrial organizations and labor unions, have been forced to downsize dramatically (Cooper, Pandey, and Campbell 2012). The idea that "bigger is better" is no longer the rule in most organizations. Instead of constantly adding new functions, and more employees, organizations are now likely to focus on their "core competencies." For example, the Ford Motor Company is focusing on manufacturing automobiles and not, as it once did, on making, among many other things, the steel for the frame and the rubber for the tires. Ford also sold off the Volvo and Jaguar lines in order to focus on the Ford brand. In essence, organizations have come to concentrate on becoming "lean and mean" (Harrison 1994). Many newer organizations such as Facebook and even Google are likely to learn lessons from the problems experienced by organizational giants like Ford. They will seek to avoid ever losing their focus or becoming too large and diverse. As a result, it is unlikely that they will ever need to downsize or simplify their organization to the degree that Ford has in order to accomplish these goals.

To adapt to a rapidly changing environment, contemporary organizations have also been forced to become more flexible and more agile than is suggested by the ideal-typical bureaucracy. For example, it appears that Ford has become flexible enough to compete with rising automobile manufacturers such as Hyundai. However, when today's organizations lack such flexibility, there is a strong likelihood that they will decline or disappear. For example, Blockbuster and its large chain of video stores failed to adapt sufficiently and fast enough to competition from Netflix and its movies-by-mail and later streaming of movies, as well as to Redbox and its video-dispensing kiosks. As a result, Blockbuster went bankrupt in 2010. Its last store closed in late 2013, but it continues to rent movies online and through its own video kiosks. However, it lags far behind Netflix and Redbox in the latter domains.

Yet another important organizational development is the increasing trend toward **outsourcing**, or the transfer of activities once performed by one organization to another organization in exchange for money (Ritzer and Lair 2007). Since the early 2000s, outsourcing has increased dramatically. For example, in 1989 U.S. companies spent between $9 billion and $12 billion a year to outsource

The 2010 Deepwater Horizon oil spill (shown here during a controlled burn process) killed 11 workers and poured millions of gallons of oil into the Gulf of Mexico for 3 months before it was capped. British Petroleum, which owned the oil rig, was widely held to be responsible for the disaster and was charged with various criminal acts in the aftermath. Its CEO resigned and the company continues to deal with the clean-up effort and resulting lawsuits.

information technology (IT) jobs (Krass 1990; Lacity and Hirscheim 1993), "from medical transcription to nanotechnology research" (Davis-Blake and Broschak 2009: 322). By 2008 that number had reached $55 billion, and it was expected to grow between 15 and 20 percent per year over the succeeding five years (Oshri, Kotlarsky, and Willcocks 2009). Companies have become more likely to outsource functions such as those handled traditionally by human resource departments (Korkki 2012). Hospitals outsource the operation of their emergency rooms to businesses that employ people—including physicians— devoted to such work. The government, including the federal government, also outsources work to other organizations, especially private businesses. An example that has received a lot of negative publicity is the U.S. government's outsourcing of many military and paramilitary activities in Iraq to a company known as Blackwater. When news media raised alarms over the company's involvement in unwarranted killings and use of unnecessary force, the company changed its name to Xe Services, and in 2011 it became Academi.

> **outsourcing** The transfer of activities once performed by one organization to another organization in exchange for money.

World Bank and IMF

Bernard Madoff

London Riots

One form of offshore outsourcing that has become familiar to many U.S. consumers is Indian call centers that provide customer service and product support for U.S. firms. Why are some employees in such centers encouraged to assume American identities?

Another recent trend in organizations not anticipated by Weber's ideal-typical bureaucracy is to turn work formerly performed by officeholders over to clients. For example, we are increasingly filling out census forms on our own, thereby doing work that used to be done by census takers. We are scanning checks into our cell phones instead of handing them to a teller, reviewing restaurants and movies online rather than reading a review by a professional critic, talking about our experiences with products or brands on social networking sites instead of passively accepting advertising messages from producers, and scanning our own groceries in self-checkout lanes. More and more, we are scanning our own groceries; the first self-checkout machine was installed in the United States in 1992. It is estimated that there will be 430,000 such machines in operation in 2014. In taking on these tasks, clients and consumers are turned into producers, at least for a time. In other words, consumers have been transformed into *prosumers,* combining the acts of consumption and production (Ritzer, Dean, and Jurgenson 2012) (see Chapter 3). This is yet another wide-ranging and pervasive change that is dramatically transforming the nature of organizations and organizational life.

Globalization and Bureaucracy

Most organizations of any significant size have become increasingly global. They are affected by numerous global realities and changes and in many cases have, themselves, become global forces and players. The global reach of McDonald's is well known. It has more than 33,000 restaurants in 119 countries throughout the world. However, in the fast-food industry, Yum! Brands (Pizza Hut, KFC, etc.) is in slightly more countries—120—and has over 5,000 more restaurants than McDonald's. Wal-Mart is another American global powerhouse with 10,700 stores in 27 countries. There are other organizations with a presence in the United States that have roots elsewhere in the world. Examples include IKEA, based in Sweden, with 301 stores in 41 countries; H&M, an apparel retailer from Sweden; T-Mobile, a telecommunications company originating in Germany; HSBC, a financial services provider from Hong Kong and Shanghai; and Zara International, a fashion retailer, whose home base is in Spain (Ritzer 2013a).

Spanning much of the globe is a challenge to any organization and forces it to adapt to global realities in innumerable ways. Ford Motor Company, for example, recognized some years ago that producing a different model car for every country or global region was very inefficient. And so it focused on the manufacture and sale of a global car, the Ford Focus.

Globalization has also accelerated the transfer of work to organizations in other countries, known as **offshore outsourcing.** It takes many forms, but the one we are most familiar with is the outsourcing of call center work. A call center is a centralized office that handles a large volume of telephone calls asking an organization for information and help. At first many U.S. organizations outsourced such work to call centers in the United States. More recently, much of that work has been outsourced offshore because it can be done outside the United States much less expensively.

McDonaldization and Bureaucracy

During the early twenty-first century the fast-food restaurant can be seen as the best example of the ongoing process of rationalization first described by Weber (Ritzer 2013a). While the fast-food restaurant is a relatively new and important organizational development, it is continuous with the bureaucracy and its basic principles: efficiency, predictability, calculability, control, and the

offshore outsourcing The transfer of work to organizations in other countries.

ACTIVE SOCIOLOGY

Are Prosumers Changing the Way We Travel?

Society is increasingly rearranging itself around our dual role as *prosumers*, that is, both consumers and producers. For instance, in the past professional travel agents guided all your trip planning, from finding the best family vacation deals or the most romantic destinations to making plane and hotel reservations. Today, whether you're embarking on a summer vacation or a Friday night date, you are the planner, and countless ideas and tools are at your fingertips. Sites like Trip Advisor (www.tripadvisor.com) allow you to purchase all your leisure and travel needs at one site—airline tickets, hotels, restaurants, and rental cars—and consult reviews and images posted by other amateur travelers. You can even take these tools on the go with a smartphone app or mobile connection to your Facebook account.

1. Browse the Trip Advisor site and make a comprehensive list of everything a user can do there.

2. How much of what you can do and see on the site is provided by a travel industry professional, and how much is provided by prosumers?

3. How do you think the participation of prosumers has changed the leisure and travel industry?

4. What other travel and leisure sites or apps do you know of that turn the customer into the prosumer?

---

seemingly inevitable irrationalities of rationality. What, then, distinguishes McDonaldized fast-food restaurants from bureaucracies?

McDonaldization is applicable to both large organizations and relatively small organizations, most of which are independent operations, not franchises. The principles of bureaucracy tended to be applied only to state governments and giant corporations like Ford and Wal-Mart. Such bureaucracies still exist, although in many cases they are much smaller than they once were. The principles of McDonaldization can be applied not only to large corporations such as Starbucks but also to small restaurants and all sorts of small enterprises. In short, the model of the McDonaldized fast-food restaurant has much wider applicability than the bureaucratic model. There is an infinitely greater number of small enterprises throughout the United States and the world than there are state governments and large corporations.

McDonaldization is applicable to both consumption-oriented organizations and production-oriented organizations. The bureaucratic model was most applicable, outside of the government, to large production-oriented corporations. However, the United States has moved away from a society dominated by work and production to one dominated by consumption. As a result, the large corporation involved in goods production has declined in importance, at least in the United States and other developed countries. In its place we have seen the rise of similarly large corporations, such as Subway, Wal-Mart, and IKEA, devoted to consumption. While the corporate structures of these organizations remain highly bureaucratized, their real heart lies in the numerous smaller outlets that constitute the source of income and profit for the organization. Thus, of greatest importance now is the McDonaldization of those outlets and not the bureaucratization of the larger organization in which they exist.

ASK YOURSELF

Employees at fast-food restaurants are trained to smile and treat customers in an overtly friendly way. Why do you think being customer-friendly is more important to McDonaldized systems than to traditional bureaucracies? What is the goal of this user friendliness, and why aren't bureaucracies more user friendly?

Despite the spread of McDonaldization, some are speculating that it, like bureaucratization, has passed its peak. For example, important online organizations such as eBay may be replacing McDonald's as models of contemporary organization. The basic dimensions of eBay are very different from those of McDonaldized organizations:

- *Variety.* eBay offers millions of products; McDonald's only a few dozen.

Outsourcing

Globalization Backlash

- *Unpredictability.* The predictable products of McDonald's are quite unlike the highly unpredictable products on eBay—for example, a Hero Chinese Symbol Engraved Stone Ocean Pebble Rock.

- *Highly specific and limited control.* Whereas eBay sellers interact directly with buyers of their products, with little involvement of the eBay organization, McDonaldized systems exercise more widespread control.

As our world continues to move in the direction of digitization, an online site such as eBay may prove to be a more useful organizational model than McDonald's.

ASK YOURSELF

Do you think the dimensions of eBayization described above are unique to eBay? Why or why not? Do you believe eBayization is a more useful concept than McDonaldization, or do you feel eBay is simply a highly McDonaldized organization? Why?

NETWORK ORGANIZATIONS

The bureaucracy and the fast-food restaurant both continue to be important in the early twenty-first century. However, organizations continue to change and to evolve. Further, entirely new organizational forms are coming into existence. One such new form is the network organization. As we will discuss in more detail below, the **network organization** is defined by its networks, especially those based on and linked together by information (Blaschke, Schoeneborn, and Seidl 2012). The network organization came about in the wake of the revolution in informational technology in the United States in the 1970s. The developments included the penetration of television deep into American life and the introduction of home computers, PDAs, and the Internet (S. Allan 2007; Van Dijk 2012). The network model is also inextricably entwined with globalization. Most of the important functions and processes in the information age are increasingly dominated by these networks, and many of them are global in scope. This revolution led, in turn, to a fundamental restructuring of the global capitalist system beginning in the 1980s. For example, multinational corporations grew in importance, in part because of great improvements in the ability to communicate globally. Those corporations that were narrowly nation-based experienced serious declines or were, themselves, transformed into multinationals.

Characteristics of the Network Organization

This new organizational form has several notable characteristics. Of greatest importance is the idea that an organization is composed of several **networks**, or "interconnected nodes." A network organization has the following characteristics:

- *Horizontal structure.* Instead of the vertical and hierarchical structures that characterize classic bureaucracies, network organizations are flatter, meaning that there are fewer positions between the top of the organization and the bottom.

- *Fuzzy boundaries.* Network organizations are **not** seen as distinct entities with clear and definite boundaries, as would be the case with a bureaucracy. Rather, organizations intertwine with one another in many ways. Most obviously, they form strategic alliances with other organizations that have similar or complementary goals.

- *Dispersed decision making.* Many of the differences between network organizations and bureaucracies stem from a number of highly successful Japanese innovations. One such innovation is more collective decision making involving many more people in the organization in the decision-making process.

- *Flexible production.* Manufacturing organizations with a network model have moved away from mass production and toward more flexible production methods, such as variable and limited production runs.

An organization with these characteristics is, in comparison with a bureaucracy, more open, more capable of expansion, more dynamic, and better able to innovate without disrupting the system.

In the global information economy, at least in developed nations, the nature of work is being transformed. Workers, including manufacturing employees, are dealing more with information and less with material processes (Caprile and Pascual 2011). This has reduced the total number of employees needed, even as output increases (see Figure 5.2). In addition, the network organization allows for new kinds

> **network organization** A new organizational form that is flat and horizontal; is intertwined with other organizations; is run and managed in very different ways than traditional organizations; uses more flexible production methods; and is composed of a series of interconnected nodes.
>
> **networks** "Interconnected nodes" that are open, capable of unlimited expansion, dynamic, and able to innovate without disrupting the system in which they exist.

of work arrangements because information can flow anywhere, especially anywhere there is a computer. Thus, for example, more people can work from the comfort of their homes, in transit on airplanes, and in hotels anyplace in the world (Alexander, Ettema, and Dijst 2010; Kaufman-Scarbrough 2006). This change is reflected in the 2009 movie *Up in the Air*, which depicts efforts to move away from firing people in person and toward doing it via videoconferencing on the computer. More personally, I now teleteach some of my graduate-level courses at the University of Maryland from my winter home in Florida.

Informationalism

The processing of knowledge, or what Manuel Castells (1996, 1997, 1998; Subramanian and Katz 2011; S. Williams 2012) calls **informationalism**, is a key feature of network organization. Forces of production and consumption, such as factories and shopping malls, are linked through knowledge and information. Thus, for example, the stocking of shelves at Wal-Mart is done nearly automatically. Computerized technology at the local Wal-Mart tracks stock on hand and transmits the information to centralized warehouses. As the stock is being depleted, new shipments are being sent out automatically so that the shelves at the local Wal-Mart will remain well stocked.

Informationalism has five basic characteristics:

- Technologies act on information, such as the depletion of stock at Wal-Mart.

- These technologies have a pervasive effect, as information transmitted to personal computers, PDAs, and smartphones increasingly becomes a part of all human activity.

- All organizations, and other systems using information technologies, are defined by a "networking logic" that allows them to affect a wide variety of processes and organizations to which they are linked. For example, Wal-Mart has linkages to its many suppliers throughout the world.

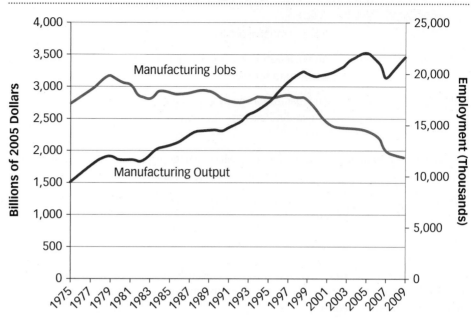

FIGURE 5.2 • U.S. Manufacturing: Output versus Jobs, 1975–2009

SOURCE: Data from Federal Reserve, Bureau of Labor Statistics, compiled by Veronique de Rugy, Mercatus Center at George Mason University. In John Lounsbury, *U.S. Trade Deficits Worth 26 Million Jobs, Credit Writedowns*, February 10, 2011. Copyright © 2011 Mercatus Center at George Mason University.

- The new technologies are highly flexible allowing them to adapt and to change constantly.

- The specific technologies associated with information are already merging into a highly integrated system that cuts across many different organizations and areas of the world. Thus, for example, the Internet, e-mail, and text messaging link innumerable global organizations.

As a result of informationalism, a new, increasingly profitable global informational economy has emerged. The productivity of firms and nations depends on their ability to generate, process, and apply knowledge-based information efficiently. Global communication systems allow those involved in this economy to operate as a unit on a worldwide scale. While it is a global system, there are regional differences, even among those areas—North America, the European Union, the Asia-Pacific—that are at the heart of the new global economy. Other regions such as sub-Saharan Africa are largely excluded, as are pockets of deprivation in the developed world, including inner cities in the United States.

The network organization, as well as the informationalism that defines it, is the latest organizational

Outsourcing Education

Manuel Castells

CHECKPOINT 5.1   TYPES OF ORGANIZATIONS

Bureaucracy	A highly rational organization characterized by efficiency.
Informal organization	An organization as it really functions, as opposed to the way it is intended to function.
Oligarchy	An organization led by a small group of people who illegitimately acquire and exercise far more power than they are entitled to have.
Gendered organization	An organization in which gender plays a large role in determining a person's position and career progression.
Network organization	An organization defined by networks based on and linked by information.

form to draw sociologists' attention, but it is certainly not the last. New organizational forms are likely to emerge as society and the world continue to change.

SOCIETIES

Sociologists have traditionally defined society as a complex pattern of social relationships that is bounded in space and persists over time (Ray 2007). This definition has two key characteristics. First, it is very abstract. Second, this abstractness allows it to encompass the gamut of social relationships. Thus, in these terms, a triad (a three-person group; see Chapter 4) and any larger group would be a kind of society, as would the United States and other countries, as well as global organizations such as the United Nations and the International Monetary Fund.

There is a long tradition in sociology of thinking about, and studying, such highly diverse societal forms. A classic analysis of this type was created by Ferdinand Toennies ([1887] 1957) who differentiated between two broad types of societies—*gemeinschaft* and *gesellschaft*. He labeled traditional societies **gemeinschaft** societies and defined them as being characterized by face-to-face relations. Toennies considered families, rural villages, and small towns to be *gemeinschaft* societies. Such societies tend to be quite small because they are based on such intimate interaction. Relationships between people were valued for their intrinsic qualities such as familiarity and closeness and not, or at least not merely, for their utility. *Gemeinschaft* societies continue to exist in many parts of the world, including the United States.

More modern societies are **gesellschaft** societies characterized by impersonal, distant, and limited social relationships. In such societies, people tend to enter relationships for what they can gain from them rather than

for their intrinsic qualities. That is, relationships are often a means to an end. *Gesellschaft* societies can be small in scale, and social groups and communities can have the characteristics of a *gesellschaft* society, such as impersonality. For instance, employees within an office may work together 40 hours or more a week, but only interact with one another in a highly businesslike way. Furthermore, after they go home to their "real life" and intimate relationships, they are likely to rarely, if ever, interact with co-workers outside of the workplace. However, *gesellschaft* societies are much more likely to be large-scale societies, or to exist within them.

Of course, *gemeinschaft* and *gesellschaft* are ideal types. In the real world, including today's world, aspects of both exist in all societies. The abstract and broad-ranging definition of society mentioned above encompasses both *gemeinschaft* and *gesellschaft* societies, and everything in between. Furthermore, both concepts can be applied to every social relationship from the smallest groups to the largest societies such as China.

Although the earlier general definition of society has its utility, *society* can be more narrowly and specifically—and usefully—defined as a relatively large population that lives in a given territory, has a social structure, and shares a culture. The United States, China, and Spain would be societies in this macro-level sense of the term. This definition also fits the thrust of this chapter, which ends with a discussion of the most macroscopic level of social organization: the global society.

One of the best-known theories of society in this sense was created by leading structural-functionalist Talcott Parsons. In fact, Parsons wrote a book titled *Societies* (Parsons 1966). As a structural-functionalist, Parsons had a very positive view of macro-level societies. He was concerned with the major structures of societies, including the economy, the political system, systems responsible for transmitting culture and its norms and values

> **gemeinschaft** societies Traditional societies characterized by face-to-face relations.
>
> **gesellschaft** societies Modern societies characterized by impersonal, distant, and limited social relationships.

(e.g., schools), and the legal system, which is responsible for the integration of society. Clearly, these are key components of society in the macro sense of the term.

RISK SOCIETY

Sociologists who study societies often ask big questions about them and their changing nature. One of the most notable of the recent efforts to think about the issues facing society as a whole is the work of the German sociologist Ulrich Beck (Anais and Hier 2012). Until recently, it was the norm to think of society as being dominated by industry. In "industrial society" the key issue was wealth and how to distribute it more evenly. This problem continues to concern many sociologists (see Chapter 7). However, Beck (1992) argues that we have moved from an industrial society to a **risk society** where the central issue is risk, especially how to prevent, minimize, and channel it. In addition, while in industrial society a central concern was equality, in risk society the focus shifts to how to remain safe in the face of increasing risk. Most importantly, there is a big difference between the two types of society in the ways in which solidarity is achieved. In an industrial society, solidarity is achieved by people joining together in the search for the positive goal of creating a more equal society. In a risk society, solidarity is achieved through the largely negative and defensive goal of being spared from danger. The implication is that risk society is weaker, more individualized, and less laudable than industrial society and its humanitarian goal of increased equality.

What accounts for the emergence of risk society? The key is that the risks are far greater today than ever before and no society is safe from them. Many societies produce various risks (air pollution, the danger from nuclear plants and weapons) that threaten not only themselves, but other societies. Furthermore, even when risks are exported, consciously or unconsciously, to other societies, they tend to boomerang back on the society that is the source of the risks. For example, terrorism is a risk to the United States and other societies. The United States has sought to cope with it by combatting it outside its own borders (e.g., in Afghanistan and more recently in North Africa). However, those efforts have provoked attacks on the United States and its interests elsewhere in the world.

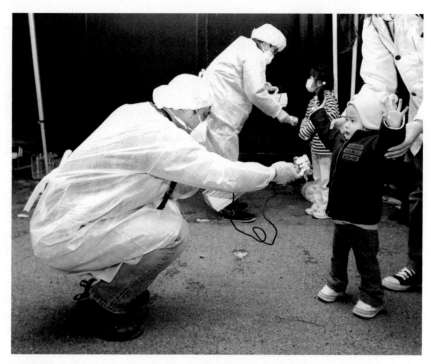

Has Japan become a risk society in the wake of the continuing leaks from its devastated Fukushima nuclear power plant? Here officials check children from the evacuation area around the plant for radiation.

Globalization is the major reason why there are far greater risks to society than ever before. Risks in one society easily flow to many other societies. For example, because of relatively easy and inexpensive air travel, a flu outbreak in one society can more easily and quickly engulf many other societies. Thus, modern risks are not easily restricted to one locale or society. A nuclear accident such as the one that occurred at Chernobyl in Russia in 1986 can release radiation that affects surrounding societies and ultimately much of the world. Modern risks are also not limited by time. The Chernobyl accident led to genetic defects in Russians and those in neighboring societies for decades after the accident.

Globalization has led some sociologists to call into question the importance of society (and the nation-state), arguing that in the contemporary world it is necessary to think about a global world. Debates about the possibility of global citizenship are one example of how the idea of globalization is reshaping how we think about the boundaries of what we call society (Kivisto and Faist 2007: 138–140). Other sociologists have suggested that globalization requires a perspective on society that sees it as more fluid and unstable than would be implied by the work of earlier sociologists. Thus, Zygmunt Bauman (2007: 1) contends that we live in "liquid times" where structures and institutions no longer "keep their shape for long."

> **risk society** A society whose central issue is preventing, minimizing, and channeling risk.

Google's Dominance

CHECKPOINT 5.2 — COMPARING TYPES OF SOCIETIES

Gemeinschaft society: A society characterized by face-to-face relationships, such as families, rural villages, and small towns.

Gesellschaft society: A society characterized by impersonal, distant, and limited social relationships governed by the desire for gain, such as a workplace.

Industrial society: A society whose central issue is wealth and its even distribution.

Risk society: A society whose central issue is risk and how to prevent, minimize, and channel it.

It is clear from the preceding discussion that sociologists who analyze societies do not stop at their borders, but also examine the relationships among and between societies. In fact, there is an entire field—international relations—that deals with these relationships. However, in recent years the focus of such scholarship has shifted beyond societies and even their interrelationships to the even more macroscopic global level.

THE GLOBAL DOMAIN

Most work on the global level does not start with the concept of a society, but rather works with a different set of basic concepts. All of these concepts are consistent with the macroscopic sense of society:

- A **nation** is a large group of people linked through common descent, culture, language, or territory. Nations can exist in contiguous geographic areas regardless of country borders. For example, the Kurds live in what is called Kurdistan, a region that overlaps Iraq, Iran, and Turkey (see Figure 5.3). Nations can also be spread throughout much of the world, such as the Roma people, or gypsies, who live throughout Europe and increasingly in the United States.

- A **state** is a political organizational structure with relatively autonomous officeholders (e.g., in the United States the president functions largely independently of Congress and the Supreme Court) and with its own rules and resources coming largely from taxes. The U.S. government is an example of a state.

- A **nation-state** is an entity that encompasses both the populations that define themselves as a nation and the organizational structure of the state. Israel is a nation-state since it has a state government and encompasses a nation of Jews (although there are large numbers of Muslims in Israel and in the occupied territories, as well).

Of greater importance in the global age is the idea that these entities, especially the nation-state, are losing influence because of globalization and broad global processes.

CONTROLLING GLOBAL FLOWS

The nation-state is under siege largely because it has lost or is losing control over a number of global flows (Cerny 2007). In many ways, it is informationalism that threatens the nation-state. E-mail and tweets, to take two examples, flow around the world readily and quickly. There is little or nothing the nation-state can do to stop or limit those flows, although China, among others, keeps trying. One example is China's Internet "firewall," which is described in the next "Digital Living" box. During the 2011 uprisings in Egypt, the government attempted to locate an "off switch" for the Internet to prevent the flow of news and images about the protests. However, it was unable to block them completely (Richtel 2011b). There are many economic, financial, and technological flows around the world that involve information of various kinds. Global information flows have the potential to subvert the authority of nation-states because they cover a much larger geographic area than the nation-state. This is especially true of information that would cast a negative light on the nation-state. One example would be the distribution of information throughout China about the great inequality that exists there or its human rights abuses.

A more specific example of the decreasing ability of nation-states to isolate themselves from global processes is the economic crisis that began in the United States in late 2007 and cascaded rapidly around the world. For example, dramatic drops in the American stock market

nation A group of people who share similar cultural, religious, ethnic, linguistic, and territorial characteristics.

state A political body organized for government and civil rule, with relatively autonomous officeholders and with its own rules and resources coming largely from taxes.

nation-state The combination of a nation with a geographic and political structure; encompasses both the populations that define themselves as a nation with various shared characteristics and the organizational structure of the state.

FIGURE 5.3 • Distribution of Kurds in the Middle East and Vicinity, 2012

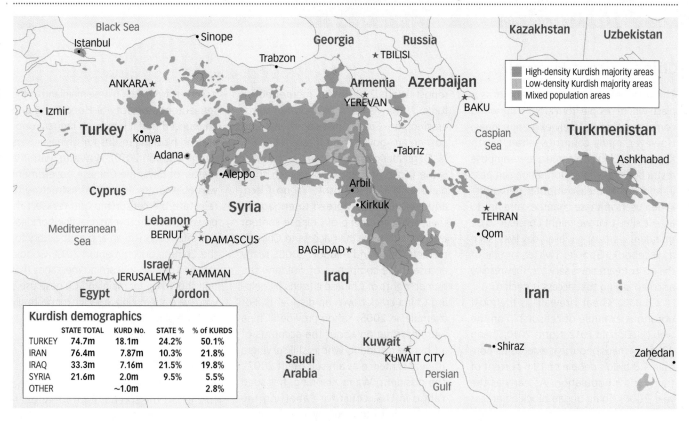

Kurdish demographics

	STATE TOTAL	KURD No.	STATE %	% of KURDS
TURKEY	74.7m	18.1m	24.2%	50.1%
IRAN	76.4m	7.87m	10.3%	21.8%
IRAQ	33.3m	7.16m	21.5%	19.8%
SYRIA	21.6m	2.0m	9.5%	5.5%
OTHER		~1.0m		2.8%

Legend:
- High-density Kurdish majority areas
- Low-density Kurdish majority areas
- Mixed population areas

SOURCE: *Distribution of Kurds in the Middle East and Vicinity, 2012*, The Gulf/2000 Project, School of International and Public Affairs, Columbia University.

(see the 2011 movie *Margin Call* for a fictionalized treatment of the origins of that economic crisis) were followed by declines in many other stock markets in the world. Similarly, bank failures in the United States were quickly followed by even more ruinous bank failures in other countries, most notably Iceland and Ireland. This series of events illustrates the importance and power of global flows, and demonstrates the inability of the nation-state to do much, if anything, to limit its impact within its borders on its economy and the lives of its citizens. "In a global financial system, national borders are porous" (Landler 2008a: C1). Global economic flows move more quickly than ever, if not instantaneously, and are so fluid that they are difficult, if not impossible, to stop with the barriers available to nation-states.

Information and economic flows are just two of the many global flows that nation-states cannot control. Among the others are flows of undocumented immigrants, new social movements, expertise in various domains, terrorists, criminals, drugs, money (including laundered money, and other financial instruments), human trafficking (as shown in Figure 5.4), and much else. Then there are global problems such as AIDS, H1N1 flu, tuberculosis, and the effects of global warming that flow around the world readily and cannot be handled very well by a nation-state operating on its own.

A great deal of evidence today indicates that the nation-state has become increasingly porous, but the fact is that no nation-state has ever been able to exercise complete control over its borders (Bauman 1992). For example, people's ability to travel from one European country to another was largely unimpeded until the World War I era when passports were introduced on a large scale for the first time. It is not the porosity of the nation-state that is new, but rather the dramatic increase in that porosity.

Thus, the largest unit of analysis in sociology has now become the globe and especially the global flows that best define globalization today. The concept of globalization appears throughout this book in an informal sense, but it is now time for the formal definition of globalization: "a transplanetary *process* or set of *processes* involving increasing *liquidity* and the growing multidirectional *flows* of people, objects, places and information as well as the *structures* they encounter and create that are *barriers* to, or

Nation-States

DIGITAL LIVING

China's Great Firewall

The Internet is often talked about as a place where people from around the world come together to freely exchange ideas. However, many countries—Iran, North Korea, and China, to name a few—impose restrictions on what information can pass in and out of their computer networks. When users in these countries attempt to access sites that we might consider to be mundane parts of our everyday lives, such as Facebook, Google, Twitter, or one of the mainstream news services, they receive a screen saying that access is denied.

China's "Great Firewall" is the most notorious example of censorship on the web (McDonald 2012; Norris 2010; Zhang 2006), perhaps because it extends to more than 1.3 billion people or 19.6 percent of the world's population. As early as the year 2000, China began blocking access to foreign news sites such as the *New York Times*, CNN, the BBC, and *Le Monde*. Named after the Great Wall of China, the Great Firewall is the world's largest form of online censorship. According to one report (Watts 2006), "An internet police force . . . trawls websites and chatrooms, erasing anti-Communist comments and posting pro-government messages."

Of greater concern to many in the West is the fact that many leading tech companies (including Microsoft, Yahoo, Cisco, and Google) have agreed to engage in their own censorship of Chinese content as a condition for their access to Chinese markets (Dann and Haddow 2008). Many accuse these companies of violating the human rights of Chinese citizens by helping China crack down on dissidents. For example, in 2005, Yahoo provided China with information about the accounts of a Chinese dissident, who is still serving a 10-year sentence as a result (Helft 2007). The dissident, Wang Xiaoning, has sued Yahoo in U.S. court for "abetting the commission of torture" by working with Chinese authorities.

In 2010, after Google's systems were hacked by agents with alleged ties to the Chinese government, the company moved its servers from the Chinese mainland to the semiautonomous city of Hong Kong and announced that it would no longer cooperate in blocking results for Chinese users (Stone and Xin 2010). However, within a matter of days, the Chinese government was able to use its own infrastructure to reinstate the censorship and reassert its power and control over global flows of ideas and information. In an apparent victory for the Chinese government in 2013, Google stopped displaying warning messages that had shown up for mainland Chinese users who were attempting to search for politically sensitive phrases (Halliday 2013).

Think About It

Are organizations like Google and Yahoo furthering the spread of informationalism, their own corporate goals, or both by attempting to operate under restrictions in China? What do you think it would take for the government of China to allow its citizens free access to the Internet?

---

expedite, those flows" (Ritzer 2010c; see also Chapter 15). Clearly, this is a view that goes beyond the nation-state and sees it enmeshed in, and subordinated to, a global set of flows and structures.

Globalization is increasingly characterized by great flows of not just information, ideas, and images but also objects and people. For example, food now flows more quickly and to more people around the world. Examples of food being sold in locales far from their source include fresh fruit from Chile (Goldfrank 2005), fresh sushi from Japan, and live lobsters from Maine. Looking at a very different kind of flow, migration within countries and from one country to another has become more common as well.

In addition, other kinds of physical objects are becoming increasingly more liquid and thus able to flow more easily. Not long ago we might have been amazed by our ability to order a book from Amazon and receive it via an express package delivery system in as little as a day. That method, however, now seems notably sluggish compared to the speed of downloading that book, in perhaps less than a minute, on a wireless device such as Amazon's Kindle or Apple's iPad. That level of liquidity and flow is a major aspect of, as well as a major contributor to, globalization.

LANDSCAPES

Although global flows and globalization contribute to some degree of homogenization of the social experience around the world, they also contribute to greater global cultural diversity and heterogeneity. A very important contribution to thinking on the latter aspects of global flows is Arjun Appadurai's (1996) work on what he calls **landscapes**—*scapes* for short. These are fluid, irregular, and variable global flows that produce different results throughout the world. As we will see below, these scapes can involve the flow of many different things, including people and ideas. At the heart of

> **landscapes** Fluid, irregular, and variable global flows that produce different results throughout the world.

Appadurai's thinking are five types of landscapes that operate independently of one another to some degree, and may even conflict with one another:

- **Ethnoscapes** involve the movement, or fantasies about movement, of various individuals and groups such as tourists and refugees. The ethnoscape of undocumented immigrants is of particular concern these days. They are often poor people who have in the main been forced to move because of poverty and poor job prospects in their home country. They also move because of the belief, sometimes the fantasy, that economic conditions will be better for them elsewhere in the world, especially in the more developed countries of the United States and Western Europe.

- **Technoscapes** involve mechanical technologies such as the containerized ships now used to transport freight, informational technologies such as the Internet, and the material such as refrigerators and e-mail that moves so quickly and freely throughout the world via those technologies.

- **Financescapes** involve the use of various financial instruments in order to allow huge sums of money and

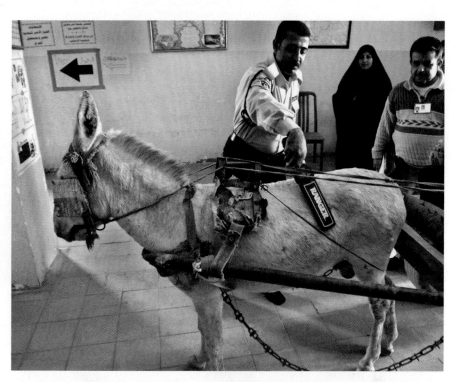

Unrest and war in Iraq have increased flows across its borders and threatened a recent election. This donkey brought a disabled man to an urban polling station, where a police officer ran a security check.

other things of economic value (e.g., stocks, bonds, precious metals [especially gold]) to move through nations and around the world at great speed, almost instantaneously. The great global economic meltdown beginning in late 2007 demonstrated quite clearly the importance and the power of financescapes in the contemporary world.

- **Mediascapes** involve both the electronic capability to produce and transmit information around the world and the images of the world that these media create and disseminate. Those who write blogs and download photos (e.g., Flickr) and videos (YouTube), global filmmakers and film distributors, global TV networks (CNN, Al Jazeera), and even old-fashioned newspapers and magazines create a variety of mediascapes.

- **Ideoscapes** are, like mediascapes, involved with images, although they are largely restricted to political images that are in line with the ideologies of nation-states. Also included here are images and counterideologies produced by social movements that are oriented toward supplanting those in power or at least gaining a portion of that power. Thus, for example, Israel has one ideoscape that disseminates

ethnoscapes Landscapes that involve the movement, or fantasies about movement, of various individuals and groups.

technoscapes Landscapes that involve mechanical and informational technologies, as well as the material that moves quickly and freely through them.

financescapes Landscapes that involve the use of various financial instruments to allow huge sums of money and other things of economic value to move into and across nations and around the world at great speed, almost instantaneously.

mediascapes Landscapes that involve the electronic capability to produce and transmit information and images around the world.

ideoscapes Landscapes that involve images, largely political images, that are often in line with the ideologies of nation-states.

China's Firewall

Arjun Appadurai

FIGURE 5.4 • Countries of Origin for Human Trafficking

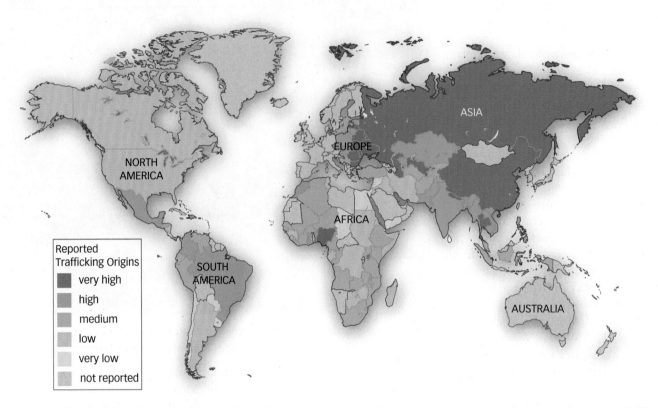

Reported Trafficking Origins
- very high
- high
- medium
- low
- very low
- not reported

NOTE: Most trafficking schemes follow three basic steps: (1) Recruitment/abduction: Some victims are lured by the promise of work, and others are recruited for their experience in the sex trade. According to the United Nations, most victims are chosen carefully and many are unmarried and uneducated.
(2) Transportation: Victims are moved along occasionally convoluted routes. Traffickers use commercial airlines, cars and vans. (3) Exploitation: The majority of exploited victims are women and girls forced into the sex trades. Men and boys are used for labor that often borders on slavery.

SOURCE: From United Nations Office on Drugs and Crime. (2006). Trafficking in persons: Global patterns.

negative images and information about the militant group Hezbollah (Israel and the United States also consider it a terrorist organization); in turn, Hezbollah has an ideoscape that responds with similarly negative images and information about Israel. News conferences by Israeli leaders attacking Hezbollah's terrorism are met by videotapes by the latter's leaders critiquing Israeli militarism. Ideoscapes may be disseminated through mediascapes and technoscapes (for example, shipping propaganda-laden books by containerized shipping throughout the world).

Further increasing the global heterogeneity that results from the interaction of these landscapes is the fact that the impact of one can be at variance, even in conflict, with another. In addition, these landscapes are interpreted differently by people and groups in different parts of the world. This depends on both the culture in which they exist and their own subjective interpretations of the scapes. Powerful forces create at least some of these scapes. Nonetheless, those who merely live in them or pass through them have the power not only to redefine them in idiosyncratic ways, but also ultimately to subvert them in many different ways. For example, those on guided tours of various parts of the world designed to show a given locale in a particularly positive light can break off from the tour and see and hear things that lead to a very different impression of the locale. When they return home, they can portray that locale in a way that contradicts the image presented by the tour creators and guides.

GLOBAL BARRIERS

The globe, and the flows that increasingly pervade it, are of central concern to sociology. However, there is another aspect of globalization that is of increasing concern to sociology, and that is the global barriers to these flows. The world is made up of not just a series of flows but also many structures such as trade agreements, regulatory agencies, borders, customs barriers, standards, and so on (Inda and Rosaldo 2008). Any thoroughgoing account of globalization needs to look at the ways in which structures

The "Flat World" of Thomas Friedman

Thomas Friedman (1953–), winner of several Pulitzer Prizes, is one of the most influential journalists in the world. In part, his influence comes via his regular columns in the *New York Times*, but more important for our purposes are his books, especially those on globalization.

In *The World Is Flat: A Brief History of the Twenty-First Century*, Friedman (2005) argues that the barriers and hurdles to competing successfully on a global scale have declined, if not completely disappeared. In other words, the global playing field has been increasingly leveled, making it possible for more and more people to play, to compete, and to win. Small companies and even individuals anywhere in the world have an unprecedented ability to compete successfully on a global basis. Friedman (2005: 231) is not just describing a trend, but praising it as well. This is clear when he says that the "world is flattening

and rising at the same time." In his view, everyone is benefiting from the flat world.

The flat world thesis implies an elimination of all barriers to free trade—and virtually everything else, for that matter. That is, in a flat world, trade is free to roam everywhere and to get there without impediments. Indeed, the opposite of a flat world is one with lots of barriers—some high, some low—that serve to impede free trade. Those barriers include tariffs, quotas, restrictions, regulations, and so on.

Many sociologists disagree (Antonio 2007) with Friedman about the desirability of all global flows, especially those associated with free trade, and the need to eliminate all barriers to them. These sociologists believe that at least some barriers are worth retaining in order to protect some individuals and structures from the ravages of free-floating global flows. Further, most sociologists

and other social scientists disagree with Friedman on the existence, or even the possibility, of a flat world (an entire 2008 issue of *Cambridge Journal of Regions, Economy and Society* is devoted to the topic: "The World Is Not Flat; Putting Globalization in Its Place"). Much of sociology is premised on the idea that those with power will erect barriers of all sorts that enhance their interests and that, in the process, adversely affect others and create great inequalities.

Think About It

Do you agree with Thomas Friedman that the world is increasingly flat, or do you see barriers being erected that, among other things, harm others and create inequality? Give specific examples to support your answer. Do you think the world *should* be flat? Why or why not?

---

both produce and enhance flows as well as alter and even block them. In other words, there is interplay between flows and structures, especially between flows and the structures that are created in an attempt to inhibit or to stop them (Shamir 2005).

As has already been mentioned, the most important and most obvious barriers to global flows are those constructed by nation-states. There are borders, gates, guards, passport controls, customs agents, health inspectors, trade regulations, and so on, in most countries in the world. Although undocumented immigrants, contraband goods, and digitized messages do get through those barriers, other phenomena that nation-states deem to be not in their national interest are successfully blocked or impeded. For example, in 2006 the U.S. government blocked a deal in which a Dubai company was to purchase an American company involved in the business of running America's ports ("DP Seeks to Calm the Storm" 2006). The government felt that such ownership would be a threat to national security since foreign nationals, perhaps enemies, could acquire information that would allow terrorists easy access to U.S. ports. As another example, in 2008 the U.S. government

blocked an effort by a Chinese company to join with an American private equity firm in purchasing 3Com, an American company that, among other things, manufactures software that prevents hacking into military computers (Weisman 2008). In 2010 the U.S. government blocked the sale by an American firm of its fiber optics business to a Chinese investment corporation on the grounds that it would constitute a threat to America's national security (Bushell-Embling 2010). Some have noted that as nations focus more on "nationalism and militarism," their openness to international trade and other formalized "flows" across borders decreases (Acemoglu and Yared 2010).

ARE GLOBAL BARRIERS EFFECTIVE?

However, many of the barriers created by nation-states are not effective. For instance, it is highly doubtful that the

Border Fences

Thomas Friedman

Digital Divide

This Palestinian boy climbing through a wall erected by Israel in Shuafat near Jerusalem demonstrates that not all global barriers are as effective as their builders wish. Should we be glad, or sorry?

such as Germany, which see the open borders as essential to European unity. Moreover, in late 2011, months after the policy was enacted, a new center-left government eliminated the controls and returned to policies in accord with other EU countries (Laegaard 2013).

ORGANIZATIONAL BARRIERS

There are many different kinds of organizations that, though they may expedite global flows for some, create all sorts of barriers for others. For example, nation-states create protectionist tariff systems (Reuveny and Thompson 2001) that help their own farmers send agricultural products (wheat) and manufacturers send goods (automobiles) across the borders of other nation-states while inhibiting the inflow of goods from their foreign competition. Another example is found in the two-tier system of passport control at international airports where citizens usually pass through quickly and easily while foreigners often wait in long lines.

Multinational corporations use market competition rather than trade policies to achieve similar results. Toyota, for instance, is devoted to optimizing the flow of its automobiles to all possible markets throughout the world. It also seeks to compete with and outperform other multinational corporations in the automobile business. If it is successful, the flow of automobiles from competing corporations is greatly reduced, further advantaging Toyota.

Labor unions are also organizations devoted to promoting the flow of some things while working against the flow of others (Bronfenbrenner 2007). Unions often oppose, for example, the flow of undocumented immigrants because they are likely to work for lower pay and fewer, if any, benefits such as health insurance than indigenous, unionized workers. Similarly, labor unions oppose the flow of goods produced in nonunion shops, in other countries as well as their own. They do so because the success of nonunion shops would put downward pressure on wages and benefits. This would adversely affect unionized shops and, in turn, hurt the union and its members. On the other hand, many employers are eager to look the other way when hiring undocumented immigrant labor. Because these laborers lack documentation, they are easy to exploit. Employers can threaten to deport them if workers demand higher wages and better working conditions, or threaten to organize.

very expensive fence that was constructed between Mexico and the United States, combined with the use of cameras, lights, satellites, and drones, will be able to curtail the flow of undocumented immigrants to the United States. It has become more difficult, costly, and dangerous to enter the country illegally, but it has not stopped such entry. Moreover, the fence has had the unintended consequence of making it harder for illegals already in the United States from moving back to Mexico. Similarly, it is not clear whether the wall between Israel and the West Bank (and more recently between Israel and Egypt) will stop the flow of terrorists into Israel the next time hostilities in the Middle East flare up. The wall is certainly not stopping Palestinians and Israelis from communicating person-to-person via digital media, as the next "Digital Living" box demonstrates.

In the European Union (EU), barriers to movement between member countries have been greatly reduced, if not eliminated. The EU has a structure that allows people and products to move much more freely and much more quickly. However, at least one country—Denmark—sought to reestablish border controls (Day 2011; "Schengen State" 2011). After more than 10 years with no border controls, the Danish government claimed that it had experienced an increase in transborder crime, and that new customs inspections would help curb organized crime. The move, however, was sharply criticized by some other EU countries,

DIGITAL LIVING

A Virtual Bridge between Palestinians and Israelis

While it is difficult to move people physically across their borders, Palestinians and Israelis can communicate virtually via the Internet. The site Facebook.com/yalaYL (*yala* is Arabic for "let's go"; YL stands for Young Leaders) was created in 2011 by an Israeli, the president of the Peres Center for Peace, who said, "All communication today is on the Internet—sex, war, business—why not peace? . . . Today we have no brave leaders on either side, so I am turning to a new generation, the Tahrir Square [the main site of the Egyptian protests in 2011 that brought down the regime of Hosni Mubarak] and Facebook generation." Even though the site is Israeli in origin, it is supported by Palestinians, including a Palestinian National Authority official who said, "Believe me, they don't know each other at all. . . . Since Israelis and Palestinians don't meet face to face anymore, this is a virtual place to meet" (Bronner 2011b: 9). More than half the active visitors to the site have been Arabs, and most of those have been Palestinians.

While lots of postings deal with common everyday interests such as music and sports, of greatest importance are those that are concerned with peace between Israelis and Palestinians. Said a Palestinian graduate student, "I joined immediately because right now, without a peace process and with Israelis and Palestinians physically separated, it is really important for us to be interacting without barriers" (Bronner

Was it inevitable that some transnational flows would be purely digital, like the website facebook.com/yalaYL? This site unites Palestinians and Israelis in an attempt to promote peace.

2011b: 9). The hope of the founder of the site is that the joint projects that develop between Israelis and Palestinians on the site will push the leaders of both sides in the direction of seeking peace.

The site also enhances the level of mutual understanding between Palestinians and Israelis. An 18-year-old Palestinian college student said, "This is my first contact with Israelis. . . . It helps me understand the differences between Israel and the occupation" (Bronner 2011b: 9). These Israelis and Palestinians are breaking through the physical borders and reconnecting in a more fluid, globally connected online world.

Inspired by the model of yalaYL, groups around the world (including the Italian government, a Barcelona soccer team, and MTV) have sought to become more involved in the processes of globalization.

Think About It

In which of Appadurai's "scapes" does the webpage Facebook.com/yalaYL operate? Do you think this virtual meeting place can ever become as powerful as the physical barriers between the Palestinian and Israeli nations? Why or why not?

Food-industry workers worldwide are taking actions that draw attention to their low wages, including these Indonesian workers blocking a road in Jakarta. Will the increased global flows of products help or hurt such workers?

ASK YOURSELF

What kinds of global flows does your college or university allow or promote? What kinds of global flows does it impede, and how?

MORE OPEN ORGANIZATIONS

Organizations of many types that seek to control global flows are facing increasing competition from organizations that are becoming more fluid and open. The best-known computer operating systems are produced by Microsoft (Vista and Windows 7 and 8). They cost a great deal and are closed. Only those who work for the company can, at least legally, work on and modify them. In contrast, a traditional closed organization—IBM— has embraced the Linux system. This is a free computer operating system that welcomes changes contributed by anyone in the world with the needed skills. IBM has also opened up more and more of its own operations to outside inputs. Another example is Apple, whose Macintosh operating system has traditionally been closed but is allowing outsiders to produce applications for its iPhone and iPad. Many other manufacturers of smartphones have followed suit. The free online encyclopedia Wikipedia and wikis more generally encourage virtually anyone, anywhere in the world, to contribute. In contrast, traditional and very costly dictionaries such as *Merriam-Webster's Collegiate Dictionary* (2008) and encyclopedias like *Encyclopedia Britannica* (2010) and the *Encyclopedia of Sociology* (Ritzer 2007a, forthcoming) are closed to contributions from anyone other than selected and invited experts.

Even with the new open systems, structural realities help some and hinder others. For example, to contribute to Linux or Wikipedia one must have a computer, computer expertise, and access, especially high-speed access to the Internet. Clearly, those without economic advantages—people in the lower classes in developed countries or people who live in the less developed countries of the Global South—are on the other side of the "digital divide" and do not have access to the required

CHECKPOINT 5.3	**TYPES OF FLOWS ACROSS AND THROUGH THE GLOBAL SOCIETY**
Globalization	An increasingly liquid and multidirectional flow of people, objects, places, and information—and the barriers they encounter—across the globe.
Ethnoscapes	Real or imagined flows of individuals and groups such as tourists and refugees in search of better living conditions.
Technoscapes	Mechanical means of transporting freight, material, and information, such as container ships and the Internet.
Financescapes	Channels that allow the global flow of huge sums of money and other valuable commodities such as stocks, bonds, and precious metals.
Mediascapes	Electronic means to produce and transmit information globally, and the content of these media transmissions.
Ideoscapes	Political images in line with the ideologies of various nation-states and social movements within them.

tools. As a result, they are unable to contribute to, or to gain from, open systems to the same degree as those in more privileged positions. The fact that women are less likely than men to contribute to Wikipedia suggests that there are additional social factors to be considered here (Cohen 2011). This further suggests that women in the Global South are doubly disadvantaged when it comes to access to these open systems—and much else.

Thus, despite the new openness, most organizations and systems remain closed to various flows. These barriers usually benefit some (elites, males) and disadvantage others (the poor, females).

SUMMARY

Much sociological work on organizations is based on Max Weber's model of bureaucracy. However, one criticism of Weber's model is that bureaucracies are not as highly rational as he believed. Their rationality is limited by the instabilities and conflicts that exist in organizations. McDonaldization has become an increasingly important model for organizations seeking to operate more rationally. This model is applicable to both large corporations and relatively small outlets that are crucial parts of these organizations, and to organizations increasingly devoted to consumption rather than production.

Compared to classic bureaucracies, networks are less hierarchical, more open and flexible, and more capable of expansion and innovation.

The next level of social organization on the micro–macro continuum is the society, a relatively large population that lives in a given territory, has a social structure, and shares a culture. Talcott Parsons identified several structures particularly important to

modern societies, including the economy, the political system, the systems responsible for transmitting culture and its norms and values, and the legal system. A key recent change is the shift from industrial to risk societies.

A key structure in global analysis is the nation-state, which combines the organizational structure of the state and a population that defines itself as a nation of people with shared characteristics. However, the nation-state as a form of social organization is under siege because of global flows over which it has little control—for example, flows of information, economic phenomena, and new social movements.

Consequently, sociologists are coming to focus more attention on the global domain, the process of globalization, and in particular the global flows that best define globalization. Arjun Appadurai focuses on five different types of global landscapes or scapes. There are also limits to global flows, mainly created by macro-level entities like nation-states and labor unions.

KEY TERMS

REVIEW QUESTIONS

1. What are the characteristics of the ideal-typical bureaucracy? What are some of the ways the ideal-typical bureaucracy is unrealistic?

2. It is often the case that those who occupy offices lower in the bureaucratic hierarchy have greater knowledge and competence than those who rank above them. What does this suggest about the ideal-typical bureaucracy? Can you think of examples from your own experiences where this has been the case?

3. According to Weber, what are the three types of legitimate authority? How is rational-legal authority related to his concept of bureaucracy?

4. Over the last several decades, what changes have bureaucratic organizations undergone? How are these changes reflective of increasing globalization?

5. What is informationalism, and how has informationalism affected the global economy? How is the emergence of informationalism related to the development of new communication technologies like the Internet, social networking sites, and smartphones?

6. How has the process of globalization threatened the nation-state? What sorts of barriers have nation-states developed to limit global flows? What sorts of flows have nation-states been unable to limit?

7. Discuss each of Appadurai's landscapes, with special focus on the conflicts (with examples) among and between them. What are the implications of these disjunctures for the process of globalization?

8. How are network organizations different from classic bureaucracies? In what ways are network organizations reflective of what Thomas Friedman would call the "flat world"?

9. Does the virtual bridge between Palestinians and Israelis offer the hope of reconciliation between them, in the not-too-distant future?

10. How are open-source technologies reflective of a more fluid and open world? What structural barriers have transnational corporations created to limit these open-source technologies? What do you think is going to be the direction of the future? Why?

APPLYING THE SOCIOLOGICAL IMAGINATION

You are at the center of two of the key issues discussed in this chapter—globalization and networks. Try to list the many ways in which your life on any given day is affected by globalization. Now enumerate the many networks in which you are involved.

How many of those networks are global in scope? Which ones? How has your involvement in each of them affected your sense and understanding of other parts of the world as well as the globe as a whole?

STUDENT STUDY SITE

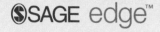

Sharpen your skills with SAGE edge at **edge.sagepub.com/ritzeressentials**

SAGE edge for students provides a personalized approach to help you accomplish your coursework goals in an easy-to-use learning environment.

"The Vampire Woman," aka Mary José Cristerna, attended the 3rd annual Venezuela Tattoo International Expo in Caracas, where hundreds of tattoo artists demonstrated their skills. Different cultures define deviance differently. Does Cristerna's appearance fit your definition of deviance, or is she simply wearing a lot of body art?

DEVIANCE AND CRIME

LEARNING OBJECTIVES

1 Define deviance.

2 Describe explanatory and constructionist approaches to theorizing about deviance.

3 Discuss crime in the context of deviance, and the purposes and effects of the criminal justice system.

In January 2011, Police Constable Michael Sanguinetti addressed a group of law students in Toronto, Canada, on the topic of crime prevention. At one point the constable said, "I've been told I'm not supposed to say this; however, women should avoid dressing like sluts in order not to be victimized."

A few months later, in April 2011, more than 3,000 women, men, and transgendered individuals responded by marching in the streets of Toronto in the country's first annual SlutWalk. The march was held to protest and to counter the misperception,

> **As a culture shifts, so too do its definitions of deviance.**

articulated in Sanguinetti's remarks, that provocative clothing encourages—and even excuses—rape and other forms of sexual abuse. Since then, SlutWalk marches, often accompanied by speeches and workshops, have been held in Australia, England, India, Brazil, South Africa, Israel, England, Poland, and several U.S. cities including Austin, Chicago, Boston, and New York. An all-volunteer SlutWalk Toronto organization maintains a website and social media presence to encourage participation, and local groups are active in other cities as well.

Sanguinetti's comments, for which he later apologized, reveal a great deal about western perceptions of sexual deviance. The negative label "slut" is applied to a woman who deviates, or is believed to deviate, from expected norms and who engages in sexual activity outside a committed relationship. Any woman who dresses in a way that deviates from a normalized presentation of sexuality may also be assumed to be a slut, no matter her actual sexual conduct. Because such women are or present themselves as sexually deviant, Sanguinetti's line of reasoning went, they should expect—and possibly deserve—to be punished by the application of negative labels.

However, a 2003 study found that victims' attire is not a significant factor in sexual assault. Instead, rapists look for signs of passivity and submissiveness, traits that are actually more likely to be associated with wearing concealing clothing. Like any disconnect between perception and reality, this one may be slow to change. Inevitably, however, as a culture shifts, so too does its definition of deviance. And as global cultures change, groups everywhere are struggling to revise or reaffirm prevailing norms and laws. Norms defining sexual deviance are no different. The SlutWalks now happening around the world may be a marker of that struggle. •

DEVIANCE

What exactly is deviance, and where is the line between deviance and nondeviance? Without giving it much thought, many people would likely express the absolutist view that certain things are deviant in all places, for all groups, and at all times (Little 2007). However, from a sociological perspective, no act, belief, or human characteristic is inherently deviant (Perrin 2007). Rather, to the sociologist, deviance is socially defined. Thus, **deviance** is any action, belief, or human characteristic that members of a society or a social group consider a violation of group norms for which the violator is likely to be censured or punished (Ben-Yehuda 2012; Goode 2007a).

If a powerful group wants to have a form of behavior defined as deviant, it is likely to be so defined. At the same time, powerful groups are likely to use their power to resist the efforts of others to define the powerful group's behaviors as deviant. For example, in the wake of the collapse of the home mortgage market in 2008, bankers fought, largely successfully, against being seen as deviant for their fraudulent predatory loan policies (Braithwaite 2010). However, borrowers who lied about their financial situation suffered far greater consequences (Nguyen and Pontell 2011). They were likely to lose their homes, often their jobs, and sometimes even their health. Social power has a great deal of influence over who gets defined as deviant and suffers the negative consequences of such a definition.

SHIFTING DEFINITIONS OF DEVIANCE

In addition to being influenced by power relationships, what is thought to be deviant will vary from one time period to another, from one geographic location to another, and from one group to another. For example, tattoos have been transformed from a form of deviance into a normal phenomenon (Dombrink and Hillyard 2007). Until a couple of decades ago, most people in the United States would have considered tattoos (and body art more generally, including body piercing [Koch et al. 2010] and "flesh hook pulling" [Horton

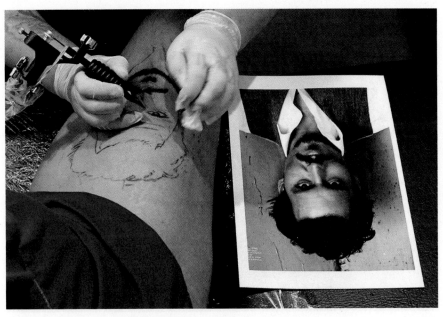

Is getting a tattoo of actor Johnny Depp on your thigh a form of deviant behavior?

2013]) "discredited bodily states." A tattoo was seen as deviant in and of itself, or it was assumed to signify membership in some deviant group, such as a biker gang. Today, a much greater proportion of Americans consider tattoos normal, and indeed about 45 million Americans have gotten tattoos themselves. In the public realm, we accept the sight of athletes—especially professional basketball players—covered with tattoos. Once associated with working-class individuals who never attended college, tattoos have become much more common today among college students. Restricted largely to men not too long ago, tattoos are more and more popular today with women. Some women, such as Kat Von D, have also gained fame as tattoo artists, a historically male-dominated occupation that has become so accepted that many in it aspire to be, or consider themselves, professionals (Maroto 2011). And tattoo parlors, once limited to the marginal areas of town, are now found on Main Street, as well as in the shopping mall, perhaps next to the maternity shop or the toy store. Tattoos have become just another product of our consumer society (Patterson and Schroeder 2010; Trebay 2008).

Another example of the movement from deviance to normality is U.S. attitudes toward premarital sex (Regnerus and Uecker 2011). Just a few decades ago, a leading textbook on the subject of deviance devoted a

> **deviance** Any action, belief, or human characteristic that members of a society or a social group consider a violation of group norms and for which the violator is likely to be censured or punished.

Body Art

If smoking is considered normal in China, is a Chinese child who smokes therefore also normal?

chapter to "premarital sex" (Bell 1971). Today, premarital sex is so common and widely accepted (or at least tolerated) that it is considered normal in most groups (Wellings et al. 2009). Furthermore, "hooking up," or having sexual relationships outside of committed romantic relations, common among youth today, was considered deviant behavior in earlier generations (Bogle 2008; Lewis et al. 2011; Manning, Giordano, and Longmore 2006). Much the same can be said about cohabitation before marriage (see Chapter 10); it once was defined as "living in sin." Today the pendulum has swung entirely in the other direction, to the point where couples who do not live together before marriage may be considered deviant. In other words, cohabitation has become normative (Popenoe 2009; Sassler and Miller 2011). Homosexuality is another form of sexual behavior that has moved away from being considered a form of deviance (see Chapter 15). Its normalization is reflected in a host of social changes such as the inclusion of same-sex partners in family benefits offered by employers, the repeal of the military's "don't ask, don't tell" policy, the growing number of U.S. states that issue same-sex marriage licenses, and the 2011 reversal of the federal government's position on the Defense of Marriage Act (Savage and Stolberg 2011).

Of course, some members of American society cringe at the idea that premarital sex, cohabitation before marriage, and homosexuality are becoming normative. Religious fundamentalists, for example, may believe in an absolute moral standard by which these behaviors are deviant, no matter how many other people consider them normal. Fundamentalists believe that only married

heterosexuals should live together and have sexual intercourse with one another (Hendershott 2002; Powell et al. 2010).

There are great differences from one geographic area to another in the way some behaviors are defined. At one time, smoking cigarettes was an accepted, even admired, form of behavior in the United States. For example, the characters in the TV show *Mad Men,* which deals with the advertising industry in New York City about half a century ago, are often seen smoking and drinking alcohol. They are doing so heavily, with great pleasure, and in their offices. Now, of course, smoking is widely considered to be deviant in the United States. However, smoking is certainly not viewed as deviant in most parts of Europe. It is considered quite normal in China (Kohrmann 2008), which consumes more tobacco than any other country in the world. In 2010 there were just over 301 million smokers in China; over half of all Chinese men were smokers (Yang et al. 2011). Smoking marijuana in public is another behavior defined differently according to geographic location. It is considered deviant by most groups in the United States, but in the Netherlands marijuana smoking, while technically illegal, is quite normal. As you will see in the next "Globalization" box, however, some changes are taking place in the Dutch attitude toward marijuana.

Even within the same society, groups differ on what is and is not considered deviant. In top-rated high schools in the United States students with high IQs are considered quite normal, but in typical or underperforming public high schools such students might be considered, and consider themselves to be, deviant (Margolin 1994).

ASK YOURSELF

Can you think of any other behaviors that were once considered deviant and are now accepted or even normative? What brought about the change in their status? Can you identify any behaviors that were once normative and are now considered deviant, such as failing to clean up after your dog?

While there are great differences in what is considered to be deviant, it is important to remember that deviance has existed for all groups, in all parts of the world, and for all times.

Rethinking the Dutch Approach to Marijuana Use

The Netherlands has long been the model of an open and tolerant society. It was the first nation in the world to allow same-sex marriage and euthanasia. However, globalization is threatening one of the things the Netherlands is most famous for: its openness to drug use in general, and especially to the sale and use of marijuana and hashish. Although marijuana is technically illegal in the Netherlands, smoking marijuana in public is not unusual, and there are "coffee shops" throughout the country where marijuana is sold openly. Many cafes have marquees, resembling those in fast-food restaurants, which offer the customer the choice of many varieties of the drug; "Amnesia," "Big Bud," and "Gold Palm" are just a few examples.

Tourists have been drawn to these shops for decades. But in recent years Dutch citizens have begun to see "drug tourism" (Uriely and Belhassen 2005) as a social problem. This is especially the case in border cities like Maastricht, which lie just a few miles from Germany, France, and Belgium. Selling marijuana is illegal in these countries, but the European Union's open borders have made it easy to drive to the Netherlands to get marijuana. As a result, Maastricht and other Dutch border cities are plagued with traffic jams, noise, and, more importantly, crime. The large numbers of visitors in search of marijuana have attracted criminals who want to sell them other, harder drugs, which are definitely illegal. What is worse, these criminals have been involved in shootouts

In an effort to limit drug tourism and encroaching drug crime, the Dutch are beginning to rein in their legendary openness about marijuana use. Is there another way they could address these new social problems?

and killings. The Dutch are shocked by this development because they saw their openness to marijuana as a way of keeping their young people safer, not endangering them in new and unforeseen ways.

As a result, the Dutch passed a law, which took effect on January 1, 2013, prohibiting the sale of marijuana to nonresidents. However, the mayor of Amsterdam announced that the 220 shops selling marijuana in that city would remain open through the end of 2013. He feared that the closure of the shops would lead to a massive increase in the illegal sale of the

drug across the city (Jolly 2012). The nationwide ban on marijuana is in effect in the Netherlands, but local officials have been given the power to override it.

Think About It

Would you say, based on their laws and their behaviors, that the Dutch see marijuana use as normative or as deviant? Do you think they are likely to be successful in their attempts to maintain an effective double standard in governing marijuana use within their borders? Why or why not?

GLOBAL FLOWS AND DEVIANCE

Deviance can be seen as a global flow. Obviously, like many others, people who are defined as being deviant can move around the world quickly and easily. In addition, definitions of deviance flow even more easily from society to society. For example, through its "war on drugs," the United States has made a strong effort to have drug use throughout the world defined as a form of deviance and to

make drug use illegal wherever possible. While there have been successes, many societies and cultures have resisted this effort and persist in viewing at least some drug use

Marijuana in the Netherlands

as normal. For example, use of the stimulant drug *khat* is normal in Yemen. The flip side of that phenomenon is that alcohol use is considered deviant in Yemen but thought to be quite normal in the United States.

Global trends toward normalizing that which was defined at one time and in some places as deviant are even clearer and more pronounced. This is particularly the case with changes in the acceptability of various forms of sexuality. Ever greater portions of the world are accepting premarital sex, cohabitation before marriage, and, to a lesser degree, homosexuality. According to the International Lesbian, Gay, Bisexual, Trans and Intersex Association (ILGA), as of 2012 "deviant" sexuality was protected by antidiscrimination laws in 57 countries, and same-sex unions were recognized in 31 countries (see the ILGA map in Figure 6.1). However, the barriers to normalizing such forms of sexual behavior remain in place and are quite powerful in large parts of the world. (The ILGA map indicates that deviant sexual behavior was punishable by imprisonment in 79 countries and death in 5.) This is especially the case in Islamic societies, which tend to be more absolutist on matters relating to sexual deviance and where deeply held religious beliefs serve as such a barrier. In spite of the barriers, these behaviors exist, often covertly, in these societies and may well be expanding in the wake of increasing global acceptance.

DEVIANCE AND CONSUMPTION

The most obvious relationship between deviance and consumption is the use of goods and services that are illegal or considered deviant. This form of consumption often involves committing deviant, or illegal, acts in order to be able to afford to consume. For example, many drug addicts are forced into committing criminal acts such as prostitution, shoplifting, mugging, and breaking and entering in order to pay for the high cost of their illegal drugs.

Poverty drives some to commit illegal and/or deviant acts so they can afford to consume that which is necessary for survival (Edin and Lein 1997; Livermore et al. 2011). There are many reasons for engaging in prostitution, including the need to pay for illegal drugs, a history of abuse and rape, and being forced through human trafficking or other coercion, as well as simply a last-ditch effort to survive (Kennedy et al. 2007; Weitzer 2009). However, many women—and men—engage in prostitution to earn the money they need to afford various conventional goods and services.

A striking example of the relationship between deviance and consumption is the "mall girls" of Warsaw, Poland, the subject of a 2010 documentary film of the same name. These teenage girls (15 years of age or younger) are so drawn to the malls and the goods and services offered there that they are willing to engage in sex in these settings (in the restrooms or outside in the parking lot), not for cash but for the goods and services themselves. Thus they exchange sex for pricey sushi dinners in the mall, as well as for Chanel scarves, "designer jeans, Nokia cell phones, even a pair of socks," especially those with brand names and expensive designer labels (Bilefsky 2010: A8). Because no money is exchanged, the girls do not see themselves as prostitutes. They call their clients "boyfriends," "benefactors," or "sponsors." This phenomenon is linked by some to a postcommunist decline in values and the declining power of the Catholic Church in Poland. The maker of the documentary film argued that "the shopping mall has become the new cathedral in Poland" (Bilefsky 2010: A8).

Defining Deviant Consumption

As with all sorts of deviance, definitions of what is deviant consumer behavior are frequently in dispute. For instance, deviant consumers often do not see a relationship between deviance and their consumption patterns. Using the services of prostitutes or smoking marijuana may well be seen by most U.S. "consumers" of prostitution or marijuana as completely justifiable and therefore not as forms of deviance. Their actions are partly due to the fact that the laws prohibiting consumption of the services of prostitutes and the use of marijuana are rarely enforced. "Johns" and "Janes" are rarely arrested, and if they are, they ordinarily get only a legal slap on the wrists. Purchasing and smoking marijuana are treated in a similar fashion, at least for the white middle class.

However, those who consume the "wrong" drugs are more likely to be considered deviant than those who consume the "right" drugs. Thus, people who consume alcohol, even if they consume it excessively, are far less likely to be considered deviant than people who use marijuana. And the purchase and use of "harder drugs" that are associated with the have-nots in society, such as methamphetamine and heroin, are dealt with more harshly than the purchase and use of either alcohol or marijuana (Chriqui et al. 2002: ix; Jackson-Jacobs 2005: 835). Similarly, there are extensive differences along racial and ethnic lines in arrests for drug offenses (Ousey and Lee 2010: 551). For example, the greatest disparity in black and white arrest rates involves drugs. Blacks are six times more likely than whites to be arrested for a drug offense (Ousey and Lee 2008).

"Dangerous Consumers"

Interestingly, in the era before the Great Recession, deviants in the realm of consumption were often considered to be the individuals who did not consume enough. They have been

FIGURE 6.1 • Lesbian and Gay Rights around the World, 2013

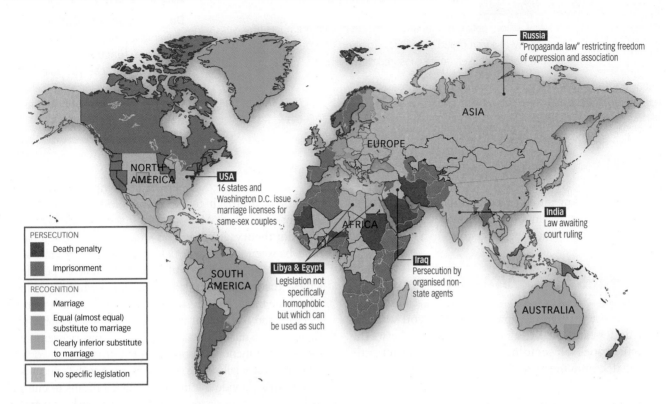

SOURCE: From *ILGA launches 2013 ILGA State-Sponsored Homophobia Report, 2013*. Reprinted by permission of the International Lesbian, Gay, Bisexual, Trans and Intersex Association.

called "dangerous consumers" (Bauman 1997; Ritzer 2001a). They included the unemployed, the poor (Hamilton 2012), "dropouts," those who voluntarily sought to simplify their lives, and those who saved rather than spent their money. Their insufficient consumption posed a threat to the success of consumer society and to an economy that had come to depend on high levels of consumption. Similarly, those who did not go into debt to the credit card companies and to banks for car and home loans were also considered to be dangers to the economy. This was the case even though lesser consumption may be better for the long-term sustainability of humanity, the environment, and even the economy.

ASK YOURSELF

Do you think those who voluntarily reduce their consumption, especially of nonrenewable energy and disposable goods that contribute to the wasteful use of finite resources, should be considered deviant? Might some forms of deviance actually be admirable? Under what circumstances?

The idea of dangerous, or deviant, consumers can be applied more broadly. Clearly, consuming illegal goods

and services is considered deviant, but consuming merely the "wrong" products and services can also be seen as a threat. For example, buying secondhand goods, or worse, obtaining such goods free of charge from charities, threatens those with a vested interest in an ever-expanding economy. Such acquisitions do little or no good for the producers of various products, those whose jobs depend on those producers, the government that collects taxes from those producers and workers, and the consumption-based economy as a whole. Similarly, the use of public or welfare services can be viewed as a deviant form of consumption because, among other things, it constitutes a drain on government coffers and on the national economy.

Recent changes in the economy demonstrate, once again, the relative nature of deviance. After the onset of the Great Recession, those who came to be defined as deviant or dangerous were those who consumed too much and who went too deeply into debt. For example, those who bought homes even though there was no way they could afford the mortgage payments, at least after an initial period

Deviance and Consumption

State Prisons

Deviance	Any action, belief, or human characteristic that members of a society or social group consider a violation of group norms for which the violator is likely to be censured or punished.
Behaviors no longer considered deviant	Tattoos, premarital sex, homosexuality.
Behaviors no longer considered nondeviant	Smoking (in the United States).

ASK YOURSELF

Do you agree with Durkheim that deviance is, in a sense, normal and therefore functional? To support this argument, can you think of an example of a deviant act or behavior that has helped society define its standards of conduct?

of uncommonly low interest rates and monthly payments, came to be seen as deviants. They had jeopardized not only their own way of life but also the economy as a whole.

THEORIES OF DEVIANCE

Deviance is a very good topic to study if you want to better understand the utility of, and contrasts between, the main types of sociological theories—structural/functional, conflict/critical, and inter/actionist.

STRUCTURAL/FUNCTIONAL THEORIES

A good place to start is with the thinking of Émile Durkheim, one of the classical sociological theorists and creator of what later came to be known as structural-functionalism. While Durkheim focused on crime, it is possible to extend his thinking to deviance more generally. His basic argument was that because deviance and crime have existed in all societies at all times (and in that sense are "normal"), they must have positive functions for the larger society and its structures. In other words, deviance would not have existed, exist, or continue to exist were it not for the fact that it was and is functional.

The most important function of deviance in Durkheim's view is that it allows societies, or groups, to define and clarify their collective beliefs—their norms and values. Were it not for deviance, norms and values would not come into existence. More importantly, the norms and values that limit or prohibit deviance would grow weak without the need to be exercised on a regular basis in response to deviant acts. The public as a whole, officials, and even potential deviants would grow progressively less aware of, and less sensitive to, the existence of these prohibitions. Thus, in a sense society needs deviance. If periodic violations of standards of conduct did not occur, those standards would become less clear to all concerned, less strongly held, and less powerful (Dentler and Erikson 1959; Jensen 1988).

Strain

A more contemporary structural-functional approach to deviance, most associated with the work of Robert Merton (1938; see below), is known as **strain theory**. According to strain theory, a discrepancy exists between the larger structure of society, especially what is valued, and the structural means available to people to achieve that which is valued. Strain exists when the culture values one thing, but the structure of society is such that not everyone can realize that value in a socially acceptable way. There are two major ways in which strain theory exemplifies a structural-functional approach. First, it is concerned with structures, especially those structures, such as the educational system, that provide the institutionalized means to cultural goals. Second, it deals with structural relationships between those goals and institutionalized means (e.g., between success and hard work).

The most obvious and important example in the United States, and in many other developed societies throughout the world, is the strain produced by the fact that although a high value is placed on material success, the structure of society does not give everyone an equal chance of attaining that success. Thus, contrary to the ideal of equal opportunity and a "level playing field," in reality most poor people in the United States have little or no chance of gaining the experience, training, education, and stable career that are the prerequisites for economic success. Nevertheless, they are still likely to value economic success, and at least some find alternative ways of achieving it (Bourgeois 2003; Duneier 1999).

For example, in poor and minority areas in the United States, and especially in its major cities, dealing drugs can be a means of making money—for some, big money. Many young men are willing to risk jail terms and even their lives selling drugs because they believe it offers

> **strain theory** Theory based on the idea that the discrepancy between the larger structure of society and the means available to people to achieve that which the society considers to be of value produces strain that may cause an individual to undertake deviant acts.

them an attainable route to economic success (Dunlap et al. 2010; Levitt and Venkatesh 2000). Sociologist Sudhir Venkatesh (2002) studied the Robert Taylor Homes housing project in Chicago. He spent a great deal of time talking to and observing J. T., a man who was able to make quite a lot of money by being a gang leader and drug dealer. J. T. was not uneducated and was a person of considerable ability. However, he had concluded that he was more likely to achieve material success through deviant, gang-related activities than he would by finishing college and pursuing a more acceptable and conventional career. Even within this deviant career, however, there was a hierarchical structure of opportunity and pay. While J. T. made a great deal of money, the dealers who worked under him barely made the equivalent of minimum wage. This wage gap explains "why drug dealers still live with their mothers" (Levitt and Dubner 2005).

Adaptations to Strain. The issue at the heart of Robert Merton's strain theory is the way people relate to the institutionalized means (such as getting a college degree and working hard) that are needed to achieve such cultural goals as economic success. Of greatest interest in this context is the strain placed on some people by the relationship of means and ends. Merton identified five possible relationships between means and ends and associated them with five types of adaptations:

- **Conformists** are people who accept both cultural goals such as making lots of money and the traditional means of achieving those goals, including hard work. Conformists are the only one of Merton's types who would not be considered deviant.

---

conformists People who accept both cultural goals and the traditional means of achieving those goals.

innovators Individuals who accept cultural goals but reject conventional means of achieving success.

ritualists Individuals who realize that they will not be able to achieve cultural goals, but who nonetheless continue to engage in the conventional behavior associated with such success.

retreatists Individuals who reject both cultural goals and the traditional routes to their attainment; they have completely given up on attaining success within the system.

rebels Individuals who reject both traditional means and goals and instead substitute nontraditional goals and means to those goals.

- **Innovators** accept the same cultural goals the conformists do, but they reject the conventional means of achieving them. Innovators are deviants in that they choose nonconventional routes to success. Bernie Madoff is one example, though an extreme one. He was highly successful as a financier, before he turned to illegal activities through which he bilked his clients out of $65 billion. Other innovators choose legal routes to success. An example is Shaun White who created and competed in the new extreme and highly dangerous sport of snowboarding. It has become a lucrative and perfectly legal career for him and others.

- **Ritualists** realize that they will not be able to achieve cultural goals, but they nonetheless continue to engage in the conventional behavior associated with such success. Thus, a low-level employee might continue to work diligently even after realizing that such work is not going to lead to much economic success. Merton sees such diligent work with no realizable goal as a form of deviance.

- **Retreatists** reject both cultural goals and the traditional routes to their attainment. Retreatists have completely given up on attaining success within the system. One example is Theodore Kaczynski, who gained notoriety as the "Unabomber." At the time of his arrest in 1996, Kaczynski had been living for some 20 years in a cabin in a remote area of Montana without water or electricity, using a bicycle as his only means of transportation. To demonstrate his anger at modern society's "industrial-technological system," he had mailed off more than a dozen bombs, which killed three people and injured 23 others. After a long and complicated trial, he was sentenced to life in prison. Kaczynski's case has many interesting aspects, including the fact that he used the U.S. mail, part of the system he despised, to deliver his bombs and thereby his antiestablishment message. Moreover, it can be argued that Kaczynski was a conformist before he became a retreatist. Prior to his withdrawal from society he had gotten a PhD from Harvard in mathematics and had begun an academic career at the University of California–Berkeley.

- **Rebels** are like retreatists in that they reject both traditional means and goals. However, in their stead they substitute nontraditional goals and

Strain Theory

Will Smith played the lead in the film *Pursuit of Happyness*, based on Chris Gardner's real-life struggle to overcome homelessness. Gardner fits Merton's description of a conformist. Preston Tucker was an innovator who made an ill-fated challenge to the Big Three automakers in the 1940s. In the film *Tucker* he was played by Jeff Bridges. The fed-up workers in the film *Office Space*, one of whom is shown here as portrayed by Stephen Root, represent ritualists, while *The Big Lebowski*'s Dude (Jeff Bridges) is a retreatist. Finally, Heath Ledger's iconic villain the Joker in the film *The Dark Knight* is a rebel figure, though a criminal one. Can you think of other examples of these five types?

means to those goals. In a sense that makes them doubly deviant. Revolutionaries such as Ernesto "Che" Guevara can be seen as fitting into the rebel category. Guevara rejected success as it was defined in Cuba in the 1950s. Instead, he chose to assist Fidel Castro in his effort to overthrow the country's dictatorial system. Furthermore, he chose unconventional means—guerrilla warfare waged from the mountains of Cuba and, eventually, Bolivia—to attain his goals.

Adaptations of means to ends exemplify a structural-functional approach because some of the adaptations are highly functional. Conformity certainly has positive consequences in the sense that it allows the social system to continue to exist without disturbance. Innovation is functional because society needs innovations in order to adapt to new external realities. No society can survive without innovation. Even rebellion can be seen as

functional because there are times when society needs more than gradual innovation—it needs to change radically. Structural-functionalism is concerned not only with functions but also with dysfunctions. For example, ritualists and retreatists can be seen as largely dysfunctional for society, or at least as having more dysfunctions than functions. The unchanging behavior of ritualists contributes little or nothing to the requirements of an ever-changing society, and retreatists contribute even less because they are uninvolved in, and have withdrawn from, the larger society.

More Recent Developments in Strain Theory. While Merton focused on specific strains often related to economic matters, Robert Agnew (1992; Patchin and Hinduja 2011) sought to develop a theory that focuses more generally on what happens to those who experience strain. Among other things, he argued, they are likely to feel frustrated and angry about the strain. Those feelings predispose them to committing more deviant and even criminal acts. While Merton focused on the strain associated with the failure to achieve positively valued goals such as economic success, Agnew added two other types of strain. One results from the loss of something. An example is unwanted termination of a romantic relationship. The second type of strain involves experiencing an adverse situation such as living with an abusive parent or spouse. While many people suffer such strains, only those who feel angry or frustrated about them are likely to engage in deviant acts. Those acts are often aimed at doing something about the source of the strain.

Another important contribution to strain theory is Stephen Messner and Richard Rosenfeld's (1997) more macroscopic approach to strain. While Agnew focuses more on individual feelings and what people seek to do about the source of their strain, Messner and Rosenfeld are concerned, as is structural-functional theory in general, with the relationship among large-scale structures. On the one side are cultural and social structural pressures to succeed, especially economically. On the other are social institutions such as the family, the political system, and religion, which are supposed to reduce these pressures. However, if the latter institutions are weak, or if they exert weak controls over the sources of pressure to succeed, then people are more likely to engage in deviant behavior to enhance their chances of success, especially economically. To put it simply, poor people are more likely to engage in deviance or crime if there is no social institution powerful enough to reduce the pressure to commit such acts in order to improve their economic position.

Social Control

Travis Hirschi's (1969) **social control theory** also is included under the heading of structural-functional theories. Hirschi's theory focuses on the reasons why people do *not* commit deviant acts. In brief, people are less likely to commit deviant acts if they have a variety of social bonds. Conversely, they are more likely to commit such acts if those bonds are weak. While Hirschi's theory

Travis Hirschi proposed that strong social bonds, such as those provided by membership in religious groups like this one in Georgia, make deviant acts less likely. Can there ever be too much social control?

has wide application to deviance in general, he was most interested in young people and juvenile delinquency.

Social control involves the structures of society and the people who formally act on behalf of those structures. In a sense, Hirschi sees those structures and the people who work on their behalf as functional for society. People who are involved in those structures and are responsive to those who act on their behalf are more likely to be conformists, and less likely to become deviants. However, those who are more likely to become deviants are not deeply involved in those structures and not responsive to their demands or to those of the people who act on their behalf. In terms of the latter, Hirschi (1969: 18) contends: "If a person does not care about the wishes and expectations of other people . . . then he is to that extent not bound by the norms. He is free to deviate." One structure of great importance to Hirschi is the school. If a young person is not involved in school and with teachers, she is likely to be more inclined to deviant behavior. More informal factors are also important. For example, those who do not have close personal relationships, or who are not involved in extracurricular activities such as sports, are also more inclined to deviance. The lack of a job and involvement in the work world has similar effects. Without such attachments and involvements, young people are less likely to accept conventional goals or internalize the norms of society. Lacking attachments to family and conventional

social control theory A theory that focuses on the reasons why people do not commit deviant acts and the stake people have in engaging in conformist behavior.

Sudhir Venkatesh

norms and goals, there is little to prevent a person from becoming a deviant, a juvenile delinquent, or even a career criminal. The lack of other vested interests such as owning a house is also likely to contribute to deviant behavior. People in such a situation have little or nothing to lose in violating norms and laws.

In later work, Hirschi (2004: 545) described these circumstances as "inhibitors," or "factors that one takes into account in deciding whether to commit a criminal act." If young people lack such inhibitors as ties to schools and teachers, they are more likely to become juvenile delinquents (Intravia, Jones, and Piquero 2011).

This view is consistent with structural-functionalism in that it focuses on larger structures (school, work, and the housing market), those who exist in those structures and act on behalf of them (teachers, supervisors), and the positions that people do or do not hold in those structures. Involvement in these structures is likely to inhibit nonconformist behavior, while a lack of such involvement makes such behavior more likely.

While acknowledging the importance of structures and those who act formally on their behalf, Sampson and Laub (1993, 2005) expanded on Hirschi's control theory, which tends to focus more on the formal aspects of social control. Sampson and Laub deal with *both* the formal and informal aspects of control. In terms of informal control, they are most interested in the interpersonal bonds that serve to control what people do that prevents them from engaging in deviance and crime. Furthermore, while Hirschi focuses on young people and delinquency, Sampson and Laub deal with the relationship between control and deviance over the full course of people's lives. Informal social control in the family, in schools, and among peers is crucial to determining whether or not young people engage in deviant behavior. A lack of such control is a key cause of juvenile delinquency. However, informal social control also plays an important role in adulthood, influencing whether or not adults engage in deviant and criminal behavior. For adults, the most important informal social controls are those that relate to the family and work. Adults with strong interpersonal ties in those contexts—and others—are less likely to engage in criminal behavior.

Interestingly, according to Sampson and Laub's research, whether or not an adult engaged in delinquent behavior as a youth does not affect the likelihood of adult criminal behavior. For both those who have and those who have not been delinquents, the key to adult behavior is the existence and nature of later informal interpersonal relationships. While what happens to children is important, social ties in adolescence and adulthood also affect later criminal behavior. That is, irrespective of childhood involvement in delinquency, informal interpersonal bonds can serve to make it more *or* less likely that adolescents and adults will commit crimes. Those who lack nurturing, supportive and controlling relationships in adulthood and throughout the life course are more likely to be persistent offenders. Those who are involved in such relationships later in life are less likely to be criminals. In other words, being a delinquent does not necessarily mean that one will be a criminal in later life. That depends, among other things, on the nature of interpersonal ties and social controls at various stages throughout the life course. In sum, informal social control is negatively associated with crime throughout the life course.

Broken Windows. A very different aspect of control as it relates to deviance and especially crime is found in the highly controversial "broken windows" theory (Harcourt and Ludwig 2006; Wilson and Kelling 1982). The theory acknowledges that people worry about criminals who have the potential to mug or rob them. However, it is also the case that in public places, especially in large cities, people also tend to be disturbed by a variety of less dangerous forms of urban disorder. This disorder is perceived by them to stem from a variety of types of people encountered far more frequently than criminals interested in doing them harm. The former include panhandlers, loiterers, prostitutes, those who are mentally disturbed, public drunks and drug addicts, and noisy teenagers. The perception is that these types of people, and others, are permitted to behave in a disorderly manner because no one, including the authorities, cares enough about the neighborhood. The same point holds in regard to buildings that are covered with graffiti and have many broken windows, as well as in regard to other signs of neighborhood deterioration such as abandoned and vandalized automobiles. Furthermore, untended broken windows and vandalized cars tend to invite more of each leading to an increasingly disorderly neighborhood. Neighborhoods that lack the informal controls needed to prevent these developments and to maintain order are those that may allow criminal elements to gain a foothold and to thrive. In other words, crime is likely to flourish in disorderly neighborhoods. The clear answer, then, is to make neighborhoods more orderly. To do so, they need to be controlled better both informally by neighbors and more formally by the police. The formal control by the police is needed to supplement informal control by neighbors. This control is designed to deal early with such things as rowdy behavior, broken windows, and abandoned automobiles so that they do not proliferate and create an environment in which more widespread criminal behavior can take root.

However, there are a variety of fears associated with the broken windows approach. For one thing, there is the concern that it gives the police wide discretion to deal with people, even arrest them, although they have done no actual harm. The other is that such police behavior will lead to discrimination against minorities. While these worries continue, the broken windows theory has enjoyed great popularity. This is especially the case in light of New York City's great success in reducing crime, at least in part because of an application of this theory (Zimring 2011). In fact, crime there dropped by about 75 percent between the early 1980s and 2013. Astoundingly, this occurred at the same time that the prison population declined (Tierney 2013). Of course, many other factors have been associated with this decline in crime such as an older population less likely to commit crimes and the moderation of the crack epidemic that caused so many crimes. One recently popular approach that may have also contributed to the decline is "hot-spot policing." Since crime seems to recur in a small number of locales, the police have tended to concentrate their attention on these "hot spots." However, in addition to the contributions of such newer approaches, it is the case that at least some of the decline may be traceable to fewer broken windows, less graffiti, and the arrests of more people for minor violations.

ASK YOURSELF

Is it likely that disordered neighborhoods are really more crime-ridden than others? Why or why not? Given your answer, do you think making neighborhoods more orderly and better controlled serves to reduce crime? If not, what might be more effective?

Self-Control. While the preceding discussion focuses on the external control exerted over those who might deviate, there is another approach that focuses on the role of self-control in deviance and crime (Gottfredson and Hirschi 1980). The central point is that those with low self-control are more likely to engage in deviant and criminal acts. Family upbringing is a key factor in the development of enough self-control to resist committing such acts. High levels of self-control are likely to develop when parents monitor their children, supervise them, and recognize and deal with their antisocial behavior. Parental failure in these and other ways is likely to lead to low self-control. A tendency to have low self-control is likely to persist throughout a person's life. Those with low self-control are unable to resist various temptations. They are also unlikely to be able to foresee the negative consequences of acting on those temptations. Of course, such actions depend on the existence of opportunities to do so. A child might be tempted by a brand-new BMW, but he is unlikely to steal it if he does not know how to drive.

Overall, it is likely that it is a combination of formal and informal external controls, in interaction with self-control, that best explains whether or not people engage in deviant and criminal behavior.

CONFLICT/CRITICAL THEORIES

Structural-functional theorists trace the source of deviance to the larger structures of society and the strains they produce or the fact that they do not exercise adequate social control over people. Conflict/critical theorists, especially conflict theorists, are also interested in those structures and their effect on people, but they adopt a different orientation to them. A major focus is the inequality that exists in those structures and the impact that it has on individuals. In conflict theorists' view, inequality causes at least some of the less powerful individuals in society to engage in deviant—and criminal—acts because they have few, if any, other ways of succeeding in society (Goode 2007b). In this, they are similar to the innovators in Merton's taxonomy of adaptations to strain. Conversely, those in power commit crimes, especially corporate or white-collar crimes (Simpson 2002; Simpson and Weisburd 2009), because the nature of their high-level positions in various social structures (business, government) makes it not only possible, but relatively easy, for them to do so. Further, conflict theorists argue, those in power in society create the laws and rules that define certain things as deviant, or illegal, while others are defined as normal. They do so in a self-serving way that advantages them and disadvantages those who lack power in society.

The conflict view of deviance has been extended to many other acts on the basis of racial, sexual, gender, age-related, and other social inequalities (Collins 1975). For example, questionable acts committed by racial minorities are more likely to be labeled as deviance or crime than are the same acts when they are committed by majority group members. Before the repeal of state antisodomy laws by the Supreme Court in 2003, police in some states could arrest homosexuals for having sex with one another in the privacy of their own homes. Heterosexuals engaging in sodomy—that is, having oral or anal sex—in their own homes would almost never be arrested for such acts even though the acts were illegal in some locales. Some geographic areas have curfews for teenagers, meaning that a teenager who is out after a certain time can be labeled as deviant. In contrast, curfews for adults are almost unheard of except during emergencies such as a natural disaster or a state of martial law. Again, this list can be extended greatly, but the point is that conflict theorists tend to see those who rank low in the system of social stratification, on any dimension, as being more likely to be labeled as deviant.

(Un)deviant Behavior

Bernie Madoff was sentenced to 150 years in prison for stealing from investors in a long-running financial fraud considered the largest ever perpetrated in the United States. Even with time off for good behavior, Madoff would have to live to be 201 to be released.

Deviance and the Poor

Conflict theories can be applied to social inequalities throughout the ages. For instance, they form the basis of research by William Chambliss (1964) on vagrancy laws in medieval England. These laws came into existence as feudalism was falling apart; the first vagrancy law was enacted in England after the Black Death, around 1348. In the feudal system, serfs were forced to provide labor for landowners, but with the end of feudalism, and therefore of serfdom, a new source of labor was needed. Not coincidentally, the former serfs now lacked a permanent home or source of income and wandered about the countryside. Those in power saw them as a likely group to provide the needed labor at little cost and created vagrancy laws. Then it became illegal for those without work or a home to loiter in public places; some of those itinerants were arrested under the new laws. As a result, many people who otherwise might not have worked for the landowners were forced to work in order to avoid arrest and imprisonment.

Contemporary conflict theorists, heavily influenced by Marxian theory, have come to see deviance as something created by the capitalist economic system. Today's definitions of deviance serve the interests of the capitalists, especially by further enriching them. Conversely, they adversely affect the proletariat, especially the poor, who grow even poorer. This view is well summed up by Jeffrey Reiman and Paul Leighton's *The Rich Get Richer and the Poor Get Prison* (2012). As the title of this book implies, the best examples of this process lie in the realm of crime rather than deviance, although to be seen as a crime an act must be first defined as deviant. For example, as we saw above, at the close of the Middle Ages it was in the interest of elite members of society to define vagrancy as deviance and as a crime. Such a definition seems fair and even-handed until we realize that elite members of society are rarely, if ever, going to be without work and a home. They are therefore unlikely to be defined as vagrants. It is only the poor who are going to find themselves in those situations, with the result that they are just about the only ones who are going to be affected by the laws against vagrancy. As the great novelist Anatole France ([1894] 2011) once commented sarcastically, "The law, in all its majestic equality, forbids the rich as well as the poor to sleep under bridges on rainy nights, to beg on the streets, and to steal bread."

Conflict theorists do not argue that have-nots never commit crimes or deviant acts. Rather, they argue that it is because of the laws (e.g., those against sleeping under bridges) created by societal elites that the actions of the have-nots are singled out for notice and for sanctions. Furthermore, the costs to society of elite deviance are much higher than the costs associated with crime and deviance among society's have-nots. Compare, for example, the approximately $65 billion the disgraced and now imprisoned Bernie Madoff cost his clients by engaging in illegal activities to the few dollars a con artist or a mugger wrests from his victims.

Deviance and the Elite

Great efforts are made to legitimize elite crimes and acts of elite deviance (Simon 2012) and, failing that, to pay little or no attention to them. Those who rank high in such hierarchies as business, government, and the military have a much greater ability to commit deviant acts (for example, to sexually harass a subordinate), to have them seen as being legitimate, and to get away with them.

However, as is clear in the imprisonment of people like Bernie Madoff, there are limits to the ability of elites to get away with deviant and criminal behavior. There are times when the acts are so extreme that they can no longer be hidden. They come to light and become great public issues. Once this happens, even the most elite members of society have a difficult time escaping negative judgment and perhaps even punishment and imprisonment.

In fact, there is a long list of scandals involving elite public figures (e.g., Richard Nixon, Tiger Woods) of various types who have been found to have committed deviant acts. In the main, their acts were so extreme, or the revelations about them became so public, that they could not be ignored. However, what has often caused difficulties for those involved has been their awkward efforts to lie about, or cover up, their offenses once they first became public. In many cases, especially in this era of the Internet, evidence is uncovered or witnesses come forward that make it clear that the public figure has been deceiving the public and the authorities. However, the view of conflict theorists is that as lengthy as this list of elite deviants and criminals might be, it is merely the tip of the iceberg. Because elites have a wide variety of means at their disposal to conceal their actions, there are many, many more acts of deviance and criminality by elites that escape detection and punishment. Such elite acts can persist for years, decades, or even a lifetime.

INTER/ACTIONIST THEORIES

The third major type of theory employed in this book, inter/actionism, can also be used to analyze deviance. For example, to the rational choice theorist, a person chooses deviance because it is a rational means to some desired goal. Gang members join gangs because of the camaraderie and perceived protection offered by the gang (Melde, Taylor, and Esbensen 2009), as well as access to a world in which the member can obtain money and achieve recognition and high status (Bell 2009; Decker and Curry 2000). Ethnomethodologists are concerned with the ways in which people "do" deviance—that is, the everyday behaviors in which they engage that produce deviance. People need to adopt methods of speech and forms of behavior that would make their deviance invisible to most others. In a classic ethnomethodological study, Harold Garfinkel (1967) describes the painstaking steps taken by Agnes, a male-to-female transgendered person, to "pass" as a woman. She not only changed her manner of dress, posture, and demeanor, but also underwent physical changes. However, there are times when those who are deviant will want to talk and act in ways that make it clear that they are deviant. For example, gang members may use certain phrases, dress in certain ways, and display certain tattoos in order to make their allegiance clear to other members of the same gang—and to members of opposing gangs (see Chapter 3). However, when they interact with the public or the police, gang members may speak and dress in a way that conceals, or at least attempts to hide, their membership in the gang.

Professional basketball player Kobe Bryant may hope to outlive the negative labels that were attached to his name when he was revealed to be cheating on his wife. Do private individuals face less risk from such labels than public figures do?

ASK YOURSELF

Has any form of deviance ever seemed rational to you, in the sense that inter/actionist theories use the term? If so, was the deviance visible or invisible to others? Did it help you (or would it have helped you) achieve a goal?

Labeling

Symbolic interactionism is of great utility in analyzing deviance and fills in many of the gaps in understanding left by structural/functional and conflict/critical theories. One variety of symbolic interactionism—labeling theory—is particularly useful in thinking about deviance. From that perspective, at least two things are needed for deviance to occur:

- A **symbol**, or in this case a "label." In the realm of deviance, a number of labels are particularly powerful negative symbols: *alcoholic, drug addict, pedophile, adulterer,* and so on. The golfer Tiger Woods is a good example of the power of labels. He had become a well-known public symbol, even a brand. His name conjured up images of not only a great golfer, but someone who seemed "squeaky-clean." In 2009 he was involved in a car crash that led to revelations of cheating on his wife with multiple women, and

> **symbol** A word, gesture, or object that stands in for something or someone (i.e., a "label").

Mortgage Crisis

a painful separation that led to divorce. The labels *adulterer* and *sex addict* were linked with his name, and his reputation and public image were badly tarnished. Even though the accusations had nothing to do with golf, several of his corporate sponsors dropped him because they no longer wanted to be associated with a person who was labeled so negatively. They feared that his spoiled reputation would extend to them and adversely affect their businesses and profits. After a slump, Woods regained much of his former greatness as a golfer. He also has regained at least some of his reputation. This was helped by, and reflected in, the fact that President Obama played golf with him in 2013. Nevertheless, those negative labels will continue to haunt him for years, if not the rest of his life.

- Interaction (see Chapter 4) between a person or group doing the labeling (the labeler) and a person or group to whom the label is applied (the labelee). During this interaction one or more of these labels is applied to the deviant. Those who do the labeling are known as **social control agents**. Some of these agents (police, psychiatrists) are performing official functions, but far more often it is friends or family who label others as, for example, *drunks* or *womanizers*. When public figures are labeled as deviant, the media and their representatives are often the ones who do the labeling.

From the perspective of **labeling theory**, a deviant is someone to whom a deviant label has been successfully applied (Becker 1963; Restivo and Lanier 2013). This stands in contrast to the view of the public and many sociologists who focus on what an individual does in order to be labeled a deviant. Also of interest in labeling theory is the way the person labeled as deviant is affected by the label (Dotter and Roebuck 1988; Gove 1980; Walsh 1990). Among other things, the label can be accepted to varying degrees, or efforts can be made to resist, reject, or shed the label. People will also vary greatly in how they react to, and feel about, being labeled a deviant. For example, some might be mortified by being labeled a sex addict, but others might take pride in it.

Labeling theory is also concerned with the actions and reactions of social control agents, as well as their interactions with those being labeled (Pontell 2007). From the labeling perspective "deviance is not a consequence of the act the person commits, but rather a consequence of the [creation and] application by others of rules and sanctions to an 'offender'" (Becker 1963: 9). A focus on social control agents, rather than deviants, leads to the view that deviant labels are not necessarily applied uniformly. Some people and some forms of deviance are more likely than others to be labeled as deviant. Thus, murderers and the act of murder are almost uniformly labeled as deviant (and criminal). However, in many other cases the process is more selective and less clear-cut: "Some men who drink too much are called alcoholics and others are not; some men who act oddly are committed to hospitals and others are not; some men who have no visible means of support are hauled into court and others are not" (Erikson 1964: 11–12). Overall, people are more likely to be socially defined as deviant when they are poor, work in low-status occupations, or are in similarly devalued circumstances (Goffman 1959). A person in a more advantageous social situation often escapes being defined or labeled as deviant, despite manifesting the same forms of behavior.

PRIMARY AND SECONDARY DEVIANCE

An important distinction that flows from labeling theory is that between primary and secondary deviance.

- **Primary deviance** involves early, random acts of deviance such as an occasional bout of drinking to excess or an act here or there that is considered to be strange or out of the ordinary. Virtually all of us commit such acts; we all have engaged in various forms of primary deviance (Wallerstein and Wyle 1947). Isolated acts of primary deviance rarely, if ever, lead to the successful application of a deviant label.

- Of far greater interest to labeling theorists is **secondary deviance** or deviant acts that persist, become more common, and eventually cause people to organize their lives and personal identities around their deviant status. Thus, if a person moves from isolated sexual encounters to being obsessed with such encounters and to seeking them out whenever and wherever possible, that person may be labeled a sex addict. It is possible, as in the case of Hank Moody (lead character on the HBO show *Californication*) and

---

social control agents Those who label a person as deviant.

labeling theory A theory contending that a deviant is someone to whom a deviant label has been successfully applied.

primary deviance Early, nonpatterned acts of deviance or an act here or there that is considered to be strange or out of the ordinary.

secondary deviance Deviant acts that persist, become more common, and eventually cause people to organize their lives and personal identities around their deviant status.

perhaps Tiger Woods, that the label of sex addict will be more important than all other definitions of the self. When that happens, sex addiction becomes a form of secondary deviance. In one recent study, body modifications such as tattoos and body piercings were shown to be acts of primary deviance that are related to forms of secondary deviance such as drug abuse and juvenile delinquency (Dukes and Stein 2011).

While labeling theory tends to focus on others labeling an individual as deviant, it is possible, or even likely, that individuals will label themselves in this way (Thoits 1985, 2011), that they will do so before anyone else does (D. Norris 2011), and that they will act in accord with their self-imposed label (Lorber 1967). This is consistent with the view of the leading symbolic interactionist, George Herbert Mead, who saw the mind as an internal conversation with oneself. Such an internalized conversation may certainly lead to labeling oneself as deviant.

KEY IDEAS IN THE LABELING PROCESS

Social control is the process by which a group or society enforces conformity to its demands and expectations. One way in which this is accomplished is through the creation and application of rules and labels. This leads to the distinction between rule creators and rule enforcers. **Rule creators** are usually elite members of society who devise its rules, norms, and laws (Ryan 1994). Without rule creators and their rules there would be no deviance. Rule creators are usually (but not always) distinct from **rule enforcers,** who threaten to enforce or actually do enforce the rules (Bryant and Higgins 2010). Another important idea here is that of **moral entrepreneurs**, or those individuals or groups of individuals who come to define an act as a moral outrage and who lead a campaign

> **social control** The process by which a group or society enforces conformity to its demands and expectations.
>
> **rule creators** Individuals who devise society's rules, norms, and laws.
>
> **rule enforcers** Individuals who threaten to, or actually, enforce the rules.
>
> **moral entrepreneurs** Individuals or groups who come to define an act as a moral outrage and who lead a campaign to have it defined as deviant and to have it made illegal and therefore subject to legal enforcement.
>
> **moral panic** A widespread, but disproportionate, reaction to a form of deviance.

to have it defined as deviant and to have it made illegal and therefore subject to legal enforcement (Becker 1963; Lauderdale 2007; Nordgren 2013). Drugs provide a good example, especially globally, since moral entrepreneurs located especially in the United States have taken it upon themselves to have them defined as illegal and their use as deviant. They have done so even though the use of many of these drugs (such as marijuana) is common and accepted not only in many societies throughout the world but also among a large portion of the American population. In addition, a number of states in the United States have legalized (medical) marijuana in one way or another, and others are likely to follow. One famous example of a moral entrepreneur was U.S. Senator Joe McCarthy who in the 1950s created a public furor over the existence of communists in the government and elsewhere (such as Hollywood). As a result, many were labeled communists (often falsely) and therefore came to be seen in a negative light, perhaps for the rest of their lives.

Moral Panics

Moral entrepreneurs can stir up such a fuss that they cause a **moral panic**, or a widespread but disproportionate reaction to the form of deviance in question (Goode and Ben-Yehuda 1994, 2009; Hier 2011; Krinsky 2013). It could be argued that today we are witnessing, both in the United States and in Europe, a moral panic over the threat posed by immigrants, especially those who are undocumented. Singled out in the United States in this panic are immigrants from Latin America, especially Mexico. In Europe—and to a lesser degree in the United States—it is Muslims who are causing a moral panic. Of course, a related moral panic involves the threat of terrorism posed by radical Islamic groups. However, it is important to remember that the vast majority of Muslims are *not* terrorists.

A good historical example of a moral panic is the witch craze that occurred in Europe between the fourteenth and sixteenth centuries (Ben-Yehuda 1980, 1985). The idea of witches had existed before this time, but it was seen as a more complex phenomenon involving both bad and good witches. In any case, no assumption had been made about a conspiracy between women and Satan to corrupt the world. However, in this era Dominican friars took the lead in defining witchcraft as such a conspiracy and as a crime subject to corporal punishment, in this case burning at the stake. The friars were the moral entrepreneurs in this case. They played a key role in generating a moral panic that came to involve large numbers of people. That panic, in turn, led to the painful deaths of hundreds of thousands of people, mostly women.

Moral Panic

Moral panics such as the witch-hunting crazes of Renaissance Europe rely in part on the use of labels to identify a perceived threat. What might help stem the development of a moral panic?

Moral panics are, by definition, exaggerated. Thus, the threat posed by witches in the fifteenth century, the communists in the 1950s, and immigrants and even terrorists today is made out by many, especially moral entrepreneurs, to be greater than it really is. One of the ways to do this is to create a "folk devil" who stands for that which is feared. In the case of communism it was Joseph Stalin or Mao Zedong; more recently terrorism made Osama bin Laden a folk devil.

Stigma

Erving Goffman's (1963) *Stigma* is a very important contribution of symbolic interactionism to our understanding of deviance. A **stigma** is a characteristic that others find, define, and often label as unusual, unpleasant, or deviant. Goffman begins his book with analyses of physically stigmatized individuals such as those missing a nose. He then introduces a wide array of other stigmas such as being on welfare. In the end, readers come to the realization that they have been reading not only about people who are unlike them, with major physical deformities, but rather about themselves: "The most fortunate of normals is likely to have his half-hidden failing, and for every little failing there is a social occasion when it will loom large, creating a shameful gap" (Goffman 1963: 127). Goffman's idea of a stigma has attracted many scholars and has been applied to many forms of deviance, such as prostitution (Scambler and Paoli 2008; Wong, Holroyd, and Bingham 2011), mental illness (Payton and Thoits 2011), and mothers of children suffering from Asperger's syndrome (Hill and Liamputtong 2011).

There are two types of stigmatized individuals. The individual with a **discredited stigma** "assumes his differentness is known about already or is evident on the spot." In contrast, those with a **discreditable stigma** assume that their stigma "is neither known about by those present nor immediately perceivable about them" (Goffman 1963: 4). An example of a discredited stigma

might be a lost limb or being a member of a minority group viewed negatively by others, while discreditable stigmas include having done poorly in school or having a prison record. As is to be expected with a symbolic interactionist perspective, of great importance is the symbolic nature of the stigma and the individual's interaction with others, especially those thought to be normal. Because the physical nature of a discreditable stigma is not visible to others, neither are its symbolic qualities. Nevertheless, the people with such a stigma want to make sure it remains secret and thus try to conceal the stigmatizing information during most interactions. However, in the case of a discredited stigma (such as being morbidly obese), those with the stigma must deal with the tension associated with interacting with people who view them negatively because of the stigma.

The idea of discreditable stigma has wide applicability to the contemporary world. For example, the court records of juvenile offenders are often hidden from the public or expunged to avoid stigmatizing otherwise promising young people for a lifetime. People with mental illness or substance abuse problems often go to great lengths to hide the real reason for unscheduled absences from work. Parents of mentally disabled children, especially the mildly impaired, "mainstream" their children in standard classrooms in part so their disability will be more likely to be discreditable than discredited. The theme of hiding stigmatizing conditions is common in popular entertainment as well: In the movie *Philadelphia* (1993), actor Tom Hanks plays a high-powered lawyer in a prestigious law firm who is diagnosed with HIV during the early years of the epidemic. As the disease progresses, he tries but ultimately fails to conceal the signs that he has the disease, such as skin blemishes associated with Kaposi's sarcoma. When it becomes clear to the leaders of his firm that he has AIDS, he is fired. This movie, unlike some, realistically portrays the painful, destructive effects of revealing a discredited stigma.

stigma A characteristic that others find, define, and often label as unusual, unpleasant, or deviant.

discredited stigma A stigma that the affected individual assumes is already known about or readily apparent.

discreditable stigma A stigma that the affected individual assumes is neither known about nor immediately perceivable.

ACTIVE SOCIOLOGY

Have You Broken a Social Norm Today?

Folkway violations—that is, mild forms of deviance—often provide good examples of humor. Several websites are devoted to sharing—for the sake of humor—acts of deviance witnessed in public. One of these is People of Walmart (www.peopleofwalmart.com). Visit the site and record your observations below. Be prepared to share and discuss them with the class.

1. How do the photos on the site demonstrate deviance? Provide a few examples.

2. Do any of the acts pictured cross the line from violation of folkways to violation of mores (see Chapter 3)? Explain your answer.

3. Is there any evidence of potentially illegal activity?

4. Have you ever posted anything to a site like this? What was the result?

5. Does the fact that deviant actions can be instantly and permanently put on view influence what you do in public? If so, how?

CRIME

While there are many ways to define it, **crime** is simply a violation of the criminal law (Whitehead 2007). As pointed out above, it is the fact that it violates the law that differentiates crime from other forms of deviance. **Criminology** is the field devoted to the study of crime (S. Brown 2007a; Maguire, Morgan, and Reiner 2012; Rosenfield 2011). Many, but certainly not all, criminologists are sociologists. (Jack Levin, one criminologist/sociologist who actively presents his views to the public, offers his thoughts on his own work in the next "Public Sociology" box.) While many criminologists are now found in departments and schools devoted to the study of criminology, a large number work in sociology departments. There is a sociology of crime, but the field also includes those from many other disciplines such as psychologists, economists, biologists, and anthropologists, as well as officials who once worked in the criminal justice system. In fact, the field today has become much more multidisciplinary, even interdisciplinary (Wellford, 2012).

> **crime** A violation of the criminal law.
>
> **criminology** The study of all aspects of crime.

CHECKPOINT 6.2 — COMPARING THEORIES OF DEVIANCE

Explanatory theories attempt to explain why deviance does or does not occur.	**Constructionist theories** attempt to describe the process by which we define and classify some behaviors as deviant and others as normal.
—Structural/functional theories: Strain theory, social control, broken windows, self-control. —Conflict/critical theories.	—Inter/actionist theories: Labeling theory.

While there is growing interdisciplinarity in the study of crime, sociology plays an important role in it. Clearly a variety of sociological factors (including social class and race [Chilton and Triplett 2007a, 2007b]) are involved in who commits crimes and which crimes they commit. The same sociological factors are involved in who gets caught, prosecuted, and incarcerated, as well as how much of the sentence they actually serve. And such factors are involved in what happens to people after they serve their sentences and whether or not they are likely to end up back in prison.

The "father of criminology" is Cesare Lombroso who published *The Criminal Man* in 1876 (McShane and Williams 2007). The title of the book reflects the fact that the focus of early criminologists was on criminals and their innate physical or psychological characteristics. Criminals were seen as being defective in various ways, and the goal was to study scientifically the defects and those who had them in

Stigma

Public Shaming

Edwin H. Sutherland

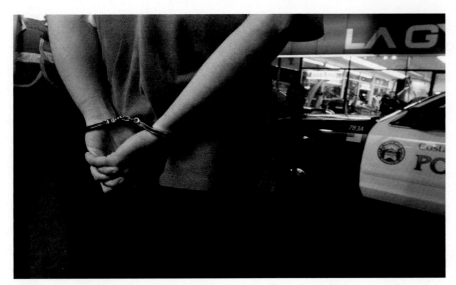

Crime worries many people despite the fact that few are actually likely to be victims of a crime. What insights does sociology bring to the study of crime?

leveled at differential association theory; even Sutherland later came to criticize it on various grounds. For example, it didn't explain why some people became criminals while others exposed to the same situations did not. One of Sutherland's own criticisms was the fact the theory did not give enough attention to the role of opportunity in committing crimes.

ASK YOURSELF

Why do some people become criminals while others exposed to the same situations do not? Consider the theories of deviance discussed above as you prepare your answer.

order to deter crime. While the major causes were considered to lie within the individual, they were seen as being beyond their control. In fact, Lombroso's main focus was on the "born criminal." Hence, the early criminologists adopted the view that such people needed the external control of the criminal justice system. Lombroso was prone to gross and indefensible generalizations such as contending that gypsies "murder in cold blood in order to rob, and were formerly suspected of cannibalism. The women are very clever at stealing" (cited in Williams and McShane 2007: 2663).

In more recent years criminology has shifted away from its focus on criminals and their defects and to a concern with the social context of criminal actions and the effect of those actions on the larger society. A key figure in bringing a sociological perspective to criminology was Edwin Sutherland. Sutherland studied a variety of issues in criminology such as white-collar crime, the death penalty, and prisons, but his greatest influence was his textbook *Criminology* (Sutherland 1924). The book went through 10 editions and was used by students for nearly 70 years. Sutherland was a symbolic interactionist. This perspective helped shift the focus in criminology from the criminal and his misdeeds to society, especially the societal reaction to those actions, including the labels placed on criminals.

Sutherland's most important contribution to the sociology of crime is **differential association** theory. The main point is that people learn criminal behavior. Therefore, who a person associates with is crucial. One's family and friends—the primary group—are important sources of attitudes toward crime, knowledge about how to commit crimes, and rationalizations that help one live with being a criminal. Today, we would need to add the fact that criminal behavior can also be learned through television, songs, and especially the Internet. Many criticisms were

While the above focuses on the causes of crime, especially those that are sociological in nature, criminology has long had a second focus on the criminal justice system (Wellford 2012). This interest is traceable to another early Italian scholar, Cesare Beccaria (1738–1794) (McShane and Williams 2007). Beccaria was a lawyer by training and received a doctorate in law. He is best known for his 1764 book, *On Crimes and Punishments,* and its concern with such issues as the origins of law and the criminal justice system. His work led not only to an interest in this system but also to whether its major components—law enforcement, courts, and corrections (Culver 2007)—were fair, effective, and just. In terms of the latter, much work has been done on the (un)fairness, especially as far as race is concerned, of arrest decisions by the police, length of sentences, and likelihood of receiving the death penalty.

CRIMINAL JUSTICE SYSTEM

The criminal justice system in the United States consists of various loosely connected government agencies and individuals who work in those agencies. It is involved in the apprehension, prosecution, and punishment of those who violate the law. It also seeks to prevent those violations before they occur. Finally, the criminal justice system has many more general responsibilities such as ensuring public safety and maintaining social order (Culver 2007: 851). The major components of the

> **differential association** A theory that focuses on the fact that people learn criminal behavior from those with whom they associate.

criminal justice system are law enforcement, the courts, and the correctional system.

An enormous number of people are in the jail and prison system. At the beginning of 2012 there were over two and a quarter million adults incarcerated in federal and state prisons, and jails. The United States has the highest rate of incarceration (about 1 percent of the adult population) in the world. It has 600,000 more prisoners than China and over 1.5 million more than Russia (see Table 6.1). Although it has only 5 percent of the world's population, the United States has 25 percent of the world's prisoners (Cullen, Jonson, and Nagin 2011). This is a very costly system to operate (Bratton 2011). It is estimated that in 2008 local, state, and federal governments spent about $75 billion on corrections, much of it on incarceration (Schmidt, Warner, and Gupta 2010). Further complicating matters is the fact that the economic problems facing the United States in general, and state and local jurisdictions in particular, mean that fewer prisons and jails are being built while an increasing number of Americans are being sentenced to them. This increasingly large number of prisoners creates other problems including the overcrowding of the prisons as well as increased violence against fellow prisoners. Given the huge numbers involved, prisons have become little more than warehouses for prisoners. As a result of the increase in numbers, there is a tendency toward the decline in the ability of prisons to rehabilitate inmates and an increase in the focus on punishment (Phelps 2011).

Beyond the over 2 million people in prisons and jails, another 4,933,667 people were under the control of the criminal justice system because they were either on parole or on probation (Bureau of Justice Statistics 2009). **Parole** involves the supervised early release of a prisoner for such things as good behavior while in prison. Parole officers work with those on parole to help them adjust to life outside prison and to be sure they are not violating the conditions of their release. If they do violate those conditions, they can have their parole revoked, and they can be sent back to prison. Those who are convicted of less serious crimes may be placed on

parole The supervised early release of a prisoner for such things as good behavior while in prison.

probation A system by which those who are convicted of less serious crimes may be released into the community, but under supervision and under certain conditions such as being involved in and completing a substance abuse program.

specific deterrence Whether the experience of punishment in general, and incarceration in particular, makes it less likely that an individual will commit crimes in the future.

TABLE 6.1 • Countries with the Highest Prison Populations, 2011

Rank	Country	Number of Prisoners
1	United States	2,239,751
2	China	1,640,000
3	Russia	688,600
4	Brazil	548,003
5	India	372,296
6	Thailand	267,834
7	Mexico	242,754
8	Iran	217,000
9	South Africa	153,000
10	Indonesia	144,332

SOURCE: From *World Prison Brief: Entire World: Prison Population Totals.* International Centre for Prison Studies.

probation whereby they are released into the community with supervision. They are also released under certain conditions such as being involved in and completing a substance abuse program. If the offender does not adhere to these conditions, is arrested, or is convicted, probation can be revoked. In that case, a new, more restrictive probation can be imposed, or the offender can be sent to prison (Culver 2007). Both parole and probation require the involvement of a bureaucracy, especially the parole and probation officers involved in it. These systems, like the prison and jail system, are very costly.

It might be argued that this enormous cost of prisons—as well as the parole and probation systems—is justifiable if they taught people that "crime does not pay." In other words, a case might be made for mass imprisonment if it rehabilitated prisoners so that they there were less likely to commit crimes after they were released. But does a prison term serve as deterrence to the commission of crimes after an inmate is released from prison? It is obvious that prisoners are deterred while imprisoned from further crime, although some seem to be able to engage in crimes while in prison. After a prisoner is released, those involved in the criminal justice system are interested in the issue of **specific deterrence**, or whether the experience of punishment in general, and incarceration in particular, makes it less likely that the ex-prisoner will commit crimes in the future. In other words, the issue is whether an individual will be "scared"

Jack Levin

PUBLIC SOCIOLOGY

Jack Levin on Crime, in His Own Words

I have published the results of my research, mainly in the areas of murder and hate crimes, in scholarly books and journals accessible to fellow and future sociologists. However, I have also had an interest in reaching an audience of laypersons and opinion leaders. While my bachelor's degree and doctorate are both in sociology, I also have a master's degree in communication research.

I am certain that effective theory and research are essential for the development of important sociological ideas, but there is much more to the mission of the field than scholarship alone. There are many sociologists who share my conviction that we must apply sociological knowledge, not as some academic exercise, but with the purpose of improving the quality of social life generally.

I have had a professional mission that contains elements of both journalism and sociology. I have sought to share sociological insights that might enhance the rationality of public discourse and the effectiveness of important policy decisions. I have written hundreds of opinion columns and have been interviewed for perhaps thousands of articles in major newspapers and magazines. In addition, I have appeared on hundreds of television programs where I was given an opportunity to apply a sociological perspective to some public controversy or breaking news event. For example:

- In the area of defending efforts at reducing illegal immigration, I suggested that our response ought to be based on facts rather than stereotypes. Research has shown that immigrants have a much lower rate of violent crime and a lower rate of incarceration than native-born Americans.

- In popular thinking, mass killers suddenly snap—go bonkers or berserk, run amok. Actually, they are almost always methodical and selective, not at all impulsive or spontaneous, planning their crimes for days, weeks, even months before they strike. In addition, few mass murderers target their victims in shopping malls or parking lots. They select family members, co-workers, or fellow students, rather than random strangers.

- I suggested that the AMBER Alert program—the practice of going public with an urgent bulletin in the most serious child-abduction cases—is "not as good as people believe." By the time law enforcement alerts the public to a truly dangerous situation, the abducted child has already returned home or has been killed.

- A few years ago, I wrote a *Boston Globe* opinion column in which I was very critical of attempts to register sex offenders. Thanks to the severity of the stigma, many offenders are forced to relocate many times to different neighborhoods and shelters. Too often, they end up living under bridges or on the streets, where control over their activities is nonexistent (see Russell Banks's 2011 novel, *Lost Memory of Skin*).

I seek to broaden the scope of the journalistic enterprise, to modify the thinking of reporters and commentators, so that the sociological perspective is never left out of the public conversation.

SOURCE: Printed with the permission of Jack Levin.

Think About It

Do you think the "public conversation" about crime to which Jack Levin refers sometimes lacks the sociological perspective? Give an example to support your answer. Do you agree with Levin that sociological knowledge should be applied to improving the quality of social life? Why or why not?

---

straight by punishment, especially incarceration (Apel and Nagin 2011).

Recidivism is the repetition of a criminal act by one who has been convicted for an offense (Smith 2007). However, most research in the field has shown that prisons do a poor job of rehabilitating prisoners and as a result do not reduce recidivism. Instead, there is evidence that prisons are "schools for crime." Those in them learn new and better criminal techniques. In other words, prisons have a "criminogenic" effect leading to more rather than less crime (Cullen, Jonson, and Nagin 2011). Nonetheless, no experts would argue for the elimination of punishments, including imprisonment, for most crimes. However, there is a need for more focused forms of specific deterrence (Braga and Weisburd 2011). Furthermore, there are important individual and situational differences that have an impact on the effectiveness of such deterrence. What is needed is a focus on what forms of specific deterrence will be effective on what types of criminals and under what circumstances (Piquero et al. 2011).

> **recidivism** The repetition of a criminal act by one who has been convicted for an offense.

General deterrence deals with the population as a whole and whether individuals will be less likely to commit crimes because of fear that they might be punished or imprisoned for their crimes (Apel and Nagin 2011). Although it is not clear how many people do not commit crimes because of fear of punishment, it is clear that it constitutes some level of deterrence to some who might otherwise become criminals.

The ultimate example of both forms of deterrence is capital punishment or the death penalty (Paternoster, Brame, and Bacon 2007). Someone who is executed clearly cannot commit another crime. However, there is evidence that even capital punishment is not a strong general deterrent to crime (Cohen-Cole et al. 2009).

Although a number of countries have abolished the death penalty, the United States is one of many countries

The last public execution in the United States was the 1936 hanging of Rainey Bethea, a 22-year-old black man, for the rape of a 70-year-old white woman in Kentucky. What arguments can be made against capital punishment?

that continue to employ it. The four leading countries in the world in terms of the number of people executed are China, Iran, North Korea, and Yemen. These are countries that the United States would not like to be associated with, especially on this issue. The United States ranks fifth with 43 executions in 2011 (Amnesty International 2012). This is fewer than the 200 or so who were executed in each of two consecutive years in the 1930s. Overall, there have been more than 15,000 known executions in the United States (Paternoster 2007). While this is a large number, capital punishment remains rare in the United States, especially when one considers the number of capital crimes (such as murder) committed every year. There has also been a trend toward more "humane," if such a thing is possible, executions. Prior to 1930, most executions were done by hanging. Many of these were mishandled resulting in those who were condemned gradually choking to death. From 1930 to 1967 the majority of executions were by electrocution. This did not seem to be much of

an improvement as the initial electrical charge, at least in some cases, did not cause death or even unconsciousness and in some cases caused the condemned to catch on fire. Beginning in 1977 there was movement toward the use of lethal injections, and about 80 percent of executions are now performed in that way.

The application of capital punishment continues to be highly controversial. In fact, many death sentences are accompanied by active campaigns against them and vigils protesting executions both before and as they occur. There are many who feel that it is morally wrong to kill anyone. Others are opposed to the death penalty because it is likely that at least some innocent people are killed in the process (Aronson and Cole 2009). Finally, there is strong evidence of bias, especially racial bias, in capital punishment. Many studies have shown that blacks, and nonwhites more generally, who are convicted of killing whites are more likely to get the death penalty than whites who kill other whites (Paternoster 2007).

TYPES OF CRIMES

Much data on crime is found in the FBI's Uniform Crime Report (UCR), which includes crimes reported to the police and police arrest statistics (see Table 6.2). Two broad types of crime are reported. **Violent crime** involves the

---

general deterrence The deterrence of the population as a whole from committing crimes for fear that the members will be punished or imprisoned for their crimes.

violent crime The threat of injury or the threat or actual use of force, including murder, rape, robbery, and aggravated assault, as well as terrorism and, globally, war crimes.

Types of Crime

Hate Crimes

TABLE 6.2 • Arrest Trends in the United States, 2002–2011

| | Number of persons arrested | | | | | | | | |
| | Total all ages | | | Under 18 years of age | | | 18 years of age and over | | |
Offense charged	2002	2011	Percent change	2002	2011	Percent change	2002	2011	Percent change
Murder and nonnegligent manslaughter	7,630	6,752	−11.5	679	500	−26.4	6,951	6,252	−10.1
Forcible rape	17,293	12,069	−30.2	2,814	1,735	−38.3	14,479	10,334	−28.6
Robbery	67,523	67,791	+0.4	15,339	14,360	−6.4	52,184	53,431	+2.4
Aggravated assault	305,232	258,765	−15.2	39,849	25,345	−36.4	265,383	233,420	−12.0
Burglary	189,315	193,993	+2.5	56,995	40,253	−29.4	132,320	153,740	+16.2
Larceny-theft	755,039	840,187	+11.3	227,824	172,003	−24.5	527,215	668,184	+26.7
Motor vehicle theft	86,046	40,876	−52.5	26,324	8,301	−68.5	59,722	32,575	−45.5
Arson	10,790	7,385	−31.6	5,616	3,210	−42.8	5,174	4,175	−19.3

SOURCE: From Federal Bureau of Investigation, Uniform Crime Report, Table 32. U.S. Department of Justice, Federal Bureau of Investigation.

threat of injury or the threat or actual use of force. The violent crimes are murder and negligent manslaughter, forcible rape, robbery, and aggravated assault. Although they do not appear in the UCR, in recent years increasing attention has been paid in the United States and elsewhere to violent crimes related to terrorism, as well as globally to war crimes (Gartner 2007). **Property crimes** do not involve injury or force, but rather are offenses that involve gaining or destroying property. While there are others such as shoplifting and forgery, the major property crimes are burglary, larceny-theft, motor-vehicle theft, and arson; about three-fourths of all U.S. crime is property crime (Copes and Null 2007). Another important way of distinguishing between crimes is by separating **felonies**, or more serious crimes punishable by a year or more in prison, from **misdemeanors**, or minor offenses punishable by imprisonment of less than a year.

Beyond these broad types, a number of more specific types of crime are important to society and to criminologists:

- **White-collar crimes** are those committed "by a person of responsibility and high social status in the course of his occupation" (Geis 2007b: 850).

- **Corporate crime** involves legal organizations that violate the law. It includes such illegal acts as antitrust violations, stock market violations such as insider trading, and false advertisements (Geis 2007a).

- **Organized crime** can involve various types of organizations, but is most often associated with syndicated organized crime, especially the Mafia, which uses violence or the threat of violence and the corruption of public officials to profit from illegal activities (Griffin 2007). Other examples of organized crime are Mexican drug cartels and the Russian Mafia.

property crimes Crimes that do not involve injury or force, but rather are offenses that involve gaining or destroying property.

felonies Serious crimes punishable by a year or more in prison.

misdemeanors Minor offenses punishable by imprisonment of less than a year.

white-collar crimes Crimes committed by responsible and (usually) high-social-status people in the course of their work.

corporate crime Violations of the law by legal organizations, including antitrust violations and stock market violations.

organized crime A type of crime that may involve various types of organizations but is most often associated with syndicated organized crime that uses violence (or its threat) and the corruption of public officials to profit from illegal activities.

- **Political crime** can be either an offense against the state to affect its policies, such as the assassination of one of its officials, especially its leader (as in the assassination of John F. Kennedy), or an offense by the state, either domestically (for example, spying on citizens) or internationally (state-sponsored terrorism; bribery of a foreign official) (Tunnell 2007).

- **Hate crimes** are those that stem, in whole or in part, from the fact that those who are being victimized are in various ways different from the perpetrators. These differences include race, religion, sexual orientation, gender, national origin, and disability status. Victims are held in contempt by the perpetrators (Levin 2007).

- **Cybercrime** (see the next "Digital Living" box) targets computers (for example, by hacking). Cybercriminals use computers to commit traditional crimes, such as stealing from a bank account or theft of a credit card number. They also use computers to transmit illegal information and images to carry out such activities as insider trading, identity theft, child pornography, plans for terrorist acts, or "cyberterrorism" (Nunn 2007).

- **Consumer crimes**, or crimes related to consumption, including shoplifting and using stolen credit cards or credit card numbers.

Although these are all classified as crimes, they are not all considered equally abhorrent. In line with the idea that deviance is defined by elites, so are crimes and criminal punishments. Thus white-collar and corporate crimes are often downplayed while the crimes usually associated with those in the lower social classes—for example, violent crimes, especially felonies, and property crimes—receive a great deal of attention from the police, the media, and the public.

ASK YOURSELF

Of the eight types of crime described above, which type do you consider most serious? Least serious? Why? What are your criteria for defining the seriousness of various types of crime?

GLOBALIZATION AND CRIME

The amount of global, or cross-border (Andreas and Nadelmann 2006; Shelley, Picarelli, and Corpora 2011), crime has increased with globalization. Globalization makes cross-border crime increasingly possible and more likely. International crime has existed for centuries in such forms as piracy on the oceans and the African slave trade. However, today there seems to be far more of it. This may be due to the fact that because of the increase in global criminal flows, much more public and government attention is devoted to these crimes. Fortunately, action against crime does flow almost as easily as the crimes themselves.

The growth in global crime is largely traceable to increasing concern about drugs in the United States in the late 1960s and early 1970s, as well as Western Europe's interest in terrorism during roughly the same period. Drugs and terrorism now top the list of global concerns as far as crime is concerned, but others include "clandestine trade in sophisticated weaponry and technology, endangered species, pornographic materials, counterfeit products, guns, ivory, toxic waste, money, people [i.e., trafficking in human beings; Farr 2005], stolen property, and art and antiquities" (Andreas and Nadelmann 2006: 5). All of these involve flows of all sorts—drugs, money, human victims (for example, those to be used as prostitutes), and human perpetrators (such as terrorists). They also include various illegal things that flow through the World Wide Web (e.g., child pornography, laundered funds, the spread of computer viruses).

These illegal flows have been aided by the decline of the nation-state and its increasing inability to reduce, or halt, them. Furthermore, global criminal cartels have come into existence to expedite illegal flows and to increase the profits that can be derived from them. The book *McMafia* attributes much of their success to increasingly sophisticated organizational methods (including economies of scale, global partnerships, and

> **political crime** Either an illegal offense against the state to affect its policies, or an offense by the state, either domestically or internationally.
>
> **hate crimes** Crimes that stem from the fact that the victims are in various ways different from, and disesteemed by, the perpetrators.
>
> **cybercrime** Crime that targets computers, uses computers to commit traditional crimes, or transmits illegal information and images.
>
> **consumer crime** Crimes related to consumption, including shoplifting and using stolen credit cards or credit card numbers

Internet Crime   Crimes on Campus

Cybercrime

Certain characteristics of the web, such as the infinite reproducibility of information and the ease of distributing that information across time and space, lend it to new modes of crime. Significantly, the Internet allows crime to become increasingly globalized. As a result, cybercrime is seldom restricted to national borders. However, it is important to remember that, while the infrastructures through which crimes are committed have changed, the social problems and individual incentives that motivate crime remain much the same. As with traditional crime, there is a wide range of crimes committed using the Internet. One of the most common and widespread Internet crimes is hacking, or illegally accessing data. Others are digital content piracy and government and industrial espionage. For example, American intelligence agencies have publicly condemned both China and Russia for using the Internet to steal valuable technology from the U.S. government and American corporations. The losses are so substantial that it is impossible to estimate their value (Shanker 2011). In fact, China's digital espionage has now escalated to such a degree that it has been called a new "Cold War in cyberspace" (Sanger 2013).

Also to be noted here is the distribution of illegal content (such as child pornography), as well as the existence of sexual harassment, through the Internet.

Are you surprised that new forms of crime have become possible with the development and worldwide use of the Internet? Is cybercrime inevitable?

While it is not a crime, also worth mentioning in this context is cyberbullying through, among other things, online social networks (Kowalski, Limber, and Agatson 2012), as well as sexting, or sending racy pictures via, for example, Snapchat.

Identity theft through phishing and hacking databases is yet another common form of crime on the Internet (Holt and Turner 2012). It is subject to intense media attention, and many businesses advertise their ability to prevent such theft. The most common form of identity theft is unauthorized use of a credit card account. It is estimated that, in a two-year period, 5 percent of American adults were the target of attempted or successful identity theft. Losses totaled $17.3 billion (Bureau of Justice Statistics 2008).

Think About It

Do you believe music file sharing is deviant? Should it be criminalized? What purpose does enforcing copyright laws serve? Who benefits, and who is harmed?

SOURCE: Printed with the permission of PJ Rey.

---

the opening of new markets) that are copied from leading legitimate businesses such as McDonald's (Glenny 2008). New technologies have also been employed to make at least some criminal flows more successful. For example, one cartel used a primitive submarine to transport drugs. The Internet has made a number of illegal flows (e.g., child pornography and Internet scams) much easier and is largely impervious to efforts at control by individual nation-states.

"Criminalization" of Global Activities

As pointed out earlier, crime (and deviance) is always a matter of social definition or social construction. So although the power of nation-states has generally declined in the global age, it continues to matter greatly as far as what come to be *defined* as global forms of deviance and crime. In the era of globalization, the nation-states of Western Europe and the United States have played the central role in criminalizing certain activities. It is *their* sense of morality

Women and Crime in Taliban-Controlled Afghanistan

In areas of Afghanistan where the Taliban are in control, women are confined to their homes or strictly supervised in public. As a result, they have little opportunity to commit most types of crime that Americans consider worthy of the name. However, women are subject to severe punishment for social offenses such as adultery and elopement. Under Islamic sharia law it is permissible to this day to stone people to death, especially women, as well as to amputate parts of the body. The practice was described in gruesome detail in the 2008 movie *The Stoning of Soraya M.*

Stoning made the news a few years ago when a couple, who had been unable to persuade the woman's family to allow them to marry, was stoned to death for eloping. The man was married with two children, but that was not the problem. Afghan men can have as many as four wives. The problem was that the woman was engaged to a relative of the man, but refused to marry him. A religious court found the couple guilty and sentenced them to death by stoning.

The couple had run away, but they were tricked into returning by family members who said that they would be allowed to marry. Once they returned, the punishment was decided upon and carried out by a group of about 200 villagers (no women allowed). When the punishment commenced, members of

An Afghan woman pleads to be released from prison in Kabul, Afghanistan, where she was jailed without trial for the crime of adultery. Why do definitions of deviance and crime vary so much from one culture to another?

the Taliban were the first to cast stones. Others, including family members (the man's father and brother and the woman's brother), soon joined them. The woman died first from multiple wounds caused by the stones; the man died soon after. The crowd was reported to be joyful and festive during the stoning because the couple was perceived to have committed a crime (Nordland 2010).

Think About It

Given that women have so few opportunities for law breaking under Taliban rule, why are the punishments so severe for the acts of which they are convicted? In what other ways could these societies resolve what they perceive to be deviant behavior? Do you think movies like *The Stoning of Soraya M.* shed a useful light on extreme practices, or, by publicizing them globally, could they actually perpetuate violent responses to behaviors considered to be crimes?

---

and *their* norms of behavior that have come to be the rule in much of the world (Andreas and Nadelmann 2006). The global criminalization of drug use is a good case in point.

However, while there have been a number of efforts to define drug use as deviant and illegal, they have not always been successful. The global drug trade has in fact expanded in spite of great efforts by the United States and other nation-states to at least reduce it.

Much of the publicity about drugs and the ways in which they are implicated in globalization involves cocaine

and heroin. Great attention is devoted to, for example, the growing of poppies in Afghanistan and drug production in Guatemala and the ways in which drugs from those areas, and many others, make their way around the world. A relatively new global drug is methamphetamine (meth), made easily and cheaply in home-based "cooking facilities" from pseudoephedrine, the main ingredient in a number of cough, cold, and allergy medications. The AMC television show *Breaking Bad* deals with the "cooking" of meth by an ex–high school chemistry teacher in New

Crime on the Mexican American Border

The United Nations Office on Drugs and Crime (2012) estimates that 203 million people globally (5 percent of the world's population, aged 15–64) used illegal substances at least once in 2010, with the largest markets in North America and Europe. Because there is no way for affluent Americans who want these drugs to obtain them legally, a lucrative black market has emerged (see Figure 6.2). Drug cartels, taking advantage of lax regulation and weak enforcement mechanisms in South and Central America, have developed a complex infrastructure to produce drugs and smuggle them into the United States. Roughly 60 percent of all illicit drugs found in the United States enter through the Mexican border (Archibold 2009). The illegal drugs most trafficked across that border include marijuana, methamphetamine, and cocaine.

The cartels, each competing for a larger share of the multibillion-dollar industry, have ignited a series of turf wars. To secure or expand their hold on profitable drug routes, they are smuggling weapons from the United States, where guns are plentiful and laws regulating their purchase are lax, to Mexico. Possessing assault rifles, grenades, and bulletproof vests, gangs are now often better armed than local police forces. Moreover, because the drug trade is so much more profitable than other industries in Mexico, cartels are often able to buy off poorly paid local police officials. Violent crime on the Mexican side of the border has become commonplace. In the peak year of 2009, about 3,400 people were killed in the border city of Ciudad Juárez alone, leading it to be defined as one of the most dangerous and deadly

Crosses were erected in the Mexican border city of Ciudad Juarez to commemorate the unsolved serial murders of women there. What does U.S. demand for drugs contribute to the wave of violent drug crime Mexico is experiencing?

cities in the entire world (Thompson and Lacey 2010). The figure dropped to 2,028 in 2011, leading some to speculate that perhaps the murder wave was ebbing. Others suspect that the reason for the decline is that for the moment one drug cartel has gained control of the drug trade. This, they note, often produces a short-lived lull in conflict (Booth 2012). In fact, the violence has gotten so bad that thousands of Mexicans are fleeing their homes—some even seeking political asylum in the United States (McKinley 2010). Violence is also spilling over the American side of the border. For example, many home invasions are directly linked to the drug trade (Archibold 2009). Police believe

that in some cases, Americans have been murdered simply for crossing paths with drug traffickers in the process of sneaking across the border (Archibold 2010).

Violence stemming from the drug trade is now so significant that it has come to dominate U.S.–Mexico relations.

Think About It

How would a conflict theorist explain the persistence of the violent drug trade occurring on the U.S.–Mexico border? How much do different definitions of deviance involving drugs and guns contribute to this ongoing problem?

FIGURE 6.2 • Trafficking Routes of Black-Market Drugs, 2007

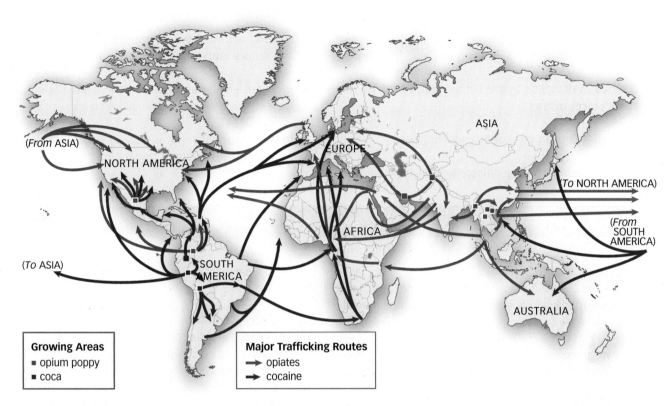

Growing Areas
- opium poppy
- coca

Major Trafficking Routes
- → opiates
- → cocaine

SOURCE: From Gilman, Nils; Jesse Goldhammer; and Steven Weber. *Deviant Globalization: Black Market Economy in the 21st Century.* Copyright © 2011 Continuum Publishing Company. Reprinted with permission.

Mexico and meth's often violent relationship to the drug trade in nearby Mexico. Once largely an American phenomenon, the production and use of methamphetamine is expanding globally. For example, it is a growing problem in the Czech Republic and Slovakia, and the fear is that it will spread from there throughout the European Union and many other parts of the world as well (Kulish 2007).

There are several aspects of crime, especially as it relates to drugs, that help to account for why global, as well as national, efforts to counter it have been largely unsuccessful. First, those who commit the crimes do not require a great many resources. Second, they do not need very much expertise to commit the crimes. Third, such crimes are easy to conceal. Fourth, in many cases the crimes are not apt to be reported to the police or other authorities. Finally, the crimes are those for which great consumer demand exists and there are no readily available alternative products (e.g., drugs) or activities (e.g., prostitution) (Andreas and Nadelmann 2006).

CHECKPOINT 6.3	**SOCIOLOGICAL CONCEPTS OF CRIME**
Crime	A violation of the criminal law.
Criminology	The study of crime.
Differential association theory	Theory that people learn criminal behavior from those with whom they associate.
Specific deterrence	Reduced likelihood of future crimes because of experiencing punishment and specifically incarceration.
General deterrence	Reduced likelihood that the population as a whole will be likely to commit crimes for fear of punishment, particularly imprisonment.

However, it would be wrong to judge global efforts to control drugs and other illegal substances and activities as complete failures. The fact is that while drugs continue to flow readily throughout the world (see Figure 6.2) for the reasons suggested above, the United States has had considerable success in internationalizing its views, laws, procedures, and efforts at enforcement. As mentioned earlier,

Mexico's Drug War

powerful societies are often able to get weaker societies to adopt their ways of doing things. Foreign governments have

- altered their laws and methods of law enforcement to more closely match U.S. laws on drugs;

- acceded to demands by the United States to sign law enforcement treaties;

- adopted American investigative techniques;

- created specialized drug enforcement agencies;

- stationed law enforcement representatives in other countries;

- enacted various laws on conspiracy, asset forfeiture, and money laundering relating to drugs; and

- provided greater assistance to the United States, and their changed laws, on financial secrecy.

In other words, we have seen an Americanization of law enforcement throughout much of the world.

SUMMARY

For sociologists, a person or action is deviant when socially defined as such. Durkheim argued that since deviance and crime have always existed in all societies, they are, in essence, normal and have positive functions for society.

Merton's strain theory is a contemporary version of structural-functionalism and argues that deviance is more likely to occur when a culture values something, such as material success, but the societal structure does not allow everyone the ability to achieve this value in a socially accepted way. Hirschi's social control theory focuses on why people do not commit deviant acts.

Conflict/critical theorists see inequality, in particular economic inequality, as the cause of much deviance. In this view, those in the lowest classes engage in deviant or criminal behavior because they otherwise have few ways of achieving normative societal goals, whereas those in the upper classes commit crimes

because the nature of their positions makes it relatively easy to do so.

From an inter/actionist perspective, deviance requires first a symbol or label, and second an interaction between a social control agent, the person or group doing the labeling, and the person or group to whom the label is applied. Another inter/actionist perspective comes from Goffman's writings on stigma, a characteristic that others find, define, and often label as unusual or deviant.

Crime is a form of deviance that violates criminal law. The major components of the criminal justice system are law enforcement, the courts, and the correctional system.

Increasing globalization has been associated with increases in global or cross-border crime, particularly the international drug trade. Illegal flows are aided by nation-states' declining ability to halt them.

KEY TERMS

Conformists, 165
Consumer crime, 181
Corporate crime, 180
Crime, 175
Criminology, 175
Cybercrime, 181
Deviance, 159
Differential association, 176
Discreditable stigma, 174
Discredited stigma, 174
Felonies, 180
General deterrence, 179
Hate crimes, 181
Innovators, 165

Labeling theory, 172
Misdemeanors, 180
Moral entrepreneurs, 173
Moral panic, 13
Organized crime, 180
Parole, 177
Political crime, 181
Primary deviance, 172
Probation, 177
Property crimes, 180
Rebels, 165
Recidivism, 178
Retreatists, 165
Ritualists, 165

Rule creators, 173
Rule enforcers, 173
Secondary deviance, 172
Social control, 173
Social control agents, 172
Social control theory, 167
Specific deterrence, 177
Stigma, 174
Strain theory, 164
Symbol, 171
Violent crime, 179
White-collar crime, 180

1. What do sociologists mean when they say that deviance is socially defined? Given a sociological approach, in what ways is tattooing deviant, and in what ways is it not?

2. How can we understand deviance as a global flow? How do countries differ in terms of their interpretation of what is deviant? In an increasingly globalized world, what are the consequences of these differing interpretations?

3. How does consuming the "wrong" products and services make someone a deviant? What does this suggest about the relationships between power and deviance?

4. Adolescents and teenagers value a certain level of independence from their parents. Often, teenagers want more control over their own lives. They want to be able to do what they want to do without the need for permission from their parents. Apply Merton's strain theory to an understanding of how teenagers might behave given this desire for more independence.

5. Why do those who rank high in such hierarchies as business, government, and the military have a much greater ability to commit deviant acts, to have them be seen as being legitimate, and to get away with them?

6. What does this elite deviance suggest about the "fairness" of deviance?

7. What are the differences between a discredited stigma and a discreditable stigma? What is an example of each?

8. How is crime different from deviance? Why do some forms of deviance become criminalized and others do not?

9. Are you hopeful of success in Mexico's drug war?

10. What sort of barriers do countries attempt to implement in order to limit the global flow of drugs? Why have these been relatively unsuccessful?

APPLYING THE SOCIOLOGICAL IMAGINATION ·····················

In this exercise you will use an ethnomethodological approach to understand the stable and orderly properties of interactions on the Internet. You will need to pay specific attention to the ways in which rules are broken on the Internet.

First select a website that allows for people to interact with one another (such as Facebook, Twitter, Snapchat, your favorite interactive blog, an online discussion forum, or the comments section of an article on your local newspaper's website). In what ways does the Internet help facilitate behavior that might be deviant elsewhere? What norms are broken on the Internet that might not be broken in face-to-face interactions? What sorts of structural barriers exist on the Internet that might limit deviant behavior? Overall, do you think deviant behavior flows more easily because of the Internet?

STUDENT STUDY SITE ·····························

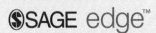

Sharpen your skills with SAGE edge at **edge.sagepub.com/ritzeressentials**

SAGE edge for students provides a personalized approach to help you accomplish your coursework goals in an easy-to-use learning environment.

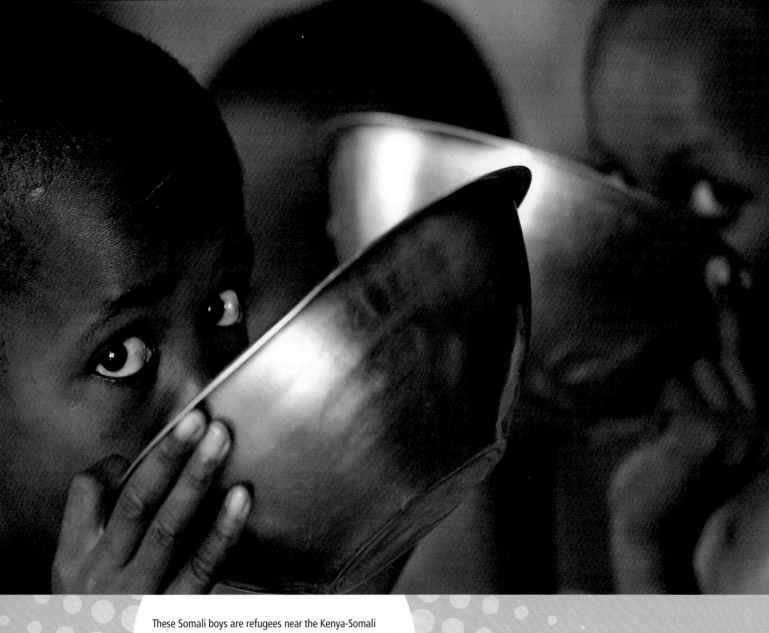

These Somali boys are refugees near the Kenya-Somali border, where famine threatens several million with starvation while people in other countries have more food than they can eat. How does sociology explain the existence of income, wealth, and other inequalities that serve to create and maintain distinct social classes?

SOCIAL STRATIFICATION

LEARNING OBJECTIVES

1 Describe the dimensions of social stratification: social class, status, and power.

2 Identify the factors involved in economic inequality, including income, wealth, and poverty.

3 Identify the types of social mobility and the forces that help and hinder them.

4 Discuss structural/functional, conflict/critical, and inter/actionist theories of social stratification.

5 Explain the relationship between consumption and social stratification.

Mark Zuckerberg, who dropped out of Harvard when the social networking site he created in his dorm room quickly became one of the most successful companies in the world, was only 22 when Yahoo offered him $900 million for Facebook. Now 29, Zuckerberg is said to be worth more than $13 billion and is still Facebook's CEO and major shareholder.

A small global class of ultra-rich elite is emerging at the top of the world's social hierarchy.

An unprecedented shift is taking place in the global socioeconomic structure. Deregulation of global trade and advances in information technology have led to the emergence of a small, ultra-rich class of elite entrepreneurs and executives who think and operate very differently than their predecessors. Some believe these fortunate few have much in common with one another, such as their tightly focused emotional and financial commitment to their business, their drive to create and innovate, and their staggering wealth and real or potential political influence. However, the elite don't always agree with each other, as the opposing views of two U.S. billionaires, investor Warren Buffett (CEO of Berkshire Hathaway) and Charles G. Koch

(CEO of Koch Industries), make clear. Buffett, the third-wealthiest person in the world, has publicly stated his belief that U.S. law should require him to pay more income tax than he does, while Koch, the sixth wealthiest, opposes the notion of higher taxes on the super-rich and believes in the power of private investments. But elites like these have much less in common with anyone else. Do they constitute a brand-new social class?

Increasing concentrations of wealth, power, and status have given an elite few the power to ascend to the very highest levels of the global system of social stratification. The norms, tastes, and beliefs they share have been shaped more by a global than a local culture. Many achieved their successes through risk-taking and hard work, rather than by being born into elite positions. They are fiercely driven and sometimes oblivious to the socioeconomic problems of the middle and lower classes of their home countries. Some observers worry that the elites' wealth allows them access to an unprecedented amount of social and political power that might be wielded with narrow self-interest.

As you read the following chapter, think about your own position in our stratified society. And—just for fun—imagine how having billions of dollars would affect your views of those below you in the social scale. •

We often hear that the world is unfair. That is, a relatively small number of people have way too much, while most of the rest, especially us, have far too little. In the United States, this unfairness is made abundantly clear when we see or read news reports about the excesses of the super-rich, such as multimillion-dollar bonuses, private jets, and mansions worth tens of millions of dollars. At the other extreme, the gap is just as clear when we encounter homeless people begging on street corners and at turn lanes on heavily traveled roads.

What is it that some people have, or are thought to have, and others lack? The most obvious answer is money and that which money buys. However, **social stratification** involves hierarchical differences not only in economic positions but also in other important areas such as status, or social honor, and power. Social stratification has a profound effect on how monetary and nonmonetary resources are distributed in American society and around the globe.

DIMENSIONS OF SOCIAL STRATIFICATION

Any sociological discussion of stratification draws on an important set of dimensions derived from the work of the great German social theorist Max Weber ([1921] 1968; Bendix and Lipset 1966; Ultee 2007a, 2007b). These three dimensions are social class, status, and power.

SOCIAL CLASS

One's economic position in the stratification system, especially one's occupation, defines one's **social class**. A person's social class position strongly determines and reflects his or her income and wealth. Those who rank close to one another in wealth and income can be said to be members of the same social class. For example, Bill Gates and Warren Buffett belong to one social class; the janitor in your university building and the mechanic who fixes your car at the corner gas station belong to another. Terms often used to describe a person's social class are *upper class* (e.g., large-scale entrepreneurs and

> **social stratification** Hierarchical differences and inequalities in economic positions, as well as in other important areas, especially political power and status, or social honor.
>
> **social class** One's economic position in the stratification system, especially one's occupation, which strongly determines and reflects one's income and wealth.

FIGURE 7.1 • Social Classes, Occupations, and Incomes in the United States

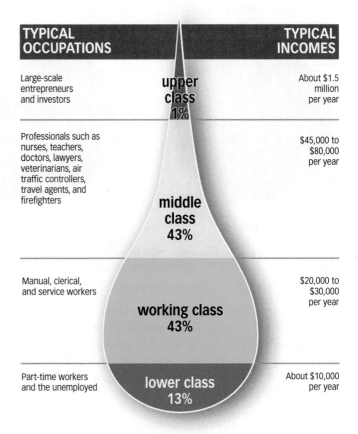

TYPICAL OCCUPATIONS		TYPICAL INCOMES
Large-scale entrepreneurs and investors	upper class 1%	About $1.5 million per year
Professionals such as nurses, teachers, doctors, lawyers, veterinarians, air traffic controllers, travel agents, and firefighters	middle class 43%	$45,000 to $80,000 per year
Manual, clerical, and service workers	working class 43%	$20,000 to $30,000 per year
Part-time workers and the unemployed	lower class 13%	About $10,000 per year

SOURCE: Adapted from Gilbert, D. L. (2011). *The American class structure in an age of growing inequality.* Thousand Oaks, CA: Pine Forge Press.

investors); *middle class* (e.g., semiprofessionals such as nurses, teachers, and firefighters); *working class* (e.g., manual, clerical, and sales workers); and *lower class* (e.g., part-time workers and the unemployed). Figure 7.1 illustrates the relationships among occupation, income, and social class in the United States. Its teardrop-like shape represents the percentage of Americans in each class; there are substantially more people in the working and lower classes than there are in the upper class. As we will soon see, the United States is even more stratified than Figure 7.1 suggests.

STATUS

The second dimension of the stratification system, *status* (introduced in Chapter 4), relates to the prestige attached

Incomes of the Top 1%

Social Class in America

FIGURE 7.2 • Who Earns More, Husbands or Wives? 1970 and 2013

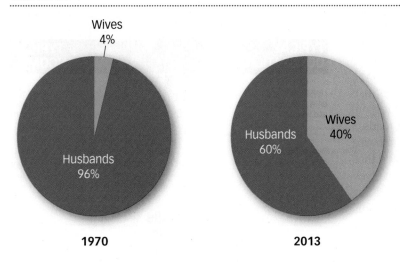

SOURCE: Reprinted with permission from "New Economics of Marriage: The Rise of Wives," Richard Fry and D'Vera Cohn, Pew Research Center, January 19, 2010.

to one's positions within society. This demonstrates that factors other than those associated with money are considered valuable in society. For example, in a 2007 Harris poll of 1,010 adult Americans, *firefighter* was ranked as the most prestigious occupation even though the pay is comparatively modest.

POWER

The third dimension of social stratification is **power**, the ability to get others to do what you want them to do, even if it is against their will. Those who have a great deal of power rank high in the stratification system, while those with little or no power are arrayed near the bottom. In politics, the president of the United States ranks very high in power, while millions of ordinary

Power, of course, is not restricted to the political system but also exists in many other institutions. Thus, top officials in large corporations have greater power than workers, religious leaders have more power than parishioners, and those who head households are more powerful than their spouses or children (Collins 1975).

Greater income is generally associated with more power, but there are exceptions to this general rule. In the late 2000s, an increasing number of media stories focused on the phenomenon of "breadwinner wives," or "alpha wives"—women who earn more than their husbands (Mundy 2013; Roberts 2010). As shown in Figure 7.2, only 4 percent of wives in 1970 had an income greater than that of their husbands, but by 2010, 40 percent of wives earned more than their husbands. In spite of their greater income, these women may not have greater power in the marital relationship and in many cases will need to be content sharing power with their husbands (Cherlin 2010). In fact, many high-earning women have great difficulty even finding a mate, and they face disapproval for breaking gender norms. Expectations regarding gender, and other types of minority status, can clearly complicate power relations.

ECONOMIC INEQUALITY

A major concern in the sociological study of stratification is **inequality**, a condition whereby some positions in society yield a great deal of money, status, and power while others yield little, if any, of these. While other bases of stratification exist, the system of stratification in the United States, and much of the contemporary world, is based largely on money. Money is not inherently valuable and desirable. It only has these characteristics when it is so defined in a money economy (Simmel [1907] 1978). In such an economy, the occupational structure is characterized by a payment system in which those

CHECKPOINT 7.1	THE DIMENSIONS OF SOCIAL STRATIFICATION
Social class	A person's economic position in the social stratification system: upper class, middle class, working class, or lower class.
Status	The prestige attached to a person's position within society.
Power	The ability to get others to do what you want them to, even if against their will.

voters have comparatively little political power. Still lower on the political power scale are disenfranchised citizens, such as convicted felons, and noncitizens, including undocumented immigrants (as well as foreign domestic workers such as those described in the next "Globalization" box).

power The ability to get others to do what you want them to do, even if it is against their will.

inequality The fact that some positions in society yield a great deal of money, status, and power while others yield little, if any, of these.

ACTIVE SOCIOLOGY

What Does Your Facebook Page Say About You?

Social class is visible in all parts of society. Even when we don't realize it, we are "doing" social class through the language, desires, style, and leisure activities we choose. As our lives become more visible on social media sites, we can even more easily see that social class is apparent in everyday life.

Examine your own Facebook timeline as well as those of three or four of your friends and record your observations below. Be prepared to discuss and share them in class.

1. How do your status updates, photos, likes, and comments illustrate your position in the stratification system? Why?

	How they illustrate my stratification position	Why
Status updates		
Photos		
Likes		
Comments		

2. How do your friends' timelines illustrate their position in the stratification system?

	How they illustrate friends' stratification position	Why
Status updates		
Photos		
Likes		
Comments		

3. Is social stratification discussed openly among any of you? If yes, how? If not, why not?

4. What do you think your posts and others' say about the display of social class and economic inequality in the United States?

in higher-level positions, and who perform well in these positions, are rewarded with larger paychecks. The use of money as a reward makes money seem valuable to people. They come to desire it for itself, as well as for what it will buy.

While other bases are possible, money remains at the root of the United States stratification system. Money can take the form of income or wealth. **Income** is the amount of money a person earns from a job, a business, or returns on various types of assets (e.g., real estate rents) and investments (e.g., dividends on stocks and bonds). Income is generally measured year by year. For example, you might have an income of $25,000 per year. **Wealth**, on the other hand, is the total amount of a person's financial assets and other properties accumulated to date less the total of various kinds of debts, or liabilities. Assets include such things as savings, investments, homes, and automobiles, while examples of debts include home mortgages, student loans,

> **income** The amount of money a person earns in a given year from a job, a business, or various types of assets and investments.
>
> **wealth** The total amount of a person's assets less the total of various kinds of debts.

Inequality in the United States

Domestic Workers in Kuwait

Kuwait is a small Persian Gulf nation-state with vast oil reserves. Because oil demands a high price on the global market, Kuwait is exceptionally wealthy. Wealth allows Kuwaitis to hire domestic workers, mostly women, from many relatively poor countries, including the Philippines, Sri Lanka, Nepal, and Indonesia (Fahim 2010).

A family might pay $2,000 to an agency to bring workers to Kuwait, but once there, the workers are under the control of their Kuwaiti employer-sponsors. While some are treated well, a large number have complained of sexual and/or physical abuse, not being paid their wages, and restrictions on their movements by, for example, withholding of their passports. In one case, a Sri Lankan maid escaped what she claimed had been 13 years of imprisonment, without pay, by her Kuwaiti employer. In another, it was reported that a Filipino maid was tortured and killed. Her employers then took her body to the desert and ran over it with a car to make her death appear to be an accident. Finally, a Filipino domestic sought help from her agency because of an abusive family. When the family members found out, they threw her out of a third-floor window, breaking her back.

With the acceleration of globalization, large numbers of poor people are traveling far from home in the hopes of finding work or, in many cases, being trafficked illegally. In many places in the world, including the United States, they

A maid sweeps the front of her employers' house in Kuwait. Laws to protect such workers have been slow in coming. Why?

have few, if any, rights and are subject to a wide range of abuses. Without rights, legal representation, or money, they are often powerless. They exist at the bottom of often very highly stratified societies.

Think About It

What accounts for the huge disparity in power between wealthy employers and the immigrants who work as their household help? Why do agencies that try to help these employees tend to focus on individual cases and not on the wider problem of power inequality? Would addressing power issues be more effective in the long run? Why or why not?

---

car loans, and amounts owed to credit card companies. If all your assets totaled $100,000, but you owed $25,000, your wealth (or net worth) would amount to $75,000. Wealth can be inherited from others, so a person can be very wealthy yet have a modest income. Many elderly widows and widowers find themselves in this position. Conversely, people can earn substantial incomes and not be very wealthy because, for example, they squander their money on expensive vacations or hobbies, or on alcohol or drugs.

INCOME INEQUALITY

Sociologists are interested in inequality in status and power, but they tend to be most concerned about economic inequality. In many parts of the world, incomes became more equitable from the late 1920s until the 1970s. However, since the 1970s, there has been a substantial increase in income inequality in many countries, with a few individuals earning a great deal more and many earning little, if any, more. Even in the United

These groups represent opposing views on economic inequality. What motivates each group?

States, which we historically and erroneously (Massey 2008) regard as an egalitarian society, the top 1 percent of Americans earned 23.5 percent of all income in 2007, up from 9 percent in 1979. The top 0.1 percent—yes, one-tenth of a percent—earned 6 percent of the nation's total income in 2007; this figure was only 2 percent in 1988 (Kocieniewski 2010).

Inequality became a hot political issue in 2011 with the release of government reports showing increasing inequality and poverty in the United States. The simple fact is that the average inflation-adjusted, after-tax family income of the top 1 percent of earners in the United States almost tripled between 1979 and 2007 (Congressional Budget Office 2011), as Figure 7.3 shows. Others in the top 20 percent (81st to 99th percentile) did well, but not nearly as well, with an increase of 65 percent in income. At the other end of the spectrum, the income for those in the bottom fifth increased by only 18 percent. The 60 percent in the middle, those between the top 20 percent and the bottom 20 percent, saw an increase of slightly less than 40 percent in income. Another way of looking at income inequality is the fact that the top 20 percent of the population had over 50 percent of all income—more than the bottom 80 percent. At the other end of the spectrum, the bottom 20 percent had only 5 percent of all income—down from 7 percent in 1979. The middle 60 percent had the rest of the income (over 40 percent), but their percentage of income had declined slightly from 1979. Between 2005 and 2007, the after-tax income of the top 20 percent was greater than the income for everyone else (the other 80 percent).

WEALTH INEQUALITY

As unfair as income inequality may seem, the greatest disparities in society—the greatest differences between the haves and the have-nots—are found to be disparities not in income but rather in the enormous differences in wealth in society. Inequality in wealth tends to be much greater than income inequality, as you can see in Figure 7.4. Like income inequality, wealth inequality has tended to increase in recent years in the United States and other western countries (Mishel and Bivens 2011; Wilterdink 2007). Over 80 percent of the wealth gain in the United States between 1983 and 2009 went to the wealthiest 5 percent of the population. In contrast, the poorest 60 percent of the population saw a 7.5 percent *decline* in its wealth. See Figure 7.5.

Those with great wealth live a lifestyle beyond the wildest dreams of those who live on the lowest rungs of the economic ladder. Wealth brings with it a wide range of advantages:

- It can be invested in stocks, bonds, real estate, and the like in order to yield greater income and to generate even greater wealth.

- It can be used to purchase material comforts of all sorts: large homes, vacation retreats, luxury cars, and custom-tailored clothes, as well as the services

Causes of Inequality

Occupy Movement

FIGURE 7.3 • Average Income Growth by Income Group, 1979–2007

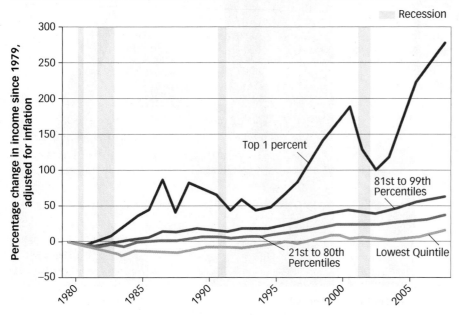

SOURCE: From *A CBO Study: Trends in the Distribution of Household Income Between 1979 and 2007.* October 2011. The Congress of the United States, Congressional Budget Office, Figure 2, page 3.

FIGURE 7.4 • Average Wealth of Americans by Quintile Rank, 2009

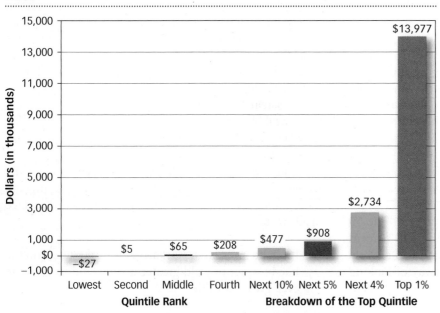

SOURCE: From Federal Reserve Board.

the means to live well for the rest of their lives.

• It purchases far more freedom and autonomy than less wealthy individuals can acquire. An example would be the freedom to leave unsatisfactory employment without worrying about how the bills will be paid.

Status, Power, and Wealth

Perhaps of greatest importance is the fact that wealth not only accords a high-level position on one dimension of stratification—social class—but it is also an important factor in gaining similar positions on the other dimensions of stratification—status and power. Those who have great wealth tend to rank high in social class because class is, to a considerable degree, defined economically and wealth is a key economic indicator of it. Those with great wealth are also generally able to buy or to otherwise acquire that which gives them high status and great power. There are exceptions, however, to the link between great wealth and high social class. An example is those who retain a high social ranking even though they have lost much or most of their wealth over time. Another exception is the nouveau riche, whose inelegant tastes and behaviors may lead others in the upper class to refuse to accept them as members of their class. However, in general, those with great wealth *are* members of the upper class.

In terms of status, the wealthy can afford more and better-quality education. They can, for example, send their children to very expensive and highly exclusive prep schools and Ivy League universities. In some elite universities, being a "legacy"—the son or daughter of an elite who attended the same school—can increase the chances of gaining admission. This practice is sometimes called "affirmative action for the rich" (Kahlenberg 2010). At Princeton, for example, 41.7 percent of legacy applicants in 2009 were admitted compared to 9.2 percent of nonlegacies. The wealthy can also purchase more of the trappings of high

of housekeepers, gardeners, mechanics, personal trainers, and so forth.

• It can afford a high level of financial security, allowing the wealthy, if they wish, to retire at an early age with

culture such as subscriptions to box seats at the opera or multimillion-dollar paintings by famous artists. The wealthy can also achieve great recognition as philanthropists by, for example, attending $1,000-a-ticket charity balls or even donating the money needed to build a new wing of a hospital.

Power over employees is a fact of life for wealthy individuals who own businesses or run other organizations. Their needs for financial, household, and personal services give the wealthy another source of power. They have the ability to direct the activities of many charities and civic groups. And if that isn't enough, the wealthy can buy more power by bribing political officials or making generous campaign contributions to favored politicians. Such contributions often give donors great behind-the-scenes power. In some cases, the wealthy choose to use their money to run for public office themselves; if successful, such families come to occupy positions that give them great power. These families can even become political dynasties with two or more generations obtaining high political office. Prescott Bush made his money on Wall Street and became a U.S. senator. His son, George H. W. Bush, became president of the United States, as did his paternal grandson, George W. Bush.

The lifestyles that large amounts of money can buy are a source of interest and fascination for many people. On MTV's *Cribs,* celebrity musicians and athletes show off their homes, pools, cars, and other trappings of wealth. Reality TV shows, such as Bravo's *Real Housewives* series and E!'s *Keeping Up With the Kardashians,* feature the daily lives of an elite group of the extremely wealthy. These shows highlight the gap between the wealthy and everyone else. The prevalence of such entertainment suggests a deep curiosity about how people with a great deal of status, money, and power live. For example, many of the real-life elites do not know how to do things that seem commonplace to many including pumping their own gasoline or waiting in line at the DMV for a driver's license.

In this political dynasty in the making are, second from left, George H. W. Bush, the 41st U.S. president, with his sons (l. to r.) Neil, Jeb (the former governor of Florida), George W. (the 43rd president), and Marvin.

The Perpetuation of Wealth

One of the great advantages of the wealthy is their ability to maintain their social class across generations. Their ability to keep their wealth, if not expand it, often allows

FIGURE 7.5 • Share of Total Wealth Gain of Americans by Quintile Rank, 1983–2009

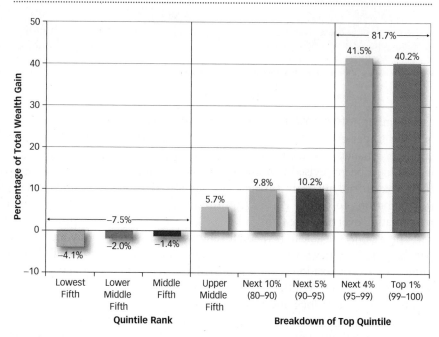

SOURCE: Adapted from *Occupy Wall Streeters Are Right about Skewed Economic Rewards in the United States,* Lawrence Mishel and Josh Bivens, Economic Policy Institute Briefing Paper #331, Figure L, p. 12.

Dalton Conley on Social Inequality

Dalton Conley published a well-known personal memoir, *Honky* (2001b), about his experience of growing up as a white child in the New York City projects. Among other things, he focused on the advantages he had over children of color growing up in the same environment.

In his many pieces for academic and public media, Conley has dealt with a wide range of issues including urban poverty, the black-white wealth gap, the family as a social stratifier, the advantages of having a randomly selected college roommate, and corporate crime. His main area of interest, however, is inequality within and across generations. In addition, he writes about the relationship between inequality and siblings, race, physical appearance, and health and biology. Let us look at the insights to be derived from some of his journalistic work:

- In a 2008 op-ed piece in the *New York Times* titled "Rich Man's Burden," Conley focuses on stratification among the most well-to-do members of society. He details how those near the top of the income hierarchy work more, more even

than those on the bottom of the stratification hierarchy. The reason is that those in the top half of the stratification system are very conscious of those above them and the fact that the latter may be pulling farther and farther ahead of them. As a result, even though they are well off, those near the top tend to work harder and longer hours in order to try to keep up, or at least to keep the gap from growing wider.

- In a 2001(a) essay in *The Nation* titled "The Black-White Wealth Gap," Conley shows that while black-white *income* differences are important, the difference between the races in their total *wealth* (net worth) is even greater. At the time he wrote this essay, among families with less than $15,000 in income, whites had an average net worth of $10,000, while blacks' net worth was zero. In middle-class families earning $40,000 a year, white families had a net worth of $80,000, while for black families the total was about half that. Among the super-rich, only two black Americans

were on the *Forbes* list of the 400 richest Americans. Today, there is only one black American—Oprah Winfrey—on that list. Winfrey's estimated net worth of $2.7 billion places her only 130th on that list. Whites have had a number of advantages such as long-term wealth, allowing assets to be passed down from one generation to the next. And, blacks have had many disadvantages including barriers to black property accumulation, especially of that most important, albeit now tarnished, component of net worth—home ownership.

Think About It

Dalton Conley (2012) has proposed that a lottery for admission to top colleges would help reduce inequality. Do you agree? Why or why not? Do you think a lottery system for other social advantages such as high-paying jobs or homes in desirable neighborhoods would help reduce inequality? Why or why not? What potential problems do you see with any of these lotteries?

---

the members of the upper class to pass their wealth, and the upper-class position that goes with it, to their children. Financial mechanisms (e.g., generation-skipping trusts) have been devised that allow the wealthy to pass their wealth on not only to the next generation, but to generations to come. Thus, wealth tends to be self-perpetuating over the long term.

The wealthy are able to perpetuate their wealth in large part because they have been able to use their money and influence to resist taxation systems designed to redistribute at least some of the wealth in society. For example, the wealthy have fought long and hard against the estate tax, which places a high tax on assets worth more than a certain amount (see below) that are left behind when they die. Many of the wealthy prefer to call the estate tax, in more negative terms, a "death tax."

A lack of wealth also tends to be self-perpetuating. Those who have little or no personal wealth can be fairly sure that their children, and generations beyond them, will also lack wealth. Of course there have been, and will be, many exceptions to this pattern, but in the main there is great consistency from generation to generation. This contradicts the Horatio Alger myth, which tells us that anyone can get ahead, or rise in the stratification system, through hard work and effort. The Horatio Alger myth is functional in that many people believe in it and continue to strive to get ahead (and some even do), often in the face of overwhelming barriers and odds. But it is also dysfunctional in that it tends to put all the burdens of achieving success on the shoulders of individuals. The vast majority of people are likely to fail and to blame themselves, rather than the unfairness of the highly stratified system, for their failures.

POVERTY

Poverty and the many problems associated with it are of great concern both to sociologists and to society as a whole (Iceland 2007, 2012). Poverty is troubling for many reasons, most importantly for its negative effect on the lives of the poor themselves. Those suffering from poverty are likely to be in poor health and to have a lower life expectancy. More generally, poverty hurts the economy in various ways. The vibrancy of the working class is reduced because poverty adversely affects at least some employees and their ability to work. They may be less productive or lose more work time due to illness. Another example is that the level of consumption in society as a whole is reduced because of the inability of the poor to consume very much. Crime, social disorder, and revolution are more likely where poverty is widespread.

The great disparity between the rich and the poor is considered by many to be a moral problem, if not a moral crisis, for society as a whole. The poor are often seen as not doing what they should, or could, to raise themselves out of poverty. They are seen as disreputable, which makes them objects of moral censure by those who have succeeded in society (Damer 1974; Matza 1966). They may be blamed for the degradation of society. However, some see poverty as an entirely different kind of moral problem. They argue that the poor should be seen as the "victims" of a system that impoverishes them (Ryan 1976). The existence of large numbers of poor people in otherwise affluent societies is a "moral stain" on that society (Harvey 2007). Something about a society that allows so much poverty must be amiss.

Those who lack the bare means of survival—food, clothing, and shelter—experience absolute poverty, although even this "absolute" standard varies from country to country. What does that variation tell us about global levels of stratification?

ASK YOURSELF

Do you believe the poor are victims? If so, of whom? Or do you believe the poor have chosen not to raise themselves from poverty? If so, what sociological factors would explain this choice?

ANALYZING POVERTY

It may be tempting to blame the poor for the existence of poverty, but a sociological perspective notes the larger social forces that create and perpetuate poverty. To the sociologist, poverty persists for three basic reasons:

- Poverty is built into the capitalist system, and virtually all societies today—even China—have a capitalist economy. Capitalist businesses seek to maximize profits. They do so by keeping wages as low as possible and by hiring as few workers as possible. When business slows, they are likely to lay people off, thrusting most of them into poverty. It is in the interest of the capitalist system to have a large number of unemployed, and therefore poor, people. This population serves as what Marx called the "reserve army of the unemployed." This is a readily available pool of people who can be drawn quickly into the labor force when business booms and more workers are needed. This reserve army also keeps existing workers in line and reluctant to demand much, if anything, from management.

- Competition among social classes encourages some elite groups of people to seek to enhance their economic position by limiting the ability of other groups even to maintain their economic positions. The elites do so by limiting the poor's access to opportunities and resources such as those afforded by various welfare systems.

> poverty line The threshold, in terms of income, below which a household is considered poor.

Public Sociology: Dalton Conley

Poverty

How are poverty and class related? Is poverty inevitable in a stratified society?

FIGURE 7.6 • Poverty in the United States, 1959–2011

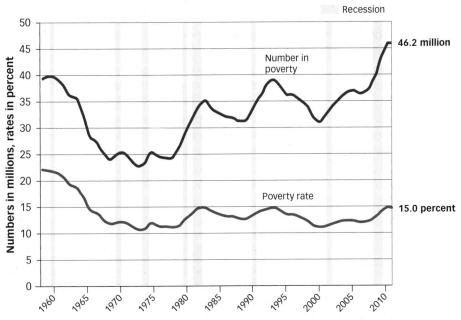

SOURCE: From DeNavas-Walt, Carmen, Bernadette D. Proctor, and Jessica C. Smith, U.S. Census Bureau, Current Population Reports, *Income, Poverty, and Health Insurance Coverage in the United States*: 2010, Fig. 4, p. 14. U.S. Government Printing Office, Washington, DC, 2011.

- Government actions to reduce poverty, or ameliorate its negative effects on people and society, are generally limited by groups of people who believe that the poor should make it on their own and not be aided by the government. They also believe that government aid reduces the incentives needed for people to do on their own what is needed to rise above the poverty line. These beliefs are fairly common among political conservatives.

Poverty in the United States

The U.S. government sets a **poverty line**, or threshold, in terms of income, and then the income of a household is compared to it. A household whose income falls below the threshold is considered poor. Poverty lines vary from country to country. In the United States, the Social Security Administration sets the poverty line. It is determined by multiplying the cost of what is deemed to be a nutritionally adequate food plan by three. This is because a family is assumed to spend a third of its budget on food. It is worth noting that many people criticize this calculation for not considering other necessary expenses, such as child care, housing, and transportation. The poverty line in 2012 for a family of four was a pretax income of $23,050, and $11,170 for a single adult. In 2010, over 15 percent of the U.S. population (46.2 million people) lived below the poverty line, and were therefore officially categorized as poor (DeNavas-Walt, Proctor, and Smith 2011). They represented about one-seventh of the U.S. population, the highest percentage since 1991.

Of course, millions who exist at or slightly above that line would also be considered poor by many people in society. There is talk in the wake of the lingering effects of the Great Recession that there should be more of a focus on the "near poor" (DeParle, Gebeloff, and Tavernise 2011). Those who have income that is less than 50 percent above the poverty line would be included in this category. Using this system, in 2011, 51 million people would have been considered near poor. If that number were combined with the number of the poor, there would be almost 100 million Americans, nearly a third of the population, who were poor or very close to it. There is no question that poverty is a huge problem in the United States. It is almost certainly far greater than we ever imagined.

FIGURE 7.7 • Poverty Rates in the United States by Family Type, 1959–2010

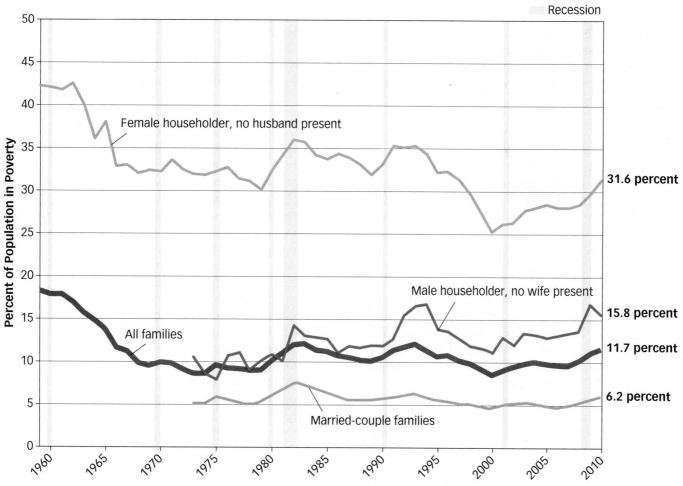

SOURCE: From DeNavas-Walt, Carmen, Bernadette D. Proctor, and Jessica C. Smith, U.S. Census Bureau, *Current Population Reports, Income, Poverty, and Health Insurance Coverage in the United States: 2010*, Fig. 1, p. 8. U.S. Government Printing Office, Washington, DC, 2011.

Looking at the longer-term trends shown in Figure 7.6, we can see that there has been considerable variation in the number of people living in poverty from year to year since 1960. What is striking, however, is the sharp increase in poverty that coincided with the beginning of the Great Recession; 2 million more households were below the poverty line in 2010 as compared to 2009. Also worth noting is that while the poverty rate is still down dramatically from 22.4 percent in 1960, there has been a significant uptick in recent years: 14.3 percent of households were below the poverty line in 2009 compared to 15.1 percent in 2010. One indicator of increasing poverty is the increase in the number of people on food stamps. At the beginning of 2010, 39 million people received food stamps; by the beginning of 2011, there were 44.2 million people receiving such aid—an increase of over 5 million people in only 12 months (Murray 2011)!

As you might expect given their disadvantages in income and wealth, minorities suffer disproportionately from poverty. While the poverty rate for non-Hispanic whites in 2010 was 9.9 percent, it was 12.5 percent for Asians—down significantly from 16.1 percent in the mid-1980s, but still higher than for non-Hispanic whites. Even more telling, the poverty rate was over 25 percent for both blacks (27.4 percent) and Hispanics (26.6 percent).

Figure 7.7 looks at poverty by family type. Families headed by females with no husband present have long had dramatically higher poverty rates than other family types, and since 2007, poverty among these families has increased sharply. Meanwhile, among married-couple families the percentage living under the poverty line has remained fairly stable. However, even among these families there has been a substantial increase in poverty since the recession.

One indication of poverty and its effect on the family is the increase in the number of families experiencing

Poverty Knowledge

"doubling up." Doubled-up families are those that include one additional adult who is over 18 years old and not in school, the householder, the spouse, or cohabiting with the householder. Between 2007 and 2011, there was a 10.7 percent increase in the number of doubled-up households. Further, there was a 25.5 percent increase during that period in 25- to 34-year-olds living with their parents. The latter trend should be especially worrisome to many readers of this book.

Feminization of Poverty

A central issue in the study of poverty is the degree to which women and children are overrepresented among the poor (Hamilton 2012; Hinze and Aliberti 2007; Morrow and Pells 2012). In 2010, 16.2 percent of American women were below the poverty line while only 14.0 percent of men lived in poverty (U.S. Census Bureau 2011b). Poverty levels vary by age: Women between the ages of 45 and 64 are less likely to be poor than those 18 and below and 65 and above. Female poverty levels also vary based on race and ethnicity: Both black and Latino women are more than twice as likely to be poor than are white women. Also, as you have seen, female-headed households with no husband present have far higher rates of poverty than families headed by married couples.

The "feminization of poverty" means that those living in poverty are increasingly more likely to be women than men (Goldberg 2010; Pearce 1978). Although in recent years the improved position of women in the work world, and increases in women's earnings, would seem to indicate that the poverty gap is narrowing, the gender gap persists (McLanahan and Kelly 1999). A variety of demographic factors and changes help to explain the feminization of poverty:

- Women are more likely to live alone because, for example, single women marry later and divorced women are less likely to remarry than men.

- Women have lower average earnings than men do. This is the case even when they do the same work.

- More children are being born to unmarried women, who tend to earn less than married women. The latter are also more likely to be fully responsible for dependents.

- Women have longer life spans than men, increasing the likelihood that older women will be living on their own.

Economically, women have suffered from a variety of disadvantages. Historically, males were considered the main breadwinners, and women, if they worked, were thought of as secondary earners. They have existed in a sex-segregated labor force in which the best and highest-paying positions have gone largely to men. The subordinate economic position of women was reinforced by the systematic wage discrimination practiced against them. They were routinely paid less than men, even for the same work. Women's incomes have also been adversely affected by the fact that they are more likely than men to work part-time, to hold temporary jobs, or to work at home (Presser 2005). Female workers have gained some ground: They earned about 61 percent of male earnings in 1960 but 77 percent in 2009 (National Committee on Pay Equity 2010), in part because of stagnation in male earnings. In spite of the improvement, the gender gap in earnings persists to this day (see Figure 7.8).

Poverty is a problem for women not only in the United States; it is a global problem. According to one estimate, about 70 percent of the women in the world are poor (UN Women 2011).

SOCIAL MOBILITY

Those who live in poverty are understandably eager to improve their lot. However, virtually everyone in a stratified system is concerned with **social mobility** (van Leeuwen and Maas 2010), or the ability or inability to change one's position in the hierarchy. *Upward mobility,* the ability to move higher (Kupfer 2012; Miles, Savage, and Bühlmann 2011), is obviously of great concern, especially for those who are poor. Upward mobility is the route out of poverty. The middle class may have an even greater desire to be mobile than the poor. This is

CHECKPOINT 7.2	FACTORS IN ECONOMIC INEQUALITY
Income inequality	Substantially higher since the 1970s, including in the United States.
Wealth inequality	Much greater than income inequality. Wealth is a key economic indicator of class that confers a wide range of material advantages as well as status and power and can be passed on for generations to come.
Poverty	Built into the capitalist system in virtually all societies and tends to disproportionately affect women and children.

social mobility The ability or inability to change one's position in the social hierarchy.

because they are likely to have experienced at least some of the possibilities associated with upward mobility. They have some class, status, and power, but they tend to want more. They often want to move into the upper class. Even those in the upper class are interested in and concerned about upward mobility. They often want to move to higher-level positions than their rivals within the upper class. They are also interested in keeping tabs on those below them who may be moving up the ladder. Those on the move up the stratification system threaten to supplant them, and perhaps even reach positions higher than their own.

People in all social classes are also concerned about *downward mobility* (Wilson, Roscigno, and Huffman 2013). That is, people worry about descending to lower levels within their social class or to lower classes (e.g., dropping from the upper to the middle or even lower class). Downward mobility causes people real hardships, but even its mere possibility is a great cause of concern. Immigrants and refugees who move to a new country almost always experience downward mobility during the first generation in their new locale. This is especially true of those who held high-level occupations in their countries of origin (Gans 2009). More generally, it is likely that, given the current economic problems in the United States and Europe, many people will experience downward mobility relative to their parents' status during their lifetimes. As one columnist put it: "Young people today are staring at a future in which they will be less well off than their elders, a reversal of fortune that should send a shudder through everyone" (Herbert 2011).

---

vertical mobility Both upward and downward mobility.

horizontal mobility Movement within one's social class.

intergenerational mobility The difference between the parents' social class position and the position achieved by their child(ren).

FIGURE 7.8 • Female-to-Male Earnings Ratio and Median Earnings of Full-Time Workers in the United States by Gender, 1960–2010

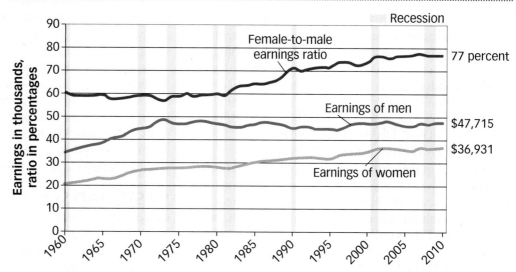

SOURCE: From U.S. Census Bureau, Current Population Survey, *1961 to 2007 Annual Social Economic Supplement,* Fig. 2, p. 7.

ASK YOURSELF

Why should the public "shudder" at the prospect that young people today will be less well off in the future than their elders? What negative effects could this future reality have on social institutions, such as schools, workplaces, and industries like banking and real estate? Would it have any positive effects, perhaps on consumerism or the natural environment? How might it affect the world standing of the United States as a society? Explain your answers.

TYPES OF SOCIAL MOBILITY

To this point, we have discussed upward and downward mobility, but there are a number of other types of social mobility as well. Upward and downward mobility are the key components of the general process of **vertical mobility**. Also of interest is **horizontal mobility**, or movement within one's social class. For example, a chief executive officer (CEO) may become CEO of a much larger corporation that brings with it much greater compensation. At the other end of the spectrum, the plumber who becomes a taxi driver also exhibits horizontal mobility (Ultee 2007a).

Sociologists are also concerned with two other types of mobility. One is **intergenerational mobility**, or the difference between the parents' social class position and the positions achieved by their children (Park and Myers 2010).

Social Mobility

Social Caste in India

Children who rise higher in the stratification system than their parents have experienced upward intergenerational mobility. Those who descend to a lower position on the ladder have experienced downward intergenerational mobility. **Intragenerational mobility** involves movement up or down the stratification system in one's lifetime. It is possible for some to start their adult lives in the lower class and to move up over the years to a higher social class. However, it is also possible to start out in the upper class and to slide down the stratification ladder to a lower class in the course of one's lifetime (Ultee 2007b).

Much of the concern with mobility relates to the work that people do or the occupations they hold. **Occupational mobility** involves changes in people's work either across or within generations (Blau and Duncan 1967; Treiman 2007). Research on occupational mobility has generally focused on men. This is the case even though occupational mobility obviously also applies to women (Mandel 2012). For example, in the case of intergenerational mobility the focus has been on the difference between a man's occupation and that of his father.

All of the above types of mobility are concerned with individual mobility. **Structural mobility** involves the effect of changes in the larger society on the position of individuals in the stratification system, especially the occupational structure (Gilbert and Kahl 1993; R. Miller 2001). For example, China under communism offered people little mobility of any type. Now that China has a booming capitalist economy, there has been a vast increase in structural mobility since many more higher-level positions (especially occupations) are now available (Vogel 2011). Millions have moved out of the peasantry and into an expanding hierarchy of nonagricultural occupations and thus higher social positions.

ACHIEVEMENT AND ASCRIPTION

Thus far, we have been describing a system of social stratification defined by status, power, and class—especially economic class. This, however, is but one type of stratification system. A chief characteristic of this system is the idea that social positions are based on **achievement**, or the accomplishments, the merit, of the individual. For example, a person becomes a physician, and thereby attains a high-level position in the stratification system, only after many years of education, hard work, and practical experience. Conversely, some people believe that a person at or near the bottom of the stratification system is there because he lacks the necessary accomplishments. These people might suggest that a homeless person is homeless because she has not worked hard enough to earn a living wage. The idea that achievement determines social class is accurate to some extent, but the fact is that where a person ends up in the stratification system may have little or nothing to do with

achievement. Instead, it can be explained by external factors over which the individual has little control.

A person's status usually has a great deal to do with **ascription**, or being born with, or inheriting, certain characteristics such as race and gender, wealth, and high status (or, conversely, poverty and low status) (Bond 2012). Thus, a person's position in the social hierarchy may be due to nothing more than the accident of being born a man or a woman, black or white. At the extremes, ascribed status has little or nothing to do with a person's accomplishments, skills, or abilities. Further, once in a given position in the stratification system, a person is likely to remain in that position during his or her lifetime.

CASTE AND SLAVERY

Caste is the most rigid and closed system of stratification based on ascription. The best-known caste system is found in India (Teltumbde 2011), but it has existed at other times and in other places. Examples include fifteenth- to nineteenth-century Japan, as well as the era of apartheid—1948 to 1994—in South Africa (Jalali 2007). Indeed, the caste system and the apartheid system of racial stratification are often seen as similar (Slate 2011).

A caste system is closed in several senses. For one, the possibility of individual mobility is severely restricted. It is almost impossible for a person to move out of the caste group into which he or she is born. There also exist limited possibilities for a change in status of the caste group as a whole. The caste system is reinforced by the fact that castes are usually *endogamous,* meaning that people marry within their own caste (see Chapter 10). Further, contact with those from other castes, especially those with a higher rank, is prohibited or greatly limited, often by elaborate rituals and customs. For example, those from lower-ranked caste groups such as the *Dalits,* the "untouchables" who

---

intragenerational mobility Movement up or down the stratification system in one's lifetime.

occupational mobility Changes in people's work either across or within generations.

structural mobility The effect of changes in the larger society on the position of individuals in the stratification system, especially the occupational structure

achievement The accomplishments, or the merit, of individuals.

ascription Being born with or inheriting certain characteristics (wealth, high status, etc.).

caste The most rigid and most closed system of stratification, usually associated with India.

Social Stratification in Once Socialist Israel

At its founding in 1947 as a homeland for Jews, especially the victims of the Holocaust, Israel was dominated by Zionism, a political movement aimed at finding a Jewish homeland. Zionists were steeped in Socialist principles. They opposed capitalism and favored social equality (at least for Jews). Israeli socialism was best exemplified by the kibbutz.

The early kibbutz was largely agricultural, although some later kibbutzim were more oriented toward manufacturing and tourism. The land was owned communally, as were all tools, machines, and even clothing. In the early decades of kibbutz life, even the children were seen as belonging to the community. They were even breast-fed by mothers other than their own. Above all, there was a strong notion of equality. Kibbutz members were all to be rewarded according to Karl Marx's (1938: 10) principle: "From each according to his ability, to each according to his need." This system began to break down for various reasons because of the declining economic importance of agriculture, the formation of capitalistic enterprises within the kibbutz, and the fact that more and more people who lived in the kibbutz began to take outside jobs. Much of this process was driven by Israel's integration, beginning in the 1980s, into the global economy (Fogiel-Bijaoui 2007, 2009). Kibbutz production systems faced competition in a market increasingly dominated by global financial systems. Property and goods were privatized, which, of course, led to increasing stratification within the kibbutz. Those who remained in, and wedded to, its socialist ideals dropped to the bottom of the stratification system within the kibbutz. As Israel became more integrated into the world economy in the 1980s and

This milk processing plant in an Israeli kibbutz is now automated. Will eliminating the need for people to perform heavy or repetitive tasks reduce or increase social stratification in a society?

1990s, its right-wing government began selling off state-owned assets. Assets were sold to capitalists who transformed many of them into highly profitable capitalist enterprises. Furthermore, some of the early capitalists began to expand into other businesses and came to control a complex web of highly profitable enterprises. Many of the owners of these webs—the "tycoons"—have become extraordinarily rich, as have those who hold high positions in them.

The high level of equality that once prevailed within Israeli society has given way to a highly stratified society in which a small number of families control the 10 largest businesses in Israel with about 30 percent of the economy. As a result, Israel now has one of the "largest gaps between rich and poor in the industrialized world" (Bronner 2011a). In fact, there is more wealth concentration in Israel than there is in Great Britain, Germany, and the United States.

Like other areas throughout the world, dissatisfaction with rising inequality, as well as high prices, led to massive protests throughout Israel in 2011. At the top of the protesters' list of objectives was "minimizing social inequalities" (Bronner 2011a). More concretely, the protesters wanted more affordable housing, food, and gasoline; lower taxes; and restoration of lost social services. Most generally, there was a feeling that the once just system (at least for Jews in Israel) had grown increasingly unjust.

Think About It

Do you think Israel's recent experience with capitalism suggests that a society characterized by collective ownership and social equality is not sustainable? Why or why not? Is the small scale of Israel's society an advantage or a disadvantage if its leaders turn their attention to its growing income inequality?

Slavery defines people like these South Carolina plantation workers of the 1860s as property and denies their rights as humans. What keeps such an extreme form of stratification in place?

An economic boom transforming much of India, urbanization, a crisis in agriculture, affirmative action policies, and political changes have prompted some sociologists to argue that the caste system is fast breaking down (Raman 2011).

Another extreme stratification system associated with ascription is slavery. **Slavery** is a system in which people are defined as property, involuntarily placed in perpetual servitude, and not given the same rights as the rest of society. Slaves, of course, exist at or near the bottom of the stratification system. This was the case, for example, in the American South before the end of the Civil War. Some forms of slavery persist to this day, such as child slavery in Southeast Asia (Rafferty 2007), a phenomenon that is at least in part related to human trafficking (see Chapter 1; Hoque 2010). Children, particularly female children, are being used not only for hard labor, but for the sexual gratification of adults. In each country where this sort of slavery occurs, existing structures shape the nature of slavery. In India, for instance, children who become sex slaves are most likely to be victims of the caste system as well (Hepburn and Simon 2010).

currently represent 16 percent of the Indian population, are often relegated to menial positions. There, they may not be permitted to eat with members of a higher-ranked caste, or even touch the food to be eaten by the latter. This poses great difficulties, especially in a modern society of fast-food restaurants. There the food eaten by persons of higher-ranking castes is likely to be prepared and served by persons of lower-ranking castes. Since membership in a caste is hereditary and various economic and social resources have been unevenly distributed among the castes, inequality is often reproduced across multiple generations. Marriages are still likely to be arranged within castes, and individual castes continue to survive as they compete for secular resources (Srinivas 2003). The poor in India are still disproportionately found among the lower-ranking castes. The caste system is also still important in rural areas, where the Dalits are, among other things, banned from temples and the use of village water wells. As a group, they continue to be desperately poor, powerless, landless, and largely illiterate.

Though caste survives in contemporary India, the caste system has been altered greatly by various social changes. After India gained independence in 1947, legal changes were instituted to address inequities among the castes. The constitution prohibited discrimination against those considered untouchables and others in public places. Affirmative action provided avenues of social mobility to the Dalits—now called the "scheduled castes" by the government. For example, positions are reserved for Dalits in universities and in the government bureaucracy.

THEORIES OF SOCIAL STRATIFICATION

Within the sociology of social stratification, the dominant theoretical approaches are structural/functional theory and conflict/critical theory. These approaches are also involved in the major theoretical controversies within this area of sociological study (de Graaf 2007). Also to be discussed here are inter/actionist theories of stratification.

As in all areas of the social world, different theories focus on different aspects of social stratification. Instead of choosing one theory over another, it may make more sense to use all of them. Structural/functional and conflict/critical theories tell us much about the macro structures

slavery A system in which people are defined as property, involuntarily placed in perpetual servitude, and not given the same rights as the rest of society.

Caste on the Internet

Caste manifests itself in many ways on the Internet. For example, it is becoming a popular medium for matrimonial services and, in the process, encouraging people to marry within their castes. Information regarding eligible brides and bridegrooms supplements offline caste-based matrimonial services and newspaper matrimonials. The Internet is also home to multiple matrimonial websites that perpetuate caste divisions by servicing multiple castes with separate sections (such as www.shaadi.com) or by servicing a single caste (for instance, www.agarwal2agarwal.org).

Members of castes also use the Internet to organize themselves into caste networks and communicate with caste members throughout the world. They may set up stand-alone websites such as www.hebbariyengar.net or use social networking websites such as Orkut or Facebook. For instance, members of the Mukkulathor caste have created a group called "Thevar Community" on Facebook (www.facebook.com/groups/bulletravi), which has more than 500 members. These websites and social networking sites also provide a forum for caste members to discuss the histories and practices of their particular castes, as well as contemporary economic, political, and social issues that they perceive as being relevant to their castes. Often, websites and groups provide safe spaces where members can raise issues that might attract censure if raised offline in public spaces. Among such issues would be a questioning of the continuation of the caste system or contemplating the end of the caste-based affirmative action policies.

Others use the Internet to attack the caste system. For instance, the group Dalit Freedom Network utilizes the Internet to protest discrimination against Dalits, to coordinate its activities, and to organize members on its website, www.dalitnetwork.org. Some groups on social networking sites, such as the Facebook group "End Caste System, End Communal Hatred, and Be a Human!" (www.facebook.com/groups/136066263161299), provide spaces for individuals who would like to end the caste system.

Think About It

How does caste segregation on the Internet differ from other forms of segregation we might observe there, such as segregation by country, by language used, or by interests (for instance, golfers may not frequent knitting websites)? Does it surprise you to learn that everyone is not equal on the Internet? Why or why not?

SOURCE: Printed with the permission of Jillet Sam.

---

of stratification, while interactionist theories offer great detail about what goes on within those structures at the micro levels.

STRUCTURAL/ FUNCTIONAL THEORY

Within structural/functional theory, it is structural-functionalism that offers the most important—and controversial—theory of stratification. It argues that all societies are, and have been, stratified. Further, the theory contends that societies need a system of stratification in order to exist and to function properly (Davis and Moore 1945). Stratification is needed first to ensure that people are motivated to occupy the less pleasant, more difficult, and more important positions in society. Second, stratification is needed to be sure that people with the right abilities and talents find their way into the appropriate positions. In other words, what is required is a good fit between people and the requirements of the positions they occupy.

CHECKPOINT 7.3	TYPES OF SOCIAL MOBILITY
Vertical	Upward or downward movement through the social hierarchy.
Horizontal	Movement within one's social class.
Intergenerational	Movement by children to a different social class than their parents'.
Intragenerational	Vertical movement over the course of one's lifetime.
Occupational	Changes in people's work across or within generations.
Structural	Changes in the larger society, particularly the occupational structure, that affect one's position in the stratification system.

Affirmative Action Bans

The structural-functional theory of stratification assumes that higher-level occupations, such as physicians and lawyers, are more important to society than such lower-level occupations as laborers and janitors. The higher-level positions are also seen as being harder to fill because of the difficulties and unpleasantness associated with them. For example, both physicians and lawyers require many years of rigorous and expensive education. Physicians are required to deal with blood, human organs, and death; lawyers have to defend those who have committed heinous crimes. It is argued that in order to motivate enough people to occupy such positions, greater rewards, such as prestige, sufficient leisure, and especially large amounts of money, need to be associated with them. The implication is that without these high rewards, high-level positions would remain understaffed or unfilled. As a result, structural-functionalists see the stratification system as functional for the larger society. In this case, it provides the physicians and lawyers needed by society.

CONFLICT/CRITICAL THEORY

Conflict/critical theories tend to take a jaundiced view of stratified social structures because they involve and promote inequality. They are especially critical of the structural-functional perspective and its view that stratification is functional for society. Conflict/critical theory takes a hard look at who benefits from the existing stratification system and how those benefits are perpetuated.

Critical theorists focus on the control that those in the upper levels of the stratification system exercise over culture (Kellner and Lewis 2007; Lash and Lury 2007). In contrast to Marx's emphasis on the economy, they see culture as of utmost importance in the contemporary world. Elites are seen as controlling such important aspects of culture as television and movies, and as seeking to exert increasing control over the Internet and such major social networking sites as Facebook and Twitter. Elites use the media to send the kinds of messages that further their control. Furthermore, the amount of time that those lower in the stratification system are led to devote to TV, video games, movies, and the Internet is so great that they have little time to mobilize and oppose, let alone overthrow, those in power.

ASK YOURSELF

Do you agree with the structural-functional perspective that stratification provides an important function for society? Or do you believe, as conflict/critical theorists do, that stratification exists to perpetuate benefits for the elite and to expand their control? Justify your choice.

Social Rewards and Status

While critical theorists focus more on culture, conflict theorists are mainly concerned with social structure (Huaco 1966; Tumin 1953). Conflict theorists ridicule the idea that higher-level positions in the social structure would go unfilled were it not for the greater rewards they offer. They ask, for example, whether higher-level positions in the stratification system are less pleasant than those at the lower end of the continuum. Is being a surgeon really less pleasant than being a garbage collector? The argument being made by structural-functionalists seems preposterous to conflict theorists and to many others.

Conflict theorists accept the idea that higher-level positions such as being a lawyer may be more difficult than lower-level positions such as being a garbage collector. However, they wonder whether these positions are always more important. Is a lawyer who engages in shady deals or who defends environmental polluters more important than a garbage collector? In fact, the garbage collector is of great importance to society. Without garbage collectors, diseases that could seriously threaten society would develop and spread.

Conflict theorists also criticize the idea that those at the upper levels of the stratification system require the large rewards offered to them. Many people would be motivated to occupy such positions as CEO of a multinational corporation or hedge fund manager without such extraordinary rewards. Fewer economic rewards for those at the top, and more for those on the bottom, would reduce the economic gap and make for a more equal society. Conflict theorists also argue that providing huge sums of money to motivate people is not the only way to get them to pursue an advanced education or whatever else is necessary to occupy high-ranking positions. For example, the status or prestige associated with those positions would be a strong motivator, as would the power that comes with them. It may even be that economic rewards motivate the wrong people to occupy these positions. That is, those interested in maximizing their income rather than doing right by their patients and clients are being motivated to become surgeons. Focusing on the rewards associated with making positive contributions to society would likely improve the way medicine, law, business, finance, and other high-status occupations function.

Gender, Race, and Class

Operating from another variant of conflict/critical theory, feminist theorists tend to focus on the issue of stratification in the work world. Because men owned the means of production in the development of capitalism, they gained positions of great power and prestige that yielded major economic rewards (Hartmann 1979). Women, by contrast, were relegated to subordinate positions. Over the years, women's position in the U.S. stratification system has improved with the entrance of more women into the workforce and greater legal protections against workplace gender discrimination. There are now many more women in such high-ranking positions as executive, physician, and lawyer. Yet, compared to men overall, women still occupy a subordinate position in the stratification system. They may also find it harder to rise very high in that system.

Feminist theorists have dealt with this issue under the heading of *occupational gender segregation*, or the unequal allocation of occupations to men and women (Reskin 1993). Women have been disadvantaged by occupational gender segregation in various ways. They have tended to get inferior occupational training and therefore to be hired at lower-level, lower-paying positions than men. Women have also tended to be hired, and to remain in, female-dominated occupations. These factors have been likely to lead women into careers in which they do not rise as high in the employing organization, and are not paid as much, as men. Women are also likely to confront more problems in the day-to-day operations and procedures of their employing organization. For example, organizational policies on day care are far more likely to have an adverse effect on female employees than on male employees. Such factors are far more likely to impede the careers of women.

While the occupational situation for women has improved in recent years, the occupational world remains segregated on the basis of gender (Gauchat, Kelly, and Wallace 2012). For example, women face a "motherhood penalty" (Budig, Misra, and Boeckman 2012; Correll, Benard, and Paik 2007) in the workplace that limits upward mobility among women with children. Mothers seeking jobs are less likely to be hired, are offered lower salaries, and are seen by others as less committed to the workplace. Illustrating how pervasive this penalty is, the wage gap between women without children and mothers is greater than the wage gap between men and women (Boushey 2008; Hausmann, Ganguli, and Viarengo 2009). Even women at the highest levels of the corporate world continue to face barriers unique to their gender. Recent research finds that women tend to give themselves lower self-ratings than do men. This internalized modesty about work performance contributes to lower upward mobility over and above external factors such as the glass ceiling (Hutson 2010) (see Chapter 5).

Yet another type of conflict/critical theory, *critical theories of race and racism*, introduced in Chapter 2, argues that a similar white-controlled stratification system has put whites on top, and kept racial minorities in subordinate positions. Minorities face huge, sometimes insurmountable, barriers to moving into, or even close to, high-level positions. As evidence of this, upward career mobility among black Americans has lagged behind that of whites (Sites and Parks 2011).

INTER/ACTIONIST THEORY

From an inter/actionist theory perspective, social stratification is not a function of macro-level structures, but of micro-level, individual actions and interactions. While both structural/functional and conflict/critical theorists see stratification as a hierarchical structure, inter/actionists see it as much more of a process or a set of processes. As a process, stratification involves interactions among people in different positions. Those who occupy higher-level positions may try to exert power in their interactions with those below them, but the latter can, and usually do, contest such exertions of power.

To the symbolic interactionist inequality ultimately depends on face-to-face interaction. It is what happens in face-to-face interaction that leads to inequality. One symbolic interactionist approach identifies four processes that produce and reproduce inequality (Schwalbe et al. 2000). First, the dominant group defines the subordinate group into existence. Second, once in existence, the subordinate group finds ways of adapting to its situation. Third, there are efforts to maintain the boundaries between the two groups. Finally, both groups must manage the emotions associated with their position in the stratification system. For example, those at the top must not show too much sympathy for those below them and those at the bottom must not display too much anger to those above them.

Symbolic interactionists see social stratification as much more fluid than do structural/functional and conflict/critical theorists. While the theories discussed above focus mainly on economic factors, symbolic interactionists are much more concerned with the struggle over things that are symbolically important to those at various positions in the stratification system. Those in higher-level positions define what they have as of great importance. Those below them may accept that definition and work to gain those symbols. However, the latter can also reject those definitions and find or create other symbols that are of importance to them and that serve to elevate them and their positions. For example, those in lower-level positions may reject the long hours and high stress associated with higher-level positions. Instead, they may place a higher value on positions that involve less responsibility and offer more reasonable hours, and therefore more time to enjoy leisure activities.

Ethnomethodologists note that people may exist within a stratified structure, but what really matters is

Glass Ceiling

Affirmative Action Bans

Global Super-Elite

CHECKPOINT 7.4 — THEORIES OF SOCIAL STRATIFICATION

Structural/functional theories	All societies need stratification to exist and to function properly.
Conflict/critical theories	Stratified social structures promote inequality and control by those in the upper levels of the stratification system.
Inter/actionist theories	Social stratification is a function of micro-level individual actions and interactions among people in different positions.

what they *do* within such a structure. As in other aspects of the social world, people use commonsense procedures to operate and make their way in such structures. These procedures are used by elites and the downtrodden alike in order to "do" their position in the system. For example, elite members of society are likely to carry themselves with authority and self-importance. In contrast, those in the bottom rungs of the stratification system are more likely to appear overburdened and to slouch through the day. In other words, one of the ways in which people do stratification is in their body language.

People can and do use the system of stratification to accomplish their goals. On the one hand, elites may get others to do their bidding merely by acting as elite members of society and sporting the trappings of that position, such as driving a Porsche. On the other hand, those at the bottom may use their position to extract handouts at street corners or from charitable agencies. Alternatively, they may use their position to obtain loans or scholarships that allow them to move up the stratification system.

CONSUMPTION AND SOCIAL STRATIFICATION

Much of this chapter relates to issues of production and work, but social stratification is also related to consumption in various ways. For one thing, different positions in the stratification system involve differences in consumption. Most obviously, those in the upper classes are able to afford to consume products (such as yachts, Maserati automobiles, and Dom Pérignon champagne) and services (such as those provided by maids, chefs, and chauffeurs) that those in the middle and especially the lower classes cannot even contemplate. For another, the nature of consumption itself forms a stratification system. The consumption of certain sorts of things accords a higher position than does consumption of other kinds of things.

STRATIFIED CONSUMPTION

Fashion is a good example of a stratified form of consumption. Georg Simmel ([1904] 1971) argued that those in higher levels of the stratification system continually seek to distinguish their consumption from those below them. This is evident in the realm of fashion where the elites adopt new fashions, thereby displaying that they can afford the latest styles. However, elites soon find that those below them have copied their fashions with cheaper, if not cheap, imitations. Thus fashion, as well as other choices by elites, has a tendency to "trickle down" the social stratification ladder to the middle and eventually the lower classes. To distinguish themselves from the masses, elites must continually move on to new and different fashions. This phenomenon most obviously applies to fashions in clothing, but there are fashions in many other things, as well, such as cars, homes, vacations, and even ideas (Lipovetsky [1987] 2002, 2005).

Simmel's contemporary Thorstein Veblen ([1899] 1994) also theorized about stratification and consumption. In Veblen's view, the elite members of society want to be "conspicuous." In the past, they were conspicuous about their accomplishments in the work world, but over time, these feats became less and less visible as they came to be concealed by factory walls and office buildings. As a result, elites shifted more toward *conspicuous consumption,* wanting others to see what they are able to consume, especially those things that serve to differentiate them from those who are in lower social classes (see Chapter 2). Thus, their money came to be invested in mansions, fancy furnishings, fine riding horses, expensive automobiles, designer dresses, and exquisite jewelry because such things can be easily seen and admired by others.

This is a key difference between Simmel's and Veblen's theories: Simmel's concept of trickle-down fashion assumes that the middle and lower classes will, in a sense, copy the consumption patterns of the elite. On the other hand, Veblen believed that because the things that the elite consume are very expensive, their consumption patterns cannot be copied so easily by those who rank lower in the stratification system. Therefore, elite status is expressed and solidified through conspicuous consumption. What appears to involve unnecessary expense has a payoff in supporting and enhancing the status of elites. In fact, in Veblen's view, the factor that distinguishes elites from others is their ability to engage in wasteful consumption.

Do you think Simmel's concept of trickle-down fashion or Veblen's notion of conspicuous consumption is a more accurate description of the relationship between consumption and social stratification? Why? Can you provide examples to support your answer?

SOCIAL CLASS, DISTINCTION, AND TASTE

Both Simmel and Veblen focus on the economic aspects of consumption, but a more contemporary French sociologist, Pierre Bourdieu (1984; Bennett et al. 2009), does a cultural analysis of consumption and stratification. What animates Bourdieu's work is the idea of **distinction**, the need to distinguish oneself from others. Both Simmel and Veblen deal with the desire of elites to distinguish their superior economic position through the wasteful things it enables them to buy. Although he too recognizes the economic factors involved, Bourdieu adds the more cultural dimension of taste to the analysis of consumption and stratification (Gronow 2007; Marsh 2012). That is, elites seek to distinguish themselves from others by their good taste. With members of the lower classes constantly imitating the tastes of the upper classes, the latter are continually forced to find new ways to achieve distinction. In other words, in Bourdieu's view, in order to achieve distinction elites are forced to become ever more refined, sophisticated, and exclusive in their tastes.

Perhaps the most important aspect of this work on distinction and taste is that it is closely related to struggles for power and position within the stratification system. On the one hand, elites use culture to obtain and maintain their position. They might do this by focusing on high culture such as opera or art. Such taste helps elites to gain high-level positions in the stratification system and to make those below them accept their lesser positions in that system. The focus of elites on high culture serves to exclude the lower classes from higher-level positions in the stratification system. It excludes them from even thinking of trying to move into those positions. Even those from the lower classes who manage to acquire

considerable wealth are not likely to have or to develop the level of cultural sophistication needed to appreciate something like ballet. Like Marxian theorists, Bourdieu and his followers see the stratification system as an arena of ongoing struggle. However, while Marxists tend to see this as largely an economic struggle, Bourdieu, although he certainly recognizes its economic aspects, sees it as a cultural struggle.

A person's taste in consumption helps in deciding the social class to which that person belongs. For example, if you read the *New York Times* (whether online or in hard copy), you are likely to be classified as in the middle or upper class. However, if you read *USA Today* or don't follow the news at all, you will be classified by most as standing lower in the stratification system. While taste can be demonstrated in the purchase and display of expensive consumer goods, it also can be shown much more subtly in the way one talks, the kind of music one listens to, and the books one reads. Good taste in these and other areas demonstrates and enhances the position of elite members of society. It supposedly shows that they have good breeding, have come from a good family, have a good education, and, especially, have the good sense to value things not simply because of how much they cost or for their monetary value. Those without such taste, who have taste for the necessary rather than the good taste of elites (Holt 2007), in music for example (Prior 2011), are likely to be relegated to the lower reaches of the stratification system.

Taste must be considered not only in terms of how others classify you, but also by how you classify yourself through your demonstration of taste, lack of taste, or, more extremely, tastelessness. For example, at a formal business luncheon, a conservative suit would show good taste, while either a tuxedo or a sports jacket would show a lack of taste; being either over- or underdressed demonstrates lack of taste regarding appropriate attire. A T-shirt and jeans would be completely tasteless, and might result in your losing a business opportunity. Demonstrations of taste or

CHECKPOINT 7.5	THEORISTS WHO RELATED CONSUMPTION TO SOCIAL STRATIFICATION
Georg Simmel	Elites in higher social levels seek to distinguish their consumption from that of those below them, but that which is consumed such as fashions trickle down.
Thorstein Veblen	Elites' status is expressed and solidified through conspicuous consumption that those below them cannot easily copy.
Pierre Bourdieu	Elites seek to distinguish themselves from those who rank below them by the refinement and exclusivity of their taste.

distinction The need to distinguish oneself from others.

tastelessness are not simply demonstrations of individuality but also demonstrate linkages to the larger social world, especially the social class system.

GLOBALIZATION AND STRATIFICATION

All societies are stratified on the basis of class, status, and power. However, it is also the case that the nations of the world form a stratified system (Wallerstein 1974). The nations at the top are those that tend to be better off economically, to wield great power in many parts of the world, and to be looked up to around the globe. Conversely, the nations at the bottom of the global stratification system are likely to be very poor, to have little power outside (and perhaps even inside) their borders, and to be looked down upon by many throughout the world. Global stratification is a macro-level phenomenon that has profound effects at the micro level of individuals' relationships and opportunities.

THE GLOBAL NORTH AND SOUTH

Stratification on the global level is often seen as a divide between those nation-states located in the northern hemisphere (more specifically, the north temperate climate zone)—the Global North—and those located in the tropics and southern hemisphere—the Global South. For centuries, the North has dominated, controlled, exploited, and oppressed the South. Today the North encompasses the nations that are the wealthiest, most powerful, and highest status in the world, such as the United States, China, Germany, France, Great Britain, and Japan. The South, on the other hand, has a disproportionate number of nations that rank at or near the bottom in terms of global wealth, power, and prestige. Most of the nations of Africa would be included here, but there are others, especially in Asia, such as Afghanistan and Yemen.

Position in the global stratification system greatly affects stratification within a given society. A nation, like the United States, that stands at or near the top of the global stratification system has a larger proportion of middle- and upper-class positions than does a low-ranking nation, like Somalia, that is dominated by lower-class positions and the poverty associated with them. This stratification has been recognized by institutions such as the International Monetary Fund, which distributes funds from countries in the Global North to those in the Global South.

THE BOTTOM BILLION

There is certainly great inequality between the North and the South, but a focus on that relationship tends to obscure the full extent of global inequality. Consider what have been called the "bottom billion" of global residents (Collier 2007). The vast majority (70 percent) of the people in the bottom billion are in Africa, but countries such as Haiti, Bolivia, and Laos are also significant contributors.

Wherever they live, the bottom billion have incomes of only about a fifth of those in other developing countries. They also have many other serious problems, such as:

- A low life expectancy of about 50 years; the average is 67 in other developing nations

- A high infant mortality rate; 14 percent of the bottom billion die before their fifth birthday, versus 4 percent in other developing countries

- A higher likelihood of showing symptoms of malnutrition; 36 percent of the bottom billion are malnourished, as opposed to 20 percent in other developing countries (Collier 2007)

RACE TO THE BOTTOM

Those nations that rank low in the global stratification system often have to engage in a so-called economic race to the bottom in order to have a chance of eventually moving up the global hierarchy. The basic method is to offer lower prices than the competition—usually other low-ranking countries. Such nations may lower prices by reducing costs, which they do by offering their citizens lower wages, poorer working conditions, longer hours, ever-escalating pressure and demands, and so on. An especially desperate nation will go further than the others to degrade wages and working conditions in order to reduce costs and attract the interest of multinational corporations. However, the "winning" less developed nation remains a favorite of the multinationals only until it is undercut by another low-ranking country eager for jobs. In other words, the countries that get the work are those that "win" the race to the bottom. These, of course, are almost always questionable victories, since the work is poorly paid and subjects workers to horrid circumstances.

ASK YOURSELF

What could the Global North do to reduce other countries' need to engage in the race to the bottom? Why have such efforts so far been few and generally ineffective? How would slowing or even ending the race to the bottom affect the trend toward consumerism in the countries of the Global North?

A similar point is made, albeit in far more general terms, by Pietra Rivoli (2005) in her study of the global market for T-shirts. If one takes the long historical view, the nations that won the race to the bottom centuries ago are now among the most successful economies in the world. In textiles, the race to the bottom was won first by England, then the United States, Japan, and Hong Kong. The most recent winner of this race was China, which now is moving up industrially and economically.

Rivoli generalizes examples from the global textile industry to argue that nations must win the race to the bottom in order ultimately to succeed. Victory in this race is, in her view, the "ignition switch" that turns the economy on and gets it rolling. Thus, she concludes, those who criticize globalization are misguided in their efforts to end this race.

Rivoli's view seems to endorse the race to the bottom for all countries interested in development. However, we must take note of the fact that it leads them deeper into poverty, for at least a time. It also greatly advantages the wealthy North, which is guaranteed a continuing source of low-priced goods and services as one country replaces another at the bottom. Winning the race to the bottom is no guarantee of moving up the global stratification system, but it is a guarantee of low wages and poverty in developing countries in the South *and* of cheap goods for the middle and upper classes in the North.

Infant mortality is common among the world's bottom billion inhabitants. Here an eight-month-old victim of cholera is buried in eastern Congo, where war has intensified life-threatening problems of crowding and sanitation.

access to the Internet, prohibitively expensive. Language represents another source of inequality on the Internet. Most webpages are in English, and very few are in languages other than English, German, Japanese, French, Spanish, or Swedish (Bowen 2001; EnglishEnglish.com n.d.). Clearly, those who do not speak any of these languages—the overwhelming majority of whom live in the Global

THE GLOBAL DIGITAL DIVIDE

The Internet allows for participation, at least theoretically, by anyone, anywhere in the global, digital economy. However, although this is true in principle, in reality there is a daunting global digital divide (Drori 2006, 2010). For example, while almost 80 percent of those in North America are Internet users, only slightly more than 10 percent of those in Africa use the Internet.

The main barriers to global equality in Internet access and use are the lack of infrastructure within less developed countries. Also important are the low incomes in those areas that make complex digital technologies, and therefore

CHECKPOINT 7.6	GLOBALIZATION ISSUES IN STRATIFICATION
Global North and South	The Global North encompasses the wealthiest and most powerful nations, which dominate, control, exploit, and oppress the Global South, which has little or no power or prestige on the global stage.
Bottom Billion	The bottom billion have incomes one-fifth of those in developing countries, lower life expectancy, higher infant mortality, and greater risk of malnutrition.
Race to the Bottom	Desperate nations compete to degrade wages and working conditions in order to reduce costs and attract multinational corporations.
Global Digital Divide	Access to the Internet in the Global South is hampered by a lack of infrastructure, as well as a language barrier.

The Digital Divide

The "race to the bottom" in the global economy is won by those countries, like China, that can produce needed goods like textiles at the lowest price. What is winning worth, however, if it means that a country's workers must accept a substandard wage?

wide-scale use of social media in the 2010–2011 Arab Spring revolutions in Tunisia, Libya, and especially Egypt (see Chapter 15). The digital divide is beginning to be bridged by the rising accessibility of relatively simple and inexpensive PDAs, iPhones, other smartphones, iPads, and Internet tablets that are essentially mini-computers. Industry analysts indicate that mobile Internet access is ramping up significantly faster than desktop Internet access ever did.

An important reason for the rapid expansion of mobile access is not only that mobile devices are relatively inexpensive, but that they do not require the expensive, hardwired infrastructure needed by traditional computers and computer systems. Cellular signal access provides Internet access at increasingly high speeds. Much of the less developed world will be able to leapfrog stages of technological development that were experienced by the developed world. Similarly, less developed nations have leapt straight to solar power rather than erecting huge power plants run by coal, oil, or nuclear energy. Some nations avoided having to build fixed phone line systems by moving straight to mobile phone technology. Leapfrogging traditional computer systems and adopting PDAs instead could greatly reduce the global digital divide in a relatively short period.

South—are at a huge disadvantage on the Internet. They may even find the Internet completely inaccessible because of the language barrier.

However, there are signs that the digital divide is being reduced significantly. This was clear, for example, in the

SUMMARY

Social stratification results in hierarchical differences and inequalities. In the money-based stratification system in the United States, wealth and income are the main determinants of social class. However, as Weber argued, status and power are also involved in social stratification.

Since the 1970s, the United States has experienced increasing income inequality. However, the greatest economic differences in U.S. society are due to differences in wealth. People with great wealth often have high class, status, and power and can usually pass most of those advantages to future generations. Those who have little have a difficult time amassing their own wealth.

In the United States, the poverty line is the level of income that people are thought to need in order to survive. Members of minority groups, women, and children are overrepresented among the poor. While individuals in the United States have generally experienced intergenerational upward mobility, it

seems likely that young people in the twenty-first century will experience downward mobility. Sociologists are also concerned with structural mobility, or changes mainly in the occupational structure.

Structural-functional theories of stratification argue that societies need a system of stratification in order to function properly. Conflict theorists challenge this assumption, particularly the idea that positions at the higher end of the stratification system are always more important. Finally, symbolic interactionists view stratification as a process or set interactions among people in different positions.

Social stratification is related to consumption in a number of ways. Those in the higher classes can afford expensive items that those in the lower classes cannot. Elites use their patterns of consumption to distinguish themselves, sometimes conspicuously, from those beneath them.

Stratification also occurs on a global level. Most often, analysts talk about a divide between the Global North and the Global South. However, we can further distinguish a very poor bottom billion. Many nations engage in a "race to the bottom" to attract investment by multinational organizations.

KEY TERMS

Achievement, 204
Ascription, 204
Caste, 204
Distinction, 211
Horizontal mobility, 203
Income, 193
Inequality, 192

Intergenerational mobility, 203
Intragenerational mobility, 204
Occupational mobility, 204
Poverty line, 199
Power, 192
Slavery, 206
Social class, 191

Social mobility, 202
Social stratification, 191
Structural mobility, 204
Vertical mobility, 203
Wealth, 193

REVIEW QUESTIONS

1. According to Max Weber, what are the various dimensions of social stratification? What are some examples of people who rank highly on each of the dimensions?

2. What is the difference between income and wealth? Which is more important to explaining the differences between the haves and the have-nots? Why?

3. What do we mean by the feminization of poverty? What factors help to explain the position of women in the system of social stratification?

4. How has the nature of individual social mobility in the United States changed since the 1900s, and in what ways are these changes related to structural mobility?

5. According to structural-functional theories, how is inequality beneficial to society? How can the income and wealth of celebrities and sports stars be used as a criticism of this model?

6. What is the motherhood penalty? How does it affect women's position in the stratification system?

7. How does stratification operate at the global level?

8. In what ways are the bottom billion disadvantaged in the global stratification system?

9. Should a less developed country get involved in the race to the bottom? Why? Why not?

10. How does access to the Internet and new technologies relate to the system of stratification? How can the Internet be used to alter the system of stratification?

APPLYING THE SOCIOLOGICAL IMAGINATION

According to Pierre Bourdieu, elites create a distinction between themselves and the masses of people by defining "good taste." For this exercise, examine how taste works in the social world by taking a look at items in an industry of your choice (such as fashion, food, art, clothing, cars, homes) that supposedly reflect "good taste."

If necessary, use the Internet to research tasteful items in the industry you chose (search words like *luxury, designer, gourmet,*

and so on). Go to different websites and pay attention to how the items are marketed and the language used to describe them. In what ways are differences created around these products? How do lower-cost items mimic these tasteful items? Do you think that globalization and the Internet are changing how taste differentiates people? Why or why not?

⑤SAGE edge™

Sharpen your skills with SAGE edge at **edge.sagepub.com/ritzeressentials**

SAGE edge for students provides a personalized approach to help you accomplish your coursework goals in an easy-to-use learning environment.

Harsh Realities of Work in the Global World

Labor-saving machines, job benefits, and laws that mandate clean and safe working conditions and prohibit child labor now characterize the work lives of many in the world's industrialized nations. These protections and benefits are not universal, however.

▲ The brutally dangerous work of breaking ships up for scrap metal occupies 15,000 people on Pakistan's seacoast, most of whom earn no more than about $4 a day at a location that has been called a death trap.

▲ Children still labor in many parts of the world. This 13-year-old boy carries engine parts in an auto workshop in Mumbai, India (left), and another child (right) works without the protection of shoes or gloves to earn a few dollars a day at a brick-making factory outside Kabul in Afghanistan.

▲ Equally dangerous work is done far above the ground. This worker services an electricity pylon in the Angui province of China.

◄ Chinese workers manually haul a boat upstream on the Wu Jiang River, a tributary of China's Yangtze River—grueling work that has been done this way for thousands of years.

THINKING ABOUT SOCIOLOGY

1. How do the conditions of the work you do, or hope to do, compare with the conditions in the photos?

2. Who benefits from the very low level of pay that characterizes the kinds of work shown here? Think globally before you answer.

3. **Essay question:** Describe the political, economic, and social forces in both the industrialized and the developing worlds that help maintain the kinds of jobs and working conditions sampled in these photos. What needs to change in order to improve the lives of workers in developing countries? What risks should be avoided in the process?

Indigenous people celebrate the first day of the 2009
World Social Forum in Belém, Brazil, near the mouth of
the Amazon River. How do ethnic and racial majority and
minority groups view one another, and where do racism and
discrimination come from? Why do they persist?

RACE AND ETHNICITY

LEARNING OBJECTIVES

1 Contrast historical and recent views of racial categories and ethnic identities in the United States.

2 Describe the effects on majority–minority relations of stereotypes, prejudice, discrimination, and the social construction of difference.

3 Discuss the foundations of racism, including xenophobia, ethnocentrism, and social structures and institutions.

4 Describe how globalization is affecting ethnic identities, ethnic conflicts, and migrations.

In 2009, Evo Morales won his second term as president of Bolivia in a landslide victory, with 64 percent of the vote. Four years earlier, the widely popular union leader and political activist had ridden to office on an unorthodox leadership style and a reformist agenda. A pioneer in many respects, Morales not only brought the democratic republic of Bolivia a new socialist mandate and a reformed constitution, but as an Aymara, he also became the developing nation's first indigenous president.

> **Denying that racism, xenophobia, and ethnocentrism exist serves only to perpetuate them.**

The Aymara are a racially and ethnically distinct people who have lived in central South America for more than 2,000 years. Conquered first by the Incas, then by Spanish colonists, they lived as an indentured minority group until Bolivia won its independence in 1825. Despite achieving legal freedom, however, the Aymara continued to be stereotyped, discriminated against, and marginalized by the country's Spanish-descended majority.

After nearly two centuries of marginalization, the Aymara rose via a number of social movements to achieve social equality and political power for Bolivia's indigenous populations. Organizations such as the militant Tupac Katari Guerrilla Army

and Evo Morales's own Movimiento al Socialismo (MAS) challenged racist norms and championed sweeping reform. Running on a string of successful MAS actions (including the ousting of the previous president) and a populist platform of farmers' rights and antimilitarism, Morales transcended old stereotypes and expectations, rising to his country's highest office.

Like Nelson Mandela before him in South Africa and Barack Obama, his U.S. contemporary, Evo Morales is a living symbol of a particular culture's ongoing struggle with prejudice, racism, and institutional discrimination. His presidency marks an important step in Bolivia's social evolution, but it by no means signifies that the Aymara have achieved social equality. Racism and ethnic discrimination have permeated Bolivia for hundreds—if not thousands—of years. During that time, the country's dominant groups have accumulated wealth, power, and prestige—assets they have been reluctant to share.

It took roughly eight generations for Bolivia to elect its first indigenous president and slightly longer for the United States to elect its first biracial one. These accomplishments have led some to suggest that we have achieved a postracial, or "color-blind," world. Racism, xenophobia, ethnic conflict, and ethnocentrism are sensitive topics for most people. However, denying that these difficult problems persist will only perpetuate them. •

A discussion of race and ethnicity flows naturally from a discussion of social stratification. Racial or ethnic difference per se is not a problem. Problems arise when these differences are defined in such a way that certain groups confront prejudicial attitudes and discriminatory conduct.

While many scholars and citizens have come to believe that racism is on the wane and the chances for racial integration and a postracial society have improved (Alba 2009; Wise 2010), there are others who contend that it not only continues to exist, but remains highly virulent (Feagin 2012; Jung, Vargas, and Bonilla-Silva 2011). In order to assess the conflicting claims, we need to put the issue of race into a broader context and define concepts basic to a sociological understanding of race, ethnicity, and majority–minority relations.

Many ethnic and other groups are more varied than we sometimes realize. These Jews demonstrating in Israel against racism and discrimination are Ethiopians.

THE CONCEPTS OF RACE AND ETHNICITY

Globally, many groups of people have been singled out for differential treatment on the basis of "race." These include people who are white, black, brown, red, and yellow—or the Roma, Jews, Semites, Arabs, Navajo, Tibetans, Finns, and Serbs. You may notice a difference between these two sets of groups. **Race** is a social definition based on some real or presumed physical, biological characteristic, such as skin color or hair texture, as well as a shared lineage (Law 2012a; Omi and Winant 1994). That is, while race is based on real or presumed bodily differences, it is more about what people define it to be than it is about any basic physical differences. **Ethnicity** is also socially defined, but on the basis of some real or presumed cultural characteristic such as language, religion, traditions, and cultural practices (see the next "Globalization" box). **Ethnic groups** have a sense of shared origins, they have relatively clear boundaries, and they tend to endure over time. These boundaries are recognized by both insiders and outsiders.

While they have been defined separately, the lines between races and ethnic groups are not always clear (Kivisto and Croll 2012: 8–13). Races are often considered ethnic groups, and ethnic groups are often considered races. For instance, *white* is a racial category that is frequently subordinated to ethnic categories such as Italian American or White Russian. Similarly, *black* has become "ethnicized." For example, Davis (1991a, 1991b) argues that blacks in the United States are now a self-conscious social group with an "ethnic identity." The creation of Kwanzaa, soul food, and the development of hip-hop all speak to the significance of *African American* as a cultural identity—not just a racial one. On the other hand, Jews, most notoriously in Nazi Germany during the Holocaust, have frequently been thought of not simply as an ethnic group, but also as a race. However, Jews do not all come from the same genetic stock; some have Semitic features, and others have European features. They do tend to share some ethnic characteristics, most notably

> **race** A social definition based on shared lineage and a real or presumed physical, biological characteristic, such as skin color.
>
> **ethnicity** A social definition based on a real or presumed cultural characteristic such as language or religion.
>
> **ethnic groups** Groups typically defined on the basis of some cultural characteristic such as language, religion, traditions, and cultural practices.

What Is Race?

Obama's America

a religion and a shared cultural history. Thus, while we will at times discuss race and ethnic groups separately in this chapter, the reader should bear in mind the strong overlap between them.

HISTORICAL THINKING ABOUT RACE

The concept of race has an ancient history. It has taken many different forms over the centuries, but it always serves as a way of differentiating among groups of people and creating hierarchies that empower some and disempower, or disadvantage, others (Song 2007). Race has also played a key role in most imperial conquests, often with whites imposing their will on, and then exploiting, other races. During the peak of the British Empire, for example, the British controlled India, the West Indies, and West Africa, all of whose dark-skinned populations were subordinated to the British. The rationalizations for this pattern of dominance included both "scientific" and cultural explanations.

"Scientific" Explanations

Following the Enlightenment, and especially in the nineteenth and early twentieth centuries, folk ideas about race were supplemented with "rational," or what today are seen as pseudoscientific, justifications for treating people of other races differently (Blatt 2007). While the Enlightenment thinkers believed in the unity of humankind, they also believed in classifying people along a continuum from primitive to modern. One result was classification schemes based on race. These schemes ranged from as few as four races, such as Carolus Linnaeus's 1740 distinction among American, European, Asiatic, and African races, to schemes identifying as many as 30 or more races (Arthur and Lemonik 2007a).

A more ominous result was to use allegedly fixed biological characteristics not simply to differentiate among groups of people, but to justify "scientifically" the unequal distribution of wealth, power, prestige, access to resources, and life chances of subordinate racial groups. In 1795, a German naturalist invented the idea of the Caucasian race as the first and most perfect race. In 1800, a French scientist argued that race was involved in social hierarchies and that whites stood on top of those hierarchies.

Evolutionary thinking spurred interest in racial categories. The idea of Social Darwinism, associated with sociologist Herbert Spencer, was taken to mean that racial differences were the result of evolutionary differences among the races. One race was better off, and another was worse off, because of evolution. Further, society was not to try to tamper with, reduce, or eliminate these differences; it was not to interfere with a natural process. Spencer (1851: 151) defined this in terms of the "survival of the fittest."

Also during the nineteenth century, Gregor Mendel's work on genetics and heredity led to the idea that the races could be distinguished from one another on the basis of their genetic makeup. This idea played a role in the development of the Eugenics movement, which notoriously argued that the human population could be improved genetically through scientific manipulation. Especially in the first half of the twentieth century and during the Nazi era, eugenicists defended racial segregation, opposed interracial marriage, and sought the restriction of immigration and the compulsory sterilization of those considered "unfit."

ASK YOURSELF

Do you think the ideas behind the Eugenics movement would be widely accepted by many people today? Why or why not?

Others criticized these extreme ideas while still arguing for genetically based racial differences in behavior. With the creation of the IQ test in the early 1900s, IQ was used not only to differentiate among races but to demonstrate racial superiority and inferiority. Later scholars argued that it is possible to make predictions based on race about intelligence (Herrnstein and Murray 1994), the likelihood of inheriting certain diseases (Hatch 2009), and the propensity to engage in criminal activities (Duster 2003). In 2007, the Nobel laureate James Watson (co-discoverer of the structure of DNA) controversially contended that races with darker skin have a stronger sex drive than those with lighter skin. He also stated that he was "gloomy about the prospect of Africa" because blacks scored lower on intelligence tests than whites. Watson later recanted, saying he did not believe that Africans were "genetically inferior" (Law 2012a).

The pseudoscientific focus on race as the source of significant social differences has gotten a recent boost because of the growing interest in genetics and the success of the international Human Genome Project, which seeks to create a map of human biological difference. However, the goal of the genome project is simply "to understand the genetic factors in human disease" and to "accelerate the pace of medical discovery" (National Institutes of Health 2011). Relative intelligence, personality types, and behaviors are *not* a focus of study.

Contemporary sociologists typically reject "scientific" explanations of race, including the view that genetic differences create socially significant differences among

Threats to the Roma

The Roma (often called gypsies) long have been, and continue to be, singled out and discriminated against. This treatment is traceable to their dark skin, mysterious origins, and Romani language; the distinctive way in which they dress; and their cultural tradition of living an itinerant lifestyle, setting up camps close to others, but refusing to become part of any society in which they find themselves. They tend to form tight-knit groups, marry within the group, and form strong family ties.

The Roma population has long been concentrated in Europe. In 2011, it was estimated that there were between 7 million and 8 million Roma in Europe (Lydaki 2012). The map in Figure 8.1 indicates where the European Roma are concentrated.

The Roma have traditionally been regarded with suspicion and hostility, and they suffer all the negative social consequences of being a powerless minority group. During World War II, the Nazis were especially brutal to the Roma, rounding them up and shipping them to concentration camps; between 200,000 and 600,000 gypsies died in the camps (Lydaki 2012). In recent years, hostility against them has again increased throughout Europe.

What is new in the era of the open borders created by the European Union is that many more Roma than ever before have made their way from Eastern Europe to wealthy Western European countries, seeking relief from poverty and limited prospects. However, because of the

FIGURE 8.1 • Roma Population in Europe, 2009

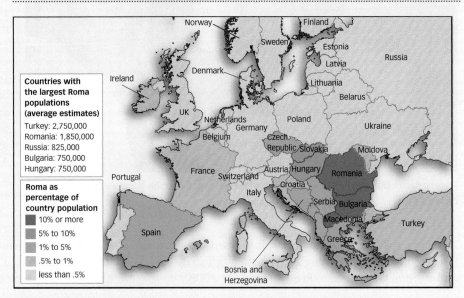

SOURCE: Data from European Roma and Travellers Forum, Council of Europe.

greater numbers of Roma and in the face of other globalizing processes, many European countries have recently violated human rights that had been guaranteed to them by a 2009 European treaty (Phillips, Connolly, and Davies 2010). Some European countries have expelled the Roma, seeing them as a threat to national identity (Bancroft 2005). In 2010, French President Nicolas Sarkozy expelled recently arrived Roma from his country and had their camps dismantled (Saltmarsh 2010).

Ironically, Roma culture is threatened by the Roma's own activities. Many are now settling down in cities, which poses a threat to their itinerant way of life. Their traditional jobs (e.g., peddling) are

being undermined by social and technological change. However, the high rate of illiteracy among the Roma persists, and children in the camps tend not to attend school. Their lack of education will almost undoubtedly lock them into a marginal position in society for the foreseeable future.

Think About It

What are some of the reasons the Roma have not assimilated into the majority culture in any of the areas in which they live? Do you agree that they are unlikely to do so in the future, despite the changes occurring in their way of life? Why or why not?

A young Barack Obama is shown here with his mother and grandfather; his father was Kenyan. Is Obama's family of origin unusual? Should we consider it so?

racial groups. Sociological research focused on genetics tends to take the stance that genes matter, but so do social and cultural factors (Guo, Roettger, and Cai 2008).

Cultural Explanations

Even though "scientific" explanations of race continue to exist, explanations based on social and cultural factors such as religion, language, and national origin are more prevalent today. In the second half of the twentieth century, ideas of cultural superiority and inferiority increasingly replaced those associated with biological superiority and inferiority. For example, African Americans have been described as having a "culture of poverty," which suggests that they have a sense of learned helplessness and powerlessness (Cohen 2010). While this argument has been used against poor people more generally, it has often been racialized to explain the disproportionately high rates of black poverty. Like "scientific" explanations, it has been used to legitimate racial differences in class position, rather than explaining these differences in terms of the lack of economic opportunity that some races have faced throughout history. Furthermore, such cultural explanations show how the concept of race increasingly resembles that of ethnicity (Eriksen 2010, 2012).

THE FLUIDITY OF RACIAL CATEGORIES

Sociologists point to the fact that racial categories are often blurred and subject to change; race is a dynamic and fluid social concept. There are many examples of the fluidity

and variability of the race concept in the United States. For example, President Barack Obama is the offspring of a white mother and a black African father. However, he is referred to as black or African American, not "half black" or "half African American." This is a legacy of the **hypodescent rule**, also known as the "one drop" rule or the "one Black ancestor rule" (Davis 1991a, 1991b). In Virginia, persons with as little as one-sixteenth African ancestry were considered by law to be black; in Florida it was one-eighth, and in Louisiana it was one-thirty-second. In the early twentieth century, several states, including Tennessee and Alabama, adopted a rule that a person with the slightest trace of African ancestry was considered black.

The amount of African blood borne by a person was considered so important to society that at various times several variations were encoded into U.S. laws (see Table 8.1): A *quadroon* (one-fourth black) was classified as black despite the fact that three of four grandparents were white. *Octoroons* (one-eighth black) were defined as black even though seven of eight immediate ancestors were white and they generally had few, if any, of the physical traits associated with people generally recognized as "black." *Mulatto* originally referred to a child with one "all white" parent and one "all black" parent, but was later changed to mean the child of one mixed parent and one white parent (Davis 1991a, 1991b).

Someone who was not white under a hypodescent rule but who had light skin and hair and Caucasoid features often tried to "pass" for white in order to reap the benefits of being in the privileged group. For example, Homer Plessy was an "octoroon" who was able to pass as "white." When it was discovered that he was "colored," Plessy was forced to leave a "white-only" train car. Plessy fought this in court. His case eventually led to the "separate but equal" doctrine in the 1896 Supreme Court decision, *Plessy v. Ferguson* that legitimized segregation until overturned by *Brown v. Board of Education of Topeka* in 1954. The fluidity and variability of the race concept is even clearer when we adopt a global perspective. In South

> **hypodescent rule** A law or judicial ruling that classifies persons with even one nonwhite ancestor, or a nonwhite ancestor within a certain number of generations, as black or colored.

TABLE 8.1 • Race in the U.S. Census, 1790–Present

Racial Category	Year(s) Used in Census	Description
White or Black	1790–1850	Only white and black categories used (mulatto also used if not "fully" black); black was divided into "free" and "slave"
Mulatto	1850–1870, 1890, 1910, 1920	Mixed race; one mixed parent and one white parent
Quadroon	1890	Mixed race, one-quarter African ancestry
Octoroon	1890	Mixed race, one-eighth African ancestry
Hindu	1910–1940	South Asian Indian
Mexican	1930	First and only time listed as a race if parents or individual was Mexican born.
Hispanic	1980–present	Anyone of Spanish-speaking descent, regardless of race or physical appearance
More than one	2000–present	First time in U.S. history when a person could identify with more than one specific racial category

SOURCE: Reprinted by permission of Lisa Speicher Muñoz.

Africa during apartheid (1948–1994), there were three racial categories: white, black, and colored. Whites were descended from Europeans and blacks from Africans. The colored category was more complex, including both those with mixed racial backgrounds (who might also have been labeled black) and those descended from Asians. In many Caribbean and Latin American countries, especially Brazil, race is a matter of gradations between black and white, with indigenous descent and social status factored in as well. In this case, it is especially clear that the color of one's skin does not determine whether a person is "black" or "white." It is also true that someone defined as black in the United States might be considered white in, say, Peru. Clearly, racial categories embrace far too much variation to claim a scientific basis.

Race data have been collected by the United States since its first census in 1790. However, these categories have changed across time, reflecting the social, economic, and political climate of the time. It was not until 1970 that individuals were allowed to choose their own race. Prior to this time, census takers filled in the race category based at times on asking the individual, and at other times on assumptions of the interviewer (Passel 2010). The 2000 census used the five racial groups established as "standard" by the U.S. government in 1997: White; Black or African American; American Indian; Asian; Native Hawaiian and Other Pacific Islander; and Some Other Race and Two or More Races. Although people have identified as "mixed

CHECKPOINT 8.1   RACE AND ETHNICITY

Race: A social definition based on shared lineage and a real or presumed physical, biological characteristic such as skin color.

Ethnicity: A social definition based on a real or presumed cultural characteristic such as language or religion.

race" for generations, it wasn't until the 2000 census that people were allowed to officially identify with two or more races. Table 8.2 shows the racial composition of the U.S. population based on data from the 2000 and 2010 censuses. In addition to the categories mentioned above, Table 8.2 separates out the Hispanic or Latino population, which is treated as an ethnic rather than a racial category. Of greatest interest in Table 8.2 is the strong increase between 2000 and 2010 in the Hispanic and Asian populations and the relatively slow growth of the black, white, and Alaska Native populations.

RACIAL AND ETHNIC IDENTITIES

Many individuals from oppressed racial and ethnic groups go to some lengths to identify with the dominant group. They might adopt the cultural values and practices of the dominant culture. For instance, linguistic assimilation—adopting English and leaving the old language behind—is almost inevitable among ethnic minority groups in the

Race in America

TABLE 8.2 • Racial Composition of the U.S. Population, 2000 and 2010

	2000		2010		Change, 2000 to 2010	
	Number	Percentage of Total Population	Number	Percentage of Total Population	Number	Percent
Total population	281,421,906	100	308,745,538	100	27,323,632	9.7
Hispanic or Latino	35,305,818	12.5	50,477,594	16.3	15,171,776	43.0
Not Hispanic or Latino	246,116,088	87.5	258,267,944	83.7	12,151,856	4.9
White alone	194,552,774	69.1	196,817,552	63.7	2,264,778	1.2
One Race	274,595,678	97.6	299,736,465	97.1	25,140,787	9.2
White	211,460,626	75.1	223,553,265	72.4	12.092,639	5.7
Black or African American	34,658,190	12.3	38,929,319	12.6	4,271,129	12.3
American Indian and Alaska Native	2,475,956	0.9	2,932,248	0.9	456,292	18.4
Asian	10,242,998	3.6	14,674,252	4.8	4,431,254	43.3
Native Hawaiian and Other Pacific Islander	398,835	0.1	540,013	0.2	141,178	35.4
Some Other Race	15,359,073	5.5	19,107,368	6.2	3,748,295	24.4
Two or More Races	6,826,228	2.4	9,009,073	2.9	2,182,845	32.0

SOURCE: U.S. Census Bureau, 2010 Census Redistricting Data (Public Law 94-171) Summary File, www.census.gov/prod/cen2010/doc/Pl94-171.Pdf (http://www.census.gov/prod/cen2010/briefs/c2010br-02.pdf).

United States. In addition, in the past it was common for individuals to change their names to have a more Anglo sound. Some individuals assigned to a subordinate race have the advantage of physically resembling the dominant race. Those who don't might go so far as to straighten, curl, or color their hair or to lighten their skin. They might go even further and consider cosmetic surgery.

At the same time, many have a strong and positive attachment to their racial or ethnic identity. This is evident in various ways, including supporting racial or ethnic organizations, participating in group-specific celebrations, and taking pride in the achievements of highly successful members of the group.

MAJORITY–MINORITY RELATIONS

Race and ethnicity can be understood in the context of a wide range of relationships that can be subsumed under the heading of majority–minority relations (Chapman and Wertheimer 1990; Farley 2009; Yetman 1991). The focus in such work is often on the difficulties experienced by minority groups. Many of these problems are traceable to majority group prejudice and discrimination (Jackson 2007). Those in a dominant group are prone to exploit and marginalize members of subordinate groups.

However, the distinction between majority and minority raises a number of questions: How can the white race, to take one example, be considered a majority group when it is outnumbered by a wide margin in the world by those in the other races? Whites are still numerically dominant in the United States, but the U.S. Census Bureau has projected that by 2042 the non-Hispanic white population in the country will be in the minority when compared to the combined nonwhite population groups, although whites will still outnumber any single racial/ethnic group (America.gov 2008). The 2010 census terms this demographic situation a **majority–minority population**, "where more than 50 percent of the population is part of a minority group." For

majority-minority population A population in which more than 50 percent of the members are part of a minority group.

California, Texas, Hawaii, New Mexico, and the District of Columbia, a majority–minority population already exists (U.S. Census Bureau 2011a).

Similarly, the U.S. Census Bureau (2012) reported 157 million women (51 percent) and 151.8 million men (49 percent) in the U.S. population. How can women be a minority when they outnumber men? The answer to this question lies in the fact that the sociological definitions of *majority* and *minority* do not rely on the numerical size of a group. Rather, these definitions are concerned with differences in levels of money, prestige, and power possessed by a group. A **minority group** is in a subordinate position in terms of wealth, power, or prestige (status), while a **majority group** is in a dominant position on those dimensions. While these three factors often vary together, a higher ranking in only one or two can be enough to accord a group majority status and, by implication, define another as a minority group. Women are a minority group because, although they are in the numerical majority, women as a group have less wealth, power, and prestige than men.

The same principles apply at other times and in other places. The British colonialists in India were a distinct numerical minority. In fact, this was true virtually anywhere that the British and other colonials went. It is something of a marvel that the British were able to control the vast land area and population of India with a comparative handful of soldiers and administrators. The British were the dominant group—with great wealth, power, and prestige in pre-independence India. In spite of their huge numbers, India's natives were the minority group.

THE SOCIAL CONSTRUCTION OF DIFFERENCE

Earlier in human history, white people discussed, quite incredibly, whether black persons had souls or whether they were more beast than human. Their descriptions said less about the observable characteristics of black people than about their own need to construct a clear boundary between black people and themselves (Wimmer 2013). Today members of the white majority no longer deny that blacks and other racial and ethnic minorities are fully human. But the insistence on significant differences between the majority and minorities persists.

We tend to think of majority and minority status as being objective in the sense that they are based on such externally observable characteristics as the color of one's skin, sex, or age. However, the fact is that all majority and minority statuses are products of social definitions, including the social definition of seemingly objective traits. This means that since they involve social definitions, majority–minority statuses also differ— because those definitions vary—over time and from one locale to another. The emphasis on social definitions is based on one of the classic arguments in sociology: "If men [sic] define situations as real, they are real in their consequences" (Thomas and Thomas 1928: 572).

ASK YOURSELF

What does it mean to say that if we define a situation as real, it is real in its consequences? How does this sociological argument apply to majority–minority statuses? To what social constructions you have studied in other chapters might it also apply?

STEREOTYPES, PREJUDICE, AND DISCRIMINATION

A **stereotype** is a generalization about an entire category of people. Stereotypes frequently appear in daily social interaction. For example, people might assume that a clean-cut young white medical student is highly trustworthy. In reality, it was just such a man, Philip Markoff, who was dubbed the Craigslist killer. In contrast, stereotypes about racial and ethnic minorities tend to work against them. In department stores, security guards may, without apparent cause, follow black customers, and sales personnel may view black shoppers with suspicion because of a stereotype about criminals tending to be black.

Stereotypes are the basis for prejudice and discrimination. **Prejudice** involves negative attitudes, beliefs, and feelings toward minorities. **Discrimination** is the unfavorable treatment of minorities arising from the negative stereotypes associated with prejudice (Law 2007). Discrimination occurs either formally (e.g., on

minority group A group in a subordinate position in terms of wealth, power, and prestige.

majority group A group in a dominant position along the dimensions of wealth, power, and prestige.

stereotype An exaggerated generalization about an entire category of people.

prejudice Negative attitudes, beliefs, and feelings toward minorities.

discrimination The unfavorable treatment of black Americans and other minorities, either formally or informally, simply because of their race or some other such characteristic.

THE MAN ON THE LEFT
IS 75 TIMES MORE LIKELY TO BE STOPPED
BY THE POLICE WHILE DRIVING THAN
THE MAN ON THE RIGHT.

It happens every day on America's highways. Police stop drivers based on their skin color rather than for the way they are driving. For example, in Florida 80% of those stopped and searched were black and Hispanic, while they constituted only 5% of all drivers. These humiliating and illegal searches are violations of the Constitution and must be fought. Help us defend your rights. Support the ACLU.

american civil liberties union
125 Broad Street, 18th Floor, NY, NY 10004 www.aclu.org

Perhaps you have seen this ACLU poster, whose message speaks for itself. With whom will you share it?

the job) or informally (e.g., in interpersonal situations). It can occur in any social realm, including schools, the workplace, and the criminal justice system. Members of the majority group unfairly deny minority group members access to opportunities and rewards that are available to the majority.

Discrimination and prejudice do not necessarily occur in concert with one another. People can be prejudiced without discriminating; they need not act on their prejudices. However, stereotypes, prejudice, and discrimination often interact with one another. For example, black women often face stereotypes that they are overly sexual and financially irresponsible (Collins 2004). These stereotypes can have negative real-life consequences. Black women who receive welfare aid have at some points in U.S. history been compelled to undergo compulsory sterilization. In some parts of the United States, children as young as 12 have been forced to undergo sterilization procedures (Flavin 2008). The assumption in these cases was that black women had too many children and were unable to support them financially. The stereotype of black men as dangerous criminals (Bolton and Feagin 2004; Ferguson 2001; Schilt 2010) has persisted from the end of slavery to the present and has created difficulties for black police

officers working with prejudiced white officers. In the United States today, much overt discrimination has been outlawed.

While blacks and other racial minorities are legally entitled to receive fair treatment in jobs, housing, and education, prejudice has been harder to root out. Many minorities still face negative stereotypes. They are constantly reminded that their social group has been defined as "different" from the majority group. George Yancy (2008: 5) has described lingering prejudice as being reinforced on a daily basis through "the white imaginary," a "perspective that carries the weight of white racist history and everyday encounters of spoken and unspoken anti-Black racism." This white imaginary, or racist social construction of "difference," has a cumulative effect that can alienate, disempower, and psychologically oppress blacks (Trepagnier 2010).

The majority does not experience discrimination or prejudice on a regular and ongoing basis and thus may have trouble empathizing with members of minority groups (Croll 2013). Members of the majority do not have to consider repeatedly whether their daily experiences reflect or do not reflect discrimination and prejudice. Peggy McIntosh (2010) sees this freedom from daily consideration of such issues as "white privilege." She defines "white privilege" as obliviousness to the sorts of challenges that minorities experience on a regular basis.

INTERSECTIONALITY

Many groups may be described as minority groups. Individuals may belong to more than one such group—for instance, Asian homosexuals or disabled Native Americans. Many of their experiences as one type of minority overlap and intersect with others common to another type of minority. Thus, these experiences need to be examined under the broader heading of *intersectionality,* or the idea that members of any given minority group are affected by the nature of their position in other arrangements of social inequality (P. Collins 1990, 2012) (see also Chapter 2). This concept was developed initially to analyze the situation confronting women of color, who face prejudice and discrimination along both gender and racial lines. It has subsequently been expanded to include other variables.

Minority group members are seen as being enmeshed in a "matrix of oppression" that involves not only race but also gender, ethnic group, sexual orientation, age, social class, religion, ability status, and the part of the globe, North or South, in which they live. The problems associated with being a member of multiple oppressed minority groups are not simply additive, but the disadvantages multiply, as do their effects (Kivisto and Croll 2012: 66).

The converse is also true. That is, a person who holds a number of statuses that are highly valued by society is likely to be extremely advantaged. One of the most esteemed groups consists of people who are male, white, Anglo-Saxon, upper class, heterosexual, and adult. This could be seen as a "matrix of power and advantage."

The allocation of Social Security benefits to the elderly yields a good illustration of the concept of intersectionality. Women rely on Social Security benefits after the age of 65 to a greater extent than men, and racial minorities rely on these benefits more than whites (Calasanti and Slevin 2001). In calculating Social Security and pensions, however, work and income history matters. People who earn more and work more during their lifetime receive higher Social Security payments in retirement. Because women and minorities face labor force discrimination and thus lower lifetime wages, their retirement income is lower. Black women are particularly vulnerable, as they face both gender and racial discrimination (Calasanti and Slevin 2001). Since black women are less likely to be married than white women, they also benefit less from spousal benefits. Whites, especially men who work for an employer without interruption for childbearing, are more likely than blacks and Hispanics to receive pensions from employers. The disadvantages of being female and a member of a racial minority thus accumulate over time.

PATTERNS OF INTERACTION

When members of majority and minority groups interact, the outcomes tend to follow one of four patterns: *pluralism, assimilation, segregation,* or *genocide*.

Pluralism exists in societies where many groups are able to coexist without any of them losing their individual qualities. For example, in pluralistic societies there might be multiple religions worshipped and many languages spoken.

Assimilation occurs when a minority group takes on the characteristics of the dominant group and leaves its old

ways behind. In the United States, assimilation occurs when immigrant groups choose to give up their native language for English or when they adopt mainstream American cultural values and customs. Sometimes, though, assimilation is forced upon groups. During the late nineteenth and early twentieth centuries, many Native Americans were forced into boarding schools where they were given new names, forced to speak English (and punished for speaking their native languages), and taught Christianity.

The United States has leaned more at times toward pluralism, and other times toward assimilation. Even when minorities feel that their differences are respected, all majority–minority relations are fraught with at least the potential for conflict. Members of the majority group act to maintain or enhance their positions, and minority group members struggle to improve theirs, or, at least, prevent them from declining any further. As a general rule, these conflicts, potential or real, are generally resolved in favor of the majority group because it has far greater resources—money, power—than the minority group.

ASK YOURSELF

If your parents or grandparents came to the United States from another country, did they arrive during a period when pluralism was the norm, or assimilation? How did this prevailing norm affect their experience as immigrants? Do you think it has had an effect on your life, or on the life of your family?

Segregation involves the physical and social separation of majority and minority groups. Historically, segregation was mandated by law. As a result, whites and minorities were not able to attend the same schools, live in the same neighborhoods, or share the same public facilities (such as restrooms, swimming pools, or courtrooms). *Brown v. Board of Education* (1954) is seen as the beginning of the end of legally mandated segregation. While levels of segregation have declined, such history set into motion practices that continue to segregate majority and minority groups. Schools are generally still segregated, a reflection of the persistence of residential segregation (Logan, Minca, and Adar 2012).

Genocide—an active, systematic attempt at eliminating an entire group of people—is a final outcome of majority–minority group relations. Some have argued that a genocidal campaign was conducted against Native Americans. This is not strictly accurate insofar as an official

pluralism The coexistence of many groups without any of them losing their individual qualities.

assimilation The integration of minorities into the dominant culture.

segregation The physical and social separation of majority and minority groups.

genocide An active, systematic attempt to eliminate an entire group of people.

Segregation in the U.S.

An S.S. guard took this photograph of children and an old woman on their way to the gas chambers at Auschwitz in 1944, victims of genocide carried out against the Jews and others. What might help prevent the rise of such an extreme form of interaction between majority and minority groups?

governmental policy of extermination did not exist. In this regard, the tragedy of the Native Americans is not the same as that which confronted Jews, the Roma, and homosexuals during the Nazi reign of terror known as the Holocaust (Berger 2012) or that which confronted the Tutsi ethnic group during the genocide in Rwanda.

RACE, ETHNICITY, AND EDUCATION

Economic success is in large part predicted by educational opportunity and achievement. As you can see in Figure 8.2, which shows the relationship between race/ethnicity and educational attainment, Hispanics are the group least likely to complete high school. That is in line with their higher-than-average rate of poverty. Hispanics (especially Mexicans) and blacks are the least likely to get a college degree or beyond. The groups that are more likely to complete a bachelor's degree or higher, Asians and whites, are also the two groups with the lowest percentage of members living below the poverty line.

Racial and ethnic inequality in learning outcomes is a critical dimension of inequality. Black and Hispanic students have lower levels of educational attainment. The most obvious explanation for these differences is that black and Hispanic students are significantly more likely to come from poor families than white students. Black and Hispanic families have lower levels of education than whites, and black children are especially likely to grow up in single-parent families. Family background is the

strongest predictor of how well a student does in school. Thus, the black-white gap in achievement is considerable in the prekindergarten years (Aud and Hannes 2011). However, among elementary school students with similar family backgrounds, black and white students have similar levels of academic achievement (Yeung and Pfeiffer 2009).

Things change as students enter high school. Many black adolescents disengage in school because they are exposed to an "oppositional" peer culture. Black students often equate doing well in school with "acting white." Consequently, to fit in with their peers and to affirm their racial identity, black students tend to exert less effort in their schoolwork and thus attain lower grades.

Black students are much more likely to attend segregated schools than whites. Seventy-two percent of black students attend schools that are 50 percent or more minority, and almost 40 percent attend schools that are 90 percent or more minority (Aud and Hannes 2011). Much of this is due to residential segregation in the United States. Black families live in predominantly black neighborhoods, and students are typically assigned to schools based on where their families live. School segregation contributes to the black-white gap in learning because data show that students learn less as the percent minority in a school increases (Hanushek and Rivkin 2006). Black students are also strongly affected by variation in school resources. Both teacher quality and class size are more important predictors of learning for black students than for white students. Thus, school-based reforms such as better teachers and smaller class size can potentially play an important role in reducing or erasing the black-white gap in learning.

The black-white achievement gap is an important reason why black students are less likely than white students to attend, and to graduate from, a four-year college (Perna 2006). Black students who attend more racially diverse schools are more likely to pursue a college degree, and are more likely to graduate.

Hispanic students share numerous disadvantages with black students, including fewer family resources than white students and attending segregated schools. However, they also face some unique challenges. First, many Hispanic students are recent immigrants to the United States. Interestingly, more recent Hispanic immigrants to the United States typically do better than those who have been here longer. Much of this "immigrant paradox" is explained by students' orientation toward school and their experience in the broader culture (Suárez-Orozco, Rhodes,

FIGURE 8.2 • Educational Attainment in the United States by Race and Ethnicity, 1970–2010

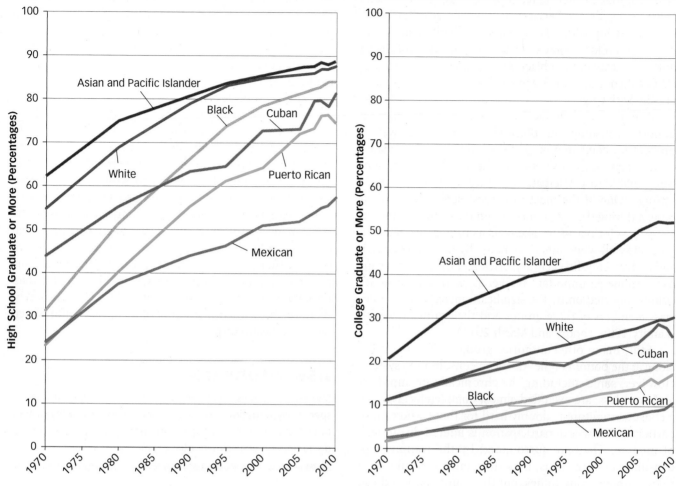

SOURCE: U.S. Census Bureau 2012.

and Milburn 2009). New immigrant families typically value hard work and see it as the key to success. In contrast, immigrants who have resided in the United States for a longer time are more aware of the structural barriers to success and do not fully believe that hard work pays off (Portes and Zhou 1993).

Second, Hispanic students have more diverse ethnic backgrounds than black students. For example, Mexican students typically have the lowest achievement among Hispanic students, while Cuban students rank highest in achievement (Reardon and Gallindo 2008). As Portes and Zhou (1993) note, Cuban students are especially advantaged because they have organized small, tightly knit enclaves that provide resources and support for immigrant children.

Finally, Hispanic students sometimes struggle in school because English is their second language. Many schools provide special bilingual programs that help students learn the curriculum in their native language until they are proficient enough in English to

enter English instruction classes. The Hispanic–white gap in learning decreases dramatically from kindergarten through fifth grade, partly reflecting increased facility with English.

RACE, ETHNICITY, AND CONSUMPTION

All races and ethnic groups are involved in consumer culture. However, there are huge differences in the nature of their involvement. Elite members of the white majority in the United States have their pick of the best and most expensive goods and services in the world. Others in the white majority also do well in consumer culture.

Some of those in racial and ethnic minorities are also actively involved in, and well served by, consumer culture.

Racism in Schools

However, minorities face some particular limits and opportunities in their consumption patterns. They also consume goods and services within their own frames of reference (Chin 2007). For example, both black and white American children may own Barbies, but the doll has a different meaning for a black American child in inner-city Detroit than it does for a white child in an upscale suburb of New York City.

The history of the races is an important influence on minority consumption. Black slaves themselves were a product for consumption. Only a little more than half a century ago, blacks and other ethnic and racial minorities were unable to participate in whites-only consumption settings. One of the most important acts of nonviolent protest during the civil rights movement of the 1950s and 1960s was for blacks to take seats as paying customers at previously all-white lunch counters. By the late twentieth and early twenty-first century, black and Latino Americans had become an important market segment for consumer culture, spurred on by the significant increase in middle-class members of these groups and their growing wealth (Landry 1988; Landry and Marsh 2011).

Still, many other minority group members scrape along at the bottom of the American consumption system. However, some, including the chronically unemployed and homeless, are excluded almost completely. Living in a consumer culture is doubly hard for those who cannot participate, or whose participation is limited due to lack of income. They are surrounded by the trappings of consumer culture. Thus, minorities must not only learn to do without many things, but they must learn to do so while they are literally surrounded by that which they cannot afford.

Marketing to Minorities

Clearly, businesses will market to the black and Latino communities as long as they believe that there is money to be made from them. Such marketing efforts lead to higher levels of consumption of various goods and services within these groups and to deeper involvement of blacks and Latinos in consumer culture.

Corporations interested in maximizing profits and the consumption of their goods and services often use race and ethnicity to sell to minority group members. Certain foods, clothing styles, cosmetics, financial services, and so on are sold exclusively, or nearly so, to particular racial or ethnic groups. In addition, advertising and marketing campaigns for goods and services sold to the more general public may also target particular racial or ethnic groups.

One example of this kind of racialized marketing is menthol cigarettes. Black smokers are four times as likely as white smokers to choose menthol cigarettes over unflavored cigarettes. This preference of menthol cigarettes has been relentlessly reinforced by advertising campaigns, creating what one research scientist called "the African Americanization of menthol cigarette use" (McNichol 2011). As early as the 1950s, makers of Kool menthol cigarettes used black sports celebrities and musicians as spokespeople. In the 1980s and 1990s, Kool sponsored jazz and hip-hop festivals—two forms of music typically consumed by blacks. In the late 2000s, the federal government considered banning menthol cigarettes. To mobilize the black community against such a ban, the makers of Newport, another popular menthol cigarette, ran ads featuring black men and women that framed such a ban as an assault on civil rights (McNichol 2011). Some leaders in the black community also fought the ban, saying that it unfairly targeted one particular racial group. The Food and Drug Administration chose not to ban menthols, though it admitted that, according to some research evidence, menthols may be more addictive than unflavored cigarettes (McNichol 2011). Unfortunately, then, the continued marketing of menthols could widen racialized health disparities.

ASK YOURSELF

Should companies be allowed to create marketing campaigns specifically targeting racial and ethnic minorities? Why or why not? Could preventing such marketing actually be a form of discrimination against minorities? Explain your answer.

White Consumption of Black Culture

Many whites are interested in consuming products associated with ethnic minorities. Consider the popularity of sushi restaurants and salsa as a condiment, among many other things. Whites have a strong, long-standing interest in consuming aspects of black culture (P. Collins 2009). There is, for example, a lengthy history of white interest in jazz, much of which comes from the black community. More recently, various aspects of black music (e.g., rap), and culture more generally (e.g., ways of dressing, talking, walking), have been of great interest to whites, especially youths.

However, white consumption of black culture has been highly selective. For example, white teenagers often want to be "black" on Saturday night in terms of things like the clothes they wear and their music preferences. However, their desire for blackness is likely limited to clothes, music, and the like, whereas the rest of the time they, and indeed whites in general, avoid and even criticize black culture.

White consumption of black culture is selective in another, more important, sense. It could be argued that whites are interested in consuming "everything but the burden" associated with black culture (cited in P. Collins 2009:

141). White entrepreneurs tend to select out of black culture only that which they think is desirable, especially what they think is marketable and from which they can earn a profit. Interestingly, whites, especially youth, seem to prefer to consume aspects of black lower-class culture. More damagingly, whites often glorify the negative aspects of black culture.

White interest in consuming "everything but the burden" could also be taken to mean that whites are unwilling to accept the burden of their responsibility for the problems that exist in the black community and that can be traced to white racism. Acceptance and consumption of a few aspects of black culture can be seen as helping to assuage white responsibility, at least collectively, for the difficulties that exist within that community.

Commercialization of Ethnicity

Minority groups sometimes seek to commercialize themselves—to sell themselves and their unusual or unique offerings to a larger public. For example, many tourists visiting Hawaii are attracted to the "luaus," marketed as unique indigenous customs. Locales like the Hollywood Forever cemetery in California draw thousands of tourists annually for the one-day "Day of the Dead" (*Dia de los Muertos*) event unique to Mexican cultural traditions. At such events, members of the ethnic group sell cultural products to the "consumers" of the experience. In this way, they can be said to be commercializing themselves.

There is an international market for cultural and ethnic products, which people in some parts of the world seek to exploit. Some ethnic groups in southern Africa have become like business corporations in their attempt to capitalize on what they have to offer to the global market (Comaroff and Comaroff 2009). Some ethnic and racial minorities go so far as to seek exclusive rights to their culture through legal means (Kasten 2004). If they control their "brand," either they can sell parts of it themselves

CHECKPOINT 8.2	MAJORITY–MINORITY RELATIONS AND THE SOCIAL CONSTRUCTION OF DIFFERENCE
Prejudice	Negative attitudes, beliefs, and feelings toward minorities.
Discrimination	Unfavorable treatment of minorities based on negative stereotypes associated with prejudice.
Pluralism	Coexistence of many groups retaining their individual qualities.
Assimilation	Process in which a minority group takes on the characteristics of the dominant group, leaving its old ways behind.
Segregation	Physical and social separation of majority and minority groups.
Genocide	Active and systematic efforts to eliminate an entire group of people.

(e.g., by sole rights to its distinctive products), or they can sell the rights to aspects of that culture to third parties (e.g., majority group tour operators taking tourists on "Zulu tours" to Africa).

RACISM

Racism involves defining a minority group as a race, attributing negative characteristics to that group, and then creating the circumstances that keep that group at a disadvantage relative to the majority (Law 2012b). Racism can be seen as a subtype of xenophobia, or "fear caused by strangers." **Xenophobia** involves the beliefs, attitudes, and prejudices that reject, exclude, and vilify groups that are not part of the dominant social group.

Note that the definition of racism used here allows us to discuss negative attitudes and treatment based on either race or ethnicity. Cultural characteristics that are different from the mainstream, the hallmark of ethnic identity, are almost always associated with racial groups, and so cultural discrimination is central to racial discrimination. In short, racism is based on *ethnocentrism* (see Chapter 3), or the belief that one's own group and its norms, values, customs, and so on are superior to other groups and their norms (S. Brown 2007b; Sumner [1906] 1940).

If you were to ask any American on the street whether he or she is racist, you are almost certain to be told that the person is not prejudiced and considers people of all races and ethnicities to be equal. Yet racist attitudes and behaviors persist. Minority members are likely to have experienced, or to know someone who has experienced,

> **racism** Defining a group as a race and attributing negative characteristics to that group.
>
> **xenophobia** Prejudices that cause people to reject, exclude, and vilify groups that are outsiders or foreigners to the dominant social group.

Xenophobia

Demonstrators gather at Columbia University to protest the racially motivated harassment of an African American professor at the school. How do ethnocentrism and xenophobia contribute to racist behavior?

comments or telling racist jokes. If they happen to be in a place where outsiders, especially minority group members, might intrude, they may use a code word or symbol instead of an overt racial slur.

FOUNDATIONS OF RACISM

Social Structure and Racism

In the United States, whites disproportionately occupy higher-level positions, and blacks are more likely to be near or at the bottom of the racial hierarchy. However, this is an overly simplistic picture of racial stratification in America (Song 2007). For one thing, there are blacks scattered throughout every level in that hierarchy, even in its highest reaches as exemplified, most notably, by Barack Obama. For another, large numbers of whites exist at or near the bottom rungs in that hierarchy. Finally, undocumented immigrants to the United States are predominantly Latino, and now they are much more likely to exist in the lowest rungs in the racial hierarchy than blacks.

One of the main indications of racial stratification is the extent to which poverty is linked to race. Figure 8.3 shows the relationship between race/ethnicity and poverty between 1959 and 2011. The fact that about a quarter of blacks and Hispanics were below the poverty line in 2011—compared with less than 12 percent of non-Hispanic whites and Asians—is a strong indicator of economic disadvantage for the first two groups. Also worth noting is the strong increase in poverty among blacks and Hispanics after the Great Recession. The historical influences of segregation and legal discrimination in generations past, coupled with the economic benefits of white privilege, help link economic disadvantage and racism.

discrimination at the hands of a white person or within the structure of an organization or society as a whole.

Erving Goffman's ideas on dramaturgy can be used to analyze this disparity (Slatton and Feagin 2012). Whites often quite unconsciously conceal or play down their racism in their front stage. However, when they are back stage with those they are confident hold similar views, they are quite comfortable making overtly racist

Culture and Racism

Some sociologists argue that a part of the larger culture of the United States involves a **white racial frame** through which whites, and to some degree blacks, view race (Feagin 2010; Slatton and Feagin 2012). The white racial frame includes an array of racist ideas, racial stereotypes, racialized stories and tales, racist

FIGURE 8.3 • Poverty Rates in the United States by Race and Hispanic Origin, 1959–2011

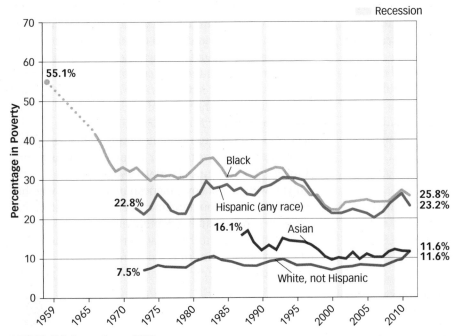

SOURCE: U.S. Census Bureau 2010.

images, powerful racial emotions, and various inclinations to discriminate against blacks. To a certain extent, blacks themselves have adopted elements of this frame. This is exemplified in "gangsta" style being identified as black culture. It is also found in such measures of success as graduating from college, gaining a professional job, or living in the suburbs being seen by black culture as selling out or "acting white." This white racial frame is largely responsible for perpetuating racial stereotypes, as is seen throughout movies, music videos, and television shows.

This set of ideas is pervasive throughout American culture and is found in and affects many, if not all, of its structures and institutions. These ideas come to "operate as a taken-for-granted, almost unconscious common sense" in the minds of the individuals who accept them (Winant 2001: 293).

Racism has often been, and can still be, a matter of physical domination of minorities by, for example, the power of the state. However, racism is now more a matter of **hegemony**. That is, one race now subordinates another more on the basis of dominant ideas, especially about cultural differences, than through force.

INSTITUTIONAL RACISM

Institutional racism is race-based discrimination that results from the day-to-day operation of social institutions and social structures and their rules, policies, and practices (Arthur and Lemonik 2007b; Bonilla-Silva 2009; Carmichael and Hamilton 1967). In other words, racism is more than attitudes (prejudice) or behavior (discrimination). It is "systemic" within society, especially American society and its most important and powerful social structures (Feagin 2006, 2010, 2013).

> **white racial frame** An array of racist ideas, racial stereotypes, racialized stories and tales, racist images, powerful racial emotions, and various inclinations to discriminate against blacks.
>
> **hegemony** The subordination by one race (or other group) of another, more on the basis of dominant ideas, especially about cultural differences, than through material constraints.
>
> **institutional racism** Race-based discrimination that results from the day-to-day operation of social institutions and social structures and their rules, policies, and practices.

Members of the Ku Klux Klan march through the streets of Sharpsburg, Maryland, in August 2004. A group of nine participants gathered at a community park near Antietam National Battlefield. The Klansmen were outnumbered by more than two dozen police officers who kept them away from scores of people gathered at a downtown intersection.

Institutional discrimination is found in many settings:

- Educational systems—for example, the underfunding of schools where the student body is disproportionately black or Latino.

- Labor markets, where equally qualified black candidates are less likely to obtain interviews and jobs than their white counterparts. Bertrand and Mullainathan (2004) sent out 5,000 résumés in response to real job ads. The only significant difference in the résumés was whether a name sounded very white (Emily or Greg) or very black (Lakisha or Jamal). The authors found that people with white-sounding names received 50 percent more callbacks than people with black-sounding names.

- The courts and prison system where drug laws and enforcement heavily penalize the selling and possession of the kinds of drugs, especially narcotics, that young black and Latino men are more likely to use or sell. In contrast, laws against the use of the drugs of preference among affluent whites—especially cocaine—are less likely to be enforced by the system (Alexander 2012).

Institutional Racism

Culture and Racism

ACTIVE SOCIOLOGY

Do You Talk About Race?

Race issues seem to be all around us, yet many people claim racism is a thing of the past. In what ways does race appear to be a salient part of your life? Use your Facebook and/or Twitter pages to examine race by studying your recent posts and answering the following questions.

1. How much do you talk about race in your posts and comments? Why? If you don't talk about race, why not?

2. How racially or ethnically diverse are your friends or the people who follow you on these pages? What do you think explains this diversity (or lack of it)?

Now consider a current issue or news event that in some way is related to race. Post something related to these issues or events on your Twitter or Facebook page and watch the responses you get.

1. What are people saying about these issues?

2. What might be going unsaid? Why?

3. How does what people are (or are not) saying influence your understanding of race and racism as they relate to the events you posted about?

- The health care system where blacks and Latinos are likely to receive no treatment at all or are more likely to receive poorer-quality treatment in, for example, emergency rooms rather than in the offices of physicians in private practice.

Most social institutions and structures in the United States are not overtly designed to discriminate on the basis of race. Many policies and practices are designed to be fair. Nevertheless, they may have an unintended discriminatory effect. Take, for example, the employment policy that favors seniority in economic downturns. This is not an unreasonable idea, but minority members are overrepresented among the less senior personnel due to historically limited opportunities. Thus such "last hired, first fired" policies have the unintended discriminatory outcome of resulting in the disproportionate firing of blacks and Latinos.

ASK YOURSELF

Do employment policies that favor seniority work against the goals of affirmative action? If so, how? What type of workplace layoff policy might be less racially and ethnically discriminatory than "last hired, first fired" when minorities lack seniority? Do you think the choice of such policies should be up to employers or mandated by law? Why?

The Role of Individuals in Institutional Racism

Often, individual racism is rooted in, and supported by, racism in institutional structures. Thus, while much research indicates that prejudice and racism at the individual level are declining (Alba 2009), the larger structures in which those attitudes and behaviors are embedded continue to operate to the detriment of blacks and other racial minorities (Bonilla-Silva 1997; Slatton and Feagin 2012).

In fact, discriminatory policies may be carried out by persons who do not actually believe in them. For example, a person may be expected to discriminate against minorities to please her superiors and to succeed on the job. Before laws against such practices were instituted, many real estate agents would not sell to black clients because they were afraid of alienating their white clients and thereby losing the income derived from selling homes to them. Selling to black clients would also anger white bosses who might fire agents who sold homes to blacks, thereby jeopardizing future sales to whites.

The "Invisibility" of Institutional Racism

Individual acts based on racism are often out in the open and easy for all to see. However, institutional discrimination is far subtler—often even invisible. Individual acts that are reflective of prejudice (e.g., shouting a racial epithet) or discrimination (a taxi driver refusing to pick up a black passenger) are easy to discern. However, the mundane operations of a large organization are often difficult to see.

In addition, large numbers of whites benefit from the racism of larger structures with higher-paying jobs, better working conditions, and power over others, including over blacks and other minorities. These beneficiaries have a deep, if perhaps unacknowledged, interest in seeing institutions continue to operate to their benefit, but to the detriment of blacks and other racial minorities.

Because their day-to-day operations are largely invisible, institutions that operate in a racist manner are much less likely to be seen as a problem than individual acts of prejudice or discrimination. This is the case in spite of the fact that institutional racism and discrimination represent far greater problems for blacks and other minorities than individual discrimination and prejudice. In addition, the comparative invisibility of institutional racism makes it far more difficult to find ways of combating it.

SOCIAL MOVEMENTS AND RACE

Hate Groups

Most hate groups in the United States are white supremacist movements, with the Ku Klux Klan (KKK) being an archetype. It is best known for its antiblack positions and activities, but the KKK originated as a nativist, anti-Catholic, and anti-Semitic group. KKK activity began at a time of high European immigration from places like Ireland, Italy, and other non-WASP (White Anglo-Saxon Protestant) nations.

Other well-known racist hate groups include the neo-Nazis and skinheads. In 2012 the Southern Poverty Law Center (SPLC) identified 1,007 active hate groups. The SPLC cited a rise in ethnic-based hate crimes following 9/11. It reports that an increasing number of hate crimes are directed toward immigrant populations, thus reflecting continued xenophobia in American society. Activities of hate groups include rallies, the maintenance of websites, and criminal activities including vandalism, arson, and sexual assaults against immigrant women. Figure 8.4 is a map of active hate groups in the United States.

FIGURE 8.4 • Active Hate Groups in the United States, 2012

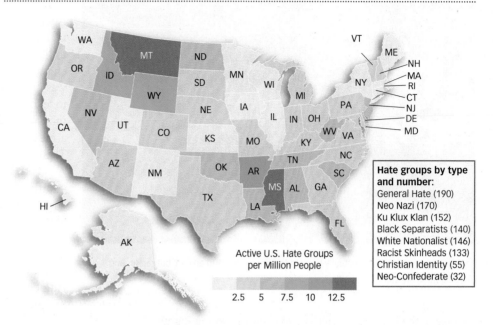

Active U.S. Hate Groups per Million People

2.5 5 7.5 10 12.5

Hate groups by type and number:
General Hate (190)
Neo Nazi (170)
Ku Klux Klan (152)
Black Separatists (140)
White Nationalist (146)
Racist Skinheads (133)
Christian Identity (55)
Neo-Confederate (32)

SOURCE: Reprinted with permission; originally appeared in *The Atlantic*: "The Geography of Hate" by Richard Florida, May 2011. Map by Zara Matheson, Martin Prosperity Institute. Data source: http://www.splcenter .org/get-information/hate-map

Civil Rights Movement

It is also the case that there has been, and continues to be, resistance to oppression by blacks and others. One major example of this is, of course, the modern civil rights movement, which arose, largely in the South, in the mid-1950s to deal with black oppression maintained by the Jim Crow system (Morris 1984, 2007). Under Jim Crow law, instituted after the Civil War and Reconstruction, blacks were denied political and social rights and were exploited economically.

Blacks and progressive allies had long opposed and fought against this system. However, it was the civil rights movement that brought Jim Crow to an end. It did so by honing a variety of techniques such as "boycotts, mass marches, mass arrests, sit-ins, freedom rides, attempts to register at all-white schools, lawsuits, and other unruly tactics" (Morris 2007: 510). For their part, racist whites and their representatives often responded with "bombings, billy clubs, high-pressure water hoses, and attack dogs" (Morris 2007: 510). These responses often took place in front of TV cameras, and this served to put pressure on the federal government and white public opinion to reform the system.

As a result, between 1955 and 1965 Jim Crow was dismantled. The civil rights movement of that era led to the

White Privilege

The civil rights movement eventually brought the Jim Crow era to an end, but racism and discrimination are still with us. Why?

Collective Identity and "Power" Movements

After the successes of the civil rights movement in the mid-1960s, several social movements arose in the late 1960s and early 1970s that sought to energize racial minorities. Winning legal rights was one thing, but many individuals continued to feel belittled and oppressed. The Black Power movement was the best-known attempt to raise a racial minority out of its sense of inferiority. Their slogan was "black is beautiful."

The visibility of the Black Power movement contributed to racialization among Hispanics. The Brown Berets saw themselves as analogous to the Black Panthers. The Brown Berets adopted the slogan "Brown Power" (and later "Viva la Raza," or "long live the race"). More recent politicized racial identities among American Latinos include the "indigena" movement, which elevates South American Indian ancestry to a matter of pride.

passage of the Civil Rights Act of 1964 and the Voting Rights Act of 1965, formally striking down legal discrimination in various aspects of public life. However, blacks today tend to suffer from many of the same problems they did before the civil rights movement, although they are caused more by institutional racism than by the law or racial hatred of individuals.

RACE AND ETHNICITY IN THE GLOBAL CONTEXT

Historically, ethnic identities have been closely tied to nation-states. For instance, until the modern era, the population of Ireland almost exclusively embraced the Gaelic language and Irish culture. However, nation-based ethnic identity has declined over time. One major factor in this decline is **diaspora**, or the dispersal, typically involuntary, of a racial or ethnic population from its traditional homeland and over a wide geographic area. In recent years, mass migration in an age of globalization has had a powerful impact on ethnic identities and reduced their association with a given nation-state.

Such population movement has led to the existence of multiple identities on the global stage. This, in

> **diaspora** Dispersal, typically involuntary, of a racial or ethnic population from its traditional homeland and over a wide geographic area.

CHECKPOINT 8.3	RACISM
Racism	Process of defining a minority group as a race, attributing negative characteristics to it, and keeping it at a disadvantage relative to the majority.
Xenophobia	Presence of beliefs, attitudes, and prejudices that reject, exclude, and vilify groups outside the dominant social group.
Ethnocentrism	The belief that your own group and its norms, values, and customs are superior to those of other groups; the basis of racism.
White racial frame	An array of racist ideas, racial stereotypes, racialized stories and tales, racist images, powerful racial emotions, and various inclinations to discriminate against blacks.
Hegemony	A situation in which one race subordinates another more on the basis of dominant ideas, especially about cultural differences, than through force.
Affirmative action	Efforts to increase diversity and opportunity by considering race and other minority-group factors when making decisions about, for example, hiring.
Institutional racism	Race-based discrimination that results from the day-to-day operation of social institutions and structures such as education and employment.

W. E. B. Du Bois and the Negro Press

W. E. B. Du Bois, the first African American to obtain a PhD from Harvard, held a variety of academic positions and published a number of important theoretical works and empirical studies. He also spent a good portion of his life as a journalist. He became a correspondent for a black newspaper, the *New York Globe*, in 1882 when he was only 15 years old. After he graduated from Harvard in 1905, he wrote for various black and white newspapers and magazines. He eventually founded *The Crisis*, the official magazine of the National Association for the Advancement of Colored People (NAACP).

Du Bois was the NAACP's director of publications and research. Through *The Crisis* Du Bois was able to disseminate his ideas widely because he was solely responsible for its editorial content. A dispute with the director of the NAACP led Du Bois to resign in 1934 because of the organization's position in favor of "voluntary segregation" to further black advancement.

Du Bois continued his journalistic career writing for, among others, the *Amsterdam News* in New York City between 1939 and 1944. During World War II, some black journalists were attacked, primarily by white journalists, for disloyalty because they criticized fascism both abroad and in the United States (at least in relationship to the treatment of black Americans). Du Bois responded to the critics by writing that "what white commentators . . . are really seeing is the intensity of feeling and resentment which is sweeping over the Negro people" (Franklin 1987: 40–44).

W. E. B. DuBois stands (top right) in the office of *The Crisis* magazine, which he founded and edited for many years, but which he eventually left over a policy disagreement with the NAACP. Would social movements be more effective, or less, if all members agreed all the time?

Think About It

Do you think that the press today expresses the real feelings of people, especially black Americans? Why or why not? Are those real feelings more likely to be expressed elsewhere today (e.g., on blogs or social networking sites)?

---

turn, has increased the possibility of people having hybrid ethnic identities. That is, an increasing number of people identify not only with, say, the ethnic group into which they were born, but also with other ethnic groups in geographic areas to which they may have migrated. Thus, migrants from India to China might see themselves as both Indian and Chinese.

- Ethnic identities are not nearly as fragile as is often believed. Ethnicity is inculcated from birth, within the family, and then, often, in school and by the surrounding culture. Thus it usually becomes part of a person's core identity.

ETHNIC IDENTITY AND GLOBALIZATION

Some see globalization as a threat to ethnic identity; they see globalization as leading toward a world of homogeneous identities. However, others disagree because:

Affirmative Action   Public Sociology: W. E. B. Du Bois

- Globalization can be a force, maybe the most significant force, in the creation and proliferation of ethnic identity (Tomlinson 2000). Ethnic groups and many aspects of their culture flow around the globe creating new pockets of ethnic identity and reinforcing that identity in particular locales. Global pressures toward a homogenized identity may also stiffen a person's resolve to maintain ties to an ethnic culture.

- Ethnic identity and globalization are part of the same modern process. For example, through the development of advanced forms of communication, globalization allows ethnic group members to stay in touch with one another for the express purpose of maintaining familiar traditions. This more powerful sense of ethnic identity can be exported back to the home country through the same global media. This is part of the broader process of transnationalism (Faist, Fauser, and Reisenauer 2013).

ASK YOURSELF

Do you believe globalization threatens ethnic identity by making the world more homogeneous through information and cultural flows? Or do you feel ethnicity is a strong enough identity factor to survive globalization, and that global communication flows can help preserve ethnic identities by keeping emigrants in touch with their home country? Explain your answer.

GLOBAL RACISM, PREJUDICE, AND DISCRIMINATION

To this point, we have focused on majority–minority relations within specific nation-states, especially the United States. But we can also examine majority–minority relations in a global context. The North–South distinction is a key factor. Most of the "bottom billion," or the poorest billion people in the world (Collier 2007, 2012), are minority group members in the Global South. Few from the bottom billion are in the North. In fact, the richest billion people in the world are largely in the Global North and are mainly members of the majority groups.

It has long been the case that the Global North and its majority groups have dominated, controlled, exploited, and oppressed the Global South and its minority groups. Historically, imperialism, colonialism, economic development, westernization, and Americanization have worked in large part to Northerners' advantage and to the disadvantage of Southerners. The system that dominates globalization today—neoliberal economics—helps those in the advantaged categories in the Global North and hurts, often badly, those in the disadvantaged categories in the Global South (Harvey 2005).

Majority groups from the Global North often "invented" minority groups in the Global South. One example is the creation of "Indians" as an oppressed minority group after the British colonized India. To that point, Indian society had its own highly developed system of majority and minority castes. Another example derives from **Orientalism**, a set of ideas and texts produced by the Global North that served as the basis of systems designed to dominate, control, and exploit the Orient (the East) and its many minority groups (Said [1979] 1994).

Racism is not exclusive to the West in general, or to the United States in particular, but exists in many societies throughout the world. For example, in Japan, differences in skin color, hair, and even body odor have been used to distinguish among races such as the Ainu and Buraku. Japanese citizens whose ancestry is partly Caucasian or African are also subject to prejudice within their own country.

GLOBAL FLOWS BASED ON RACE AND ETHNICITY

One way to think about globalized majority–minority relations is in terms of global flows. Both race and ethnicity can be said to flow around the world. One manifestation is the migration of people of various races and ethnic groups who move around the world today with greater ease and rapidity than ever before. People from the North are more likely to be tourists, or retirees who visit or take up residence in the nations of the South, because of the good weather and a low cost of living (Croucher 2009). In contrast, residents of the South typically migrate to wealthy nations in the North in search of employment, be it in low-skilled or high-skilled positions (Kivisto and Faist 2010: 49–54).

Another form of global flow involves the social and cultural aspects of race and ethnicity. As we have seen, neither race nor ethnicity is defined by objective characteristics such as "blood," genes, or skin color. Rather, both are defined socially and culturally. As social constructions and as ideas, race and ethnicity flow across borders and around the world effortlessly. A good example is the global spread of anti-Muslim prejudice today. Globalized mass communication helps to spread these ideas, but they are also carried by people who are taking advantage of inexpensive means of travel, especially by air.

> **Orientalism** A set of ideas and texts produced in the West that served as the basis for dominating, controlling, and exploiting the Orient (the East) and its many minority groups.

Paul Gilroy's (1993) *The Black Atlantic: Modernity and Double Consciousness* is an important work on majority–minority relations that stresses global flows. As the title makes clear, Gilroy is particularly interested in the flows that relate to blacks in the Atlantic region (Figure 8.5 shows that flow, as well as other flows of slaves from Africa to other parts of the world): "I have settled on an image of ships across the spaces between Europe, America, Africa and the Caribbean as a central organizing symbol. . . . The image of a ship . . . in motion" (Gilroy 1993: 4). This image encompasses the flow of slaves from Africa to the eastern coast of the Americas and the later return of some blacks to Africa. It also encompasses the circulation of activists, ideas, books, works of art, and the like that relate to blacks and race relations. All are seen as involved in "displacements, migrations, and journeys" (Gilroy 1993: 111). Gilroy argues that in trying to understand global flows based on race we should focus not on national boundaries but rather on the Black Atlantic, which he portrays as a transnational space.

A woman who opened a temporary mosque in Temecula, California, offers a flower in response to protestors across the street from the site of a planned Islamic Center. How have the increased flows of globalization affected your community?

Positive and Negative Flows

Those in the Global North are able to create structures that greatly enhance positive or protective flows. For example, in the United States, the 911 phone system quickly summons help; even elderly people who cannot get to a telephone have medical alert buttons. Setting up the complex network to handle these emergencies is expensive. Minorities, especially in the Global South, have little or no access to such networks and therefore to the positive flows expedited by them. Those in the minority categories are far less likely to participate in the globe's positive flows of money, commodities, food, health care, technologies, and the like. Conversely, those in the majority categories are likely to be in the thick of these positive flows, both as creators and as beneficiaries.

On the other hand, the structures that expedite negative flows are more likely to dump into, and to be found in, areas dominated by minority groups. For example, illegal structures allow the relatively free flow of weapons into and through many poor areas of the world. Much stronger structures are in place to prevent their flow into the wealthier regions of the globe. Another example is the tendency for people in the Global South to live in close proximity to disease vectors such as malaria-bearing mosquitoes and chickens carrying avian flu. The result is that they are at greater risk of contracting vector-borne diseases. In contrast, majority group members in the Global North are far more likely to live at some distance from, or to be heavily protected from, disease-carrying mosquitoes or live chickens, to say nothing of the vectors for many other diseases.

Those in minority groups throughout the world are more likely to be on the receiving end of such negative flows as borderless diseases, crime, corruption, war, and most environmental problems. Those in the majority groups certainly cannot completely avoid these negative flows, but they are far better able to insulate and protect themselves from them. Furthermore, those in majority groups often initiate negative flows (armaments, global warming) that have profoundly negative effects on minority groups.

Racism itself can be seen as having wide-ranging negative consequences for minority group members as the ideas and practices associated with it flow around the world (D. Goldberg 2009). This flow of racism around the world has been referred to as the "racialization of the globe" (Dikötter 2008). Nevertheless, racist ideas and practices are certainly not the same throughout the world, but rather are adapted and modified in each locale. They are affected by local ideas, as well as local economic, political, and

Orientalism

FIGURE 8.5 • Slave Trade Routes, 1518–1850

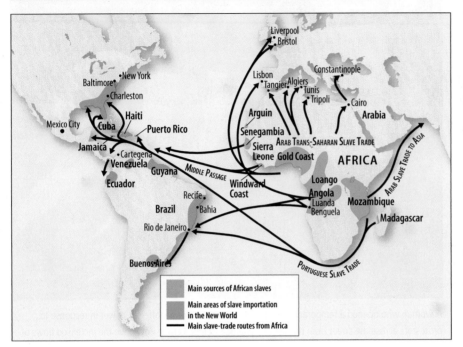

Main sources of African slaves

Main areas of slave importation in the New World

Main slave-trade routes from Africa

military realities. As a result, racism as it involves blacks is not the same in Great Britain, Ghana, or the United States.

Racial and Ethnic Barriers

As with all aspects of globalization, there are not only flows of various kinds, but also barriers to flows. Thus members of racial and ethnic minorities may be locked into a particular racial or ethnic identity, or they may be physically unable to move from a particular area (e.g., a ghetto) that defines them in a certain way. They are also likely to reside in countries in the South from which it may be difficult to move (because, for example, of poverty).

Just as majority groups have the advantage when it comes to positive flows, they are better able than minority groups to create barriers between themselves and negative flows. These barriers can include border controls in the nation-states dominated by advantaged groups, local actions such as creating gated communities patrolled by guards, and even individual actions such as having alarm systems installed in one's home. Minorities can afford few, if any, of these kinds of protective barriers.

Minority group statuses are likely, in and of themselves, to serve as "subtle" barriers that impede many positive flows. People in those categories are not likely to participate, or at least participate equally, in such positive flows. For example, there are no physical barriers, no walls, between Muslims and Christians in Europe, or Hispanics and Anglos in the United States,

but the mere fact of being a Muslim or a Hispanic, or being perceived as such, serves as a barrier to all sorts of positive flows (e.g., of jobs, useful information) for members of these minority groups.

ETHNIC CONFLICT WITHIN NATION-STATES

Greater ethnic diversity has increased the possibility of ethnic conflict within many nation-states. Of course, such ethnic conflict is not new. Among the most notable examples in the twentieth and twenty-first centuries have been conflicts between Turks and Armenians in Turkey; Germans, especially Nazis, and Jews in Germany; Tamils and Sinhalese in Sri Lanka; the Tutsi and Hutu in Burundi and Rwanda; Arabs and ethnic Africans in Darfur, and the conflict between various ethnic groups—Slovenes, Croatians, Serbs, Bosnians, Montenegrins, Macedonians, and Albanians—after the breakup of Yugoslavia in 1991. However, today with more members of ethnic groups in more and more countries, there is the potential for a great increase in the number, if not the intensity, of ethnic conflicts.

One example occurred in Paris in 2008 (Erlanger 2008: A11). The 19th Arrondissement on the edge of Paris is very large, poor, and ethnically and racially diverse, and it has high crime rates. The area is divided into three enclaves, dominated by Arabs largely from North Africa, blacks mainly from Mali and Congo, and Jews. Youth gangs in each area are major factors in the conflict. The youths not only live in separate enclaves, but they also go to separate schools. According to the deputy mayor in charge of youth affairs, this creates a situation in which "the kids don't know each other and that creates a logic of rivalry" (quoted in Erlanger 2008: A11). The conflict reached a peak with the beating of a 17-year-old Jewish youth who was attacked and put into a coma by a group of young blacks and Arabs because he was wearing a skullcap.

This episode is consistent with hate crime patterns in the United States, where whites are least likely to be victimized and where, when minority group members are aggressors, they tend to victimize members of other minority groups (Bodinger-deUriarte 1992: 24).

The most disturbing examples of ethnic conflict tend to involve the majority group's efforts to "deal" with ethnic minorities through expulsion, ethnic cleansing, and genocide.

Expulsion, or the removal of a group from a territory, may seem relatively benign because minorities are not purposely injured or killed in order to get rid of them. Expulsion can take two forms (Simpson and Yinger 1985). In *direct expulsion*, minority ethnic groups are ejected by the majority through military and other government action. In *voluntary expulsion*, a minority group leaves of its "own volition" because it is being harassed, discriminated against, and persecuted. Of course, in the real world these two forms of expulsion occur in concert with one another. And although physical harm may be relatively light, social and economic harm can be considerable. The people who are forced to leave typically lose much of their property, and their social networks are often irretrievably broken.

Many of those racial and ethnic groups involved in diasporas have experienced both forms of expulsion. This is particularly true of Jews and Roma, who have often moved both because they have been forcibly ejected (e.g., Jews by the Romans from Jerusalem in the second century AD and Spain and Portugal in the fifteenth century AD) and moved voluntarily (e.g., those Jews who left the Stalinist Soviet Union because of harassment).

Ethnic cleansing is the establishment by the dominant group of policies that allow or require the forcible removal, abuse, and even murder of people of another ethnic group (Oberschall 2012; Sekulic 2007a: 1450–52).

Ethnic cleansing achieved recent notoriety during the wars that were associated with the dissolution of Yugoslavia in 1991. The ethnic groups that dominated various regions sought to create areas that were ethnically homogeneous, and they did this by expelling and even

U.S. citizens of Japanese descent were forced into internment camps during World War II in actions upheld by the Supreme Court at that time but now seen as discriminatory. Contrast these camps with steps the government is taking today to try to ensure national security.

killing members of other ethnic groups. For example, Croatians were expelled from parts of Croatia inhabited by Serbs. Bosnia, which declared independence in 1992, was composed of three major ethnic groups—Slavic Muslims (the largest single group), Serbs, and Croats. Serbian armed forces created ethnically homogeneous enclaves by forcibly removing and murdering members of the other ethnic groups, especially Muslims.

In situations of ethnic cleansing, women and girls often have been targeted with physical violence and murder, as well as, in many cases, sexual violence. In Bosnia in the 1990s, Serbian men systematically raped an estimated 50,000 Muslim and Croatian women as part of their campaign of terror. Since the Serbian police were in positions of power, it was difficult, if not impossible, for the women who were victims of rape to get help or to prosecute their attackers. As of 2010, only 12 of the potential 50,000 cases had been prosecuted (Cerkez 2010).

Mass rape as a weapon of war has also occurred in the region of Darfur within Sudan, with the government-supported janjaweed militiamen raping Darfuri women and girls held in refugee camps. In 2008, Sudan's president, Omar Hassan Ahmad al-Bashir, was accused by

expulsion Removal of a minority group from a territory, either by forcible ejection through military and other government action or by "voluntary" emigration due to the majority's harassment, discrimination, and persecution.

ethnic cleansing The establishment by the dominant group of policies that allow or require the forcible removal of people of another ethnic group.

Leadership and Racism

FIGURE 8.6 • Select Genocides Around the World, 1914–Present

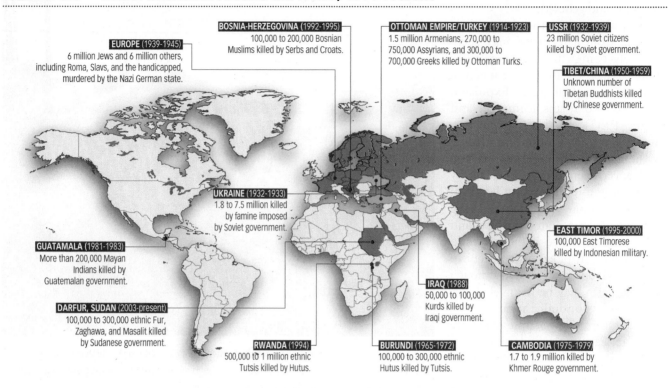

EUROPE (1939-1945)
6 million Jews and 6 million others, including Roma, Slavs, and the handicapped, murdered by the Nazi German state.

BOSNIA-HERZEGOVINA (1992-1995)
100,000 to 200,000 Bosnian Muslims killed by Serbs and Croats.

OTTOMAN EMPIRE/TURKEY (1914-1923)
1.5 million Armenians, 270,000 to 750,000 Assyrians, and 300,000 to 700,000 Greeks killed by Ottoman Turks.

USSR (1932-1939)
23 million Soviet citizens killed by Soviet government.

TIBET/CHINA (1950-1959)
Unknown number of Tibetan Buddhists killed by Chinese government.

UKRAINE (1932-1933)
1.8 to 7.5 million killed by famine imposed by Soviet government.

EAST TIMOR (1995-2000)
100,000 East Timorese killed by Indonesian military.

GUATAMALA (1981-1983)
More than 200,000 Mayan Indians killed by Guatemalan government.

IRAQ (1988)
50,000 to 100,000 Kurds killed by Iraqi government.

DARFUR, SUDAN (2003-present)
100,000 to 300,000 ethnic Fur, Zaghawa, and Masalit killed by Sudanese government.

RWANDA (1994)
500,000 to 1 million ethnic Tutsis killed by Hutus.

BURUNDI (1965-1972)
100,000 to 300,000 ethnic Hutus killed by Tutsis.

CAMBODIA (1975-1979)
1.7 to 1.9 million killed by Khmer Rouge government.

SOURCE: Copyright © Genocide Studies Program, Yale University. Used with permission.

the prosecutor of the International Criminal Court at the Hague of not only mass genocide but also propagating rape as a weapon of war and terror (Scheffer 2008). As of 2013, this case has not been tried (Simons 2010c).

The most extreme cases of ethnic conflict involve an active, systematic attempt at eliminating an entire group of people, or *genocide*. Genocide is seen as the crime of the twentieth century, and it shows every sign of continuing to define the twenty-first century.

Figure 8.6 shows select genocides of the twentieth and twenty-first centuries. The earliest genocide depicted here dates back to 1914, but there were many other instances of genocide long before that.

The 1948 UN convention on genocide was prompted by the Nazi Holocaust (Karstedt 2007: 1909–10). At first, the Holocaust occurred within the confines of Germany, but it later spread to the European countries allied with, or conquered by, Germany. It was in that sense transnational, and it would have undoubtedly become far more of a global phenomenon had the Nazis achieved their goal of world conquest. For example, had the Nazis succeeded in conquering the United States, we would have undoubtedly seen the genocide of American Jews.

A parallel example of large-scale genocide was the mass killings, during the era of the rule of Joseph Stalin, that took place throughout the then-vast Soviet Empire. In the main, though, genocide continues to be practiced within nation-states. Examples include the murder of millions by the Khmer Rouge in Cambodia in the mid to late 1970s, the Bosnian Serb murder of tens of thousands

CHECKPOINT 8.4	RACE AND ETHNICITY IN THE GLOBAL CONTEXT
Diaspora	Dispersal, often involuntary, of a racial or population group from its homeland.
Orientalism	Ideas and texts produced by the Global North to dominate and exploit the East.
Positive flows	Flows of money, commodities, food, health care, technologies, and the like, often created by and benefiting the majority.
Negative flows	Flows of disease, crime, corruption, war, and environmental damage, which especially affect minorities around the world.
Expulsion	The removal of a group from a territory.
Ethnic cleansing	Policies established by the dominant group to allow or require the forced removal, abuse, or murder of another ethnic group.

of Bosnians and Croats in the 1990s, and the killing of hundreds of thousands of ethnic Africans in Sudan since 2003 by the ethnic Arabs.

The global age has brought with it the globalization of genocide as instances of it have flowed around the world (Karstedt 2012). That is, genocide has become another negative flow making its way from one part of the world to another. Genocide may become more likely in the future because of proliferating and accelerating global flows of ideas, agitators, and arms. Added to this is the increased inability of nation-states to block many of these flows.

SUMMARY

Race has historically been defined on the basis of a shared lineage and some real or presumed physical or biological characteristic. In the second half of the twentieth century, race began to be defined more as a cultural phenomenon, making it more akin to the concept of ethnicity. Ethnic groups are typically defined on the basis of some real or presumed cultural characteristic such as language, religion, traditions, and cultural practices.

Race and ethnicity have always served as a way of stratifying individuals into groups with more or less power. The majority group, even if it has fewer members, has more money, prestige, and power and is likely to exploit members of minority groups. Intersectionality, or belonging to more than one type of minority (e.g., being black and female), often compounds disparities.

All races and ethnic groups are active in consumer culture, though engagement may be difficult for minorities, surrounded by things they cannot afford and subjected to aggressive marketing for products, some of which are harmful. Members of the majority may appropriate elements of minority culture—as when whites adopt the clothing, jargon, and music of black culture.

Majority–minority relations devolve into racism when the majority defines a group as a race and attributes negative characteristics to that group. It is the combination of xenophobia and ethnocentrism that makes racism so powerful. Current racism is more often a matter of hegemony, or the majority group foisting its culture on the minority, than of legal and material constraints on minority groups.

There is some evidence that individual-level prejudice and racism against African Americans and other minority groups in the United States are on the decline. However, institutional racism persists, and the white cultural frame is pervasive throughout American society and its structures and institutions.

Putting majority–minority relations in a global context, the North has more majority group members and dominates and oppresses those in the South. Majority groups are also better positioned than minority groups to create structures that enhance positive or protective global flows.

Greater ethnic diversity within nation-states has opened up more possibilities for internal ethnic conflicts. At the extreme, ethnic conflict leads to expulsion, ethnic cleansing, and genocide of minorities by the majority within a territory.

KEY TERMS

Diaspora, 240
Discrimination, 230
Ethnic cleansing, 245
Ethnic group, 223
Ethnicity, 223
Expulsion, 245
Genocide, 231
Hegemony, 237

Hypodescent rule, 226
Institutional racism, 237
Majority group, 229
Majority–minority population, 229
Minority group, 299
Orientalism, 242
Pluralism, 231
Prejudice, 230

Race, 223
Racism, 235
Segregation, 231
Stereotype, 229
White racial frame, 237
Xenophobia, 235

REVIEW QUESTIONS

1. What is the difference between race and ethnicity? What are the similarities? How have biological and cultural explanations helped to create racial and ethnic differences?

2. Barack Obama is the offspring of a white mother and a black African father, but more often than not he is referred to as black. What does this suggest about the nature of race in the United States? What are the consequences of this perception?

3. What criteria do sociologists use to define a majority group? How do majority groups maintain their positions of privilege?

4. Considering some of the examples provided in this chapter, do your consumption patterns reflect racial and ethnic identity?

5. Do you think that it is a good idea for ethnic groups to commercialize ethnicity? What do they stand to gain? What do they stand to lose in the process? Are the gains worth the costs?

6. What are the different motivations for racism? What are some mechanisms that minorities have used to resist racism?

7. What is institutional racism, and what are some examples of institutional racism? In what ways is institutional racism more problematic than individual racism?

8. How would you characterize majority–minority relations on a global level? What sort of advantages do majority groups have on the global level?

9. How is globalization changing the nature of ethnicity on a global scale? In what ways have ethnic groups been able to use advances in communication and media to retain their ethnic identity?

10. Do you agree that globalization is creating a universal culture?

APPLYING THE SOCIOLOGICAL IMAGINATION

There are scholars and citizens who have come to believe that racism is declining and the chances for racial integration have improved, but we also know that corporations pay attention to racial and ethnic differences when marketing their products.

For this activity, conduct a qualitative content analysis of advertisements in two different magazines: a mainstream magazine part of the dominant culture (e.g., *Vanity Fair, Cosmopolitan, Businessweek*) and a traditionally black magazine (e.g., *Essence,*

Ebony, Jet, Black Enterprise). Compare and contrast the ads in the magazines. Can you identify any differences between the magazines in terms of the products or themes of their ads? What sorts of images are used in each of the magazines? In what ways are the advertisements reflective of larger majority–minority group relationships in the United States? How can we use this exercise to explain the relationship between stratification and consumption?

STUDENT STUDY SITE

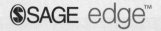

Sharpen your skills with SAGE edge at **edge.sagepub.com/ritzeressentials**

SAGE edge for students provides a personalized approach to help you accomplish your coursework goals in an easy-to-use learning environment.

This Jordanian girl's Western-style doll wears traditional clothing to match her own. Our culturally influenced notions of sex and gender are increasingly affected by the forces of globalization. Are men and women fundamentally the same? What dictates our behavior as men and as women?

GENDER AND SEXUALITY

9

LEARNING OBJECTIVES

1   Describe the continuum of sexual identities and orientations and define sexual deviance.

2   Discuss the many ways people enact gender as well as the cultural influences on gender.

3   Describe the effect of globalization on sexuality and sexual and gender-related behavior.

One day in 2011, several dozen Saudi Arabian women entered their family cars and drove to various locations throughout the country, performing errands and meeting up for social dates. While this may sound like an ordinary day to most of us, the undertaking made a bold and controversial statement about equality, civil rights, and gender relationships in the conservative Middle Eastern kingdom. The reason? Throughout Saudi Arabia, a fundamentalist interpretation of Islamic law, enforced by the *mutaween* (morality police), subjects all women to strict norms and laws, including a ban on driving.

Sex and gender are powerful determinants of our interactions with others.

As a measure of how strictly such laws are upheld, consider that while most of the women apprehended for participating in the protest were escorted home by police with only a warning, one was convicted of driving without permission and sentenced to 10 lashes with a whip. The sentence was overturned by Saudi Arabian king Abdullah bin Abdul-Aziz Al Saud, who had also just granted women the right to vote in the country's next municipal election.

For a person to be prohibited from driving simply because she was born a female may seem unreasonable to you, but our culture's sex and gender norms likely seem equally unreasonable to others around the world.

Attitudes toward sex and gender shift not only across space but also over time. Globalization, technological advancements in communication, and the feminization of labor, among other important factors, are changing what we perceive as appropriate sexual behavior and gender performance. As King Abdullah and the female drivers watched neighboring nations being shaken by violent public demonstrations during the Arab Spring, they saw an opportunity and perhaps an imperative for reform. The full extent of that reform is yet to be seen. For the people of Saudi Arabia, however, the ongoing struggle between religious tradition and sexual freedom is exhilarating and terrifying, joyful and heart wrenching. For sociologists, it's a testament to the intricate beauty of a living, breathing culture.

Sex and gender are two of the most decisive—and divisive—factors in determining how we interact with those around us. Culture frames our thoughts and actions about sex and gender, as well as the way we are perceived and treated by others. A person who challenges a cultural norm by expressing an uncommon sexual preference or protesting patriarchal rules may be labeled deviant and be subject to legal repercussions—or worse. ●

*S*ex and *gender* are terms that are often used interchangeably and confused with one another. However, it is important that they be distinguished clearly. **Sex** is principally a biological distinction between males and females based on fundamental differences in their reproductive organs and functions. **Gender** is based on what, given a person's sex, are considered appropriate physical, behavioral, and personality characteristics. The key difference is that sex is based *mainly* on biological differences, whereas gender is based on social distinctions (Ryan 2007). But both have important similarities from a sociological perspective. This chapter will describe how sociology approaches questions of sex and gender.

Qian Jinfan, 84 years old and shown holding a photo of herself at 59, always felt she was a woman. She began experimenting with hormone treatments at the age of 60. A retired official of the Chinese Communist Party who prefers to be known as "Yiling," she has gone public in hopes of breaking down traditional assumptions about transsexuals.

SEX AND SEXUALITY

Although we tend to think in terms of two—and *only* two—biological sexes, in fact there is a continuum between male and female anatomy (Fausto-Sterling 1999). In the middle are individuals with some combination of both male and female genitalia. In the past, such people were called hermaphrodites, and doctors altered infants' genital structures to better match the typical male or female anatomy (Coventry 2006). Today people with ambiguous genitalia are usually referred to as **intersexed**. They are more often spared surgery, at least until they are old enough to be identified, or to identify themselves, with one sex or the other (Zeiler and Wickstrom 2009). Also in the middle are **transsexuals**, those who may have the genitalia of one sex or the other, but who believe that they are locked into the wrong body. While some remain, often uncomfortably, in those bodies, others take hormones to change their sexes, and some

> **sex** A mainly biological distinction between males and females based on fundamental differences in their reproductive functions.
>
> **gender** The physical, behavioral, and personality characteristics considered appropriate for one's sex.
>
> **intersexed** People who have some combination of the genitalia of both males and females.
>
> **transsexuals** Individuals whose genitalia are of the sex opposite to the one with which he or she identifies and who may undergo treatment or surgery to acquire the physical characteristics of the self-identified sex.

undergo genital reassignment surgery. Such a biological transformation must be accompanied by the careful management of one's new sex status. Sex needs to be seen not as a given but as something to be achieved. This point was made by Harold Garfinkel (1967: 116–185) in his famous study of a transsexual he called "Agnes." It has been illustrated autobiographically by the well-known economic historian Deirdre McCloskey (2000), who was Donald until reassignment surgery at age 53.

This idea of a sexual continuum extends to male and female hormones as well. For example, both males and females have the hormones estrogen and testosterone. However, the amounts vary greatly from individual to individual within and between sexes, as well as over time (Kimmel 2004). Both sexes also have breasts. Although women typically have larger breasts than men do, the size of some men's breasts exceeds that of some women's. Breast cancer is largely a disease of women, but some men contract the disease. Facial hair is usually thought of as a male characteristic, but some women grow enough facial hair to need to shave regularly. Biologically, there are no absolutely clear-cut differences between men and women.

Also pointing against the idea that there are simply two sexes is the fact that at a global level there are a number of cultures in which there exists a "third gender" (Ryan 2012). This is socially defined as a truly distinct gender, neither man nor woman, nor a combination of the two. Examples include the hijras of India (see Chapter 2), the berdache of a number of Indian cultures, Thailand's kathoeys, and the fa'afafine of Samoa.

SEXUAL SELVES

Of central interest to sociologists is **sexuality**, or the ways in which people think about, and behave toward, themselves and others as sexual beings (Plummer 1975). Sex and sexuality are not identical. A person who is biologically female (or who believes she should be in a female body) may engage in sexual behavior with either men or women, or for that matter with both or neither. Given the multiple dimensions of both sex and sexuality, there is much variation among individuals.

There is now a huge and growing body of literature on the sociology of sexuality (Plummer 2012). While bodies and biology are deeply involved, the bulk of this work deals with the social, social-psychological, and cultural aspects of sexuality. Sociologists have become more interested in sexuality for a number of reasons:

- the growing number of sexually linked social problems, including the HIV/AIDS epidemic and sexual violence;

- the greater visibility of sex-related social movements, especially those associated with gays and lesbians;

- technological change, such as the arrival of erectile dysfunction drugs like Viagra and Cialis, and the media's presentation of sex in its many forms;

- the globalization of sexuality, for example sex tourism and sex trafficking (Frank 2012a);

- more overt expressions of sexuality in consumer culture—not only widespread commerce in sexual activity but also the use of sexuality to sell virtually everything; and

- the development of the Internet, where sexuality is readily available and a vibrant commercial sex culture has developed.

People express their sexualities for many different reasons; it is rarely simply a matter of sexual release. Culture gives us patterns, rules, and codes to manage our sexualities and their expression. Gender roles and power dynamics affect our sexualities, as do race and class (Scott and Schwartz 2008). What people do and do not do is symbolically important to them and to others in society. The stories that people tell and do not tell about their sexualities are of great significance to them. These stories are of great symbolic importance. They tell us much about not only the storytellers and their listeners, but also the societies in which they live.

Sexuality is also a prime area for the sociological study of emotions (Stets and Turner 2007). To the individual, sexuality is emotionally "hot," but there are various social forces that seek to cool it off. This was a concern to Max Weber who saw the process of rationalization as an "iron cage," as described in Chapter 2, that served to limit many things, including sexual expression.

Sexual Identities and Orientations

We all have sexual identities. One element of sexual identity is **sexual orientation**, which involves whom you desire, with whom you want to have sexual relations, and with whom you have a sense of connectedness (Scott and Schwartz 2008). Sexual orientation is typically divided into four categories: **heterosexuality**, or sexual desire for the opposite sex; **homosexuality**, or desire to have sexual relations with someone of the same sex (Ryan 2012); **bisexuality**, or a desire for sexual relations with both sexes; and **asexuality**, or a lack of sexual desire (E. Kim 2011). Expression of these orientations varies among individuals; for example, one heterosexual is not like all others in the degree of desire for members of the opposite sex. In addition, a person's sexual orientation and romantic tendencies may differ. For example, a bisexual may have sexual relations with people of both sexes but prefer romantic relationships with members of the opposite sex. Layered onto sexual orientation are a variety of other sexual identities, such as sex addict (like the main character in the TV series *Californication*), sex worker, or celibate. Sexual identity adds considerable complexity to the male–female sex continuum.

Sexual identities reflect changes in the larger society, and they have a profound effect on the individuals with those identities, as well as on those to whom the individuals relate. These identities, and feelings about them, are not static. The best-known example is the increasing openness about identifying as gay or lesbian. In many environments, it is no longer necessary to hide those identities, and it is in fact possible, even likely, to be very public, and to feel

---

sexuality The ways in which people think about, and behave toward, themselves and others as sexual beings.

sexual orientation Preferences based on whom one desires sexually, with whom one wants to engage in sexual relations, and to whom one feels connected—typically categorized as heterosexual, homosexual, bisexual, or asexual.

heterosexuality Desire to have sexual relations with someone of the opposite sex.

homosexuality Desire to have sexual relations with someone of the same sex.

bisexuality A desire to have sexual relations with individuals of both the opposite sex and the same sex.

asexuality A lack of sexual desire.

very good, about one's gay or lesbian identity (Plummer 2007a). The development of TV channels such as LOGO, which are geared toward the LGBTQ (lesbian, gay, bisexual, transsexual, and queer) community, reflects a wider acceptance of diverse forms of sexuality within mainstream media outlets.

Sexual identities encompass a wide range, and growing number, of sexual subcultures. These subcultures include those associated with cross-dressing ("drag"), polyamory (multiple love relationships), and BDSM (bondage, domination, submission, and masochism). The BDSM subculture has entered mainstream culture, at least vicariously, through the enormous popularity of E. L. James's *Fifty Shades of Grey*. Furthermore, there are multiple subcultures that are constantly coming together and splitting apart (Bauer 2008; Gates 1999). Thus, for example, there are many gay subcultures, including drag kings and queens, and gay Christians.

The increasing multiplicity of sexualities and sexual communities makes conflicts over the boundaries of sexualities increasingly likely (Kollen 2013). Young adults often experiment with sexuality and sexual behavior in an effort to discover those boundaries for themselves. To make things more complicated, some individuals engage in same-sex practices while rejecting the label *gay* or *lesbian*.

Gendered Sexual Scripts

The differences between men and women in sexuality are perhaps greater than in any other aspect of our intimate lives (Naples and Gurr 2012). Although biological differences play a role in gender differences in sexuality, the sociological view is that social and cultural factors are of far greater importance. Socialization plays an especially key role. Men and women learn sexual behavior by observing and learning from others. Of special importance is the learning of gender-appropriate **sexual scripts**, or the generally known ideas about what one ought to do and what one ought not to do as far as sexual behavior is concerned.

The male script focuses on the penis as the basic "tool" to be used in sexual relations. Sexuality is defined, then, as coitus, because it involves the use of the penis and its insertion into the vagina. Therefore, the primary expression of sexuality as far as most men are concerned is coitus; it is the way to use the penis appropriately and to achieve pleasure. This does not rule out oral or anal sex as alternatives to vaginal sex. However, excluded are many nongenital forms of sexuality since the only "true" form of sexuality for males, like the penis itself, is outside one's self.

> **sexual scripts** Generally known ideas about what one ought to do and not do as far as sexual behavior is concerned.

Men are also supposed to approach sexuality like work. They are supposed to be knowledgeable about it and good at it, to operate efficiently, and to be in control of both their own bodies and those of their partners. For women, by contrast, sexuality is more like play, efficiency is devalued, and there is no strong need to be in control. Given the internal nature of the vagina, the sexual script for women is much more inwardly focused. It is also broader, involving many more acceptable ways of experiencing real sexuality and thinking of many more nongenital parts of the body as sexual in nature.

The social aspect of sexual behavior is also gender-driven. Men are expected to be in charge of arousal; women are expected to be aroused. Men are expected to be driven by lust and desire while women are supposed to be aroused by that and not to arrive at a sexual encounter "in lust." Susan M. Shaw and Janet Lee (2009: 179) argue that men engage in "instrumental sex (sex for its own sake) . . . and women engage in expressive sex (sex involving emotional attachments)."

There are great differences in these male and female scripts. Nonetheless, such scripts are widely shared. Learning these scripts, and the scripts themselves, better account for gender differences in sexuality than do biological differences.

ASK YOURSELF

Where and how do we learn sexual scripts? Do you think we can unlearn them, or learn new ones? Why or why not?

SOCIAL CONSTRAINTS ON SEXUALITY

There is an increasing sense, not without reason, that sexuality has grown increasingly free of social constraints. This is clear in many realms of the social world, but one example is the way the media treat sexuality. An MTV reality show titled *16 and Pregnant* deals with younger teens going through the trials and tribulations of pregnancy. Other broadcasts with similar themes are the TV movie *The Pregnancy Pact* and, on occasion, the network TV program *Glee*. These programs demonstrate a relaxed attitude toward teenage sexuality: that it is OK for teenagers to have sexual relations, maybe even unprotected relations; to become pregnant; and perhaps even to have the babies that may result.

Acceptance of LGBTQs   Sexual Minorities Online

While there is much to support the idea of increasing sexual freedom, human sexuality is never totally free. For example, a public school in Mississippi canceled its senior prom because a lesbian student wanted to bring her girlfriend as a date (Joyner 2010a, 2010b).

Society contains structures such as school, family, law, police, and religion, as well as customs that constrain sexuality. In addition, constraints on sexuality are closely linked to larger social phenomena and hierarchies. One of the most important of these is minority status.

Generally speaking, the sexuality of oppressed minorities is more likely to be constrained than is the sexuality of the dominant group. For example, men have historically been freer to express their sexuality, while women have been subjected to a number of physical and social traditions that discourage them from the free exercise of their sexuality. More extremely, women are more likely to be abused and raped and to sell their sexuality while men are more likely to be sex offenders and sex addicts and to buy sexual relations.

Culture and Consent

Important to a discussion of social constraints on sexuality are the concepts of consensual sex, sexual assault, and rape. All involve issues of the relative power of the individuals involved in sexual activity. **Consensual sex** is defined as sexual intercourse that is agreed upon by the participants in an informed process. **Sexual assault** encompasses sexual acts of domination usually enacted by men against women. Such assaults can occur between strangers, but they usually occur between acquaintances. **Rape**, also a form of domination, is violent sexual intercourse (Rudrappa 2012).

Communities vary in terms of the probability of sexual violence and the effectiveness of constraints on the kinds of behaviors that often lead to such violence. In many religious communities, strong expectations for modesty and sexuality only within marriage keep sexual violence to a minimum. In contrast, the nature of sexuality in colleges can promote a "rape culture" (Argiero et al. 2010; Boswell and Spade 1996), an environment conducive to rape. Rape cultures tend to be prevalent in and around college campuses due to the overpowering presence of alcohol and drugs and the youth of the population.

Sexual assaults have very serious consequences. According to the World Health Organization (WHO) and the Rape, Abuse, and Incest National Network (RAINN), the largest anti–sexual violence network in the United States, survivors are 3 times more likely than those who have not been assaulted to suffer from depression, 4 times more likely to contemplate suicide, 6 times more likely to suffer from post-traumatic stress disorder (PTSD), 26 times more likely to abuse drugs, and 13 times more

likely to abuse alcohol as a coping mechanism (RAINN 2009b). Moreover, a host of physical maladies can persist, including tension headaches, fatigue, gastrointestinal upset, difficulty urinating, and a variety of vaginal and rectal problems.

SEX AND CONSUMPTION

Regardless of the constraints on sexuality, everyday life has been sexualized to a large degree. The world has been "made sexy" (Rutherford 2007). In our consumer society, sex is used to encourage consumption of all sorts of things that are not inherently sexual. Advertisements use sexualized images to promote innumerable products, from cars to toothpaste and from clothing to soft drinks. The implication in many of these ads is that use of the product leads to sexual relationships. The well-known media adage that "sex sells" shows no signs of going out of fashion. However, researchers have found that women usually have a strong negative reaction to explicit sexual content in advertising and are less likely to buy merchandise promoted with these types of ads (Dahl, Sengupta, and Vohs 2009). In comparison, men tend to feel positively toward such ads.

More blatant than the use of sexual images to sell products and services is the way in which human sexualities themselves have been increasingly marketed as commodities (Y. Taylor 2007). Of course, the consumption of sex is nothing new. After all, prostitution is often referred to as the "oldest profession." What is new since the mid twentieth century is the rise of a huge sex industry, one whose outreach spans the globe. This sexual marketplace can be seen as being composed of five interlocking markets (Plummer 2007b):

- *Bodies and sexual acts*. This market includes prostitution and other forms of sex work, such as stripping and table and lap dancing. "Real sex" involving "real bodies" is available for purchase by those with the ability to pay.

- *Pornography and erotica*. The production, distribution, sale, and consumption of pornography—by both men and women—are increasingly taking place on the Internet.

---

consensual sex Sexual intercourse that is agreed upon by the participants in an informed process.

sexual assault Sexual acts of domination usually enacted by men against women.

rape A form of domination; violent sexual intercourse.

PUBLIC SOCIOLOGY

Pepper Schwartz on Sexuality

Pepper Schwartz is a sociologist who focuses on sexuality and sexual relationships. She has published many scholarly articles and books (most notably, in 1983, *American Couples: Money, Work and Sex* with Philip Blumstein). However, Schwartz does not limit herself to dry academic tracts or scholarly topics. She is also well known to the general public through the articles and columns she has contributed to many magazines and newspapers, including monthly columns "Sex and Health" for *Glamour* magazine (with Janet Lever) and "Talking About Sex" in *American Baby* magazine. She also blogs on MedHelp.org and PerfectMatch.com and has appeared regularly on KIRO-TV in Seattle. Schwartz currently serves as a consultant and advice counselor for AARP (formerly the American Association of Retired Persons).

For all they learn growing up and from the media about sexuality and sexual scripts, people still have many questions.

The following is a sampling of Schwartz's journalistic advice:

Orgasms are greatly affected by our thoughts and emotions. If you finally get an evening alone with your partner after a period of abstinence . . . [i]t doesn't take much technique to get you over the top.

At other times, as you know, technique matters. A woman's arousal is heightened when her partner stimulates erogenous zones in addition to her breasts and genitals. . . . Direct clitoral stimulation, instead of just vaginal intercourse, also results in more vaginal contractions, which is why some women claim their vibrator gives them the most intense orgasms. *(Glamour)*

Children are so absorbing that it's easy to have them become the focus of your marriage, but you risk falling into the role of parents rather than lovers. Reinvesting in your relationship should be a priority. Taking care of your emotional intimacy isn't a luxury but a necessity. (*American Baby*)

Schwartz has recently discussed some of her own sexual adventures in *Prime: Adventures and Advice in Sex, Love, and the Sensual Years* (2007), a book aimed at a popular audience. She is interested not only in revealing much about herself, but also in continuing to offer advice on sexuality and on relationships, sexual and otherwise.

Think About It

Are younger generations more knowledgeable about sex and sexuality than their elders, or less? If your peers have questions about sex, whom do they ask? Could they benefit from reading Schwartz's work?

- *Sexualized objects.* Sexualized objects include sex toys (e.g., inflated blow-up dolls), drugs that are thought to enhance sexual sensations ("poppers" or nitrate inhalers), vibrators, and lingerie (Coulmont and Hubbard 2010).

- *Sexualized technologies.* People around the world increasingly consume contraceptives as well as drugs like Viagra and Cialis (Katsulis 2010). Other sexualized technologies range from surgeries to make oneself more sexually attractive (breast-enhancement surgery, revirgination/vaginal rejuvenation, penile enlargement) to changing one's sex (sex-reassignment surgery). Digital technologies, such as smartphones and the Internet, have been similarly sexualized.

- *Sexualized relationships.* Help for improving a sexualized relationship can be purchased from highly paid sex therapists, from self-help books of all sorts, and increasingly from websites across the Internet.

SEXUAL DEVIANCE

As is the case with deviance in general, what is considered sexual deviance varies greatly from place to place, from time to time, and among different individuals and groups. There is no universal definition of sexual deviance. (For an example of place-based definitions of sexual deviance, see the next "Globalization" box.) An example of sexual historical fluidity in definitions of sexual deviance is marital rape. There was no notion of marital rape for most of human history. Wives did not have the right to deny the advances, even the forcible advances, of their husbands. However, largely as a result of the women's movement, marital rape has come to be seen in many parts of the world as a deviant act and, in some cases, even illegal. Marital rape is defined by most state laws as "any unwanted intercourse or penetration (vaginal, anal, or oral) obtained

Public Sociology: Peter Schwartz   Legal Definitions of Rape

Violence against Women in India

India and much of the world were galvanized by the horrific gang rape and death of a 23-year-old Indian female medical student in New Delhi in December 2012.

The woman and a male friend had been to the movies and were seeking a ride when a bus pulled over and they were waved on board. The couple had been tricked into believing that it was a public bus. Six men, including the driver and another posing as a conductor, were out for a joy ride. The woman was harassed and her companion was beaten with a metal rod. The woman was then repeatedly raped, and she was penetrated by the metal rod as the bus circled the city. Eventually, the naked couple was dumped by the side of a highway on the outskirts of the city (Mandhana and Trivedi 2012). The woman survived for almost two weeks but then died as a result of internal injuries.

The case brought attention to a broader pattern of murder and other forms of violence against women in India including killings over dowry disputes, sexual violence, family conflicts, and discriminatory treatment of both infant girls and elderly women (Harris 2013). Sexual harassment is common and rape is a daily occurrence in New Delhi and elsewhere in India.

This rape of the medical student was followed, a month later, by what was apparently a well-planned attack in the north

The death of a rape victim in India drew the world's attention to a widespread pattern of sexual harassment and violence against women there. Is this an Indian problem?

Indian state of Punjab. A woman was assaulted after accepting a motorcycle ride from the driver of a bus on which she had been riding. He took her to a nearby village where she was raped repeatedly by six men: the driver himself, the conductor, and four other men (Timmons and Kumar 2013).

Recent rapes have attracted global attention and spurred protests and demonstrations in India (Timmons and Gottipati 2012). It remains to be seen whether anything changes, and whether

Indian women will become less subject to rape and other forms of sexual violence and harassment.

Think About It

What cultural forces in India contribute to an atmosphere in which rape is so commonplace? What economic forces might also be contributing to this social problem in India? What needs to change in order for rape and other sexual violence to grow less common there?

---

by force, threat of force, or when the wife is unable to consent" (RAINN 2009a). It occurs when a spouse is forced to take part in sexual acts without her (or his) consent. In the United States, as of 1993, marital rape is considered a crime in all states.

Marital rape is but one example of what has been described as "defining deviancy up" (Karmen 1994). This occurs over time as behaviors that were once overlooked or tolerated come to be increasingly discouraged, deterred, forbidden, and outlawed (Scott

and Schwartz 2008). Another good example is *sexual harassment*, which involves unwanted sexual attention, such as sexually oriented remarks and jokes, advances, and requests that take place in the workplace or in other settings (Zippel 2007). This, too, was considered quite normal not too long ago, but the women's movement has also helped to redefine sexual harassment as a form of sexual deviance.

The whole idea of sexual deviance, as well as many specific behaviors that have in the past been considered

Sexting

Sexuality has become increasingly mobile, thanks to sexting, or the ability to e-mail or text explicitly sexual material primarily via smartphones. Sexting may be fun, but it is not harmless. In 2011, Anthony Weiner, for example, was forced to resign as a U.S. congressman when it was disclosed that he had been tweeting close-up photos of his erect penis concealed by his under-shorts to a young woman. There have also been a number of scandals involving high school students sexting and then living to regret it.

A survey of 1,200 teenage respondents found that more than a quarter of them admitted to some form of sexting (Grier 2010). Some have discovered the disadvantages of sexting. Some girls perceive that, paradoxically, "the Internet is making boys more aggressive sexually—more accepting of graphic images or violence toward women, brasher, more demanding—but it is also making them less so, or at least less interested in the standard-issue, flesh-and-bone girls they encounter in real life who may not exactly have *Penthouse* proportions or porn-star inclinations" (Morris 2011).

Middle school girls have confessed that they send suggestive photos of themselves to boys to "mess with other girls' boyfriends." Furthermore, nearly one out of five teens who received sext messages said they passed them on to someone else; 50 percent of them admitted they forwarded the images to multiple recipients (Grier 2010). The forwarding of sext messages may expose those in the photos to ridicule, scorn, and even retaliation by aggrieved boyfriends and girlfriends.

Think About It

What do you think is the lure of sexting? What are the risks? Do you think it is a deviant activity? Why or why not? What, if anything, might dissuade young people from participating in this activity?

---

deviant, is being contested with the increasing acceptance of a very wide range of sexual activities. However, there are still people, groups, and societies that regard at least some forms of sexual behavior as deviant. Many people with conservative social values consider homosexuality to be deviant. However, public opinion is changing rapidly, and the percentage of people holding such views is declining. In contrast, strong negative reactions to instances of pedophilia indicate that it is definitely considered a deviant practice by most Americans.

Four criteria have been used to define a given form of sexual behavior as deviant (Tewksbury 2007):

- *Degree of consent of those involved.* Sexual relations are more likely to be considered deviant when one of the parties does not agree to, or even resists, the acts involved. Rape is the most obvious form of nonconsensual sexual relations (Brownmiller 1975; L. Kelly 2007).

- *Nature of the person involved in the sex act.* Sex with children is considered deviant because they are not capable of consensual sex in the eyes of the law and public opinion. Likewise, having sex with an individual who is too drunk to offer informed consent constitutes rape, as the jury concluded in a recent Steubenville, Ohio, case involving a teenaged female and two high school football players.

- *Nature of the action involved or the body part employed.* The use of body parts in the sexual act not usually thought of as sexual—feet, the nose, the ear—would also be considered deviant, at least by most.

- *Place in which the sexual act takes place.* Even "normal" sex acts would be considered deviant if they occurred in, for example, a church, synagogue, or mosque.

GENDER

As explained at the beginning of this chapter, sex is largely biologically based (although it is also powerfully affected by social and cultural factors), whereas gender is a social distinction and social definition. However, gender can be enacted in many different ways, and in recent years that range of behaviors has increased greatly. Thus gender is a social construction that is subject to change, sometimes quite dramatically, over time (Dongen, 2012).

Although we do learn sexualities, sex is usually more of a given. In contrast, gender is a largely learned behavior. To a great degree, we *learn* to be men and women. For

Sexting

World Gender Categories

Crowd Licentiousness in China

Ma Yaohai is a Chinese professor of computer science whose online name was "Roaring Virile Fire." Ma was sentenced to three-and-a-half years in prison in 2010 for what was called "crowd licentiousness" (Wong 2010). The "crime" involved the organization of orgies where an informal club of swingers engaged in group sex and partner swapping. The law under which the professor was prosecuted was left over from an old Chinese law against "hooliganism," or sex outside of marriage, which was abandoned in 1997. Before the old law was dropped, the leader of a swingers club was executed for his crimes under the "crowd licentiousness" law.

The punishment of Ma Yaohai is out of step with contemporary China where sexual content is readily available online, brothels are proliferating, and premarital sexual relations are common among young people. The website Happy Village has a chat room devoted to swinging. Love and sex are discussed more openly on radio and television (Scott and Schwartz 2008).

At his trial Ma exclaimed, "How can I disturb social order? What happens in my house is a private matter" (Wong 2010: A8). Nevertheless, he was sentenced to prison.

This case is not only out of step with current realities in China, but it is even more distant from the realities of sexual life in

Ma Yaohai (center) is shown entering the courtroom for his trial in Nanjing. Do you consider orgies and group sex to be deviant sexual behaviors?

many parts of the world. Like them, China has clearly grown increasingly "sexy," but its laws have certainly not kept pace. This is a case of "cultural lag" (Ogburn 1922). Chinese law is also out of step with the behavior of the Chinese people and with the norms and values in Chinese culture as they relate to sexual behavior. Since many Chinese are going to resist efforts to make their lives less "sexy," it seems likely that

the law will change or, at least, never be enforced again.

Think About It

What social function(s) do laws against certain types of sexual behavior serve? Do such laws benefit anyone? Who? Do you agree that China's law against "crowd licentiousness" is unlikely to be enforced again? Why or why not?

---

example, we learn the appropriate physical appearance, behavior, and personality for a man or a woman. Learning, understanding, and viewing one another as male and female are social processes. Our parents believe certain ideas about gender-appropriate behavior, and attempt to pass those ideas on to us. Later we learn gender through socialization in schools. Expected behavior is further reinforced within same-sex social circles, during a period when boys tend to play only with boys and girls tend to play only with girls (Kimmel 2011). Of course, the media—print, television, and Internet—also have a great effect on our sense of gender-appropriate behavior.

FEMININITY AND MASCULINITY

Useful in this context is the distinction between "femininity" and "masculinity." These are gender identities—what it means to be a "woman" or a "man"—acquired during the socialization process (Laurie et al. 1999; Lind 2007). There is a tendency to develop stereotypes about what it means to be a woman (mother, nurturant, emotional) and a man (father, tough, unemotional). In reality, however, these stereotypes are not natural or biological but rather socially constructed. As Simone de Beauvoir (1973: 301) famously put it, "One is not born, but rather becomes, a woman." The same is true, of course, for a man. Furthermore, these categories are fluid, have wide ranges, and differ greatly both historically and geographically.

ASK YOURSELF

What did Simone de Beauvoir mean by saying, "One is not born, but rather becomes, a woman"? Do you agree with her view? Why or why not? Do you think she would say the same thing today?

CHECKPOINT 9.1 — SEX AND SEXUALITY

Sex: Mainly a biological distinction between males and females based on fundamental differences in their reproductive organs and functions.	**Gender:** Social distinctions based on the physical, behavioral, and personality characteristics considered appropriate for one's sex.
Intersexed individuals: People with some combination of male and female genitalia.	**Transsexuals:** People with the genitalia of one sex who believe they are a member of the opposite sex and are trapped in the wrong body.
Heterosexuality: Sexual desire for people of the opposite sex.	**Homosexuality:** Sexual desire for people of the same sex.
Bisexuality: Sexual desire for both sexes.	**Asexuality:** Lack of sexual desire.

Yet the distinction between masculine and feminine persists. An effort to explain its persistence is found in the work of Raewyn (née Robert W.) Connell (1987, 1997, 2009). Connell coined the terms *hegemonic masculinity* and *emphasized femininity* and analyzed the roles these ideas have played in global gender inequality. **Hegemonic masculinity**, linked to patriarchy, is a set of socially constructed ideas about masculinity that focuses on the interests and desires of men. Characteristics associated with hegemonic masculinity include being white, tall, athletic, Protestant, young, married, northern, heterosexual, a father, college educated, and fully employed, as well as having a good complexion and weight and being successful in sports. Emphasized femininity is a set of socially constructed ideas that accommodates the interests of men and patriarchy and involves the compliance of females. **Emphasized femininity** focuses on social ability rather than intellect, on ego stroking, and on acceptance of the roles of mother and wife (Kimmel 2011).

Hegemonic masculinity acts in concert with emphasized femininity to subordinate women. It also serves to subordinate men who do not live up to the stereotype of hegemonic masculinity, including men who are nonwhite, homosexual, or poor. In addition, just as many men are subordinated by hegemonic masculinity, many women do not live up to the ideals associated with emphasized femininity and are adversely affected by the stereotypes (Butler 1990). Of note in this context are **transgender** individuals, whose gender identity does not conform to the sex to which they were assigned at birth and who move across the gender line in behavior by, for example, cross-dressing. Thus transgender individuals also challenge mainstream ideas of masculinity and femininity.

Interestingly, while men benefit greatly from hegemonic masculinity, it has, at least until recently, been largely invisible to them. Not having to think about masculinity is one of the dividends of gender inequality for men. In contrast, women think a great deal about masculinity since they are so oppressed by it in many different ways.

It is important to remember that masculinity and femininity need to be detached, at least to some degree, from sex and the body. That is, men can act in feminine ways, perhaps by nurturing others, and women can behave in a masculine manner, perhaps by competing aggressively. At the beginning of this chapter, the continuum between the male and female sexes was discussed. Similarly, we should not think in simple, dualistic terms about gender; there is a continuum between masculinity and femininity, which results in part from the variety of socialization patterns that both women and men experience over the life course. Moreover, individuals can be high in both masculinity *and* femininity, or low in both. Therefore, we must think of gender performance as being fluid rather than static.

hegemonic masculinity A set of ideas about the characteristics of men that focuses on the interests and desires of men and is linked to patriarchy.

emphasized femininity A set of socially constructed ideas that accommodates to the interests of men and to patriarchy and involves the compliance of females.

transgender An umbrella term describing individuals whose gender identity does not conform to the sex to which they were assigned at birth and whose behavior challenges gender norms.

Transgender Issues

FIGURE 9.1 • Gender, Marital Status, and Household Income in the United States, 1970–2007

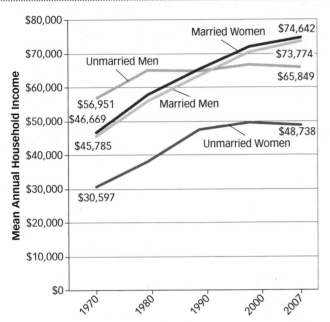

SOURCE: Gender, Marital Status, and Household Income, 1970–2007 is reprinted with permission from *Women, Men and the New Economics of Marriage* by Richard Fry and D'Vera Cohn. Copyright © 2010 Pew Research Center, Social & Demographic Trends Project.

NOTE: Includes only native-born 30- to 44-year-olds. Incomes adjusted for household size, scaled to reflect a three-person household, and then adjusted to 2007 dollars.

GENDER, WORK, AND FAMILY

The relationship among gender, work, and family is one of the most studied issues in the field of gender (Thorn 2007). The main concern is the ways in which the intersection of work and family varies by gender. For example, it has been shown that married or cohabiting males do better at work and are more productive, at least in part, because their wives are handling more of the responsibilities in the home. Men's wages also tend to increase when they marry or cohabit (Ahituv and Lerman 2007; Korenman and Neumark 1991). As you can see in Figure 9.1, married men have tended, at least since 1990, to earn somewhat more than men who are not married. However, unmarried women's household income is far below that of all men and of married women. Many of these inequities are based on traditional gender roles in the family.

The Decline of Separate Spheres

Since the mid twentieth century, the once clear-cut, gender-based differentiation between the public and private spheres has been breaking down. Now women are more likely not only to be in the work world (England 2010) but, increasingly, to be the principal—or even the only—wage

earner in the family. The family characterized by a division between male/breadwinner and female/homemaker has increasingly given way to more blended roles, and even to role reversals, especially in dual-earner families.

Dual-Earner Households

A key issue in the study of gender, work, and family is the difference in the way men and women use their time in the era of dual-earner families. Arlie Hochschild (2003) argues that in dual-earner families with children, wives who take jobs outside the home tend to be saddled with a second body of work—their traditional tasks of child care and housework—when they get home from their paid job. Such women can be said to be working a "second shift." Figure 9.2 presents 2010 data on gender differences in performing two specific household tasks: preparing and cleaning up after meals and cleaning the house. While on an average day 68 percent of women did food preparation or cleanup, only 41 percent of men performed these tasks. More extremely, 49 percent of women did housework on an average day while only 20 percent of men did such work.

ASK YOURSELF

Did your mother or grandmother work a "second shift"? How many women do you know who are doing so now? Do you know any men who could be said to be working a "second shift" to the same degree?

This male tendency to handle far less domestic work than women (Lachance-Grzela and Bouchard 2010; Miller and Sassler 2010) has been attributed to a "stalled revolution" (England 2010). There has certainly been a revolution in the labor force in the past half-century or so, with women participating at much higher rates. The revolution has stalled because a high percentage of men still do not share traditionally female work in the home.

However, recent research indicates that the differences between women and men are narrowing (Bianchi, Robinson, and Milkie 2006). While the second shift continues to exist for women, they are now spending more time at work and less at home. Thus they have less time for, and are less involved in, the second shift. The reverse is the case for men, who are spending less time at work and more time at home and participating more in the tasks associated with the second shift. It may be that the stalled revolution has regained its momentum. It is having a wider effect on society as a whole, on both men and women in the labor force and in the family. However, it would be premature to argue that the revolution is now complete, that the second shift has ended for women, or that there is true equality in men's and women's work, both in the labor force and in the home.

According to a 2010 United Nations (UN) report, women worldwide shoulder vastly more household responsibilities than men. As you can see in Figure 9.3, however, American women have the lightest burden among women in all regions. Perhaps the major explanation for this is the greater affluence of American women and their ability to afford more and more sophisticated household appliances, to consume more meals in restaurants, and to hire people to help with household tasks more often.

GENDER AND EDUCATION

Gender inequality in access to, and experience in, educational systems is an important source of gender inequality throughout American society and across the globe. Historically, families invested relatively little in the education of females because they were expected to stay at home as wives and mothers. Thus, there was a gender gap in education in many countries, including the United States. Increasing awareness of this gap has led to significant efforts to overcome the problem and subsequently to great gains for women in education (Dorius and Firebaugh 2010).

This is not to say that all the traditional male advantages in education have disappeared. While gender differences in courses taken in American high schools are declining, females are still less likely to take advanced computer classes and more likely to take courses in word processing and data entry. Such differences persist in college where women are more likely to be in fields such as education, English, and nursing and less likely to be in areas such as science, technology, and engineering that are more likely to lead to higher pay. This kind of sex typing in education is a global phenomenon.

Educational Achievement and Attainment

When boys and girls begin school, there are few substantial differences in their levels of achievement (Aud and Hannes 2011). However, from 4th through 12th grade, female students consistently score higher than male students on both reading and writing assessments. Recent data indicate that by the end of high school males hold a very small

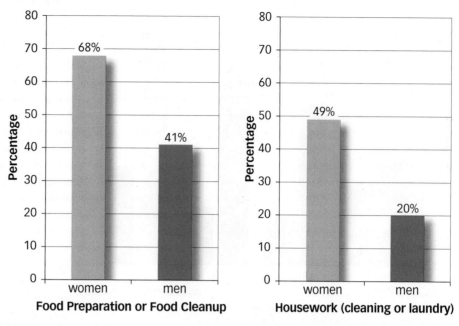

FIGURE 9.2 • Division of Household Labor in the United States by Gender, 2010

SOURCE: Daily Household Labor in the United States by Gender from *American Time Use Survey News Release*, June 22, 2011. U.S. Department of Labor, Bureau of Labor Statistics.

advantage over females in math, and a larger advantage in science. International comparisons indicate that the male–female gap in math in the United States is relatively small compared to that in other industrialized nations (Aud and Hannes 2011).

Today gender differences in educational attainment generally favor females. Females are significantly more likely than males to graduate from high school and to attend either a two- or four-year college (Carbonaro and Covay 2010). In 1960, women represented less than 40 percent of college undergraduates in the United States. Today, roughly 57 percent of students at both two- and four-year colleges are female (Goldin, Katz, and Kuziemko 2006). Women are more likely than men to receive a bachelor's or master's degree (Alon and Gelbgiser 2011; Buchmann and DiPrete 2006). Changing societal attitudes about gender roles and declining sexism have had dramatic effects on women's educational attainment. We can see this most clearly in the dramatic increases in law and medical degrees earned by women. However, men continue to be more likely to be trained in the most prestigious colleges and universities and to obtain doctoral degrees. A significant gender gap in pay remains even with female gains in education (Charles and Bradley 2009; Jacobs 1996).

Dual-Career Families   Men and Masculinity

FIGURE 9.3 • Average Hours per Day Spent on Housework by World Region and Gender, 2010

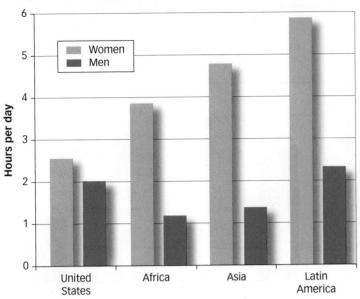

SOURCE: Average Hours per Day Spent on Housework, by World Region and Gender, 2010. United Nations Statistics Division; Bureau of Labor Statistics.

One of the explanations for overall female success in schooling outcomes is the fact that females are more engaged in school and more likely to comply with school rules such as doing homework and responding to teacher requests. They are less likely to get in trouble than males (Buchmann and DiPrete 2006). These "noncognitive" skills are strong predictors of academic success. They partly explain why females outperform male students on most academic indicators. Another explanation of female success in school is that many occupations tend to be segregated by gender. Most male-segregated occupations, such as truck drivers, auto mechanics, and firefighters, do not require postsecondary schooling, while most female-segregated occupations, for example preschool teachers, registered nurses, and dental hygienists, require schooling beyond high school. This occupational segregation is increasingly responsible for female advantages in educational attainment (Jacobs 1996).

Gender, Education, and Race

Overall, both males and females of color, especially those from the working class, have greater difficulties in school than do white males and females (Morris 2005, 2008). For example, white, middle-class boys do better in school than boys from the working class and of color (Willis 1977). African American working-class girls are sometimes seen as troublemakers because they do not live up to white, middle-class standards of femininity and are seen as assertive and outspoken (Bettie 2003; Morris 2007).

Because of media images that have depicted black male youth as pathological and criminal, black youth are often viewed as insufficiently childlike by teachers and school administrators (Ferguson 2001). In other words, black male and female children are "adultified." Consequently, their mistakes in school are often considered intentional, and sometimes sinister, rather than merely youthfully inept. Moreover, African American girls are thought to be more sexually advanced than their white peers, a characteristic that is seen as needing to be controlled. At the same time, black boys are not allowed to be "naturally naughty." Physical expressions of masculinity that would be considered typical among their white peers are viewed as insubordinate. As a result, in school black boys learn that to act obedient is to survive and that disobedience will lead to disciplinary action.

Schools have a wide range of expectations for students from different demographic groups, "allocating girls to home economics and sewing courses, lower-class youngsters to slower tracks, and black children to compensatory programs" (Hare 2001: 97). These practices have long-term effects on educational and occupational attainment, including being relegated to low-skill and low-paying jobs.

WOMEN AND CONSUMER CULTURE

In consumption, like much else in the social world, there are gender differences and inequalities. Since the Industrial Revolution, production has been centered outside the household and has primarily been the function of men. Women, relegated to the home, have been assigned the role of being consumers (Williams and Sauceda 2007). This is both different and unequal since historically production has been far more highly valued than consumption.

Consumption, Work, and Family

Women were not only defined as the prime consumers, but their consumer practices were also closely tied to their domestic practices and their roles in the home. Women consumed goods and services to care for, and on behalf of, their families (DeVault 1991). More extremely, much of women's shopping was related to love, especially their love of family members (Miller 1998). In one way or another, women generally made purchases for their families and to fulfill their responsibilities in the home and to those who lived there.

However, as more women have entered the work world in recent years, their consumption patterns have changed. For one thing, they are now more likely to consume an array of subcontracted services such as cleaning and child care. Much of this work is done by other women. Women are subcontracting work to other women (Bowman and Cole 2009). For another, they are more likely to consume for themselves rather than for others. For example, greater involvement in the work world requires the consumption of a wider variety of clothing.

Advertising and Gender

Much of advertising and marketing is targeted at either women or men. Advertising targeted at women in the first half of the twentieth century focused on household products, those that helped them with their responsibilities to home and family. As more women entered the labor force, at least some advertising came to focus on the needs of working women for such things as labor-saving devices in the home.

Feminist critiques of advertising beginning in the 1970s attacked the emphasis in advertisements on weight, especially slimness, and beauty. The main argument was— and is—that these advertisements set up ideals that few women could approximate, thereby adversely affecting their self-esteem (Bordo 1993).

As mentioned previously, the media have a propensity to influence both working and at-home mothers to focus on maintaining domestic happiness (Douglas and Michaels 2006). More recently, advertising has focused more on allowing women to purchase what they need in order to be unique individuals (Zukin 2004). Of course, there is a huge contradiction involved in offering generally available, brand-name products as a way of achieving uniqueness (Maguire and Stanway 2008).

Interrelated aspects of consumer culture, and the social world more generally, come together to control women's and men's consumption behavior. For example, gender ideals in advertising are reinforced by the spatial segregation of women's and men's television networks (Lifetime mainly for women, Spike mainly for men); in television shows (*The Bachelor/Bachelorette* vs. *Monday Night Football*); in movies ("chick flicks" vs. action movies); in lifestyle magazines (*Vogue* and *O, The Oprah Magazine* vs. *GQ*); and in departments in department stores and shops in the malls. However, as with consumption in general, adult women and men are not simply passive in the face of these pressures. They are able to resist, or even actively reconstruct, the messages being communicated to them (Zlatunich 2009).

Gender differences in educational achievement seem to arise in primary school and persist through high school and even beyond. Why do women still experience a pay gap when their academic achievements are usually higher than men's?

ASK YOURSELF

Have you ever resisted or reconstructed advertising messages directed at you as a man or a woman? What was the product or service advertised? Why did you resist the message, and how?

Women and Girls as Consumers

"For a large number of girls in modern America, participating in the consumer realm is the defining feature of life as a girl" (Best 2007: 724). In earlier periods, girls' involvement in consumer culture had more to do with the roles they were playing, and were likely to play, as adults in the family. As girls have gained more freedom from those expectations, and are spending more of their own money, they have been courted more aggressively and differently by advertisers and marketers (Deutsch and Theodorou 2010). This is particularly clear in the efforts made by the cosmetics and clothing industries to sell to young women by, among other things, advertising in magazines (*Seventeen, Teen Vogue*) aimed at them as well as through pop-up advertisements on the Internet. Among the unfortunate consequences of this for young girls is increased rates of eating disorders and body dysmorphia— an obsession with perceived flaws in one's body—as well as the hypersexualization of their lives (Hesse-Biber 1996; Kimmel 2011).

Gender Socialization

Women as Consumers in Popular Culture

Gender and the Internet

Sociologists interested in the early, male-dominated Internet wondered whether it allowed people to be free of ascribed statuses and identities such as gender and race (Hornsby 2013: 61–64). For example, users of MUDs ("multiuser dungeons") freely selected their name, their gender, and even their species. In *Life on the Screen*, Sherry Turkle (1995: 10) argued that identity in cyberspace may be "decentered, multiple and fragmented" and that cyberspace plays a prominent role in "eroding boundaries." Many theorists thought "gender" would be a category that would erode in cyberspace (Stone 1991).

In time, the Internet started to include equal numbers of women, and users not necessarily interested in technology but who simply wanted to use technology to socialize, to shop, and to interact. As a result, our understanding of how gender online interacts with gender offline changed. The rise of sites such as Facebook, which require people to use their real names and make it easy to post many pictures of themselves, has made gender even more prominent.

Most current research finds that women and men tend to replicate certain offline gender patterns online. Women who tend to do most of the work of kinship and socializing tend to do so online as well, and women are prominent users of social networking sites. Women interacted more

Why doesn't gender disappear in the online environment?

with their close friends and family whereas men were more likely to be searching for other people. This reflects gender patterns we see in the offline world.

Women and men portray themselves differently online, and women are rewarded for posting sexualized photographs of themselves. Female students are more likely than males to have private profiles (Lewis et al. 2011). It looks like cyberspace does not completely free us from gender, after all, and that life on the screen looks somewhat like life off the screen.

Think About It

Are you surprised that early predictions about the likely users of the Internet were proven wrong? What social factors drew women online in such unexpected numbers? Why do you think men's and women's different patterns of communication and social interaction in the real world have simply migrated to the Internet essentially unchanged? Could things have been different?

SOURCE: Printed with the permission of Zeynep Tufekci.

Several historical events mark the development of greater interest in girls, and children more generally, as consumers (Cook 2007). One was the emergence of the department store in the middle and late 1800s and the celebration of Christmas, and its associated gifts, by department stores. Children's consumer culture gained great impetus when department stores began to have separate departments for toys and, more importantly, separate departments for boys' and girls' clothing. At

about the same time, the media and entertainment began to focus more attention on children, again often divided along gender lines. Movies, television programs, and more recently television networks—Nickelodeon, for example—are increasingly dedicated to children. Now, of course, children and teenagers are being targeted on their computers, their iPhones, and myriad other new and yet-to-be created technologies (Kahlenberg and Hein 2010; Sheldon 2004).

GENDER AND SPORTS

Historically, boys and men have been far more likely than girls and women to be encouraged to participate in sports. As a result, males participate more in organized competitive sports, and they dominate coaching and administrative positions in the sports world. Sports teach, perpetuate, and celebrate hegemonic masculinity, including competitiveness, physical aggression, and dominance over one's opponent. Females have been defined as inferior in the world of sports (Mansfield 2007), because they did not generally live up to masculine ideals in terms of strength, speed, jumping ability, toughness, and so on. Thus, in general, females have not participated as much, or as ardently, in sports as males and have not risen as high as males in most administrative hierarchies in the sports world.

Ronda Rousey (left) and Liz Carmouche faced off in the first-ever women's bout at UFC 157. Do you think of some sports as typically masculine and others as typically feminine?

However, this began to change in the 1970s as a result, in large part, of protests by feminists. In addition, greater knowledge of the importance of sports and fitness to health led to the promotion of physical activity for women. As a result, female opportunities and participation rates in sports have increased. Legal changes, most notably Title IX of the Education Amendments of the Civil Rights Act (1972), served to reduce discrimination against females in sports and to prevent or remove barriers to their participation in sports (Brown and Connolly 2010).

The masculine ideal in sports is powerful throughout the social world. In detention facilities, for example, where incarcerated males need to project hegemonic masculinity to avoid being persecuted, physical prowess is viewed as largely the only way for men to demonstrate their masculinity. Sports and fitness activities in prison allow male prisoners to "do masculinity" (Sabo 2005: 110). Sports images play a role in efforts by the all-volunteer military to project particular images of masculinity in recruiting advertisements (Brown 2012).

Sports often serve to shape gender identity for men. However, the need to live up to the masculine ideal can limit men and prevent them from being all they can be in sports and in much else. Those males who do not excel, or who do not participate, in sports are likely to have their masculinity, even their heterosexuality, questioned. This overemphasis on hegemonic masculinity is rooted, sometimes to males' own detriment, in how males are socialized to participate in sports by their fathers (White, Young, and McTeer 1995). Participation in sports engenders an ideology that physical prowess is an exhibition of masculinity, and that pain and injuries should be ignored, hidden, normalized, or disrespected. These coping mechanisms for dealing with pain are internalized by men to the detriment of their overall health.

And, for those men who participate in athletic programs that are not considered sports, such as ballet, there are larger pressures to "do masculinity" when interacting with other males. For example, in a study of the ballet world, males reported that they constantly dealt with homophobic stereotypes (McEwen and Young 2011). These dancers see their participation in dance as "challenges [to] dominant notions of appropriate ways of doing gender and being a man" (McEwen and Young 2011: 15). They cope by redefining dance as a masculine athletic endeavor that requires even more physical prowess than sports. Both men and women are forced to confront hegemonic masculine ideals when involved in athletics or the arts.

GENDER, HEALTH, AND MORTALITY

Women tend to have significantly longer life spans than men, especially in developed countries. There is great

Women's Sports

TABLE 9.1 • U.S. Life Expectancy by Gender, 1900–2010

Year	Both Sexes	Male	Female
2010	78.7	76.2	81.1
2006	77.7	75.1	80.2
2000	76.8	74.1	79.3
1990	75.4	71.8	78.8
1980	73.7	70.0	77.4
1970	70.8	67.1	74.7
1960	69.7	66.6	73.1
1950	68.2	65.6	71.1
1940	62.9	60.8	65.2
1930	59.7	58.1	61.6
1920	54.1	53.6	54.6
1910	50.0	48.4	51.8
1900	47.3	46.3	48.3

SOURCE: U.S. Life Expectancy by Gender, 1900–2020 from Arias, E. United States life tables, 2006. *National Vital Statistics Reports*: Vol. 58, No. 21, Hyattsville, MD: National Center for Health Statistics. 2010: U.S. Census Bureau, *Statistical Abstract of the United States: 2012.*

variation between the genders in life expectancy around the world; in 2000 the range was from 81.1 years in Japan—where women lived until age 84.7 while men lived until 77.5—to 37.5 years in Malawi—where women lived until age 37.8 and men until 37.1. In the United States, women live until about 81.1 years of age and men until 76.2 (Bianchi and Wight 2012).

Table 9.1 shows that the life span for both males and females increased in the United States between 1900 and 2010. However, it has increased more for females than for males. While in 1900 women lived, on average, two years longer than men, in 2010 the gap had widened to almost five years. The major factor in the increase of the life span of women is the great reduction in the number of deaths in childbirth (Larsen 2007; World Health Organization 2003).

However, women suffer from more illness and other health-related problems than men. The greatest difference between the genders is in depression; females are almost twice as likely as men to suffer from this disease. Men are more likely to suffer from HIV/AIDS (Centers for Disease Control and Prevention 2012) and coronary heart disease (American Heart Association 2010), while women have slightly higher rates of cerebrovascular disease such as stroke (American Heart Association 2010).

Over the course of illness, women are more likely to be confined to bed, to take sick leave, and to visit doctors and hospitals, and they report more symptoms than men. There is some doubt that women are actually more likely to be ill than men, but it is clear that women are more likely to admit that they are sick and to report that fact to others.

Researchers do not fully understand gender differences in life span and ill health, but the major factors involved are biological differences, behavioral differences, and psychosocial factors related to symptoms and behavior when ill, including seeking health care. Socialization patterns appear to push women into more behaviors that maintain health, such as monitoring of diseases and having physicals and checkups.

GENDER, CRIME, AND DEVIANCE

Across cultures, gender is the strongest predictor of crime. Males are most likely to commit crimes (Messerschmidt 2007). As an example of the discrepancy, Table 9.2 depicts the gender differences in arrests for property crimes in the United States. It clearly shows that more males than females committed property crimes in both 2000 and 2011. However, the table also shows that property crime committed by American females actually increased over that period while property crime by males decreased slightly. At the same time, men continue to commit violent crimes at a much higher rate than women.

Various ideas have been put forth to explain why males are overrepresented in crime and deviance:

- *Family socialization:* Females are more controlled by their mothers during childhood than are males and are therefore less likely to engage in criminal behavior when they are older (Hagan 1989).

- *Strain:* Males and females face different expectations, and the inability to meet those expectations leads to strain. For example, males are under greater pressure than females to succeed materially, and the strain that is created when they fail to achieve material success can lead to higher rates of property crime (Agnew 2001).

- *Response to adversity:* Men are more likely to blame others for their failures while women are more likely to blame themselves. As a result, males are likely to see their masculinity as being affirmed by being angry and striking out at others through property crimes and violent crimes.

SEXUALITY, GENDER, AND GLOBALIZATION

Globalization has affected sexuality, sexual behavior, and gender-related expectations and behaviors, as it has affected every other aspect of social life.

SOCIAL CHANGE AND THE GLOBALIZATION OF SEXUALITY

Globalization is one of a number of forces that are changing sexuality in the twenty-first century (Plummer 2012). The globalization of sexuality is linked to a variety of social changes that are altering not only sexuality, but much of what transpires in the social world:

CHECKPOINT 9.2	GENDER
Hegemonic masculinity	A set of socially constructed ideas about masculinity, linked to patriarchy, that focuses on the interests and desires of men.
Emphasized femininity	A set of socially constructed ideas that focus on social ability rather than intellect and that emphasize ego stroking and acceptance of the roles of wife and mother.
Separate spheres	The idea that men are the breadwinners in the public world of work, while women are relegated to a submissive role in the private sphere of the home.
The second shift	The set of traditional child care tasks and housework women working outside the home face when they return from their paid job.

- *Globalization of media:* Sexuality is a growing presence in the global media. The Internet, and the social networks that it has engendered, is most important. However, photos, movies, music, advertising, and television have also gone global. These media have been sexualized; they can even be said to have undergone a process of "pornographication" (McNair 2002).

- *Increasing urbanization:* Urbanization has contributed both to increased freedom of sexual expression and to the globalization of sexuality (Bell 2007). Cities are at the center of freedoms of all sorts (Simmel [1903] 1971), including sexual freedoms. Residents of global cities learn a great deal from one another about the latest developments in sexuality. Further, sex trafficking and sex tourism take place primarily in the world's cities. The world's major cities, including London, Hong Kong, and Shanghai, are the nodes in global "sex-scapes" (Kong 2010).

- *Globalization of social movements:* Global social movements dealing with issues relating to sexualities

have become increasingly important. Among them are the women's and gay movements (see Chapter 15), as well as more specific movements focused on such issues as repressive sex laws. The personnel and the ideas associated with these movements flow easily around the globe.

- *Increased mobility:* It is relatively easy now for people to travel to locales far from home. Sexual intercourse has become a global phenomenon, with large numbers of people in various parts of the world increasingly having sex with one another (Altman 2001; Frank 2012a).

Sexuality is flowing around the world in a multitude of other ways such as via sex trafficking, sex tourism, and the sexual diaspora as members of various sexual subcultures move easily around the world and from one society to another. In addition, all sorts of sexual goods and services are being shipped and sold globally, especially via the Internet.

Sex has also become a global phenomenon politically. There are now a number of laws that operate globally, such as laws against the sexual exploitation of children.

TABLE 9.2 • Arrests for Property Crimes by Gender, 2000 and 2011

Year	Total Arrests	Number of Men Arrested	Number of Women Arrested	Male Percentage	Female Percentage
2000	978,552	682,562	295,990	69.75%	30.25%
2011	1,082,441	674,716	407,725	62.33%	37.675%

SOURCE: Arrests for Property Crimes by Gender, 2000–2011 from "Crime in the United States," *Uniform Crime Reports*, U.S. Department of Justice, Federal Bureau of Investigation, September 2012.

Global organizations like UNICEF monitor these laws and seek to protect the vulnerable from sexual predators. Laws around the world dealing with various sexual crimes such as rape have grown increasingly similar (DiMaggio and Powell 1983).

At a cultural level, norms and values about sex have been changing, and those changes have tended to flow around the world. As a result, such norms and values have grown increasingly similar in many parts of the world. For example, there has been a general movement away from trying to control sexuality as a way to maintain the collective order and procreation. At the same time, there has been a movement toward viewing sexuality as a series of acts that are mainly about pleasure and self-expression. Nonmarital sex has also become increasingly normative in many (but certainly not all) parts of the world. Another example of global cultural change involves the global diffusion of such sexual identities as straight, gay, and bisexual. Almost anywhere you go in the world, you will find similar identities, norms, and values relating to sexuality.

Sexual Minorities in Global Context

A key issue for sexual minorities in the context of globalization is the barriers that inhibit their movement around the world or encourage their flow from one place to another (Altman 2001; Binnie 2004; Carrara 2007). Those barriers may be erected within their home country, as well as between countries. Barriers at home that might push them to migrate include legal prohibitions of consensual sex acts with same-sex partners, a lack of equal opportunity in the workplace, and bans on same-sex marriages. A variety of other problems, such as physical assaults, and even murders, of sexual minorities, can force them to seek a better life elsewhere in the world. They can also be pulled elsewhere in the world by better conditions, such as more opportunities to work and marry. Urban environments are attractive because large and visible groups of sexual minorities are often accepted by the majority group in cities.

Other aspects of globalization such as inexpensive air travel, the Internet, and sex tourism have made it easier for sexual minorities to communicate and to be with those who share their orientation and lifestyle. Globalization has also contributed to the rise of gay and lesbian global social movements and to the increasing acceptance in large parts of the world of same-sex sexual relationships (Frank and McEneaney 1999).

While globalization has aided sexual minorities, globalization has also assisted the spread of homophobia and other forms of prejudice and discrimination (Binnie 2004). Globalization has not been an unmitigated good as far as sexual minorities are concerned.

Global Sex Industry

The sexuality industry has become increasingly important to global capitalism. Bars, massage parlors, the pornography industry, and the tourist industry create, and help to meet, the demand for sex labor around the globe. It is almost impossible to get accurate numbers on those involved in the global sex industry, and at least some of the data are likely fabricated (Steinfatt 2011). The 2010 annual report of the U.S. State Department estimated that 12.3 million adults and children were in forced labor, bonded labor, and forced prostitution around the world. The UN Global Initiative to Fight Human Trafficking (2007) estimated that sex trafficking yields annual profits of $31.6 billion. Most of the countries of the Global South and Eastern Europe have experienced an unparalleled growth in prostitution. Many of these prostitutes find their way to the developed nations of the Global North.

The global sex tourism industry has grown to be a multibillion-dollar enterprise (Weitzer 2012; Wortmann 2007). The flow of people in the global sex industry not only moves from the South to the North, but also in the other direction. While there is some sex tourism that moves in the direction of the developed countries of the North (for example, to Amsterdam in the Netherlands), much of it involves the flow of customers from the North to the less developed countries of the South (Katsulis 2010). For example, Thailand receives millions of sex tourists every year from the United States, Western Europe, Australia, and Japan, bringing in billions of dollars (Bales 1999). Several factors have contributed to the rise of sex tourism. Poverty leads large numbers of women in sex-tourist destinations to participate in the industry. Low-cost travel has permitted more sex tourists to circle the globe in search of sexual relations (Brennan 2004). Finally, the Internet expedites sex tourism as well. Information about havens for those interested in sex tourism is readily available through websites, chat rooms, blogs, and guidebooks (Wortman 2007). Advice is accessible and readily obtainable on the best tourist sites to visit, the best sex workers at those sites, how to arrange a visit, and even how to negotiate the lowest price for various sexual services (Katsulis 2010). It is even possible through the Internet to organize a customized package tour of the best locations in the world for sex tourism.

GLOBAL MIGRATION AND GENDER

The global economy has contributed to an unprecedented increase in female migration: "Women are on the move as never before in history" (Ehrenreich and Hochschild 2002: 2). Some have referred to this trend as the "feminization of migration." Much of this global flow involves women from the South moving, legally and illegally, to the North to handle work that was historically performed by northern women (Runyon 2012). Nine of the largest countries from which women are emigrating are China, India, Indonesia,

ACTIVE SOCIOLOGY

What Do You Know about Trafficking?

The globalization of sexuality has contributed to a rise in sex trafficking and the forced prostitution of women around the world. Visit the website of one antitrafficking organization, Stop Trafficking, at www.stopenslavement.org, and complete the following exercises:

1. Click on the current issue of the organization's newsletter. Does this issue have a theme? What is it?

2. Review the list of sponsors on the front page. Why do you think they are mostly groups of women? What role do you think men could or should play in preventing trafficking?

3. How does the newsletter help promote the organization's goals of raising awareness, creating advocacy, and taking action? What resources does it provide?

4. Do you think an online newsletter is a good way to achieve these goals? Why or why not? What other media or avenues do you think might help reach more people or be more effective in creating change around trafficking, and why?

5. Skim two or three articles and list some suggested actions readers of the newsletter could take to promote awareness, advocacy, or action. Which of these would you be willing to take, and why?

Myanmar, Pakistan, the Philippines, Sri Lanka, Thailand, and Bangladesh. The migrants largely become nannies (Cheever 2002), maids (Ehrenreich 2002), and sex workers (Brennan 2002).

This migrant labor enriches the North and enhances its already elevated lifestyle. Many female labor immigrants clean and care for largely affluent children and their families while also trying to send money to their families in their home country (Faist, Fauser, and Reisenauer 2013; Hondagneu-Sotelo 2000). Domestic work is now considered the largest labor market for women worldwide. See Figure 9.4 for the 10 countries from which the most women emigrate to the United States (Immigration Policy Center 2010).

Undocumented and informal female migration, which is common for women migrating to the North for domestic work, exposes women to the worst forms of discrimination, exploitation, and abuse (Bach 2003; Jones 2008; UN 2006). They can be held as debt hostages by recruitment agencies until their transportation and placement fees are paid, locked up in the houses of their employers, treated inhumanely, and sometimes even murdered. An increasing number of migrant women are victims of sexual abuse, sex trafficking, and prostitution.

FEMINIZATION OF LABOR

There has been a notable increase in women's labor force participation rates worldwide (see Figure 9.5), particularly

FIGURE 9.4 • Female Emigration to the United States: Countries of Origin, 2008

- Mexico 27%
- All other countries 43%
- China 5%
- Philippines 5%
- India 4%
- Vietnam 3%
- Korea 3%
- El Salvador 3%
- Cuba 3%
- Dominican Republic 2%
- Canada 2%

SOURCE: Figure 1, Female Foreign-Born Population by Country or Origin, 2008 is reprinted with permission from *Immigrant Women in the United States: A Portrait of Demographic Diversity*. Immigration Policy Center, American Immigration Council.

The STEM Gender Gap

FIGURE 9.5 • Global Employment by Gender, 1962–2010

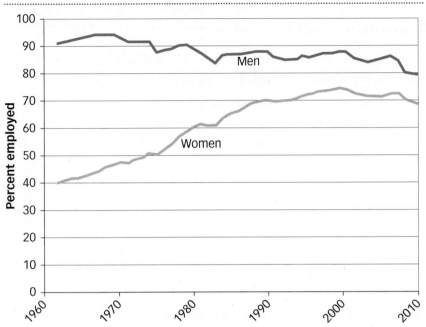

SOURCE: Based on "End of the Gender Revolution," Reeve Vanneman, Department of Sociology, University of Maryland. Authors' calculations from Current Population Survey (CPS) data provided by the Integrated Public Use Microdata (IPUMS) files.

in the Americas and Western Europe. Even though there are significant variations within and across regions, women's labor force participation has also risen substantially in sub-Saharan Africa, North Africa, Eastern Europe, Southeast Asia, and East Asia (Cagatay and Ozler 1995; Heintz 2006; Moghadam 1999; Kivisto and Faist 2010). While the progress in women's employment status is linked, at least in part, to gender equality movements, the key factor in this change is the better integration of an increasing number of areas into the world economy through trade and production.

The increasing participation of women in the labor force has been termed the **feminization of labor** (Standing 1989), or the rise of female labor participation in all sectors and the movement of women into jobs traditionally held by men. This global trend has occurred in both developing and developed countries.

In many developed countries, educated middle-class women have made inroads into professional and managerial employment. However, in the global paid-labor market, women are heavily employed in agriculture (Preibisch and Grez 2010), as well as in the labor-intensive manufacture of products such as garments, sportswear, and electronics. Women predominate in such office jobs as data entry, word processing, and telecommunications (Freeman 2001; Gaio 1995; Pearson 2000). They are likely to work as teachers and university professors, as nurses and doctors in public hospitals, and as workers and administrators in government offices (Moghadam

1999). Women have also made inroads in professional services such as law, banking, accounting, computing, and architecture.

Women and Informal Employment

At the same time as some women are finding success in the work world, others are being limited by the nature of their arrangements with employers. Informal employment, which has increased in many countries, includes temporary work without fixed employers, paid employment from home, domestic work for households (de Regt 2009), and industrial work for subcontractors. Informal sectors are characterized by low pay and a lack of secure contracts, worker benefits, and social protection. Workers in the informal economy do not have wage agreements, employment contracts, regular working hours, or health insurance or unemployment benefits. They often earn below legal minimum wage and may not be paid on time. Many formal jobs have been replaced by informal ones as lower labor and production costs have increasingly become the major organizing factor in global production.

While greater informal employment characterizes both the male and female labor force globally, women and men are concentrated in different types of informal work. Men are concentrated mainly in informal wage-based jobs and agricultural employment, while women are typically concentrated in nonagricultural employment, domestic work, and unpaid work in family enterprises. Compared to men's informal employment, women's employment is much more likely to have lower hourly wages and less stability. In order to reduce labor costs, most multinational corporations establish subcontracting networks with local manufacturers employing low-paid workers, mostly women, who can be terminated quickly and easily. In these production networks, women are likely to work in small workshops or from home. Many women accept the lower wages and less formal working arrangements of home-based work in order to be able to continue to carry out household responsibilities.

> **feminization of labor** The rise of female labor participation in all sectors and the movement of women into jobs traditionally held by men.

Feminization of Poverty and Female Proletarianization

The feminization of labor, especially in the developing economies, is often accompanied by **female proletarianization**, as an increasing number of women are channeled into low-status, poorly paid manual work. Female proletarianization is closely related to the **feminization of poverty** (Brady and Kall 2008). Globally, more women are being drawn into labor-intensive and low-paying industries such as textiles, apparel, leather products, food processing, and electronics (Villareal and Yu 2007). Jobs in these industries are characterized by the flexible use of labor, high turnover rates, part-time and temporary employment, and a lack of security and benefits. Women are preferred in these industries because of the persistence of a number of stereotypes that often have little basis in reality. Such stereotypes include the idea that they will typically work for lower wages, and they are easier for male employers and managers to supervise. They are considered not only to be more docile, but also to have greater patience and more dexterity than men in performing standardized and repetitive work. Female employment is also characterized by poorer and more dangerous working conditions and more compulsory overtime with no extra pay.

These women are hand-picking beans in a quality-control operation in Nicaragua. They belong to a progressive farming cooperative with several women in senior management positions, including the CEO, but most women in agricultural societies are still employed in low-level positions.

ASK YOURSELF

What is the relationship between the feminization of labor and the feminization of poverty? Is this relationship inevitable? What social, structural, and gender-related factors might account for it?

A great deal of attention has been focused on the place of women on the "global assembly line" (Collins 2003). While high-status research and management jobs are likely to be found in the North, assembly-line work is relegated to the less developed nations of the South (Ward 1990). Women are much more likely to be employed in the latter than in the higher-level positions in the developed countries.

In the corporate economic centers, especially global cities, large amounts of low-wage labor are required, and again women often fill the bill. They help to maintain the offices and lifestyles of entrepreneurs, managers, and professionals through clerical, cleaning, and repair work and labor for companies providing software, copying paper, office furniture, and even toilet paper (Sassen 2004). Furthermore, the vast majority of provisioning and cleaning of offices, child tending, and caring for the elderly and for homes is done by immigrants, primarily women (Acker 2004).

> **female proletarianization** The channeling of an increasing number of women into low-status, poorly paid manual work.
>
> **feminization of poverty** The rise in the number of women falling below the poverty line.

GENDER, WAR, AND VIOLENCE

Men are certainly more likely to be killed or wounded in warfare than women. However, a 2004 Amnesty International report described women as "bearing the brunt of war." More specifically, women are more likely than men to be the noncombatant victims of organized collective violence including multinational and bilateral wars, wars of liberation, and civil wars (Gerami and Lehnerer 2007).

Several changes have made it more likely that women will be the victims of international violence. One is the change in the nature of warfare. For example, "asymmetric warfare" involving forces of unequal capabilities often takes

Women in the Military

We Can Do It!

WAR PRODUCTION CO-ORDINATING COMMITTEE

Rosie the Riveter symbolized the many women who, from necessity, entered the blue-collar workforce during World War II. How is her influence still felt today?

"Globalization" box). They have long been used to weaken and demoralize the nation-states and ethnic enclaves in which the victims live. One example occurred in the war in Bosnia (1992–1995) where Bosnian Serb soldiers and officers systematically raped Bosnian women. The Serbs set up camps where the goal was the impregnation of Bosnian women (Salzman 2000). This is one technique of ethnic cleansing. By giving birth to children with Serbian "blood," the children born to Bosnian women as a consequence of rape would no longer have "pure" Bosnian "blood." Ultimately the number of the invader's descendants in the invaded country would rise. Rape as a tool of war is also used to traumatize the victims and to humiliate the enemy by "taking" their women. As is true with rape in general (Rudrappa 2012), rape in warfare is not a sexual act, but rather is an act of power (Brownmiller 1975). Beyond rape and sexual assault, forced prostitution and slavery are also used against women in times of warfare.

Women can sometimes benefit from warfare. Among other things, they can gain greater economic independence, more freedom to act, and greater mobility. With the norms and values of society disrupted, women can acquire a more public role in the community and society, gain greater responsibility for decision making, and acquire more power. Such was the case in World War II, when labor shortages caused by the mobilization of men for military service resulted in work opportunities for women.

THE GLOBAL WOMEN'S MOVEMENT

As you have seen, globalization and the rise of a global economy have created or exacerbated a variety of inequalities

the form of shootouts in the streets. Obviously, civilians—women, but also children and the elderly—are more likely to be victims than when conventional ground battles take place. This is evident, for example, in the brutal civil war that at this writing continues to engulf Syria. Generally, the line between combatants and civilians has blurred with the result that more civilians, including women, have become the victims of warfare. Finally, more women are in the armed forces in various countries, and this greatly increases their chances of being the victims of violence.

A consequence of war that also affects women is the use of rape and sexual assault as weapons (see the next

CHECKPOINT 9.3	EFFECTS OF GLOBALIZATION
Sexuality	Sexuality is a growing presence in the global media, including through the influence of "sexperts" and social movements such as women's and gay movements.
Sexual minorities	Helped by ease of travel and the Internet, minorities are finding both greater acceptance and the rise of homophobia.
Sex industry	Millions of adults and children are likely in forced labor and prostitution around the world.
Feminization of migration	Globalization brings women from the South to the North in search of work.
Feminization of labor	Women are participating in the workforce in increasing numbers worldwide.
Feminization of poverty	Increasing numbers of women are channeled into low-status, poorly paid manual work.
War and violence	Women are bearing the brunt of war worldwide, including the effects of rape as a tool of war.

Rape as a Weapon of War

The use of rape as a weapon of war has been so virulent in the African nation of the Democratic Republic of Congo that the United Nations representative called it the "rape capital" of the world (Mawathe 2010). The conflict in the Congo persists because of the existence of many different rebel groups, an army that is in disarray, a UN peacekeeping force that is ineffectual, and the battle over valuable minerals (tin, gold, etc.). The warring groups often use women's bodies as a battleground, where rape is a sign of power of one group over another. Groups may also use rape in the hopes of gaining concessions from those in power (Hochschild 2011).

In one case, four armed rebels barged into a hut and repeatedly raped an 80-year-old grandmother in the presence of children. The rapists themselves were so much younger than the woman that she cried out: "Grandsons . . . Get off me!" (Gettleman 2010). They eventually did, but with about 300 other rebels from at least two different groups, they went from hut to hut gang-raping about 200 women. After the rapes, women said they heard hollering throughout the night. It sounded as if the rebels were celebrating. The grandmother

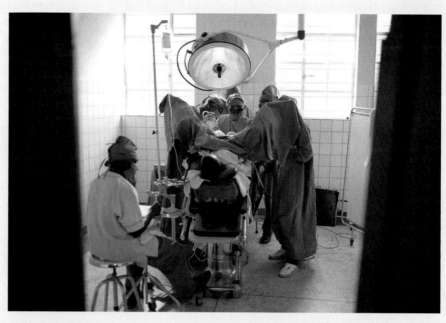

Gynecologist Denis Mukwege observes as his assistants perform reconstructive surgery on one of the many women and girls raped and abused by soldiers on both sides of the ongoing conflict in the Democratic Republic of Congo.

lay bleeding on the floor listening to the celebration.

Many women who are raped are rejected by their husbands, who call them "dirty" (Mawathe 2010). Other survivors are severely injured. The psychological trauma leaves some women entirely emotionless.

Think About It

Why does rape as a tool of war persist? Is it an act of sex, or one of power and violence? Can its incidence be reduced? If so, how?

---

faced by women. One response has been the expansion of the international women's movement (see Chapter 15) in recent years because of problems created for women by globalization. It has also expanded because of the increased ability of those working on behalf of the movement to travel and communicate globally. The international women's movement has a long history traceable back to the late 1800s (Rupp 1997). It has focused on issues such as reproductive rights, labor issues, and sexual harassment. Its greatest triumphs have related to women's right to vote in countries around the world (Ramirez, Soysal, and Shanahan 1997).

A key event was the UN International Women's Year in 1975 and four related world conferences—Mexico City (1975), Copenhagen (1980), Nairobi (1985), and Beijing

(1995) (Alter Chen 1995). Given its dominance mainly by patriarchal males, the UN is an "unlikely godmother" of the women's movement (Snyder 2006). However, these meetings created interpersonal networks throughout the globe, and the expansion of the Internet has greatly increased the ability of women to interact and to mobilize on a global basis.

The focus of the UN meetings as well as the larger global movement was on human rights (Yuval-Davis 2006), economic concerns, health care issues, and violence against women. The movement has also come

Rape

to focus on the adverse effects of global capitalism, the lack of women's voices in global civil society, the growth of antifeminist fundamentalist movements (the Taliban, for one), and the HIV/AIDS epidemic. More generally, the international women's movement has focused attention on issues of global justice for women and other minorities. It has had a strong impact on the UN and has helped to create strong linkages between the UN, national governments, and nongovernmental organizations (George 2007).

Women throughout the world have not only been involved in the global women's movement, but they have responded at local and regional levels to common problems caused by globalization. They also localize global political activities undertaken by the international women's movement and global human rights groups. In addition, they organize against global activities such as militarism and conflict and use global organizations (such as the UN and international nongovernmental organizations) to help in local and regional activities (Naples and Desai 2002). However, even the activities that have been primarily or exclusively local in nature have had a profound effect globally. Even with all the local variations, feminism can be seen as "a truly global phenomenon" (Marx Ferree and Tripp 2006: viii).

SUMMARY

Sex is primarily a biological distinction between males and females and exists on a continuum; gender is based on the physical, behavioral, and personality characteristics considered appropriate given a person's biological category. Humans enact a wide variation of expressions of both sex and sexuality—people are not simply female or male, homosexual or heterosexual. However, everyone's behavior is controlled to a great extent by learned sexual scripts, which account more clearly for gender differences in sexuality than biological differences do.

What is considered sexually deviant varies among times and places. Today behavior is generally judged on the basis of four criteria: the degree of consent, the nature of the person or object involved, the nature of the action or body part employed, and the place where the act takes place.

Hegemonic masculinity works in concert with emphasized femininity to subordinate women and create gender inequality. In gendered organizations and institutions, men and women are placed in different domains, and gender inequality is built in.

The male breadwinner–female homemaker model is not as prevalent in developed countries as it once was, although women still tend to do more housework and child care than men, even when both are working. In schools, girls often excel academically, but boys get more attention. Although female undergraduates outnumber males, men are more likely to graduate from more prestigious schools and earn more money than women. Women and men are prone to different diseases, and women tend to live longer than men. Being male is the strongest predictor of crime, though arrests for crime among women are increasing.

Globalization reinforces but also destabilizes preexisting gender structures on a global scale. Further, norms and values about sex have flowed across the world and grown increasingly similar over time. The greater flow of people also creates more opportunity for traffickers to transport women and children for sexual exploitation. Globalization is linked to the increasing number of women working in the Global South, although many are drawn into low-status, poorly paid, and sometimes dangerous manual work. On the global level, women are also suffering as rape has become a prominent weapon of war. The international women's movement has gained strength since the UN celebrated the International Women's Year in 1975.

KEY TERMS

Asexuality, 254
Bisexuality, 254
Consensual sex, 256
Emphasized femininity, 261
Female proletarianization, 273
Feminization of labor, 272
Feminization of poverty, 273

Gender, 253
Hegemonic masculinity, 261
Heterosexuality, 254
Homosexuality, 254
Intersexed, 253
Rape, 256
Sex, 253

Sexual assault, 256
Sexual orientation, 254
Sexual scripts, 255
Sexuality, 254
Transgender, 261
Transsexual, 253

REVIEW QUESTIONS

1. What do sociologists mean when they say that there are no clear-cut biological differences between men and women?

2. What are the differences in the ways that men and women approach sexuality? How are the differences in approaches related to the socialization process? Do you think that increasing equality between men and women will affect these approaches?

3. What is the relationship between consumption and sexuality and our sexual identity?

4. What is the difference between sex and gender? How does sex affect gender? How does gender affect sexuality?

5. What are the differences in the ways that men and women experience "hegemonic masculinity" and "emphasized femininity"? How do these constructs help create and reinforce gender stratification?

6. How do men and women differ in terms of their educational experiences?

7. Why are women and men treated differently as consumers? What events in recent decades have changed the way women are thought of as consumers?

8. In what ways has the sex industry become increasingly important to global capitalism? How is this sex industry reflective of gender stratification? How is it reflective of inequalities between the Global North and South?

9. What do sociologists mean by the "feminization of labor"? What are the benefits and disadvantages of the feminization of labor? How has the feminization of labor influenced female migration?

10. What types of violence are women most likely to experience when they live in places experiencing war and other types of armed conflict?

APPLYING THE SOCIOLOGICAL IMAGINATION

According to the chapter, the United Nations is the "unlikely godmother" of the global women's movement. Despite being led primarily by men, the UN has been a key ally in the global women's movement. In fact, the UN is responsible for the most complete international agreement on the basic human rights for women, the Convention on the Elimination of All Forms of Discrimination against Women, also known as CEDAW.

For this activity, do research on the history of CEDAW. How does CEDAW define discrimination against women? What are the basic principles of the articles of the convention? How do these relate to the issues discussed in this chapter? What countries have ratified CEDAW? What sort of success has CEDAW had in addressing issues of global gender stratification?

STUDENT STUDY SITE

$SAGE edge™

Sharpen your skills with SAGE edge at **edge.sagepub.com/ritzeressentials**

SAGE edge for students provides a personalized approach to help you accomplish your coursework goals in an easy-to-use learning environment.

A mother and her child at an emergency feeding center in Tahoua, Niger, are the subjects of this prize-winning news photo. Even as new global flows of money, people, and ideas affect an increasing number of families, the very definition of family is changing. Who is in your family?

THE FAMILY

10

LEARNING OBJECTIVES

1 Explain basic sociological concepts of the family, marriage, and intimate relationships.

2 Describe trends leading to the decline in marriage rates and changes in the family household including increases in single parenting, blended families, and lesbian and gay families.

3 Describe types of family conflict, forms of abuse and violence within the family, and the effects of poverty on family life.

4 Identify the effects of globalization and global flows on the family today.

The groundbreaking series *An American Family*, aired on public television in the 1970s, is widely credited with being the medium's first reality show. It intended simply to chronicle the happy, mundane lives of husband and wife Bill and Pat Loud and their five children. Over the course of the series, however, cracks in the California family's calm and stable facade became apparent. The cement that had held the Louds together eventually began to crumble, exposing events never seen on U.S. television before. The public witnessed Bill and Pat's real-life separation and subsequent divorce, for example, and eldest son Lance's coming out as television's first openly gay person.

Families are a universal social institution, our first group and primary socializer.

Since then, family-based reality television shows have flourished, forcing contemporary series to focus on exceptional families in order to distinguish themselves. Some have spotlighted celebrities (*Keeping Up With the Kardashians*), families with many children (*19 Kids and Counting*), or the wealthy (*My Super Sweet 16* and the *Real Housewives* series).

It should come as no surprise that family-based reality shows are so enormously popular. Family, after all, is a universal social institution.

It constitutes a person's first group and primary socializer and, for many, a lifelong source of companionship and security. Because the institution of family is such a central part of life, it is natural to be fascinated by—and even to feel connected to—the intimate relationships and conflicts forged in other people's families.

As reality television indicates, the structure of a family can take a great number of forms. Extended and nuclear families have proven popular over the last 100 years, but recent social changes have opened a wide variety of other options. Some couples marry for love, others marry for purely economic reasons, and an increasing number choose not to marry at all. Some have children in the double digits, while others have one or none. Some maintain exclusive partnerships until death, others remarry, and still others incorporate new members into existing relationships.

Family-based reality shows paint a picture of domestic dynamics that is captivating and intriguing but by no means complete. They largely sidestep issues critical to sociology, such as poverty, gender inequality, and the prevalence of domestic abuse. Also unlike sociology, they have not adopted a global perspective, choosing instead to focus on traditional upper- and middle-class western family structures. That leaves us with much to learn and study. ●

This chapter examines a variety of topics and issues of concern to sociologists—and almost everyone else—interested in the family.

FAMILY, MARRIAGE, AND INTIMATE RELATIONSHIPS

The **family** is a group of people who are related by descent, marriage, or adoption. It is especially important in socializing children so that they are better able to fit into the larger society. Sociologists view the family as a universal social institution that is central to social life (Powell and Branden 2007). Sociologists are interested in such issues as the relationship between family and marriage, the different forms taken by families, and how families are formed and maintained, expand and contract, and even dissolve (Farrell, VandeVusse, and Ocobock 2012).

Mohd Miqdad Ashaari has three wives (two are pictured here) and six children. He is a member of Malaysia's Polygamy Club. Do polygamous families bear any unusual burdens?

SOME BASIC CONCEPTS

In this section, we will define such basic concepts and ideas as marriage, intimate relationships, and love and explore their roles in the family.

---

family A group of people who are related by descent, marriage, or adoption.

marriage The socially acknowledged, approved, and often legal union of two people allowing them to live together and to have children by birth or adoption.

monogamy Marriage between one wife and one husband (or two wives or two husbands).

polygamy Marriage to multiple wives (polygyny) or multiple husbands (polyandry).

polygyny Marriage (of a husband) to multiple wives.

polyandry Marriage (of a wife) to multiple husbands.

cenogamy Group marriage.

endogamy Marriage to someone with similar characteristics in terms of race, ethnicity, religion, education level, social class, and so on.

exogamy Marriage to someone with dissimilar characteristics in terms of race, ethnicity, religion, education level, social class, and so on.

Marriage

Marriage is the socially acknowledged and approved and often legal union of two people, allowing them to live together and to have children by birth or adoption. Families govern various issues that relate to marriage such as the "meanings of marriage" as well as "the number of marriage partners" (Shaw and Lee 2009:378). **Monogamy** is a marriage between one wife and one husband (however, given changing laws related to gay marriage, monogamy might involve two wives or two husbands). **Polygamy** involves multiple spouses. **Polygyny**, in which a single husband has multiple wives, is a more common form of polygamy than **polyandry**, in which a single wife has multiple husbands. **Cenogamy** involves group marriage.

Key to understanding the family is the concept of **endogamy**, or marriage to one with similar characteristics in terms of race, ethnicity, religion, education level, social class, and so on. In contrast, **exogamy** involves marriage to someone with characteristics that are dissimilar on these dimensions. Throughout history, families have been defined much more by endogamy than by exogamy. In recent years, endogamy has declined in importance, and there is more exogamy. For example, there has been an increasing tendency of Americans to marry those of another

An American Family

Marriage

race (Qian and Lichter 2011). However, as a general rule, families continue to be characterized more by endogamy than by exogamy.

In the last several decades, the nature of family and marriage has undergone a series of rapid and dizzying changes. It is less and less clear exactly what constitutes marriage or a family. One thing is clear, however: Whatever they are today, the close linkage between marriage and the family has been greatly reduced, if not broken. Nevertheless, most people in the United States are involved in one or more marriages during their lifetime. And those who do marry create families, although they may not stay together as long as families did in the past. Being married and in a family does not mean that the same people will remain in them for the duration of their lives. Marriage and the family will remain important and intimate, but they will not be the only, or even the dominant, forms of intimacy in the future.

Intimate Relationships

An **intimate relationship** involves partners who have a close, personal, and domestic relationship with one another. This intimate relationship is a by-product of courtship rituals in which two people are attracted to each other, develop intimacy, enjoy each other's company, and identify as a couple.

The nature of intimacy is not static, but changes over time. Fifty or a hundred years ago, couples could be intimate without necessarily sharing very much about themselves with each other, especially their most private thoughts. However, in western culture today, intimacy increasingly involves disclosing much, if not everything, about oneself to one's partner (Jamieson 2007). Levels of disclosure tend to be gendered (Kimmel 2011). Women tend to function as emotional caretakers within heterosexual relationships. They do so because they are generally socialized to engage in communication in which they express their emotions, whereas males are socialized to suppress their emotions and communicate little about them. In other words, women tend to be the ones to share first and to help males to share by drawing them out. The assumption made by most women is that such self-disclosure will strengthen a relationship because there are no secrets and therefore there will be no surprises, or at least there will be fewer of them, as the relationship develops.

Love

Intimacy in domestic relationships is, of course, often associated with love (Frieze 2007). **Passionate love** has a sudden onset, involves strong sexual feelings, and tends to include idealization of the one who is loved (Hatfield, Bensman, and Rapson 2012). Passionate love brings with it great intimacy, but it is an intimacy that is very likely to be short-lived. In contrast, **companionate love** develops more gradually, is not necessarily tied to sexual passion, and is based on more rational assessments of the one who is loved. Companionate love is more likely than passionate love to lead to long-lasting intimate relationships. However, these two types of love are not clearly distinguished from one another. This is clearest in the fact that long-term intimate relationships often start out with passionate love, but in those that succeed over time it tends to be combined with, or even supplanted by, companionate love.

Zygmunt Bauman (2003) has sought to get at the essence of love in the contemporary world in his book *Liquid Love*. On the cover of that book is a heart drawn in the sand. However, the sea is nearby, and the implication is that love will soon be washed away by the waves. To Bauman, love, like everything else in today's liquid society, is fleeting. This clearly applies to passionate love, but to Bauman even companionate love is today constantly at risk of erosion and disappearance. This represents a major challenge to all intimate relationships, especially marriage, and to all of those involved in them. However, liquid love can also be seen as offering people freedom from lifelong, loveless relationships. It also offers the possibility of innumerable experiences with love and the possibility of many different relationships built on love.

ASK YOURSELF

What do you think of Bauman's concept of "liquid love"? Do you agree that love is fleeting, and that this impermanence is a reflection of a society in which nothing lasts? Why or why not? Would you find the experience of liquid love troubling, or liberating? Why?

It can be argued that our main concerns in this chapter—family and marriage—are also increasingly liquid. Because they are now so liquid, the borders of marriage and the family are increasingly difficult to define. More importantly, many traditional forms of marriage and the family are confronting the possibility of being washed away. As a result, many sociologists have moved away

> **intimate relationship** A close, personal, and domestic relationship between partners.
>
> **passionate love** A type of love that develops suddenly and includes strong sexual feelings and idealization of the one who is loved; romantic love.
>
> **companionate love** A type of love that develops gradually and is not necessarily tied to sexual passion but is based on more rational assessments of the one who is loved.

from a focus on the family and marriage and prefer to discuss, instead, vaguer phenomena such as "relationships" and "personal life." Nevertheless, most people, including most sociologists, continue to think in terms of marriage and the family (Powell et al. 2010). We will do the same in this chapter, but with an understanding that both are changing dramatically and refer to phenomena that are far more liquid than they were in the past.

DECLINE OF MARRIAGE

In 1960, married couples constituted 71 percent of all households (see Figure 10.1); by 2010, only 52 percent of all American households were married couples. Similarly, the traditional **nuclear family** involving two adults and one or more children dropped from 43 percent of all households in 1950 to only about a fifth of all households in 2010.

Another way to get a sense of the dramatic change in marriage and the family is to look at the percentage of those who have ever been married (see Figure 10.2). In 1960, 60 percent of 20- to 24-year-olds had ever married, but by 2010 that number had dwindled to 14 percent. Among 25- to 29-year-olds, the decline from 84 percent to 42 percent in those ever married was also steep, but not as dramatic. It remains the case that as people age, they are more likely to marry, but even in the 30–34 and 35–39 age groups there was a decline between 1960 and 2010 of those ever married. Further declines are expected in most, if not all, age categories.

Perspectives on the Decline in Marriage

The decline in marriage (and the family) has led to some fascinating new perspectives on the status of marriage today.

Would you find passionate love or companionate love to be more fulfilling in the long term? Can they coexist?

CHECKPOINT 10.1	FAMILY, MARRIAGE, AND INTIMATE RELATIONSHIPS
Marriage	The socially acknowledged and approved and often legal union of two people, allowing them to live together and to have children by birth or adoption.
Monogamy	Marriage between one wife and one husband (or two wives or two husbands).
Polygamy	Marriage to multiple wives (polygyny) or multiple husbands (polyandry).
Cenogamy	Group marriage.
Endogamy	Marriage to someone of a similar race, ethnicity, religion, education level, social class, and so on.
Exogamy	Marriage to someone of a dissimilar race, ethnicity, religion, education level, social class, or other such characteristics.
Passionate love	Type of love that develops suddenly and includes strong sexual feelings and idealization of the one who is loved; romantic love.
Companionate love	Type of love that develops gradually and is not necessarily tied to sexual passion but is based on more rational assessments of the one who is loved.

> **nuclear family** A family consisting of two married adults and one or more children.

Intimate Relationships

Traditional Families

FIGURE 10.1 • Marital Status in the United States, 1960–2010

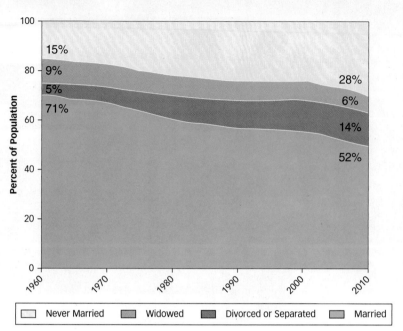

SOURCE: Reprinted with permission from "New Marriages Down 5% from 2009 to 2010: Barely Half of U.S. Adults Are Married—A Record Low," by Paul Taylor et al., December 14, 2011. Pew Research Center analysis of Decennial Census (1960–2000) and American Community Survey data (2008, 2010), IPUMS.

The Deinstitutionalization of Marriage. Andrew Cherlin (2004) focuses on the "deinstitutionalization of American marriage." By **deinstitutionalization** he means that the social norms relating to marriage have weakened. As a result, people increasingly question their actions, or those of others, as they relate to marriage. While Cherlin focuses on this deinstitutionalization in the United States, he recognizes that a similar process is occurring in much of Europe, as well as in Canada. In the mid twentieth century, especially in the United States, few questioned marriage and the creation of a nuclear family. As a result, most plunged into both, sometimes successfully, but more often with dubious or even disastrous results. Now, with marriage and perhaps the nuclear family and the family household deinstitutionalized, it is much easier for people *not* to rush into such an arrangement. They are freer to experiment with many other arrangements.

Five factors are involved in the deinstitutionalization of marriage. First, as more women entered the labor force, the clear division of labor in the family between homemaker and breadwinner began to break down. The once clear norms about what men and women were to do in a marital relationship were eroding. This contributed a more general lack of clarity about marriage as well as the family. Second, the norms about having children within the context of marriage and the family were also eroding. This was demonstrated in the dramatic increase in childbirth outside of marriage, which increased from one out of six in the late 1970s to

one out of three in the early twenty-first century. Third, the high and increasing divorce rate between 1960 and the mid 1980s contributed to the deinstitutionalization of marriage (see Figure 10.3). Although the divorce rate has declined in recent decades, the high rate between 1960 and the mid 1980s had a seemingly irreversible impact on attitudes toward marriage. Fourth is the growth in cohabitation, which began in the 1970s and accelerated as the twentieth century ended. Finally, same-sex marriage flowered in the 1990s and has grown further in the twenty-first century.

These ideas on deinstitutionalization are embedded in a long-term model of change. In the early twentieth century, **institutional marriage** was the predominant form. The focus in such a marriage was on the maintenance of the institution of marriage itself. There was less concern that those involved would love or be good companions to one another. Today, many see the time of institutional marriage as past; but there are also those who see it as alive and well and as having a future (Lauer and Yodanis 2010).

By the middle of the twentieth century, a model of **companionate marriage** (see above section on companionate love) had become predominant (Amato 2012; Amato et al. 2007; Burgess and Locke 1945). Companionate marriage meshed well with the nuclear family. It involved a clear division of labor between the single-earner breadwinner—almost always the male—and the female homemaker. In spite, or perhaps because, of the strict division of labor, husbands and wives were held together by bonds of sentiment, friendship, and sexuality. They were supposed to be each other's companions, which included being each other's friends, confidants, and lovers. Romantic love was an essential component of companionate marriage.

In the 1960s, a dramatic shift began to take place in the direction of the **individualized marriage** (Lauer and Yodanis 2011). The goal of the companionate marriage was the satisfaction of the couple, the family as a whole,

deinstitutionalization Weakened social norms especially with regard to the institution of marriage.

institutional marriage A marriage focused on maintaining the institution of marriage itself.

companionate marriage A marriage emphasizing a clear division of labor between a breadwinner and a homemaker and held together by sentiment, friendship, and sexuality.

and the roles the couple played in the family. However, that focus began to shift increasingly in the direction of the satisfaction of each individual involved, as well as toward individuals' ability to develop and express their selves. In addition, instead of being as rigid as companionate marriage, individualized marriage became increasingly open and flexible. Furthermore, couples were becoming more open with each other in communicating about and dealing with problems. Many of those involved, as well as many observers, applauded the greater freedoms and sensitivities associated with individualized marriage.

A major factor in the rise of individualized marriage was the changing place of women in society. For example, as more women went to work, they were no longer restricted to the homemaker role and reliant on the male breadwinner. As more women obtained a higher education, their occupational prospects were enhanced. This put them in a context where ideas associated with companionate marriage were increasingly open to question. The greater access of women to contraception and to abortion freed more women from the constraints of companionate marriage as they related to producing and socializing children.

As a result of all of these changes, people today feel freer to never marry, to marry later, to end unhappy marriages more readily, and especially to engage in many other types of intimate relationships. Yet, in spite of all of the change, the vast majority of people—perhaps as many as 90 percent—will eventually marry, although many of their marriages will end long before the "till death do us part" stage is reached. Thus, marriage has not been deinstitutionalized to the degree anticipated by Cherlin.

Marriage as a Carousel. In *The Marriage-Go-Round*, Cherlin (2009) adopts a somewhat different perspective involving a "carousel of intimate partners." Some of those intimate partners are to be found in marriages, but

FIGURE 10.2 • Percentage of Americans Currently or Formerly Married, by Age, 1960 and 2010

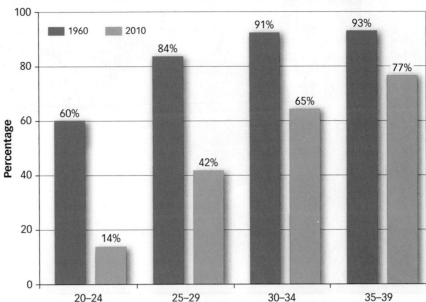

SOURCE: Reprinted with permission from "New Marriages Down 5% from 2009 to 2010: Barely Half of U.S. Adults Are Married—A Record Low," by Paul Taylor et al., December 14, 2011. Pew Research Center analysis of Decennial Census (1960–2000) and American Community Survey data (2008, 2010), IPUMS.

FIGURE 10.3 • U.S. Divorce Rate, 1950–2012

SOURCE: Divorce Rate 1950–2009, CDC/National Vital Statistics Reports 2010.

> **individualized marriage** A marriage characterized by greater freedom for the partners to develop and express themselves and seek satisfaction.

The Meaning of Marriage for Young Adults

A Japanese couple smashed their wedding ring before filing for divorce following the 2011 earthquake and tsunami disasters that reportedly led many Japanese to rethink their values and their marriages. Would such reevaluations have been cause for divorce a generation ago?

Self-Disclosing Intimacy and Pure Relationships. British sociologist Anthony Giddens (1992) offers an ambivalent view on the new individualized forms of marriage and of relationships more generally. The key to this new form of relationship is what Giddens calls "self-disclosing intimacy." Couples are disclosing much more to each other. As a result, much more intimate relationships are likely to develop. This is contrasted with companionate marriages, which were more likely to be based on secrets and half-truths. Thus, companionate marriages in the past, and even the many that continue today, may survive for decades or a lifetime even though they may be based on deceptions that leave one or both partners in the dark. The partners often remain in such marriages for reasons other than their openness and honesty. They may stay together because of social norms against divorce or "for the sake of the children."

Giddens recognizes the advantages of self-disclosing intimacy, but he also argues that intimate relationships based on full disclosure are made much more fragile by such disclosures, especially as the disclosures continue and proliferate over time. The more weaknesses one reveals to a partner, the more likely that partner is to become disappointed with the relationship. Despite this, Giddens, as well as many others today, seems to prefer relationships based on mutual disclosure because he believes they are likely to be more mutually satisfying, equal, and democratic. Further, he contends that almost anything is preferable to being locked into the kind of dishonest and unsatisfying relationship often associated with companionate marriage.

Since marriage of any kind can be confining and limiting, Giddens (1992) coined the term *pure relationships* to describe a new reality. A **pure relationship** is one that is entered into for its own sake, or for what each partner can get from it, and those involved remain in it only as long as each derives enough satisfaction from it.

those marriages are more likely to end; people are likely to remarry, perhaps more than once. Rounds of separation and divorce add to the merry-go-round and its increasingly dizzying speed. Then there may be a series of cohabitations into and out of which people move. Thus, many people have not given up on the idea and even the practice of marriage, but they exist side-by-side with the often-conflicting notion of individualism. People want to be legally defined as couples and as families, but they also want to be free of constraints and to act as they wish as individuals. Current sociological research underscores this paradox. On the one hand, researchers are told that most people, including young adults, want an "exclusive, lifelong intimate partnership, most commonly a marriage" (Hull, Meier, and Ortyl 2010: 37). On the other hand, people often indicate by their behavior that they want to be free of such bonds. Americans remain committed to the ideal of marriage, but in reality they spend fewer of their adult years married than previous generations did.

ASK YOURSELF

Which do most of your peers seem to want, an exclusive lifelong partnership such as marriage, or the freedom to live and act as an individual? What might account for their preference? Which is your preference?

> **pure relationship** A relationship entered into for its own sake or for what each partner can get from it, maintained only as long as each derives enough satisfaction from the other.

While pure relationships can exist within marriage, they are more likely to exist outside of such a legal relationship. As a result of the increasing predominance of this idea, at least among young people, a relationship is likely to be ended when couples no longer find their relationship satisfying. It is also likely that another, different pure relationship (or several) will be formed in relatively short order, or perhaps even simultaneously with the existing one. This fits with the increasing individualization of contemporary society as well as the closely related phenomenon of individuals wanting more choices and greater freedom of choice. It represents a greater degree of individualization than even that found in individualized marriage. Less constrained by marriage, or more likely not married at all, couples are free to individualize their lives to a much greater degree. Marriage is seen as just one of a wide range of lifestyle choices open to couples. In whatever type of intimate relationship people find themselves today, the possibility that it will dissolve is never very far from their consciousness.

The idea of the pure relationship had its origins in western society, although like many such ideas in the global age, it has flowed readily around the world to many locales.

Questioning the New Ideas on Marriage and Relationships. There are those who have questioned the range of new ideas, like those discussed above, about intimate relationships. For example, Lynn Jamieson (1998) has questioned the importance of self-disclosing intimacy. There are many forms of intimacy other than those based on self-disclosure, and good relationships are based on more than such disclosures. For example, negotiating an equitable division of labor in the home may do more for increasing intimacy than a wide range of self-disclosures.

Interestingly, a major critique of these new ideas on marriage and the family is implicit in the work of one of sociology's classic social theorists, Georg Simmel (see Chapters 1, 2, and 4). In his famous essay on secrecy, Simmel ([1906] 1950) argues that while there is always a temptation to reveal all to a partner in an intimate relationship, especially marriage, such revelations would be a big mistake. In his view, all relationships require a certain proportion of both openness and secrecy, and marriage is no exception. Even if it were possible to disclose everything about one's self, and it almost certainly isn't, this would only serve to make marriage boring and matter-of-fact because all possibility of the unexpected would be eliminated. Finally, most of us have limited internal resources, and every revelation reduces the (secret) treasures that we have to offer our mates. Only those few with great storehouses of personal assets and accomplishments can afford numerous revelations to a marriage partner. All others are left denuded—and perhaps less interesting—by excessive self-revelation. The contrast is striking between Simmel's ideas, written over a century ago, and the current thinking of many who emphasize the importance of revealing all to intimate partners.

The Resilience of Marriage. In spite of all of the changes discussed above, there are those who remain committed to the traditional notion of marriage. "Marriage naturalists" view "marriage as the *natural* expected outcome of a relationship that has endured for a period of time" (Kefalas et al. 2011: 847). In contrast, "marriage planners" need to deal with a number of practical realities before they can consider marriage. These include finding a well-paying job and being able to create and support a separate household. *Marriage naturalists* "see marriage as being a prerequisite to being an adult," and *marriage planners* "want to establish themselves as adults *before* they wed" (Kefalas et al. 2011: 870). In either case, however, the goal is to marry.

While they are going about creating those realities, marriage planners and marriage naturalists may have premarital sexual/romantic relationships, cohabit, and bear children out of marriage. All of the latter phenomena have been found by sociological researchers to have risen in recent years. Kefalas et al. (2011) found that the marriage naturalists were more likely to be rural, while the marriage planners had to arrange their intimate lives around the realities of urban life. In addition, the marriage naturalists were closer to the realities of marriage in the mid-twentieth-century United States, while the marriage planners better fit the realities of postindustrial America and the wait-and-see attitude more characteristic of the early twenty-first century.

Only about one-fifth of the young adults studied by Kefalas et al. (2011) were marriage naturalists; the rest were marriage planners. However, the marriage planners, even those who regarded marriage as only a distant possibility, still desired to marry eventually. More striking is the fact that there was little discussion among young adults of passion or love.

ASK YOURSELF

Among the married couples you know, how many were marriage naturalists, and how many were marriage planners? Have you observed other approaches to marriage among those who are committed to the institution? If so, what are they?

Today there is a debate between those who see marriage as being in decline and those who emphasize its resilience

Nuclear family	Family consisting of two married adults and one or more children, now only about 20 percent of households.
Deinstitutionalization of marriage	Weakening of the social norms relating to marriage.
Institutional marriage	A marriage focused on maintaining the institution of marriage itself.
Companionate marriage	A marriage emphasizing a clear division of labor between a breadwinner and a homemaker and held together by sentiment, friendship, and sexuality.
Individualized marriage	A marriage characterized by greater freedom for the partners to develop and express themselves and seek satisfaction.
Pure relationship	A relationship entered into for its own sake or for what each partner can get from it, maintained only as long as each derives enough satisfaction from the other.

(Amato 2004). Those who see marriage as in decline focus on such things as the rising divorce rate and the increase in the number of children born out of wedlock. These are seen as problems in themselves and as indicators of larger problems, such as an excessive focus on the individual and an inadequate concern for the collectivity. Those who focus on the resilience of marriage argue, for example, that divorce allows people to escape from marriages from which people ought to escape, especially marriages that are dysfunctional in various ways, such as abusive marriages. Having children out of wedlock may have the positive effect that fewer children will be locked into families in which they are socialized poorly or even abused physically and psychologically.

ALTERNATIVE FORMS OF FAMILIES

A **family household** comprises two or more people who occupy a given domicile and are related by blood, marriage, or adoption. It is distinguished by the fact that those involved are related but not necessarily married, and by their occupation of a specific domicile. One member of the family household—the *householder*—owns or rents the property as well as maintains it.

As a form of an intimate relationship, the family household, like the family itself, has been declining in the United States and in the Global North more generally. For example, in 1940, 90 percent of households were family households, but that declined to 81 percent in 1970 and to 66.4 percent in 2010. This means, of course, a corresponding increase in nonfamily households over

this period of time (Casper 2007; Jacobsen, Mather, and Dupuis 2012).

Recent social changes have made it possible for people to choose a nontraditional family structure for themselves, including nonfamily households, cohabitation, single-parent families, and lesbian and gay families.

NONFAMILY HOUSEHOLDS AND "GOING SOLO"

Nonfamily households are those in which a person lives either alone or with nonrelatives. Of greatest interest is the growth of one-person households, or people living alone. As is clear in Figure 10.4, we have witnessed an increase in such households from 13 percent in 1970 to over 27 percent of all households in 2011.

One-person households, or "singletons," are the subject of Eric Klinenberg's (2012) *Going Solo: The Extraordinary Rise and Surprising Appeal of Living Alone*. Detailed in this work is the long-term increase in the number of people living alone. The number grew from 9 percent of all households in 1950 to 3 times that many today. Overall, 31 million Americans now live alone. The fastest-growing segment of the population going solo is young adults between 18 and 34. In 1950, only a half-million of those in this age group lived alone, while today the total of 5 million is 10 times the number in the mid twentieth century. Fifteen million of those who are middle-aged (35–64) live alone, while 10 million of the elderly are singletons. More women (17 million) than men (14 million) live alone. Going solo is mainly an urban phenomenon; more than half of dwellings in Manhattan are one-person residences.

There are several reasons for the increase in singletons. First, increasing economic affluence has made it possible for more people to afford the greater costs associated with

family household A household comprising two or more people who occupy a given domicile and are related by blood, marriage, or adoption.

nonfamily household A household consisting of a person who lives either alone or with nonrelatives.

living alone than sharing expenses with others. Second, it is consistent with the growth of individualism in the United States and much of the developed world. Third, there is the rising status of women and their higher levels of education and their higher-paying jobs (although their wages continue to be lower than men's wages and they are more likely than men to be poor). With greater independence, they are more likely to marry later, separate, or divorce. Fourth, the communications revolution has allowed people to communicate with other people, and be entertained, while they are home alone. Fifth, mass urbanization has made the active social life of the city available to more people. Finally, there is the aging of the population and the fact that as people live longer they are more likely to find themselves alone.

While in the past living alone might well have been considered a problem, Klinenberg argues that increasing numbers of people are coming to prefer going solo. It allows people to pursue "individual freedom, personal control, and self-realization. . . . It allows us to do what we want, when we want, on our own terms" (Klinenberg 2012: 17–18). Interestingly, singletons may also be more socially active than those who live with others. It is certainly true that those who live alone have problems, but so do those who live with partners.

Cohabitation

Cohabitation is defined as couples sharing a home and a bed without being legally married (Manning and Cohen 2012; Sassler 2010; Thornton, Axinn, and Xie 2007). There are clearly more cohabiting couples today than there were previously, although they still compose a small percentage (about 4 percent) of all households (Casper 2007). Among 30- to 44-year-olds in the United States, the percentage of cohabiting couples more than doubled from slightly more than 3 percent in 1995 to 7 percent in 2010 (see Figure 10.5). Nevertheless, the United

FIGURE 10.4 • Percentage of Single-Person Households in the United States, 1960–2011

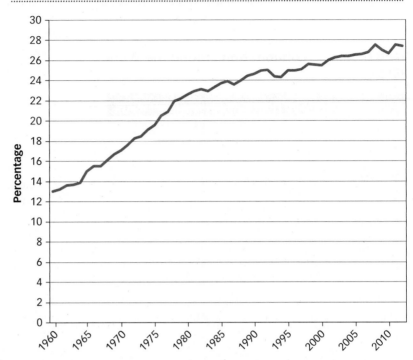

SOURCE: U.S. Census Bureau, Current Population Survey, 1960 to 2011. Annual Social and Economic Supplements.

FIGURE 10.5 • Cohabitation Rate Among 30- to 44-Year-Olds in the United States, 1995–2010

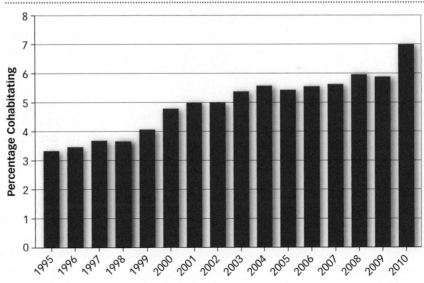

SOURCE: From Richard Fry and D'Vera Cohn, *Living Together: The Economics of Cohabitation*, Pew Research Center: Social & Demographic Trends. June 27, 2011, p. 9. Reprinted with permission.

cohabitation A couple sharing a home and a bed without being legally married.

Alternative Families

Cohabitation

States still only ranks in the middle globally in terms of cohabitation. For example, cohabitation is more common in France, Sweden, Argentina, South Africa, and Canada (see Table 10.1).

TABLE 10.1 • Cohabitation around the World, 2005–2009

Country	Percent of Adults Cohabiting
Colombia	31
Peru	25
Sweden	18
France	16
Argentina	15
Canada	12
Philippiness	11
South Africa	11
Chile	10
Mexico	10
New Zealand	10
United Kingdom	9
Australia	8
Germany	8
United States	7
Italy	5
Spain	5
Kenya	4
India	4
Poland	3
Japan	2
Malaysia	2
China	1
Nigeria	1
Egypt	<1
Saudi Arabia	<1
South Korea	<1
Indonesia	<1
Taiwan	<1

SOURCE: From *The Sustainable Demographic Dividend: What Do Marriage and Fertility Have to Do with the Economy?* National Marriage Project.

It is unclear exactly how many people are involved in such relationships because cohabitation is not a formally constituted relationship and it leaves no legal records. Furthermore, it is not clear how many nights, weeks, months, or years a couple must be together to be categorized as cohabiting. It is clear, however, that more young men and women (especially between 25 and 35) are living together outside of marriage even if they are not considered, or do not consider themselves, a cohabiting couple. Living together has come to be considered a common tryout for, and pathway to, marriage, although few people plan to marry when they begin cohabiting. Then again, marriage may never occur or even be discussed, and cohabiting couples may break up and move on to other relationships. A declining number—less than 50 percent—of cohabiting couples end up getting married.

At one time cohabitation was associated with being poor, less educated, or in the lower classes; it was seen as the "poor man's marriage." More recently, cohabitation has become increasingly common among those with advanced education, even college degrees. Blacks are more likely to cohabit than are whites, and both are more likely to cohabit than Hispanics, although there are differences among these groups in the function of cohabitation. For instance, for blacks, cohabitation is more likely to be an alternative to marriage; for whites, it is more likely a prelude to marriage (England and Edin 2009; Smock and Manning 2004).

In a recent study, Huang et al. (2011) sought to better understand why young adults have cohabited or would cohabit. The percentage of women who had ever cohabited ranged from 40.0 percent (Latinas) to 53.8 percent (both white and black women) and was consistent with previous studies of this phenomenon. Perhaps the most interesting results of the study related to gender difference in terms of the ways in which cohabiting enhanced the relationship: Women focused on love while men focused on sex. As one man put it, "Most girls want to have the connection with the guy and know it's a relationship. 'Cause women, their number one thing in life is to have good relationships with people. . . . Guys, the thing they strive for is sex, so it's kind of a tradeoff" (Huang et al. 2011: 887).

The biggest gender differences revolved around cohabitation's disadvantages. Women saw it as less legitimate and as entailing less commitment than marriage. Men were most concerned about the decline in freedom compared to being single. In terms of the latter, men focused on their loss of personal autonomy with regard to space, social activities, choice of friends, and sexual freedom. Overall, however, for both men and women the benefits of cohabitation outweighed the disadvantages.

Cohabitation varies greatly around the globe. Sweden has a long history of cohabitation, and the process is well institutionalized there. In excess of 90 percent of first partnerships are cohabitations, and over 40 percent of all first births are to cohabiting couples (Perelli-Harris and Gassen 2012). The legal status, or the rights and privileges, of those who cohabit is virtually the same as that of married couples in terms of such things as social security and taxes (Wilk, Bernhardt, and Noack 2010). The high rate of cohabitation has led to a decline in the importance of marriage and of the customs, rituals, and ceremonies associated with it. Couples that cohabit and then marry might well give the date they met as their anniversary. Instead of making a decisive break, young people are likely to drift away from their families of orientation, perhaps in stages, and then settle down and cohabit with someone else (Popenoe 1987). However, since 1998, there has been evidence of a change in this pattern, as more Swedes are marrying. This reverses a long-term decline in marriage in Sweden between the 1960s and the 1990s (Ohlsson-Wijk 2011). Other, mainly Catholic, European countries—Italy and Spain—have much lower rates of cohabitation. There is evidence of the spread of cohabitation throughout much of Europe, including Eastern Europe, and elsewhere.

Single-Parent Families

Among the developed countries, the United States has the highest rate of single-parent families (29.5 percent of all households with children), while Japan has the lowest (10.2 percent) (see Table 10.2). In Europe, the northern countries—for example, the United Kingdom (25 percent), Ireland (22.6 percent), and Denmark and Germany (both 21.7 percent)—have the highest rates of single-parent families. It is mainly the southern European countries—Greece and Spain (5 percent), Portugal (6 percent), and Italy (7 percent)—that have the lowest rates of such families (Rowlingson 2007).

Lesbian and Gay Families

It is very difficult to get accurate numbers on the gay and lesbian population as a whole, let alone on those involved in long-term relationships, including those in which children are present. Gays and lesbians were largely invisible half a century ago due to cultural and legal biases and sanctions against them. That began to change in the era of sexual liberation of the 1960s and 1970s.

A major factor in the gay and lesbian community in general, and in gay and lesbian family formation in particular, has been the HIV/AIDS epidemic that emerged in the 1980s (Heaphy 2007a). The gay and lesbian community reacted by building institutions to better deal not only with HIV/AIDS, but with many other concerns as well. One of the institutions that was buttressed in this period was the gay and lesbian family. Previously, gay and lesbian couples had often come together because of the need for support and comfort in the face of a hostile

TABLE 10.2 • Single-Parent Households in Select Countries

Country	Percent of Single-Parent Households
United States	29.5%
United Kingdom	25%
Canada	24.6%
Ireland	22.6%
Germany	21.7%
Denmark	21.7%
France	19.8%
Sweden	18.7%
Netherlands	16%
Japan	10.2%

SOURCE: U.S. Census Bureau, *Statistical Abstract of the United States: 2012.*

environment. Today, such linkages have become more affirmative in nature, especially as the larger society has become more accepting of homosexuality and of gay and lesbian families as an institution. Lesbian and gay politics have devoted more attention to these individuals' right to marry, adopt children, and be parents.

Gay and lesbian couples have various similarities with, as well as differences from, straight families. One important difference is that gay and lesbian couples tend to be more reflexive and democratic in their family decisions and practices than straight couples. This is particularly the case in the way in which domestic duties are negotiated and organized in dual-labor straight families. Gay and lesbian couples are less constrained by gender roles with the result that they are freer in their negotiations over couple and family practices. Another difference is over monogamy. Although the latter is assumed (but often violated) by straight couples, same-sex male couples are not as wedded to the idea or practice of sexual exclusivity. They negotiate over this issue and develop clear ground rules on nonmonogamous sexual relationships. Gay male relationships tend to be more fragile while lesbian relationships tend to be far more stable. Some of the reasons for these gender differences are related to the previous discussion in Chapter 9 about gender socialization patterns and sexual scripts (Kimmel 2011).

Single-Parent Homes   Nontraditional Families

states in the United States have legalized same-sex marriages (California, Connecticut, Delaware, Iowa, Maine, Maryland, Massachusetts, Minnesota, New Hampshire, New Jersey, New York, Rhode Island, Vermont, and Washington, as well as the District of Columbia) (Freedom to Marry 2013). However, the contentiousness of this issue is reflected in the pushback against it; dozens of other states have enacted legislation banning such marriages. The polar views on same-sex marriage are, on the one hand, that it is an expression of greater tolerance in the population as a whole and, on the other hand, that it is yet another threat to religion, morality, and heterosexual marriage.

Jeri (left) and Amy Andrews holding their marriage license in Seattle after Washington state legalized same-sex matrimony in December 2012. Do you think the ability to marry is, on balance, a benefit to gays and lesbians, or a surrender to conformity?

Studies of children of same-sex couples have tended to indicate that growing up in these families does not have adverse effects on children such as psychological or developmental problems, or at least any more or different adverse effects than growing up in straight families. However, most of this research has been done on children brought into a same-sex family but conceived, and having spent at least some time, in a previous heterosexual family. Now, however, same-sex couples are more likely to become parents themselves in various ways, such as artificial insemination (Mamo 2007), adoption, becoming foster parents, or becoming surrogate parents. While we do not yet know much about such children, there is no reason to assume they will be adversely affected by these methods of achieving same-sex parenthood. In fact, there is every reason to believe that they will do at least as well as children raised in traditional heterosexual families.

Same-sex marriage is a major issue these days (Biblarz and Stacey 2010; Heaphy 2007b). As late as the 1990s, there was no legal recognition of such marriages *anywhere in the world*. Furthermore, such marriages face considerable hostility and intolerance. A key event occurred in September 2000 in the Netherlands when the right to marry was extended to same-sex couples. In the ensuing decade, a number of other countries throughout the world (Argentina, Canada, France, Belgium, Norway, Portugal, Sweden, Spain, South Africa, and Uruguay, as well as Mexico City) came to permit same-sex marriages. In recent years, a number of

ASK YOURSELF

Do you believe same-sex marriage will eventually be legal in all 50 states? Why or why not? Is it legal in your state? Why or why not?

PROBLEMS IN THE FAMILY

There is a wide variety of family troubles, but we will focus on a few of the major ones in this section.

ABUSE AND VIOLENCE WITHIN THE FAMILY

Heightened conflict within the family can lead to abuse and violence. This can take various forms, but the most common are parental abuse of children and violence by husbands against their wives (who are considered "battered women") (Dunn 2005). Far less common are women abusing and behaving in a violent manner toward their children and even their husbands. Violence within the family can take emotional or psychological forms. It can also involve physical and sexual abuse (Carmody 2007). Although norms that relate to the acceptability of such behavior have changed in recent years, such abuse and violence are still common and accepted in some groups and parts of the

ACTIVE SOCIOLOGY

Do You Know Your Family History?

Genealogy is a popular subject, and sites like www.ancestry.com have helped many people become prosumers in their quest to discover their family history. Explore as much of the ancestry.com website as you can (some areas are limited to members only, and membership is not free). Record your observations by answering these questions, and share your responses with the class.

1. What assumptions does the site make about families? List as many as you notice.

2. How does the site normalize certain structures and functions of the family?

3. Are nonbiological families represented?

4. What are some possible reasons for the site's assumptions about family structures?

Start your own family tree on this site (you can make a beginning without being a member).

1. How do the site's assumptions limit your ability to tell your own family story?

2. How might you compensate for these drawbacks?

world. In such cases, parents feel justified in abusing children, and husbands think it is acceptable to batter their wives. While there are exceptions, we should remember that the vast majority of those who engage in such behavior are not considered deranged (Straus 1980).

Child Abuse

Hundreds of millions of children throughout the world are abused, as well as maltreated and exploited (Bell 2011). According to the World Health Organization, "child abuse or maltreatment constitutes all forms of physical and/or emotional ill-treatment, sexual abuse, neglect, or negligent treatment or commercial or other exploitation, resulting in actual or potential harm to the child's health, survival, development, or dignity in the context of a relationship of responsibility, trust, or power" (cited in Polonko 2007: 448). In the United States alone, official reports indicate that several million children (15 percent) have been severely maltreated, but this number deals only with official reports, and the actual number is much higher. Furthermore, it only includes those who have been the

CHECKPOINT 10.3	ALTERNATIVE FORMS OF FAMILY
Family household	A household comprising two or more people who are related by blood, marriage, or adoption.
Nonfamily household	A household consisting of a person who lives either alone or with nonrelatives.
Cohabitation	A couple sharing a home and a bed without being legally married.

victims of severe abuse and who clearly have been injured. The most common forms of child abuse are parents hitting their child with an object (20 percent); kicking or biting their child or hitting their child with their fists (10 percent); and physically beating up their child (5 percent) (Kimmel 2011). Fathers or father surrogates are most likely to commit these offenses.

The impact of child abuse is great, especially for the children involved, but also for the parents (or adults) and the larger society. Physical and emotional abuse

Curing Child Abuse

Domestic Violence

The Family and the Internet

There is great concern that the Internet, as well as the technologies needed to access it such as the computer, the iPhone, the iPad, and the like, has radically altered many things, including family life. Today people consume an average 12 hours of media a day at home compared to 5 hours a day in 1960. In the remainder of this box, we look at the impact of the Internet and related technologies on one upper-middle-class family.

Mr. and Mrs. Campbell live in a rented four-bedroom home in an affluent suburb of San Francisco (Richtel 2010a). The Campbells have two children, ages 16 and 8. Mr. Campbell has been involved in successful Internet businesses. Operating from home, he works with three computer screens simultaneously (sometimes adding a laptop and an iPad). His involvement, even obsession, with computer technology (he falls asleep with either a laptop or an iPhone on his chest and goes online as soon as he opens his eyes in the morning) has had a negative effect on his family.

When things are tough emotionally for Mr. Campbell, he deals with it by escaping into video games. When the family goes on vacation, he has a difficult time putting his devices aside and staying away from e-mail and the Internet. Both mother and daughter complain that Mr. Campbell prefers technology to his family.

With media consumption reaching an all-time high, how can families keep the Internet from taking over the time they would otherwise spend together? Should they be concerned about losing this time together?

Although Mrs. Campbell spends a lot of time on the Internet texting, on Facebook, and checking her own e-mail many times a day, she would love to see her husband spend less time with his technologies and more time with his family. However, she knows that he gets "crotchety" if he does not get his technology "fix." She feels she must accept the role that technology plays in their lives. Her understanding, however, does not contradict the fact that these technologies and the Internet have contributed to the innumerable stresses and conflicts in the family life of the Campbells and in the lives of many other families.

Think About It

Do you know people like Mr. and Mrs. Campbell? If so, what effect does their need to engage with technology have on their families? Do you know families in which technology plays a less prominent role? What differentiates these families from others?

and violence toward children can lead to an increased likelihood of cognitive impairment (lower IQ and levels of educational attainment), impaired ability to reason morally (a weakly developed conscience), and a greater likelihood of engaging in violence and crime. Such children are themselves more likely to be violent toward other children, including siblings, and later in life to abuse their own children, their spouse, and even elderly parents.

There is often a cycle of violence and abuse toward children that stretches across several generations (Steinmetz 1987). Many of the parents who mistreat and abuse their children were themselves victims as children and, as a result, may have developed mental and substance abuse problems that can increase their own likelihood of mistreating others.

There is also a cost to society; in the United States alone, the cost has been put at over $12 billion. These costs are traceable to social services provided to families, the lesser contributions of victims to society, and related criminal justice and health care activities. While there

Andrew Cherlin on Public Sociology, in His Own Words

I have written for, and spoken to, the print and electronic media about family and demographic issues since I took a job as an assistant professor of sociology at Johns Hopkins University in the late 1970s. . . .

To write for newspapers . . . I had to learn how to (1) engage the reader's interest, (2) make a single point, and (3) present my interpretation, all in about 700 words. I also had to be willing to accept failure. During my career, I have submitted more than 20 op-ed pieces to the *New York Times*, and the editors have accepted nine of them. That's actually a good batting average . . .

My early newspaper and magazine pieces led to telephone calls from reporters who wanted a quote from an academic expert for a story they were writing. Here I had to develop another skill: how to say something that helps the reader understand the topic in 25 words or less. It's harder than you might think to get to the heart of an issue in a sentence or two.

I have found that print (and now online) reporters can usually be trusted to put my remarks in the proper context. Many reporters cover family and demographic issues day after day, and they become quite knowledgeable. . . . Television, however, is another story. Typically, a harried producer who rarely covers the family will be given an assignment at 10:00 a.m., call me at 10:30, send a crew to film me by 2:00, and then splice five or ten seconds of my remarks into a piece that will run on the evening news at 6:30. Sometimes the producer will include nothing if the piece has to be shortened at the last minute. I often feel used and discarded by television, in contrast to my generally positive experiences with print, online, and radio media.

Overall, though, my work with the media has served me well. It has allowed me to place my ideas before a broad audience. It has also expanded the reach of my academic work.

SOURCE: Printed with the permission of Andrew Cherlin.

Think About It

Is there a need for sociologists who study the family, as Andrew Cherlin does, to share their ideas and findings directly with the public as well as with their peers? What do family members gain from such exposure to public sociology? What about legislators and policy makers on issues affecting the family?

---

are things that can be done to deal with adults involved in terms of intervention and prevention, the structure of society as a whole needs to be addressed in various ways. Of greatest importance is the need to change a culture where children are viewed as property that parents and other adults can treat, and abuse, in any way they want. Children also need to be seen as having human rights. In addition, children need to be better protected, helped, and treated by the various agencies involved. More generally, society and the government need to believe in and support a wide range of policies that are of benefit to children such as more and better child care.

Domestic Violence

Domestic violence entails the exertion of power over a partner in an intimate relationship through behavior that is intimidating, threatening, harassing, or harmful

(Carmody 2007). The spouse can be harmed physically, as well as sexually, emotionally, and psychologically; the violence can occur multiple times (Goodlin and Dunn 2011). A debate in this area is whether the concept of domestic violence should be restricted to physical violence, or whether abuse in all of these areas qualifies as domestic violence.

A great deal of research has been done on domestic violence, and several general conclusions can be drawn from this work:

- Women are about five times more likely than men to be victims.

- Women are about six times more likely to be assaulted by those they are intimate with (partner or former partner) than by strangers.

> **domestic violence** The exertion of power over a partner in an intimate relationship through behavior that is intimidating, threatening, harassing, or harmful.

Andrew Cherlin

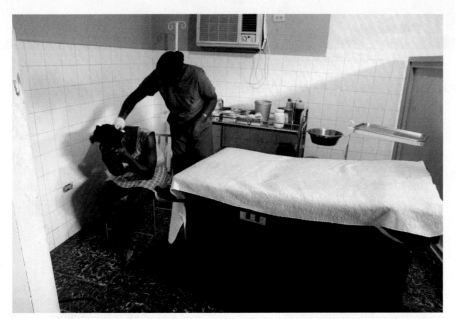

A victim of domestic violence in Haiti is treated at a hospital. Though police held her partner in custody, she wanted him freed and would not press charges. What makes some abused women reluctant to seek more effective help?

- One of the leading causes of injury to women is domestic violence.

- Among minority groups, blacks have the highest rate of such violence.

- Most likely to be victims are poor females between 16 and 24 years of age.

- It is difficult to leave a violent relationship, and the risk of serious, even fatal, injury is greatest when one does try to leave such a relationship.

- Domestic violence is a major cause of homelessness.

- About a third of all female homicide victims are killed by those who are intimates.

Because gender socialization often leads men to see violence as an appropriate means of communication, it follows that most abusers tend to be male. In addition to being very costly to victims and their families, domestic violence is costly to society. Those abused are not likely to be able to function as well in the larger society as those who are not victimized. For example, the abused have higher levels of absenteeism from work. Furthermore, society often needs to pay the costs associated with medical treatment, police involvement, court expenses, and shelters for those who have been victimized.

Elder Abuse

The elderly do not escape abuse merely because of their advanced age. This is certainly an ancient problem, although it has come to wide-scale public attention only in the last half century. In a large national study, about 10 percent of elderly respondents reported some type of abuse (Acierno et al. 2010). The elderly are abused in various ways including physically, psychologically, financially, sexually, and through neglect. Among other things, we know that elderly women are more likely to be abused than men, the very elderly (over 80 years of age) are most likely to be victims, and adult children and spouses are most likely to perpetrate the abuse. Beyond the elder abuse committed by family members, there is the fact that such abuse also takes place in residential care facilities for the elderly.

ASK YOURSELF

What do you think accounts for the fact that elder abuse is most often committed by members of the victim's family? Does your reason suggest any ways society can reduce this problem? How?

POVERTY AND THE FAMILY

There is a close relationship between family structure and poverty (Lichter 2007). For example, the poverty rate in 2010 in the United States for married-couple families was 8.8 percent, but for female-headed families it was almost five times as much (40.7 percent). The likelihood of poverty for female-headed families is much less in many other developed countries largely because of more generous social welfare programs. This concentration of poverty among female-headed households tends largely to reflect consequences of gender inequality.

The big debate here is not over the facts, but over whether the family structure causes poverty or whether poverty causes problems within the family. On the one hand, the argument is made that a weak family structure, one for example where women are left alone to raise children, causes poverty. Such women are apt to be poor because they are unlikely to be able to work, and the children are poor because they are not adequately supported by these women or their absent fathers. On the other hand, it is contended that poverty causes families to crumble. Women are left alone to raise children as the men leave because they cannot support them or because the mothers are more likely to qualify for welfare if the father is absent. The emotional and economic stresses associated with being poor are likely to put intolerable strains on the family.

Being unmarried is likely to be associated with poverty for women with children. Divorce is also likely to drive women, especially those who are already in a marginal economic situation, into poverty. More generally, divorce is likely to affect almost all women adversely. The only debate in this area is how badly women will be affected and how much they will be hurt economically, as well as in other ways.

This Waco, Texas, family's possessions are on the street because the parents and their five children have been evicted. The Great Recession has brought economic and other hardships to many U.S. families.

THE FAMILY AND CONSUMPTION

The lingering effects of the Great Recession have caused many changes in American society and throughout the world. The family is certainly no exception. While the family was affected in many different ways in various locales, the concern here is changes in the consumption patterns of American families. For many families, these changes have been made necessary by lost jobs, reductions in pay, declines in home values and even foreclosures, and the withering of investment accounts, retirement funds, and college savings plans.

Clearly, many families have had less, sometimes a lot less, to spend on consumption of all kinds, especially consumption of that which is not needed for survival. The latter includes items besides food, shelter, and (some) clothing. Even if the family's economic position has not declined markedly, a perception has still emerged among many that they could, or at least should, not consume the way they did in the boom period of the early twenty-first century. Many families responded not only by consuming less, but also by reducing their level of debt and by saving much more. The savings rate in the United States increased from an average of about 1 to 2 percent of income in 2000 to about 8 percent in 2010 before declining to about 4 percent in 2011 (see Figure 10.6).

Some families are not only buying less but also concentrating more on engaging in family activities, especially those that cost little or nothing (Cave 2010). Activities such as watching television together (or alone), reading, socializing with friends or family, and going to museums are more in vogue in these more difficult economic times. In addition, family members are more willing to discuss their reduced circumstances and changed patterns of consumption among themselves as well as with those in other families. While such topics may have been a source of embarrassment at one time, the realization that many families are in the same situation has made it easier to discuss them publicly. For example, it is easier for many to tell their children that the family needs to eat out far less often and to tell friends that they cannot afford to go out to dinner. Families are also willing to discuss more openly their financial straits and even to share stories about the bad economic decisions they might have made in the past (Tugend 2010).

Some families are even more willing to reevaluate the whole idea of the consumer culture in which they were so immersed before the Great Recession. There is even a questioning of what Juliet Schor (1998) called the "work-and-spend" syndrome that many had embraced. That is, families are wondering whether one or both partners really have to work as long and as hard as they did in the past just to be able to consume more—to buy more expensive

Homeless Families

FIGURE 10.6 • Household Savings Rates in the United States, 1959–2012

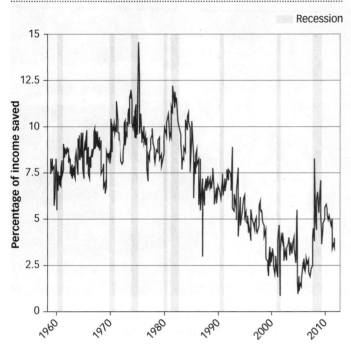

SOURCE: FRED® Economic Data, U.S. Department of Commerce: Bureau of Economic Analysis, Personal Income, and Outlays.

goods, services, and experiences. Some families are even coming to accept the ideas of the "voluntary simplicity" movement (Elgin 2010) by downsizing their homes, getting rid of all sorts of things they may have never needed in the first place, and in the end living a simpler, far less expensive lifestyle. Many are coming to realize that "the acquisition of material goods doesn't bring happiness" (Rosenbloom 2010).

GENDER INEQUALITIES

Intimate relationships, especially marriages, are unequal as far as the men and women involved are concerned. Marriages from the point of view of men and women can be so different that they seem like completely different systems. These inequalities take several forms (Shehan and Cody 2007).

The first is inequality in the amount of time devoted to household tasks. Although there is evidence that this gap is shrinking, especially because men are spending more time on housework (Sayer 2005), at least until recently women on average spent about twice as much time (19 hours a week) on housework as men (10 hours). However, we know that the intersection of race and class can impact the likelihood of further involvement by men in housework. In addition, men spend more time on tasks that are discretionary, at least

to some degree, while women are more likely to perform regular, repetitive labor. Mothers are more likely to maintain the children, while fathers are more likely to engage in recreational activities with the children. The disparity is even greater when it comes to the care of the ill and the elderly; this is almost always the near-total responsibility of females.

Then there are various gender inequalities in power and decision making. As in sociology in general, power here is defined as the ability to impose one's will on others despite their opposition. This can involve forcing a spouse to do something or to define a situation in a particular way. In heterosexual marriages, men are favored in terms of power within the marital relationship because of their greater size and strength, they are likely to earn more money, and they are likely to dominate conversations, thereby swinging decisions their way. In addition, male power tends to be institutionalized and supported by religions and their customs (especially by Evangelical Christians, Hasidic Jews, the Amish, and Mormons) as well as by governments and their policies. The latter often assume that husbands are the household heads and are responsible for the support of wives and children, and that wives are supposed to take care of the household and the children.

As we saw above, women are more likely to be the victims of intimate violence than men even though men are more likely to be victimized by violence in general. Globally, in 1993, the United Nations adopted the Declaration on the Elimination of Violence against Women. Within the United Nations, UN Women (previously UNIFEM) is particularly concerned about the violence perpetrated globally against women and girls, especially in the family. There is a strong preference for male children throughout much of the world with the result that female embryos are more likely to be aborted, female infants are more likely to be the victims of infanticide, and female children are more likely to be the victims of violence.

Globally, wife-beating is the most common form of family violence. In some parts of the world, this is taken to extreme lengths in which wives are beaten to death. Brides may be burned to death because of (supposed) infidelity, or even because the bride's family was unable to pay the dowry in full to the husband. In some parts of the world, women are stoned to death for such offenses. The movie *The Stoning of Soraya M.* (2008), based on a 1994 novel of the same name, tells the true story of an Iranian woman who was stoned to death by members of the community, including her father and sons, on the basis of a false accusation by her husband—who wanted another woman—that she had been unfaithful to him. Some cultures support honor killings, or the killing of females because they have engaged in such "dishonorable" behaviors as infidelity, same-sex sexual relations, wanting out of an arranged marriage, seeking a marriage on their own, or even refusing to adhere to the dress code. There has been a good deal of publicity about, and public uproar over, honor killings in places like Pakistan, Egypt, Turkey, and Iran.

DIVORCE

Divorce increased in western nations during the twentieth century. The United States has one of the highest divorce rates in the world (Amato and James 2010) (see Table 10.3); however, the often-repeated "statistic" that half of all U.S. marriages end in divorce is inaccurate.

The once dramatic differences between the United States and Europe have declined, mostly because of increases in the divorce rate across Europe; Europe has become more like the United States in terms of divorce. For example, "between 1971 and 2007, the crude divorce rate increased from 0.73 to 2.8 in Belgium, from 0.88 to 2.0 in the Netherlands, from 1.2 to 2.4 in the United Kingdom, from 0.42 to 1.2 in Greece, and from 0.32 to 0.80 in Italy" (Amato and James 2010: 3).

Factors in Divorce

Regardless of how prevalent or rare it is, divorce is the best-known way of leaving a marriage. Divorce is a formal and legal mechanism that relates to legal marriages. Many marriages end with separations that become permanent without a divorce. Other intimate relationships, even those that last a long time, do not require a divorce; they end as informally as they began.

Divorce is often the result of a litany of family problems, for example, violence and abuse, that may occur over a long period of time before a divorce is ever contemplated, let alone takes place. Divorce itself can be seen as a problem, as well as one that creates many other problems, but it also can be seen as a solution to many problems. Divorce allows a spouse to get out of a bad, even disastrous, relationship. In fact, to some, it is the relationship, especially a "bad" marriage, that is the problem and not the divorce. Thus, we should not simply assume—as many do—that divorce is in itself a problem.

An important factor in divorce today in the United States, and in the Global North in general, is the increasing emphasis on the self and individualism. This is also linked to the idea of the pure relationship

Women in Mexico City recently staged a one-day strike against housework, so some men, including Robert Delgadillo shown here with his wife Maria Aguirre, had to pick up the slack. Do you know any couples who spend equal amounts of time on housework?

TABLE 10.3 • Countries with the Highest Divorce Rates, 2008

Country	Crude Divorce Rate (number of divorces per 1,000 population)	Divorce to Marriage Ratio
Russia	4.7	51%
Belarus	4.1	45%
United States	3.6	53%
Gibraltar	3.2	48%
Moldova	3.1	42%
Belgium	3.0	71%
Lithuania	3.0	53%
Cuba	2.9	56%
Czech Republic	2.9	66%
Switzerland	2.8	51%

discussed above. As we saw, in such relationships, including marital relationships, the partners do not necessarily feel that they are locked into them for a lifetime, or even an extended period of time. Rather,

Gender Prejudice

　TYPES OF FAMILY CONFLICT

Child abuse	Child abuse can lead to impaired cognitive and moral reasoning abilities in victims as well as a greater likelihood of engaging in violence toward others throughout life.
Elder abuse	Abuse and neglect of the elderly is most likely to be committed by family members; women and the very old are most often victims.
Domestic violence	Women are far more likely than men to be victims; domestic violence is a major cause of homelessness.
Poverty	Female-headed families are far more likely to be poor.
Gender inequalities	Mothers spend more time caring for children, the ill, and the elderly than men; many religious traditions grant men more power in marital relationships.
Divorce	Divorce has grown more common and more acceptable, in part because of no-fault laws and women's increasing financial independence.

they feel that they are in a relationship as long as it continues to work for *them*. Once individuals come to the conclusion that the relationship is no longer working for them, they are free to leave. Indeed, some take the view that they have an obligation to themselves to leave because they should not jeopardize their own need to have a satisfying life.

In the past, there was a tendency to value positively all marriages that remained intact—that did not end in divorce or in other ways. In many ways, a bad marriage can be a far greater problem than one that ends in divorce. For example, children in unhappily married families tend to feel highly neglected and humiliated (Kimmel 2011: 179). As acceptance of divorce has spread, the negative attitudes and social sanctions aimed at those who divorce have declined.

ASK YOURSELF

What are some of the reasons that divorce has become more socially acceptable? What specific norms and values about individuals, families, and the institution of marriage have changed to make this acceptance possible? Do you think the increase in the number of divorces has had an impact on society at large? If so, what sort of impact?

Not only have negative attitudes, norms, and values as they relate to divorce declined, but so have the material circumstances surrounding divorce. Of prime importance is the fact that women today are likely to be better equipped materially to handle divorce. Among

other things, they are better educated and more likely to be in the labor force. Thus, they may be more willing to seek a divorce because they can better afford to be on their own. Furthermore, dissatisfied husbands are more likely to leave a marriage when they know that their wives can not only survive it economically, but be financially independent after the divorce. Changes in the law are another important material factor that has followed from changes in the norms and values that relate to divorce. One important example is no-fault divorce, which not only has made it easier for people to divorce but also seems to be associated with an increase in the divorce rate. This law has also acted on the larger culture, helping it to become even more accepting of divorce.

A long list of risk factors has been associated with the likelihood of divorce, including having relatively little education, marrying as a teenager, whether or not the couple cohabited before marriage, poverty, having divorced parents, infidelity, alcohol or drug abuse, mismanaged finances, and domestic violence. The reasons for divorce in Europe are very similar to those found in the United States. In terms of the nature of the relationship, marriages are more likely to be stable, and less likely to end in divorce, when couples handle their disagreements and anger well, such as by having a sense of humor about disagreements. Conversely, divorce is more likely when couples are contemptuous of, or belligerent toward, one another, or react defensively to disagreements (Gottman et al. 1998; Hetherington 2003).

GLOBAL FAMILIES

Just as the nation-state is eroding in the face of globalization, it could be argued that the traditional family, deeply embedded in a national context, is also declining. It is no longer necessary that family members live in the same country, have the same passport, be of the same ethnicity, or share a household in a given locale. Characteristics that used to separate people, and make creating global families difficult or impossible, are less important in the global age. National hostilities, religious differences, and even great geographic distances matter less to family formation today than they did in the past (Beck and Beck-Gernsheim 2012).

On the one hand, this clearly makes possible, and even highly likely, a wide range of new family types and configurations. For example, it is increasingly possible for family members, even spouses, to live in different countries, even on different continents, and to function quite well (Nobles 2011).

On the other hand, these new realities also create many new possibilities for conflict within the family. That is, family members are now bringing to the family new and far broader stresses and strains of various types; clashes of different languages,

Madonna and her adopted Malawian daughter Mercy James visited Malawi on a charity tour in 2010. The increased ease of some global flows have made families like Madonna's more possible.

cultures, religions, and races create all new points of potential conflict and hostility. However, these differences are also likely to enrich the family, as well as the larger society, in various significant ways. As globalization increases, new hybrid forms of the family will be created, resulting in innovative and interesting differences within and between families. New combinations of, and interactions between, hybrid cultures will result in unforeseen sociological developments, such as wholly new customs and traditions. Another way of putting this is to say that global families are increasingly liquid (Bauman 2000). That is, they no longer—if they ever did—form solid and immutable structures that are impervious to outside, especially global, influences. Families are subject to global flows of all types, and they and their members are increasingly part of those global flows.

While there are great variations in family forms throughout the world, there are also great commonalities. Thus, many of the general ideas discussed throughout this chapter apply globally. It is well beyond the scope of this section to describe similarities and differences in the family throughout the world. There are sociologists, engaged in the comparative analysis of families in various societies, who spend their entire careers doing just that (Goode 1963; Ingoldsby and Smith 2006). Globalization on the whole is more about global flows and how these flows relate to the family than it is about comparing families across the world (Ritzer 2010c). In this section, then, we will examine at least some of the global flows that involve or affect the family. It is clear that many families are actively

involved in global flows of one kind or another, and that no family is totally unaffected by those global flows (Karraker 2008; Trask 2010).

GLOBAL FLOWS THAT INVOLVE THE FAMILY

Global flows that involve the family take four major forms. First, entire families, even extended families, can move from one part of the globe to another with relative ease (assuming they have the resources to do so). They can do so on vacation, in relationship to a temporary job change, or permanently.

Second, individual family members can move to a different part of the world and then bring the rest of the family along later. It is ordinarily the case that males are those doing the moving. Once they are secure enough economically in their new location, they are then able to bring over the rest of the family. Of course, it is possible that males will make new lives for themselves in the new locale and leave their families behind in their countries of origin. With increasing economic independence, more women are now moving first and then bringing the remainder of their family over (or not). However, many women move globally in low-paying, low-status jobs, for example, as a care worker or, by force, in the global sex trade. Such women are unlikely to be in a strong enough economic position to enable other family members to join them.

Third, individuals can immigrate to create a new family. For example, there are many marriage bureaus in developed countries that are in the business of bringing together men

TABLE 10.5 • Top 10 Countries of Origin for Adoptions to the United States, 2011

Country of Origin	Number of Adoptions
China	2,587
Ethiopia	1,732
Russia	952
South Korea	736
Ukraine	640
Philippines	229
India	226
Colombia	216
Uganda	207
Taiwan	205

SOURCE: From *Intercountry Adoption Report*, Bureau of Consular Affairs, U.S. Department of State, 2011.

from those countries with women who are usually from less developed countries. Great differences between such men and women often create enormous problems for the relationship, however. For one, there is great economic disparity between the spouses. For another, the women often come from societies that are unstable politically and economically, and this makes it difficult for them to adapt to a more stable environment. Finally, marriage bureaus often portray the women as fitting traditional gender expectations, but when they arrive it may turn out that they do not really measure up to those expectations. Overall, these differences put females in a weak position vis-à-vis the males, and they are therefore more vulnerable to abuse of various kinds.

Fourth, transnational adoptions generally involve the flow of children from less to more developed countries (Marre and Briggs 2009). The United States is the world leader in the adoption of children from other countries, while very few American children are adopted elsewhere. See Table 10.5 for adoptions to the United States. Adopting a child from another part of the world transforms the family in many ways. There are also various problems associated with this, such as the health risks associated with being born, and having spent at least some time, in less developed countries. There are also stresses involved in the differences between the cultures from which the children came and the cultures of the countries to which they have been sent. This is especially a problem if the adopted children are not infants.

GLOBAL FLOWS THAT AFFECT THE FAMILY

As a liquid phenomenon in a liquid world, the global family is affected by, and affects, all of the other liquid phenomena that make up the global world. We will examine just two of them in this section.

Global Migration

The global family is affected by population flows of various kinds. Of utmost importance is the high rate of global migration, both legal and illegal (see Chapter 14). Among other things, this means that very different people from very different parts of the world are coming together in greater numbers than ever before. Some will settle and marry in diasporic communities composed of people like them; many others will not. Those who do not are likely to create families with mates who are very different from themselves in terms of place of origin, race, ethnicity, religion, and the like (Qian and Lichter 2011). As you recently learned, those entering hybrid families are likely to encounter various difficulties and hostilities. Such problems are likely to be greatest for undocumented immigrants, whose family problems are compounded by the fact that they are in the country illegally.

Global Trafficking

Human trafficking involves selling and buying humans as products. It is likely to affect the family in many ways (Jakobi 2012). Children are sometimes trafficked for the purpose of illegal adoption. As with legal adoption, the children generally flow from poor, weak countries to those that are rich and powerful. Recall from Chapter 1 that women are trafficked for purposes of prostitution and forced marriage, both of which have the potential to disrupt family life. Then there is the illegal global traffic in human organs. Family members in developed countries who cannot obtain needed organs locally are better able to survive because of this traffic. Poor people in less developed countries sell organs not critical to their lives, which are then transported to developed countries and implanted into well-to-do recipients (Scheper-Hughes 2001). Although the poor in less developed countries do receive some money for their organs, this is but another form of exploitation of the global poor by the global rich. It is a particularly heinous form of exploitation since the poor must sacrifice one or more of the things that make them human in order to survive.

The main point is that the family today is an integral part of globalization, which it is both affecting and being affected by. There is no such thing as a typical global family; at best, there are many global families. More to the point, those people involved in today's families are at

The Role of Families in Improving Relations between the United States and Cuba

Relations between the United States and Cuba began to unravel when a communist regime headed by Fidel Castro took power in 1959. By 1962, the United States had placed an embargo on Cuba, and by 1963, all travel between the two countries had been banned.

A number of Cubans had fled the country for the United States prior to the travel embargo, and others fled later either illegally or as a result of temporary thaws in the relationship between Cuba and the United States. Most of these Cubans settled in South Florida. Almost a million of them live there today, and they represent a potent economic and political force. Many, especially the early immigrants, were middle-class and opposed to Castro and communism, which sought to redistribute their wealth more equitably among Cubans. For decades they resisted bettering relations with Cuba, but in recent years those relations have improved somewhat, especially among the younger Cuban Americans who arrived after the mid-1990s as a result of a special visa program.

Many Cuban Americans left family members in Cuba, and for decades it was difficult or impossible for them to see those they had left behind. However, in the last decade, and especially in the last few years, travel restrictions for family members have eased considerably. In 2009, President Obama loosened restrictions on shipping and travel between the two countries; there are no longer any restrictions on flights by Cuban Americans to visit family members in Cuba. For its part, Cuba now allows its citizens to own cell phones and computers, thereby

This mural in Florida reflects the influence of Cuban immigrants and the fact that Hispanics make up about 13 percent of the state's registered voters. Can families seeking to preserve their ties to relatives overseas succeed on their own in improving relationships between the United States and Cuba?

easing contact with family members in the United States.

Cuba has also made it easier for Cubans to buy homes and businesses. As a result, Cuban Americans are sending all sorts of products to their families in Cuba, thus making it possible for those family members to open an array of small businesses. Furthermore, increasing amounts of money are flowing to Cuba to help family members buy (and sell) property.

There are still those in the United States (and undoubtedly in Cuba) who would like to reinstitute restrictions on travel and shipping. Some Americans, especially Cuban Americans in Congress, fear that the Cuban regime is being strengthened by these contacts.

Regardless of politics, it is the drive to connect to family members that is doing much to overcome the lingering hostility between the two nations. As one expert on Cuba put it, "In Washington the whole debate over normalizing relations in Cuba is dead in the water. . . . Meanwhile, in Miami, Cuban-Americans are normalizing relations one by one" (Alvarez 2011: A3).

Think About It

How many different types of global flows are helping Cuban and Cuban American families "normalize" their relationships? Why are younger family members more open to using these flows?

EFFECTS OF GLOBALIZATION ON THE FAMILY

Voluntary global flows	Physical moves, such as for vacation, a job change, adoption of a child, or migration.
Human trafficking	The buying and selling of humans as products.

the intersection of innumerable global flows and are, as a result, enmeshed in constantly changing intimate relationships of all sorts. This may be as good a definition as any of the family in the global age.

SUMMARY

The family is a crucial social institution that has changed in many ways over the last century. Marriage is a legal union of two people, but it can involve not only monogamy, but also polygamy and cenogamy. In an intimate relationship, partners have a close, personal, and domestic relationship with one another.

The traditional nuclear family now accounts for only about a fifth of all households. To explain the decline of the nuclear family, Cherlin focuses on the deinstitutionalization of marriage, while Giddens posits that pure relationships are more fragile than other forms of marriage. Simmel suggests that some degree of secrecy is necessary to a successful marriage.

The structure of intimate relationships has changed over time. Cohabitation and single-parent households have increased in the United States, and gay and lesbian families are more visible.

Abuse and domestic violence severely affect many families, as does poverty. Gender inequality in marriages is visible in partners' decision making and power distribution, and in the different amounts of time they devote to household tasks.

Global flows that affect the family take four major forms: Entire families can move from one part of the globe to another with relative ease; individual family members can move to a different part of the world and bring the rest of the family later; individuals can emigrate to create a new family; and transnational adoptions can bring children from less developed to more developed countries. Global migration, trafficking, economics, and conflict all affect the global family.

KEY TERMS

Cenogamy, 281
Cohabitation, 289
Companionate love, 282
Companionate marriage, 284
Deinstitutionalization, 283
Domestic violence, 294
Endogamy, 281
Exogamy, 281

Family, 281
Family household, 288
Individualized marriage, 284
Institutional marriage, 284
Intimate relationship, 282
Marriage, 281
Monogamy, 281
Nonfamily household, 288

Nuclear family, 283
Passionate love, 282
Polyandry, 281
Polygamy, 281
Polygyny, 281
Pure relationship, 286

REVIEW QUESTIONS

1. How has the structure of the family changed in the United States since 1900?

2. In spite of the changes, in what ways does the family seem resilient?

3. What about marriage makes it important? Despite its importance, what are some problems that arise from marriage and the families formed through marriage?

4. What forms can intimate relationships take? Do you think that some forms of relationships in the United States are valued more highly than others? Do you think these values will change in the future? Why or why not?

5. Recent studies show that one out of every six relationships is started on an Internet dating site. In what ways are these dating sites reflective of the changes in marriage in the United States?

6. What are the causes of divorce? Do you agree with the view that there is too much divorce in the United States today?

7. What are some general conclusions sociologists have made about domestic violence? Where is there still debate? What are some other common problems that arise within families?

8. Many sociologists see a close relationship between family structure and poverty. What is this relationship? What role does gender play? What are some contrasting viewpoints?

9. How have the Internet and new social media changed relationships in the family?

10. How do global flows such as migration and trafficking affect the family?

APPLYING THE SOCIOLOGICAL IMAGINATION

The television program *Modern Family* depicts a diversity of intimate relationships and family structures. Nontraditional family structures have become increasingly prevalent in the United States. For this exercise, choose two other currently popular television shows and describe how they portray the types of relationships discussed in this chapter. What are the differences in how familial relationships are portrayed in each show? Despite the differences, what similarities do the familial relationships have? What structural factors (e.g., network, time of day aired, target audience) could lead to the portrayal of differences that you noted?

STUDENT STUDY SITE

Sharpen your skills with SAGE edge at **edge.sagepub.com/ritzeressentials**

SAGE edge for students provides a personalized approach to help you accomplish your coursework goals in an easy-to-use learning environment.

Students recite the Koran, the holy book of Islam, near an important shrine west of Tripoli (Libya). Sociologists are concerned not with the truth of any particular religion but rather with the role belief and ritual play in human lives. Does religion have a role in your life?

RELIGION AND EDUCATION

11

LEARNING OBJECTIVES

1 Identify the major components of religion—beliefs, rituals, and experiences.

2 Describe the types of religious institutions.

3 Describe the relationship between globalization and the world's major religions.

4 Discuss the relationship between education, commercialization, and consumption.

5 Describe inequality in education, its sources, and its effects.

Proposed by Charles Darwin in 1859 and affirmed by countless twentieth-century biologists and geneticists, the theory of evolution has achieved scientific consensus as an explanation of the natural origin of humankind over time. In contrast, the idea of intelligent design sees the overwhelming complexity of the universe as the work of a rational, omnipotent designer, whether a god, an alien, or some other source.

Since 1925, U.S. laws and court cases have challenged the teaching of first evolution, then religious creationism (essentially, the belief that the biblical God created the universe), and finally intelligent design in public schools. Advocates of evolution-only science programs cite the First Amendment's Establishment Clause, which sets forth the separation of church and state, as well as the imperative to offer ideas that are scientifically valid in the classroom. Intelligent design proponents believe evolution and intelligent design should be taught equally, and that students should be encouraged to decide the controversy for themselves.

Sociology studies the central role of religion as a force in many lives.

Even though intelligent design was developed to sidestep the religious nature of the creationism argument, its acceptance of an otherworldly, untestable force is deeply rooted in religious belief and a nonscientific framing of the world. Humans have explained life as the work of an omnipotent, sentient god or gods since before recorded history, passing creation myths down across many centuries and even millennia of socialization. Many advocates of evolution thus contend that intelligent design has no place in educational courses dedicated to evidence-based knowledge.

While the debate over evolution has been going on for more than a century, it is but one indication of a larger phenomenon in the modern world: our efforts to define the relationship between science and religion. One view of this relationship privileges science over religion, saying that science undermines the credibility of religion and leads us to abandon it as an outdated worldview characteristic of premodern times. Another view does the opposite, saying that when science challenges religious convictions—such as literal interpretations of the biblical creation story—we should reject science in favor of a religious perspective. Yet another position calls for treating science and religion as each having its own proper place, rejecting the idea that making such a choice is necessary or wise.

We'll see in this chapter that sociology takes no position in the debate. Its purpose in studying religion is rather to understand the role it plays as a central force in many lives. ●

Religion has been a central feature in the evolution of the human species and continues to be of great importance today (Bellah 2011). For that reason, it is one of sociology's longest-running concerns. Indeed, the early giants in the field were all affected by, and interested in, religion. Given this history, and the importance of religion to society, it is not surprising that religion became a central concern within later sociology.

RELIGION

The definition of religion employed in this chapter is largely derived from Durkheim's ([1912] 1965) classic statement: **Religion** is a social phenomenon that consists of beliefs about the sacred; the experiences, practices, and rituals that reinforce those beliefs; and the community that shares similar beliefs and practices (Kurtz 2012).

COMPONENTS OF RELIGION

Three of the major components of religion are beliefs, rituals, and experiences.

Beliefs

Every religion has a set of interrelated **beliefs**, or ideas that explain the world and identify what should be sacred or held in awe, that is, the religion's "ultimate concerns." Religious beliefs have been shaped over thousands of years, and both are embedded in religious traditions and serve as the "raw material" for new religions.

Durkheim ([1912] 1965: 14) wrote that religion deals with "things which surpass the limits of our knowledge." Others have used such words as *holy, supernatural,* or *sacred* to describe this realm. Durkheim preferred the last of these terms. He argued that all human experience could be divided into two categories, the **sacred**, or what is of ultimate concern, and the **profane**, or the ordinary and mundane. People can come to *believe* that virtually anything is sacred—a deity, a place (Jerusalem or Mecca),

---

> **religion** A social phenomenon that consists of beliefs about the sacred; the experiences, practices, and rituals that reinforce those beliefs; and the community that shares similar beliefs and practices.
>
> **beliefs** Ideas that explain the world and identify what should be sacred or held in awe, that is, a religion's ultimate concerns.
>
> **sacred** To Durkheim, that which has been defined as being of ultimate concern.
>
> **profane** To Durkheim, that which has not been defined as sacred, or that which is ordinary and mundane.

---

a particular time or season (Ramadan or Diwali), an idea (freedom), or even a thing (an animal, a mountain, a tree, a canyon, a flag, or a rock). The sacred is treated with respect, and one's relation to it is often defined in rituals (see below): You might bow when passing in front of an altar or take off your shoes when entering a temple. People believe that anything that is not considered sacred is profane.

Each religious tradition weaves together many different and interdependent beliefs. These include beliefs about creation and suffering, as well as ethical standards for judging proper behavior. For example, when Muslims declare in their daily prayers that they believe God is the Most Merciful and the Most Compassionate, it means that their behavior must reflect God's mercy (Abd-Allah 2005).

Beliefs are often presented in sacred stories and scriptures. They address questions about the origin and meaning of life, theories about why the world was created, and explanations of suffering and death. They first express a *worldview*—that is, a culture's most comprehensive image of the ways in which life—nature, self, and society—is ordered (Geertz 1973). That worldview, in turn, shapes an *ethos*, which "expresses a culture's and a people's basic attitude about themselves and the world in general" (Geertz 1973: 173).

These beliefs are models both of and for reality. They provide believers with information and a framework for interpreting the world around them. As models *for* reality, however, beliefs show how the world should be versus how it really is, often prompting the believer to act. Mahatma Gandhi believed that the world was ultimately grounded in truth and nonviolence, and that a just god ruled the world. His noncooperation with the British Empire on behalf of the struggle for Indian independence was not only political resistance but also an act of faith. He saw no reason to be fearful of unjust political powers that were simply under the illusion that they were in control of the world. Hindu and Buddhist theories of *ahimsa,* nonharmfulness or nonviolence, not only explained the real power behind the universe for Gandhi but also gave him a guide for how to act.

Most religious belief systems include a *cosmogony,* a story about how and why the world was created, which usually links the believers to the act of creation.

Finally, every religious tradition provides a *theodicy,* an explanation for the presence of evil, suffering, and death. Most explanations of this type identify the source of evil in the world. How a religion recommends confronting evil may affect everything from individual beliefs and decisions to a nation's foreign policy. We can find a wide range of

Religious Involvement

The city of Mecca in Saudi Arabia is a sacred place. The birthplace of Muhammad, it is the holiest city in Islam and the site of a mandatory pilgrimage for all who are able. Non-Muslims are forbidden to enter.

explanations in the world's religions for the existence of suffering: It may be seen as punishment for sinful behavior, the result of a battle between evil and good, or just part of the natural cycles of life and death.

One of the most difficult dilemmas for any religion is to explain why good people suffer and bad people sometimes flourish. While the suffering of the righteous is problematic, most religious explanations suggest that ethical behavior will eventually be rewarded. Most mainstream religions suggest that suffering is just part of the way the universe functions, so everyone is subject to it at one time or another. It is how you deal with suffering that is most important.

Rituals

In most religious traditions, simply believing is never enough; one also has to act. The belief systems of religious traditions are loaded with rituals that reinforce those beliefs, serve as reminders, and help believers enact their beliefs in the world. A **ritual** is a set of regularly repeated, prescribed, and traditional behaviors that serve to symbolize some value or belief (Kurtz 2012). Rituals are enacted during ceremonies and festivals, such as funerals and weddings. In other words, rituals are part of the **rites of passage** that surround major transitions in life, such as marriage and death. Also included under the heading of rituals are spiritual practices such as personal prayer and attending worship services.

Rituals come in many forms. Some, such as prayer, chanting, singing, and dancing, help people communicate or show devotion to the gods. Some, such as mantras and meditations, help believers organize their personal and

social lives. Some frame daily life, like those relating to diet, hygiene, and sexual practices, while others celebrate cycles of nature and build community, like holidays and seasonal festivals.

Rituals solve problems of personal and collective life by providing time-tested actions, words, and sentiments for every occasion. When addressing serious problems, such as death, violence, natural disasters, or social crises, people often use rituals to

1. identify the source of the problem,

2. characterize it as evil,

3. mark boundaries between "us" and "others," and

4. give them some means of working toward a solution, or at least the satisfaction that they are doing something about the problem.

In times of crisis, rituals can help people transform tragedy into opportunity. They build a sense of solidarity

> **ritual** A set of regularly repeated, prescribed, and traditional behaviors that serve to symbolize some value or belief.
>
> **rites of passage** Rituals that surround major transitions in life, such as birth, puberty, marriage, and death.

that provides support for the suffering and reinforces the authority of the social order and the institutions that sponsor the rituals, especially when they are threatened. Rituals provide a theory of evil and focus participants' attention on some abstract issue, a personified devil or mythical figure, or a human enemy who needs to be denounced or attacked.

ASK YOURSELF

Which religious rituals have you been involved in or witnessed in your life? Consider those of your own religion, if any, and those of other religions to which you have been exposed through friends or relatives. What was the stated purpose of these rituals? Were there other reasons for these rituals that were less obvious? If so, what were they?

Most religions are marked by ritual, including those like Christian baptism that signal an individual's entry into the community of the faithful. What religious rituals have you witnessed or participated in?

Participants usually believe that their rituals are effective and remember the stories from their culture or religion that remind them of their efficacy. Although partly a rational process, rituals as symbols also evoke sentiments and emotions that go beyond rationality. When a traditional ritual is used to solve personal or social troubles, it gains new authority and helps to sustain old habits and preserves the society and its institutions.

Religious rituals are also crucial for social change and cultural innovation, especially when traditional rituals can be transformed for revolutionary purposes. One example is Gandhi's use of religious processions, prayers, and scripture readings to mobilize his fellow Indians, as brothers and sisters of the same god, to demand their freedom from the British Empire. In another example, in 2011 and 2013, the Muslim Friday prayers in Egypt became occasions for large gatherings on Friday afternoons that moved from prayer to protest.

Moreover, religious rituals often mark a **liminal period**, or a special time set apart from ordinary reality (Turner 1967). The sacred time during a religious ceremony may involve an inversion of apparent reality, giving hope for the oppressed that they will be liberated, for the sad that they will be comforted, and for the last that they shall be first. In the traditional Catholic Carnival ritual preceding Lent

(a period of penitence), the norms of appropriate behavior appear to be suspended as the celebrants sing, dance, and drink to excess. This helps encourage the revelers to overthrow authority. In the liminal period where authority is defeated by youthful energy, the cycles of nature replace winter with spring, resurrecting hope in the hearts of the celebrants.

Experience

The combination of beliefs, rituals, and other practices forms the variety of religious experiences for believers regardless of which tradition they celebrate. Much of the human community views the world through a religious lens and constructs an identity around religious affiliation and experiences, such as prayer or attendance at religious services. In a survey of 40 countries, large numbers of people, especially in Africa, Latin America, and parts of Asia, reported religion and religious experiences to be very important in their lives (see Figure 11.1).

Even in the United States, 59 percent of respondents report that religion is very important to them. Moreover, 58 percent say that they pray daily. Approximately two-thirds of American women, people over 65, and people earning less than $30,000 a year report that they pray daily (see Figure 11.2).

> **liminal period** A period, or a special time, set apart from ordinary reality.

Religion and Cultural Studies

FIGURE 11.1 • Importance of Religion Worldwide

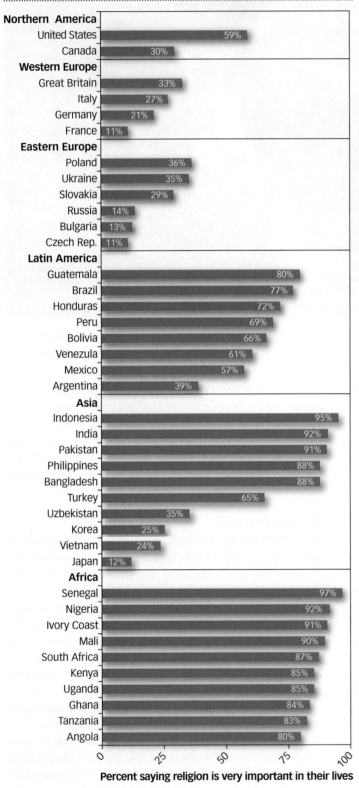

Northern America
- United States: 59%
- Canada: 30%

Western Europe
- Great Britain: 33%
- Italy: 27%
- Germany: 21%
- France: 11%

Eastern Europe
- Poland: 36%
- Ukraine: 35%
- Slovakia: 29%
- Russia: 14%
- Bulgaria: 13%
- Czech Rep.: 11%

Latin America
- Guatemala: 80%
- Brazil: 77%
- Honduras: 72%
- Peru: 69%
- Bolivia: 66%
- Venezuela: 61%
- Mexico: 57%
- Argentina: 39%

Asia
- Indonesia: 95%
- India: 92%
- Pakistan: 91%
- Philippines: 88%
- Bangladesh: 88%
- Turkey: 65%
- Uzbekistan: 35%
- Korea: 25%
- Vietnam: 24%
- Japan: 12%

Africa
- Senegal: 97%
- Nigeria: 92%
- Ivory Coast: 91%
- Mali: 90%
- South Africa: 87%
- Kenya: 85%
- Uganda: 85%
- Ghana: 84%
- Tanzania: 83%
- Angola: 80%

(Scale: 0, 25, 50, 75, 100)

Percent saying religion is very important in their lives

SOURCE: *U.S. Stands Alone in Its Embrace of Religion among Wealthy Nations*, December 19, 2002. Pew Global Attitudes Project, Pew Research Center.

Interestingly, a negative relationship exists between wealth and religiosity, with people living in poorer nations being more religious than those in wealthy countries (see Figure 11.3). The major exception is the United States. Religion is much more important to Americans than it is to people living in other wealthy nations. In African countries, no fewer than eight in ten report religion as very important, as do a majority of all Latin Americans (except Argentinians). Nine in ten of those in the predominantly Muslim countries (e.g., Indonesia, Pakistan, Mali, and Senegal) view religion as very important.

CIVIL RELIGION

The experiences discussed to this point in this section relate to organized religion. However, many religious experiences occur outside of, and side-by-side with, those that occur in those religions. One set of such experiences has been particularly important to Americans—**civil religion**, or the beliefs, practices, and symbols that a nation holds sacred (Yamane 2007). This idea has a long history in philosophy and sociology. However, it was an essay by Robert Bellah in 1967 that gave this idea broad visibility. He argued that civil religion has existed in American society since its founding. It exists, among other places, in presidential addresses from George Washington to Barack Obama (Gorski 2011), texts like the Constitution, revered geographical locations like the battlefield at Gettysburg, and community rituals like fireworks on July 4. Civil religion becomes especially prominent and important in difficult times, such as after 9/11. In the immediate aftermath of this tragedy, many Americans sought to express their shared national identity by flying flags. This was a powerful moment during which people felt a deep bond with their fellow Americans. The site of the main attack on the World Trade Center has become a sacred geographical area.

What is the function of civil religion? As the example above illustrates, it provides a sense of a collective national identity. It does so by promoting shared ideas and ideals that are reaffirmed in various ceremonies and rituals. It reinforces a sense of solidarity, defining who the "we" is in "we the people." Of course, at the same time it creates a boundary. By defining who falls into the category of "we," it also establishes the category of "they." As such, religion becomes a source of patriotism.

> **civil religion** The beliefs, practices, and symbols that a nation holds sacred.

FIGURE 11.2 • Daily Prayer in the United States, 2011

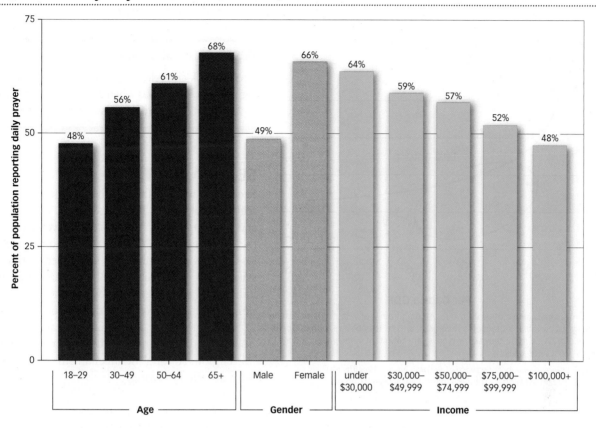

SOURCE: National Day of Prayer, April 28, 2011. The Pew Forum on Religion and Public Life, Pew Research Center.

America's civil religion is not rooted in a particular religion, as is true in Britain, where the Anglican Church links church and state. The separation of church and state in the United States means that no one particular religion can become the official religion of the nation. Rather, the civil religion has to be broader than any one religious tradition.

This being said, the nation's founding groups were overwhelmingly Protestants of one denomination or another. This is significant for two reasons. First, certain ideas about America and its place in the world derive from those earliest settlers. Thus, the ideas that the nation has a covenant with God and that it is a model for other nations—a beacon on a hill—are deeply rooted in the country's history. Second, Protestants, as the "insiders," have often been unwilling to accept the idea that other religious traditions, and nonreligious traditions, should be considered part of the civil religion. From the nineteenth century into the twentieth, the two largest non-Protestant groups were Catholics and Jews. Both faced considerable hostility and opposition. For example, Catholics were described as unfit to be citizens in a democracy because of their loyalty to the Pope. Meanwhile, virulent anti-Semitism condemned Jews and sought to prevent them from being accepted.

Over time, the "we" category has been revised to become more inclusive. Nonetheless, by the second half of the twentieth century, prejudice against Catholics and Jews had declined considerably. As a result, these groups were included under the canopy of civil religion (Berger 1969). It became fashionable to describe the United States as a "Judeo-Christian" nation (Herberg [1955] 1983). The extent to which this new tolerance and inclusiveness extends to religious traditions that are neither Christian nor Jewish is not entirely clear, nor is the place of those who profess no religious beliefs. In terms of the former, Rhys Williams (2011) argues that there is some evidence that efforts are being made to include Muslims. Thus, defining Islam as sharing a history with Judaism and Christianity because they are all "Abrahamic religions" (after the Old Testament figure) is an attempt to find room for them under the canopy. However, some sociologists concluded that in contemporary America, the ultimate "other" is the self-professed atheist (Edgell, Gerteis, and Hartmann 2006).

Civil Religion

FIGURE 11.3 • Wealth and Religiosity

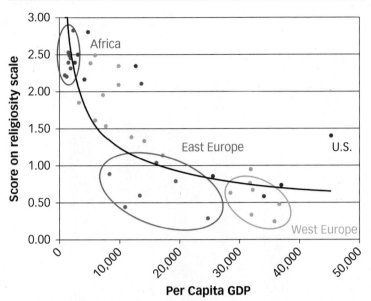

Religiosity is measured using a three-item index ranging from 0-3, with "3" representing the most religious position. Respondents were given a "1" if they believe faith in God is necessary for morality; a "1" if they say religion is very important in their lives; and a "1" if they pray at least once a day.

SOURCE: *U.S. Stands Alone in Its Embrace of Religion among Wealthy Nations,* December 19, 2002. Pew Global Attitudes Project, Pew Research Center.

Many Americans experience civil religion by reading the sacred texts, visiting key places in the nation's history, and participating in rituals such as those associated with July 4. By actively participating in this distinctive American religion, Americans serve to legitimate the state (Bloom 1992). While many Americans continue to believe in the country's civil religion, others contend that it is less important today. For one thing, there has been a resurgence of traditional religions as well as the emergence of new religions that appear to dwarf civil religion in importance, for at least some people. For another, divisions within American society, especially between liberals and conservatives, suggest that there may no longer be a consensus on the major components of America's civil religion. While this divide makes consensus difficult, Bellah actually was aware of this possibility. In fact, during the era of the civil rights movement and the Vietnam War, the nation was also highly divided. In fact, it was likely more divided. He wrote about this era as one of a "broken covenant," but he believed that it could be fixed (Bellah 1975). Of course, another crisis such as the one associated with 9/11 would serve to reduce those differences and lead to a reaffirmation of America's civil religion. But even beyond moments of national crisis, as long as nations continue to exist, citizens of those nations need to share

certain values and beliefs, which are the glue that holds the country together.

ASK YOURSELF

Do you think civil religion is more important to American society now than it was when, say, you were a child? Why or why not? Give examples to support your answer.

SECULARIZATION

Secularization is defined as the declining significance of religion (Dobbelaere 2007). It occurs at both the societal and individual levels. At the societal level, it can involve the declining power of organized religion, as well as the loss by religion of functions, such as education, to the state. At the individual level, secularization means that individual experiences with religion are less intense and less important than other kinds of experiences.

Secularization refers to historical developments in the modern world that undermine the authority of religion. Among the mechanisms that contribute to it are the following:

1. The rise of scientific thinking as an alternative way of interpreting the world that encourages skepticism and doubt, thereby challenging the certainty of religious belief.

2. The development of industrial society, particularly when it results in relative affluence and thus encourages materialism and downplays otherworldly concerns.

3. The rise of governments that do not mandate or promote an established religion.

4. The encouragement of religious tolerance, which leads to a "watering down" of religion in general and religious differences in particular.

5. The existence of competing secular moral ideologies, such as humanism (Smelser 1994: 305–306).

Given the combined impact of these developments, by the 1960s, proponents of secularization theory (e.g., Berger 1969; Wilson 1966) assumed that religion would continue to decline. People would be less likely to attend religious services, join religious institutions, or embrace

secularization The declining significance of religion.

religious beliefs. What was happening in the wealthy industrial nations, the first to become "modern," would inevitably happen elsewhere too at some point in the future. Western Europe seemed to exemplify this trend because the churches were empty and religious convictions were waning. But even as these views were being presented, the United States remained a highly religious nation. In the 1980s, sociologist and priest Andrew Greeley (1989; see next Public Sociology box) found that more than 90 percent of Americans said they believed in God and 40 percent reported that they attended religious services every week. This appeared to be an exception to what was expected to happen. But given the vibrancy of religion in most of the world, Europe increasingly looked like the exception.

Lavish celebrations of the Fourth of July are popular rituals in the U.S. civil religion. What others can you identify?

There are still some proponents of the original secularization thesis such as Scottish sociologist Steve Bruce in his provocatively titled book *God Is Dead* (2002; Bruce 2013). However, more sociologists have embraced the idea of a "postsecular" society. The idea is that two contradictory trends can be observed: increasing religiosity *and* entrenched and expanding secularization (Goldstein 2009; Gorski et al. 2012).

RELIGION AS A FORM OF CONSUMPTION

A religious marketplace exists in societies that have a great deal of religious diversity and in which people are free to choose. Roger Finke and Rodney Stark (2005) have built on this idea by describing religious institutions in terms of a "religious economy" operating like a commercial economy. In this view, religious institutions are like business firms seeking to serve a market. In so doing, they enter into competitive relationships with other "firms" for market share.

Religious consumers have different tastes, which can be influenced by class, race, gender, educational attainment, age, region, and similar factors. Consumers "purchase" a religious institution for different reasons. Some seek a family-friendly place with quality child care on the premises, some might emphasize very traditional worship, others may value contemporary worship formats, and still others might place a premium on the religious leaders' stances on various social and moral issues.

One measure of the degree to which the leaders of religious organizations have become conscious of the need to market their "product" can be seen in the increasing stress placed on treating potential members as customers engaged in a particular form of consumption. Religion thus can be seen as an arena in which to market religious experiences (Drane 2008). Like all other aspects of consumer culture, religions need to respond to the demands of those who consume them and advertise what they have to offer (Roof 2001). Among the more obvious examples are the efforts to sell all sorts of goods and services linked to religion (Moore 1997). All major holidays are associated with one form of consumption or another, but this is most clearly true of Christmas (Belk 1987). There are even religious theme parks devoted to consumption (O'Guinn and Belk 1989). For example, in Pigeon Forge, Tennessee, the "Biblical Times Theater" offers dinner theater performances of biblical stories not far from Dolly Parton's Dollywood. In Orlando, near Disney World, the Trinity Broadcasting Network runs the "Holy Land Experience" where customers can visit the Garden of Eden and Bethlehem.

Less obvious is the fact that religion itself has become another form of consumption. That is, in the United States and elsewhere, people "shop" for religion much as they shop for most other things (Gonzalez 2010; Warner 1993). In this context, religions must compete for consumers of religion in much the same way that manufacturers and shopping malls compete for customers. This occurs in what sociologist Wade Clark Roof (2001) calls the "spiritual marketplace."

Many churches, especially the large megachurches, are increasingly oriented to making themselves consumer friendly. Megachurches are defined as churches having at least 2,000 people in attendance at worship services each week. Among the more well-known megachurches are

ACTIVE SOCIOLOGY

Does Religion Work on the Web?

One quality that interests sociologists about religion is its ability to create a sense of community or solidarity. While television and radio broadcasts have long brought church services to many who cannot attend in person, churches like Calvary Chapel in Fort Lauderdale go a step further. Visit the website of this evangelical church's "digital and media ministry" (www.calvaryftl.org) and record your observations by answering the following questions. Be ready to share your information with the class.

1. What areas or features of the website might encourage online visitors to feel connected to others in the church's community? List as many as you find.

2. What characteristics of the website suggest institutional aspects of religion as opposed to spiritual aspects? Be specific.

Now click the Media tab on the homepage to view a live service, or select the Sermon Library if no live service is being streamed. Sample as much of a real-time or recorded service as you like.

1. What aspects of the service do you think contribute to on-site participants' sense of community? List as many as you observe.

2. What aspects of the video or streaming feed contribute to the website user's sense of community? List as many as you observe.

3. Do you think a religious organization's website can succeed in fostering a feeling of belonging to a community? Why or why not?

Willow Creek Community Church in suburban Chicago, Saddleback Church in Southern California, and Lakewood Church in Houston. These churches and others like them "have created sanctuaries that can only be intended to be entertainment spaces complete with stages, lighting, and even theatre-style seats" (Drane 2000: 90–91). The fanciest megachurches have aerobics classes, food courts, and bowling alleys, as well as multimedia bible classes that are presented in ways that resemble MTV videos (Niebuhr 1995). At crusades, and in some cases churches themselves (such as Canterbury Cathedral in England), people exit through a bookstore/gift shop that sells all sorts of religious and nonreligious items. On Sunday morning, big screens project scripture verses and lyrics to pop-style religious songs so that everyone in the congregation can follow along (Niebuhr 1995). The pastor of one Baptist church who sought to make services more "fun" urged his staff to study Disney World's techniques (Barron 1995).

While religion has become more like secular forms of consumption, consumption has become our new religion. As a result, shopping malls and fast-food restaurants, among many other settings, have become places where people go to practice their consumer religion. For example, at the opening of a McDonald's in Moscow, a worker spoke of it "as if it were the Cathedral at Chartres . . . a place to experience 'celestial joy'" (Keller 1990). A trip to Disney World has been described as the "middle class hajj, the compulsory visit to the sunbaked city" (Garfield 1991).

Shopping malls have much in common with traditional religious centers (Zepp 1997). Like religious centers, malls fulfill various human needs such as connecting with other people; gaining a sense of community as well as receiving community services; being in the presence of nature in the form of water, trees, and flowers found in the atriums; and participating in the nonstop festivals that are, and that take place in, shopping malls. Malls also provide the centeredness associated with temples. They are also characterized by a similar balance, order, and symmetry. Play is generally an integral part of religious practice, and malls are certainly places to play. Similarly, malls offer a place where people can partake of ceremonial meals. In these and other ways, the

CHECKPOINT 11.1   THREE COMPONENTS OF RELIGION

Beliefs	Ideas that explain the world and identify what should be held sacred.
Rituals	Sets of regularly repeated, prescribed, and traditional behaviors that symbolize a value or belief.
Experiences	Combinations of beliefs, rituals, and other religious practices such as prayer and services.

shopping mall has religious qualities and therefore can truly be considered a "cathedral of consumption" (Ritzer 2010a). In those cathedrals and in the process of consumption, many people have what can only be described as religious experiences.

TYPES OF RELIGIOUS INSTITUTIONS

Various typologies describe the most common religious institutions. Much of this work distinguishes between *sects* and *churches* (Swatos 2007b, n.d.; Troeltsch 1932). These two terms are the poles of a continuum from the sect at one end to the church on the other.

In the most traditional Amish sects clothing is plain and modest, and outside contacts and influences are minimal. What advantages and disadvantages do sects present for their members?

SECT

A **sect** is a small group of people who have joined the group consciously and voluntarily to have a personal religious experience. They see themselves as the "true believers" who have privileged access to religious truths, which makes them critical of other religious institutions. Their religious experiences and behavior tend to be spontaneous and unregimented. A sect's leadership is usually composed of laypersons rather than those with specialized training. As such, the organizational structure is nonbureaucratic and nonhierarchical. Leaders often arise because they are seen as possessing charisma, and thus should be obeyed without question. Sects tend to be antiestablishment, and the members often feel alienated from, and as a result are prone to reject, society and the status quo. In fact, sects can be seen as breakaway, dissident groups that leave established religious institutions. They do so because they think such institutions have compromised too much with "the world" and therefore have polluted the religion's teachings.

Sects frequently draw their membership from the lower classes who are more interested either in changing society or in remaining apart from it rather than maintaining the status quo. Sects tend to set themselves apart from the larger society and only admit those who rigorously conform to the group's norms. There is a demand for high levels of commitment on the part of members. Likewise, doctrinal purity is emphasized, and diversity of opinions within the group about such matters is not permitted. Sects frequently set themselves apart from society in terms of such things as how they dress and what they eat. In addition, they might even segregate themselves physically and live in areas that are largely isolated from the rest of the community. Sect members may not be in a position to effectively challenge religious competition, but they do not believe in tolerating other religious organizations.

Numerous sects within the Christian tradition have long histories in the United States, including the Puritans, Amish, Seventh-Day Adventists, and Jehovah's Witnesses. Within Judaism, Hasidic Jews are an example of a sect.

CHURCH

A **church** is a large group of religiously oriented people that one is usually born into rather than joins consciously and voluntarily. The church's leadership is composed of professionals who have highly specialized training. The church tends to have a highly bureaucratic structure and a complex division of labor (Diotallevi 2007).

> **sect** A small group of people who have joined the group consciously and voluntarily to have a personal religious experience.
>
> **church** A large group of religiously oriented people that one is usually born into rather than joins consciously and voluntarily.

God in America

Andrew M. Greeley: Sociologist, Priest, Novelist

Andrew M. Greeley was a unique person and a unique public sociologist. He obtained degrees in theology in the early 1950s and served as an assistant priest at a church in Chicago. He also studied sociology at the University of Chicago and received his PhD from there in 1962.

As a priest, Greeley used sociology to raise a variety of social issues that needed to be faced by his parishioners, the Catholic Church, and society as a whole. He wrote a weekly column for the *Chicago Sun-Times* and was a frequent contributor to other newspapers including the *New York Times*.

What most distinguished Greeley as a public sociologist was the fact that he published many best-selling novels including *The Bishop in the West Wing* (2003) and *The Priestly Sins* (2005). Although these tell good stories, they also often deal with important sociological issues. However, it would be wrong to conclude that Greeley's main goal in his novels was to teach sociological lessons. Rather, as a priest his major objective was to teach moral and religious lessons both to laypeople and to those who labored in the church hierarchy.

In 2008, Greeley suffered a devastating brain injury when his coat got caught in the door of a moving taxicab. He was under 24-hour care for years, had difficulty speaking, and was no longer able to write. Andrew Greeley died on May 29, 2013.

Does Andrew M. Greeley fit your idea of what a priest should be? Of what a sociologist should be?

Think About It

Do you agree that fiction can serve a public sociological purpose? Why or why not?

Churches tend to draw members from throughout society and across all social classes. While a sect tends to restrict membership to true believers, a church seeks to include as many people as possible. Churches often actively seek out new members, sometimes by employing missionaries. A church's belief systems tend to be highly codified, and rituals are often elaborate and performed in a highly prescribed manner. In comparison to members of sects, church members tend to have a lower level of commitment, and much less is expected of them. While sects tend to reject the status quo, churches accept the status quo.

The Roman Catholic Church during the Middle Ages is perhaps the best illustration of the strict meaning of church, existing in relatively pure form. It still has the status of church in some Western European nations.

While *sect* and *church* are presented here as if they are totally distinct, in reality there is no clear dividing line between them. In fact, over time there is a tendency for sects to take on the organizational features of a church. As sects become larger, they need ever-larger bureaucratic structures with less charismatic leadership and more leadership based on expertise. The behavior of sect members becomes less spontaneous and more formal.

CULTS AND NEW RELIGIOUS MOVEMENTS

A cult resembles a sect in many ways, but it is important to distinguish between them (Stark and Bainbridge 1979). While a sect is a religious group that breaks off from a more established religion as a result of a schism in order to revive it and rediscover the original beliefs and practices of that organization, a **cult** is a new, innovative, small, voluntary, and exclusive religious tradition that was never associated with any religious organization. A cult is often at odds with established religions as well as the larger society. Those who found a cult tend to be religious radicals who want to go back to religion's origins, to import ideas from other religions, or to create totally new ideas. Like sects, cults demand high levels of commitment and involvement on the part of members. Because they are new, cults even more than sects tend to be led by charismatic figures.

> **cult** A new, innovative, small, voluntary, and exclusive religious tradition that was never associated with any religious organization.

The term *cult* has fallen out of favor in sociology because it has come to be associated in the popular mind and press with such destructive groups as Charles Manson and his "family," who murdered a number of people including actress Sharon Tate in 1969. The Manson cult was not actually a religious organization. But a number of religiously based cults have proven to be very destructive. These include Jim Jones's People's Temple, David Koresh's Branch Davidians, and Heaven's Gate. All of these groups ended in tragedy. In the case of the People's Temple, the end involved the 1979 mass suicide and murder of 918 of Jones's followers in their jungle compound in Guyana. In the case of the Branch Davidians, the leader and membership died in a controversial confrontation with federal officials from the Bureau of Alcohol, Tobacco, and Firearms (Juergensmeyer 2009).

However, none of these are true cults in the sense of the definition offered above. Among those that better fit the definition are more benign groups such as Baha'i, the International Society for Krishna Consciousness (commonly known as *Hare Krishnas*), and Rastafarians. The best-known cult is the Unification Church, founded by South Korean reverend Sun Myung Moon. Given the negative connotations associated with the term *cult*, many sociologists today have discontinued using it. However, others continue to view it as a useful sociological concept (Gary Shepard 2007).

Some sociologists prefer to use the term *new religious movements* to encompass sects, cults, and a wide array of other innovative religious groups. **New religious movements** are typified by their zealous religious converts, their charismatic leaders, their appeal to an atypical portion of the population, a tendency to differentiate between "us"

About 3,500 couples were married in this mass wedding ceremony of the Unification Church that took place recently in Seoul, Korea. Why do so many people consider this church to be a cult?

CHECKPOINT 11.2 — TYPES OF RELIGIOUS ORGANIZATIONS

Sect	A small group of people who see themselves as true believers and who voluntarily join a group, usually broken off from a more established religion, to have a personal religious experience.
Church	A large group of religiously oriented people that members are usually born into rather than consciously join.
Cult	A small, new, and exclusive group whose religious tradition has never been associated with and is often at odds with any established religious organization.
Denomination	A religious group that exhibits a general spirit of tolerance and acceptance of other religious bodies.

and "them," distrust of others, and being prone to rapid fundamental changes (Barker 2007). The use of the term *new religious movement* eliminates or reduces the negative connotations associated with cults. It also emphasizes the idea that each unconventional religious organization should be examined objectively. The uproar around Scientology

---

new religious movements Movements that attract zealous religious converts, follow charismatic leaders, appeal to an atypical portion of the population, have a tendency to differentiate between "us" and "them," are characterized by distrust of others, and are prone to rapid fundamental changes.

Andrew Greeley

New Age Religion

FIGURE 11.4 • The World's Dominant Religions by Percentage of Adherents

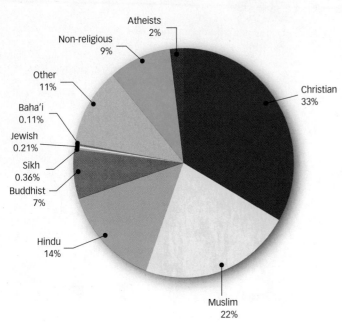

- Atheists 2%
- Non-religious 9%
- Other 11%
- Baha'i 0.11%
- Jewish 0.21%
- Sikh 0.36%
- Buddhist 7%
- Hindu 14%
- Muslim 22%
- Christian 33%

SOURCE: CIA World Factbook, 2012. Retrieved May 31, 2012, from https://www.cia.gov/library/publications/the-world-factbook/geos/xx.html.

suggests that controversy cannot be eliminated by simply opting for a different term to describe it. For example, in 2012, Russian courts upheld a ban on the publication and distribution of Scientologist books, citing them as extremist literature. Scientology has provoked considerable controversy in this country, too (L. Wright 2013).

DENOMINATIONS

Like a church, a **denomination** is an organized form of religious expression that is usually supportive of the social order and of other religious forms. Unlike a sect, a conversion experience—such as being born again—is not required. Religious services of denominations, like those of churches, are formal and reserved, with an emphasis on teaching rather than on an emotional religious experience.

Like churches, denominations are hierarchical and bureaucratic. Local churches are not independent, but part of a larger regional or national institutional structure. They rely on a specialized, professionally trained, full-time clergy. The clergy are generally trained in seminaries run by the denomination to ensure conformity to doctrines.

Among the major Christian denominations today are Protestant groups such as Baptists, Episcopalians, Lutherans, Methodists, Presbyterians, and Unitarians. This list would also include Roman Catholics and Eastern Orthodox. Denominationalism accepts a pluralistic view of religion.

RELIGION AND GLOBALIZATION

Every major religious tradition was originally a local, even tribal, expression of faith that grew out of a specific environment and then diffused across regions and eventually the globe. All of the global religions originated in Asia. The eastern religions, including Hinduism, Buddhism, Confucianism, and Taoism, originated in South Asia and then spread east into China and East and South Asia. The western religions, including Judaism, Christianity, and Islam, came from West Asia, or the Middle East.

Today, over two billion people in the world identify as Christians (Britannica 2012; Kurtz 2012: 46). Over one and a half billion people are Muslims, there are almost a billion Hindus, and a similar number practice Buddhism or Chinese folk religions. All other religions, including Judaism and Sikhism, are minuscule in comparison (see Figure 11.4).

It is clear that religion globalized before anything else. We can focus on institutional religion and on two aspects of its relationship to globalization.

First, there is the issue of the importance of religion in transnational migration in the bringing of institutional religion to new locales. Migrants transplant religions into new places, making those places more multireligious. They also generate in those locales new and different versions of the local religions even as the migrants' versions are influenced and altered by local religions. This, in turn, can alter religion in the migrants' homeland. Thus, transnational migration globalizes religion spatially and contributes to the further pluralization of religion around the world. Migrants also help to unify various parts of the world by, for example, making pilgrimages to religious sites like Mecca and the Wailing Wall, posting prayers in cyberspace, and sending money to religious centers in their homelands.

Second is the spread of religious organizations and movements through independent missions. Here the Christian Church, especially the Roman Catholic Church, has played a central role through its missionaries. In fact, Christianity became the first worldwide religion.

> **denomination** A religious group not linked to the state that exhibits a general spirit of tolerance and acceptance of other religious bodies.

FIGURE 11.5 • Majority Religions, by Country

Christianity
Islam
Hinduism
Buddhism
Judaism
Chinese religions
(Buddhism, Taoism, Confucianism)
Japanese religions
(Shinto, Buddhism)
Other

SOURCE: World Religion Map. 2012. Retrieved May 31, 2012 from http://www.mapsofworld.com/world-religion-map.htm.

Messengers for Islam created the most global system prior to the modern era (see page 322).

ASK YOURSELF

Have any other social institutions spread as widely as religion? What do you think accounts for religion's staying power in the places to which it has been transported? Why are religions still expanding globally today?

THE MOST SIGNIFICANT GLOBAL RELIGIONS

The religions we will deal with in this section are those that have spread furthest throughout the world: Judaism, Buddhism, Hinduism, Islam, and Christianity (see Figure 11.5). Although it is not a large global religion, we will also examine Mormonism. We do so because of its very contemporary efforts to become a global religion.

Judaism

Founded more than 3,000 years ago, Judaism is today one of the smallest of the world's religions with roughly 13.4 million people in the world defining themselves as Jews (Goldberg 2007; Goldscheider 2012). However, for a variety of reasons Judaism's importance both historically and contemporaneously has been far greater than one would think looking simply at the numbers. By the late nineteenth century, there were 12 million Jews in the world who had migrated from the Middle East and were

spread in mostly small enclaves throughout the world. There was and continued to be a large concentration of Jews in Europe, but migrations to North America, as well as to Palestine (then under Ottoman control), began during this period. By the onset of World War II, the number of Jews in the world had grown to 16.6 million, but the atrocities of the Nazis led to a reduction in the population to about 10 million. The founding of Israel in 1948 marked an important turning point for Jews, and its population is now approaching 6 million people. Another large concentration of Jews—approximately 6 million—lives in North America, mostly in the United States. The vast majority of all of the over 13 million Jews alive today live in either North America or Israel with fewer than 2 million living elsewhere, especially in Europe. Just a few of the factors that make Judaism of great global significance are the spread of Jews throughout the world, Zionism (which helped lead to the founding of Israel), the Holocaust, anti-Semitism, and the conflict between Israel and its Arab neighbors over Palestine.

Hinduism

Although there is no precise starting date, Hinduism began sometime between 800 and 200 BCE (Abrutyn 2012). While it had ancient origins, Hinduism became firmly established in India as it opposed foreign occupations of Muslims (999–1757) and later the British

Religion and Globalization

The Hindu Holi festival, or the festival of colors, occurs in the spring and celebrates the love of Krishna and Radha.

(1757–1947). Today, the vast majority of Hindus (about 800 million) live in India. Hinduism is strongly defined by the *Vedas,* which are both historical documents and enumerations of incantations needed for successful rituals.

While it continues to be heavily concentrated in India, Hinduism is a global religion spread across six continents. It is spread by both migrants and itinerate religious teachers (Madan 2007). Although it is heavily concentrated geographically, Hinduism has been important as part of the "Easternization of the West" (Campbell 2007) in, for example, the spread of yoga, transcendental meditation, and so on.

Buddhism

Buddhism arose in the Indus Ganges Basin in about the sixth century BCE and began to have a transnational influence about three centuries later (Nichols 2012; J. Taylor 2007). Today, there are nearly 500 million Buddhists across the globe, although the vast majority are in Asia. China has the largest number of Buddhists followed by Japan. Other Asian countries with majority Buddhist populations include Thailand, Cambodia, Myanmar, Bhutan, Sri Lanka, Laos, and Vietnam.

Islam

Islam was founded by Muhammad (570–632 CE) on the Arabian Peninsula. The lands encompassed by Islam were seen as the center of the world with all else subordinate to it. Important to its spread (see Figure 11.6) was its universalistic worldview; Muslims did not view themselves as a chosen people but believed that they and all of humanity had a common destiny. Islam's universalistic ideas (God-given standards that led everyone to search for goodness) had to be diffused throughout the world. Such beliefs led to a global mission to rid the world of competing idea systems such as idolatry and superstition. On the other hand, it saw itself as building on, but going beyond, Judaism and Christianity. Thus, "Islam was the first of the world's great religious civilizations to understand itself as one religion among others" (Keane 2003: 42).

Believers in Islam, as well as their armies, spread westward into Spain and France and eastward into Byzantium, Persia, and eventually India and China. They traveled with the belief that they were the messengers and that everyone was eagerly awaiting their message. Thus, the belief emerged that "Islam would prevail among the world's peoples, either by willing acceptance, or by spiritual fervour, or (in the face of violent resistances) by conquest" (Keane 2003: 42). Because there was only one God and therefore only one law according to Islam, such a view—and mission—meant that followers of Islam took no notice of nation-states and their borders.

In the end, the efforts of Islam's early missionaries were thwarted. One factor was the efforts of alternative religions, especially Christianity and its various militaristic campaigns against Islam. Another was that the principle of *jihad,* or the duty to struggle on behalf of God against those who doubted him or were his enemies, was rarely pursued unconditionally. Thus, Islam was willing to compromise with its opponents, and this proved fatal to its ambitions. Furthermore, because ultimate victory was ensured, Muslims believed that contact with nonbelievers was acceptable, even encouraged. These efforts were ultimately only a limited success because of the Crusades, as well as because of military defeats that forced Muslims out of Italy, Spain, and Portugal. However, the history of such efforts remains strong among many devotees of Islam and helps to inform the contemporary thinking of jihadists and Islamic fundamentalists (Sayyid 2012).

Christianity

Christianity and Islam are the two fastest-growing religions in the world today (Garrett 2007; Thomas 2012).

FIGURE 11.6 • The Global Expansion of Islam

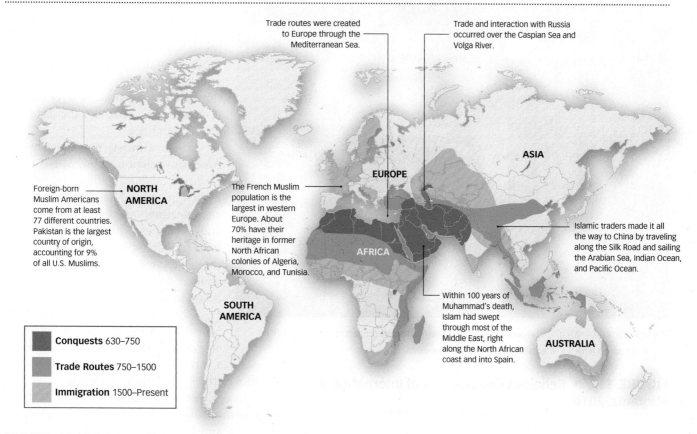

Trade routes were created to Europe through the Mediterranean Sea.

Trade and interaction with Russia occurred over the Caspian Sea and Volga River.

ASIA

EUROPE

Foreign-born Muslim Americans come from at least 77 different countries. Pakistan is the largest country of origin, accounting for 9% of all U.S. Muslims.

NORTH AMERICA

The French Muslim population is the largest in western Europe. About 70% have their heritage in former North African colonies of Algeria, Morocco, and Tunisia.

AFRICA

Islamic traders made it all the way to China by traveling along the Silk Road and sailing the Arabian Sea, Indian Ocean, and Pacific Ocean.

SOUTH AMERICA

Within 100 years of Muhammad's death, Islam had swept through most of the Middle East, right along the North African coast and into Spain.

AUSTRALIA

Conquests 630–750

Trade Routes 750–1500

Immigration 1500–Present

SOURCE: The World of Islam—Version 2.0, 2001, Editor: J. Dudley Woodberry, General Mapping International.

Christianity spread in the Middle East following the death of Jesus. By 1000 CE, a schism developed between Roman Catholicism in the West and Orthodoxy in the East, with more Christians living in the East than the West. A major series of events in the history of globalization was the Crusades, which began in 1095 CE and lasted for centuries. The Crusades were designed to liberate the Holy Land from Muslims and others who had gained control of Jerusalem in 638 CE. This is still a sensitive issue for Muslims as reflected in protests that erupted when President George W. Bush used the word *crusades* in a speech shortly after the 9/11 terrorist attacks.

Christianity today is declining in Europe, but that is more than compensated for by strong growth in the Global South, including parts of Asia, Africa, and Latin America. Growth is so strong in the Global South that it is predicted that, by 2050, 80 percent of the world's Christians will be Hispanic. Southern Christianity is "more . . . morally conservative, and evangelical" (Garrett 2007: 143).

Pentecostalism, a charismatic movement, offers another example of the spread of Christianity around the globe. This religion had its origins in poor black and white revivals held in Los Angeles in 1906. It is now the second-largest and fastest-growing form of Christianity, with somewhere between 150 million and 400 million adherents. It has come to exceed in size all forms of Christianity except Catholicism. Its growth has been especially great in Asia, Africa, and Latin America (Lechner and Boli 2005). Missionaries from there now often travel back to the United States and to Europe. It has produced many variations and localized forms that are linked through publications, conferences, electronic media, and travel.

Mormonism

Mormonism, or the Church of Jesus Christ of Latter-Day Saints, has shown substantial growth in the last 50 years. Founded in the United States in the nineteenth century, Mormonism had fewer than 2 million members in 1960, but today that number has risen to approximately 13 million.

World's Religions

The Bella Vista Assembly of God church in Arkansas is one of a loosely connected group of churches that make up the largest Pentecostal denomination in the world.

FIGURE 11.7 • Religious Composition of International Migrants, 2010

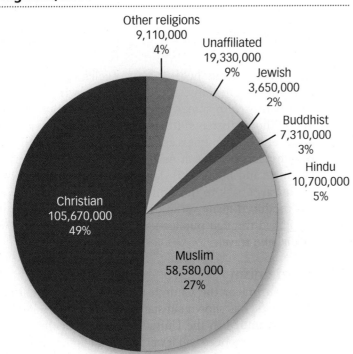

Other religions
9,110,000
4%

Unaffiliated
19,330,000
9%

Jewish
3,650,000
2%

Buddhist
7,310,000
3%

Hindu
10,700,000
5%

Christian
105,670,000
49%

Muslim
58,580,000
27%

SOURCE: "Faith on the Move: The Religious Affiliation of International Migrants," March 8, 2012. The Pew Forum on Religion and Public Life, Pew Research Center.

The Church of Jesus Christ of Latter-Day Saints is centrally controlled from its headquarters in Salt Lake City, Utah. The organization exercises considerable oversight over its churches in the United States and around the world from these headquarters. It also transmits much content, such as conferences and leadership training, via satellite throughout the world. And, of course, it maintains websites for the use of its global members.

Once almost exclusively an American religion, today it has more members (about 7 million) outside the United States and has 8,400 churches and meetinghouses in 178 countries and territories. Although it had a ban on blacks becoming priests until 1978, today it is growing rapidly in Africa with about a quarter of a million members there (Jordan 2007).

The global expansion of Mormonism is not only an example of globalization but also the result of a variety of global processes. First, as noted above, the church has made extensive use of the Internet, especially its well-known website (www.mormon.org). Second, church services, conferences, and leadership training conducted at the church's headquarters are broadcast via satellite to 6,000 of its churches around the world. Third, it continues to follow the traditional path of global and globalizing religions by sending tens of thousands of missionaries around the world. The global acceptance and expansion of Mormonism is especially notable because of its sect-like character and practices. For example, the church has a history of polygamy and the marriage of preteen girls to older men—practices that some fundamentalist branches of Mormonism continue to this day. Such traditions are not easily accepted in many cultures and parts of the world. Other unusual practices include having a family "sealed" so that it can stay together after death, and *tithing* whereby one-tenth of one's income is given to the church.

In contrast to other globally successful religions, Mormonism has not significantly adapted to local customs and realities. For example, unlike the far more rapidly expanding Pentecostalism, Mormonism has *not* incorporated a variety of indigenous customs (such as drumming and dancing) into its African Sunday services. Said one member who had moved to Nigeria and married a Nigerian: "No matter where you go in the world, the service is the same . . . the buildings, baptismal fonts, services and hymns in Lagos were nearly identical to those back home in the United States" (Jordan 2007: A13). Through watching Salt Lake City services via satellite, worshippers elsewhere in the world can easily see that the services and the teachings are the same—or at least very similar.

FUNDAMENTALISM

Religious **fundamentalism** is a strongly held belief in the foundational precepts of any religion (Stolow 2004). It is also characterized by a rejection of the modern secular world (Kivisto 2012a). Fundamentalism is involved in globalization in at least two major senses (Lechner 1993). First, it is often expansionistic seeking to extend its reach and power into more and more areas of the world. Second, it is profoundly affected by various globalizations. For example, the globalization of one fundamentalist religion, such as Islamic militants, is likely to lead to a counterreaction by another, such as Hasidic Jews. Another important reaction involves that against various forces seen as emanating from the modern world, including secularism, popular culture, rationalization, and the United States and the West in general. Much of the momentum for the recent rise of fundamentalism can be seen as traceable to a reaction against such forces. In a subtler sense, it has become a global expectation that people develop a communal identity through involvement in fundamentalism.

FAITH ON THE MOVE

The globalization of religion is also the result of the movement of people. The United Nations estimates that in 2010 there were 214 million immigrants globally. This represents just over 3 percent of the total world population. Recently, an attempt was made to determine what that movement of people means in terms of the movement of religions across

MackRandy Wolford, pastor of the fundamentalist Church of the Lord Jesus in Jolo, West Virginia, died after refusing medical treatment for a rattlesnake bite he suffered during a sermon.

international borders. Figure 11.7 provides a broad overview of the movement of people associated with the major world religions (Connor 2012). The world's two largest religions—Christianity and Islam—contribute the largest numbers of immigrants. Christians account for nearly a half of all immigrants. Muslim immigrants amount to 27 percent of all immigrants. Hindus account for 5 percent, Buddhists 3 percent, and Jews 2 percent of immigrants.

EDUCATION

The sociology of education is concerned primarily with studying those institutions—collectively known as schools—created by modern societies that function to prepare young people for future roles in various careers and as citizens. As such, considerable attention is focused

---

CHECKPOINT 11.3   **RELIGION AND GLOBALIZATION**

Migrants transplant religion to new places.

Religious organizations and movements spread through independent missions.

> **fundamentalism** A strongly held belief in the fundamental or foundational precepts of any religion, or a rejection of the modern secular world.

Religious Fundamentalism

Classrooms in Egypt, Bolivia, the Philippines, and Israel (l. to r.) demonstrate the similarities and differences in educational systems around the world. How do sociologists explain the functions of education in society?

on examining and comparing various ways of organizing schools. In addition, sociologists examine the learning and social outcomes for students of the educational experience.

Education is closely related to the process of socialization discussed in Chapter 4. In fact, there is no clear line between the two, since both involve the learning process. Socialization tends to be a more informal process while education takes place more formally in schools of various types (Zerelli 2007). Much socialization—for example, learning not to eat with one's hands—takes place, largely within the family, in a child's early years. However, a good deal of education takes place during those years as well, with children learning to talk and in many cases to read before they begin their formal schooling. In adulthood, much new learning takes place during socialization processes, such as when starting a new job, but adults also increasingly participate in adult education programs. Overall, some education takes place during socialization processes, and socialization (e.g., orientation when beginning college) occurs in educational settings.

Historically, in the United States, when a child has reached about five years of age, the focus has shifted from the highly informal process of socialization in the family to the more formal educational process in schools. However, an increasing number of American children, and more recently children elsewhere in the world, are being homeschooled (Stevens 2001, 2007). This, like many other changes in education, is spurred on by the digital revolution, which is making homeschooling, and indeed schooling in any setting, much easier and more effective than was the case in the past (Collins and Halverson 2009).

While five years of age is the norm for starting school in the United States and in other developed countries, much younger children are increasingly entering preschools. Infants as young as a few months old are being placed in day care centers. While all schools involve a shift away from parents to others in the processes of socialization and education, a number of issues arise when many two- to three-year-olds, and especially two- to three-month-olds, are turned over to schools for large portions of the day.

FIGURE 11.8 • The Relationship between National Gross Domestic Product and Average Years of Schooling, 2000

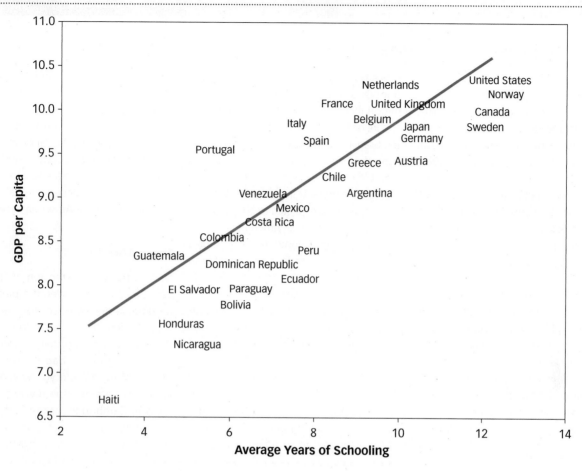

SOURCE: Adapted from Campante, Filipe and Edward Glaeser. 2009. "Yet Another Tale of Two Cities: Buenos Aires and Chicago." Working Paper 15104, National Bureau of Economic Research: Cambridge, MA.

Of course, this only touches on the beginnings of the educational process. In the United States, as in all other advanced industrial countries, education goes on for years through grade school, high school, college, graduate school, and professional school, and even beyond in formal adult socialization programs (Kotarba 2007). Most people do not progress through all of these stages. Where one ends one's formal education has profound implications for one's future. Clearly, educational attainment and lifetime earnings are closely related. While there are many other measures of success in life, levels of education and earnings are obviously of great importance (Blau and Duncan 1967). In addition to being associated with higher earnings, higher levels of education serve as protection against unemployment. During the recession that began in 2008, the hardest-hit segment of the population was people with less than a high school diploma. Least negatively impacted were those with doctoral and advanced professional degrees.

The unemployment rate in 2012 for individuals with doctoral degrees was 2.5 percent, and for those with advanced professional degrees it was 2.1 percent. The rate for individuals with less than a high school diploma was 12.4 percent, whereas it was 8.3 percent for people with no more than a high school diploma (U.S. Department of Labor, Bureau of Labor Statistics 2013).

Education makes a huge difference not only at the individual level but also at the level of the nation-state. Thus, if we compare nation-states on a global basis, nations with strong educational systems and high levels of education tend to be more economically prosperous. There are other benefits as well, such as being better off in terms of overall health and tending to be more open politically (Bills 2007; Buchmann and Hannum 2001). As Figure 11.8 shows, nations with populations characterized by higher levels of schooling are much more likely to have a more prosperous economy as measured by gross domestic product per person.

GL🌐BALIZATION

American Universities Overseas

A relatively recent development has been the rush toward the construction of branch campuses of American universities in China, India, Singapore, and most importantly the Middle East, especially the Persian Gulf area (Clotfelter 2010; Lewin 2008a, 2008b, 2008c). Why there? The obvious answer is that the nations in that area are awash with oil money and can afford such educational centers. For example, New York University was led to create a branch campus in Abu Dhabi by a $50 million gift from its government.

Universities are becoming *global universities*. Faculty and students move back and forth around the globe to the various branch campuses of a university. Students from Education City in Doha, Qatar, are able to study at branch campuses of leading universities, such as Weill Medical College of Cornell University, Georgetown, and Carnegie Mellon.

The expansion of American universities overseas raises a number of interesting issues from the point of view of globalization. One is to what degree these international campuses will reflect American culture or the culture of the nation in which the branch campus exists. This was highlighted when Yale University announced it would enter into a joint venture to create Yale–National University of Singapore College, which is expected to open in 2015. Critics, including faculty members on the Yale campus, questioned the institution's commitment to freedom and equality in entering into this alliance in a city-state known for its excessive control over people and institutions. Thus, for example, students at Yale-NUS will be prohibited from involvement in political parties or protest movements (Gooch 2012).

Another issue is whether it is in America's interest to export its educational systems. There are those who believe that training people from other nations will serve to adversely affect America's ability to compete globally. Then there is the matter of what will happen to these campuses, especially as they expand in the future, if, for example, Abu Dhabi falls to a radical Islamic regime hostile to the United States. Still another issue is whether these transplanted universities will come to generate great hostility as a new version of American imperialism.

Think About It

Do you think the extension of U.S. universities abroad is overall a positive or a negative development for the societies in which they are opening? Why? Is the cultural and informational flow they represent good or bad for the United States? Why? Would you welcome the arrival of an extension division of, say, Oxford, Cambridge, or the Sorbonne in your state? What about Cairo University or Qatar University? Why or why not?

EDUCATION AND CONSUMPTION

Students have always been consumers of education. What is different today is the emergence of an all-encompassing consumer society, as well as the increasing commercialization of education (T. Norris 2011a). Although students have always consumed education, they have not always done so in ways that yield profits to commercial enterprises.

COMMERCIALIZATION AND CONSUMPTION

Education takes place in various societies where consumption is pervasive. American society is a prime example. Consumption is not restricted to obvious places like the shopping mall, but is manifest throughout society. Students are deeply immersed in that society and can't help but bring its ethos into the educational setting. At the college level, education, or at least the degree, is increasingly seen as a product to be purchased and consumed. As with most consumption, the emphasis is on evaluating educational alternatives to find the one that promises the greatest return for the least amount of money. Parents who are likely to foot the bill for most college expenses are especially oriented toward looking at college education from a cost-benefit perspective.

CHECKPOINT 11.4 — EDUCATION, COMMERCIALIZATION, AND CONSUMPTION

Education today is seen as a product to be purchased and consumed.

Like any other product, education is being evaluated based on what provides the greatest return for the lowest cost.

Profit-making organizations have intruded in various ways into the schools.

DIGITAL LIVING

Student Plagiarism in the Internet Age

Plagiarism among students and the role of the Internet in it are of huge concern in the educational system, especially in colleges and universities (Blum 2009). In the Internet age, plagiarism has become much more common, much easier, and much more difficult to detect (Gabriel 2010). Text can simply be "cut" from an Internet site and "pasted" on a student's paper. However, what is most different today is that it seems less clear, at least to students, what is their own work and what is that of others.

A key factor here is the idea of "crowd-sourcing" (Howe 2008); that is, much of what appears on the Internet has been produced by a large number of people. For example, all entries on Wikipedia are written and rewritten by hundreds, perhaps thousands, of people. It may even be the case, although it would be highly unusual, that the student plagiarizing part of a Wikipedia entry was one of the contributors to it. The "author" of much of the material on the user-generated Internet is unclear. Some students may believe that it is not necessary to cite work for which no author is indicated. If the whole idea of an author is unclear, and crowdsourcing is increasingly the norm, then it should come as no surprise that at least some students are not clear about what is their work and what constitutes the illegitimate use of others' work. In addition, there is an increasing sense that what is on the

Websites like Turnitin.com attempt to stop student plagiarism before it starts. Are there any drawbacks for teachers or students of relying on digital systems to ensure honesty?

Internet is common property. It therefore seems that everyone is free to do what he or she wants with material on the Internet. Even if students are consciously engaging in plagiarism, they may simply believe that it is just not much of a "crime."

Students should be aware of the fact that both professors and university administrators expend considerable effort going after plagiarists. Universities post information about what constitutes plagiarism and what the consequences are if one is caught plagiarizing. A typical syllabus also reminds students of the perils of using the work of others without attribution. An increasing number of faculty members also use sophisticated software packages designed to detect plagiarism.

Think About It

Has technology made plagiarism more widespread simply because the copying process is now easier, or because the Internet's ability to support crowdsourcing has blurred the norms that define authorship? Or is it both? Defend your answer. What is your own definition of plagiarism? Does it agree with the standards of your school or university?

As a result, at least in part, of the pervasiveness of consumer culture, we are witnessing the increasing commercialization of the educational system itself. There is, for example, the increase in for-profit education in corporations such as the University of Phoenix. It is the largest for-profit university in the United States with over 300,000 students (including 50,000 students at the postgraduate level), about a third of whom are online students. Overall, this is estimated to be a $30 billion-a-year industry. About 3 million students take courses from for-profit colleges either online or on traditional campuses. For-profit colleges have been accused of luring students into programs such as cosmetology with false promises of careers following completion of the program (Lichtblau 2011). These institutions have relied on the easy availability of federally subsidized student loans and generally operate with open-admissions policies. Critics complain that many students brought into these institutions are not adequately prepared for higher education. This fact is borne out by the high attrition rate and, linked to it, the high rate of

FIGURE 11.9 • Reading and Math Achievement among U.S. 17-Year-Olds by Parental Education, 2008

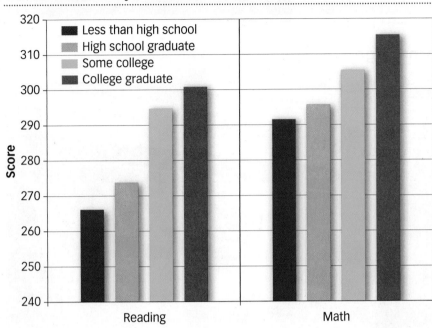

SOURCE: Data from Aud, Susan and Gretchen Hannes, editors. 2011. *The Condition of Education 2011 in Brief* (NCES 2011-034). Washington, DC: U.S. Department of Education, National Center for Education Statistics

NOTE: NAEP = National Assessment of Educational Progress. NAEP scores range from 0 to 500. For reading, students scoring 250 are able to search for specific information, interrelate ideas, and make generalizations about literature, science, and social studies materials. Students scoring 300 are able to find, understand, summarize, and explain relatively complicated literary and informational material. For math, a score of 250 indicates ability to carry out simple multiplicative reasoning and two-step problem solving. A score of 300 indicates ability to perform reasoning and problem solving involving fractions, decimals, percentages, elementary geometry, and simple algebra.

default on student loans. Then there are corporations such as Kaplan and Sylvan that run for-profit learning centers. They perform a variety of educational functions such as tutoring children with problems in school. However, their big money makers are the courses that prepare students for such national tests as the SAT.

Perhaps of greater importance is the increasing intrusion of profit-making corporations into traditional public schools. This accelerated after the Great Recession as a funding crisis hit schools and they grew desperate for funds. Corporations were willing to fill the economic void, at least in part, as long as they could use the opportunity to advertise their products in the schools. For example, one local retailer of high-tech products donated computers to some schools in the Toronto school system. In return, the retailer required the schools to repaint classrooms in the colors and patterns of its logo. In addition, the only schools that received computers were those within shopping distance of one of the retailer's stores (T. Norris 2011b).

The best-known example of the intrusion of commercialization into education is Channel One News, a corporation that donates equipment to schools in return

for the right to broadcast programming into the schools. News is interspersed with commercials, and students are often unable to differentiate between the two. Furthermore, because the commercials are being shown in a school setting, they are seen as more credible than when they are viewed outside the school setting (T. Norris 2011a, 2011b). In many ways, schools are becoming just one more setting dominated by the media and infused with consumer culture.

INEQUALITY IN EDUCATION

A **meritocracy** is a dominant ideology involving the widely shared belief that all people have an equal chance of succeeding economically based on their hard work and skills (see Chapter 3). It also requires that people's social origins, such as class background, and ascribed characteristics, such as race and gender, be unrelated to their opportunities to move up in the social system. Education is a centrally important institution in a meritocracy because it has the potential to level the playing field and provide equal opportunities for students to learn, work hard, and compete to move up in the social hierarchy.

WHO SUCCEEDS IN SCHOOL?

In a meritocratic society, we would expect to find that social origins and ascribed characteristics have little effect on how much students learn and how far they go in school. However, there is a clear pattern of inequality in the United States that suggests that our educational system is *not* meritocratic. In Figure 11.9, we see that students with the highest reading and math scores at the end of high school are those whose parents have the most education. The same pattern is evident if we look at family income and parental occupational status. In terms of race/ethnicity, we see in Figure 11.10 that Asian and white students have

meritocracy A dominant ideology involving the widely shared belief that all people have an equal chance of succeeding economically based on their hard work and skills.

much higher achievement scores than black and Hispanic students. Finally, looking at sex differences in Figure 11.11, we see that females outperform males in reading (but males and females are more nearly equal in math).

The same patterns are observed when we look at educational attainment, or how far students go in school, in Figures 11.12 through 11.14. Figure 11.12 shows how educational attainment is related to family background, using a measure of socioeconomic status (SES), which is a combination of parental education, occupation, and family income. Students from the most socioeconomically advantaged (high-SES) families are the most likely to attain a bachelor's degree (60.4 percent) and the least likely to drop out of high school (0.3 percent). In contrast, children from low-SES families are actually more likely to drop out of high school (19.9 percent) than attain a bachelor's degree (7.3 percent). Likewise, black students are much less likely than white students (17.1 percent versus 34.6 percent) to graduate from college and are much more likely to fail to finish high school. Hispanic students are the most disadvantaged group in terms of attainment; they are also slightly more likely to drop out of high school than to complete a bachelor's degree (see Figure 11.14). Finally, women are significantly more likely than men to attain both high school and college degrees.

Clearly, social origins and ascribed characteristics are strongly related to educational outcomes. This suggests that American society is decidedly unmeritocratic.

THE COLEMAN REPORT: HOW MUCH DO SCHOOLS MATTER?

The first large-scale study of American schools was conducted in the 1960s by James Coleman. Coleman's findings were a surprise, and they changed the way that sociologists understand educational inequality. They led to a rethinking of the assumption that educational institutions could create equal opportunities that would overcome existing class and racial inequalities in the larger society.

First, Coleman (1966) estimated how much schools differ in "quality." He collected data on such things as teachers' salaries, teacher quality, the number of books in

FIGURE 11.10 • Reading and Math Achievement among U.S. 17-Year-Olds by Race, 2008

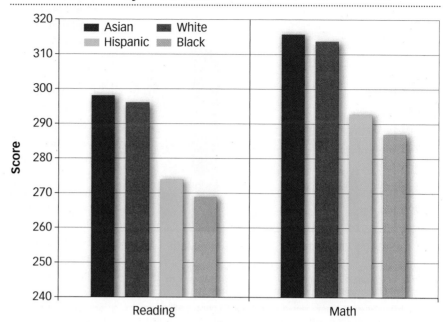

SOURCE: Data from Aud, Susan and Gretchen Hannes, editors. 2011. *The Condition of Education 2011 in Brief* (NCES 2011-034). Washington, DC: U.S. Department of Education, National Center for Education Statistics.

NOTE: NAEP = National Assessment of Educational Progress. NAEP scores range from 0 to 500. For reading, students scoring 250 are able to search for specific information, interrelate ideas, and make generalizations about literature, science, and social studies materials. Students scoring 300 are able to find, understand, summarize, and explain relatively complicated literary and informational material. For math, a score of 250 indicates ability to carry out simple multiplicative reasoning and two-step problem solving. A score of 300 indicates ability to perform reasoning and problem solving involving fractions, decimals, percentages, elementary geometry, and simple algebra.

the library, the age of school buildings, and the curriculum. Schools were much more similar in these respects than was commonly believed. Subsequent research has supported this finding, and reforms in the past half century have made schools even more similar than they were when Coleman conducted his study.

Second, Coleman found few school characteristics that were related to student learning. School resources, such as per-pupil spending, the books in a library, and so on, did not predict student achievement. In terms of achievement, Coleman found that the most important school characteristics were teacher quality and the family background and racial composition of the students attending the school. Students learned more in schools with better teachers and white, middle-class peers. Finally, Coleman found that the most important predictor of student learning was a student's family background.

Higher Education and Race   School Segregation

FIGURE 11.11 • Reading and Math Achievement among U.S. 17-Year-Olds by Gender, 2008

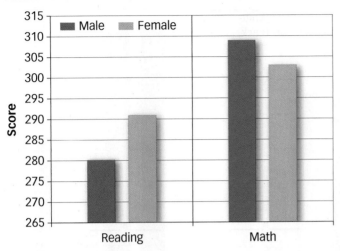

SOURCE: Data from Aud, Susan and Gretchen Hannes, editors. 2011. *The Condition of Education 2011 in Brief* (NCES 2011-034). Washington, DC: U.S. Department of Education, National Center for Education Statistics.

NOTE: NAEP = National Assessment of Educational Progress. NAEP scores range from 0 to 500. For reading, students scoring 250 are able to search for specific information, interrelate ideas, and make generalizations about literature, science, and social studies materials. Students scoring 300 are able to find, understand, summarize, and explain relatively complicated literary and informational material. For math, a score of 250 indicates ability to carry out simple multiplicative reasoning and two-step problem solving. A score of 300 indicates ability to perform reasoning and problem solving involving fractions, decimals, percentages, elementary geometry, and simple algebra.

ASK YOURSELF

What resources—social, material, and other—does the institution of the family provide to account for Coleman's finding that family background is the most important predictor of student learning? Does it surprise you to learn that schools are very similar in terms of their physical and material features? Why or why not?

Recent research on "school effects" has generally been supportive of Coleman's conclusion that school differences in resources contribute less to educational inequality than has often been assumed. The key point is that schools play a role secondary to that of the different levels of cultural capital students bring to the classroom due to their socioeconomic backgrounds. There have been many studies of the importance of school funding for student learning, and generally the results have been mixed.

Finally, recent large-scale surveys indicate that socioeconomic and racial and ethnic differences in student ability are sizable when children *begin* kindergarten. Furthermore, these differences can be detected when children are as young as two years of age (Aud and Hannes 2011). Clearly, schools cannot be implicated in producing educational inequalities if the inequalities are present *before students even enter school!* In short, Coleman's study and subsequent research undermine the simplistic explanation that educational inequality merely reflects unequal opportunities available to students while they are in school.

This is not to argue that schools are irrelevant. Indeed, they play a significant role. Since his study was conducted during the height of the civil rights movement, one of Coleman's concerns was the impact of segregated schools. Using standardized test results, he observed that blacks did not do as well as whites. However, he found that black students did best when they were in integrated schools rather than in predominantly black ones. Integration, in other words, was a resource just like teacher quality. Unfortunately, efforts aimed at school integration led to massive white flight. The integration of public schools peaked in the 1980s, and since then the nation has witnessed the resegregation of schools (Orfield 2001). The educational achievement gap between blacks and whites narrowed between the 1960s and 1990s, but since that time it has remained basically unchanged (Gamoran and Long 2006).

INTELLIGENCE AND SCHOOL SUCCESS

One possible explanation for Coleman's findings, and those of others, is innate differences in intelligence. In *The Bell Curve*, Herrnstein and Murray (1994) argued that educational inequalities are due mostly to "natural" differences in intelligence in human populations rather than systematic differences in educational opportunities.

Herrnstein and Murray claimed that differences in learning and schooling are largely determined by differences in intelligence. In addition, they argued that differences in intelligence are largely inherited (up to 80 percent) and fixed. Two of those claims will be evaluated here. If intelligence determines how much students learn and intelligence is largely inherited and fixed, then efforts to equalize opportunities in schools are futile, and nothing much can be done to eliminate differences in student learning.

Herrnstein and Murray's claim that learning and school success are determined by intelligence is consistent with the finding that students who learn more in school have higher IQs. However, intelligence is by no means the only, or even the most important, predictor of learning. Duckworth and Seligman (2005) conducted a study in which students' "self-discipline," such as their work habits, perseverance, and intelligence, was measured and correlated with their grades at the end of the year. They found that a student's self-discipline had a substantially greater impact than intelligence on that student's grades at the end of the year. These findings suggest that students who master the school's "hidden curriculum" by, for example, developing the best work habits are the most likely to be rewarded in school.

Herrnstein and Murray's claim that intelligence is largely inherited and fixed has been vigorously challenged by many researchers. Herrnstein and Murray rely on data on identical twins raised in separate families to derive their estimates of the high "heritability" of IQ. The IQs of identical twins raised in different families are almost as similar as the IQs of those who are raised in the same families. These findings suggest that intelligence is affected more strongly by a person's genes than by the family in which a person is raised.

However, several recent studies have raised doubts about this conclusion. First, a high percentage of adoptive families are upper middle class; almost none are lower class (Stoolmiller 1999). In addition, adoptive family environments are much more similar than those of nonadoptive families. Thus, twins reared apart are likely raised in very similar family environments. This makes it unsurprising that they have similar IQs. Second, a French study examining IQs among children who were adopted into upper- and lower-class families found that being born to upper-class parents boosted a child's IQ by about 12 points (Capron and Duyme 1989). However, being adopted by and raised in an upper-class family also raised a child's IQ by 12 points. Finally, scores on intelligence tests have increased dramatically in many nations in the past 50 years (Flynn 2007). Such dramatic increases in intelligence across generations in so short a time are inconsistent with the claim that intelligence is largely genetically determined and fixed.

Far more troubling and controversial were Herrnstein and Murray's conclusions about racial differences. They claimed that whites had discernibly higher intelligence levels than blacks and Latinos. Their research has been subjected to rigorous analyses by numerous social scientists who have found that Herrnstein and Murray's conclusions were based on a number of methodological and interpretive errors. The consensus of the social scientific community is that there are no grounds for contending that there are innate intelligence differences along racial lines (Fischer et al. 1996).

FIGURE 11.12 • Educational Attainment in the United States by Family Socioeconomic (SES) Background, 2000

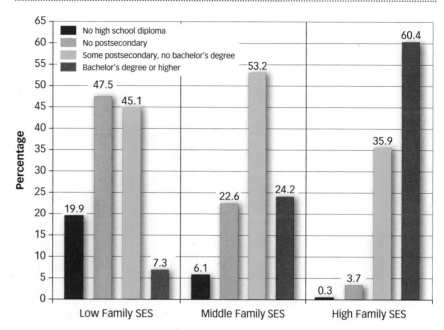

SOURCE: Data from Aud, Susan and Gretchen Hannes, editors. 2011. *The Condition of Education 2011 in Brief* (NCES 2011-034). Washington, DC: U.S. Department of Education, National Center for Education Statistics.

NOTE: Socioeconomic status (SES) is a composite measure of parental education and occupational status and family status. Low-SES families are below the 25th percentile, and high-SES families are above the 75th percentile. Respondents were followed for eight years after they were supposed to finish high school. (At the end of the eight years, in 2000, most of them were 25 years old.)

CLASS DIFFERENCES IN EARLY CHILDHOOD

If both school-based and "natural" explanations of educational inequality fail, what remains? Many social scientists have turned their attention to inequalities in children's earliest experiences—the home environment. Hart and Risley (1995) performed an in-depth study of 42 families and their children. The study began when each child studied was seven to nine months old. The researchers visited each family once every month until the children were three years old. For each hour-long visit, Hart and Risley recorded every spoken word and took notes on what happened. They found that the three types of families in their study—professional, working class, and welfare—differed markedly in how they spoke to and interacted with their children. By the time the children were three years of age, there were massive differences in the number of words that had been addressed to them among these different families: 35 million words in professional families,

Changing Educational Paradigms   Expanding Higher Education

FIGURE 11.13 • Percentage of U.S. High School Dropouts by Race and Gender, 2009

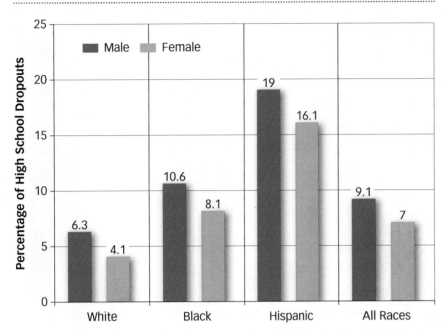

SOURCE: Data from Aud, Susan and Gretchen Hannes, editors. 2011. *The Condition of Education 2011 in Brief* (NCES 2011-034). Washington, DC: U.S. Department of Education, National Center for Education Statistics.

FIGURE 11.14 • U.S. Educational Attainment by Race and Gender, 2008

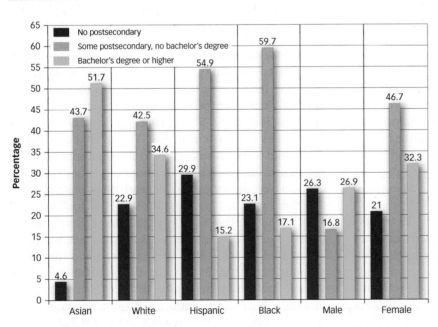

SOURCE: Data from Aud, Susan and Gretchen Hannes, editors. 2011. *The Condition of Education 2011 in Brief* (NCES 2011-034). Washington, DC: U.S. Department of Education, National Center for Education Statistics.

NOTE: Respondents were followed for eight years after they were supposed to finish high school. (At the end of those eight years, in 2000, most of them were 25 years old.)

20 million in working-class families, and fewer than 10 million in welfare families. Children in professional families experienced the most encouragement and least discouragement by their parents, as well as the greatest diversity in language. In terms of interaction styles, parents in professional families tended to use questions rather than commands to direct children's behavior. They were also more responsive to their children's requests.

Did these differences in home environments matter for early learning outcomes? By age three, children's exposure to differences in parenting practices and styles is highly correlated with vocabulary growth, vocabulary use, and intelligence. These effects persist when intelligence is measured at ages nine and ten. In addition, class differences in early cognitive outcomes are almost entirely explained by differences in parenting. Hart and Risley's classic study provides compelling evidence that children enter formal schooling with large differences in ability because they are exposed to very different home environments from an early age.

Preschool

Can we change children's educational outcomes by changing the cognitive culture that they experience when they are very young? From 1962 to 1967, 123 black children whose families were living in poverty in Ypsilanti, Michigan, participated in a fascinating policy experiment (Schweinhart, Barnett, and Belfield 2005). Half of the children were assigned to an enriched preschool program, while the other half—the control group—received no preschooling (Stoolmiller 1999). By the time the program ended, children who had attended the Perry Preschool program for two years were experiencing larger gains in intelligence than the control group. However, this IQ advantage faded away only a few years after the program ended. The Perry students performed better in school because they were more motivated to learn. Researchers followed these two groups of students well into adulthood (age 40), and found that the Perry students did substantially better as adults than the control group. The Perry students were more likely to finish high school and college and to hold a steady job, and they had higher earnings than the control group.

ASK YOURSELF

How strong do you think the connection is between social skills learned in preschool and adult success? Why? What advice would you give educational policy makers based on your conclusions?

James Heckman (2006) has estimated that in the long run every dollar spent on the Perry Preschool program saved $7 in tax revenue. Since the differences in cognitive ability between the two groups were negligible, he attributed the success enjoyed by Perry students as adults to the better social skills they learned in preschool.

Preschool is believed to benefit young students well into adulthood. Are there ethical ways to test this hypothesis?

INEQUALITY WITHIN SCHOOLS: TRACKING AND STUDENT OUTCOMES

Many studies have examined whether students who attend the same school receive similar learning opportunities. It is common at all levels of schooling in the United States to group students by ability, which is typically measured by standardized test scores and/or grades. This is commonly known as tracking. Barr and Dreeben (1983) examined first-grade reading groups in which students were grouped by their reading ability at the beginning of the year. Students in higher-ability groups learned more new words and improved their reading skills more rapidly than students in low-ability groups. Better readers were placed in high-ability groups at the beginning of the year. They received more instructional time, were exposed to more new words, and experienced a faster pace of instruction than students placed in low-ability groups. In short, higher-performing students received more learning opportunities than lower-performing students. Consequently, the gap between high- and low-achieving students grew larger during the year. This process is known as **cumulative**

advantage—the most advantaged individuals are awarded the best opportunities, and this increases inequality over time (DiPrete et al. 2006).

ASK YOURSELF

Do you thinking tracking is a good thing? If yes, what are its downsides? If not what are some alternatives to it?

As students progress through middle and secondary school, curricular differentiation takes the form of different classes with different content. Traditionally, these curricular tracks are aligned with students' future ambitions: The "high" track entails course work that prepares students for four-year colleges and professional careers. The "low" track focuses on basic and/or vocational skills for semiskilled occupations that do not require a college degree. Research consistently finds that high-track classes offer better learning opportunities to students because they are taught by more experienced, higher-quality teachers who have higher expectations of their students (Kelly 2004). Higher-track classes cover more material, and students receive higher-quality instruction (Gamoran et al. 1995). Students in high-track classes are more engaged and exert greater effort in school (Carbonaro 2005), which also helps them learn at a faster rate. Research consistently shows that

> **cumulative advantage** The process by which the most advantaged individuals are awarded the best opportunities, which increases inequality over time.

Global Illiteracy

Sara Gustoff of Iowa reads to her children as part of their homeschooling education. Should homeschooling be more heavily regulated by the government, or less?

parents were also much more integrated into social networks in the school—through parent-teacher associations and volunteering, for example. They used these connections to gain information about classes and teachers in the school. Finally, college-educated parents influenced their children in selecting classes by encouraging them to challenge themselves and think about the long-term consequences of their choices.

ALTERNATIVES TO TRADITIONAL PUBLIC SCHOOLS

Not everyone in the United States attends public schools. Three alternatives to public schools have emerged in the past few decades: vouchers, homeschooling, and charter schools. Proponents of each are highly critical of existing public schools, either for what they claim are shortcomings in educational achievement or for promoting values at odds with particular beliefs.

Vouchers

Vouchers are government-issued certificates that allow students to use public tax dollars to pay tuition at a private school. Parents seeking to remove their children from underperforming public schools find vouchers an attractive alternative.

Many voucher schools are religious schools. This raises constitutional issues about the separation of church and state. Moreover, whereas public schools are required by law to accept all students, this does not apply to private schools.

Proponents of voucher schools argue that parents—particularly poor parents—are provided with options for their children's educations that they otherwise would not have. In addition, they contend that the increased competition that the local public schools face from private schools stimulates them to enact changes to improve their educational programs. Opponents counter that vouchers encourage the creaming off of the best students from public schools. They also express a concern that vouchers will reduce funding levels of already underfunded public schools.

There has been limited research on whether students in voucher schools do better than their counterparts in public schools. In a study in Florida, Rudolfo Abella (2006) found that over a two-year period, voucher students did about as well as students remaining in public schools.

otherwise similar students learn more when placed in a higher-track class because of higher expectations, greater effort, and better learning opportunities. Ultimately, high-track students are more likely to attend college than low-track students.

What determines how students are assigned to different ability groups, tracks, and classes? In a meritocracy, achieved characteristics—hard work and prior academic success—should determine which students have access to high-track classes. Most studies show that prior achievement and grades are indeed the most important predictors of track placement. Since students from high-SES families are more likely to be high achievers, they are much more likely to take high-track classes than low-SES students. However, when students with the same test scores and grades are compared, students from higher-SES families are still more likely to be enrolled in high-track classes than low-SES students (Gamoran and Mare 1989). Thus, high-SES students are doubly advantaged in the track placement process.

What accounts for the SES advantage in track placement? Useem (1992) studied how families affect students' placement in middle school math classes. She found that college-educated parents had several key advantages in the placement process that ensured that their children would end up in the high-level classes. First, college-educated parents were much more knowledgeable about which classes were the most demanding and which ones were linked to high-level classes in high school. Indeed, some less educated parents seemed unaware that math classes were tracked. College-educated parents also better understood how the placement process worked, and they knew how to intervene successfully on their child's behalf. Second, college-educated

Homeschooling

Some parents decide that rather than sending their children to the local public school or to an alternative private school, they would prefer to educate their children at home. The popularity of homeschooling has grown over the years. About 1.5 million students were being homeschooled in the United States in 2007, the most recent year for which data have been provided (U.S. Department of Education, National Center for Education Statistics 2009).

Most homeschooled students come from two-parent families, only one of whom is in the labor force. The main reason that parents give for homeschooling their children is to ensure that they receive a religious or moral education that they do not think can be found outside the home. Related to this, they express concerns about the safety of schools, citing crime, drugs, and negative peer pressure. Some parents think the public schools do not adequately challenge their children, while others opt for homeschooling because their child has a disability, has a special need, or has had behavioral problems in public school settings.

As the number of homeschooled students has risen, universities have begun to address the need to assess such students as they apply for admission in increasing numbers. Based on standardized tests, homeschooled children may on average perform slightly better than their public school counterparts. Critics identify two topics that standardized tests do not address. The first has to do with whether homeschooled students have the social skills to function in a diverse society. The second raises concerns about their critical abilities and whether they look at the world unreflectively, embracing their parents' worldview.

ASK YOURSELF

Why might homeschooled children be at risk of lacking the social skills and worldview necessary to succeed in a diverse society? Is it important for homeschooling parents to address this risk? Does your answer to this question agree with your thoughts about the connection between social skills learned in preschool and adult success? Why or why not?

Charter Schools

Charter schools are intended to be an alternative to the traditional public school, but they remain part of the public school system. They receive public tax dollars, although they can also receive private funding. Charter schools were intended to be schools of choice, alternatives for parents dissatisfied with the local public school and interested in sending their children to schools over which they had greater control. The ideal of charter schools was that they would be more responsive to the concerns of parents and more accountable in terms of ensuring solid student outcomes.

These schools are granted greater autonomy than traditional public schools. They define their own mission and establish criteria for determining whether or not they achieve their objectives. Charter schools have a sponsor, and they are accountable to it and to the state in which they are located. One of the chief objectives of early proponents of charter schools was to reduce racial segregation in schools. At the same time, since the traditional public schools would end up competing with charter schools, proponents argued that they would be forced to improve to remain viable.

The results from a quarter century of experience with charter schools are mixed at best. For one thing, the schools have experienced managerial problems. Somewhere between 10 and 15 percent of charter schools have failed and closed. This has led some to propose larger-scale administrative organizations that would overcome some of the shortcomings of existing local charter management (Farrell, Wohlstetter, and Smith 2012). Second, racial segregation is not being reduced by charter schools. On the contrary, it appears that the self-selection process built into the idea of choice actually increases levels of racial segregation (Garcia 2008; Jacobs 2013). Third, there is no evidence to support the idea that competition from charter schools results in improved performance of traditional public schools (Zimmer and Buddin 2009).

A recent study found that charter schools are improving. But there are wide differences across states. While in some states charter schools achieve better results than their traditional counterparts, in other states their results are much worse. Overall, 31 percent of charter schools have actually been found to offer a *less* successful education than regular public schools (Berends et al. 2010; Rich 2013).

One of the reasons for these disparities is that charter schools have not overcome the differential funding levels that exist in the traditional public school sector, where wealthier suburban communities have greater financial resources to tap into compared to their inner-city counterparts. An ethnographic study of three charter schools in California—one serving a predominantly white suburb, another a working-class Latino community, and the third an inner-city African American neighborhood—showed that they had very different experiences. Charter schools in the wealthier community were far more capable of achieving their educational goals than those in the two poorer

For-Profit Schools

College Online

FIGURE 11.15 • U.S. Students Attaining at Least a Bachelor's Degree by Family Background and Academic Ability, 2000

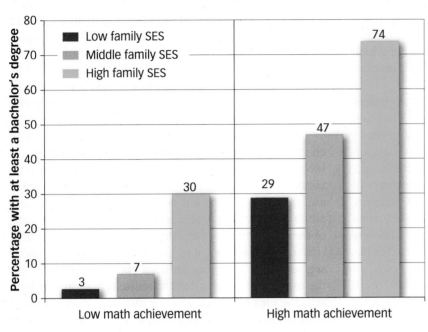

SOURCE: Data from Aud, Susan and Gretchen Hannes, editors. 2011. *The Condition of Education 2011 in Brief* (NCES 2011-034). Washington, DC: U.S. Department of Education, National Center for Education Statistics.

NOTE: Socioeconomic status (SES) is a composite measure of parental education and occupational status and family status. Low-SES families are below the 25th percentile, and high-SES families are above the 75th percentile. Respondents were followed for eight years after they were supposed to finish high school. (At the end of those eight years, most of them were 25 years old.)

neighborhoods. The charter schools in the African American community fared the worst (Bancroft 2009).

WHO GOES TO COLLEGE?

Figure 11.15 shows that students with more advantaged family backgrounds are more likely to graduate from high school and college. White students are also more likely to successfully make these educational transitions.

Do these advantages in educational attainment merely reflect differences in student learning? Test scores and grades are strong predictors of who finishes high school and goes to college. This partly explains why advantaged students attain more schooling. However, Figure 11.15 shows that student achievement does not fully account for the advantages of family background. In this figure, we compare students' chance of getting a bachelor's degree based on both their family background and their academic achievements in mathematics. We see that among both high- and low-SES students, high-achieving students are considerably more likely to attain a bachelor's degree. A high-SES student is more than twice as likely to

get a bachelor's degree when he or she is high achieving rather than low achieving (74 percent versus 30 percent). For low-SES students, high achievers are actually 10 times more likely to get a bachelor's degree than low achievers (29 percent versus 3 percent). Thus, it appears that merit—what students accomplish—is rewarded in the American educational system. However, the figure also attests to the power of ascriptive characteristics in educational attainment. We see that high-SES students who are low achievers have virtually the same chance of attaining a bachelor's degree as high-achieving low-SES students—roughly 30 percent. In contrast, low-achieving students from low-SES families have virtually no chance of getting a baccalaureate degree (3 percent).

Why does family background matter so much for college attainment, above and beyond academic achievement? Studies from the 1950s through the 1980s found that students from high-SES families had a greater likelihood of receiving a college degree. More recent studies, however, suggest that virtually all students—regardless of family background—want and expect to complete a college degree (Schneider and Stevenson 1999). This trend reflects a "college-for-all" mentality by policy makers, counselors, and the general public (Rosenbaum 2001, 2011).

However, higher-SES students are more likely to attend and to graduate from college because they encounter a "college-going habitus" at home and in school. A **habitus** is an internalized set of preferences and dispositions that are learned through experience and social interactions in specific social contexts (Bourdieu and Passeron 1977). For example, children raised in families with highly educated parents may constantly be exposed to justifications regarding the importance of education in adult life. They may also hear dismissive and derogatory comments that devalue people with less education. It may become clear that education is a critical part of being accepted as a member of the group. Ultimately, children in this situation may not

> **habitus** An internalized set of preferences and dispositions that are learned through experience and social interactions in specific social contexts.

DIGITAL LIVING

Massive Open Online Courses (MOOCs)

"Massive Open Online Courses," or MOOCs, are designed to enroll a *massive* number of students, to be *open* to anyone, to exist only *online* and be accessible only to those with a computer and access to the Internet, and to offer *courses* designed to educate.

The first true MOOC arrived in 2008. Three years later, three Stanford University MOOCs each enrolled more than 100,000 students from nearly every country in the world. A corporation named Coursera emerged out of this experience, which by 2012 had enrolled over 2 million students. Other corporations have also been created, including Udacity and edX. A growing number of universities are exploring the possibility of offering MOOCs. They are likely to spread rapidly and to alter higher education dramatically. A major driving force is the increasing costs of traditional higher education; MOOCs are able to reach a far greater number of students at much lower costs.

One MOOC is an Introduction to Sociology course taught by Professor Mitch Duneier from Princeton University and offered to approximately 40,000 students worldwide. As in most of the early MOOCs, less than 5 percent of the students who began the course completed it and took the final exam. However, there was a lot of student involvement, and Duneier found, "within three weeks, I had more feedback on my sociological ideas than I'd had in my whole teaching career" (Lewin 2012). Feedback came through global exchanges on an online discussion, a video chat room, and study groups that formed throughout the world.

However, there are a variety of problems associated with MOOCs beyond the fact that such a small percentage of students actually complete the courses. One is the difficulties involved in creating a web-based course that has the high production values students are accustomed to in video games and movies. Another is that the requirements of being a good teacher mediated by the computer are different from those required in the classroom; few professors are trained to teach in this way. Then there is the issue of evaluating the work of thousands of students and the need for a professor to have a small army of assistants. One of the ways this is dealt with at the moment is to have students evaluate each other. It is not clear that these courses will ever become part of programs that lead to receipt of a degree from elite universities, which are wary about devaluing their highly sought-after degrees. In addition, the business model for MOOCs remains murky. How to collect fees and what to charge remain unanswered questions (Lewin 2012).

Finally, there is the worry that MOOCs will lead to an even more stratified educational system. On the one hand, students in less developed countries, as well as students in community colleges and lower-tier colleges in the United States, will be exposed to elite educators and courses, and thus MOOCs seem likely to democratize education and reduce levels of educational inequality. On the other, these same students will be exposed to such institutions *only* via MOOCs. Higher-achieving students who get accepted to elite universities will continue to have the benefit of life on their campuses and the opportunities for sustained face-to-face encounters with famous professors. This latter group will continue to have the opportunity to earn a prestigious degree while it remains unclear whether similar opportunities will be granted to those obtaining their education via MOOCs.

Think About It

Have you ever attended a MOOC or another type of online course? If so, was your purpose to enhance your knowledge in your major area of study or in another field? Why did you choose an online flow of information for this purpose, and how did your experience in the course differ from your experiences in the traditional classroom setting?

---

see the pursuit of a college degree as "choice"; rather, they may see it as an obligation. As students experience different social contexts that correspond with their family backgrounds, they will form different ideas about the importance of college and the role it plays in their lives.

GLOBALIZATION AND EDUCATION

We have spent much time discussing educational inequality in learning outcomes in the United States. Is the American system typical? How do other school systems around the world differ and with what consequences?

PISA Rankings

PISA refers to the Program for International Student Assessment, a worldwide study of student educational performance. Since 2000, it has measured the proficiency of 15-year-olds in reading, math, and science every three years. Table 11.1 provides a list of the top-performing nations in 2012.

World Poverty and Education   Underground College in Iran

TABLE 11.1 • PISA Rankings, 2012

Education ranking	Country	Public spending on education	
		as % of GDP	as % of gov't spending
1	Finland	6.8	12.1
2	South Korea	4.8	15.8
3	Hong Kong	3.5	20.1
4	Japan	3.4	9.4
5	Singapore	3.5	21.4
6	Britain	5.6	11.3
7	Netherlands	5.9	11.5
8	New Zealand	5.6	16.1
9	Switzerland	5.5	16.2
10	Canada	5.0	12.3
11	Denmark	8.7	15.1
12	Australia	5.1	12.9
13	Poland	5.1	11.4
14	Germany	5.1	10.5
15	United States	5.4	13.1

SOURCE: Pearson UNESCO.

As has been true in previous years, Finland tops the table, followed by South Korea. Educational experts have been especially fascinated by Finland's top ranking.

What does the Finnish educational system look like? First, teachers are well trained. Gaining acceptance into teacher-training programs in universities is competitive. Teachers are well paid, and the teaching profession remains highly respected. Teachers are unionized, which undercuts an argument of conservatives in the United States and elsewhere that teachers' unions have been detrimental to the delivery of quality education.

Second, Finland has not embraced any of the policies pursued in recent decades in the United States, including charter schools, vouchers, merit pay for teachers, and evaluation of teachers and schools in terms of how well they perform on standardized tests (Ravitch 2012: 19).

Third, Finnish schools perform at remarkably similar levels; there is less variation in achievement across the educational system than there is in other countries (Sahlberg 2011). Diane Ravitch (2012: 19) concluded that Finland comes "closest to achieving equality of educational opportunity." School funding is uniform and equitable. The

school system reflects the larger national culture, which has been shaped for many decades by a social democratic commitment to equality and to a welfare system that promotes it.

To appreciate the fact that different societies have tackled educating future generations differently, we turn to three large industrial societies: the United States, Germany, and Japan. Their 2012 PISA rankings were, respectively, 15, 14, and 4.

U.S., German, and Japanese Education Systems

In Germany, all elementary school students attend Grundschule, which does not practice ability grouping; all children are exposed to the same curriculum. At the end of fourth grade, teachers make recommendations to families regarding the type of secondary school a given child should attend based on his or her test scores and their subjective assessments of the student's ability. There are three types of schools that represent academic and vocational tracks: lower-level "gymnasium" (the college track), "realschule" (the middle track), and "hauptschule" (the lowest track). Each of these schools has its own curriculum designed to correspond with the future occupational trajectories of its students. Only 30 percent of students are placed in the gymnasium level. Transferring to a different track is possible, but it is difficult and rare. Between-school tracking continues at the next level of schooling. Only students who attend upper-level gymnasium can proceed to the university system and attain the equivalent of a baccalaureate degree.

From school entry through ninth grade in Japan, there is little or no ability grouping among students either between or within schools. For the first nine years of school, Japanese students are exposed to a remarkably uniform curriculum. At the end of ninth grade, Japanese students take a high-stakes test that determines which type of high school they will attend. About 75 percent of students attend "futsuuka," which has a college preparatory curriculum. The remaining 25 percent of students attend a variety of technical and vocational schools. Family background still plays an important role in educational success for Japanese students because of a "shadow education" system, in which informal schooling opportunities outside of school give more advantaged students better preparation for both high school and college entrance exams.

All American students, regardless of their class origins and their future aspirations, attend the same types of schools. Tracking occurs within schools, not between schools. The United States also has more variability in school quality by geographical region. The German and Japanese systems are much more centralized than the United States. The United States has 50 different educational systems (one run by each state) with different levels of funding and varying curricula. In the United States, more so than in Japan and Germany, the quality and character of students' education is likely to be affected by where their family lives.

These differences have implications for achievement outcomes in each nation (Montt 2011). Germany has the highest levels of achievement inequality because of its highly stratified system. Japan has higher average achievement than Germany but much less inequality in outcomes because it does not practice curricular differentiation until very late. The United States actually has the lowest average achievement and the least variability of these three nations.

CHECKPOINT 11.5 INEQUALITY IN EDUCATION

Patterns of inequality	—High-scoring U.S. students are those whose parents have the most education. —Black students are much less likely than white students to finish high school or graduate from college. —Hispanic students are the most disadvantaged in terms of attainment. —Women are much more likely to finish both high school and college than men.
The Coleman Report	—Schools differ in quality much less than previously thought. —School resources do not predict student achievement. —Teacher quality, family background, and racial composition of a school's population are the most important indicators of achievement.
The Bell Curve	Students who learn more in school have higher IQs (but later research has shown that work habits and perseverance have even greater impact).
Effects of preschool	Attendance at preschool programs confers only temporary gains in intelligence but lifetime gains in social skills.
Voucher schools	Many are religious schools that can provide opportunities for poorer students but may blur the separation of church and state and skim off resources and students from the public system.
Homeschooling	Increasingly popular, homeschooling raises questions about students' development of social skills and their potentially limited worldviews.
Charter schools	Publicly funded but privately operated, charter schools define their own mission and criteria but have experienced administrative failings and rely on self-selection that may increase racial segregation.
College success	High-achieving students at all socioeconomic levels are more likely to attain a bachelor's degree.

SUMMARY

The components of religion include a set of interrelated beliefs, a variety of rituals, and religious experiences. While religion can be separate in many respects from the rest of society, it is also often interconnected. This is true of civil religion, which uses religious values and rituals to promote national identity and patriotism.

Sociologists have identified different types of religious institutions. These include sects, small cults of "true believers"; churches, large groups into which members are usually born; cults, exclusive small groups often at odds with established religions; and denominations, groups not linked to the state that generally tolerate other religious organizations. Some sociologists prefer to use the term *new religious movements* to encompass sects, cults, and a wide array of other innovative religious groups.

The spread of religion is not new, but it has accelerated with increased globalization. Christianity and Islam are the two largest religions in the world and are growing, while Judaism is the smallest. The vast majority of Buddhists reside in Asia, and the majority of Hindus live in one particular country: India. However, Buddhism and Hinduism have been spreading to other places around the globe. Mormons have aggressively expanded globally using modern techniques and technologies. One factor contributing to growing global religious diversity is global migration.

Education is closely related to the process of socialization, although it most often takes place more formally in schools. Coleman found that teacher quality, family background, and racial composition of the student body were the most important factors affecting student achievement. Herrnstein and Murray later argued that inherited differences account for different levels of achievement. However, other researchers have convincingly shown that differences in the home environment of very young children better explain differences in educational ability and attainment.

The use of tracking in schools often leads to cumulative advantage for students placed in higher tracks. These most advantaged students are consequently awarded the best opportunities for learning, which in turn increases inequality over time. Further increasing inequality is the fact that students from higher-SES families are more often placed in higher tracks than their low-SES peers, regardless of ability. Differences in SES also affect college attainment. Great differences in educational inequality remain around the world.

KEY TERMS

Beliefs, 309
Church, 317
Civil religion, 312
Cult, 318
Cumulative advantage, 335
Denominations, 319
Fundamentalism, 325

Habitus, 338
Liminal period, 311
Meritocracy, 330
New religious movements, 319
Profane, 309
Religion, 309
Rites of passage, 310

Ritual, 310
Sacred, 309
Sect, 317
Secularization, 314
Vouchers, 336

REVIEW QUESTIONS

1. How do we define religion? What are the basic elements and components of religious institutions? In what ways have religions changed over time?

2. What are the major religions of the world? How are people distributed among the major religions of the world? In what ways are religions global?

3. What is the difference between a sect and a church? Provide one example of a sect and one of a church. Why has the term *cult* fallen out of favor with sociologists of religion?

4. What is ritual? Why is it an important component of religion? Offer examples of ritual practice from one of the major global religions discussed in the chapter. Provide another example, this time from a new religious movement.

5. Provide a definition of civil religion and discuss its function. The text describes several examples of civil religion. Offer additional examples.

6. What is a meritocracy, and why is the educational system an important component of a meritocratic society? In what ways is the U.S. education system meritocratic, and in what ways is it not meritocratic?

7. According to the Coleman Report, how important is the quality of schools to the quality of student achievement? What other factors affect student achievement? What factors have not been found to affect student achievement to any great extent?

8. Describe overall trends in student achievement by race and ethnicity and by gender. In what ways are these changes reflective of larger societal changes? Do you think that new technologies can be used to close achievement gaps across groups? Why or why not?

9. Compare and contrast the American, German, and Japanese educational systems. How do these systems' differences affect achievement outcomes in these countries? How do their attitudes toward grouping reflect their respective cultural norms and values?

10. MOOCs have burst onto the higher education scene in recent years, with some courses enrolling more than 100,000 students from around the world. While advocates see such course offerings as the future of higher education, skeptics think that this will be a passing fad. What do you think, and why?

APPLYING THE SOCIOLOGICAL IMAGINATION ....

1. This chapter pointed out that a large and increasing number of people in the world today consider themselves nonreligious. For this activity, think of yourself as someone who is nonreligious seeking to become a member of one of the major world religions. Use the Internet (Google search, Twitter hashtags) to learn more about the major world religions and to determine the pros and cons of trying to adopt and participate in a specific religion. What would you do to facilitate your membership? How is choosing a religion different from choosing to buy a certain product or join a certain gym?

2. As this chapter indicated, an increasing number of people seeking alternatives to conventional public schools have opted to homeschool their children. As a result, a number of organizations have emerged that are designed to promote homeschooling and to ensure that parents doing the homeschooling are provided with necessary training and instructional resources. Use the Internet to examine some of the websites of these organizations to get a better understanding of the messages they convey about the rationales for homeschooling and the audiences to which they are targeting these messages. Given that parents engaged in homeschooling are prosumers (producing education for their children), how do the messages attempt to convince them that they are capable of doing so? Are the criticisms of public schools made explicitly or implicitly? Do you find the claims convincing? What would you want to know before you could make a sociologically informed assessment of the homeschooling alternative?

STUDENT STUDY SITE ....

Sharpen your skills with SAGE edge at **edge.sagepub.com/ritzeressentials**

SAGE edge for students provides a personalized approach to help you accomplish your coursework goals in an easy-to-use learning environment.

This Chinese worker has been painting a new crane at a port in Shanghai. China's political system retains many elements of Communism, but its economy has been growing quite rapidly by adopting the business practices of capitalism. What does China's growth mean for members of the world's other economies?

POLITICS AND THE ECONOMY

12

The worldwide economic collapse of 2008 set off a chain reaction that devastated much of the international economy, triggering a global recession whose effects, including stagnant wages and widespread unemployment, are still being felt today. Most of the world's industrialized economies, like those of the United States and the European Union countries, stumbled badly. Ireland, Jamaica, Venezuela, North Korea, Madagascar, and Croatia even experienced negative economic growth as their economies unexpectedly shrank rather than expanded.

Sociology studies our political and economic choices, their relationship, and their consequences.

The global financial crisis is an issue not just of economics, but also of politics. In fact, in many ways these two fundamental social institutions are inseparable, and this chapter considers them together. A nation's political system—and the policy makers who populate it—have an enormous impact on the way money and resources are distributed, spent, and saved at every level of society. The basic economic questions of what goods and services society will produce, how it will produce them, and who will consume them have yielded answers as different in their political philosophies and effects as communism, socialism, and capitalism.

"Command" economic systems, such as communism, gather society's resources under a central government authority that makes all decisions about production, pricing, and distribution, ideally ensuring fairness to all. In contrast, laissez-faire ("leave it alone") systems, like unregulated capitalism, allow buyers and sellers to make their own profit-motivated decisions about how to use society's resources, avoiding government regulation in the belief that "the market knows best" how to manage production and consumption. Socialism, in turn, emphasizes common or cooperative ownership of society's resources, distributes what society produces according to what individuals have contributed to make it, and discourages the accumulation of profit. No country's system is a pure version of any of these systems, of course, and today communism has all but disappeared.

Given the political philosophies behind these economic systems, you can see that their relationship is complex, and that political conflict and social change can have serious long-term economic consequences. The global financial crisis has taught a hard, perhaps inevitable, lesson about globalization: We are all connected, and as success flows, so too does failure. This is particularly so for the middle and lower classes, who are hardest hit by unemployment, wage stagnation, and rising prices. Sociology looks at how we make the political and economic choices we do, and how we as a society deal with the consequences. •

This chapter deals with two key social institutions—politics and the economy.

POLITICS: POWER AND CONTROL

Society can be seen as a collection of overlapping groups that compete to meet their own objectives. When groups go through established governmental channels to do so, this competition is referred to as **politics**. The state is the political body organized for government and civil rule (see Chapter 5). By putting pressure on the state, a group can advance a given position or have enacted a policy that benefits its members. Therefore, politics is one way of exercising power in society.

As you saw in Chapter 7, power is the ability to get others to do what you want them to do, even if it is against their will. It is often expressed formally by, among others, police officers, professors, and business executives. However, it is also expressed in subtler, more informal ways, such as in casual social relationships. When it is legitimated by a social structure such as a government, university, or corporate hierarchy, power is referred to as authority (see Chapter 5). Because authority is a legitimate form of domination, there is a strong likelihood that commands will be considered appropriate—and will be obeyed—by subordinates.

> **politics** Societal competition through established governmental channels to advance a position or enact a policy to benefit the group's members.
>
> **democracy** A political system in which people within a given state vote to choose their leaders and in some cases vote on legislation.
>
> **representative democracy** A political system in which people, as a whole body, do not actually rule themselves but rather have some say in who will best represent them in the state.
>
> **direct democracy** A political system in which people directly affected by a given decision have a say in that decision.
>
> **citizens** The people represented by a given state, most often born within its territories.
>
> **citizenship** The idea that people of a given state can vote for their representatives within the state, but also that they have access to rights and responsibilities as citizens.
>
> **dictatorships** States that are usually totalitarian and ruled either by a single individual or by a small group of people.

DEMOCRACY: CITIZENSHIP AS A RADICAL IDEA

Democracies are political systems in which people within a given state vote to choose their leaders and in some cases vote on legislation as well. In modern democracies, people vote to choose their legislators rather than actually effectively managing their own political affairs and directly making decisions about the things that affect their lives. Nevertheless, contemporary theorists of democracy often suggest that the power to rule in democracies comes from the *consent* of the people.

Sometimes these systems are called **representative democracies**. The people, as a whole body, do not actually rule themselves but rather have some say in who will best represent them in the state. In **direct democracies**, by contrast, the people have a say in decisions that directly affect them.

Democratic states are organized into bureaucracies (see Chapter 5) with clear hierarchies, as well as established and written codes, laws, and rules. The authority that legislators have in democracies is based on legal codes that confer this authority on them. Democracies tend to extend rights to **citizens**, the people represented by the state and most often born within its territories. **Citizenship** means that the people of a given state can vote for their representatives and that they have rights and responsibilities as citizens (Soysal 2012; Turner 2011). Under *universal citizenship*, these rights are generally conferred on most people residing in a given state's territory. At times, however, citizenship is denied to groups of immigrants residing within that territory. In the United States, citizens have certain rights and can vote on who will be president and on who will represent them in Congress.

Most democratic states guarantee citizens the right to freely express dissent, the right to due process and equality before the law, the right to freedom of speech and of the press, and the right to privacy. These rights and others are sometimes extended to noncitizens.

Democracies are not without their critics, even from within. For example, it is argued that voters are typically uninformed about many political issues. Similarly, there is the belief that liberal democracies extend *too many* rights and tend to allow too much diversity of thought and interest, making them unstable.

DICTATORSHIP: THE SEIZURE OF POWER

Dictatorships are states that are usually totalitarian and ruled either by a single individual or by a small group of people. They are governments *without* the consent of the people being governed. In the modern period, dictatorships

Social Change/Social Media

The Red Scare

DIGITAL LIVING

The State and the Power of the Internet

Power is something that we usually associate with the state, but it is not unusual for that power to be threatened or overthrown in social revolutions. In the last few years, a new threat to the state has arisen in the form of the power of the crowd as manifest in social revolutions made possible in large part by social media, the so-called Twitter and Facebook revolutions. If threatened with such a revolution, the state has essentially four choices: repression, censorship, the use of propaganda, or to try to remain off the grid:

1. Muammar Gaddafi sought unsuccessfully to *repress* the revolution in Libya, and as I write, Bashar al-Assad is in the third year of attempting to use his military to suppress the growing revolution in Syria. The problem with repression is that it usually serves to heighten the opposition and to fuel the revolution. It can even serve to radicalize those who are for the regime, or hurt the society in other ways, for example, by slowing down the economy.

2. In the old days, newspapers, radio programs, and television shows were censored, but such *censorship* was easy to achieve compared to the difficulties involved in censoring the Internet.

3. The state might resort to *propaganda* delivered via the media, perhaps even the Internet, in an effort to counter the messages being put forth by the rebels.

An illuminated portrait of Kim Il-sung, North Korea's late founder, hangs on a building in the capital city of Pyongyang. The country is almost entirely insulated from the online world, since its people are not permitted access to the Internet. What factors motivate such a decision by the government?

4. Finally, it is possible, as in the case of North Korea, to *stay off the grid* almost completely and to deny people access to the Internet.

While many see social media as a revolutionary force (see, for example, the "Digital Living" box in Chapter 15), there are those (e.g., Gladwell 2010) who see it as fostering "slacktivism" rather than activism. Some potential activists might be more inclined to blog than to take to the streets. However, even if these activists are unlikely to become revolutionaries, social media are likely to increase solidarity among those involved (Woods 2011). Another view is that state officials will make better use of social media than the crowd, and that the state's position will be strengthened, not jeopardized, by it (Morozov 2011).

Think About It

Do you feel that social media inspire slacktivism rather than activism? Why or why not? Do you think states may eventually be able to use social media for their own agendas and purposes, appropriating the power of the crowd? What qualities or characteristics of the state as an organization might make this possible?

---

are often formed in formerly democratic states that have been seized by small groups of political fanatics.

In the years just before and during World War II, the world saw an alliance of dictatorships based on fascist principles. These dictatorships shared some very basic institutional arrangements and principles. They

- were totalitarian because they attempted to control every facet of social life;

- had a **cult of masculinity** that organized political life and the public sphere around men and punished perceived deficiencies in masculinity such as homosexuality;

> **cult of masculinity** A social practice that organizes political life and the public sphere around men and punishes perceived deficiencies in masculinity in men.

- saw conflict and war as natural states and methods for human betterment; and

- were viciously opposed to liberalism, anarchism, and any form of socialism or communism.

Dictatorships did not end with the defeat of the fascist powers in World War II. Indeed, in the postwar era, the Soviet Union and its satellites in the Eastern Bloc were often organized as dictatorships, with small groups of Communist Party officials controlling society. Further, the United States has often sponsored dictatorships and fought against democracy. This has occurred particularly where a democratically elected leader might indicate a turn toward socialism and, thus, become a thorn in the side of American business interests (Chomsky 1985).

THE U.S. POLITICAL SYSTEM

The U.S. political system is a **two-party system** in which members of two parties hold nearly all positions of political power. In **multiparty systems,** by contrast, more than two parties hold political office (e.g., in Germany, Canada, and Taiwan). In **single-party systems**, the ruling party holds all offices (e.g., in China and Singapore). The single-party system outlaws, or heavily restricts, opposing parties.

Two-party systems can actually narrow political options (Disch 2002). They certainly afford more breadth for discussion, debate, and policy than single-party

A couple in Kyrgystan, in Central Asia, exercise one of citizenship's basic rights, the right to vote. Do you plan to vote in the next election?

CHECKPOINT 12.1	DEMOCRACY VS. DICTATORSHIP
Democracy	A political system in which people in a given state vote to choose their leaders and in some cases vote on legislation.
Dictatorship	States that are usually totalitarian and ruled either by a single individual or by a small group of people.

systems. However, two-party systems create a "race to the center" whereby parties compete for the majority of the vote without alienating voters with extreme positions. This means that minority points of view are often ignored by the ruling parties. Third parties do at times run candidates and on very few occasions win office, but they typically "play . . . the role of spoiler, drawing votes from one of the two major parties" (Glasberg and Shannon 2011: 91).

POLITICAL PARTIES AND ELECTIONS

In the United States' two-party system, Democrats and Republicans are the major political players. The **Democrats** are typically seen as the liberal party. They tend to seek larger and more generous welfare and social assistance programs, such as universal health care. They also tend to support social reforms, such as gay marriage and the right

> **two-party system** A political system in which two parties hold nearly all positions of political power in a given nation.
>
> **multiparty systems** A political system in which more than two parties enjoy public support and hold political office in a nation.
>
> **single-party systems** A political system in which the ruling party outlaws, or heavily restricts, opposing parties.
>
> **Democrats** Members of a political party within the U.S. two-party system, typically seen as the liberal party.

Forms of Government

The United States' two-party system is dominated by the Democrats and the Republicans, whose candidates in the 2012 presidential election were, respectively, the incumbent president Barack Obama (right) and challenger Mitt Romney. If a third party were to succeed in the United States, what sort of political platform would it likely promote?

Because of the race to the center, the parties have not historically looked that much different when it comes to the legislation that they support or sign into law. So it might be overly simplistic to think of the Democrats as a liberal party and the Republicans as its conservative opposition. A simple binary understanding of the two ruling parties often disguises more than it illuminates in terms of actual legislation and policy.

However, the two parties seem to have drawn further apart in recent years. This is largely because Republicans have become more conservative. As a result, there has been a stalemate at the highest reaches of the American government. It has proven difficult or impossible to agree on important legal changes or on ways to reduce the national deficit.

of women to have abortions. The **Republicans** are often seen as the conservative party, seeking less government spending and waste as well as restrictions on abortions and gay marriage.

FIGURE 12.1 • Voter Turnouts in U.S. Presidential Elections, 1948–2012

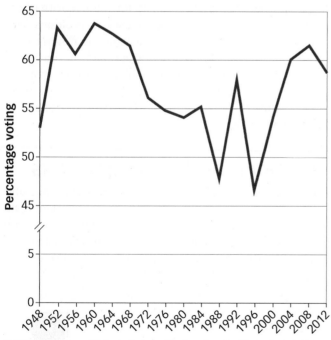

SOURCE: Data from UC Santa Barbara, The American Presidency Project, Voter Turnout in Presidential Elections: 1828–2012.

ASK YOURSELF

Would the existence of a third major political party in the United States reduce the likelihood of stalemates in government, such as the one the country is currently experiencing? Why or why not? What obstacles might stand in the way of the formation of such a party? For the United States, are there any disadvantages of a multiparty system?

Demographics and Voting Patterns

Supporters of representative democracies typically point to the vote as a critical source of power for citizens. It is curious, then, that so few people in the United States actually go to the polls. Even in the elections where the most eligible Americans vote—presidential elections—little more than half of eligible voters typically bother to cast a ballot. And when Americans choose their local, congressional, and state leaders, turnouts are even smaller (see Chapter 3).

As Figure 12.1 illustrates, voter turnout varies over time. Studies of voter turnout ask questions about who votes and why or why not. They also ask what election processes offer citizens in terms of power over their lives and the nation's political directions. In the United States, this

> **Republicans** Members of a political party within the U.S. two-party system; typically seen as the conservative party.

often means looking at groupings of people to investigate voting patterns. This also allows political sociologists to formulate theories about why people may or may not vote. They also theorize about whether people feel invested in the political process or, perhaps, feel disenfranchised from it and alienated to the extent that they may not participate.

One might be tempted to believe that the people most likely to vote are those most disadvantaged in a given society. If voting is a way an engaged citizenry exercises its power, then voting allows those people to attempt to improve their lot. By most measures, the exact opposite is the case with voting patterns in the United States. Indeed, those with jobs, those with higher incomes, older people, those with more education, and women are more likely to cast ballots than are their counterparts (U.S. Census Bureau 2009; Wattenberg 2002). With the exception of women, this means that the most advantaged are the most likely to vote.

This leaves sociologists with the task of explaining why there is low voter turnout in general and why political participation and turnout tend to be lower in disadvantaged groups (Hajnal and Lee 2011). Some studies have suggested that participation in organizations linked with electoral processes allows for political education for their members and that this might translate into higher rates of voter participation. For example, belonging to unions might provide important political education for the working class. The decline of unions might also explain decreases in working-class participation in electoral processes (Kerrissey and Schofer 2013; Radcliff 2001).

However, organizational participation can lead to forms of political activity outside of the electoral process, such as protests or community and workplace organizing (R. McVeigh and Smith 1999). This could point to alienation from the electoral process. Individuals who take the time to learn about politics within these organizations often put their energies elsewhere. Some potential voters may feel alienated from the process as a result of the lack of community structures that encourage meaningful political participation (Docherty, Goodlad, and Paddison 2001). Still others, due to widespread unemployment, political scandals, their disenfranchisement, and the like, might question the very legitimacy of the political institutions under which they live (Bay and Blekesaune 2002).

Media play an enormous role in the political life of the United States, not only during elections but throughout the year. From which media source do you get your political news? Is it fair and unbiased? How do you know?

This sense of alienation and disenfranchisement from the electoral process is increased by racism. For example, amid widespread disputes over ballot-counting in Florida in the 2000 election contest between George W. Bush and Al Gore, it was found that in largely white precincts about 1 in 14 ballots were invalid while in largely black precincts 1 in 5 ballots were declared invalid (Lichtman 2003). To make matters worse, the state disqualified thousands of voters—more than half of whom were black—from registration without notifying them (U.S. Commission on Civil Rights 2000). This occurred in an election where 90 percent of black Americans cast their ballots for Gore and whites made up 95 percent of pro-Bush voters (Wing 2001).

MEDIA AND THE POLITICAL PROCESS

The media influence what people consider "important political issues" as well as pointing out who they think is responsible for social conflicts (Barnhurst and Wartella 1998; Iyengar 1990). Through media concentration, wealthy and powerful people are given much more access to this primary means of socialization *and* persuasion. They are able to set the political agenda and create news that reflects their interests. Herman and Chomsky (1988; Downing 2011) note how news media concentration also serves to legitimate our class system. This is certainly a boon to the wealthy, who benefit from people seeing material inequalities as natural and normal.

Voter Turnout in Democracies

Big Donors

In addition to wealthy interests that exert inordinate control over the news media, *political* elites have great power over, and access to, the media. News media rely on the state's acceptance of their activities and are regulated by the political system in terms of both ownership and content. News media also rely on the state for source material. Studies have consistently shown that government officials are the source of most news, in many cases subtly and not so subtly shaping the content (Gans 1979, 2003; Herman and Chomsky 1988; McChesney 1999; Shehata 2010).

Similarly, government officials rely on news media to circulate information. Politicians seeking votes or a particular public image, legislators seeking support for political decisions, and governments desiring to inform citizens about social policy, conflict, or in some cases public hazards all rely on news media to disseminate information in a way that clearly articulates their position. Thus, the relationship between news media and government is *symbiotic*, each relying on the other in important ways. The wealthy corporations that own most news media also exist in a symbiotic relationship with government, further solidifying the links between political elites and the wealthy.

The tendency of media to showcase ideas that are acceptable to wealthy and powerful elites, especially those who are conservative, may seem obvious. Yet there is a popular belief in the United States that mass media, and news media in particular, have a liberal bias (Groseclose 2011). Studies, however, have shown quite the opposite. Howard (2002) concluded that network news tends to accord centrality to the views of powerful political and economic leaders. However, it gives comparatively little access to liberals—and others—who challenge those leaders and their views.

Despite unequal access to media and the great concentrations of ownership of mass media, the delivery or acceptance of the messages of elites is in no way guaranteed. The media can be, and are, used to challenge the status quo (Black and Allen 2001). For example, pictures of innocent children injured or killed by U.S. missile and drone attacks fueled opposition to the war in Afghanistan. And although critics of society's dominant institutions are most often relegated to independent media, there are times when they slip through into mass media. One example is the 2006 film *V for Vendetta* with anarchist-inspired themes in opposition to capitalism and the state.

Elites also have little control over how their perspectives are received. For example, despite attempts at "encoding" a given message into media, people often "decode" those messages in very different ways (Hall 1980). Likewise, political messages in media "can neither produce a single and homogenous audience nor create a single effect on people" (Gans 2003: 70).

WHO RULES THE UNITED STATES?

The issue of who rules the United States is a source of continuing debate among sociologists.

The Structural/Functional Perspective: Pluralism

Within structural-functionalism, **political pluralism** is the typical position put forward regarding who rules America. This is the view that the United States is characterized by a number of powerful competing interest groups, but no one of them is in control all of the time. In other words, there is a kind of balance of power among these interest groups. In addition, there is a **separation of powers** in the government. The different branches of government are separate and counterbalance one another so that there is little danger that any one branch of government can wield too much power.

Among pluralists, there are two major strands of thought. **Group pluralism** focuses on society's many different interest groups and organizations and how they compete for access to political power in an attempt to further their interests (Drache 2008; Fung 2004). For group pluralists, this jockeying for power by various organizations provides stability for society. They see a *balance of group power,* where no one group retains power indefinitely and any group can always be challenged by another group. Further, there are *crosscutting group memberships,* by which group members belong to a variety of organizations that see to their needs and interests. This allows people to be political actors in a variety of collective processes. Group pluralists also believe that there tends to be a general *consensus of values* in society. As a result, the state is expected and pressured to legislate according to the common good and according to the cultural values largely held in common by members of society.

Group pluralists not only focus on existing organizations and groups that act for their political interests in society, but also see *potential groups* as a source of stability. If, for example, the state expects that legislation might mobilize a group in opposition to it, that threat might hold political actors back from taking action. This group might not yet be an interest group, but the *mobilization of their latent interests* can serve to pressure politicians

---

political pluralism Within structural-functionalism, the typical position put forward regarding who rules America.

separation of powers The separation and counterbalancing of different branches of government so that no one branch of government can wield too much power.

group pluralism The competition of society's various interest groups and organizations for access to political power in an attempt to further their interests.

to legislate in the common good. To group pluralists, then, organizations do not have to exist to help create societal stability. The mere threat of the *possibility* of future organizations can have the same effect.

Elite pluralism focuses specifically on how political elites form similar interest groups and organizations that vie for power (Highley and Burton 2006; Lipset 1981; Rose 1967). While voters may decide which elites represent them, the ultimate decision-making power rests in the hands of those elites. Similar to group pluralists, elite pluralists look at political elites as a diverse social body that organizes into groups to compete with one another for votes. This competition for votes ensures that no one group retains political power indefinitely. Stability is achieved in the system because these political elites must forge agreements with one another in order to pass legislation. This allows for a diversity of interests to be satisfied through those agreements, which tend to represent the common values of the larger society.

In his college days George H. W. Bush (standing nearest the clock, on the left) belonged to the elite and secret Yale University society called Skull and Bones. How does membership in such groups confer advantage on members later in life?

The Conflict/Critical Perspective: The Power Elite

Pluralism is often juxtaposed with a theory produced by conflict/critical theorists. C. Wright Mills's (1956) **power elite theory** holds that power is not dispersed throughout a stable society—either among citizen groups or among elite groups. Rather, power is concentrated among a small number of people who control the major institutions of the state, the corporate economy, and the military. The powerful people who make up these institutions might have minor disagreements about policy, but for the most part they are unified in their interests and in the business of owning and operating much of American society.

These elites develop a common worldview. First, elites undergo a process of *co-optation* whereby they are taught the common ideology of the elite. Further, they forge a shared ideology through their common *class identity*. That

> **elite pluralism** The formation by political elites of similar interest groups and organizations that vie for power.
>
> **power elite theory** A theory holding that power is not dispersed throughout a stable society but is concentrated in a small number of people who control the major institutions of the state, the corporate economy, and the military.

is, members of the power elite tend to come from wealthy families, go to similar schools, and belong to similar clubs. Those clubs count as their members many of the most powerful people in the world, including corporate leaders, politicians, and top military brass. The clubs provide a private space where friendships and common policies are forged (Clogher 1981; Domhoff 1974).

The power elite within the military, the state, and the corporate world are also often *interchangeable*. That is, the people who hold leadership positions within these three major institutions play a sort of institutional "musical chairs," switching from one powerful institution to another. In sum, to power elite theorists, the state is not some neutral institution existing in a stable society where everyone (or every group) has an equal chance of having their interests met. Rather, the state is an institution that is controlled by the elites.

Which Perspective Is Correct?

One can see strengths and weaknesses in both pluralism and power elite theory. The pluralist idea that latent interests influence politicians cannot be verified empirically. The assumption that society is stable is also problematic. It avoids questions such as for whom society might be stable and in which contexts. Finally, pluralism assumes that the state is a neutral institution, rather than an institution with its own interests and one that tends to be controlled by wealthy elites.

Power elite theory also has various problems. For example, it assumes that elites share a common worldview and interests to an extent that may not match reality.

Political Ideology

Two-party system	Political system in which members of two parties (in the United States, the Republican and Democratic parties) hold nearly all positions of political power.
Voter turnout	Low in the United States, particularly among disadvantaged groups, perhaps due to a decline in union membership (unions provide political education for the working class) or alienation from the electoral process.
Media	Concentration of media ownership gives the wealthy much greater access to means to set political agendas, create news, and legitimate the class system.
Structural/ functional perspective	The United States has many powerful and competing interest groups, but pluralism ensures that no one of these is in control all the time.
Conflict/critical perspective	Power elite theory suggests that power is concentrated among a few who control the major institutions of the state, the corporate economy, and the military.

Indeed, can we assume that the power elite is monolithic and with little diversity of thought? Further, is the power elite untouchable by the masses of people? Does the power elite control society to the extent that theorists would have us believe, or are there avenues for changing society from below that those theorists are ignoring? And if the power elite all but control our society, how is it that legislation is passed that benefits some sections of society at their expense? How did we end up with minimum wage laws, social welfare, Medicaid, "Obamacare," and so on?

IMPLEMENTING POLITICAL OBJECTIVES: LEGITIMATE VIOLENCE, WAR, AND TERRORISM

When authority rests in the hands of the state, it maintains order through its claim to the legitimate use of violence in a given territory. Thus, through the police force and the military, the state is able to legitimate violence to enforce order. Much of the power of the state rests in this monopoly on legitimate violence.

The state also legitimates the forms of violence that might be used by people not directly acting as its agents. Private security firms can legitimately use violence, provided the state sees this use as legitimate. These firms operate both domestically, as in security details for private corporations, and abroad. The state also determines when private citizens have the right to use violence. If someone uses violence against another and it is deemed self-defense by the courts, then that violence is seen as legitimate. The state creates and maintains the regulations and rules that one must abide by to commit an act of violence. At times, this is in defense of oneself, but in some cases it is in defense of one's property. There are also legal codes dealing with when people can use violence in defense of someone else or of another person's property.

War

War occurs when nations use their military in an attempt to impose their will on others outside the nation. It also occurs in cases of civil war, when a nation uses its military to impose its political will within its confines. War is one method of "doing politics," or dealing with political disagreements.

Why does war occur? First, there needs to be a cultural tradition of war. Second, a situation must exist in which two political actors have objectives that are incompatible. Finally, a "fuel" must bring the situation from thinking about war to actually *making war* (Timasheff 1965).

In the United States, the cultural tradition of war is all around us. We are often taught in our history classes about our involvement in foreign wars in which we are depicted as saviors, the bringers of democracy, and so on. In our own history, we can see antagonistic situations that have brought us into military conflict with other nations or peoples. Acts of aggression such as the Japanese attack on Pearl Harbor and the September 11 terrorist attacks, respectively, served as the fuel that ignited war.

Terrorism

Terrorism typically refers to nongovernmental actors engaging in acts of violence targeting noncombatants, property, or even military personnel to influence politics. *Terrorism* is often a controversial term because it is usually the powerful who define who is and who is not a terrorist. Consider, for example, that if property destruction as a way to express political grievances is terrorism, then the people who were part of the Boston Tea Party fit the description. And where is the line between terrorists and revolutionaries

---

war Armed conflict in which a nation uses its military to attempt to impose its will on others.

terrorism Acts of violence by nongovernmental actors who engage in acts of violence that targets noncombatants, property, or military personnel to influence politics.

fighting against invading or occupying armies? Who gets to draw that line, and why? Can states be terrorists?

Nevertheless, all over the world, people refer to acts like suicide bombings and the targeting of civilians of enemy nations or groups as examples of terrorism. More specifically, in the West today, a group is more likely to be labeled as terrorist if it has a history of engaging in violence against the citizens of a government, is Islamic, and targets airplanes (Beck and Minor 2013). Terrorist attacks are quite common in the early twenty-first century and do not seem to be on the decline. This is particularly the case in settings where one nation occupies another and attempts to police its population.

ASK YOURSELF

It is often pointed out that those revered in U.S. history as the instigators of the American Revolution could be characterized as terrorists in another light. Do you agree with this characterization? What is the difference between a terrorist and a revolutionary hero?

When you think of terrorism, you may think only of the attacks on the World Trade Center (pictured) and the Pentagon that took place September 11, 2001. Terrorism occurs around the world, however.

GLOBAL POLITICS

Geopolitics entail political relationships that involve broad geographic areas, including the globe as a whole (Steinmetz 2012). On the one hand, geopolitics is concerned with how politics affects geography. One example is the ways in which national borders are redrawn after the end of a war. On the other hand, geopolitics is concerned with the ways in which geography affects politics. One example is the constant low-level warfare between Israel and its neighbors. This conflict occurs, at least to some degree, because Israel is a tiny nation surrounded by much larger hostile nations. After World War II, much of geopolitics focused on the relationship between the United States and the Soviet Union and their allies. There was great concern over the global expansion of communism. The United States and the Soviet Union clashed, usually indirectly, over their political influence in Germany, Korea, Cuba, Vietnam, and so on. While the Soviet Union sought to expand geopolitically, the United States followed a policy of containment of Soviet efforts to expand communism.

> **geopolitics** Political relationships that involve large geographic areas or the globe as a whole.

For decades, the United States adopted what was known as the *domino theory*; if one nation was allowed to fall to communism, many neighboring nations would also fall. For example, in the 1960s and early 1970s, the United States feared that if Vietnam fell to the communists, neighboring countries like Laos and Cambodia would be next.

THE NATION AND THE NATION-STATE

Geopolitics relates to core concerns in the global age, especially the future of the nation and the nation-state (see Chapter 5). A nation is a group of people who share, often over a long period of time, similar cultural, religious, ethnic, and linguistic characteristics (Chernilo 2012). Jews are a nation by this definition, and, ironically, so are their frequent geopolitical enemies, the Palestinians. While many Jews and Palestinians live in the Middle East, many others, especially Jews, are spread throughout the world. They are scattered or dispersed; as described in Chapter 8, they exist in a *diaspora* (Fiddian-Qasmiyeh 2012). All diasporas share certain characteristics. First, they involve people who have been dispersed from their homeland. Second, the people in the diaspora retain a collective and idealized memory

The United Nations

Palestinian demonstrators protest Israel's construction of a controversial West Bank barrier near Hebron. What makes Jews a nation? What makes Palestinians a nation?

so on—easily pierce the borders of nation-states and serve to erode their national sovereignties. Second, even if it does not threaten national sovereignty, globalization serves to alter the nation-state's structure and functions. For example, corporations have become increasingly important on the global stage and have come to operate more autonomously from the state. Third, the government itself has to change to adjust to global changes. For example, the United States created the Department of Homeland Security in 2002 to deal with, among other things, the global threat of terrorism. Fourth, there is the possibility that global flows can strengthen the nation-state. For example, external threats can lead citizens to put their differences aside, at least for the time being, and rally around the government and the nation-state more broadly.

In spite of changes such as those described above, we continue to think of nation-states as being all-powerful. However, not only do we have states experiencing the kinds of problems described here, but a number of them have failed, or are on the verge of failing, the "basic conditions and responsibilities" of a sovereign state (Boas 2012: 633). Among the characteristics of a *failed state* are a "lack of control over own territory, widespread corruption and criminality, huge economic recession and/or hyperinflation, failure to provide basic services, and large flows of refugees and internally displaced persons" (Boas 2012: 633). In addition, states that do not have economic and political institutions that include a broad segment of society are more likely to fail. Failed states also tend to exploit one segment of society (e.g., the middle and lower classes) for the benefit of another subset, especially the rich (Acemoglu and Robinson 2012). The best-known failed state in the world today is Somalia, but Afghanistan is often placed in this category as well. Failed states cause many problems for themselves and their residents, but from a global perspective, it is the problems they cause for others that are the main concern. For example, pirates based in Somalia roam the high seas and have succeeded in a number of acts of high-stakes piracy, such as holding huge oil tankers for millions of dollars in ransom. The Somalian government, to the extent that it exists, is unable to control the pirates or their activities.

of the homeland that they transmit to their offspring as well as to other members of the diaspora. Third, as a result of this idealization, they are often alienated from their host country; the realities of the latter cannot measure up to the idealizations associated with the homeland. Fourth, those in the diaspora often take as a political goal the idea and the objective of returning to the homeland (Cohen 1997).

Many of those involved in a nation, especially those in the diaspora, may have no direct contact with the homeland or with those who live there. Their linkages to them may be largely or purely imaginary. In other words, they exist in what Benedict Anderson (1991; Roudometof 2012) called **imagined communities**, or communities that are socially constructed by those who see themselves as part of them. Thus, Jews who have never been to Israel, or who may never even want to visit there, may still be part of an imagined community rooted in Israel. The same is true of the relationship between Palestine and many Palestinians scattered throughout the world.

The nation-state combines the nation with a geographic and political structure. In other words, in addition to encompassing people with a shared identity and culture, a nation-state exists in a bounded physical location and encompasses a government to administer the locale.

Nation-states exist within a global context, but they are affected, even threatened, by globalization in various ways (Hershkovitz 2012). First, global flows of various kinds—undocumented immigrants, drugs, terrorists, and

> **imagined communities** Communities that are socially constructed by those who see themselves as part of them.

THE U.S. ECONOMY: PRODUCTION AND CONSUMPTION

The **economy** is the social system involved in the production, consumption, and distribution of goods and services. The economy is the first and longest-running concern of sociology (Ramella 2007). All of the major figures in early sociology had a focal interest in the economy: Marx, of course, was interested in capitalism, Weber in the rationalization of the economy, Durkheim in the economic division of labor, Simmel in money, and Veblen in consumption (see Chapter 2). Today, the subfield of economic sociology continues to be quite vibrant (Granovetter and Swedberg 2011; Swedberg 2007).

HISTORICAL CHANGES IN THE ECONOMY

Over the last 200 years, the U.S. economy has undergone major changes.

The Industrial Revolution

The nineteenth-century Industrial Revolution (see Figure 12.2) introduced the factory system of production (Hobsbawm and Wrigley 1999). Instead of making products alone at home or in small groups in workshops, large numbers of workers were brought together in factories. Eventually, manual factory work with hand tools gave way to work in conjunction with machines. In addition, human and animal power were replaced by power supplied by steam and other energy sources. While there were skilled

> **economy** The social system involved in the production and distribution of a wide range of goods and services.
>
> **mass production** Production characterized by large numbers of standardized products, highly specialized workers, interchangeable machine parts, precision tools, a high-volume mechanized production process, and the synchronization of the flow of materials used in production, with the entire process made as continuous as possible.
>
> **scientific management** The application of scientific principles and methods to management.

CHECKPOINT 12.3   GLOBAL POLITICS

War	Occurs when nations use their military to impose their will on others.
Terrorism	Occurs when nongovernmental actors engage in violence against noncombatants, property, or the military to influence politics.
Geopolitics	Political relationships that affect broad geographical areas, even the entire globe.
Nation	A group of people who share cultural, religious, ethnic, and linguistic characteristics.
Imagined community	A community socially constructed by those who see themselves as part of it.
Nation-state	A political entity that combines the nation with a geographic and political structure.

workers in these early factories, they tended over time to be replaced because skills were increasingly likely to be built into the machinery. This meant that less skilled or even unskilled workers, less well-trained and lower-paid workers, and even children could be—and were—hired to do the work. They tended to work increasingly long hours in harsh working conditions and at ever lower pay. Another defining characteristic of this factory system was an elaborate division of labor by which a single product was produced by a number of workers, each performing a small step in the overall process.

The factories of the early Industrial Revolution were quite primitive, but over time they grew much larger, more efficient, more technologically advanced, and more oriented toward the mass production of a wide variety of goods. **Mass production** involves large numbers of standardized products; highly specialized workers; interchangeable machine parts; precision tools; a high-volume mechanized production process; and the synchronization of the flow of materials used in production, with the entire process made as continuous as possible. The logical outcome of this was the assembly line, which came to fruition in the early twentieth century in the mass production of Ford automobiles. By the mid twentieth century these systems had reached their fullest application in the United States and had spread to many other parts of the world. Japan, and later other nations such as Korea, adopted these American innovations and came to outstrip the United States in many areas, most notably the production of electronics and automobiles.

Scientific Management

American industry has been dominated by principles created in the late nineteenth and early twentieth centuries, primarily by Frederick W. Taylor. Taylor championed **scientific management**, or the application of scientific principles

FIGURE 12.2 • Timeline of the Industrial Revolution, 1712–1903

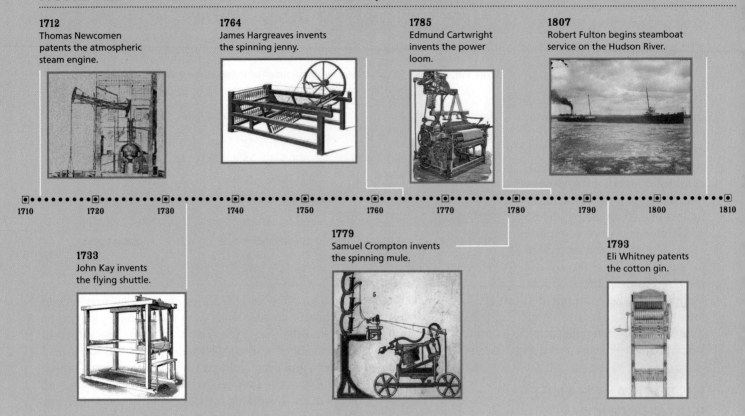

1712
Thomas Newcomen patents the atmospheric steam engine.

1764
James Hargreaves invents the spinning jenny.

1785
Edmund Cartwright invents the power loom.

1807
Robert Fulton begins steamboat service on the Hudson River.

1710   1720   1730   1740   1750   1760   1770   1780   1790   1800   1810

1733
John Kay invents the flying shuttle.

1779
Samuel Crompton invents the spinning mule.

1793
Eli Whitney patents the cotton gin.

SOURCE: Adapted from *Industrial Revolution: Timeline, Facts, and Resources*. Research by B. Sobey, TheFreeResource.com.

and methods to management. These principles came to be known as "Taylorism" (Prechel 2007) and were designed to rationalize work by making it more efficient. Those who applied these ideas were called "efficiency experts," and they sought to discover the "one best way" to do a job.

Scientific management certainly helped to rationalize work and to make it more efficient, but it had its irrationalities. Above all, it separated the conception of work from its execution. That is, managers—with the help of efficiency experts—were to conceive how the work was to be done. Workers were expected to do what they were told to do in an unthinking manner. Because workers were asked to do only one or a few repetitive tasks, most of the skills and abilities that made them human, including the ability to think, were not used. This was a dehumanizing system. Workers were expendable. They were hired and fired at will. This had a series of disastrous consequences. For example, workers' full capabilities were ignored, dissatisfied employees performed poorly and sabotaged the production process, and workers quit in large numbers, leading to high costs associated with significant turnover. For this reason, among many others, by the 1980s at least some American industries found themselves outstripped by their Japanese counterparts, which had discovered ways of using the abilities of its workers more fully. Today, as

Japan declines as an industrial power, its neighbor China is rising dramatically (see Figure 12.3).

One hears little these days about Taylor's efficiency experts. However, their impact remains strong in various manufacturing industries as well as in other sectors of the economy. In the fast-food industry, restaurants strive to discover and implement the "one best way" to grill hamburgers, cook French fries, prepare shakes, and process customers. The most efficient ways of handling a variety of tasks have been codified in training manuals and taught to managers who, in turn, teach them to new employees. The design of the fast-food restaurant and its various technologies have been put in place to aid in the attainment of the most efficient means to the end of feeding large numbers of people. This could be called "McDonaldism" rather than Taylorism. Whatever it is called, the basic ideas of scientific management are alive and well in the fast-food restaurant, as well as in many other work settings (Ritzer 1997).

ASK YOURSELF

What influence do you think the legacy of Taylorism might have on the process of McDonaldization, described in several places in this book? How do you think the two are different?

1837
Samuel Morse invents the telegraph.

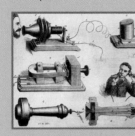

1876
Alexander Graham Bell invents the telephone.

1879
Thomas Edison invents the incandescent light bulb.

1900
The zeppelin invented by Count Ferdinand von Zeppelin.

1903
The Wright Brothers make the first successful airplane flight.

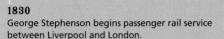

1820   1830   1840   1850   1860   1870   1880   1890   1900   1910

1830
George Stephenson begins passenger rail service between Liverpool and London.

1866
Cyrus Field lays the first successful transatlantic cable.

1892
Rudolf Diesel invents the diesel-fueled internal combustion engine.

1896
Henry Ford manufactures his first motorcar.

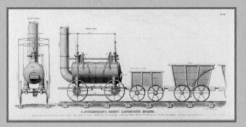

From Fordism to Post-Fordism

Fordism includes the ideas, principles, and systems created by Henry Ford and his associates at the turn of the twentieth century. Ford is generally credited with the development of the modern mass production system, primarily through the creation of the automobile assembly line. Among the characteristics associated with Fordism are the mass production of homogeneous products; reliance on inflexible technologies such as the assembly line; the use of Tayloristic, standardized work routines; economies of scale; and the creation of a mass market for the products, like automobiles, that flow from the assembly line (Beynon and Nichol 2006; Bonanno 2012).

Fordism dominated much of the twentieth-century American automobile industry and many others. It declined in the 1970s, especially with the 1973 oil crisis and the rise of the Japanese automobile industry. It was also done in by the fact that consumers were no longer content with homogeneous products. They demanded greater choice in their automobiles and their components.

Post-Fordism is associated with smaller production runs of more specialized products, especially those high in style and quality, more flexible machinery made possible by advances in technology largely traceable to the computer, more skilled workers with greater flexibility and autonomy, less reliance on economies of scale, and more differentiated markets for those more specialized products (Amin 1994; Prechel 2007).

> **Fordism** The ideas, principles, and systems created by Henry Ford (who is credited with the development of the modern mass production system) and his associates at the turn of the twentieth century.
>
> **Post-Fordism** A production environment associated with smaller production runs of more specialized products, especially those high in style and quality; more flexible machinery made possible by advances in technology largely traceable to the computer; more skilled workers with greater flexibility and autonomy; less reliance on economies of scale; and more differentiated markets for those more specialized products.

SOCIALISM, COMMUNISM AND CAPITALISM

While the Industrial Revolution is associated with capitalism, it is important to see it not only in

Communism Today

FIGURE 12.3 • Economic Comparison of China and Japan, 1992–2010

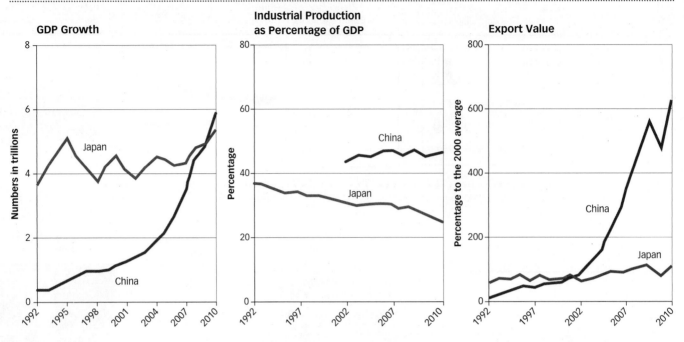

SOURCE: World Bank.

NOTE: Export values are the current value of exports (f.o.b.) converted to U.S. dollars and expressed as a percentage of the average for the base period (2000). For example, the value 297 indicates the export value of that certain country is 297 percent of the average export value in 2000.

that context, but also in relation to socialism and communism.

Socialism and Communism

Socialism and communism are often used more or less interchangeably. However, it is important to differentiate between them.

Communism is an economic system oriented to the collective, rather than the private, ownership of the means of production (Lovell 2007). Recall from Chapter 2 that the means of production are the tools, machines, and factories that in capitalism are owned by the capitalists and are needed by the workers—the proletariat in Marx's terms—to produce. Marx hoped that the exploitation of the proletariat would lead them to revolt against the capitalist system. That, in turn, would lead to collective rather than private ownership of the means of production, resulting in a communist economy. Control of the economic base would lead to control of everything else of importance, including the political system.

From a Marxian perspective, **socialism** can be seen as a historical stage following communism. It involves the effort by society to plan and organize production consciously and rationally so that all members of society benefit from it (Cox 2007; Shevchenko 2012). The collective control of the means of production in communism is a first step, but in itself is not enough to run a society. Once in control of the means of production, the collectivity must set about the task of creating a rational centralized economy (and

society) that operates for the good of all and creates social and economic equality.

The ideas associated with communism and socialism are less important today than they were only a few decades ago before the fall of the Soviet empire in late 1991. With its demise, there is little that passes for communism in the world today. Cuba continues to see itself as a communist society, and China does as well, even though it has a highly capitalistic economic system.

Welfare States. Socialism is more vibrant in the contemporary world than communism. However, even Israel, not long ago a strongly socialist economy, has moved decidedly in the direction of capitalism (Ram 2007; Zilberfarb 2005). Although there are no fully socialist societies in the world today, many societies have socialistic elements. Many Western European countries have become **welfare states** (Cousins 2005). They have

> **socialism** A historical stage following communism involving the effort by society to plan and organize production consciously and rationally so that all members of society benefit from it.
>
> **welfare states** States that seek both to run their economic markets efficiently, as capitalism does, and to do so more equitably, which capitalism does not do.

Fordlandia in Brazil

Beginning in the late 1920s, Henry Ford decided he needed greater control over the supply of rubber required for his tires. The best and closest source of rubber was a remote jungle area near the Amazon River in Brazil. This was a wild and untamed area inhabited by people unaccustomed to the modern, standardized, and rationalized world that Ford had played such a huge role in creating.

Ford sought to apply the principles and methods that had made him successful in the production of automobiles to his Brazilian rubber plantations. However, the wilds of the Amazon were far from the urban realities of Detroit. They proved far more resistant to Ford's methods of operation.

Ford created a town—"Fordlandia"— as the hub of rubber operations in Brazil (Grandin 2010). This was a version of small-town America with suburban-type houses built in perfect rows along neatly laid-out streets. It was out of place in the jungles of Brazil. For example, the houses that already existed there had thatched roofs. They functioned reasonably well in the extremely hot and humid climate because they allowed hot air to escape easily. Ford had his new houses built with modern metal roofs lined with asbestos. They retained much more heat than did those with thatched roofs and were transformed into ovens.

In the wild, rubber trees tend to grow in a haphazard manner and at some distance from one another. This makes obtaining the rubber very time-consuming. However, it is also more difficult for diseases and insects to attack trees that are widely dispersed throughout the jungle. The Ford people had their rubber trees planted close to one another in neat rows. This made it much easier for the trees to contract disease and to be assaulted by insects. Many of the trees died, and Ford's rubber plantation eventually failed.

Fordlandia represented the battle to apply modern techniques to a wilderness and to a people who operated on the basis of their own, very different, principles. In the short run, the wilderness and the natives and their ways won out. However, in more recent years, Brazil has become one of the world's rising economic powerhouses, a good portion of the Amazon has undergone deforestation, and major metropolises have burst forth out of the forest. It may be that Henry Ford was just way ahead of his time.

Think About It

Could Ford's management have prevented any of the problems that arose in Fordlandia? If so, how? Why did plans for the settlement fail to take account of the area's biological, environmental, and cultural realities? If they had done so, would the result have been different? Why or why not?

---

powerful social welfare programs that are socialistic in nature because they are run consciously and rationally by centralized authorities. Welfare states seek both to operate their economic markets efficiently, as capitalism does, and to do so equitably, which capitalism does *not* do (Esping-Anderson 1990; Gangl 2007). Their goal is to provide for the welfare—the well-being—of their citizens (Peoples 2012). There are many examples of social welfare programs including national health plans, old age plans, child care and parental leave systems, and social safety nets of one kind or another (e.g., unemployment insurance).

Even the United States has social welfare programs such as unemployment insurance, Social Security, and Medicare. However, the United States lags far behind leaders in Western Europe (and Canada) in these kinds of programs. And there are powerful forces in the United States aligned with capitalism that strongly resist efforts to expand social welfare programs. For example, President Barack Obama was criticized for being a socialist because of his attempts to reform the American health care system. Still, for all the criticism in the United States, socialism remains alive and well in many parts of the world today.

While the United States struggles to implement more social welfare programs, the most developed social welfare states in Europe are experiencing something of a crisis and finding it difficult to maintain existing programs (Kangas 2007). In fact, some, especially Great Britain, are retrenching in various ways such as offering less generous benefits and programs, making it more difficult for people to qualify for them, and making people take greater responsibility for providing for their own welfare. Threats to, and declines in, social welfare programs have spread throughout Europe as a result of both the Great Recession and the euro crisis (see below) that have threatened the European economies. Those countries worst hit by the latter—Greece and Spain—have had to cut back on these programs. Programs are even in danger in countries such as Sweden, which have long been at the forefront in social welfare programs.

Welfare states have been threatened before. However, they are much more threatened today by the realities of the global economy. With today's markets for virtually everything becoming increasingly global and highly competitive, the lion's share of global business is very likely to go to the countries, and the industries in them, where costs are lowest

This political cartoon by Frederick Burr Opper shows the nineteenth-century U.S. railroad magnates Cornelius Vanderbilt, Jay Gould, Russell Sage, and Cyrus Field dividing the country between them. What does this image say about monopoly capitalism?

(see Chapter 7). This advantages countries like China, India, and Vietnam, where social welfare costs are minimal or nonexistent. By contrast, the costs of production in Western European countries are far higher, in part because of the extraordinary social welfare expenses that must be factored into their cost structure. This has made Western Europe, and the United States to a lesser degree, less competitive or even uncompetitive in various global markets. This is seen by many as a profound threat to these economies and societies. Some argue that these countries must reduce social welfare expenditures to compete in the global marketplace. Others contend that the more generous welfare states must lower costs of business in some sectors and help make the workforce more productive (Hall and Soskice 2001). Greater spending on social welfare programs can contribute to a more educated, healthier, and more flexible workforce.

CAPITALISM

From its inception, the Industrial Revolution was capitalist in nature. As is the case with heavy industries such as automobiles, the United States is beginning to lose its grip on the position of being the preeminent capitalist society in the world. China is already outstripping the United States in many areas, and it is projected that China will replace the United States as the dominant force in global capitalism by the middle of the twenty-first century (Jacques 2009). This is ironic because of China's recent history as a communist power and the fact that it continues to think of and

describe itself, as least politically, as a communist nation.

Karl Marx lived during the era of **competitive capitalism,** characterized by a large number of relatively small firms. No single firm or small subset of firms could completely dominate and control a given area of the economy. The capitalism of Marx's day was highly competitive.

However, in the late nineteenth century and into much of the twentieth century, this situation changed. Huge corporations would emerge and, alone or in combination with a few other similarly sized corporations, come to dominate, or monopolize, a market. This was **monopoly capitalism** (Baran and Sweezy 1966). Perhaps the best example was the American automobile industry, which for much of the twentieth century was dominated by three huge corporations—General Motors, Ford, and Chrysler.

Of course, capitalism has changed once again, as is clear in the decline of these automobile companies in the early twenty-first century. In addition, a number of foreign companies (Toyota, Honda, Nissan, Hyundai, BMW, Mercedes) now compete successfully with the U.S. firms. We may have seen the end of monopoly capitalism in the United States. However, it is likely that we will see the emergence of a global system of monopoly capitalism in which a small number of corporations come to dominate a global, not just a national, market.

Whether or not capitalism once again becomes monopolistic, in recent years it has certainly become increasingly global. This can be seen as **transnational capitalism** where it is no longer national, but transnational,

competitive capitalism A form of capitalism where there are a large number of relatively small firms with the result that no one, or no small subset, of them can completely dominate and control a given area of the economy.

monopoly capitalism A form of capitalism in which huge corporations monopolize the market.

transnational capitalism An economic system in which transnational economic practices predominate.

FIGURE 12.4 • The U.S. Rust Belt

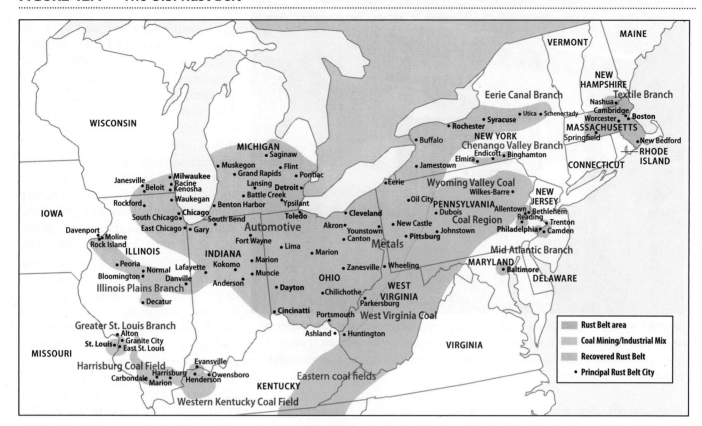

economic practices that predominate (Sklair 2002). Thus, the global flow of automobiles and even money has become far more important than their existence and movement within national boundaries.

It could also be argued that the center of capitalism no longer lies in production but rather lies in consumption (see Chapter 1). That is, the focus is on inducing large numbers of people throughout the world to consume at high levels. While the capitalism of Marx's day was described as producer capitalism, we now live more in the era of consumer capitalism. Within the realm of consumption, some of the leading transnational corporations are Wal-Mart, IKEA, H&M clothing, and McDonald's.

DEINDUSTRIALIZATION IN THE UNITED STATES

Industry and industrial employment were clearly crucial to economic development in the United States and other developed nations. However, a number of developed nations, especially the United States, have been undergoing

> **deindustrialization** The decline of manufacturing as well as a corresponding increase in various types of services.

a process of deindustrialization. **Deindustrialization** involves the decline of manufacturing, as well as a corresponding increase in various types of services (Bluestone and Harrison 1984; Dandaneau 2012; Wren 2013).

We tend to think of deindustrialization in the United States as a process that has been going on for decades, is now far advanced, and may even be near completion. The focus tends to be on the *Rust Belt* in middle America and the demise, beginning in the 1960s, of such steel cities as Pittsburgh, Youngstown, and Bethlehem, Pennsylvania, as well as Akron, Ohio, the heart of the rubber industry (see Figure 12.4). These industries are all but gone, and these cities have suffered greatly, although in a few cases such as Pittsburgh they have been able to reinvent themselves.

The decline of the auto industry began a bit later, but it, too, has clearly undergone massive deindustrialization. This is reflected in the decline of many American cities, but in no city is it more evident than in Detroit, Michigan. In early 2013, conditions had gotten so bad in Detroit that the state of Michigan appointed an emergency manager to take control of the city's finances (Vlasic 2013). However, deindustrialization

Deindustrialization

Foxconn is one of the biggest Chinese manufacturers today, employing thousands of young workers to cheaply produce goods for Apple and other U.S. electronics companies. Will recent publicity about the grueling and sometimes dangerous working conditions there sway U.S. companies to switch suppliers even if that raises their costs?

in the United States has not yet run its course, and other industries, such as the glass industry, are now experiencing this process (Uchitelle 2010).

Factors in Deindustrialization

There are several factors responsible for deindustrialization in the United States. First was the aging technology in many American industries. This made them vulnerable to foreign competitors, which were often building new, state-of-the-art factories. Another technological factor was the rise of automation, which greatly reduced the need for many blue-collar workers (Noble 2011). Furthermore, the increased efficiency of automated technologies made it possible to close unnecessary factories, thus cutting many more jobs.

Second was globalization, which brought with it industrial competition from low-wage workers in less developed countries. This was especially true in the early years of the emergence of China as an industrial power. Now, of course, China is developing rapidly, but its low wages and seemingly endless stream of workers will make it nearly impossible for American industries to compete with Chinese industries. For example, most of the work on Apple's iPhone is done in China at Foxconn City (Duhigg and Bradsher 2012). About 230,000 people work there, often six days a week and for as many as 12 hours a day. Workers sleep in on-site barracks provided by the company, and many earn less than $17 a day. How many

American workers would be willing to work in such enormous factories, to work such long hours, and to live in company barracks, all for $17 a day?

A third factor was the rise of consumer society and the increasing demand for goods of all types. This should have helped American industries. However, it led many more foreign manufacturers to become anxious to sell products to that consumer market. American industries have had great difficulty competing with them. In terms of the demand for goods, there arose, partly as a result of the low prices offered by foreign manufacturers, a mania among American consumers for ever-lower prices. This worked to the advantage of foreign manufacturers because of their much lower cost structures, especially their lower labor costs. The consumer obsession with lower prices has led to the *high cost of low price* (Spotts and Greenwald 2005), or the unfortunate unanticipated consequences of such low prices. Among those consequences are the heightened exploitation of foreign workers, an increasing preference for goods produced by low-cost foreign manufacturers, and a decline in the number of American manufacturers and the jobs they offer.

A fourth factor responsible for deindustrialization was the rise of the service sector in the United States (as well as other developed countries [Wren 2013]). In the last half of the twentieth century, an increasingly affluent U.S. population demanded not only more and cheaper goods, but also a dramatic increase in services of all types (Kollmeyer 2009). Increasingly wealthy Americans seemed to prefer spending their newfound money on services rather than on industrial products. Among other things, this led to the expansion of service industries, such as the health, education, and personal and social services industries. More recently, other service industries have come to the fore, such as the financial, real estate, tourism, and hospitality (e.g., hotels, cruise ships) industries.

Many service jobs proliferated, and some were not so desirable. The best example is the millions of jobs in the fast-food industry (Leidner 1993). In addition, millions of jobs created for Americans of all age groups, even senior citizens, opened in the retail sector, most notably in retail giants such as Wal-Mart and Target. Women are disproportionally represented in these service careers.

Closely related to deindustrialization is the decline of labor unions in the United States (Fantasia and Voss 2007; Timms 2012; Western and Rosenfeld 2012). The American labor movement grew from 3 percent of the labor force in 1900 to 23 percent by the close of World War II. A decline began in the 1960s, at about the same time as the onset of deindustrialization and the rise of the service sector. As of 2010, only 11.9 percent of the U.S. labor force belonged to labor unions (see Figure 12.5).

ASK YOURSELF

How would a structural/functionalist explain the steady progress of deindustrialization in the United States? What about a conflict/critical theorist? Are there are factors in this development about which they would agree?

FIGURE 12.5 • U.S. Union Membership by Sector, 1973–2011

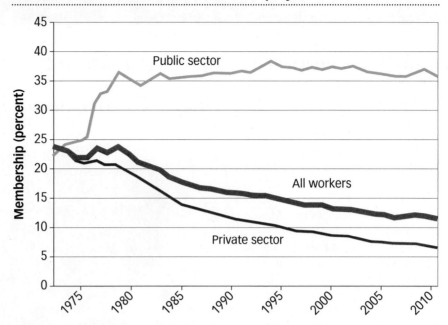

SOURCE: Adapted from Barry T. Hirsch and David A. Macpherson, "Union Membership and Coverage Database From the Current Population Survey: Note," *Industrial and Labor Relations Review*, Vol. 56, No. 2, January 2003, pp. 349–54.

THE POSTINDUSTRIAL SOCIETY

Clearly, deindustrialization and the decline of unions set the stage for the emergence of postindustrialism in the United States and in the developed world in general. An increasing emphasis on consumption and the dramatic growth in service jobs, many of which exist to serve a consumer-oriented society, pushed the United States even further from industrialization and toward a truly postindustrial society (Bell 1973; Cohen 2008; Hage and Powers 1992; Smart 2011).

A **postindustrial society** is one that was at one time industrial, but where the focus on the manufacture of goods has been replaced by an increase in service work. The latter is work in which people provide services for one another rather than producing goods. It encompasses a wide range of service-oriented occupations including lawyer, physician, teacher, financial adviser, and computer geek as well as salesperson, clerk, and counter person at a fast-food restaurant. Employment in such occupations has increased dramatically in the United

> **postindustrial society** A society that was at one time industrial, but where the focus on the manufacture of goods has been replaced by an increase, at least initially, in service work; that is, work in which people are involved in providing services for one another rather than producing goods.

States in the last century while there has been a similarly dramatic decline in work relating to goods production. Agricultural work had declined earlier and even more steeply.

WORK AND CONSUMPTION

Much of the preceding deals with the economy in terms of general trends and developments. However, most people connect to the economy either through their work or through the process of consumption, to be discussed below. The relationship between people and their work is undergoing rapid change.

EMPLOYMENT, UNEMPLOYMENT, AND UNDEREMPLOYMENT

Not long ago, we tended to think of people as taking a job, perhaps in a large and stable organization, and embarking on a lifelong career. That career entailed at least some upward mobility, sufficient earnings for workers and their families to live on, and retirement in their early 60s with an ample pension, perhaps in sunny Florida or Arizona.

Low-Wage Labor

Barbara Ehrenreich and Being "Nickel and Dimed" at Work

In the popular book *Nickel and Dimed: On (Not) Getting By in America* (2001), Barbara Ehrenreich (1941–) focuses on the low-paying jobs that millions of American women (and men) are forced to take.

Ehrenreich adopted the time-honored sociological research method of becoming a participant observer and took a number of low-paying, entry-level jobs. Indeed, she actually worked in several of them, including being a waitress, working for a cleaning service, and working for Wal-Mart. In these jobs, she was often paid between $6 and $7 an hour. One of her goals was to determine whether this work truly paid a living wage. What she found, of course, was that it did not. In fact, it provided only about a quarter of the income needed to live. (Figure 12.6 shows that in no state can a minimum-wage worker afford a two-bedroom unit at fair market rent, working a standard 40-hour workweek.) Living conditions on such an income were dismal, eating well was problematic, and there was little if anything left for savings or for leisure activities. The work was often hard, even backbreaking.

Perhaps worst of all, there were innumerable humiliations along the way. For example, as a house cleaner, Ehrenreich found herself in a humiliating relationship with the "woman of the house," who closely watched what she did and insisted that she do such things as wash the floor on her hands and knees.

Ehrenreich found that the "nickels and dimes" that millions of American women and men are paid to work are grossly inadequate. This forces them to, and even beyond, the edge of poverty and into a wide variety of humiliating circumstances and experiences.

FIGURE 12.6 • Hours at Minimum Wage Needed to Afford Rent, 2012

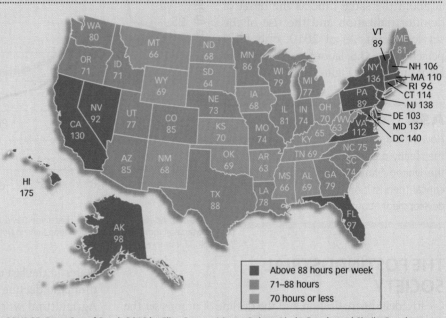

SOURCE: From *Out of Reach 2012* by Elina Bravve, Megan Bolton, Linda Couch, and Sheila Crowley. Copyright © 2012 by The National Low-Income Housing Coalition.

Think About It

Why, given the reporting of Ehrenreich and others, has there not been a revolutionary change in the working conditions and salary many U.S. workers must accept with their jobs? What function is served by the existence of such low-paying jobs, and why are women most often hired for them? What kinds of conflict are likely to be fostered by the expansion of these jobs and the predominance of women in them?

However, there are several problems with this romantic scenario. Even in its heyday from about 1950 to 1990, it applied to only a very small proportion of the population. Employment has ebbed and flowed over time. It has always been the case that a number of people have been unable to get any jobs at all. In the United States, **unemployment** is defined as being economically active and in the labor force (e.g., not retired), able and willing to work, and seeking employment, but unable to find a job (Nordenmark 2007). The unemployment rate in the United States has generally run at about 5 percent of the labor force, but in 2009, in the midst of the recession, it reached 9.7 percent, and at the end of 2013, it was still at an unusually high 7.9 percent (see Figure 12.7).

> **unemployment** The state of being economically active and in the labor force, being able and willing to work, and seeking employment, but being unable to find a job.

The government's reported rate of unemployment includes those who are actively seeking employment. Why do you suppose it does *not* include those who have given up looking for work, or who have settled for less employment than they need or would like, such as part-time instead of full-time work? What would happen to the unemployment picture if the reported unemployment rate did include these people, and how might that difference affect economic policy making about labor?

William Julius Wilson (1997) focuses on the problems that long-term unemployment creates for black Americans. Black Americans have suffered disproportionately from many different problems, so it is not surprising that they experience greater unemployment as well as a long list of difficulties associated with it. For example, they have more children born out of wedlock or without involved fathers, and have greater problems with drugs, crime, and gang violence. Many observers have seen these as structural problems that are difficult if not impossible to solve. In linking them to unemployment, Wilson sees them as solvable through a number of reforms, including creating more work for black Americans.

A large number of Americans must also cope with the problem of **underemployment** (Dooley and Prause 2009). This involves (a) being in jobs that are beneath one's training and ability, such as a college professor working as a day laborer; (b) being an involuntary part-time worker, that is, working part-time because one cannot find full-time work; or (c) working, but in jobs that are not fully occupying, such as in a seasonal industry like agriculture where work slows down dramatically or disappears in the off-season.

The welfare states of Europe have done better in dealing with these problems, but even there, these problems and

> **underemployment** Employment in jobs that are beneath one's training and ability, as a part-time worker when one is capable and desirous of full-time work, or in jobs that are not fully occupying.

CHECKPOINT 12.4 THE U.S. ECONOMY

Industrial Revolution	Introduced the factory system of production, leading to the assembly line and mechanized mass production.
Scientific management	The application of scientific principles and methods, promoted by Frederick Taylor, in search of the "one best way" to do a job.
Fordism	The modern mass production system promoted by Henry Ford, relying on machines, routines, economies of scale, and inflexible technologies like the assembly line.
Post-Fordism	A production system for more specialized products in differentiated markets, relying on smaller production runs, more flexible machinery including the computer, and skilled workers.
Socialism	The historical stage following communism and characterized by society's effort to consciously and rationally plan and organize production so all members of society benefit from it.
Welfare state	Nations with powerful social welfare programs run by centralized authorities. Welfare states seek both to operate their economic markets efficiently and to do so equitably.
Competitive capitalism	An economic system characterized by a large number of relatively small firms.
Monopoly capitalism	An economic system characterized by a few large corporations that dominate or monopolize a market.
Transnational capitalism	An economic system characterized by the prevalence of transnational economic practices rather than national ones.
Deindustrialization	The decline of manufacturing and a corresponding increase in the provision of services.
Postindustrial society	A onetime industrial society in which the focus on manufacturing has been replaced by an increase in service work.

others are on the rise. In part, this is because of the large influx of immigrants, many of them illegal, who are much more likely to have difficulty finding work. Employment difficulties in Europe are also related to the continent-wide economic crisis and the myriad problems being experienced with the euro—but more on that in the next section.

Being without a job is a major problem. However, as pointed out above, most Americans who want jobs have them, although they might not always have the jobs that they want. An even bigger problem is that many jobs (especially

Global Consumption

Many who thought their jobs and futures were secure have been devastated by the recent recession and the widespread unemployment that followed. Has the global economy failed job-seekers like these?

FIGURE 12.7 • Unemployment in the U.S., 2002–2013

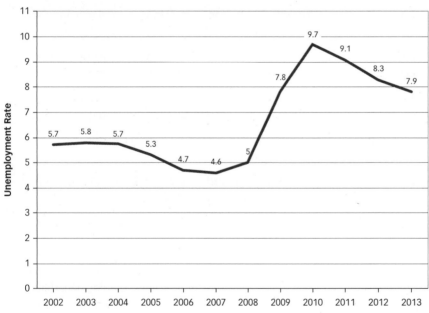

SOURCE: U.S. Bureau of Labor Statistics (2013). Labor Force Statistics from the *Current Population Survey.*

process involving the interrelationship among consumer objects and services, consumers, the consumption process, and consumption sites (Ritzer, Goodman, and Wiedenhoft 2001). First, consumption involves that which is to be consumed, largely consumer objects (e.g., clothes, cars, electronic gear) and services (e.g., help from computer experts, medical services). Second, consumption requires consumers, or people who do the consuming. Third, there must be a process of consumption (e.g., shopping). Fourth, this process often takes place in consumption sites, such as shopping at a farmers' market, wandering through a shopping mall, enjoying yourself at a theme park, or setting off on a cruise ship.

The latter three sites can be seen as **cathedrals of consumption** (Ritzer 2010a). These are the large and lavish consumption sites created mostly in the United States in the last half of the twentieth century and into the early twenty-first century. The use of the term *cathedrals* is meant to indicate the fact that consumption has in many ways become today's religion. We go to the cathedrals of consumption to practice that religion. Thus, for example, many middle-class children make a pilgrimage to Disney World at least once in their lives.

Outdoor strip malls are traceable to the 1920s, and the first indoor malls were built in the 1950s, but it is the megamall, which arrived in the 1980s and 1990s (for example, Mall of America in Minneapolis in 1992), that is the crucial innovation here. What defines the megamall is the combination under one roof of a number of cathedrals of consumption, especially a shopping mall and a theme park. The theme park itself is a second cathedral of consumption. The first landmark development was the opening of Disneyland in southern California in 1955. Third is the

service jobs) do not pay a *living wage,* an income that is high enough to meet the most basic family expenses.

CONSUMPTION

Recall from Chapter 1 that consumption is the process by which people obtain and utilize goods and services (Brandle and Ryan 2012; Sassatelli 2007). More specifically, it is a

> **cathedrals of consumption** Large and lavish consumption sites, created mostly in the United States in the last half of the twentieth century and into the early twenty-first century.

modern cruise ship, the first of which set sail in 1966 (Clancy 2012). The final major cathedral of consumption is the casino hotel, most notably those that define Las Vegas. The first of these—the Flamingo—was built in 1946. It was the idea of the mobster Bugsy Siegel, as dramatized in the 1991 movie *Bugsy*.

ASK YOURSELF

Why is a farmers' market not a cathedral of consumption? What other places in which you can engage in consumption are not cathedrals of consumption? Is the Internet a cathedral of consumption? Why or why not? If not, could it ever become one?

Of course, there are many other important cathedrals of consumption—superstores such as Bed Bath & Beyond and Best Buy, huge discounters such as Wal-Mart and Costco, and now online retailers and malls such as Amazon .com and eBay. These cathedrals, along with other consumption sites, especially chain stores such as McDonald's and Starbucks, have come to define not only the sites themselves, but much of consumption as a whole.

Consumption and Postmodern Society

Consumption is generally considered to be the hallmark of postmodern society. That is, while modernity is defined by production and work, postmodernity is defined by consumption. This change is best seen in the United States, which moved from being the preeminent industrial society in the world in the mid twentieth century to being the world's most important consumer society in the late twentieth and early twenty-first century. This is reflected, for example, in the fact that consumption accounts for approximately 70 percent of the U.S. economy today.

Consumption is central to the idea of a postmodern society precisely because it represents a shift from the focus on production in modern society. However, in another sense, there is such a thing as postmodern consumption that is different from, and stands in contrast to, modern consumption (Hamouda and Abderrazak 2013; Venkatesh 2007). In modernity, consumption is seen as a secondary activity, as well as something to be avoided as much as possible so that people can focus on the far more important activities of

> **consumerism** A value-laden term indicating an obsession with consumption.

One of the oldest shopping malls in the world, the Galleria Vittorio Emaneuele II in Milan offers four floors of luxury stores, cafés, and restaurants. What message does this structure convey by its size and elaborate architecture?

production and work. This, of course, was the view associated with Max Weber's ([1904–1905] 1958) famous conception of the Protestant ethic. According to this ethic, people were to concentrate on work because it was there, especially in being successful in one's work, that the signs of religious salvation could be found. People were expected to consume minimally, to be frugal, to save their money, and to reinvest what they earned from productive activities.

Postmodern consumption is best thought of as **consumerism**, an obsession with consumption (Barber 2007; see also the documentary *Shop 'Til You Drop: The Crisis of Consumerism*). We have become consumed by consumption. This reflects the view, outlined in Chapter 2, that postmodern theory can be seen as a new kind of critical theory. For example, Baudrillard ([1970] 1998) argues against the conventional view that consumption is about the satisfaction of needs. He contends that if that were the case, consumption would cease when one's needs were satisfied. However, in contemporary consumerism, as soon as one need is satisfied, a new and different need comes to the fore, requiring additional consumption. Baudrillard further argues that what consumption is really about is difference. That is, it is through consumption that people seek to demonstrate that they are different from others in, for example, their taste in clothes or in cars. In the postmodern world where an endless and ever-expanding

A billboard by the British street artist Bansky sums up one view of the future as the euro crisis continues to affect member countries of the European Union, including those, like Britain, that did not adopt the euro. What factors affect nations' policy choices in difficult times?

CHECKPOINT 12.5	EMPLOYMENT AND CONSUMPTION
Unemployment	The state of those in the labor force who are able and willing to work and are seeking employment but are unable to find a job.
Underemployment	The state of workers who are involuntarily working only part-time, working beneath their training and ability, or not fully occupied, as in a seasonal industry.
Living wage	An income high enough to meet the most basic family expenses.
Cathedrals of consumption	Large and lavish consumption sites such as shopping malls, theme parks, and cruise ships.
Consumerism	An obsession with consumption.
Hyperconsumption	Buying more than you want, need, or can afford.
Hyperdebt	Borrowing more than you can repay.

set of differences is created, consumption becomes a never-ending process of demonstrating those differences.

Postmodernists are very prone to append the prefix *hyper-* to many things (Lipovetsky 2005). Appending *hyper-* to any modern characteristic tends to turn it into something associated with, and critical of, the postmodern world. For example, the postmodern world is associated with hyperconsumption (see Chapter 2), or buying more than you want, need, and can afford (Ritzer 2001a). Related to the idea of hyperconsumption, especially consuming more than you can afford, is the idea of **hyperdebt**, or borrowing more than you should, thereby owing more than you will be able to repay.

However, some postmodernists have a complex view of consumption, whereby a more positive perspective coexists with this critical orientation (Venkatesh 2007). For example, they tend to see consumption as an aesthetic undertaking, as a kind of work of art. Consumers are seen as artists in, for example, buying, and putting together in highly creative ways, the various elements of an outfit. This is particularly related to the postmodern idea of *pastiche*, or the mixing together of various elements, especially those that most would not see as fitting together. While a modern consumer might purchase an outfit composed of matching elements (e.g., skirt and top) predesigned and preselected by the manufacturer, the postmodern consumer is seen as creatively and artistically putting together components from a wide range of manufacturers and styles. Furthermore, new and used clothing, or clothing from different time periods, is combined in unique ways to create outfits that can be seen as works of art.

GLOBALIZATION AND THE ECONOMY

Globalization is associated with many changes in the economy. In this section, we will focus on macrofinance.

MACROFINANCE: GLOBALIZATION OF MONEY AND FINANCE

One of the most remarkable changes associated with the global economy has been in **macrofinance**, or globalization as it relates to money and finance. Not long ago, money

> **hyperdebt** Borrowing more than one should, thereby owing more than one will be able to pay back.
>
> **macrofinance** The globalization of money and finance.

and finance were closely tied to the nation-state that issued the money and to the financial transactions that took place therein. Moving money and financial instruments—for example, stocks and bonds, as well new instruments such as derivatives—from one part of the world to another was difficult and cumbersome. Travelers would need to change their own country's currency into the currency of a country to which they were traveling. And if they were going to many different countries, this transaction had to be repeated over and over. Now, however, all a traveler needs is a debit card, which can be used in most nations in the world to rapidly and efficiently obtain the currencies of each of the nations visited. As Dodd (2012: 1446) puts it, "We are witnessing the end of money's geography."

As a result, money is increasingly liquid, and it flows around the world quite readily. This is clearly true for tourists and businesspeople, but it is true in other ways as well: Substantial flows of money are associated with the informal economy, criminal networks, the international drug trade, and money laundering. To take another example, much money flows in the form of remittances, largely from migrants in the Global North to family and friends back home in the Global South. In fact, in 2010, recorded remittances—much more probably went unreported—totaled $325 billion (Ratha and Mohapatra 2012). While this sounds like a great deal of money, it pales in comparison to other types of global financial transactions. For example, in only one aspect of the global financial market, the market for the world's currencies, about $4 trillion changes hands *every day* (Knorr-Cetina 2012).

The largest amounts of money by far flow easily and quickly through electronic transmissions associated with global financial markets (Knorr-Cetina 2012). People and businesses are increasingly dependent on electronic transfers for the credit needed in today's world. Individuals usually need credit to purchase such things as homes and automobiles. Credit is also central to the growth and investments of corporations and governments.

Even more important is global trade in a series of obscure financial instruments. Banking practices tied to the U.S. housing market and such financial instruments set off a chain reaction that devastated international economic flows and triggered a global recession. Central to these problems was the fact that financial markets in both the United States and much of the rest of the world were deregulated to a great degree. Without governmental oversight, many of these markets were allowed to run wild. For example, there was wild speculation in exotic financial instruments, producing an economic bubble that

burst violently, causing the recession to develop and gather momentum.

The bursting of the bubble created a global liquidity crisis because nations and their banks were reluctant to lend to one another. They were afraid the economic crisis would render other nations and banks unable to repay their loans. Without these loans, many nations were plunged into deep recessions. This was especially true in the European countries that constitute the *eurozone*, the 17 of 27 European nations that use the euro as a common currency.

Over the years, this led to the *euro crisis*, which continues to this day, although it grew particularly intense in late 2011 and early 2012 (Riera-Crichton 2012). The wealthier European societies, especially Germany, were able to deal with the recession well. Other countries, especially Greece, Portugal, Ireland, Spain, and later Italy and Cyprus, were not. They suffered huge economic problems, such as the collapse of their housing markets and high unemployment. Several of these countries have had their credit ratings reduced. In such a situation, the typical course of action for a country is to devalue its currency, thereby reducing its costs. This makes its products cheaper and more competitive in the global economy, allowing the economy to begin to grow again. However, because those troubled countries were part of the eurozone, they were unable to devalue their currency. The troubled European economies were left without the traditional method of dealing with recessions and depression.

Further worsening the situation for these countries was the fact that it became more difficult for them to borrow money to keep their economies functioning. Lenders increasingly believed that the troubled nations might not be able to repay those loans. The result was that the troubled eurozone countries had to pay ever higher interest rates in order to get the loans. In the short run, countries like Ireland, Greece, and Cyprus had to get bailouts from European

CHECKPOINT 12.6	GLOBALIZATION AND THE WORLD ECONOMY
Macrofinance	A globalization process that relates to money and finance.
Deregulation	Lifting of government oversight of banking practices, allowing wild speculation and economic bubbles that worsened the recession.
Eurozone	The 17 European nations that use the euro as their currency.
Euro crisis	Deep recession in the eurozone.

Microfinance

ACTIVE SOCIOLOGY

Would You Give Up Your Day Job for Etsy?

The nature of work has changed in response to shifts in the economy. For instance, digital technology allows almost anyone with a business idea to market products and services anywhere in the world. This means that even small businesses can grow in a global society. Check out the marketplace website Etsy (www.etsy.com) as an example of this phenomenon by answering the following questions. Compare your responses with those of others in the class.

1. Browse two or three product categories listed on the homepage. What kinds of goods and services are for sale? What can you discover about the range of prices?

Category	Type of goods and services for sale	Price range

2. Review the Seller Handbook under the "Blog" tab on the homepage.

   • What kind of help and support does the site offer to sellers?

   • How do sellers help each other?

3. Who do you think are most likely to be buyers on this site? Why?

4. Who benefits most from a site like Etsy—the buyers, the sellers, or the site owners? Why?

5. What is the function of the business owner/seller on a marketplace site like Etsy? What roles or tasks must he or she perform?

6. How is this work different from that in a typical job?

Now consider a product or service that you could make or provide for sale on Etsy.

1. What steps would you have to take to begin your business?

2. What resources would you need to be successful? Consider tangible resources like cash, raw materials, a work space, or tools, as well as intangibles such as your own expertise or the advice of others. Be as specific as you can.

Tangible resources I would need	Intangible resources I would need

Would you be able to make this your full-time job? Why or why not?

sources. In exchange for those bailouts, they had to agree to practice greater austerity. For example, they fired government employees and cut back welfare programs. Paradoxically, this austerity further weakened their economies, at least in the short run, because many people had less money to spend.

While the dangers associated with the euro crisis ebbed in early 2012 with the bailout of Greece, the basic problems with the euro remain, and the crisis flared again in early 2013 in Cyprus. There are many fears associated with a euro crisis. First, those living in the countries most affected by the crisis faced unavoidable economic hardships. Second, at least some of the affected countries might find it necessary to abandon the euro and return to the currencies they used before the creation of the euro, which began circulating in 2002. This could lead to huge internal economic problems for those countries in the short term and, in the long term, to the collapse of the eurozone. This could, in turn, lead to a return to the era in which European nations fought horrendous wars against one another. Third, there is a fear that affected countries would drag the rest of the eurozone countries, and eventually much of the rest of the world, down economically. Fourth, there is the worry that people in the most affected countries could grow increasingly disaffected, leading to political revolutions. Among the fears is the possibility, in the face of looming insurrections, of the rise of right-wing governments and the possibly of the emergence of new dictatorships. This is what happened as a result of economic disruption after World War I and the Great Depression, which, among other things, led to the rise of fascism in Europe and eventually to World War II (Thomas 2011).

SUMMARY

Politics is one way to advance a given position or policy through the use of, or by putting pressure on, the state. Democracy is a political system in which people within a given state vote to choose their leaders and, in some cases, to approve legislation. This is in contrast to dictatorships, which are usually totalitarian government operating without the consent of the governed.

The United States is a democracy with a two-party system; the parties are the Republicans and the Democrats. Voting is one way of influencing politics, but there are several others. Structural/functionalist sociologists emphasize political pluralism, while conflict/critical sociologists focus on power elite theory. One way of dealing with political disagreements is through war. Terrorism refers to nongovernmental actors engaging in violence targeting noncombatants, property, or military personnel.

Sociologists define the economy as the social system that ensures the production and distribution of goods and services. In the last 200 years, the capitalist U.S. economy has transitioned from the Industrial Revolution to industrialization to deindustrialization. Communism is an economic system oriented to the collective, and socialism, which followed it historically, is characterized by a society's efforts to plan and organize production consciously and rationally. The United States has some social welfare programs but still lags far behind more developed welfare states in what it provides.

In addition to general shifts in the U.S. economy, there have been dramatic changes in the nation's labor force. The number of unemployed and underemployed workers rose during the recent recession. Deindustrialization and the decline of labor unions, as well as the growth of service jobs and an increasing focus on consumption, set the stage for a postindustrial society, in which the focus on the manufacture of goods has been replaced by an increase in service work.

Consumption is generally considered to be the hallmark of postmodern society. Consumerism indicates an obsession with consumption. Cathedrals of consumption show that consumption has in many ways become today's religion. The postmodern world is also associated with hyperconsumption and hyperdebt.

Capitalism has become increasingly global in that transnational, not national, economic practices predominate. The eurozone has faced, and may again confront, a euro crisis that threatens to destabilize Europe and possibly the world.

KEY TERMS

REVIEW QUESTIONS

1. What factors help to explain the emergence of democratic political systems? How is democracy related to bureaucracy and rational-legal concepts that you learned about in previous chapters?

2. In what ways is citizenship an important component of a democratic political system? Do you think that low voter turn-out in the United States is due to a failure of its citizens? Or do nonvoters in the United States express their political interests in other ways? In what ways could new technologies facilitate political involvement?

3. The question of who rules the United States is still being debated. In what ways does a political pluralist understanding of power and politics in the United States differ from the power elite perspective? Do you think globalization has an effect on who rules the United States? Why or why not?

4. What are socialism and communism? In what ways are they alternatives to capitalism?

5. What lessons are to be learned from the failure of Fordlandia in Brazil? In what ways may it have been ahead of its time?

6. What elements of welfare states are socialistic, and what forces in the United States are resistant to social welfare programs?

7. What factors help to explain deindustrialization in the United States, and how does deindustrialization relate to the decline of unions? What effects has deindustrialization had on other countries?

8. In what ways has work in postindustrial societies become increasingly oriented to providing services rather than producing products?

9. How is our society characterized by rampant and insatiable consumerism? How do we use consumption to satisfy our needs in the world today? Do you agree that we tend to consume beyond our needs? In what ways is consumption today the new religion?

10. In what ways are you personally involved in macrofinance? How are you affected by crises in global finance such as the euro crisis?

APPLYING THE SOCIOLOGICAL IMAGINATION

1. This chapter poses the question "Who rules the United States?" According to the power elite perspective, power is concentrated in the hands of a small number of people who control the major institutions of the state, the corporate economy, and the military. The powerful people who make up these institutions might have minor disagreements about policy, but for the most part they are unified in their interests and in owning and operating much of American society.

For this activity, choose an organization from the top 10 of the Fortune 500. Use the Internet to find the most up-to-date data. After selecting the company, go to its website to find information on its board of directors. A good place to start is the company's annual report. For the most part, annual reports are made available on a company's website or its "About Us" page. Finally, select two members from the company's board of directors and answer the following questions:

- What are their racial or ethnic backgrounds?

- What are their educational backgrounds? Where did they go to school?

- What are their primary occupations?

- Do they have military backgrounds?

- Have they held formal positions in government?

- Do they have affiliations with other organizations? If so, which ones?

- Are they outspoken members of particular political parties?

- Do they belong to any specific social clubs?

- Are they often mentioned in news reports? What types of mention?

Do you think the answers to these questions provide evidence for or against the power elite perspective? How might a group pluralist or elite pluralist respond to the limited evidence you have compiled here?

2. How can you use the clothes on your back to understand the nature of globalization? As has been explored throughout the textbook, the things we consume say a lot about who we are and how we want others to perceive us. Rarely, however, do we pay attention to how these individual choices are situated within larger global processes. For this activity, choose five of your favorite articles of clothing and check their tags to see where they were made. Then, do research on the companies and their production sites in these various countries. In what ways are the clothes you wear part of an increasingly globalized economy? What are the benefits of such an economy for you? What are the benefits and disadvantages for the workers producing the clothes? What are the consequences for each of the different countries?

STUDENT STUDY SITE

ⓈSAGE edge™

Sharpen your skills with SAGE edge at **edge.sagepub.com/ritzeressentials**

SAGE edge for students provides a personalized approach to help you accomplish your coursework goals in an easy-to-use learning environment.

CATHEDRALS OF CONSUMPTION

Outdoor markets and bazaars are traditional exchanges in many countries, and you can even think of a multi-family garage sale as a descendant of this venerable form of commerce. "Cathedrals of consumption," on the other hand, are large and lavish sites, such as theme parks and shopping malls, that celebrate a level of consumption approaching a form of religion for some.

▲ The Disney Dreams show, created to celebrate the 20th anniversary of the Disneyland theme park resort outside Paris, was an extravaganza of special effects months in preparation. It featured fireworks, music, fountains, lasers, and projection mapping on the surface of the park's castle.

▲ Sihlcity (left), a recently opened shopping mall in Zurich, Switzerland, offers consumers 100,000 square meters of stores, restaurants, apartments, and offices and houses a multiplex movie theater, fitness area, nightclub, hotel, and chapel. At the multi-billion-dollar Marina Bay Sands in Singapore (right), the largest atrium casino in the world accommodates thousands of guests and is only one of many luxury attractions.

▲ Vegetable vendors wait for customers at a wholesale produce market in northern India.

◄ Most of the developing world still trades at outdoor markets. Produce sellers at a floating market on Dal Lake in Srinagar, Kashmir (India).

THINKING ABOUT SOCIOLOGY

1. Do informal markets in developing countries share any characteristics of Western "cathedrals of consumption?" If so, what are they?

2. What social and cultural functions do malls and markets serve, besides providing for the economic exchange of goods and services? Do online stores serve the same functions?

3. **Essay question:** Describe the ways in which malls encourage us to shop for reasons other than need. What makes such consumption possible? What would make it easier to resist the pressure to consume?

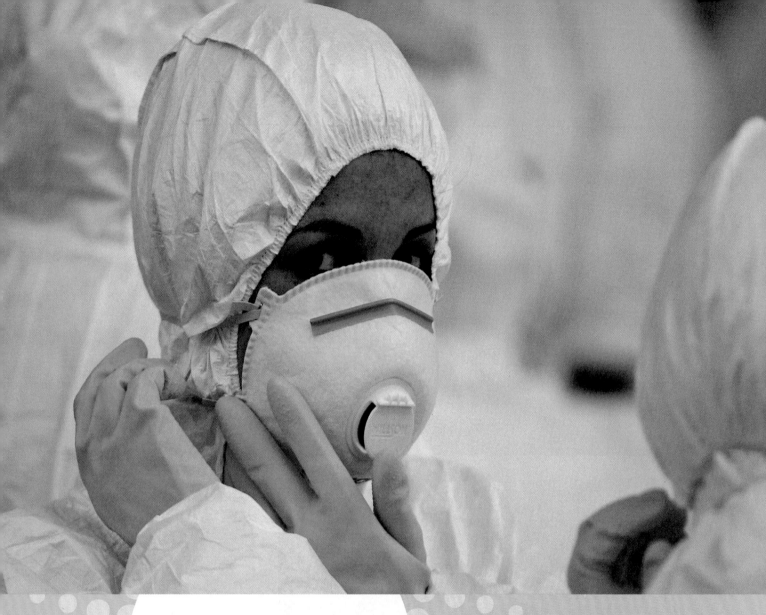

A Romanian sanitation worker adjusts her face mask inside a quarantined area in Bucharest, during an outbreak of avian flu. As sociologists study health care and health care systems, they confront the effects of globalization in the form of new borderless diseases. How do you protect your own health?

THE BODY, MEDICINE, HEALTH, AND HEALTH CARE

13

LEARNING OBJECTIVES

1 Discuss sociological concepts that relate to the body, including sexuality, health and beauty, body modifications, and risky behaviors.

2 Outline the issues studied in medical sociology, including the sick role, the U.S. medical professional, the health care system and its weaknesses and inequities, and the influence of technology on the practice of medicine.

3 Discuss the influence of globalization on health, illness and disease, and health care.

The popularity of designer drugs with brand names like K2 and Spice has exploded. These synthetic blends resemble marijuana in composition, use, and effect and are often legal, sold online and in specialty stores as incense or bath salts, and labeled "not for human consumption." Law enforcement agencies around the world have been struggling to understand and control them since they appeared in 2006. In the meantime, while the sale of these substances has grown to generate nearly $5 billion in annual revenue in North America, increasing numbers of users are finding out that their being legal and available does not mean they are safe.

> **The way we perceive and treat our bodies reflects our socialization and cultural norms.**

The psychoactive compounds in synthetic marijuana are so new that most have not been tested for their long-term health effects, such as their potential to cause cancer and other diseases. Still, as their popularity has risen, so too have reports of dangerous short-term side effects. In 2011, for instance, three 16-year-old boys were hospitalized after suffering heart attacks apparently caused by the ingestion of a synthetic incense blend.

Researchers have begun studying some of the most prevalent active chemicals found in synthetic marijuana. However, for-profit laboratories are continually developing new compounds with slightly modified chemical structures and shipping them to Internet-based distributors around the world. This efficient, interconnected global network is not only maddening to law enforcement agencies working to ban specific compounds, but it is also frustrating to health care professionals who seek to understand the chemicals, effects, and dangers associated with synthetic marijuana.

The popularity of synthetic marijuana in the United States is shaped by, among other factors, the illegality of organic marijuana in most states, the depressed economy, and the convenience and confidentiality of online consumption. It is a considerable national and international health concern, but it is far from the only one. The way we perceive and treat our bodies is a reflection of our socialization and the cultural norms we have internalized. Some of us try to maximize our body's functionality and appearance. Perhaps we work out, eat a vegetarian diet, dress to impress, or color and style our hair. Perhaps we jeopardize our bodies with risky, sometimes self-destructive, behavior like binge drinking, extreme diets, unprotected sex, or texting while driving. Some people dabble at both extremes. This chapter takes a sociological view of a number of health- and health-care-related challenges that matter to society and to you. ●

The central concerns of this chapter—the body, medicine, health (including, albeit briefly, mental health), and health care—are at the top of the social, as well as almost everyone's personal, agenda. Globally, there is much concern about epidemics such as AIDS, malaria, the flu, and SARS-like viruses, as well as the great inequalities in health and health care that exist throughout the world. At the societal level, the United States is wracked by an acrimonious debate over reforms of health care ("Obamacare"). Some changes in health care have been instituted and others will follow, but they have been far less significant than many hoped. Millions of Americans will still not have health care even after the major reforms take effect in 2014. These global and societal issues affect the health and health care of individuals. Among those most concerned about such issues are those who are or will be patients—that is, virtually everyone—as well as the large and growing number of people who work in health care.

Ultimately, much of the interest in health comes down to a growing focus on, and concern about, the state of our bodies. However, interest in the body manifests itself in different ways for various social groups. If you are young, your main concerns, and those of your friends, are likely to be how to remain good-looking, healthy, and fit through diet, exercise, and perhaps even a nip or a tuck here or there. These are likely to be lifelong concerns. However, as you age your focus will shift to the increasing likelihood of various diseases—breast cancer for women and prostate cancer for men, as well as heart disease for both men and women. You will also become increasingly concerned about how to avoid those diseases, if possible. Health-protective behaviors include screenings, self-examinations, and regular checkups. Gender affects the types of health-protective behaviors that you employ. Women tend to be more active participants in their health maintenance than men. If you contract a disease, your focus will be on how to deal with it—*if* it can be dealt with.

Some of you will fall ill, be hospitalized, and perhaps die in middle age (or even earlier). However, most of you will face health-related issues with increasing frequency and intensity as you move into old age. New health-related concerns will emerge when you attain that age, such as the possibility of developing Alzheimer's disease. As shown in Figure 13.1, the estimated number of people with Alzheimer's disease will almost triple between 2000 and 2050. The number of people 85 years of age and over with

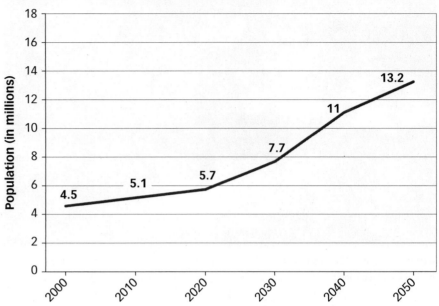

FIGURE 13.1 • Projected Number of Americans Age 65 and Over with Alzheimer's Disease, 2000–2050

SOURCE: From *2013 Alzheimer's Disease Facts and Figures*. Reprinted with permission from the Alzheimer's Association.

the disease—and there will be many more in that age group in the coming years—will quadruple. As you age, there will also be increasing worry about how you will die and whether you will be able to die with dignity. Then there are issues of whether you are going to have the funds, or the insurance, needed to pay the often-astronomical health care costs associated with the inevitable illnesses of your last years.

For these reasons as well as others, the body has emerged in recent years as a major concern in sociology (Moore and Kosut 2010; Schilling 2012; B. Turner 2008). However, before discussing the body, it is important to remember that the mind and mental processes have long been of concern and of interest to many sociologists. While the introduction to this chapter has focused on physical illnesses, mental illnesses such as depression, schizophrenia, and attention deficit/hyperactivity disorder (ADHD) are also major concerns at the global, national, and individual levels (Rogers and Pilgrim 2010). There is no clear line between the mind and the body. The brain, which houses the mind, is, after all, a body part. Mental processes affect the body (such as through psychosomatic illnesses), and the body affects the mind. One example of the latter is the emergence of postpartum depression, caused, at

Aging Population   Synthetic Marijuana

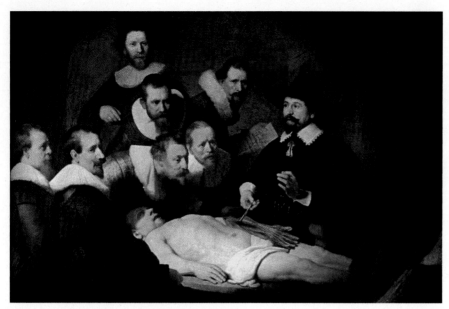

Rembrandt's famous 1632 group portrait, *The Anatomy Lesson of Dr. Nicolaas Tulp,* shows the state of medical knowledge and research of his day. How is the study of medicine different today?

to be more humane treatment in prison. There, prisoners' bodies were contained and controlled rather than being tortured. However, Foucault argues that in some ways, the prison system was far *less* humane than the earlier systems of physical torture. Imprisonment, as well as the continual surveillance associated with it, involved constant mental torture of what Foucault called the "soul" of the prisoner. Today, it can be argued that the souls of prisoners and nonprisoners alike are being tortured to an increasing degree because surveillance is so much more pervasive (Bauman and Lyon 2012). We are being watched by ever-present video cameras, through scanners at airports, and on the computer, where Google and others keep tabs on the websites we visit (Andrejevic 2009).

In *The Birth of the Clinic* (1975), Foucault begins with an analysis of medicine prior to the nineteenth century. At this time, to diagnose a disease, doctors focused on lists of diseases and their associated symptoms. However, in the nineteenth century, the gaze of doctors shifted from such lists to human beings, especially their bodies and the diseases that afflicted them. Of great importance was the ability to see and touch diseased or dead bodies. In terms of the latter, the focus shifted to performing autopsies—cutting into bodies and body parts—to learn about diseases, their courses, and their effects on bodies and their organs.

The Sexual Body

In *The History of Sexuality,* Foucault (1978) emphasized the importance of sexuality and the role of the body in obtaining sexual pleasure. He believed that society used sexuality, and restrictions on it, to gain access to the body to control, discipline, and govern it. He suggested that people reject such constraints on the body as well as constricted forms of sexuality. Instead, Foucault urged people to focus on sexuality that was about "bodies and pleasures" (Foucault 1978: 157). One way to do that, he wrote, was to push one's body to the limit in sexual experiences—to make sexuality a limit experience. While most people do not come close to Foucault's limit experiences in the realm of sexuality, there is today much more openness and freedom as far as sexuality is concerned.

With the work of Foucault and many others as a base, the study of the body has become increasingly important. It is defined by a general focus on the relationship among the body, society, and culture (B. Turner 2007a, 2007b). It also includes a wide range of more specific concerns including the gendered body, sexuality, body modifications

least in part, by hormonal imbalances (Benoit et al. 2007). Another is the development of depression after one learns of a diagnosis of prostate cancer or heart disease (Luo 2010). However, it is important to remember that mental processes can also have a positive effect on the body and its well-being. A strong sense of self-efficacy can help when quitting smoking, losing weight, or recovering from a heart attack, among other things.

THE BODY

While sociology has always had some interest in the body, the recent explosion of interest in it is largely traceable to the work of French social theorist Michel Foucault.

THE THINKING OF MICHEL FOUCAULT

In *Discipline and Punish: The Birth of the Prison*, Foucault ([1975] 1979) is concerned, at least initially, with the punishment of the criminal's body. The book opens with a description of the punishment inflicted on a condemned murderer in 1757: "[His flesh was] . . . torn from his breasts, arms, thighs and calves with red-hot pincers, his right hand . . . burnt with sulphur . . . and then his body drawn and quartered by four horses . . . when that did not suffice, they were forced to cut off the wretch's thighs, to sever the sinews and hack at the joints" (Foucault [1975] 1979: 3). Clearly, at this point in the history of punishment, the focus was on the body.

Between 1757 and the 1830s, the abysmal treatment of criminals and their bodies gave way to the rise of what seemed

like tattooing, bodily pain, abominations of the body (such as stigma; see Chapter 6), and so on. The issue of the body is also central to the main focus of this chapter, the sociology of health and medicine.

THE HEALTHY BODY: LIFESTYLE, BEAUTY, AND FITNESS

You live in an increasingly reflexive society. In the context of health, reflexivity involves a heightened awareness of your body and of yourself more generally. Many of you engage in risky behaviors that endanger your health, the way you look, and your physical fitness. However, many of you focus on creating a lifestyle that you hope will make you fit, attractive, and healthy. You may feel a responsibility to take care of yourself, and especially to do everything possible to avoid becoming sick and dying. Your body and its health have become "projects" to be worked on continually. In spite of this, there is no shortage of times—that trip to the fast-food restaurant, one too many beers on Saturday night—during which health and the body take a backseat. You are likely to mold, and perhaps even alter, your body throughout the course of your life. While this is increasingly true for most people in the developed North, it is particularly characteristic of adolescent girls (Brumberg 1998; Strandbu and Kvalem 2013).

ASK YOURSELF

Do you view your body and health as "projects" you work on? Do you know others who do? What beliefs and activities can you identify that characterize this outlook on the body and health?

Reflexivity often leads to dissatisfaction with your body, especially in comparison to those portrayed in the media. This is particularly true of women who are likely to see themselves as not being thin enough. Adolescent girls are often dissatisfied with their bodies. This is true of preadolescent girls ages 8 to 11 and even girls 5 to 8 years of age (Dohnt and Tiggemann 2006). Among the latter, there is a significant increase in the desire for thinness among 6-year-old girls, perhaps reflecting the influence of peers during the first year of school.

Beauty: The Myth

The issue of beauty became a much more popular topic in society and in sociology after the publication of Naomi Wolf's ([1991] 2002) *The Beauty Myth*. Wolf argues that the media confront the vast majority of people with an unattainable standard of beauty. This standard of beauty is referred to as the "male gaze," since it is males who dominate the media (Kimmel 2009). This standard is rooted in patriarchal and Eurocentric ideals of beauty and attractiveness.

Some argue that the importance of beauty has its roots in evolution (Singh and Singh 2011). That is, beauty may be an indicator of health and fertility with the result that women with those characteristics are more likely to be selected for mating. They are also more likely to have children who are beautiful and have a greater chance of survival and success. In any case, both women and men use beauty as means of determining who is attractive and how to be attractive to the opposite sex, as well as to members of the same sex. Efforts oriented toward attaining a high standard of beauty include excessive dieting, bingeing, and purging. These often lead to failure, a negative self-image, and low self-esteem (Daniels 2009; Rosenberg 1979). Similarly, increased media attention to men's bodies leads to a preoccupation with ideas about the ideal male form. Consequently, many men feel ashamed to enter locker rooms fearing criticism of their bodies. Some homosexual men feel compelled to diet excessively to fit the "twink" body type, a very slender form that is often deemed more attractive within the queer community (Kimmel 2009).

The Quest for the Ideal

Yet, the rewards for being beautiful are so great that many continue to try to at least approximate the mythic ideal. This is clear, for example, in the enormous sums of money spent on cosmetics, on fitness workouts and in fitness centers, on clothing, and, most extremely, on cosmetic surgeries of all sorts (Gimlin 2007). As is clear in Figure 13.2, the most popular cosmetic surgeries are breast augmentation, lipoplasty (liposuction), abdominoplasty (tummy tuck), blepheroplasty (cosmetic eye surgery), and breast reduction. Genital reconstruction is a cosmetic surgery that is increasing in frequency among both women and men (Kimmel 2009). One example is a surgical procedure aimed at obtaining the "perfect vagina."

The Consumption of Beauty

In our consumer culture, beauty has become a commodity that can be bought (or at least we think it can) almost always through expenditures of large sums of money. This interest in how we (and others) look has grown dramatically in this era of increasing reflexivity. We are more conscious not only that we can do things to improve our appearance, but also of what alternatives are available to us for doing so. The increase in pure relationships (see Chapter 10) also adds greater importance to this focus on appearance since others are more likely to leave a relationship with us if they are dissatisfied with how we look (and vice versa).

Pleasure   Commodification of the Body

Fitness is possible at any age. What does your fitness routine consist of?

Fitness and the Healthy Body

Closely related to the emphasis on beauty is the focus on both female and male physical activity, physical fitness, sports, and body building (Klein 1993; Scott 2011). All of these are seen, at least in part, as ways of obtaining a body that is not only more beautiful but also healthier (Waddington 2007)—or at least one that appears that way. However, it is important to distinguish among the methods employed to achieve a healthy body. The clearest linkage is between physical activity and a healthy body. Walking, cycling, and jogging are clearly good for one's health. These sports typically do not involve competition. One may develop a better-looking body as a result of involvement in sports. However, the increasingly competitive nature of many sports may actually adversely affect the health of one's body and its appearance. Such sports require great exertion and are often violent. They can be damaging, and even dangerous, to the body. There is an increased likelihood of exercise-related injuries in sports, especially in "contact sports." This is clear in the increasing alarm over concussions in various sports, especially professional football. See, for example, the extensive coverage of this topic by the *New York Times* ("Head Injuries in Football" 2010, as well as regular coverage since then).

Some contact sports, such as wrestling and boxing, require competitors to qualify for, and remain in, very restrictive weight classes. This can lead to bouts of starvation and dehydration to "make the weight." This, in turn, can evolve into what has been called "manorexia," a male analogue of the mainly female practice of anorexia, by which one strives to attain a slimmer body (Kershaw 2008). There is also a phenomenon known as "bigorexia," or the Adonis complex (Kimmel 2009). This affects men who might have grown up with photos of Arnold Schwarzenegger as a body builder and who aspire to have

FIGURE 13.2 • The Five Most Popular Cosmetic Procedures in the United States, 2012

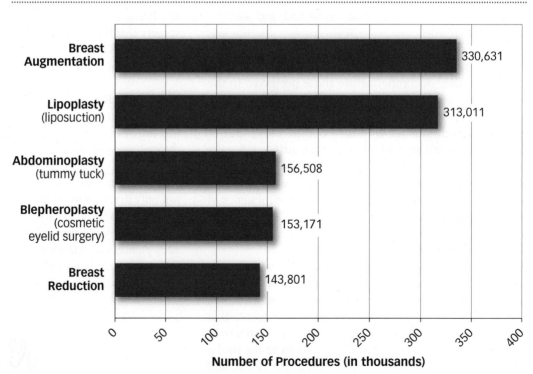

SOURCE: Reprinted with the permission of American Society for Aesthetic Plastic Surgery.

similar physiques. They are likely to feel that their biceps, to take one example, are inadequate in comparison to those of such idealized models. Such men might be led to lift weights obsessively and to consume mainly, or only, proteins. Involvement in some sports can have a variety of deleterious effects on the body in both the short and the long term.

Exercise, sports, and physical activity often take as their goal the improvement of the body and of one's health more generally. They are increasingly oriented toward *outcomes* such as losing weight and strengthening muscles. However, what is often forgotten these days is the importance of the fun associated with exercise (Wellard 2012). As a result, people do not explore the full potential of various kinds of physical activities.

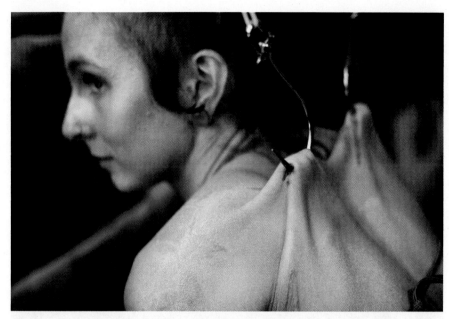

Alice Newstead is a British performance artist who has hung suspended from shark hooks in staged events around the world to call attention to the brutal methods of shark hunters. Does the person's motivation matter in your reaction to body modifications like scarring?

ASK YOURSELF

Consider any and all sports you have played in your life so far. What was your goal? Were you forced to play during gym or fitness class, or did you play for fun, or to earn a college scholarship? What effect did your motives have on your level of engagement and the outcomes for your health? Do you still play?

BODY MODIFICATIONS

Body modifications (Ferreira 2011; Pitts 2003) have been nearly universal across societies and throughout history. However, in recent years, there has been a boom in such modifications in the United States and elsewhere. There are several major forms of body modification including tattooing (Atkinson 2003; Dukes and Stein 2011), scarification (scarring or cutting the skin; see Inckle 2007), piercing (Vail 2007), and even intentional self-injury (Adler and Adler 2011). At one time, body modification was associated with deviants (see Chapter 6) of various types, including gangbangers, outlaw motorcycle gang members, prisoners, and prostitutes.

Today, body modifications, especially tattoos, not only have become more widespread and common but are now even mainstream (Adams 2009). For example, tattooing occurs these days in tattoo parlors found in shopping malls. The media are full of images of movie stars and especially star athletes (e.g., basketball players Amar'e Stoudemire and J. R. Smith) adorned, if not covered, with tattoos. Usually associated with men, body modification now seems to be much more common among women (Botz-Bornstein 2012; Laumann and Derick 2006). Parents seem less likely to reject the idea of tattoos on their children. They may even have tattoos themselves, though perhaps usually concealed by clothing. In many ways, body modification is now in fashion, and is itself a fashion statement.

Body modification reflects the increase in reflexivity. Ever greater reflexivity is required with each succeeding decision about which new form or style of body modification to have. Among the issues to be decided are whether the modification, say a new tattoo, should be visible; where it should be placed; and how traditional or creative and unique it should be. Furthermore, a variety of different tastes in tattooing have emerged. For example, gang members prefer tattoos that identify them as such and that have autobiographical elements. Various groups also gain status for different types of tattoos. For example, a full-back tattoo, a "back piece," is highly valued in artistic circles.

ASK YOURSELF

Thinking back on the definition of deviance, can you identify body modifications you think are deviant, if any? What about modifications others might see as deviant that are normal to you? What makes the difference between these two categories?

Tattoos

Some jobs are inherently risky. Would you look forward to going to work at this job every day?

As tattoos have grown more mainstream, and even common in some circles, the people originally drawn to them have sought other ways of distinguishing their bodies from those of others. Many have been drawn to piercings of various types (Schorzman et al. 2007). Most common are tongue and eyebrow piercings. However, as those, too, have become more common, there are more piercings of other parts of the body, even the genitals, and an increase in the number of piercings adorning one's body.

RISKY BEHAVIOR

Ulrich Beck ([1986] 1992) argues that we live in a "risk society." The idea of risk has become a central concern in many areas of sociology, and one of those is the way in which it relates to the body and to health. Interestingly, this meshes well with Foucault's ideas on limit experiences since it is in such experiences that the risks are greatest. Indeed, it is the risks that draw people to them (Lupton 2007).

People take a wide range of risks that have the potential to jeopardize their health. On the one hand, there are the things people do *not* do such as see their physicians, have regular medical checkups, be vaccinated, and take prescribed medicines. On the other hand, people engage in many behaviors that they know pose health risks; cigarette smoking is at, or near, the top of the list. Other examples include:

- Taking illegal drugs of various sorts, especially those that are addictive.

- Drinking alcohol to excess or driving (or boating) under the influence of alcohol. Especially dangerous are the cocktails that combine alcohol and caffeine (Goodnough 2010). The natural inclination with alcohol consumption is to grow sleepy and stop drinking, but it is counteracted by the caffeine. The result is that some people go on drinking well beyond normal inebriation.

- Consuming energy drinks such as Red Bull and 5-Hour Energy. There has been a dramatic growth in visits to emergency rooms associated with these drinks because of irregular heartbeats and even heart attacks (Meier 2013).

- Having unprotected sex. This is highly risky, especially with multiple partners, and having such sex has been linked to other risky behaviors such as drug and alcohol abuse.

- Overeating, allowing oneself to become obese, and staying that way even though there is overwhelming evidence linking obesity to various illnesses.

- Talking on cell phones, or texting, while driving. People do so even though the increased risk of having an accident associated with such actions has received a great deal of publicity (see, e.g., Newman 2011; Watkins 2009).

In some cases, the nature of one's work is risky. One example involves nuclear workers and their exposure to radiation that can make them ill and perhaps kill them (Cable, Shriver, and Mix 2008). Of course, there are many occupations that carry with them a variety of health risks.

It is worth noting that there is another side to risky behavior. It may well be that taking some risks makes one happier and mentally, and perhaps even physically, healthier. This may help to account for the growing interest in extreme sports such as surfing and snowboarding. Of course, this does not negate the fact that such sports involve extraordinary physical and health risks. This was borne out by the death of snowmobiler Caleb Moore after he attempted a backflip during the 2013 Winter X Games (Branch 2013).

THE SOCIOLOGY OF HEALTH AND MEDICINE

Medical sociology is the largest specialty area within sociology (Cockerham 2012). It is concerned with the "social causes and consequences of health and illness" (Cockerham 2007: 2932). Social factors are also deeply involved in the delivery of health care. Medical sociology addresses a wide variety of specific issues, including:

- Racial/ethnic differences in health care.

- The basic causes of health inequalities by social class, gender, and race/ethnicity.

- The linkage between stress and health.

- The relationship between patients and health care providers.

- The increasing use of advanced medical technology.

- The astronomical and spiraling cost of medical care.

- The changing nature of the medical profession (Hankin and Wright 2010).

THE SICK ROLE

Having a body and focusing on it is one thing, but having a sick body is quite another thing. One link between a concern for the body and its sicknesses and the sociology of this phenomenon is the concept of the **sick role**, or expectations about the way sick people are supposed to act (Parsons 1951; Twaddle 2007). Like all roles, the sick role is defined by the expectations associated with it. A sick person is:

- Exempted, within limits, from normal role obligations. That is, if you are sick, you can ignore some family responsibilities, at least for a time.

CHECKPOINT 13.1	THE SOCIOLOGY OF HEALTH AND MEDICINE
Sexuality	Foucault believed that society used and restricted sexuality to control, discipline, and govern the body and that people should reject such constraints in search of "limit experiences."
Health and beauty	In an increasingly reflexive society, the body and its health have become "projects" that are continually worked on, particularly among women who see themselves as not thin or attractive enough.
Body modification	Tattooing, scarification, and piercing have become mainstream, another manifestation of reflexivity.
Risky behavior	Reflecting Foucault's notion of "limit experiences," many today take actions that endanger their health, their bodies, and their lives.

- Not expected to take responsibility for being ill; the sick person did not cause the illness and needs help in dealing with it.

- Expected to want to get well.

- Expected to seek help from those with medical expertise.

The idea of the sick role has been criticized on various grounds. For one thing, at least some people clearly do not conform to the sick role. For example, they may ignore the exemptions associated with being sick and insist on handling their usual responsibilities, blame others for making them sick, not want to get well because of the benefits of being considered sick, and not seek help or seek the "wrong" kind of help (e.g., from a "quack" doctor). For another, the sick role is associated with a theory, structural-functionalism (see Chapter 2), that gives too much power to the larger social structure, the roles that are part of it, and the expectations associated with them. In this case, it gives too much weight to the expectations associated with the sick role. Of special importance is the fact that it grants too much power to the medical profession and *too little power* to the patients. Finally, the idea of the sick role does not fit the changing realities of medicine in the twenty-first century. Patients have grown more powerful while the medical profession has weakened. Physicians are less able to enforce the sick role, and patients are less willing to accept it (Burnham 2012). While the concept of the sick role has its problems and its critics, the fact is that many people continue to behave in accordance with its expectations.

> **medical sociology** A field concerned with the social causes and consequences of health and illness.
>
> **sick role** Expectations about the way sick people are supposed to act.

Preventing Diseases

FIGURE 13.3 • U.S. Physician Starting Salaries by Gender, 1999–2008

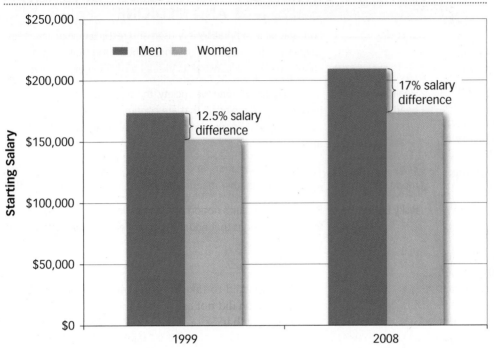

SOURCE: Anthony T. Lo Sasso, Michael R. Richards, Chiu-Fang Chou, and Susan E. Gerber, "The $16,819 Pay Gap for Newly Trained Physicians: The Unexplained Trend of Men Earning More Than Women," *Health Affairs* 30, no. 2 (2011):193–201. Copyright © 2011 Project HOPE. Reprinted with permission.

THE MEDICAL PROFESSION

In the mid twentieth century, a great deal of power was accorded to the health care system and especially to the medical profession. Physicians exercised great power over virtually everyone involved in the health care system—nurses, hospital administrators, and so on (Hafferty and Castellani 2011). They also gained and retained great power over birth and death. This was an era in which the professions of medicine not only exercised great power but also acquired great autonomy. In fact, a **profession** is distinguished from other occupations by its great power and considerable autonomy.

Physicians have been disproportionately male. One of the areas in which male physicians' power is evident is their persistently higher starting salaries. As illustrated in Figure 13.3, the starting salaries of male physicians have been consistently higher than those of their female counterparts. In fact, female physicians' 2008 starting salaries were about the same as those of male physicians in 1999.

The professions generally, and the medical profession in particular, continue to enjoy considerable power, autonomy, and high status. However, there has been a marked decline in all of those dimensions in the last half century. In fact, what has characterized professions in the last several decades has been a process of **deprofessionalization**. That is, their power and autonomy, as well as their high status and great wealth, have declined (Brooks 2011). A variety of factors are involved in the declining power of the medical profession, especially the increasing power of patients, third-party payers such as the government through Medicare and Medicaid, and the pharmaceutical industry. However, while the medical profession is weaker than it once was, it remains a powerful force in the practice of medicine and in the larger society (Timmermans and Oh 2010).

How do we account for the deprofessionalization of physicians? First, they simply had acquired too much power to sustain it at that level for very long. Second, the public, which had granted the medical profession that power and autonomy, came to question it. One basis of this increasing doubt was a growing awareness of the extraordinary wealth and power acquired by many physicians. Another was the revelation of medical malpractice, which demonstrated that physicians did not always adhere to their own code of ethics (Ocloo 2010). The growth in malpractice suits was aided, if not instigated, by the other major profession, law, which reaped great economic rewards from medical malpractice lawsuits. Third, the government came to exert more power over the medical profession through, for example, Medicare and Medicaid. Fourth, patients became much more active and aggressive consumers of physician services as well as of other aspects of the medical system. Fifth, and perhaps most importantly, private health insurance companies like United Healthcare became the most powerful players in the medical care system. Among other things, the insurance companies squeezed physicians' income by reimbursing them for office visits and medical services at a much lower rate than the amount billed.

profession An occupation distinguished from other occupations by its power and considerable autonomy.

deprofessionalization The process whereby a profession's power and autonomy, as well as high status and great wealth, have declined, at least relative to the exalted position it once held.

WEAKNESSES IN THE U.S. HEALTH CARE SYSTEM

There is broad consensus that the American system of health care is badly flawed (Galston, Kull, and Ramsay 2009). One major problem is high and rapidly rising costs. The United States spends about 16 percent of its gross domestic product on health care, and that is expected to rise to almost 20 percent by 2017. Of all the countries in the world, only East Timor spends more in percentage terms. In 2009, the United States spent $2.5 trillion, or over $8,000 per person, on health care. Costs of health insurance are rising rapidly. Many people are forced into bankruptcy because of their inability to pay their medical bills. Among the reasons for the high cost of American medicine are:

- The American love affair with expensive advanced medical technologies like magnetic resonance imaging (MRI).

- The cultural notion that Americans have a right to the best health care possible.

- An aging population that spends more proportionately on health care than other age groups.

- The fact that costs for all are driven up by large numbers of well-off Americans willing to spend almost anything to remain healthy or to recover from illness.

In spite of spending more than almost any other country absolutely and per capita, the U.S. health care system fares poorly in comparison to the health care systems in other countries. Life expectancy in the United States is lowest among the high-income nations in the world (Woolf and Aron 2013). The United States ranks 50th in the world in terms of life expectancy (Central Intelligence Agency 2012d). Infant mortality is higher in the United States than in most other industrialized countries (Central Intelligence Agency 2012d). Tens of thousands of Americans die each year because of a lack of medical care (Wilper et al. 2009).

FIGURE 13.4 • Health Insurance Coverage in the United States, 1987–2011

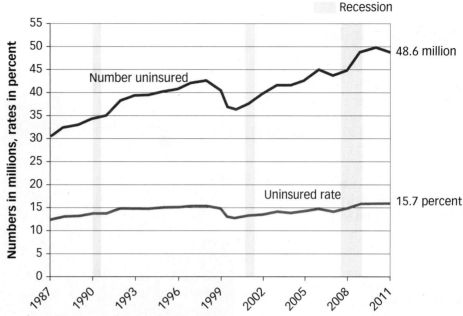

SOURCE: DeNavas-Walt, Carmen, Bernadette D. Proctor, and Jessica C. Smith, U.S. Census Bureau, Current Population Reports, P60-239, *Income, Poverty, and Health Insurance Coverage in the United States: 2010*, U.S. Government Printing Office, Washington, DC, 2011.

ASK YOURSELF

Why do you suppose the U.S. health care system achieves such comparatively low-quality outcomes considering the huge financial costs it imposes on U.S. society? Why do Americans accept such poor-quality health care? What might be standing in the way of achieving the level of care experienced in other industrialized societies? What can be done to remedy this situation?

Inequalities in U.S. Health Care

There are great inequalities in the American health care system. The well-off in the United States can afford any medical care they wish as well as "Cadillac" health insurance policies that will pay at least some of the costs. In contrast, more than 16 percent of Americans have little or no money to pay for health care, and almost 50 million have no health insurance (see Figure 13.4).

The inequalities that exist in the United States in health and health care are unjust, artificial, undesirable, and likely avoidable (Lahelma 2007). Among the major inequalities are those based on social class, race, and gender.

Inequalities in Health Care

Health Care in Mexico

The lack of universal health care in the United States, even with the reforms currently under way, is often compared unfavorably to the more universal health care available in other countries, especially in Europe (Russell 2006). However, much closer to home, Mexico also has, at least theoretically, a universal health plan (De Ferrante and Frenk 2012).

In 2000, about half of all Mexicans were not covered by health insurance. Those who held salaried jobs were covered by the Mexican Social Security Institute, and a small number of the wealthiest Mexicans had private insurance. Excluded from coverage, however, were many people, including farmers, those who were self-employed, part-time workers, and the like. In 2006, the government passed legislation that had as its goal the provision of health care for all Mexicans. At least on paper, all Mexicans who have been without health care coverage are, or soon will be, enrolled in the health insurance plan. In fact, many poor Mexicans are already receiving medical treatment that they would not have been able to afford in the past.

Since 2004, all Mexicans have had the option of signing up for the Seguro Popular, or "popular insurance." This covers a wide range of medical services and medicines, and offers some coverage in cases of catastrophic illness. People are supposed to pay an annual fee for the program, but few actually do. The program is underfunded, and its budget allows for only about $200 per patient. Furthermore, the money is not distributed equally throughout the country. The money is allocated to the states based on the numbers enrolled in the program in each state. It is in the states' interest to sign up as many people as possible, but they are not held accountable for how the money is spent. As a result, as the

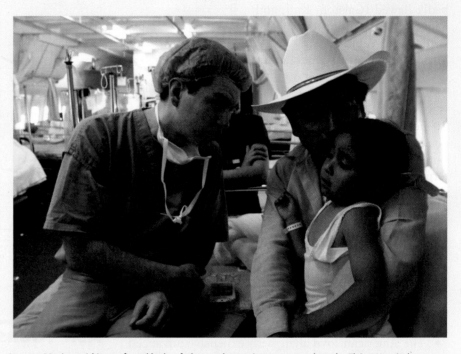

A young Mexican girl is comforted by her father as she receives eye care aboard a Flying Hospital, a humanitarian medical charity. Mexico recently passed legislation intended to provide health insurance and thus better access to care for all.

director of a watchdog group said, "You have people signed up on paper, but there are no doctors, no medicine, no hospital beds" (Malkin 2011). There is great variability in health care from one Mexican state to another. To get adequate care, some people may have to go to another state and camp out there until care is available and until it is completed. As a result, the health care facilities in some states are overwhelmed by people who come there from other states. Health care in Mexico is still far from universal; it is a work in progress.

While Mexico continues to struggle to implement its attempt for universal health care, both developed and developing countries have provided universal care much more effectively (World Health Organization [WHO] 2000, 2010b). For example, Thailand is able to provide universal coverage to its citizens

for an average of $136 per capita. It offers broader care for a lower price than Mexico or the United States (WHO 2010b). Because of the quality of care in Thailand and some other developing countries, they are now major destinations in a global system of "medical tourism." Patients from developed countries travel to these countries for more affordable, high-quality health care (L. Turner 2007). Some Americans are now even traveling to Mexico for health care (Medina 2012).

Think About It

What lessons about universal health care might the United States learn from Mexico's experience? Do cultural differences prevent such lessons from being applied across countries? Why or why not?

Social Class and Health. The lower one's social class, the poorer one's health is likely to be (Elo 2009; Warren and Hernandez 2007). This holds across countries and over time. Inequalities based on social class have generally increased over the years.

There are a number of causes of social class differences in health (Lahelma 2007). First, the conditions in which children live matter a great deal since early differences may have long-lasting health consequences. Thus, living in poverty or in a broken home can contribute to ill health in childhood and therefore later in life (Duncan, Ziol-Guest, and Kalil 2010). Second, conditions in the adult years also affect health. Contributors to poor physical and mental health among adults include poor living conditions, especially those associated with living in unhealthy urban neighborhoods (Cockerham 2012), working lives that are unrewarding economically and psychologically, and high levels of stress. Third, a variety of health-related behaviors contribute to inequalities in health. These include the greater likelihood that those in the lower classes will use illegal drugs, smoke, drink to excess, and become obese as a result of poor eating habits and a lack of exercise. Finally, the presence or absence of quality health care can play a huge role in health inequalities (Gawande 2011).

A good example of the relationship between social class and health is the adverse health consequences associated with smoking (Marmor 2005). In the 1950s, those in the upper social classes were more likely than those in the lower classes to smoke (Kimmel 2009). However, by the 1960s, it was those in the lower social classes who were more likely to smoke. It was during this period that medical knowledge about the adverse health effects of smoking became better known and publicized. However, while that knowledge was disseminated quickly in the upper classes, it had a much harder time working its way to and through the lower classes (Phelan et al. 2004: 269; Phelan, Link, and Tehranifar 2010). A key factor here is the lower educational levels in the lower classes and thus a greater inability to access and understand the research and data available on the negative effects of smoking (Layte and Whelan 2009). In any case, to this day the lower classes suffer much more from the ill effects of smoking than do the upper classes.

Race and Health. The relationship between race and health is closely related to that between social class and health. In the United States, for example, whites are more likely to be in the middle and upper classes while blacks and Hispanics are disproportionately in the lower classes. Overall, whites tend to have better health than blacks (and Hispanics). As a result, blacks have a life expectancy that is 4.8 years *shorter* than that of whites (Centers for Disease Control and Prevention 2011; Olshansky et al. 2012).

An ad from the 1930s promotes smoking as a healthy enough pastime for even nurses to adopt. Why are there class differences in the numbers of those who smoke today, and in the severity of the health effects they suffer?

Why do blacks have poorer health than whites? Racism, both today and as a legacy of the past, plays a major role. Due to experiments on black women's bodies during slavery, as well as notoriously unethical clinical trials such as the Tuskegee experiments (see Chapter 2), many black women and men have great distrust of the American medical system because of what they see as its practice of medical racism (Collins and Williams 2004). Blacks have great difficulty getting the education they need to gain higher-status occupations and the higher incomes associated with them (U.S. Census Bureau 2011b, 2011c). Even if they are able to get such an education, they may still not be able to obtain those jobs and the income that comes with them. As a result, they are less likely to have the best health insurance, or any at all. They are also less likely to have the money to visit health care professionals, at least on a regular basis. The health care they do get from hospital emergency rooms, public hospitals, or more marginal physicians is likely to be inferior. Even if they can afford better care, offices and centers that offer such health care may be far away or in forbidding white middle- and upper-class neighborhoods. Blacks are also more likely to be poorly treated, or even mistreated, by the health care system (Perloff et al. 2006; Wasserman, Flannery, and Clair 2007). As a result, they are more likely to underutilize that system, to not utilize it at all, or to use

Income Inequality and Health

alternative medicines (e.g., folk and faith healers). They are also likely to be put off by the underrepresentation of blacks in high-status health care positions and occupations. Blacks are more likely to be relegated to neighborhoods and conditions that adversely affect their health. Examples include living near waste dumps where the land, air, and water are contaminated and in apartments or houses with lead-based paint that poses a health risk, especially to young children (Crowder and Downey 2010). Stress associated with racism throughout the life course adversely affects the mortality rates of black women and infants (Nuru-Jeter et al. 2008).

ASK YOURSELF

What could social institutions like schools, employers, the insurance industry, the medical profession, and local governments do to reduce the racial disparities in health we observe in the United States? What costs would such efforts incur, and who is likely to bear them? Does anyone benefit from these health disparities? If so, who, and how?

Conditions may improve for blacks and other racial minorities beginning in 2014 when many health reforms come into effect. Also pointing in the direction of such improvement is the fact that unless researchers receive a special dispensation, research funded by the National Institutes of Health must now include proportionate numbers of racial minorities (Epstein 2009). Knowing more about the distinctive health problems of blacks should lead to improved prevention and treatment.

Gender and Health. On the surface, inequality in health does not appear to be a problem that afflicts females since their life expectancy throughout the western world exceeds that of males by a significant margin. However, as we saw in Chapter 9, while women live longer, there is a widespread, although not fully accepted, view that they have poorer health than men during their lifetimes (Shinberg 2007).

A good example of an area in which women *are* disadvantaged in comparison to men is coronary heart disease. Men are more likely to have this disease than women, but the gap is narrowing as more women are smoking—a major risk factor in heart disease. Doctors are less likely to give women with coronary symptoms close attention and the needed diagnostic tests (Adams et al. 2008; Ayanian and Epstein 1991). Women are more likely not to get treatment until the disease is well advanced. They are also more likely to have emergency surgery for it. Less is known about heart disease in women because they have tended not to be included in epidemiological studies and clinical trials. Even though the disease is somewhat

different in women and men, findings from research on men have simply been extended to women.

Coronary heart disease is related to stress, and women appear to experience more stress. This is largely because they are less likely to be in control of the settings in which they find themselves. At work, they are more likely to be in lower-status jobs that give them less control over what they do, as well as offering less security and fewer financial rewards. When women work, there is for many the additional stress of having to continue to handle household responsibilities, including child rearing (see Chapter 9).

Women have experienced a process of the medicalization of aspects of their lives that are specific to them. **Medicalization** involves the tendency to label as an illness a phenomenon or syndrome that was not previously considered an illness. It also involves a tendency to exaggerate the ability of medicine to deal with that phenomenon or syndrome (Conrad 1986; Conrad, Mackie, and Mehrota 2010; Conrad and Schneider 1980). Medicalization is particularly clear in the case of childbirth. Perhaps the most infamous example of a female condition being medicalized is the female orgasm. This was long seen not as a natural aspect of female sexuality, but rather as a "hysterical" disease that required medical attention (Maines 2001). Many other aspects of women's health have been medicalized including premenstrual syndrome (PMS), infertility, and menopause. Overall, it could be argued that women receive too little medical attention in some crucial areas (e.g., coronary care) and too much medical attention in other areas (e.g., childbirth).

CONSUMERISM AND HEALTH CARE

Historically, thinking about health care involved a tendency to focus on the "producers" of health care, especially physicians and other health care workers, hospitals, and government agencies. While much attention continues to be paid to all of those producers of health care, the focus began to shift several decades ago in the direction of the consumers of that care. Larger numbers of patients began to realize that they did not simply have to accept what was offered to them by physicians, hospitals, and others. They came to the recognition that they were consumers of those services in much the same way that they were consumers of many other services (and goods).

This was due, in part, to the deprofessionalization of physicians. As physicians came to be seen as less powerful professionals, it was increasingly easy for patients to

> **medicalization** The tendency to label as an illness a phenomenon or syndrome that was not previously considered an illness, as well as to exaggerate the ability of medicine to deal with that phenomenon or syndrome.

question them. At the same time, the increasing questioning furthered physicians' decline in status and power. The entry of consumerism into medicine led to an increase in shopping around for physicians and to questioning their diagnoses and treatment recommendations.

The best example of increasing consumerism in contemporary medicine is associated with pharmaceutical companies' decision to increase the sales of prescription drugs through a direct appeal to consumers using catchy advertisements in newspapers, in magazines, online, and on television. The avalanche started in 1997 when the Food and Drug Administration (FDA) began to relax restrictions on direct-to-consumer prescription drug advertisements. The pharmaceutical companies have increasingly supplemented their marketing to physicians through advertisements in medical journals, salespeople, free samples, and other media. Direct marketing targets the ultimate consumer of the pharmaceuticals—the patients (S. G. Morgan 2007). The irony is that, in general, patients cannot go out and obtain these drugs on their own. They need prescriptions from their physicians. Thus the idea is to motivate patients to ask their doctors for, and in some cases demand, the desired prescriptions. The evidence is that this works, and as a result the pharmaceutical companies have become increasing presences in the media (e.g., Singer 2009).

We are all familiar with endless advertisements for the leading and most profitable prescription drugs, such as Lipitor (to treat high cholesterol), Nexium (for heartburn), and Advair (an asthma inhaler), and especially the seemingly ubiquitous advertisements for the drugs that treat erectile dysfunction, such as Viagra and Cialis. All of these ads suggest either directly or indirectly that viewers ask their physicians to prescribe these medications for them.

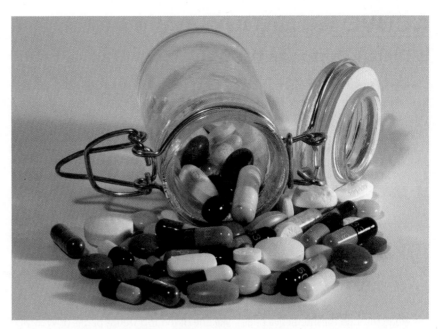

Have you ever been influenced by advertising to ask your doctor for a certain prescription drug? Is such a request a positive form of medical consumerism?

ASK YOURSELF

Overall, do you think the shift to consumerism is a positive or a negative development for patients? Why? What about for the medical profession? Why? Would a structural/functionalist see medical consumerism as functional for society? Why or why not?

CHECKPOINT 13.2	**THE SOCIOLOGY OF HEALTH AND MEDICINE**
Sick role	Social expectations about the way sick people are supposed to act.
Deprofessionalization of the medical profession	A decline in the power, autonomy, status, and wealth of the professions in general and of the medical profession in particular.
U.S. health care system	Despite per-capita costs that are higher than those in almost any other country, the U.S. health care system fares poorly in terms of outcomes and life expectancy and perpetuates serious inequalities of social class, race, and gender.

GLOBALIZATION AND HEALTH

A nearly endless array of issues could be discussed under the heading of globalization and health (Linn and Wilson 2012). We can do little more than touch on a few of them in this section.

GROWING GLOBAL INEQUALITY

While globalization has been associated with increased aggregate life expectancy, it also has tended to widen global disparities in health (Yach and Yashemian 2007). Women and children tend to be the most vulnerable populations globally

Health Care in Poor Nations

ACTIVE SOCIOLOGY

Is There a Doctor on the Web?

Many websites provide information about health and wellness, one of which is WebMD (www.webmd.com). Visit the site and answer the following questions about it to explore the way health is constructed. Discuss your results with the class.

1. What is considered healthy, and what is considered sick? Give examples from the site.

2. What types of illnesses are presented in general, and how are they described?

3. How are constructions of beauty embedded in the site? Provide some examples.

4. From a sociological perspective, why might someone use a site like WebMD instead of going to a doctor?

5. Read through the interactive pages, like one of the Top Trends pages or WebMD Experts & Blogs. Who is sharing information here?

6. How does this site reflect the prosumer perspective?

To participate in the site yourself, create your own account.

1. What medical advice or knowledge are you allowed to create or contribute?

2. What are the pros and cons of being a prosumer on this site?

---

due to their lower social positions and poor access to health care (Fillipi et al. 2006). People in poor nations tend to have poorer health as a result of limited access to health care services, education, sanitation, and adequate nutrition and housing. Conversely, poor health tends to limit economic growth in those nations mainly by adversely affecting productivity. Developing countries have a disproportionate share of mortality and morbidity, much of which could be prevented inexpensively and treated effectively if the money was available. Of the total burden of disease, 90 percent is concentrated in low- and middle-income countries. Yet, only 10 percent of total global health care expenditures occur in those countries, the ones that need the money the most. Only 10 percent of the research money in the United States is devoted to the health problems that account for 90 percent of the global disease burden (Al-Tuwaijri et al. 2003).

For these and other reasons, there is a 19-year gap in life expectancy between high- and low-income countries. The improvements in developing countries tend to be in countries more deeply and successfully involved

in economic globalization, such as Brazil, Egypt, and Malaysia. However, for most of the rest, especially the least-developed countries in the Global South, globalization has brought with it a decline in economic growth, an increase in poverty, and, as a result, a decline in health.

Disease

The vast majority of not only acute, but also chronic, diseases occur at younger ages and in low- and middle-income countries. The rising cost of dealing with chronic diseases in developing countries will adversely affect their ability to deal with acute infectious diseases. Of special importance from the point of view of globalization is the increasing global marketing of tobacco, alcohol, sugar, and fat—the latter two especially aimed at children—and the consequent global spread of the diseases associated with these products.

Malnutrition

Countries in the Global South suffer disproportionately from hunger and malnutrition (Van de Poel et al. 2008).

Roughly 850 million people there are affected by these problems. The causes include inadequate, or totally unavailable, food supplies, and poor and unbalanced diets. Dealing with hunger and malnutrition is especially important for children because those who are underweight are, as adults, likely to be less physically and intellectually productive and to experience more chronic illnesses and disabilities. This carries on across generations as the ability of such adults to provide adequate nutrition for their children is compromised.

Undernutrition is a form of malnutrition involving an inadequate intake of nutrients, including calories, vitamins, and minerals. The other form of malnutrition involves obesity, which is caused by an excessive intake of nutrients, especially calories. Developing countries now increasingly suffer from a "double nutritional burden." This involves *both* those who do not have enough to eat *and* those who eat too much, especially of the wrong kinds of food (e.g., food that is high in fat and cholesterol) (Kelishadi 2007; Prentice 2006). However, although the latter is increasing in the less developed world, undernutrition is the greatest problem there. It is especially a problem for mothers and children. Problems stemming from undernutrition continue through the life cycle and are responsible for stunted growth, less schooling, lower productivity, giving birth to lower-weight infants, and chronic diseases. It is even linked to rapid weight gain and obesity among formerly underweight children (Serra-Majem and Ngo 2012).

Undernutrition is related to problems not only for individuals, but also for societies as a whole. It leads to underdevelopment and tends to perpetuate poverty. Without adequate nutrition, the human capital needed for economic development cannot develop.

Food insecurity is an important cause of undernutrition. Such insecurity exists when people do not have sufficient access to safe and nutritious food. There are many causes of food insecurity, but one of the most important is a lack of adequate agricultural development. A number of global programs have been undertaken to help deal with the problem, such as the creation of community gardens, farmers' markets, agricultural diversification programs, and the like.

---

undernutrition A form of malnutrition involving an inadequate intake of nutrients, including calories, vitamins, and minerals.

food insecurity Lack of sufficient access to safe and nutritious food.

Smoking

Smoking is an important cause of health problems around the world. Nevertheless, a highly profitable tobacco industry continues to be central to the global economy (Fulbrook 2007). According to a 2013 World Health Organization estimate, nearly 6 million people die each year from tobacco use, and unless there are dramatic changes, that number will rise to 8 million by 2030. It is also projected that 1 billion people will die in the twenty-first century from smoking-related diseases.

With the western market for cigarettes shrinking because of growing awareness of the risks associated with smoking, the tobacco corporations have shifted their focus to Africa and Asia. India accounts for almost a third of the world's tobacco-related deaths. China is now the world's biggest market for cigarettes (Gu et al. 2009) with 1.7 trillion cigarettes smoked every year. The Chinese consume about 30 percent of the world's cigarettes, although China has about 20 percent of the world's population. Many Chinese appear to have little knowledge of the health hazards associated with smoking (WHO 2010a). For their part, the western powers are the major exporters of cigarettes to the rest of the world. The United States is the single largest exporter of cigarettes as well as of globally recognized cigarette advertisements and brands.

ASK YOURSELF

The hazards of smoking are well known in the United States. Should it be legal for tobacco companies to export their products to markets where such information is not widely known or is disregarded? Why or why not? What would a conflict/critical theorist say is happening here?

BORDERLESS DISEASES

Another negative aspect of globalization as far as health is concerned is the flow of borderless diseases (Ali 2012). While borderless diseases have become much more common in recent years, they are not a new phenomenon. Tuberculosis (TB) was known in ancient times. Today the World Health Organization estimates that more than a third of the world's population are infected with the cause of the disease—the TB bacillus (Linn and Wilson 2012). Sexually transmitted infections (STIs) of various types have long diffused globally. A specific example of the latter is syphilis, which has spread globally, and continues to circulate, especially throughout a number of less developed countries. However, the roots of the disease were probably in Europe, and it was spread by European colonialism and military exploits.

Then there is the increasing prevalence of other borderless diseases, many of them relatively new. Examples include severe acute respiratory syndrome (SARS); avian

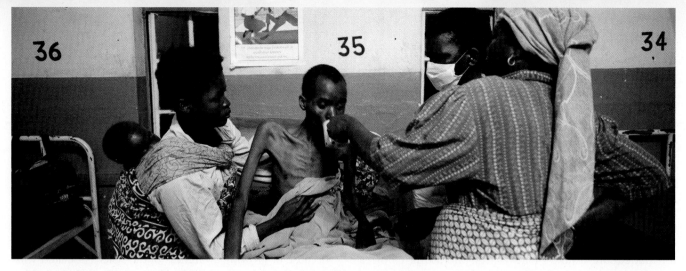

A night nurse gives medicine to a tuberculosis patient at a hospital in Malawi (Africa). How should countries protect their citizens from such widespread and contagious diseases as TB?

and SARS-like flu; and HIV/AIDS. The nature of these diseases and their spread, either in fact (HIV/AIDS) or merely, at least so far, as a frightening possibility (newer forms of flu), tells us a great deal about the nature and reality of globalization in the twenty-first century. The pathogens that cause these diseases flow, or have the potential to flow, readily throughout the globe.

Several factors help explain the great and increasing global mobility of borderless diseases. First, there is the increase in global travel and the increasing rapidity of that travel (Rosenthal 2007b). Second, there is growing human migration and the ease with which people can cross borders. As a result, they often bring with them diseases that are not detected at the nation's borders. Third, the expansion of massive urban areas has created vast mixing bowls where large numbers of people in close and frequent proximity can easily infect one another. Fourth is increasing human involvement in natural habitats previously untouched by human beings. There, people can have contact with pathogens for which they have no immunity and that they can spread rapidly throughout the world (Ali 2012).

The flow of efforts to deal with these diseases must be equally global. That is, there is a need for global responses to the increasing likelihood of the spread of various diseases. However, some nations have proven unable or unwilling to be responsive to this global need. For example, China and Vietnam were unwilling to provide the WHO with samples of the avian flu that had become a serious problem in those countries. Such samples were needed to study the spread of the disease and the ways in which the flu was evolving. This information could have been useful in heading off the further spread of the disease and might have speeded up the development of a vaccine to prevent it.

HIV/AIDS

HIV/AIDS was first recognized in the United States in 1981 and has since been acknowledged as a scourge throughout not only the United States, but much of the world (Whiteside 2008, 2012). In 2010, it was estimated that 25 million people had died from AIDS while another 33 million, many of whom will die from the disease, were suffering from AIDS. The numbers of people infected with HIV and living with AIDS vary greatly around the world (see Figure 13.5).

HIV/AIDS cannot be contracted through casual contact with people who have the disease. The disease spreads only through intimate human contact with body fluids, especially through unprotected sex and intravenous drug use. Thus, in spite of the large numbers of people with AIDS, it is *not* an easy disease to contract. For instance, fellow passengers on an international flight will not contract AIDS simply because they sit next to, or talk with, a fellow passenger with the disease.

The spread of AIDS is linked to globalization, especially the increased global mobility associated with tourism (notably, sex tourism), the greater migration rates of workers, increased legal and illegal immigration, much greater rates of commercial and business travel, the movement (sometimes on a mass basis) of refugees, military interventions and the movement of military personnel, and so on.

People who have the disease can travel great distances over a period of years without knowing they have the disease. They therefore have the ability to transmit the disease to many others in widely scattered locales. Thus, when people with HIV/AIDS have sexual contact with people in other countries, they are likely to transmit the disease to at least some of them. Similarly, those without the disease can travel to nations where HIV/AIDS is prevalent, contract it, and then bring it back to their home country. In either case, the disease moves from region to region, country to country, and ultimately globally, carried by human vectors.

More and more people, especially in the Global South, are contracting the disease. Sub-Saharan Africa has been especially hard-hit (Nolan 2006). About

FIGURE 13.5 • HIV/AIDS Prevalence Worldwide, 2010

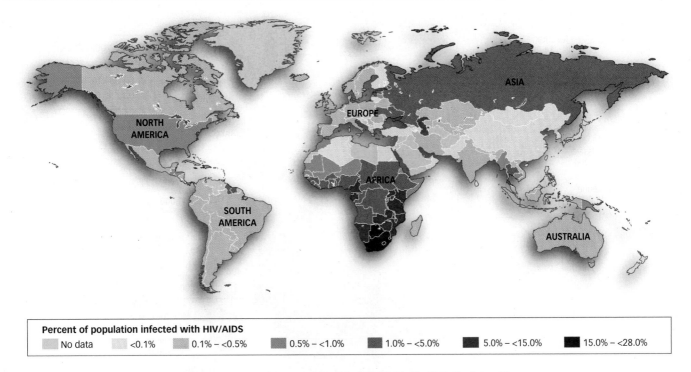

Percent of population infected with HIV/AIDS

No data   <0.1%   0.1% – <0.5%   0.5% – <1.0%   1.0% – <5.0%   5.0% – <15.0%   15.0% – <28.0%

SOURCE: Data from HIV Prevalence Map. *Global Report: UNAIDS Report of the Global AIDS Epidemic, 2010.* Fig. 2.4, p. 23.

two-thirds of all adults and children living with the disease live in sub-Saharan Africa (see Figure 13.6). Auguring poorly for the future of sub-Saharan Africa is the fact that about two-thirds of all new HIV/AIDS infections in 2009 occurred there. The data on specific countries in the southern part of Africa are sobering. For example:

- As of 2008, about 19 percent of Swazis were HIV positive. In the U.S. context, that would translate into 57 million infected Americans.

- Life expectancy in Swaziland was 54 years in 1980 and 58 in 1990, but fell to 40 in 2007. Most of the decline in life expectancy is traceable to HIV/AIDS and to the early age at which HIV/AIDS victims are likely to die.

- In South Africa, 180,000 people died from HIV/AIDS in 2000, but by 2007 the number of deaths had risen to 350,000.

- It is estimated that 6 million South Africans—about 13 percent of the population—will have perished from HIV/AIDS by 2015 (UNAIDS 2008; Whiteside 2012).

The disease, and the many burdens associated with it, is having an adverse effect on all aspects of social and economic life throughout Africa.

The greater prevalence of AIDS in Africa is just one example of the greater vulnerability of the world's have-nots to this and many other borderless diseases. Compounding the problem is the fact that it is precisely this *most* vulnerable population that is also *least* likely to have access to the high-quality health care and the very expensive drugs that can slow the disease for years, or even decades.

Malaria

Like many borderless diseases, and indeed most diseases, malaria has its greatest impact on the less well-off and most vulnerable populations in the developing world (Hall 2012a). While nearly half of the world's population live in countries that have at least some incidence of malaria, the greatest risk of disease has been in Africa, Southern Asia, and South America's equatorial regions. However, as is clear in Figure 13.7, the disease has become primarily an African disease. According to the WHO, in 2008 there were nearly 250 million cases of malaria, and 863,000 deaths were attributed to the disease. Of this total, 85,000 deaths were

Conquering AIDS

FIGURE 13.6 • The Prevalence of AIDS in Sub-Saharan Africa, 2009

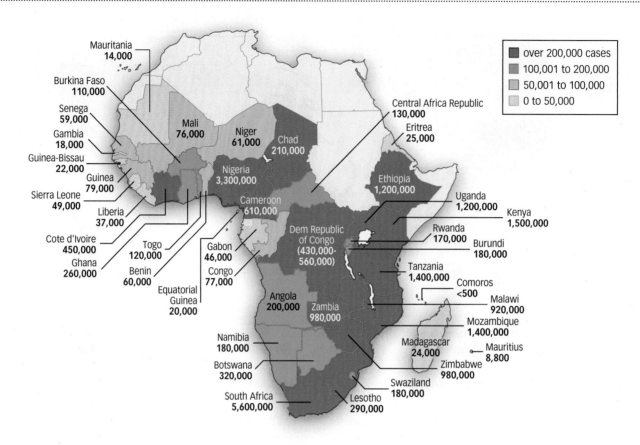

SOURCE: Data from Sub-Saharan Africa HIV and AIDS Statistics, AVERT, and International HIV and AIDS Charity.

of children under five years of age. Beyond the illnesses and deaths, other costs involve lost work and income, lost school days, and expenditures on public health that limit money that can be spent on other pressing health needs.

There is no vaccine for malaria, but efforts to control the mosquitoes that carry the disease can help. Insecticide-treated nets reduce the number of bites while people are asleep, and indoor spraying of homes helps a great deal. However, it is possible that mosquitoes can develop resistance to the chemicals.

Dealing with malaria is complicated by the great mobility characteristic of the global age. New arrivals, especially those without immunity, have a higher risk of contracting the disease. New centers of disease can develop as the disease is passed from infected individuals to previously uninfected mosquitoes, which then are able to infect other humans in a new area. This can lead to renewed outbreaks in areas that had previously been cleared of the disease. The global health community has engaged in a concerted effort to reduce the incidence of malaria. Progress has been made, but elimination of the disease is a distant hope.

New Forms of Flu

In 2009 and 2010 the world witnessed an avian flu pandemic (H1N1), but it proved to be a relatively mild form of the disease. Prior to that, there had been fear of a pandemic of a potentially far more deadly strain of avian flu. Because we live in a global age, the spread of the flu would be faster and more extensive than that of earlier pandemics. However, it is also the case that the ability to deal with such a pandemic is enhanced as a result of globalization. For example, global monitoring has increased, and there is greater ability to get health workers and pharmaceuticals rapidly to the site of an outbreak.

Some flu subtypes can spread through casual human contact with an infected animal, but there is little evidence of human-to-human spread of the avian flu virus. The relatively small number of humans in the world who have gotten the disease, including the even smaller number who have died from it, contracted the disease through direct contact with birds infected with the disease. Those in less developed nations are more likely to have direct contact with their birds—some literally live with the birds. In

FIGURE 13.7 • Areas at High Risk for Malaria, 2010

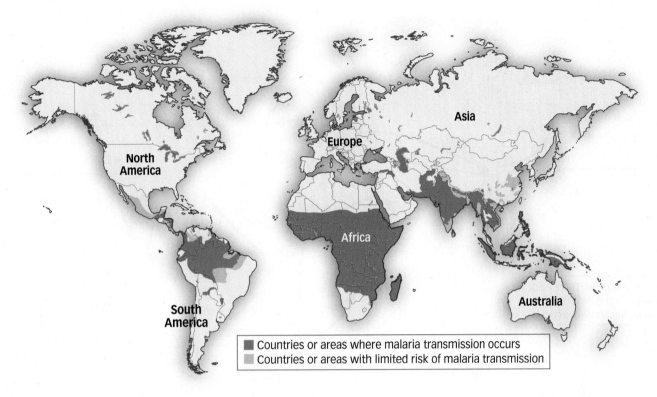

Countries or areas where malaria transmission occurs
Countries or areas with limited risk of malaria transmission

SOURCE: Data from *World Malaria Report, 2011*. World Health Organization.

contrast, relatively few people in the developed world have direct contact with birds, and so they are highly unlikely to contract bird flu in this way.

There is some fear, however, that the virus that causes bird flu might eventually transform itself into a strain that can be spread by casual human-to-human contact. This fear stems from the fact that viruses have taken this route before and caused global human pandemics such as the infamous "Spanish flu" of 1918–1920, which killed half a million people in the United States and tens of millions worldwide (see Figure 13.8) (Kolata 1999). Were this virus transformation to occur, the increased global mobility of people would lead to a rapid spread of the disease.

In late 2011, an alarm was raised over the creation in the laboratory of an avian flu (H5N1) that had previously not been thought to be easily communicable by human-to-human contact. Researchers were able to modify the virus so that it could be spread through the air. The virus has the potential, if it gets out of control, to spread around the world, and it could prove far more deadly than even the Spanish flu since it has an extraordinarily high death rate (Grady and Broad 2011). In fact, the U.S. government made highly unusual and controversial efforts to limit publication of the full results

of the research for fear that the information could be used by terrorists to create a global pandemic. The argument against such censoring is that access to the results of the research could lead to greater understanding of the virus and better ways to prevent and treat the disease. In early 2012, a decision was made to allow the research results to be published. The argument was that the danger of terrorists using the information to start an epidemic was less than the danger of the virus itself undergoing a mutation that could cause an epidemic. The hope is that the publication of the results will lead to methods to prevent or ameliorate such an epidemic.

The most recent scare of this type occurred in mid-2013 over a SARS-like virus (Middle East respiratory syndrome coronavirus, or MERS-CoV). There had been a relatively small SARS pandemic in 2002–2003. Some form of SARS or of avian flu could become a global pandemic that proves to be worse than the Spanish flu.

Foreign Medications

FIGURE 13.8 • The Spread of Spanish Flu, First and Second Waves, 1918, 1920

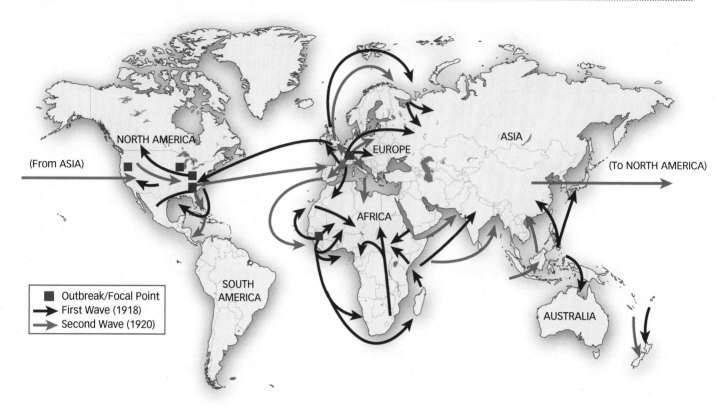

SOURCE: Inverness Medical Innovations, Inc. Spanish Flu 2009.

ASK YOURSELF

Could medical practitioners or governments have anticipated the possibility that germs and viruses might begin to flow more easily around the world, along with people, goods, and information? Communicable diseases have always existed, so why is their ability to travel globally of such concern? Does the Global North bear any particular responsibility for dealing with potential outbreaks? Why or why not?

GLOBALIZATION AND IMPROVEMENTS IN HEALTH AND HEALTH CARE

Globalization has also brought with it an array of developments that have improved, or at least should improve, the quality of health throughout the world. One example is the growth of global health-related organizations such as the Red Cross and *Médecins Sans Frontières* (Inoue and Drori 2006). Of course, as with much else about globalization, the effects have been uneven and affected by a variety of local circumstances.

Increasing interpersonal relations among and between various regions throughout the world means that positive developments in one part of the world are likely to find their way to most other parts of the world, and quite rapidly. In addition, there is a ready flow of new ideas associated with health and health care. In the era of the Internet and online journals—in this case medical journals—information about new medical developments flashes around the world virtually instantaneously. Of course, how those ideas are received and whether, and how quickly, they can be implemented vary enormously. There is great variability around the world in the number of professionals able to comprehend and utilize such information. Furthermore, the institutions in place in which such ideas can be implemented also vary greatly. Thus, hospitals in developed countries would be able to implement changes to reduce the risks of hospital-based infections, but those in less developed countries would find such changes difficult or impossible because of the costs involved.

New medical products clearly flow around the world much more slowly than new ideas, but because of global improvements in transport they are much more mobile than ever before. Included under this heading would be pharmaceuticals of all types. Clearly, the superstars of the pharmaceutical industry are global phenomena. In fact, while the United States accounted for about $325 billion of the $880 billion in pharmaceutical sales expected worldwide in 2011, sales in emerging markets outside the United States are growing more rapidly than U.S. sales (Alazraki 2010; Herper and Kang 2006). As new drugs are approved and come to be seen as effective, they are likely to flow around the world, especially to developed countries and to the elites in less developed countries.

Of course, the drugs that are most likely to be produced and distributed globally are those considered likely to be most profitable. Those drugs address the health problems of the wealthier members of global society, such as hypertension, high cholesterol, arthritis, mental health problems, impotence, hair loss, and so on. The well-to-do are most able to afford the diets that lead to high cholesterol, acid reflux, and heartburn, and they are therefore the likely consumers of Lipitor, Zocor, Nexium, and Prevacid. Because they produce the greatest earnings for pharmaceutical companies, these drugs are most likely to achieve global distribution.

Conversely, drugs that might save many lives are not apt to be produced (Moran et al. 2009). Few, if any, of the pharmaceutical companies surveyed devote research and development money to creating drugs that would help those in less developed countries who suffer from diseases such as malaria. Such drugs are unlikely to yield great profits because those who need them are mainly the poor in less developed countries. If the drugs are produced, their flow to those parts of the globe is likely to be minimal. Thus, as we have seen, Africa is a hotbed of many diseases, such as malaria, some of them killing millions of people each year. However, these are largely poor people in impoverished countries, and the major drug companies based primarily in the wealthy developed countries are little interested in doing the research and paying for the start-up and production costs necessary to produce drugs that are not likely to be profitable.

A similar point can be made about the flow of advanced medical technologies, including MRIs and CAT scans throughout the world. These are extraordinarily expensive technologies found largely in the wealthy developed countries of the Global North. The machines are not only more likely to exist in these developed countries, but they are more likely to be used extensively there because patients, either on their own or because of health insurance, are able to afford the very expensive scans and tests associated with them. Figure 13.9 shows the 2010 world leaders in number of MRI exams per 1,000 people. The United States is at the top with 91.2 per 1,000; all of the other countries are in the Global North. In contrast, relatively few of these technologies flow to less developed, southern countries; they are used there less extensively; and there are relatively few trained people there capable of conducting the tests and interpreting the results (Debas 2010; WHO 2010b).

FIGURE 13.9 • MRI Exams by Country, 2010

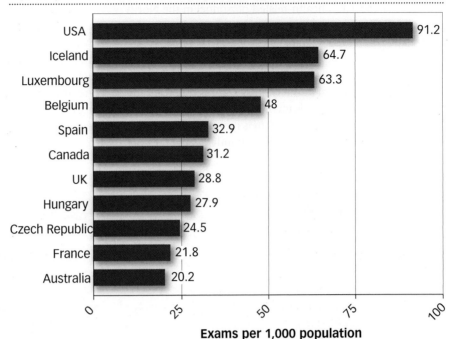

Exams per 1,000 population

SOURCE: From "World Population Prospects: The 2010 Revision," Department of Economic and Social Affairs, Population Division, United Nations.

CHECKPOINT 13.3   GLOBALIZATION AND HEALTH

Inequality	Women and children are the most vulnerable global populations, facing malnutrition, disease, and food insecurity with poor access to health care.
Borderless diseases	Flu, among other diseases, demonstrates how easily pathogens can flow throughout the globe.
HIV/AIDS	The spread of AIDS is linked to globalization via sex tourism, legal and illegal immigration, and the movement of refugees, war, and increased commercial and business travel.
Medical technologies	Expensive diagnostic technologies like MRIs and CAT scans are found largely in the Global North where many patients can afford them.

In terms of networks of people, much the same picture emerges. Medical and health-related personnel in the North are tightly linked through an array of professional networks. As a result, personnel can move about within those networks. More importantly, the latest findings and developments in health and medicine are rapidly disseminated through those networks. The problem in the Global South is that not only are there fewer professionals involved in these networks, but the flow of new information to them is more limited (Godlee et al. 2004; Horton 2000). More importantly, even if they are able to get the information, they generally lack the resources and infrastructure to use it, or to use it adequately.

At a more general level, we can say that the health and medical institutions in the North are highly interconnected while those in the South are only weakly interconnected with those in the North, as well as with one another (Buss and Ferreira 2010). This is another, more general, reason for the fact that important new developments in health and medicine do not flow rapidly to the Global South.

SUMMARY

In many ways, beauty has become a commodity that can be bought. The emphasis on beauty has also led to more attention to physical activity and its linkages to healthy bodies. Body modification, such as tattoos and piercing, is an example of society's increase in reflexivity and has become more common over the last several decades. The explosion of sociological interest in the body can be traced to Michel Foucault, whose work formed the foundation of the sociological study of the body. This field is defined by a general focus on the relationship between the body, society, and culture. It encompasses a wide range of concerns such as the gendered body, sexuality, and bodily pain.

The medical profession has gone through a process of deprofessionalization, characterized by a decline in power and autonomy, as well as status and wealth among members. There is broad consensus that the U.S. health care system is seriously flawed, with higher costs and lower outcomes than in the rest of the developed world. Health disadvantages are often linked with social class, race, and gender.

Global disparities in health and health care have often been tied to globalization. Individuals in the Global South suffer disproportionately from hunger and malnutrition, including obesity and undernutrition. The spread of AIDS is linked to globalization and increased global mobility. However, although the ability to implement new technologies and afford new treatments clearly varies by region, globalization also allows information about new medical developments to flow more quickly around the world.

KEY TERMS

Deprofessionalization, 388
Food insecurity, 395
Medical sociology, 387

Medicalization, 392
Profession, 388
Sick role, 387

Undernutrition, 395

REVIEW QUESTIONS

1. We live in an increasingly reflexive society with a heightened awareness of our bodies. According to Naomi Wolf, how does the beauty myth perpetuate such reflexivity?

2. How is risk-taking behavior related to Michel Foucault's idea of limit experiences? What satisfaction do people get out of risk-taking behavior?

3. You decide to go to a party with friends on the night before a big exam. You end up drinking too much and sleep through your alarm clock. According to Parsons's idea of the sick role, why would your professor be justified in deciding not to give you a makeup exam? What would you have to change to be excused?

4. What are the characteristics of a profession? What factors can help explain why physicians have become increasingly deprofessionalized?

5. What are the weaknesses of the health care system in the United States? How are these weaknesses related to systems of stratification?

6. What are some of the disadvantages of patients having access to more information about health care?

7. How has globalization tended to widen global disparities in health care?

8. What kinds of health problems are you most likely to find in the Global South? What could be done to deal with some of these problems?

9. How has globalization improved the quality of health care around the world?

10. In what ways has technology been an important factor in the improvement of global health? Are there ways in which technologies have made global health worse?

APPLYING THE SOCIOLOGICAL IMAGINATION

This chapter highlights the inequalities in U.S. health care and health care around the world. For this activity, compare the United States to two other countries—one from the Global North and one from the Global South—based on their health care spending and health outcomes (e.g., life expectancy and infant mortality). Use the Internet to locate data from the World Health Organization. What do the data suggest about health in each of the countries? How is this reflective of global stratification? How could globalization be used to help change the outcomes in each of these countries?

STUDENT STUDY SITE

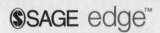

Sharpen your skills with SAGE edge at **edge.sagepub.com/ritzeressentials**

SAGE edge for students provides a personalized approach to help you accomplish your coursework goals in an easy-to-use learning environment.

A woman of Tianjin, China, braves a sandstorm with a scarf covering her face. Sand blowing in from China's interior deserts can reduce the air quality to "hazardous," compounding the industrial pollution that already plagues the country. Are societies prepared to face the environmental problems of the future?

POPULATION, URBANIZATION, AND THE ENVIRONMENT

14

At two minutes to midnight on October 30, 2011, the world's population reached 7 billion. While it would have been impossible to identify the actual 7 billionth living human among the several hundred born around the world at that moment, Danica May Camacho, born in Manila, Philippines, was the first of several babies chosen by the United Nations to represent this major milestone in population growth. A series of media events and press conferences were held throughout the following day, which the United Nations dubbed "The Day of 7 Billion" in an effort to draw attention to the challenges posed by an ever growing population.

> **Population growth and demographic change will challenge the way we interact with our environment.**

For media outlets around the world, reaching the 7 billion mark proved a fascinating but passing diversion. Some reports were celebratory, others contemplative, but most were over once the next big news story broke. For sociologists, demographers, ecologists, and other scientists, however, the growing global population is a major and ongoing social phenomenon that has had—and will continue to have—enormous consequences on where and how we live. Along with environmentalists, these scientists have voiced serious concerns about what continued population growth means for the "carrying capacity" of the planet, with its finite and fragile resources.

Population growth and other demographic changes over the last 150 years, such as the changing proportions of young and old in many countries and the increasing concentrations of people in urban environments, have helped give rise to new patterns of living. Urbanization, for instance, has brought with it the emergence of megacities, edge cities, and megalopolises. The rising global consumption that accompanies population growth has contributed to serious environmental problems on a worldwide scale, such as climate change, unchecked pollution, the rapid accumulation of human and manufactured waste, and a new scarcity of potable water. These effects will further challenge the way we perceive and interact with our environments, both natural and social.

While Danica May Camacho's birth will not have a direct effect on urbanization trends or the environment, the rapid growth of the global population that her arrival represents most certainly will. Efforts to reduce fertility and limit family size have had some effect on the world's growing population, but not enough to slow or reverse projected gains. As long as new births outpace deaths and the population climbs, Earth's environment will be challenged, and we will need to adapt. •

This chapter covers three broad topics—population, urbanization, and the environment. While each is important in its own right, they are covered together here because of the many ways in which they interrelate.

POPULATION

Demography is the scientific study of population (Bianchi and Wight 2012; Weeks 2011; Wight 2007), especially its growth and decline, as well as the movement of people. Those who study these population dynamics are **demographers**. Demography is both a distinct field of study and a subfield within sociology.

POPULATION GROWTH

A great deal of attention has been devoted to population growth and the idea of a population explosion, or the "population bomb" (Ehrlich 1968). Some of that fear has dissipated in recent years. This is, at least in part, because of the ability of the world's most populous country, China, to slow its population growth through, among other things, its one-child policy. Nevertheless, China's population is huge and continues to grow. However, China will soon be surpassed by India in population size. Population increases are important and of interest not only in themselves, but also because of the need for greater resources to support a growing population. Also of concern is the strain such increases place on national and city services, as well as on the environment.

While overall fertility rates are dropping globally, the world's population continues to increase, although at a declining rate. It was not until the early 1800s that the global population exceeded 1 billion people; it reached 2 billion in just one century (1930), then 3 billion by 1960. In the next 14 years, it reached 4 billion (1974); 13 years more, and it was 5 billion (1987); and in another 12 years, it reached 6 billion (1999) (Roberts 2009). In 2011, the world's population exceeded 7 billion people—37 percent of them in China and India alone (Population Reference Bureau 2010). Projections are that the next milestone will be achieved in 2025 with a global population of 8 billion people. While the overall trend is a slowing of population

> **demography** The scientific study of population, especially its growth and decline, as well as the movement of people.
>
> **demographers** Those who study population dynamics.
>
> **birthrate** The number of births per 1,000 people per year.

growth, there remain many countries (e.g., Ethiopia and Niger) where population growth continues to accelerate. In fact, in spite of the ravages of warfare and of diseases such as malaria and AIDS, the population of Africa as a whole is expected to double by 2050. As shown in Figure 14.1, nearly all future population growth will be in the world's less developed countries.

Rapid growth after World War II led to dire predictions about the future of population growth. At one time, projections were for a global population of about 16 billion people by 2050. However, it is now estimated that *only* about 9 billion people will be in the world by that time (Bianchi and Wight 2012). While this is a dramatic reduction in future estimates, it still represents a major increase in the world's population. This growth is occurring in spite of high death rates in many parts of the world due to high infant mortality, war, starvation, disease, and natural disasters. The death rate may increase dramatically in the twenty-first century if, as many expect, the disastrous effects of global warming accelerate, although that increase is unlikely to have much of an impact on overall population projections. Nevertheless, while there is less talk these days about a population explosion, there is little doubt that the world's population is increasing, perhaps at an unsustainable rate.

POPULATION DECLINE

Historically, population decline has not been considered as important as growth, but it has recently come to the fore in various parts of the world, especially in a number of European countries (e.g., Italy, Germany, Russia) and Japan (Coleman and Rowthorn 2011). By 2050, the population of Germany is projected to *drop* from 82.4 million to 71.5 million, while Japan's population is projected to decline from 127.7 million to 107.1 million (Coleman and Rowthorn 2011: 220; U.S. Census Bureau 2013a). Perhaps of greatest concern is the decline expected to occur in Russia from 142.8 million to 109.1 million in 2050. A variety of problems such as high alcoholism rates and greatly unequal development across the country have led to predictions of the "depopulation" of Russia. Even greater declines, and problems, are expected in a number of ex–Soviet Bloc countries such as the Ukraine, Bulgaria, and Latvia. Population decline can be caused by a low **birthrate**, the number of childbirths per 1,000 people per year. It can also be caused by a high death rate, more emigration than immigration, or some combination of the

Population Growth

Population Decline

A train is packed with Muslims preparing for the festival of Eid-al-Adha in Bangladesh's capital city of Dhaka. Have the dangers of population growth been overstated?

total number of productive workers. Third, the fact that population decline is generally accompanied by an aging population brings with it various problems including a "financial time bomb." This is because of a dramatic increase in the cost of caring for the elderly—especially government pensions and health-related expenses. A parallel decline in the number of younger people in the labor force means that there are fewer people who are able to help pay those costs through taxes (N. Singer 2010). Among other things, this financial time bomb will bring with it a great increase in national debt. This, of course, is already a concern in many countries. However, there are actions that can be taken to mitigate this problem such as raising the retirement age so that older people can support themselves longer. Another possibility, although it is difficult politically, is for nations to reduce pensions and medical coverage.

FIGURE 14.1 • World Population Growth, 1950–2050

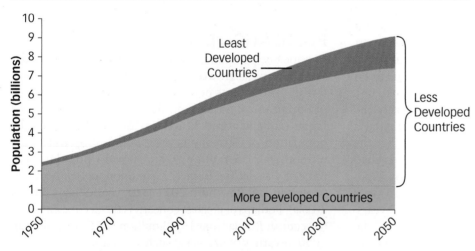

SOURCE: From United Nations Population Division, *World Population Prospects: The 2010 Revision*, medium variant (2011).

ASK YOURSELF

What are some of the problems nations would face in reducing expensive government benefits in attempts to defuse the "financial time bomb" of an aging population? Who would benefit from such reductions? Who would be harmed, and how could governments protect them?

It would be wrong to conclude that population decline brings with it only problems. Among the gains would be a reduction of the ecological problems caused by a growing population. For example, a smaller population would produce fewer automobile emissions and create less pollution. In addition, the pressure on the world's diminishing supplies of oil, water, and food would be reduced.

three. In countries with aging populations, birthrates are often below the level needed to maintain the population.

Of interest here are not only the various causes of such declines but also their impact on society as a whole. For one thing, population decline can weaken nations in various ways, including militarily. The power of nations is often associated with having large populations; a smaller population generally translates into a smaller military (Israel is an exception). For another, population decline can weaken a nation's economy because of the decline of the

While some nations will be hurt by an aging population, others, especially developing countries, will get a "demographic dividend" (Desai 2010; R. D. Lee 2007) because they have a favorable ratio between those who are able to work and those who are dependents, such as the aged and children. The dividend is due, in part, to a large younger population able to work and earn money. At the same time, there are relatively few in need of their support.

THE PROCESSES OF POPULATION CHANGE

Three basic processes are of concern to demographers. The first is **fertility**, or people's reproductive behavior, especially the number of births. Key to understanding fertility is the birthrate. Second is **mortality**, or deaths and death rates within a population. Finally, there is **migration**, or the movements of people, or *migrants,* and the impact of these movements on both the sending and receiving locales (Bianchi and Wight 2012; Faist, Fauser, and Reisenauer 2013). While these are dynamic processes, demographers are also concerned about more structural issues such as population composition, especially the age and sex characteristics of a population.

Mothers bring their babies for free checkups at a government health center in Manila. The president of the Philippines, a Catholic in a heavily Catholic country, supports laws to provide for sex education and free birth control. What obstacles does such legislation face?

Fertility

Theoretically, women could average as many as 16 births throughout their reproductive years. In reality, women rarely reach that number. Today, fertility levels vary widely from less than one birth per woman in Macao to almost eight births per woman in Niger. In this section, we deal with the economic and social factors affecting fertility, regional differences in fertility, and fertility trends in the United States.

Economic Factors. Fertility is affected by a variety of economic factors. For example, we know that record low points in population growth were associated with the Great Depression. Low points were also recorded in the 1970s, when an oil crisis led to a dramatic jump in oil prices and rampant inflation.

Social Factors. Fertility is also affected by a variety of social factors. For instance, there is the obvious impact of age on fertility. Most childbearing involves women between the ages of 15 and 45. Especially important in the context of age is the fertility and childbearing of adolescents (less than 20 years old). Globally, adolescents give birth to an estimated 15 million

> **fertility** People's reproductive behavior, especially the number of births.
>
> **mortality** Deaths and death rates within a population.
>
> **migration** The movements of people and their impact on the sending and receiving locales.

babies a year: The rate is as high as 200 per 1,000 births in some African countries, 24 per 1,000 in most developed countries, and only 5 or fewer per 1,000 in China, Japan, and Korea (Cooksey 2007). The "United States has the highest rates of births to teenage mothers of all industrial nations—double that of the next highest country, the United Kingdom" (Kimmel 2011: 170). Among the concerns about the high birthrate among adolescents is that they, as well as their children, experience more birth-related health complications and that they may not be ready to care for their children. Adolescent mothers generally lack the knowledge and power needed to make informed decisions on childbearing and child rearing (Weiss and Lonnquist 2009).

A second, and related, issue is the broader category of nonmarital fertility; not all of such fertility is accounted for by adolescents (Musick 2007). Nonmarital fertility has increased dramatically in the United States, rising from only 5 percent of all births in 1960 to a third in 2000; it now accounts for about 40 percent of all births (Bianchi and Wight 2012). The United States is not unique among western industrialized countries in this; its rate of nonmarital fertility is higher than some, such as Germany's; on a par with others, such as Ireland's; and lower than others, such as Scandinavia's. For a look at fertility rates around the world, see Figure 14.2.

Regional Factors. While those in many less developed areas of the world still worry about high birthrates, officials

FIGURE 14.2 • Global Fertility Rates, 2010–2015

Median Projections of Total Fertility, 2010–2015

- 6.5–7.5
- 5.5–6.5
- 4.5–5.5
- 3.5–4.5
- 2.5–3.5
- 2–2.5
- 0.8–2

SOURCE: Population Division of the Department of Economic and Social Affairs of the United Nations Secretariat (2007). *World Population Prospects: The 2006 Revision, Highlights*. New York: United Nations.

in many developed countries have grown increasingly concerned about their *low* birthrates. A birthrate of 2.1 is needed to replace an existing population. However, in the early twenty-first century, the average fertility in developed countries was 1.6 children for each woman; in some of those countries, it approached "lowest low fertility" of less than 1.3 children (in Russia, it was 1.1). In other words, the birthrates there are inadequate to replace the current population. This is a particular concern throughout Western Europe and has led to worry over the issues discussed above in terms of an aging population. Another concern is the future of the historical cultures of various European countries where the birthrates of immigrants (especially Muslims) far exceed those of "natives" (Caldwell 2009). This fact has contributed to increasing animosity between natives and immigrants and a growing likelihood of conflict between them.

U.S. Fertility Trends. When the United States was founded, the average birthrate was slightly less than 8 per woman; that rate declined throughout the nineteenth century and throughout most of the first half of the twentieth century. Then World War II led to an increase in the birthrate, and it remained high throughout the 1950s. In fact, the rise in the birthrate between 1946 and 1960 is referred to as the *baby boom*. The peak in fertility in the United States

was reached in 1957, after which the birthrate declined for almost two decades. It reached a low of 1.7 in 1976, and has gradually increased since then so that today the birthrate is slightly above 2. In other words, fertility in the United States is at "replacement level"—the number needed to replace its population.

Mortality

As an indicator of change, a population's mortality—or death rate—is as important to demographers as its birthrate. A population's death rate is measured as the number of deaths per 1,000 people. Life expectancy is the number of years an individual can be expected to live, given the population's mortality rate.

Life Expectancy. In prehistoric times, life expectancy in the world ranged between 20 and 30 years; by 1900, that number had hardly increased at all, but today it has reached 69 years. Nearly half of the decline in mortality in developed countries took place in the twentieth century. Life expectancy is now 77 years in the more developed countries, 67 years in less developed countries, and 56 years in the least developed countries (Bianchi and Wight 2012) (see Figure 14.3). Life expectancy in Africa is only 50 years (Elo 2007). As we saw in Chapter 9, the highest life expectancy is found in Japan, where women live an average of 84.7 years and men are apt to live 77.5 years. Life expectancy for women in the United States is about 81 years; for men it is 76.2 years (Bianchi and Wight, 2012). By 2050, American women can expect to live between 89.2 and 93.3 years, while men can expect to live between 83.2 and 85.9 years.

Macro-Social Factors. Although death is, of course, a biological inevitability, increased life expectancy and lower death rates in a population can be affected by a variety of macro-social factors (Elo 2007):

- A general improvement in standard of living (better housing quality, improved nutrition)

- Better public health (improved sanitation, cleaner drinking water)

- Cultural and behavioral factors (stronger norms regarding healthy lifestyles)

- Advances in medicine and medical technologies that not only lead to an aging population, but also reduce infant mortality rates (antibiotics and newer drugs, immunizations, improved surgical techniques)

- Government actions (control of diseases such as malaria)

Other important factors keep death rates high (including infectious diseases such as malaria and AIDS), and still others loom on the horizon that could increase the death rate, including global flu epidemics.

Mortality is greatly affected by one's position in the system of social stratification (see Chapter 7). In the United States, those in the lower classes are likely to have shorter life spans than those who rank higher in the stratification system. As for race, blacks have a lower life expectancy than whites, but black males are more disadvantaged in comparison to white males than black females are compared to white females. Lower life expectancies among black men are the result of the fact that they are less likely to seek health care, are at higher risk of death by homicide, and are more likely to engage in substance abuse (Sabo 1998).

In terms of gender, females have a longer life expectancy than males in spite of the various disadvantages they confront stemming from gender stratification (see Chapter 9). This difference is due, in part, to the fact that women engage in more health-protective behaviors than men, such as more frequent visits to physicians. Gender roles also tend to protect women from fatal disease and injury (Rieker and Bird 2000). For example, women are

FIGURE 14.3 • Global Life Expectancy, 1950–2050

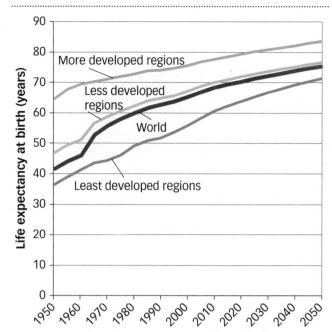

SOURCE: United Nations, Department of Economic and Social Affairs, Population Division (2007). *World Population Prospects: The 2006 Revision, Highlights*, Working Paper No. ESA/P/WP.202. Figure 4, p. 19.

less likely than men to engage in potentially disabling or deadly activities such as using illegal drugs, driving dangerously, and engaging in violent behavior. Higher death rates for male fetuses, as well as for male infants in the first four months of life, suggest that females may be more viable organisms than males. However, in general, "women now live longer than men not because their biology has changed, but because their social position and access to resources have changed" (Weitz 2010: 52). Nevertheless, there are some areas of the world such as India and Pakistan in which females have a lower life expectancy than males. This is traceable, at least in part, to the fact that females in some regions are more likely to die in infancy, perhaps because of parental neglect or female infanticide, or when giving birth to their own children.

Micro-Social Factors. Mortality is also affected by a number of micro-social factors, especially those associated with poor lifestyle choices including smoking, failing to exercise, overeating, and eating unhealthy foods. Obesity has long been related to higher death rates from heart disease and stroke. A more recent discovery is the linkage between obesity and death from various forms of cancer, including breast and endometrial cancer. More than 100,000 new cases of cancer per year in the United States, and perhaps more, can be traced to obesity. Conversely, healthy lifestyle choices can lead to longer lives. For

FIGURE 14.4 • The Three Stages of Demographic Transition

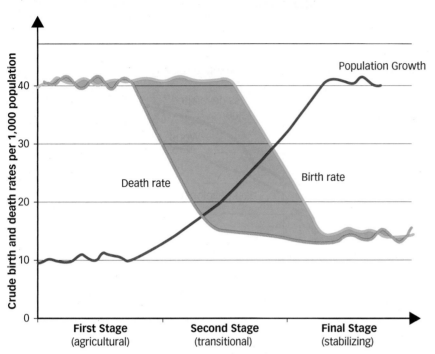

SOURCE: Adapted from *A Dictionary of Geography*, 2nd edition by Susan Mayhew (1997). Figure 20, p. 122. By permission of Oxford University Press.

example, religious groups that restrict the use of tobacco products, alcohol, coffee, and addictive drugs, such as the Mormons, tend to have longer life expectancies. Globally, the lifestyle of the Japanese, which includes eating more fish and less red meat, is closely related to their greater longevity.

The Demographic Transition

According to *demographic transition* theory, population changes are related to the shift from an agricultural society to a more industrialized and urbanized society (Davis 1945; Weeks 2007). Three stages are associated with the demographic transition (see Figure 14.4). In the first, or agricultural, stage, there is a rough balance between high death rates (mortality) and high birthrates (fertility). As a result, the population is fairly stable or grows only very slowly. In the second, or transitional, stage, the death rate declines while the birthrate remains high or declines more slowly than the death rate. The total population grows rapidly under these circumstances. In this stage, death rates decline first in developed countries for various reasons, including improvement in the standard of living, a better-informed population, improved hygiene, better health care, and so on. This was the situation in most of the developed countries of Europe beginning in the eighteenth century. In the final, stabilizing stage, the decline in the death rate leads to more children in the family and the community. As a result, people begin to think about limiting the number of children. In addition, fewer children are required because not as many workers are needed on the family farms. Many family members move into the cities and take jobs in industries and other organizations. For these and other reasons, it is to the family's advantage to limit family size. Eventually, the birthrate drops to a level roughly equal to the death rate. As a result, in this third stage, population growth once again slows or stabilizes.

As a general rule, birthrates drop more slowly than death rates largely because it is difficult to overcome the positive value individuals and cultures place on children and on life more generally. In contrast, reducing the death rate is relatively easy, at least when the means to do so exist, because postponing death *is* consistent with valuing life. This contradicts the myth that a population grows because of a rise in the birthrate. Rather, such growth is better attributed to a decline in death rates with birthrates remaining largely unchanged.

In Western Europe, the entire demographic transition took about 200 years, from the mid-1800s until the mid twentieth century. The process continues today in much of the rest of the world. However, in recent years, in less developed countries, the process has taken much less time. This is traceable to the much more rapid decline in the death rate because of the importation of advanced, especially medical, technologies from developed countries. Since birthrates have remained high while death rates have declined, population growth in less developed countries has been extraordinarily high.

Given this recent rapid population growth in less developed countries, the issue is what can be done about it, especially in the areas of the world where fertility remains high. In other words, how can the birthrate be reduced in those areas?

ASK YOURSELF

What happens to families that depend on children's earnings for survival when those children are required to attend school instead of working? Should society help address the loss of income to such families, and if so, how? Should companies that hired child workers in the past be responsible for these families' survival? Why or why not?

Reducing Fertility. Adopting the view that development is the best contraceptive, one approach to reducing fertility is to stress economic development. This follows from what has been learned from the demographic transition in Europe and the United States where economic development did lead to lower fertility. A second approach is voluntary family planning. This includes providing people with information about reproductive physiology and the use of contraceptive techniques, actually providing such things as birth control pills and condoms, and developing societal or local informational programs to support the use of contraception and the ideal of a small(er) family. The third approach involves a change in the society as a whole, especially where large numbers of children have been considered both advantageous and desirable. In many societies, children are still needed to work for the family to survive and to provide for the parents in their old age. Changes such as compulsory childhood education and child labor laws can counter the fact that these realities lead families to have large numbers of children. They serve to make children less valuable economically because they cannot work when they are in school and they are kept out of the labor force for years by child labor laws. As a result, at least some parents have fewer children. Another important step is to be sure that women acquire public roles beyond the family realm. With greater educational and occupational opportunities, there is a decline in female fertility, and families have fewer children (Fillipi et al. 2006). However, solutions that involve changing cultural ideas about women and reproduction can be difficult and slow to achieve.

Infanticide is an unfortunate practice impacting fertility. The selective killing of female fetuses, also known as *femicide,* directly affects fertility because of the reduction of females in a population (Bhatnagar, Dube, and Dube 2006). Infanticide is most common in South and East Asia, although it is also found in other areas of the world, including North Africa and the Middle East (United Nations 2006).

A Second Demographic Transition. In the 1980s, some scholars began thinking in terms of a second demographic transition to describe the general decline in the fertility rate and of population growth, especially in developed countries (Lesthaeghe 2010; Lesthaeghe and van de Kaa 1986). This decline is linked to parents

What effect will this Afghan girl's ability to complete her education likely have on her childbearing decisions?

coming to focus more on the quality of life of one child, or a few children, as well as on the quality of their own lives. Better occupational prospects, and therefore a more affluent lifestyle, have come to be associated with having fewer children.

Like the first demographic transition, the second is seen as involving three stages, but it is the first stage, between 1955 and 1970, that is of greatest importance. The key factor during this period was the end of the baby boom aided by the revolution in contraception that made it less likely that people would have unwanted children. Also beginning at this time was the gender revolution, which meant, among other things, that women began to marry later and to divorce more. They also entered the work world in greater numbers. This tended to reduce the birthrate as did the fact that there were fewer women at home to care for children. These and other factors can be said to be associated with a second demographic transition involving subreplacement fertility, lower birthrates, and a declining rate of population growth (Lesthaeghe 2007). This transition has also been accompanied by the proliferation of a variety of living arrangements other than marriage and an increasing disconnect between marriage and procreation (Klinenberg 2012).

Demographic Shifts

Why do countries attempt to control access to their borders today when they often didn't in the past?

Migration

Although migration certainly takes place within national borders (Crowder and Hall 2007), our primary concern here is with cross-border, international (Kritz 2007), or global migration (Faist 2012; Scherschel 2007).

Controlling Migration. Prior to the beginning of the fifteenth century, people moved across borders rather freely, although they were greatly hampered by limitations in transportation. However, with the rise of the nation-state in the fifteenth century, much more notice was taken of such movement, and many more barriers were erected to limit and control it (Hollifield and Jacobson 2012). Nevertheless, as late as the end of the nineteenth century, there was still much freedom of movement, most notably in the great Atlantic migration to the United States from Europe. It is estimated that about 50 million people left Europe for the United States between 1820 and the end of the nineteenth century (Moses 2006). Prior to 1880, entry into the United States was largely unregulated—virtually anyone could get in. In 1889, an International Emigration Conference declared: "We affirm the right of the individual to the fundamental liberty accorded to him by every civilized nation to come and go and dispose of his person and his destinies as he pleases" (cited in Moses 2006: 47). World War I changed attitudes and the situation dramatically; nation-states began to impose drastic restrictions on the global movement of people. Today, while there is variation among nation-states, "there is not a single state that allows free access to all immigrants" (Moses 2006: 54). With legal migration being restricted in various ways and border controls being more stringent, one unintended consequence (Massey and Pren 2012) has been an increase in illegal immigration (Hadjicostandi 2007) often involving human smugglers (Shane and Gordon 2008).

There has been a great deal of population movement associated with globalization (Kritz 2008; Kritz, Lim, and Zlotnik 1992). In the early twenty-first century, about 3 percent of the global population was on the move ("Keep the Borders Open" 2008). To some observers, this represents a large and growing number and, in fact, constitutes a substantial increase of 36 percent since 1990. However, to other observers, the sense that we live in a global era of unprecedented international migration is exaggerated because the actual rate was higher in the late nineteenth and early twentieth centuries (Guhathakurta, Jacobson, and DelSordi 2007).

While it is true that the rate is lower than it was a century ago, migrants do make up a significant percentage of the population of many countries (Kivisto and Faist 2010). For example, in 2005, migrants accounted for almost a quarter of the population of Australia and Switzerland (Australian Government 2011; Swiss Federal Statistical Office 2012), just under 20 percent of Germany's population, and 12 percent of the U.S. population (Roberts 2008), while in Great Britain and France migrants represent just under 10 percent of the population ("Keep the Borders Open" 2008). In the case of the United States, the percentage of migrants in the total population will reach 15 percent between 2020 and 2025, and it will rise to 19 percent by 2050, but only if the migratory wave persists. This will exceed the previous high of nearly 15 percent achieved in the late nineteenth century (Roberts 2008).

There are several interesting and important changes that have affected the nature of today's international migrants. For one thing, the proportion of such migrants from the developed world has actually declined. For another, there has been a large increase in the number of migrants from the developing world, and a very significant proportion of them (70 to 90 percent) are moving to North America.

Figure 14.5 offers a more general view of global migration. It shows the countries taking in the highest percentage of immigrants and those with the most emigrants leaving.

FIGURE 14.5 • Total Immigrant and Emigrant Population by Region, 2007

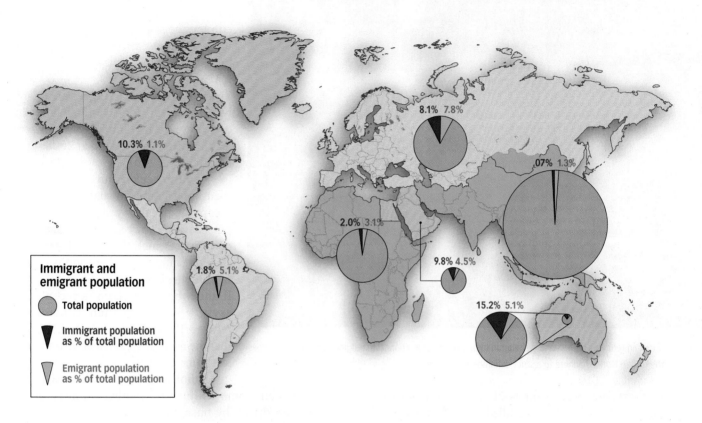

Immigrant and emigrant population

- ⬤ Total population
- ▼ Immigrant population as % of total population
- ▽ Emigrant population as % of total population

SOURCE: Map 1, p. 523, from *World Migration 2008: Managing Labour Mobility in the Evolving Global Economy.* Volume 4, IOM World Migration Report. Reprinted by permission of the International Organization for Migration.

While we almost always focus on migration from the Global South to the Global North, there is also some North-to-South migration.

Unlike much else in the modern world (trade, finance, investment), restrictions on the migration of people, especially labor migration, have *not* been liberalized (Tan 2007). The major exception is within the European Union (EU), and only for the citizens of member nations. Elsewhere in the world restrictions on migration remain in place, as they do in the EU for non-EU citizens. In some places, and for some less welcome migrants, restrictions have not only been increased (Schuster 2012b) but have also been militarized in some cases.

ASK YOURSELF

What social function do restrictions on immigration serve? What kinds of conflicts are caused by the privatization of immigration controls?

However, there are daunting problems involved in attempting to control global human migration. For one

thing, there is the problem of the sheer numbers of such people. According to one estimate, "tens of millions of people cross borders on a daily basis" (Hollifield and Jacobson 2012: 1390). The greatest pressure is on the United States and Europe, which are the most desirable destinations for migrants, both legal and illegal. For another thing, controls are very costly, and few nations can afford to engage in much more than token efforts. Then, there is the fact that attempts to control migration inevitably lead to heightened and more sophisticated efforts to evade those controls. A lucrative market opens up for those, such as smugglers, who are in the business of transporting people across borders illegally. Finally, the increased efforts at control lead to increasingly desperate efforts to evade them. This, in turn, leads to more deaths and injuries. For example, in 2012, there were 477 known deaths of people who sought to cross the U.S.–Mexican border illegally.

To prosper economically, a nation-state must try to retain its own labor force, comprising highly paid skilled

Types of Migrants

Christian refugees gathered at a shelter in India seeking protection from religious violence. Why does the United Nations adhere to a strict definition of *refugee*?

phones and the Internet (especially e-mail and Skype) or through more informal family and social networks that might well employ the same technologies. All of this makes it much easier to migrate and to be more comfortable in new settings.

Types of Migrants. **Refugees** are migrants who are forced to leave their homeland, or who leave involuntarily because they fear for their safety (Haddad 2008; Kivisto 2012b; Loyal 2007).

Asylum seekers are people who flee their home country usually in an effort to escape political oppression or religious persecution. They seek to remain in the country to which they fled. They are in a state of limbo until a decision is made on their request for asylum (Schuster 2012a). If and when that claim is accepted, the asylum seeker is then considered a refugee. If the claim is rejected, it is likely that the asylum seeker will be returned to the home country.

Labor migrants are those who move from their home country to another country because they are driven by push and pull factors associated with work (Kritz 2008). An example of labor migrants is the Mexican and South American women who immigrate to the United States to find work as domestics. Among the push factors for such women are "tenuous and scarce job opportunities," civil wars, and economic crises in their home countries (Hondagneu-Sotelo and Avila 2005: 308). The major pull factor is the existence of jobs paying higher wages than those back home.

Figure 14.6 shows the sources of immigrants to the United States by region of birth. Latin America and the Caribbean are the major sources of such migrants, but there is a strong flow of migrants from Asia as well.

workers and professionals of various types as well as masses of low-paid semiskilled and unskilled workers. If a nation-state routinely lost large numbers of either of these types of workers, but especially the former, its ability to compete in the global marketplace would suffer. However, nation-states also need both skilled and less skilled workers from other locales, and it is in their interest to allow them entry either legally or illegally.

Explaining Migration. A combination of push and pull factors is usually used to explain migration. Among the *push* factors are the desire of migrants for a better or safer life; problems in the home country, such as unemployment and low pay, making it difficult or impossible for migrants to achieve their goals; and major disruptions, such as war, famine, political persecution, or economic depression. Then there are such *pull* factors in the host country as a favorable immigration policy, higher pay and lower unemployment, formal and informal networks in countries that cater to immigrants, labor shortages, and a similarity in language and culture between the home and host countries.

In addition to these traditional factors are those specific to the global age. There is, for example, the global diffusion of information making it easier to find out about, and become comfortable in, a host country. Then there is the interaction of global-local networks, either through formal networks mediated by modern technologies like mobile

refugees Migrants who are forced to leave their homeland, or who leave involuntarily, because they fear for their safety.

asylum seekers People who flee their home country, usually in an effort to escape political oppression or religious persecution.

labor migrants Those who migrate because they are driven by either "push" factors (a lack of work, low pay) in their homeland or "pull" factors (jobs and higher pay available elsewhere).

Undocumented immigrants are those residing in a receiving country without valid authorization (Torpey 2012; Yamamoto 2012). This category overlaps with some of the above types of migrants; both asylum seekers and labor migrants may be undocumented immigrants. There are three broad types of undocumented immigrants. The first are those who manage to gain entry without passing through a checkpoint or without undergoing the required inspection. The second type comprises those who gain entry legally, but then stay beyond the period of time permitted by their visa. Third, there are those who immigrate on the basis of false documents. Estimates of the number of undocumented immigrants in the world range from several million to as many as 40 million people.

It is estimated that more than 10 percent of Mexico's total population lives in the United States. As of 2009, about 6.7 million Mexicans, the majority of Mexican immigrants, were in the United States illegally (Hoefer, Rytina, and Baker 2010). They come because although they may be paid poverty wages by U.S. standards, that may be as much as four times what they could earn in Mexico (Preston 2006a). Furthermore, there are more jobs and better future job opportunities in the United States than there are in Mexico.

Another reason many immigrants enter the United States is for educational opportunities not available in their home countries. Many become undocumented students. Harmon and colleagues (2010: 69) estimate that "approximately 1.8 million undocumented immigrants are under 18 years of age with an estimated 65,000 students graduating from public high schools annually." Furthermore, because the U.S. Supreme Court holds that states cannot deny undocumented students access to primary and secondary education, "education plays a central role in social mobility" for this outlaw culture (Harmon et al. 2010: 75).

The Case against Migration Restrictions. Public opinion is divided over immigration policies in general and dealing with the undocumented in particular. The case against restrictions on international migration can be divided into economic, political, and moral arguments (Moses 2006).

Economically, immigration has had a positive, *not* a negative, effect on the economy of the United States as well as on that of other developed nations. Contrary to what many believe, it is not clear that immigrants compete with

> **undocumented immigrants** Those residing in a receiving country without valid authorization.

FIGURE 14.6 • Foreign-Born Population by Region of Birth, 2011

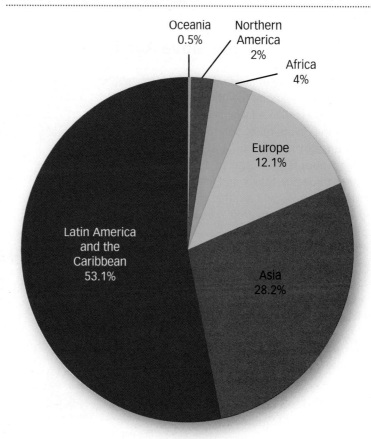

SOURCE: Data from "The Foreign-Born Population in the United States: 2010." *American Community Survey Reports.* May 2012. United States Census Bureau.

natives for jobs. It is also not clear that immigrants have less skill than natives. While the wages of native, less skilled workers may be negatively affected, wages overall are not affected. Immigrants are not a drain on public finances and may even pay more in taxes and into Social Security than they cost in services. A very strong economic argument in support of more open immigration in developed countries is the fact that because these countries are dominated by aging workforces, they need an influx of young, vibrant, and "hungry" workers. Yet another economic argument relates to the high cost of border controls to restrict immigration. If border controls were eased, this money could be put to other uses.

Politically, freer immigration can contribute in various ways to greater democratization. In terms of sending countries, the fact that people, especially the most highly educated and skilled, can and do leave because of a lack of democracy puts pressure on their political systems to reform themselves. More generally, it strengthens the ability of individuals to influence political regimes and to push them

Irish Migrants on the Move Again

One of the best-known mass migrations occurred in the mid nineteenth century when Ireland experienced a famine resulting from the failure of its potato crops, a key source of food for the Irish. Over a million people migrated to several countries throughout the world (many to the United States), and another million died, leading to a sharp drop in Ireland's population.

Conditions seemed to have changed dramatically beginning in the late 1980s and early 1990s. Ireland's economy boomed, and that boom continued until the beginning of the Great Recession. In fact, in the decade leading up to 2007, property values in Ireland grew more than those in any other developed country in the world. Emigration from Ireland remained low, and immigration into Ireland rose dramatically, peaking between 2006 and 2008.

However, the Great Recession had an enormous effect on Ireland. The Irish economy shrank by 20 percent between 2007 and 2010 ("Irish Economy Shrank" 2011). Home values dropped 50 percent from their peak in 2007. In late 2010, Ireland had to borrow 85 billion euros to stay afloat economically. As Ireland's economy tanked, immigration to the country dropped dramatically. On the other hand, emigration from Ireland rose substantially. At first, many of these migrants were those who had come from elsewhere earlier and were returning to their home countries. However, more

This mural in Yonkers, New York, celebrates scenes of Irish life, appropriate because many Irish have settled in New York and in the Northeast generally. Why do immigrants concentrate in specific geographic areas?

recently, it is the Irish themselves who are, once again, leaving Ireland. Many feel that they have little economic future there.

Although migration is difficult, especially when it is forced by such things as economic hardship, the Irish may be better able to cope with it than others. Aiding migration today are the new global technologies. As one woman said, "It's not like when we were waving goodbye from a dock. . . . There are lots of ways to stay in touch—Google, Facebook" (cited in Daley 2010b: 4).

Think About It

Do you agree that social networks can pave the way and ease the pain of parting for Irish men and women who choose to leave their country today? Why or why not? Will their departure be an economic benefit to those left behind under a regime of austerity, or a burden? Why?

in the direction of increased democratization. In a world of freer movement, nation-states also compete with one another to be better able both to keep their best people and to attract those from elsewhere. This could make nation-states the world over more democratic and enhance international exchanges.

There are two basic moral arguments in support of freer migration. First, as an end in itself, free mobility is "a universal and basic human right" (Moses 2006: 58). Second, instrumentally, free migration is a means of achieving greater economic and political justice. In terms of the latter, greater freedom of movement would lead to a reduction in global economic inequality and would mitigate global tyranny.

We turn now to a discussion of urban areas, the destination for many migrants and the locales most affected by population changes of various types.

URBANIZATION

The world has, until very recently, been predominantly rural; even in 1800, there were only a handful of large urban areas in the world. As late as 1850, only about 2 percent of the world's population lived in cities of more than 100,000 residents. Urban areas have, of course, grown rapidly since then. In the first decade of the present century, a "watershed in human history" occurred as, for "the first time[,] the urban population of the Earth" outnumbered the rural population (Davis 2007: 1). However, there are great differences among the nations of the world in terms of their degrees of urban development: In the United Kingdom, 90 percent of the population is urban, and in the United States, 79 percent is, while only 5 percent of Rwanda's population is urban.

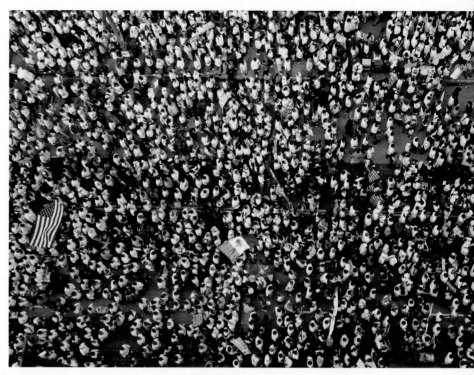

Thousands of people demonstrated in Los Angeles to protest legislation meant to crack down on illegal immigrants, who come mainly from Mexico. What arguments would you make for joining the protest?

CHECKPOINT 14.1	**POPULATION GROWTH AND DECLINE; IMMIGRATION**
Population growth	The world's population continues to increase but at a declining rate.
Population decline	Populations in some countries are expected to drop due to low birthrates, high death rates, and/or more emigration than immigration.
Demographic transition	Population changes occur as death rates and then birthrates eventually decline in the shift from an agricultural to a more industrialized and urbanized society.
Migration	Cross-border migration is a central aspect of globalization, but restrictions on it have been increasing except among members of the European Union.

> **cities** Large, permanent, and spatially concentrated human settlements.

It is projected that by 2050, 70 percent of the world's population will live in urban areas. For the more developed areas of the world, 86 percent of the population will live in cities, and 67 percent of those in the less developed world will be urban dwellers.

The importance of **cities**, or large, permanent, and spatially concentrated human settlements, has progressively increased. Even when there were not very many of them, cities were at the heart of many societies. Max Weber ([1921] 1968) accorded great importance to the rise of the city in the West in the Middle Ages. The city became increasingly central, and it has become much more important in the context of today's "global" cities (see discussion below).

The term *urban* generally refers to city dwelling (Coward 2012). However, the term has a more specific and technical meaning, although what is considered urban varies from society to society (Parrillo 2007). To be considered **urban** in the United States, an area must have more than 50,000 inhabitants. In comparison, to be classified as urban in, say, Iceland, an area need have only 200 residents. The U.S. government labels a city of 50,000 residents or greater an "urbanized area," or a "metropolitan statistical area" (Farley 2007). **Urbanization** is the process by which an increasing percentage of a society's population comes to be located in relatively densely populated urban areas (Orum 2007). It is clear that urbanization occurred even in ancient times when large numbers of people moved to Rome, Cairo, and Peking; however, it has accelerated greatly in the modern era. **Urbanism** is the way of life that emerges in, and is closely associated with, urban areas. That way of life includes distinctive lifestyles, attitudes, and social relationships. In terms of the latter, one example would be the greater likelihood of relating to strangers (Elliott 2012).

EVER LARGER URBAN AREAS

Cities have grown considerably larger in recent decades. After 1920 in the United States (and later elsewhere), there emerged a new urban form—the **metropolis**—a large, powerful, and culturally influential urban area that contains a central city and its surrounding communities, known as **suburbs,** that are economically and socially linked to the center but located outside the city's political boundaries (Friedman 2007). They often create bandlike structures around cities. While suburbs in the United States have tended to be middle class, cities in other societies, such as France and South American cities, are more likely to be dominated by the lower class, including many recent immigrants. A **megalopolis** is a cluster of highly populated cities that can stretch over great distances (Gotham 2007; Gottman 1961). There are currently 18 megalopolises in the United States with the area between Boston and Washington, DC, being the classic example. Another now stretches from San Diego to San Francisco and ultimately may extend as far as Seattle and even Vancouver.

SUBURBANIZATION

The process of **suburbanization** occurs when large numbers of people move out of the city and into nearby, less densely populated, environs. They are often impelled by urban problems such as crime, pollution, poverty, homelessness, and poor schools. The "American dream" of the last half of the twentieth century of an affordable one-family home was more likely to be found in the suburbs than in the city.

Various criticisms have been directed at suburbanization. One is that it led to the creation of vast areas characterized by a seemingly endless sprawl of tract houses and the businesses created to serve them (Duány, Plater-Zyberk, and Speck 2010). Another critique renamed suburbia "Disturbia," describing the suburban home as a "split-level trap" (Gordon, Gordon, and Gunther 1960). More recently, many others have noted the problem of suburban sprawl, which promotes high levels of traffic congestion and environmental degradation. However, there were others, especially many who lived in such homes and communities, who found much merit in suburbia (Gans 1967: 432).

Suburban developments have changed over the years and are no longer the homogeneous communities they once were (Dullea 1991). More importantly, many suburban developers have learned from previous mistakes. They have, among other things, created communities in which the houses have at least several different styles, even though they may at base be similar.

---

urban City dwelling; in the United States, to be considered urban, an area must have more than 50,000 inhabitants.

urbanization The process by which an increasing percentage of a society's population comes to be located in relatively densely populated urban areas.

urbanism The distinctive way of life (lifestyles, attitudes, social relationships) that emerges in, and is closely associated with, urban areas.

metropolis A large, powerful, and culturally influential urban area that contains a central city and surrounding communities that are economically and socially linked to the center.

suburbs Communities that are adjacent to, but outside the political boundaries of, large central cities.

megalopolis A cluster of highly populated cities that can stretch over great distances.

suburbanization The process whereby large numbers of people move out of the city and into nearby, less densely populated, environs.

A more recent suburban development has been the emergence of **gated communities**. In these communities, gates, surveillance cameras, and guards provide home owners with greater security from dangers they think they have left behind in the city (Atkinson and Blandy 2005; Blakely and Snyder 1997). However, Low (2003) finds that such communities tend to produce a heightened sense of fear and insecurity among community members.

While the early suburban communities had small ranch-style houses, the boom years running up to the late 2007 recession witnessed the birth and expansion of suburban communities populated by "McMansions" (Lowell 1998; Rogers 1995). These are huge private homes that have at least 5,000 square feet of living space, and often much more. They are built on tracts of land of one, two, or even more acres. They are dubbed McMansions because even though they are expensive ($1 million to $2 million or more), they are built on the same principles (efficiency and predictability) as suburban tract houses. McMansions are little more than huge and luxuriously appointed tract homes built on the basis of a limited number of models.

Suburbanization was first associated with the United States, though it is now a global phenomenon. However, there is considerable variation around the world in this process and the nature of suburbs. It would be a mistake to simply assume the American model fits suburbs elsewhere in the world (Clapson and Hutchison 2010).

The Postsuburban Era

Suburbanization in the United States peaked in the late twentieth century. Today, there is much talk about the decline of the suburbs and the idea that we live in a postsuburban era. In part, this is related to the growing realization that a way of life that includes large, energy-devouring private homes and vast thirsty lawns is ecologically unsustainable. It is also a result of the Great

The G.I. Bill helped many returning soldiers start families in homes built in the suburbs after World War II. Suburbs are often criticized, but what are some of their advantages?

Recession in the early twenty-first century and the collapse of housing prices. The American dream of investing in and owning a home turned into a disaster for many whose homes are "underwater." That is, they owe more on the mortgage on the home than the value of their home (although home values had rebounded somewhat by late 2013). Related to this are high gasoline prices and home heating and air-conditioning costs that further help to make the cost of a suburban home prohibitive for many. Renting an apartment and moving back into or close to the city is back in vogue.

ASK YOURSELF

Some home owners who are "underwater" in regard to their mortgages have abandoned their homes rather than continuing to pay more for them than they are currently worth. What happens to a community when people walk away from their homes? Who should attempt to solve this problem? How and why?

Exurbia. Cities and suburbs continue to push outward where land and housing costs are lower. Developments in these outlying areas, the crabgrass frontiers between the

> **gated communities** Communities in which gates, surveillance cameras, and guards provide the owners of homes or condominiums greater security from the problems (crime, panhandling) that they think they left behind in the city.

The DREAM Act

Suburbanization

suburbs and rural areas, are called **exurbia** (Crump 2007). These are generally upper-middle-class communities and may have enormous, custom-built homes (rather than McMansions) on large, heavily treed lots.

Edge Cities. Associated with the rise of exurbia is the emergence of what have come to be called edge cities (Garreau 1991; Phelps and Wood 2011). As the name suggests, **edge cities** are developments at the outermost rings surrounding large cities that in many ways function more like cities than suburbs. As part of exurbia, edge cities become indistinguishable from the hinterlands, giving rise to the idea of the "edgeless city." Just as suburbanization did, the phenomenon of edge cities originated in the United States, but there are signs that these cities are becoming increasingly global (Bontje and Burdack 2011).

THE DECLINE OF MAJOR U.S. CITIES

Many major American cities that developed with the industrialization of the nation have undergone substantial deterioration as a result of deindustrialization, or the decline in the manufacturing sector. This decline was accompanied by the exodus of whites from cities, which has been called white flight. This has led not only to highly segregated urban areas, but also to areas that have a declining tax base and a deteriorating infrastructure (roads, water and sewage systems, public transportation) and thus a declining ability to provide basic services for residents (Williams 1999).

In some cases, cities have rebuilt at least some of their infrastructure in a process of urban renewal (Crowley 2007). A related process is **gentrification**, in which real estate capital is reinvested in blighted inner-city areas to refurbish housing for the upwardly mobile middle class (Lees, Slater, and Wyly 2010; Patch and Brenner 2007). One prominent example is the borough of Brooklyn, New York, which in the 1940s and 1950s was largely shunned by New Yorkers because of its industrial-era slums. Today, however, much of Brooklyn and its famous brownstones have been transformed into a model postindustrial landscape. Its townhouses and condominiums have been renovated and are ultraexpensive. Restaurants, bars, and other businesses catering to the new residents have sprung up all over the borough (Osman 2011). Pioneers in the process of gentrification are often young professionals, many of them gays, and artists (Zukin 1969). Gentrification allows the wealthier residents (the "gentry") who grew up in the suburbs to return to the city. The expectation is that they will rebuild its depressed

areas not only physically, but also economically, socially, and culturally. In the process, working-class and poor residents are often forced out.

ASK YOURSELF

Does gentrification serve a social purpose? If so, what is it? Does conflict/critical theory apply to the fate of the working class and the poor in this process? If so, how?

CITIES AND GLOBALIZATION

From the beginning, cities have been central to both scholarly and popular work on globalization (Sassen 2012; Timberlake and Ma 2007). Cities are seen as being **cosmopolitan**, or open to a variety of external and global influences (Beck 2007). In contrast, small towns and rural areas are more likely to be viewed as **local**, or inward rather than outward looking. Cities therefore came to be seen as inherently global, and they grew more so as they came to encompass a range of populations, cultures, ethnicities, languages, and consumer products from around the world. Cities also exerted a powerful influence over surrounding areas.

Cities today are part of global flows of people, products, information, and more. This has been described as "mobile urbanism" (McCann and Ward 2011). Urban policies and ideas on how to improve the city flow easily throughout the world's urban areas. The many city-based organizations are linked through elaborate networks to organizations in other cities throughout the home country and the world. Furthermore, the people in those cities are themselves involved in a wide range of global networks and are linked to people throughout the world.

Global Cities

At the top of the world's hierarchy of cities are the global cities of New York City, London, and Tokyo (Sassen 1991).

---

exurbia Outlying upper-middle-class areas between the suburbs and rural areas.

edge cities Developments at the outermost rings surrounding large cities.

gentrification The reinvestment of real estate capital in blighted inner-city areas to rebuild residences and create a new infrastructure for the well-to-do.

cosmopolitan Being open to a variety of external and global influences.

local Inward rather than outward looking.

Global cities are embedded in the process of economic (capitalistic) globalization. Priority is accorded to the three cities mentioned above on the basis of their place in the world economy. Specifically, they are **global cities** because they are

- the key locations for leading industries and marketplaces and the high-level management and specialized services they require;

- the centers of the production and creation of innovative, cutting-edge financial services;

- the homes of new financial, legal, and accountancy products; and

- the settings from which businesses and organizations exercise global command and control.

Much of what global cities achieve is made possible by a wide range of new electronic technologies. In light of the Great Recession, we also know that these cities, with their great financial centers, are likely to be at the epicenter of monumental collapses in the global economy and, presumably, of economic renaissances.

Global cities are central nodes in a new international division of labor. Of great importance are the linkages among and between these global cities and the flows, both positive and negative, among and between them. In many ways, the global cities have more in common with one another than with the smaller cities and the hinterlands within their own country. They are also more integrated into the global economy than those hinterlands. The direct linkages between global cities point to the fact that nation-states are less important in the global age than previously. They are unable to control the flows between global cities. As Sassen (2012: 189) puts it, the global city "engages the global directly, often bypassing the national." In addition, the nation-state is unable to stem such global flows as undocumented immigrants and illegal drugs.

A fire destroyed 500 shanties that were homes to poor workers in Dhaka, Bangaldesh. How can societies avoid the kind of urban blight that leaves so many people living in slums?

> **global cities** Key locations for leading industries, centers of production, and centers of innovative financial services from which businesses and organizations exercise global command and control.
>
> **megacities** Cities with a population greater than 10 million people.

Megacities (and Beyond)

Megacities are defined as cities with a population greater than 10 million people. Of course, the global cities discussed above meet that criterion, but what is striking is the large and growing number of cities in the less developed world that can be defined as megacities (Krass 2012). In 2012, there were 26 urban areas qualifying as megacities, led by Tokyo with 37.1 million people, Jakarta with 26.1 million, and Seoul with 22.5 million (Worldatlas 2012). And these cities are expected to grow dramatically in the coming years.

Such population concentrations bring with them enormous problems associated with the large number of very poor people living in these cities, especially in the third world. Mike Davis (2007: 19) envisions a planet of urban slums that are a far cry from what early urban visionaries had in mind:

> The cities of the future, rather than being made out of glass and steel as envisioned by earlier generations of urbanists, are instead largely constructed out of crude brick, straw, recycled plastic, cement blocks and scrap wood. Instead of cities of light soaring toward heaven, much of the twenty-first-century urban world squats in squalor, surrounded by pollution, excrement, and decay.

Revitalizing Cities

Of course, these megacities, even the most blighted of them, have wealthy residents as well, and thus they are sites of some of the most profound inequalities in the world. A stunning example of this inequality is found in Mumbai where Mukesh Ambani, the richest person in India, built a 27-story, single-family home that may be valued at as much as $1 billion. Among other things, it has nine elevators, a six-level garage, helipads, "airborne swimming pools," a spa, hanging gardens, a 50-person theater, and a grand ballroom. The structure requires hundreds of servants and staff. All of this is found in a city noted for its poverty, where about 60 percent of the population lives in slums (Yardley 2010).

The Main Site of Global Problems

Global cities are home to the rich and powerful, the main beneficiaries of globalization. However, it is also the case that cities, including the global, are especially hard hit by a wide range of global problems. Among other things, some of the world's great cities have been the main targets of major terrorist attacks; the destination for large numbers of immigrants, many of them undocumented; the settings where large numbers of those affected by global health problems are likely to end up in search of medical help; and so on. Zygmunt Bauman (2003: 101) contends that "cities have become dumping grounds for globally forgotten problems."

In spite of their global nature and source, dealing with these problems becomes a local political problem, and city officials often lack the economic resources needed to address them. For example, the mayor of London is limited in what he can do to deal with the forces that lead many to migrate to his city, the roots of terrorism in the tribal territories of Pakistan, the global HIV/AIDS epidemic, or air pollution generated elsewhere. "Local politics—and particularly urban politics—has become hopelessly overloaded" (Bauman 2003: 102).

The Center of Culture and Consumption

Much of this discussion of the city tends to emphasize its problems, or dark side. However, it is also the case that cities have played a highly positive role in the development of societies throughout the world. Much of what we think of as culture, especially "high culture," has its origins, and has become centered, in the city. Thus, a great number of the world's great universities, museums, symphony orchestras, opera companies, theaters, restaurants, and so on are found in the world's great cities. It is also the case that much of pop culture emanates from the city.

The city is also the source of many developments in the world of consumption. For example, shopping arcades (Benjamin 1999), world's fairs, and department stores had their origins in nineteenth-century Paris and other European cities (Williams [1982] 1991). In the twentieth century,

U.S. cities became the world leaders in such consumption sites, most notably New York City with its world-famous department stores (Macy's and Gimbels), as well as the 1939 and 1964 World's Fairs. When those who lived outside the city could afford to travel, and wanted to consume, they often made regular treks to the city to shop, go to the theater, and so on. Cities like Paris and New York also played other key roles in consumption, such as being national and global centers of fashion (Lipovetsky [1987] 2002; Simmel [1904] 1971). Furthermore, cities, especially New York and its famed Madison Avenue, became centers for the advertising industry that functions to drive consumption (Schudson 1987). A number of cities have become more specialized centers of consumption, the most notable examples being gambling centers such as Las Vegas and Macau. Dubai has undergone a massive building boom in an effort to become the commercial and consumption center for a good part of the world stretching from Cairo to Tokyo.

Fantasy City. A **fantasy city** is one in which great emphasis is placed on creating a spectacle, especially in the areas of consumption, leisure, tourism, and real estate dominated by impressive buildings and other developments. Hannigan (1998, 2007) sees only two cities as full-scale fantasy cities: Las Vegas, Nevada, and Orlando, Florida (home of Disney World and many other tourist attractions). However, many others, especially Dubai, have moved more in that direction (see the next "Globalization" box).

Fantasy cities are characterized by an infrastructure dominated by such "cathedrals of consumption" (Ritzer 2010a) as "themed restaurants, nightclubs, shopping malls, multiplex cinemas, virtual reality arcades, casino-hotels . . . sports stadiums and arenas, and other urban entertainment centers" (Hannigan 2007: 1641). The whole idea is to draw people, especially tourists, to fantasy cities and once they are there to lure them into the various cathedrals of consumption where they will spend large sums of money. Like many developments in the realm of consumption, the fantasy city was largely a U.S. creation, but it has now become increasingly global.

Although people are drawn to fantasy cities to consume, what they find especially attractive is the spectacle of the city. For example, many American cities have built huge and spectacular new sports arenas (the new $1 billion–plus Yankee Stadium in New York is a prime example) as places in which to spend large sums of money (Hoffman, Fainstein, and Judd 2003). In Las Vegas, the

> **fantasy city** A city in which great emphasis is placed on creating a spectacle, especially in the areas of consumption, leisure, tourism, and impressive buildings and other real estate developments.

spectacle is the famous Strip, Las Vegas Boulevard, with its themed casino-hotels such as the Paris (with replicas of the Eiffel Tower and Arc de Triomphe), the Venetian (with its canals and gondolas), Bellagio (including its famous fountains), and Treasure Island (with its regular outdoor sea battles). Other cities have sought to draw tourists and consumers in similar ways.

Decline. In recent years, the central role of cities, especially in consumption, has been reduced. First, suburban shopping malls supplanted urban shopping centers and department stores as the prime destination for many shoppers. More recently, the shopping malls themselves have been being supplanted by online shopping (Amazon .com, eBay). Globally, such major players in the world of consumption as IKEA (from Sweden with Dutch ownership) and Carrefour (French) are most likely to be located outside the city. Entertainment giant Disney has placed its theme parks outside of some of the world's great cities.

In many ways, roles have been reversed, and instead of being the source of innovations in consumption, external developments are increasingly finding their way into the cities. They are making the distinction between cities, suburbs, edge cities, and other geographic areas less clear and meaningful. For example, fast-food restaurants (especially McDonald's) were originally suburban and small-town phenomena, but they have increasingly become urban phenomena, as well. In the process, they have tended to displace distinctive urban cafes and restaurants, driving many of the latter out of business and into oblivion. Similarly, discount chains (Target and Kohl's) have increasingly made their way into American cities. Even New York City, long known for its highly distinctive consumption sites, has come to look more and more like the rest of the United States (and much of the world) with its large numbers of McDonald's, Kentucky Fried Chicken, and now even Kohl's stores.

THE ENVIRONMENT

A concern for the natural environment is part of a broader concern for **ecology**, or the study of people and their relationship to one another as well as to the larger context in which they live (Sanford 2007).

Because of the explosive growth of a wide range of environmental problems in recent years, as well as the growing attention to, concern over, and even fear of those problems, many sociologists have been drawn to the

> **ecology** The study of people and their relationship to one another as well as to the larger context (including the natural environment) in which they live.

study of the environment, and especially to an analysis of environmental problems (Antonio and Brulle 2012; Dunlap 2007; Dunlap and Jorgenson 2012). They were inspired, as was the public as a whole, by such highly influential books as Rachel Carson's (1962) *Silent Spring*, which focused on poisons such as insecticides and weed killers and the threats they posed to the human food supply. There is now a large and growing group of environmental sociologists, as well as a relatively new specialty, environmental sociology (York and Dunlap 2012).

GLOBALIZATION AND THE ENVIRONMENT

The environment performs three general functions for humans and other species (Dunlap and Catton 2002; Dunlap and Jorgenson 2012). First, the environment is kind of a "supply depot" that provides us with the natural resources needed for life to exist. Among the renewable and nonrenewable resources provided are air, water, food, shelter, and the resources needed for industries to operate. However, overuse of such renewable resources as water and such nonrenewable resources as fossil fuels can deplete, if not empty, the supply depot.

Second, in consuming those resources, humans produce wastes of various kinds. The environment serves as a "sink" to absorb or dispose of the waste. However, it is possible to produce so much waste that the environment cannot absorb it all. For example, too much sewage can lead to water pollution.

Third, the environment provides us with living space, or "habitat—where we live, work, play, and travel" (Dunlap and Jorgenson 2012: 530). However, having too many people in a living space creates numerous problems associated with overcrowding and overpopulation.

In terms of all three functions, it could be argued that humans are beginning to exceed the "carrying capacity" of Earth.

There is great global inequality in these three functions. Basically, the developed nations adversely affect the ability of the less developed nations to perform these functions. For example, they use less developed nations as supply depots for natural resources for which they have historically underpaid. In the process, they often adversely affect the ability of the less developed nations to continue to produce these resources. Developed nations also often ship e-waste—that is, discarded electronic equipment— to developing countries, polluting them and their people with the minerals and chemicals in this dangerous debris.

Environmental Problems

Dubai as a Fantasy City

Dubai is a major city in the United Arab Emirates (UAE), a federation of states in the Middle East. Of particular note is the ambitious effort by Dubai to become a fantasy city. It did so by building several cathedrals of consumption, including an impressive set of skyscrapers. These are highlighted by the tallest building in the world, the 211-story Burj Khalifa, which opened in late 2009 and was scaled by Tom Cruise in the 2012 movie *Mission: Impossible—Ghost Protocol.* Dubai is also noted for its grand hotels, such as the Burj Al Arab, which proclaims itself the most luxurious and highest-rated hotel in the world. (See the "Globalization" box in Chapter 1, page XXX.)

However, perhaps the most spectacular development, and the greatest fantasy, in Dubai is the Palm Islands—Palm Jumeirah, Palm Jebel Ali, and Palm Deira. These are to be the world's three largest artificial (simulated) islands and the result of the largest land reclamation project ever undertaken. All three are to be shaped, albeit somewhat differently, as palm trees. All three are spectacular because of their size; the largest, Palm Deira, is planned to be bigger than Paris. Also spectacular is the way in which they were, and are, being created, by massive and unprecedented dredging of sand from the bottom of the Persian Gulf and by hauling sand in from the surrounding desert. Of course, the developers are not content with the spectacle of the islands themselves, but they are each to have their own cathedrals of consumption—luxury hotels, theme parks, shopping malls, and the like.

These massive development projects have been fueled by the UAE's enormous oil wealth—the country is the fourth-largest exporter of oil in the world. Much of the labor to build the fantasy city has been performed by immigrants from South Asia. This made Dubai a major destination for migrant labor during its rapid expansion in the early 2000s and contributed to the UAE's massive immigration flows. Because of Dubai's growth, its standard of living now rivals that of many developed nations in the world, but migrant laborers have been exploited throughout the development process (Davis 2006).

More recently, Dubai was badly hurt by the Great Recession. It was announced at the end of 2009 that Dubai was unable to make payments due on an estimated $100 billion debt incurred to build the fantasy city. Planned projects are on hold, construction cranes are stilled, and the city is littered with many unfinished buildings and other projects. Many of the migrant laborers have left the city and returned to their home countries (Worth 2009). Dubai's future depends, as do the futures of all the fantasy cities, on the state of the economy. A specific factor in Dubai's case is the willingness of oil-rich neighbors such as Abu Dhabi—Dubai itself has little oil—to continue to bankroll it.

Burj Dubai, in the emirate of Dubai, is the tallest tower in the world and only one of the extravagant structures in this fantasy city. Dubai has incurred enormous debts to build some of these projects. Was it worth it?

Think About It

What is the purpose of transforming Dubai into a fantasy city? Who benefits from this development of the city? Who is harmed?

This, in turn, despoils the living space and the ecosystem of those developing countries.

While environmental problems can and do affect specific countries, the vast majority of these problems are global in nature and scope. As a result, one of the most enduring and important issues in the study of the environment involves its relationship to globalization (Stevis 2005). The environment is inherently global. That is, we all share the atmosphere, are warmed by the Sun, and are connected by the oceans (Yearley 2007). Further, much that relates to the environment has an impact on and flows around the world, or at least large portions of it (e.g., through weather patterns).

Global Issues Challenged

Although the idea that environmental problems are global issues may seem indisputable, this view has been challenged in various ways:

- Not everyone or every part of the world is equally to blame for the most pressing global environmental problems. It is clear that those from the most developed countries are disproportionately responsible for them.

- Such problems do not, and will not, affect everyone and all areas of the world in the same way. For example, the rise of the level of the seas as a result of global warming will mostly affect those who live in coastal areas or on islands. Such areas will also be most affected by the expected increase in the number and severity of hurricanes. Tornadoes are also expected to increase, although they are likely to affect some geographic areas, such as the American

Does society hold business and industry sufficiently accountable for their impact on the environment? Here engine fuel is cleared from a beach near Gibraltar after a commercial ship ran aground there in a storm.

CHECKPOINT 14.2   URBANIZATION

Urbanization	The process by which an increasing percentage of a society's population comes to be located in relatively densely populated urban areas.
Metropolis	A large, powerful, and culturally influential urban area consisting of a central city and surrounding suburbs.
Megalopolis	A cluster of highly populated cities that can stretch over great distances.
Suburbanization	The process by which large numbers of people move out of the city and into nearby, less densely populated areas.
Gated communities	Communities in which gates, surveillance cameras, and guards provide home owners with security.
Exurbia	Upper-middle-class communities between the suburbs and rural areas.
Edge cities	Developments at the outermost rings surrounding large cities.
Gentrification	The process in which real estate capital is reinvested in blighted inner-city areas to refurbish housing for the upwardly mobile middle class.
Global cities	Key locations for leading industries, centers of production, and centers of innovative financial services from which business and organizations exercise global command and control.
Megacities	Cities with populations greater than 10 million people.
Fantasy city	A city in which great emphasis is placed on creating a spectacle, especially for consumption, leisure, and tourism.

ACTIVE SOCIOLOGY

What's It Worth to You?

Sociologists want to know how our understanding of environmental issues affects our social behavior, norms, and policies. As our society has become increasingly materialistic, for example, we increasingly need to deal with our discarded items. In that context, do you feel that websites like Craigslist, eBay, and Listia have been influenced by our awareness of environmental issues? Could these sites serve an environmental function, and if so, how?

Go to each of these sites and explore the types of *used* items for sale. Choose one category of item (say, electronics, clothing, or toys) and track examples listed for sale over the course of a few days. Record your observations by answering the following questions, and compare your results to those of the rest of the class.

1. What was the age and condition of each item you tracked?

2. How much did each item end up selling for? How did this price compare to the asking price? To the price of equivalent new items?

3. If there were many items for sale in your categories, why do you think people still buy new instead of used?

4. Do you think an increasing awareness of environmental issues encourages people to buy used goods? Why or why not?

5. List an item you no longer need on one of these sites. Does there appear to be high demand for it? Why or why not?

Midwest, more than others. In addition, because of their greater wealth, those in the Global North will be better able than those in the Global South to find ways of avoiding or dealing with all but the most catastrophic of the problems caused by global warming.

- There are global differences in the importance accorded to, and the dangers associated with, these problems. For example, many in the developed North are highly concerned about global warming, while many in the Global South feel that they are faced with many more pressing problems, such as health problems related to disease and malnutrition, as well as the decline of available drinking water.

- The main sources of environmental problems change. For example, the center of manufacturing, with its associated pollutants, has moved from the United States to China.

ASK YOURSELF

Do you think environmental problems are local, global, or both? Why? If we are to solve those problems, do you think it matters who is responsible for creating them? Why or why not?

THE LEADING ENVIRONMENTAL PROBLEMS

There are many important environmental problems, and we touched on several in the preceding sections. In this section, we deal with a few in more depth, including the destruction of natural habitats, global warming, and the decline in freshwater.

Destruction of Natural Habitats

Natural habitats such as the "forests, wetlands, coral reefs, and the ocean bottom" are being destroyed across the globe, often as the result of population growth and the conversion of some of those natural habitats into human habitats (Diamond 2006: 487). Today, the most notable deforestation in the world is taking place in the Amazon rain forest (mostly in Brazil) ("Welcome to Our Shrinking Jungle" 2008), but other parts of the world are also destroying or losing their forests. The Amazon forest is being decimated to allow the area to be "developed"—to create farms and areas for livestock to graze—and for the creation of more human settlements. Brazil's forests are so huge, and they play such a large role in the global ecology, that their destruction will have negative effects on the world as a whole. For example, the burning of all of those felled trees releases huge amounts of carbon dioxide that drift into the atmosphere and flow around the globe, contributing to global warming. The loss of the forest leads to other problems for humans, including a diminished supply of timber and of other raw materials. This is of great concern also because, especially in the areas undergoing deforestation, forests protect against soil erosion, are essential to the water cycle, and provide habitats for many plants and animals. The loss of the other natural habitats such as wetlands, coral reefs, and the ocean bottom will also have a variety of negative consequences for life on Earth. For example, the decline of coral reefs due to runoff from agriculture adversely affects the sea life that exists in and around them.

Marine life in the world's oceans has been greatly diminished by overfishing. According to the United Nations Food and Agricultural Organization, 69 percent of the world's most important fisheries can be considered either "fully exploited" or "overexploited." An early twenty-first-century study concluded that industrial fishing had led to a 90 percent decline in swordfish, tuna, and marlin populations (Khatchadourian 2007).

A major culprit in the decimation of marine life is industrial fishing. As the amount of sea life declines, the fishing industry compensates by using much more industrialized and intensive techniques. Among these industrial techniques is the use of huge nets that catch large numbers of fish, including many that are not wanted and are discarded. Modern industrial fishing is also characterized by the use of factory ships that process the fish on board rather than waiting until the ships return to port. These technologies contribute to overfishing and in the process destroy complex ecosystems.

Global Warming

Humans have produced greenhouse gases that have damaged the atmosphere and in the view of most experts are leading to a dramatic rise in the temperature of Earth. During the twentieth century, Earth's temperature rose by about 0.74 degrees centigrade; projections for the twenty-first century are for a rise of between 2 and 8 degrees centigrade. Because of the accumulation of greenhouse gases, heat generated by the Sun that would ordinarily be reflected back into the atmosphere is trapped and "radiated back to the Earth at a greater rate than before" (Beer 2012). Great concern these days is focused on the burning of fossil fuels (coal, gas, oil), the resulting emission of carbon dioxide, and the role that this plays in the accumulation of greenhouse gases and global warming. Rates of carbon dioxide emissions, mainly from industrialized countries, increased by 80 percent between 1970 and 2004 and have grown by 3 percent a year since 2000.

There is little or no doubt, at least among scientists, that global warming is a real phenomenon with man-made causes. Furthermore, the predominant view is that global warming is already well advanced and is progressing rapidly. Many scientists have further added that some negative effects of global warming, such as the thawing of *permafrost,* soil that has been at or below the freezing point of water for more than two years, will be irreversible once they start.

However, there are still a few scientists and many lay dissenters who take the view that global warming and the resulting climate changes that are now occurring are not the result of human actions but simply part of a natural cycle. Further, they argue that we will soon return to the cold part of the cycle when, for example, much of the ice in the Arctic and Antarctica will refreeze, as will the glaciers atop the world's highest mountains. Some believe that the rise in global temperature is traceable to changes in the energy output of the Sun; they also question the computer models that are being used to make future projections about temperature rise. However, scientific data that measure global surface temperatures 650,000 years into the past show that our world is warmer now than it ever has been through the many cycles of warming and cooling in the past (Lüthi et al. 2008).

Global warming is expected to adversely affect humans in a number of different ways (D. Brown 2007). It will bring with it more, and more intense, heat waves, and excessive heat can be deadly. A heat wave in Europe in 2003, the worst in almost 500 years, caused about 30,000 deaths from heat-related illnesses. The aging of the population throughout much of the developed world makes more people vulnerable to being made ill and dying due to excessive heat. Urbanization also increases the likelihood of death since cities can become heat islands. Other factors making death from excessive heat more likely are being very young, ill, poor, or someone who lacks the ability to move away from superheated areas. However, things can be done to mitigate the dangers of heat stress, such as greater use of air-conditioning, although many people in the world have no access to it or cannot afford it, and furthermore it causes other problems such as huge demand on energy resources.

Rising temperatures will speed up chemical reactions and worsen pollution from ozone and soot. Deaths from ozone pollution (mostly among those with lung or heart problems) could increase by 5 percent by 2050. Pollen production could increase, adversely affecting those with asthma and other allergies.

Waterborne diseases (e.g., cholera) will increase with higher temperatures and more torrential rains. Food-borne infections (e.g., salmonella) will also increase with hotter weather.

Diseases caused by animals and insects may increase. For example, it is expected that there will be an increase in malaria and dengue borne by mosquitoes. Exposure to malaria is expected to increase by 25 percent in Africa by 2100. However, as noted in Chapter 13, actions can

Hundreds of Belizians and supporters from around the world gathered to spell out an ecological message on a Barrier Reef island. Could climate change submerge this island some day?

be taken to mitigate the problem, such as by controlling the mosquito population with pesticides, greater use of bed nets (especially by pregnant women and children), and better medical care. Other diseases of this type that are likely to become more prevalent are yellow fever, also carried by mosquitoes, and Lyme disease, which is carried by ticks (D. Brown 2007).

Global warming will make some parts of the world wetter, but other parts will grow drier. As a general rule, already wet areas will grow wetter, already dry areas drier; both floods and droughts will intensify. Sea levels are projected to rise dramatically especially as the glaciers melt. During the twenty-first century a conservative estimate is that sea levels will rise about one meter. Approximately 100 million people in the world, mostly in Asia and on island nations, live within a meter of sea level, and their homes would be washed away by such a rise in the sea level. However, this does not take into account the melting of the Greenland and West Antarctic ice sheets that could add 10 or more meters to the rising seas. In such a case, much larger areas of both the less developed and developed worlds would be inundated.

Experts contend that because warmer air holds more moisture, heavy precipitation is expected to increase in some regions as a result of global warming, and the increased flooding will lead to more deaths. One example of this phenomenon is the death of almost 140,000 people in Myanmar as a result of a typhoon in 2008. The residents

of coastal areas are in particular danger due to storm surges. Extreme variations in weather may lead to more droughts and shortages of water. Food production may not increase as rapidly as expected with the result that the number of the world's hungry will increase.

The melting of mountaintop glaciers that are an important source of the supply of drinking water to many people in the world will cause great problems. As those glaciers melt and fail to re-form fully, they will produce less and less water for those who need the water to survive.

More generally, in the areas made drier by global warming, we are likely to see increasingly desperate and expensive efforts to find water by, for example, drilling ever deeper for underground water supplies (Struck 2007). Among the areas likely to grow drier are southern Europe, the Middle East, South Australia, Patagonia, and the southwestern United States. In May 2008, Barcelona became the first major city in the world to begin importing large amounts of water by ship to help deal with a long-term drought and a precipitous drop in water resources.

There are predictions of Dust Bowl–like conditions in the American Southwest and the resulting possibility of mass migrations. In Mexico, similar conditions may lead to mass migrations to Mexican cities and to the United States. Such an increase threatens to create far greater problems and animosities than already exist in the United States as a result of legal, and especially undocumented, immigration from Mexico. In more general terms, we are increasingly likely to see the emergence of an entirely new group of people in the world—climate refugees (Gray and Mueller 2012). They are apt to come into conflict with residents of the still water-rich areas to which they are likely to move.

The Decline in Freshwater

Water is becoming an increasingly critical global issue (Conca 2006; Hoekstra 2012). There are many who talk in terms of an imminent "water crisis" in some parts of the world, including California and Nevada in the United States (Subramaniam, Whitlock, and Williford 2012). However, it is the less developed countries in the world that are most likely to be negatively affected by a water crisis as water-dependent manufacturing industries locate themselves within their borders. In addition, they are the least likely to have environmental regulations to prevent problems or to be able to do very much about the problems once they begin. Among the concerns about water are the following:

- *Water inequality.* The United States has a water footprint double that of the world average and four times that of China. While many in the world have little access to water, many Americans "water their gardens, fill their swimming pools, and . . . consume considerably more meat than the world average, which significantly enlarges their water footprint" (Hoekstra 2012: 2207).

- *Water pollution.* Humans contribute to the pollution of water through manufacturing processes, mining, agriculture, and not adequately treating and managing waste (especially fecal matter). One result of this pollution is an increase in waterborne diseases, especially those that affect children (Jorgenson and Givens 2012).

This young girl collects water from a pond shared with animals in a drought-stricken town on the border between Ethiopia and Kenya. What can Western nations do to protect the world's fresh water supplies?

- *Marine pollution.* This involves "a disruption to the natural ecology of water systems, particularly oceans, as a direct or indirect result of human activity" (Burns 2012: 1324). Among the most important causes of marine pollution is the dumping into the oceans of the herbicides, pesticides, and fertilizers used in modern, industrial agriculture.

- *An increasing scarcity of water.* There is a possibility that the flow of water could slow or stop completely, at least in some locales. Some nations are forced to choose between essential uses of water, such as drinking and irrigating crops (Martin 2008). There are tensions within nations and between nations—and even the possibility of war—over increasingly scarce water supplies.

Desertification is the decline in the water supply as a result of the degradation and deterioration of soil and vegetation (Glantz 1977). Water, once considered a public good, is increasingly becoming a valuable and privatized commodity as many places run low on drinkable water. Another preventable decline in water supply is caused by wasting those supplies; for example,

nearly two-thirds of all water used for irrigation, in addition to as much as half of city water supplies, is wasted due to leaky pipes.

Although we usually think of water as abundant and readily accessible, the fact is that over a billion people do not have reliable sources of safe drinking water and more than 2 billion do not have adequate sanitation systems (Conca 2007). The poorest areas of the globe and the poorest people within those areas experience a disproportionate share of water-related problems. The situation is apt to grow worse in coming years; it is possible that half the world's population will be faced with water-related problems by the 2030s.

A less visible water problem involves international trade, especially in agricultural and industrial products. For example, when Japan buys crops (which are water-intensive) produced in the United States, pressure is put on American water supplies. People throughout the world are using water from elsewhere on the globe. This is called "virtual water" because almost all the water has been used in production of some commodity. If people do not realize they are using or abusing water, how can they do anything about it?

Astounding quantities of water may be used to produce commodities consumed as much as halfway around the world. For example, according to one estimate, it takes about 140 liters of rainwater to produce enough coffee beans to make one cup of coffee. We begin to get a

> **desertification** A decline in the water supply as a result of the degradation and deterioration of soil and vegetation.

Sustainable Development

Destruction of natural habitats	Burning of biologically valuable forests contributes to climate change, diminishes supplies of raw materials, and destroys plant and animal habitats.
Adverse effects on marine life	Overfishing has led to 90 percent declines in some fish populations.
Decline in freshwater supply	Water is becoming increasingly scarce due to industrialization, and some foresee a water crisis in some parts of the world including the western United States.
Global warming	Human-produced greenhouse gases have damaged the atmosphere and are increasing the temperature of the Earth.

sense of the magnitude of the water problem produced by the consumption of virtual water when we multiply that level of water consumption by the many cups of coffee, to say nothing of all the other commodities, that people consume on a daily basis throughout the world (Hoekstra and Chapagain 2008).

ASK YOURSELF

What can individuals do to help alleviate potential problems in the world's freshwater supply? Is it realistic to think that individuals can make a difference in this environmental challenge? Why or why not?

GLOBAL RESPONSES

Many global environmental problems, especially global warming, are traceable to capitalist economic development (Antonio and Brulle 2012). That is, as economies grow and generate greater wealth, they are likely to do increasing damage to the environment. As concerned as nation-states are becoming about damage to the environment, they are not about to either give up the fruits of economic development or cease seeking to become more developed.

As a result, a variety of efforts have arisen to at least reduce the magnitude of environmental problems. We have seen the emergence of a variety of environmental movements such as Greenpeace oriented to this goal (Caniglia 2012). Involved in these movements, but more general in nature, is the increase in environmental activism (Fisher 2012). Activists are generally interested in either protecting some aspect of the environment, such as a coral reef or a virgin forest, or protesting environmental hazards, such as toxic waste or the site of a garbage dump. In terms of globalization, either activists can oppose the global exportation of environmental problems, or they can support international efforts and treaties to mitigate these problems. While some

environmental movements and activists may want to slow or stop economic development, many favor sustainable development.

Sustainable Development

Sustainable development involves economic and environmental changes that meet the needs of the present, especially of the world's poor, without jeopardizing the needs of the future. While the focus of sustainable development is on physical sustainability, there must also be a concern for equity within the current generation and for future generations.

Globalization can be seen as either a threat or a boon to sustainability. As a threat, globalization can lead to unsustainable development by reducing the regulatory capacities of governments over environmental threats. Globalization can aid sustainable development by the spread of modern, less environmentally destructive technologies and the creation of standards for more efficient resource utilization. Globalization can also lead to a greater demand for cleaner environments.

There are a number of dimensions to the relationship between globalization and sustainability. First, there is the *economic* dimension and the issue of whether economic development irretrievably destroys the environment or whether with economic development comes the desire and the ability to better control the factors that are adversely affecting the environment. Second, *technology* can be seen as both producing environmental degradation and creating the possibility of limiting the damage. Third, there is the dimension of *awareness* and whether the global media create greater awareness of environmental problems and their causes, or whether consumerism, also pushed by the global media, increases people's blindness to these issues. Finally, there is the *politics* of environmentalism with some global organizations, such as the World Trade Organization (WTO), pushing for more economic growth, while many others, like Greenpeace, are seeking to reduce it or to limit its negative impact on the environment. Overall, then, many aspects of globalization adversely affect efforts at sustainable development.

> **sustainable development** Economic and environmental changes that meet the needs of the present, especially of the world's poor, without jeopardizing the needs of the future.

SUMMARY

While overall fertility rates are dropping globally, the world's population continues to increase, although at a declining rate. Population decline can weaken nations in various ways, but it can also have benefits. Demographers focus on three main processes: fertility, people's reproductive behavior; mortality, death or death rates within a population; and migration, the movements of people and the impact of these movements on both sending and receiving societies.

Urbanization is the process by which an increasing percentage of a society's population comes to be located in relatively densely populated urban areas. Cities are large, permanent settlements that are cosmopolitan in that they are open to a variety of external, including global, influences. Despite some problems, they play a positive role in the development of societies around the world. The most important of the world's cities are global cities. Megacities have populations greater than 10 million.

Suburbs are communities adjacent to, but outside the political boundaries of, central cities. Edge cities are on or near major highways, house large corporate offices, and have important commercial and consumption centers such as shopping malls. Looking for cheaper land and housing, people have pushed even farther out into areas between the suburbs and rural areas, known as exurbia. Major American cities have seen significant declines as they have lost the industries they once relied on. Gentrification has lured some white, middle-class residents back to cities' urban centers.

Increasing environmental problems have led sociologists to examine the environment more closely. Most environmental problems are global in nature and scope.

Global climate change is likely to make already wet parts of the world wetter, while already dry places are likely to get even drier. The relationship between globalization and sustainability has a number of dimensions including economic, technological, and political awareness.

KEY TERMS

Asylum seekers,   416
Birthrate,   407
Cities,   419
Cosmopolitan,   422
Demographers,   407
Demography,   407
Desertification,   431
Ecology,   425
Edge cities,   422
Exurbia,   422

Fantasy city,   424
Fertility,   409
Gated communities,   421
Gentrification,   422
Global cities,   423
Labor migrants,   416
Local,   422
Megacities,   423
Megalopolis,   420
Metropolis,   420

Migration,   409
Mortality,   409
Refugees,   416
Suburbanization,   420
Suburbs,   420
Sustainable development,   432
Undocumented immigrants,   417
Urban,   420
Urbanism,   420
Urbanization,   420

REVIEW QUESTIONS

1. How does the "demographic dividend" differ from the "financial time bomb"? Overall, is the United States in a period of a demographic dividend or a financial time bomb? Why?

2. According to demographic transition theory, what role do technological advances play in changing demographics? Why is "development the best contraceptive"?

3. How does the nature of today's migrants differ from the nature of migrants in the past? In contrast, how are the barriers to migration consistent with those of the past? How have the "push" and "pull" factors changed in the global age?

4. What are the arguments against restrictions on international migration? How do these fit into today's popular and political dialogue regarding immigration in the United States?

5. How is the creation of new residential and commercial models related to the decline of major U.S. cities?

6. How are McMansions and strip malls signs of the McDonaldization of society?

7. What makes cities cultural and consumption centers? How is a "fantasy city" different from a traditional urban area? In what ways are fantasy cities related to processes of Americanization?

8. How can sustainable development create a more ecologically friendly city? How would this development differ from that of the last 200 years?

9. In what ways does economic development contribute to environmental destruction? How could economic development be changed to reduce that destruction?

10. Do you think that globalization is ultimately a threat or a boon to sustainability? What current evidence would you cite to support your position?

APPLYING THE SOCIOLOGICAL IMAGINATION

This chapter examines global differences in perception of environmental issues. For this activity, choose one highly developed and one less developed country, and compare and contrast their environmental policies with that of the United States. How does each country approach global warming? Based on the chapter, why do you suppose these countries have similar or different approaches to environmental policy? How does this reflect their positions in a global system of stratification? What are the potential consequences of their positions?

STUDENT STUDY SITE

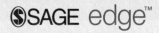

Sharpen your skills with SAGE edge at **edge.sagepub.com/ritzeressentials**

SAGE edge for students provides a personalized approach to help you accomplish your coursework goals in an easy-to-use learning environment.

RESISTANCE WORLDWIDE

Protests have grown in number, significance, and impact around the globe. Europeans rallied against government austerity, women in India marched against widespread sexual aggression toward women and girls, and citizens challenged corruption in China and Russia. In Brazil, even soccer fans protested the government's lavish spending on the World Cup as schools and hospitals fell into neglect.

▲ Chilean riot police arrest a student protestor in Santiago. Students say the government is using the state education system for profiteering.

▲ Riot police in Athens (left) clash with antigovernment protestors opposed to the government's austerity plans. Police restrain Indian student protestors (right) angered by the recent rape and murder of a young college student.

▲ Amsterdam's gay community depicts Russian president Vladimir Putin with makeup in a protest against Russia's stringently enforced laws against homosexuality.

◄ In the heart of Brazil's Amazon region, some 200 peasants, including this woman carrying her child, used bows and arrows against police with tear gas and dogs in a vain protest against eviction from a privately owned tract of land.

THINKING ABOUT SOCIOLOGY

1. Are social movements and mass protests inextricably linked? Or can one occur without the other?

2. Have you ever participated, or would you participate, in a public protest? Do you feel it is an effective way of stating opposition or accomplishing change? Why or why not?

3. **Essay question:** The world faces a number of global threats, including overpopulation, climate change, and food and water shortages, whose impact will be serious but difficult to forecast with precision. Are mass protests an effective way to bring about global government action to reduce the impact of these events? If so, explain why and what they would accomplish, and if not, propose and defend the course of action you recommend.

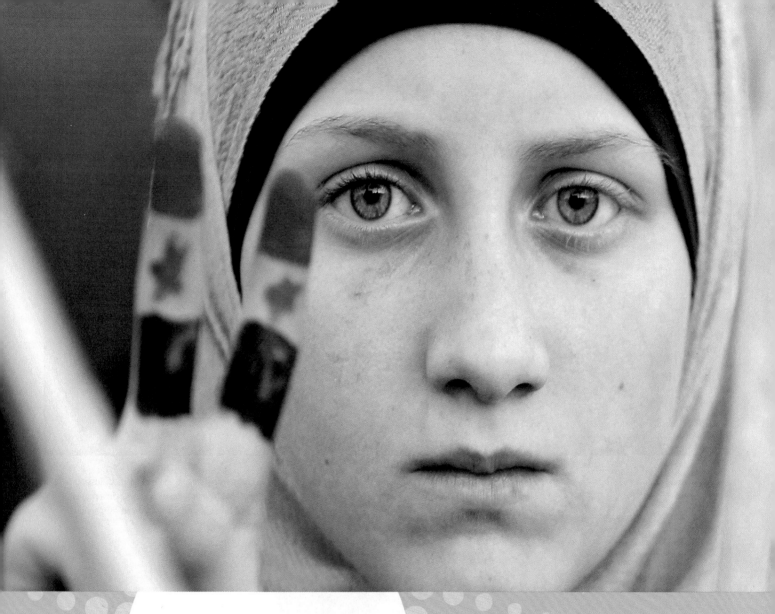

A Syrian girl gestures with fingers painted in the colors of her national flag during a protest in Jordan against Syrian president Bashar Al-Assad. Public protests provide an outlet for anger and frustration and a forum for ideas and support. Do they also bring about real change?

SOCIAL CHANGE, SOCIAL MOVEMENTS, AND COLLECTIVE ACTION

15

LEARNING OBJECTIVES

1 Use sociological concepts to explain the rise and impact of social movements such as the women's movement, the gay and lesbian movement, the civil rights movement, and the Tea Party.

2 Contrast social movements and other types of collective action, such as crowds, riots, and disasters.

3 Describe the process of social change, particularly the interactions of globalization, consumption, and the rise of the Internet.

Social movements come and go. Sometimes they have powerful impacts, as did those that led to the French and Russian Revolutions. More often, they have a limited or local effect and then recede and ultimately disappear into the mists of history. For now, at least, this seems to be the fate of the Occupy movement that not long ago garnered so much media and global attention.

On September 17, 2011, social and political activists took to New York City's Zuccotti Park to bring attention to the mounting struggles of the lower classes, and to end governmental partiality toward corporate and upper-class interests. Calling their budding social movement Occupy Wall Street, the group established a semipermanent encampment that served as home base for a series

> **Social movements can have powerful, if sometimes temporary, global impacts.**

of demonstrations, marches, and speeches in the city's bustling financial district. Media attention and support from large labor unions bolstered the movement's legitimacy—and its numbers. Large crowds gave rise to a unique culture with distinct roles, norms, values, and social institutions.

As the Wall Street encampment endured the chill of winter, Occupy movements fashioned after the original began to appear across the United States and, soon after, around the world. More than 1,000 were documented globally, including several dozen large encampments across the Americas, Europe, Australia, and Asia. Splinter groups' diverse regional cultures played a significant role in shaping the way they operated, what they valued, and the way they were perceived and treated by local populations and authority figures. The nearly instantaneous dissemination of up-to-the-minute news and videos across social media networks, combined with the sheer number of these interconnected protests, marked Occupy as a truly global social movement, at least for a short time.

Clashes at several Occupy protest sites, caught by viral videos depicting police use of riot gear, pepper spray, and semiautomatic weapons, drew international media attention and affected the way some viewed the movement. Some of the largest encampments, including Occupy Wall Street, were forcibly emptied by police—although some re-formed in different locations. By late 2012, however, the Occupy movement seemed to have become a historical footnote, although the Wall Street group later shifted gears to help victims of Hurricane Sandy. Whether or not it survives, the original Occupy movement was certainly successful for a time in bringing its members' concerns to the forefront of public attention. •

Social change involves variations over time in every aspect of the social world, ranging from changes affecting individuals to transformations having a global impact (Sekulic 2007b; Sztompka 1993; Weinstein 2010). Sociologists are concerned about social changes affecting the self-concepts of individuals, the structures of the United States, the global economic and political systems, and much more.

The issue of social change has been at the heart of sociology since its inception. This interest continues to this day and will be at least as true, if not truer, in the future. Social movements in Arab countries that began in late 2010 and continue to this day have dramatically changed much of the world. These movements are referred to collectively as the "Arab Spring" and have been discussed several times throughout this text.

This rebel fighter has just lost a comrade in the continuing violence in Syria. Few expected that the influence of the Arab Spring, which began in 2010, would be so widespread or so long-lasting.

The most important change wrought by the Arab Spring was the overthrow in 2011 of longtime Egyptian dictator Hosni Mubarak and the coming to power of a former leader of the Islamic Brotherhood, Mohamed Morsi. However, Morsi's rule was uneasy and marked by much protest and disorder. In fact, Morsi was overthrown in a military coup in July 2013. Egypt today is far from stable. The dictator of Tunisia, Zine El Abidine Ben Ali, was also overthrown in 2011, but his successor Hamadi Jebali was forced from office in early 2013 as a result of a continuing conflict between Islamists and secularists. In Libya, another dictator, Muammar Gaddafi, was killed in 2011; Libya now has a weak and highly unstable political system. President Ali Abdullah Saleh of Yemen was badly injured in a bomb attack and was forced out of office in late 2011. The new government of Yemen has struggled to maintain control over the country. An extremely bloody rebellion in Syria sparked by the Arab Spring is well into its third year in late 2013 with President Bashar al-Assad clinging to control over part of the country. The protagonists in this conflict, as in much of the Muslim world, are Shiites (in this case, an offshoot, the Alawites) and Sunnis. The conflict in Syria is spreading across the border into an already highly unstable Lebanon. Syria also abuts Israel, which has been drawn into the conflict in various ways (attacking weapons shipments) and could be drawn in much more deeply, especially if Arabs in the Occupied Territories grow restive. Many other countries throughout the region have been, and continue to be, affected by the Arab Spring. The social movements associated with the Arab Spring continue, and their effects reverberate throughout, especially, the Middle East (Lynch 2013: Moss 2013).

The effects of the Arab Spring spread southward to an area of Africa known as the Sahel. This is a band of land that stretches from the Atlantic Ocean to the Red Sea and encompasses parts of a number of nations. In late 2012 and 2013, violence associated with the disorder accompanying the Arab Spring occurred in Mali and Algeria. In Mali in late 2012, Islamic militants nearly succeeded in taking over the entire country. The French intervened and drove them back into the mountains where they remain a threat to the country. In Algeria, Islamic militants occupied an oil refinery in early 2013, and 23 hostages were killed in the process.

What is most important for our purposes is that the Arab Spring is an excellent illustration of the major sociological ideas to be discussed in this chapter. It brought about *social change*, and it exemplifies both *collective action* and *social movements*. We begin this discussion with the latter idea.

The Age of Protest

Arab Spring Bloggers

Is the Tea Party a social movement, a political party in the making, or a flash in the pan? This rally in California launched the group's "Reclaiming America" tour.

SOCIAL MOVEMENTS

A **social movement** is a sustained and intentional collective effort, usually operating outside of established institutional channels, either to bring about or to retard social change (Cross and Snow 2012; Snow 2013b; Snow et al. 2013). Having already touched on the Arab Spring movements, we discuss other examples of social movements in this chapter—the Tea Party, the women's movement, the gay and lesbian movements, and the civil rights movement. Following brief overviews of those movements, we will discuss various sociological concepts and ideas that help us to better understand these social movements. Finally, although we will not deal with them here, it is worth noting (given the focus in this book on consumption) that there have also been important *consumer* social movements, such as the National Consumers League and the Consumers Union (Forno 2013; Glickman 2009).

THE TEA PARTY

The Tea Party (www.teaparty.org) is a national movement named after the Boston Tea Party of 1773. In the contemporary context, *tea* stands for "taxed enough already." The Tea Party is *not* a political party, but it wields great power over and within the Republican Party. It emerged in the United States in 2009 as a protest against high taxes and other government actions (Pullum 2013). It especially targeted the Obama administration's efforts to address the Great Recession and the associated housing crisis, as well as its efforts to stimulate the economy through the American Recovery and Reinvestment Act of 2009. It

also opposed the Patient Protection and Affordable Care Act (known pejoratively as "Obamacare") (Barstow 2010), which was signed into law in 2010 and is scheduled to be implemented to a large degree in 2014 (see Chapter 13).

The initial impetus for the Tea Party movement was a February 19, 2009, on-air rant by commentator Rick Santelli on the conservative and pro-business cable TV network CNBC. Among other things, Santelli said, "The government is promoting bad behavior. . . . How many of you people want to pay your neighbor's mortgage, that has an extra bathroom, and can't pay their bills? Raise their hand! . . . we're thinking of having a Chicago Tea Party in July . . . I'm going to start organizing" (cited in Williamson, Skocpol, and Coggin 2011: 37).

Interest in the Tea Party boomed in the ensuing year. However, it remains a loosely organized group of local and national conservative organizations. According to one estimate, there are only a few hundred active Tea Party groups in the United States, and only a fraction of them have more than 500 members (Williamson et al. 2011). The organization's impact was greatly magnified by the media, especially the "advocacy journalism" of cable television news networks. Whatever else such overheated media coverage managed to accomplish, it brought a degree of attention and influence to the Tea Party far out of proportion to the number of active participants in the movement.

The Tea Party had almost immediate success when on April 15, 2010, there were hundreds of Tax Day protests throughout the United States with between 5,000 and 10,000 people participating in the main protest in Washington, DC. The Tea Party's greatest success occurred in the November 2010 congressional elections when candidates linked to the movement won 39 of 129 races for the House of Representatives and 5 of 9 races for the Senate (Karpowitz et al. 2011).

The Tea Party could become a new political party rather than just a faction within the Republican Party. Although not impossible, this is not likely, because the United States has been dominated by a two-party political system. If the Tea

> **social movement** Sustained and intentional collective efforts, usually operating outside of established institutional channels, either to bring about or to retard social change.

The Role of Social Media in the Arab Spring

The self-immolation of Mohamed Bouazizi in Tunisia that started the Arab Spring movement was preceded by a similar incident three months before (Khondker 2011). However, since that event was not filmed, it could not appear on any social media. The filming of Bouazizi's suicide made possible its wide dissemination through social media (Moss 2013). Further, social media had boomed in Tunisia, going from about 28,000 users of Facebook in 2008 to 2 million users in 2010. At least in part as a result of this explosion in social media, the 2010 protest led to the downfall of the government while a 2008 protest had been crushed. Although social media triggered the revolution, other factors were also important. For one thing, old media, especially television coverage by Qatar-based Al Jazeera, were a significant force in the revolution. Second, the social and economic conditions in Tunisia were ripe for revolution. Finally, the police and the military were no longer able to contain the revolutionary activities.

The revolution spilled over into Egypt where social media may have played an even larger role (see Chapter 2) (Gardner 2013). As one leading figure in cyber-activism in Egypt put it, "If you want to free a society just give them Internet access" (cited in Khondker 2011: 676). A good example of the role of social media occurred in the case of Khaled Said, an Egyptian blogger. In mid-2010, Said was dragged from a cybercafé in Alexandria and beaten to death by police

Would the Arab Spring have been possible without social media? Thousands of Egyptians used cell phones to record the celebrations in Cairo after the overthrow of President Hosni Mubarak in 2011.

officers. Afterward, the café owner gave a filmed interview that appeared online along with pictures of the blogger's shattered face. Soon an Egyptian and Google executive created a Facebook page titled "We Are All Khaled Said." Within six months, it had 350,000 members.

Social media were not only of great importance in Egypt, but they came to play specialized roles there and elsewhere. As an Egyptian activist indicated in a tweet, "We use Facebook to schedule the protests, Twitter to coordinate,

and YouTube to tell the world" (cited in Khondker 2011: 677).

Think About It

Social movements such as the drive for women's right to vote occurred long before the existence of the Internet. What do you think accounted for their success when they lacked the advantages social media can provide? Are there any disadvantages to the use of social media in promoting a social movement? If so, what are they?

Party were to become a full-fledged political party and became institutionalized, it would no longer be a social movement. It would also no longer be a social movement if it petered out and died. It is also possible that it will remain what it is, a social movement, for some time to come.

Like the other examples to be discussed later, the Tea Party has *the basic characteristics of a social movement*:

- It is *a collective effort* since it *involves a significant number of people* from throughout the United States.

- It has been *sustained* for several years.

- It was certainly *brought into being intentionally.*

- It is *outside established institutional channels* since it is not formally affiliated with either political party.

- It is an *effort to retard some political changes*, such as tax increases and President Obama's stimulus program and health care reform act.

A Sociologist Debates a Journalist: The Internet and Social Movements

Malcolm Gladwell is a journalist who draws on many different fields in his work, especially a number of social sciences, including sociology. (See Chapter 4 for a discussion of his work on the "tipping point" in social change.) In October 2010, before the height of the Arab Spring, he wrote an essay for the *New Yorker* titled "Small Change: Why the Revolution Will Not Be Tweeted." He argued *against* the notion that social activism had been radically transformed by the new social media. More generally, he contested the idea that "Facebook and Twitter and the like upended the traditional relationship between political authority and popular will, consequently making it easier for the less powerful to engage in collective action."

Gladwell based this view on the sociological argument that social media are built on the basis of people who have only "weak ties" with one another (Granovetter 1973) (see Chapter 4). He went on to argue that people who are not strongly related to one another are unlikely to come together to engage in high-risk behaviors such as a social revolution. I knew that the assertion that social media relationships involve only people with weak ties to one another was wrong (Tufekci 2010). In fact, extensive research shows that people use social media to relate to those with whom they have *both* strong and weak ties. Most people use Facebook to interact with close friends and family as well as with acquaintances with whom they do not have close ties.

In a blog post on www.technosociology .org, I argued that social media could well

A student-run Facebook page simulates splashes of blood on the Tunisian flag after the Tunisian government closed schools and universities in an effort to end violent clashes with police. Does contact that occurs on the Internet foster strong interpersonal ties?

be a major contributor to social change by facilitating connections and collective action among ordinary people, which would otherwise be very hard to coordinate. Also, the Internet allows citizens to circumvent censorship and to express their preferences. Unlike television, which is primarily a one-way medium, ordinary citizens can have a voice via the Internet.

Just a few months after I wrote this blog entry, revolutions in Tunisia and Egypt burst onto the world scene. It was clear that the activists involved in these revolutions were using Facebook, Twitter, YouTube, and other platforms to disseminate information that would otherwise be censored. They were communicating with people with whom they were weakly *and* strongly connected to

mobilize the masses ultimately to overthrow the existing regimes. Contrary to Gladwell's argument, it was clear in these instances, and in many others, that social media can enable collective action and facilitate social change.

SOURCE: Printed with the permission of Zeynep Tufekci.

Think About It

Do people who have strong links to leaders of a social movement react differently to social media messages about the movement than people with weak links? Why or why not? Consider your close friends and your distant acquaintances. Do they react differently to your Facebook messages? Why or why not?

- It is an *attempt to bring about substantial political change* in the Republican Party and the government as a whole. The Tea Party seeks to change the Republican Party by moving it further to the right and to change the American government by forcing it to reduce taxes, better control government spending and debt, and shrink its size and power.

WOMEN'S MOVEMENTS

Women's movements are based on **feminism**, or the belief that women are equal to men, especially socially, politically, and economically (see Chapter 9). They have all of the characteristics of a social movement outlined above (Crossley and Hurwitz 2013). It certainly was the intention of many of the (primarily) women involved to bring the movement into being and to maintain it. Women's movements have, at least until recently, had to work outside established institutional channels because women were generally denied access to these channels by the men in control of the institutions. The movements have certainly demonstrated durability, as you will soon learn, both in the United States and around the world (Basu 2010). And, they are oriented toward improving dramatically the position of women throughout the world.

The Women's Movement in the United States

The first wave of the women's movement in the United States is traceable to the 1840s (Reger 2007). It was focused largely on the issue of suffrage, or gaining the right to vote for women. It had its roots in the early involvement of women in the antialcohol (temperance) movement and especially the antislavery movement. However, women were largely subordinated and ignored in these movements. Anger about such treatment led to the 1848 Seneca Falls Convention. The meetings focused on such issues as restrictions on women's roles within the family, women's rights in terms of education and property, and, especially, women's suffrage (Wellman 2004). Various meetings and conventions followed, and several national organizations were formed to push forward women's right to vote. Feminists introduced the Nineteenth Amendment giving women that right as early as 1848, but it did not become law until August 26, 1920.

The second wave began in the 1960s. It drew from the first wave, but went beyond it in various ways. Several key books, including Simone de Beauvoir's (1952) *The Second Sex* and Betty Friedan's (1963) *The Feminine Mystique*, had a strong effect on the movement and articulated a number of its key ideas. More practically, the second wave, like the first, grew out of the dissatisfaction of activists with their involvement in other social movements, especially the civil rights movement (discussed later in the chapter) (Houck and Dixon 2011), and their failure to deal with gender issues. Activists were also angered by the fact that these movements themselves were patriarchal. An important event in the midst of the second wave was the founding of the National Organization for Women (NOW) on October 29, 1966. The founders were women in government dissatisfied with its failure to deal with sex discrimination against women in the workplace. NOW eventually came to focus on a much wider range of issues, such as discrimination against women in education, the rights of women within the family, and the problems of poor women.

The second wave reached its peak between 1972 and 1982. A number of developments occurred during this period including the founding of *Ms.* magazine; the appearance of women's studies programs on college campuses; the passage of Title IX, ending discrimination on the basis of sex in publicly funded education; and the 1973 Supreme Court decision *Roe v. Wade*, legalizing abortion. However, the second wave was soon wracked by internal conflicts as minority women—women of color, lesbians, working-class women—protested the fact that their interests were not being adequately reflected in, or addressed by, the women's movement (Roth 2004). These internal conflicts resulted in a polarization of feminism. More conservative feminists, the reformists, were primarily concerned about gender equality in the workplace (hooks 2000). Revolutionary feminists criticized the limited goals of the reformists, who focused primarily on the concerns of white middle-class women. They also emphasized the ways in which conservative feminists often acted in a patriarchal and sexist manner toward other women.

In addition, feminism lost its edge because of a decline among women engaging in feminist dialogue in "consciousness-raising" groups (hooks 2000). College campuses had served as one of the few arenas in which feminist politics were discussed. Consequently, feminist politics grew stunted, and some dissatisfied radical feminists left the movement. The rise of opposition groups and the emergence of a powerful conservative movement in the United States in the 1980s contributed to the development of a sense, at least among some observers and participants, that we had entered a postfeminist era (Hall and Rodriguez 2003).

> **feminism** The belief that women are equal to men, especially socially, politically, and economically.

Global Women's Movement

How different might today's society be if women had been able to vote as long as men have? Would there have been a women's movement?

By the early 1990s, it was clear that feminism was once again alive and well as a third wave of the women's movement emerged. It has been marked by a reaction against the problems confronted by the movement in the 1980s. The defining characteristics of the third wave have been greater racial and ethnic inclusivity and more of a focus on the problems of minority women, such as racism, classism, and homophobia. The focus has also shifted to the place of women in the larger culture and to a variety of specific issues such as sexual harassment, violence against and sexual abuse of women, and women's body image. The turn to the Internet, and the rise of cyberfeminism (Carty 2013; Haraway 1991; Wajcman 2010), can also be seen as part of the third wave. While it is using the latest technologies and is far more internally differentiated than ever before, the third wave continues to draw on the first two waves (Snyder 2008). It is fusing the old and the new in an effort to adapt feminism to the rapidly changing realities of the twenty-first century.

The Global Women's Movement

Organizing women on a transnational basis began between the 1830s and the 1860s (Berkovitch 1999, 2012). At first this was highly informal, but formal organizations did emerge, such as the World Woman's Christian Temperance Union (WWCTU), founded in 1874. While the WWCTU focused on the problem of alcohol, it was concerned about other issues as well, such as political equality for women. By the time of its first international convention in 1891,

the WWCTU had branches in 26 countries. Members adopted the view that "universal sisterhood" existed and that women throughout the world experienced a common fate. Suffrage became an increasingly important issue globally, and that led to the founding of the International Woman Suffrage Alliance (IWSA) in 1904 (Rupp and Taylor 1999). One of the most striking events in the early twentieth century was the gathering of more than a thousand women in the Netherlands in 1915 at an International Congress of Women. This meeting took place in spite of the fact that World War I raged around the attendees, which made it very difficult to pass through national borders. The main goal of the meeting was to find ways to resolve conflicts and prevent future wars. After World War I, the founding of the League of Nations and the International Labour Organization (ILO) created new opportunities for global action by women (and others). However, women's activities in and through these organizations achieved few tangible results, in part because leaders within these organizations tended to be "elite, White, Christian women from Northern and Western Europe" (Freedman 2009: 48). Many women within these groups supported colonialism despite the presence of fellow members who suffered under colonial rule. Moreover, the reproduction of colonial relationships within the movement was yet another facet of the contentious beginnings of an international women's movement. In reaction to this, black women from Africa and the United States formed the International Council of Women of the Darker Races in 1920. It called for support of a struggle not only for personal, but also for national, independence from colonial domination (Freedman 2009).

Much greater strides were made as a result of the founding of the United Nations (UN) after World War II. Instrumental in this progress was the UN Commission on the Status of Women. Its initiative led to a world conference on women in 1975 and to the declaration of that year as the UN International Women's Year. Yet, at the 1975 conference, men dominated the speeches and leadership positions; they tended to represent the interests of their respective governments rather than those of women's organizations. But women continued to press for equality and were eventually granted more leadership roles to foster discussions about the gaps between male and female opportunities. This was followed by the UN Decade for Women (1976–1985), conferences during that decade, and follow-up conferences held in 1995 (30,000 people attended the UN Fourth World Conference on Women in Beijing) and 2005. Because of such meetings, women from all over the world were able to interact on a face-to-face basis and to develop various transnational interpersonal ties (Davis [1991] 1999). As a result of these associations, many local and transnational women's organizations emerged. In addition to these formal organizations, many transnational feminist networks have developed in recent years (Ferree and Tripp 2006). These are more fluid organizational forms, which lack formal membership and a bureaucratic structure. They have been aided in their formation and interaction by new communication technologies, especially the Internet. However, rather than leading to a single global sisterhood, fractures and divisions have grown stronger in the global women's movement. For example, women of the Global South often resist initiatives from women of the Global North. This resistance is due in part to a need to prevent the imposition of northern notions of superiority and to recognize that injustice and emancipation can take various forms (Freedman 2009). In spite of this, the women's movement is far more global than ever and is not only having an impact on the position of women throughout the world, but also shaping, and being shaped by, globalization (Basu 2010; Crossley and Hurwitz 2013). This can be seen, for example, in arguments over the meaning(s) of feminism and women's rights during the war in Afghanistan and America's participation in other international conflicts (Ali 2010).

What arguments do opponents of gay and lesbian rights make to support their beliefs?

ASK YOURSELF

Does it surprise you to learn that the women's movement and its global arm are characterized by fractures? What might heal these divisions? Do men need to play a role in women's movements? Why or why not?

THE GAY AND LESBIAN MOVEMENTS

Although the origins of U.S.-based gay and lesbian movements can be traced back to as early as the 1890s (Shroedel and Fiber 2000), space limitations restrict us to a discussion of developments during and after World War II. Further, this overview focuses mainly on the United States

(Valocchi 2013). However, it is important to note that there were earlier gay and lesbian movements in other places, such as Germany (Newton 2009), and there are, of course, gay and lesbian movements throughout the world today (de la Dehesa 2010).

World War II and the Lavender Scare

The World War II era has been described as something of a golden age for gays and lesbians in the United States. Men and women engaged in new experiences as they left home, settled in new living situations, and found themselves in same-sex milieus in the military or civilian workplace. This period has been described as "somewhat of a nationwide coming out experience" (Bérubé, as cited in Johnson 2004: 51). The war years allowed for increased possibilities and opportunities for sexual encounters, as well as an "anything goes" mentality. However, beginning in 1948, the United States entered a period of mounting public criticism of the "moral decay" of both communism and homosexuality.

What came to be known as the "Lavender Scare" signaled a turning point for the history of gay and lesbian

SOURCE: The *Gay and Lesbian Movements* section is printed with the permission of Tracy Royce and Danielle Antoinette Hidalgo.

Stonewall Inn

movements in the United States. The Lavender Scare constituted a government-sponsored attack on sexual minorities and those who engaged in same-sex sexual behaviors. Large numbers of those in government service were vulnerable to being labeled as "security risks" if they were suspected of engaging in "sexual perversions" or homosexuality. Those who posed a "security risk" were discharged from the government. Given the governmental tactics used to persecute those engaged, or assumed to be engaged, in same-sex behavior, many Americans lost their jobs, and some committed suicide. However, this institutionalized attack on homosexuality also sparked political organization among gays and lesbians. Thus, the "crackdown" on homosexuals, "perverts," and those engaged in "immoral" sexual relations paradoxically fostered a long-lasting collective movement to fight for the rights of gays and lesbians.

The U.S.-Based Homophile Movement

Early gay rights organizing in the form of "homophile" movements crystallized in the formation of the Mattachine Society. The Daughters of Bilitis (DOB), an offshoot of the Mattachine Society and a space for gay women, was founded in 1955 (Rutledge 1992; Valocchi 2007). These organizations emphasized education and largely embraced assimilationist strategies to gain mainstream acceptance. Although gay and lesbian activists worked alongside each other, gender privilege (particularly male) remained and was a source of dissatisfaction for lesbians active in the homophile movement. As one lesbian activist stated, "There wasn't a Women's Movement yet. . . . We knew our place— we were always the coffee makers" (Shroedel and Fiber 2000: 99).

Stonewall

The 1969 uprisings at Greenwich Village's Mafia-owned Stonewall are regarded by many as pivotal in the twentieth-century struggle for gay rights, and denote the beginning of the modern gay rights movement (Armstrong and Crage 2006, 2013; Duberman 1994). At the time, police raids of gay bars, and other forms of government-sponsored persecution, were commonplace. Despite ongoing arrests, harassment, and police brutality, gays had responded to this repression with only minimal resistance. However, the patrons of the Stonewall Inn reacted violently to a police raid on this gay space. Law enforcement officials and members of the gay community alike credited this event with inspiring gays to more aggressively demand equality and freedom from abuse. Today, gay pride days and marches continue to commemorate the assertion of collective gay identity and entitlement to rights that emerged as a result of Stonewall. However, some question

gay history's emphasis on the Stonewall uprisings. They remind us that new forms of the gay and lesbian movement owe much to the foundational work of homophile groups, as well as to twentieth-century civil rights, antiwar, and feminist organizations (Jay 1999).

Lesbian Herstory

Given the underlying male privilege that was embodied in groups such as the Mattachine Society, many lesbians were dissatisfied with their organizing experiences alongside gay men. And although lesbians found a respite from sexism in the mainstream second-wave women's movement, the heterosexism and sometimes overt hostility encountered by lesbians in feminist groups made these organizing spaces less than hospitable. Consequently, many lesbians split off from the mainstream gay and feminist movements. Numerous lesbian separatist groups emerged, such as the Furies, who framed lesbianism as a political choice in opposition to male supremacy.

Not all lesbians politicized their sexual identities in this way. For women who desired other women in butch/ femme (traditionally male/traditionally female) space, a masculine–feminine relationship continued. But lesbian separatists argued that to truly be a feminist, women had to remove themselves completely from the male sphere. In practice, this resulted in the formation of women-only communities or "womyn's lands" and lesbian-driven, woman-centered activism. These women "wanted to create entirely new institutions and to shape a women's culture that would embody all of the best values that were not male" (Faderman 1991: 216).

ASK YOURSELF

Why do all gays and lesbians not have the same goals or try to achieve equality by the same means? Do their philosophical and practical divisions help or hinder their efforts? Why?

HIV/AIDS, ACT UP, and Queer Nation

The recognition of HIV/AIDS in 1981 by the Centers for Disease Control and Prevention (CDC) had a tremendous impact on gay and lesbian politics and communities. The activism that emerged from this period was embodied in the early efforts of the AIDS Coalition to Unleash Power (ACT UP) (Stockdill 2013). In 1989, ACT UP pressured the pharmaceutical company, Burroughs Wellcome, to make its new antiretroviral drug, AZT, more affordable for HIV-positive patients. ACT UP embodied a new kind of activism, which included civil disobedience, activist art, and other forms of creative activities and representations. ACT UP chapters opened throughout the nation. In 1990, some ACT UP activists formed a new group, Queer Nation, which, although short-lived, served as the beginning of a public and direct representation of LGBTQ (lesbian, gay, bisexual, transgender, and queer) issues. Out of HIV/AIDS activism and via the efforts of Queer Nation, the gay and lesbian movement shifted into a politics of queer spaces and identities.

The Ongoing Fight for Marriage Equality

Same-sex couples currently enjoy the legal right to marry in Argentina, Belgium, Brazil, Canada, Denmark, France, Iceland, the Netherlands, New Zealand, Norway, Portugal, Spain, South Africa, Sweden, Uruguay, some jurisdictions in Mexico, and, at the time of this writing, 14 U.S. states and the District of Columbia (Freedom to Marry 2013). Gays and lesbians in the United States continue to fight for the right to marry their same-sex partners, including by legally challenging the 1996 Defense of Marriage Act. Gay and lesbian proponents of marriage equality in the United States seek formal recognition of their coupled relationships. They also want many of the federal and state benefits that are automatically conferred upon heterosexual couples who benefit from the legal recognition of their marriages.

Resistance to the legalization of gay marriage comes from both outside and within the gay rights movement. Religious conservatives oppose same-sex marriages, arguing that they threaten the sanctity of marriage and the traditional family. But queer-identified groups have also offered criticisms of gay marriage. For example, emphasizing the central importance of securing legal marriage is criticized for failing to address the inequalities inherent in the institution of marriage itself (www .beyondmarriage.org). The rights associated with marriage do not benefit everyone equally. Nor do they compensate fully for unjust deficiencies in contemporary public policy, such as the lack of a national health care program. To challenge the institution of marriage and to address the needs of varied family forms across the LGBTQ community, a number of alternatives to the mainstream LGBTQ movement's focus on marriage are suggested:

- Legal recognition for a diverse range of relationships and family forms

Should some people not be allowed to marry? This sign appeared outside the San Francisco county clerk's office on the first day same-sex marriage was once again legal there.

- Basic resources such as health care and housing for all persons, regardless of their marital or citizenship status

- Separation of church and state in all matters

- Freedom from state regulation of sexual lives and gender choices

The gay marriage debate and activist efforts relating to it continue to be fraught with tension both within and beyond the LGBTQ community. While the gay and lesbian movements discussed in this section are global in scope, the movements have had mixed success globally. While at least some forms of homosexuality are legal in some parts of the world, either it is illegal or same-sex couples are not recognized in a much larger part of the world. There are even parts of the world, mostly Islamic, where homosexuality is subject to large penalties, life in prison, or even death.

THE CIVIL RIGHTS MOVEMENT

Arguably, the most notable social movement in the United States was, and may still be, the civil rights movement (Andrews 2013; Morris 1984, 2007). (Others would contend that the anticolonial [Schock 2013] and the labor movements [Fantasia, Voss, and Eidlin 2013], among others, were of greater importance, especially globally.)

The Civil Rights Movement

Reverend Martin Luther King Jr. (center) leading the 1965 protest march from Selma to Montgomery (Alabama). Has the civil rights movement accomplished its objectives?

Perhaps the key event in its history was the successful 1955 Montgomery, Alabama, boycott of segregated city buses. At the time, blacks had to ride in the back of public buses. While the movement was organized locally, it was led by Martin Luther King Jr. ([1958] 2010). His success there catapulted him into the leadership position of the national civil rights movement. The Montgomery boycott served as a model for future civil rights action and all other subsequent social movements. It emphasized nonviolent action, made it clear that the black community could overcome internal divisions to become an effective force for change, showed the central role that the black church could play in such a social movement, and demonstrated that the black community was able to finance these actions with little or no outside help.

The success of the Montgomery bus boycott led black organizations to become more involved in civil rights organizations. These included the National Association for the Advancement of Colored People (NAACP), formed in 1910, and the Congress of Racial Equality (CORE), organized in 1942. It also led to the formation of new organizations, especially the Southern Christian Leadership Conference (SCLC), and to the creation and active involvement of innumerable local groups. The actions spurred on by these groups and organizations encountered significant opposition from whites, sometimes leading to violence. A key development in 1960 was the large-scale involvement of black college students in sit-ins at segregated lunch counters throughout the South. These students were crucial to the

formation of another new organization, the Student Nonviolent Coordinating Committee (SNCC), in 1960. It, in turn, drew many white students into the movement.

In the 1960s, the civil rights movement became a significant force through boycotts, sit-ins, freedom rides, mass marches, and mass arrests. These involved both blacks and their white allies. In some cases, vicious attacks against black activists gave the movement great visibility and elicited much sympathy from those not initially inclined to support it.

Many of the "invisible leaders" of the civil rights movement were black women such as Fannie Lou Hamer, Septima Poinsette Clark, and Ella Baker. Their invisibility in leadership positions was an unfortunate by-product of the gender hierarchy as it existed in the 1950s. When women spearheaded successful civil rights campaigns, more "visible" men in the movement took the credit and usurped women's leadership positions (Olson 2002). The many women who participated in the movement served as volunteers, and their numbers far outweighed those of their male counterparts. Even within the radical Black Panther Party, female leadership was greatly limited despite the fact that women, like Elaine Brown, were prominent participants in the party's outreach and advocacy programs (Brown 1992).

ASK YOURSELF

Why are the black women who served as "invisible leaders" of the civil rights movement not more widely known today? Do you think women who are fighting racism today, whatever their color, are sufficiently recognized by the public? Why or why not?

The movement had great success, especially the Civil Rights Act of 1964 banning discrimination on the basis not only of race, but also of sex, religion, and national identity. Of course, the larger goal of eliminating racism in the United States eluded the civil rights movement and continues to elude it to this day (Pager, Western, and Bonikowski 2009).

The global nature of the civil rights movement is especially clear in the antiapartheid movement led by Nelson Mandela in South Africa (Van Kessel 2013). Apartheid was a system of racial separation that had been made legal in 1948. Soon thereafter a social movement against it emerged, led by the African National Congress. It garnered great international support and succeeded in achieving its goals in less than half a century (Waldmeir [1997] 2001). By 1994, both apartheid and white hegemony in South Africa had ended.

EMERGENCE, MOBILIZATION, AND IMPACT OF SOCIAL MOVEMENTS

A variety of conditions determine whether or not a social movement will emerge. To start with, there must be grievances, or matters that large numbers of people find troublesome (Snow 2013a). In the case of the Tea Party, for example, grievances included those against high taxes, the economic stimulus, and health care reform. The grievances about the unfair treatment of women, gays and lesbians, and blacks animated the other social movements discussed above. However, grievances alone are not sufficient for a social movement to arise. Individuals and organizations must be mobilized to do something about them. All of the movements discussed above were successful in mobilizing people to act.

South African schoolchildren stand before a mural of Nelson Mandela, who led the antiapartheid movement.

Factors in the Emergence of a Social Movement

Assuming a set of grievances and efforts at mobilization, certain other conditions must exist for a social movement to emerge. First, there must be openings or opportunities within the political system. For example, a deep and stubborn recession, high unemployment rates, a massive bailout of banks and large corporations, and a dramatic escalation in the national debt provided an opening for the rise of the Tea Party (MacDonald 2010; Pace 2010). That opening was widened as these and related problems, as well as public concern about them, increased (Crutsinger 2010).

A second factor involves various spatial arrangements, such as the physical proximity of those involved. Clearly,

social movements develop more easily when those who at least have the potential to become involved come into contact with one another fairly easily or on a regular basis. Another spatial factor is whether or not there are "free spaces" where those involved can meet. It is in such spaces that the movement can develop out of the limelight and free of external surveillance and control. Women on college campuses existed in close proximity to one another, and this helped in the formation of the women's movement, while free spaces such as churches were especially important to the development of the civil rights movement.

A third factor is the availability of resources. This is the concern of **resource mobilization theory**, one of the most popular approaches to understanding social movements today (Edwards and Gillham 2013; Jenkins 1983; Walder 2009). The focus is on what groups of people need to do in order to mobilize effectively to bring about social change. This theory assumes that there is some strain within the larger society and that there are groups of people who have grievances that result from those strains. One of the most important works in this tradition is that of Jack Goldstone (1991; Rojas and Goodwin 2013) on *revolutions*. These are social movements in which the strains produced by state breakdown (e.g., failure of the government to function properly, fiscal distress) play a key role in the development of revolutionary movements. Major examples of revolutions include the French, American, and Russian Revolutions. Once a strain exists, the issue, then, is what resources are needed for these groups to become social movements, perhaps even successful social movements.

> **resource mobilization theory** An approach to understanding social movements that focuses on what groups of people need to do to bring about social change.

Resources and Mobilization of Social Movements

Five types of resources have been identified as important to the mobilization of social movements. First are *material resources,* such as money, property, and equipment. It is costly to mount a successful social movement, and money and other material resources are mandatory (Snow, Soule, and Cress 2005). Notable in this regard is the backing of the Tea Party by conservative billionaires. Second are *social-organizational resources,* which include infrastructure (Internet access is especially important today, as discussed later in this chapter), social networks (insiders with access to important groups and organizations), and the organizations that are formed by the social movement (Tea Party, NAACP, ACT UP) (Stepan-Norris and Southworth 2007). Third are *human resources,* such as the leadership, expertise, skills, and day-to-day labor of those in the organization (Tsutsui and Wotipka 2004). More specific resources might be dynamic public speakers (e.g., Martin Luther King Jr.) and spokespersons, skilled web designers, or those skilled in organizational dynamics. Fourth are *moral resources* such as the degree to which the larger public regards the movement as legitimate. Other moral resources involve a sense that there is a high level of integrity among the leaders, as well as in the membership as a whole (Lowe 2002). Finally, there are *cultural resources,* such as bodies of knowledge or skills that are tacitly shared by at least some members of the movement. These might include knowledge of how to organize a protest, hold a news conference, or run a meeting. Overall, the keys to the success or failure of a social movement are the available resources and the ability to use some or all of them to mobilize effectively to pursue desired social change.

Another important issue is the source of such resources. One source is simply having members who are able to produce the resources by, for example, raising money, developing networks, or socializing their children to become part of the movement as adults. Another is aggregating external resources, such as soliciting donations from a wide range of donors. Also of importance is the need to locate patrons who can be relied on to support the group monetarily and in many other ways (e.g., by providing staff members). Finally, a social movement can co-opt the resources of other organizations. For example, social movements in the United States have often co-opted the resources of churches by using their buildings, their staff, and their moral authority.

Participation. Once a social movement is under way, methods must be found to ensure member participation. First, people need to be asked to participate. For that to occur, they need to be embedded in social networks involving other movement members. Second, a variety of social-psychological factors are involved. These include personally identifying with the movement and its causes, being aroused emotionally by the issues involved and becoming committed to dealing with them, and being at a point in life—retired, unemployed, in college—where one is available to participate in the movement. Third, incentives need to be offered so that the gains to members for their involvement outweigh the risks and costs. For example, the achievement of greater rights for blacks outweighed the risk of being beaten or murdered and the cost of lost time and income for participants in the civil rights movement. While material incentives are important, of far greater importance are the social incentives associated with joining with others as part of the movement, as well as the moral incentives of being involved in something one believes in strongly (Quadagno and Rohlinger 2009).

Goals, Strategy, and Tactics. Once formed, a social movement needs to have goals, a strategy, and a variety of tactics to succeed. Goals relate to what the movement seeks to do, such as cut taxes or make society more equal. Strategy involves the movement's long-term plan for achieving its goals. Once a strategy is in place, tactics become important. Tactics are more short-term in nature. They need to be quite fluid and able to adapt quickly in light of changes taking place in the immediate or larger environment. In the case of the civil rights movement, the strategy was to create situations that brought the plight of black Americans, especially those who lived in the South, to the attention of the media, the public, and political leaders. Tactics, in this case, involved engaging in *civil disobedience,* or nonviolent public acts that are against the law and aimed at changing it or government policies (Tescione 2013). For example, blacks attempted to order food at segregated lunch counters. The acts of civil disobedience produced reactions (e.g., white protests, police action) that attracted media and public attention and eventually public outrage. Of particular importance are the actions of countermovements and government officials. For example, the civil rights movement had to adapt to the hostile actions of both white supremacists and hostile local government officials.

Factors in Success. A variety of factors help to determine whether or not a social movement will succeed (Cross and Snow 2012; Rochon 1990). One is its sheer *size.* All social movements start small, but those that succeed are likely to have recruited large numbers of activists and supporters. Another is *novelty,* or the uniqueness of the movement and its goals. Uniqueness and size are important because they lead to a great deal of media attention, which, in turn, is likely to generate additional supporters and funds. The latter are two of the many *resources* social movements need to succeed (see above). *Violence,* as in the case of the Stonewall riots, can be useful in achieving results. However, it also can be counterproductive by turning off potential supporters and members. Perhaps more importantly, it can lead to violent reactions that can end in the suppression of the movement. *Militancy* can also be double-edged, since a highly militant social movement might be able to achieve its goals quickly, but militancy, like violence, can lead to counterreactions and suppression. *Nonviolence* has been a successful method for social movements because it avoids the powerful counterreactions engendered by violent and militant social movements. The nonviolent approach is traceable largely to Mahatma Gandhi and his use of such means as noncooperation with the British-controlled government to gain Indian independence in 1947.

In a widely criticized action, University of California, Davis, police pepper-sprayed students during a peaceful "Occupy" sit-in in 2011. Have you ever taken part in an act of civil disobedience?

Today, a large number of social movements, including the Tea Party and the women's, civil rights, and gay and lesbian movements, have adopted a nonviolent approach. Globally, many organizations associated with the environmental movement, as well as those associated with the World Social Forum (see below) and operating in opposition to at least some aspects of globalization, rely almost exclusively on nonviolent methods.

Although various aspects of social movements themselves strongly affect whether or not they will be successful, many other factors are involved in this. Of great importance is the ability of individuals, groups, or the state (especially the police and the military) to suppress a social movement (Earl 2007). Efforts at suppressing social movements can be covert, such as the FBI's wiretapping of the phones of members of dissident groups, especially suspected communist and civil rights groups in the United States in the mid-1950s through the early 1970s. They can also be overt, a major example being the violent suppression in 1989 of antigovernment protests in Tiananmen Square by the Chinese government and the military. Another example is the violence committed by local law enforcement officers and white supremacists against civil rights activists in the United States in the 1960s. Yet another example is the police raids of public bathhouses frequented by homosexuals in the 1960s (Clendinen and Nagourney 1999).

Impact of Social Movements

Whether or not they are successful, social movements often leave their mark, which is sometimes a quite powerful imprint. A government may be able to suppress a social movement, but it is likely that aspects of the government and the way it operates will be affected by the movement as well as the efforts to suppress it. For example, in the 1940s and 1950s, the U.S. government was able to suppress efforts to increase the influence of communism throughout the country. However, while it was successful in those efforts, it engaged in a variety of highly questionable actions. Major examples include the activities of the House Un-American Activities Committee (HUAC) and especially those of the infamous Senator Joseph McCarthy. Recall from Chapter 6 that McCarthy conducted hearings with the ostensible goal of rooting communists out of the government and elsewhere, most notably Hollywood and the U.S. Army. McCarthy and his associates often made wild public accusations without presenting any supporting evidence. Long-lasting changes were brought about in the government as a result of the public's revulsion over the reprehensible tactics used by McCarthy and his supporters. Since that time, government actions that even hint at the kind taken during the 1940s and 1950s are labeled "McCarthyism" and, as a result, are unlikely to succeed.

Social movements, especially those that achieve some success, often leave a strong legacy for, and have a powerful impact on, later movements. For example, the civil rights movement was an inspiration and a model for many later movements in the United States, such as the student, antiwar, environmental, gay and lesbian, and disability movements. Social movements outside the United States— for example, South Africa's antiapartheid movement, the Solidarity movement in Poland, and the democracy

An unknown man temporarily stopped a row of tanks near Tiananmen Square in Beijing during an iconic moment in China's ill-fated 1989 pro-democracy movement. *Time* magazine called the man one of the "100 most important people of the century," but his fate is unknown and few in China appear to be aware of the photo, which was suppressed there, or its significance.

movement in China—were also strongly affected by the civil rights movement.

While social movements are oriented toward changing society, they also have a strong impact on the individuals involved in a social movement, either members of the movement or those who oppose it. The greatest impact is usually on the large numbers of people actively involved in the movement (Roth 2007). Their attitudes, and perhaps the entire course of their lives, are often altered greatly by active involvement in social movements. Much the same is true of those who take an active role in opposing social movements. Senator McCarthy, for example, was embittered by his failures and died soon after he was discredited.

THE INTERNET, GLOBALIZATION, AND SOCIAL MOVEMENTS

Two of the most important recent developments as far as social movements are concerned relate to globalization (Agrikoliansky, 2013; Maiba 2005) and the Internet (Carty 2013), as well as other new media such as smartphones (Castells 2008).

The Internet has proven to be an important way of involving and organizing large numbers of people, perhaps millions of them, who are widely separated from one another, perhaps even in different parts of the world. In other words, people no longer need to be in close

physical proximity to be involved in social movements. People can also now communicate more easily through the use of mobile phones, even from the site of an event. This offers new possibilities for mobilizing those involved in a social movement. It is possible not only to communicate verbally with others in the movement, but also to snap pictures or shoot videos with one's smartphone and send them instantaneously via YouTube or Facebook to large numbers of interested parties. This allows them to see for themselves what is transpiring in the social movement. There are also now online activists (e-activists) who are creating electronic social movements (e-movements). At least some e-movements have the possibility of becoming social movements in the material world.

The Internet and other technologies enable social movements to cover wide geographic areas, and even to become global. Like much else in the world today, social movements are less constrained than ever before by national borders. It seems likely that the future will bring with it an increasing number of global social movements. We will discuss the Internet and globalization further later in this chapter.

COLLECTIVE ACTION

Collective action is generated, or engaged in, by a group of people. It serves to encourage or retard social change (Oliver 2013: 210). A social movement is one kind of collective action; others include crowds, riots, and disasters. Like all other forms of collective action, social movements usually occur outside of established institutional channels. However, social movements are different from all other forms of collective action in at least two ways. First, most forms of collective action are short-lived compared to social movements. Thus, a crowd, for example, can come together and disperse within hours, but a social movement can be sustained for years or decades. Second, a social movement is intentional; other forms of collective action are not. For example, a community that comes together immediately after a disaster such as an earthquake or

---

collective action Action generated, or engaged in, by a group of people.

a flood does not do so intentionally. It has been brought together and springs into action because of some unanticipated external event. After the 2011 earthquake and tsunami in northern Japan, newspapers reported that a strong sense of community had emerged and helped people survive the aftermath (Fackler 2011).

While social movements have been theorized separately and somewhat differently (resource mobilization theory), the dominant approach to thinking about other forms of collective action is **emergent norm theory** (Arthur and Lemonik 2013; Turner and Killian 1987). This theory is based on the idea that new norms emerge in light of some precipitating event. They guide the often-nontraditional actions that characterize collective behavior. Implicit in this theory is the idea that in collective behavior, conventional norms cease to be as effective or as important, at least to some degree. Contrary to popular opinion, however, collective behavior is not irrational, random, or out of control. It is rational and guided by the new norms that develop in the situation.

This flash mob in Kiev, Russia, consisted of about 100 young people throwing flour at each other. What kind of flash mob would you participate in if the opportunity arose?

CROWDS

The clearest application of emergent norm theory to collective action involves the case of a **crowd**, a temporary gathering of a relatively large number of people in a common geographic location and at a given time (McPhail 2007; Snow and Owens 2013). We are all familiar with all sorts of crowds, such as those that gather at the site of a celebration or a catastrophe, but a relatively new type is the flash crowd (or flash mob). Flash crowds

have become easier to generate as a result of the Internet and e-mails and social networking sites. A flash crowd might gather, for example, to engage in a pillow fight. In fact, in 2008, a kind of a global pillow fight took place, involving participants in two-dozen cities around the world. In recent years, largely teenage flash crowds have come together in Philadelphia; they have been disorderly, gotten into fights, attacked bystanders, and been cracked

> **emergent norm theory** A theory arguing that, in light of some precipitating event, new norms emerge that guide the often-nontraditional actions that characterize collective behavior.
>
> **crowd** A temporary gathering of a relatively large number of people in a common geographic location and at a given time.

Collective Behavior

RIOTS

A **riot** is temporary unruly collective action that causes damage to persons or property (Myers 2007, 2013). There have been a number of major riots in the last half century in the United States, including race riots in the 1960s in Watts (Los Angeles), Detroit, and Washington, DC. One notable race riot occurred in Los Angeles in 1992 following the beating of Rodney King by a number of police officers. Riots, of course, have happened elsewhere in the world; they are a global phenomenon. For example, significant rioting and extensive looting and arson took place in London and in other cities in England in August 2011. Five people died in the riots (see the next "Globalization" box).

Looting and rioting broke out in Los Angeles following a 1992 incident in which a black man named Rodney King was videotaped being beaten by police. What turns a gathering into a riot?

Negative Views of Riots

We are likely to have negative views of riots and rioters. However, riots may not be irrational outbursts. Rather, they may be motivated by frustrations over various kinds of abuses and the inability to do much about them under normal circumstances (Auyero and Moran 2007). It is hard to generalize about rioters, but there is little support in the research for the idea that rioters are more likely to be criminals, unemployed, or uneducated. A few things seem clear about those who participate in riots. They are more likely to be men, to be young, to have been physically close to where the riots occur, and to feel that their actions can make a difference. The literature on police involvement is also ambiguous, with police being seen as having the ability both to quell riots and to incite them further with their repressive actions.

It is also worth noting that the mass media can contribute to rioting through the ways in which they treat riots. For one thing, live coverage of riots can inflame them by drawing others into them. Live, immediate media reports are also more likely to be inaccurate and to involve inflammatory reporting. For another thing, media reports of riots can suggest that this is a form of action to be emulated at other places and times. Social media can also quickly draw large numbers of people to a riot site.

Positive Effects of Riots

Riots can have positive effects. The Rodney King riots of 1992 undoubtedly led to changes and improvements in the way

down upon in unnecessarily aggressive ways by the police (Massarro and Mullaney 2011).

One concern in the literature on crowds is the degree to which individuals behave differently in crowds than they do in other social contexts. Emergent norm theory suggests that they do behave differently, but that is because they are conforming to a different set of norms than exist elsewhere in the social world. That is more comforting than the alternative view, which sees people in crowds as losing control of their cognitive processes, complying blindly with the suggestions of crowd leaders, and copying mindlessly what is done by those around them in the crowd. A large body of research has failed to find any support for the latter view (Postmes and Spears 1998).

However, it is possible that flash crowds brought together by messages on Twitter do operate differently and may be more in line with the alternative, discomforting view of crowds. It might be that because they have been brought together so impersonally, and might well not know one another when they do come together, they do not have time to develop norms.

ASK YOURSELF

Do you behave differently when in a crowd than you do when alone? How, and why? Have you ever been in a flash mob? What was the experience like?

> **riot** Temporary unruly collective behavior that causes damage to persons or property.

Riots in Paris, France

Riots broke out in the Paris suburbs of Argenteuil in 2005 and in Villiers-le-Bel in late 2007. They occurred in areas dominated by the working and lower classes and were associated with large immigrant groups, especially Arabs and Africans (Sciolino 2007). The riots revealed that racism, which had long been most associated with the United States, was also a French, if not a global, problem. In fact, racism in France is much more blatant now than it is in the United States. Racism in France resembles the racism that existed in the United States decades ago. Among other things, at the behest of landlords, French real estate agents seek out white-only tenants, *pâtisseries* sell chocolate-covered cakes called *tête de nègre* (head of Negroes), TV programs are dominated by white actors and actresses, and women from Africa and Asia are seen in the wealthy areas of town as "nannies" accompanying well-dressed children to and from school. Racial and ethnic minorities in France primarily work in poorly paid manual jobs that are likely to involve cleaning, pushing, serving, digging, or carrying. Higher-level, higher-paid positions in virtually every sector of the economy are out of the reach of most

minorities, even those with adequate education and training. While the unemployment rate for French university graduates is 5 percent, it is more than 25 percent for university graduates from North African communities. Minorities are almost totally absent among the elites in almost every walk of life in France. The situation facing minorities in France shows no signs of improving. The French electorate has (so far) not elected far-right politicians to its top positions. However, many of France's politicians, as well as its public philosophers, have moved in the direction of right-wing ideas that stand in opposition to social welfare and public assistance (Murray 2006).

Racial and ethnic minorities in France experience a variety of other problems. They generally are housed in suburban, government-run "projects," many built in the 1960s. These are not American-style suburbs with well-manicured lawns, but dull expanses of concrete and asphalt. The suburbs are generally isolated from the city center, and it takes a great deal of time and several changes of buses and/or trains to get there.

Jobs are few in the suburbs, especially since many factories have been shuttered

as a result of globalization. Unemployment in the suburbs can be as high as 40 percent. The result is poverty and hopelessness, especially among the young who represented the vast majority of the rioters in the Paris suburbs. There is great tension with the police who are apt to harass minority group members, address them rudely, call them names, treat them brutally, and on occasion kill them.

These riots can be seen as being linked to globalization, especially large-scale migration, at least some of it undocumented. Thus, the rioting by the minorities outside Paris can be seen as resistance both to the way they are treated in France and more generally to the negative effects and consequences of globalization. This unplanned collective action, therefore, is underpinned by dramatic structural inequality as a result of both national and global processes.

Think About It

Were the Paris riots inevitable? Why or why not? What might the French learn from the U.S. experience with racism? Might cultural differences between France and the United States prove a barrier to such learning? Why or why not?

---

the police deal with suspects and the general public, although similar incidents continue to be reported. More generally, riots have at times led to various programs designed to deal with the conditions that were seen to be at their source, such as poverty and unemployment. However, the lasting power of these changes is unclear, and in any case, people are injured and die, and communities are ruined in riots. In some cases, it takes decades for riot sites to recover (Cannon 1997; Schoch and Lin 2007; Spencer 2004).

> **disasters** Events that suddenly, unexpectedly, and severely disrupt and harm the environment, the social structure, people, and their property.

DISASTERS

Disasters are events that suddenly, unexpectedly, and severely disrupt and harm the environment, the social structure, people, and their property (Silver 2007). They are distinguished from accidents (e.g., automobile and airplane crashes) by their far greater impact. Many U.S. disasters cause billions of dollars' worth of damage (see Figure 15.1). One disaster much in the news in 2010 was the earthquake in Haiti that decimated a significant portion of that Caribbean nation, which shares an island (Hispaniola) with the Dominican Republic. No one knows the exact numbers, but it is estimated that more than 200,000 people were killed and another 300,000 were injured. Innumerable poorly constructed homes, schools,

FIGURE 15.1 • Billion-Dollar Weather and Climate Disasters in the United States, 1980–2011

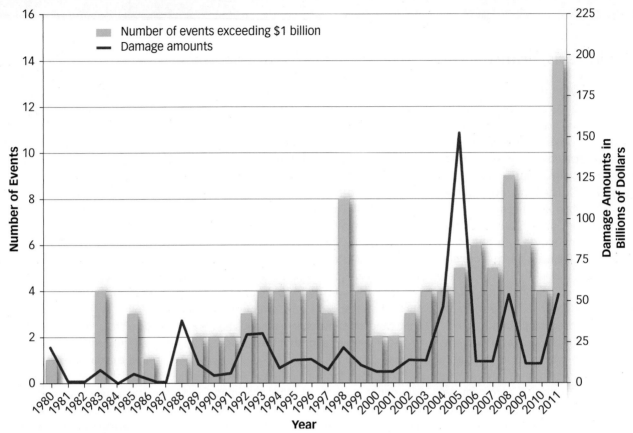

SOURCE: Billion Dollar Weather and Climate Disasters in the United States, 1980–2011, National Climatic Data Center.

and other buildings were destroyed. The government virtually ceased functioning as its offices collapsed, literally and figuratively, and many officials were killed or injured (Bhatty 2010). By the end of 2012, little progress had been made in rebuilding homes and the infrastructure in Haiti (Sontag 2012). While it is a stark example, the earthquake in Haiti represents just one of many natural disasters that occurred in 2010. As is evident in Figure 15.2, such disasters occur all around the world every year. At the time of this writing, perhaps the largest typhoon in history struck the Philippines on November 8, 2013, causing massive destruction. Early estimates are that over 5,000 people were killed by the storm.

Human Involvement in Disasters

Disasters such as earthquakes are natural phenomena, but humans often play a role in bringing them about and in exacerbating their consequences. People frequently build in areas—for example, on geological fault lines or on floodplains—where there should be no significant building. Furthermore, what they build is often quite flimsy and likely to be destroyed in a natural disaster. Building stronger structures can be very costly, and impoverished

nations such as Haiti simply cannot afford it ("Why the Palace Fell" 2010).

There are, of course, disasters that are the result of human error or corruption. Recall that on April 20, 2010, a huge explosion on a BP/Deepwater Horizon oil rig in the Gulf of Mexico killed 11 workers and unleashed a gusher of oil ("Louisiana Oil Rig Explosion" 2010). There had been warnings for decades about the dangers associated with deep-sea drilling and oil wells. However, the drilling was pushed forward by the desire for ever escalating profits by corporations like BP and the voracious need for oil in the United States and other developed nations. Once the oil gusher occurred, it became clear that no one quite knew how to go about stopping it. The well was finally capped on July 15. However, by that time about 5 million barrels of oil had flowed into the surrounding waters ("Gulf Oil Spill" 2010). The oil caused great damage to the Gulf's marine life, its beaches, and the businesses that depend on tourists drawn to the area.

Recall from Chapter 5 that the space shuttle *Challenger* disintegrated a little over a minute into its flight, killing all seven crew members (Vaughan 1996). To get needed funds

FIGURE 15.2 • Natural Catastrophes Worldwide, 2012

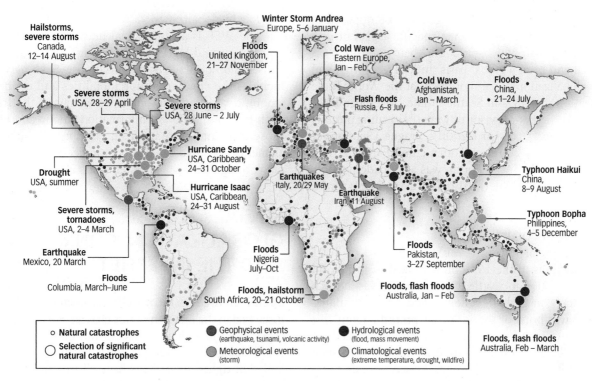

SOURCE: Natural Catastrophes, 2012 World Map. © 2013 Münchener Rückversicherungs-Gesellschaft, Geo Risks Research, NatCatSERVICE.

and to launch space shuttles in a timely manner, NASA had ignored warnings, taken risks, and tolerated mistakes and deception. While Vaughan (1996) saw this disaster as a unique occurrence, Charles Perrow (1999) sees such accidents as "normal." That is, highly complex systems such as those associated with NASA and the space shuttle will inevitably have such disasters, although they happen only rarely.

Human-made disasters also can be political in nature, and they are associated with revolutions, riots, and acts of terrorism. For example, in mid-2010, the center of Bangkok, Thailand, was ravaged by riots aimed at overthrowing the government. And then, of course, there was the 9/11 disaster caused by hijackers crashing planes into the World Trade Center towers and the Pentagon, as well as downing one plane before it reached its target. These terrorist attacks resulted in the death of nearly 3,000 people.

The Effects of Disasters

Disasters have enormous negative long-term consequences for the people and areas involved. Individuals and collectivities are traumatized for long periods after a disaster (Erikson 1978). People's lives are disrupted for years, if not decades, as are the social networks in which they are enmeshed. Disasters also worsen existing inequalities. For

example, females in Haiti have suffered disproportionately from the effects of the 2010 hurricane. Furthermore, they have been less likely than males to receive humanitarian aid in the aftermath of the hurricane. Haitian women are more likely to live in tents that, among other things, provide them little protection and security. They are especially vulnerable to "unwanted sexual advances and assault" (Jean-Charles 2010).

However, some people and groups are in a position to handle disasters better than others. Disaster can also be a time when people and communities come together in unprecedented ways to deal with the disaster and its aftereffects. The heroism of many of those involved in helping after the 9/11 disaster—firefighters, police officers, and citizens—is one example of this (Fritsch 2001; Rozdeba 2011; Saxon 2003). Within Haiti, a number of aid agencies are working to continue to provide aid to women and girls such as the UN Population Fund, the World Food Programme, and World Vision. In addition, "cash for work" programs, instituted by the Haitian Ministry of Women's Affairs, have helped 100,000 women living in the camps to survive (Jean-Charles 2010). Moreover, in response to the increased vulnerability of women and girls, the Femmes Citoyennes Haiti Solidaire, or Women Citizens Haiti United, has formed an alliance of activists to continue addressing gender inequality and injustices within Haiti.

GLOBALIZATION AND CYBER-ACTIVISM

The existence of the Internet has given those opposed to globalization in general, or some specific aspect of it, a powerful tool with which to mount their opposition on a regional and even a global basis. Indeed, the origins of the antiglobalization social movement at the World Trade Organization meetings in Seattle in late November 1999 were based on cyber-activism, as were the ensuing protests in Washington, DC (April 2000), Prague (September 2000), Genoa (July 2001), and other cities (Pleyers 2010). Further, the World Social Forum was also made possible by such activism (Kohler 2012; Sen et al. 2004; Smith et al. 2011).

World Social Forum

The World Social Forum (WSF) was formed in 2001 and had its roots in the 1999 protests against the World Trade Organization in Seattle. A key concern was the lack of democracy in global economic and political affairs. The WSF was born of the idea that protests about this problem were insufficient. That is, there was a need for more positive and concrete proposals to deal with such issues, as well as a forum in which these proposals could be generated. The WSF's slogan has been "Another World Is Possible" (Teivainen 2007). That is, there must be, and there is, an alternative to the free-market capitalism that has dominated the world economically and politically (Smith 2008). Although the slogan is powerful and has facilitated the coordination of large and diverse groups, the WSF has not yet produced concrete actions and policies to make "another world" a reality.

ASK YOURSELF

What would it take to make an alternative to free-market capitalism a reality? What would such a system be like? Would it be viable for the long term? Why or why not?

The initial, 2001 meeting of the WSF in Porto Alegre, Brazil (Byrd 2005), drew about 5,000 participants, and the number of participants grew to 100,000 at the meetings in 2004 in Mumbai, India, and in 2005 in Porto Alegre. In 2006, the meeting was decentralized and held on three continents, and many local, national, and regional meetings have developed. In 2011, a centralized meeting in Dakar, Senegal, drew 75,000 participants.

The WSF is, by design, not a social movement but merely an arena in which like-minded people can exchange ideas on specific social movements and global issues. The very diversity of the movements and people involved in the WSF makes the development of concrete political proposals, not to mention actions, difficult. The WSF continues to struggle with this issue and its identity and role in globalization.

The WSF is a huge social network, and it is based on the "cultural logic of networking" (see Chapter 5 for a discussion of network organizations). Such networking includes the creation of horizontal ties and connections among diverse and autonomous elements, the free and open communication of information among and between those elements, decentralized coordination among the elements that involves democratic decision making, and networking that is self-directed (Juris 2005).

SOCIAL CHANGE: GLOBALIZATION, CONSUMPTION, AND THE INTERNET

Social change is intimately connected to the topics discussed in the first part of this chapter. Social movements, especially those that are successful, often lead to major social changes. For example, the women's, gay and lesbian, and civil rights movements have all led, and continue to lead, to such social changes. Collective action is less likely to lead to social change, but there have certainly been many examples of crowd behavior, riots, and disasters that have led to change. For example, the Los Angeles race riots of 1992 led to changes not only in police behavior but also in efforts to deal with the underlying causes of the riots.

Although social change occurs throughout the social world, it is particularly characteristic of the three areas that are the signature concerns of this book—globalization, consumption, and the Internet. Globalization is, of course, a social process of relatively recent origin; it is changing the world in which we live and likely to lead to a variety of even more dramatic changes in the future. For example, the changing nature of the global economy, especially the shift of its center away from the United States and in the direction of China and Asia more generally, means that the job prospects of Americans are changing and apt to change even more in the future. Some economic prospects have declined, especially those that relate to the production of goods and the jobs associated with it. However, others have improved. New jobs have arisen—especially those that involve computers

> **social change** Variations over time in every aspect of the social world ranging from changes affecting individuals to transformations having an impact on the globe as a whole.

and the Internet. Clearly, the Internet is important not only in this sense but also because it is an arena in which great and extremely rapid change has taken place in recent years. It is an arena that will certainly continue to change and to affect our lives in innumerable ways. The changes discussed here—globalization, the economy, and the Internet—are related to the changing nature of our other core concern—consumption.

Consumption has itself become increasingly global as, for example, more of the things we buy come from outside the United States. The U.S. economy has shifted away from one dominated by production to one dominated by consumption. It is clear that more consumption is taking place through the Internet, and that trend can only accelerate in the future.

GLOBALIZATION AS THE ULTIMATE SOCIAL CHANGE

Prior to the current epoch of globalization, one of the things that characterized people, things, information, places, and much else was their greater solidity. That is, all of them tended to (figuratively) harden over time and therefore, among other things, to remain largely in place. As a result, people did not venture very far from where they were born and raised. Their social relationships were limited to those who were nearby. Much the same could be said of most objects (tools, food), which tended to be used where they were produced. The solidity of most material manifestations of information (stone tablets, books) also made them at least somewhat difficult to move very far. Furthermore, since people didn't move very far, neither did information. Places, too, not only were quite solid and immovable but tended to be surrounded by solid barriers (mountains, oceans, walls, borders) that made it difficult for people and things to exit or to enter.

Global "Liquids"

At an increasing rate over the last few centuries, and especially in the last several decades, that which once seemed so solid has tended to "melt." Instead of thinking of people, objects, information, and places as being like solid blocks of ice, we need to see them as tending to melt and as becoming increasingly liquid (Beilharz 2012). Needless to say, it is far more difficult to move blocks of ice than it is to move the water that is produced when those blocks melt. Of course, to extend the metaphor, there continue to exist blocks of ice, even glaciers, in the contemporary world that have not melted, at least not completely. Solid material realities, such as people, cargo, and newspapers, continue to exist, but because of a wide range of technological developments in transportation, communication, and the Internet, they can move across the globe far more readily.

Thus, following the work of Zygmunt Bauman (2000, 2003, 2005, 2006), the perspective on globalization presented here involves increasing liquidity (Lakoff 2008; Ritzer 2010c). However, there is a constant interplay between liquidity and solidity, with increases in that which is liquid (e.g., terrorist attacks launched against Israel from the West Bank) leading to counterreactions and the erection of new solid forms (a fence between Israel and the West Bank). However, at the moment and for the foreseeable future, the momentum lies with increasing and proliferating global liquidity.

Global "Flows"

Closely related to the idea of liquidity, and integral to it, is another key concept in thinking about globalization, the idea of "flows" (Appadurai 1996; Inda 2012). After all, liquids flow easily, far more easily, than solids. Because so much of the world has "melted," or is in the process of "melting," globalization is increasingly characterized by great flows of increasingly liquid phenomena of all types, including people, objects, information, decisions, places, and so on. In many cases, the flows have become raging floods that are increasingly less likely to be impeded by place-based barriers of any kind, including the oceans, the mountains, and especially the borders of nation-states. This was demonstrated once again in late 2008 in the spread of the American credit and financial crisis to Europe and elsewhere: "In a global financial system, national borders are porous" (Landler 2008a: C1).

Globalization Backlash

ACTIVE SOCIOLOGY

Can Petitions Effect Change?

The wave of social and political uprisings we now call the Arab Spring (2011) showcased the influence of social media on collective action and social movements. Information that used to take hours or even days to spread is now shared in real time on Facebook and Twitter, often as minute-by-minute updates of unfolding events. Change.org is a site that promotes active citizenship by allowing you, the user, to create positions and gain public support for your cause. Visit this site (www.change.org) and view some current petitions. What are the top causes right now?

Choose a petition you think is important. Sign it and share with your friends via Facebook or Twitter. Now record your observations by answering these questions and sharing your responses with the class.

1. Track the petition and observe its outcome, or its progress over the next several days. What happened?

2. How does this site allow for individual participation in social change?

3. What are the pros and cons of the site's ease of use? List as many as you can think of.

4. After you sign and track a petition, will you continue following that cause or take any further action related to it? Why or why not?

5. Do you think other signers of petitions on the site often take additional actions to further the cause they support? Why or why not?

Think about a current issue (local, national, or global) that you think calls for social change. Start a petition on this site and see where it goes.

Looking at a very different kind of flow, as we saw in Chapter 14, many people in many parts of the world believe that they are being swamped by migrants, especially poor undocumented migrants (Moses 2006). Whether or not these are actually floods, they have come to be seen as such by many people, often aided by politicians and media personalities who have established their reputations by portraying migrants in that way. Places, too, can be said to be flowing around the world, for example, as immigrants re-create the places from which they come in new locales (Logan, Alba, and Zhang 2002). Ideas, images, and information, both legal (blogs) and illegal (child pornography), flow everywhere undoubtedly because of their immateriality. They do so through interpersonal contact and the media, especially now via the Internet. Much of what would have been considered the height of global liquidity only a few years ago now seems increasingly sludge-like. This is especially the case when we focus on the impact of the computer and the Internet on the global flow of all sorts of things. For example, instead of scouring an import VHS catalog and waiting weeks for an anime movie to ship from Japan, a person can simply open the Netflix app on her Xbox 360 and stream any number of anime movies instantly.

ASK YOURSELF

What aspects of your life can you imagine as "liquids"? Which seem like "flows"? What do you imagine these elements looked like 20 years ago, before the advent of globalization?

GLOBALIZATION AND THE INTERNET

Since its birth in the 1990s, the Internet has profoundly affected almost every aspect of life, especially in the developed world. The Internet has expedited the globalization of many different things and is, itself, a profound form and aspect of globalization (Powell 2012). The Internet is global in several senses, but the most important is that while its users are not equally divided between North and South, rich and poor, and so on, they *do* exist virtually everywhere in the world (Drori 2006, 2012). It is also global in the sense that it was produced and is maintained by a number of global and transnational corporations and organizations, including multinational corporations (such as Intel), intergovernmental organizations, and international nongovernmental organizations. For instance, the World Intellectual Property Organization regulates intellectual property rights; the Internet Corporation for Assigned Names and Numbers coordinates domain names; and the UN Educational, Scientific, and Cultural Organization promotes computer and Internet use in schools throughout the world.

Computer Viruses

The idea of a computer virus made its first appearance in science fiction in the late 1960s and early 1970s. Over a decade later, a graduate student wrote the first program that was able to replicate and propagate itself. His professor, seeing its similarity to a biological phenomenon, suggested it be called a "computer virus." The first global computer virus was likely created in Pakistan in 1986. Since then, of course, many different viruses—some benign, some malicious ("malware")—have been created, circled the globe, and in some cases caused great damage to computer systems. For example, some of these viruses (Win32/Fareit, Mariposa) "infect" personal computers and access users' information, such as credit card numbers, which the cyberthief then uses to purchase all sorts of goods and services illegally. At the same time, global organizations, including law enforcement agencies, have emerged to try to warn people about new viruses and malware—the so-called *trojans* and *worms*—and to develop countermeasures to protect against them (Chanda 2007). To the degree that they are successful, the latter are barriers to the largely free flow of computer viruses around the globe.

It is clear that no change has done more to further the process of globalization than the Internet (Subramanian 2012). It occupies pride of place in many analyses of globalization. Perhaps the most famous is Thomas Friedman's (2005) analysis of globalization as involving a "flat world" (see the "Public Sociology" box in Chapter 5); the major example of such a world is the Internet. The Internet is flat in the sense that virtually anyone anywhere can, at least theoretically, become

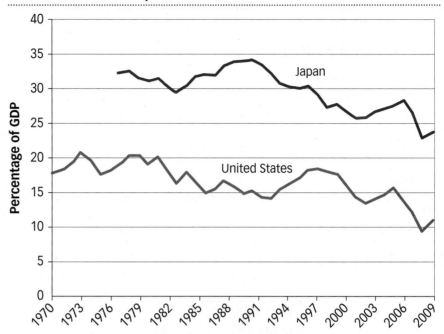

FIGURE 15.3 • Gross Savings as Percentage of GDP in the United States and Japan, 1970–2009

SOURCE: Adapted from The World Bank, Data: Gross Savings (% of GDP).

involved in it. However, it is important to remember that many poor and undeveloped communities still lack Internet access.

CONSUMPTION AND GLOBALIZATION

The emphasis in the global economy is to greatly increase flows of everything related to consumption and to greatly decrease any barriers to those flows. Especially important is expediting global flows of consumer goods and services of all types and of the financial processes and instruments that facilitate those flows. Thus, for example, the relatively small number of credit card brands with origins in the United States, especially Visa and MasterCard, are increasingly accepted and used throughout the world (Ritzer 1995). This serves to expedite not only global

CHECKPOINT 15.3	SOCIAL CHANGE
Globalization	The ultimate social change.
The Internet	A profound form and aspect of globalization that has affected almost every aspect of life.
Consumption	Closely associated with U.S. culture and now exported around the world.

Naomi Klein: *No Logo*

In *No Logo*, Naomi Klein ([2000] 2010) offers an unrelenting critique of the role of branding in the world of consumption. Among Klein's favorite targets are Nike, McDonald's, Microsoft, and Tommy Hilfiger, as well as celebrity brands such as Michael Jordan. In the context of an American society that has shifted from the dominance of production to the preeminence of consumption, corporations have discovered that the key to success is no longer what they manufacture but the creation and dissemination of a brand. While it concentrates on its brand, the modern corporation often outsources production to subcontractors in less developed parts of the world. Those who do the work in such places are paid a small percentage of what their counterparts in more developed nations would be paid. Klein is especially critical of the work done in free-enterprise zones in less developed countries where corporations and subcontractors are able to do as they wish, free of local government control. In those settings, wages are particularly low and working conditions especially harsh.

Given these realities in less developed countries, it is clearly in the interest of corporations to produce little or nothing in high-wage, developed countries. With production costs minuscule in less developed countries, these corporations can spend lavishly on their brands and the associated logos such as Nike's swoosh and the McDonald's Golden Arches. Low production costs also allow for great profits and make it possible for corporate leaders to be paid unconscionable sums of money. Especially egregious is the contrast between the wealth of Phil Knight, founder and chairman of Nike, and the economic situation experienced by those who work in development zone factories to produce Nike products, including some trafficked workers who function as modern-day slaves and are forced to work in Nike factories against their will. Similarly egregious is the sums of money paid to celebrities like Michael Jordan to advertise products and, in the process, to become brands themselves. Once someone like Jordan achieves such a status, a synergy develops between the person and the corporation so that viewing one immediately brings to mind the other. Michael Jordan and Nike have become brands that have mutually supported and literally enriched one another.

Think About It

Would the conditions Naomi Klein criticizes be possible without the implied consent of consumers in western countries? Do you look for logos when you shop? Why or why not?

---

consumption but also the flow of global consumers, including tourists.

Local and Regional Differences

Local areas have certainly not always, or perhaps ever, been overwhelmed by American imports but have integrated them into the local cultural and economic realities. Furthermore, other nations and regions have been significant exporters of important aspects of consumer society, such as Mercedes-Benz and BMW automobiles from Germany. Finally, much of consumption remains largely, if not totally, local in character. One example is the growing consumption of a mild stimulant, khat, or *qat,* in Kenya, where it is defined in a highly positive way locally. In addition, there is active resistance to external definitions of it, especially the U.S. definition of khat as a dangerous drug (Anderson and Carrier 2006).

Consumption also plays itself out differently in different parts of the world. For example, both the United States and Japan can be seen as consumer societies, but Japanese consumers differ from their U.S. counterparts in many ways. For example, the Japanese never fully embraced the idea of a consumer society. More specifically, unlike Americans, the Japanese continue to manage to save a significant amount of money (see Figure 15.3) (Garon 2006).

While many consumer objects and services remain highly local (e.g., the khat mentioned above, the services of street-based letter writers for illiterate Indians), an increasing number have been globalized. On the one hand, there are, for example, such global objects as automobiles from the United States, Germany, and Japan. On the other hand, there are such global services as those offered by accounting firms like KPMG International, as well as package delivery services like DHL.

Global Brands

A **brand** is a symbol that serves to identify and differentiate one product or service from the others. A brand can be contrasted with, and seeks to contrast itself to, generic

> **brand** A symbol that serves to identify and differentiate one product or service from the others.

commodities such as flour or soap (Arviddson 2012; Holt 2004; Muniz 2007). The process of branding a product or service is undertaken because, if successful, not only is a brand distinguished from the basic commodity, but more of it can be sold and at a higher price. We are all familiar with the most successful brands in the world (Apple, Coca-Cola, McDonald's, Wal-Mart, Mercedes, etc.), and much consumption is oriented to the purchase of brand-name products and services. Furthermore, even people come to be brand names (Michael Jordan, Angelina Jolie) and as such are "consumed" globally to a large degree. As brands themselves, they come to be closely associated with various brand-name products, with the best-known example being the association of Michael Jordan with Nike and Hanes (Andrews and Mower 2012).

Nike is one of those brands that has made itself so important that it can be said to have created a Nike culture. To some degree, we can be said to live in such a culture (Goldman and Papson 1998; Hollister 2008); however, it is but a part of the larger *brand culture* in which we live. That is, brands are a key part of the larger culture, they infuse it with meaning, and contemporary society as a whole is profoundly affected by brands (Schroeder 2007).

This young Maasai boy carries refreshments to a coming-of-age ceremony in Kenya. Global brands like Coca-Cola, Nike, and Toyota are known throughout the world. Is their economic power a positive or a negative force overall?

Brands are of great importance not only within the United States and many other nations, but also globally. Indeed, much money and effort is invested in creating brand names that are recognized and trusted throughout the world. Klein ([2000] 2010) details the importance of brands in the contemporary world and the degree to which they are both globalized—corporate logos are virtually an international language—and having a global impact.

SUMMARY

Social change creates variations over time in every aspect of the social world. Social movements are sustained and intentional collective efforts, usually operating outside established institutional channels, either to bring about social change or to retard it. Prominent social movements include the Tea Party, the women's movement, the civil rights movement, and the gay and lesbian movement.

The emergence of a social movement requires a set of grievances, efforts at mobilization, opportunities within the political system, the proximity of people, the availability of free space to meet, and the availability of resources. Factors that affect the success of a social movement include its size and uniqueness as well as other groups' ability to suppress the movement. When successful, social movements can leave a lasting legacy.

A social movement is one type of collective behavior. Collective behavior is action generated, or engaged in, by a group of people. Emergent norm theory, based on the idea that new norms emerge in light of some precipitating event and guide the often-nontraditional actions that characterize behavior, is the dominant theoretical approach to examining types of collective behavior. Other types of collective behavior include crowds and riots and responses to disasters.

Social change is particularly characteristic of globalization, consumption, and the Internet. Globalization is arguably the most important change in human history and characterized by great flows of liquid phenomena across the globe. The Internet is both a form and an aspect of globalization and has expedited globalization. The global economy focuses on increasing the flows of everything related to consumption and reducing the barriers to these flows.

KEY TERMS

REVIEW QUESTIONS

1. What about the Tea Party makes it a social movement? What were the conditions that brought about the emergence of the Tea Party movement?

2. What have been the three different waves of the women's movement? How did the goals and strategies of the women's movement change during each of these three waves?

3. How have new communication technologies like the Internet and social networking sites (Facebook and Twitter) aided global social movements? What types of resources move more easily because of these new technologies?

4. According to resource mobilization theory, what do groups of people need to mobilize effectively? How can we apply this theory to the discussion of the civil rights movement in this chapter?

5. What mechanisms do social movements use to ensure member participation? How can you apply these mechanisms to the gay and lesbian movement discussed in this chapter?

6. What factors are used to determine whether a social movement is successful? How has the Tea Party movement been successful to date? Has there been any resistance to the movement? How might this affect the movement's future success?

7. According to emergent norm theory, why are individuals likely to behave differently when they are in crowds? How can we explain some deviant behavior in bars (e.g., fighting, public displays of affection) using emergent norm theory?

8. The 2011 earthquake and tsunami in Japan and the 2013 typhoon in the Philippines are examples of disasters. In what ways did humans exacerbate the consequences of these natural disasters? What sorts of negative long-term consequences can be expected from disasters like these?

9. In what ways is globalization the "ultimate social change"? How has the world become more liquid because of globalization? What role have new communication technologies played in making the world more liquid?

10. Why is branding an important process to transnational corporations? In what ways is branding reflective of the process of Americanization?

APPLYING THE SOCIOLOGICAL IMAGINATION

The last few years have been very important for social movements around the world. Using what you have learned about social movements in this chapter, do some research on one of the social movements in the Arab world. What are some of the reasons that the social movement emerged? What resources was the social movement able to mobilize? What mechanisms did the social movement use to encourage member participation? How did the processes of globalization affect the movement? How was the movement been affected by new communication technologies like the Internet and social networking sites? As it stands now, was the social movement successful? Is it likely to be successful in the long run?

STUDENT STUDY SITE

⑤SAGE edge™

Sharpen your skills with SAGE edge at **edge.sagepub.com/ritzeressentials**

SAGE edge for students provides a personalized approach to help you accomplish your coursework goals in an easy-to-use learning environment.

GLOSSARY

Achieved status: A position acquired by people on the basis of what they accomplish or the nature of their capacities.

Achievement: The accomplishments, or the merit, of individuals.

Agency: Individual social power and capacity for creativity; the potential to disrupt or destroy the structures in which one finds oneself.

Agents of socialization: Those who do the socializing.

Alienation: In a capitalist system, being unconnected to one's work, products, fellow workers, and human nature.

Americanization: The importation by other countries of products, images, technologies, practices, norms, values, and behaviors that are closely associated with the United States.

Anomie: The feeling of not knowing what is expected of one in society or of being adrift in society without any clear, secure moorings.

Anti-Americanism: An aversion to America in general, as well as to the influence of its culture abroad.

Anticipatory socialization: The teaching (and learning) of what will be expected of one in the future.

Ascribed status: A position in which individuals are placed, or to which they move, that has nothing to do with what they have done or their capacities or accomplishments.

Ascription: Being born with or inheriting certain characteristics (wealth, high status, etc.).

Asexuality: A lack of sexual desire.

Assimilation: The integration of minorities into the dominant culture.

Asylum seekers: People who flee their home country, usually in an effort to escape political oppression or religious persecution.

Authority: A particular type of domination: legitimate domination.

Back stage: The part of the social world where people feel free to express themselves in ways that are suppressed in the front stage.

Beliefs: Ideas that explain the world and identify what should be sacred or held in awe, that is, a religion's ultimate concerns.

Birthrate: The number of births per 1,000 people per year.

Bisexuality: A desire to have sexual relations with individuals of both the opposite sex and the same sex.

Bounded rationality: Rationality limited by, among other things, instabilities and conflicts within most, if not all, organizations, as well as by the limited human capacity to think and act in a rational manner.

Brand: A symbol that serves to identify and differentiate one product or service from the others.

Bureaucracy: A highly rational organization characterized by efficiency.

Bureaucratic personality: A type of bureaucrat who slavishly follows the rules of the organization to such an extent that the ability to achieve organizational goals is subverted.

Butterfly effect: The far-ranging or even global impact of a small change in a specific location, over both time and distance.

Capitalism: In Marx's view, an economic system based on one group of people—the capitalists (owners)—owning what is needed for production and a second group—the proletariat (workers)—owning little but their capacity for work.

Capitalists: Those who own what is needed for production—factories, machines, tools—in a capitalist system.

Caste: The most rigid and most closed system of stratification, usually associated with India.

Cathedrals of consumption: Large and lavish consumption sites, created mostly in the United States in the last half of the twentieth century and into the early twenty-first century.

Cenogamy: Group marriage.

Charismatic authority: Authority based on the devotion of the followers to what they define as the exceptional characteristics, such as heroism, of the leaders.

Church: A large group of religiously oriented people that one is usually born into rather than joins consciously and voluntarily.

Cities: Large, permanent, and spatially concentrated human settlements.

Citizens: The people represented by a given state, most often born within its territories.

Citizenship: The idea that people of a given state can vote for their representatives within the state, but also that they have access to rights and responsibilities as citizens.

Civil religion: The beliefs, practices, and symbols that a nation holds sacred.

Cohabitation: A couple sharing a home and a bed without being legally married.

Collective action: Action generated, or engaged in, by a group of people to encourage or retard social change.

Collective conscience: The set of beliefs shared by people throughout society.

Companionate love: A type of love that develops gradually and is not necessarily tied to sexual passion but is based on more rational assessments of the one who is loved.

Companionate marriage: A marriage emphasizing a clear division of labor between a breadwinner and a homemaker and held together by sentiment, friendship, and sexuality.

Competitive capitalism: A form of capitalism where there are a large number of relatively small firms with the result that no one, or no small subset, of them can completely dominate and control a given area of the economy.

Conflict theory: A set of ideas focusing on the sources of conflict within society; this theory sees society as held together by coercion and focuses on its negative aspects.

Conformists: People who accept both cultural goals and the traditional means of achieving those goals.

Consensual sex: Sexual intercourse that is agreed upon by the participants in an informed process.

Conspicuous consumption: The public demonstration of wealth through consumption that one is able to waste money—for example, by flaunting the use of expensive, high-status goods and services (mansions, yachts, personal assistants, etc.).

Consumer crime: Crimes related to consumption, including shoplifting and using stolen credit cards or credit card numbers.

Consumer culture: A culture in which the core ideas and material objects relate to consumption and in which consumption is a primary source of meaning in life.

Consumerism: A value-laden term indicating an obsession with consumption.

Consumption: The process by which people obtain goods and services.

Convenience sample: A readily available group of people who fit the criteria for participating in a research project.

Corporate crime: Violations of the law by legal organizations, including antitrust violations and stock market violations.

Cosmopolitan: Being open to a variety of external and global influences.

Counterculture: A group whose culture not only differs in certain ways from the dominant culture, but whose norms and values may be incompatible with those of the dominant culture.

Crime: A violation of the criminal law.

Criminology: The study of all aspects of crime.

Critical theories of race and racism: A set of ideas arguing that race continues to matter and that racism continues to exist and adversely affect blacks.

Critical theory: A set of critical ideas derived from Marxian theory but focusing on culture rather than the economy.

Crowd: A temporary gathering of a relatively large number of people in a common geographic location and at a given time.

Cult: A new, innovative, small, voluntary, and exclusive religious tradition that was never associated with any religious organization.

Cult of masculinity: A social practice that organizes political life and the public sphere around men and punishes perceived deficiencies in masculinity in men.

Cultural hybrid: A cultural phenomenon combining inputs and impositions from other cultures with local realities.

Cultural imperialism: The imposition of one culture, more or less consciously, on other cultures.

Cultural relativism: The idea that aspects of culture such as norms and values need to be understood within the context of a person's own culture and that there are no universally accepted norms and values.

Culture: A collection of ideas, values, practices, and material objects that mean a great deal to a group of people, even an entire society, and that allow them to carry out their collective lives in relative order and harmony.

Culture industry: The rationalized and bureaucratized structures that control modern culture.

Culture jamming: The radical transformation of an intended message in popular culture, especially one associated with the mass media, to protest underlying realities of which consumers may be unaware.

Culture war: A conflict that pits subcultures and countercultures against the dominant culture or that pits dominant groups within society against each other.

Cumulative advantage: The process by which the most advantaged individuals are awarded the best opportunities, which increases inequality over time.

Cybercrime: Crime that targets computers, uses computers to commit traditional crimes, or transmits illegal information and images.

Cyberculture: An emerging online culture that has the characteristics of all culture, including distinctive values and norms.

Dangerous giant: An entity that has agency.

Debunking: Looking beneath and beyond the surface of social structures, which are seen as facades that conceal what is truly important.

Deindustrialization: The decline of manufacturing as well as a corresponding increase in various types of services.

Deinstitutionalization: Weakened social norms especially with regard to the institution of marriage.

Democracy: A political system in which people within a given state vote to choose their leaders and in some cases vote on legislation.

Democrats: Members of a political party within the U.S. two-party system, typically seen as the liberal party.

Demographers: Those who study population dynamics.

Demography: The scientific study of population, especially its growth and decline, as well as the movement of people.

Denomination: A religious group not linked to the state that exhibits a general spirit of tolerance and acceptance of other religious bodies.

Dependent variable: A characteristic or measurement that is the result of manipulating an independent variable.

Deprofessionalization: The process whereby a profession's power and autonomy, as well as high status and great wealth, have declined, at least relative to the exalted position it once held.

Descriptive statistics: Numerical data that allow researchers to see trends over time or compare differences between groups, to describe some particular collection of data that is based on a phenomenon in the real world.

Descriptive survey: A questionnaire or interview used to gather accurate information about those in a group, people in a given geographic area, or members of organizations.

Desertification: A decline in the water supply as a result of the degradation and deterioration of soil and vegetation.

Deviance: Any action, belief, or human characteristic that members of a society or a social group consider a violation of group norms and for which the violator is likely to be censured or punished.

Diaspora: Dispersal, typically involuntary, of a racial or ethnic population from its traditional homeland and over a wide geographic area.

Dictatorships: States that are usually totalitarian and ruled either by a single individual or by a small group of people.

Differential association: A theory that focuses on the fact that people learn criminal behavior from those with whom they associate.

Direct democracy: A political system in which people directly affected by a given decision have a say in that decision.

Disasters: Events that suddenly, unexpectedly, and severely disrupt and harm the environment, the social structure, people, and their property.

Discreditable stigma: A stigma that the affected individual assumes is neither known about nor immediately perceivable.

Discredited stigma: A stigma that the affected individual assumes is already known about or readily apparent.

Discrimination: The unfavorable treatment of black Americans and other minorities, either formally or informally, simply because of their race or some other such characteristic.

Distinction: The need to distinguish oneself from others.

Domestic violence: The exertion of power over a partner in an intimate relationship through behavior that is intimidating, threatening, harassing, or harmful.

Domination: The probability or likelihood that commands will be obeyed by subordinates.

Double-consciousness: Among black Americans, the sense of "two-ness," of being both black and American.

Dramaturgy: The view that social life is a series of dramatic performances akin to those that take place in a theater and on a stage.

Dyad: A two-person group.

Dysfunction: An observable consequence that negatively affects the ability of a given system to survive, adapt, or adjust.

Ecology: The study of people and their relationship to one another as well as to the larger context (including the natural environment) in which they live.

Economy: The social system involved in the production and distribution of a wide range of goods and services.

Edge cities: Developments at the outermost rings surrounding large cities.

Elite pluralism: The formation by political elites of similar interest groups and organizations that vie for power.

Emergent norm theory: A theory arguing that, in light of some precipitating event, new norms emerge that guide the often-nontraditional actions that characterize collective behavior.

Emphasized femininity: A set of socially constructed ideas that accommodates to the interests of men and to patriarchy and involves the compliance of females.

Empiricism: The gathering of information and evidence using one's senses, especially one's eyes and ears, to experience the social world.

Endogamy: Marriage to someone with similar characteristics in terms of race, ethnicity, religion, education level, social class, and so on.

Ethics: A set of beliefs concerning right and wrong in the choices that people make and the ways those choices are justified.

Ethnic cleansing: The establishment by the dominant group of policies that allow or require the forcible removal of people of another ethnic group.

Ethnic group: A group typically defined on the basis of some cultural characteristic such as language, religion, traditions, and cultural practices.

Ethnicity: A social definition based on a real or presumed cultural characteristic such as language or religion.

Ethnocentrism: The belief that one's own group or culture—including its norms, values, customs, and so on—is superior to, or better than, others.

Ethnography: Observational research, often intensive and over lengthy periods, that leads to an account of what people do and how they live.

Ethnomethodology: A theory focusing on what people do rather than on what they think.

Ethnoscapes: Landscapes that involve the movement, or fantasies about movement, of various individuals and groups.

Exchange relationship: A stable and persistent bond between individuals who interact, generally formed because their interactions are rewarding.

Exchange theory: A set of ideas related to the rewards and costs associated with human behavior.

Exogamy: Marriage to someone with dissimilar characteristics in terms of race, ethnicity, religion, education level, social class, and so on.

Experiment: The manipulation of a characteristic under study (an independent variable) to examine its effect on another characteristic (the dependent variable).

Explanatory survey: A questionnaire or interview used to uncover potential causes for some observation.

Exploitation: A feature of capitalism in which the workers (proletariat) produce virtually everything but get few rewards, while the capitalists, who do little, reap the vast majority of the rewards.

Expulsion: Removal of a minority group from a territory, either by forcible ejection through military and other government action or by "voluntary" emigration due to the majority's harassment, discrimination, and persecution.

Exurbia: Outlying upper-middle-class areas between the suburbs and rural areas.

False consciousness: Regarding the proletariat in capitalism, the lack of understanding of capitalism's nature and the erroneous belief that capitalism operates to workers' benefit; exists when large numbers of people do not have a clear and correct sense of their true interests.

Family: A group of people who are related by descent, marriage, or adoption.

Family household: A household comprising two or more people who occupy a given domicile and are related by blood, marriage, or adoption.

Fantasy city: A city in which great emphasis is placed on creating a spectacle, especially in the areas of consumption, leisure, tourism, and impressive buildings and other real estate developments.

Felonies: Serious crimes punishable by a year or more in prison.

Female proletarianization: The channeling of an increasing number of women into low-status, poorly paid manual work.

Feminism: The belief that women are equal to men, especially socially, politically, and economically.

Feminist theory: A set of ideas critical of the social situation confronting women and offering solutions for improving, if not revolutionizing, their situation.

Feminization of labor: The rise of female labor participation in all sectors and the movement of women into jobs traditionally held by men.

Feminization of poverty: The rise in the number of women falling below the poverty line.

Fertility: People's reproductive behavior, especially the number of births.

Field experiment: Research that occurs in natural situations but that allows researchers to exert at least some control over who participates and what happens during the experiment.

Financescapes: Landscapes that involve the use of various financial instruments to allow huge sums of money and other things of economic value to move into and across nations and around the world at great speed, almost instantaneously.

Folkway: A norm that is relatively unimportant and, if violated, carries few if any sanctions.

Food insecurity: Lack of sufficient access to safe and nutritious food.

Fordism: The ideas, principles, and systems created by Henry Ford (who is credited with the development of the modern mass production system) and his associates at the turn of the twentieth century.

Front stage: The part of the social world where the social performance is idealized and designed to define the situation for those who observe it.

Function: An observable, positive consequence that helps a system survive, adapt, or adjust.

Fundamentalism: A strongly held belief in the fundamental or foundational precepts of any religion, or a rejection of the modern secular world.

Game stage: Mead's second stage in the socialization process in which a child develops a self in the full sense of the term, because it is then that the child begins to take on the role of a group of people simultaneously rather than the roles of discrete individuals.

Gated communities: Communities in which gates, surveillance cameras, and guards provide the owners of homes or condominiums greater security from the problems (crime, panhandling) that they think they left behind in the city.

Gemeinschaft societies: Traditional societies characterized by face-to-face relations.

Gender: The physical, behavioral, and personality characteristics considered appropriate for one's sex.

General deterrence: The deterrence of the population as a whole from committing crimes for fear that the members will be punished or imprisoned for their crimes.

Generalized other: The attitude of the entire group or community adopted by individuals.

Genocide: An active, systematic attempt to eliminate an entire group of people.

Gentrification: The reinvestment of real estate capital in blighted inner-city areas to rebuild residences and create a new infrastructure for the well-to-do.

Geopolitics: Political relationships that involve large geographic areas or the globe as a whole.

Gesellschaft societies: Modern societies characterized by impersonal, distant, and limited social relationships.

Gesture: A movement of one animal or human that elicits a mindless, automatic, and appropriate response from another animal or human.

Global cities: Key locations for leading industries, centers of production, and centers of innovative financial services from which businesses and organizations exercise global command and control.

Global ethnography: A type of ethnography that is "grounded" in various parts of the world and that seeks to understand globalization as it exists in people's social lives.

Globalization: "A transplanetary *process* or set of *processes* involving increasing *liquidity* and the growing multidirectional *flows* of people, objects, places and information as well as the *structures* they encounter and create that are *barriers* to, or *expedite,* those flows" (Ritzer 2010c).

Group: A relatively small number of people who over time develop a patterned relationship based on interaction with one another.

Group pluralism: The competition of society's various interest groups and organizations for access to political power in an attempt to further their interests.

Habitus: An internalized set of preferences and dispositions that are learned through experience and social interactions in specific social contexts.

Hate crimes: Crimes that stem from the fact that the victims are in various ways different from, and disesteemed by, the perpetrators.

Hegemonic masculinity: A set of ideas about the characteristics of men that focuses on the interests and desires of men and is linked to patriarchy.

Hegemony: The subordination by one race (or other group) of another, more on the basis of dominant ideas, especially about cultural differences, than through material constraints.

Heterosexuality: Desire to have sexual relations with someone of the opposite sex.

Historical-comparative research: A research methodology that contrasts how different historical events and conditions in various societies (or components of societies) lead to different societal outcomes.

Homosexuality: Desire to have sexual relations with someone of the same sex.

Horizontal mobility: Movement within one's social class.

Hyperconsumption: Consumption of more than one needs, really wants, and can afford.

Hyperdebt: Borrowing more than one should, thereby owing more than one will be able to pay back.

Hypodescent rule: A law or judicial ruling that classified persons with even one nonwhite ancestor, or a nonwhite ancestor within a certain number of generations, as black or colored.

"I": The immediate response of an individual to others; the part of the self that is incalculable, unpredictable, and creative.

Ideal culture: Norms and values indicating what members of a society should believe in and do.

Ideal type: An exaggeratedly rational model that is used to study real-world phenomena.

Identity politics: The use of a minority group's power to strengthen the position of the cultural group with which it identifies.

Ideoscapes: Landscapes that involve images, largely political images, that are often in line with the ideologies of nation-states.

Imagined communities: Communities that are socially constructed by those who see themselves as part of them.

Impression management: People's use of a variety of techniques to control the image of themselves that they want to project during their social performances.

Income: The amount of money a person earns in a given year from a job, a business, or various types of assets and investments.

Independent variable: In an experiment, a condition that can be independently manipulated by the researcher with the goal of producing a change in some other variable.

Individualized marriage: A marriage characterized by greater freedom for the partners to develop and express themselves and seek satisfaction.

Inequality: The fact that some positions in society yield a great deal of money, status, and power while others yield little, if any, of these.

Inferential statistics: Numerical data that allow researchers to use data from a small group to speculate with some level of certainty about a larger group.

Informal organization: An organization as it really functions as opposed to the way it is intended to function.

Informationalism: The processing of knowledge.

In-group: A group to which people belong and with which they identify, perhaps strongly.

Innovators: Individuals who accept cultural goals but reject conventional means of achieving success.

Institutional marriage: A marriage focused on maintaining the institution of marriage itself.

Institutional racism: Race-based discrimination that results from the day-to-day operation of social institutions and social structures and their rules, policies, and practices.

Interaction: A social engagement that involves two, or more, individuals who perceive, and orient their actions to, one another.

Interaction order: An area of interaction that is organized and orderly, but in which the order is created informally by those involved in the interaction rather than by some formal structure.

Intergenerational mobility: The difference between the parents' social class position and the position achieved by their child(ren).

Intersectionality: The confluence, or intersection, of various social statuses and the inequality and oppression associated with each in combination with others.

Intersexed: People who have some combination of the genitalia of both males and females.

Interview: A research method in which information is sought from participants (respondents) who are asked a series of questions that have been spelled out, at least to some degree, before the research is conducted.

Intimate relationship: A close, personal, and domestic relationship between partners.

Intragenerational mobility: Movement up or down the stratification system in one's lifetime.

Labeling theory: A theory contending that a deviant is someone to whom a deviant label has been successfully applied.

Labor migrants: Those who migrate because they are driven by either "push" factors (a lack of work, low pay) in their homeland or "pull" factors (jobs and higher pay available elsewhere).

Laboratory experiment: Research that occurs in a laboratory, giving the researcher great control over both the selection of the participants to be studied and the conditions to which they are exposed.

Landscapes (scapes): Fluid, irregular, and variable global flows that produce different results throughout the world.

Language: A set of meaningful symbols that makes possible the communication of culture as well as communication more generally within a given culture, and that calls out the same meaning in the person to whom an utterance is aimed as it does to the person making the utterance.

Latent functions: Unintended positive consequences.

Law: A norm that has been codified, or written down, and is formally enforced through institutions such as the state.

Liminal period: A period, or a special time, set apart from ordinary reality.

Local: Inward rather than outward looking.

Looking-glass self: The self-image that reflects how others respond to a person, particularly as a child.

Macro: Macroscopic; used to describe large-scale social phenomena, such as groups, organizations, cultures, society, and the globe.

Macrofinance: The globalization of money and finance.

Majority group: A group in a dominant position along the dimensions of wealth, power, and prestige.

Majority–minority population: A population in which more than 50 percent of the members are part of a minority group.

Manifest functions: Positive consequences that are brought about consciously and purposely.

Marriage: The socially acknowledged, approved, and often legal union of two people allowing them to live together and to have children by birth or adoption.

Mass culture: Cultural elements that are administered by large organizations, lack spontaneity, and are phony.

Mass production: Production characterized by large numbers of standardized products, highly specialized workers, interchangeable machine parts, precision tools, a high-volume mechanized production process, and the synchronization of the flow of materials used in production, with the entire process made as continuous as possible.

Master status: A position that is more important than any others both for the person in the position and for all others involved.

Material culture: All of the material objects that are reflections or manifestations of a culture.

McDonaldization: The process by which the rational principles of the fast-food restaurant are coming to dominate more and more sectors of society and more societies throughout the world.

"Me": The organized set of others' attitudes assumed by the individual; it involves the adoption by the individual of the generalized other.

Mechanical solidarity: Cohesion among a group of people based on the fact that they all do essentially the same things.

Mediascapes: Landscapes that involve the electronic capability to produce and transmit information and images around the world.

Medical sociology: A field concerned with the social causes and consequences of health and illness.

Medicalization: The tendency to label as an illness a phenomenon or syndrome that was not previously considered an illness, as well as to exaggerate the ability of medicine to deal with that phenomenon or syndrome.

Megacities: Cities with a population greater than 10 million people.

Megalopolis: A cluster of highly populated cities that can stretch over great distances.

Meritocracy: A dominant ideology involving the widely shared belief that all people have an equal chance of succeeding economically based on their hard work and skills.

Metropolis: A large, powerful, and culturally influential urban area that contains a central city and surrounding communities that are economically and socially linked to the center.

Micro: Microscopic; used to describe small-scale social phenomena such as individuals and their thoughts and actions.

Micro–macro continuum: The range of social entities from the individual, even the mind and self, to the interaction among individuals, the groups often formed by that interaction, formally structured organizations, societies, and increasingly the global domain.

Migration: The movements of people and their impact on the sending and receiving locales.

Mind: An internal conversation that arises in relation to, and is continuous with, interactions, especially conversations that one has with others in the social world.

Minority group: A group in a subordinate position in terms of wealth, power, and prestige.

Misdemeanors: Minor offenses punishable by imprisonment of less than a year.

Monogamy: Marriage between one wife and one husband (or two wives or two husbands).

Monopoly capitalism: A form of capitalism in which huge corporations monopolize the market.

Moral entrepreneurs: Individuals or groups who come to define an act as a moral outrage and who lead a campaign to have it defined as deviant and to have it made illegal and therefore subject to legal enforcement.

Moral panic: A widespread, but disproportionate, reaction to a form of deviance.

More: An important norm whose violation is likely to be met with severe sanctions.

Mortality: Deaths and death rates within a population.

Multiculturalism: The encouragement of cultural differences within a given environment, both by the state and by the majority group.

Multiparty system: A political system in which more than two parties enjoy public support and hold political office in a nation.

Nation: A group of people who share similar cultural, religious, ethnic, linguistic, and territorial characteristics.

Nation-state: The combination of a nation with a geographic and political structure; encompasses both the populations that define themselves as a nation with various shared characteristics and the organizational structure of the state.

Natural experiment: An experiment that occurs when researchers take advantage of a naturally occurring event to study its effect on one or more dependent variables.

Netnography: An ethnographic method in which the Internet becomes the research site and what transpires there is the sociologist's research interest.

Network organization: A new organizational form that is flat and horizontal; is intertwined with other organizations; is run and managed in very different ways than traditional organizations; uses more flexible production methods; and is composed of a series of interconnected nodes.

Networks: "Interconnected nodes" that are open, capable of unlimited expansion, dynamic, and able to innovate without disrupting the system in which they exist.

New religious movements: Movements that attract zealous religious converts, follow charismatic leaders, appeal to an atypical portion of the population, have a tendency to differentiate between "us" and "them," are characterized by distrust of others, and are prone to rapid fundamental changes.

Nonfamily household: A household consisting of a person who lives either alone or with nonrelatives.

Nonparticipant observation: A research method in which the sociologist plays little or no role in what is being observed.

Norm: An informal rule that guides what a member of a culture does in a given situation and how that person lives.

Nuclear family: A family consisting of two married adults and one or more children.

Observation: A research method that involves systematically watching, listening to, and recording what takes place in a natural social setting over some period of time.

Occupational mobility: Changes in people's work either across or within generations.

Offshore outsourcing: The transfer of work to organizations in other countries.

Oligarchy: An organization led by a small group of people who illegitimately acquire and exercise far more power than they are entitled to have.

Organic solidarity: Cohesion among a group of people based on their differences.

Organization: A collective purposely constructed to achieve particular ends.

Organized crime: A type of crime that may involve various types of organizations but is most often associated with syndicated organized crime that uses violence (or its threat) and the corruption of public officials to profit from illegal activities.

Orientalism: A set of ideas and texts produced in the West that served as the basis for dominating, controlling, and exploiting the Orient (the East) and its many minority groups.

Out-group: A group to which outsiders (at least from the perspective of the in-group) belong.

Outsourcing: The transfer of activities once performed by one organization to another organization in exchange for money.

Parole: The supervised early release of a prisoner for such things as good behavior while in prison.

Participant observation: A research method in which the researcher actually plays a role, usually a minor one, in the group or setting being observed.

Passionate love: A type of love that develops suddenly and includes strong sexual feelings and idealization of the one who is loved; romantic love.

Play stage: Mead's first stage in the socialization process where children learn to take on the attitudes of specific others toward themselves.

Pluralism: The coexistence of many groups without any of them losing their individual qualities.

Political crime: Either an illegal offense against the state to affect its policies, or an offense by the state, either domestically or internationally.

Political pluralism: Within structural-functionalism, the typical position put forward regarding who rules America.

Politics: Societal competition through established governmental channels to advance a position or enact a policy to benefit the group's members.

Polyandry: Marriage (of a wife) to multiple husbands.

Polygamy: Marriage to multiple wives (polygyny) or multiple husbands (polyandry).

Polygyny: Marriage (of a husband) to multiple wives.

Post-Fordism: A production environment associated with smaller production runs of more specialized products, especially those high in style and quality; more flexible machinery made possible by advances in technology largely traceable to the computer; more skilled workers with greater flexibility and autonomy; less reliance on economies of scale; and more differentiated markets for those more specialized products.

Postindustrial society: A society that was at one time industrial, but where the focus on the manufacture of goods has been replaced by an increase, at least initially, in service work; that is, work in which people are involved in providing services for one another rather than producing goods.

Postmodern theory: A set of ideas oriented in opposition to modern theory by, for example, rejecting or deconstructing the grand narratives of modern social theory.

Postmodernism: The emergence of new and different cultural forms in music, movies, art, architecture, and the like.

Poverty line: The threshold, in terms of income, below which a household is considered poor.

Power: The ability to get others to do what you want them to do, even if it is against their will.

Power elite theory: A theory holding that power is not dispersed throughout a stable society but is concentrated in a small number of people who control the major institutions of the state, the corporate economy, and the military.

Prejudice: Negative attitudes, beliefs, and feelings toward minorities.

Primary deviance: Early, nonpatterned acts of deviance or an act here or there that is considered to be strange or out of the ordinary.

Primary groups: Groups that are small, are close-knit, and have intimate face-to-face interaction.

Primary socialization: The acquisition of language, identities, gender roles, cultural routines, norms, and values from parents and other family members at the earliest stages of an individual's life.

Probation: A system by which those who are convicted of less serious crimes may be released into the community, but under supervision and under certain conditions such as being involved in and completing a substance abuse program.

Profane: To Durkheim, that which has not been defined as sacred, or that which is ordinary and mundane.

Profession: An occupation distinguished from other occupations by its power and considerable autonomy.

Proletariat: Workers as a group, or those in the capitalist system who own little or nothing except for their capacity for work (labor), which they must sell to the capitalists to survive.

Property crimes: Crimes that do not involve injury or force, but rather are offenses that involve gaining or destroying property.

Prosumer: One who combines the acts of consumption and production.

Protestant ethic: A belief in hard work, frugality, and good work as means to achieve both economic success and heavenly salvation.

Public sociology: Sociological work addressing a wide range of audiences, most of which are outside the academy, including a variety of local, national, and global groups.

Pure relationship: A relationship entered into for its own sake or for what each partner can get from it, maintained only as long as each derives enough satisfaction from the other.

Qualitative research: Any research method that does not require statistical methods for collecting and reporting data.

Quantitative research: Any research method that involves the analysis of numerical data derived usually from surveys and experiments.

Queer theory: A theory based on the idea that there are no fixed and stable identities (such as "heterosexual" or "homosexual") that determine who we are.

Questionnaire: A self-administered, written set of questions.

Race: A social definition based on shared lineage and a real or presumed physical, biological characteristic, such as skin color.

Racism: Defining a group as a race and attributing negative characteristics to that group.

Random sample: A subset of a population in which every member of the group has an equal chance of being included.

Rape: A form of domination; violent sexual intercourse.

Rational choice theory: A set of ideas that sees people as rational and as acting purposively to achieve their goals.

Rational-legal authority: Authority that is legitimated on the basis of legally enacted rules and the right of those with authority under those rules to issue commands.

Rationalization: The process by which social structures are increasingly characterized by the most direct and efficient means to their ends.

Real culture: What people actually think and do in their everyday lives.

Rebels: Individuals who reject both traditional means and goals and instead substitute nontraditional goals and means to those goals.

Recidivism: The repetition of a criminal act by one who has been convicted for an offense.

Reciprocity: The expectation that those involved in an interaction will give and receive rewards of roughly equal value.

Reference groups: Groups that people take into consideration in evaluating themselves.

Refugees: Migrants who are forced to leave their homeland, or who leave involuntarily, because they fear for their safety.

Reliability: The degree to which a given question (or another kind of measure) produces the same results time after time.

Religion: A social phenomenon that consists of beliefs about the sacred; the experiences, practices, and rituals that reinforce those beliefs; and the community that shares similar beliefs and practices.

Representative democracy: A political system in which people, as a whole body, do not actually rule themselves but rather have some say in who will best represent them in the state.

Republicans: Members of a political party within the U.S. two-party system; typically seen as the conservative party.

Resocialization: The unlearning of old behaviors, norms, and values and the learning of new ones.

Resource mobilization theory: An approach to understanding social movements that focuses on what groups of people need to do to mobilize to bring about social change.

Retreatists: Individuals who reject both cultural goals and the traditional routes to their attainment; they have completely given up on attaining success within the system.

Reverse socialization: The socialization of those who normally do the socializing—for example, children socializing their parents.

Riot: Temporary unruly collective behavior that causes damage to persons or property.

Risk society: A society whose central issue is preventing, minimizing, and channeling risk.

Rites of passage: Rituals that surround major transitions in life, such as birth, puberty, marriage, and death.

Ritual: A set of regularly repeated, prescribed, and traditional behaviors that serve to symbolize some value or belief.

Ritualists: Individuals who realize that they will not be able to achieve cultural goals, but who nonetheless continue to engage in the conventional behavior associated with such success.

Role: What is generally expected of a person who occupies a given status.

Role conflict: Conflicting expectations associated with a given position or multiple positions.

Role making: The ability of people to modify their roles, at least to some degree.

Role overload: Confrontation with more expectations than a person can possibly handle.

Rule creators: Individuals who devise society's rules, norms, and laws.

Rule enforcers: Individuals who threaten to, or actually, enforce the rules.

Sacred: To Durkheim, that which has been defined as being of ultimate concern.

Sample: A representative portion of the overall population.

Sanctions: The application of rewards (positive sanctions) or punishments (negative sanctions) when norms are accepted or violated.

Scientific management: The application of scientific principles and methods to management.

Scientific method: A structured way to find answers to questions about the world.

Secondary data analysis: Reanalysis of data, often survey data, collected by others, including other sociologists.

Secondary deviance: Deviant acts that persist, become more common, and eventually cause people to organize their lives and personal identities around their deviant status.

Secondary groups: Generally large, impersonal groups in which ties are relatively weak and members do not know one another very well, and whose impact on members is typically not very powerful.

Sect: A small group of people who have joined the group consciously and voluntarily to have a personal religious experience.

Secularization: The declining significance of religion.

Segregation: The physical and social separation of majority and minority groups.

Self: The sense of oneself as an object.

Separation of powers: The separation and counterbalancing of different branches of government so that no one branch of government can wield too much power.

Sex: A mainly biological distinction between males and females based on fundamental differences in their reproductive functions.

Sexual assault: Sexual acts of domination usually enacted by men against women.

Sexual harassment: Unwanted sexual attention that takes place in the workplace or other settings.

Sexual orientation: Preferences based on whom one desires sexually, with whom one wants to engage in sexual relations, and to whom one feels connected—typically categorized as heterosexual, homosexual, bisexual, or asexual.

Sexual scripts: Generally known ideas about what one ought to do and not do as far as sexual behavior is concerned.

Sexuality: The ways in which people think about, and behave toward, themselves and others as sexual beings.

Sick role: Expectations about the way sick people are supposed to act.

Significant symbol: A gesture that arouses in the individual the same kind of response, although it need not be identical, as it is supposed to elicit from those to whom the gesture is addressed.

Simulation: An inauthentic or fake version of something.

Single-party system: A political system in which the ruling party outlaws, or heavily restricts, opposing parties.

Slavery: A system in which people are defined as property, involuntarily placed in perpetual servitude, and not given the same rights as the rest of society.

Social change: Variations over time in every aspect of the social world ranging from changes affecting individuals to transformations having an impact on the globe as a whole.

Social class: One's economic position in the stratification system, especially one's occupation, which strongly determines and reflects one's income and wealth.

Social construction of reality: The continuous process of individual creation of structural realities and the constraint and coercion exercised by those structures.

Social control: The process by which a group or society enforces conformity to its demands and expectations.

Social control agents: Those who label a person as deviant.

Social control theory: A theory that focuses on the reasons why people do not commit deviant acts and the stake people have in engaging in conformist behavior.

Social facts: Macro-level phenomena—social structures and cultural norms and values—that stand apart from and impose themselves on people.

Social mobility: The ability or inability to change one's position in the social hierarchy.

Social movements: Sustained and intentional collective efforts, usually operating outside of established institutional channels, either to bring about or to retard social change.

Social processes: Dynamic and changing aspects of the social world.

Social stratification: Hierarchical differences and inequalities in economic positions, as well as in other important areas, especially political power and status, or social honor.

Social structures: Enduring and regular social arrangements, such as the family and the state, based on persistent patterns of interaction and social relationships.

Socialism: A historical stage following communism involving the effort by society to plan and organize production consciously and rationally so that all members of society benefit from it.

Socialization: The process through which a person learns and generally comes to accept the ways of a group or of society as a whole.

Society: A complex pattern of social relationships that is bounded in space and persists over time.

Sociological imagination: A unique perspective that gives sociologists a distinctive way of looking at data and reflecting on the world around them.

Sociology: The systematic study of the ways in which people are affected by, and affect, the social structures and social processes that are associated with the groups, organizations, cultures, societies, and world in which they exist.

Specific deterrence: Whether the experience of punishment in general, and incarceration

in particular, makes it less likely that an individual will commit crimes in the future.

State: A political body organized for government and civil rule, with relatively autonomous officeholders and with its own rules and resources coming largely from taxes.

Status: A dimension of the social stratification system that relates to the prestige attached to people's positions within society.

Statistics: The mathematical method used to analyze numerical data.

Stereotype: An exaggerated generalization about an entire category of people.

Stigma: A characteristic that others find, define, and often label as unusual, unpleasant, or deviant.

Strain theory: Theory based on the idea that the discrepancy between the larger structure of society and the means available to people to achieve that which the society considers to be of value produces strain that may cause an individual to undertake deviant acts.

Stratified sample: A sample created when a larger group is divided into a series of subgroups and then random samples are taken within each of these groups.

Structural-functionalism: A set of ideas focused on social structures as well as the functions and dysfunctions that such structures perform.

Structural mobility: The effect of changes in the larger society on the position of individuals in the stratification system, especially the occupational structure.

Structuralism: Social theory interested in the social impact of hidden or underlying structures.

Subculture: A group of people who accept much of the dominant culture but are set apart from it by one or more culturally significant characteristics.

Suburbanization: The process whereby large numbers of people move out of the city and into nearby, less densely populated, environs.

Suburbs: Communities that are adjacent to, but outside the political boundaries of, large central cities.

Survey research: A research methodology that involves the collection of information from a population, or more usually a

representative portion of a population, through the use of interviews and, more importantly, questionnaires.

Sustainable development: Economic and environmental changes that meet the needs of the present, especially of the world's poor, without jeopardizing the needs of the future.

Symbol: A word, gesture, or object that stands in for something, or someone (i.e., a "label").

Symbolic culture: Aspects of culture that exist in nonmaterial forms.

Symbolic interaction: Interaction on the basis of not only gestures but also significant symbols.

Symbolic interactionism: A sociological perspective focusing on the role of symbols and how their meanings are shared and understood by those involved in human interaction.

Technology: The interplay of machines, tools, skills, and procedures for the accomplishment of tasks.

Technoscapes: Landscapes that involve mechanical and informational technologies, as well as the material that moves quickly and freely through them.

Terrorism: Acts of violence by nongovernmental actors that target noncombatants, property, or military personnel to influence politics.

Theory: A set of interrelated ideas that have a wide range of application, deal with centrally important issues, and have stood the test of time.

Total institution: A closed, all-encompassing place of residence and work set off from the rest of society that meets all of the needs of those enclosed within it.

Traditional authority: Authority based on a belief in long-running traditions.

Transgender: An umbrella term describing individuals whose gender identity does not conform to the sex to which they were assigned at birth and whose behavior challenges gender norms.

Transnational capitalism: An economic system in which transnational economic practices predominate.

Transsexual: An individual whose genitalia are of the sex opposite to the one with which he or she identifies and who may undergo treatment or surgery to acquire the physical characteristics of the self-identified sex.

Triad: A three-person group.

Two-party system: A political system in which two parties hold nearly all positions of political power in a given nation.

Unanticipated consequence: An unexpected social effect, especially a negative effect.

Underemployment: Employment in jobs that are beneath one's training and ability, as a part-time worker when one is capable and desirous of full-time work, or in jobs that are not fully occupying.

Undernutrition: A form of malnutrition involving an inadequate intake of nutrients, including calories, vitamins, and minerals.

Undocumented immigrants: Those residing in a receiving country without valid authorization.

Unemployment: The state of being economically active and in the labor force, being able and willing to work, and seeking employment, but being unable to find a job.

Urban: City dwelling; in the United States, to be considered urban, an area must have more than 50,000 inhabitants.

Urbanism: The distinctive way of life (lifestyles, attitudes, social relationships) that emerges in, and is closely associated with, urban areas.

Urbanization: The process by which an increasing percentage of a society's population comes to be located in relatively densely populated urban areas.

Validity: The degree to which a question (or another kind of measure) gets an accurate response, or measures what it is supposed to measure.

Values: General and abstract standards defining what a group or society as a whole considers good, desirable, right, or important—in short, its ideals.

Vertical mobility: Both upward and downward mobility.

Violent crime: The threat of injury or the threat or actual use of force, including murder, rape, robbery, and aggravated assault, as well as terrorism and, globally, war crimes.

Vouchers: Government-issued certificates that allow students to use public tax dollars to pay tuition at a private school.

War: Armed conflict in which a nation uses its military to attempt to impose its will on others.

Wealth: The total amount of a person's assets less the total of various kinds of debts.

Welfare states: States that seek both to run their economic markets efficiently, as capitalism does, and to do so more equitably, which capitalism does not do.

White-collar crime: Crimes committed by responsible and (usually) high-social-status people in the course of their work.

White racial frame: An array of racist ideas, racial stereotypes, racialized stories and tales, racist images, powerful racial emotions, and various inclinations to discriminate against blacks.

Xenophobia: Prejudices that cause people to reject, exclude, and vilify groups that are outsiders or foreigners to the dominant social group.

REFERENCES
Chapter-Opening Vignettes

CHAPTER 1

Ryan, Yasmine. 2011. "How Tunisia's Revolution Began." *Al Jazeera English*. Retrieved May 5, 2011 (http://english.aljazeera.net/indepth/features/2011/01/2011126121815985483.html).

Staff. 2011. "Tunisia Protests against Ben Ali Left 200 Dead, Says UN." *BBC News*. Retrieved May 5, 2011 (http://www.bbc.co.uk/news/world-africa-12335692).

CHAPTER 2

Freedman, Andrew. 2011. "Public Remains Confused about Global Warming, but Less So." *Washington Post*, June 14. Retrieved June 15, 2011 (http://www.washingtonpost.com/blogs/capital-weather-gang/post/public-remains-confused-about-global-warming-but-less-so/2011/06/13/AG04TaUH_blog.html).

Oreskes, Naomi. 2004. "The Scientific Consensus on Climate Change." *Science*, December. Retrieved June 15, 2011 (http://www.sciencemag.org/content/306/5702/1686.full).

CHAPTER 3

Carr, Ian. 1998. *Miles Davis: The Definitive Biography*. New York: Thunder Mouth Press.

Smith, Jeff and Jean Wylie. 2004. "China's Youth Define 'Cool.'" *China Business Review*. Retrieved June 17, 2011 (http://www.chinabusinessreview.com/public/0407/smith.html).

Thompson, Robert Farris. 1973. "An Aesthetic of the Cool." *African Arts* 7(1). Retrieved June 16, 2011 (http://www.jstor.org/pss/3334749).

CHAPTER 4

Landler, Mark. 2013. "Obama Awards Medal of Honor to Former Army Sergeant." *New York Times*, February 12, p. A18.

CHAPTER 5

Castle, Stephen. 2013. "Report of U.S. Spying Angers European Allies." *New York Times*, June 30. Retrieved October 11, 2013 (http://www.nytimes.com/2013/07/01/world/europe/europeans-angered-by-report-of-us-spying.html?pagewanted=all).

Neuman, William and Randal C. Archibold. 2013. "U.S. Is Pressuring Latin Americans to Reject Snowden." *New York Times*, July 12. Retrieved October 11, 2013 (http://www.nytimes.com/2013/07/12/world/americas/us-is-pressing-latin-americans-to-reject-snowden.html?pagewanted=1&ref=todayspaper).

CHAPTER 6

Beiner, Theresa M. 2007. "Sexy Dressing Revisited: Does Target Dress Play a Part in Sexual Harassment Cases?" *Duke Journal of Gender Law & Policy* 14(1). Retrieved August 24, 2011 (http://www.law.duke.edu/shell/cite.pl?14+Duke+J.+Gender+L.+&+Pol%27y+125).

"'SlutWalk' Marches Sparked by Toronto Officer's Remarks." 2011. *BBC News*. Retrieved August 24, 2011 (http://www.bbc.co.uk/news/world-us-canada-13320785).

CHAPTER 7

Buffett, Warren E. 2011. "Stop Coddling the Super-Rich." *New York Times*, August 14. Retrieved August 26, 2011 (http://www.nytimes.com/2011/08/15/opinion/stop-coddling-the-super-rich.html?_r=3&hp).

Foster, Daniel. 2011. "Koch Responds to Buffett's Call for Tax Hikes." *National Review Online*, August 19. Retrieved August 26, 2011 (http://www.nationalreview.com/corner/275099/koch-responds-buffetts-call-tax-hikes-daniel-foster#).

Freeland, Chrystia. 2011. "The Rise of the New Global Elite." *The Atlantic*, January/February. Retrieved August 26, 2011 (http://www.theatlantic.com/magazine/print/2011/01/the-rise-of-the-new-global-elite/8343/).

CHAPTER 8

"Profile: Bolivia's President Evo Morales." 2011. *BBC News*, January 12. Retrieved October 21, 2011 (http://www.bbc.co.uk/news/world-latin-america-12166905).

Romero, Simon. 2009. "In Bolivia, a Force for Change Endures." *New York Times*, December 5. Retrieved October 21, 2011 (http://www.nytimes.com/2009/12/06/world/americas/06bolivia.html?ref=evomorales).

Webber, Jeffery R. 2011. *From Rebellion to Reform in Bolivia: Class Struggle, Indigenous Liberation, and the Politics of Evo Morales*. Chicago: Haymarket Books.

CHAPTER 9

Hussain, Lubna. 2011. "Saudi Woman Driver Spared 10 Lashes after King Intervenes." *The Independent*, September 30. Retrieved October 13, 2011 (http://www.independent.co.uk/news/world/middle-east/saudi-woman-driver-spared-10-lashes-after-king-intervenes-2363197.html).

MacFarquhar, Neil. 2011. "In a Scattered Protest, Saudi Women Take the Wheel." *The New York Times*, June 17. Retrieved October 13, 2011 (http://www.nytimes.com/2011/06/18/world/middleeast/18saudi.html?_r=2).

CHAPTER 10

"Lance Loud! A Death in *An American Family*." 2011. *PBS*. Retrieved November 18, 2011 (http://www.pbs.org/lanceloud/american/).

Winer, Laurie. 2011. "Reality Replay." *The New Yorker*, April 25. Retrieved November 18, 2011 (http://www.newyorker.com/talk/2011/04/25/110425ta_talk_winer).

CHAPTER 11

Associated Press. 2005. "Judge Rules against 'Intelligent Design.'" *MSNBC*, December 20. Retrieved December 1, 2011 (http://www.msnbc.msn.com/id/10545387/ns/technology_and_science-science/t/judge-rules-against-intelligent-design/).

Staff. 2011. "Muslim Medical Students Boycotting Lectures on Evolution . . . Because It 'Clashes with the Koran.'" *The Daily Mail Online*, November 28. Retrieved December 1, 2011 (http://www.dailymail.co.uk/news/article-2066795/Muslim-students-walking-lectures-Darwinism-clashes-Koran.html).

Timpane, John. 2011. "The Politics of Science: Evolution and Climate Change Are Shortcuts Conveying Broader Messages." *The Philadelphia Enquirer*, August 23. Retrieved December 1, 2011 (http://articles.philly.com/2011-08-23/news/29917822_1_climate-change-evolution-presidential-candidate-jon-huntsman).

Webley, Kayla. 2010. "Brief History: The Textbook Wars." *Time*, March 29. Retrieved December 1, 2011 (http://www.time.com/time/magazine/article/0,9171,1973276,00.html).

CHAPTER 12

Central Intelligence Agency. 2011. "The World Factbook: GDP—Real Growth Rate." Retrieved November 30, 2011 (https://www.cia.gov/library/publications/the-world-factbook/rankorder/2003rank.html).

Chan, Sewell. 2011. "Financial Crisis Was Avoidable, Inquiry Finds." *New York Times*, January 25. Retrieved November 30, 2011 (http://www.nytimes.com/2011/01/26/business/economy/26inquiry.html).

International Monetary Fund. 2010. "World Economic Outlook Update." Retrieved November 30, 2011 (http://www.imf.org/external/pubs/ft/weo/2010/update/01/).

Reuters. 2011. "S&P May Lower Outlook on France's Credit Rating." *Chicago Tribune*, November 29. Retrieved November 30, 2011 (http://www.chicagotribune.com/business/breaking/chi-sp-may-lower-outlook-on-frances-credit-rating-20111129,0,7620009.story).

Sappenfield, Mark. 2011. "S&P Downgrade of US Credit Rating Sends Clear Message to Congress: Shape Up." *The Christian Science Monitor*, August 6. Retrieved November 30, 2011 (http://www.csmonitor.com/USA/Politics/2011/0806/S-P-downgrade-of-US-credit-rating-sends-clear-message-to-Congress-shape-up).

CHAPTER 13

American Association of Poison Control Centers. 2011. "Synthetic Marijuana Data: Updated November 3, 2011." Retrieved November 22, 2011 (http://www.aapcc.org/dnn/Portals/0/Synthetic%20Marijuana%20Data%20for%20Website%2011.03.2011.pdf).

Paynter, Ben. 2011. "The Big Business of Synthetic Highs." *Bloomberg Businessweek*. Retrieved November 22, 2011 (http://www.businessweek.com/print/magazine/content/11_26/b4234058348635.htm).

Roan, Shari. 2011. "Synthetic Marijuana Linked to Heart Attacks in Teens." *Los Angeles Times*. Retrieved November 22, 2011 (http://www.latimes.com/health/boostershots/la-heb-marijuana-heart-attacks-20111108,0,2439807.story).

CHAPTER 14

Coleman, Jasmine. 2011. "World's 'Seven Billionth Baby' Is Born." *The Guardian*. Retrieved November 17, 2011 (http://www.guardian.co.uk/world/2011/oct/31/seven-billionth-baby-born-philippines).

Development Data Group. 2011. "World Development Indicators." Washington, DC: World Bank. Retrieved November 17, 2011 (http://data.worldbank.org/data-catalog/world-development-indicators?cid=GPD_WDI).

McQueeney, Kerry. 2011. "Welcome to a Very Full World, Danica: Was This the World's Seven Billionth Baby?" *The Daily Mail Online*. Retrieved November 17, 2011 (http://www.dailymail.co.uk/news/article-2055419/Danica-Camacho-Seven-billionth-baby-born-Philippines.html).

Newcomb, Alyssa. 2011. "7 Billion People: What Number Are You?" *ABC News*. Retrieved November 17, 2011 (http://abcnews.go.com/blogs/headlines/2011/10/7-billion-people-what-number-are-you/).

CHAPTER 15

Nir, Sarah Maslin. 2012. "Helping Hands Also Expose a New York Divide." *New York Times*, November 16.

Sorkin, Andrew Ross. 2012. "Occupy Wall Street: A Frenzy that Fizzled." *New York Times*, September 18.

REFERENCES
Comprehensive List

Abd-Allah, Umar F. 2005. "Mercy: The Stamp of Creation." A Nawawi Foundation Paper, p. 6. Retrieved March 28, 2012 (http://www.nawawi.org/downloads/article1.pdf).

Abella, Rudolfo. 2006. "An Analysis of the Academic Performance of Voucher Students in the Opportunity Scholarship Program." *Education and Urban Society* 38(40): 406–418.

Abrutyn, Seth. 2012. "Hinduism." Pp. 932–937 in *The Wiley-Blackwell Encyclopedia of Globalization*, edited by G. Ritzer. Malden, MA: Wiley-Blackwell.

Acemoglu, Daron, and James A. Robinson. 2012. *Why Nations Fail: The Origins of Power, Prosperity, and Poverty*. New York: Crown Business.

Acemoglu, Daron and Pierre Yared. 2010. "Political Limits to Globalization." Working Paper 15694. Retrieved March 28, 2012 (http://www.nber.org/papers/w15694).

Acierno, Ron, Melba A. Hernandez, Ananda B. Amstadter, Heidi S. Resnick, Kenneth Steve, Wendy Muzzy, and Dean G. Kilpatrick. 2010. "Prevalence and Correlates of Emotional, Physical, Sexual, and Financial Abuse and Potential Neglect in the United States: The National Elder Mistreatment Study." *American Journal of Public Health* 100: 292–297.

Acker, Joan. 1990. "Hierarchies, Jobs, and Bodies: A Theory of Gendered Organizations." *Gender and Society* 4(2): 139–158.

Acker, Joan. 2004. "Gender, Capitalism and Globalization." *Critical Sociology* 30(1): 17–41.

Acker, Joan. 2009. "From Glass Ceiling to Inequality Regimes." *Sociologie du Travail* 51(2): 199–217.

Adams, Josh. 2009. "Bodies of Change: A Comparative Analysis of Media Representations of Body Modification Practices." *Sociological Perspectives* 52: 103–129.

Adams, Ann, Christopher D. Buckingham, Antje Lindenmeyer, John B. McKinlay, Carol Link, Lisa Marceau, and Sara Arber. 2008. "The Influence of Patient and Doctor Gender on Diagnosing Coronary Heart Disease." *Sociology of Health and Illness* 30(1): 1–18.

Adler, Patricia A. and Peter Adler. 2011. *The Tender Cut: Inside the Hidden World of Self-Injury*. New York: New York University Press.

Adler, Patricia A. and Peter Adler. 2012. "Tales from the Field: Reflections on Four Decades of Ethnography." *Qualitative Sociology* 8: 10–32.

Adorno, Theodor and Max Horkheimer. 1997. *Dialectic of Enlightenment*. London: Verso.

Agnew, Robert. 1992. "Foundation for a General Strain Theory of Crime and Delinquency." *Criminology* 30: 47–88.

Agnew, Robert. 2001. "An Overview of General Strain Theory." Pp. 161–174 in *Explaining Criminals and Crime: Essays in Contemporary Criminological Theory,* edited by R. Paternoster and R. Bachman. Los Angeles: Roxbury.

Agrikoliansky, Eric. 2013. "Globalization and Movements." Pp. 528–531 in *The Wiley-Blackwell Encyclopedia of Social and Political Movements*, 3 vols., edited by D. A. Snow, D. Della Porta, B. Klandermans, and D. McAdam. Malden, MA: Wiley-Blackwell.

Aguirre, B. E., Manuel R. Torres, Kimberly B. Gill, and H. Lawrence Hotchkiss. 2011. "Normative Collective Behavior in the Station Building Fire." *Social Science Quarterly* 92: 100–118.

Ahemba, Tume. 2007. "Lagos Rejects Nigeria Census, Says Has 17.5 Million." *Reuters*, February 6. Retrieved February 28, 2012 (http://uk.reuters.com/article/2007/02/06/nigeria-lagos-idUKL0674057420070206).

Ahituv, Avner and Robert I. Lerman. 2007. "How Do Marital Status, Work Effort, and Wage Rates Interact?" *Demography* 44(3): 623–647

Ahuvia, Aaron and Elif Izberk-Bilgin. 2011. "Limits of the McDonaldization Thesis: EBayization and Ascendant Trends in Post-industrial Consumer Culture." *Consumption, Markets and Culture* 14: 361–364.

Ajrouch, Kristine A. 2007. "Reference Groups." Pp. 3828–3829 in *The Blackwell Encyclopedia of Sociology,* edited by G. Ritzer. Malden, MA: Blackwell.

Akers, Donald S. 1967. "On Measuring the Marriage Squeeze." *Demography* 4: 907–924.

Alatas, Farid. 2011. "Ibn Khaldun." Pp. 12–29 in *The Wiley-Blackwell Companion to Major Social Theorists: Volume 1. Classical Theorists*, edited by G. Ritzer and J. Stepnisky. Malden, MA: Wiley-Blackwell.

Alazraki, Melly. 2010. "Global Pharmaceutical Sales Expected to Rise to $880 Billion in 2011." *Daily Finance*. Retrieved January 25, 2012 (http://www.dailyfinance.com/2010/10/07/global-pharmaceutical-sales-expected-to-rise-to-880-billion-in/).

Alba, Richard. 2009. *Blurring the Color Line: The New Chance for a More Integrated America*. Cambridge, MA: Harvard University Press.

Albrow, Martin. 1996. *The Global Age*. Cambridge, UK: Polity Press.

Aleman, Ana M. and Katherine Link Wartman. 2008. *Online Social Networking on Campus: Understanding What Matters in Student Culture*. New York: Routledge.

Alexander, Bayarma, Dick Ettema, and Martin Dijst. 2010. "Fragmentation of Work Activity as a Multi-dimensional Construct and Its Association with ICT, Employment and Sociodemographic Characteristics." *Journal of Transport Geography* 18(1): 55–64.

Alexander, Douglas. 2010. "The Impact of the Economic Crisis on the World's Poorest Countries." *Global Policy* 1: 118–120.

Alexander, Jeffrey C. 2013. "Struggling over the Mode of Incorporation: Backlash against Multiculturalism in Europe." *Ethnic and Racial Studies*. doi:10.1080/01419870.2012.752515.

Alexander, Michelle. 2012. *The New Jim Crow: Mass Incarceration in the Age of Colorblindness*. New York: The New Press.

Ali, Ayann Hirsi. 2010. "Not the Child My Grandmother Wanted." *New York Times*, December 2. Retrieved May 28, 2012 (http://www.nytimes.com/2010/12/02/opinion/global/02iht-GA13ali.html?_r=2).

Ali, S. Harris. 2012. "Diseases, Borderless." Pp. 446–449 in *The Wiley-Blackwell Encyclopedia of Globalization,* edited by G. Ritzer. Malden, MA: Wiley-Blackwell.

Allan, Graham. 2007. "Family Structure." Pp. 1618–1621 in *The Blackwell Encyclopedia of Sociology*, edited by G. Ritzer. Malden, MA: Blackwell.

Allan, Stuart. 2007. "Network Society." Pp. 3180–3182 in *The Blackwell Encyclopedia of Sociology*, edited by G. Ritzer. Malden, MA: Blackwell.

Allen, I. Elaine and Jeff Seaman. 2010. *Learning on Demand: Online Education in the United States, 2009*. Needham, MA: Sloan Center for Online Education.

Allmendinger, Jutta. 2007. "Unemployment as a Social Problem." Pp. 5092–5096 in *The Blackwell Encyclopedia of Sociology*, edited by G. Ritzer. Malden, MA: Blackwell.

Alon, Sigal and Dafne Gelbgiser. 2011. *Social Science Research* 40(1): 107–119.

Alter Chen, Martha. 1995. "Engendering World Conference: The International Women's Movement and the United Nations." *Third World Quarterly* 16(3): 477–494.

Altman, Dennis. 1996. "Rupture or Continuity? The Internationalization of Gay Identities." *Social Text* 48.

Altman, Dennis. 2001. *Global Sex*. Chicago: University of Chicago Press.

Al-Tuwaijri, Sameera, Louis J. Currat, Sheila Davey, Andrés de Francisco, Abdul Ghaffar, Susan Jupp, and Christine Mauroux. 2003. *The 10/90 Report on Health Research 2003–2004*. Geneva: Global Forum for Health Research.

Alvarez, Lizette. 2006a. "A Growing Stream of Illegal Immigrants Choose to Remain Despite the Risks." *New York Times*, December 20.

Alvarez, Lizette. 2006b. "Fear and Hope in Immigrant's Furtive Existence." *New York Times*, December 20.

Alvarez, Lizette. 2011. "Pull of Family Reshapes U.S.-Cuban Relations." *New York Times*, November 22, pp. A1, A3.

Alvesson, Mats and Yvonne Due Billing. 2009. *Understanding Gender and Organizations*. 2nd ed. London: Sage.

Amato, Paul R. 2000. "The Consequences of Divorce for Adults and Children." *Journal of Marriage and Family* 62(4): 1269–1287.

Amato, Paul R. 2004. "Tension between Institutional and Individual Views of Marriage." *Journal of Marriage and the Family* 66: 959–965.

Amato, Paul. 2012. "Institutional, Companionate and Individualized Marriages: Change over Time and Implications for Marital Quality." Pp. 107–124 in *Marriage at the Crossroads: Law, Policy, and the Brave New World of Twenty-First-Century Families*, edited by M. Garrison and E. Scott. Cambridge, UK: Cambridge University Press.

Amato, Paul R., Alan Booth, David R. Johnson, and Stacy J. Rogers. 2007. *Alone Together: How Marriage in America Is Changing*. Cambridge, MA: Harvard University Press.

Amato, Paul R. and Spencer James. 2010. "Divorce in Europe and the United States: Commonalities and Differences across Nations." *Family Science* 1: 2–13.

America.gov. 2008. "U.S. Minorities Will Be the Majority by 2042, Census Bureau Says." *Archive*, August 15. Retrieved April 14, 2011 (http://www.america.gov/st/peopleplace-english/2008/August/20080815140005xlrennef0.1078106.html).

American Heart Association. 2010. "Heart and Stroke Update." Retrieved March 28, 2012 (http://www.americanheart.org/downloadable/heart/1265665152970DS-3241%20HeartStrokeUpdate_2010.pdf).

Amin, Ash, ed. 1994. *Post-Fordism*. Oxford: Blackwell.

Amnesty International. 2004. "Lives Blown Apart: Crimes against Women in Times of Conflict: Stop Violence against Women." Retrieved March 28, 2012 (http://www.amnesty.org/en/library/info/ACT77/075/2004/en).

Amnesty International. 2011. "Death Sentences and Executions, 2010." London: Author. Retrieved March 28, 2012 (http://www.amnesty.org/en/library/asset/ACT50/001/2011/en/ea1b6b25-a62a-4074-927d-ba51e88df2e9/act500012011en.pdf).

Amnesty International. 2012. *Death Sentences and Executions 2011*. London: Author.

Anais, Seantel and Sean P. Hier. 2012. "Risk Society and *Current Sociology*." *Current Sociology* 60: 1–3.

Anderson, Benedict. 1991. *Imagined Communities: Reflections on the Origin and Spread of Nationalism*. 2nd ed. London: Verso.

Anderson, Chris. 2009. *Free: The Future of a Radical Price*. New York: Hyperion.

Anderson, David M. and Carrier Neil. 2006. "'Flower of Paradise' or 'Polluting the Nation': Contested Narratives of Khat Consumption." Pp. 145–66 in *Consuming Cultures, Global Perspectives: Historical Trajectories, Transnational Exchanges*, edited by J. Brewer and F. Trentmann. Oxford: Berg.

Anderson, Elijah. 1999. *Code of the Street: Decency, Violence, and the Moral Life of the Inner City*. New York: Norton.

Anderson, Eric. 2005. "Orthodox and Inclusive Masculinity: Competing Masculinities among Heterosexual Men in a Feminized Terrain." *Sociological Perspectives* 48(3): 337–355.

Anderson, Sam. 2010. "The Human Shuffle." *New York Magazine*, February 5. Retrieved May 26, 2011 (http://nymag.com/news/media/63663/).

Andreas, Peter and Ethan Nadelmann. 2006. *Policing the Globe: Criminalization and Crime Control in International Relations*. New York: Oxford University Press.

Andrejevic, Mark. 2009. *Spy: Surveillance and Power in the Interactive Era*. Lawrence: University of Kansas Press.

Andrews, David L. and Ron L. Mower. 2012. "Spectres of Jordan." *Ethnic and Racial Studies* 35: 1059–1077.

Andrews, Geoff. 2008. *The Slow Food Story: Politics and Pleasure*. Montreal: McGill University Press.

Andrews, Judy A., Elizabeth Tildesley, Hyman Hops, and Fuzhong Z. Li. 2002. "The Influence of Peers on Young Adult Substance Use." *Health Psychology* 4: 349–357.

Andrews, Kenneth T. 2013. "Civil Rights Movement." Pp. 193–199 in *The Wiley-Blackwell Encyclopedia of Social and Political Movements*, 3 vols., edited by D. A. Snow, D. Della Porta, B. Klandermans, and D. McAdam. Malden, MA: Wiley-Blackwell.

Androff, David K. and Kyoko Y. Tavassoli. 2012. "Deaths in the Desert: The Human Rights Crisis on the U.S.–Mexico Border." *Social Work* 57: 165–173.

Anspach, Renee and Nissim Mizrachi. 2006. "The Field Worker's Fields: Ethics, Ethnography and Medical Sociology." *Sociology of Health and Illness* 28(6): 713–731.

Antonio, Robert. 2007. "The Cultural Construction of Neoliberal Globalization." Pp. 67–83 in *The Blackwell Companion to Globalization*, edited by G. Ritzer. Malden, MA: Blackwell.

Antonio, Robert J. 2011. "Karl Marx." Pp. 115–164 in *The Wiley-Blackwell Companion to Major Social Theorists: Volume 1. Classical Theorists*, edited by G. Ritzer and J. Stepnisky. Malden, MA: Wiley-Blackwell.

Antonio, Robert J. and Robert J. Brulle. 2012. "Ecological Problems." Pp. 476–484 in *The Wiley-Blackwell Companion to Sociology*, edited by G. Ritzer. Malden, MA: Wiley-Blackwell.

Apel, Robert S. and Daniel Nagin. 2011. "General Deterrence: A Review of Recent Literature." Pp. 411–436 in *Crime and Public Policy*, edited by J. Q. Wilson and J. Petersilia. Oxford: Oxford University Press.

Apesoa-Varano, Ester Carolina. 2007. "Educated Caring: The Emergence of Professional Identity among Nurses." *Qualitative Sociology* 30: 249–274.

Appadurai, Arjun. 1996. *Modernity at Large: Cultural Dimensions of Globalization*. Minneapolis: University of Minnesota Press.

Appelbaum, Steven H., Neveen Asham, and Kamal Argheyd. 2011a. "Is the Glass Ceiling Cracked in Information Technology? A Quantitative Analysis: Part 1." *Industrial and Commercial Training* 43(6): 354–361.

Appelbaum, Steven H., Neveen Asham, and Kamal Argheyd. 2011b. "Is the Glass Ceiling Cracked in Information Technology? A Quantitative Analysis: Part 2." *Industrial and Commercial Training* 43(7): 451–459.

Archibold, Randal C. 2009. "Mexican Drug Cartel Violence Spills Over, Alarming U.S." *New York Times*, March 22. Retrieved September 10, 2013 (http://www.nytimes.com/2009/03/23/us/23border.html?pagewanted=all).

Archibold, Randal C. 2010. "Ranchers Alarmed by Killing Near Border." *New York Times*, April 4.

Argiero, Sarah J., Jessica L. Dyrdahl. Sarah S. Fernandez, Laura E. Whitney, and Robert J. Woodring. 2010. "A Cultural Perspective for Understanding How Campus Environments Perpetuate Rape-Supportive Culture." *Journal of the Indiana University Student Personnel Association* 43: 26–40.

Aries, Phillipe. 1978. "La Famille et La Ville." *Esprit* 1: 3–12.

Aries, Philippe. 1980. "Two Successive Motivations for the Declining Birth Rates in the West." *Population and Development Review* 6(4): 645–650.

Armstrong, Elizabeth and Suzanna M. Crage. 2006. "Movements and Memory: The Making of the Stonewall Myth." *American Sociological Review* 71(5): 724–751.

Armstrong, Elizabeth A. and Suzanna M. Crage. 2013. "Stonewall Riots." Pp. 1251–1253 in *The Wiley-Blackwell Encyclopedia of Social and Political Movements*, 3 vols., edited by D. A. Snow, D. Della Porta, B. Klandermans, and D. McAdam. Malden, MA: Wiley-Blackwell.

Armstrong-Coben, Anne. 2009. "The Computer Will See You Now." *New York Times,* March 6.

Arnold, Tom. 2011. "Major Gain for Dubai Non-oil Trade." *The National*, May 19. Retrieved May 19, 2011 (www.thenational.ae/business/markets/major-gain-for-dubai-non-oil-trade).

Arnquist, Sarah. 2009. "Research Trove: Patients' Online Data." *New York Times*, August 25, p. D1.

Aronson, Jay D. and Simon A. Cole. 2009. "Science and the Death Penalty: DNA, Innocence, and the Debate over Capital Punishment in the United States." *Law and Social Inquiry* 34: 603–633.

Arriola, Elvia R. 2006–2007. "Accountability for Murder in the Maquiladoras: Linking Corporate Indifference to Gender Violence at the U.S.-Mexico Border." *Seattle Journal for Social Justice* 603(5).

Arthur, Mikaila Mariel Lemonik. 2007a. "Race." Pp. 3731–3734 in *The Blackwell Encyclopedia of Sociology*, edited by G. Ritzer. Malden, MA: Blackwell.

Arthur, Mikaila Mariel Lemonik. 2007b. "Racism, Structural and Institutional." Pp. 3765–3767 in *The Blackwell Encyclopedia of Sociology*, edited by G. Ritzer. Malden, MA: Blackwell.

Arthur, Mikaila Mariel Lemonik. 2013. "Emergent Norm Theory." Pp. 397–399 in *The Wiley-Blackwell Encyclopedia of Social and Political Movements*, 3 vols., edited by D. A. Snow, D. Della Porta, B. Klandermans, and D. McAdam. Malden, MA: Wiley-Blackwell.

Arvidsson, Adam. 2012. "Brands." Pp. 135–38 in *The Wiley-Blackwell Encyclopedia of Globalization,* edited by G. Ritzer. Malden, MA: Wiley-Blackwell.

Asch, Solomon Eliot. 1952. *Social Psychology*. New York: Prentice-Hall.

Ashmore, Richard, Lee Jussim, and David Wilder. 2001. *Social Identity, Intergroup Conflict, and Conflict Resolution*. Oxford, UK: Oxford University Press.

Atkinson, Michael. 2003. *Tattooed: The Sociogenesis of a Body Art*. Toronto, ON: University of Toronto Press.

Atkinson, Rowland and Sarah Blandy. 2005. "Introduction: International Perspectives on the New Enclavism and the Rise of Gated Communities." *Housing Studies* 20: 177–186.

Aud, Susan and Gretchen Hannes, eds. 2011. *The Condition of Education 2011 in Brief* (NCES 2011-034). Washington, DC: U.S. Department of Education, National Center for Education Statistics.

Australian Government. 2011. "Trends in Migration: Australia 2010–11." Department of Immigration and Citizenship. Retrieved February 28, 2012 (http://www.immi.gov.au/media/publications/statistics/trends-in-migration/trends-in-migration-2010-11.pdf).

Auyero, Javier and Timothy Patrick Moran. 2007. "The Dynamics of Collective Violence: Dissecting Food Riots in Contemporary Argentina." *Social Forces* 85(3): 1341–1367.

Avishai, Orit. 2007. "Managing the Lactating Body: The Breast-Feeding Project and the Privileged Mother." *Qualitative Sociology* 30: 135–142.

Ayanian, John Z. and Arnold M. Epstein. 1991. "Differences in the Use of Procedures between Men and Women Hospitalized for Coronary Heart Disease." *The New England Journal of Medicine* 325(1): 221–225.

Ayres, Tammy C. and James Treadwell. 2012. "Bars, Drugs and Football Thugs: Alcohol, Cocaine Use and Violence in the Night Time Economy among English Football Firms." *Criminology and Criminal Justice* 12: 83–100.

Babb, Sarah. 2005. "The Social Consequences of Structural Adjustment: Recent Evidence and Current Debates." *Annual Review of Sociology* 31: 199–222.

Babones, Salvatore. 2007. "Studying Globalization: Methodological Issues." Pp. 144–161 in *The Blackwell Companion to Globalization,* edited by G. Ritzer. Malden, MA: Blackwell.

Bach, Stephen. 2003. *International Migration of Health Workers: Labour and Social Issues* (Working Paper No. 209). Geneva: International Labour Office.

Baehr, Peter. 2001. "The 'Iron Cage' and the 'Shell as Hard as Steel': Parsons, Weber, and the Stahlhartes Gehäuse Metaphor in the Protestant Ethic and the Spirit of Capitalism." *History and Theory* 40(2): 153–169.

Baehr, Peter and Daniel Gordon. 2012. "Unmasking and Disclosure as Sociological practices: Contrasting Modes for Understanding Religious and Other Beliefs." *Journal of Sociology* 48: 380–396.

Bair, Jennifer and Gary Gereffi. 2003. "Upgrading, Uneven Development, and Jobs in the North American Apparel Industry." *Global Networks* 3(2): 143–169.

Bajaj, Vikas. 2011. "Philippines Replaces India as Companies Seek American English." *New York Times*, November 26, pp. B1, B4.

Baker, Carolyn. 1997. "Ethnomethodological Studies of Talk in Educational Settings." Pp. 43–52 in *Encyclopedia of Language and Education: Volume 3. Oral Discourse and Education,* edited by B. Davies and D. Corson. Netherlands: Kluwer.

Baker, Peter. 2010. "Book Says Afghanistan Divided White House." *New York Times*, September 22, p. A12.

Bales, Kevin. 1999. *Disposable People: New Slavery in the Economy*. Berkeley: University of California Press.

Bancroft, Angus. 2005. *Roma and Gypsy-Travellers in Europe: Modernity, Race, Space, and Exclusion*. Burlington, VT: Ashgate.

Bancroft, Kim. 2009. "To Have and to Have Not: The Socioeconomics of Charter Schools." *Education and Urban Society* 41(2): 248–279.

Bandura, Albert, Claudio Barbaranelli, Gian Vittorio Caprara, and Concetta Pastorelli. 1996. "Mechanisms of Moral Disengagement in the Exercise of Moral Agency." *Journal of Personality and Social Psychology* 71: 364–374.

Banks, Russell. 2011. *Lost Memory of Skin*. New York: HarperCollins.

Bannon, Lisa and Bob Davis. 2009. "Spendthrift to Penny Pincher: A Vision of the New Consumer." *Wall Street Journal*, December 17, pp. A1, A24.

Bar, Stephen J., Chao-Chin Lu, and Jonathan H. Westover. 2007. "Divorce." Pp. 1206–1210 in *The Blackwell Encyclopedia of Sociology,* edited by G. Ritzer. Malden, MA: Blackwell.

Baran, Paul A. and Paul M. Sweezy. 1966. *Monopoly Capital: An Essay on American Economic and Social Order*. New York: Modern Reader Paperbacks.

Barber, Benjamin R. 1995. *Jihad vs. McWorld*. New York: Times Books.

Barber, Benjamin R. 2007. *Consumed: How Markets Corrupt Children, Infantilize Adults, and Swallow Citizens Whole*. New York: MTM Publishing.

Barboza, David. 2008. "China Surpasses U.S. in Number of Internet Users." *New York Times,* July 26. Retrieved May 23, 2011 (http://www.nytimes.com/2008/07/26/business/worldbusiness/26internet.html).

Barboza, David. 2010. "China Passes Japan as Second-Largest Economy." *New York Times*, August 15. Retrieved May 29, 2011 (http://www.nytimes.com/2010/08/16/business/global/16yuan.html).

Barkan, Elliott R., Hasia Diner, and Alan M. Kraut, eds. 2008. *From Arrival to Incorporation: Migrants to the US in a Global Era*. New York: New York University Press.

Barker, Eileen. 2007. "New Religious Movements." Pp. 3201–3206 in *The Blackwell Encyclopedia of Sociology*, edited by G. Ritzer. Malden, MA: Blackwell.

Barnes, Brooks. 2010. "Disney Selling Film Tickets on Facebook." *New York Times*, June 2, pp. B1, B4.

Barnhurst, Kevin G. and Ellen Wartella. 1998. "Young Citizens, American TV Newscasts and the Collective Memory." *Critical Studies in Mass Communication* 15(3): 279–305.

Barr, Rebecca and Robert Dreeben. 1983. *How Schools Work*. Chicago: University of Chicago Press.

Barron, James. 1995. "A Church's Chief Executive Seeks the Target Audience." *New York Times,* April 18, p. A20.

Barstow, David. 2010. "Tea Party Lights Fuse for Rebellion on the Right." *New York Times,* February 16.

Bartky, Sandra. 1990. *Femininity and Domination.* New York: Routledge.

Basu, Amrita, ed. 1995. *The Challenge of Local Feminisms: Women's Movements in Global Perspective.* Boulder, CO: Westview Press.

Basu, Amrita, ed. 2010. *Women's Movements in the Global Era: The Power of Local Feminisms.* Westview Press.

Baudrillard, Jean. [1968] 1996. *The System of Objects.* London: Verso Books.

Baudrillard, Jean. [1970] 1998. *The Consumer Society.* London: Sage.

Baudrillard, Jean. [1976] 1993. *Symbolic Exchange and Death.* London: Sage.

Baudrillard, Jean. [1983] 1990. *Fatal Strategies.* New York: Semiotext(e).

Baudrillard, Jean. [1991] 1995. *The Gulf War Did Not Take Place.* Bloomington: Indiana University Press.

Bauer, Robin. 2008. "Transgressive and Transformative Gendered Sexual Practices and White Privileges: The Case of the Dyke/Trans BDSM Communities." *Women's Studies Quarterly* 36(3–4): 233–253.

Bauman, Zygmunt. 1989. *Modernity and the Holocaust.* Ithaca, NY: Cornell University Press.

Bauman, Zygmunt. 1992. *Intimations of Postmodernity.* London: Routledge.

Bauman, Zygmunt. 1997. *Postmodernity and Its Discontents.* Cambridge, UK: Polity Press.

Bauman, Zygmunt. 1998. *Globalization: The Human Consequences.* New York: Columbia University Press.

Bauman, Zygmunt. 1999. "The Self in Consumer Society." *Hedgehog Review* Fall: 35–40.

Bauman, Zygmunt. 2000. *Liquid Modernity.* Cambridge, UK: Polity Press.

Bauman, Zygmunt. 2003. *Liquid Love.* Cambridge, UK: Polity Press.

Bauman, Zygmunt. 2005. *Liquid Life.* Cambridge, UK: Polity Press.

Bauman, Zygmunt. 2006. *Liquid Fear.* Cambridge, UK: Polity Press.

Bauman, Zygmunt. 2007. *Liquid Times: Living in an Age of Uncertainty.* Cambridge: Polity.

Bauman, Zygmunt and David Lyon. 2012. *Liquid Surveillance: A Conversation.* London: Polity.

Baumer, Eric P. and Janet L. Lauritsen. 2010. "Reporting Crime to the Police, 1973–2005: A Multivariate Analysis of Long-Term Trends in the National Crime Survey (NCS) and National Crime Victimization Survey (NCVS)." *Criminology* 48(1): 131–185.

Bay, Ann-Helen. and Morten Blekesaune. 2002. "Youth, Unemployment and Political Marginalisation." *International Journal of Social Welfare* 11(2): 132–139.

Baym, Nancy. 2010. *Personal Connections in the Digital Age.* Cambridge, UK: Polity Press.

Beaglehole, Robert, Alec Irwin, and Thomson Prentice. 2003. *World Health Report: Shaping the Future.* Geneva: World Health Organization.

Beauvoir, Simone de. [1949] 1957. *The Second Sex.* New York: Vintage.

Beauvoir, Simone de. 1952. *The Second Sex,* translated by H. M. Parshley. New York: Vintage.

Beauvoir, Simone de. 1973. *The Second Sex.* New York: Vintage.

Beauvoir, Simone de. [1980] 1989. *The Second Sex.* New York: Vintage.

Beccaria, Cesare. [1764] 1986. *On Crimes and Punishments.* Indianapolis, IN: Hackett.

Beck, Colin and Emily Minor. "Who Gets Designated a Terrorist and Why?" *Social Forces* 91, 2013: 837-872.

Beck, Ulrich. [1986] 1992. *Risk Society: Towards a New Modernity.* London: Sage.

Beck, Ulrich. 2007. "Cosmopolitanism: A Critical Theory for the Twenty-First Century." Pp. 162–176 in *The Blackwell Companion to Globalization,* edited by G. Ritzer. Malden, MA: Blackwell.

Beck, Ulrich and Elisabeth Beck-Gernsheim. 1995. *The Normal Chaos of Love.* Cambridge, UK: Polity Press.

Beck, Ulrich and Elisabeth Beck-Gernsheim. 2002. *Individualization: Institutionalized Individualism and its Social and Political Consequences.* London: Sage.

Beck, Ulrich and Elisabeth Beck-Gernsheim. 2012. "Families." Pp. 637–639 in *The Wiley-Blackwell Encyclopedia of Globalization,* edited by G. Ritzer. Malden, MA: Wiley-Blackwell.

Becker, Gary S. 1992. "Human Capital and the Economy." *Proceedings of the American Philosophical Society* 136(1): 85–92.

Becker, Howard. 1953. "Becoming a Marihuana User." *American Journal of Sociology* 59(3): 232–242.

Becker, Howard S. 1963. *Outsiders: Studies in the Sociology of Deviance.* New York: Free Press.

Becker, Howard and Blanche Geer. 1958. "The Fate of Idealism in Medical School." *American Sociological Review* 23: 50–56.

Becker, Howard, Blanche Geer, Everett Hughes, and Anselm Strauss. 1961. *Boys in White: Student Culture in Medical School.* Chicago: University of Chicago Press.

Becker, Penny Edgell and Phyllis Moen. 1999. "Scaling Back: Dual Earner Couples' Work-Family Strategies." *Journal of Marriage and Family* 61: 995–1007.

Beer, David and Roger Burrows. 2007. "Sociology and, of and in Web 2.0: Some Initial Considerations." *Sociological Research Online* 12(5). Retrieved March 29, 2012 (socresonline.org.uk/12/5/17.html).

Beer, Todd. 2012. "Global Warming." Pp. 841–844 in *The Wiley-Blackwell Companion to Sociology,* edited by G. Ritzer. Malden, MA: Wiley-Blackwell.

Beilharz, Peter. 2012. "Liquidity." Pp. 1299–1230 in *Wiley-Blackwell Encyclopedia of Globalization,* edited by G. Ritzer. Malden, MA: Wiley-Blackwell.

Belk, Russell W. 1987. "A Child's Christmas in America: Santa Claus as Deity, Consumption as Religion." *Journal of American Culture* 10(1): 87–100.

Belk, Russell W. 2007. "Consumption, Mass Consumption, and Consumer Culture." Pp. 737–746 in *The Blackwell Encyclopedia of Sociology,* edited by G. Ritzer. Malden, MA: Blackwell.

Bell, Daniel. 1973. *The Coming of Post-industrial Society: A Venture in Social Forecasting.* New York: Basic Books.

Bell, David. 2007. "Sexualities, Cities and." Pp. 4254–4256 in *The Blackwell Encyclopedia of Sociology,* edited by G. Ritzer. Malden, MA: Blackwell.

Bell, Kerryn. 2009. "Gender and Gangs: A Quantitative Comparison." *Crime and Delinquency* 55: 363–387.

Bell, Robert R. 1971. *Social Deviance: A Substantive Analysis.* Homewood, IL: Dorsey.

Bell, Sheri. 2011. "Through a Foucauldian Lens: A Genealogy of Child Abuse." *Journal of Family Violence* 26: 101–108.

Bellah, Robert N. 1967. "Civil Religion in America." *Daedalus,* Winter.

Bellah, Robert N. 1975. *The Broken Covenant: American Civil Religion in Time of Trial.* New York: Seabury.

Bellah, Robert N. 1985. *Habits of the Heart: Individualism and Commitment in American Life.* Berkeley: University of California Press.

Bellah, Robert N. 2011. *Religion in Human Evolution: From the Paleolithic to the Axial Age.* Cambridge, MA: Harvard University Press.

Bendix, Reinhard and Seymour Martin Lipset, eds. 1966. *Class, Status and Power.* 2nd rev. ed. Glencoe, IL: Free Press.

Benjamin, Walter. 1999. *The Arcades Project.* Cambridge, MA: Belknap.

Bennett, Tony, Mike Savage, Elizabeth Silva, Alan Warde, Modesto Gayo-Cal, and David Wright. 2009. *Culture, Class, Distinction.* London: Routledge.

Bennett, M. Daniel and Mark W. Fraser. 2000. "Urban Violence among African American Males: Integrating Family, Neighborhood, and Peer Perspectives." *Journal of Sociology and Social Welfare* 27: 93–117.

Bennett, Isabella. 2011. "Media Censorship in China." Council on Foreign Relations. Retrieved May 23, 2011 (http://www.cfr.org/china/media-censorship-china/p11515).

Bennhold, Katrin. 2008. "A Veil Closes France's Door to Citizenship." *New York Times,* July 19, pp. A1, A2.

Bennhold, Katrin and Stephen Castle. 2010. "E.U. Calls France's Roma Expulsions a 'Disgrace.'" *New York Times,* September 14.

Benoit, Cecilia, Rachel Westfall, Adrienne E. B. Treloar, Rachel Phillips, and S. Mikael Jansson. 2007. "Social Factors Linked to Postpartum Depression: A Mixed-Methods Longitudinal Study." *Journal of Mental Health* 16: 719–730.

Ben-Yehuda, Nachman. 1980. "The European Witch Craze of the 14th to 17th Centuries: A Sociologist's Perspective." *American Journal of Sociology* 86(1): 1–31.

Ben-Yehuda, Nachman. 1985. *Deviance and Moral Boundaries.* Chicago: University of Chicago Press.

Ben-Yehuda, Nachman. 2012. "Deviance: A Sociology of Unconventionalities." Pp. 197–211 in *The Wiley-Blackwell Companion to Sociology,* edited by G. Ritzer. Malden, MA: Wiley-Blackwell.

Berard, Tim J. 2007. "Deviant Subcultures." Pp. 4872–4877 in *The Blackwell Encyclopedia of Sociology,* edited by G. Ritzer. Malden, MA: Blackwell.

Berends, Mark, Ellen Goldring, Marc Stein, and Xiu Cravens. 2010. "Instructional Conditions in Charter Schools and Students' Mathematics Achievement Gains." *American Journal of Education* 116: 123–156.

Berger, Peter. 1963. *Invitation to Sociology.* New York: Doubleday.

Berger, Peter. 1969. *The Sacred Canopy: Elements of a Sociological Theory of Religion.* New York: Doubleday.

Berger, Peter L. and Thomas Luckmann. 1967. *The Social Construction of Reality: A Treatise in the Sociology of Knowledge.* New York: Anchor Books.

Berger, Ronald. 2012. *The Holocaust, Religion, and the Politics of Collective Memory: Beyond Sociology.* New Brunswick, NJ: Transaction Publishers.

Bergquist, Magnus. 2003. "Open-Source Software Development as Gift Culture: Work and Identity Formation in an Internet Community." In *New Technologies at Work: People, Screens, and Social Virtuality,* edited by C. Garsten and H. Wulff. New York: Berg.

Berkovitch, Nitza. 1999. *From Motherhood to Citizenship: Women's Rights and International Organizations.* Baltimore: Johns Hopkins Press.

Berkovitch, Nitza. 2012. "Women's Movement(s), Transnational." Pp. 2233–2242 in *The Wiley-Blackwell Encyclopedia of Globalization,* edited by G. Ritzer. Malden, MA: Wiley-Blackwell.

Bernard, Jessie. 1972. *The Future of Marriage.* 2nd ed. New Haven, CT: Yale University Press.

Bernhardt, Annette, Martina Morris, Mark S. Handcock, and Marc A. Scott. 2001. *Divergent Paths: Economic Mobility in the New American Labor Market.* New York: Russell Sage Foundation.

Berton, Justin. 2007. "Continent-Size Toxic Stew of Plastic Trash Fouling Swath of Pacific Ocean." *San Francisco Chronicle,* October 19. Retrieved May 25, 2011 (http://www.sfgate.com/cgi-bin/article.cgi?f=/c/a/2007/10/19/SS6JS8RH0.DTL).

Bertrand, Marianne and Sendhil Mullainathan. 2004. "Are Emily and Greg More Employable than Lakisha and Jamal? A Field Experiment on Labor Market Discrimination." *The American Economic Review* 94(4): 991–1013.

Best, Amy L. 2007. "Consumption, Girls' Culture and." Pp. 724–727 in *The Blackwell Encyclopedia of Sociology,* edited by G. Ritzer. Malden, MA: Blackwell.

Bestor, Theodore C. 2005. "How Sushi Went Global." Pp. 13–20 in *The Cultural Politics of Food and Eating: A Reader,* edited by J. L. Watson and M. L. Caldwell. Malden, MA: Blackwell.

Betancur, John. 2011. "Gentrification and Community Fabric in Chicago." *Urban Studies* 48: 383–406.

Betegeri, Aarti. 2011. "Cricket World Cup Final: You May Not Care, But India Sure Does." *Christian Science Monitor,* March 29. Retrieved March 29, 2012 (http://www.csmonitor.com/World/Global-News/2011/0329/Cricket-World-Cup-final-You-may-not-care-but-India-sure-does).

Bettie, Julie. 2003. *Women Without Class: Girls, Race, and Identity.* Berkeley: University of California Press.

Beyer, Peter. 2006. *Religion and Globalization.* London: Sage.

Beynon, Huw and Theo Nichol, eds. 2006. *The Fordism of Ford and Modern Management: Fordism and Post-Fordism.* Cheltenham, UK: Elgar.

Bhambra, Gurminder K. 2007a. *Rethinking Modernity: Postcolonialism and the Sociological Imagination.* Houndsmills, UK: Palgrave Macmillan.

Bhambra, Gurminder K. 2007b. "Sociology and Postcolonialism: Another 'Missing' Revolution?" *Sociology* 41: 871–884.

Bhanoo, Sindya N. 2010. "Denmark Leads the Way in Digital Care." *New York Times,* January 12, p. D5.

Bhatnagar, Rashmi, Renu Dube, and Reena Dube. 2006. *Female Infanticide in India: A Feminist Cultural History.* New York: SUNY Press.

Bhatty, Ayesha. 2010. "Haiti Devastation Exposes Shoddy Construction." BBC News. Retrieved March 31, 2012 (http://news.bbc.co.uk/2/hi/8460042.stm).

Bhaumik, Subir. 2010. "India to Deploy 36,000 Extra Troops on Chinese Border." BBC News. Retrieved May 26, 2011 (http://www.bbc.co.uk/news/world-south-asia-11818840).

Bian, Yanjie. 1997. "Bringing Strong Ties Back In: Indirect Ties, Network Bridges, and Job Searches in China." *American Sociological Review* 62: 366–385.

Bianchi, Stefania. 2010. "Leak at Dubai Mall Aquarium Forces Evacuation." *Wall Street Journal,* March 1. Retrieved May 19, 2011 (http://online.wsj.com/article/SB10001424052748704479404575087122447511764.htm).

Bianchi, Suzanne and Melissa Milkie. 2010. "Work and Family Research in the First Decade of the 21st Century." *Journal of Marriage and Family* 72: 705–725.

Bianchi, Suzanne M., John R. Robinson, and Melissa A. Milkie. 2006. *Changing Rhythms of American Family Life.* New York: Russell Sage Foundation.

Bianchi, Suzanne M. and Vanessa Wight. 2012. "Population." Pp. 470–487 in *The Wiley-Blackwell Companion to Sociology,* edited by G. Ritzer. Malden, MA: Wiley-Blackwell.

Biblarz, Timothy J. and Judith Stacey. 2010. "How Does the Gender of Parents Matter?" *Journal of Marriage and Family* 72(1): 3–22.

Bihagen, Erik. 2007. "Class Origin Effects on Downward Career Mobility in Sweden 1982–2001." *Acta Sociologica* 50(4): 415–430.

Bilefsky, Dan. 2010. "Dark Film on Teenagers Echoes From Mall to Church." *New York Times,* March 4, p. A8.

Bills, David. 2007. "Educational Attainment." Pp. 1333–1336 in *The Blackwell Encyclopedia of Sociology,* edited by G. Ritzer. Malden, MA: Blackwell.

Binkley, Sam. 2007. "Counterculture." Pp. 809–810 in *The Blackwell Encyclopedia of Sociology,* edited by G. Ritzer. Malden, MA: Blackwell.

Binnie, Jon. 2004. *The Globalization of Sexuality.* London: Sage.

Bishop, Ryan. 2006. "The Global University." *Theory, Culture and Society* 23: 563–566.

Black, Amy E. and Jamie L. Allen. 2001. "Tracing the Legacy of Anita Hill: The Thomas/Hill Hearings and Media Coverage of Sexual Harassment." *Gender Issues* 19(1): 33–52.

Blackburn, George L. and W. Allan Walker. 2005. "Science-Based Solutions to Obesity: What Are the Roles of Academia, Government, Industry, and Health Care?" *The American Journal of Clinical Nutrition* 82(1): 207–210.

Blackman, Shane. 2007. "'Hidden Ethnography': Crossing Emotional Borders in Accounts of Young People's Lives." *Sociology* 41: 699–716.

Blair-Loy, Mary. 2003. *Competing Devotions.* Cambridge, MA: Harvard University Press.

Blakely, Edward J. and Mary G. Snyder. 1997. *Fortress America: Gated Communities in the United States.* Washington DC: Brookings Institution Press.

Blaschke, Steffen, Dennis Schoeneborn, and David Seidl. 2012. "Organizations as Networks of Communication Episodes: Turning the Network Perspective Inside Out." *Organization Studies* 33: 879–906

Blatt, Jessica. 2007. "Scientific Racism." Pp. 4113–4115 in *The Blackwell Encyclopedia of Sociology,* edited by G. Ritzer. Malden, MA: Blackwell.

Blau, Peter. 1963. *The Dynamics of Bureaucracy.* Chicago: University of Chicago Press.

Blau, Peter. 1964. *Exchange and Power in Social Life.* New York: Wiley.

Blau, Peter and Otis D. Duncan. 1967. *The American Occupational Structure.* New York: Wiley.

Blauner, Robert. 1964. *Alienation and Freedom: The Factory Worker and His Industry.* Chicago: University of Chicago Press.

Blee, Kathleen. 2002. *Inside Organized Racism.* Berkeley: University of California Press.

Blee, Kathleen M. 2007. "Racist Movement." Pp. 3767–3771 in *The Blackwell Encyclopedia of Sociology,* edited by G. Ritzer. Malden, MA: Blackwell.

Blight, James G. and Janet M. Lang. 2005. *The Fog of War: Lessons from the Life of Robert S. McNamara.* Lanham, MD: Rowman and Littlefield.

Bloom, Harold. 1992. *The American Religion: The Emergence of a Post-Christian Nation.* New York: Simon and Schuster.

Bluestone, Barry and Bennett Harrison. 1984. *The Deindustrialization of America: Plant Closings, Community Abandonment, and the Dismantling of Basic Industry.* New York: Basic Books.

Blum, Linda. 2000. *At the Breast: Ideologies of Breastfeeding and Motherhood in the Contemporary United States.* Boston: Beacon Press.

Blum, Susan. 2009. *My Word! Plagiarism and College Culture.* Ithaca, NY: Cornell University Press.

Blumenberg, Werner. 2008. *Karl Marx: An Illustrated Biography.* New York: Verso.

Boas, Morten. 2012. "Failed States." Pp. 633–635 in *The Wiley-Blackwell Encyclopedia of Globalization,* edited by G. Ritzer. Malden, MA: Wiley-Blackwell.

Bocian, Debbie Gruenstein, Wei Li, and Keith S. Ernst. 2010. *Foreclosures by Race and Ethnicity: The Demographics of a Crisis.* Durham, NC: Center for Responsible Lending.

Bodinger-deUriarte, Cristina. 1992. *Hate Crime Sourcebook for Schools.* Philadelphia: RBS.

Boehlin, W. 1992. "Street Corner Society: Cornerville Revisited." *Journal of Contemporary Ethnography* 21: 11–51.

Bogdanich, Walt. 2007. "Free Trade Zones Ease Passage of Counterfeit Drugs to US." *New York Times,* December 17.

Bogle, Kathleen. 2008. *Hooking Up: Sex, Dating, and Relationships on Campus.* New York: New York University Press.

Bolton, Kenneth and Joe Feagin. 2004. *Black in Blue: African American Police Officers and Racism.* New York: Routledge.

Bonanno, Alessandro. 2012. "Fordism Post Fordism." Pp. 680–682 in *The Wiley-Blackwell Encyclopedia of Globalization,* edited by G. Ritzer. Malden, MA: Wiley-Blackwell.

Bond, Matthew. 2012. "The Bases of Elite Social Behaviour: Patterns of Club Affiliation among Members of the House of Lords." *Sociology* 46: 613–632.

Bonilla-Silva, Eduardo. 1997. "Rethinking Racism: Toward a Structural Interpretation." *American Sociological Review* 62: 465–480.

Bonilla-Silva, Eduardo. 2009. *Racism without Racists: Color-Blind Racism and the Persistence of Racial Inequality in the United States.* Lanham, MD: Rowman and Littlefield.

Bontje, Marco and Joachim Burdack. 2011. "Edge Cities, European-Style: Examples from Paris and the Randstad." *Urban Studies* 48: 2591–2610.

Booth, William. 2012. "In Mexico's Murder City, the War Appears Over." *Washington Post.* Retrieved March 12, 2013 (www.articles.washingtonpost/2012-08-20/world/3549288-1).

Bordo, Susan. 1993. *Unbearable Weight: Feminism, Western Culture, and the Body.* Berkeley: University of California Press.

Bose, Christine E. and Edna Acosta-Belen, eds. 1995. *Women in the Latin American Development Process.* Philadelphia: Temple University Press.

Bosick, Stacey. 2009. "Operationalizing Crime over the Life Course." *Crime and Delinquency* 55: 472–496.

Boswell, A. Ayres and Joan Z. Spade. 1996. "Fraternities and Collegiate Rape Culture: Why Are Some Fraternities More Dangerous Places for Women?" *Gender and Society* 10(2): 133–147.

Botz-Bornstein, Thorsten. 2012. "From the Stigmatized Tattoo to the Graffitied Body: Femininity in the Tattoo Renaissance." *Gender, Place and Culture: A Journal of Feminist Geography* 20(2): 236–252.

Bourdieu, Pierre. 1984. *Distinction: A Social Critique of the Judgment of Taste.* Cambridge, MA: Harvard University Press.

Bourdieu, Pierre. 1992. *The Logic of Practice.* Palo Alto, CA: Stanford University Press.

Bourdieu, Pierre and Jean-Claude Passeron. [1970] 1990. *Reproduction in Education, Society and Culture.* London: Sage.

Bourdieu, Pierre and Jean-Claude Passeron. 1977. *Reproduction: In Education, Society, and Culture.* Beverly Hills, CA: Sage.

Bourgeois, Phillippe. 2003. *In Search of Respect: Selling Crack in El Barrio.* Cambridge, UK: Cambridge University Press.

Boushey, Heather. 2008. "Motherhood Penalty and Women's Earnings, Opting out? The Effect of Children on Women's Employment in the United States." *Feminist Economics* 14(1): 1–36.

Bowen, Ted Smalley. 2001. "English Could Snowball on Net." *Technology Research News,* November 21. Retrieved January 3, 2012 (http://www.trnmag.com/Stories/2001/112101/English_could_snowball_on_Net_112101.html).

Bowles Samuel and Herbert Gintis. 1976. *Schooling in Capitalist America: Educational Reform and the Contradictions of Economic Life.* New York: Basic Books.

Bowling, Ben and James W. E. Sheptycki. 2012. *Global Policing.* London: Sage.

Bowman, John R. and Alyson Cole. 2009. "Do Working Mothers Oppress Other Women? The Swedish 'Maid Debate' and the Welfare State Politics of Gender Equality." *Signs* 35(1): 157–184.

boyd, danah. 2010. "White Flight in Networked Publics? How Race and Class Shaped American Teen Engagement With MySpace and Facebook." In *Digital Race Anthology,* edited by L. Nakamura and P. Chow-White. New York: Routledge.

Boykoff, Jules and Eulalie Laschever. 2011. "The Tea Party Movement, Framing, and the U.S. Media." *Social Movement Studies* 10: 341–366.

Brady, David and Denise Kall. 2008. "Nearly Universal, but Somewhat Distinct: The Feminization of Poverty in Affluent Western Democracies, 1969–2000." *Social Science Research* 37(3): 976–1007.

Braga, Anthony A. and David L. Weisburd. 2011. "The Effects of Focused Deterrence Strategies on Crime: A Systematic Review and Meta-Analysis of the Empirical Evidence." *Journal of Research in Crime and Delinquency.* Retrieved March 29, 2012 (http://jrc.sagepub.com/content/early/2011/09/08/0022427811419368.abstract).

Braithwaite, John. 1997. "Conferencing and Plurality—Reply to Blagg." *British Journal of Criminology* 37:502–506.

Braithwaite, John. 2010. "Diagnostics of White-Collar Crime Prevention." *Criminology and Public Policy* 9: 621–626.

Branch, John. 2013. "The X Games, Driven by Risk, Have First Death." *New York Times,* January 31.

Brandle, Gaspar and J. Michael Ryan. 2012. "Consumption." Pp. 289–295 in *The Encyclopedia of Globalization,* edited by G. Ritzer. Malden, MA: Wiley-Blackwell.

Branisa, Boris, Stephan Klasen, and Maria Ziegler. 2009. "New Measures of Gender Inequality: The Social Institutions and Gender Index (SIGI) and Its Subindices." Courant Research Centre Discussion Paper #10. Retrieved March 29, 2012 (http://www2.vwl.wiso.uni-goettingen.de/courant-papers/CRC-PEG_DP_10.pdf).

Bratton, William J. 2011. "Reducing Crime through Prevention Not Incarceration." *Criminology and Public Policy* 10: 63–68.

Braveman, Paula A., Catherine Cubbin, Susan Egerter, Sekai Chideya, Kristen S. Marchi, Marilyn Metzler, and Samuel Posner. 2005. "Socioeconomic Status in Health Research: One Size Does Not Fit All." *Journal of the American Medical Association* 294(22): 2879–2888.

Brennan, Denise. 2002. "Selling Sex for Visas: Sex Tourism as a Stepping-stone to International Migration." In *Global Woman: Nannies, Maids and Sex Workers in the New Economy,* edited by B. Ehrenreich and A. Hochschild. New York: Henry Holt.

Brennan, Denise. 2004. *What's Love Got to Do with It? Transnational Desires and Sex Tourism in the Dominican Republic.* Durham: NC: Duke University Press.

Brents, Barbara, Crystal A. Jackson, and Kate Hausbeck. 2009. *The State of Sex: Tourism, Sex and Sin in the New American Heartland.* New York: Routledge.

Brewer, John and Frank Trentmann. 2006. "Introduction: Space, Time and Value in Consuming Cultures." Pp. 1–17 in *Consuming Cultures, Global Perspectives: Historical Trajectories, Transnational Exchanges,* edited by J. Brewer and F. Trentmann. Oxford, UK: Berg.

Brim, Orville. 1968. "Adult Socialization." Pp. 182–1226 in *Socialization and Society,* edited by J. A. Clausen. Boston: Little, Brown.

Brimeyer, Ted M., JoAnn Miller, and Robert Perrucci. 2006. "Social Class Sentiments in Formation: Influence of Class Socialization, College Socialization, and Class Aspirations." *The Sociological Quarterly* 47: 471–495.

Brinkley, Douglas. 2006. *The Great Deluge: Hurricane Katrina, New Orleans, and the Mississippi Gulf Coast.* New York: Harper Perennial.

Britannica. 2012. "Religion: Year in Review 2010." In *Britannica Book of the Year.* Retrieved May 29, 2012 (http://www.britannica.com/EBchecked/topic/1731588/religion-Year-In-Review-2010).

Broder, John M. 2009. "Seeking to Save the Planet, with a Thesaurus." *New York Times,* May 1. Retrieved March 29, 2012 (http://www.nytimes.com/2009/05/02/us/politics/02enviro.html).

Brody, Jane E. 2009. "Buyer Beware of Home DNA Tests." *New York Times,* September 1, p. D6.

Bronfenbrenner, Kate, ed. 2007. *Global Unions: Challenging Transnational Capital through Cross-Border Campaigns.* Ithaca, NY: Cornell University Press.

Bronner, Ethan. 2011a. "Protests Force Israel to Confront the Wealth Gap." *New York Times,* August 11. Retrieved March 29, 2012 (http://www.nytimes.com/2011/08/12/world/middleeast/12israel.html?pagewanted=all).

Bronner, Ethan. 2011b. "Virtual Bridge Allows Strangers in Mideast to Seem Less Strange." *New York Times,* July 10. Retrieved March 29, 2012 (http://www.nytimes.com/2011/07/10/world/middleeast/10mideast.html).

Brooks, Robert A. 2011. *Cheaper by the Hour: Temporary Lawyers and the Deprofessionalization of the Law.* Philadelphia: Temple University Press.

Brown, David. 2007. "As Temperature Rise, Health Could Decline." *Washington Post,* December 17, p. A7.

Brown, Elaine. 1992. *A Taste of Power: A Black Woman's Story.* New York: Doubleday.

Brown, Katrina and Catherine Connolly. 2010. "The Role of Law in Promoting Women in Elite Athletics: An Examination of Four Nations." *International Review for the Sociology of Sport* 45(1): 3–21.

Brown, Melissa T. 2012. *Enlisting Masculinity: The Construction of Gender in US Military Recruiting Advertising during the All-Volunteer Force.* New York: Oxford University Press.

Brown, Stephen E. 2007a. "Criminology." Pp. 856–860 in *The Blackwell Encyclopedia of Sociology,* edited by G. Ritzer. Malden, MA: Blackwell.

Brown, Stephen E. 2007b. "Ethnocentrism." Pp. 1478–1479 in *The Blackwell Encyclopedia of Sociology,* edited by G. Ritzer. Malden, MA: Blackwell.

Brown Timothy C., William B. Bankston, and Craig Forsyth. 2013. "'A Service Town': An Examination of the Offshore Oil Industry, Local Entrepreneurs, and the Civic Community Thesis." *Sociological Spectrum* 33: 1–15.

Brownmiller, Susan. 1975. *Against Our Will: Men, Women, and Rape.* New York: Simon and Schuster.

Broyard, Bliss. 2007. *One Drop: My Father's Hidden Life.* New York: Little, Brown.

Bruce, Steve. 2002. *God Is Dead: Secularization in the West.*

Bruce, Steve. 2013. *Secularization: An Unfashionable Theory.* New York: Oxford University Press.

Brumberg, Joan Jacobs. 1998. *The Body Project: An Intimate History of American Girls.* New York: Vintage.

Bryant, Melanie and Vaughan Higgins. 2010. "Self-confessed Troublemakers: An Interactionist View of Deviance During Organizational Change." *Human Relations* 63: 249–277.

Bryk, Anthony, Valerie Lee, and Peter Holland. 1993. *Catholic Schools and the Common Good.* Cambridge, MA: Harvard University Press.

Bryman, Alan. 2004. *The Disneyization of Society.* London: Sage.

Buchmann, Claudia and Thomas DiPrete. 2006. "The Growing Female Advantage in College Completion: The Role of Family Background and Academic Achievement." *American Sociological Review* 71(4): 515–541.

Buchmann, Claudia and Emily Hannum. 2001. "Education and Stratification in Developing Countries: A Review of Theories and Research." *Annual Review of Sociology* 27: 77–102.

Buckingham, David, ed. 2008. *Youth, Identity and Digital Media.* Cambridge, MA: MIT Press.

Buckley, Cara. 2009. "For Uninsured Young Adults, Do-It-Yourself Medical Care." *New York Times,* February 18.

Buddha, Gautama. N.d. "Dhammapada 1: The Twin Verses (Yamakavaggo)," translated by V. Nàrada. Retrieved March 29, 2012 (http://www.metta.lk/tipitaka/2Sutta-Pitaka/5Khuddaka-Nikaya/02Dhammapada/01-Yamakavaggo-e2.html).

Budig, Michelle J., Joya Misra, and Irene Boeckman. 2012. "The Motherhood Penalty in Cross-National Perspective: The Importance of Work–Family Policies and Cultural Attitudes." *Social Politics* 19: 163–193.

Bulman, Philip. 2009. "Using Technology to Make Prison Safer." *National Institute of Justice Journal* 262.

Burawoy, Michael. 1979. *Manufacturing Consent: Changes in the Labor Process under Monopoly Capitalism.* Chicago: University of Chicago Press.

Burawoy, Michael. 2000. "Introduction: Reaching for the Global." Pp. 1–40 in *Global Ethnography: Forces, Connections, and Imaginations in a Postmodern World,* edited by M. Burawoy, J. A. Blum, S. George, Z. Gille, T. Gowan, L. Haney, M. Klawiter, S. H. Lopez, S. Ó Riain, and M. Thayer. Berkeley: University of California Press.

Burawoy, Michael. 2005. "For Public Sociology." *American Sociological Review* 70(1): 4–28.

Bureau of Justice Statistics. 2008. "Identity Theft." Retrieved November 6, 2011 (http://www.bjs.gov/index.cfm?ty=tp&tid=42).

Bureau of Justice Statistics. 2009. "Sourcebook of Criminal Justice Statistics" (Section 6: Persons Under Criminal Supervision).

Retrieved December 21, 2011 (http://www.albany.edu/sourcebook/tost_6.html#6_e).

Bureau of Labor Statistics. 2008. "Chart Book: Occupational Employment and Wages." Retrieved January 31, 2010 (http://bls.gov/oes/2008/may/chartbook.htm).

Burger, Jerry. 2009. "Replicating Milgram: Would People Still Obey Today?" *American Psychologist* 64(1): 1–11.

Burgess, Ernest W. and Harvey J. Locke. 1945. *The Family: From Institution to Companionship.* New York: American Book.

Burke, Peter J. 1991. "Identity Processes and Social Stress." *American Sociological Review* 56: 836–849.

Burke, Peter J. and Donald C. Reitzes. 1981. "The Link between Identity and Role Performance." *Social Psychology* 44(2): 83–92.

Burke, Peter J. and Donald C. Reitzes. 1991. "An Identity Theory Approach to Commitment." *Social Psychology* 54(3): 239–251.

Burke, Peter J. and Jan E. Stets. 1999. "Trust and Commitment through Self-Verification." *Social Psychology Quarterly* 62: 347–366.

Burnham, John. 2012. "The Death of the Sick Role." *Social History of Medicine* 25(4): 761.

Burns, John F. 2011. "Founder Says WikiLeaks, Starved of Cash, May Close." *New York Times,* October 24. Retrieved March 29, 2012 (http://www.nytimes.com/2011/10/25/world/europe/blocks-on-wikileaks-donations-may-force-its-end-julian-assange-warns.html?_r=1&ref=wikileaks).

Burns, John F. and Ravi Somaiya. 2010a. "Hackers Attack Sites Considered WikiLeaks Foes." *New York Times,* December 9, p. A1.

Burns, John and Ravi Somaiya. 2010b. "WikiLeaks Founder on the Run, Trailed by Notoriety." *New York Times,* October 23. Retrieved March 29, 2012 (http://www.nytimes.com/2010/10/24/world/24assange.html).

Burns, Thomas J. 2012. "Marine Pollution." Pp. 1324–1325 in *The Wiley-Blackwell Companion to Sociology,* edited by G. Ritzer. Malden, MA: Wiley-Blackwell.

Buse, Kent. 2007. "World Health Organization." P. 1277 in *Encyclopedia of Globalization,* edited by J. A. Scholte and R. Robertson. New York: MTM Publishing.

Bushell-Embling, Dylan. 2010. "US Blocks Chinese Fiber Deal over National Security Fears." *TelecomsEurope,* June 30. Accessed December 7, 2011 (www.telecomseurope.net/content/us-blocks-chinese-fiber-deal-over-national-security-fears).

Buss, Paulo and Jose Roberto Ferreira. 2010. "Developing Global Public Health Links." *UN Chronicle* XLVII(2). Retrieved March 29, 2012 (http://www.un.org/wcm/content/site/chronicle/cache/bypass/home/archive/issues2010/achieving_global_health/developingpublichealthlinks?ctnscroll_articleContainerList=1_0&ctnlistpagination_articleContainerList=true).

Butler, Judith. 1990. *Gender Trouble: Feminism and the Subversion of Identity.* New York: Routledge.

Byles, Jeff. 2003. "Profile of the President. Tales of the Kefir Furnaceman: Michael Burawoy." *Footnotes* 21(7).

Byrd, Scott. 2005. "The Porto Alegre Consensus: Theorizing the Forum Movement." *Globalizations* 2(1): 151–163.

Cable, Sherry, Thomas E. Shriver, and Tamara L. Mix. 2008. "Risk Society and Contested Illness: The Case of Nuclear Weapons Workers." *American Sociological Review* 73: 380–401.

Cagatay, Nilufer and Sule Ozler. 1995. "Feminization of the Labor Force: The Effect of Long Term Development and Structural Adjustment." *World Development* 23(11): 1827–1836.

Cahill, Spencer, William Distler, Cynthia Lachowetz, Andrea Meany, Robyn Tarallo, and Teena Willard. 1985. "Meanwhile Backstage: Public Bathrooms and the Interaction Order." *Journal of Contemporary Ethnography* 14: 33–58.

Calasanti, Toni and Kathleen Slevin. 2001. *Gender, Social Inequality and Aging.* Walnut Creek, CA: AltaMira Press.

Caldwell, Christopher. 2009. *Reflections on the Revolution in Europe: Immigration, Islam, and the West.* New York: Doubleday.

Callinicos, Alex. 2004. *The Revolutionary Ideas of Karl Marx.* London: Bookmarks.

Calvin, John. 1536. *Institutes of the Christian Religion.* Basel, Switzerland.

Campbell, Colin. 1987. *The Romantic Ethic and the Spirit of Modern Consumerism.* Oxford, UK: Blackwell.

Campbell, Colin. 2007. *The Easternization of the West: A Thematic Account of Cultural Change in the Modern Era.* Boulder, CO: Paradigm Press.

Caniglia, Beth. 2012. "Environmental Protection Movement." Pp. 536–541 in *The Wiley-Blackwell Encyclopedia of Globalization*, edited by G. Ritzer. Malden, MA: Wiley-Blackwell.

Cannon, Lou. 1997. "Scars Remain Five Years after Los Angeles Riots." Special to the *Washington Post*, April 28. Retrieved March 28, 2012 (http://www.washingtonpost.com/wp-srv/national/longterm/lariots/lariots.htm).

Caprile, Maria and Amparo Serrano Pascual. 2011. "The Move towards the Knowledge-Based Society: A Gender Approach." *Work and Organization* 18: 48–72.

Capron, Christiane and Michel Duyme. 1989. "Assessment of the Effects of Socioeconomic Status on IQ in a Full Cross-Fostering Study." *Nature* 340: 552–554.

Carbonaro, William. 2005. "Tracking, Student Effort, and Academic Achievement." *Sociology of Education* 78: 27–49.

Carbonaro, William and Elizabeth Covay. 2010. "School Sector and Student Achievement in the Era of Standards Based Reforms." *Sociology of Education* 83: 160–182.

Carey, Stephen. 2011. *A Beginner's Guide to Scientific Method.* Boston: Wadsworth.

Carmichael, Stokely and Charles V. Hamilton. 1967. *Black Power: The Politics of Liberation.* New York: Vintage Books.

Carmody, Dianne Cyr. 2007. "Domestic Violence." Pp. 1219–1220 in *The Blackwell Encyclopedia of Sociology*, edited by G. Ritzer. Malden, MA: Blackwell.

Carnevale, Anthony P., Stephen J. Rose, and Ban Cheah. 2009. *The College Payoff: Education, Occupations, Lifetime Earnings.* Retrieved March 29, 2012 (http://www9.georgetown.edu/grad/gppi/hpi/cew/pdfs/collegepayoff-complete.pdf).

Carrara, Sergio. 2007. "Sexual Minorities." In *Encyclopedia of Globalization,* edited by J. A. Scholte and R. Robertson. New York: MTM Publishing.

Carroll, William K. and Colin Carson. 2003. "The Network of Global Corporations and Elite Policy Groups: A Structure for Transnational Capitalist Class Formation?" *Global Networks* 3(1): 29–57.

Carson, Rachel. 1962. *Silent Spring.* New York: Houghton Mifflin.

Carter, Bill and Tanzia Vega. 2011. "In Shift, Ads Try to Entice Over-55 Set." *New York Times,* May 13.

Carty, Victoria. 2013. "Internet and Social Movements." Pp. 620–623 in *The Wiley-Blackwell Encyclopedia of Social and Political Movements*, 3 vols., edited by D. A. Snow, D. Della Porta, B. Klandermans, and D. McAdam. Malden, MA: Wiley-Blackwell.

Casey, Emma. 2006. "Domesticating Gambling: Gender, Caring the UK National Lottery." *Leisure Studies* 25(1).

Casper, Lynne M. 2007. "Family Demography." Pp. 1583–1589 in *The Blackwell Encyclopedia of Sociology*, edited by G. Ritzer. Malden, MA: Blackwell.

Castells, Manuel. [1972] 1977. *The Urban Question: A Marxist Approach,* translated by A. Sheridan. London: Edward Arnold.

Castells, Manuel. 1996. *The Rise of the Network Society.* The Information Age: Economy, Society and Culture, Vol. 1. Oxford, UK: Blackwell.

Castells, Manuel. 1997. *The Power of Identity.* The Information Age: Economy, Society, and Culture, Vol. 2. Oxford, UK: Blackwell.

Castells, Manuel. 1998. *End of Millennium.* The Information Age: Economy, Society, and Culture, Vol. 3. Oxford, UK: Blackwell.

Castells, Manuel. 2008. *The New Public Sphere: Global Civil Society, Communication Networks, and Global Governance.* Los Angeles: University of Southern California.

Castells, Manuel. 2010. *The Rise of the Network Society.* The Information Age: Economy, Society and Culture, Vol. 1. 2nd ed. Malden, MA: Wiley-Blackwell.

Castle, Stephen. 2010. "France Faces European Action after Expulsions." *New York Times,* September 29.

Cavanagh, Allison. 2007. *Sociology in the Age of the Internet.* Maidenhead, UK: Open University Press.

Cave, Damien. 2010. "In Recession, Americans Doing More, Buying Less." *New York Times,* January 3.

Cave, Damien. 2011. "Mexico Turns to Social Media for Information and Survival." *New York Times,* September 25, p. 5.

Centers for Disease Control and Prevention. 2004. "Leading Causes of Death by Age Group, Black Males—United States." Retrieved March 29, 2012 (http://www.cdc.gov/men/lcod/2004/04black.pdf).

Centers for Disease Control and Prevention. 2011. "Life Expectancy at Birth, by Race and Sex—United States, 2000–2009." *Morbidity and Mortality Weekly Report* 60(18): 588.

Centers for Disease Control and Prevention. 2012. "HIV in the United States: At a Glance." Retrieved March 29, 2012 (http://www.cdc.gov/hiv/resources/factsheets/us.htm).

Central Intelligence Agency. 2012a. "East and Southeast Asia: Singapore." *The World Factbook,* March 22. Retrieved March 29, 2012 (https://www.cia.gov/library/publications/the-world-factbook/geos/sn.html).

Central Intelligence Agency. 2012b. "North America: United States." *The World Factbook.* Retrieved March 29, 2012 (https://www.cia.gov/library/publications/the-world-factbook/geos/us.html).

Central Intelligence Agency. 2012c. "Qatar." *The World Factbook,* March 20. Retrieved March 29, 2012 (https://www.cia.gov/library/publications/the-world-factbook/geos/qa.html).

Central Intelligence Agency. 2012d. *The World Factbook.* Washington, DC: U.S. Government Printing Office.

Cerkez, Aida. 2010. "UN Official: Bosnia War Rapes Must Be Prosecuted." *Washington Post,* November 26.

Cerny, Phillip G. 2007. "Nation-State." In *Encyclopedia of Globalization,* edited by J. A. Scholte and R. Robertson. New York: MTM Publishing.

Chakravorti, Robi. 1993. "Marx the Journalist." *Economic and Political Weekly* 28(September 4): 1856–1859.

Chambers, Erve. 2010. *Native Tours: The Anthropology of Travel and Tourism.* Prospect Heights, IL: Waveland Press.

Chambliss, William J. 1964. "A Sociological Analysis of the Law of Vagrancy." *Social Problems* 12: 67–77.

Chammartin, Gloria Moreno-Fontes. 2005. "Domestic Workers: Little Protection for the Underpaid." *Migration Information Source.* Retrieved June 2, 2011 (http://www.migrationinformation.org/Feature/display.cfm?id=300).

Chanda, Nayan. 2007. *Bound Together: How Traders, Preachers, Adventurers, and Warriors Shaped Globalization.* New Haven, CT: Yale University Press.

Chandy, Laurence and Geoffrey Gertz. 2011. "Poverty in Numbers: The Changing State of Global Poverty from 2005 to 2015." The Brookings Institution. Retrieved March 29, 2012 (http://www.brookings.edu/~/media/Files/rc/papers/2011/01_global_poverty_chandy/01_global_poverty_chandy.pdf).

Chapman, John and Alan Wertheimer, eds. 1990. *Majorities and Minorities: Nomos XXXII.* New York: New York University Press.

Charles, Maria and Karen Bradley. 2009. "Indulging Our Gendered Selves: Sex Segregation by Field of Study in 44 Countries." *American Journal of Sociology* 114: 924–976.

Cheal, David. 2007. "Family Theory." Pp. 1630–1634 in *The Blackwell Encyclopedia of Sociology*, edited by G. Ritzer. Malden, MA: Blackwell.

Cheever, Susan. 2002. "The Nanny Dilemma." Pp. 31–38 in *Global Woman: Nannies, Maids and Sex Workers in the New Economy*, edited by B. Ehrenreich and A. Hochschild. New York: Henry Holt.

Chen, Katherine. 2009. *Enabling Creative Chaos: The Organization behind the Burning Man Event.* Chicago: University of Chicago Press.

Chen, Pauline W. 2010. "Are Doctors Ready for Virtual Visits?" *New York Times*, January 7.

Cherlin, Andrew J. 1978. "Remarriage as an Incomplete Institution." *American Journal of Sociology* 84: 634–650.

Cherlin, Andrew J. 2004. "The Deinstitutionalization of American Marriage." *Journal of Marriage and the Family* 66: 848–861.

Cherlin, Andrew J. 2009. *The Marriage-Go-Round: The State of Marriage and the Family in America Today.* New York: Knopf.

Cherlin, Andrew J. 2010. "The Houswife Anomaly." *New York Times*, January 24.

Chernilo, Daniel. 2012. "Nation." Pp. 1485–1492 in *The Wiley-Blackwell Encyclopedia of Globalization*, edited by G. Ritzer. Malden, MA: Wiley-Blackwell.

Chilton, Roland and Ruth Triplett. 2007a. "Class and Crime." Pp. 542–545 in *The Blackwell Encyclopedia of Sociology*, edited by G. Ritzer. Malden, MA: Blackwell.

Chilton, Roland and Ruth Triplett. 2007b. "Race and Crime." Pp. 3734–3737 in *The Blackwell Encyclopedia of Sociology*, edited by G. Ritzer. Malden, MA: Blackwell.

Chin, Elizabeth. 2007. "Consumption, African Americans." Pp. 706–709 in *The Blackwell Encyclopedia of Sociology*, edited by G. Ritzer. Malden, MA: Blackwell.

Chin, Margaret. 2005. *Sewing Women: Immigrants and the New York City Garment Industry.* New York: Columbia University Press.

Chin, Tiffani and Meredith Phillips. 2004. "Social Reproduction and Child-Rearing Practices: Social Class, Children's Agency, and the Summer Activity Gap." *Sociology of Education* 77: 185–210.

China Internet Network Information Center. 2010. "Statistical Report on Internet Development in China." Retrieved June 17, 2011 (http://www.cnnic.cn/uploadfiles/pdf/2010/8/24/93145.pdf).

Chodorow, Nancy. 1978. *The Reproduction of Mothering.* Berkeley: University of California Press.

Chodorow, Nancy. 1988. *Psychoanalytic Theory and Feminism.* Cambridge, UK: Polity Press.

Chomsky, N. 1985. *Turning the Tide: U.S. Intervention in Central America and the Struggle for Peace.* Boston: South End Press.

Chriqui, James F., Rosalie Liccardo Pacula, Duane C. McBride, Deborah A. Reichmann, Curtis J. Vanderwaal, and Yvonne Terry-McElrath. 2002. *Illicit Drug Policies: Selected Laws from the 50 States.* Princeton, NJ: Robert Wood Johnson Foundation.

Chriss, James J. 2007. "Networks." Pp. 3182–3185 in *The Blackwell Encyclopedia of Sociology*, edited by G. Ritzer. Malden, MA: Blackwell.

Clammer, John. 1997. *Contemporary Urban Japan: A Sociology of Consumption.* Oxford, UK: Blackwell.

Clancy, Michael. 2012. "Cruise Tourism." Pp. 360–362 in *The Wiley-Blackwell Encyclopedia of Globalization*, edited by G. Ritzer. Malden, MA: Wiley-Blackwell.

Clapson, Mark and Ray Hutchison, eds. 2010. *Suburbanization in Global Society.* United Kingdom: Emerald Publishing Group.

Clark, Nancy L. and William H. Worger. 2004. *South Africa: The Rise and Fall of Apartheid.* New York: Longman.

Clawson Dan, Alan Neustadtl, and Mark Weller. 1998. *Dollars and Votes: How Business Campaign Contributions Subvert Democracy.* Philadelphia: Temple University Press.

Clawson, Dan, Robert Zussman, Joya Misra, Naomi Gerstel, and Randall Stokes. 2007. *Public Sociology: Fifteen Eminent Sociologists Debate Politics and the Profession in the Twenty-First Century.* Berkeley: University of California Press.

Cleary, Thomas, trans. 2004. *The Qur'an: A New Translation.* Chicago: Starlatch Press.

Clegg, Stewart. 2007. "Ideal Type." Pp. 2201–2202 in *The Blackwell Encyclopedia of Sociology*, edited by G. Ritzer. Malden, MA: Blackwell.

Clegg, Stewart and Michael Lounsbury. 2009. "Sintering the Iron Cage: Translation, Domination and Rationalization." Pp. 118–145 in *The Oxford Handbook of Sociology and Organization Studies: Classical Foundations*, edited by P. S. Adler. Oxford, UK: Oxford University Press.

Clendinen, Dudley and Adam Nagourney. 1999. *Out for Good: The Struggle to Build a Gay Rights Movement in America.* New York: Simon and Schuster.

Clogher, R. 1981. "Weaving Spiders Come Not Here: Bohemian Grove: Inside the Secret Retreat of the Power Elite." *Mother Jones* (August): 28–35.

Clotfelter, Charles T. 2010. *American Universities in a Global Market.* Chicago: University of Chicago Press.

Clough, Patricia Ticineto. 2013. "The Digital, Labor, and Measure Beyond Politics." Pp. 112–126 in *Digital Labor: The Internet as Playground and Factory*, edited by T. Scholz. New York: Routledge.

Clougherty, Jane E., Kerry Souza, and Mark R. Cullen. 2010. "Work and Its Role in Shaping the Social Gradients in Health." *Annals of the New York Academy of Sciences* 1186: 102–124.

Coakley, Jay. 2007. "Socialization and Sport." Pp. 4576–4579 in *The Blackwell Encyclopedia of Sociology*, edited by G. Ritzer. Malden, MA: Blackwell.

Cockerham, William C. 2007. "Medical Sociology." Pp. 2932–2936 in *The Blackwell Encyclopedia of Sociology*, edited by G. Ritzer. Malden, MA: Blackwell.

Cockerham, William. 2012. "Current Directions in Medical Sociology." Pp. 385–401 in *The Wiley-Blackwell Companion to Sociology*, edited by G. Ritzer. Malden, MA: Wiley-Blackwell.

Cohen, Daniel. 2008. *Three Lectures on Post-industrial Society.* Cambridge, MA: MIT Press.

Cohen, Lizabeth. 2004. *A Consumer Republic: The Politics of Mass Consumption in Post War America.* Chicago: University of Chicago Press.

Cohen, Noam. 2011. "Define Gender Gap? Look Up Wikipedia's Contributor List." *New York Times*, January 30. Accessed on December 3, 2011 (http://www.nytimes.com/2011/01/31/business/media/31link.html).

Cohen, Patricia. 2010. "'Culture of Poverty' Makes a Comeback." *New York Times*, October 17. Retrieved March 29, 2012 (http://www.nytimes.com/2010/10/18/us/18poverty.html).

Cohen, Philip and Matt Huffman. 2007. "Working for the Woman? Female Managers and the Gender Wage Gap." *American Sociological Review* 72: 681–704.

Cohen, Richard. 2008. "The Election that LBJ Won." *Washington Post*, November 4, p. A17.

Cohen, Robin. 1997. *Global Diasporas: An Introduction.* London: Routledge.

Cohen-Cole, Ethan, Steven Durlauf, Jeffrey Fagan, and Daniel Nagin. 2009. "Model Uncertainty and the Deterrent Effect of Capital Punishment." *American Law and Economics Review* 11: 335–369.

Cole, Ellen and Jessica H. Daniel. 2005. *Featuring Females: Feminist Analyses of Media.* Washington DC: American Psychological Association.

Coleman, David and Robert Rowthorn. 2011. "Who's Afraid of Population Decline? A Critical Examination of Its Consequences." *Population and Development Review* 37: 217–248.

Coleman, James. 1966. *Equality of Educational Opportunity.* Washington, DC: U.S. Department of Health, Education, and Welfare.

Coleman, James. 1990. *Foundations of Social Theory.* Cambridge MA: Belknap Press of Harvard University Press.

Coleman, Marilyn and Lawrence H. Ganong. 2007a. "Stepfamilies." Pp. 4765–4768 in *The Blackwell Encyclopedia of Sociology*, edited by G. Ritzer. Malden, MA: Blackwell.

Coleman, Marilyn and Lawrence H. Ganong. 2007b. "Stepmothering." Pp. 4770–4772 in *The Blackwell Encyclopedia of Sociology*, edited by G. Ritzer. Malden, MA: Blackwell.

Collet, Francois. 2009. "Does Habitus Matter? A Comparative Review of Bourdieu's Habitus and Simon's Bounded Rationality with Some Implications for Economic Sociology." *Sociological Theory* 27: 419–434.

Collier, Paul. 2007. *The Bottom Billion: Why the Poorest Countries Are Failing and What Can Be Done about It.* New York: Oxford University Press.

Collier, Paul. 2012. "The Bottom Billion." Pp. 126–130 in *The Wiley-Blackwell Encyclopedia of Globalization*, edited by G. Ritzer. Malden, MA: Wiley-Blackwell.

Collins, Allan and Richard Halverson. 2009. *Rethinking Education in the Age of Technology: The Digital Revolution and the Schools.* New York: Teachers College Press.

Collins, Chiquita and David R. Williams. 2004. "Segregation and Mortality: The Deadly Effects of Racism?" *Sociological Forum* 45: 265–285.

Collins, James. 2009. "Social Reproduction in Classrooms and Schools." *Annual Review of Anthropology* 38: 33–48.

Collins, Jane L. 2003. *Threads: Gender, Labor, and Power in the Global Apparel Industry.* Chicago: University of Chicago Press.

Collins, Patricia Hill. 1990. *Black Feminist Thought: Knowledge, Consciousness, and the Politics of Empowerment.* Boston: Unwin Hyman.

Collins, Patricia Hill. 2000. *Black Feminist Thought: Knowledge, Consciousness, and the Politics of Empowerment.* 2nd ed. New York: Routledge.

Collins, Patricia Hill. 2004. *Black Sexual Politics: African-Americans, Gender and the New Racism.* New York: Routledge.

Collins, Patricia Hill. 2009. *Another Kind of Public Education: Race, the Media, Schools, and Democratic Possibilities.* Boston: Beacon Press.

Collins, Patricia Hill. 2012. "Looking Back, Moving Ahead Scholarship in Service to Social Justice." *Gender and Society* 26: 14–22.

Collins, Randall. 1975. *Conflict Society: Toward an Explanatory Science.* New York: Academic Press.

Collins, Randall. 1979. *The Credential Society: An Historical Sociology of Education and Stratification.* New York: Academic Press.

Collins, Randall. 1990. "Conflict Theory and The Advance of Macro-historical Sociology." In *Frontiers of Social Theory*, edited by G. Ritzer. New York: Columbia University Press.

Collins, Randall. 2008. *Violence: A Micro-sociological Theory.* Princeton, NJ: Princeton University Press.

Collins, Randall. 2009. "Micro and Macro Causes of Violence." *International Journal of Conflict and Violence* 3: 9–22.

Collins, Randall. 2012. "C-Escalation and D-Escalation: A Theory of the Time-Dynamics of Conflict." *American Sociological Review* 77: 1–20.

Colosi, Rachel. 2010. *Dirty Dancing? An Ethnography of Lap-Dancing.* Abingdon: Willam Publishing.

Comaroff, John L. and Jean Comaroff. 2009. *Ethnicity, Inc.* Chicago: University of Chicago Press.

Comstock, George and Erica Scharrer. 2007. *Media and the American Child.* Burlington, MA: Academic Press.

Conca, Ken. 2006. *Governing Water: Contentious Transnational Political and Global Institution Building.* Cambridge, MA: MIT Press.

Conca, Ken. 2007. "Water." In *Encyclopedia of Globalization*, edited by J. A. Scholte and R. Robertson. New York: MTM Publishing.

Congressional Budget Office. 2011. "Trends in the Distribution of Household Income between 1979 and 2007." Retrieved March 29, 2012 (http://www.cbo.gov/ftpdocs/124xx/doc12485/10-25-HouseholdIncome.pdf).

Conley, Dalton. 2001a. "The Black-White Wealth Gap." *The Nation*, March 26. Retrieved March 29, 2012 (http://www.thenation.com/article/black-white-wealth-gap).

Conley, Dalton. 2001b. *Honky.* New York: Vintage Books.

Conley, Dalton. 2004. "For Siblings, Inequality Starts at Home." *Chronicle Review*, March 4. Retrieved March 29, 2012 (http://chronicle.com/article/For-Siblings-Inequality/7314/).

Conley, Dalton. 2008. "Rich Man's Burden." *New York Times*, September 2. Retrieved March 29, 2012 (http://www.nytimes.com/2008/09/02/opinion/02conley.html).

Conley, Dalton. 2012. "Harvard by Lottery." *Chronicle Review*, April 1. Retrieved October 3, 2013 (http://chronicle.com/article/Harvard-by-Lottery/131322/).

Conley, Dalton and Brian J. McCabe. 2011. "Body Mass Index and Physical Attractiveness: Evidence from a Combination of Image-Alteration/List Experiment." *Sociological Methods and Research* 40: 6–31.

Connell, Robert W. 1987. *Gender and Power: Society, the Person and Sexual Politics.* Palo Alto, CA: Stanford University Press.

Connell, Robert W. 1995. *Masculinities.* Berkeley: University of California Press.

Connell, Robert W. 1997. "Hegemonic Masculinity and Emphasized Femininity." Pp. 22–25 in *Feminist Frontiers IV*, edited by L. Richardson, V. Taylor, and N. Whittier. New York: McGraw-Hill.

Connell, Robert W. 2005. *Masculinities.* 2nd ed. Berkeley: University of California Press.

Connell, Raewynn. 2009. *Gender.* Cambridge: Polity Press.

Connor, Phillip. 2012. *Faith on the Move: The Religious Affiliation of International Migrants.* Washington, DC: Pew Research Center.

Conrad, Peter. 1986. "Problems in Health Care." Pp. 415–450 in *Social Problems*, edited by G. Ritzer. 2nd ed. New York: Random House.

Conrad, Peter, Thomas Mackie, and Ateev Mehrota. 2010. "Estimating the Costs of Medicalization." *Social Science and Medicine* 70: 1943–1947.

Conrad, Peter and Joseph W. Schneider. 1980. *Deviance and Medicalization: From Badness to Sickness.* St. Louis, MO: Mosby.

Considine, Austin. 2012. "Gay Marriage Victory Still Shadowed by AIDS." *New York Times* Sunday Styles, January 1, pp. 1, 2.

Cook, Daniel T. 2004. *The Commodification of Childhood: The Children's Clothing Industry and the Rise of the Child Consumer.* Durham, NC: Duke University Press.

Cook, Daniel T. 2007. "Consumer Culture, Children's." Pp. 693–697 in *The Blackwell Encyclopedia of Sociology*, edited by G. Ritzer. Malden, MA: Blackwell.

Cook, Karen S., Richard M. Emerson, Mary B. Gilmore, and Toshio Yamagishi. 1983. "The Distribution of Power in Exchange Networks: Theory and Experimental Results." *American Journal of Sociology* 89: 275–305.

Cooksey, Elizabeth. 2007. "Fertility: Adolescent." Pp. 1725–1729 in *The Blackwell Encyclopedia of Sociology*, edited by G. Ritzer. Malden, MA: Blackwell.

Cooley, Charles Horton. 1909. *Social Organization: A Study of the Larger Mind.* New York: Charles Scribner's Sons.

Cooper, Cary L., Alankrita Pandey, and James Quick Campbell, eds. 2012. *Downsizing: Is Less Still More?* Cambridge, UK: Cambridge University Press.

Copes, Heith and Crystal Null. 2007. "Property Crime." Pp. 3675–3676 in *The Blackwell Encyclopedia of Sociology*, edited by G. Ritzer. Malden, MA: Blackwell.

Correll, Shelley J. 2001. "Gender and the Career Choice Process: The Role of Biased Self Assessments." *American Journal of Sociology* 106(6).

Correll, Shelley J. 2004. "Constraints into Preferences: Gender, Status, and Emerging Career Aspirations." *American Sociological Review* 69(1): 93–113.

Correll, Shelley J., Stephen Benard, and In Paik. 2007. "Getting a Job: Is There a Motherhood Penalty?" *American Journal of Sociology* 112: 1297–1338.

Corsaro, William A. and Peggy J. Miller, eds. 1992. "Interpretive Approaches to Children's Socialization." Special Edition of *New Directions for Child Development* 58(Winter).

Corwin, Zoe Blumberg and William G. Tierney. 2007. "Institutional Review Boards and Sociological Research." Pp. 2345–2351 in *The Blackwell Encyclopedia of Sociology*, edited by G. Ritzer. Malden, MA: Blackwell.

Cosenza, Vicenzo. 2011. "World Map of Social Networks." Retrieved August 27, 2011 (www.vincos.it/world-map-of-social-networks/).

Coser, Lewis. 1956. *The Functions of Social Conflict.* New York: Free Press.

Cotter, David A., Joan M. Hermsen, Seth Ovadia, and Reeve Vanneman. 2001. "The Glass Ceiling Effect." *Social Forces* 80(2): 655–682.

Coulmont, Baptiste and Phil Hubbard. 2010. "Consuming Sex: Socio-legal Shifts in the Space and Place of Sex Shops." *Journal of Law and Society* 37(1): 189–209.

Cousins, Mel. 2005. *European Welfare States: Comparative Perspectives*. London: Sage.

Coventry, Martha. 2006. "Tyranny of the Esthetic: Surgery's Most Intimate Violation." Pp. 203–211 in *Estelle Disch's Reconstructing Gender: A Multicultural Anthology*. New York: McGraw-Hill Education.

"Covering J. R. Smith: A Knick Talks About His Tattoos." 2012. *New York Times,* December 28.

Coward, Martin. 2012. "Urban." Pp. 2130–2134 in *The Wiley-Blackwell Encyclopedia of Globalization*, edited by G. Ritzer. Malden, MA: Wiley-Blackwell.

Cox, Lloyd. 2007. "Socialism." Pp. 4549–4554 in *The Blackwell Encyclopedia of Sociology*, edited by G. Ritzer. Malden, MA: Blackwell.

Cox, Richard Henry and Albert Schilthuis. 2012. "Governance." Pp. 885–888 in *The Wiley-Blackwell Encyclopedia of Globalization*, edited by G. Ritzer. Malden, MA: Wiley-Blackwell.

Creswell, John. 2008. *Research Design: Qualitative, Quantitative, and Mixed Methods Approaches*. Thousand Oaks, CA: Sage.

Crissey, Sarah. 2009. *Educational Attainment in the US: 2007*. Washington, DC: U.S. Census Bureau.

Croll, Paul R. 2013. "Explanations for Racial Disadvantage: Beliefs about Both Sides of Inequality in America." *Ethnic and Racial Studies* 36(1): 47–74.

Cronk, Christine and Paul Sarvela. 1997. "Alcohol, Tobacco, and Other Drug Use among Rural/Small Town and Urban Youth: A Secondary Analysis of the Monitoring the Future Data Set." *American Journal of Public Health* 87(5): 760–764.

Cross, Remy and David Snow. 2012. "Social Movements." Pp. 522–544 in *The Wiley-Blackwell Companion to Sociology*, edited by G. Ritzer. Malden, MA: Wiley-Blackwell.

Crossley, Alison Dahl and Heather McKee Hurwitz. 2013. "Women's Movements." Pp. 1402–1408 in *The Wiley-Blackwell Encyclopedia of Social and Political Movements*, 3 vols., edited by D. A. Snow, D. Della Porta, B. Klandermans, and D. McAdam. Malden, MA: Wiley-Blackwell.

Crothers, Charles. 2011. "Robert K. Merton." Pp. 65–88 in *Major Social Theorists: Volume II. Contemporary Social Theorists,* edited by G. Ritzer and J. Stepnisky. West Sussex, UK: Wiley-Blackwell.

Crothers, Lane. 2010. *Globalization and American Popular Culture*. 2nd ed. Lanham, MD: Rowman Littlefield.

Croucher, Sheila. 2009. *The Other Side of the Fence: American Migrants in Mexico*. Austin: University of Texas Press.

Crouse, Janice Shaw. 2010. "Cohabitation Nation." *Washington Times*, November 22, p. 1.

Crowder, Kyle and Liam Downey. 2010. "Interneighborhood Migration, Race, and Environmental Hazards: Modeling Microlevel Processes of Environmental Inequality." *The American Journal of Sociology* 115(4): 1110–1149.

Crowder, Kyle and Matthew Hall. 2007. "Migration, Internal." Pp. 3014–3019 in *The Blackwell Encyclopedia of Sociology*, edited by G. Ritzer. Malden. MA: Blackwell.

Crowley, Gregory J. 2007. "Urban Renewal and Development." Pp. 5128–5132 in *The Blackwell Encyclopedia of Sociology*, edited by G. Ritzer. Malden, MA: Blackwell.

Crowley, Martha, Daniel Tope, Lindsey Joyce Chamberlain, and Randy Hodson. 2010. "Neo-Taylorism at Work: Occupational Change in the Post-Fordist Era." *Social Problems* 57: 421–447.

Crump, Jeff. 2007. "Exurbia." Pp. 1549–1551 in *The Blackwell Encyclopedia of Sociology*, edited by G. Ritzer. Malden, MA: Blackwell.

Crutsinger, Martin. 2010. "G20 Leaders Facing Worries About Rising Deficits." Retrieved March 29, 2012 (http://www.businessweek.com/ap/financialnews/D9GHNNI81.htm).

Cullen, Francis T., Cheryl Lero Jonson, Daniel S. Nagin. 2011. "Prisons Do Not Reduce Recidivism: The High Cost of Ignoring Science." *The Prison Journal* 91: 48S–65S.

Culver, Leigh. 2007. "Criminal Justice System." Pp. 851–856 in *The Blackwell Encyclopedia of Sociology*, edited by G. Ritzer. Malden, MA: Blackwell.

Cummings, Elijah E. 2013. "Justice Scalia's Staggering Assertion of Judicial Activism." *The Hill*, March 8. Retrieved November 13, 2013 (http://thehill.com/blogs/congress-blog/judicial/287037-justice-scalias-staggering-assertion-of-judicial-activism).

Cunningham, Carolyn, Nicholas Brody, and Daniel C. Davis. 2012. *Social Networking and Impression Management: Self-Presentation in the Digital Age*. Lexington Books.

Curtiss, Susan. 1977. *Genie: A Psycholinguistic Study of a Modern-Day "Wild Child."* New York: Academic Press.

Cyert, Richard Michael and James G. March. 1963. *A Behavioral Theory of the Firm*. Englewood Cliffs, NJ: Prentice-Hall.

Dahl, Darren, Jaideep Sengupta, and Kathleen D. Vohs. 2009. "Sex in Advertising: Gender Differences and the Role of Relationship Commitment." *Journal of Consumer Research* 36(2): 215–231.

Dahlberg, Lincoln. 2010. "Cyber-libertarianism 2.0: A Discourse Theory/Critical Political Economy Examination." *Cultural Politics* 6: 331–356

Dahrendorf, Ralf. 1959. *Class and Class Conflict in Industrial Society*. Stanford, CA: Stanford University Press.

Daipha, Phaedra. 2012. "Weathering Risk: Uncertainty, Weather Forecasting, and Expertise." *Sociological Compass* 6: 15–25.

D'Alessio, Dave and Mike Allen. 2000. "Media Bias in Presidential Elections: A Meta-analysis." *Journal of Communication* 50(4): 133–156.

Daley, Suzanne. 1999, October 12. "Montredon Journal; French See a Hero in War on 'McDomination.'" Retrieved March 29, 2012 (http://www.nytimes.com/1999/10/12/world/montredon-journal-french-see-a-hero-in-war-on-mcdomination.html).

Daley, Suzanne. 2010a. "A Dutch City Seeks to End Drug Tourism." *New York Times*, August 18, pp. A1, A12.

Daley, Suzanne. 2010b. "The Hunt for Jobs Send the Irish Abroad, Again." *New York Times*, November 21, p. 4.

Damer, Sean. 1974. "Wine Alley: The Sociology of a Dreadful Enclosure." *Sociological Review* 22: 221–248.

Dandaneau, Steven P. 2007. "Norms." Pp. 3229–3322 in *The Blackwell Encyclopedia of Sociology*, edited by G. Ritzer. Malden, MA: Blackwell.

Dandaneau, Steven P. 2012. "Deindustrialization." Pp. 385–387 in *The Wiley-Blackwell Encyclopedia of Globalization*, edited by G. Ritzer. Malden, MA: Wiley-Blackwell.

Daniels, Jessie. 2009. *Cyber Racism: White Supremacy Online and the New Attack on Civil Rights*. Lanham, MD: Rowman and Littlefield.

Dann, Gary Elijah and Neil Haddow. 2008. "Just Doing Business or Doing Just Business: Google, Microsoft, Yahoo! and the Business of Censoring China's Internet." *Journal of Business Ethics* 79: 219–234.

Danseco, Evangeline, Paul Kingery, and Mark Coggeshall. 1999. "Perceived Risk of Harm from Marijuana Use among Youth in the USA." *School Psychology International* 20(1): 39–56.

Dant, Tim. 2007. "Material Culture." P. 2835 in *The Blackwell Encyclopedia of Sociology*, edited by G. Ritzer. Malden, MA: Blackwell.

"The Dark Side of Organizations: Mistake, Misconduct, and Disaster." 1999. *Annual Review of Sociology* 25: 271–305.

D'Arma, Alessandro. 2011. "Global Media, Business and Politics: A Comparative Analysis of News Corporation's Strategy in Italy and the UK." *International Communication Gazette* 73(8): 670–684.

Darwin, Charles. [1859] 2003. *On the Origin of Species*. London: Signet Classics.

Datar, Srikant, David A. Garvin, and Patrick G. Cullen. 2010. *Rethinking the MBA: Business Education at a Crossroads*. Cambridge, MA: Harvard Business Review Press.

David, Mathew and Peter Millwood. 2012. "Football's Coming Home? Digital Reterritorialization, Contradictions in the Transnational Coverage of Sport and the Sociology of Alternative Football Broadcasts." *The British Journal of Sociology* 63: 349–369.

Davidson, Christopher M. 2008. *Dubai: The Vulnerability of Success*. New York: Columbia University Press.

Davidson, Julia O'Connell. 2005. *Children in the Global Sex Trade*. Cambridge, UK: Polity Press.

Davis, F. James. 1991a. *Who Is Black? One Nation's Definition*. Philadelphia: Penn State University Press.

Davis, F. James. 1991b. "Who Is Black? One Nation's Definition." Retrieved January 27, 2012 (http://www.pbs.org/wgbh/pages/frontline/shows/jefferson/mixed/onedrop.html).

Davis, Flora. [1991] 1999. *Moving the Mountain: The Women's Movement in America since 1960.* New York: Simon and Schuster.

Davis, Kingsley. 1940. "Extreme Social Isolation of a Child." *American Journal of Sociology* 45(4): 554–565.

Davis, Kingsley. 1945. "The World Demographic Transition." *Annals of the American Academy of Political and Social Science* 237: 1–110.

Davis, Kingsley. 1947. "Final Note on a Case of Extreme Isolation." *American Journal of Sociology* 50: 432–437.

Davis, Kingsley and Wilbert E. Moore. 1945. "Some Principles of Stratification." *American Sociological Review* 10.

Davis, Mike. 2006. "Fear and Money in Dubai." *New Left Review* 41(September/October).

Davis, Mike. 2007. *Planet of Slums.* London: Verso.

Davis-Blake, Allison and Joseph P. Broschak. 2009. "Outsourcing and the Changing Nature of Work." *Annual Review of Sociology* 35: 321–340.

Day, Jennifer Cheeseman and Eric C. Newburger. 2002. "The Big Payoff: Educational Attainment and Synthetic Estimates of Work-Life Earnings." *Current Population Reports* (July): 1–13.

Dean, Cornelia. 2007. "Experts Discuss Engineering Feats, Like Space Mirror, to Slow Climate Change." *New York Times,* November 10, p. A11.

Debas, Haile T. 2010. "Global Health: Priority Agenda for the 21st Century." *UN Chronicle* XLVII(2). Retrieved March 29, 2012 (http://www.un.org/wcm/content/site/chronicle/cache/bypass/home/archive/issues2010/achieving_global_health/globalhealth_priorityagendaforthe21stcentury?ctnscroll_articleContainerList=1_0&ctnlistpagination_articleContainerList=true).

Decker, Scott H. and G. David Curry. 2000. "Addressing Key Features of Gang Membership: Measuring the Involvement of Young Members." *Journal of Criminal Justice* 28: 473–482.

De Ferrante, David and Julio Frenk. 2012. "Toward Universal Health Coverage." *New York Times,* April 5.

De Graaf, Nan D., Paul M. De Graaf, and Gerbert Kraaykamp. 2000. "Parental Cultural Capital and Educational Attainment in the Netherlands." *Sociology of Education* 73: 92–111.

De Graaf, Paul M. 2007. "Stratification: Functional and Conflict Theories." Pp. 4797–4799 in *The Blackwell Encyclopedia of Sociology,* edited by G. Ritzer. Malden, MA: Blackwell.

De la Dehesa, Rafael. 2010. *Queering the Public Sphere in Mexico and Brazil: Sexual Rights Movements in Emerging Democracies.* Durham, NC: Duke University Press.

D'Elia, Valarie. 2011. "Developers Have Big Plans for NJ Mega Mall." *NY1,* May 19. Retrieved May 19, 2011 (http://bronx.ny1.com/content/ny1_living/travel/139387/developers-have-big-plans-for-nj-mega-mall).

De Lollis, Barbara and Laura Petrecca. 2005. "Four Years after 9/11, New York Is Back." *USA Today,* September 8. Retrieved March 31, 2012 (http://www.usatoday.com/travel/news/2005-09-08-new-york-usat_x.htm).

DeNavas-Walt, Carmen, Bernadette D. Proctor, and Jessica C. Smith. 2010. "Income, Poverty, and Health Insurance Coverage In the United States: 2009" (Table A-3). *Current Population Reports: Current Income.* U.S. Census Bureau, U.S. Department of Commerce.

DeNavas-Walt, Carmen, Bernadette D. Proctor, and Jessica C. Smith. 2011. "Income, Poverty, and Health Insurance Coverage in the United States: 2010." *Current Population Reports: Consumer Income* (September): P60–239. Retrieved March 29, 2012 (http://www.census.gov/prod/2011pubs/p60-239.pdf).

Denegri-Knott, Janice and Detlev Zwick. 2012. "Tracking Prosumption Work on eBay: Reproduction of Desire and the Challenge of Slow Re-McDonaldization." *American Behavioral Scientist* 56: 439–458.

Dentler, Robert A. and Kai T. Erickson. 1959. "The Function of Deviance in Small Groups." *Social Problems* 7: 98–107.

Denzin, Norman K. and Yvonna S. Lincoln. 2011. "Introduction: The Discipline and Practice of Qualitative Research." Pp. 1–20 in *The SAGE Handbook of Qualitative Research,* edited by N. K. Denzin and Y. S. Lincoln. 4th ed. Thousand Oaks, CA: Sage.

DeParle, Jason, Robert Gebeloff, and Sabrina Tavernise. 2011. "Older, Suburban and Struggling." *New York Times,* November 19, pp. A1, A13.

Desai, Sonalde. 2010. "The Other Half of the Demographic Dividend." *Economic and Political Weekly* 14: 12–14.

De Silva, Dakshina G., Robert P. McComb, Young-Kyu Moh, Anita R. Schiller, and Andres J. Vargas. 2010. "The Effect of Migration on Wages: Evidence From a Natural Experiment." *American Economic Review: Papers and Proceedings* 100(May): 321–326.

Desmond, Matthew. 2010. *The Dynamics of Eviction in Inner-City Milwaukee.* PhD dissertation, University of Wisconsin.

Deutsch, Claudia H. 2007. "For Fiji Water, a Big List of Green Goals." *New York Times,* November 7, p. C3.

Deutsch, Nancy and Eleni Theodorou. 2010. "Aspiring, Consuming, Becoming: Youth Identity in a Culture of Consumption." *Youth and Society* 42(2): 229–254.

DeVault, Marjorie. 1991. *Feeding the Family: The Social Organization of Caring as Gendered Work.* Chicago: University of Chicago Press.

Dey EL. 1997. "Undergraduate Political Attitudes: Peer Influence in Changing Social Contexts." *Journal of Higher Education* 68: 398–416.

Diamond, Jared. 2006. *Collapse: How Societies Choose to Fail or Succeed.* New York: Penguin.

Dicke, Thomas S. 1992. *Franchising in America: The Development of a Business Method, 1840–1980.* Chapel Hill: University of North Carolina Press.

Dikötter, Frank. 2008. "The Racialization of the Globe: An Interactive Interpretation." *Ethnic and Racial Studies* 31(8): 1478–1496.

Dilworth-Anderson, Peggye and Gracie Boswell. 2007. "Cultural Diversity and Aging: Ethnicity, Minorities and Subcultures." Pp. 898–902 in *The Blackwell Encyclopedia of Sociology,* edited by G. Ritzer. Malden, MA: Blackwell.

DiMaggio, Paul. 1987. "Classification in Art." *American Sociological Review* 52: 440–455.

DiMaggio, Paul, Eszter Hargittai, W. Russell Neuman, and John P. Robinson. 2001. "Social Implications of the Internet." *Annual Review of Sociology* 27: 307–336.

DiMaggio, Paul J. and Walter W. Powell. 1983. "'The Iron Cage Revisited': Institutional Isomorphism and Collective Rationality in Organizational Fields." *American Sociological Review* 48(2): 147–160.

Diotallevi, Luca. 2007. "Church." Pp. 483–489 in *The Blackwell Encyclopedia of Sociology,* edited by G. Ritzer. Malden, MA: Blackwell.

DiPrete, Thomas A., Gregory M. Eirich, Karen S. Cook, and Douglas S. Massey. 2006. "Cumulative Advantage as a Mechanism for Inequality: A Review of Theoretical and Empirical Developments." *Annual Review of Sociology* 32: 271–297.

Disch, Lisa J. 2002. *The Tyranny of the Two-Party System.* New York: Columbia University Press.

Dobbelaere, Karel. 2007. "Secularization." Pp. 4140–4148 in *The Blackwell Encyclopedia of Sociology,* edited by G. Ritzer. Malden, MA: Blackwell.

Docherty, Iain, Robina Goodlad, and Ronan Paddison. 2001. "Civic Culture, Community and Citizen Participation in Contrasting Neighbourhoods." *Urban Studies* 38(12): 2225–2250.

Dodd, Nigel. 2012. "Money." Pp. 1444–1448 in *The Wiley-Blackwell Encyclopedia of Globalization,* edited by G. Ritzer. Malden, MA: Wiley-Blackwell.

Dohnt, Hayley K. and Marika Tiggeman. 2006. "Body Image Concerns in Young Girls: The Role of Peers and Media Prior to Adolescence." *Journal of Youth and Adolescence* 35: 21–33.

Dombrink, John and Daniel Hillyard. 2007. *Sin No More: From Abortion to Stem Cells, Understanding Crime, Law and Morality in America.* New York: New York University Press.

Domhoff, G. William. 1974. *The Bohemian Grove and Other Retreats: A Study in Ruling-Class Cohesiveness.* New York: Harper and Row.

Dominguez, Jorge I., Rafael Hernandez, and Lorena Barberia, eds. 2011. *Debating U.S.-Cuban Relations: Shall We Play Ball?*

Contemporary Inter-American Relations Series. London: Routledge.

Donadio, Rachel. 2008. "Italy's Attacks on Migrants Fuel Debate on Racism." *New York Times*, October 2.

Donadio, Rachel. 2010. "Looking Past The Façade of Italian City After Riots." *New York Times*, January 13, p. A6.

Dongen, Stefan. 2012. "Fluctuating Asymmetry and Masculinity/Femininity in Humans: A Meta-analysis." *Archives of Sexual Behavior* 41(6): 1453–1460.

Dooley, David and JoAnn Prause. 2009. *The Social Costs of Underemployment: Inadequate Employment as Disguised Unemployment*. Cambridge, UK: Cambridge University Press.

Dorius, Shawn and Glenn Firebaugh. 2010. "Trends in Global Gender Inequality." *Social Forces* 88(5): 1941–1968.

Dotter, Daniel L. and Julian B. Roebuck. 1988. "The Labeling Approach Re-examined: Interactionism and the Components of Deviance." *Deviant Behavior* 9(1): 19–32.

Douglas, Susan J. and Meredith W. Michaels. 2006. "The New Momism." Pp. 226–238 in *Reconstructing Gender: A Multicultural Anthology*, edited by E. Disch. New York: McGraw-Hill Education.

Downes, David and Paul Rock. 2011. *Understanding Deviance: A Guide to the Sociology of Crime and Rule-Breaking*. Oxford, UK: Oxford University Press.

Downey, Douglas B., Paul T. von Hippel, and Beckett A. Broh. 2004. "Are Schools the Great Equalizer? Cognitive Inequality during the Summer Months and the School Year." *American Sociological Review* 69: 613–635.

Downing, John D. H. 2011. "Media Ownership, Concentration, and Control: The Evolution of Debate." In *The Handbook of Political Economy of Communications*, edited by J. Wasko, G. Murdock, and H. Sousa. Oxford, UK: Wiley-Blackwell.

Doyle, Thomas P. 2003. "Roman Catholic Clericalism, Religious Duress, and Clergy Sexual Abuse." *Pastoral Psychology* 51(3): 189–231.

"DP Seeks to Calm the Storm Over Ports." 2006. *The Economist*, March 10. Retrieved March 29, 2012 (http://www.economist.com/node/5620236).

Drache, D. (with M. D. Froese). 2008. *Defiant Publics: The Unprecedented Reach of the Global Citizen*. Cambridge, UK: Polity Press.

Drane, John. 2000. *The McDonaldization of the Church: Spirituality, Creativity, and the Future of the Church*. London: Darton, Longman and Todd.

Drane, John. 2001. *The McDonaldization of the Church*. London: Darton, Longman, Todd.

Drane, John. 2008. *After McDonaldization: Mission, Ministry, and Christian Discipleship in an Age of Uncertainty*. Grand Rapids, MI: Baker.

Dreeben, Robert. 1968. *On What Is Learned in School*. Reading, MA: Addison-Wesley.

Drew, Christopher. 2010. "The War Chatroom." *New York Times*, June 8, p. B1.

Drori, Gili. 2006. *Global E-litism: Digital Technology, Social Inequality, and Transnationality*. New York: Worth.

Drori, Gili S. 2010. "Globalization and Technology Divides: Bifurcation of Policy Between the 'Digital Divide' and the 'Innovation Divide.'" *Sociological Inquiry* 80: 63–91.

Drori, Gili. 2012. "Digital Divide." Pp. 435–438 in *Wiley-Blackwell Encyclopedia of Globalization*, edited by G. Ritzer. Malden, MA: Wiley-Blackwell.

Duány, Andrés and Elizabeth Plater-Zyberk. 1990. "Projects of Villages, Towns and Cities, Territories, and Codes." In *Towns and Town-making Principles*, edited by A. Krieger and W. Lennertz. New York: Rizzoli.

Duány, Andres, Elizabeth Plater-Zyberk, and Jeff Speck. 2010. *Suburban Nation: The Rise of Sprawl and the Decline of the American Dream*. 10th anniversary ed. North Point Press.

Duberman, Martin B. 1994. *Stonewall*. New York: Plume.

Du Bois W. E. B. [1899] 1996. *The Philadelphia Negro: A Social Study*. Philadelphia: University of Pennsylvania Press.

Du Bois, W. E. B. [1903] 1966. *The Souls of Black Folk*. New York: Modern Library.

Duckworth, Angela and Martin Seligman. 2005. "Self-Discipline Outdoes IQ Predicting Academic Performance in Adolescents." *Psychological Science* 16: 939–944.

Duhigg, Charles and Keith Bradsher. 2012. "How the U.S. Lost Out on iPhone Work." *New York Times*, January 22, pp. A1, A22.

Dullea, Georgia. 1991. "The Tract House as Landmark." *New York Times*, October 17, pp. C1, C8.

Dukes, Richard L. and Judith A. Stein. 2011. "Ink and Holes Correlates and Predictive Associations of Body Modification among Adolescents." *Youth and Society* 43: 1547–1569.

Dumazadier, Joffre. 1967. *Toward a Society of Leisure*. New York: Free Press.

Duncan, Greg J., Kathleen M. Ziol-Guest, and Ariel Kalil. 2010. "Early-Childhood Poverty and Adult Attainment, Behavior, and Health." *Child Development* 81: 306–325.

Duneier, Mitchell. 1999. *Sidewalk*. New York: Farrar, Strauss, Giroux.

Dunlap, Eloise, Bruce D. Johnson, Joseph A. Kotarba, and Jennifer L. Fackler. 2010. "Macro-Level Social Forces and Micro-Level Consequences: Poverty, Alternate Occupations, and Drug Dealing." *Journal of Ethnicity in Substance Abuse* 9(2): 115–127.

Dunlap, Riley E. 2007. "Environment, Sociology of the." Pp. 1417–1422 in *The Blackwell Encyclopedia of Sociology*, edited by G. Ritzer. Malden, MA: Blackwell.

Dunlap, Riley E. and William R. Catton Jr. 2002. "Which Functions of the Environment Do We Study? A Comparison of Environmental and Natural Resource Sociology." *Society and Natural Resources* 15: 239–249.

Dunlap, Riley E. and Andrew K. Jorgenson. 2012. "Environmental Problems." Pp. 529–536 in *The Wiley-Blackwell Companion to Sociology*, edited by G. Ritzer. Malden, MA: Wiley-Blackwell.

Dunn, Jennifer L. 2005. "'Victims' and 'Survivors': Emerging Vocabularies of Motive for 'Battered Women Who Stay.'" *Sociological Inquiry* 75: 1–30.

Dunning, Eric, Patrick Murphy, and John Williams. 1986. *The Roots of Football Hooliganism*. London: Routledge and Kegan Paul.

Durkheim, Émile. [1893] 1964. *The Division of Labor in Society*. New York: Free Press.

Durkheim, Émile. [1895] 1982. *The Rules of Sociological Method*. New York: Free Press.

Durkheim, Émile. [1897] 1951. *Suicide*. New York: Free Press.

Durkheim, Émile. [1912] 1965. *Elementary Forms of Religious Life*. New York: Free Press.

Durkheim, Émile. 1956. *Education and Society*. Glencoe, IL: Free Press.

Durkheim, Émile. 1973. *Moral Education*. New York: Free Press.

Duster, Troy. 2003. *Backdoor to Eugenics*. New York: Routledge.

Dustin, Donna. 2007. *The McDonaldization of Social Work*. Burlington, VT: Ashgate.

Dworkin, Andrea. 1974. *Woman Hating*. New York: E. P. Dutton.

Earl, Jennifer. 2007. "Social Movements, Repression of." Pp. 4475–4479 in *The Blackwell Encyclopedia of Sociology*, edited by G. Ritzer. Malden, MA: Blackwell.

Eckholm, Erik. 2010. "Recession Raises U.S. Poverty Rate to a 1-Year High." *New York Times*, September 17, pp. A1, A3.

Edgell, Penny, Joseph Gerteis, and Douglas Hartmann. 2006. "Atheists as 'Other': Moral Boundaries and Cultural Membership in American Society." *American Sociological Review*, 71(2): 211–234.

Edin, Kathryn and Laura Lein. 1997. *Making Ends Meet: How Single Mothers Survive Welfare and Low-Wage Work*. New York: Russell Sage.

Edwards, Bob. 2007. "Resource Mobilization Theory." Pp. 3893–3898 in *The Blackwell Encyclopedia of Sociology*, edited by G. Ritzer. Malden, MA: Blackwell.

Edwards, Bob and Patrick F. Gillham. 2013. "Resource Mobilization Theory." Pp. 1096–1101 in *The Wiley-Blackwell Encyclopedia of Social and Political Movements*, 3 vols., edited by D. A. Snow, D. Della Porta, B. Klandermans, and D. McAdam. Malden, MA: Wiley-Blackwell.

Edwards, Rosalind and Lucy Hadfield. 2007. "Stepfathering." Pp. 4768–4770 in *The Blackwell Encyclopedia of Sociology*, edited by G. Ritzer. Malden, MA: Blackwell.

Ehrenreich, Barbara. 2001. *Nickel and Dimed: On (Not) Getting By in America*. New York: Henry Holt.

Ehrenreich, Barbara. 2002. "Maid to Order." In *Global Woman: Nannies, Maids and Sex Workers in the New Economy*, edited by B. Ehrenreich and A. Hochschild. New York: Henry Holt.

Ehrenreich, Barbara. 2008. *Nickel and Dimed: On (Not) Getting By in America.* New York: Holt Paperbacks.

Ehrenreich, Barbara and Arlie Hochschild. 2002. "Introduction." In *Global Woman: Nannies, Maids and Sex Workers in the New Economy,* edited by B. Ehrenreich and A. Hochschild. New York: Henry Holt.

Ehrlich, Paul. 1968. *The Population Bomb.* New York: Ballantine.

Ekland-Olson, Sheldon. 2012. *Who Lives, Who Dies, Who Decides.* New York: Routledge.

Elgin, Duane. 2010. *Voluntary Simplicity: Toward a Way of Life that Is Outwardly Simple, Inwardly Rich.* 2nd ed. New York: Quill.

Elliott, Anthony and John Urry. 2010. *Mobile Lives.* London: Routledge.

Elliott, David L. 2012. "Urbanism." Pp. 2134–2136 in *The Wiley-Blackwell Encyclopedia of Globalization,* edited by G. Ritzer. Malden, MA: Wiley-Blackwell.

Elliott, Diana B., Rebekah Young, and Jane Lawler Dye. 2011. "Variation in the Formation of Complex Family Households During the Recession" (SEHSD Working Paper Number 2011-32). Paper presented at the National Council on Family Relations 73rd Annual Conference, Orlando, FL, November 16–19.

Ellison, Christopher G. 1999. "Introduction to Symposium: Religion, Health, Well-being." *Journal for the Scientific Study of Religion* 37: 692–693.

Elo, Irma T. 2007. "Mortality: Transitions and Measures." Pp. 3096–102 in *The Blackwell Encyclopedia of Sociology,* edited by George Ritzer. Malden, MA: Blackwell.

Elo, Irma. 2009. "Social Class Differentials in Health and Mortality: Patterns and Explanations in Comparative Perspective." *Annual Review of Sociology* 35: 553–572.

Elster, Jon. 1999. *An Introduction to Karl Marx.* New York: Cambridge University Press.

Emerson, R., ed. 2001. *Contemporary Field Research: Perspectives and Formulations.* 2nd ed. Longrove, IL: Waveland Press.

Emery, Robert E. 1999. *Marriage, Divorce and Children's Adjustment.* 2nd ed. Thousand Oaks, CA: Sage.

Encyclopedia Britannica Inc. 2010. *The Encyclopedia Britannica.* Chicago.

Engels, Friedrich. [1884] 1970. *The Origins of the Family, Private Property and the State.* New York: International Publishers.

Engels, Friedrich. [1884] 2010. *The Origin of the Family, Private Property and the State.* New York: Penguin Classics.

England, Paula. 2010. "The Gender Revolution: Uneven and Stalled." *Gender and Society* 24(2): 149–166.

England, Paula and Kathryn Edin. 2009. "Briefing Paper: Unmarried Couples With Children: Why Don't They Marry? How Can Policy-Makers Promote More Stable Relationships?" Pp. 307–312 in *Families as They Really Are,* edited by B. J. Risman. New York: Norton.

EnglishEnglish.com. N.d. "The English Language: Facts and Figures." Retrieved January 3, 2012 (http://www.englishenglish.com/english_facts_8.htm).

Entwhistle, Joanne. 2009. *The Aesthetic Economy of Fashion: Markets and Value in Clothing and Modelling (Dress, Body, Culture).* New York: Berg.

Entwisle, Doris, Karl Alexander, and Linda Olson. 1998. *Children, Schools, and Inequality.* Boulder, CO: Westview Press.

Epstein, Cynthia Fuchs. 1988. *Deceptive Distinctions: Sex, Gender, and the Social Order.* New Haven, CT: Yale University Press.

Epstein, Steve. 2009. *Inclusion: The Politics of Difference in Medical Research.* Chicago: University of Chicago Press.

Eriksen, Thomas Hylland. 2007. "Steps to an Ecology of Transnational Sports." In *Globalization and Sport,* edited by R. Giulianotti and R. Robertson. Malden, MA: Blackwell.

Eriksen, Thomas Hylland. 2010. *Ethnicity and Nationalism: Anthropological Perspectives.* 3rd ed. Sidmouth, England: Pluto Press.

Eriksen, Thomas Hylland. 2012. "Ethnicity." Pp. 551–558 in *The Wiley-Blackwell Encyclopedia of Globalization,* edited by G. Ritzer. Malden, MA: Wiley-Blackwell.

Erikson, Erik. 1994. *Identity and the Life Cycle.* New York: Norton.

Erikson, Kai T. 1964. "Notes on the Sociology of Deviance." In *The Other Side: Perspectives on Deviance,* edited by H. S. Becker. New York: Free Press.

Erikson, Kai. 1978. *Everything in Its Path.* New York: Simon and Schuster Paperbacks.

Erlanger, Steven. 2008. "Tense Rivalries Threaten a Melting-Pot District." *New York Times,* September 24, p. A11.

Erlanger, Steven. 2010a. "Expulsion of Roma Raises Questions in France." *New York Times,* August 19.

Erlanger, Steven. 2010b. "A French Castle Built of Stone and Dreams." *New York Times,* August 1.

Erlanger, Steven. 2010c. "Utopian Dream Becomes Battleground in France." *New York Times,* August 9, p. A7.

Ertman, Thomas. 1997. *Birth of the Leviathan.* Cambridge: Cambridge University Press.

Esping-Anderson, Gosta. 1990. *The Three Worlds of Welfare Capitalism.* Princeton, NJ: Princeton University Press.

Etzioni, Amitai, ed. 1969. *The Semi-professions and Their Organization: Teachers, Nurses, and Social Workers.* New York: Free Press.

Ezzy, Douglas. 1993. "Unemployment and Mental Health: A Critical Review." *Social Science and Medicine* 37: 41–52.

Fackler, Martin. 2008. "Losing an Edge, Japanese Envy India's Schools." *New York Times,* January 2, pp. A1, A9.

Fackler, Martin. 2011. "Severed from the World, Villagers Survive on Tight Bonds and To-Do Lists." *New York Times,* March 23. Retrieved March 29, 2012 (http://www.nytimes.com/2011/03/24/world/asia/24isolated.html?adxnnl=1&adxnnlx=1332612166-pPLwIe5hgFAW4cQM2m4bWQ).

Faderman, Lillian. 1991. *Odd Girls and Twilight Lovers: A History of Lesbian Life in Twentieth Century America.* New York: Penguin.

Fadiman, Anne. 1997. *The Spirit Catches You and You Fall Down: A Hmong Child, Her Doctors, and the Collision of Two Cultures.* New York: Farrar, Strauss, Giroux.

Fahim, Kareem. 2010. "Away From Home, Fleeing Domestic Life: Immigrant Maids Suffer Abuse in Kuwait." *New York Times,* August 2, pp. A4, A8.

Faist, Thomas. 2012. "Migration." Pp. 1384–1388 in *The Wiley-Blackwell Encyclopedia of Globalization,* edited by G. Ritzer. Malden, MA: Wiley-Blackwell.

Faist, Thomas, Margit Fauser, and Eveline Reisenauer. 2013. *Transnational Migration.* Cambridge: Polity.

"Family Caregiver Role Acquisition: Role-Making through Situated Interaction." 1995. *Research and Theory for Nursing Practice* 9(3): 211–226.

Fantasia, Rick. 1992. "The Assault on American Labor." In *Social Problems,* edited by C. Calhoun and G. Ritzer. New York: McGraw-Hill.

Fantasia, Rick and Kim Voss. 2007. "Labor Movement." Pp. 2518–2521 in *The Blackwell Encyclopedia of Sociology,* edited by G. Ritzer. Malden, MA: Blackwell.

Fantasia, Rick, Kim Voss and Barry Eidlin. 2013. "Labor Movement." Pp. 665–671 in *The Wiley-Blackwell Encyclopedia of Social and Political Movements,* 3 vols., edited by D. A. Snow, D. Della Porta, B. Klandermans, and D. McAdam. Malden, MA: Wiley-Blackwell.

Farber, Henry. 2011. "Job Loss in the Great Recession: Historical Perspective From Displaced Workers Survey, 1984–2010." Paper presented at a Federal Reserve Conference, San Francisco, May.

Farley, John E. 2007. "Metropolitan Statistical Area." Pp. 2993–2996 in *The Blackwell Encyclopedia of Sociology,* edited by G. Ritzer. Malden, MA: Blackwell.

Farley, John E. 2009. *Majority-Minority Relations.* 6th ed. New Jersey: Prentice-Hall.

Farmer, Charles M. 2003. "Reliability of Police-Reported Information for Determining Crash and Injury Severity." *Traffic Injury Prevention* 4(1).

Farr, Kathryn. 2005. *Sex Trafficking: The Global Market in Women and Children.* New York: Worth.

Farrell, Betty, Alicia VandeVusse, and Abigail Ocobock. 2012. "Family Change and the State of Family Sociology." *Current Sociology* 60: 283–301.

Farrell, Caitlin, Priscilla Wohlstetter, and Joanna Smith. 2012. "Charter Management Organizations: An Emering Approach to Scaling Up What Work." *Educational Policy* 26(4): 499–532.

Farrell, Dan and James C. Peterson. 2010. "The Growth of Internet Research Methods and the Reluctant Sociologist." *Sociological Inquiry* 80: 114–125.

Fassmann, Heinz and Rainer Munz. 1992. "Patterns and Trends of International Migration in Western Europe." *Population and Development Review* 18: 457–480.

Fausto-Sterling, A. 1999. "The Five Sexes: Why Female and Male Are Not Enough." *The Sciences* (March/April): 20–24.

Feagin, Joe R. 2006. *Systemic Racism: A Theory of Oppression*. New York: Routledge.

Feagin, Joe R. 2010. *The White Racial Frame: Centuries of Racial Framing and Counter-Framing*. New York: Routledge.

Feagin, Joe R. 2012. *White Party, White Government: Race, Class, and U.S. Politics*. New York: Routledge.

Feagin, Joe R. 2013. *The White Racial Frame: Centuries of Racial Framing and Counter-Framing*. New York: Routledge.

Feagin, Joe R. and Harlan Hahn. 1973. *Ghetto Revolts: The Politics of Violence in American Cities*. New York: Macmillan.

Feagin, Joe, Anthony Orum, and Gideon Sjoberg, eds. 1991. *A Case for the Case Study*. North Carolina: University of North Carolina Press.

Feagin, Joe R. and Brittany Chevon Slatton. 2012. "Racial and Ethnic Issues: Critical Race Approaches in the United States." In *The New Blackwell Companion to Sociology*, edited by G. Ritzer. Malden, MA: Wiley-Blackwell.

Federal Bureau of Investigation. 2002–2005. "Terrorism." Retrieved March 29, 2012 (http://www.fbi.gov/stats-services/publications/terrorism-2002-2005/terror02_05).

Federal Bureau of Investigation. 2009. "Crime in the United States 2008." Retrieved April 21, 2010 (http://www.fbi.gov/ucr/cius2008/arrests/index.html).

Federal Bureau of Investigation. 2010. "Crime in the United States, 2009." Retrieved December 21, 2011 (http://www2.fbi.gov/ucr/cius2009/data/table_29.html).

Fehr, Ernst, Urs Fischbacher, and Simon Gächter. 2002. "Strong Reciprocity, Human Cooperation, and the Enforcement of Social Norms." *Human Nature* 13(1): 1–25.

Ferguson, Ann Arnett. 2001. *Bad Boys: Public Schools in the Making of Black Masculinity*. University of Michigan Press.

Fernandez, Bina. 2010. "Cheap and Disposable? The Impact of the Global Economic Crisis on the Migration of Ethiopian Women Domestic Workers to the Gulf." *Gender and Development* 8(2): 249–262.

Ferraro, Emilia. 2001. "Trueque: An Ethnographic Account of Barter, Trade and Money in Andean Ecuador." *The Journal of Latin American and Caribbean Anthropology* 16: 168–184.

Ferreira, Vitor Sergio. 2011. "Becoming a Heavily Tattooed Young Body: From a Bodily Experience to a Body Project." *Youth and Society* (November): 1–35.

Fiddian-Qasmiyeh, Elena. 2012. "Diaspora." Pp. 430–433 in *The Wiley-Blackwell Encyclopedia of Globalization*, edited by G. Ritzer. Malden, MA: Wiley-Blackwell.

Fielding, A. J. 1989. "Migration and Urbanization in Western Europe Since 1950." *The Geographical Journal* 155: 60–69.

Fields, Echo. 1988. "Qualitative Content Analysis of Television News: Systematic Techniques." *Qualitative Sociology* 11(3): 183–193.

Fillipi, Veronique, Carine Ronsman, Oona MR Campbell, Wendy J. Graham, Anne Mills, Jo Borghi, Marjorie Koblinsky, and David Osrin. 2006. "Maternal Health in Poor Countries: The Broader Context and a Call for Action." *The Lancet* 368: 1525–1541.

Fine, Gary. 1987. *With the Boys: Little League Baseball and Preadolescent Culture*. Chicago: University of Chicago.

Fine, Gary Alan. 2010. *Authors of the Storm: Meteorologists and the Culture of Prediction*. Chicago: University of Chicago Press.

Fine, Gary. 2012. "Group Culture and the Interaction Order: Local Sociology on the Meso-Level." *Annual Review of Sociology* 38: 159–179.

Fine, Mark A. 2007. "Children and Divorce." Pp. 467–471 in *The Blackwell Encyclopedia of Sociology*, edited by G. Ritzer. Malden, MA: Blackwell.

Finke, Roger and Rodney Stark. 2005. *The Churching of America, 1776–2005: Winners and Losers in Our Religious Economy*. New Brunswick, NJ: Rutgers University Press.

Firebaugh, Glenn and Brian Goesling. 2007. "Globalization and Global Inequalities: Recent Trends." Pp. 549–564 in *The Blackwell Companion to Globalization*, edited by George Ritzer. Malden, MA: Blackwell.

Fischer, Claude S., Michael Hout, Martin Sanchez Jankowski, and Samuel R. Lucas, eds. 1996. *Inequality by Design: Cracking the Bell Curve Myth*. Princeton, NJ: Princeton University Press.

Fisher, Dana. 2012. "Environmental Activism." Pp. 517–519 in *The Wiley-Blackwell Encyclopedia of Globalization*, edited by G. Ritzer. Malden, MA: Wiley-Blackwell.

Fisher, William F. and Thomas Ponniah. 2003. *Another World Is Possible: Popular Alternatives to Globalization at the World Social Forum*. London: Zed Books.

Fitzgerald, Patrick and Brian Lambkin. 2008. *Migration in Irish History 1607–2007*. New York: Palgrave Macmillan.

Flanigan, James. 2008. "Passports Essential for the M.B.A.'s." *New York Times*, February 21, p. C5.

Flavin, Jeanne. 2008. *Our Bodies, Our Crimes*. New York: New York University Press.

Florida, Richard, Tim Gulden, and Charlotta Mellander. 2007. *The Rise of the Mega-region*. Joseph L. Rotman School of Management, The Martin Prosperity Institute, University of Toronto.

Flynn, Nicole. 2007. "Deindustrialization." Pp. 992–994 in *The Blackwell Encyclopedia of Sociology*, edited by G. Ritzer. Malden, MA: Blackwell.

Flynn, Sean. 2011. "The Sex Trade." Pp. 41–66 in *Deviant Globalization: Black Market Economy in the 21st Century*, edited by N. Gilman, J. Goldhammer, and S. Weber. London: Continuum.

FM Signal. 2010. "Morgan Stanley: Internet Trends." *SlideShare*, June 7. Retrieved March 31, 2012 (http://www.slideshare.net/CMSummit/ms-internet-trends060710final).

Fogiel-Bijaoui, Sylvie. 2007. "Women in the Kibbutz: The 'Mixed Blessing' of Neo-Liberalism." *Nashim: A Journal of Jewish Women's Studies and Gender Issues* 13(Spring): 102–122.

Fogiel-Bijaoui, Sylvie. 2009. "Kibbutz." *Jewish Women: A Comprehensive Historical Encyclopedia*, March 1. Jewish Women's Archive. Retrieved September 10, 2011 (http://jwa.org/encyclopedia/article/kibbutz).

Fontana, Andrea. 2007. "Interviewing, Structured, Unstructured, and Postmodern." Pp. 2407–2411 in *The Blackwell Encyclopedia of Sociology*, edited by George Ritzer. Malden, MA: Blackwell.

Forno, Francesca. 2013. "Consumer Movements." Pp. 253–256 in *The Wiley-Blackwell Encyclopedia of Social and Political Movements*, 3 vols., edited by D. A. Snow, D. Della Porta, B. Klandermans, and D. McAdam. Malden, MA: Wiley-Blackwell.

Foucault, Michel. 1975. *The Birth of the Clinic: An Archaeology of Medical Perception*. New York: Vintage.

Foucault, Michel. [1975] 1979. *Discipline and Punish: The Birth of the Prison*. New York: Vintage.

Foucault, Michel. 1978. *The History of Sexuality: Volume 1. An Introduction*. New York: Vintage.

Fourcade, Marion. 2009. *Economists and Societies: Discipline and Profession in the United States, Britain, and France, 1890s to 1990s*. Princeton, NJ: Princeton University Press.

Fourcade-Gourinchas, Marion. 2007. "Culture, Economy and." Pp. 932–936 in *The Blackwell Encyclopedia of Sociology*, edited by George Ritzer. Malden, MA: Blackwell.

"14 Cool Vending Machines from Japan." 2009. *Toxel.com*, June 8. Retrieved August 25, 2011 (www.toxel.com/tech/2009/06/08/14-cool-vending-machines-from-Japan/).

Fox, Susannah, Kathryn Zickuhr, and Aaron Smith. 2009. "Twitter and Status Updating." *Pew Internet and American Life Project*, October 21. Retrieved March 29, 2012 (http://www.pewinternet.org/Reports/2009/17-Twitter-and-Status-Updating-Fall-2009.aspx?r=1).

Frailing, Kelly, Jr., and Dee Wood Harper. 2010. "The Social Construction of Deviance, Conflict and the Criminalization of Midwives, New Orleans: 1940s and 1950s." *Deviant Behavior* 31: 729–755.

France, Anatole. [1894] 2011. *The Red Lily*. Kindle edition.

Francis, Mark. 2011. "Herbert Spencer." Pp. 165–184 in *The Wiley-Blackwell Companion to Major Social Theorists: Volume 1. Classical Theorists*, edited by G. Ritzer and J. Stepnisky. Malden, MA: Wiley-Blackwell.

Frank, David John. 2012a. "Global Sex." In *The Wiley-Blackwell Encyclopedia of Globalization*, edited by G. Ritzer. Malden, MA: Wiley-Blackwell.

Frank, David John. 2012b. "Sex." Pp. 1843–1847 in *The Wiley-Blackwell Companion to Sociology*, edited by G. Ritzer. Malden, MA: Wiley-Blackwell.

Frank, David John and Elizabeth H. McEneaney. 1999. "The Individualization of Society and the Liberalization of State Policies on Same Sex Sexual Relations, 1984–1995." *Social Forces* 77: 911–944.

Frank, Robert H. 2011. *The Darwin Economy: Liberty, Competition, and the Common Good*. Princeton, NJ: Princeton University Press.

Frank, Robert H. and Philip J. Cook. 1995. *The Winner-Take-All Society*. New York: Penguin.

Franklin, V. P. 1987. "W. E. B. Du Bois as Journalist." *The Journal of Negro Education* 56(Spring): 40–44.

Freedman, Russell. 2009. *Freedom Walkers: The Story of the Montgomery Bus Boycott*. Holiday House.

Freedom to Marry. 2013. *States*. Retrieved October 24, 2013 (http://www.freedomtomarry.org/states/).

Freeman, Carla. 2001. "Is Local: Global as Feminine: Masculine? Rethinking the Gender of Globalization." *Signs: Journal of Women in Culture and Society* 26(4): 1007–1037.

Freeman, Richard B. and James L. Medoff. 1984. *What Do Unions Do?* New York: Basic Books.

Freidrichs, Robert. 1970. *A Sociology of Sociology*. New York: Free Press.

Freidson, Eliot. 1970a. *Profession of Medicine*. New York: Dodd, Mead.

Freidson, Eliot. 1970b. *Professional Dominance*. New York: Atheron.

French, Howard W. 2008. "Great Firewall of China Faces Online Rebels." *New York Times*, February 4.

Freud, Sigmund. 2006. *The Penguin Freud Reader*. New York: Penguin.

Freudenheim, Milt. 2009. "Tool in Cystic Fibrosis Fight: A Registry." *New York Times*, December 22, p. D1.

Freudenheim, Milt. 2010. "In Haiti, Practicing Medicine from Afar." *New York Times*, February 9.

Friedan, Betty. 1963. *The Feminine Mystique*. New York: Dell.

Frieden, Jeffry A. 2006. *Global Capitalism: Its Fall and Rise in the Twentieth Century*. New York: Norton.

Friedkin, N. E. 2001. "Norm Formation in Social Influence Networks." *Social Networks* 23(3): 167–189.

Friedman, Debra and Michael Hechter. 1988. "The Contribution of Rational Choice Theory to Macrosociological Research." *Sociological Theory* 6: 201–218.

Friedman, Jonathan. 1986. "The World City Hypothesis." *Development and Change* 17.

Friedman, Jonathan. 1994. *Culture Identity and Global Processes*. London: Sage.

Friedman, Judith J. 2007. "Suburbs." Pp. 4878–4881 in *The Blackwell Encyclopedia of Sociology*, edited by G. Ritzer. Malden, MA: Blackwell.

Friedman, Thomas. 1999. *The Lexus and the Olive Tree*. New York: Farrar, Strauss, Giroux.

Friedman, Thomas. 2005. *The World Is Flat: A Brief History of the Twenty-First Century*. New York: Farrar, Strauss, Giroux.

Friedrichs, David O. 2007. "Organizational Deviance." Pp. 3303–3306 in *The Blackwell Encyclopedia of Sociology*, edited by G. Ritzer. Malden, MA: Blackwell.

Friedrichs, Robert. 1970. *A Sociology of Sociology*. New York: Free Press.

Frieze, Irene Hanson. 2007. "Love and Commitment." Pp. 2671–2674 in *The Blackwell Encyclopedia of Sociology*, edited by G. Ritzer. Malden, MA: Blackwell.

Fritsch, Jane. 2001. "A Day of Terror: The Response; Rescue Workers Rush In, and Many Do Not Return." *New York Times*, September 12. Retrieved March 29, 2012 (http://www.nytimes.com/2001/09/12/us/a-day-of-terror-the-response-rescue-workers-rush-in-and-many-do-not-return.html?ref=sept112001).

Fulbrook, Julian. 2007. "Tobacco." Pp. 1146–1149 in *Encyclopedia of Globalization*, edited by J. A. Scholte and R. Robertson. New York: MTM Publishing.

Fung, A. 2004. *Empowered Participation: Reinventing Urban Democracy*. Princeton, NJ: Princeton University Press.

Gabriel, Trip. 2010. "For Students in Internet Age, No Shame in Copy and Paste." *New York Times*, August 2, pp. A1, A10.

Gadsden, Gloria. 2007. "Gender, Deviance and." Pp. 1856–1858 in *The Blackwell Encyclopedia of Sociology*, edited by G. Ritzer. Malden, MA: Blackwell.

Gaio, Fatima Janine. 1995. "Women in Software Programming: The Experience in Brazil." In *Women Encounter Technology*, edited by S. Mitter and S. Rowbotham. London: Routledge.

Gallegos, Jodi. 2008. "Basic Skateboarding Terminology: Beginner's Terms for Skateboard Tricks and Styles." Outdoor and Recreation Suite 101, ExtremeSports, March 5. Retrieved August 26, 2011 (www.suite101.com/content/basic-skateboarding-terminology-a46799).

Galston, William A., Steven Kull, and Clay Ramsay. 2009. *Battleground or Common Ground? American Public Opinion on Health Care Reform*. Washington, DC: Brookings Institution.

Gambino, Matthew. 2013. "Erving Goffman's Asylums and Institutional Culture in the Mid-Twentieth-Century United States." *Harvard Review of Psychiatry* 21: 52–57.

Gamoran, Adam and Daniel A. Long. 2006. *Equality of Educational Opportunity: A 40-Year Retrospective* [WCER Working Paper No. 2006-9]. Madison: Wisconsin Center for Education Research. Retrieved July 13, 2013 (http://www.wcer.wisc.edu).

Gamoran, Adam and Robert D. Mare. 1989. "Secondary School Tracking and Educational Inequality: Compensation, Reinforcement, or Neutrality?" *American Journal of Sociology* 94: 1146–1183.

Gamoran, Adam, Martin Nystrand, Mark Berends, and Paul C. LePore. 1995. "An Organizational Analysis of the Effects of Ability Grouping." *American Educational Research Journal* 32: 687–715.

Gangl, Markus. 2007. "Welfare State." Pp. 5242–5246 in *The Blackwell Encyclopedia of Sociology*, edited by G. Ritzer. Malden, MA: Blackwell.

Gans, Herbert. 1962. *The Urban Villagers*. New York: Free Press.

Gans, Herbert. 1967. *The Levittowners*. New York: Columbia University Press.

Gans, Herbert. 1979. *Deciding What's News*. New York: Pantheon.

Gans, Herbert. 1999. *Popular Culture and High Culture: An Analysis and Evaluation of Taste*. New York: Basic Books.

Gans, Herbert J. 2003. *Democracy and the News*. New York: Oxford University Press.

Gans, Herbert J. 2009. "First Generation Decline: Downward Mobility among Refugees and Immigrants." *Ethnic and Racial Studies* 32: 1658–1670.

Garcia, David. 2008. "The Impact of School Choice on Racial Segregation in Charter Schools." *Educational Policy* 22(6): 805–829.

Gardner, Beth Gharrity. 2013. "Social Media." Pp. 1191–1193 in *The Wiley-Blackwell Encyclopedia of Social and Political Movements*, 3 vols., edited by D. A. Snow, D. Della Porta, B. Klandermans, and D. McAdam. Malden, MA: Wiley-Blackwell.

Gardner, Margo and Laurence Steinberg. 2005. "Peer Influence on Risk Taking, Risk Preference, and Risky Decision Making in Adolescence and Adulthood: An Experimental Study." *Developmental Psychology* 41: 625–635.

Garfield, Bob. 1991. "How I Spent (and Spent and Spent) My Disney Vacation." *Washington Post*, July 7, p. B5.

Garfinkel, Harold. 1967. *Studies in Ethnomethodology*. Malden, MA: Blackwell.

Garon, Sheldon. 2006. "Japan Post-War 'Consumer Revolution,' or 'Striking a Balance' between Consumption and Saving." In *Consuming Cultures, Global Perspectives: Historical Trajectories, Transnational Exchanges*, edited by J. Brewer and F. Trentmann. Oxford: Berg.

Garreau, Joel. 1991. *Edge City: Life on the New Frontier*. New York: Doubleday.

Garrett, William R. 2007. "Christianity." Pp. 139–144 in *Encyclopedia of Globalization*, edited by J. A. Scholte and R. Robertson. New York: MTM Publishing.

Gartner, Rosemary. 2007. "Violent Crime." Pp. 5206–5208 in *The Blackwell Encyclopedia of Sociology*, edited by G. Ritzer. Malden, MA: Blackwell.

Gates, Katherine. 1999. *Deviant Desires: Incredibly Strange Sex*. New York: Juno Books.

Gauchat, Gordon, Maura Kelly and Michael Wallace. 2012. "Occupational Gender Segregation, Globalization, and Gender Earnings Inequality in U.S. Metropolitan Areas." *Gender and Society* 26: 718–747.

Gawande, Atul. 2011. "The Hot Spotters." *New Yorker*, January 24.

Geertz, Clifford. 1973. *The Interpretation of Cultures.* New York: Basic Books.

Geis, Gilbert. 2007a. "Crime, Corporate." Pp. 826–828 in *The Blackwell Encyclopedia of Sociology,* edited by G. Ritzer. Malden, MA: Blackwell.

Geis, Gilbert. 2007b. "Crime, White-Collar." Pp. 850–851 in *The Blackwell Encyclopedia of Sociology,* edited by G. Ritzer. Malden, MA: Blackwell.

Genosko, Gary. 1994. *Baudrillard and Signs: Signification Ablaze.* London: Routledge.

Gentina, Elodie and Isabelle Muratore. 2012. "Environmentalism at Home: The Process of Ecological Resocialization by Teenagers." *Journal of Consumer Behaviour* 11: 162–169.

George, Kimberly. 2007. "Woman's Movements." Pp. 1257–1260 in *Encyclopedia of Globalization,* edited by J. A. Scholte and R. Robertson. New York: MTM Publishing.

George, Sheba. 2000. "'Dirty Nurses' and 'Men Who Play': Gender and Class in Transnational Migration." Pp. 144–174 in *Global Ethnography: Forces, Connections, and Imaginations in a Postmodern World,* edited by M. Burawoy, J. A. Blum, S. George, Z. Gille, T. Gowan, L. Haney, M. Klawiter, S. H. Lopez, S. Ó Riain, and M. Thayer. Berkeley: University of California Press.

Gerami, Shahin and Melodye Lehnerer. 2007. "Gendered Aspects of War and International Violence." Pp. 1885–1888 in *The Blackwell Encyclopedia of Sociology,* edited by G. Ritzer. Malden, MA: Blackwell.

Gereffi, Gary. 2005. "The Global Economy: Organization, Governance, and Development." In *Handbook of Economic Sociology,* edited by N. Smelser and R. Swedberg. Princeton, NJ: Princeton University Press.

Gereffi, Gary. 2009. "Development Models and Industrial Upgrading in China and Mexico." *European Sociological Review* 25: 37–51.

Gerhardt, H. Carl and Franz Huber. 2002. *Acoustic Communication in Insects and Anurans: Common Problems and Diverse Solutions.* Chicago: University of Chicago Press.

Gershon, Ilana. 2010. *The Break-Up 2.0.* Ithaca, NY: Cornell University Press.

Gerth, Hans and C. Wright Mills, eds. 1958. *From Max Weber.* New York: Oxford University Press.

Gettleman, Jeffrey. 2010. "4-Day Frenzy of Rape in Congo Reveals U.N. Troops' Weakness." *New York Times,* October 4, pp. A1, A3.

Giddens, Anthony 1984. *The Constitution of Society: Outline of the Theory of Structuration.* Berkeley: University of California Press.

Giddens, Anthony. 1992. *The Transformation of Intimacy: Sexuality, Love and Eroticism in Modern Societies.* Stanford, CA: Stanford University Press.

Gilbert, Dennis. 2011. *The American Class Structure in an Age of Growing Inequality.* 8th ed. Thousand Oaks, CA: Pine Forge Press.

Gilbert, Dennis and Joseph A. Kahl. 1993. *The American Class Structure: A New Synthesis.* Belmont, CA: Wadsworth.

Gilman, Nils, Jesse Goldhammer, and Steven Weber. 2011. *Deviant Globalization: Black Market Economy in the 21st Century.* London: Continuum.

Gilroy, Paul. 1993. *The Black Atlantic: Modernity and Double Consciousness.* London: Verso.

Gimlin, Debra. 2000. "Cosmetic Surgery: Beauty as Commodity." *Qualitative Sociology* 23(1): 77–98.

Gimlin, Debra. 2007. "Accounting for Cosmetic Surgery in the USA and Great Britain: A Cross-Cultural Analysis of Women's Narratives." *Body and Society* 13: 41–60.

Giridharadas, Anand. 2010. "Getting In (and Out of) Line." *New York Times,* August 8. Retrieved November 9, 2011 (http://www.nytimes.com/2010/08/07/world/asia/07iht-currents.html).

Giridharadas, Anand and Keith Bradsher. 2006. "Microloan Pioneer and His Bank Win Nobel Peace Prize." *New York Times,* October 13.

Giroux, Henry and David E. Purpel, eds. 1983. *The Hidden Curriculum and Moral Education.* Berkeley, CA: McCutchan.

Gitlin, Todd. 1980. *The Whole World Is Watching.* Berkeley: University of California Press.

Gitlin, Todd. 1993. *The Sixties: Years of Hope, Days of Rage.* New York: Bantam.

Gittins, Diana. 1993. *The Family in Question.* New York: Macmillan.

Gladwell, Malcolm. 2000. *The Tipping Point.* New York: Little, Brown.

Gladwell, Malcolm. 2009. *What the Dog Saw.* New York: Little, Brown.

Gladwell, Malcolm. 2010. "Small Change: Why the Revolution Will Not Be Tweeted." *The New Yorker,* October. Retrieved November 9, 2013 (http://www.newyorker.com/reporting/2010/10/04/101004fa_fact_gladwell).

Glantz, Michael H. 1977. *Desertification.* Boulder, CO: Westview.

Glasberg, Davita S. and Deric Shannon. 2011. *Political Sociology: Oppression, Resistance, and the State.* Thousand Oaks, CA: Pine Forge Press.

Glaze, Lauren E. 2011. "Correctional Population in the United States, 2010." Washington, DC: U.S. Department of Justice.

Glenny, Misha. 2008. *McMafia: A Journey through the Global Criminal Underworld.* New York: Knopf.

Glickman, Lawrence B. 2009. *Buying Power: A History of Consumer Activism in America.* Chicago: University of Chicago Press.

Gloor, Peter and Scott Cooper. 2007. *Coolhunting: Chasing Down the Next Big Thing.* New York: AMACOM.

Gmelch, Sharon Bohn, ed. 2010. *Tourists and Tourism: A Reader.* Prospect Heights, IL: Waveland Press.

Godlee, Fiona, Neil Pakenham-Walsh, Dan Ncayiyana, Barbara Cohen, and Abel Packer. 2004. "Can We Achieve Health Information for All by 2015?" *The Lancet* 364: 295–300.

Godwyn, Mary and Jody Hoffer Gittell, eds. 2011. *Sociology of Organizations: Structures and Relationships.* Thousand Oaks, CA: Pine Forge Press.

Goffman, Erving. 1959. *The Presentation of Self in Everyday Life.* Garden City, NY: Anchor Books.

Goffman, Erving. 1961a. *Asylums: Essays on the Social Situations of Mental Patients and Other Inmates.* Garden City, NY: Anchor Books.

Goffman, Erving. 1961b. *Encounters.* Indianapolis: Bobbs-Merrill.

Goffman, Erving. 1963. *Stigma: Notes on the Management of Spoiled Identity.* Englewood Cliffs, NJ: Prentice-Hall/Spectrum.

Goffman, E. 1979. *Gender Advertisements.* New York: Harper.

Goffman, Erving. 1983. "The Interaction Order." *American Sociological Review* 48: 1–17.

Golani, Helena Yakovlev. 2011. "Two Decades of the Russian Federation's Foreign Policy in the Commonwealth of Independent States: The Cases of Belarus and Ukraine." The European Forum at the Hebrew University of Jerusalem. Retrieved March 29, 2012 (http://www.ef.huji.ac.il/publications/Yakovlev%20Golani.pdf).

Goldberg, David Theo. 2009. "Racial Comparisons, Relational Racisms: Some Thoughts on Method." *Ethnic and Racial Studies* 32: 1271–1282.

Goldberg, Gertrude Schaffner, ed. 2010. *Poor Women in Rich Countries: The Feminization of Poverty over the Life Course.* New York: Oxford University Press.

Goldberg, Harvey E. 2007. "Judaism." Pp. 690–693 in *Encyclopedia of Globalization,* edited by J. A. Scholte and Roland Robertson. New York: MTM Publishing.

Goldberger, Paul. 2010. "What Happens in Vegas." *The New Yorker,* October 4, pp. 95–96.

Goldburg, Rebecca J. 2008. "Aquaculture, Trade, and Fisheries Linkages: Unexpected Synergies." *Globalization* 5(2): 143–150.

Goldfield, Michael. 1987. *The Decline of Organized Labor.* Chicago: University of Chicago Press.

Goldfrank, Walter. 2005. "Fresh Demand: The Consumption of Chilean Produce in the United States." Pp. 42–53 in *The Cultural Politics of Food and Eating: A Reader,* edited by J. L. Watson and M. L. Caldwell. Malden, MA: Blackwell.

Goldin, Claudia, Lawrence F. Katz, and Ilyana Kuziemko. 2006. "The Homecoming of American College Women: The Reversal of the College Gender Gap." *Journal of Economic Perspectives* 20: 133–56.

Goldman, R. 2008. "Do It Yourself! Amateur Porn Stars Make Bank." Retrieved October 18, 2010 (http://abcnews.go.com/Business/SmallBiz/story?id=4151592&page=1).

Goldman, Robert and Stephen Papson. 1998. *Nike Culture*. London: Sage.

Goldscheider, Calvin. 2012. "Judaism." Pp. 1225–1234 in *Wiley-Blackwell Encyclopedia of Globalization*, edited by G. Ritzer. Malden, MA: Wiley-Blackwell.

Goldstein, Warren. 2009. "Secularization Patterns in the Old Paradigm." *Sociology of Religion* 70: 157–178.

Goldstone, Jack. 1991. *Revolution and Rebellion in the Early Modern World*. Berkeley: University of California Press.

Gonzalez, Michelle A. 2010. *Shopping*. Fortress Press.

Gooch, Liz. 2012. "With Opening Near, Yale Defends Singapore Venture." *New York Times*, August 27. Retrieved July 5, 2013 (www.nytimes.com/2012/08/27/world/asia).

Goode, Erich. 1996. "Gender and Courtship Entitlement: Responses to Personal Ads." *Sex Roles* 3–4: 141–169.

Goode, Erich. 2002. "Sexual Involvement and Social Research in a Fat Civil Rights Organization." *Qualitative Sociology* 25(4): 501–534.

Goode, Erich. 2007a. "Deviance." Pp. 1075–1082 in *The Blackwell Encyclopedia of Sociology*, edited by G. Ritzer. Malden, MA: Blackwell.

Goode, Erich. 2007b. "Deviance: Explanatory Theories of." Pp. 1100–1107 in *The Blackwell Encyclopedia of Sociology*, edited by G. Ritzer. Malden, MA: Blackwell.

Goode, Erich and Nachman Ben-Yehuda. 1994. *Moral Panics: The Social Construction of Deviance*. Oxford, UK: Blackwell.

Goode, Erich and Nachman Ben-Yehuda. 2009. *Moral Panics: The Social Construction of Deviance*. 2nd ed. Malden, MA: Blackwell.

Goode, Erich and Alex Thio. 2007. "Deviance, Crime and." Pp. 1092–1095 in *The Blackwell Encyclopedia of Sociology*, edited by G. Ritzer. Malden, MA: Blackwell.

Goode, Erich and D. Angus Vail. 2007. *Extreme Deviance*. Thousand Oaks, CA: Pine Forge Press.

Goode, William J. 1963. *World Revolution and Family Patterns*. New York: Free Press.

Goode, Williams J. 1959. "The Theoretical Importance of Love." *American Sociological Review* 24: 38–47.

Goodlin, Wendi E. and Christopher S. Dunn. 2011. "Three Patterns of Domestic Violence in Households: Single Victimization, Repeat Victimization, and Co-occurring Victimization." *Journal of Family Violence* 26: 101–108.

Goodnough, Abby. 2010. "Doctors Point to Caffeinated Alcoholic Drinks' Dangers." *New York Times*, October 27, p. A12.

Goodwin, Jennifer. 2011. "US Rates of Autism, ADHD Continue to Rise: Report." *US News*, May 23. Retrieved May 25, 2011 (http://health.usnews.com/health-news/family-health/brain-and-behavior/articles/2011/05/23/us-rates-of-autism-adhd-continue-to-rise-report).

Gordon, Richard E., Katherine K. Gordon, and Max Gunther. 1960. *The Split-Level Trap*. New York: Gilbert Geis Associates.

Gorman, Elizabeth H. and Julie A. Kmec. 2009. "Hierarchical Rank and Women's Organizational Mobility: Glass Ceilings in Corporate Law Firms." *American Journal of Sociology* 114: 1428–1474.

Gorski, Philip S. 2011. "Barack Obama and Civil Religion." Pp. 179–214 in *Rethinking Obama Political Power and Social Theory* (Vol. 22), edited by J. Go. Bingley, UK: Emerald Group Publishing.

Gorski, Philip S., David Kyuman Kim, John Torpey, and Jonathan VanAntwerpen, eds. 2012. *The Post-secular Question: Religion in Contemporary Society*. New York: New York University Press and the Social Science Research Council.

Gotham Kevin Fox. 2007. "Megalopolis." Pp. 2942–2944 in *The Blackwell Encyclopedia of Sociology*, edited by G. Ritzer. Malden, MA: Blackwell.

Gotham, Kevin. 2012. "Urbanization." Pp. 488–503 in *The Wiley-Blackwell Companion to Sociology*, edited by George Ritzer. Malden, MA: Wiley-Blackwell.

Gottdiener, Mark. 2001. *The Theming of America*. 2nd ed. Westview Press.

Gottdiener, Mark, Claudia C. Collins, and David R. Dickens. 1999. *Las Vegas: The Social Production of an All-American City*. Malden, MA: Blackwell.

Gottfredson, Michael R. and Travis Hirschi. 1990. *A General Theory of Crime*. Stanford, CA: Stanford University Press.

Gottman, Jean. 1961. *Megalopolis: The Urbanized Northeastern Seaboard of the United States*. New York: Twentieth Century Fund.

Gottman, John M., Tames Coan, Sybil Carrere, and Catherine Swanson. 1998. "Predicting Marital Happiness and Stability from Newly Wed Interactions." *Journal of Marriage and the Family* 60: 5–22.

Gottschalk, Simon. 2010. "The Presentation of Avatars in Second Life: Self and Interaction in Social Virtual Spaces." *Symbolic Interaction* 33(4): 501–525.

Gould, Kenneth, David N. Pellow, and Allan Schnaiberg. 2008. *The Treadmill of Production: Injustice and Unsustainability in the Global Economy*. Boulder, CO: Paradigm.

Gould, Stephen Jay. 1981. *The Mismeasure of Man*. New York: Norton.

Gouldner, Alvin W. 1960. "The Norm of Reciprocity: A Preliminary Statement." *American Sociological Review* 25(2): 161–178.

Gouldner, Alvin. 1962. "Anti-Minotaur: The Myth of a Value Free Sociology." *Social Problems* Winter: 199–213.

Gove, Walter R. and Michael Hughes. 1979. "Possible Causes of the Apparent Sex Differences in Physical Health: An Empirical Investigation." *American Sociological Review* 44: 126–146.

Gove, Walter R. 1980. *The Labelling of Deviance*. Beverly Hills, CA: Sage.

Gowan, Teresa. 2000. "Excavating 'Globalization' from Street Level: Homeless Men Recycle Their Pasts." Pp. 74–105 in *Global Ethnography: Forces, Connections, and Imaginations in a Postmodern World*, edited by M. Burawoy, J. A. Blum, S. George, Z. Gille, T. Gowan, L. Haney, M. Klawiter, S. H. Lopez, S. Ó Riain, and M. Thayer. Berkeley: University of California Press.

Grady, Denise and William J. Broad. 2011. "Seeing Terror Risk, U.S. Asks Journals to Cut Flu Study Facts." *New York Times*, December 20 (http://www.nytimes.com/2011/12/21/health/fearing-terrorism-us-asks-journals-to-censor-articles-on-virus.html?pagewanted=all).

Grandin, Greg. 2009. *Fordlandia: The Rise and Fall of Henry Ford's Forgotten Jungle City*. New York: Metropolitan Book.

Grandin, Greg. 2010. *Fordlandia: The Rise and Fall of Henry Ford's Forgotten Jungle City*. New York: Picador.

Granfield, Robert. 1992. *Making Elite Lawyers: Visions of Law at Harvard and Beyond*. New York: Routledge, Chapman and Hall.

Granovetter, Mark. 1973. "The Strength of Weak Ties." *American Journal of Sociology* 78(6): 1360–1380.

Granovetter, Mark. 1974. *Getting a Job: A Study of Contacts and Careers*. Cambridge, MA: Harvard University Press.

Granovetter, Mark and Richard Swedberg, eds. 2011. *The Sociology of Economic Life*. 3rd ed. Boulder, CO: Westview Press.

Gray, Clark and Valerie Mueller. 2012. "Drought and Population Mobility in Rural Ethiopia." *World Development,* 40(1): 134–145.

Gray, Louise. 2009. "McDonald's Waste Makes Up Largest Proportion of Fast Food Litter on Streets." *The Telegraph*, January 13. Retrieved May 26, 2011 (http://www.telegraph.co.uk/earth/earthnews/4223106/McDonalds-waste-makes-up-largest-proportion-of-fast-food-litter-on-streets.html).

Greeley, Andrew M. 1976. "The Ethnic Miracle." *The Public Interest* 45: 20–36.

Greeley, Andrew. 1989. *Religious Change in America*. Cambridge, MA: Harvard University Press.

Greeley, Andrew. 2003. *The Bishop in the West Wing*.

Greeley, Andrew. 2005. *The Priestly Sins*.

Greenberg, Andy. 2010. "WikiLeaks' Julian Assange Wants to Spill Your Corporate Secrets." *Forbes* (December): 70–86.

Greenberg, Miriam. 2007. *Branding New York: How a City in Crisis Was Sold to the World*. New York: Routledge.

Greenfeld, Lawrence A. and Steven K. Smith. 1999. "American Indians and Crime" (NCJ 173386, Table 3). Office of Justice Programs, Bureau of Justice Statistics. Retrieved March 31, 2012 (http://bjs.ojp.usdoj.gov/content/pub/ascii/aic.txt).

Greenhouse, Steven. 2011. "Union Membership in U.S. Fell to a 70-Year Low Last Year." *New York Times*, January 21.

Gressman, Eugene. 2005. "Judgments Judged and Wrongs Remembered: Examining the

Japanese American Civil Liberties Cases on Their Sixtieth Anniversary." *Law and Contemporary Problems* 68: 15–27.

Grice, Elizabeth. 2006. "Cry of an Enfant Sauvage." *Daily Telegraph*, July 17.

Grier, Ronelle. 2010. "Teen Sexting: Technological Trend Can Lead to Tragic Consequences." *Daily Tribune*. Retrieved March 29, 2012 (http://www.dailytribune.com/articles/2010/01/27/news/srv0000007438542.txt?viewmode=fullstory).

Griffin, Sean Patrick. 2007. "Crime, Organized." Pp. 833–834 in *The Blackwell Encyclopedia of Sociology*, edited by G. Ritzer. Malden, MA: Blackwell.

Grigsby, Mary. 2004. *Buying Time and Getting By: The Voluntary Simplicity Movement*. Albany: State University of New York Press.

Groenemeyer, Axel. 2007. "Deviant Careers." Pp. 1142–1145 in *The Blackwell Encyclopedia of Sociology*, edited by G. Ritzer. Malden, MA: Blackwell.

Gronow, Jukka. 2007. "Taste, Sociology of." Pp. 4930–4935 in *The Blackwell Encyclopedia of Sociology*, edited by G. Ritzer. Malden, MA: Blackwell.

Groseclose, Tim. 2011. *Left Turn: How Liberal Media Bias Distorts the American Mind*. New York: St. Martin's Press.

Gu, Dongfeng, Tanika N. Kelly, Xigui Wu, Jing Chen, Jonathan M. Samet, Jian-feng Huang, Manlu Zhu, Ji-chun Chen, Chung-shiuan Chen, Xiufang Duan, Michael J. Klag, and Jiang He. 2009. "Mortality Attributable to Smoking in China." *New England Journal of Medicine* 360: 150–159.

Gubrium, Jaber, James A. Holstein, Amir B. Marvasti, and Karyn D. McKinney. 2012. *The SAGE Handbook of Interview Research: The Complexity of the Craft*. 2nd ed. Thousand Oaks, CA: Sage.

Guhathakurta, Subhrajit, David Jacobson, and Nicholas C. DelSordi. 2007. "The End of Globalization? The Implications of Migration for State, Society and Economy." Pp. 201–215 in *The Blackwell Companion to Globalization*, edited by G. Ritzer. Malden, MA: Blackwell.

Guillen, Mario F. 2010. "Classical Sociological Approaches to the Study of Leadership." Pp. 223–238 in *Handbook of Leadership Theory and Practice*, edited by N. Nohria and R. Khurana. Boston: Harvard University Press.

Gulati, Ranjay and Phanish Puranam. 2009. "Renewal through Reorganization: The Value of Inconsistencies Between Formal and Informal Organization." *Organization Science* 20: 422–440.

"Gulf Oil Spill Declared 'Effectively Dead.'" 2010. *CBS News*, September 20. Retrieved March 29, 2012 (http://www.cbsnews.com/stories/2010/09/19/national/main6881308.shtml).

Guo, Guang, Michael E. Roettger, and Tianji Cai. 2008. "The Integration of Genetic Propensities into Social-Control Models of Delinquency and Violence Among Male Youths." *American Sociological Review* 73(4): 543–568.

Habermas, Jurgen. 1975. *Legitimation Crisis*. Boston: Beacon Press.

Haddad, Emma. 2008. "The Refugee: The Individual between Sovereigns." *Global Society* 17(3).

Hadden, Wilbur C. and Raul D. Rockswold. 2008. "Increasing Differential Mortality by Educational Attainment in Adults in the United States." *IJHS* 38(1): 47–61.

Hadjicostandi, Joanna. 2007. "Migration: Undocumented/Illegal." Pp. 3031–3034 in *The Blackwell Encyclopedia of Sociology*, edited by G. Ritzer. Malden. MA: Blackwell.

Hafferty, Frederic W. 2009. "Professionalism and the Socialization of Medical Students." In *Teaching Medical Professionalism*, edited by R. L. Cruess, S. R. Cruess, and Y. Steinert. New York: Cambridge University Press.

Hafferty, Frederic and Brian Castellani. 2011. "Two Cultures: Two Ships: The Rise of a Professionalism Movement within Modern Medicine and Medical Sociology's Disappearance from the Professionalism Debate." Pp. 201–220 in *Handbook of the Sociology of Health, Illness, and Healing: A Blueprint for the 21st Century*, edited by B. A. Pescosolido, J. K. Martin, J. D. McLeod, and A. Rogers. Dordrecht, Netherlands: Springer.

Hagan, John. 1989. *Structural Criminology*. New Brunswick, NJ: Rutgers University Press.

Hage, Jerald and Charles H. Powers. 1992. *Post-industrial Lives: Roles and Relationships in the 21st Century*. Newbury Park, CA: Sage.

Hajnal, Zoltan L. and Taeku Lee. 2011. *Why Americans Don't Join the Party: Race, Immigration, and the Failure (of Political Parties) to Engage the Electorate*. Princeton, NJ: Princeton University Press.

Hall, Elaine J. and Marnie Salupo Rodriguez. 2003. "The Myth of Postfeminism." *Gender and Society* 17(6): 878–902.

Hall, Jason K. 2012a. "Malaria." Pp. 1319–1320 in *The Wiley-Blackwell Encyclopedia of Globalization*, edited by G. Ritzer. Malden, MA: Wiley-Blackwell.

Hall, Jason K. 2012b. "Tuberculosis." Pp. 2051–2053 in *The Wiley-Blackwell Encyclopedia of Globalization*, edited by G. Ritzer. Malden, MA: Wiley-Blackwell.

Hall, Peter and David Soskice, eds. 2001. *Varieties of Capitalism: The Institutional Foundations of Comparative Advantage*. Oxford University Press.

Hall, Stuart. 1980. "Encoding and Decoding." In *Culture, Media, Language: Working Papers in Cultural Studies*. London: Hutchinson.

Halle, David. [1993] 2007. *Inside Culture*. Chicago: University of Chicago Press.

Halle, David. 2007. "Highbrow/Lowbrow." Pp. 2123–2126 in *The Blackwell Encyclopedia of Sociology*, edited by G. Ritzer. Malden, MA: Blackwell.

Halliday, Josh. 2013. "Google's Dropped Anti-censorship Warning Marks Quiet Defeat in China." *The Guardian*, January 7. Retrieved October 11, 2013 (http://www.theguardian.com/technology/2013/jan/04/google-defeat-china-censorship-battle).

Hamilton, Kathy. 2012. "Low-Income Families and Coping through Brands: Inclusion or Stigma?" *Sociology* 46: 74–90.

Hamilton, Laura and Brian Powell. 2007. "Hidden Curriculum." Pp. 2116–2118 in *The Blackwell Encyclopedia of Sociology*, edited by G. Ritzer. Malden, MA: Blackwell.

Hamilton, Mykol C., David Anderson, Michelle Broaddus, and Kate Young. 2006. "Gender Stereotyping and Under-representation of Female Characters in 200 Popular Children's Picture Books: A Twenty-First Century Update." *Sex Roles* 55: 757–765.

Hammersley, Martyn. 2007. "Ethnography." Pp. 1479–1483 in *The Blackwell Encyclopedia of Sociology*, edited by G. Ritzer. Malden, MA: Blackwell.

Hamouda, Manel and Gharbi Abderrazak. 2013. "The Postmodern Consumer: An Identity Constructor?" *International Journal of Marketing Studies* 5.

Handelman, Jay M. and Robert V. Kozinets. 2007. "Culture Jamming." Pp. 945–946 in *The Blackwell Encyclopedia of Sociology*, edited by G. Ritzer. Malden, MA: Blackwell.

Hankin, Janet R. and Eric R. Wright. 2010. "Reflections on Fifty Years of Medical Sociology." *Journal of Health and Social Behavior* 51: S10–S14.

Hannigan, John. 1998. *Fantasy City: Pleasure and Profit in the Postmodern Metropolis*. London: Routledge.

Hannigan, John. 2007. "Fantasy City." Pp. 1641–1644 in *The Blackwell Encyclopedia of Sociology*, edited by G. Ritzer. Malden, MA: Blackwell.

Hanson, Andrew and Zackary Hawley. 2011. "Do Landlords Discriminate in the Rental Housing Market? Evidence From an Internet Field Experiment in US Cities." *Journal of Urban Economics*. Retrieved March 30, 2012 (http://www.sciencedirect.com/science/article/pii/S0094119008000181).

Hanushek, Eric and Steven Rivkin. 2006. "School Quality and the Black-White Achievement Gap" (Working Paper No. 12651). Cambridge, MA: National Bureau of Economic Research.

Haraway, Donna. 1991. "A Cyborg Manifesto: Science, Technology, and Socialist-Feminism in the Late Twentieth Century." Pp. 149–81 in *Simians, Cyborgs and Women: The Reinvention of Nature*. New York: Routledge.

Harcourt, Bernard E. and Jens Ludwig. 2006. "Broken Windows: New Evidence from New York City and a Five-City Social Experiment." *The University of Chicago Law Review* 73: 271–320.

Harding, David. 2010. *Living the Drama: Community, Conflict, and Culture Among Inner-City Boys*. Chicago: University of Chicago Press.

Hare, Bruce. 2001. "Black Youth at Risk." Pp. 97–113 in *Race Odyssey: African Americans and Sociology*, edited by B. Hare. Syracuse, NY: Syracuse University Press.

Hargrove, Barbara. 1989. *Sociology of Religion: Classical and Contemporary Approaches.* 2nd ed. Arlington Heights, IL: Harlan Davidson.

Harmon, Corinne, Glenda Carne, Kristina Lizardy-Hajbi, and Eugene Wilkerson. 2010. "Access to Higher Education for Undocumented Students: 'Outlaws' of Social Justice, Equity, and Equality." *Journal of Praxis in Multicultural Education* 5(1): 67–82.

Harper, Douglas. 1982. *Good Company.* Chicago: University of Chicago Press.

Harris, Gardiner. "India's New Focus on Rape Shows Only the Surface of Women's Perils." *New York Times* January 13, 2013.

Harrison, B. 1994. *Lean and Mean: The Changing Landscape of Corporate Power in the Age of Flexibility.* New York: Basic Books.

Harrison, Michelle. 1982. *A Woman in Residence.* New York: Random House.

Hart, Betty and Todd Risley. 1995. *Meaningful Differences in the Everyday Experience of Young American Children.* Baltimore: Paul H. Brookes Publishing.

Hart, Sarah V. 2003. "Making Prison Safer through Technology." *Corrections Today* 65(2).

Hartmann, Heidi. 1979. "Capitalism, Patriarchy and Job Segregation by Sex." Pp. 206–247 in *Capitalist Patriarchy and the Case for Socialist Feminism,* edited by Z. Eisenstein. New York: Monthly Review Press.

Harvey, Adia Wingfield. 2009. "Racializing the Glass Escalator: Reconsidering Men's Experiences with Women's Work." *Gender and Society* 23(1): 5–26.

Harvey, David. 2000. *Spaces of Hope.* Berkeley: University of California Press.

Harvey, David. 2003. *The New Imperialism.* New York: Oxford University Press.

Harvey, David. 2005. *A Brief History of NeoLiberalism.* Oxford, UK: Oxford University Press.

Harvey, David. 2007. "Poverty and Disrepute." Pp. 3589–3594 in *The Blackwell Encyclopedia of Sociology,* edited by G. Ritzer. Malden, MA: Blackwell.

Haslam, Alexander and Michelle K. Ryan. 2008. "The Road to the Glass Cliff." *Leadership Quarterly* 19: 530–546.

Hatch, Anthony. 2009. *The Politics of Metabolism: The Metabolic Syndrome and the Reproduction of Race and Racism in the United States.* PhD dissertation, University of Maryland.

Hatfield, Elaine, Lisamarie Bensman, and Richard L. Rapson. "A Brief History of Social Scientists' Attempts to Measure Passionate Love." *Journal of Social and Personal Relationships* 29, 2012: 143-164.

Hatton, Erin and Mary Nell Trautner. "Equal Opportunity Objectification? The Sexualization of Men and Women on the Cover of *Rolling Stone.*" *Sexuality and Culture* 15, 2011: 256-278

Haug, Marie. 1973. "Deprofessionalization: An Alternative Hypothesis for the Future." *Sociological Review Monograph.*

Hausbeck, Kathryn and Barbara G. Brents. 2008. *The State of Sex: Nevada's Brothel Industry.* New York: Routledge.

Hausbeck, Kathryn and Barbara G. Brents. 2010. "McDonaldization of the Sex Industries? The Business of Sex." Pp. 102–117 in *McDonaldization: The Reader,* edited by G. Ritzer. 3rd ed. Thousand Oaks, CA: Pine Forge Press.

Hausmann, Ricardo, Ina Ganguli, and Martina Viarengo. 2009. "The Dynamics of the Gender Gap: How Do Countries Rank in Terms of Making Marriage and Motherhood Compatible with Work." Pp. 27–29 in *Global Gender Gap Report,* edited by R. Hausmann, L. D. Tyson, and S. Zahidi. Geneva: World Economic Forum.

Hawley, Amos. 1950. *Human Ecology: A Theory of Community Structure.* New York: Ronald Press.

Hayes, Dennis and Robin Wynyard, eds. 2002. *The McDonaldization of Higher Education.* Westport, CT: Bergin and Garvey.

Haynie, L. 2001. "Delinquent Peers Revisited: Does Network Structure Matter?" *American Journal of Sociology* 106: 1013–1057.

Hays, Sharon. 1998. *The Cultural Contradictions of Motherhood.* New Haven, CT: Yale University Press.

"Head Injuries in Football." 2010. *New York Times,* October 21. Retrieved March 30, 2012 (topics.nytimes.com/top/reference/timestopics/subjects/f/football/head_injuries/index.html).

Heaphy, Brian. 2007a. "Lesbian and Gay Families." Pp. 2606–2609 in *The Blackwell Encyclopedia of Sociology,* edited by G. Ritzer. Malden, MA: Blackwell.

Heaphy, Brian. 2007b. "Same-Sex Marriage/Civil Unions." Pp. 3995–98 in *The Blackwell Encyclopedia of Sociology,* edited by George Ritzer. Malden, MA: Blackwell.

Hecht, L. M. 2001. "Role Conflict and Role Overload: Different Concepts, Different. Consequences." *Sociological Inquiry* 71(1): 111–121.

Heckman, James. 2006. "Skill Formation and the Economics of Investing in Disadvantaged Children." *Science* 312: 1900–1902.

Hedenus, Anna. 2011. "Finding Prosperity as a Lottery Winner: Presentations of Self After Acquisition of Sudden Wealth." *Sociology* 46(1): 22–37.

Heintz, James. 2006. "Globalization, Economic Policy and Employment: Poverty and Gender Implications." Employment Strategy Unit, International Labor Organization. Retrieved March 30, 3012 (http://www.ilo.org/empelm/pubs/WCMS_114024/lang—en/index.htm).

Heise, David R. 1979. *Understanding Events.* Cambridge, UK: Cambridge University Press.

Heise, David R. 2007. *Expressive Order: Confirming Sentiments in Social Actions.* New York: Springer.

Helft, Miguel. 2007. "Chinese Political Prisoner Sues in U.S. Court, Saying Yahoo Helped Identify Dissidents." *New York Times,* April 19.

Heller, Joseph. 1955. *Catch-22.* New York: Knopf.

Heller, Nathan. "Laptop U". *New Yorker* May 20, 2013: 80ff.

Helweg-Larsen, Marie and Barbara L. LoMonaco. 2008. "Queuing Among U2 Fans: Reactions to Social Norm Violations." *Journal of Applied Social Psychology* 38(9): 2378–2393.

Hendershott, Anne. 2002. *The Politics of Deviance.* San Francisco: Encounter Books.

Henriques, Diana. 2009. "Madoff Is Sentenced to 150 Years for Ponzi Scheme." *New York Times,* June 29. Retrieved March 30, 3012 (http://www.nytimes.com/2009/06/30/business/30madoff.html?pagewanted=all).

Henriques, Diana B. 2011. "From Prison, Madoff Says Banks 'Had to Know' of Fraud." *New York Times,* February 15. Accessed December 20, 2011 (http://www.nytimes.com/2011/02/16/business/madoff-prison-interview.html?pagewanted=all).

Henry J. Kaiser Family Foundation. 2010. "Generation M2: Media in the Lives of 8- to 18-Year-Olds." Retrieved March 30, 3012 (http://www.kff.org/entmedia/mh012010pkg.cfm).

Henry, Stuart. 2007. "Deviance, Constructionist Perspectives." Pp. 1086–92 in *The Blackwell Encyclopedia of Sociology,* edited by George Ritzer. Malden, MA: Blackwell.

Hepburn, Stephanie and Rita Simon. 2010. Hidden in Plain Sight: Human Trafficking in the United States." *Gender Issues* 27(1/2):1–26.

Herberg, Will. [1955] 1983. *Protestant-Catholic-Jew: An Essay in American Religious Sociology.* Chicago: University of Chicago Press.

Herbert, Bob. 2011. "Losing Our Way." *New York Times,* March 25. Retrieved March 30, 3012 (http://www.nytimes.com/2011/03/26/opinion/26herbert.html).

Herman, Edward S. and Noam Chomsky. 1988. *Manufacturing Consent: The Political Economy of the Mass Media.* New York: Pantheon.

Herod, Andrew. 2009. *Geographies of Globalization: A Critical Introduction.* Malden, MA: Wiley-Blackwell.

Herper, Matthew and Peter Kang. 2006. "The World's Ten Best-Selling Drugs." *Forbes,* March 22. Retrieved January 25, 2012 (http://www.forbes.com/2006/03/21/pfizer-merck-amgen-cx_mh_pk_0321topdrugs.html).

Herrnstein, Richard J. and Charles Murray. 1994. *The Bell Curve: Intelligence and Class Structure in American Life.* New York: Free Press.

Hershkovitz, Shay. 2012. "Nation-State." Pp. 1492–1496 in *The Wiley-Blackwell Encyclopedia of Globalization,* edited by G. Ritzer. Malden, MA: Wiley-Blackwell.

Hesse-Biber, Sharlene. 1996. *Am I Thin Enough Yet? The Cult of Thinness and Commercialization of Identity.* London: Oxford University Press.

Hetherington, E. Mavis. 2003. "Intimate Pathways: Changing Patterns in Close Personal Relationships across Time." *Family Relations* 52: 183–206.

Hibel, Jacob, George Farkas, and Paul Morgan. 2010. "Who Is Placed Into Special

Education?" *Sociology of Education* 83(4): 312–332.

Hier, Sean P. 2011. "Tightening the Focus: Moral Panic, Moral Regulation and Liberal Government." *The British Journal of Sociology* 62: 523–541.

Highley, John and Michael Burton. 2006. *Elite Foundations of Liberal Democracy.* Lanham, MD: Rowman and Littlefield.

Hill, Jessica and Pranee Liamputtong. 2011. "Being the Mother of a Child With Asperger's Syndrome: Women's Experiences of Stigma." *Health Care for Women International* 32: 708–722.

Hillman, Arye L. and Eva Jenkner. 2004. "Educating Children in Poor Countries." International Monetary Fund. Retrieved March 30, 2012 (http://www.imf.org/external/pubs/ft/issues/issues33/index.htm).

Hillyard, Daniel. 2007. "Deviance, Criminalization of." Pp. 1095–1100 in *The Blackwell Encyclopedia of Sociology*, edited by G. Ritzer. Malden, MA: Blackwell.

Himanen, Pekka. 2001. *The Hacker Ethic, and the Spirit of the Information Age.* New York: Random House.

Hindin, Michelle J. 2007. "Role Theory." Pp. 3951–3954 in *The Blackwell Encyclopedia of Sociology*, edited by George Ritzer. Malden, MA: Blackwell.

Hindmarsh, Jon, Christian Heath, and Mike Fraser. 2006. "(Im)materiality, Virtual Reality and Interaction: Grounding the 'Virtual' in Studies of Technology in Action." *Sociological Review* 54(4): 795–817.

Hinze, Susan W. and Dawn Aliberti. 2007. "Feminization of Poverty." Pp. 1718–1725 in *The Blackwell Encyclopedia of Sociology*, edited by G. Ritzer. Malden, MA: Blackwell.

Hirschi, Travis. 1969. *The Causes of Delinquency.* Berkeley: University of California Press.

Hirschi, Travis. 2004. "Self-Control and Crime." Pp. 537–552 in *Handbook of Self-Regulation: Research, Theory and Application*, edited by R. F. Baumeister and K. D. Vohs. New York: Guilford.

Hobsbawm, Eric J. and Chris Wrigley. 1999. *Industry and Empire: The Birth of the Industrial Revolution.* New York: New Press.

Hochschild, Adam. 2011. "Explaining Congo's Endless Civil War." *New York Times* Book Review, April 1. Accessed January 29, 2012 (http://www.nytimes.com/2011/04/03/books/review/book-review-dancing-in-the-glory-of-monsters-the-collapse-of-the-congo-and-the-great-war-of-africa-by-jason-k-stearns.html?pagewanted=all).

Hochschild, Arlie R. 1979. "Emotion Work, Feeling Rules and Social Structure." *American Journal of Sociology* 85: 551–575.

Hochschild, Arlie. 1983. *The Managed Heart.* Berkeley: University of California Press.

Hochschild, Arlie. 1989. *The Second Shift.* New York: Viking.

Hochschild, Arlie. 1997. *The Time Bind.* New York: Holt.

Hochschild, Arlie. 2000. "Global Care Chains and Emotional Surplus Value." Pp. 130–146 in *On the Edge: Living with Global Capitalism*, edited by W. Hutton and A. Giddens. London: Jonathan Cape.

Hochschild, Arlie R. (with A. Machung). 2003. *The Second Shift.* New York: Penguin.

Hodge, David. 2008. "Sexual Trafficking in the US: A Domestic Problem With Transnational Dimensions." *Social Work* 53(2): 143–152.

Hodson, Randy. 2001. *Dignity at Work.* Cambridge, UK: Cambridge University Press.

Hoecker-Drysdale, Susan. 2011. "Harriet Martineau." Pp. 61–95 in *The Wiley-Blackwell Companion to Major Social Theorists: Volume 1. Classical Theorists*, edited by G. Ritzer and J. Stepnisky. Malden, MA: Wiley-Blackwell.

Hoefer, Michael, Nancy Rytina, and Bryan C. Baker. 2010. "Estimates of the Unauthorized Immigrant Population Residing in the United States: January 2009." U.S. Department of Homeland Security. Retrieved February 28, 2012 (http://www.dhs.gov/xlibrary/assets/statistics/publications/ois_ill_pe_2009.pdf).

Hoekstra, Arjen J. 2012. "Water." Pp. 2202–2210 in *The Wiley-Blackwell Companion to Sociology*, edited by G. Ritzer. Malden, MA: Wiley-Blackwell.

Hoekstra, Arjen Y. and Ashok K. Chapagain. 2008. *Globalization of Water: Sharing the Planet's Freshwater Resources.* Malden, MA: Blackwell.

Hoff, Erika, Brett Laursen, and Twila Tardiff. 2002. "Socioeconomic Status and Parenting." Pp. 231–252 in *Handbook of Parenting, Volume 2. Biology and Ecology of Parenting*, edited by M. H. Bornstein. 2nd ed. Mahwah, NJ: Erlbaum.

Hoffman, Lily M., Susan S. Fainstein, and Dennis R. Judd, eds. 2003. *Cities and Visitors: Regulating People, Markets, and City Space.* New York: Blackwell.

Hollander, Jason. 2003. "Renowned Columbia Sociologist and National Medal of Science Winner Robert K. Merton Dies at 92." Retrieved April 1, 2012 (http://www.columbia.edu/cu/news/03/02/robertKMerton.html).

Hollifield, James E. and David Jacobson. 2012. "Migration and the State." Pp. 1390–1400 in *The Wiley-Blackwell Encyclopedia of Globalization*, edited by G. Ritzer. Malden, MA: Wiley-Blackwell.

Hollister, Geoff. 2008. *Out of Nowhere: The Inside Story of How Nike Marketed the Culture of Running.* Maidenhead, UK: Meyer and Meyer Sport.

Holmes, Mary. 2007. "Couples Living Apart Together." Pp. 810–812 in *The Blackwell Encyclopedia of Sociology*, edited by G. Ritzer. Malden, MA: Blackwell.

Holt, Douglas. 2004. *How Brands Become Icons: Principles of Cultural Branding.* Cambridge, MA: Harvard Business School Press.

Holt, Douglas B. 2007. "Distinction." Pp. 1189–1191 in *The Blackwell Encyclopedia of Sociology*, edited by G. Ritzer. Malden, MA: Blackwell.

Holt, Thomas J. and Michael G. Turner. 2012. "Examining Risks and Protective Factors of On-line Identity Theft." *Deviant Behavior* 33: 308–323.

Holton, Robert. 2011. *Globalization and the Nation State.* 2nd ed. New York: Palgrave Macmillan.

Homans, George. 1961. *Social Behavior: Its Elementary Forms.* New York: Harcourt, Brace, and World.

Hondagneu-Sotelo, Pierette. 2000. *Doméstica: Immigrant Workers Cleaning and Caring in the Shadows of Affluence.* Berkeley: University of California Press.

Honwana, Alcinda. 2007. *The Child Soldiers in Africa.* Philadelphia: University of Pennsylvania Press.

hooks, bell. 2000. *Feminist Thought: From Margin to Center.* Cambridge, UK: South End Press.

Hondagneu-Sotelo, Pierette and Ernestine Avila. 2005. "I'm Here, but I'm There": The Meanings of Latina Transnational Motherhood." In *Gender through a Prism of Difference*, edited by M. Baca Zinn, P. Hondagneu-Sotelo, and M. Messner. New York: Oxford University Press.

Hoque, Sajjadul N. 2010. "Female Child Trafficking From Bangladesh: A New Form of Slavery." *Canadian Social Science* 6(1): 45–58.

Hornsby, Anne M. 2013. "Surfing the Net for Community: A Durkheimian Analysis of Electronic Gatherings." Pp. 51–94 in *Illuminating Social Life: Classical and Contemporary Revisited*, edited by Peter Kivisto. Thousand Oaks, CA: Sage.

Horovitz, Bruce. 2002. "Fast-Food World Says Drive-Thru Is the Way to Go." *USA Today*, April 3. Retrieved May 26, 2011 (http://www.usatoday.com/money/covers/2002-04-03-drive-thru.htm).

Horrey, William J. and Christopher D. Wickens. 2006. "Examining the Impact of Cell Phone Conversations on Driving Using Meta-analytic Techniques." *Human Factors: The Journal of the Human Factors and Ergonomics Society* 48: 196–205.

Horrigan, John. 2008. *Online Shopping.* Washington, DC: Pew Internet and American Life Project.

Horrigan, John. 2009. "Wireless Internet Use." Retrieved January 27, 2012 (http://pewinternet.org/Reports/2009/12-Wireless-Internet-Use.aspx).

Horton, Alicia D. 2013. "Flesh Hook Pulling: Motivations and Meaning-Making from the 'Body Side' of Life." *Deviant Behavior* 34: 115–134.

Horton, Richard. 2000. "North and South: Bridging the Information Gap." *The Lancet* 355(9222): 2231–2236.

Houck, Davis W. and David E. Dixon, eds. 2011. *Women and the Civil Rights Movement, 1954–1965.* Jackson: University of Mississippi Press.

Howard, I. 2002. "Power Sources: On Party, Gender, Race and Class, TV News Looks to the Most Powerful Groups." Retrieved March 30, 2012 (http://www.fair.org/index.php?page=1109).

Howe, Jeff. 2008. *Crowdsourcing: Why the Power of the Crowd Is Driving the Future of Business.* New York: Three Rivers Press.

Huaco, George. 1966. "The Functionalist Theory of Stratification: Two Decades of Controversy." *Inquiry* 9: 215–240.

Huang, Penelope M., Pamela J. Smock, Wendy D. Manning, and Cara A. Bergstrom-Lynch. 2011. "He Says, She Says: Gender and Cohabitation." *Journal of Family Issues* 32: 876–905.

Hughes, Donna M. 1999. "Pimps and Predators on the Internet-Globalizing the Sexual Exploitation of Women and Children." Kingston, RI: Coalition Against Trafficking in Women. Retrieved March 30, 2012 (http://www.uri.edu/artsci/wms/hughes/pprep.pdf).

Hughes, Donna M. 2000. "Welcome to the Rape Camp: Sexual Exploitation and the Internet in Cambodia." *Journal of Sexual Aggression* 6: 1–23.

Hughes, Gerald and Doug Degher. 1993. "Coping with a Deviant Identity." *Deviant Behavior* 14: 297–315.

Hull, Kathleen E., Ann Meier, and Timothy Ortyl. 2010. "The Changing Landscape of Love and Marriage." *Contexts* 9: 32–37.

Humphreys, Laud. 1970. *Tearoom Trade: A Study of Homosexual Encounters in Public Places.* Chicago: Aldine.

Humphreys, Laud. 1972. *Out of the Closets: The Sociology of Homosexual Liberation.* Upper Saddle River, NJ: Prentice Hall Trade.

Humphreys, Laud. 1975. *Tearoom Trade: Impersonal Sex in Public Places.* Enlarged ed. Chicago: Aldine.

Humphreys, Lee. 2005. "Cellphones in Public: Social Interactions in a Wireless Era." *New Media and Society* 7: 810–833.

Humphry, Derek. 2002. *Final Exit: The Practicalities of Self-Deliverance and Assisted Suicide for the Dying.* 3rd ed. New York: Delta.

Hunt, Stephen. 2007. "Social Structure." Pp. 4524–4526 in *The Blackwell Encyclopedia of Sociology*, edited by G. Ritzer. Malden, MA: Blackwell.

Hunter, James Davison. 1992. *Culture Wars: The Struggle to Control the Family, Art, Education, Law, And Politics in America.* New York: Basic Books.

Huntington, Samuel P. 1996. *The Clash of Civilizations and the Remaking of the World Order.* New York: Simon and Schuster.

Hurley, Dan. 2005. "Divorce Rate: It's Not as High as You Think." *New York Times*, April 19.

Hutson, Brittany. 2010. "Overcoming Gender Differences." *Black Enterprise* 40(8): 56–57.

Iceland, John. 2003. *Poverty in America.* Berkeley: University of California Press.

Iceland, John. 2007. "Poverty." Pp. 3587–3588 in *The Blackwell Encyclopedia of Sociology*, edited by G. Ritzer. Malden, MA: Blackwell.

Iceland, John. 2012. *Poverty in America: A Handbook.* Updated ed. Berkeley: University of California Press.

Illouz, Eva. 2007. *Cold Intimacies: The Making of Emotional Capitalism.* Cambridge, UK: Polity.

Illouz, Eva. 2008. *Saving the Modern Soul: Therapy, Emotions and the Culture of Self Help.* Berkeley: University of California Press.

Immigration Policy Center. 2010. *Immigrant Women in the United States: A Portrait of Demographic Diversity.* Retrieved October 21, 2013 (www.immigrationpolicy.org/just-facts/immigrant-women-united-states-portrait-demographic-diversity).

Inckle, Kay. 2007. *Writing on the Body? Thinking through Gendered Embodiment and Marked Flesh.* Newcastle, UK: Cambridge Scholars.

Inda, Jonathan Xavier. 2012. "Flows." Pp. 668–670 in *Wiley-Blackwell Encyclopedia of Globalization*, edited by G. Ritzer. Malden, MA: Wiley-Blackwell.

Inda, Jonathan Xavier and Renato Rosaldo. 2008. *The Anthropology of Globalization: A Reader.* 2nd ed. Malden, MA: Blackwell.

Inglehart, Ronald and Wayne E. Baker. 2000. "Modernization, Cultural Change, and the Persistence of Traditional Values." *American Sociological Review* 65: 19–51.

Inglehart, Ronald, Roberto Foa, Christopher Peterson, and Christian Welzel. 2008. "Development, Freedom, and Rising Happiness: A Global Perspective (1981–2007)." *Perspectives on Psychological Science* 3(4): 264–285.

Ingoldsby, Bron B. and Suzanna D. Smith. 2006. *Families in Global and Multicultural Perspective.* 2nd ed. Thousand Oaks, CA: Sage.

Inoue, Keiko and Gili S. Drori. 2006. "The Global Institutionalization of Health as a Social Concern." *International Sociology* 21(1): 199–219.

Insch, Gary S., Nancy McIntyre, and Nancy C. Napier. 2008. "The Expatriate Glass Ceiling: The Second Layer of Glass." *Journal of Business Ethics* 83: 19–28.

Institute of International Studies, University of California at Berkeley. 2001. "Conversations with History: Manuel Castells." Retrieved April 1, 2012 (http://globetrotter.berkeley.edu/people/Castells/castells-con0.html).

Intergovernmental Panel on Climate Change. 2007. "Summary for Policymakers." In *Climate Change 2007: The Physical Science Basis*, edited by S. Solomon, D. Qin, M. Manning, Z. Chen, M. Marquis, K. B. Averyt, M. Tignor, and H. L. Miller. Contribution of Working Group I to the Fourth Assessment Report of the Intergovernmental Panel on Climate Change. Cambridge, UK: Cambridge University Press.

International Confederation of Free Trade Unions. 2004. "The Informal Economy: Women on the Frontline." *Trade Union World Briefing* 2, March 2. Retrieved March 30, 2012 (www.ilo.org/public/english/region/ampro/cinterfor/temas/informal/doc/womflin.pdf).

International Federation of the Phonographic Industry. 2012. "Music Market Statistics." March 30, 2012 (http://www.ifpi.org/content/section_statistics/index.html).

International Labour Office. 2005. *A Global Alliance against Forced Labour: Global Report under the Follow-up to the ILO Declaration on Fundamental Principles and Rights at Work: 2005* (Report I [B]), pp. 55–56. International Labour Conference, 93rd Session.

International Monetary Fund. 2011. "WEO Data: April 2011 Edition." Retrieved May 26, 2011 (http://www.imf.org/external/pubs/ft/weo/2011/01/weodata/WEOApr2011all.xls).

International Organization for Migration. 2005. "World Migration 2005: Costs and Benefits of International Migration." Retrieved March 30, 2012 (http://www.iom.int/jahia/Jahia/cache/offonce/pid/1674?entryId=932).

International Pacific Research Center. 2011. "Where Will the Debris from Japan's Tsunami Drift in the Ocean?" April 5. Retrieved May 25, 2011 (http://www.soest.hawaii.edu/iprc/news/press_releases/2011/maximenko_tsunami_debris.pdf).

"The Internet in China." 2008. *The Economist*, January 31. Retrieved March 29, 2012 (http://www.economist.com/node/10608655).

Intravia, Jonathan, Shayne Jones, and Alex R. Piquero. 2011. "The Roles of Social Bonds, Personality, and Perceived Costs: An Empirical Investigation into Hirschi's 'New' Social Control Theory." *International Journal of Offender Therapy and Comparative Criminology* [Published online before print September 26]. doi:10.1177/0306624X11422998.

Introvigne, Masimo. 2007. "New Age." Pp. 3189–3192 in *The Blackwell Encyclopedia of Sociology*, edited by G. Ritzer. Malden, MA: Blackwell.

Ioffe, Julia. 2010. "Roulette Russian: The Teenager Behind Chatroulette." *The New Yorker*, May 17, p. 54.

"Irish Economy Shrank by One Fifth During Recession." 2011. *BBC News*, September 19. Retrieved February 28, 2012 (http://www.bbc.co.uk/news/uk-northern-ireland-14976439).

Iyengar, S. 1990. "The Accessibility Bias in Politics: Television News and Public Opinion." *International Journal of Public Opinion Research* 2(1): 1–15.

Jackson, Shirley A. 2007. "Majorities." Pp. 2701–2702 in *The Blackwell Encyclopedia of Sociology*, edited by G. Ritzer. Malden, MA: Blackwell.

Jackson-Jacobs, Curtis. 2005. "Hard Drugs in a Soft Context: Managing Trouble and Crack Use on a College Campus." *Sociological Quarterly* 45(4): 835–856.

Jacobs, Andrew. 2010. "China Seeks End to Public Shaming." *New York Times*, July 27, pp. A1, A3.

Jacobs, Jerry. 1996. "Gender Inequality and Higher Education." *Annual Review of Sociology* 22: 153–185.

Jacobs, Mark D. 2007. "Interaction Order." Pp. 2365–66 in *The Blackwell Encyclopedia of Sociology,* edited by George Ritzer. Malden, MA: Blackwell.

Jacobs, Nicholas. 2013. "Racial, Economic, and Linguistic Segregation: Analyzing Market Supports in the District of Columbia's Public Charter Schools." *Education and Urban Society,* 45(1): 120-141.

Jacobsen, Linda A., Mark Mather and Genevieve Dupuis. "Household Change in the United States." *Population Bulletin* 67, 1: 2012.

Jacques, Martin. 2009. *When China Rules the World: The End of the Western World and the Birth of a New Global Order.* London: Penguin.

Jagannathan, S. 1984. *Hinduism: An Introduction.* Bombay, India: Vakils, Feffer, and Simons.

Jakobi, Anja P. 2012. "Human Trafficking." Pp. 953–956 in *The Wiley-Blackwell Encyclopedia of Globalization,* edited by G. Ritzer. Malden, MA: Wiley-Blackwell.

Jalali, Rita. 2007. "Caste: Inequalities Past and Present." Pp. 404–406 in *The Blackwell Encyclopedia of Sociology,* edited by G. Ritzer. Malden, MA: Blackwell.

James, William. [1902] 1960. *The Varieties of Religious Experience.* New York: Random House.

Jamieson, Kathleen. 1996. *Packaging the Presidency: A History and Criticism of Presidential Campaign Advertising.* New York: Oxford.

Jamieson, Lynn. 1998. *Intimacy: Personal Relationships in Modern Societies.* Cambridge, UK: Polity Press.

Jamieson, Lynn. 2007. "Intimacy." Pp. 2411–2414 in *The Blackwell Encyclopedia of Sociology,* edited by G. Ritzer. Malden, MA: Blackwell.

Jansen, Jim. 2010. "Online Product Research." *The Pew Research Center,* September 29. Retrieved May 27, 2011 (http://www.pewinternet.org/~/media//Files/Reports/2010/PIP%20Online%20Product%20Research%20final.pdf).

Jasper, James M. 2007. "Social Movement." Pp. 4443–4451 in *The Blackwell Encyclopedia of Sociology,* edited by G. Ritzer. Malden, MA: Blackwell.

Jay, Karla. 1999. *Tales of the Lavender Menace: A Memoir of Liberation.* New York: Basic Books.

Jay, Martin. 1973. *The Dialectical Imagination.* Boston: Little Brown.

Jean-Charles, Régine Michelle. 2010. "Cracks of Gender Inequality: Haitian Women after the Earthquake." Retrieved March 30, 2012 (http://www.ssrc.org/features/pages/haiti-now-and-next/1338/1428/).

Jefferson, Gail. 1979. "A Technique for Inviting Laughter and Its Subsequent Acceptance Declination." Pp. 79–96 in *Everyday Language: Studies in Ethnomethodology,* edited by G. Psathas. New York: Irvington.

Jeffreys, Sheila. 2005. *Beauty and Misogyny: Harmful Cultural Practices in the West.* New York: Routledge.

Jeffries, Ian. 2011. *Economic Developments in Contemporary Russia.* New York: Routledge.

Jekielek, Susan M. and Kristin A. Moore. 2007. "Family Structure and Child Outcomes." Pp. 1621–1626 in *The Blackwell Encyclopedia of Sociology,* edited by G. Ritzer. Malden, MA: Blackwell.

Jenkins, J. C. 1983. "Resource Mobilization Theory and the Study of Social Movements." *Annual Review of Sociology* 9: 248–267.

Jenness, Valerie. 2004. "Explaining Criminalization: From Demography and Status Politics to Globalization and Modernization." *Annual Review of Sociology* 30: 141–171.

Jensen, Gary F. 1988. "Functional Perspectives on Deviance: A Critical Assessment and Guide for the Future." *Deviant Behavior* 9: 1–17.

Jerolmack, C. 2009. Special Issue (Part 1). *Ethnography* 10(4): 435–457.

Jerolmack C. 2009. "Humans, Animals, and Play: Theorizing Interaction When Intersubjectivity Is Problematic." *Sociological Theory* 27(4): 371–389.

Jimenez, Maria. 2009. "Humanitarian Crisis: Migrant Deaths at the U.S.-Mexican Border." Retrieved March 30, 2012 (http://www.aclu.org/files/pdfs/immigrants/humanitariancrisisreport.pdf).

Johnson, Carrie. 2009. "Justice Department Turning Attention toward Native American Crime Issues." *The Washington Post,* June 15.

Johnson, Cathryn, Rebecca Ford, and Joanne Kaufman. 2000. "Emotional Reactions to Conflict: Do Dependence and Legitimacy Matter?" *Social Forces* 79(1): 107–137.

Johnson, David K. 2004. *The Lavender Scare: The Cold War Persecution of Gays and Lesbians in the Federal Government.* Chicago: University of Chicago Press.

Johnson, Kevin and Mimi Hall. 2010. "Officials, Analysts Flay WikiLeaks Release of Key U.S. Security Sites." *USA Today,* December 7, p. 6A.

Johnson, Naomi. 2010. "Consuming Desires: Consumption, Romance, and Sexuality in Best-Selling Teen Romance Novels." *Women's Studies in Communication* 33: 54–73.

Jolly, David. 2012. "Amsterdam Shops Selling Marijuana to Stay Open." *New York Times,* November 1.

Jones, Adele. 2008. "A Silent but Mighty River: The Costs of Women's Economic Migration." *Journal of Women in Culture and Society* 33(4): 761–769.

Jones, Steven T. 2011. *The Tribes of Burning Man: How an Experimental City in the Desert Is Shaping the New American Counterculture.* San Francisco: Consortium of Collective Consciousness.

Jordan, Mary. 2007. "The New Face of Global Mormonism: Tech-Savvy Missionary Church Thrives as Far Afield as Africa." *Washington Post,* November 19, pp. A1, A13.

Jorgenson, Andrew and Jennifer Givens. 2012. "Pollution, Water." P. 1674 in *The Wiley-Blackwell Companion to Sociology,* edited by G. Ritzer. Malden, MA: Wiley-Blackwell.

Joyner, Chris. 2010a. "Miss. Prom Canceled." *Signs* 33(4): 761–769.

Joyner, Chris. 2010b. "Miss. Prom Canceled After Lesbian's Date Request." *USA Today,* March 11. Retrieved March 30, 2012 (http://www.usatoday.com/news/nation/2010-03-10-noprom_N.htm).

Juergensmeyer, Mark. 2009. *Global Rebellion: Religious Challenges to the Secular State, from Christian Militias to al Qaeda.* Berkeley: University of California Press.

Jung, Moon-Kie, Joao Costa Vargas, and Eduardo Bonilla-Silva, eds. 2011. *State of White Supremacy: Racism, Governance, and the United States.* Stanford CA: Stanford University Press.

Jurgenson, Nathan. 2012. "When Atoms Meet Bits: Social Media, the Mobile Web and Augmented Revolution." *Future Internet* 4: 83–91.

Juris, Jeffrey. 2005. "The New Digital Media and Activist Networking Within Anti-corporate Globalization Movements." *Annals* 597(January):189–208.

Kadushin, Charles. 2012. *Understanding Social Networks: Theories, Concepts, and Findings.* New York: Oxford University Press.

Kahlenberg, Richard D., ed. 2010. *Affirmative Action for the Rich: Legacy Preferences in College Admissions.* Washington, DC: Brookings Institution Press.

Kahlenberg, Susan G. and Michelle M. Hein. 2010. "Progression on Nickelodeon? Gender-Role Stereotypes in Toy Commercials." *Sex Roles: A Journal of Research* 62(11–12): 830–847.

Kahn, Joseph and Mark Landler. 2007. "China Grabs West's Smoke-Spewing Factories." *New York Times,* December 21.

Kahn, Richard and Douglas Kellner. 2007. "Resisting Globalization." Pp. 662–674 in *The Blackwell Companion to Globalization,* edited by G. Ritzer. Malden, MA: Blackwell.

Kalberg, Stephen. 1980. "Max Weber's Type of Rationality: Cornerstones for the Analysis of Rationalization Processes in History." *American Journal of Sociology* 85.

Kalberg, Stephen. 2011. "Max Weber." Pp. 305–372 in *The Wiley-Blackwell Companion to Major Social Theorists: Volume 1. Classical Theorists,* edited by G. Ritzer and J. Stepnisky. Malden, MA: Wiley-Blackwell.

Kalev, Alexandra. 2009. "Cracking the Glass Cages? Restructuring and Ascriptive Inequality at Work." *American Journal of Sociology* 114: 1591–1643.

Kalleberg, Arne. 2009. "Precarious Work, Insecure Workers: Employment Relations in Transition." *American Sociological Review* 74: 1–22.

Kalra, Gurvinder. 2012. "*Hijras*: The Unique Transgender Culture of India." *International Journal of Culture and Mental Health* 5: 121–126.

Kane, Emily. 2006. "'No Way My Boys Are Going to Be Like That!' Parents' Responses to Children's Gender Nonconformity." *Gender and Society* 20(2): 149–176.

Kangas, Olli E. 2007. "Welfare State, Retrenchment of." Pp. 5247–5249 in *The Blackwell Encyclopedia of Sociology*, edited by G. Ritzer. Malden, MA: Blackwell.

Kanter, Rosabeth Moss. 1993. *Men and Women of the Corporation*. New York: Basic Books.

Karmen, A. 1994. "Defining Deviancy Down: How Senator Moynihan's Misleading Praise about Criminal Justice Is Rapidly Being Incorporated Into Popular Culture." *Journal of Criminal Justice and Popular Culture* (October): 99–127.

Karon, Tony. 2001. "Why Courts Don't Deter France's Anti-McDonald's 'Astérix.'" *Time*, February 15. Retrieved March 30, 2012 (http://www.time.com/time/world/article/0,8599,99592,00.html).

Karpowitz, Christopher F., Quin J. Monson, Kelly D. Patterson, and Jeremy C. Pope. 2011. "Tea Time in America? The Impact of the Tea Party Movement on the 2010 Midterm Elections." *PS* (April): 303–309.

Karraker, Meg Wilkes. 2008. *Global Families*. Boston: Pearson.

Karstedt, Susanne. 2007. "Genocide." Pp. 1909–1913 in *The Blackwell Encyclopedia of Sociology*, edited by G. Ritzer. Malden, MA: Blackwell.

Karstedt, Susanne. 2012. "Genocide." Pp. 793–797 in *The Wiley-Blackwell Encyclopedia of Globalization*, edited by G. Ritzer. Malden, MA: Wiley-Blackwell.

Kasarda, John D. and Greg Lindsay. 2011. *Aerotropolis: The Way We'll Live Next*. New York: Farrar, Straus, Giroux.

Kasten, Erich. 2004. *Properties of Culture, Culture as Property: Pathways to Reform in Post-Soviet Siberia*. Berlin: Reimer.

Katsulis, Yasmina. 2010. "'Living like a King': Conspicuous Consumption, Virtual Communities, and the Social Construction of Paid Sexual Encounters by U.S. Sex Tourists." *Men and Masculinities* 27: 1–18.

Katz-Gerro, Tally and Mads Meier Jaeger. 2011. "Top of the Pops, Ascend of the Omnivores, Defeat of the Couch Potatoes: Cultural Consumption Profiles in Denmark 1975–2004." *European Sociological Review*.

Kaufman, Jason and Orlando Patterson. 2005. "Cross-National Cultural Diffusion: The Global Spread of Cricket." *American Sociological Review* 70:82–110.

Kaufman, Michael T. 2003. "Robert K. Merton, Versatile Sociologist and Father of the Focus Group, Dies at 92." *New York Times* Obituaries, February 24. Retrieved March 30, 2012 (http://www.nytimes.com/2003/02/24/nyregion/robert-k-merton-versatile-sociologist-and-father-of-the-focus-group-dies-at-92.html?pagewanted=all&src=pm).

Kaufman-Scarbrough, Carol. 2006. "Time Use and the Impact of Technology: Examining Workspaces in the Home." *Time and Society* 15(1): 57–80.

Keane, John. 2003. *Global Civil Society*. Cambridge, UK: Cambridge University Press.

"Keep the Borders Open." 2008. *The Economist*, January 3. Retrieved March 7, 2012 (http://www.economist.com/node/10430282).

Kefalas, Maria J., Frank F. Furstenberg, Patrick J. Carr, and Laura Napolitano. 2011. "'Marriage Is More than Being Together': The Meaning of Marriage for Young Adults." *Journal of Family Issues* 32: 845–875.

Kelishadi, Roya. 2007. "Childhood Overweight, Obesity, and the Metabolic Syndrome in Developing Countries." *Epidemiologic Reviews* 29(1): 62–76.

Keller, Bill. 1990. "Of Famous Arches, Been Meks and Rubles." *New York Times*, January 28, Section 1, p. 12.

Kellerhals, Jean. 2007. "Family Conflict." Pp. 1580–1583 in *The Blackwell Encyclopedia of Sociology*, edited by G. Ritzer. Malden, MA: Blackwell.

Kellner, Douglas and Tyson E. Lewis. 2007. "Cultural Critique." Pp. 896–898 in *The Blackwell Encyclopedia of Sociology*, edited by G. Ritzer. Malden, MA: Blackwell.

Kelly, Liz. 2007. "Sexual Violence and Rape." Pp. 4249–4254 in *The Blackwell Encyclopedia of Sociology*, edited by G. Ritzer. Malden, MA: Blackwell.

Kelly, William W., ed. 2004. *Fanning the Flames: Fans and Consumer Culture in Contemporary Japan*. New York: State University of New York Press.

Kelly, William W. 2007. "Is Baseball a Global Sport? America's 'National Pastime' as a Global Field and International Sport." Pp. 79–93 in *Globalization and Sport*, edited by R. Giulianotti and R. Robertson. Malden, MA: Blackwell.

Kelso, Alicia. 2011. "NRA 2011: McCafé Digital Menu Board Project Largest in World." QSR Web. Retrieved May 25, 2011 (http://www.qsrweb.com/article/181495/NRA-2011-McCaf-digital-menu-board-project-largest-in-world).

Kempadoo, Kamala and Jo Doezema, eds. 1998. *Global Sex Workers: Rights, Resistance, and Redefinition*. London: Routledge.

Kemper, Theodore D. 1991. "Predicting Emotions From Social Relations." *Social Psychology Quarterly* 54: 330–342.

Kennedy, John. 2007. "China: Blogger Goes to Court." *Global Voices*. Retrieved May 23, 2011 (http://globalvoicesonline.org/2007/08/06/china-blogger-goes-to-court/).

Kennedy, M. Alexis, Carolin Klein, Jessica T. K. Bristowe, Barry S. Cooper, and John C. Yuille. 2007. "Routes of Recruitment: Pimps' Techniques and Other Circumstances That Lead to Street Prostitution." *Journal of Aggression, Maltreatment and Trauma* 15(2): 1–19.

Kennedy, Randall. 2003. *Nigger: The Strange Career of a Troublesome Word*. New York: Vintage Books.

Kerber, Linda K. 1988. "Separate Spheres, Female Worlds, Woman's Place: The Rhetoric of Women's History." *The Journal of American History* 75(1): 9–39.

Kerrissey, Jasmine and Evan Schofer. 2013. "Union Membership and Political Participation in the United States." *Social Forces* 91: 895–928.

Kerry L. Preibisch and Evelyn Encalada Grez. 2010. "The Other Side of el Otro Lado: Mexican Migrant Women and Labor Flexibility in Canadian Agriculture." *Signs* 35(2): 289–316.

Kershaw, Sarah. 2008. "Starving Themselves, Cocktail in Hand." *New York Times*, March 2. Retrieved January 1, 2012 (http://www.nytimes.com/2008/03/02/fashion/02drunk.html).

Kestnbaum, Meyer. 2012. "Organized Coercion and Political Authority: Armed Conflict in a World of States." Pp. 588–608 in *The Wiley-Blackwell Companion to Sociology*, edited by G. Ritzer. Malden, MA: Wiley-Blackwell.

Khan, Rana Ejaz Ali and Muhammad Zahir Faridi. 2008. "Impact of Globalization and Economic Growth on Income Distribution: A Case Study of Pakistan." *IUB Journal of Social Sciences and Humanities* 6(2): 7–33.

Khatchadourian, Raffi. 2007. "Neptune's Navy." *The New Yorker*, November 5.

Khondker, Habibul Haque. 2011. "Role of the New Media in Arab Spring." *Globalizations* 8: 675–679.

Kiaye, Risper Enid and Anesh Maniraj Singh. 2013. "The Glass Ceiling: A Perspective of Women Working in Durban." *Gender in Management: An International Journal* 28: 28–42.

Kidder, Jeffrey L. 2012. "Parkour: The Affective Appropriation of Urban Space, and the Real/Virtual Dialectic." *City and Community* 11: 229–253.

Kienle, Eberhard. 2012. "Egypt without Mubarak, Tunisia after Bin Ali: Theory, History and the 'Arab Spring.'" *Economy and Society* 41: 532–557.

Kilgannon, Corey and Jeffrey E. Singer. 2010. "Stores' Treatment of Shoplifters Tests Rights." *New York Times*, June 21. Accessed December 20, 2011 (http://www.nytimes.com/2010/06/22/nyregion/22shoplift.html?pagewanted=all).

Kim, Eunjung. 2011. "Asexuality in Disability Narratives." *Sexualities* 24: 479–493.

Kimmel, Michael S. 2004. *The Gendered Society*. New York: Oxford University Press.

Kimmel, Michael. 2009. *The Gendered Society*. New York: Oxford University Press.

Kimmel, Michael. 2011. *The Gendered Society*. New York: Oxford University Press.

King, Anthony. 2004. *The Structure of Social Theory*. London: Routledge.

King, Martin Luther Jr. [1958] 2010. *Stride toward Freedom: The Montgomery Story*. Boston: Beacon Press.

Kinney, William J. 2007. "Asch Experiments." Pp. 189–191 in *The Blackwell Encyclopedia of Sociology*, edited by G. Ritzer. Malden, MA: Blackwell.

Kirk, Roger E. 2007. "Experimental Design." Pp. 1533–1537 in *The Blackwell Encyclopedia of Sociology*, edited by G. Ritzer. Malden, MA: Blackwell.

Kirton, Gill. 2007. "Gendered Enterprise." Pp. 1888–1891 in *The Blackwell Encyclopedia of Sociology*, edited by G. Ritzer. Malden, MA: Blackwell.

Kivisto, Peter. 2012a. "Fundamentalism." Pp. 709–713 in *The Wiley-Blackwell Encyclopedia of Globalization*, edited by G. Ritzer. Malden, MA: Wiley-Blackwell.

Kivisto, Peter. 2012b. "Refugees." Pp. 1761–1765 in *The Wiley-Blackwell Encyclopedia of Globalization*, edited by G. Ritzer. Malden, MA: Wiley-Blackwell.

Kivisto, Peter. 2012c. "We *Really* Are All Multiculturalists Now." *The Sociological Quarterly* 53(1): 1–24.

Kivisto, Peter and Paul R. Croll. 2012. *Race and Ethnicity: The Basics*. New York: Routledge.

Kivisto, Peter and Thomas Faist. 2007. *Citizenship: Discourse, Theory, and Transnational Prospects*. Malden, MA: Blackwell.

Kivisto, Peter and Thomas Faist. 2010. *Beyond a Border: The Causes and Consequences of Contemporary Immigration*. Thousand Oaks, CA: Pine Forge/Sage.

Klein, Alan. 1993. *Little Big Men: Bodybuilding Subculture and Gender Construction*. Albany: State University of New York Press.

Klein, Naomi. [2000] 2010. *No Logo: Taking Aim at the Brand Bullies*. Toronto: Vintage, Canada.

Kleinfeld, J. 1979. *Eskimo School on the Andreafsky: A Study of Effective Bicultural Education*. Praeger.

Klinenberg, Eric. 2012. *Going Solo: The Extraordinary Rise and Surprising Appeal of Living Alone*. New York: Penguin.

Klingmann, Anna. 2007. *Brandscapes: Architecture in the Experience Economy*. Cambridge, MA: MIT Press.

Knorr Cetina, Karin. 2012. "Financial Markets." Pp. 653–664 in *The Encyclopedia of Globalization*, edited by G. Ritzer. Malden, MA: Wiley-Blackwell.

Koch, Jerome R., Alden E. Roberts, Myrna L. Armstrong, and Donna C. Owen. 2010. "Body Art, Deviance, and American College Students." *The Social Science Journal* 47: 151–161.

Kochel, Tammy Rinehart, David B. Wilson, and Stephen D. Mastrofski. 2011. "Effect of Suspect Race on Officers' Arrest Decisions." *Criminology* 49: 473–512.

Kocieniewski, David. 2010. "In Tax Cut Plan, Debate over the Definition of the Rich." *New York Times*, September 29. Accessed December 28, 2011 (http://www.nytimes.com/2010/09/30/business/30rich.html?pagewanted=all).

Kohlberg, Lawrence. 1966. "A Cognitive-Development Analysis of Sex-Role Concepts and Attitudes." In *The Development of Sex Differences*, edited by E. Maccoby. Berkeley: University of California Press.

Kohler, Kristopher. 2012. "World Social Forum." Pp. 2325–2327 in *The Wiley-Blackwell Encyclopedia of Globalization*, edited by G. Ritzer. Malden, MA: Wiley-Blackwell.

Kohm, Steve. 2009. "Naming, Shaming and Criminal Justice: Mass-Mediated Humiliation as Entertainment and Punishment." *Crime Media Culture* 5(2): 188–205.

Kohn, Melvin L. (with Joanne Miller, Karen A. Miller, Carrie Schoenbach, and Ronald Schoenberg). 1983. *Work and Personality: An Inquiry into the Impact of Social Stratification*. Norwood, NJ: Ablex.

Kohrmann, M. 2008. "Smoking among Doctors: Governmentality, Embodiment, and the Diversion of Blame in Contemporary China." *Medical Anthropology* 27(1): 9–42.

Kolata, Gina. 1999. *The Flu: The Story of the Great Influenza Pandemic of 1918 and the Search for the Virus that Caused It*. New York: Touchstone.

Kollen, Thomas. 2013. "Bisexuality and Diversity Management: Addressing the B in LGBT as a Relevant 'Sexual Orientation in the Workplace." *Journal of Bisexuality* 13(1): 122–137.

Koller, Daphne. 2011. "Death Knell for the Lecture: Technology as a Passport to Personalized Education." *New York Times*, December 5.

Kollmeyer, Christopher. 2009. "Explaining Deindustrialization: How Affluence, Productivity Growth, and Globalization Diminish Manufacturing Employment." *American Journal of Sociology* 114: 1644–1674.

Kong, Travis. 2010. *Chinese Male Homosexualities*. London: Routledge.

Konrad, Waleca. 2009. "Seeking the Best Medical Care Prices." *New York Times*, November 28, p. B5.

Koppell, Jonathan G. S. 2010. *World Rule: Accountability, Legitimacy and the Design of Global Governance*. Chicago: University of Chicago Press.

Korda, Andrew. 2006. "The Nazi Medical Experiments." *ADF Health* 7 (April): 33–37.

Korenman, Sanders D. and David Neumark. 1991. "Does Marriage Really Make Men More Productive?" *Journal of Human Resources* 26: 282–307.

Korkki, Phyllis. 2012. "When the H.R. Office Leaves the Building." *New York Times*, December 12.

Kortenhaus, Carole M. and Jack Demarest. 1993. "Gender Role Stereotyping in Children's Literature: An Update." *Sex Roles* 28: 219–232.

Kosic, Ankica, Arie W. Kruglanski, Antonio Pierro, and Lucia Mannetti. 2004. "The Social Cognition of Immigrants' Acculturation: Effects of the Need for Closure and the Reference Group at Entry." *Journal of Personality and Social Psychology* 86: 796–813.

Kotarba, Joseph A. 2007. "Socialization, Adult." Pp. 4563–4566 in *The Blackwell Encyclopedia of Sociology*, edited by G. Ritzer. Malden, MA: Blackwell.

Kotarba, Joseph, Andrea Salvini, and Bryce Merrill, eds. 2010. *The Present and Future of Symbolic Interactionism. Proceedings of the International Symposium*. Pisa: Franco Angeli.

Kottak, Conrad P. 2010. "What Is Hypodescent?" Human Diversity and "Race" Online Learning, McGraw-Hill. Retrieved April 15, 2011 (http://highered.mcgraw-hill.com/sites/0072500506/student_view0/chapter5/faqs.html).

Kowalski, Robin W., Susan P. Limber, and Patricia W. Agatson. 2012. *Cyberbullying: Bullying in the Digital Age*, 2nd ed. Malden, MA: Wiley-Blackwell.

Kozinets, Robert V. 1998. "On Netnography: Initial Reflections on Consumer Research Investigations of Cyberculture." Pp. 366–371 in *Advances in Consumer Research*, edited by J. Alba and W. Hutchinson. Provo, UT: Association for Consumer Research.

Kozinets, Robert V. 2002a. "Can Consumers Escape the Market? Emancipatory Illuminations from Burning Man." *Journal of Consumer Research* 29: 20–38.

Kozinets, Robert V. 2002b. "The Field behind the Screen: Using Netnography for Marketing Research in Online Communities." *Journal of Marketing Research* 39: 61–72.

Kozinets, Robert V. 2009. *Netnography: Doing Ethnographic Research Online*. Thousand Oaks, CA: Sage.

Kozol, Jonathan. 1991. *Savage Inequalities: Children in America's Schools*. New York: Harper Perennial.

Kozol, Jonathan. 2006. *The Shame of the Nation: The Restoration of Apartheid Schooling in America*. New York: Broadway.

Kramer, Andrew E. 2011. "Delivering on Demand: American Fast Food Meets a Warm Reception in Russia." *New York Times*, August 4, pp. B1, B4.

Krass, Frauke, ed. 2012. *Megacities: Our Global Urban Future*. New York: Springer.

Krass, P. 1990. "The Dollars and Sense of Outsourcing." *Information Week*, February 26, pp. 26–31.

Krauss, Clifford. 2004. "Internet Drug Exporters Feel Pressure in Canada." *New York Times*, December 11. Retrieved March 30, 2012 (http://query.nytimes.com/gst/fullpage.html?res=9F04EED81131F932A25751C1A9629C8B63&&scp=4&sq=pharmaceutical%20purchase%20over%20internet&st=cse).

Kreager Derek. 2007. "Unnecessary Roughness? School Sports, Peer Networks, and Male Adolescent Violence." *American Sociological Review* 72(5): 705–724.

Krings, Torben, Alicja Bobek, Elaine Moriarty, Justyna Salamonska, and James Wickham. 2009. "Migration and Recession: Polish Migrants in Post-Celtic Tiger Ireland." *Sociological Research Online* 14(2): 9. Retrieved March 30, 2012 (http://www.socresonline.org.uk/14/2/9.html).

Krinsky, Charles, ed. 2013. *The Ashgate Research Companion to Moral Panics*. Burlington, VT: Ashgate.

Kritz, Mary M. 2007. "Migration, International." Pp. 3019–3025 in *The Blackwell Encyclopedia of Sociology*, edited by G. Ritzer. Malden, MA: Blackwell.

Kritz, Mary M. 2008. "International Migration." In *The Blackwell Encyclopedia of Sociology Online*, edited by G. Ritzer. Malden, MA: Blackwell.

Kritz, Mary M., Lin Lean Lim, and Hania Zlotnik. 1992. *International Migration Systems: A Global Approach*. Oxford: Oxford University Press.

Kroen, Sheryl. 2006. "Negotiations with the American Way: The Consumer and the Social Contract in Post-war Europe." Pp. 251–278 in *Consuming Cultures, Global Perspectives: Historical Trajectories, Transnational Exchanges*, edited by J. Brewer and F. Trentmann. Oxford: Berg.

Kroneberg, Clemens and Frank Kalter. 2012. "Rational Choice Theory and Empirical Research: Methodological and Theoretical Contributions in Europe." *Annual Review of Sociology* 38: 73–92.

Kuhn, Thomas. [1962] 1970. *The Structure of Scientific Revolutions*. 2nd ed. Chicago: University of Chicago Press.

Kuisel, Richard. 1993. *Seducing the French: The Dilemma of Americanization*. Berkeley, CA: Berkeley University Press.

Kulish, Nicholas. 2007. "Europe Fears that Meth Foothold Is Expanding." *New York Times*, November 23.

Kupfer, Antonia. 2012. "A Theoretical Concept of Educational Upward Mobility." *International Studies in Sociology of Education* 22: 57–72.

Kurtz, Lester R. 2005. "From Heresies to Holy Wars: Toward a Theory of Religious Conflict." *Ahimsa Nonviolence* 1(March–April): 143–157.

Kurtz, Lester. 2012. *Gods in the Global Village*. Thousand Oaks, CA: Sage.

Kurzban. 2006. "Post-Sept. 11, 2001." Kurzban's *Immigration Law Sourcebook* (pp. xxi–xxiii). 10th ed. Washington, DC: American Immigration Law Foundation.

Kurzman, Charles. 2002. "Bin Laden and Other Thoroughly Modern Muslims." *Contexts*, Fall/Winter.

Lacey, Marc. 2009. "Money Trickles North as Mexicans Help Relatives." *New York Times*, November 16, p. A1.

Lacey, Marc. 2011. "Rift in Arizona as Latino Class Is Found Illegal." *New York Times*, January 7. Retrieved March 30, 2012 (http://www.nytimes.com/2011/01/08/us/08ethnic.html).

Lachance-Grzela, Mylene and Genevieve Bouchard. 2010. "Why Do Women Do the Lion's Share of Housework? A Decade of Research." *Sex Roles: A Journal of Research* 63(11–12): 767–780.

Lacharite, Jason. 2002. "Electronic Decentralisation in China: A Critical Analysis of Internet Filtering Policies in the People's Republic of China." *Australian Journal of Political Science* 37(2): 333–346.

Lacity, Mary Cecelia and R. A. Hirschheim. 1993. *Information Systems Outsourcing: Myths, Metaphors and Realities*. New York: Wiley.

Laegaard, Sune. 2013. "Danish Anti-Multiculturalism? The Significance of the Political Framing of Diversity." In *Debating Multiculturalism in the Nordic Welfare States*, edited by P. Kivisto and Ö. Wahlbeck. Basingstoke: Palgrave Macmillan.

Lahelma, Eero. 2007. "Health and Social Class." Pp. 2086–2091 in *The Blackwell Encyclopedia of Sociology*, edited by G. Ritzer. Malden, MA: Blackwell.

Lakoff, Andrew. 2008. "Diagnostic Liquidity: Mental Illness and the Global Trade in DNA." Pp. 277–300 in *The Anthropology of Globalization: A Reader*, edited by J. X. Inda and R. Rosaldo. 2nd ed. Malden, MA: Blackwell.

Lal, Dinesh. 2008. *Indo-Tibet-China Conflict*. Delhi, India: Kalpaz Publications.

Landler, Mark. 2008a. "Credit Cards Tighten Grip Outside US." *New York Times*, August 30, p. C1.

Landler, Mark. 2008b. "At Tipping Point." *New York Times*, October 1.

Landry, Bart. 1988. *The New Black Middle Class*. Berkeley: University of California Press.

Landry, Bart and Kris Marsh. 2011. "The Evolution of the New Black Middle Class." *Annual Review of Sociology* 37: 373–394.

Lane, Harlan. 1975. *The Wild Boy of Aveyron*. Cambridge, MA: Harvard University Press.

Lareau, Annette. [1989] 2000. *Home Advantage: Social Class and Parental Intervention in Elementary Education*. 2nd ed. Lanham, MD: Rowan and Littlefield.

Lareau, Annette. 2003. *Unequal Childhoods: Class, Race, and Family Life*. Berkeley: University of California Press.

Larsen, Ulla. 2007. "Gender, Health, and Morality." Pp. 1864–1867 in *The Blackwell Encyclopedia of Sociology*, edited by G. Ritzer. Malden, MA: Blackwell.

Lasn, Kalle. 2000. *Culture Jam: How to Reverse America's Suicidal Consumer Binge—And Why We Must*. Morrow.

Lash, Scott Lash and Celia Lury. 2007. *Global Culture Industry*. Cambridge, UK: Polity Press.

Lauderdale, Pat. 2007. "Deviance, Moral Boundaries and." Pp. 1114–1116 in *The Blackwell Encyclopedia of Sociology*, edited by G. Ritzer. Malden, MA: Blackwell.

Laumann, Anne E. and Amy J. Derick. 2006. "Tattoos and Body Piercings in the United States: A National Data Set." *Journal of the American Academy of Dermatology* 55: 413–421.

Lauer, Sean and Carrie Yodanis. 2010. "The Deinstitutionalization of Marriage Revisited: A New Institutional Approach to Marriage." *Journal of Family Theory and Review* 2: 58–72.

Lauer, Sean and Carrie Yodanis. 2011. "Individualized Marriage and the Integration of Resources." *Journal of Marriage and Family* 73: 669–683.

Laurie, Nina, Claire Dwyer, Sarah Holloway, and Fiona Smith. 1999. *Geographies of New Femininities*. London: Longman.

Law, Ian. 2007. "Discrimination." Pp. 1182–1184 in *The Blackwell Encyclopedia of Sociology*, edited by G. Ritzer. Malden, MA: Blackwell.

Law, Ian. 2010. *Racism and Ethnicity: Global Debates, Dilemmas*. London: Pearson.

Law, Ian. 2012a. "Race." Pp. 1737–1743 in *The Wiley-Blackwell Encyclopedia of Globalization*, edited by G. Ritzer. Malden, MA: Wiley-Blackwell.

Law, Ian. 2012b. "Racism." Pp. 1743–1746 in *The Wiley-Blackwell Encyclopedia of Globalization*, edited by G. Ritzer. Malden, MA: Wiley-Blackwell.

Law, John and John Hassard, eds. 1999. *Actor Network Theory and After*. Oxford, UK: Blackwell.

Layte, Richard and Christopher T. Whelan. 2009. "Explaining Social Class Inequalities in Smoking: The Role of Education, Self-Efficacy, and Deprivation." *European Sociological Review* 25: 399–410.

Le Gales, Patrick. 2007. "Cities in Europe." Pp. 493–497 in *The Blackwell Encyclopedia of Sociology*, edited by G. Ritzer. Malden, MA: Blackwell.

Leavitt, Alex and Tim Hwang. 2010. "ChatRoulette: An Initial Survey." *Web Ecology Project*, March 1. Retrieved March 30, 2012 (http://www.slideshare.net/GuiM_/chatroulette-an-initial-survey).

Leavitt, Judith Walzer. 1986. *Brought to Bed: Childbearing in America*. New York: Oxford University Press.

Lechner, Frank J. 1993. "Global Fundamentalism." In *A Future for Religion?* edited by W. H. Swatos. Thousand Oaks, CA: Sage.

Lechner, Frank. 2008. *The Netherlands: Globalization and National Identity*. New York: Routledge.

Lechner, Frank and John Boli. 2005. *World Culture: Origins and Consequences*. Oxford, UK: Blackwell.

Ledbetter, James. 2011. *Unwarranted Influence: Dwight D. Eisenhower and the Military-Industrial Complex*. New Haven, CT: Yale University Press.

Lee, Ching Kwan. 1999. *Gender and the South China Miracle*. Berkeley: University of California Press.

Lee, Ronald D. 2007. *Global Population Aging and Its Economic Consequences*. Washington, DC: American Enterprise Institute Press.

Lee, Susan Hagood. 2007. "Female Genital Mutilation." Pp. 1653–1657 in *The Blackwell Encyclopedia of Sociology*, edited by G. Ritzer. Malden, MA: Blackwell.

Lee, Susan Hagood. 2012a. "Genital Mutilation." Pp. 791–793 in *The Wiley-Blackwell Companion to Sociology*, edited by G. Ritzer. Malden, MA: Wiley-Blackwell.

Lee, Susan Hagood. 2012b. "Sex Trafficking." In *The Wiley-Blackwell Encyclopedia of Globalization*, edited by G. Ritzer. Malden, MA: Wiley-Blackwell.

Lees, Loretta, Tom Slater, and Elvin Wyly, eds. 2010. *The Gentrification Reader.* New York: Routledge.

Legerski, Elizabeth Miklya. 2012. "The Cost of Instability: The Effects of Family, Work, and Welfare Change on Low-Income Women's Health Insurance Status." *Sociological Forum* 27: 641–657.

Leicht, Kevin and Scott Fitzgerald. 2006. *Postindustrial Peasants: The Illusion of Middle-Class Prosperity.* New York: Worth.

Leidner, Robin. 1993. *Fast Food, Fast Talk.* Berkeley: University of California Press.

Leitch, Alison. 2003. "Slow Food and the Politics of Pork Fat: Italian Food and European Identity." *Ethnos* 68(4): 437–462.

Leitch, Alison. 2010. "Slow Food and the Politics of 'Virtuous Globalization.'" Pp. 45–64 in *The Globalization of Food*, edited by D. Inglis and D. Gimlin. Oxford, UK: Berg.

Lemert, Charles and Anthony Elliott. 2006. *Deadly Worlds: The Emotional Costs of Globalization.* Lanham, MD: Rowman and Littlefield.

Lengermann, Patricia Madoo and Gillian Niebrugge. 2008. "Contemporary Feminist Theory." Pp. 450–497 in *Sociological Theory*, edited by G. Ritzer. New York: McGraw-Hill.

Lengermann, Patricia Madoo and Gillian Niebrugge. 2014. "Feminist Theory." In *Sociological Theory*, edited by G. Ritzer and J. Stepnisky. 9th ed. New York: McGraw-Hill.

Lenhart, Amanda, Rich Ling, Scott Campbell, and Kristen Purcell. 2010. "Teens and Mobile Phones." Pew Research Center, Pew Internet and American Life Project, April 20.

Lenin, Vladimir. [1917] 1939. *Imperialism: The Highest Stage of Capitalism.* New York: International Publishers.

Lenski, Gerhard. 1954. "Status Crystallization: A Non-vertical Dimension of Stratification." *American Sociological Review* 19: 405–413.

Lesthaeghe, Ron J. 2007. "Second Demographic." Pp. 4123–4127 in *The Blackwell Encyclopedia of Sociology*, edited by G. Ritzer. Malden, MA: Blackwell.

Lesthaeghe, Ron. 2010. "The Unfolding Story of the Second Demographic Transition." *Population and Development Review* 36: 211–251.

Lesthaeghe, Ron and D. J. van de Kaa. 1986. "Twee Demografische Transities?" Pp. 9–24 in *Bevolking: Groei en Krimp, Mens en Maatschappij* (Book Supplement), edited by R. Lesthaeghe and D. J. van de Kaa. Deventer: Van Loghum, Slaterus.

Levin, Jack. 2007. "Hate Crimes." Pp. 2048–2050 in *The Blackwell Encyclopedia of Sociology*, edited by George Ritzer. Malden, MA: Blackwell.

Levitt, Peggy. 2001. *The Transnational Villagers.* Berkeley: University of California Press.

Levitt, Steven. 1998. "The Relationship between Crime Reporting and Police: Implications for the Use of Uniform Crime Reports." *Journal of Quantitative Criminology* 14(1). Retrieved March 30, 2012 (http://

pricetheory.uchicago.edu/levitt/Papers/LevittTheRelationshipBetweenCrime1998.pdf).

Levitt, Steven D. and Stephen J. Dubner. 2005. *Freakonomics: A Rogue Economist Explores the Hidden Side of Everything.* New York: HarperCollins.

Levitt, Steven D. and Sudhir A. Venkatesh. 2000. "An Economic Analysis of a Drug-Selling Gang's Finances." *Quarterly Journal of Economics* 115(3): 755–789.

Levy, Frank. 1987. *Dollars and Dreams: Changing American Income Distribution.* New York: Russell Sage.

Levy, Frank. 1999. *The New Dollars and Dreams: American Incomes and Economic Change.* New York: Russell Sage.

Levy, Steven. 2010. *Hackers: Heroes of the Computer Revolution.* 25th anniversary ed. Sebastopol, CA: O'Reilly Media.

Lewin, Tamar. 2008a. "Oil Money Cultivates a Mideast Ivy League." *New York Times*, February 11, p. A12.

Lewin, Tamar. 2008b. "Universities Rush to Set Up Outposts Abroad." *New York Times*, February 10, pp. 1–8.

Lewin, Tamar. 2008c. "U.S. Universities Join Saudis in Partnerships." *New York Times*, March 6, p. A19.

Lewin, Tamar. 2010. "Children Awake? Then They're Probably Online." *New York Times*, January 20, pp. A1, A3.

Lewin, Tamar. 2012. "College of Future Could Be Come One, Come All." *New York Times*, November 19.

Lewis, C. S. 1960. *The Four Loves.* New York: Harcourt, Brace.

Lewis, Melissa A., Hollie Granato, Jessica A. Blayney, Ty W. Lostutter, and Jason R. Kilmer. 2011. "Predictors of Hooking Up Sexual Behaviors and Emotional Reactions Among U.S. College Students." *Archives of Sexual Behavior*, Online First™, July 28.

Lichtblau, Eric. 2011. "With Lobbying Blitz, Profit-Making Colleges Diluted New Rules." *New York Times*, December 10, pp. A1, A3.

Lichter, Daniel T. 2007. "Family Structure and Poverty." Pp. 1463–1465 in *The Blackwell Encyclopedia of Sociology*, edited by G. Ritzer. Malden, MA: Blackwell.

Lichtman, Allan J. 2003. "What Really Happened in Florida's 2000 Presidential Election?" *Journal of Legal Studies* 32(1): 221–243.

Liebow, Elliot. 1967. *Tally's Corner: A Study of Negro Streetcorner Men.* New York: Little, Brown.

Liftin, Karen T. 2007. "Ozone Depletion." Pp. 927–930 *Encyclopedia of Globalization*, edited by J. A. Scholte and R. Robertson. New York: MTM Publishing.

Light, Donald W. 2007. "Professional Dominance in Medicine." Pp. 3656–3660 in *The Blackwell Encyclopedia of Sociology*, edited by in G. Ritzer. Malden, MA: Blackwell.

Lin, Jan. 2012. "World Cities." Pp. 2254–2262 in *The Wiley-Blackwell Encyclopedia of Globalization*, edited by G. Ritzer. Malden, MA: Wiley-Blackwell.

Lin, Nan. 1999. "Social Networks and Status Attainment." *Annual Review of Sociology* 25: 467–487.

Lin, Nan and Yanjie Bian. 1991. "Getting Ahead in Urban China." *American Journal of Sociology* 97: 657–688.

Lin, Nan, Walter M. Ensel, and John C. Vaughn. 1981. "Social Resources and Strength of Ties: Structural Factors in Occupational-Status Attainment." *American Sociological Review* 46: 393–403.

Lind, Amy. 2007. "Femininities/Masculinities." Pp. 1662–1666 in *The Blackwell Encyclopedia of Sociology*, edited by G. Ritzer. Malden, MA: Blackwell.

Linn, James G. and Debra Rose Wilson. 2012. "Health." Pp. 910–923 in *The Wiley-Blackwell Encyclopedia of Globalization*, edited by G. Ritzer. Malden, MA: Wiley-Blackwell.

Lipovetsky, Gilles. [1987] 2002. *The Empire of Fashion: Dressing Modern Democracy.* Princeton, NJ: Princeton University Press.

Lipovetsky, Gilles. 2005. *Hypermodern Times.* Cambridge, UK: Polity Press.

Lipset, Seymour M. 1981. *Political Man.* Expanded ed. Baltimore: Johns Hopkins University Press.

Little, Craig B. 2007. "Deviance, Absolutist Definitions of." Pp. 1082–1084 in *The Blackwell Encyclopedia of Sociology*, edited by G. Ritzer. Malden, MA: Blackwell.

Liu, Yu Cheng. 2012. "Ethnomethodology Reconsidered: The Practical Logic of Social Systems Theory." *Current Sociology* 60: 581–598.

Livermore, Michelle, Rebecca S. Powers, Belinda Creel Davis, and Younghee Lim. 2011. "Failing to Make Ends Meet: Dubious Financial Success among Employed Former Welfare to Work Program Participants." *Journal of Family Economic Issues* 32: 73–83.

Loewen, James. 1996. *Lies My Teacher Told Me.* New York: Touchstone.

Logan, John, Richard Alba, and Wenquan Zhang. 2002. "Immigrant Enclaves and Ethnic Communities in New York and Los Angeles." *American Sociological Review* 67(2): 299–322.

Logan, John R., Elisabeta Minca, and Sinem Adar. 2012. "The Geography of Inequality: Why Separate Means Unequal in American Public Schools." *Sociology of Education* 85(3): 287–301.

Lohr, Steve. 2009. "A Web Site Devoted to Your Health." *New York Times*, October 6.

Lopez, Steven H., Randy Hodson, and Vincent J. Roscigno. 2009. "Power, Status, and Abuse at Work: General and Sexual Harassment Compared." *The Sociological Quarterly* 50: 3–27.

Lorber, Judith. 1967. "Deviance as Performance: The Case of Illness." *Social Problems* 14: 302–310.

Lorber, Judith. 1994. *Paradoxes of Gender*. New Haven, CT: Yale University Press.

Lorber, Judith. 2000. "Using Gender to Undo Gender: A Feminist Degendering Movement." *Feminist Theory* 1(1): 79–95.

Lorber, Judith and Lisa Jean Moore. 2002. *Gender and the Social Construction of Illness*. Lanham, MD: AltaMira Press.

Lorenz, Edward. 1995. *The Essence of Chaos*. Seattle: University of Washington Press.

"Louisiana Oil Rig Explosion: Underwater Machines Attempt to Plug Leak." 2010. *Telegraph*, April 26. Retrieved March 31, 2012 (http://www.telegraph.co.uk/finance/newsbysector/energy/oilandgas/7633286/Louisiana-oil-rig-explosion-Underwater-machines-attempt-to-plug-leak.html).

Lovell, David W. 2007. "Communism." Pp. 612–617 in *The Blackwell Encyclopedia of Sociology*, edited by G. Ritzer. Malden, MA: Blackwell.

Low, Setha. 2003. *Behind the Gates: Life, Security, and the Pursuit of Happiness in Fortress America*. New York: Routledge.

Lowe, Brian. 2002. "Hearts and Minds and Morality: Analyzing Moral Vocabularies in Qualitative Studies." *Qualitative Sociology* 25(1): 105–112.

Lowell, B. Lindsay, Micah Bump, and Susan Martin. 2007. "Foreign Students Coming to America: The Impact of Policy, Procedures, and Economic Competition." Retrieved May 31, 2011 (http://www12.georgetown.edu/sfs/isim/Publications/SloanMaterials/Foreign%20Students%20Coming%20to%20America.pdf).

Lowell, Rebecca. 1998. "Modular Homes Move Up." *Wall Street Journal*, October 23, p. W10.

Loyal, Steve. 2007. "Refugees." Pp. 3837–3838 in *The Blackwell Encyclopedia of Sociology*, edited by G. Ritzer. Malden, MA: Blackwell.

Lubbers, Marcel, Eva Jaspers, and Wout Ultee. 2009. "Primary and Secondary Socialization Impacts on Support for Same-Sex Marriage after Legalization in the Netherlands." *Journal of Family Issues* 30: 1714–1745.

Lubienski, Christopher. 2006. "School Sector and Academic Achievement: A Multilevel Analysis of NAEP Mathematics Data." *American Educational Research Journal* 43: 651–698.

Lucas, Jeffrey W., Corina Graif, and Michael J. Lovaglia. 2008. "Can You Study a Legal System in a Laboratory?" Pp. 119–136 in *Experiments in Criminology and Law: A Research Revolution*, edited by C. Horne and M. J. Lovaglia. Lanham, MD: Rowman and Littlefield.

Lukacs, George. [1922] 1968. *History and Class Consciousness*. Cambridge, MA: MIT Press.

Luker, Kristin. 1984. *Abortion and the Politics of Motherhood*. Berkeley: University of California Press.

Lukes, Steven. 1974. *Power: A Radical View*. London: Macmillan.

Lutfey, Karen and Jeylan Mortimer. 2006. "Development and Socialization through the Adult Life Course." In *Handbook of Social Psychology*, edited by J. Delamater. New York: Kluwer Academic/Plenum Publishers.

Lunneborg, Clifford E. 2007. "Convenience Sample." Pp. 788–790 in *The Blackwell Encyclopedia of Sociology*, edited by G. Ritzer. Malden, MA: Blackwell.

Luo, Michael. 2010. "At Closing Plant, Ordeal Included Heart Attacks." *New York Times*, February 24.

Lupton, Deborah. 2007. "Health Risk Behavior." Pp. 2083–2085 in *The Blackwell Encyclopedia of Sociology*, edited by G. Ritzer. Malden, MA: Blackwell.

Lüthi, Dieter, Martine Le Floch, Bernhard Bereiter, Thomas Blunier, Jean-Marc Barnola, Urs Siegenthaler, Dominique Raynaud, Jean Jouzel, Hubertus Fischer, Kenji Kawamura, and Thomas F. Stocker. 2008. "High-Resolution Carbon Dioxide Concentration Record 650,000–800,000 Years before Present." *Nature* 453: 379–382.

Luttrell, Mike. 2010. "Never-ending iTunes Sales Tally Hits 10 Billion." *TG Daily*. Retrieved November 6, 2011 (http://www.tgdaily.com/consumer-electronics-brief/48578-never-ending-itunes-sales-tally-hits-10-billion).

Luxton, David D., Jennifer D. June, and Julie T. Kinn. 2011. "Technology-Based Suicide Prevention: Current Applications and Future Directions." *Telemedicine and e-Health* 17(1): 50–54.

"Luxury: Cheaper Suites and Empty Beds." 2009. *Executive*, July. Retrieved September 6, 2011 (http://www.executive-magazine.com/getarticle.php?article=12045).

Lyall, Sarah. 2011. "Scandal Shifts British Media's and Political Landscape." *New York Times*, July 7.

Lydaki, Anna. 2012. "Gypsies." In *The Wiley-Blackwell Encyclopedia of Sociology Online*, edited by G. Ritzer. Malden, MA: Wiley-Blackwell.

Lynch, Marc. 2013. *The Arab Uprising: The Unfinished Revolutions of the New Middle East*. New York: Public Affairs.

Lyotard, Jean-Francois. [1979] 1984. *The Postmodern Condition: A Report on Knowledge*. Minneapolis: University of Minnesota Press.

Maahs, Jeff. 2007. "Juvenile Delinquency." Pp. 2454–2455 in *The Blackwell Encyclopedia of Sociology*, edited by G. Ritzer. Malden, MA: Blackwell.

MacDonald, Keith and George Ritzer. 1988. "The Sociology of the Professions: Dead or Alive?" *Work and Occupations* (August): 251–272.

MacDonald, Neil. 2010. "The Tea Party's Freak Show." Retrieved March 31, 2012 (http://www.cbc.ca/news/world/story/2010/09/24/f-rfa-macdonald.html).

MacFarquhar, Neil. 2008. "To Muslim Girls, Scouts Offer a Chance to Fit In." *New York Times*, November 28.

Machida, Satoshi. 2012. "Does Globalization Render People More Ethnocentric? Globalization and People's Views on Cultures." *American Journal of Economics and Sociology* 71: 436–469.

Mackenzie, Adrian. 2005. "The Problem of the Attractor: A Singular Generality between Sciences and Social Theory." *Theory, Culture and Society*: 45–65.

MacKinnon, Neil J. and David R. Heise. 2010. *Self, Identity, and Social Institutions*. New York: Palgrave Macmillan.

Madan, Triloki N. 2007. "Hinduism." Pp. 571–573 in *Encyclopedia of Globalization*, edited by J. A. Scholte and R. Robertson. New York: MTM Publishing.

Madood, Tariq. 2007. "Multiculturalism." Pp. 3105–3108 in *The Blackwell Encyclopedia of Sociology*, edited by G. Ritzer. Malden, MA: Blackwell.

Maguire, Jennifer and Kim Stanway. 2008. "Looking Good: Consumption and the Problems of Self-Production." *European Journal of Cultural Studies* 11: 63.

Maguire, Mike, Rob Morgan, and Robert Reiner, eds. 2012. *The Oxford Handbook of Criminology*. 5th ed. New York: Oxford.

Mahoney, James and Dietrich Rueschmeyer. 2003. *Comparative Historical Analysis in the Social Sciences*. Cambridge, MA: Cambridge University Press.

Maiba, Herman. 2005. "Grassroots Transnational Social Movement Activism: The Case of Peoples' Global Action." *Sociological Focus* 38(1): 41–63.

Maines, Rachel. 2001. *The Technology of Orgasm: "Hysteria, the Vibrator and Women's Sexual Satisfaction."* Baltimore: Johns Hopkins University Press.

Majora Carter Group. 2009. "Majora Carter Group." Retrieved February 28, 2012 (http://www.majoracartergroup.com).

Mak, Athena H. N., Margaret Lumbers, and Anita Eves. 2012. "Globalisation and Food Consumption in Tourism." *Annals of Tourism Research* 39: 171–196.

Malik, Ved. 2011. "Too Close for Comfort." *Hindustan Times*, April 7. Retrieved May 26, 2011 (http://www.hindustantimes.com/News-Feed/columnsothers/Too-close-for-comfort/Article1-682474.aspx).

Malkin, Elisabeth. 2011. "Mexico's Universal Health Care Is Work in Progress." *New York Times*, January 29. Retrieved March 30, 2012 (http://www.nytimes.com/2011/01/30/world/americas/30mexico.html?pagewanted=all).

Mall of the Emirates. 2010. "About Mall of the Emirates." Retrieved May 19, 2011 (www.malloftheemirates.com/MOE/En/MainMenu/AboutMOE/tabid/64/Default.aspx).

Mamo, Laura. 2007. *Queering Reproduction: Achieving Pregnancy in the Age of Technoscience*. Durham, NC: Duke University Press.

Mampaey, Luc and Jean-Philippe Renaud. 2000. *Prison Technologies: An Appraisal of Technologies of Political Control*. European Parliament.

Mandel, Hadas. 2012. "Occupational Mobility of American Women: Compositional and

Structural Changes, 1980–2007." *Research in Social Stratification and Mobility* 30: 5–16.

Mandhana, Niharika and Anjani Trivedi. 2012. "Indians Outraged over Rape on Moving Bus in New Delhi." *New York Times India Ink*, December 18.

Manicas, Peter. 2007. "Globalization and Higher Education." Pp. 461–477 in *The Blackwell Companion to Globalization*, edited by G. Ritzer. Malden, MA: Blackwell.

Mankekar, Purnima. 2005. "'India Shopping': Indian Grocery Stores and Transnational Configurations of Belonging." Pp. 197–214 in *The Cultural Politics of Food and Eating: A Reader*, edited by J. L. Watson and M. L. Caldwell. Malden, MA: Blackwell.

Mannheim, Karl. [1931] 1936. *Ideology and Utopia*. New York: Harcourt, Brace, and World.

Manning, Peter. 2005. "Impression Management." Pp. 397–399 in *The Encyclopedia of Social Theory*, edited by G. Ritzer. Thousand Oaks, CA: Sage.

Manning, Peter. 2007. "Dramaturgy." Pp. 1226–1229 in *The Blackwell Encyclopedia of Sociology*, edited by G. Ritzer. Malden, MA: Blackwell.

Manning, Robert D. 2001. *Credit Card Nation: The Consequences of America's Addiction to Debt*. New York: Basic Books.

Manning, Wendy D. and Jessica A. Cohen. 2012. "Premarital Cohabitation and Marital Dissolution: An Examination of Recent Marriages." *Journal of Marriage and the Family* 74: 377–387.

Manning, Wendy Peggy Giordano and Monica Longmore. 2006. "Hooking Up: The Relationship Contexts of 'Non-Relationship' Sex." *Journal of Adolescent Research* 21: 459–483.

Mansfield, Louise. 2007. "Gender, Sport and." Pp. 1875–1880 in *The Blackwell Encyclopedia of Sociology*, edited by G. Ritzer. Malden, MA: Blackwell.

Manzo, John. 2010. "Coffee, Connoisseurship, and an Ethnomethodologically Informed Sociology of Taste." *Human Studies* 33(2): 141–155.

Marger, Martin. 2008. *Social Inequality: Patterns and Processes*. Boston: McGraw-Hill.

Margolin, Leslie. 1994. *Goodness Personified: The Emergence of Gifted Children*. New York: Aldine de Gruyter.

Markoff, John. 2007. "Comparative Analysis." Pp. 193–196 in *Encyclopedia of Globalization*, edited by J. A. Scholte and R. Robertson. New York: MTM Publishing.

Marmor, Michael. 2005. *The Status Syndrome: How Social Standing Affects Our Health and Longevity*. New York: Holt.

Maroto, Michelle Lee. 2011. "Professionalizing Body Art: A Marginalized Occupational Group's Use of Informal and Formal Strategies of Control." *Work and Occupations* 38: 101–138.

Marre, Diana and Laura Briggs. 2009. *International Adoption: Global Inequalities and the Circulation of Children*. New York: New York University Press.

Marron, Donncha. 2009. *Consumer Credit in the United States: A Sociological Perspective from the 19th Century to the Present*. New York: Palgrave Macmillan.

Marsden, Peter V. and Elizabeth H. Gorman. 2001. "Social Networks, Job Changes, and Recruitment." Pp. 467–502 in *Sourcebook on Labor Markets: Evolving Structures and Processes*, edited by I. Berg and A. L. Kalleberg. New York: Kluwer Academic/Plenum Publishers.

Marsh, Robert M. 2012. "Musical Taste and Social Structure in Taiwan." *Comparative Sociology* 11: 493–525.

Marshall, Catherine and Gretchen Rossman. 2010. *Designing Qualitative Research*. Thousand Oaks, CA: Sage.

Martin, Andrew. 2008. "Mideast Facing Difficult Choice, Crops or Water." *New York Times*, July 21.

Marx, Karl. [1842] 1977. "Communism and the Augsburger Allegemeine Zeitung." P. 20 in *Karl Marx: Selected Writings*, edited by D. McLellan. New York: Oxford University Press.

Marx, Karl. [1843] 1970. "A Contribution to the Critique of Hegel's Philosophy of Right." Pp. 3–129 in *Marx/Engels Collected Works* (Vol. 3). New York: International Publishers.

Marx, Karl. [1857–1858] 1964. *Pre-capitalist Economic Formations*. New York: International Publishers.

Marx. Karl. [1859] 1970. *A Contribution to the Critique of Political Economy*. New York: International Publishers.

Marx, Karl. 1938. *Critique of the Gotha Programme*. New York: International Publishers.

Marx, Karl and Friedrich Engels. 1848. *The Communist Manifesto*. London: Communist League.

Marx Ferree, Myra and Aili Mari Tripp. 2006. "Preface." Pp. vii–ix in *Global Feminism: Transnational Women's Activism, Organizing, and Human Rights*, edited by M. Marx Ferree and A. Mari Tripp. New York: New York University Press.

Massaro, Vanessa A. and Emma Gaalaas Mullaney. 2011. "Philly's 'Flash Mob Riots' and the Banality of Post-9/11 Securitization." *City* 15: 591–604.

Massey, Douglas. 2003. *Beyond Smoke and Mirrors: Mexican Immigration in an Era of Economic Integration*. New York: Russell Sage Foundation.

Massey, Douglas. 2008. *Categorically Unequal: The American Stratification System*. New York: Russell Sage.

Massey, Douglas and Karen Pren. 2012. "Unintended Consequences of US Immigration Policy: Explaining the Post-1965 Surge from Latin America." *Population and Development Review*, 38(1): 1–29.

Mastekaasa, Arne. 1994. "Marital Status, Distress, and Well-Being: An International Comparison." *Journal of Comparative Family Studies* 23: 183–206.

Mather, Mark. 2009. *Reports on America; Children in Immigrant Families Chart New Path*. Washington, DC: Population Reference Bureau.

Matza, David. 1966. "The Disreputable Poor." Pp. 289–302 in *Class, Status, and Power: Social Stratification in Comparative Perspective*, edited by R. Bendix and S. M. Lipset. 2nd ed. New York: Free Press.

Mawathe, Anne. 2010. "Haunted by Congo Rape Dilemma." *BBC News*, May 15. Retrieved January 29, 2012 (http://news.bbc.co.uk/2/hi/africa/8677637.stm).

Mayer Brown. 2010. "The United States Blocks on National Security Grounds a Chinese Investment in a US Telecommunications and Solar Technology Firm." Retrieved December 3, 2011 (http://www.mayerbrown.com/publications/article.asp?id=9297&nid=6).

McAdams, Dan P., Michelle Albaugh, Emily Farber, Jennifer Daniels, Regina L. Logan, and Brad Olson. 2008. "Family Metaphors and Moral Intuitions: How Conservatives and Liberals Narrate Their Lives." *Journal of Personality and Social Psychology* 95: 978–990.

McBride, Sarah and Ethan Smith. 2008. "Music Industry to Abandon Mass Suits." *Wall Street Journal*, December 19.

McCann, Eugene and Kevin Ward, eds. 2011. *Mobile Urbanism: Cities and Policymaking in the Global Age*. Minneapolis: University of Minnesota Press.

McCann, P. J. and Peter Conrad. 2007. "Deviance, Medicalization of." Pp. 1110–1113 in *The Blackwell Encyclopedia of Sociology*, edited by G. Ritzer. Malden, MA: Blackwell.

McChesney, Robert W. 1999. *Rich Media, Poor Democracy: Communication Politics in Dubious Times*. New York: New Press.

McChesney, Robert. 2003. "The New Global Media." Pp. 260–268 in *The Global Transformations Reader*, edited by D. Held and A. G. McGrew. Malden, MA: Wiley-Blackwell.

McCloskey, Deirdre N. 2000. *Crossing: A Memoir*. Chicago: University of Chicago Press.

McCormick, Ken. 2011. "Thorstein Veblen." Pp. 185–204 in *The Wiley-Blackwell Companion to Major Social Theorists: Volume 1. Classical Theorists*, edited by G. Ritzer and J. Stepnisky. Malden, MA: Wiley-Blackwell.

McCurdy, David W. and James P. Spradley, eds. 1979. *Issues in Cultural Anthropology: Selected Readings*. Boston: Little, Brown.

McDonald, Mark. 2012. "Adding More Bricks to the Great Firewall of China." *New York Times*, December 23.

McDonald, Michael. 2010. "Voter Turnout." U.S. Elections Project. Retrieved September 14, 2011 (http://elections.gmu.edu/voter_turnout.htm).

McDonald, Michael. 2011. "2010 General Election Turnout Rates." *U.S. Elections Project*, January 28. Retrieved September 14, 2011 (http://elections.gmu.edu/Turnout_2010G.html).

McDonald, Michael. 2013. "2012 General Election Turnout Rates." *U.S. Elections Project*, July 22. Retrieved September 16, 2011 (http://elections.gmu.edu/Turnout_2012g.html).

McDonald's. 2010. "Financial Highlights." Retrieved August 24, 2011 (http://www.aboutmcdonalds.com/mcd/investors/publications/2010_Financial_Highlights.html).

McEwen, Krista and Kevin Young. 2011. "Ballet and Pain: Reflections from a Risk-Dance Culture." Paper presented at the Annual Meetings of the Pacific Sociological Association, Seattle, March 10–13.

McGrew, Ken. 2011. "A Review of Class-Based Theories of Student Resistance in Education." *Review of Educational Research* 81: 234–266.

McHale, Susan, Ann C. Crouter, and Shawn D. Whiteman. 2003. "The Family Contexts of Gender Development in Childhood and Adolescence Social Development." *Social Development* 12: 125–148.

McIntosh, Peggy. 2010. "White Privilege: Unpacking the Invisible Knapsack." Pp. 172–177 in *Race, Class and Gender in the United States*, edited by P. S. Rothenberg. 8th ed. New York: Worth.

McKinlay, John B. and Joan Arches. 1985. "Towards the Proletarianization of Physicians." *International Journal of Health Services* 15(2).

McKinley, James C., Jr. 2008. "Cyber-Rebels in Cuba Defy State's Limits." *New York Times*, March 6.

McKinley, James C., Jr. 2010. "Fleeing Drug Violence, Mexicans Pour into U.S." *New York Times*, April 17.

McKnight, David. 2011. "'You're All a Bunch of Pinkos': Rupert Murdoch and the Politics of HarperCollins." *Media Culture Society* 33: 835–850.

McLanahan, Sara. 1999. "Father Absence and the Welfare of Children." In *Coping with Divorce, Single Parenting and Remarriage*, edited by E. M. Hetherington. Mahwah, NJ: Erlbaum.

McLanahan, Sara S. and Erin L. Kelly. 1999. "The Feminization of Poverty: Past and Future." Pp. 127–145 in *Handbook of the Sociology of Gender*, edited by J. Saltzman Chafetz. New York: Kluwer Academic/Plenum.

McNair, B. 2002. *Striptease Culture: Sex, Media and the Democratization of Desire*. London: Routledge.

McNeil, Donald G., Jr. 2008a. "A Pandemic that Wasn't but Might Be." *New York Times*, January 22, pp. D1, D4.

McNeil, Donald G., Jr. 2008b. "W.H.O Official Complains of Gates Foundation Dominance in Malaria Research." *New York Times*, February 16, p. A6.

McNeil, Donald G., Jr. 2009. "New Web Site Seeks to Fight Myths about Circumcision and H.I.V." *New York Times*, March 3.

McNeil, Donald G., Jr. 2010. "At Front Lines, Global War on AIDS Is Falling Apart." *New York Times*, May 10.

McNichol, Tom. 2011. "Mint that Kills: The Curious Life of Menthol Cigarettes." *Atlantic Monthly*, March 25.

McPhail, Clark. 2007. "Crowd Behavior." Pp. 880–883 in *The Blackwell Encyclopedia of Sociology*, edited by G. Ritzer. Malden, MA: Blackwell.

McShane, Marilyn D. and Frank P. Williams. 2007. "Beccaria, Cesare (1738–94)." Pp. 255–256 in *The Blackwell Encyclopedia of Sociology* (Vol. 1), edited by G. Ritzer. Malden, MA: Blackwell.

McVeigh, Rory and Christian Smith. 1999. "Who Protests in America: An Analysis of Three Political Alternatives—Inaction, Institutionalized Politics, or Protest." *Sociological Forum* 14(4): 685–702.

McVeigh, Tracy. 2011. "Charity President Says Aid Groups Are Misleading the Public on Somalia." *The Guardian*, September 3. Retrieved March 30, 2012 (http://www.guardian.co.uk/global-development/2011/sep/03/charity-aid-groups-misleading-somalia).

Mead, George Herbert. [1934] 1962. *Mind, Self, and Society: From the Standpoint of a Social Behaviorist*. Chicago: University of Chicago Press.

Medina, Jennifer. 2012. "Mexicali Tour, from Tummy Tuck to Root Canal." *New York Times*, June 27.

Meier, Barry. 2013. "More Emergency Visits Linked to Energy Drinks." *New York Times*, January 11.

Meier, Robert F. 2007a. "Deviance, Normative Definitions of." Pp. 1116–1117 in *The Blackwell Encyclopedia of Sociology*, edited by G. Ritzer. Malden, MA: Blackwell.

Meier, Robert F. 2007b. "Deviance, Positivist Theories of." Pp. 1117–1121 in *The Blackwell Encyclopedia of Sociology*, edited by G. Ritzer. Malden, MA: Blackwell.

Meikle, James. 2009. "Fast Food Firms Taken to Task after Survey of Street Litter." *The Guardian*, January 13.

Meister, Sandra. 2012. *Brand Communities for Fast-Moving Consumer Goods*. Weisbaden, Germany: Gabler Verlag.

Melde, Chris, Terrance J. Taylor, and Finn Aage Esbensen. 2009. "'I Got Your Back': An Examination of the Protective Function of Gang Membership in Adolescence." *Criminology* 47(2): 565–594.

Melnick, Merrill L. and Daniel L. Wann. 2011. "An Examination of Sport Fandom in Australia: Socialization, Team Identification, and Fan Behavior." *International Review for the Sociology of Sport* 46: 456–470.

Menkes, Suzy. 2008. "Is Fast Fashion Going Out of Fashion?" *New York Times*, September 21.

Merriam-Webster. 2008. *Merriam-Webster's Collegiate Dictionary*. 11th ed. Merriam-Webster, Inc.

Mersland, Roy and R. Øystein Strøm. 2010. "Microfinance Mission Drift?" *World Development* 38(1): 28.

Merton, Robert. 1938. "Social Structure and Anomie." *American Sociological Review* 3: 672–682.

Merton, Robert. [1949] 1968. *Social Theory and Social Structure*. 3rd ed. New York: Free Press.

Merton, Robert K. 1957. *Social Theory and Social Structure*. Rev. ed. Glencoe, IL: Free Press.

Merton, Robert and Alice S. Kitt. 1950. "Contributions to the Theory of Reference Group Behavior." In *Continuities in Social Research*, edited by R. K. Merton and P. F. Lazarsfeld. Glencoe, IL: Free Press.

Messerschmidt, James W. 2007. "Masculinities, Crime and." Pp. 2818–2821 in *The Blackwell Encyclopedia of Sociology*, edited by G. Ritzer. Malden, MA: Blackwell.

Messner, Stephen F. and Richard Rosenfeld. 1997. "Political Restraint of the Market and Levels of Criminal Homicide: A Cross-National Application of Institutional-Anomie Theory." *Social Forces* 75: 1393–1416.

Meszaros, Istvan. 2006. *Marx's Theory of Alienation*. London: Merlin Press.

Metzl, Jonathan. 2009. *The Protest Psychosis*. Boston: Beacon Press.

Meyer, John, John Boli, and Francisco Ramirez. 1997. "World Society and the Nation State." *American Journal of Sociology* 103: 144–181.

Michael I. Norton and Dan Ariely. 2011. "Building a Better America—One Wealth Quintile at a Time." *Perspectives on Psychological Science*, January, pp. 9–12.

Michels, Robert. [1915] 1962. *Political Parties*. New York: Collier Books.

Miles, Andrew, Mike Savage, and Felix Bühlmann. 2011. "Telling a Modest Story: Accounts of Men's Upward Mobility from the National Child Development Study." *The British Journal of Sociology* 62: 418–441.

Milgram, Stanley. 1974. *Obedience to Authority: An Experimental View*. New York: Harper and Row.

Milibrandt, Tara and Frank Pearce. 2011. "Emile Durkheim." Pp. 236–282 in *The Wiley-Blackwell Companion to Major Social Theorists: Vol. 1. Classical Theorists*, edited by G. Ritzer and J. Stepnisky. Malden, MA: Wiley-Blackwell.

Milkie, Melissa A. 1999. "Social Comparisons, Reflected Appraisals, and Mass Media: The Impact of Pervasive Beauty Images on Black and White Girls' Self-Concepts." *Social Psychology Quarterly* 62: 190–210.

Miller, Amanda and Sharon Sassler. 2010. "Stability and Change in the Division of Labor among Cohabiting Couples." *Sociological Forum* 25(4): 677–702.

Miller, Claire Cain. 2009. "The Virtual Visit May Expand Access to Doctors." *New York Times*, December 21, p. B4.

Miller, Daniel. 1998. *A Theory of Shopping*. Ithaca, NY: Cornell University Press.

Miller, Daniel and Donald Slater. 2000. *The Internet: An Ethnographic Approach*. London: Berg.

Miller, Gale and James A. Holstein, eds. 1993. *Constructionist Controversies: Issues in Social Problems Theory*. New York: Aldine De Gruyter.

Miller, J. Mitchell and Richard Tewksbury, eds. 2001. *Extreme Methods: Innovative Approaches to Social Science Research.* Boston: Allyn and Bacon.

Miller, Jody. 2001. *One of the Guys: Girls, Gangs and Gender.* New York: Oxford University Press.

Miller, Robert. 2001. "The Industrial Context of Occupational Mobility: Change in Structure." *Research in Social Stratification and Mobility* 18: 313–353.

Mills, C. Wright. 1951. *White Collar.* New York: Oxford University Press.

Mills, C. Wright. 1956. *The Power Elite.* New York: Oxford University Press.

Mills, C. Wright. 1959. *The Sociological Imagination.* New York: Oxford University Press.

Mindlin, Alex. 2006. "Seems Somebody Is Clicking on that Spam." *New York Times,* July 3.

Mirchandani, Kiran. 2004. "Practices of Global Capital: Gaps, Cracks and Ironies in Transnational Call Centres in India." *Global Networks* 4(4): 355–373.

Mishell, Lawrence and Josh Bivens. 2011. "Occupy Wall Streeters Are Right about Skewed Economic Rewards in the United States." Economic Policy Institute Briefing Paper #331, October 26. Retrieved March 31, 2012 (http://www.epi.org/files/2011/BriefingPaper331.pdf).

Mitchell, Juliet. 1975. *Psychoanalysis and Feminism.* New York: Random House.

Mitford, Jessica. 1993. *The American Way of Birth.* New York: Plume.

"Mixed Views of Obama at Year's End." 2009. Pew Research Center for the People and the Press, December 16. Retrieved March 31, 2012 (http://people-press.org/report/572/mixed-views-of-obama-at-year-end).

Modood, Tariq. 2007. "Multiculturalism." Pp. 3105–3108 in *The Blackwell Encyclopedia of Sociology,* edited by G. Ritzer. Malden, MA: Blackwell.

Moffitt, Terrie E. 1993. "'Life Course-Persistent' and 'Adolescence-Limited' Antisocial Behavior: A Developmental Taxonomy." *Psychological Review* 100: 674–701.

Moghadam, Valentine. 1999. "Gender and Globalization: Female Labor and Women's Mobilization." *Journal of World-Systems Research* 5(2): 367–388.

Molm, Linda D. 2007. "Power-Dependence Theory." Pp. 3598–3602 in *The Blackwell Encyclopedia of Sociology,* edited by G. Ritzer. Oxford: Blackwell.

Molm, Linda D. 2010. "The Structure of Reciprocity." *Social Psychology Quarterly* 73: 119–131.

Molm, Linda D. and Karen S. Cook. 1995. "Social Exchange and Exchange Networks." Pp. 209–235 in *Sociological Perspective on Social Psychology,* edited by K. S. Cook, G. A. Fine, and J. S. House. Boston: Allyn and Bacon.

Molm, Linda, Monica M. Whithama, and David Melameda. 2012. "Forms of Exchange and Integrative Bonds: Effects of History and Embeddedness." *American Sociological Review* 77: 141–165.

Molotch, Harvey. 2003. *Where Stuff Comes From.* New York: Routledge.

Monaghan, Lee F. 2007. "McDonaldizing Men's Bodies? Slimming, Associated (Ir) Rationalities and Resistances." *Body and Society* 13: 67–93.

Monaghan, Lee F. Robert Hollands and Gary Pritchard. 2010. "Obesity Epidemic Entrepreneurs: Types, Practices and Interests." *Body and Society* 16: 37–71.

Monbiot, George and Todd Gitlin. 2011. "How to Be Radical? An Interview with Todd Gitlin and George Monbiot." *OpenDemocracy,* April 5. Retrieved November 9, 2011 (http://www.opendemocracy.net/democracy-vision_reflections/article_1462.jsp).

Montt, Guillermo. 2011. "Cross-National Differences in Educational Inequality." *Sociology of Education* 84: 49–68.

Montaigne, Fen. 2009. "The Ice Retreat: Global Warming and the Adelie Penguin." *The New Yorker,* December 21, p. 72.

Montopoli, Brian. 2010. "Jon Stewart Rally Attracts Estimated 215,000." *CBS News,* October 30. Retrieved March 31, 2012 (http://www.cbsnews.com/8301-503544_162-20021284-503544.html).

Montoya, Isaac D. 2005. "Effect of Peers on Employment and Implications for Drug Treatment." *American Journal of Drug and Alcohol Abuse* 31: 657–668.

Moore, D. 1995. "Role Conflict: Not Only for Women? A Comparative Analysis of 5 Nations." *International Journal of Comparative Sociology* 36(1–2): 17–35.

Moore, Elizabeth Armstrong. 2010. "Harvard Health Expert Calls Facebook 'Wild West.'" CNET News. Retrieved February 27, 2012 (http://news.cnet.com/8301-27083_3-20021519-247.html).

Moore, Lisa Jean and Mary Kosut, eds. 2010. *The Body Reader: Essential Social and Cultural Readings.* New York: New York University Press.

Moore, R. Laurence. 1997. *Selling God: American Religion in the Marketplace of Culture.* Oxford: Oxford University Press.

Moran, Mary, Javier Guzman, Anne-Laure Ropars, Alina McDonald, Nicole Jameson, Brenda Omune, Sam Ryan, and Lindsey Wu. 2009. "Neglected Disease Research and Development: How Much Are We Really Spending?" *PLoS Med* 6(2): e1000030.

Morelli, M. 1983. "Milgram's Dilemma of Obedience." *Metaphilosophy* 14: 183.

Morgan, David H. J. 2007. "Marriage." Pp. 2789–2791 in *The Blackwell Encyclopedia of Sociology,* edited by G. Ritzer. Malden, MA: Blackwell.

Morgan, S. Philip. 2007. "Fertility, Low." Pp. 1729–1733 in *The Blackwell Encyclopedia of Sociology,* edited by G. Ritzer. Malden, MA: Blackwell.

Morgan, Stephen G. 2007. "Direct-to-Consumer Advertising and Expenditures on Prescription Drugs: A Comparison of Experiences in the United States and Canada." *Open Medicine* 1(1): e37–e45.

Moriarty, Sandra and Mark Popovich. 1989. "Newsmagazine Visual and the 1988 Presidential Election." Paper presented at the Annual Meeting of the Association for Education in Journalism and Mass Communication, Washington, DC, August 10–13.

Morozov, Evgeny. 2011. *The Net Delusion: The Dark Side of Internet Freedom.* Public Affairs.

Morris, Aldon. 1984. *The Origins of the Civil Rights Movement: Black Communities Organizing for Change.* New York: Free Press.

Morris, Alex. 2011. "They Know What Boys Want: Why Learning about Sex from the Web Comes with Drawbacks." *New York Magazine.* Retrieved March 31, 2012 (http://nymag.com/news/features/70977/).

Morris, Aldon. 2007. "Civil Rights Movement." Pp. 507–512 in *The Blackwell Encyclopedia of Sociology,* edited by G. Ritzer. Malden, MA: Blackwell.

Morris, Edward W. 2005. "Tuck in that Shirt!" Race, Class, Gender and Discipline in an Urban School." *Sociological Perspectives* 48: 25–48.

Morris, Edward. 2008. "'Rednecks,' 'Rutters,' and 'Rithmetic': Social Class, Masculinity, and Schooling in a Rural Context." *Gender and Society* 22(6): 728–751.

Morrow, Virginia and Kirilly Pells. 2012. "Integrating Children's Human Rights and Child Poverty Debates: Examples from *Young Lives* in Ethiopia and India." *Sociology* 46: 906–920.

Moses, Jonathon W. 2006. *International Migration: Globalization's Last Frontier.* London: Zed Books.

Moss, Dana M. 2013. "Arab Spring." Pp. 118–125 in *The Wiley-Blackwell Encyclopedia of Social and Political Movements,* 3 vols., edited by D. A. Snow, D. Della Porta, B. Klandermans, and D. McAdam. Malden, MA: Wiley-Blackwell.

Mugarask, Larry. 2011. *Buffalo Law Review* 83(1):1.

Mundy, Liza. 2013. *The Richer Sex: How the New Majority of Female Breadwinners Is Transforming Sex, Love, and Family.* New York: Free Press.

Munford, Monty. 2010. "India Digs a Tunnel at the Top of the World as China Bids Its Time." *The Telegraph,* August 11. Retrieved May 26, 2011 (http://blogs.telegraph.co.uk/news/montymunford1/100050206/india-digs-a-tunnel-at-the-top-of-the-world-as-china-bides-its-time/).

Muniz, Albert M., Jr. 2007. "Brands and Branding." Pp. 357–360 in *The Blackwell Encyclopedia of Sociology,* edited by G. Ritzer. Malden, MA: Blackwell.

Muniz, Albert M., Jr., and Thomas C. O'Guinn. 2001. "Brand Community." *Journal of Consumer Research* 27: 412–432.

Munton, Don and Ken Wilkening. 2007. "Acid Rain." In *Encyclopedia of Globalization*, edited by J. A. Scholte and R. Robertson, eds. New York: MTM Publishing.

Murray, Graham. 2006. "France: The Riots and the Republic." *Race and Class* 47: 26–45.

Murray, Sara. 2011. "About 1 in 7 in US Receive Food Stamps." *Wall Street Journal*, May 3. Retrieved March 31, 2012 (http://blogs.wsj.com/economics/2011/05/03/about-1-in-7-americans-receive-food-stamps/).

Murthy, Dhiraj. 2008. "Digital Ethnography: An Examination of the Use of New Technologies for Social Research." *Sociology* 42: 837–855.

Musick, Kelly. 2007. "Fertility: Nonmarital." Pp. 1734–1737 in *The Blackwell Encyclopedia of Sociology*, edited by G. Ritzer. Malden, MA: Blackwell.

Mydans, Seth. 2008. "Indonesian Chickens, and People, Hard Hit by Bird Flu." *New York Times*, February 1, p. A3.

Myers, Daniel J. 2007. "Riots." Pp. 3921–3926 in *The Blackwell Encyclopedia of Sociology*, edited by G. Ritzer. Malden, MA: Blackwell.

Myers, Daniel J. 2013. "Riots." Pp. 1124–1129 in *The Wiley-Blackwell Encyclopedia of Social and Political Movements*, 3 vols., edited by D. A. Snow, D. Della Porta, B. Klandermans, and D. McAdam. Malden, MA: Wiley-Blackwell.

Nagourney, Adam. 2013. "Unfinished Luxury Tower Is Stark Reminder of Las Vegas's Economic Reversal." *New York Times*, January 22.

Nakano-Glenn, Evelyn. 2000. "The Social Construction and Institutionalization of Gender and Race." Pp. 3–43 in *Revisioning Gender*, edited by M. M. Ferree, J. Lorber, and B. B. Hess. Thousand Oaks, CA: Sage.

Nanda, Serena. 1999. *Neither Man Nor Woman: The Hijras of India*. 2nd ed. Belmont, CA: Wadsworth.

Naples, Nancy A. 2009. "Presidential Address: Crossing Borders: Community Activism, Globalization, and Social Justice." *Social Problems* 56: 2–20.

Naples, Nancy A. and Manisha Desai. 2002. "Women's Local and Transnational Responses: An Introduction to the Volume." In *Women's Activism and Globalization: Linking Local Struggles and Transnational Politics*, edited by N. A. Naples and M. Desai. New York: Routledge.

Naples, Nancy A. and Barbara Gurr. 2012. "Genders and Sexualities in Global Context: An Intersectional Assessment of Contemporary Scholarship." Pp. 304–332 in *The Wiley-Blackwell Companion to Sociology*, edited by G. Ritzer. Malden, MA: Wiley-Blackwell.

Napoli, Lisa. 1999. "Dispensing of Drugs on Internet Stirs Debate." *New York Times*, April 6. Retrieved March 31, 2012 (http://query.nytimes.com/gst/fullpage.html?res=9B02E1D61139F935A35757C0A96F958260&scp=8&sq=pharmaceutical%20purchase%20over%20internet&st=cse).

Naquin, Charles E., Terri R. Kurtzberg, and Liuba Y. Belkin. 2008. "E-mail Communication and Group Cooperation in Mixed Motive Contexts." *Social Justice Research* 21: 470–489.

Nasar, Jack L., Jennifer S. Evans-Cowley, and Vicente Mantero. 2007. "McMansions: The Extent and Regulation of Supersized Houses." *Journal of Urban Design* 12: 339–358.

National Center for Health Statistics. 2011. "Health, United States, 2010." U.S. Department of Health and Human Services. Retrieved February 28, 2012 (http://www.cdc.gov/nchs/data/hus/hus10.pdf).

National Committee on Pay Equity. 2010. "The Wage Gap over Time: In Real Dollars, Women See a Continuing Gap." Retrieved May 7, 2011 (http://www.pay-equity.org/info-time.html).

National Institutes of Health. 2011. "Human Genome Project." Retrieved April 15, 2011 (http://report.nih.gov/NIHfactsheets/ViewFactSheet.aspx?csid=45&key=H#H).

National Poverty Center. 2011. "Poverty in the United States." Retrieved March 31, 2012 (http://npc.umich.edu/poverty/).

Navarro, Mireya. 2006. "For Divided Family, Border Is Sorrowful Barrier." *New York Times*, December 21.

Nayyer, Deepak. 2010. "China, India, Brazil, and South Africa in the World Economy: Engines of Growth?" In *Southern Engines of Global Growth*, edited by A. U. Santos-Paulino and G. Wan. Oxford.

Nederveen Pieterse, Jan. 2009. *Globalization and Culture: Global Melange*. 2nd ed. Lanham, MD: Rowman and Littlefield.

"Netherlands: High-Grade Marijuana to Be Declassified." 2011. *New York Times*, October 7. Accessed December 20, 2011 (http://www.nytimes.com/2011/10/08/world/europe/netherlands-high-grade-marijuana-to-be-reclassified.html).

Neuendorf, Kimberly A. Thomas D. Gore, Amy Dalessandro, Patricie Janstova, and Sharon Snyder-Suh. 2009. "Shaken and Stirred: A Content Analysis of Women's Portrayals in James Bond Film." *Sex Roles* 62: 747–776.

Neuwirth, Robert. 2011. *Stealth of Nations: The Global Rise of the Informal Economy*. New York: Pantheon.

Newman, Andy. 2011. "Go Hands-Free, or Risk Points on Your License." *New York Times*, February 16. Retrieved March 31, 2012 (http://cityroom.blogs.nytimes.com/2011/02/16/go-hands-free-or-risk-points-on-your-license/?ref=andynewman&gwh=E21FA99531426B5BDF47E03EBF34EAF7).

Newman, Jerry. 2007. *My Secret Life on the McJob: Lessons from Behind the Counter Guaranteed to Supersize Any Management Style*. New York: McGraw-Hill.

Newman, Otto. 1968. "The Sociology of the Betting Shop." *The British Journal of Sociology* 19(1): 17–33.

Newton, David E. 2009. *Gay and Lesbian Rights: A Reference Handbook*. Santa Barbara, CA: ABC-CLIO.

Newton, Isaac (with Stephen Hawking). [1687] 2005. *Principia (On the Shoulders of Giants)*. Philadelphia: Running Press.

Newton, Michael. 2002. *Savage Girls and Wild Boys: A History of Feral Children*. London: Faber and Faber.

New York University Institute for Public Knowledge. 2011. "Arjun Appadurai: IPK Senior Fellow." Retrieved December 3, 2011 (http://www.nyu.edu/ipk/people/arjun-appadurai).

New York University Steinhardt School of Culture, Education, and Human Development. 2012. "Arjun Appadurai." Retrieved April 1, 2012 (http://steinhardt.nyu.edu/faculty_bios/view/Arjun_Appadurai).

Nguyen, Tomson H. and Henry N. Pontell. 2011. "Fraud and Inequality in the Subprime Mortgage Crisis." Pp. 3–24 in *Economic Crisis and Crime (Sociology of Crime Law and Deviance, Volume 16)*, edited by M. Deflem. Bingley, UK: Emerald Group.

Nichols, Brian J. 2012. "Buddhism." Pp. 142–145 in *The Wiley-Blackwell Encyclopedia of Globalization*, edited by G. Ritzer. Malden, MA: Wiley-Blackwell.

Nicholson, Linda. 2008. *Identity before Identity Politics*. Cambridge, UK: Cambridge University Press.

Niebuhr, Gustav. 1995. "Where Shopping-Mall Culture Gets a Big Dose of Religion." *New York Times*, April 16, pp. 1, 14.

Ninomiya, Akira, Jane Knight, and Aya Watanabe. 2009. "The Past, Present, and Future of Internationalization in Japan." *Journal of Studies in International Education* 13(2): 117–124.

Noble, David F. 2011. *Forces of Production: A Social History of Industrial Automation*. Transaction.

Nobles, Jenna. 2011. "Parenting from Abroad: Migration, Nonresident Father Involvement, and Children's Education in Mexico." *Journal of Marriage and Family* 73: 729–746.

Nolan, Stephanie. 2006. "The African State: An AIDS Survivor." *Globe and Mail* (Toronto), August 10, p. A7.

Nordenmark, Mikael. 2007. "Unemployment." Pp. 5090–5091 in *The Blackwell Encyclopedia of Sociology*, edited by G. Ritzer. Malden, MA: Blackwell.

Nordgren, Johan. 2013. "The Moral Entrepreneurship of Anti-khat Campaigners in Sweden—A Critical Discourse Analysis." *Drugs and Alcohol Today* 13(1): 20–27.

Nordland, Rod. 2010. "Taliban Order Stoning Deaths in Bold Display." *New York Times*, August 17, pp. A1, A10.

Nordland, Rod and Taimoor Shah. 2010. "Arrest Made in Afghan Disfigurement Case." *New York Times*, December 7. Retrieved March 31, 2012 (http://www.nytimes.com/2010/12/08/world/asia/08afghan.html).

Nordstrom, Carolyn. 2007. *Global Outlaws: Crime, Money, and Power in the Contemporary World.* Berkeley: University of California Press.

Norris, Dawn. 2011. "Interactions that Trigger Self-Labeling: The Case of Older Undergraduates." *Symbolic Interaction* 34: 173–197.

Norris, Pippa. 2001. "Global Governance and Cosmopolitan Citizens." Pp. 155–177 in *Governance in a Globalizing World,* edited by J. S. Nye and J. D. Donahue. Washington, DC: Brookings University Press.

Norris, Pippa. 2010. *Public Sentinel: News Media and Governance Reform.* Washington, DC: World Bank Publications.

Norris, Trevor. 2011a. *Consuming Schools: Commercialism and the End of Politics.* Toronto, ON: University of Toronto Press.

Norris, Trevor. 2011b. "Response to David Waddington's Review of *Consuming Schools: Commercialization and the End of Politics.*" *Studies in the Philosophy of Education* 30: 93–96.

Nossiter, Adam. 2010. "Shaken by a Promise of Riches." *International Herald Tribune,* August 20, p. 2.

Noueihed, Lin and Alex Warren. 2012. *The Battle for the Arab Spring: Revolution, Counter-revolution and the Making of a New Era.* New Haven, CT: Yale University Press.

Novek, Joel. 1992. "The Labour Process and Workplace Injuries in the Canadian Meat-Packing Industry." *Canadian Review of Sociology and Anthropology* 29(1): 17–37.

Nuland, Sherwin. 1994. *How We Die: Reflections on Life's Final Chapter.* New York: Knopf.

Nunn, Samuel. 2007. "Cybercrime." Pp. 960–961 in *The Blackwell Encyclopedia of Sociology,* edited by G. Ritzer. Malden, MA: Blackwell.

Nuru-Jeter, Amani, Tyan Parker Dominguez, Wizdom Powell Hammond, Janxin Leu, Marilyn Skaff, Susan Egerter, Camara P. Jones, and Paula Braveman. 2008. "It's the Skin You're In: African American Women Talk about Their Experiences of Racism. An Exploratory Study to Develop Measures of Racism for Birth Outcome Studies." *Maternal Child Health Journal.*

Nyden, Philip W., Leslie H. Hossfeld, and Gwendolyn E. Nyden. 2011. *Public Sociology: Research, Action, and Change.* Thousand Oaks, CA: Sage.

O'Byrne, Darren and Alexander Hensby. 2011. *Theorizing Global Studies.* Palgrave Macmillan.

O'Connell Davidson, Julia. 2005. *Children in Global Sex Trade.* Cambridge, UK: Polity Press.

O'Connor, Brendan and Martin Griffiths. 2005. *The Rise of Anti-Americanism.* London: Routledge.

O'Dell, Jolie. 2010. "12 Chatroulette Clones You Should Try." *Mashable.* Retrieved April 27, 2011 (http://mashable.com/2010/04/12/12-chatroulette-clones-you-should-try/).

O'Leary, Ann. 1985. "Self-Efficacy and Health." *Behaviour Research and Therapy* 23(4): 437–451.

O'Reilly, Tim. 2005. "What Is Web 2.0?" Retrieved March 31, 2012 (http://www.oreillynet.com/pub/a/oreilly/tim/news/2005/09/30/what-is-web-20.html).

Oakes, Jennie. 2005. *Keeping Track: How Schools Structure Inequality.* 2nd ed. New Haven, CT: Yale University Press.

Oakes, Jeannie and Gretchen Guiton. 1995. "The Dynamics of High School Tracking Decisions." *American Educational Research Journal* 32: 3–33.

Oberschall, Anthony. 2012. "Ethnic Cleansing." Pp. 547–551 in *The Wiley-Blackwell Encyclopedia of Globalization,* edited by G. Ritzer. Malden, MA: Wiley-Blackwell.

Ocloo, Josephine Enyonam. 2010. "Harmed Patients Gaining Voice: Challenging Dominant Perspectives in the Construction of Medical Harm and Patient Safety Reforms." *Social Science and Medicine* 71: 510–516.

Offutt, Michael. 2012. "Microfinance." Pp. 1373–1377 in *The Wiley-Blackwell Encyclopedia of Globalization,* edited by G. Ritzer. Malden, MA: Wiley-Blackwell.

Ogburn, William F. 1922. *Social Change.* New York: The Viking Press.

O'Guinn, Thomas C. and Russel W. Belk. 1989. "Heaven on Earth: Consumption at Heritage Village, USA." *Journal of Consumer Research* 16: 227–238.

Ohlsson-Wijk, Sofi. 2011. "Sweden's Marriage Revival: An Analysis of the New-Millennium Switch from Long-Term Decline to Increasing Popularity." *Population Studies* 65: 183–200.

Oliver, Pamela. 2013. "Collective Action (Collective Behavior)." Pp. 210–215 in *The Wiley-Blackwell Encyclopedia of Social and Political Movements,* 3 vols., edited by D. A. Snow, D. Della Porta, B. Klandermans, and D. McAdam. Malden, MA: Wiley-Blackwell.

Olshansky, S. Jay, Toni Antonucci, Lisa Berkman, Robert H. Binstock, Axel Boersch-Supan, John T. Cacioppo, Bruce A. Carnes, Laura L. Carstensen, Linda P. Fried, Dana P. Goldman, James Jackson, Martin Kohli, John Rother, Yuhui Zheng, and John Rowe. 2012. "Differences in Life Expectancy Due to Race and Educational Differences Are Widening, and Many May Not Catch Up." *Health Affairs* 31: 1803–1813.

Olson, Lynn. 2002. *Freedom's Daughters: The Unsung Heroines of the Civil Rights Movements from 1830 to 1970.* New York: Scribner.

Omi, Michael and Howard Winant. 1994. *Racial Formation in the United States: From the 1960s to the 1990s.* New York: Routledge.

Ong, Aihwa. 2003. "Cyberpublics and Diaspora Politics among Transnational Chinese." *Interventions* 5(1): 82–100.

Ong, Paul. 2007. "Bovine Spongiform Encephalopathy." Pp. 102–106 in *Encyclopedia of Globalization,* edited by J. A. Scholte and R. Robertson. New York: MTM Publishing.

Onishi, Norimitsu. 2010. "Toiling Far from Home for Philippine Dreams." *New York Times,* September 19, p. 5.

Opsal, Tara D. 2011. "Women Disrupting a Marginalized Identity: Subverting the Parolee Identity through Narrative." *Journal of Contemporary Ethnography,* 40(2): 135–167.

Orfield, Gary. 2001. *Schools More Separate: Consequences of a Decade of Resegregation.* Cambridge, MA: Harvard University, The Civil Rights Project. Retrieved July 8, 2013 (http://www.civilrightsproject.harvard.edu/research/deseg/Schools_More_Separate.pdf).

Orkin, Haris. 2011. "Did Dead Island's Powerful Announcement Trailer Misrepresent the Highly Anticipated Video Game?" *PRWeb.* Retrieved May 27, 2011 (http://www.prweb.com/releases/prweb2011/5/prweb8482799.htm).

Orlikowski, Wanda J. 2010. "Technology and Organization: Contingency All the Way Down." Pp. 239–246 in *Technology and Organization: Essays in Honour of Joan Woodward (Research in the Sociology of Organizations, Volume 29),* edited by N. Phillips, G. Sewell, and D. Griffiths. Bingley, UK: Emerald Group.

Orloff, Ann S. 1993. *The Politics of Pensions: A Comparative Analysis of Britain, Canada and the United States, 1880s–1940.* Madison: University of Wisconsin Press.

Orr, Martin. 2012. "Great Recession." Pp. 890–891 in *The Encyclopedia of Globalization,* edited by G. Ritzer. Malden, MA: Wiley-Blackwell.

Ortiz, Susan Y. and Vincent J. Roscigno. 2009. "Discrimination, Women, and Work: Processes and Variations by Race and Class." *The Sociological Quarterly* 50(2): 336–359.

Ortmeyer, David L. and Michael A. Quinn. 2012. "Coyotes, Migration Duration, and Remittances." *The Journal of Developing Areas* 46: 185–203.

Orum, Anthony M. 2007. "Urbanization." Pp. 5151–5154 in *The Blackwell Encyclopedia of Sociology,* edited by G. Ritzer. Malden, MA: Blackwell.

Orwell, George. 1949. *Nineteen Eighty-Four.* London: Secker and Warburg.

Oshri, Ilan, Julia Kotlarsky, and Leslie Willcocks. 2009. *The Handbook of Global Outsourcing and Offshoring.* Basingstoke, UK: Palgrave Macmillan.

Osman, Suleiman. 2011. *The Invention of Brownstone Brooklyn: Gentrification and the Search for Authenticity in Postwar New York.* New York: Oxford University Press.

Otnes, Cele C., and Linda Tuncay Zayre, eds. 2012. *Gender, Culture, and Consumer Behavior.* Routledge,.

Ousey, Graham C. and Matthew R. Lee. 2008. "Racial Disparity in Formal Social Control: An Investigation of Alternative Explanations of Arrest Rate Inequality." *Research in Crime and Delinquency* 45: 322–255.

Outlaw, Lucius T. 2012. "Toward a Critical Theory of Race." Pp. 140–159 in *Arguing about Science,* edited by A. Bird and J. Ladyman. New York: Routledge.

Ovaska, Tomi and Ryo Takashima. 2010. "Does a Rising Tide Lift All the Boats? Explaining the National Inequality of Happiness." *Journal of Economic Issues* XLIV(1): 205–223.

Pace, Julie. 2010. "Obama Takes on Election-Year Fears over Big Debt." Retrieved March 31, 2012 (http://www.cbsnews.com/stories/2010/09/19/national/main6881308.shtml).

Packer, George. 2006. "The Megacity: Decoding the Chaos of Lagos." *The New Yorker*, November 12.

Pager, Devah. 2003. "The Mark of a Criminal Record." *American Journal of Sociology*, pp. 937–975.

Pager, Devah. 2009. *Marked: Race, Crime, and Finding Work in an Era of Mass Incarceration.* Chicago: University of Chicago.

Pager, Devah and Bruce Western. 2012. "Identifying Discrimination at Work: The Use of Field Experiments." *Journal of Social Issues* 68: 221–237.

Pager, Devah, Bruce Western, and Bart Bonikowski. 2009. "Discrimination in a Low-Wage Labor Market: A Field Experiment." *American Sociological Review* 74(5): 777–799.

Panitch, Leo. 2009. "Thoroughly Modern Marx." *Foreign Policy*, April 15.

Pantzar, Mike and Elizabeth Shove. 2010. "Understanding Innovation in Practice: A Discussion of the Production and Re-production of Nordic Walking." *Technology Analysis and Strategic Management* 22: 447–461.

Park, Julie and Dowell Myers. 2010. "Intergenerational Mobility in the Post-1965 Immigration Era: Estimates by an Immigrant Generation Cohort Method." *Demography* 47: 369–392.

Park, Robert E. [1927] 1973. "Life History." *American Journal of Sociology* 79: 251–260.

Park, Robert, Ernest Burgess, and R. D. McKenzie. [1925] 1967. *The City: Suggestions for Investigation of Human Behavior in the Urban Environment.* Chicago: University of Chicago Press.

Parker, David and Miri Song. 2006. "New Ethnicities Online: Reflexive Racialisation and the Internet." *The Sociological Review* 54: 575–594.

Parker, Stanley. 1971. *The Future of Work and Leisure.* London: MacGibbon and Kee.

Parkinson, Cyril Northcote. 1955. "Parkinson's Law." *The Economist*, November 19.

Parreñas, Rhacel. 2001. *Servants of Globalization: Women, Migration, and Domestic Work.* Stanford, CA: Stanford University Press.

Parrillo, Vincent N. 2007. "Urban." Pp. 5101–5104 in *The Blackwell Encyclopedia of Sociology*, edited by G. Ritzer. Malden, MA: Blackwell.

Parsons, Talcott. 1943. "The Kinship System of the Contemporary United States." *American Anthropologist* 43: 22–38.

Parsons, Talcott. 1951. *The Social System.* Glencoe, IL: Free Press.

Parsons, Talcott. 1966. *Societies.* Englewood Cliffs, NJ: Prentice-Hall.

Pascoe, C. J. 2007. *Dude, You're a Fag.* Berkeley: University of California Press.

Passel, Jeffrey. 2010. "Race and the Census: The 'Negro' Controversy." *Pew Research Center Online*, January 21. Retrieved January 16, 2012 (http://www.pewsocialtrends.org/2010/01/21/race-and-the-census-the-%E2%80%9Cnegro%E2%80%9D-controversy/).

Patch, Jason and Neil Brenner. 2007. "Gentrification." Pp. 1917–1920 in *The Blackwell Encyclopedia of Sociology*, edited by G. Ritzer. Malden, MA: Blackwell.

Patchin, Justin W. and Sameer Hinduja. 2010. "Trends in Online Social Networking: Adolescent Use of MySpace over Time." *New Media and Society* 12: 197–216.

Patchin, Justin W. and Sameer Hinduja. 2011. "Traditional and Nontraditional Bullying among Youth: A Test of General Strain Theory." *Youth Society* 43: 727–751.

Patel, Reena. 2010. *Working the Night Shift: Women in India's Call Centers.* Palo Alto, CA: Stanford University Press.

Paternoster, Raymond. 1992. *Capital Punishment in America.* Lexington, MA: Lexington Books.

Paternoster, Raymond. 2007. "Capital Punishment." Pp. 385–388 in *The Blackwell Encyclopedia of Sociology* (Vol. 2), edited by G. Ritzer. Malden, MA: Blackwell.

Paternoster, Raymond, Robert Brame, and Sarah Bacon. 2007. *The Death Penalty: America's Experience with Capital Punishment.* Oxford: Oxford University Press.

Patterson, Maurice and Jonathan Schroeder. 2010. "Borderlines: Skin, Tattoos and Consumer Culture Theory." *Marketing Theory* 10: 253–267.

Patton, Peter L. 1998. "The Gangstas in Our Midst." *Urban Review* 30: 49–76.

Pavalko, Eliza K and Glen H. Elder. 1990. "World War II and Divorce: A Life-Course Perspective." *American Journal of Sociology* 95: 1213–1234.

Payton, Andrew and Peggy A. Thoits. 2011. "Medicalization, Direct-to-Consumer Advertising, and Mental Illness Stigma." *Society and Mental Health* 1: 55–70.

PBS. 2010. *Frontline: Digital Nation.* Retrieved May 25, 2011 (http://www.pbs.org/wgbh/pages/frontline/digitalnation/view/).

PBS NewsHour. 2006. "Tracking Nuclear Proliferation: Country Profiles." Retrieved May 26, 2011 (http://www.pbs.org/newshour/indepth_coverage/military/proliferation/profiles.html).

Pearce, Diane. 1978. "The Feminization of Poverty: Women, Work, and Welfare." *Urban and Social Change Review* 11: 28–36.

Pearlin, Leonard I. 1989. "The Sociological Study of Stress." *Journal of Health and Social Behavior* 30: 241–256.

Pearson, Ruth. 1992. "Gender Issues in Industrialization." In *Industrialization and Development*, edited by T. Hewitt, J. Johnson, and D. Wield. Oxford: Oxford University Press.

Pearson, Ruth. 2000. "Moving the Goalposts: Gender and Globalization in the Twenty-First Century." *Gender and Development* 8(1): 10–19.

Pegg, Rayne. 2010. "Survey Says: Farmers Markets on the Rise." *USDA Blog.* Retrieved May 27, 2011 (http://blogs.usda.gov/2010/08/04/survey-says-farmers-markets-on-the-rise/).

People v. Hall 4 Cal. 399. 1854. Supreme Court of the State of California.

Peoples, Clayton D. 2012. "Welfare State." Pp. 2218–2221 in *The Encyclopedia of Globalization*, edited by G. Ritzer. Malden, MA: Wiley-Blackwell.

Perchel, Harland. 2007. "Taylorism." Pp. 4939–4940 in *The Blackwell Encyclopedia of Sociology*, edited by G. Ritzer. Malden, MA: Blackwell.

Perelli-Harris, Brienna and Nora Sanchez Gassen. 2012. "How Similar Are Cohabitation and Marriage? Legal Approaches to Cohabitation across Western Europe." *Population and Development Review* 38: 435–467.

Perkins, Harvey C. and David C. Thorns. 2001. "Gazing or Performing? Reflections on Urry's Tourist Gaze in the Context of Contemporary Experience in the Antipodes." *International Sociology* 16(2): 185–204.

Perloff, Richard M., Bette Bonder, George B. Ray, Eileen Berlin Ray, and Laura A Siminoff. 2006. "Doctor-Patient Communication, Cultural Competence, and Minority Health: Theoretical and Empirical Perspectives." *American Behavioral Scientist* 49(6): 835–852.

Perna, Laura W. 2006. "Studying College Access and Choice: A Proposed Conceptual Model." Pp. 99–157 in *Higher Education: Handbook of Theory and Research* (Vol. 21), edited by J. Smart. The Netherlands: Springer.

Perrin, Robin D. 2007. "Deviant Beliefs/Cognitive Deviance." Pp. 1140–1142 in *The Blackwell Encyclopedia of Sociology*, edited by G. Ritzer. Malden, MA: Blackwell.

Perrow, Charles. 1999. *Normal Accidents.* Princeton, NJ: Princeton University Press.

Pescosolido, Bernice A., Elizabeth Grauerholz, and Melissa A. Milkie. 1997. "Culture and Conflict: The Portrayal of Blacks in U.S. Children's Picture Books Through the Mid- and Late-twentieth Century." *American Sociological Review*, 62: 443–464.

Peter, Lawrence J. and Raymond Hull. 1969. *The Peter Principle: Why Things Always Go Wrong.* New York: William Morrow and Company.

Peterson, Richard A. and Roger M. Kern. 1996. "Changing Highbrow Taste: From Snob to Omnivore." *American Sociological Review* 61: 900–907.

Petit, Becky and Bruce Western. 2004. "Mass Imprisonment and the Life Course: Race and Class Inequality in U.S. Incarceration." *American Sociological Review* 69: 151–169.

Pew Research Center for the People and the Press. 2009. "Public More Optimistic about the Economy, but Still Reluctant to

Spend." June 19. Retrieved March 31, 2012 (http://pewresearch.org/pubs/1260/more-optimistic-about-economy-but-reluctant-to-spend).

Pfeffer, Max J. and Pilar A. Parra. 2009. "Strong Ties, Weak Ties, and Human Capital: Latino Immigrant Employment Outside the Enclave." *Rural Sociology* 74(2): 241–269.

Phelan, Jo C., Bruce G. Link, and Parisa Tehranifar. 2004. "'Fundamental Causes' of Social Inequalities in Mortality: A Test of the Theory." *Journal of Health and Social Behavior* 45: 265–285.

Phelan, Jo C., Bruce G. Link, and Parisa Tehranifar. 2010. "Social Conditions as Fundamental Causes of Health Inequalities: Theory, Evidence, and Policy Implications." *Journal of Health and Social Behavior* 51: S28–S40.

Phelps, Michelle S. 2011. "Rehabilitation in the Punitive Era: The Gap between Rhetoric and Reality in U.S. Prison Programs." *Law and Society Review* 45: 33–68.

Phelps, Nicholas and Andrew M. Wood. 2011. "The New Post-suburban Politics?" *Urban Studies* 48: 2591–2610.

Phillips, Leigh, Kate Connolly, and Lizzy Davies. 2010. "EU Turning Blind Eye to Discrimination against Roma, Say Human Rights Groups." *The Guardian*, July 30. Retrieved November 29, 2011 (http://www.guardian.co.uk/world/2010/jul/30/european-union-roma-human-rights).

Piaget, Jean and Barbel Inhelder. 1972. *The Psychology of the Child*. New York: Basic Books.

Picca, Leslie H. and Joe R. Feagin. 2007. *Two-Faced Racism: Whites in the Backstage and Frontstage*. New York: Routledge.

Pickering, Mary. 2011. "Auguste Comte." Pp. 30–60 in *The Wiley-Blackwell Companion to Major Social Theorists: Volume 1. Classical Theorists*, edited by G. Ritzer and J. Stepnisky. Malden, MA: Wiley-Blackwell.

Pinker, Stephen. 2009. "Book Review: 'What the Dog Saw—And Other Adventures,' by Malcolm Gladwell." *New York Times Book Review*, November 9, p. 12.

Piquero, Alex R. and Zenta Gomez-Smith. 2007. "Crime, Life Course Theory of." Pp. 830–833 in *The Blackwell Encyclopedia of Sociology*, edited by G. Ritzer. Malden, MA: Blackwell.

Piquero, Alex R., Raymond Paternoster, Greg Pogarsky, and Thomas Loughran. 2011. "Elaborating the Individual Difference Component in Deterrence Theory." *Annual Review of Law and Social Science* 7: 335–360.

Piquero, Alex R., Terence P. Thornberry, Marvin D. Krohn, Alan J. Lizotte, and Nicole Leeper Piquero. 2012. *Measuring Crime and Delinquency over the Life Course*. New York: Springer.

Pitts, Victoria. 2003. *In the Flesh: The Cultural Politics of Body Modification*. New York: Palgrave Macmillan.

Plant, Rebecca F. and Michael S. Kimmel. 2007. "Sexuality, Masculinity and." Pp. 4272–4275 in *The Blackwell Encyclopedia of Sociology*, edited by G. Ritzer. Malden, MA: Blackwell.

Pleyers, Geoffrey. 2010. *Alter-Globalization: Becoming Actors in the Global Age*. Cambridge, UK: Polity.

Plummer, Ken. 1975. *Sexual Stigma: An Interactionist Account*. London: Routledge.

Plummer, Ken. 1992. *Modern Homosexualities: Fragments of Lesbian and Gay Experience*. New York: Routledge.

Plummer, Ken. 2007a. "Sexual Identities." Pp. 4238–4242 in *The Blackwell Encyclopedia of Sociology*, edited by G. Ritzer. Malden, MA: Blackwell.

Plummer, Ken. 2007b. "Sexual Markets, Commodification, and Consumption." Pp. 4242–4244 in *The Blackwell Encyclopedia of Sociology*, edited by G. Ritzer. Malden, MA: Blackwell.

Plummer, Ken. 2012. "Critical Sexuality Studies." Pp. 243–268 in *The Wiley-Blackwell Companion to Sociology*, edited by G. Ritzer. Malden, MA: Wiley-Blackwell.

Pocock, Emil. 2011. "World's Largest Shopping Malls." Shopping Center Studies at Eastern Connecticut State University. Retrieved May 19, 2011 (www.easternct.edu/~pocock/MallsWorld.htm).

Poff, Deborah. 2010. "Ethical Leadership and Global Citizenship: Considerations for a Just and Sustainable Future." *Journal of Business Ethics* 93: 9–14.

Polgreen, Lydia. 2010a. "India Digs under the Top of the World to Match a Rival." *New York Times*, August 1. Retrieved May 26, 2011 (http://www.nytimes.com/2010/08/01/world/asia/01pass.html).

Polgreen, Lydia. 2010b. "New Business Class Rises in Ashes of South India's Caste System." *New York Times*, September 11, p. A4.

Polgreen, Lydia. 2010c. "One Bride for Multiple Brothers: A Himalayan Custom Fades." *New York Times*, July 17, pp. A4, A6.

Pollack, Andrew. 2010. "Firm Brings Gene Tests to Masses." *New York Times*, January 29.

Pollock, Jocelyn M. 2001. *Women, Prison and Crime*. New York: Wadsworth.

Polonko, Karen. 2007. "Child Abuse." Pp. 448–451 in *The Blackwell Encyclopedia of Sociology*, edited by G. Ritzer. Malden, MA: Blackwell.

Pontell, Henry L. 2007. "Deviance, Reactivist Definitions of." Pp. 1123–1126 in *The Blackwell Encyclopedia of Sociology*, edited by G. Ritzer. Malden, MA: Blackwell.

Popenoe, David. 1987. "Beyond the Nuclear Family: A Statistical Portrait of the Changing Family in Sweden." *Journal of Marriage and the Family* 49: 173–183.

Popenoe, David. 1993. "American Family Decline, 1960–1990: A Review and Appraisal." *Journal of Marriage and Family* 55: 527–542.

Popenoe, David. 2009. "Cohabitation, Marriage, and Child Wellbeing: A Cross-National Perspective." *Society* 46: 429–436.

Popham, James and Kenneth Sirotnik. 1973. *Educational Statistics: Use and Interpretation*. New York: Harper and Row.

Population Reference Bureau. 2010. "World Population Data Sheet." Retrieved October 28, 2010 (www.prb.org/Publications/Datasheets/2010/2010wpds.aspx).

Portes, Alejandro and Min Zhou. 1993. "The New Second Generation: Segmented Assimilation and Its Variants." *Annals of the American Academy of Political and Social Science* 530: 75–96.

Poster, Winnifred. 2007. "Who's on the Line? Indian Call Center Agents Pose as Americans for U.S.-Outsourced Firms." *Industrial Relations: A Journal of Economy and Society* 46(2): 271–304.

Postmes, Tom and Russell Spears. 1998. "Deindividuation and Anti-Normative Behavior." *Psychological Bulletin* 123: 238–259.

Povoledo, Elisabetta. 2010. "Behind Venice's Walls of Ads, the Restoration of Heritage." *New York Times*, September 19, p. 18.

Powell, Brian, Catherine Bolzendahl, Claudia Geist, and Lala Carr Steelman. 2010. *Counted Out: Same-Sex Relations and Americans' Definitions of Family*. New York: Russell Sage Foundation.

Powell, Jason L. 2012. "Internet." Pp. 1188–1190 in *Wiley-Blackwell Encyclopedia of Globalization*, edited by G. Ritzer. Malden, MA: Wiley-Blackwell.

Powell, Joe and Karen Branden. 2007. "Family, Sociology of." Pp. 1614–1618 in *The Blackwell Encyclopedia of Sociology*, edited by G. Ritzer. Malden, MA: Blackwell.

Prall, Kevin H. 2011. *Rupert Murdoch and the News International Phone Hacking Scandal: How It All Went Down*. Kindle Edition.

Prechel, Harlan. 2007. "Taylorism." Pp. 4939–4940 in *The Blackwell Encyclopedia of Sociology*, edited by G. Ritzer. Malden, MA: Blackwell.

Preibisch, Kerry L. and Evelyn Encalada Grez. 2010. "The Other Side of el Otro Lado: Mexican Migrant Women and Labor Flexibility in Canadian Agriculture." *Signs* 35(2): 289–316.

Preisendorfer, Peter and Andreas Diekmann. 2007. "Ecological Problems." Pp. 1281–1286 in *The Blackwell Encyclopedia of Sociology*, edited by G. Ritzer. Malden, MA: Blackwell.

Prell, C., M. Reed, L. Racin, and K. Hubacek. 2010. "Competing Structure, Competing Views: The Role of Formal and Informal Social Structures in Shaping Stakeholder Perceptions." *Ecology and Society* 15(4): 34.

Premack, David. 2007. "Human and Animal Cognition: Continuity and Discontinuity." *Proceedings of the National Academy of Sciences* 104: 13861–13867.

Prentice, Andrew. 2006. "The Emerging Epidemic of Obesity in Developing Countries." *International Journal of Epidemiology* 35(1): 93–99.

Presser, Harriet B. 2005. *Working in a 24/7 Economy*. New York: Russell Sage.

Presser, Stanley. 1995. "Informed Consent and Confidentiality in Survey Research." *Public Opinion Quarterly* 58: 446–459.

Preston, Julia. 2006a. "Low-Wage Workers from Mexico Dominate Latest Great Wave of Immigrants." *New York Times*, December 19.

Preston, Julia. 2006b. "Making a Life in the United States, but Feeling Mexico's Tug." *New York Times*, December 19.

Prevost, Gary and Carlos Oliva Campos, eds. 2011. *Cuban-Latin American Relations in the Context of a Changing Hemisphere.* Amherst, New York: Cambria Press.

Prior, Nick. 2011. "Critique and Renewal in the Sociology of Music: Bourdieu and Beyond." *Cultural Sociology* 5: 121–138.

Prokos, Anastasia and Irene Padavic. 2005. "An Examination of Competing Explanations for the Pay Gap Among Scientists and Engineers." *Gender and Society* 19(4): 523–543.

Public Culture. 2011. "Arjun Appadurai." Accessed December 3, 2011 (http://publicculture.org/people/view/arjun-appadurai).

Pugh, Allison. 2009. *Longing and Belonging: Parents, Children and Consumer Culture.* Berkeley: University of California Press.

Pugh, Derek S., David Hickson, Christopher R. Hinings, and Christopher Turner. 1968. "The Context of Organizational Structures." *Administrative Science Quarterly* 14: 91–114.

Pullum, Amanda. 2013. "Tea Party Movement (United States)." Pp. 1327–1328 in *The Wiley-Blackwell Encyclopedia of Social and Political Movements*, 3 vols., edited by D. A. Snow, D. Della Porta, B. Klandermans, and D. McAdam. Malden, MA: Wiley-Blackwell.

Pun, Nagi. 1995. "Theoretical Discussions on The Impact of Industrial Restructuring in Asia." In *Silk and Steel: Asia Women Workers Confront Challenges of Industrial Restructuring.* Hong Kong: CAW.

Putnam, Robert. 2001. *Bowling Alone.* New York: Simon and Schuster.

Qian, Zhenchao and Daniel T. Lichter. 2011. "Changing Patterns of Interracial Marriage in a Multiracial Society." *Journal of Marriage and Family* 73: 1065–1084.

Quadagno, Jill and Deana Rohlinger. 2009. "Religious Conservatives in U.S. Welfare State Politics." Pp. 236–266 in *The Western Welfare State and Its Religious Roots*, edited by K. van Kersbergen and P. Manow. New York: Cambridge University Press.

Rabin, Roni Caryn. 2009. "Tool to Offer Fast Help for H.I.V. Exposure." *New York Times*, September 8.

Raby, C. R., D. M. Alexis, A. Dickenson, and N. S. Clayton. 2007. "Planning for the Future by Western Planning for the Future by Western Scrub-Jays." *Nature* 445: 919–921.

Racial Integrity Act of 1924, Article 5. State of Virginia.

Radcliff, Benjamin. 2001. "Organized Labor and Electoral Participation in American National Elections." *Journal of Labor Research* 22(2): 405–414.

Rafferty, Yvonne. 2007. "Children for Sale: Child Trafficking in Southeast Asia." *Child Abuse Review* 16: 401–422.

Ragin, Charles. 1987. *The Comparative Method: Moving Beyond Qualitative and Quantitative Strategies.* Berkeley: University of California Press.

Raley, Sara. 2010. "McDonaldization and the Family." Pp. 138–148 in *McDonaldization: The Reader*, edited by G. Ritzer. 3rd ed. Thousand Oaks, CA: Pine Forge Press.

Ram, Uri. 2007. *The Globalization of Israel: McWorld in Tel Aviv, Jihad in Jerusalem.* London: Routledge.

Raman, Anuradha. 2011. "Dalit Crorepatis: The Other Temple Entry." *Outlook*, May 2. Retrieved March 31, 2012 (http://www.outlookindia.com/article.aspx?271501).

Ramella, Francesco. 2007. "Political Economy." Pp. 3433–3436 in *The Blackwell Encyclopedia of Sociology*, edited by G. Ritzer. Malden, MA: Blackwell.

Ramirez, Francisco O., Yasemin Soysal, and Suzanne Shanahan. 1997. "The Changing Logic of Political Citizenship: Cross-National Acquisition of Women's Suffrage Rights, 1890–1990." *American Sociological Review* 62: 735–745.

Rankin, James and Kyle Brown. 2011. "Personal Income and Outlays, April 2011." *Bureau of Economic Analysis*, May 27. Accessed June 22, 2011 (http://www.bea.gov/newsreleases/national/pi/pinewsrelease.htm).

Rao, Leena. 2010. "TinyChat Launches Grouped Version of Chatroulette." *TechCrunch.* Retrieved May 27, 2011 (http://techcrunch.com/2010/02/16/tinychat-launches-grouped-version-of-chatroulette/).

Rape, Abuse, and Incest National Network. 2009a. "Marital Rape." Retrieved March 31, 2012 (http://www.rainn.org/public-policy/sexual-assault-issues/marital-rape).

Rape, Abuse, and Incest National Network. 2009b. "Who Are the Victims?" Retrieved March 31, 2012 (http://www.rainn.org/get-information/statistics/sexual-assault-victims).

Ratha, Dilip and Sanket Mohapatra. 2012. "Remittances and Development." Pp. 1782–1792 in *The Wiley-Blackwell Encyclopedia of Globalization*, edited by G. Ritzer. Malden, MA: Wiley-Blackwell.

Rauscher, Lauren. 2007. "Gendered Organizations/Institutions." Pp. 1892–1895 in *The Blackwell Encyclopedia of Sociology*, edited by G. Ritzer. Malden, MA: Blackwell.

Ravitch, Diane. 2012. "Schools We Can Envy." *New York Review of Books*, March 8, pp. 19–20.

Rawls, Anne. 2011. "Harold Garfinkel." Pp. 89–124 in *The Wiley-Blackwell Companion to Major Social Theorists: Volume II. Contemporary Sociological Theorists*, edited by G. Ritzer and J. Stepnisky. Malden, MA: Wiley-Blackwell.

Ray, Larry. 2007. "Civil Society." Pp. 512–513 in *The Blackwell Encyclopedia of Sociology*, edited by G. Ritzer. Malden, MA: Blackwell.

Reardon, Sean F. and Claudia Galindo. 2008. "The Hispanic-White Achievement Gap in Math and Reading in the Elementary Grades" (Working Paper No. 2008-01). Stanford University, Institute for Research on Education Policy and Practice.

Recording Industry Association of America (RIAA). 2012. "Piracy Online Facts." Retrieved March 31, 2012 (http://www.riaa.com/physicalpiracy.php?content_selector=piracy-online-scope-of-the-problem).

Reger, Jo. 2007. "Feminism, First, Second, and Third Waves." Pp. 1672–1681 in *The Blackwell Encyclopedia of Sociology*, edited by G. Ritzer. Malden, MA: Blackwell.

Regnerus, Mark and Jeremy Uecker. 2011. *Premarital Sex in America: How Young Americans Meet, Mate, and Think about Marrying.* Oxford, UK: Oxford University Press.

Regt, Marina de. 2009. "Preferences and Prejudices: Employers' Views on Domestic Workers in the Republic of Yemen." *Signs* 34(3): 559–581.

Reid, Colleen. 2004. "Advancing Women's Social Justice Agendas: A Feminist Action Research Framework." *International Journal of Qualitative Methods* 3(3): 1–15.

Reiman, Jeffrey H. and Paul Leighton. 2012. *The Rich Get Richer and the Poor Get Prison: Ideology, Class, and Criminal Justice.* 10th ed. Boston: Prentice Hall.

Reinberg, Steven. 2011. "Survey Finds Many Young Adults Oblivious to Heart Health." *U.S. News and World Report*, May 2. Retrieved May 23, 2011 (http://health.usnews.com/health-news/family-health/heart/articles/2011/05/02/survey-finds-many-young-adults-oblivious-to-heart-health).

Reskin, Barbara. 1993. "Sex Segregation in the Workplace." *Annual Review of Sociology* 19: 241–270.

Restivo, Emily and Mark M. Lanier. 2013. "Measuring the Contextual Effects and Mitigating Factors of Labeling Theory." *Justice Quarterly*, January.

Reuveny, Rafael and William R. Thompson. 2001. "Leading Sectors, Lead Economies and Economic Growth." *Review of International Political Economy* 8(4): 689–719.

Reverby, Susan. 2009. *Examining Tuskegee: The Infamous Syphilis Study and Its Legacy.* Chapel Hill: University of North Carolina Press.

Reyhner, Jon A. and Jeanne M. O. Eder. 2006. *American Indian Education: A History.* Norman: University of Oklahoma Press.

Rhinoplasty Online. 2011. "African American (Black) Rhinoplasty." Retrieved March 31, 2012 (http://www.rhinoplastyonline.com/africanamerican.html).

Rich, Motoko. 2013. "Charter Schools Are Improving, a Study Says." *New York Times*, June 25, p. A15.

Richtel, Matt. 2007. "For Pornographers, Internet's Virtues Turn to Vices." *New York Times*, June 2.

Richtel, Matt. 2010a. "Attached to Technology and Paying a Price." *New York Times*, June 6.

Richtel, Matt. 2010b. "Hooked on Gadgets, and Paying a Mental Price." *New York Times*, June 7, pp. A1, A12–13.

Richtel, Matt. 2011a. "In Classroom of the Future, Stagnant Scores." *New York Times*, September 3.

Richtel, Matt. 2011b. "Egypt Cuts Off Most Internet and Cell Service." *New York Times*, January 28. Accessed December 3, 2011 (http://www.nytimes.com/2011/01/29/technology/internet/29cutoff.html).

Rideout, Victoria J., Ulla G. Foehr, and Donald F. Roberts. 2010. *Generation M2: Media in the Lives of 8-to 18-Year-Olds*. Menlo Park, CA: Kaiser Family Foundation.

Ridgeway, Cecilia L. and Shelley L. Correll. 2004. "Unpacking the Gender System: A Theoretical Perspective on Gender Beliefs and Social Relations." *Gender and Society* 18(4): 510–553.

Rieger, Jon H. 2007. "Key Informant." Pp. 2457–2458 in *The Blackwell Encyclopedia of Sociology*, edited by G. Ritzer. Malden, MA: Blackwell.

Rieker, Patricia R. and Chloe E. Bird. 2000. "Sociological Explanations of Gender Differences in Mental and Physical Health." In *Handbook of Medical Sociology*, edited by C. E. Bird, P. Conrad, and A. Freemont. New York: Prentice Hall.

Riera-Crichton, Daniel. 2012. "Euro Crisis." Pp. 566–570 in *The Encyclopedia of Globalization*, edited by G. Ritzer. Malden, MA: Wiley-Blackwell.

Rifkin, Jeremy. 1995. *The End of Work*. New York: Putnam.

Riger, Stefanie. 1992. "Epistemological Debates, Feminist Voices: Science, Social Values, and the Study of Women." *American Psychologist* 47(6): 730–740.

Riis, Ole. 2012. "Combining Quantitative and Qualitative Methods in the Sociology of Religion." Pp. 91–116 in *Annual Review of the Sociology of Religion: New Methods in Sociology of Religion 2012*, edited by L. Berzano and O. Preben Riis. Leiden: Brill.

Rippeyoug, Phyllis L. F. and Mary C. Noonan. 2012. "Is Breastfeeding Truly Cost Free? Income Consequences of Breastfeeding for Women." *American Sociological Review* 77: 244–267.

Riska, Elianne. 2007. "Health Professions and Occupations." Pp. 2075–2078 in *The Blackwell Encyclopedia of Sociology*, edited by G. Ritzer. Malden, MA: Blackwell.

Ristau, Carolyn A. 1983. "Language, Cognition, and Awareness in Animals." *Annals of the New York Academy of Sciences* 406: 170–186.

Ritzer, George. 1972. *Man and His Work: Conflict and Change*. New York: Appleton-Century-Crafts.

Ritzer, George. 1975. *Sociology: A Multiple Paradigm Science*. Boston: Allyn and Bacon.

Ritzer, George. 1981. "Paradigm Analysis in Sociology: Clarifying the Issues." *American Sociological Review* 46(2): 245–248.

Ritzer, George. 1995. *Expressing America: A Critique of the Global Credit Card Society*. Thousand Oaks, CA: Pine Forge Press.

Ritzer, George. 1997. *The McDonaldization Thesis*. London: Sage.

Ritzer, George. 2001a. *Explorations in the Sociology of Consumption: Fast Food, Credit Cards, and Casinos*. London: Sage.

Ritzer, George. 2001b. "Hyperrationality: An Extension of Weberian and Neo-Weberian Theory." In *Explorations in Social Theory*, edited by G. Ritzer. London: Sage.

Ritzer, George. 2006. "Who's a Public Intellectual?" *British Journal of Sociology* 57: 209–213.

Ritzer, George, ed. 2007a. *The Blackwell Encyclopedia of Sociology*. Malden, MA: Blackwell.

Ritzer, George. 2007b. *The Globalization of Nothing*. 2nd ed. Thousand Oaks, CA: Sage Publications.

Ritzer, George. 2008. *Sociological Theory*. 7th ed. New York: McGraw-Hill.

Ritzer, George. 2010a. "Cathedrals of Consumption: Rationalization, Enchantment, and Disenchantment." Pp. 234–239 in *McDonaldization: The Reader*, edited by G. Ritzer. 3rd ed. Thousands Oaks, CA: Pine Forge Press.

Ritzer, George. 2010b. *Enchanting a Disenchanted World: Continuity and Change in the Cathedrals of Consumption*. Thousand Oaks, CA: Sage.

Ritzer, George. 2010c. *Globalization: A Basic Text*. Malden, MA: Wiley-Blackwell.

Ritzer, George, ed. 2010d. *The McDonaldization of Society: The Reader*. 3rd ed. Thousand Oaks, CA: Pine Forge Press.

Ritzer, George, ed. 2012. *The Wiley-Blackwell Encyclopedia of Globalization*, 5 volumes. Malden, MA: Wiley Blackwell.

Ritzer, George. 2013a. *The McDonaldization of Society*. 7th ed. Thousand Oaks, CA: Sage.

Ritzer, George. 2013b. "The 'New' Prosumer: Collaboration on the Digital and Material 'New Means of Prosumption.'" Paper Presented at the Meetings of the Eastern Sociological Society, March, Boston.

Ritzer, George. Forthcoming. *The Wiley-Blackwell Encyclopedia of Sociology*. 2nd ed. Malden. MA: Wiley-Blackwell.

Ritzer, George and Zeynep Atalay, eds. 2010. *Reading in Globalization: Key Concepts and Major Debates*. West Sussex, UK: Wiley-Blackwell.

Ritzer, George, Paul Dean, and Nathan Jurgenson. 2012. "The Coming of Age of the Prosumer." *American Behavioral Scientist* (Special Issue): 379–640.

Ritzer, George, Douglas Goodman, and Wendy Wiedenhoft. 2001. "Theories of Consumption." Pp. 410–427 in *Handbook of Social Theory*, edited by G. Ritzer and B. Smart. London: Sage.

Ritzer, George and Nathan Jurgenson. 2010. "Production, Consumption, Prosumption: The Nature of Capitalism in the Age of the Digital 'Prosumer.'" *Journal of Consumer Culture* 10(1): 13–36.

Ritzer, George and Craig Lair. 2007. "Outsourcing: Globalization and Beyond." Pp. 307–329 in *The Blackwell Companion to Globalization*, edited by G. Ritzer. Malden, MA: Blackwell.

Ritzer, George and Craig Lair. Forthcoming. *The Outsourcing of Everything*. New York: Oxford University Press.

Ritzer, George and Jeff Stepnisky. 2014. *Sociological Theory*. 9th ed. New York: McGraw-Hill.

Ritzer, George and David Walczak. 1988. "Rationalization and the Deprofessionalization of Physicians." *Social Forces* 67: 1–22.

Rivoli, Pietra. 2005. *The Travels of a T-Shirt in the Global Economy: An Economist Examines the Markets, Power, and Politics of World Trade*. Hoboken, NJ: Wiley.

Rizvi, Fazal. 2012. "Bollywood." Pp. 120–121 in *The Wiley-Blackwell Encyclopedia of Globalization*, edited by G. Ritzer. Malden, MA: Wiley-Blackwell.

Roberts, Sam. 2009. "In 2025, India to Pass China in Population, U.S. Estimates." *New York Times*, December 16, p. MB2.

Roberts, Sam. 2008. "Study Foresees the Fall of an Immigration Record that Has Lasted a Century." *New York Times*, February 12, p. A11.

Roberts, Sam. 2010. "More Men Marrying Wealthy Women." *New York Times*, January 19.

Robertson, Craig. 2010. *The Passport in America: The History of a Document*. New York: Oxford University Press.

Robinson, Matthew B. 2010. "McDonaldization of America's Police, Courts, and Corrections." Pp. 85–100 in *McDonaldization: The Reader*, edited by G. Ritzer. 3rd ed. Los Angeles: Pine Forge Press.

Rochon, T. R. 1990. "The West European Peace Movements and the Theory of Social Movements." In *Challenging the Political Order*, edited by R. Dalton and M. Kuchler. Cambridge, UK: Polity Press.

Rockloff, Matthew and Victoria Dyer. 2007. "An Experiment on the Social Facilitation of Gambling Behavior." *Journal of Gambling Studies* 23(1): 1–12.

Roehling, Patricia, Loma Hernandez Jarvis, and Heather Swope. 2005. "Variations in Negative Work-Family Spillover among White, Black, and Hispanic American Men and Women." *Journal of Family Issues* 26(6): 840–865.

Rogers, Ann and David Pilgrim. 2010. *A Sociology of Mental Health and Illness*. London: Open University Press.

Rogers, Patricia Dane. 1995. "Building a Dream House." *Washington Post*, February 2, pp. 12, 15.

Rohlinger, Deana A. 2007. "Socialization, Gender." Pp. 4571–4574 in *The Blackwell Encyclopedia of Sociology*, edited by G. Ritzer. Malden, MA: Blackwell.

Rojas, Rene and Jeff Goodwin. 2013. "Revolutions." Pp. 1102–1110 in *The Wiley-Blackwell Encyclopedia of Social and Political Movements*, 3 vols., edited by D. A. Snow, D. Della Porta, B. Klandermans, and D. McAdam. Malden, MA: Wiley-Blackwell.

Rojek, Chris. 2005. *Leisure Theory: Principles and Practice*. Palgrave MacMillan.

Rojek, Chris. 2007a. "George Ritzer and the Crisis of the Public Intellectual." *Review of Education, Pedagogy and Cultural Studies* 29: 3–21.

Rojek, Chris. 2007b. *The Labour of Leisure: The Culture of Free Time.* London: Sage.

Romero, Simon. 2010. "Left Behind in Venezuela to Piece Lives from Scraps." *New York Times,* September 19, p. 10.

Ronai, Carol R. and Carolyn Ellis. 1989. "Turn-ons for Money: Interactional Strategies of the Table Dancer." *Journal of Contemporary Ethnography* 18: 271–298.

Roof, Wade Clark. 2001. *Spiritual Marketplace: Baby Boomers and the Remaking of American Religion.* Princeton, NJ: Princeton University Press.

Room, Graham. 2011. "Social Mobility and Complexity Theory: Towards a Critique of the Sociological Mainstream." *Policy Studies* 32(2): 109–126.

Rootes, Christopher, ed. 1999. *Environmental Movements: Local, National and Global.* London: Routledge.

Roscigno, Vincent J. and M. Keith Kimble. 1995. "Elite Power, Race, and the Persistence of Low Unionization in the South." *Work and Occupations* 22.

Rose, Arnold. 1967. *The Power Structure.* New York: Oxford University Press.

Rose, Claire. 2010. *Making, Selling and Wearing Boys' Clothes in Late-Victorian England.* Burlington, VT: Ashgate.

Rosenbaum, James. 2001. *Beyond College for All: Career Paths for the Forgotten Half.* New York: Russell Sage Foundation.

Rosenbaum, James. 2011. "The Complexities of College for All: Beyond Fairy-Tale Dreams." *Sociology of Education* 84: 113–117.

Rosenberg, Morris. 1979. *Conceiving the Self.* New York: Basic Books.

Rosenbloom, Stephanie. 2010. "But Will It Make You Happy?" *New York Times,* August 7.

Rosenfield, Richard. 2011. "The Big Picture: 2010 Presidential Address to the American Society of Criminology." *Criminology* 49: 1–26.

Rosenstein, Judith E. 2008. "Individual Threat, Group Threat, and Racial Policy: Exploring the Relationship between Threat and Racial Attitudes." *Social Science Research* 37: 1130–1146.

Rosenthal, Elisabeth. 2007a. "As Earth Warms Up, Virus From Tropics Moves to Italy." *New York Times,* December 23, p. 21.

Rosenthal, Elisabeth. 2007b. "W.H.O. Urges Effort to Fight Fast-Spreading Disease." *New York Times,* August 27, p. A9.

Rossi, Alice. 1983. "Gender and Parenthood." *American Sociological Review* 49: 1–19.

Roszak, Theodore. [1968] 1995. *The Making of a Counter Culture: Reflections on the Technocratic Society and Its Youthful Opposition.* Berkeley: University of California Press.

Roszak, Theodore. 1969. *The Making of a Counter Culture.* New York: Anchor.

Rotella, Carlo. 2010. "Class Warrior: Arne Duncan's Bid to Shake Up Schools." *The New Yorker,* February 10, p. 24.

Roth, Benita. 2004. *Separate Roads to Feminism: Black, Chicana and White Feminist Movements in America's Second Wave.* Cambridge, UK: Cambridge University Press

Roth, Julius A. 1963. *Timetables: Structuring the Passage of Time in Hospital Treatment and Other Careers.* Indianapolis: Bobbs-Merrill.

Roth, Philip. [1969] 1994. *Portnoy's Complaint.* New York: Vintage.

Roth, Silke. 2007. "Social Movements, Biographical Consequences of." Pp. 4451–4453 in *The Blackwell Encyclopedia of Sociology,* edited by G. Ritzer. Malden, MA: Blackwell.

Rothman, Barbara. 2000. *Recreating Motherhood.* 2nd ed. New Brunswick, NJ: Rutgers University Press.

Roudometof, Victor. 2012. "Imagined Communities." Pp. 996–998 in *The Wiley-Blackwell Encyclopedia of Globalization,* edited by G. Ritzer. Malden, MA: Wiley-Blackwell.

Rousseau, Denise M. and Andrea Rivero. 2003. "Democracy: A Way of Organizing in a Knowledge Economy." *Journal of Management Inquiry* 12(2): 115–134.

Rowlingson, Karen. 2007. "Lone-Parent Families." Pp. 2663–2667 in *The Blackwell Encyclopedia of Sociology,* edited by G. Ritzer. Malden, MA: Blackwell.

Roxburgh, Susan. 2004. "There Just Aren't Enough Hours in the Day: The Mental Health Consequences of Time Pressures." *Journal of Health and Social Behavior* 45: 115–131.

Roy, Olivier. 2004. *Globalized Islam: The Search for a New Ummah.* New York: Columbia University Press.

Rozdeba, Suzanne. 2011. "Firefighters Recall Spirit of 9/11 Hero." Retrieved March 31, 2012 (http://eastvillage.thelocal.nytimes.com/2011/01/10/firefighters-recall-spirit-of-911-hero/?scp=3&rsq=9/11%20heroism&rst=cse).

Rudrappa, Sharmila. 2012. "Rape." Pp. 1748–1751 in *The Wiley-Blackwell Encyclopedia of Globalization,* edited by G. Ritzer. Malden, MA: Wiley-Blackwell.

Rueschemeyer, Dietrich, Evelyne Stephens, and John Stephens. 1992. *Capitalist Development and Democracy.* Chicago: University of Chicago Press.

Runyon, Anne Sisson. 2012. "Gender." Pp. 725–734 in *The Wiley-Blackwell Encyclopedia of Globalization,* edited by G. Ritzer. Malden, MA: Wiley-Blackwell.

Rupp, Leila J. 1997. *Worlds of Women: The Making of an International Women's Movement.* Princeton, NJ: Princeton University Press.

Rupp, Leila and Verta Taylor. 1999. "Forging Feminist Identity in an International Movement: A Collective Identity Approach to Twentieth-Century Feminism." *Signs* 24(2): 363–386.

Russell, James. 2006. *Double Standard: Social Policy in Europe and the United States.* Lanham, MD: Rowman and Littlefield.

Rutherford, Alexandra, Kelli Vaughn-Blount, and Laura C. Ball. 2010. "Responsible, Disruptive Voices: Science, Social Change, and the History of Feminist Psychology." *Psychology of Women Quarterly* 34(4): 460–473.

Rutherford, Paul. 2007. *The World Made Sexy: Freud to Madonna.* Toronto, ON: University of Toronto Press.

Rutledge, Leigh W. 1992. *The Gay Decades: From Stonewall to the Present.* New York: Plume.

Ryan, Barbara. 2007. "Sex and Gender." Pp. 4196–4198 in *The Blackwell Encyclopedia of Sociology,* edited by G. Ritzer. Malden, MA: Blackwell.

Ryan, J. Michael. 2012. "Homosexuality." Pp. 941–944 in *The Wiley-Blackwell Encyclopedia of Globalization,* edited by G. Ritzer. Malden, MA: Wiley-Blackwell.

Ryan, Kevin. 1994. "Technicians and Interpreters in Moral Crusades: The Case of the Drug Courier Profile." *Deviant Behavior* 15: 217–240.

Ryan, Michelle K. and S. Alexander Haslam. 2005. "The Glass Cliff: Evidence That Women Are Over-represented in Precarious Leadership Positions." *British Journal of Management* 16: 81–90.

Ryan, William. 1976. *Blaming the Victim.* New York: Pantheon.

Ryave, A. Lincoln and James N. Schenkein. 1974. "Notes on the Art of Walking." Pp. 265–275 in *Ethnomethodology: Selected Readings,* edited by R. Turner. Harmondsworth, UK: Penguin.

Sabo, Don. 1998. "Masculinities and Men's Health: Moving towards Post-Superman Era Prevention." In *Men's Lives,* edited by M. Kimmel and M. Messner. Needham Heights, MA: Allyn and Bacon.

Sabo, Don. 2005. "Doing Time, Doing Masculinity." Pp. 108–112 in *Gender through a Prism of Difference,* edited by M. Baca Zinn, P. Hondagneu-Sotelo, and M. Messner. New York: Oxford University Press.

Sack, Kevin. 2009. "Despite Recession, Personalized Health Care Remains in Demand." *New York Times,* May 11, p. A12.

Sadker, Myra and David Sadker. 1994. *Failing at Fairness: How Our Schools Cheat Girls.* New York: Simon and Schuster.

Sagi-Schwartz, Abraham. 2008. "The Well Being of Children Living in War Zones: The Palestinian-Israeli Case." *International Journal of Behavioral Development* 32(4): 322–336.

Sahlberg, Pasi. 2011. *Finnish Lessons: What Can the World Learn from Educational Change in Finland?* New York: Teachers College Press.

Said, Edward W. [1979] 1994. *Orientalism.* New York: Knopf.

Salkind, Neil. 2004. *Statistics for People Who (Think They) Hate Statistics.* Thousand Oaks, CA: Sage.

Sallaz, Jeffrey. 2010. "Talking Race, Marketing Culture: The Racial Habitus in and out of Apartheid." *Social Problems* 57(2): 294–314.

Saltmarsh, Matthew. 2010. "Sarkozy Toughens on Illegal Roma." *New York Times,* July 29, p. A7.

Salzman, Todd. 2000. "Rape Camps, Forced Impregnation, and Ethnic Cleansing." Pp. 63–92 in *War's Dirty Secret: Rape, Prostitution and Other Crimes against Women*, edited by A. L. Barstow. Ohio: Pilgrim Press.

Samnani, Hina and Lolla Mohammed Nur. 2011. "Crowdmapping Arab Spring—Next Social Media Breakthrough?" *Voice of America*, June 28. Retrieved August 12, 2011 (www.voanews.com/english/news/middle-east/Crowdmapping-Arab-Spring-Next-Social-Media-Breakthrough—124662649.html).

Sampson, Robert J. and John H. Laub. 1993. *Crime in the Making: Pathways and Turning Points through Life*. Cambridge, MA: Harvard University Press.

Sampson, Robert J. and John H. Laub. 2005. "A General Age-Graded Theory of Crime: Lessons Learned and the Future of Life-Course Criminology." Pp. 165–182 in *Integrated Developmental and Life-Course Theories of Offending*, edited by D. P. Farrington. New Brunswick, NJ: Transaction.

Samuel, Laurie. 2007. "Race and the Criminal Justice System." Pp. 3737–3740 in *The Blackwell Encyclopedia of Sociology*, edited by G. Ritzer. Malden, MA: Blackwell.

Sanders, Teela. 2007. "Becoming an Ex–Sex Worker Making Transitions Out of a Deviant Career." *Feminist Criminology* 2: 74–95.

Sanford, Marc M. 2007. "Ecology." Pp. 1289–1291 in *The Blackwell Encyclopedia of Sociology*, edited by G. Ritzer. Malden, MA: Blackwell.

Sanger, David. 2013. "In Cyberspace, New Cold War." *New York Times*, February 24.

Santini, Cristina, Samuel Rabino, and Lorenzo Zanni. 2011. "Chinese Immigrants Socio-economic Enclave in an Italian Industrial District: The Case of Prato." *World Review of Entrepreneurship, Management and Sustainable Development* 7(1): 30–51.

Sarroub, Loukia K. 2005. *All American Yemeni Girls: Being Muslim in a Public School*. Philadelphia: University of Pennsylvania Press.

Sassatelli, Roberta. 2007. *Consumer Culture: History, Theory and Politics*. London: Sage.

Sassen, Saskia. 1991. *The Global City: New York, London, Tokyo*. Princeton, NJ: Princeton University Press.

Sassen, Saskia. 2004. "Local Actors in Global Politics." *Current Sociology* 52(4): 649–670.

Sassen, Saskia. 2012. "Cities." Pp. 187–202 in *The Wiley-Blackwell Encyclopedia of Globalization*, edited by G. Ritzer. Malden, MA: Wiley-Blackwell.

Sassler, Sharon. 2010. "Partnering across the Life Course: Sex, Relationships, and Mate Selection." *Journal of Marriage and Family* 72: 557–575.

Sassler, Sharon and Amanda J. Miller. 2011. "Class Differences in Cohabitation Processes." *Family Relations* 60: 163–177.

Saussure, Ferdinand de. [1916] 1966. *Course in General Linguistics*. New York: McGraw-Hill.

Savage, C. 2010. "U.S. Prosecutors, Weighing WikiLeaks Charges, Hit the Law Books." *New York Times*, December 8, p. A10.

Savage, Charlie and Cheryl Gay Stolberg. 2011. "In Shift, U.S. Says Marriage Act Blocks Gay Rights." *New York Times*, February 23. Accessed December 20, 2011 (http://www.nytimes.com/2011/02/24/us/24marriage.html).

Saviano, Roberto. 2006/2007. *Gomorrah: A Personal Journey Into the Violent International Empire of Naples' Organized Crime System*. New York: Picador.

Sayer, L. C. 2005. "Gender, Time, and Inequality: Trends in Women's and Men's Paid Work, Unpaid Work, and Free Time." *Social Forces* 84: 285–303.

Sayyid, Salman. 2012. "Political Islam." Pp. 1202–1204 in *The Wiley-Blackwell Encyclopedia of Globalization*, edited by G. Ritzer. Malden, MA: Wiley-Blackwell.

Saxon, Wolfgang. 2003. "Adm. Richard E. Bennis, A Hero of 9/11, Dies at 52." *New York Times*, August 9. Retrieved March 31, 2012 (http://www.nytimes.com/2003/08/09/nyregion/adm-richard-e-bennis-a-hero-of-9-11-dies-at-52.html).

Scaff, Lawrence A. 2011. "Georg Simmel." Pp. 205–235 in *The Wiley-Blackwell Companion to Major Social Theorists: Volume 1. Classical Theorists*, edited by G. Ritzer and J. Stepnisky. Malden, MA: Wiley-Blackwell.

Scambler, Graham and Frederique Paoli. 2008. "Health Work, Female Sex Workers and HIV/AIDS: Global and Local Dimensions of Stigma and Deviance as Barriers to Effective Interventions." *Social Science and Medicine* 66: 1848–1862.

Schaefer, David R. 2012. "Homophily through Nonreciprocity: Results of an Experiment." *Social Forces* 90: 1271–1295.

Schafer, Markus H. and Kenneth F. Ferraro. 2011. "The Stigma of Obesity: Does Perceived Weight Discrimination Affect Identity and Physical Health?" *Social Psychology Quarterly* 74: 76–97.

Schauer, Edward J. and Elizabeth M. Wheaton. 2006. "Sex Trafficking into the United States: A Literature Review." *Criminal Justice Review* 31(2): 146–169.

Scheffer, David. 2008. "Rape as Genocide in Darfur." *Los Angeles Times*, November 13.

Schemo, Diana Jean. 2003. "Rate of Rape at Academy Is Put at 12% in Survey." *New York Times*, August 23. Retrieved December 3, 2011 (http://www.nytimes.com/2003/08/29/national/29ACAD.html?th).

"Schengen State Denmark to Re-impose Border Controls." 2011. *BBC News*, May 11. Retrieved March 29, 2012 (http://www.bbc.co.uk/news/world-europe-13366047).

Scheper-Hughes, Nancy. 2001. "Commodity Fetishism in Organs Trafficking." *Body and Society* 7: 31–62.

Scherschel, Karin. 2007. "Migration, Ethnic Conflicts, and Racism." Pp. 3011–3014 in *The Blackwell Encyclopedia of Sociology*, edited by G. Ritzer. Malden, MA: Blackwell.

Shevchenko, Olga. 2012. "Socialism." Pp. 1882–1886 in *The Wiley-Blackwell Encyclopedia of Globalization*, edited by G. Ritzer. Malden, MA: Wiley-Blackwell.

Schilling, Chris. 2012. *The Body and Social Theory*. 3rd ed. London: Sage.

Schlosser, Eric. 2001. *Fast Food Nation*. New York: Harper Perennial.

Schlueter Elmar and Peer Scheepers. 2010. "The Relationship between Outgroup Size and Anti-Outgroup Attitudes: A Theoretical Synthesis and Empirical Test of Group Threat and Intergroup Contact Theory." *Social Science Research* 39(2): 285–295.

Schilt, Kristen. 2010. *Just One of the Guys? Transgender Men and the Persistence of Inequality*. University of Chicago Press.

Schmidt, John, Kris Warner, and Sarika Gupta. 2010. *The High Budgetary Cost of Incarceration*. Washington, DC: Center for Economic and Policy Research.

Schmitt, Vanessa and Julia Fischer. 2009. "Inferential Reasoning and Modality Dependent Discrimination Learning in Olive Baboons (*Papio hamadryas anubis*)." *Journal of Comparative Psychology* 123(3): 316–325.

Schneider, Barbara and David Stevenson. 1999. *The Ambitious Generation: America's Teenagers, Motivated but Directionless*. New Haven, CT: Yale University Press.

Schneider, Silke L. 2008. "Anti-Immigrant Attitudes in Europe: Outgroup Size and Perceived Ethnic Threat." *European Sociological Review* 24(1): 53–67.

Schoch, Deborah and Rong-Gong Lin II. 2007. "15 Years After L.A. Riots, Tension Still High; Promises Made in the Wake of Three Days of Violence Remain Unfulfilled, Residents Tell City Officials at South Los Angeles Events." Retrieved March 31, 2012 (http://pqasb.pqarchiver.com/latimes/access/1261997281.html?dids=1261997281:1261997281&FMT=ABS&FMTS=ABS:FT&type=current&date=Apr+29%2C+2007&author=Deborah+Schoch%3B+Rong-Gong+Lin+II&pub=Los+Angeles+Times&desc=15+years+after+L.A.+riots%2C+tension+still+high%3B+Promises+made+in+the+wake+of+three+days+of+violence+remain+unfulfilled%2C+residents+tell+city+officials+at+South+Los+Angeles+events.&pqatl=google).

Schock, Kurt. 2013. "Anticolonial Movements." Pp. 66–70 in *The Wiley-Blackwell Encyclopedia of Social and Political Movements*, 3 vols., by D. A. Snow, D. Della Porta, B. Klandermans, and D. McAdam. Malden, MA: Wiley-Blackwell.

Scholz, Trebor, ed. *Digital Labor: The Internet as Playground and Factory*. NY: Routledge, 2013.

Schor, Juliet. 1993. *The Overworked American: The Unexpected Decline of Leisure*. New York: Basic Books.

Schor, Juliet. 1998. *The Overspent American: Why We Want What We Don't Need*. New York: Basic Books.

Schor, Juliet. 2005. *Born to Buy: The Commercialized Child and the New Consumer Culture*. New York: Scribner.

Schorzman, Cindy M., et al. 2007. "Body Art: Attitudes and Practices Regarding Body Piercing Among Urban Undergraduates." *Journal of the American Osteopathic Association* 107: 432–438.

Schroeder, Jonathan E. 2007. "Brand Culture." Pp. 351–353 in *The Blackwell Encyclopedia of Sociology*, edited by G. Ritzer. Malden, MA: Blackwell.

Schroyer, Trent. 1970. "Toward a Critical Theory of Advanced Industrial Society." Pp. 210–234 in *Recent Sociology: No. 2*, edited by H. P. Dreitzel. New York: Macmillan.

Schudson, Michael. 1989. "The Sociology of New Production." *Media, Culture and Society* 11: 263–282.

Schudson, Michael. 1987. *Advertising, the Uneasy Persuasion: Its Dubious Impact on American Society.* New York: Basic Books.

Schumpeter, Joseph. 1976. *Capitalism, Socialism and Democracy.* 5th ed. London: George Allen and Unwin.

Schuster, Liza. 2012a. "Asylum-seekers." Pp. 89–92 in *The Wiley-Blackwell Encyclopedia of Globalization,* edited by George Ritzer. Malden, MA: Wiley-Blackwell.

Schuster, Liza. 2012b. "Migration Controls." Pp. 1388–90 in *The Wiley-Blackwell Encyclopedia of Globalization,* edited by George Ritzer. Malden, MA: Wiley-Blackwell.

Schutt, Russell K. 2007. "Secondary Data Analysis." Pp. 4127–29 in *The Blackwell Encyclopedia of Sociology,* edited by George Ritzer. Malden. MA: Blackwell.

Schwalbe, Michael, Sandra Godwin, Daphne Holden, Douglas Schrock, Shealy Thompson, and Michele Wolkomir. 2000. "Generic Processes in the Reproduction of Inequality: An Interactionist Analysis." *Social Forces* 79: 419–452.

Schwartz, H. 1986. *Never Satisfied: a Cultural History of Diets, Fantasies and Fat.* New York: Anchor Books.

Schwartz, Pepper (with Richard Feller, Elaine Fox, and Dr. Philip Sarrel Feller). 1970. *Sex and the Yale Student.* Committee on Human Sexuality, Yale University.

Schwartz, Pepper. 2007. *Prime: Adventures and Advice in Sex, Love, and the Sensual Years.* New York: HarperCollins.

Schwartz, Pepper and Philip Blumstein. 1983. *American Couples: Money, Work and Sex.* New York: Morrow.

Schwartz, Pepper. 1971. *The Student Guide to Sex on Campus,* by the Student Committee on Human Sexuality at Yale, edited by R. Feller, E. Fox, and P. Schwartz. Signet Books.

Schweinhart, Lawrence J. W., Steven Barnett, and Clive R. Belfield. 2005. *Lifetime Effects: The High/Scope Perry Preschool Study Through Age 40.* High/Scope Press.

Schwirian, Kent. 2007. "Ecological Models of Urban Form: Concentric Zone Model, the Sector Model, and the Multiple Nuclei Model." Pp. 1277–1281 in *The Blackwell Encyclopedia of Sociology,* edited by G. Ritzer. Malden, MA: Blackwell.

Schwirtz, Michael. 2010. "In Information War, Documentary is the Latest Salvo." *New York Times,* August 1, p. 10.

Sciolino, Elaine. 2007. "Sarkozy Pledges Crackdown on Rioters." *New York Times,* November 29, p. A8.

Scott, Amy. 2011. "Pumping Up the Pomp: An Exploration of Femininity and Female Bodybuilding." *Explorations in Anthropology* 11: 70–88.

Scott, Austin. 1982. "The Media's Treatment of Blacks: A Story of Distortion." *Los Angeles Times,* September 5.

Scott, Barbara Marliene and Mary Ann A. Schwartz. 2008. *Sociology: Making Sense of the Social World.* New York: Allyn and Bacon.

Scott, W. Richard. 2008. *Institutions and Organisations: Ideas and Interests.* 3rd ed. Thousand Oaks: Sage.

Scraton, Sheila. 2007. "Leisure." Pp. 2588–2592 in *The Blackwell Encyclopedia of Sociology,* edited by G. Ritzer. Malden, MA: Blackwell.

Sedgwick, Eve Kasofsky. 1991. *The Epistemology of the Closet.* London: Harvester Wheatsheaf.

Segal, David. 2010. "Is Italy Too Italian?" *New York Times Business,* August 1, pp. 1, 6.

Segan, Sascha. 2011. "Life Behind the Great Firewall of China." *PCMag.com,* June 27. Retrieved September 12, 2011 (http://www.pcmag.com/slideshow/story/266213/life-behind-the-great-firewall-of-china).

Sekulic, Dusko. 2007a. "Ethic Cleansing." Pp. 1450–1452 in *The Blackwell Encyclopedia of Sociology,* edited by G. Ritzer. Malden, MA: Blackwell.

Sekulic, Dusko. 2007b. "Social Change." Pp. 4360–4364 in *The Blackwell Encyclopedia of Sociology,* edited by G. Ritzer. Malden, MA: Blackwell.

Sekulic, Dusko. 2007c. "Values; Global." Pp. 5172–5176 in *The Blackwell Encyclopedia of Sociology,* edited by G. Ritzer. Malden, MA: Blackwell.

Seltzer, Judith A. 2007. "Intimate Union Formation and Dissolution." Pp. 2414–2418 in *The Blackwell Encyclopedia of Sociology,* edited by G. Ritzer. Malden, MA: Blackwell.

Sen, Amartya. 2011. "Quality of Life: India vs. China." *New York Review of Books,* May 12. Retrieved June 5, 2011 (http://www.nybooks.com/articles/archives/2011/may/12/quality-life-india-vs-china/).

Sen, Jai, Anita Anand, Arturo Escobar, and Peter Waterman, eds. 2004. *World Social Forum: Challenging Empires.* New Delhi: Viveka Foundation.

Sengupta, Somini. 2012. "With a Billion Birthdays on File, Facebook Adds a Gift Store." *New York Times,* November 27.

Serra-Majem, Luis and Joy Ngo. 2012. "Undernurition." Pp. 2055–2058 in *The Wiley Blackwell Encyclopedia of Globalization,* edited by G. Ritzer. Oxford: Blackwell.

Serrano, Alfonso. 2006. "E. Coli Outbreak Linked to Taco Bell." *CBS News,* December 4. Retrieved May 26, 2011 (http://www.cbsnews.com/stories/2006/12/04/health/main2227678.shtml).

Settle, Jaime E., Christopher T. Dawes, Nicholas A. Christakis, and James H. Fowler. 2010. "Friendships Moderate an Association between a Dopamine Gene Variant and Political Ideology." *The Journal of Politics* 72: 1189–1198.

Shahbaz, Muhammad. 2010. "Income Inequality, Economic Growth and Non-linearity: A Case of Pakistan." *International Journal of Social Economics* 37(8): 613–636.

Shamir, Ronen. 2005. "Without Borders? Notes on Globalization as a Mobility Regime." *Sociological Theory* 23(2): 197–217.

Shane, Scott. 2010. "Keeping Secrets WikiSafe." *New York Times,* December 12, p. WK1.

Shane, Scott and Michael Gordon. 2008. "Dissident's Tale of Epic Escape from Iran's Vise." *New York Times,* July 13.

Shanker, T., 2011. "U.S. Accuses China and Russia of Internet Espionage." *New York Times.* Retrieved November 6, 2011 (http://www.nytimes.com/2011/11/04/world/us-report-accuses-china-and-russia-of-internet-spying.html?scp=2&sq=china%20russia&st=cse).

Shattuck, Roger. 1980. *The Forbidden Experiment: The Story of the Wild Boy.* New York: Kodansha Globe.

Shauman, Kimberlee A. 2010. "Gender Asymmetry in Family Migration: Occupational Inequality or Interspousal Comparative Advantage?" *Journal of Marriage and Family* 72: 375–392.

Shavit, Yossi. 1990. "Segregation, Tracking, and the Educational Attainment of Minorities: Arabs and Oriental Jews in Israel." *American Sociological Review* 55: 115–126.

Shaw, Susan and Janet Lee. 2009. *Women's Voices, Feminist Visions.* New York: McGraw-Hill.

Shear, Michael D. 2013. "Obama Calls for 'Moral Courage' at Naval Academy Graduation." *New York Times,* May 24.

Shehan, Constance and Susan Cody. 2007. "Inequalities in Marriage." Pp. 2301–2304 in *The Blackwell Encyclopedia of Sociology,* edited by G. Ritzer. Malden, MA: Blackwell.

Shehata, Adam. 2010. "'Marking Journalistic Independence: Official Dominance and the Rule of Product Substitution in Swedish Press Coverage." *European Journal of Communication* 25: 123–137.

Sheldon, Jane. 2004. "Gender Stereotypes in Educational Software for Young Children." *Sex Roles* 51(7/8).

Shell, Ellen Ruppel. 2009. *Cheap: The High Cost of Discount Culture.* New York: Penguin.

Shelley, Louise, John Picarelli, and Chris Corpora. 2011. "Global Crime Inc." Pp. 141–169 in *Beyond Sovereignty: Issues for a Global Agenda,* edited by M. Cusimano Love. 4th ed. Boston: Wadsworth, Cengage Learning.

Shepard, Gary. 2007. "Cults: Social Psychological Concepts." Pp. 884–887 in *The Blackwell Encyclopedia of Sociology,* edited by G. Ritzer. Malden, MA: Blackwell.

Shepard, Gordon. 2007. "Socialization, Anticipatory." Pp. 4569–4570 in *The Blackwell Encyclopedia of Sociology*, edited by G. Ritzer. Malden, MA: Blackwell.

Sherif, Muzafer, O. J. Harvey, William R. Hood, Carolyn W. Sherif, and Jack White. [1954] 1961. *Intergroup Conflict and Cooperation: The Robbers Cave Experiment*. Norman: University of Oklahoma Book Exchange.

Shinberg, Diane S. 2007. "Women's Health." Pp. 5275–5279 in *The Blackwell Encyclopedia of Sociology*, edited by G. Ritzer. Malden, MA: Blackwell.

Shirky, Clay. 2011. "The Political Power of Social Media." *Foreign Affairs*, January/February.

Shiva, Vandana. 2002. *Water Wars: Privatization, Pollution, and Profit*. Cambridge, MA: South End Press.

Shock, Kurt. 2007. "Social Movements, Nonviolent." Pp. 4458–4463 in *The Blackwell Encyclopedia of Sociology*, edited by G. Ritzer. Malden, MA: Blackwell.

Shroedel, Jean Reith and Pamela Fiber. 2000. "Lesbian and Gay Policy Priorities: Commonality and Difference." Pp. 97–118 in *The Politics of Gay Rights*, edited by C. A. Rimmerman, K. D. Wald, and C. Wilcox. Chicago: University of Chicago Press.

Shwirian, Kent. 2007. "Ecological Models of Urban Form: Concentric Zone Model, the Sector Model, and the Multiple Nuclei Model." Pp. 1277–1281 in *The Blackwell Encyclopedia of Sociology*, edited by G. Ritzer. Malden, MA: Blackwell.

Sica, Alan. 2008. "Robert K. Merton." Pp. 151–167 in *Key Sociological Thinkers*, edited by R. Stones. 2nd ed. Basingstoke, UK: Palgrave Macmillan.

Siebold, Guy L. 2007. "The Essence of Military Cohesion." *Armed Forces and Society* 33(2): 286–295.

Silver, Hilary. 2007. "Disasters." Pp. 1174–1176 in *The Blackwell Encyclopedia of Sociology*, edited by G. Ritzer. Malden, MA: Blackwell.

Silvestri, Marisa and Crowther-Dowey Chris. 2008. *Gender and Crime*. Thousand Oaks, CA: Sage.

Simmel, Georg. [1903] 1971. "The Metropolis and Mental Life." In *Georg Simmel: On Individuality and Social Forms*, edited by D. Levine. Chicago: University of Chicago Press.

Simmel, Georg. [1904] 1971. "Fashion." Pp. 294–323 in *Georg Simmel: On Individuality and Social Forms*, edited by D. Levine. Chicago: University of Chicago Press.

Simmel, Georg. [1906] 1950. "The Secret and the Secret Society." Pp. 307–376 in *The Sociology of Georg Simmel*, edited by K. H. Wolff. New York: Free Press.

Simmel, Georg. [1907] 1978. *The Philosophy of Money*, edited and translated by T. Bottomore and D. Frisby. London: Routledge and Kegan Paul.

Simmel, Georg. [1908] 1971a. "Domination." Pp. 96–120 in *Georg Simmel: On Individuality and Social Forms*, edited by D. Levine. Chicago: University of Chicago Press.

Simmel, Georg. [1908] 1971b. "The Poor." Pp. 150–178 in *Georg Simmel: On Individuality and Social Forms*, edited by D. Levine. Chicago: University of Chicago Press.

Simmel, Georg. [1908] 1971c. "The Stranger." Pp. 143–149 in *Georg Simmel: On Individuality and Social Forms*, edited by D. Levine. Chicago: University of Chicago Press.

Simmel, Georg. 1950. *The Sociology of Georg Simmel*, edited and translated by K. Wolff. New York: Free Press.

Simon, Bryant. 2009. *Everything but the Coffee: Learning about America from Starbucks*. Berkeley: University of California Press.

Simon, Bryant. 2011. *Everything but the Coffee: Learning about America from Starbucks*. Berkeley: University of California Press.

Simon, David R. 2012. *Elite Deviance*. 10th ed. Boston: Pearson/Allyn and Bacon.

Simon, Herbert A. [1945] 1976. *Administrative Behavior*. New York: Macmillan.

Simon, Rita J. and Jean Landis. 1991. *The Crimes Women Commit, the Punishments They Receive*. Lexington: Lexington Books.

Simons, Marlise. 2010a. "France: Roma Policy Challenged." *New York Times*, August 28.

Simons, Marlise. 2010b. "International Court Adds Genocide to Charges against Sudan Leader." (http://www.nytimes.com/2010/07/13/world/africa/13hague.html).

Simons, Marlise. 2010c. "Rights Panel Criticizes France over Roma Policy." *New York Times*, August 27.

Simpson, Colton. 2006. *Inside the Crips: Life Inside L.A.'s Most Notorious Gang*. St. Martin's Griffin.

Simpson, George Eaton and J. Milton Yinger. 1985. *Racial and Cultural Minorities: An Analysis of Prejudice and Discrimination*. 5th ed. New York: Plenum Press.

Simpson, Sally S. 2002. *Corporate Crime, Law, and Social Control*. New York: Cambridge University Press.

Simpson, Sally and David Weisburd, eds. 2009. *The Criminology of White-Collar Crime*. New York: Springer.

Sims, Barbara. 2007. "Crime, Radical/Marxist Theories of." Pp. 839–842 in *The Blackwell Encyclopedia of Sociology*, edited by G. Ritzer. Malden, MA: Blackwell.

Singer, Natasha. 2009. "Lawmakers Seek to Curb Drug Commercials." *New York Times*, July 27.

Singer, Natasha. 2010. "The Financial Time Bomb of Longer Lives." *New York Times*, October 16.

Singer, Peter. 1996. *Marx: A Very Short Introduction*. New York: Oxford University Press.

Singh, Devendra and Dorian Singh. 2011. "Shape and Significance of Feminine Beauty: An Evolutionary Perspective." *Sex Roles* 64: 723–731.

Sirkin, Monroe G., Rosemarie Hirsch, William Mosher, Chris Moriarty, and Nancy Sonnenfeld. 2011. "Changing Methods of NCHS Surveys: 1960–2010 and Beyond." *Morbidity and Mortality Weekly Report Supplements* 60(7): 42–48.

Sisario, B., 2011. "Master of the Media Marketplace, and Its Demanding Gatekeeper." *New York Times*. Retrieved November 5, 2011 (http://www.nytimes.com/2011/10/07/business/media/master-of-the-media-marketplace-and-its-demanding-gatekeeper.html?scp=5&sq=music%20industry&st=cse).

Sites, William and Virginia Parks. 2011. "What Do We Really Know about Racial Inequality? Labor Markets, Politics, and the Historical Basis of Black Economic Fortunes." *Politics and Society* 39(1): 40–73.

Sitton, John F., ed. 2010. *Marx Today: Selected Works and Recent Debates*. New York: Palgrave Macmillan.

Sivalingam, G. 1994. *The Economic and Social Impact of Expert Processing Zones: The Case of Malaysia*. Geneva: International Labor Organization.

Skiba, Russel, Horner, Russel, Chung, Choong-Geun, Rausch, M. Karega, May, Seth, and Tobin, Tary. 2011. "Race Is Not Neutral: A National Investigation of African American and Latino Disproportionality in School Discipline." *School Psychology Review* 40(1): 85–107.

Skinner, Quentin, ed. 1985. *The Return of Grand Theories in the Human Sciences*. Cambridge, UK: Cambridge University Press.

Sklair, Leslie. 2002. *Globalization: Capitalism and Its Alternatives*. Oxford, UK: Oxford University Press.

Sklair, Leslie. 2012a. "Culture-Ideology of Consumerism." Pp. 377–379 in *The Wiley-Blackwell Encyclopedia of Globalization*, edited by G. Ritzer. Malden, MA: Wiley-Blackwell.

Sklair, Leslie. 2012b. "Transnational Capitalist Class." Pp. 2017–2019 in *The Wiley-Blackwell Encyclopedia of Globalization*, edited by G. Ritzer. Malden, MA: Wiley-Blackwell.

Sklair, Leslie. 2012c. "Transnational Corporations." Pp. 2019–2021 in *The Encyclopedia of Globalization*, edited by G. Ritzer. Malden, MA: Wiley-Blackwell.

Skloot, Rebecca. 2011. *The Immortal Life of Henrietta Lacks*. Broadway Edition.

Slackman, Michael. 2010a. "Citizens of Qatar, a Land of Affluence, Seek What Money Cannot Buy." *New York Times*, May 14, p. A7.

Slackman, Michael. 2010b. "Piercing the Sky Amid a Deflating Economy." *New York Times*, January 14, p. A10.

Slate, Nico. 2011. "Translating Race and Caste." *Journal of Historical Sociology* 24(1): 62–79.

Slater, Don. 1997. *Consumer Culture and Modernity*. Cambridge: Polity Press.

Slatton, Brittany Chevon and Joe R. Feagin. 2012. "Racial and Ethnic Issues: Critical Race Approaches in the United States." Pp. 287–303 in *The Wiley-Blackwell Companion to Sociology*, edited by G. Ritzer. Malden, MA: Wiley-Blackwell.

Smart, Barry, ed. 2011. *Post-industrial Society*. London: Sage.

Smelser, Neil. 1994. *Sociology*. Cambridge, MA: Blackwell.

Smith, Anthony D. 1990. "Towards a Global Culture?" Pp. 171–192 in *Global Culture: Nationalism, Globalization and Modernity*, edited by M. Featherstone. London: Sage.

Smith, David, Norman, Brock Ternes, James P. Ordner, Russell Schloemer, Gabriela Moran, Chris Goode, Joshua Homan, Anna Kern, Lucas Keefer, Nathan Moser, Kevin McCannon, Kaela Byers, Daniel Sullivan, and Rachel Craft. 2011. "Mapping the Great Recession: A Reader's Guide to the First Crisis of 21st Century Capita." *New Political Science* 33.

Smith, Dorothy. 2000. "Schooling for Inequality." *Signs* 25(4): 1147–1151.

Smith, Jackie. 2008. *Social Movements for Global Democracy*. Baltimore: Johns Hopkins University Press.

Smith, Jackie and Marina Karides. 2008. *Global Democracy and the World Social Forums*. Boulder, CO: Paradigm.

Smith, Paula. 2007. "Recidivism." Pp. 3818–3819 in *The Blackwell Encyclopedia of Sociology*, edited by G. Ritzer. Malden, MA: Blackwell.

Smith, Vicki. 1997. "New Forms of Work Organization." *Annual Review of Sociology* 23: 315–339.

Smock, Pamela L. and Wendy Manning. 2004. "Living Together Unmarried in the United States: Demographic Perspectives and Implications for Family Policy." *Law and Policy* 26(1): 87–117.

Smyth, Bruce. 2007. "Non-Resident Parents." Pp. 3223–3227 in *The Blackwell Encyclopedia of Sociology*, edited by George Ritzer. Malden, MA: Blackwell.

Snow, David A. 2013a. "Grievances, Individual and Mobilizing." Pp. 540–542 in *The Wiley-Blackwell Encyclopedia of Social and Political Movements*, 3 vols., edited by D. A. Snow, D. Della Porta, B. Klandermans, and D. McAdam. Malden, MA: Wiley-Blackwell.

Snow, David. 2013b. "Social Movements." Pp. 1200–1204 in *The Wiley-Blackwell Encyclopedia of Social and Political Movements*, 3 vols., edited by D. A. Snow, D. Della Porta, B. Klandermans, and D. McAdam. Malden, MA: Wiley-Blackwell.

Snow, David, Donatella Della Porta, Bert Klandermans, and Doug McAdam. 2013c. *The Wiley-Blackwell Encyclopedia of Social and Political Movements*, 3 vols. Malden, MA: Wiley-Blackwell.

Snow, David A. and Peter B. Owens. 2013. "Crowds (Gatherings) and Collective Behavior (Action)." Pp. 289–296 in *The Wiley-Blackwell Encyclopedia of Social and Political Movements*, 3 vols., edited by D. A. Snow, D. Della Porta, B. Klandermans, and D. McAdam. Malden, MA: Wiley-Blackwell.

Snow, David A., Sarah A. Soule, and Daniel M. Cress. 2005. "Identifying the Precipitants of Homeless Protest Across 17 U.S. Cities, 1980 to 1990." *Social Forces* 83: 1183–1210.

Snow, David, Sarah A. Soule, and Hanspeter Kriesi. 2008. *The Blackwell Companion to Social Movements*. Malden, MA: Blackwell.

Snyder, Margaret. 2006. "Unlikely Godmother: The UN and the Global Women's Movement." In *Global Feminism: Transnational Women's Activism, Organizing, and Human Rights*, edited by M. Marx Ferree and A. M. Tripp. New York: New York University Press.

Snyder, Patricia. 2007. "Survey Research." Pp. 4898–4900 in *The Blackwell Encyclopedia of Sociology*, edited by G. Ritzer. Malden, MA: Blackwell.

Snyder, R. Claire. 2008. "What Is Third-Wave Feminism? A New Directions Essay." *Signs* 34(1): 175–196.

Soja, Edward W. 1989. *Postmodern Geographies: The Reassertion of Space in Critical Social Theory*. London: Verso.

Song, Miri. 2007. "Racial Hierarchy." Pp. 3360–3364 in *The Blackwell Encyclopedia of Sociology*, edited by G. Ritzer. Malden, MA: Blackwell.

Sontag, Deborah. 2012. "Rebuilding in Haiti Lags After Billions in Post-Quake Aid." *New York Times*, December 23.

Southern Poverty Law Center (SPLC). 2012. "Hate Map." Retrieved March 31, 2011 (http://www.splcenter.org/get-informed/hate-map).

Soysal, Yasemin Nuhoglu. 2012. "Citizenship, Immigration, and the European Social Project: Rights and Obligations of Individuality." *The British Journal of Sociology* 63: 1–21.

"Special Forum on the Arab Revolutions." 2011. *Globalizations* 5(8).

Spector, Michael. 2007. "Damn Spam: The Losing War on Junk E-mail." *The New Yorker*, August 6.

Speicher Muñoz, Lisa. 2011. *Difference, Inequality, and Change: Social Diversity in the U.S.* Dubuque: Kendall Hunt.

Spencer, Herbert. 1851. *Social Statics*. London: Chapman.

Spencer, James H. 2004. "Los Angeles Since 1992: How Did the Economic Base of Riot-Torn Neighborhoods Fare After the Unrest?" *Race, Gender and Class* 11(1): 94–115.

Spitz, Herman H. 1999. "Beleaguered Pygmalion: A History of the Controversy over Claims that Teacher Expectancy Raises Intelligence." *Intelligence* 27(3): 199–234.

Spitz, Vivien. 2005. *Doctors from Hell: The Horrific Account of Nazi Experiments on Humans*. Boulder, CO: Sentient Publications.

Spotts, Greg and Robert Greenwald. 2005. *Wal-Mart: The High Cost of Low Price*. New York: Disinformation Press.

Srinivas, M. N. 2003. "An Obituary on Caste as a System." *Economic and Political Weekly* 38(5): 455–459.

Srivastava, Rahul and Matias Echanove. 2008. "Airoots Interviews Arjun Appadurai." Retrieved April 1, 2012 (http://www.airoots.org/2008/09/airoots-interviews-arjun-appadurai/).

Stacey, Judith. 1998. *Brave New Families*. Berkeley: University of California Press.

Stack, Carol B. 1974. *All Our Kin: Strategies for Survival in a Black Community*. New York: Basic Books.

Staff. 2002. "Another Addition to Dubai's Malls." *Gulf News*, October 30. Retrieved May 19, 2011 (http://gulfnews.com/news/gulf/uae/general/another-addition-to-dubai-s-malls-1.402095).

Staff. 2008. "Dubai Mall Set for August 28 Opening." *Gulf News*, April 9. Retrieved May 19, 2011 (http://gulfnews.com/business/construction/dubai-mall-set-for-august-28-opening-1.97114).

Standing, Guy. 1989. "Global Feminization through Flexible Labor: A Theme Revisited." *World Development* 27(3): 583–602.

Stark, Rodney and William Sims Bainbridge. 1979. "Of Churches, Sects, and Cults: Preliminary Concepts for a Theory of Religious Movements." *Journal for the Scientific Study of Religion* 18.

Starr, Paul. 1983. *The Social Transformation of American Medicine*. New York: Basic Books.

Starr, Paul. 2009. "Fighting the Wrong Health Care Battle." *New York Times*, November 29.

Starr, Paul. 2011a. "The Medicare Bind." *The American Prospect*, September 30. Retrieved March 31, 2012 (http://prospect.org/article/medicare-bind).

Starr, Paul. 2011b. *Remedy and Reaction: The Peculiar American Struggle over Health Care Reform*. New Haven, CT: Yale University Press.

Stearns, Cindy. 2009. "The Work of Breastfeeding." *Women's Studies Quarterly* 37: 63–80.

Stearns, Cindy A. 2011. "Cautionary Tale about Extended Breastfeeding and Weaning." *Health Care for Women International* 32: 538–554.

Stebbins, Robert. 1977. "The Meaning of Academic Performance: How Teachers Define a Classroom Situation." In *School Experience*, edited by P. Woods and M. Hammersly. New York: St. Martin's Press.

Stebbins, Robert A. 2007. "Leisure, Popular Culture and." Pp. 2596–2600 in *The Blackwell Encyclopedia of Sociology*, edited by G. Ritzer. Malden, MA: Blackwell.

Steele, Valerie. 2011. "The Homogenization Effect." *New York Times*, August 21.

Steinberg, Laurence and Kathryn C. Monahan. 2007. "Age Differences in Resistance to Peer Influence." *Developmental Psychology* 43: 1531–1543.

Steinfatt, Thomas. 2011. "Sex Trafficking in Cambodia: Fabricated Numbers Versus Empirical Evidence." *Crime, Law and Social Change* 56: 443–462.

Steinmetz, George. 2012. "Geopolitics." Pp. 800–823 in *The Wiley-Blackwell Encyclopedia of Globalization*, edited by G. Ritzer. Malden, MA: Wiley-Blackwell.

Steinmetz, Suzanne K. 1987. "Family Violence." In *Handbook of Marriage and the Family*, edited by M. B. Sussman and S. K. Steinmetz. New York: Plenum Press.

Steketee, Gail and Randy Frost. 2011. *Stuff: Compulsive Hoarding and the Meaning of Things*. Boston: Mariner Books.

Stepan-Norris, Judith and Caleb Southworth. 2007. "Churches as Organizational Resources: A

Case Study in the Geography of Religion and Political Voting in Postwar Detroit." *Social Science History* 31(3): 343–380.

Stets, Jan E. and Jonathan H. Turner, eds. 2007. *Handbook of the Sociology of Emotions.* New York: Springer.

Stevens, Mitchell L. 2001. *Kingdom of Children: Culture and Controversy in the Home Schooling Movement.* Princeton, NJ: Princeton University Press.

Stevens, Mitchell L. 2007. "Schooling, Home." Pp. 4032–4034 in *The Blackwell Encyclopedia of Sociology,* edited by G. Ritzer. Malden, MA: Blackwell.

Stevis, Dimitris. 2005. "The Globalization of Environment." *Globalizations* 2(3): 323–333.

Stewart, Lathonia Denise, and Richard Perlow. 2001. "Applicant Race, Job Status, and Racial Attitude as Predictors of Employment Discrimination." *Journal of Business and Psychology* 16(2): 259–275.

Stockdill, Brett C. 2013. "ACT UP (AIDS Coalition to Unleash Power)." Pp. 5–9 in *The Wiley-Blackwell Encyclopedia of Social and Political Movements,* 3 vols., edited by D. A. Snow, D. Della Porta, B. Klandermans, and D. McAdam. Malden, MA: Wiley-Blackwell.

Stokoe, Elizabeth. 2006. "On Ethnomethodology, Feminism, and the Analysis of Categorical Reference to Gender in Talk-in-Interaction." *The Sociological Review* 54: 3.

Stolow, Jeremy. 2004. "Transnationalism and the New Religio-politics: Reflections on a Jewish Orthodox Case." *Theory, Culture and Society* 21(2): 109–137.

Stone, Brad. 2009. "Spam Back to 94% of All E-Mail." *New York Times,* March 31.

Stone, Brad. 2010. "Chatroulette's Creator, 17, Introduces Himself." *New York Times,* February 13. Retrieved May 26, 2011 (http://bits.blogs.nytimes.com/2010/02/13/chatroulettes-founder-17-introduces-himself/).

Stone, Allucquère Rosanne. 1991. "Will the Real Body Please Stand Up?" In *Cyberspace: First Steps,* edited by M. Benedikt. Cambridge, MA: MIT Press.

Stone, Richard and Hao Xin. 2010. "Google Plots Exit Strategy as China Shores Up 'Great Firewall.'" *Science* 327: 402–403.

Stoolmiller, Michael. 1999. "Implications of the Restricted Range of Family Environments for Estimates of Heritability and Nonshared Environments in Behavior-Genetic Adoption Studies." *Psychological Bulletin* 125: 392-409.

Stouffer, Samuel A., Edward A. Suchman, Leland C. DeVinney, Shirley A. Star, and Robin M. Williams. 1949. *The American Soldier: Adjustment During Army Life.* Vol. 1. Princeton, NJ: Princeton University Press.

Strandbu, Ase and Ingela Lundin Kvalem. 2013. "Body Talk and Body Ideals among Adolescent Boys and Girls: A Mixed-Gender Focus Group Study." *Youth Society,* May.

Straus, Murry A. 1980. "Victims and Aggressors in Marital Violence." *American Behavioral Scientist* 23: 681–704.

Strauss, Anselm and Juliet Corbin. 1998. *Basics of Qualitative Research.* Thousand Oaks, CA: Sage.

Strobel, Frederick R. 1993. *Upward Dreams, Downward Mobility: The Economic Decline of the American Middle Class.* Lanham, MD: Rowman and Littlefield

Struck, Doug. 2007. "Warming Will Exacerbate Global Water Conflicts." *Washington Post,* October 22.

Stryker, Sheldon and Anne Statham Macke. 1978. "Status Inconsistency and Role Conflict." *Annual Review of Sociology* 4: 57–90.

Stryker, Sheldon and Richard T. Serpe. 1994. "Identity Salience and Psychological Centrality: Equivalent, Overlapping, or Complementary Concepts?" *Social Psychology Quarterly* 57: 16–35.

Stryker, Sheldon. 1980. *Symbolic Interactionism: A Social Structural Version.* Menlo Park, CA: Benjamin/Cummings.

Stuber, J. 2009. "Class, Culture, and Participation in the Collegiate Extra-Curriculum." *Sociological Forum* 4: 877–900.

Suárez-Orozco, Carola, Jean Rhodes, and Michael Milburn. 2009. "Unraveling the Immigrant Paradox: Academic Engagement and Disengagement among Recently Arrived Immigrant Youth." *Youth and Society* 41(2): 151–185.

Subramaniam, Mangala, David Whitlock, and Beth Williford. 2012. "Water Crisis." Pp. 2210–2212 in *The Wiley-Blackwell Encyclopedia of Globalization,* edited by G. Ritzer. Malden, MA: Wiley-Blackwell.

Subramanian, Ramesh. 2012. "Computer Viruses." Pp. 270–274 in *Wiley-Blackwell Encyclopedia of Globalization,* edited by G. Ritzer. Malden, MA: Wiley-Blackwell.

Subramanian, Ramesh and Eddan Katz, eds. 2011. *The Global Flow of Information: Legal, Social, and Cultural Perspectives.* New York: New York University Press.

Sullivan, Robert. 2011. "Swamp Dreams." *New York Magazine,* August 21.

Sullivan, John. 2010. "Attacks on Journalists and 'New Media' in Mexico's Drug War: A Power and Counter Power Assessment." Retrieved March 31, 2012 (http://smallwarsjournal.com/jrnl/art/attacks-on-journalists-and-new-media-in-mexicos-drug-war).

Sumner, Colin. 1994. *The Sociology of Deviance: An Obituary.* New York: Continuum.

Sumner, William Graham. [1906] 1940. *Folkways: A Study of the Sociological Implications of Usages, Manners, Customs, Mores and Morals.* Boston: Ginn.

Suroor, Hasan. 2011. "U.K. to Raise Diplomatic Profile in India, China." *The Hindu,* May 11. Retrieved May 26, 2011 (http://www.thehindu.com/news/article2009518.ece).

Sutherland, Edwin H. 1947. *Criminology.* 4th ed. Philadelphia: Lippincott.

Sutherland, Edwin H. 1924. *Principles of Criminology.* Chicago: University of Chicago Press.

Swatos, William H., Jr. N.d. "Church-Sect Theory." In the *Encyclopedia of Religion and Society,* edited by W. H. Swatos Jr. Retrieved January 25, 2012 (http://hirr.hartsem.edu/ency/cstheory.htm).

Swatos, William H., Jr. 2007a. "Denomination." Pp. 1051–1056 in The *Blackwell Encyclopedia of Sociology,* edited by G. Ritzer. Malden, MA: Blackwell.

Swatos, William H., Jr. 2007b. "Sect." Pp. 4135–4140 in *The Blackwell Encyclopedia of Sociology,* edited by G. Ritzer. Malden, MA: Blackwell.

Swedberg, Richard. 2007. *Principles of Economic Sociology.* Princeton, NJ: Princeton University Press.

Swiss Federal Statistical Office. 2012. "Swiss Statistics: The Statistical Encyclopedia." Retrieved February 28, 2012 (http://www.bfs.admin.ch/bfs/portal/en/index/infothek/lexikon.topic.1.html).

Sykes, Gresham. [1958] 2007. *The Society of Captives: A Study of a Maximum Security Prison.* Princeton, NJ: Princeton University Press.

Symantec. 2009. *MessageLabs Intelligence (Symantec) Report.* Mountain View, CA: Author.

Sztompka, Piotr. 1993. *The Sociology of Social Change.* West Sussex, UK: Wiley-Blackwell.

Tabuchi, Hiroko. 2010. "Beef Bowl Economics: In Japan, a Price War at Popular Restaurants Is the Face of Deflation." *New York Times,* January 30, pp. B1, B6.

Tan, Celine. 2007. "Liberalization." Pp. 735–739 in *Encyclopedia of Globalization,* edited by J. A. Scholte and R. Robertson. New York: MTM Publishing.

Tansey, Oisín. 2006. "Process Tracing and Elite Interviewing." Paper presented at the annual meeting of the American Political Science Association, Philadelphia, August 31.

Tavernise, Sabrina. 2010. "Pakistan's Elite Pay Few Taxes, Widening Gap." *New York Times,* July 19, pp. A1, A9.

Taylor, J. L. 2007. "Buddhism." Pp. 108–113 in *Encyclopedia of Globalization,* edited by J. A. Scholte and R. Robertson. New York: MTM.

Taylor, Paul C. 2011. "William Edward Burghardt Du Bois." Pp. 426–447 in *The Wiley-Blackwell Companion to Major Social Theorists: Volume 1. Classical Theorists,* edited by G. Ritzer and J. Stepnisky. Malden, MA: Wiley-Blackwell.

Taylor, Paul, Cary Funk, and April Clark. 2007. *From 1997 to 2007, Fewer Mothers Prefer Full-Time Work.* Washington, DC: Pew Research Center.

Taylor, Yvette. 2007. "Sexualities and Consumption." Pp. 4256–4260 in *The Blackwell Encyclopedia of Sociology,* edited by G. Ritzer. Malden, MA: Blackwell.

Teivainen, Teivo. 2007. "World Social Forum." Pp. 1302–1304 in *Encyclopedia of Globalization,* edited by J. A. Scholte and R. Robertson. New York: MTM.

Teltumbde, Anand. 2011. *The Persistence of Caste: India's Hidden Apartheid and the Khairlanji Murders.* London: Zed Books.

Terranova, Tiziana. 2013. "Free Labor." Pp. 33–57 in *Digital Labor: The Internet as Playground and Factory*, edited by T. Scholz. New York: Routledge.

Tescione, Sara. 2013. "Civil Disobedience." Pp. 191–193 in *The Wiley-Blackwell Encyclopedia of Social and Political Movements*, 3 vols., edited by D. A. Snow, D. Della Porta, B. Klandermans, and D. McAdam. Malden, MA: Wiley-Blackwell.

Tewksbury, Richard. 2007. "Sexual Deviance." Pp. 4230–32 in *The Blackwell Encyclopedia of Sociology,* edited by George Ritzer. Malden, MA: Blackwell.

"That Pesky Glass Ceiling." 2011. *Diverse: Issues in Higher Education* 27: 7.

Thoits, Peggy A. 1985. "Self-Labeling Processes in Mental Illness: The Role of Emotional Deviance." *American Journal of Sociology* 91(2): 221–249.

Thoits, Peggy. 2011. "Perceived Social Support and the Voluntary, Mixed, or Pressured Use of Mental Health Services." *Society and Mental Health* 1: 4–19.

Thomas, George. 2012. "Christianity." Pp. 179–187 in *The Wiley-Blackwell Encyclopedia of Globalization*, edited by G. Ritzer. Malden, MA: Wiley-Blackwell.

Thomas, Landon, Jr. 2011. "Pondering a Day: Leaving the Euro." *New York Times*, December 13, pp. B1, B8.

Thomas, Samuel S. 2009. "Early Modern Midwifery: Splitting the Profession, Connecting the History." *Journal of Social History* 43: 115–138.

Thomas, William I. and Dorothy S. Thomas. 1928. *The Child in America: Behavior Problems and Programs.* New York: Knopf.

Thompson, Ginger and Marc Lacey. 2010. "U.S. and Mexico Revise Joint Antidrug Strategy." *New York Times*, March 23. Retrieved March 31, 2012 (http://www.nytimes.com/2010/03/24/world/americas/24mexico.html).

Thompson, Ginger. 2008. "Fewer People Are Entering US Illegally, Report Says." *New York Times*, October 3.

Thorn, Elizabeth. 2007. "Gender, Work, and Family." Pp. 1880–1885 in *The Blackwell Encyclopedia of Sociology*, edited by G. Ritzer. Malden, MA: Blackwell.

Thorne, Barrie. 1993. *Gender Play: Girls and Boys in School.* New Brunswick, NJ: Rutgers University Press.

Thornton, Arland, William Axinn, and Y. Xie. 2007. *Marriage and Cohabitation.* Chicago: University of Chicago Press.

Thornton, Alex and Katherine McAuliffe. 2006. "Teaching in Wild Meerkats." *Science* 313: 227–229.

Thornton, S. 1995. *Club Culture: Music, Media and Subcultural Capital.* Cambridge, UK: Polity Press.

Thrane, Lisa E. and Xiaojin Chen. 2010. "Impact of Running Away on Girls' Sexual Onset." *Journal of Adolescent Health* 46(1): 32–36.

Tibi, Bassam. 2002. *The Challenge of Fundamentalism: Political Islam and the New World Order.* Berkeley: University of California Press.

Tibi, Bassam. 2007. *Political Islam, World Politics and Europe.* London: Routledge.

Tierney, John. 2013. "Prison Population Can Shrink When Police Crowd Streets." *New York Times*, January 25.

Timasheff, N. S. 1965. *War and Revolution.* New York: Sheed and Ward.

Timberlake, Michael and Xiulian Ma. 2007. "Cities and Globalization." Pp. 254–271 in *The Blackwell Companion to Globalization*, edited by G. Ritzer. Malden, MA: Blackwell.

"Timeline: China's Net Censorship." 2010. *BBC News*, June 29. Retrieved May 23, 2011 (http://www.bbc.co.uk/news/10449139).

Timmermans, Stefan and Hyeyoung Oh. 2010. "The Continued Social Transformation of the Medical Profession." *Journal of Health and Social Behavior* 51: S94–S106.

Timmons, Heather and Sruthi Gottipati. 2012. "Indian Women March: 'That Girl Could Have Been Any of Us.'" *New York Times*, December 30.

Timmons, Heather and Hari Kumar. 2013. "Indian Woman Is Gang-Raped after Bus Ride." *New York Times*, January 13.

Timms, Jill. 2012. "Labor Movements." Pp. 1259–1261 in *The Encyclopedia of Globalization*, edited by G. Ritzer. Malden, MA: Wiley-Blackwell.

Tobacco Public Policy Center at Capital University Law School. 2006. "Ohio's Tobacco Law Resource." Retrieved May 23, 2011 (http://www.law.capital.edu/tobacco/federal_laws.asp).

Tocqueville, Alex de. [1835–1840] 1969. *Democracy in America.* Garden City, NY: Doubleday.

Toennies, Ferdinand. [1887] 1957. *Community and Society.* New York: Harper Torchbooks.

Tomlinson, John. 1999. *Globalization and Culture.* Chicago: University of Chicago Press.

Tomlinson, John. 2000. "Globalization and Cultural Identity." Pp. 269–277 in *The Global Transformations Reader*, edited by D. Held and A. McGrew. Cambridge: Polity.

Tomlinson, John. 2012. "Cultural Imperialism." Pp. 371–374 in *The Wiley-Blackwell Encyclopedia of Globalization*, edited by G. Ritzer. Malden, MA: Wiley-Blackwell.

Tong, Rosemarie. 2009. *Feminist Thought: A More Comprehensive Introduction.* 3rd ed. Boulder: Westview Press.

Tönnies, F. [1887] 1963. *Community and Society.* New York: Harper and Row.

Toobin, Jeffrey. 2009. "The Celebrity Defense." *The New Yorker*, December 14: 50.

"Top Sites in China." 2011. *Alexa.* Retrieved June 20, 2011 (http://www.alexa.com/topsites/countries/CN).

Torpey, John C. 2000. *The Invention of the Passport: Citizenship, Surveillance, and the State.* New York: Cambridge University Press.

Torpey, John. 2012. "Passports." Pp. 1644–1647 in *The Wiley-Blackwell Encyclopedia of Globalization*, edited by G. Ritzer. Malden, MA: Wiley-Blackwell.

Townsend, Peter. 2010. "The Meaning of Poverty." *British Journal of Sociology* 61: 85–102.

Trask, Bahira Sherif. 2010. *Globalization and Families: Accelerated Systemic Social Change.* New York: Springer.

Trebay, Guy. 2008. "Tattoos Gain Even More Visibility." *New York Times*, September 24. Accessed December 20, 2011 (http://www.nytimes.com/2008/09/25/fashion/25tattoo.html?scp=1&sq=September%2025,%202008%20tattoo&st=cse).

Treiman, Donald J. 2007. "Occupational Mobility." Pp. 3240–3244 in *The Blackwell Encyclopedia of Sociology*, edited by G. Ritzer. Malden, MA: Blackwell.

Trepagnier, Barbara. 2010. *Silent Racism: How Well-Meaning People Perpetuate the Racial Divide.* Boulder, CO: Paradigm.

Troeltsch, Ernst. 1932. *The Social Teaching of the Christian Churches*, translated by O. Wyon. New York: Macmillan.

Tsutsui, Kiyoteru and Christine Min Wotipka. 2004. "Global Civil Society and the International Human Rights Movement: Citizen Participation in Human Rights International Nongovernmental Organizations." *Social Forces* 83(2): 587–620.

Tuchman, Gaye. 1972. "Objectivity as Strategic Ritual: An Examination of Newsmen's Notions of Objectivity." *American Journal of Sociology* 77(4): 660–679.

Tufekci, Zeynep. 2010. "Internet Use and Social Ties of Americans: An Analysis of General Social Survey Data." Paper presented at Meetings of the American Sociological Association, Atlanta, Georgia.

Tugend, Alina. 2010. "Spending Less in a Recession, and Talking about It, Too." *New York Times*, February 13.

Tumber, Howard and Frank Webster. 2006. *Journalists under Fire: Information War and Journalistic Practices.* London: Sage.

Tumin, Melvin E. 1953. "Some Principles of Stratification: A Critical Analysis." *American Sociological Review* 18: 387–394.

Tunnell, Kenneth D. 2007. "Crime, Political." Pp. 835–836 in *The Blackwell Encyclopedia of Sociology*, edited by G. Ritzer. Malden, MA: Blackwell.

Turkle, Sherry. 1995. *Life on Screen: Identity in the Age of the Internet.* New York: Simon and Schuster.

Turkle, Sherry. 1997. *Life on Screen: Identity in the Age of the Internet.* New York: Touchstone.

Turkle, Sherry. 2011. *Alone Together: Why We Expect More from Technology and Less from Each Other.* New York: Basic Books.

Turner, Bryan S. 2007a. "Body and Cultural Sociology." Pp. 324–328 in *The Blackwell Encyclopedia of Sociology*, edited by G. Ritzer. Malden, MA: Blackwell.

Turner, Bryan S. 2007b. "Body and Society." Pp. 335–338 in *The Blackwell Encyclopedia of Sociology*, edited by G. Ritzer. Malden, MA: Blackwell.

Turner, Bryan. 2008. *The Body and Society: Explorations in Social Theory.* London: Sage.

Turner, Bryan S. 2010. "McCitizens: Risk, Coolness, and Irony in Contemporary Politics." Pp. 229–232 in *McDonaldization: The Reader,* edited by G. Ritzer. Thousand Oaks, CA: Pine Forge Press.

Turner, Bryan S. 2011. *Religion and Modern Society: Citizenship, Secularisation and the State.* Cambridge, UK: Cambridge University Press.

Turner, Fred. 2008. *From Counterculture to Cyberculture: Stewart Brand, the Whole Earth Network, and the Rise of Digital Utopianism.* Chicago: University of Chicago Press.

Turner, Jonathan. 2005. "A New Approach for Theoretically Integrating Micro and Macro Analysis." Pp. 403–422 in *The Sage Handbook of Sociology,* edited by C. Calhoun, C. Rojek, and B. Turner. London: Sage.

Turner, Jonathan. 2009. "A New Approach for Theoretically Integrating Micro and Macro Analysis." Pp. 403–422 in *The Sage Handbook of Sociology,* edited by C. Calhoun, C. Rojek, and B. Turner. London: Sage.

Turner, Jonathan H. 2010. "The Micro Basis of the Meso and Macro Social Realms." *Theoretical Principles of Sociology* 2: 271–301.

Turner, Jonathan and Barry Markovsky. 2007. "Micro-Macro Links." Pp. 2997–3004 in *The Blackwell Encyclopedia of Sociology,* edited by G. Ritzer. Malden, MA: Blackwell.

Turner, Leigh. 2007. "'First World Health Care at Third World Prices': Globalization, Bioethics and Medical Tourism." *BioSocieties* 2: 303–325.

Turner, Ralph H. 1978. "The Role and the Person." *American Journal of Sociology* 84: 1–23.

Turner, Ralph H. and Lewis M. Killian. 1987. *Collective Behavior.* 3rd ed. Englewood Cliffs, NJ: Prentice-Hall.

Turner, Victor. 1967. *The Forest of Symbols: Aspects of Ndembu Ritual.* Ithaca, NY: Cornell University Press.

Twaddle, Andrew C. 2007. "Sick Role." Pp. 4317–4320 in *The Blackwell Encyclopedia of Sociology,* edited by G. Ritzer. Malden, MA: Blackwell.

Tyerman, Andrew and Christopher Spencer. 1983. "A Critical Test of the Sherifs' Robber's Cave Experiments." *Small Group Research* 14(4): 515–531.

Tyrell, Hartmann. 2010. "History and Sociology—the First Century. From Ranke to Weber." *InterDisciplines: Journal of History and Sociology* 1(1): 94–111.

Uchitelle, Louis. 2010. "Another Shifting Industry." *New York Times,* January 19, pp. B1, B5.

Ultee, Wout. 2007a. "Mobility, Horizontal and Vertical." Pp. 3060–3061 in *The Blackwell Encyclopedia of Sociology,* edited by G. Ritzer. Malden, MA: Blackwell.

Ultee, Wout. 2007b. "Mobility, Intergenerational and Intragenerational." Pp. 3061–3062 in *The Blackwell Encyclopedia of Sociology,* edited by G. Ritzer. Malden, MA: Blackwell.

UNAIDS. 2008. "Report on the Global AIDS Epidemic." Geneva: Author.

UNAIDS. 2010. "Report on the Global AIDS Epidemic." Geneva: Author.

Ungar, Sheldon. 2012. "Ozone Depletion." Pp. 1630–1634 in *The Wiley-Blackwell Encyclopedia of Globalization,* edited by G. Ritzer. Malden, MA: Wiley-Blackwell.

United Nations. 2006. "Ending Violence against Women: From Words to Action Study of the Secretary-General, Fact Sheet." Retrieved March 31, 2012 (http://www.un.org/womenwatch/daw/vaw/launch/english/v.a.w-exeE-use.pdf).

United Nations Department of Economic and Social Affairs. 2010. *The World's Women 2010: Trends and Statistics.* New York: United Nations.

United Nations Global Initiative to Fight Human Trafficking. 2007. "Human Trafficking: The Facts." Retrieved March 31, 2012 (http://www.unglobalcompact.org/docs/issues_doc/labour/Forced_labour/HUMAN_TRAFFICKING_-_THE_FACTS_-_final.pdf).

United Nations Office on Drugs and Crime. 2010. "World Drug Report." Retrieved March 31, 2012 (http://www.unodc.org/unodc/en/data-and-analysis/WDR-2010.html).

United Nations Office on Drugs and Crime. 2012. *World Drug Report 2012* (United Nations publication, Sales No. E.12.XI.1).

UN Women. 2011. "Women, Poverty and Economics." Accessed December 29, 2011 (http://www.unifem.org/gender_issues/women_poverty_economics/).

Uriely, Natan and Yaniv Belhassen. 2005. "Drugs and Tourists' Experiences." *Journal of Travel Research* February 43(3): 238–246.

Urry, John. 2007. *Mobilities.* Cambridge: Polity.

U.S. Census Bureau. 2004. *American Community Survey: Selected Population Profiles,* S0201.

U.S. Census Bureau. 2009. "Statistical Abstracts of the United States, 2009." Retrieved March 31, 2012 (http://www.census.gov/compendia/statab).

U.S. Census Bureau. 2011a. "2010 Census Shows America's Diversity." Retrieved April 14, 2011 (http://2010.census.gov/news/releases/operations/cb11-cn125.html).

U.S. Census Bureau. 2011b. "Poverty." *Current Population Survey: Annual Social and Economic Supplement.* Retrieved March 31, 2012 (http://www.census.gov/hhes/www/cpstables/032011/pov/new01_100_01.htm).

U.S. Census Bureau. 2011c. "Statistical Abstract of the United States 2011" (Tables 225 and 226). Retrieved March 31, 2012 (http://www.census.gov/compendia/statab/2011/tables/11s0225.pdf).

U.S. Census Bureau. 2011d. "Statistical Abstract of the United States 2011" (Tables 227 and 228). Retrieved March 31, 2012 (http://www.census.gov/compendia/statab/2011/tables/11s0228.pdf).

U.S. Census Bureau. 2012. "Population." *The 2011 Statistical Abstract.* Retrieved March 31, 2012 (http://www.census.gov/compendia/statab/cats/population.html).

U.S. Census Bureau. 2013a. "International Programs." Retrieved October 27, 2013 (http://0-www.census.gov.iii-server.ualr.edu/population/international/).

U.S. Census Bureau. 2013b. "Trade in Goods with China." Retrieved February 14, 2013 (http://www.census.gov/foreign-trade/balance/c5700.html).

U.S. Census Bureau International Programs. 2012. "International Data Base." U.S. Census Bureau. Retrieved February 28, 2012 (http://www.census.gov/population/international/data/idb/country.php).

U.S. Commission on Civil Rights. 2000. "Voting Irregularities in Florida During the 2000 Presidential Election." Retrieved March 31, 2012 (http://www.usccr.gov/pubs/vote2000/report/exesum.htm).

U.S. Department of Commerce Economics and Statistics Administration, Executive Office of the President Office of Management and Budget, and White House Council on Women and Girls. 2011. "Women in America: Indicators of Economic and Social Well-being." Retrieved May 25, 2011 (http://www.whitehouse.gov/sites/default/files/rss_viewer/Women_in_America.pdf).

U.S. Department of Education, National Center for Education Statistics. 2009. *The Condition of Education 2009* (NCES 2009-081). Retrieved July 8, 2013 (www.nces.ed.gov/fast/facts/display.asp?id=91).

U.S. Department of Justice Office of Justice Programs. 2007. "Black Victims of Violent Crime." Washington, DC: U.S. Department of Justice.

U.S. Department of Labor, U.S. Bureau of Labor Statistics. 2009. "Ranks of Discouraged Workers and Others Marginally Attached to the Labor Force Rise during Recession." *Issues in Labor Statistics,* April.

U.S. Department of Labor, U.S. Bureau of Labor Statistics. 2013. "Earnings and Unemployment Rates by Educational Attainment." *Current Population Survey.* Office of Occupational Statistics and Employment Projections. Retrieved June 26, 2013 (www.bls.gov/emp/ep_chart_001.htm).

U.S. State Department. 2010. "Trafficking in Persons Report." Retrieved March 31, 2012 (www.state.gov/documents/organization/142980.pdf).

USA Today. 2005. "Sexual Assaults in Military Bring Shame, Not Action." Editorial/Opinion, March 27. Retrieved December 3, 2011 (http://www.usatoday.com/news/opinion/editorials/2005-03-27-our-view_x.htm).

Useem, Elizabeth L. 1992. "Middle Schools and Math Groups: Parents' Involvement in Children's Placement." *Sociology of Education* 65: 263–279.

Vago, Steven. 2004. *Social Change.* Upper Saddle River, NJ: Prentice Hall.

Vaidhyanathan, Siva. 2011. *The Googlization of Everything (and Why We Should Worry).* Berkeley: University of California Press.

Vail, D. Angus. 1999. "Tattoos Are Like Potato Chips . . . You Can't Have Just One: The Process of Becoming and Being a Collector." *Deviant Behavior* 20: 253–273.

Vail, D. Angus. 2007. "Body Modification." Pp. 328–330 in *The Blackwell Encyclopedia of Sociology*, edited by G. Ritzer. Malden, MA: Blackwell.

Vallone, Robert, Lee Ross, and Mark Lepper. 1985. "The Hostile Media Phenomenon: Biased Perception and Perceptions of Media Bias in Coverage of the Beirut Massacre." *Journal of Personality and Social Psychology* 49(3): 577–585.

Valocchi, Stephen. 2007. "Gay and Lesbian Movement." Pp. 1833–1838 in *The Blackwell Encyclopedia of Sociology*, edited by G. Ritzer. Malden, MA: Blackwell.

Valocchi, Stephen. 2013. "Gay and Lesbian Movement." Pp. 498–503 in *The Wiley-Blackwell Encyclopedia of Social and Political Movements*, 3 vols., edited by D. A. Snow, D. Della Porta, B. Klandermans, and D. McAdam. Malden, MA: Wiley-Blackwell.

Van De Belt, Thomas H, Lucien Engelen, Sivera Berben, and Lisette Schoonhoven. 2010. "Definition of Heath 2.0 and Medicine 2.0: A Systematic Review." *Journal of Medical Internet Research* 12, April–June. Retrieved March 31, 2012 (http://www.jmir.org/2010/2/e18/).

Van de Poel, Ellen, Ahmad Reza Hosseinpoor, Niko Speybroeck, Tom Van Ourti, and Jeanette Vega. 2008. "Socioeconomic Inequality in Malnutrition in Developing Countries." *Bulletin of the World Health Organization*.

Van de Werfhorst, Herman G. and Jonathan J. B. Mij. 2010. "Achievement Inequality and the Institutional Structure of Educational Systems: A Comparative Perspective." *Annual Review of Sociology* 36: 407–428.

Van den Berghe, Pierre L. 2007. "Race (Racism)." Pp. 3749–3751 in *The Blackwell Encyclopedia of Sociology*, edited by G. Ritzer. Malden, MA: Blackwell.

Van der Lippe, Tanja, Vincent Frey, and Milena Tsvetkova. 2012. "Outsourcing of Domestic Tasks: A Matter of Preferences?" *Journal of Family Issues*, December 6.

Van Dijk, Jan A. G. M. *The Network Society*. 3rd ed. Thousand Oaks, CA: Sage.

Van Gennep, Arnold. [1908] 1960. *The Rites of Passage*. London: Routledge and Kegan Paul.

Van Kessel, Ineke. 2013. "Antiapartheid Movements (South Africa)." Pp. 60–66 in *The Wiley-Blackwell Encyclopedia of Social and Political Movements*, 3 vols., edited by D. A. Snow, D. Della Porta, B. Klandermans, and D. McAdam. Malden, MA: Wiley-Blackwell.

Van Leeuwen, Marco H. D. and Ineke Maas. 2010. "Historical Studies of Social Mobility and Stratification." *Annual Review of Sociology* 36: 429–451.

Van Maanen, J. 1983. "The Moral Fix: On the Ethics of Field Work." In *Contemporary Field Research: Perspectives and Formulations*, edited by R. M. Emerson. Longrove, IL: Waveland Press.

Van Valen, L. 1974. "Brain Size and Intelligence in Man." *American Journal of Physical Anthropology* 40: 417–423.

Varcoe, Ian. 2007. "Historical and Comparative Methods." Pp. 2133–2136 in *The Blackwell Encyclopedia of Sociology*, edited by G. Ritzer. Malden, MA: Blackwell.

Vaughan, Diane. 1996. *The Challenger Launch Decision: Risky Technology, Culture, and Deviance at NASA*. Chicago: University of Chicago Press.

Veblen, Thorstein. [1899] 1994. *The Theory of the Leisure Class*. New York: Penguin Books.

Venkatesh, Alladi. 2007. "Postmodern Consumption." Pp. 3552–3556 in *The Blackwell Encyclopedia of Sociology*, edited by G. Ritzer. Malden, MA: Blackwell.

Venkatesh, Sudhir. 1994. "Learnin' the Trade: Conversations With a Gangsta." *Public Culture* 6: 319–341.

Venkatesh, Sudhir. 2002. "'Doin' the Hustle': Constructing the Ethnographer in the American Ghetto." *Ethnography* 3: 91–111.

Venkatesh, Sudhir. 2008. *Gang Leader for a Day: A Rogue Sociologist Takes to the Streets*. New York: Penguin.

Venturi, Robert, Denise Scott Brown, and Steven Izenour. 1972. *Learning From Las Vegas: The Forgotten Symbolism of Architectural Form*. Cambridge, MA: MIT Press.

Verkaik, Robert. 2006. "Sex Harassment in Armed Forces Is Rife, Say Women." *The Independent*, May 26. Retrieved December 3, 2011 (http://www.independent.co.uk/news/uk/crime/sex-harassment-in-armed-forces-is-rife-say-women-479769.html).

Vidal, John. 1997. *McLibel: Burger Culture on Trial*. New Press.

Villareal, Andres and Wei-hsin Yu. 2007. "Economic Globalization and Women's Employment: The Case of Manufacturing in Mexico." *American Sociological Review* 72(3): 365–389.

Vlasic, Bill. 2013. "Lawyer Outlines Challenges in New Job Fixing Detroit." *New York Times*, March 25.

Voas, David and Fenella Fleischman. 2012. "Islam Moves West: Religious Change in the First and Second Generations." *Annual Review of Sociology* 38: 525–545.

Vobejda, B. 1996. "Clinton Signs Welfare Bill Amid Division." *Washington Post*. Retrieved June 29, 2011 (http://www.washingtonpost.com/wp-srv/politics/special/welfare/stories/wf082396.htm).

Vogel, Ezra F. 2011. *Deng Xiaoping and the Transformation of China*. Cambridge, MA: Belknap Press of Harvard University Press.

Vom Lehn, Dirk. 2007. "Interaction." Pp. 2361–2365 in *The Blackwell Encyclopedia of Sociology*, edited by G. Ritzer. Malden, MA: Blackwell.

Waddington, Ivan. 2007. "Health and Sport." Pp. 2091–2095 in *The Blackwell Encyclopedia of Sociology*, edited by G. Ritzer. Malden, MA: Blackwell.

Wafi. 2009. "Wafi." Retrieved May 19, 2011 (www.wafi.com/page.aspx?id=3417&TID=216).

Wajcman, Judy. 2010. "Feminist Theories of Technology." *Cambridge Journal of Economics* 34: 143–152.

Wakefield, Sara and Christopher Uggen. 2010. "Incarceration and Stratification." *Annual Review of Sociology* 36: 387–346.

Walder, Andrew. 2009. "Political Sociology and Social Movements." *Annual Review of Sociology* 35: 393–412.

Waldmeir, Patti. [1997] 2001. *Anatomy of a Miracle: The End of Apartheid and the Birth of a New South Africa*. New Brunswick, NJ: Rutgers University Press.

Walker, Henry A. and David Willer. 2007. "Experimental Methods." Pp. 1537–1541 in *The Blackwell Encyclopedia of Sociology*, edited by G. Ritzer. Malden, MA: Blackwell.

Walker, Janet. 2007. "Child Custody and Child Support." Pp. 451–455 in *The Blackwell Encyclopedia of Sociology*, edited by G. Ritzer. Malden, MA: Blackwell.

Walker, Samuel, Cassia Spohn, and Miriam DeLone. 2000. *The Color of Justice: Race, Ethnicity and Crime in America*. 2nd ed. Belmont, CA: Wadsworth Thomson.

Wallerstein, Immanuel. 1974. *The Modern World-System*. New York: Academic Press.

Wallerstein, James S. and Clement J. Wyle. 1947. "Our Law-Abiding Law-Breakers." *Federal Probation* 25: 107–112.

Walsh, Anthony. 1990. "Twice Labeled: The Effect of Psychiatric Labeling on the Sentencing of Sex Offenders." *Social Problems* 37: 375–389.

Walters, Glenn D. 2003. "Changes in Criminal Thinking and Identity in Novice and Experienced Inmates: Prisonization Revisited." *Criminal Justice and Behavior* 30(4): 399–421.

Ward, Kathryn. 1990. "Introduction and Overview." Pp. 1–24 in *Women Workers and Global Restructuring*, edited by K. Ward. Ithaca, NY: ILR Press.

Warner, R. Steven. 1993. "Work in Progress toward a New Paradigm for the Sociological Study of Religion in the United States." *American Journal of Sociology* 98: 1044–1093.

Warren, John Robert and Elaine M. Hernandez. 2007. "Did Socioeconomic Inequalities in Morbidity and Mortality Change in the United States over the Course of the Twentieth Century?" *Journal of Health and Social Behavior* 48: 335–351.

Wasserman, J., M. A. Flannery, and J. M. Clair. 2007. "Raising the Ivory Tower: The Production of Knowledge and Distrust of Medicine among African Americans." *Journal of Medical Ethics* 33(3): 177–180.

Wasson, Leslie. 2007. "Identity Politics/Relational Politics." Pp. 2214–2215 in *The Blackwell Encyclopedia of Sociology*, edited by G. Ritzer. Malden, MA: Blackwell.

Watkins, S. Craig. 2009. *The Young and the Digital: What the Migration to Social Network Sites, Games, and Anytime, Anywhere Media Means for Our Future*. Boston: Beacon Press.

Watson, Matthew and Elizabeth Shove. 2008. "Product, Competence, Project and Practice: DIY and the Dynamics of Craft

Consumption." *Journal of Consumer Culture* 8: 69–89.

Wattenberg, Martin P. 2002. *Where Have All the Voters Gone?* Cambridge, MA: Harvard University Press.

Watts, Jonathan. 2006. "Internet Censorship." *The Guardian*, January 25.

Wax, Emily. 2007. "An Ancient Indian Craft Left in Tatters." *The Washington Post*, June 6.

Way, Sandra. 2007. "School Discipline." Pp. 4019–4023 in *The Blackwell Encyclopedia of Sociology*, edited by G. Ritzer. Malden, MA: Blackwell.

Wayne, Leslie. 2009. "Dubious Claims for H1N1 Cures Are Rife Online." *New York Times*, November 6.

Weber, Max. [1904] 1949. *The Methodology of the Social Sciences*. New York: Free Press.

Weber, Max. [1921] 1968. *Economy and Society: An Outline of Interpretative Sociology*, edited by Guenther Roth and Claus Wittich. Totowa, NJ: Bedminster Press.

Weber, Max. 1963. *The Sociology of Religion*, translated by E. Fischoff. Boston: Beacon Press.

Weber, Max. [1903–1917] 1949. *The Methodology of the Social Sciences*. New York: Free Press.

Weber, Max. [1904–1905] 1958. *The Protestant Ethic and the Spirit of Capitalism*. New York: Scribner.

Webster, Murray and Jane Sell. 2012. "Groups and Institutions, Structures and Processes." Pp. 139–163 in *The Wiley-Blackwell Companion to Sociology*, edited by G. Ritzer. Malden, MA: Wiley-Blackwell.

Weeks, John R. 2007. "Demographic Transition Theory." Pp. 1033–1038 in *The Blackwell Encyclopedia of Sociology*, edited by G. Ritzer. Malden, MA: Blackwell.

Weeks, John R. 2011. *Population: An Introduction to Concepts and Issues*. 11th ed. Belmont, CA: Wadsworth.

Wegener, B. 1991. "Job Mobility and Social Ties: Social Resources, Prior Job, and Status Attainment." *American Sociological Review* 56: 60–71.

Weiler, Bernd. 2007. "Cultural Relativism." Pp. 908–910 in *The Blackwell Encyclopedia of Sociology*, edited by G. Ritzer. Malden, MA: Blackwell.

Weininger, Elliot B. and A. Lareau. 2009. "Paradoxical Pathways: An Ethnographic Extension of Kohn's Findings on Class and Childrearing." *Journal of Marriage and the Family* 71: 680–695.

Weinstein, Jay. 2010. *Social Change*. 3rd ed. Lanham, MD: Rowman and Littlefield.

Weisman, Steven R. 2008. "U.S. Security Concerns Block China's 3Com Deal." *New York Times*, February 21.

Weiss, Gregory L. and Lonnquist, Lynne E. 2009. *Sociology of Health, Healing, and Illness*. Upper Saddle River, NJ: Pearson/Prentice Hall.

Weitz, Rose. 2010. *The Sociology of Health, Illness, and Health Care: A Critical Approach*. Boston: Wadsworth Cengage.

Weitzer, Ronald. 2009. "Sociology of Sex Work." *Annual Review of Sociology* 35: 213–34.

Weitzman, Lenore J., Deborah Eifler, Elizabeth Hokada, and Catherine Ross. 1972. "Sex-Role Socialization in Picture Books for Preschool Children." *The American Journal of Sociology* 77: 1125–1150.

"Welcome to Our Shrinking Jungle." 2008. *The Economist*, June 5. Retrieved March 9, 2012 (http://www.economist.com/node/11496950).

Wellard, Ian. 2012. "Body-Reflexive Pleasures: Exploring Bodily Experiences within the Context of Sport and Physical Activity." *Sport, Education and Society* 17: 21–33.

Wellford, Charles. 2012. "Criminology." Pp. 229–242 in *The Wiley-Blackwell Companion to Sociology*, edited by G. Ritzer. Malden, MA: Wiley-Blackwell.

Wellings, Kaye, Martine Collumbien, Emma Slaymaker, Susheela Singh, Zoe Hodges, Dhavai Patel, and Nathalie Bajos. 2009. "Sexual Behavior in Context: A Global Perspective." *The Lancet* 368: 349–358.

Wellman, Elizabeth. 2004. *The Road to Seneca Falls: Elizabeth Cady Stanton and the First Woman's Rights Convention*. Champaign: University of Illinois Press.

Welter, Barbara. 1966. "The Cult of True Womanhood: 1820–1860." *American Quarterly* 18(2,1): 151–174.

Welzel, Christian and Ronald Inglehart. 2009. "Mass Beliefs and Democratization." Chapter 9 in *Democratization*, edited by C. W. Haerpfer, P. Bernhagen, R. F. Inglehart, and C. Welzel. Oxford, UK: Oxford University Press.

Wentzel, Kathryn and Lisa Looney. 2007. "Socialization in School Settings." In *Handbook of Socialization: Theory and Research*, edited by J. E. Grusec and P. David Hastings. New York: Guilford Press.

Wernick, Andrew. 2006. "University." *Theory, Culture and Society* 23: 557–563.

West, Candace and Don Zimmerman. 1987. "Doing Gender." *Gender and Society* 1: 125–151.

Western, Bruce and Jake Rosenfeld. 2012. "Workers of the World Divide: The Decline of Labor and the Future of the Middle Class." *Foreign Affairs*, May/June.

Wharton, Amy S. and Mary Blair-Loy. 2006. "Long Work Hours and Family Life: A Cross-National Study of Employees' Concerns." *Family Issues* 27(3): 415–436.

White, Michael J. and Ann H. Kim. 2007. "Urban Ecology." Pp. 5109–5112 in *The Blackwell Encyclopedia of Sociology*, edited by G. Ritzer. Malden, MA: Blackwell.

White, Phillip, Kevin Young, and William G. McTeer. 1995. "Sport, Masculinity, and the Injured Body." Pp. 158–182 in *Men's Health and Illness*, edited by D. Sabo and F. Gordon. Thousand Oaks, CA: Sage.

Whitehead, John T. 2007. "Crime." Pp. 818–822 in *The Blackwell Encyclopedia of Sociology*, edited by G. Ritzer. Malden, MA: Blackwell.

Whiteside, Alan. 2008. *A Very Short Introduction to HIV/AIDS*. Oxford: Oxford University Press.

Whiteside, Alan. 2012. "AIDS." Pp. 45–49 in *The Wiley-Blackwell Encyclopedia of Globalization*, edited by G. Ritzer. Malden, MA: Wiley-Blackwell.

"Why the Palace Fell: Lessons Learned from the Destruction of Haiti's Presidential Home." 2010. *Newsweek*, January 20. Retrieved March 31, 2012 (http://www.thedailybeast.com/newsweek/2010/01/20/why-the-palace-fell.html).

Whyte, William Foote. 1943. *Street Corner Society: The Social Structure of an Italian Slum*. Chicago: University of Chicago.

Wight, Vanessa R. 2007. "Demography." Pp. 1038–1045 in *The Blackwell Encyclopedia of Sociology*, edited by G. Ritzer. Malden, MA: Blackwell.

"WikiLeaks." 2010. Retrieved December 12, 2010 (http://213.251.145.96/about.html).

Wiklund, Maria, Carita Bengs, Eva-Britt Malmgren-Olsson, and Ann Öhman. 2010. "Young Women Facing Multiple and Intersecting Stressors of Modernity, Gender Orders and Youth." *Social Science Medicine* 71(9): 1567–1575.

Wilk, Kenneth Aarskaug, Eva Bernhardt, and Turid Noack. 2010. "Love or Money? Marriage Intentions Among Young Cohabitors in Norway and Sweden." *Acta Sociologica* 53: 269–287.

Wilk, Richard. 2006a. "Bottled Water: The Pure Commodity in the Age of Branding." *Journal of Consumer Culture* 6(3): 303–325.

Wilk, Richard. 2006b. "Consumer Culture and Extractive Industry on the Margins of the World System." Pp. 123–144 in *Consuming Cultures, Global Perspectives: Historical Trajectories, Transnational Exchanges*, edited by J. Brewer and F. Trentmann. Oxford, UK: Berg.

Wilkinson, Gary. 2006. "McSchools for McWorld? Mediating Global Pressures With a McDonaldizing Education Policy Response." *Cambridge Journal of Education* 36: 81–98.

Williams, Christine. 1995. *Still a Man's World*. Berkeley: University of California Press.

Williams, Christine. 2006. *Inside Toyland: Working, Shopping, and Social Inequality*. Berkeley: University of California Press.

Williams, Christine, Chandra Muller, and Kristine Kilanski. 2012. "Gendered Organizations in the New Economy." *Gender and Society* 26: 549–573.

Williams, Christine and Laura Sauceda. 2007. "Gender, Consumption and." Pp. 1848–1852 in *The Blackwell Encyclopedia of Sociology*, edited by G. Ritzer. Malden, MA: Blackwell.

Williams, David R. 1999. "Race, Socioeconomic Status and Health: The Added Effects of Racism and Discrimination." *Annals of the New York Academy of Sciences*, pp. 173–88.

Williams, Erica. 2012. Sex Work." Pp. 1856–1858 in *The Wiley-Blackwell Encyclopedia of Globalization*, edited by G. Ritzer. Malden, MA: Wiley Blackwell.

Williams, Frank P. and Marilyn D. McShane. 2007. "Lombroso, Cesare (1835–1909)." Pp. 2662–2663 in *The Blackwell Encyclopedia of Sociology* (Vol. 6), edited by G. Ritzer. Malden, MA: Blackwell.

Williams, Joan. 2001. *Unbending Gender: Why Family and Work Conflict and What to Do about It*. New York: Oxford University Press.

Williams, Patrick and Laura Chrisman, eds. 1994a. *Colonial Discourse and Post-Colonial Theory: A Reader*. New York: Columbia University Press.

Williams, Patrick and Laura Chrisman, eds. 1994b. "Introduction." *Colonial Discourse and Post-Colonial Theory: A Reader*. New York: Columbia University Press.

Williams, Rhys. 2011. "Creating an American Islam: Thoughts on Religion, Identity, and Place." *Sociology of Religion* 72(2): 127–153.

Williams, Rosalind. [1982] 1991. *Dream Worlds: Mass Consumption In Late Nineteenth-Century France*. Berkeley: University of California Press.

Williams, Simon J. 2012. "Health and Medicine in the Information Age: Castells, Informationalism and the Network Society." Pp. 167–192 in *Contemporary Theorists for Medical Sociology*, edited by G. Scambler. London: Routledge.

Williamson, Oliver E. 1975. *Markets and Hierarchies: Analysis and Antitrust Implications*. New York: Free Press.

Williamson, Oliver E. 1985. *The Economic Institutions of Capitalism*. New York: Free Press.

Williamson, Vanessa, Theda Skocpol, and John Coggin. 2011. "The Tea Party and the Remaking of Republican Conservativism." *Perspectives on Politics* 9: 25–43.

Willis, Leigh A. 2007. "Health and Race." Pp. 2078–2081 in *The Blackwell Encyclopedia of Sociology*, edited by G. Ritzer. Malden, MA: Blackwell.

Willis, P. 1977. *Learning to Labor: How Working Class Kids Get Working Class Jobs*. New York: Teachers College Press.

Wilper, Andrew P., Steffie Woolhandler, Karen E. Lasser, Danny McCormick, David H. Bor, and David U. Himmelstein. 2009. "Health Insurance and Mortality in US Adults." Retrieved April 1, 2012 (http://pnhp.org/excessdeaths/health-insurance-and-mortality-in-US-adults.pdf).

Wilson, Bryan R. 1966. *Religion and Secular Society*. London: Watts.

Wilson, George, Vincent J. Roscigno, and Matt L. Huffman. 2013. "Public Sector Transformation, Racial Inequality and Downward Occupational Mobility." *Social Forces* 91: 975–1006.

Wilson, James Q. and George Kelling. 1982. "The Police and Neighborhood Safety: BrokenWindows." *The Atlantic Monthly* 127: 29–38.

Wilson, Stephen R. 1984. "Becoming a Yogi: Resocialization and Deconditioning as Conversion Processes." *Sociological Analysis* 45(4): 301–314.

Wilson, William Julius. 1978. *The Declining Significance of Race: Blacks and Changing American Institutions*. Chicago: University of Chicago Press.

Wilson, William Julius. 1987. *The Truly Disadvantaged: The Inner City, the Underclass, and Public Policy*. Chicago: University of Chicago Press.

Wilson, William Julius. 1997. *When Work Disappears: The World of the New Urban Poor*. New York: Vintage.

Wilson, William Julius. 2009. *More than Just Race: Being Black and Poor in the Inner City*. New York: Norton.

Wilterdink, Nico. 2007. "Inequality, Wealth." Pp. 2310–2313 in *The Blackwell Encyclopedia of Sociology*, edited by G. Ritzer. Malden, MA: Blackwell.

Wimmer, Andreas. 2013. *Ethnic Boundary Making: Institutions, Power, Networks*. New York: Oxford University Press.

Winant, Howard. 2001. *The World Is a Ghetto: Race and Democracy Since World War II*. New York: Basic Books.

Wines, Michael. 2010. "China Keeps 7 Million Tireless Eyes on Its People." *New York Times*, August 3, pp. A1, A7.

Wines, Michael. 2011. "Picking Brand Names in China Is a Business Itself." *New York Times*, November 11. Retrieved April 1, 2012 (http://www.nytimes.com/2011/11/12/world/asia/picking-brand-names-in-china-is-a-business-itself.html).

Wing, Bob. 2001. "White Power in Election 2000." Retrieved April 1, 2012 (http://www.colorlines.com/archives/2001/03/white_power_in_election_2000.html).

Winlow, Simon, Dick Hobbs, Stuart Lister, and Philip Hadfield. 2001. "Get Ready to Duck: Bouncers and the Realities of Ethnographic Research on Violent Groups." *British Journal of Criminology* 41: 536–548.

Wirth, Louis. [1928] 1997. *The Ghetto*. Transaction Books.

Wirth, Louis. 1938. "Urbanism as a Way of Life." *American Journal of Sociology* 44(1).

Wise, Tim. 2010. *Colorblind: The Rise of Post-Racial Politics and the Retreat from Racial Equity*. San Francisco: City Lights.

Witz, Ann. 1992. *Professions and Patriarchy*. London: Routledge.

Wolf, Diane L., ed. 1996. *Feminist Dilemmas in Fieldwork*. Boulder, CO: Westview Press.

Wolf, Naomi. [1991] 2002. *The Beauty Myth: How Images of Beauty Are Used against Women*. New York: Anchor Books.

Wolff, Kristina. 2007. "Content Analysis." Pp. 776–779 in *The Blackwell Encyclopedia of Sociology*, edited by G. Ritzer. Malden. MA: Blackwell.

Wolfsfeld, Gadi, Elad Segev, and Ramir Sheafer. 2013. "Social Media and the Arab Spring: Politics Comes First." *The International Journal of Press/Politics*, January 16.

Wolfson, Andrew. 2005. "A Hoax Most Cruel." *The Courier-Journal*, October 9.

Wong, Edward. 2010. "18 Orgies Later, China Swinger Gets Prison Bed." *New York Times*, May 21, pp. A1, A8.

Wong, William C. W., Eleanor Holroyd, and Amie Bingham. 2011. "Stigma and Sex Work from the Perspective of Female Sex Workers in Hong Kong." *Sociology of Health and Illness* 33: 50–65.

Wood, Robert T. 2006. *Straightedge Youth: Complexity and Contradictions of a Subculture*. Syracuse: Syracuse University Press.

Woodruff, Guy and David Premack. 1979. "Intentional Communication in the Chimpanzee: The Development of Deception." *Cognition* 7: 333–362.

Woods, Andrew. 2011. "These Revolutions Are Not All Twitter." *New York Times*, February 1.

Woodward, Bob. 2010. *Obama's Wars*. New York: Simon and Schuster.

Wooffitt, Robin. 2006. *The Language of Mediums and Psychics: The Social Organization of Everyday Miracles*. Aldershot, UK: Ashgate.

Woolf, Steven H. and Laudan Y. Aron. 2013. "The US Health Disadvantage Relative to Other High-Income Countries Findings from a National Research Council/Institute of Medicine Report." *JAMA* 309(8): 8.

Worldatlas. 2012. "Largest Cities of the World." Retrieved February 28, 2012 (http://www.worldatlas.com/citypops.htm).

World Bank. 2011. "GNI per Capita, PPP (Current International $)." Retrieved June 5, 2011 (http://data.worldbank.org/indicator/NY.GNP.PCAP.PP.CD?cid=GPD_8).

World Health Organization. 2000. "World Health Report: Health Systems: Improving Performance." Retrieved March 16, 2012 (http://www.who.int/whr/2000/en/).

World Health Organization. 2003. "World Health Report: Shaping the Future." Geneva: Author.

World Health Organization 2010a. "Tobacco Free Initiative: China Releases Its Global Adult Tobacco Survey Data." Retrieved April 1, 2012 (http://www.who.int/tobacco/surveillance/gats_china/en/index.html).

World Health Organization 2010b. "World Health Report: Health Systems Financing: The Path to Universal Coverage." Geneva: Author. Retrieved April 1, 2012 (http://whqlibdoc.who.int/whr/2010/9789241564021_eng.pdf).

World Health Organization. 2011. "Tobacco." Retrieved April 1, 2012 (http://www.who.int/mediacentre/factsheets/fs339/en/).

World Health Organization. 2013. "Tobacco." Retrieved October 2013 (www.who.int/mediacentre/factsheets/fs339/en/index.html).

"The World Is Not Flat: Putting Globalization in Its Place." 2008. *Cambridge Journal of Regions, Economy and Society* 1(3):Chapter 6.

World Scripture. N.d. "Chapter 19: Live for Others—Love Your Enemy." Retrieved March 28, 2012 (www.origin.org/ucs/ws/theme144.cfm).

World Values Survey. N.d. "Values Change the World." Retrieved April 1, 2012 (http://www.worldvaluessurvey.org/wvs/articles/folder_published/article_base_110/files/WVSbrochure5-2008_11.pdf).

Worth, Robert. 2009. "Laid-Off Foreigners Flee as Dubai Spirals Down." *New York Times*, February 11.

Wortham, Jenna. 2010. "Chatroulette Gives Rise to a Genre." *New York Times*, November 22, pp. B2, B2.

Wortham, Jenna. 2013. "A Growing App Lets You See It, Then You Don't." *New York Times*, February 9, pp. A1, A3.

Wortmann, Susan L. 2007. "Sex Tourism." Pp. 4200–4203 in *The Blackwell Encyclopedia of Sociology*, edited by G. Ritzer. Malden, MA: Blackwell.

Wren, Anne. 2013. *The Political Economy of the Service Transition*. New York: Oxford University Press.

Wright, Eric Olin. 2010. *Envisioning Real Utopias*. London: Verso.

Wright, Eric Olin. 2013. "Transforming Capitalism through Real Utopias." *American Sociological Review* 78(1): 1–25.

Wright, Lawrence. 2013. *Going Clear: Scientology, Hollywood, and the Prison of Belief*. New York: Knopf.

Wright, Will. 2001. *The Wild West: The Mythical Cowboy and Social Theory*. London: Sage.

Wu, Bin and Jackie Sheehan. 2011. "Globalization and Vulnerability of Chinese Migrant Workers in Italy: Empirical Evidence on Working Conditions and their Consequences." *Journal of Contemporary China* 20(68): 135–152.

Wunder, Delores F. 2007. "Agents, Socialization of." Pp. 4566–4568 in *The Blackwell Encyclopedia of Sociology*, edited by G. Ritzer. Malden, MA: Blackwell.

Wylie, Lana. 2010. *Perceptions of Cuba: Canadian and American Policies in Comparative Perspective*. Toronto, ON: University of Toronto Press.

Wysocki, Diane Kholos and Cheryl D. Childers. 2011. "'Let My Fingers Do the Talking': Sexting and Infidelity in Cyberspace." *Sexuality and Culture* 15: 217–239.

Yach, Derek and Farnoosh Yashemian. 2007. "Public Health in a Globalizing World." Pp. 516–538 in *The Blackwell Companion to Globalization*, edited by G. Ritzer. Malden, MA: Blackwell.

Yamamoto, Ryoko. 2012. "Undocumented Immigrants." Pp. 1005–1008 in *The Wiley-Blackwell Encyclopedia of Globalization*, edited by G. Ritzer. Malden, MA: Wiley-Blackwell.

Yamane, David. 2007. "Civil Religion." Pp. 506–507 in *The Blackwell Encyclopedia of Sociology*, edited by G. Ritzer. Malden, MA: Blackwell.

Yancy, George. 2008. *Black Bodies, White Gazes: The Continuing Significance of Race*. Lanham, MD: Rowman and Littlefield.

Yang, Lian, Hai-Yen Sung, Zhengzhong Mao, Teh-wei Hu, and Keqin Rao. 2011. "Economic Costs Attributable to Smoking in China: Update and an 8-year Comparison, 2000–2008." *Tobacco Control* 20: 266–272.

Yardley, Jim. 2010. "Soaring above India's Poverty, a 27-Story Single-Family Home." *New York Times*, October 29, pp. A1, A9.

Ye, Juliet. 2008. "In China, Internet Users Prefer to Say It by 'IM.'" *Wall Street Journal*, May 22. Retrieved May 23, 2011 (http://online .wsj.com/article/SB121139669127611315. html).

Yearley, Steve. 2007. "Globalization and the Environment." Pp. 239–253 in *The Blackwell Companion to Globalization*, edited by G. Ritzer. Malden, MA: Blackwell.

Yeates, Nicola. 2009. *Globalizing Care Economies and Migrant Workers: Explorations in Global Care Chains*. Palgrave Macmillan.

Yeates, Nicola. 2012. "Care Chain." Pp. 161–164 in *The Wiley-Blackwell Encyclopedia of Globalization*, edited by G. Ritzer. Malden, MA: Wiley-Blackwell.

Yetman, Norman R., ed. 1991. *Majority and Minority: The Dynamics of Race and Ethnicity in American Life*. 5th ed. Boston: Allyn and Bacon.

Yetman, Norman, ed. 1999. *Life Voices from Slavery: 100 Authentic Slave Narratives*. Dover.

Yeung, Wei-Jun J. and Kathryn M. Pfeiffer. 2009. "The Black–White Test Score Gap and Early Home Environment." *Social Science Research* 38: 412–437.

Yew, Lee Kuan. 2000. *From Third World to First: The Singapore Story: 1965–2000*. New York: Harper.

York, Richard and Riley E. Dunlap. 2012. "Environmental Sociology." Pp. 504–521 in *The Wiley-Blackwell Companion to Sociology*, edited by G. Ritzer. Malden, MA: Wiley-Blackwell.

York, Richard and Eugene A. Rosa. 2007. "Environment and Urbanization." Pp. 1423–1426 in *The Blackwell Encyclopedia of Sociology*, edited by G. Ritzer. Malden, MA: Blackwell.

Yunus, Mohammed. 2003. *Banker to the Poor: Micro-Lending and the Battle against World Poverty*. Public Affairs.

Yuval-Davis, Nira. 2006. "Human/Women's Rights and Feminist Transversal Politics." In *Global Feminism: Transnational Women's Activism, Organizing, and Human Rights*, edited by M. Marx Ferree and A. Mari Tripp. New York: New York University Press.

Zafirovski, Milan. 2013. "Beneath Rational Choice: Elements of 'Irrational Choice Theory.'" *Current Sociology* 61: 3–21.

Zeiler, Kristin and Annette Wickstrom. 2009. "Why Do 'We' Perform Surgery on Newborn Intersexed Children? The Phenomenology of the Parental Experience of Having a Child with Intersex Anatomies." *Feminist Theory* 10: 359–377.

Zelizer, Viviana. 1997. *Social Meaning of Money*. Princeton, NJ: Princeton University Press.

Zellner, William W. 1995. *Counterculture: A Sociological Analysis*. New York: St. Martin's Press.

Zeni, Jane. 2007. "Ethics, Fieldwork." Pp. 1442–1447 in *The Blackwell Encyclopedia of Sociology*, edited by G. Ritzer. Malden. MA: Blackwell.

Zepp, Ira G., Jr. 1997. *The New Religious Image of Urban America: The Shopping Mall as Ceremonial Center*. 2nd ed. Niwot: University Press of Colorado.

Zerelli, Sal. 2007. "Socialization." Pp. 4558–4563 in *The Blackwell Encyclopedia of Sociology*, edited by George Ritzer. Malden, MA: Blackwell.

Zhang, Lena. 2006. "Behind the 'Great Firewall': Decoding China's Internet Media Policies from the Inside." *Convergence* 12: 271–291.

Zhang, Yuanyuan, Travis L. Dixon, and Kate Conrad. 2010. "Female Body Image as a Function of Themes in Rap Music Videos: A Content Analysis." *Sex Roles* 62: 787–797.

Zhou, Min. 2009. *Contemporary Chinese America: Immigration, Ethnicity, and Community Transformation*. Philadelphia: Temple University Press.

Zilberfarb, Ben-Zion. 2005. "From Socialism to Free Market: The Israeli Economy, 1948–2003." *Israel Affairs* 11: 12–22.

Zimbardo, Philip. 1973. "On the Ethics of Intervention in Human Psychological Research: With Special Reference to the Stanford Prison Experiment." *Cognition* 2: 243–256.

Zimmer, Ron and Richard Buddin. 2009. "Is Charter School Competition in California Improving the Performance of Traditional Public Schools?" *Public Administration Review*, 69(5): 831–845.

Zimmerman, Don. 1988. "The Conversation: The Conversation Analytic Perspective." *Communication Yearbook* 11: 406–432.

Zimring, Franklin E. 2011. *The City that Became Safe New York's Lessons for Urban Crime and Its Control*. NY: Oxford University Press.

Zinn, Maxine Baca. "Patricia Hill Collins: Past and Future Innovations." *Gender and Society* 26, 2012: 28-32.

Zippel, Kathrin. 2007. "Sexual Harassment." Pp. 4233–4234 in *The Blackwell Encyclopedia of Sociology*, edited by G. Ritzer. Malden, MA: Blackwell.

Zlatunich, Nichole. 2009. "Prom Dreams and Prom Reality: Girls Negotiating 'Perfection' at the High School Prom." *Sociological Inquiry* 79(3): 351–375.

Zola, Irving Kenneth. 1963. "Observations on Gambling in a Lower-Class Setting." *Social Problems* 10(4): 353–361.

Zukin, Sharon. 1969. *Loft Living: Culture and Capital in Urban Change*. New Brunswick, NJ: Rutgers University Press.

Zukin, Sharon. 2004. *Point of Purchase: How Shopping Changed American Culture*. New York: Routledge.

Zukin, Sharon. 2009. *Naked City: The Death and Life of Authentic Urban Places*. Oxford, UK: Oxford University Press.

Zureik, Elia. 2011. "Colonialism, Surveillance and Population Control: Israel/Palestine." Pp. 3–46 in *Surveillance and Control in Israel/Palestine*, edited by E. Zureik, D. Lyon, and Y. Abu-Laban. New York: Routledge.

PHOTO CREDITS

INDEX

◉SAGE research**methods**

The essential online tool for researchers from the world's leading methods publisher

Find exactly what you are looking for, from basic explanations to advanced discussion

More content and new features added this year!

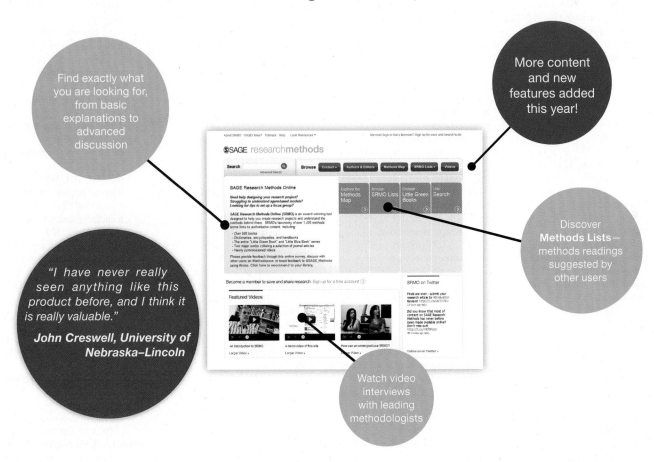

Discover **Methods Lists**— methods readings suggested by other users

"I have never really seen anything like this product before, and I think it is really valuable."

John Creswell, University of Nebraska–Lincoln

Watch video interviews with leading methodologists

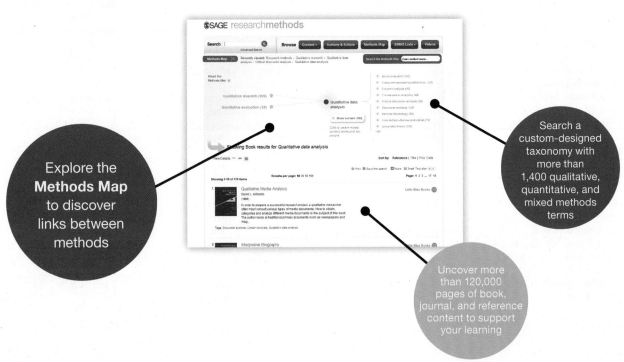

Explore the **Methods Map** to discover links between methods

Search a custom-designed taxonomy with more than 1,400 qualitative, quantitative, and mixed methods terms

Uncover more than 120,000 pages of book, journal, and reference content to support your learning

Find out more at
www.sageresearchmethods.com